# Prepare, Apply, and Confirm

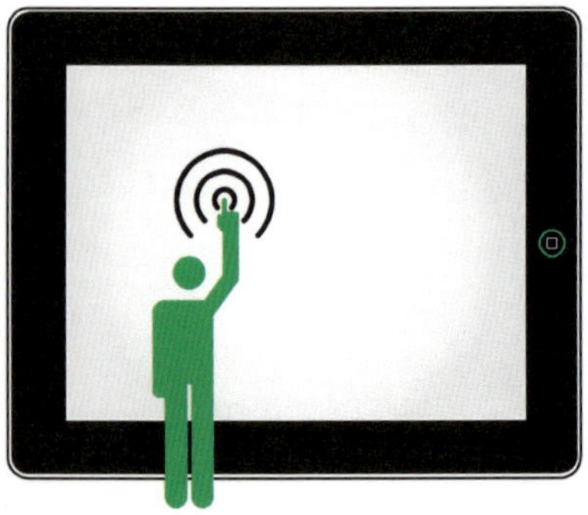

- **Enhanced eText Features**—Keep students engaged in learning on their own time, while helping them achieve greater conceptual understanding of course material through author-created solutions videos, opportunities to Try It!, and live exhibits.

- **Accounting Cycle Tutorial**—Accessed by computer, smartphone, or tablet, provides students with brief explanations of each concept of the accounting cycle through engaging videos and/or animations.

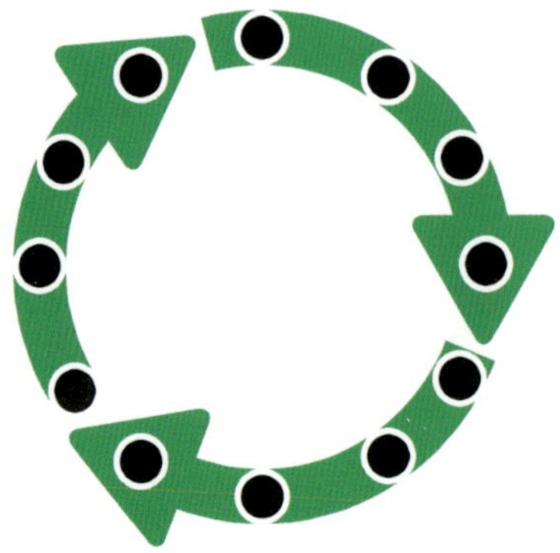

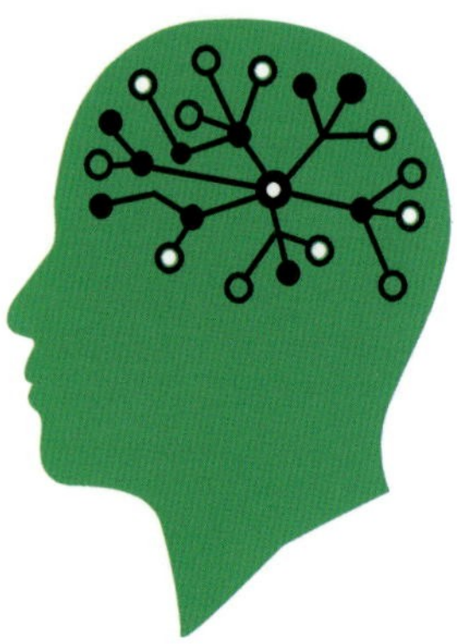

- **Dynamic Study Modules**—Work by continuously assessing student performance and activity, then using data and analytics to provide personalized content in real time to reinforce concepts that target each student's particular strengths and weaknesses.

- **Animated Lectures**—Pre-class introduction to or post-class refresher of key concepts throughout the chapter. These audio and animated lectures explain critical information and provide worked problems that students can view on their own time at their own pace.

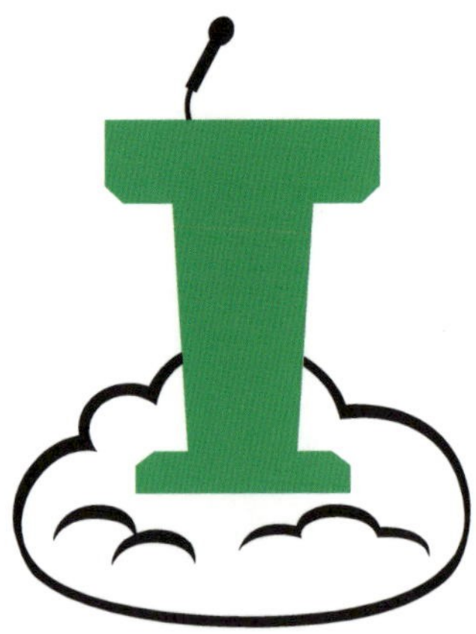

# with MyAccountingLab®

- **Hallmark Features**—Personalized Learning Aids, like Help Me Solve This, Demo Docs, and instant feedback are available for further practice and mastery when students need the help most!

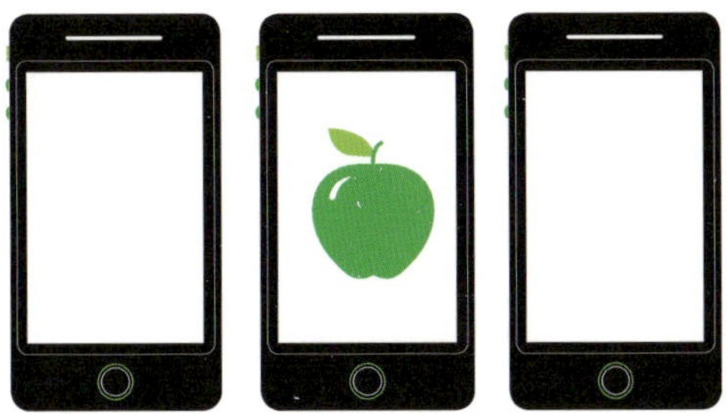

- **Learning Catalytics**—Generates classroom discussion, guides lecture, and promotes peer-to-peer learning with real-time analytics. Now, students can use any device to interact in the classroom.

- **Adaptive Study Plan**—Assists students in monitoring their own progress by offering them a customized study plan powered by Knewton, based on Homework, Quiz, and Test results. Includes regenerated exercises with unlimited practice and the opportunity to prove mastery through quizzes on recommended learning objectives.

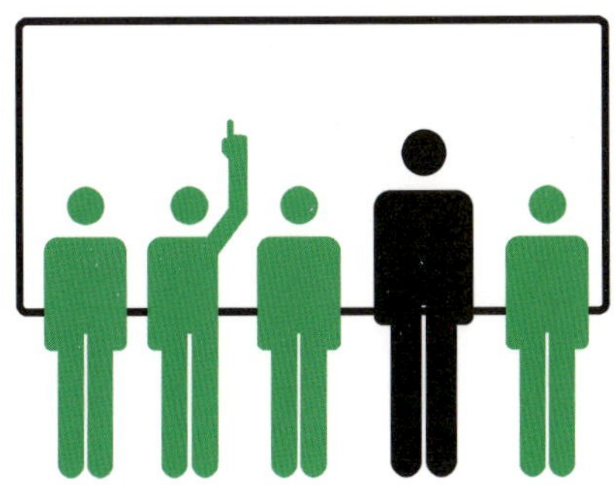

- **Worked Solutions**—Provide step-by-step explanations on how to solve select problems using the exact numbers and data that were presented in the problem. Instructors will have access to the Worked Out Solutions in preview and review mode.

PEARSON

# Prepare, Apply, and Confirm with MyAccountingLab®

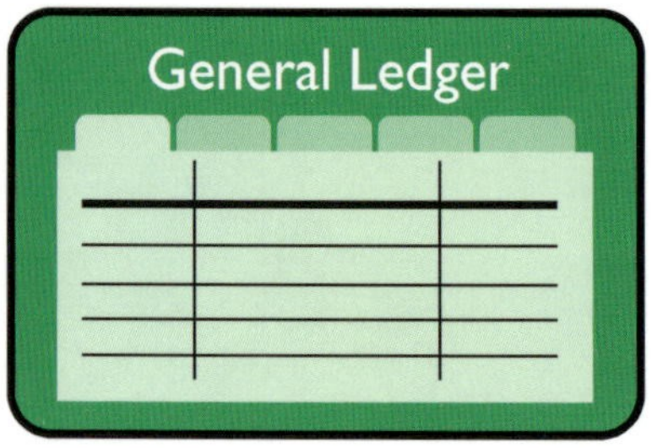


- **General Ledger**—Students can launch General Ledger software in MyAccountingLab, where they will be able to record transactions and adjusting entries, post to the ledger, close periods, and see the effects in the ledger accounts. Their work will be auto-graded, and grades will then automatically flow to the MyAccountingLab Gradebook.

- **Algorithmic Test Bank**—Instructors have the ability to create multiple versions of a test or extra practice for students.

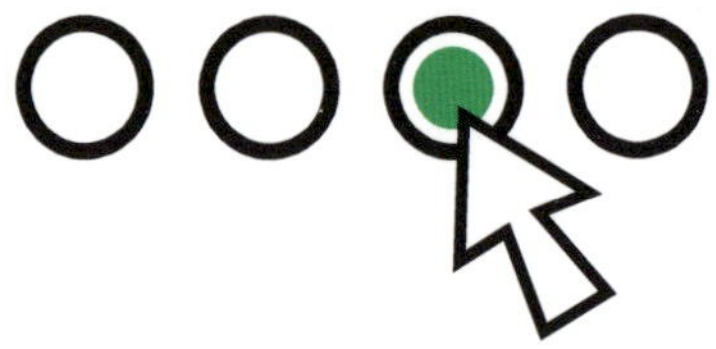

- **Reporting Dashboard**—View, analyze, and report learning outcomes clearly and easily. Available via the Gradebook and fully mobile-ready, the Reporting Dashboard presents student performance data at the class, section, and program levels in an accessible, visual manner.

- **LMS Integration**—Link from any LMS platform to access assignments, rosters, and resources, and synchronize MyLab grades with your LMS gradebook. For students, new direct, single sign-on provides access to all the personalized learning MyLab resources that make studying more efficient and effective.

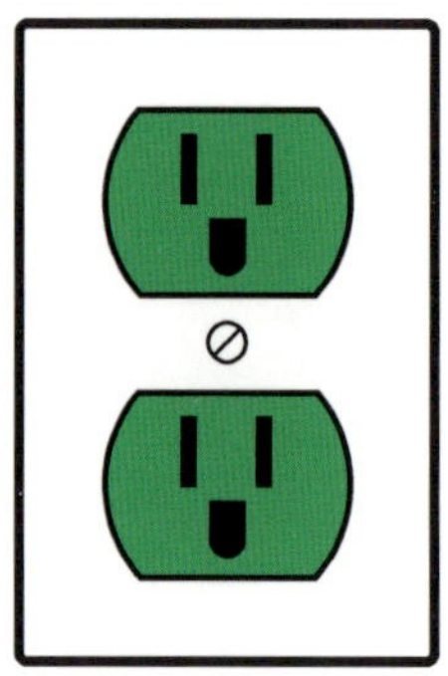

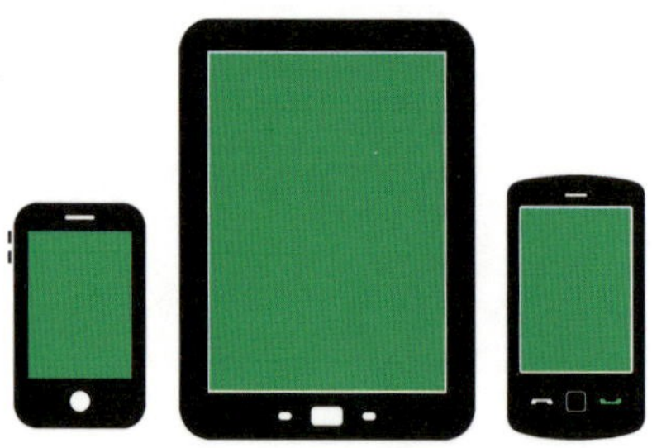

- **Mobile Ready**—Students and instructors can access multimedia resources and complete assessments right at their fingertips, on any mobile device.

HORNGREN'S

# Financial & Managerial Accounting

## THE FINANCIAL CHAPTERS

FIFTH EDITION

**Tracie Miller-Nobles**
*Austin Community College*

**Brenda Mattison**
*Tri-County Technical College*

**Ella Mae Matsumura**
*University of Wisconsin-Madison*

PEARSON

Boston Columbus Indianapolis New York San Francisco Hoboken
Amsterdam Cape Town Dubai London Madrid Milan Munich Paris Montréal Toronto
Delhi Mexico City São Paulo Sydney Hong Kong Seoul Singapore Taipei Tokyo

*Vice President, Business Publishing*: Donna Battista
*Senior Acquisitions Editor:* Lacey Vitetta
*Editorial Assistant*: Christine Donovan
*Vice President, Product Marketing*: Maggie Moylan
*Director of Marketing, Digital Services and Products*: Jeanette Koskinas
*Senior Product Marketing Manager*: Alison Haskins
*Executive Field Marketing Manager*: Lori DeShazo
*Senior Strategic Marketing Manager*: Erin Gardner
*Team Lead, Program Management*: Ashley Santora
*Program Manager*: Mary Kate Murray
*Team Lead, Project Management*: Jeff Holcomb
*Project Manager*: Roberta Sherman
*Supplements Project Manager*: Andra Skaalrud
*Operations Specialist*: Carol Melville
*Creative Director*: Blair Brown
*Art Director*: Jon Boylan
*Vice President, Director of Digital Strategy and Assessment*: Paul Gentile
*Manager of Learning Applications*: Paul Deluca
*Digital Editor*: Sarah Peterson
*Director, Digital Studio*: Sacha Laustsen
*Digital Studio Manager*: Diane Lombardo
*Product Manager*: James Bateman
*Digital Content Team Lead*: Noel Lotz
*Digital Content Project Lead*: Martha LaChance
*Full-Service Project Management and Composition*: Integra Software Services Pvt. Ltd.
*Interior Designer*: Jon Boylan
*Cover Designer*: Jon Boylan
*Cover Art*: Determined/Fotolia
*Printer/Binder*: R.R. Donnelley
*Cover Printer:* R.R. Donnelley
*Typeface*: 11/13, Adobe Garamond Pro Regular



**Library of Congress Cataloging-in-Publication Data**

Miller-Nobles, Tracie L.
Horngren's financial & managerial accounting: the financial chapters / Tracie Nobles, Texas State University / San Marcos, Brenda Mattison, Tri-County Technical College, Ella Mae Matsumura, University of Wisconsin/Madison.—Fifth Edition.
pages cm
title: Financial and managerial accounting
Includes index.
ISBN 978-0-13-385125-0
1. Accounting. 2. Managerial accounting. I. Mattison, Brenda. II. Matsumura, Ella Mae, 1952– III. Title. IV. Title: Financial and managerial accounting.
HF5636.H67 2016b
657—dc23

201404380

4 16

PEARSON

ISBN-13: 978-0-13-385125-0
ISBN-10: 0-13-385125-7

# About the Authors

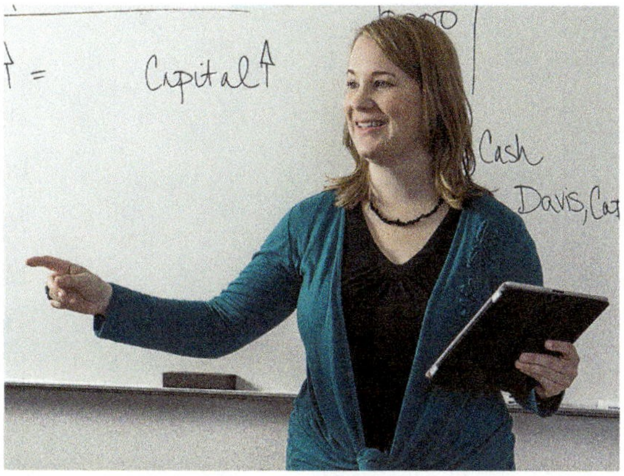


**Tracie L. Miller-Nobles, CPA,** received her bachelor's and master's degrees in accounting from Texas A&M University and is currently pursuing her Ph.D. in adult learning also at Texas A&M University. She is an Associate Professor at Austin Community College, Austin, TX. Previously she served as a Senior Lecturer at Texas State University, San Marcos, TX, and has served as department chair of the Accounting, Business, Computer Information Systems, and Marketing/Management department at Aims Community College, Greeley, CO. In addition, Tracie has taught as an adjunct professor at University of Texas and has public accounting experience with Deloitte Tax LLP and Sample & Bailey, CPAs.

Tracie is a recipient of the Texas Society of CPAs Rising Star Award, TSCPAs Outstanding Accounting Educator Award, NISOD Teaching Excellence Award and the Aims Community College Excellence in Teaching Award. She is a member of the Teachers of Accounting at Two Year Colleges, the American Accounting Association, the American Institute of Certified Public Accountants, and the Texas State Society of Certified Public Accountants. She is currently serving on the Board of Directors as secretary/webmaster of Teachers of Accounting at Two Year Colleges, as a member of the American Institute of Certified Public Accountants nominations committee, and as chair of the Texas Society of CPAs Relations with Education Institutions committee. In addition, Tracie served on the Commission on Accounting Higher Education: Pathways to a Profession.

Tracie has spoken on such topics as using technology in the classroom, motivating non-business majors to learn accounting, and incorporating active learning in the classroom at numerous conferences. In her spare time she enjoys spending time with her friends and family and camping, kayaking, and quilting.

**Brenda L. Mattison** has a bachelor's degree in education and a master's degree in accounting, both from Clemson University. She is currently an Accounting Instructor at Tri-County Technical College in Pendleton, South Carolina. Brenda previously served as Accounting Program Coordinator at TCTC and has prior experience teaching accounting at Robeson Community College, Lumberton, North Carolina; University of South Carolina Upstate, Spartanburg, South Carolina; and Rasmussen Business College, Eagan, Minnesota. She also has accounting work experience in retail and manufacturing businesses.

Brenda is a member of Teachers of Accounting at Two Year Colleges and the American Accounting Association. She is currently serving on the board of directors as Vice President of Conference Administration of Teachers of Accounting at Two Year Colleges.

Brenda previously served as Faculty Fellow at Tri-County Technical College. She has presented at several conferences on topics including active learning, course development, and student engagement.

In her spare time, Brenda enjoys reading and spending time with her family. She is also an active volunteer in the community, serving her church and other organizations.

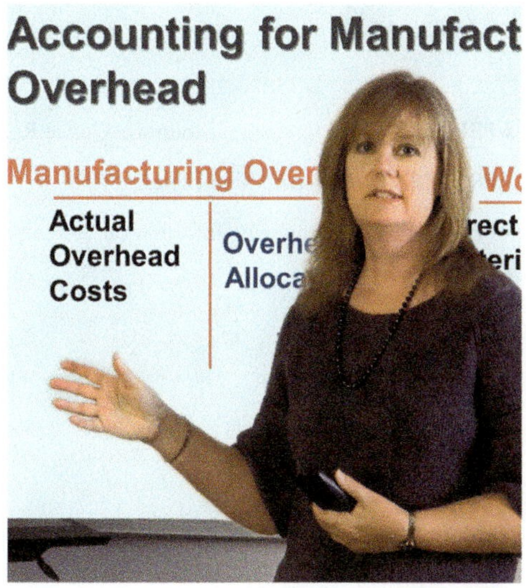


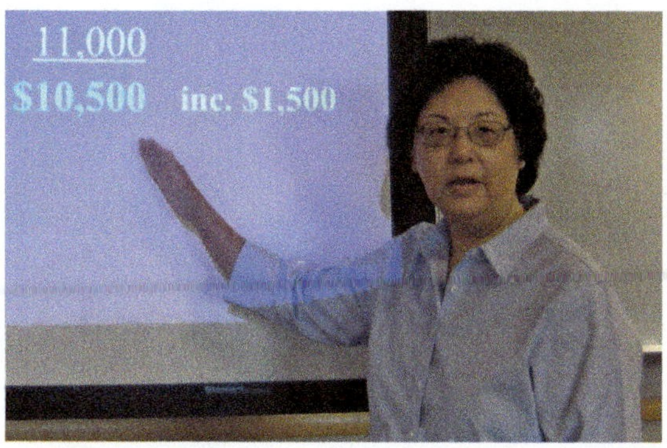


**Ella Mae Matsumura, Ph.D.** is a professor in the Department of Accounting and Information Systems in the School of Business at the University of Wisconsin–Madison, and is affiliated with the university's Center for Quick Response Manufacturing. She received an A.B. in mathematics from the University of California, Berkeley, and M.Sc. and Ph.D. degrees from the University of British Columbia. Ella Mae has won two teaching excellence awards at the University of Wisconsin–Madison and was elected as a lifetime fellow of the university's Teaching Academy, formed to promote effective teaching. She is a member of the university team awarded an IBM Total Quality Management Partnership grant to develop curriculum for total quality management education.

Ella Mae was a co-winner of the 2010 Notable Contributions to Management Accounting Literature Award. She has served in numerous leadership positions in the American Accounting Association (AAA). She was coeditor of *Accounting Horizons* and has chaired and served on numerous AAA committees. She has been secretary-treasurer and president of the AAA's Management Accounting Section. Her past and current research articles focus on decision making, performance evaluation, compensation, supply chain relationships, and sustainability. She coauthored a monograph on customer profitability analysis in credit unions.

# Brief Contents

# Contents

# Changes to This Edition

### General
Revised end-of-chapter short exercises, exercises, problems, continuing problems, comprehensive problems, and critical thinking cases.
**NEW!** Added three comprehensive problems in managerial chapters.

### Chapter 1

**NEW!** Added discussion of the Pathways Commission and incorporated the Pathways' Vision Model.
Clarified and simplified the financial statement presentation.

### Chapter 3
**NEW!** Added discussion of the new revenue recognition principle.
Replaced the word *prepaids* with *deferrals* to better align with the presentation of the other types of adjusting entries.

### Chapter 4
Increased the usage of the classified balance sheet as a requirement for end-of-chapter problems.

### Chapter 5
**NEW!** Added section on income tax expense and updated income statement presentation.

### Chapter 9
Expanded the discussion on partial-year depreciation.

### Chapter 11
**NEW!** Added a discussion on income taxes payable.
Updated the payroll section for consistency with current payroll laws at the time of printing.

### Chapter 13
Moved coverage of treasury stock before dividends to increase students' understanding of dividend transactions.
Modified the presentation of dividends to match the material presented in earlier chapters (Chapters 1–4).

# Financial & Managerial Accounting… Expanding on Proven Success

## New to the Enhanced eText

The Enhanced eText keeps students engaged in learning on their own time, while helping them achieve greater conceptual understanding of course material. The worked examples bring learning to life, and algorithmic practice allows students to apply the very concepts they are reading about. Combining resources that illuminate content with accessible self-assessment, MyAccountingLab with Enhanced eText provides students with a complete digital learning experience—all in one place.

NEW! **Try It! Solution Videos**—Author recorded solution videos accompany Try Its! Just click on the Try It! box and watch the author will walk students through the problem and the solution.

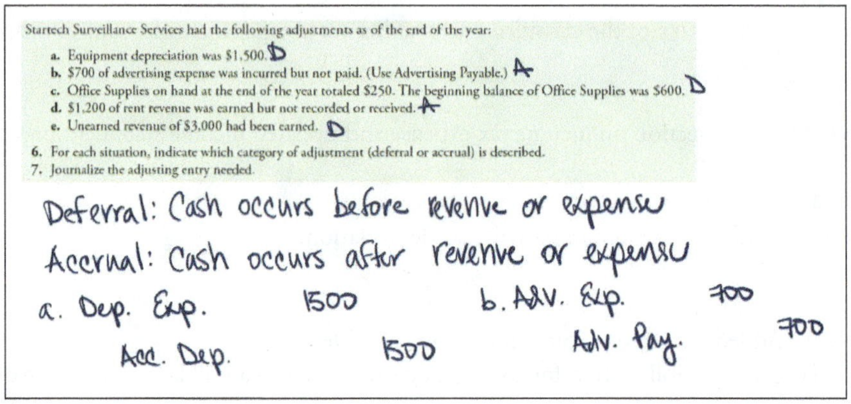
Startech Surveillance Services had the following adjustments as of the end of the year:

a. Equipment depreciation was $1,500. D
b. $700 of advertising expense was incurred but not paid. (Use Advertising Payable.) A
c. Office Supplies on hand at the end of the year totaled $250. The beginning balance of Office Supplies was $600. D
d. $1,200 of rent revenue was earned but not recorded or received. A
e. Unearned revenue of $3,000 had been earned. D

6. For each situation, indicate which category of adjustment (deferral or accrual) is described.
7. Journalize the adjusting entry needed.

Deferral: Cash occurs before revenve or expensu
Accrual: Cash occurs after revenve or expensu
a. Dep. Exp. 1500 b. Adv. Exp. 700
Acc. Dep. 1500 Adv. Pay. 700

NEW! **Accounting Cycle Tutorial**—MyAccountingLab's new interactive tutorial helps students master the Accounting Cycle for early and continued success in the introduction to Accounting course. The tutorial, accessed by computer, Smartphone, or tablet, provides students with brief explanations of each concept of the Accounting Cycle through engaging videos and/or animations. Students are immediately assessed on their understanding and their performance is recorded in the MyAccountingLab grade book. Whether the Accounting Cycle Tutorial is used as a remediation self-study tool or course assignment, students have yet another resource within MyAccountingLab to help them be successful with the accounting cycle.

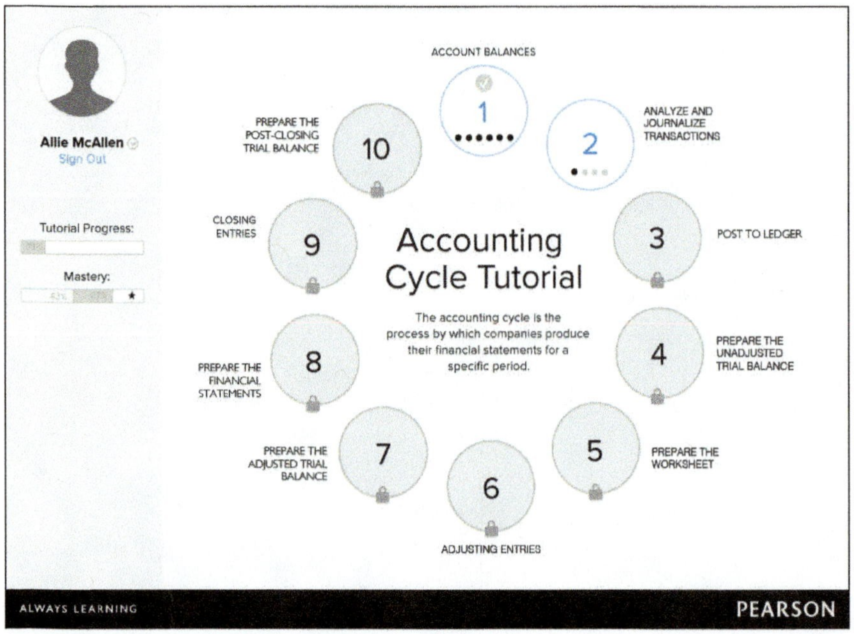

**NEW!** **Learning Catalytics**—A "bring your own device" assessment and classroom activity system that expands the possibilities for student engagement. Using Learning Catalytics, you can deliver a wide range of auto-gradable or open-ended questions that test content knowledge and build critical thinking skills. Eighteen different answer types provide great flexibility, including graphical, numerical, textual input, and more.

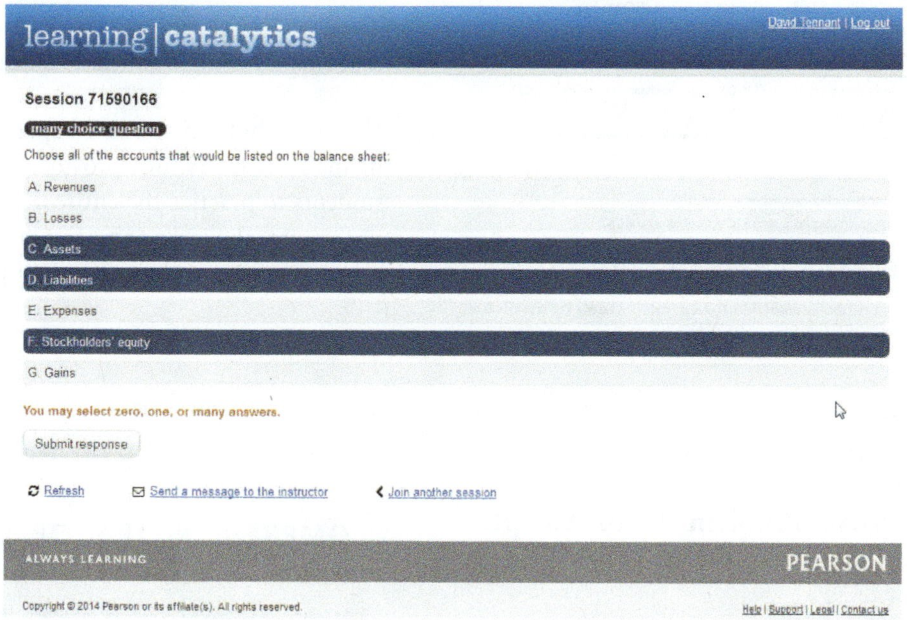


**NEW!** **Animated Lectures**—These pre-class learning aids are available for every learning objective and are professor-narrated PowerPoint summaries that will help students prepare for class. These can be used in an online or flipped classroom experience or simply to get students ready for lecture.

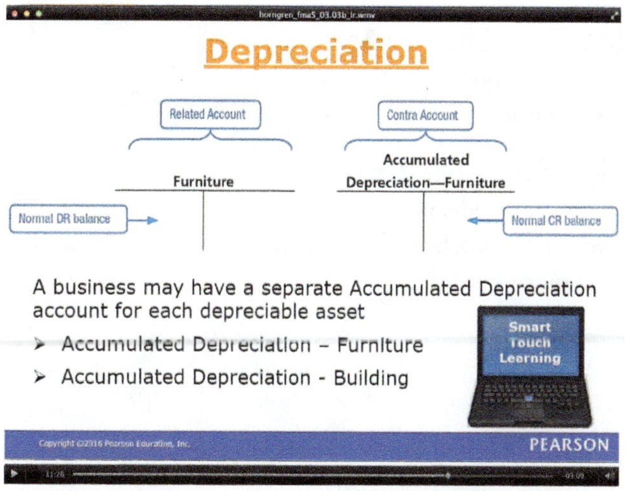

# End-of-Chapter Continuing and Comprehensive Problems

> **Continuing Problem**

Problem P1-54 is the first problem in a sequence that begins an accounting cycle. The cycle is continued in Chapter 2 and completed in Chapter 5.

**P1-54 Using the accounting equation for transaction analysis, preparing financial statements, and calculating return on assets (ROA)**

Daniels Consulting began operations and completed the following transactions during December 2016:

| | |
|---|---|
| Dec. 2 | Stockholders contributed $20,000 cash in exchange for common stock. |
| 2 | Paid monthly office rent, $2,000. |
| 3 | Paid cash for a computer, $3,600. This equipment is expected to remain in service for five years. |
| 4 | Purchased office furniture on account, $3,000. The furniture should last for five years. |
| 5 | Purchased office supplies on account, $800. |
| 9 | Performed consulting service for a client on account, $2,500. |
| 12 | Paid utilities expenses, $150. |
| 18 | Performed service for a client and received cash of $2,100. |
| 21 | Received $2,400 in advance for client service to be performed in the future. (This increases the Unearned Revenue account, which is a liability. This account will be explained in more detail in Chapter 2.) |

**Continuing Problem**—Starts in Chapter 1 and runs through the entire book exposing students to recording entries for a service company and then moving into recording transactions for a merchandiser later in the text. The managerial chapters emphasize the relevant topics for that chapter using a continuous company.

**Practice Set**—Starts in Chapter 2 and goes through the financial chapters and provides another opportunity for students to practice the entire accounting cycle. The practice set uses the same company in each chapter but is often not as extensive as the continuing problem.

**Comprehensive Problem 1 for Chapters 1–4**—Covers the entire accounting cycle for a service company.

**Comprehensive Problem 2 for Chapters 1–4**—A continuation of Comprehensive Problem 1. It requires the student to record transactions for the month after the closing process.

**Comprehensive Problem for Chapters 1–5**—Covers the entire accounting cycle for a merchandise company.

**Comprehensive Problem for Chapter 15**—Students use trend analysis and ratios to analyze a company for its investment potential.

**Comprehensive Problem for Appendix C**—Uses special journals and subsidiary ledgers and covers the entire accounting cycle for a merchandise company. Students can complete this comprehensive problem using the MyAccountingLab General Ledger or Quickbooks™ software.

## COMPREHENSIVE PROBLEMS

> **Comprehensive Problem 1 for Chapters 1–4**

Miller Delivery Service completed the following transactions during December 2016:

| | |
|---|---|
| Dec. 1 | Miller Delivery Service began operations by receiving $10,000 cash and a truck with a fair value of $20,000 from Robert Miller. The business issued Miller shares of common stock in exchange for this contribution. |
| 1 | Paid $1,000 cash for a four-month insurance policy. The policy begins December 1. |
| 4 | Paid $500 cash for office supplies. |
| 12 | Performed delivery services for a customer and received $2,000 cash. |
| 15 | Completed a large delivery job, billed the customer, $2,500, and received a promise to collect the $2,500 within one week. |
| 18 | Paid employee salary, $1,000. |
| 20 | Received $15,000 cash for performing delivery services. |
| 22 | Collected $800 in advance for delivery service to be performed later. |
| 25 | Collected $2,500 cash from customer on account. |
| 27 | Purchased fuel for the truck, paying $300 on account. (Credit Accounts Payable) |
| 28 | Performed delivery services on account, $700. |
| 29 | Paid office rent, $1,600, for the month of December. |
| 30 | Paid $300 on account. |
| 31 | Cash dividends of $3,000 were paid to stockholders. |

**Requirements**

1. Record each transaction in the journal using the following chart of accounts. Explanations are not required.

## Chapter Openers

Chapter openers set up the concepts to be covered in the chapter using stories students can relate to. The implications of those concepts on a company's reporting and decision making processes are then discussed.

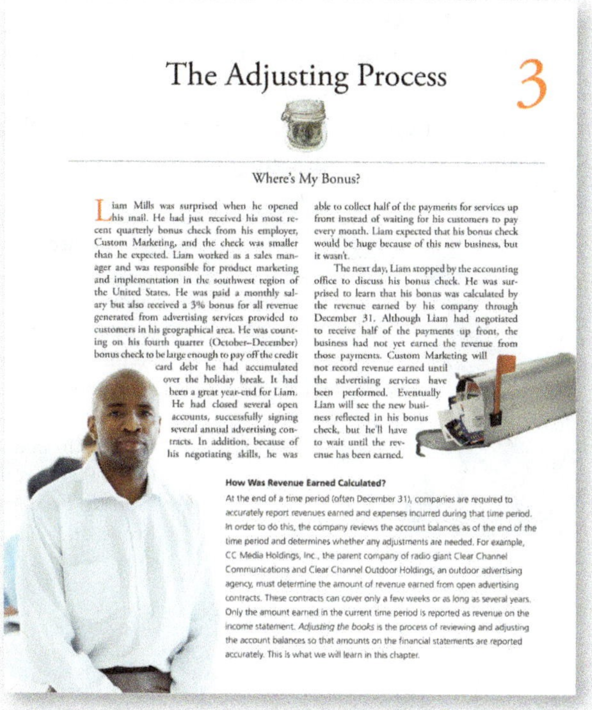

# The Adjusting Process 3

### Where's My Bonus?

Liam Mills was surprised when he opened his mail. He had just received his most recent quarterly bonus check from his employer, Custom Marketing, and the check was smaller than he expected. Liam worked as a sales manager and was responsible for product marketing and implementation in the southwest region of the United States. He was paid a monthly salary but also received a 3% bonus for all revenue generated from advertising services provided to customers in his geographical area. He was counting on his fourth quarter (October–December) bonus check to be large enough to pay off the credit card debt he had accumulated over the holiday break. It had been a great year-end for Liam. He had closed several open accounts, successfully signing several annual advertising contracts. In addition, because of his negotiating skills, he was able to collect half of the payments for services up front instead of waiting for his customers to pay every month. Liam expected that his bonus check would be huge because of this new business, but it wasn't.

The next day, Liam stopped by the accounting office to discuss his bonus check. He was surprised to learn that his bonus was calculated by the revenue earned by his company through December 31. Although Liam had negotiated to receive half of the payments up front, the business had not yet earned the revenue from those payments. Custom Marketing will not record revenue earned until the advertising services have been performed. Eventually Liam will see the new business reflected in his bonus check, but he'll have to wait until the revenue has been earned.

**How Was Revenue Earned Calculated?**

At the end of a time period (often December 31), companies are required to accurately report revenues earned and expenses incurred during that time period. In order to do this, the company reviews the account balances as of the end of the time period and determines whether any adjustments are needed. For example, CC Media Holdings, Inc., the parent company of radio giant Clear Channel Communications and Clear Channel Outdoor Holdings, an outdoor advertising agency, must determine the amount of revenue earned from open advertising contracts. These contracts can cover only a few weeks or as long as several years. Only the amount earned in the current time period is reported as revenue on the income statement. *Adjusting the books* is the process of reviewing and adjusting the account balances so that amounts on the financial statements are reported accurately. This is what we will learn in this chapter.

## Effect on the Accounting Equation

Next to every journal entry, these illustrations help reinforce the connections between recording transactions and the effect those transactions have on the accounting equation.

On November 10, Smart Touch Learning performed services for clients, for which the clients will pay the company later. The business earned $3,000 of service revenue on account.

This transaction increased Accounts Receivable, so we debit this asset. Service Revenue is increased with a credit.

**A↑**: Accounts Receivable↑ } = { **L** + **E↑**: Service Revenue↑

| Date | Accounts and Explanation | Debit | Credit |
|---|---|---|---|
| Nov. 10 | Accounts Receivable | 3,000 | |
| | Service Revenue | | 3,000 |
| | *Performed services on account.* | | |

## Instructor Tips & Tricks

Found throughout the text, these handwritten notes mimic the experience of having an experienced teacher walk a student through concepts on the "board." Many include mnemonic devices or examples to help students remember the rules of accounting.

**A↓**: Accumulated Depreciation—Building↑ } = { **L** + **E↓**: Depreciation Expense—Building↑

| Date | Accounts and Explanation | Debit | Credit |
|---|---|---|---|
| Dec. 31 | Depreciation Expense—Building | 250 | |
| | Accumulated Depreciation—Building | | 250 |
| | *To record depreciation on building.* | | |

*Remember, an increase in a contra asset, such as Accumulated Depreciation, decreases total assets. This is because a contra asset has a credit balance and credits decrease assets.*

## Common Questions, Answered

Our authors have spent years in the classroom answering students' questions and have found patterns in the concepts or rules that consistently confuse students. These commonly asked questions are located in the margin of the text next to where the answer or clarification can be found highlighted in orange text.

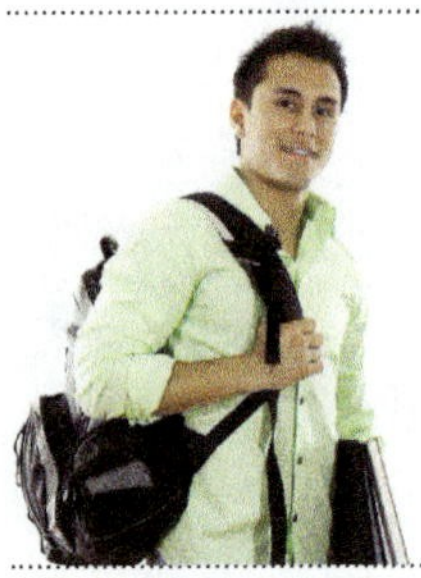

Why was the account Patent credited instead of Accumulated Amortization—Patent?

Notice that Smart Touch Learning credited the amortization directly to the intangible asset, Patent, instead of using an Accumulated Amortization account. A company may credit an intangible asset directly when recording amortization expense, or it may use the account Accumulated Amortization. **Companies frequently choose to credit the asset account directly because the residual value is generally zero and there is no physical asset to dispose of at the end of its useful life, so the asset essentially removes itself from the books through the process of amortization.**

At the end of the first year, Smart Touch Learning will report this patent at $160,000 ($200,000 cost minus first-year amortization of $40,000), the next year at $120,000, and so forth. Each year for five years the value of the patent will be reduced until the end of its five-year life, at which point its book value will be $0.

## Try It! Boxes

Found after each learning objective, Try Its! give students the opportunity to apply the concept they just learned to an accounting problem. Deep linking in the eText will allow students to practice in MyAccountingLab without interrupting their interaction with the eText.

### Try It!

Total Pool Services earned $130,000 of service revenue during 2016. Of the $130,000 earned, the business received $105,000 in cash. The remaining amount, $25,000, was still owed by customers as of December 31. In addition, Total Pool Services incurred $85,000 of expenses during the year. As of December 31, $10,000 of the expenses still needed to be paid. In addition, Total Pool Services prepaid $5,000 cash in December 2016 for expenses incurred during the next year.

1. Determine the amount of service revenue and expenses for 2016 using a cash basis accounting system.
2. Determine the amount of service revenue and expenses for 2016 using an accrual basis accounting system.

**Check your answers online in MyAccountingLab or at http://www.pearsonhighered.com/Horngren.**

For more practice, see Short Exercises S3-1 and S3-2. MyAccountingLab

## Redesigned

The redesign includes clean and consistent art for T-accounts, journal entries, financial statements, and the accounting equation. New art types include clear explanations and connection arrows to help students follow the transaction process.

| | | | | | | | | | | |
|---|---|---|---|---|---|---|---|---|---|---|
| **ASSETS** | = | **LIABILITIES +** | **EQUITY** | | | | | | | |
| | | | **Contributed Capital** | **+** | **Retained Earnings** | | | | | |
| | | | Common Stock | | − | Dividends | + | Revenues | − | Expenses |

## IFRS

Information on IFRS provides guidance on how IFRS differs from U.S. GAAP throughout the financial chapters.

## Decision Boxes

This feature provides common questions and potential solutions business owners face. Students are asked to determine the course of action they would take based on concepts covered in the chapter and are then given potential solutions.

**DECISIONS**

### Which depreciation method should be selected?

Three Junes Weaving has just purchased an automated weaving machine and is trying to figure out which depreciation method to use: straight-line, units-of-production, or double-declining-balance. Ira Glasier, the controller, is interested in using a depreciation method that approximates the usage of the weaving machine. He also expects that the weaving machine will have increasing repairs and maintenance as the asset ages. Which method should Ira choose?

#### Solution

If Ira is interested in using a depreciation method that approximates the usage of the weaving machine, he should use the units-of-production method to depreciate the asset. He could use number of machine hours as the unit of output. This method would best match the usage of the machine to the amount of expense recorded. Ira should be aware, though, that this method could produce varying amounts of depreciation expense each year. For example, if Three Junes Weaving does not use the weaving machine in one year, no depreciation expense would be recorded. This could cause net income to vary significantly from year to year. Because Ira expects the weaving machine to need more repairs as the asset ages, Ira might consider using the double-declining-balance method instead. The double-declining-balance method records a higher amount of depreciation in the early years and less later. This method works well for assets that are expected to have increasing repairs and maintenance in their later years because the total expense (depreciation and repairs and maintenance) can be spread out equally over the life of the asset.

## Things You Should Know

Provides students with a brief review of each learning objective presented in a question and answer format.

### > Things You Should Know

**1. How do we prepare financial statements?**

- Financial statements are prepared from the adjusted trial balance in the following order:
  1. Income statement—reports revenues and expenses and calculates net income or net loss during the period
  2. Statement of retained earnings—shows how retained earnings changed during the period due to net income or net loss and dividends
  3. Balance sheet—reports assets, liabilities, and stockholders' equity as of the last day of the period
- A classified balance sheet classifies each asset and each liability into specific categories.

**2. How could a worksheet help in preparing financial statements?**

- The columns of a worksheet can be extended to help in preparing the financial statements.
- The income statement section will include only revenue and expense accounts.
- The balance sheet section will include asset and liability accounts and all equity accounts except revenues and expenses.

Dear Colleague,

Thank you for taking time, out of what we know is a busy schedule, to review the newest edition of *Horngren's Financial and Managerial Accounting*. We are excited to share our innovations with you as we expand on the proven success of our significant revision to the Horngren franchise. Using what we have learned from focus groups, market feedback, and our colleagues, we've designed this edition to focus on several goals.

First, we made certain that our content was clear, consistent, and above all, accurate. As authors, we reviewed each chapter to ensure that students understand what they are reading and that there is consistency from chapter to chapter. In addition, our textbook goes through a multi-level accuracy check which includes the author team working every single accounting problem and having a team of accounting professors from across the nation review for accuracy. Next, through ongoing conversations with our colleagues and our time engaged at professional conferences, we confirmed that our pedagogy and content represents the leading methods used in the classroom and provides your students with the foundation they need to be successful in their future academic and professional careers. Lastly, we concentrated on student success and providing resources for professors to create an active and engaging classroom.

***Student success.*** Using our experience as educators, our team carefully considered how students learn, what they learn, and where they struggle the most. We understand that sometimes there is a gap in students' understanding between the textbook content and what is done in the classroom or in an online environment, so we have included in the textbook and enhanced eText several great learning aids for students. *Instructor Tips and Tricks* and *Common Questions Answered* address areas that are typically challenging for students. These aids provide handy memory tools or address common student misconceptions or confusion. We also realized that students use our enhanced eText to study on their own time and we have built in many new features to bring learning to life and to allow students to apply the concepts they are reading about outside of the classroom. Available through MyAccountingLab, students have the opportunity to watch author recorded solution videos, practice the accounting cycle using an interactive tutorial, and watch in-depth author-driven animated lectures that cover every learning objective.

***Professor expectations.*** As professors, we know it's critical to have excellent end-of-chapter material and instructor resources. With these expectations, all end-of-chapter problems have been revised and our author team, along with our trusted accuracy checkers, have checked every problem for accuracy and consistency. In addition to financial comprehensive problems, three NEW comprehensive problems have been added to the managerial content. These problems cover multiple chapters and encourage students to think reflectively about prior material learned and the connections between accounting concepts. We have also reviewed and updated ALL instructor resources to accompany this edition of the book. In addition, the PowerPoint presentations and Test Bank have had significant revisions based upon your feedback and needs.

**Expanding on the proven success** of our last edition, we believe that our enhancements to *Horngren's Financial and Managerial Accounting*, along with MyAccountingLab, will help your students achieve success in accounting. We welcome your feedback, suggestions, and comments. Please don't hesitate to contact us at *HorngrensAccounting@pearson.com*.

Tracie L. Miller-Nobles, CPA Brenda Mattison Ella Mae Matsumura, PhD

# Instructor and Student Resources

**Each supplement, including the resources in MyAccountingLab, has been reviewed by the author team to ensure accuracy and consistency with the text. Given their personal involvement, you can be assured of the high quality and accuracy of all supplements.**

## For Instructors

MyAccountingLab

### Online Homework and Assessment Manager: http://www.myaccountinglab.com

### Instructor Resource Center: http://www.pearsonhighered.com/Horngren

For the instructor's convenience, the instructor resources can be downloaded from the textbook's catalog page (http://www.pearsonhighered.com/Horngren) and MyAccountingLab. Available resources include the following:

**Online Instructor's Resource Manual:**

***Course Content:***

- Tips for Taking Your Course from Traditional to Hybrid, Blended, or Online
- Standard Syllabi for Financial Accounting (10-week & 16-week)
- Standard Syllabi for Managerial Accounting (10-week & 16-week)
- Sample Syllabi for 10- and 16-week courses
- "First Day of Class" student handouts include:
  - Student Walk-Through to Set-up MyAccountingLab
  - Tips on How to Get an A in This Class

***Chapter Content:***

- Chapter Overview
  - Contains a brief synopsis and overview of each chapter.
- Learning Objectives
- Teaching Outline with Lecture Notes
  - Revised to combine the Teaching Outline and the Lecture Outline Topics, so instructors only have one document to review.
  - Walks instructors through what material to cover and what examples to use when addressing certain items within the chapter.
- Handout for Student Notes
  - An outline to assist students in taking notes on the chapter.
- Student Chapter Summary
  - Aids students in their comprehension of the chapter.
- Assignment Grid
  - Indicates the corresponding Learning Objective for each exercise and problem.
- Answer Key to Chapter Quiz
- Ten-Minute Quiz
  - To quickly assess students' understanding of the chapter material.
- Extra Critical Thinking Problems and Solutions
  - Critical Thinking Problems removed from this edition of the text were moved to the IRM so instructors can continue to use their favorite problems.
- NEW Guide to Classroom Engagement Questions
  - Author-created element will offer tips and tricks to instructors in order to help them use the Learning Catalytic questions in class.

**Online Instructor's Solutions Manual:**

- Contains solutions to all end-of-chapter questions, short exercises, exercises, and problems.
- The Try It! Solutions, previously found at the end of each chapter, are now available for download with the ISM.
- All solutions were thoroughly reviewed by the author team and other professors.

**Online Test Bank:**

- Includes more than 3,900 questions.
- Both conceptual and computational problems are available in true/false, multiple choice, and open-ended formats.
- Algorithmic test bank is available in MyAccountingLab.

**PowerPoint Presentations:**

*Instructor PowerPoint Presentations:*

- Complete with lecture notes.
- Mirrors the organization of the text and includes key exhibits.

*Student PowerPoint Presentations:*

- Abridged versions of the Instructor PowerPoint Presentations.
- Can be used as a study tool or note-taking tool for students.

*Demonstration Problem PowerPoint Presentations:*

- Offers instructors the opportunity to review in class the exercises and problems from the chapter using different companies and numbers.

*Clicker Response System (CRS) PowerPoint Presentations:*

- 10 multiple-choice questions to use with a Clicker Response System.

*Image Library:*

- All image files from the text to assist instructors in modifying our supplied PowerPoint presentations or in creating their own PowerPoint presentations.

**Working Papers and Solutions:**

- Available in Excel format.
- Templates for students to use to complete exercises and problems in the text.

**Data and Solutions Files:**

- Select end-of-chapter problems have been set up in different software applications, including QuickBooks and General Ledger.
- Corresponding solution files are provided for QuickBooks.

## For Students

MyAccountingLab

### Online Homework and Assessment Manager: http://www.myaccountinglab.com

- Pearson Enhanced eText
- Data Files
- Animated Lectures
- Demo Docs
- Working Papers
- Student PowerPoint® Presentations
- Accounting Cycle Tutorial
- Flash Cards

### Student Resource Web site: http://www.pearsonhighered.com/Horngren

The book's Web site contains the following:

- Data Files: Select end-of-chapter problems have been set up in QuickBooks software and the related files are available for download.
- Working Papers
- Try It! Solutions: The solutions to all in-chapter Try Its! are available for download.

http://www.pearsonhighered.com/Horngren

# Acknowledgments


## Acknowledgments for This Edition:

*Tracie Miller–Nobles would like to thank her parents and sister: Kipp and Sylvia Miller and Michelle Miller. She would also like to express her gratitude to her many colleagues and friends who encourage and support her. In addition, she would like to thank Kevin Morris for always making her laugh and for being the best camping buddy she could ever ask for. Here's to many more trails.*

*Brenda Mattison has always had the loving support of her family and wishes to express her gratitude to them, especially her husband, Grant Mattison, who has been a constant and stable influence and inspiration for more than 25 years. Her family's faith in her, along with her faith in God, provided the solid foundation that allowed her to develop her gift of teaching and achieve her dreams while helping others to achieve theirs.*

*Ella Mae Matsumura thanks her family for their longstanding love and support in her endeavors: husband, Kam-Wah Tsui; son, David Tsui; sister and late parents, Linda, Lester, and Eda Matsumura. She would also like to express her appreciation to: the numerous colleagues and friends who have encouraged her and helped her grow as a scholar and a person; the many students who have provided constructive feedback that has shaped her teaching; and her faith community for its enduring love and affirmation.*

*The authors would like to sincerely thank Lacey Vitetta, Roberta Sherman, Mary Kate Murray, Andra Skaalrud, Alison Haskins, and Donna Battista for their unwavering support of this edition. They express their extreme pleasure in working with each of them and are appreciative of their guidance, patience, and belief in the success of this project.*

## Contributor:

Lori Hatchell, *Aims Community College*

## Advisory Panels, Focus Group Participants, and Reviewers:

Samad Adams, *Bristol Community College*
Sharon Agee, *Rollins College*
Markus Ahrens, *St. Louis Community College*
Janice Akao, *Butler County Community College*
Anna Alexander, *Caldwell Community College and Technical Institute*
Sheila Ammons, *Austin Community College*
Sidney Askew, *Borough of Manhattan Community College*
Michael Barendse, *Grossmont College*
Vikki Bentz, *Yavapai College*
Jennifer Cainas, *University of South Florida*
Anne Cardozo, *Broward College*
Elizabeth Carlson, *University of South Florida Sarasota-Manatee*
Martha Cavalaris, *Miami Dade College*
Donna Chadwick, *Sinclair Community College*
Colleen Chung, *Miami Dade College*
Tom Clement, *University of North Dakota*
Geoffrey Danzig, *Miami Dade College–North*
Judy Daulton, *Piedmont Technical College*
Michelle Davidowitz, *Kingsborough Community College*
Annette Fisher Davis, *Glendale Community College*
Anthony Dellarte, *Luzerne County Community College*
Crystal Drum, *Guilford Technical Community College*
Mary Ewanechko, *Monroe Community College*
Elisa Fernandez, *Miami Dade College*
Lori Grady, *Bucks County Community College*
Marina Grau, *Houston Community College*
Gloria Grayless, *Sam Houston State University*
Dawn D. Hart, *Darton State College*
Lori Hatchell, *Aims Community College*
Shauna Hatfield, *Salt Lake Community College*
Patricia Holmes, *Des Moines Area Community College*
Cynthia Johnson, *University of Arkansas, Little Rock*
Jeffrey Jones, *The College of Southern Nevada*
Thomas K. Y. Kam, *Hawaii Pacific University*
Anne Kenner, *Brevard Community College*
Stephanie (Sam) King, *Edison State College*
Paul Koulakov, *Nashville State Community College*
Christy Land, *Catawba Valley Community College*
Wayne Lewis, *Hudson Valley Community College*
Mabel Machin, *Valencia College*
Mostafa Maksy, *Kutztown University*
Richard Mandau, *Piedmont Technical College*
Maria C. Mari, *Miami Dade College*
Cynthia J. Miller, *University of Kentucky*
Joanne Orabone, *Community College of Rhode Island*
Kimberly Perkins, *Austin Community College*
William Quilliam, *Florida Southern College*
Marcela Raphael, *Chippewa Valley Technical College*
Ryan Rees, *Salt Lake Community College*
Cecile Robert, *Community College of Rhode Island*
Shani Nicole Robinson, *Sam Houston State University*
Carol Rowey, *Community College of Rhode Island*
Amanda J. Salinas, *Palo Alto College*

Dennis Shea, *Southern New Hampshire University*
Jaye Simpson, *Tarrant County*
John Stancil, *Florida Southern*
Diana Sullivan, *Portland Community College*
Annette Taggart, *Texas A&M University–Commerce*
Linda Tarrago, *Hillsborough Community College*
Teresa Thompson, *Chaffey College*
Judy Toland, *Bucks County Community College*
Robin D. Turner, *Rowan-Cabarrus Community College*
William Van Glabek, *Edison State College*
Stanley Walker, *Georgia Northwestern Tech*
Deb Weber, *Hawkeye Community College*
Denise A. White, *Austin Community College*
Donald R. Wilke, *Northwest Florida State College*
Wanda Wong, *Chabot College*
Judy Zander, *Grossmont College*

## Accuracy Checkers:

James L. Baker, *Harford Community College*
Nancy Emerson, *North Dakota State University*
Richard Mandau, *Piedmont Technical College*
Carolyn Streuly
Carol Hughes, *Asheville-Buncombe Technical Community College*

## Supplements Authors and Reviewers:

David Dearman, *Piedmont Technical College*
Kelly Damron, *Glendale Community College*
Helen Brubeck, *Saint Mary-of-the-Woods College*
Brett Killion, *Lakeland College*
Sheila Ammons, *Austin Community College*
Dave Alldredge, *Salt Lake Community College*
Michelle Suminski, *Marygrove College*
Connie Belden, *Butler Community College*
Kate Demarest, *Carroll Community College*

The authors would like to express their gratitude for the diligent and exemplary work of all of our contributors, reviewers, accuracy checkers, and supplement authors. Each of you played a part in making this book successful! Thank you!

# Accounting and the Business Environment 1

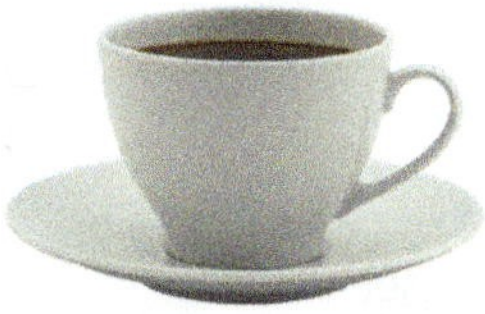

## Coffee, Anyone?

Aiden Jackson stared at the list the banker had given him during their meeting. *Business plan, cash flow projections, financial statements, tax returns.* Aiden had visited with the banker because he had a dream of opening a coffee shop near campus. He knew there was a need; students were always looking for a place to study and visit with their friends. He also had the experience. He had worked for the past three years as a manager of a coffee shop in a neighboring town. Aiden needed one thing, though—money. He had saved a small amount of money from his job and received several contributions from family and friends, but he still didn't have enough to open the business. He had decided the best option was to get a loan from his bank. After the meeting, Aiden felt overwhelmed and unsure of the future of his business.

You might think that Aiden was facing an impossible situation, but you'd be wrong. Almost every new business faces a similar situation. The owner starts with an inspiration, and then he or she needs to provide enough continuous cash flow to build the business. In addition, the owner has to make decisions such as: *Should we expand to another location? Do we have enough money to purchase a new coffee roaster? How do I know if the business made a profit?*

So how does Aiden get started? Keep reading. That's what accounting teaches you.

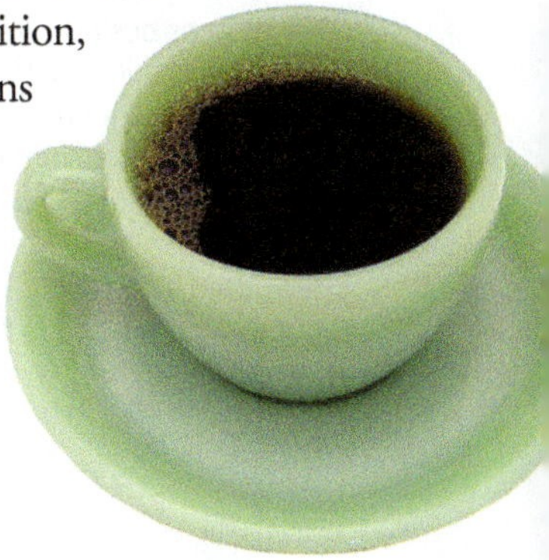

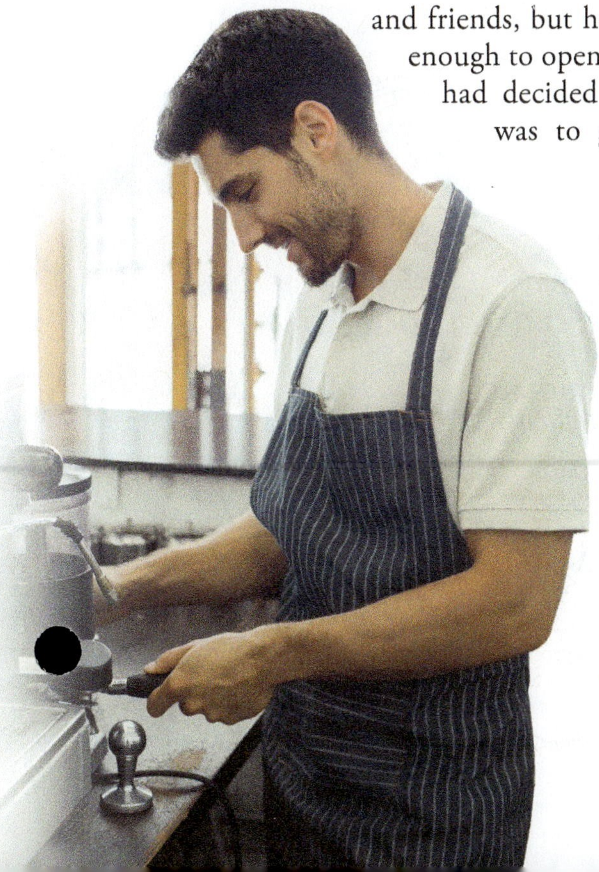

### Why Study Accounting?

The situation that Aiden faced is similar to the situations faced in the founding of most businesses. **Starbucks Corporation**, for example, first opened its doors in Seattle, Washington, in 1971. Three partners, Jerry Baldwin, Zev Siegl, and Gordon Bowker, were inspired by a dream of selling high-quality coffee. We know their dream was successful because Starbucks currently has more than 19,000 stores in 60 countries. How did Starbucks grow from a small one-store shop to what it is today? The partners understood accounting—the language of business. They understood how to measure the activities of the business, process that information into reports (financial statements), and then use those reports to make business decisions. Your knowledge of accounting will help you better understand businesses. It will make you a better business owner, employee, or investor.

# Chapter 1 Learning Objectives

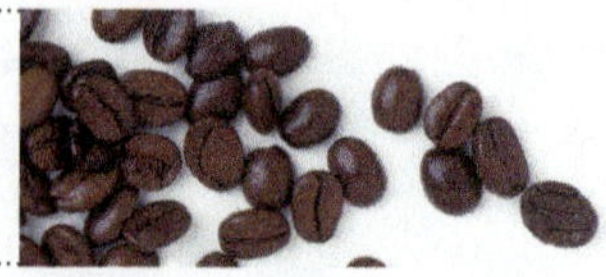

1. Explain why accounting is important and list the users of accounting information
2. Describe the organizations and rules that govern accounting
3. Describe the accounting equation and define assets, liabilities, and equity
4. Use the accounting equation to analyze transactions
5. Prepare financial statements
6. Use financial statements and return on assets (ROA) to evaluate business performance

## WHY IS ACCOUNTING IMPORTANT?

**Learning Objective 1**
Explain why accounting is important and list the users of accounting information

**Accounting**
The information system that measures business activities, processes the information into reports, and communicates the results to decision makers.

You've heard the term *accounting*, but what exactly is it? **Accounting** is the information system that measures business activities, processes the information into reports, and communicates the results to decision makers. Accounting is the language of business. The better you understand the language of business, the better you can manage your own business, be a valuable employee, or make wise investments.

We tend to think of accountants as boring and dry. However, accounting is much more than simple recordkeeping or bookkeeping. Today's accountants participate in a broad range of activities such as the investigation of financial evidence, the development of computer programs to process accounting information, and the communication of financial results to interested parties. The knowledge of accounting is used every day to help make business decisions.

Recently, leaders from across the accounting community, called the Pathways Commission, came together to create a vision model (see Exhibit 1-1) to help students and

**Exhibit 1-1 | Pathways Vision Model**

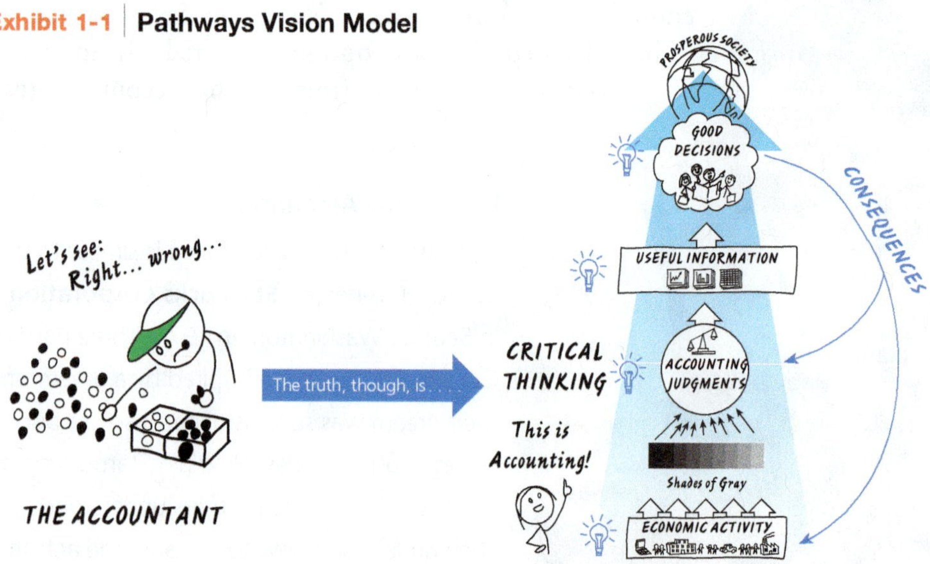


We tend to think of accountants as boring and dry.

Accountants are instrumental in helping to create a prosperous society.

the public understand what accounting is. The model is intended to explain in a visual way what accountants really do. Accounting starts with economic activities that accountants review and evaluate using critical thinking and judgment to create useful information that helps individuals make good decisions. The model emphasizes that good decisions have an impact on accounting judgments and economic activity, thus creating a circular flow of cause and effect. Accountants are more than boring, tedious number crunchers. Instead, accountants play a critical role in supporting a prosperous society.

## Decision Makers: The Users of Accounting Information

We can divide accounting into two major fields: financial accounting and managerial accounting. **Financial accounting** provides information for external decision makers, such as outside investors, lenders, customers, and the federal government. **Managerial accounting** focuses on information for internal decision makers, such as the company's managers and employees.

**Financial Accounting**
The field of accounting that focuses on providing information for external decision makers.

**Managerial Accounting**
The field of accounting that focuses on providing information for internal decision makers.

Exhibit 1-2 illustrates the difference between financial accounting and managerial accounting. Regardless of whether they are external or internal to the company, all decision makers need information to make the best choices. The bigger the decision, the more information decision makers need. Let's look at some ways in which various people use accounting information to make important decisions.

IFRS

Accounting is alive! As businesses evolve and the type of business transactions change, so must the language of business. The most significant changes in the business world in the last decade have been the huge increases in international commerce. Because more business is conducted internationally, decision makers are looking for an international accounting language.

Look for more information about International Financial Reporting Standards (IFRS) anywhere that you see this image.

**Exhibit 1-2 | Decision Making: Financial Versus Managerial Accounting**

**Financial Accounting**

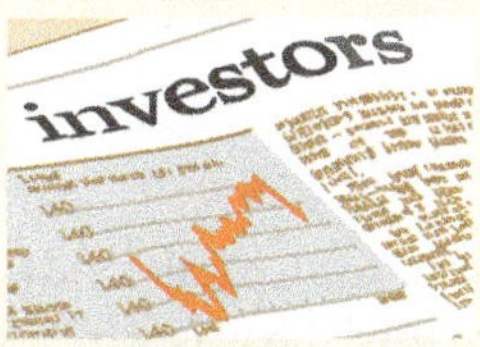


**External Decision Makers:**

Should I invest in the business?
Is the business profitable?
Should we lend money to the business?
Can the business pay us back?

**Managerial Accounting**

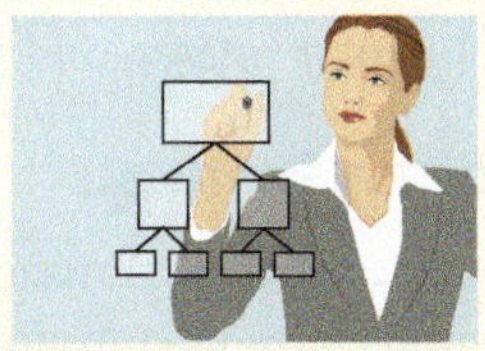

**Internal Decision Makers:**

How much money should the business budget for production?
Should the business expand to a new location?
How do actual costs compare to budgeted costs?

### Individuals

How much cash do you have? How much do you need to save each month to retire at a certain age or pay for your children's college education? Accounting can help you answer questions like these. By using accounting information, you can manage your money, evaluate a new job, and better decide whether you can afford to buy a new computer. Businesses need accounting information to make similar decisions.

### Businesses

Business owners use accounting information to set goals, measure progress toward those goals, and make adjustments when needed. The financial statements give owners the information they need to help make those decisions. Financial statements are helpful when, for example, a business owner wants to know whether his or her business has enough cash to purchase another computer.

### Investors

Outside investors who have some ownership interest often provide the money to get a business going. Suppose you're considering investing in a business. How would you decide whether it is a good investment? In making this decision, you might try to predict the amount of income you would earn on the investment. Also, after making an investment, investors can use a company's financial statements to analyze how their investment is performing.

You might have the opportunity to invest in the stock market through your company's retirement plan. Which investments should you pick? Understanding a company's financial statements will help you decide. You can view the financial statements of large companies that report to the SEC by logging on to **http://www.finance.yahoo.com**, **http://www.google.com/finance**, or the Security and Exchange Commission's EDGAR database (**http://www.sec.gov/edgar.shtml**).

### Creditors

**Creditor**
Any person or business to whom a business owes money.

Any person or business to whom a business owes money is a **creditor**. Before extending credit to a business, a creditor evaluates the company's ability to make the payments by reviewing its financial statements. Creditors follow the same process when you need to borrow money for a new car or a house. The creditor reviews accounting data to determine your ability to make the loan payments. What does your financial position tell the creditor about your ability to pay the loan? Are you a good risk for the bank?

### Taxing Authorities

Local, state, and federal governments levy taxes. Income tax is calculated using accounting information. Good accounting records can help individuals and businesses take advantage of lawful deductions. Without good records, the IRS can disallow tax deductions, resulting in a higher tax bill plus interest and penalties.

## The Accounting Profession

What do businesses such as Amazon.com, Walmart, or even your local sandwich shop across from campus have in common? They all need accountants! That is why a degree in accounting opens so many doors upon graduation.

**Certified Public Accountants (CPAs)**
Licensed professional accountants who serve the general public.

You've probably heard of a CPA before. **Certified Public Accountants**, or **CPAs**, are licensed professional accountants who serve the general public. CPAs work for public accounting firms, businesses, government entities, or educational institutions. What does it take to be a CPA? Although requirements vary between states, to be certified in a profession, one must meet the educational and/or experience requirements *and* pass a qualifying exam. **The American Institute of Certified Public Accountants (AICPA) Web site (http://www.thiswaytocpa.com) contains a wealth of information about becoming a CPA, career opportunities, and exam requirements.**

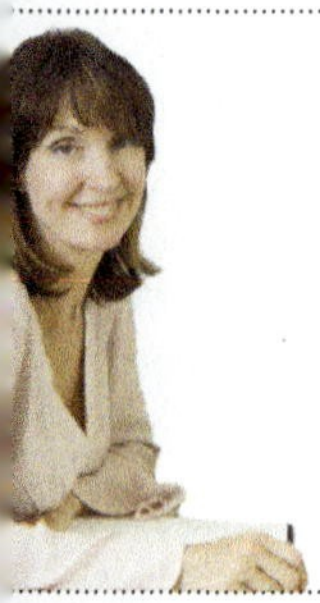

What if I want more information about becoming a CPA or CMA?

**Certified Management Accountants**, or **CMAs**, are certified professionals who specialize in accounting and financial management knowledge. Generally, CMAs work for a single company. **You can find information about becoming a CMA, how a CMA differs from a CPA, and why employers are recognizing the CMA certification on the Institute of Management Accountants (IMA) Web site (http://www.imanet.org).** It's worth spending the time and energy for accountants to get certified—certified accountants generally make 10–15% more than their noncertified colleagues when they enter the workforce.

**Certified Management Accountants (CMAs)**
Certified professionals who specialize in accounting and financial management knowledge. They typically work for a single company.

Studying accounting and becoming certified professionally can lead to a financially secure job. According to Robert Half's *2014 Salary Guide*, the top positions in demand that rely on accounting skills are controllers, financial analysts, tax accountants, auditors, cost accountants, and business systems analysts. How much do these types of accountants make? Exhibit 1-3 provides a snapshot of the earning potential for key positions.

**Exhibit 1-3** | **Comparison of Accounting Positions**

| Position | Job Description | Salary Range |
|---|---|---|
| **Controllers** | Compile financial statements, interact with auditors, and oversee regulatory reporting. | $89,000–$216,000 |
| **Financial analysts** | Review financial data and help to explain the story behind the numbers. | $41,250–$125,000 |
| **Business systems analysts** | Use accounting knowledge to create computer systems. | $44,250–$107,250 |
| **Tax accountants** | Help companies navigate tax laws. | $44,000–$190,750 |
| **Auditors** | Perform reviews of companies to ensure compliance to rules and regulations. | $44,500–$184,750 |
| **Cost accountants** | Typically work in a manufacturing business. Help analyze accounting data. | $43,000–$113,000 |
| **Paraprofessional/ Bookkeeper** | Record financial transactions and help prepare financial records. | $39,750–$59,250 |

Accountants generally work either in public, private, or governmental accounting. Public accounting involves services such as auditing and tax preparation. Well-known public accounting firms include Ernst & Young, Deloitte, PwC, and KPMG. Private accounting involves working for a single company such as Amazon.com, Walmart, or Dell. Other accountants work for the federal or state governments. Wherever accountants work, demand for their services is high. According to the U.S. Bureau of Labor Statistics, employment of accountants and auditors is expected to grow 13% from 2012–2022.

IFRS

Recently, the AICPA added a certification program in international accounting for those CPAs who want to specialize in global commerce.

## Try It!

Match the accounting terminology to the definitions.

1. Certified management accountants
2. Accounting
3. Managerial accounting
4. Certified public accountants
5. Financial accounting
6. Creditor

**a.** the information system that measures business activities, processes that information into reports, and communicates the results to decision makers

**b.** licensed professional accountants who serve the general public

**c.** any person or business to whom a business owes money

**d.** the field of accounting that focuses on providing information for internal decision makers

**e.** certified professionals who work for a single company

**f.** the field of accounting that focuses on providing information for external decision makers

**Check your answers online in MyAccountingLab or at http://www.pearsonhighered.com/Horngren.**

For more practice, see Short Exercise S1-1. MyAccountingLab

# WHAT ARE THE ORGANIZATIONS AND RULES THAT GOVERN ACCOUNTING?

**Learning Objective 2**

Describe the organizations and rules that govern accounting

**Financial Accounting Standards Board (FASB)**
The private organization that oversees the creation and governance of accounting standards in the United States.

**Securities and Exchange Commission (SEC)**
U.S. governmental agency that oversees the U.S. financial markets.

**Generally Accepted Accounting Principles (GAAP)**
Accounting guidelines, currently formulated by the *Financial Accounting Standards Board (FASB)*; the main U.S. accounting rule book.

**Economic Entity Assumption**
An organization that stands apart as a separate economic unit.

All professions have regulations. Let's look at the organizations and rules that govern the accounting profession.

## Governing Organizations

In the United States, the **Financial Accounting Standards Board (FASB)**, a privately funded organization, oversees the creation and governance of accounting standards. The FASB works with governmental regulatory agencies like the **Securities and Exchange Commission (SEC)**. The SEC is the U.S. governmental agency that oversees the U.S. financial markets. It also oversees those organizations that set standards (like the FASB). The FASB also works with congressionally created groups like the Public Company Accounting Oversight Board (PCAOB) and private groups like the AICPA, IMA, and International Accounting Standards Board (IASB).

## Generally Accepted Accounting Principles

The guidelines for accounting information are called **Generally Accepted Accounting Principles (GAAP)**. GAAP is the main U.S. accounting rule book and is currently created and governed by the FASB. In order to use and prepare financial statements, it's important that we understand GAAP. GAAP rests on a conceptual framework that identifies the objectives, characteristics, elements, and implementation of financial statements and creates the acceptable accounting practices. The primary objective of financial reporting is to provide information useful for making investment and lending decisions. To be useful, information must be relevant and have faithful representation.[1] Relevant information allows users of the information to make a decision. Information that is faithfully representative is complete, neutral, and free from error. These basic accounting assumptions and principles are part of the foundation for the financial reports that companies present.

## The Economic Entity Assumption

The most basic concept in accounting is that of the **economic entity assumption**. An economic (business) entity is an organization that stands apart as a separate economic unit. We draw boundaries around each entity to keep its affairs distinct from those of other entities. An entity refers to one business, separate from its owners.

A business can be organized as a sole proprietorship, partnership, corporation, or limited-liability company (LLC). Exhibit 1-4 summarizes the similarities and differences among the four types of business organizations.

### Distinguishing Characteristics and Organization of a Corporation

In this book, we spend most of our time studying accounting for corporations. There are several features that distinguish a corporation from other types of business organizations. Let's look at them now.

**Separate Legal Entity** A corporation is a business entity formed under state law. The state grants a charter (also called *articles of incorporation*), which is the document that gives

[1] This wording was changed from relevant and reliable by the *Statement of Financial Accounting Concepts No. 8.*

**Exhibit 1-4 | Business Organizations**

| | Sole Proprietorship | Partnership | Corporation | Limited-Liability Company (LLC) |
|---|---|---|---|---|
| **Definition** | A business with a single owner | A business with two or more owners and not organized as a corporation | A business organized under state law that is a separate legal entity | A company in which each member is only liable for his or her own actions |
| **Number of owners** | One (called the proprietor) | Two or more (called partners) | One or more (called stockholders) | One or more (called members or partners) |
| **Life of the organization** | Terminates at owner's choice or death | Terminates at a partner's choice or death | Indefinite | Indefinite |
| **Personal liability of the owner(s) for the business's debts** | Owner is personally liable | Partners are personally liable | Stockholders are not personally liable | Members are not personally liable |
| **Taxation** | Not separate taxable entities. The owner pays tax on the proprietorship's earnings. | Partnership is not taxed. Instead partners pay tax on their share of the earnings. | Separate taxable entity. Corporation pays tax. | LLC is not taxed. Instead members pay tax on their share of earnings. |
| **Type of business** | Small businesses | Professional organizations of physicians, attorneys, and accountants | Large multinational businesses | An alternative to the partnership |

the state's permission to form a corporation. This is called authorization because the state "authorizes" or approves the establishment of the corporate entity.

A corporation is a distinct entity from a legal perspective. It is an entity that exists apart from its owners, who are called the **stockholders** or *shareholders*. However, the corporation has many of the rights that a person has. For example, a corporation may buy, own, and sell property; enter into contracts; sue; and be sued. Items that the business owns (its assets) and those items that the business has to pay later (its liabilities) belong to the corporation and not to the individual stockholders.

The ownership interest of a corporation is divided into shares of stock. A person becomes a stockholder by purchasing the stock of the corporation. The corporate charter specifies how much stock the corporation is authorized to issue (sell) to the public. Due to this fact, it is usually easier for corporations to raise capital.

**Continuous Life and Transferability of Ownership** Stockholders may transfer stock as they wish—by selling or trading the stock to another person, giving the stock away, bequeathing it in a will, or disposing of the stock in any other way. Because corporations have continuous lives regardless of changes in the ownership of their stock, the transfer of the stock has no effect on the continuity of the corporation. Sole proprietorships and partnerships, in contrast, end when their ownership changes for any reason. A corporation's life is not dependent on a specific individual's ownership.

**No Mutual Agency** No mutual agency means that the stockholder of a corporation cannot commit the corporation to a contract unless that stockholder is acting in a different role, such as an officer in the business. Mutual agency of the owners is not present in a corporation as it is in a partnership.

**Sole Proprietorship**
A business with a single owner.

**Partnership**
A business with two or more owners and not organized as a corporation.

**Corporation**
A business organized under state law that is a separate legal entity.

**Limited-Liability Company (LLC)**
A company in which each member is only liable for his or her own actions.

**Stockholder**
A person who owns stock in a corporation.

**Limited Liability of Stockholders** A stockholder has limited liability for the corporation's debts. The most that stockholders can lose is the amount they originally paid for the stock. (Depending on state law, this limited liability would also apply to a limited-liability company member; however, conversely, sole proprietors and partners are personally liable for the debts of their businesses.)

The combination of limited liability and no mutual agency means that persons can invest unlimited amounts in a corporation with only the fear of losing whatever amount the individual has invested if the business fails. This attractive feature enables a corporation to raise more money than proprietorships and partnerships.

**Separation of Ownership and Management** Stockholders own the business, but a board of directors—elected by the stockholders—appoints corporate officers to manage the business. Thus, stockholders do not have to disrupt their personal affairs to manage the business.

This separation between stockholders (owners of the corporation) and management may create problems. Corporate officers may decide to run the business for their own benefit rather than for the benefit of the company. Stockholders may find it difficult to lodge an effective protest against management because of the distance between them and the top managers.

**Corporate Taxation** Corporations are separate taxable entities. They pay a variety of taxes not paid by sole proprietorships or partnerships. Depending on the state in which the organization incorporated and the state(s) in which the corporation operates, the taxes could include one or both of the following:

- Federal and state income taxes. Corporate earnings are subject to double taxation. First, corporations pay their own income tax on corporate income. Then, the stockholders pay personal income tax on the dividends that they receive from corporations. This is different from sole proprietorships and partnerships, which pay no business income tax. Instead, the tax falls solely on the individual owners.
- Annual franchise tax levied by the state. The franchise tax is paid to keep the corporation charter in force and enables the corporation to continue in business.

**Government Regulation** To protect persons who loan money to a corporation or who invest in its stock, states monitor the actions of corporations. Corporations are subjected to more governmental regulation than other forms of business, which is a disadvantage for corporations and can be expensive.

**Organization of a Corporation** As noted earlier, creation of a corporation begins when its organizers, called the incorporators, obtain a charter from the state. The charter includes the authorization for the corporation to issue a certain number of shares of stock, which represent the ownership in the corporation. The incorporators pay fees, sign the charter, and file the required documents with the state. Once the first share of stock is issued, the corporation comes into existence. The incorporators agree to a set of bylaws, which act as the constitution for governing the corporation. Bylaws are the rule book that guides the corporation.

The ultimate control of the corporation rests with the stockholders, who normally receive one vote for each share of stock they own. The stockholders elect the members of the board of directors, which sets policy for the corporation and appoints the officers. The board elects a chairperson, who usually is the most powerful person in the corporation. The board also designates the president, who as chief operating officer manages day-to-day operations. Most corporations also have vice presidents in charge of sales, operations, accounting and finance, and other key areas. Exhibit 1-5 shows the authority structure in a corporation.

**Exhibit 1-5 | Structure of a Corporation**

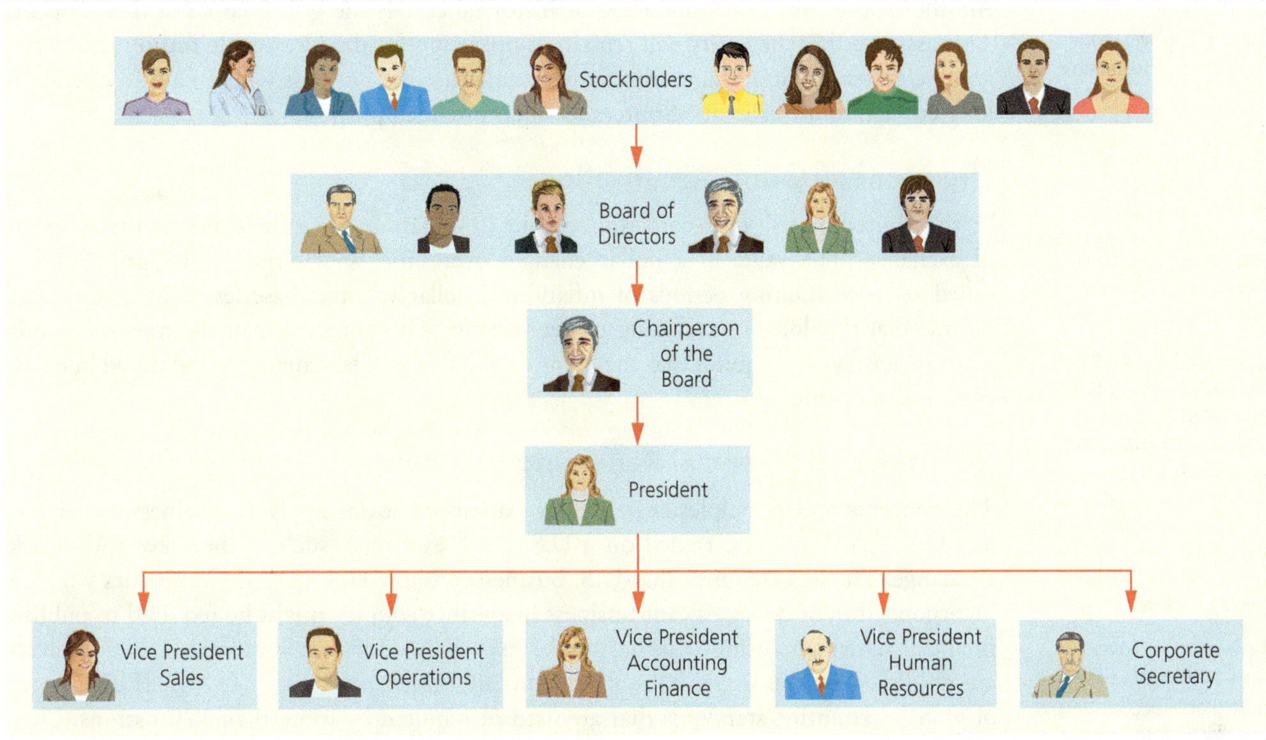


In order to demonstrate the economic entity assumption and several other concepts in this chapter, we will use a fictitious corporation—Smart Touch Learning—an e-learning business that specializes in providing online courses in accounting, economics, marketing, and management. This fictitious business will be used often throughout the book.

Assume Sheena Bright started the business by organizing it as a corporation. She contributed cash of $30,000 in exchange for stock of $30,000. Following the economic entity assumption, the $30,000 is recorded separately from Sheena's personal assets, such as her clothing and car. To mix the $30,000 of business cash with Sheena's personal assets would make it difficult to measure the success or failure of Smart Touch Learning. The economic entity assumption requires that each organization be separate from other businesses and from the owners.

**Cost Principle**
A principle that states that acquired assets and services should be recorded at their actual cost.

## The Cost Principle

The **cost principle** states that acquired assets and services should be recorded at their actual cost (also called *historical cost*). The cost principle means we record a transaction at the amount shown on the receipt—the actual amount paid. Even though the purchaser may believe the price is a bargain, the item is recorded at the price actually paid and not at the "expected" cost. For example, assume our fictitious company Smart Touch Learning purchased land for $20,000. The business might believe the land is instead worth $25,000. The cost principle requires that Smart Touch Learning record the land at $20,000, not $25,000.

The cost principle also holds that the accounting records should continue reporting the historical cost of an asset over its useful life. Why? Because cost is a reliable measure. Suppose Smart Touch Learning holds the land for six months. During that time land prices rise, and the land could be sold for $30,000. Should its accounting value—the figure on the books—be the actual cost of $20,000 or the current market value of $30,000? According to the cost principle, the accounting value of the land would remain at the actual cost of $20,000.

IFRS

Under international reporting standards, the company would be allowed to restate and report the land at $30,000. The ability to report some assets and liabilities at their current fair value each year under international standards is a significant difference from U.S. rules.

## The Going Concern Assumption

**Going Concern Assumption**
Assumes that the entity will remain in operation for the foreseeable future.

Another reason for measuring assets at historical cost is the **going concern assumption**. This assumes that the entity will remain in operation for the foreseeable future. Under the going concern assumption, accountants assume that the business will remain in operation long enough to use existing resources for their intended purpose.

## The Monetary Unit Assumption

**Monetary Unit Assumption**
The assumption that requires the items on the financial statements to be measured in terms of a monetary unit.

In the United States, we record transactions in dollars because the dollar is the medium of exchange. The value of a dollar changes over time, and a rise in the price level is called *inflation*. During periods of inflation, a dollar will purchase less. But accountants assume that the dollar's purchasing power is stable. This is the basis of the **monetary unit assumption**, which requires that the items on the financial statements be measured in terms of a monetary unit.

## International Financial Reporting Standards

**International Financial Reporting Standards (IFRS)**
A set of global accounting guidelines, formulated by the *International Accounting Standards Board (IASB).*

**International Accounting Standards Board (IASB)**
The private organization that oversees the creation and governance of *International Financial Reporting Standards (IFRS).*

The concepts and principles that we have discussed so far apply to businesses that follow U.S. GAAP and are traded on a U.S. stock exchange, such as the New York Stock Exchange. The SEC requires that U.S. businesses follow U.S. GAAP. Companies who are incorporated in or do significant business in another country might be required to publish financial statements using **International Financial Reporting Standards (IFRS)**, which are published by the **International Accounting Standards Board (IASB)**. IFRS is a set of global accounting standards that are used or required by more than 120 nations. They are generally less specific and based more on principle than U.S. GAAP. IFRS leaves more room for professional judgment. For example, unlike U.S. GAAP, IFRS allows periodic revaluation of certain assets and liabilities to restate them to market value, rather than keeping them at historical cost. At one point in time it was thought that the SEC would endorse IFRS. However, the SEC has backed away from this strategy and is currently considering whether a single set of global accounting standards is achievable.

## Ethics in Accounting and Business

Ethical considerations affect accounting. Investors and creditors need relevant and faithfully representative information about a company that they are investing in or lending money to. Companies want to be profitable and financially strong to attract investors and attempt to present their financial statements in a manner that portrays the business in the best possible way. Sometimes these two opposing viewpoints can cause conflicts of interest. For example, imagine a company that is facing a potential million-dollar lawsuit due to a defective product. The company might not want to share this information with investors because it would potentially hurt the business's profitability. On the other hand, investors would want to know about the pending lawsuit so that they could make an informed decision about investing in the business. To handle these conflicts of interest and to provide reliable information, the SEC requires publicly held companies to have their financial statements audited by independent accountants. An **audit** is an examination of a company's financial statements and records. The independent accountants then issue an opinion that states whether the financial statements give a fair picture of the company's financial situation.

**Audit**
An examination of a company's financial statements and records.

The vast majority of accountants do their jobs professionally and ethically, but we often don't hear about them. Unfortunately, only those who cheat make the headlines. In recent years, we have seen many accounting scandals.

In response to the Enron and WorldCom reporting scandals, the U.S. government took swift action. It passed the **Sarbanes-Oxley Act (SOX)**, intended to curb financial scandals. SOX requires companies to review internal control and take responsibility for the accuracy and completeness of their financial reports. In addition, SOX made it a criminal offense to falsify financial statements. The Sarbanes-Oxley Act also created a new watchdog agency, the Public Company Accounting Oversight Board (PCAOB), to monitor the work of independent accountants who audit public companies. More recent scandals, such as the Bernie Madoff scandal in which Mr. Madoff pleaded guilty to defrauding thousands of investors by filing falsified trading reports, have further undermined the public's faith in financial reporting. This may result in more legislation for future reporting.

**Sarbanes-Oxley Act (SOX)**
Requires companies to review internal control and take responsibility for the accuracy and completeness of their financial reports.

## Try It!

Match the accounting terminology to the definitions.

| | |
|---|---|
| 7. Cost principle | a. oversees the creation and governance of accounting standards in the United States |
| 8. GAAP | b. requires an organization to be a separate economic unit |
| 9. Faithful representation | c. oversees U.S. financial markets |
| 10. SEC | d. states that acquired assets and services should be recorded at their actual cost |
| 11. FASB | e. creates International Financial Reporting Standards |
| 12. Monetary unit assumption | f. the main U.S. accounting rule book |
| 13. Economic entity assumption | g. assumes that an entity will remain in operation for the foreseeable future |
| 14. Going concern assumption | h. assumes that items on the financial statements are recorded in a monetary unit |
| 15. IASB | i. requires information to be complete, neutral, and free from material error |

**Check your answers online in MyAccountingLab or at http://www.pearsonhighered.com/Horngren.**

For more practice, see Short Exercises S1-2 through S1-5. MyAccountingLab

## WHAT IS THE ACCOUNTING EQUATION?

**Learning Objective 3**
Describe the accounting equation, and define assets, liabilities, and equity

The basic tool of accounting is the **accounting equation**. It measures the resources of a business (what the business owns or has control of) and the claims to those resources (what the business owes to creditors and to the owners). The accounting equation is made up of three parts—assets, liabilities, and equity—and shows how these three parts are related. Assets appear on the left side of the equation, and the liabilities and equity appear on the right side.

**Accounting Equation**
The basic tool of accounting, measuring the resources of the business (what the business owns or has control of) and the claims to those resources (what the business owes to creditors and to the owners). Assets = Liabilities + Equity.

**Assets = Liabilities + Equity**

*Remember, the accounting equation is an equation—so the left side of the equation always equals the right side of the equation.*

**Example:** If a business has assets of $230,000 and liabilities of $120,000, its equity must be $110,000 ($230,000 − $120,000).

| **Assets** | = | **Liabilities** | + | **Equity** |
|---|---|---|---|---|
| $230,000 | = | $120,000 | + | ? |
| $230,000 | = | $120,000 | + | $110,000 |

## Assets

**Assets**
Economic resources that are expected to benefit the business in the future. Something the business owns or has control of.

An **asset** is an economic resource that is expected to benefit the business in the future. Assets are something of value that the business owns or has control of. Cash, merchandise inventory, furniture, and land are examples of assets.

## Liabilities

**Liabilities**
Debts that are owed to *creditors*.

Claims to those assets come from two sources: liabilities and equity. **Liabilities** are debts that are owed to creditors. Liabilities are something the business owes and represent the creditors' claims on the business's assets. For example, a creditor who has loaned money to a business has a claim to some of the business's assets until the business pays the debt. Many liabilities have the word *payable* in their titles. Examples include accounts payable, notes payable, and salaries payable.

## Equity

**Equity**
The owners' claims to the assets of the business.

**Contributed Capital**
Owner contributions to a corporation.

**Revenues**
Amounts earned from delivering goods or services to customers.

**Expenses**
The cost of selling goods or services.

**Dividend**
A distribution of a corporation's earnings to stockholders.

**Common Stock**
Represents the basic ownership of a corporation.

**Retained Earnings**
Equity earned by profitable operations of a corporation that is not distributed to stockholders.

The owners of a corporation are referred to as stockholders (also called *shareholders*). The owners' claims to the assets of the business are called **equity** (also called *stockholders' equity*). Equity represents the amount of assets that are left over after the company has paid its liabilities. It is the company's net worth.

Equity increases with owner contributions and revenues. Owner contributions to a corporation are referred to as **contributed capital**. A stockholder can contribute cash or other assets (such as equipment) to the business and receive capital. Equity is also increased by revenues. **Revenues** are earnings that result from delivering goods or services to customers. Examples of revenues are sales revenue, service revenue, and rent revenue.

Equity decreases with expenses and distributions to owners. **Expenses** are the cost of selling goods or services. Expenses are the opposite of revenues and, therefore, decrease equity. Examples of expenses are rent expense, salaries expense, advertising expense, and utilities expense.

A profitable corporation may make distributions to stockholders in the form of **dividends**. Dividends can be paid in the form of cash, stock, or other property. Dividends are not expenses. A corporation may or may not make dividend payments to the stockholders. Dividends are the opposite of owner contributions and, therefore, decrease equity.

Equity consists of two main components: contributed capital and retained earnings. Contributed capital (also called *paid-in capital*) is the amount invested in the corporation by its owners, the stockholders. The basic element of contributed capital is stock, which the corporation issues to the stockholders as evidence of their ownership. **Common stock** represents the basic ownership of every corporation.

**Retained earnings** is the equity earned by profitable operations that is not distributed to stockholders. There are three types of events that affect retained earnings: dividends, revenues, and expenses. Dividends represent decreases in retained earnings through the distribution of cash, stock, or other property to stockholders. Revenues are increases in retained earnings from delivering goods or services to customers. Revenues are earnings. For example, if Smart Touch Learning provided e-learning services and earned $5,500 of revenue, the business's retained earnings increased by $5,500. Expenses are the decreases in retained earnings that result from operations. For example, Smart Touch Learning paid salaries of $1,200 to its employees, and that is an expense that decreases retained earnings.

The accounting equation can now be expanded to show the components of equity.

**ASSETS** = **LIABILITIES +** **EQUITY**

**Contributed Capital** + **Retained Earnings**

Common Stock − Dividends + Revenues − Expenses

**Net Income**
The result of operations that occurs when total revenues are greater than total expenses.

**Net Loss**
The result of operations that occurs when total expenses are greater than total revenues.

Businesses strive for net income. When revenues are greater than expenses, the result of operations is a profit or **net income**. When expenses are greater than revenues, the result is a **net loss**.

**Try It!**

**16.** Using the expanded accounting equation, solve for the missing amount.

| | |
|---|---|
| Assets | $ 71,288 |
| Liabilities | 2,260 |
| Common Stock | ? |
| Dividends | 14,420 |
| Revenues | 53,085 |
| Expenses | 28,675 |

**Check your answer online in MyAccountingLab or at http://www.pearsonhighered.com/Horngren.**

For more practice, see Short Exercises S1-6 through S1-8. MyAccountingLab

## HOW DO YOU ANALYZE A TRANSACTION?

**Learning Objective 4**
Use the accounting equation to analyze transactions

Accounting is based on actual transactions. A **transaction** is any event that affects the financial position of the business *and* can be measured with faithful representation. Transactions affect what the company has or owes or its net worth. Many events affect a company, including economic booms and recessions. Accountants, however, do not record the effects of those events. An accountant records only those events that have dollar amounts that can be measured reliably, such as the purchase of a building, a sale of merchandise, and the payment of rent.

**Transaction**
An event that affects the financial position of the business and can be measured with faithful representation

### Transaction Analysis for Smart Touch Learning

To illustrate accounting for a business, we'll use Smart Touch Learning, the business introduced earlier. We'll account for the transactions of Smart Touch Learning during November 2016 and show how each transaction affects the accounting equation.

### Transaction 1—Owner Contribution

Assume Sheena Bright contributes $30,000 cash to Smart Touch Learning, a corporation, in exchange for stock. The e-learning business receives $30,000 cash and issues common stock to Sheena Bright. The effect of this transaction on the accounting equation of the business is as follows:

| | **ASSETS** | | **LIABILITIES** + | **EQUITY** |
|---|---|---|---|---|
| | | | | **Contributed Capital** |
| | Cash | = | | Common Stock |
| (1) | +30,000 | | | +30,000 |

Let's take a close look at the transaction above following these steps:

**Step 1: Identify the accounts and the account type.** Each transaction must have at least two accounts but could have more. *The two accounts involved are Cash (Asset) and Common Stock (Equity).*

**Step 2: Decide if each account increases or decreases.** Remember to always view this from the *business's* perspective, not from the stockholders' or customers' perspective. *Cash increases.* The business has more cash than it had before. *Common Stock increases.* The business received a $30,000 contribution and issued stock.

**Step 3: Determine if the accounting equation is in balance.** For each transaction, the amount on the left side of the equation must equal the amount on the right side. *$30,000 = $30,000*

### Transaction 2—Purchase of Land for Cash

The business purchases land for an office location, paying cash of $20,000. This transaction affects the accounting equation of Smart Touch Learning as follows:

| | **ASSETS** | | | | **LIABILITIES** | + | **EQUITY** |
|---|---|---|---|---|---|---|---|
| | | | | | | | **Contributed Capital** |
| | Cash | + | Land | = | | + | Common Stock |
| Bal. | $30,000 | | | | | | $30,000 |
| (2) | −20,000 | | +20,000 | | | | |
| Bal. | $10,000 | + | $20,000 | | | | $30,000 |

Let's review the transaction using the steps we learned:

**Step 1: Identify the accounts and the account type.** *The two accounts involved are Cash (Asset) and Land (Asset).*

**Step 2: Decide if each account increases or decreases.** *Cash decreases.* The business paid cash. *Land increases.* The business now has land.

**Step 3: Determine if the accounting equation is in balance.** *$10,000 + $20,000 = $30,000*

### Transaction 3—Purchase of Office Supplies on Account

Smart Touch Learning buys office supplies on account (credit), agreeing to pay $500 within 30 days. This transaction increases both the assets and the liabilities of the business as follows:

| | ASSETS | | | | | | LIABILITIES | + | EQUITY |
|---|---|---|---|---|---|---|---|---|---|
| | | | | | | | | | Contributed Capital |
| | Cash | + | Office Supplies | + | Land | = | Accounts Payable | + | Common Stock |
| Bal. | $10,000 | | | + | $20,000 | | | | $30,000 |
| (3) | | | +500 | | | | +500 | | |
| Bal. | $10,000 | + | $500 | + | $20,000 | | $500 | + | $30,000 |

**Step 1: Identify the accounts and the account type.** *The two accounts involved are Office Supplies (Asset) and Accounts Payable (Liability).* Office Supplies is an asset, not an expense, because the supplies aren't used up yet but will be in the future. The liability created by purchasing "on account" is an **accounts payable**, which is a short-term liability that will be paid in the future. A payable is always a liability.

**Accounts Payable**
A short-term liability that will be paid in the future.

**Step 2: Decide if each account increases or decreases.** *Office Supplies increases.* The business now has more office supplies than it had before. *Accounts Payable increases.* The business now owes more debt than it did before.

**Step 3: Determine if the accounting equation is in balance.** *$10,000 + $500 + $20,000 = $500 + $30,000*

> Notice how the steps help when analyzing transactions. It's important that, as you are learning, you use the steps to complete the transactions. Moving forward, try writing the steps out yourself before looking at the transaction analysis.

## Transaction 4—Earning of Service Revenue for Cash

Smart Touch Learning earns service revenue by providing training services for clients. The business earns $5,500 of revenue and collects this amount in cash. The effect on the accounting equation is an increase in Cash and an increase in Service Revenue as follows:

| | ASSETS | | | | | | LIABILITIES | + | EQUITY | | |
|---|---|---|---|---|---|---|---|---|---|---|---|
| | | | | | | | | | Contributed Capital | + | Retained Earnings |
| | Cash | + | Office Supplies | + | Land | = | Accounts Payable | + | Common Stock | + | Service Revenue |
| Bal. | $10,000 | + | $500 | + | $20,000 | | $500 | + | $30,000 | | |
| (4) | +5,500 | | | | | | | | | | +5,500 |
| Bal. | $15,500 | + | $500 | + | $20,000 | | $500 | + | $30,000 | + | $5,500 |

A revenue transaction grows the business, as shown by the increases in assets and equity.

## Transaction 5—Earning of Service Revenue on Account

Smart Touch Learning performs a service for clients who do not pay immediately. The business receives the clients' promise to pay $3,000 within one month. This promise is an asset, an **accounts receivable**, because the business expects to collect the cash in the future. In accounting, we say that Smart Touch Learning performed this service *on account*. It is in performing the service (doing the work), not collecting the cash, that the company *earns*

**Accounts Receivable**
The right to receive cash in the future from customers for goods sold or for services performed.

the revenue. As in Transaction 4, increasing revenue increases equity. Smart Touch Learning records the earning of $3,000 of revenue on account as follows:

| | ASSETS | | | | | | | | LIABILITIES + | | EQUITY | | |
|---|---|---|---|---|---|---|---|---|---|---|---|---|---|
| | | | | | | | | | | | Contributed Capital | + | Retained Earnings |
| | Cash | + | Accounts Receivable | + | Office Supplies | + | Land | = | Accounts Payable | + | Common Stock | + | Service Revenue |
| Bal. | $15,500 | | | + | $500 | + | $20,000 | | $500 | + | $30,000 | + | $5,500 |
| (5) | | | +3,000 | | | | | | | | | | +3,000 |
| Bal. | $15,500 | + | $3,000 | + | $500 | + | $20,000 | | $500 | + | $30,000 | + | $8,500 |

> *The term "on account" can be used to represent either Accounts Receivable or Accounts Payable. If the business will be receiving cash in the future, the company will record an Accounts Receivable. If the business will be paying cash in the future, the company will record an Accounts Payable.*

### Transaction 6—Payment of Expenses with Cash

The business pays $3,200 in cash expenses: $2,000 for office rent and $1,200 for employee salaries. The effects on the accounting equation are as follows:

| | ASSETS | | | | | | | | LIABILITIES + | | EQUITY | | | | | | |
|---|---|---|---|---|---|---|---|---|---|---|---|---|---|---|---|---|---|
| | | | | | | | | | | | Contributed Capital | + | Retained Earnings | | | | |
| | Cash | + | Accounts Receivable | + | Office Supplies | + | Land | = | Accounts Payable | + | Common Stock | + | Service Revenue | − | Rent Expense | − | Salaries Expense |
| Bal. | $15,500 | + | $3,000 | + | $500 | + | $20,000 | | $500 | + | $30,000 | + | $8,500 | | | | |
| (6) | −3,200 | | | | | | | | | | | | | | −2,000 | | −1,200 |
| Bal. | $12,300 | + | $3,000 | + | $500 | + | $20,000 | | $500 | + | $30,000 | + | $8,500 | − | $2,000 | − | $1,200 |

Expenses have the opposite effect of revenues. Expenses shrink the business, as shown by the decreased balances of assets and equity. Each expense is recorded separately. We record the cash payment in a single amount for the sum of the expenses: $3,200 ($2,000 + $1,200). Notice that the accounting equation remains in balance ($12,300 + $3,000 + $500 + $20,000 = $500 + $30,000 + $8,500 − $2,000 − $1,200).

### Transaction 7—Payment on Account (Accounts Payable)

The business pays $300 to the store from which it purchased office supplies in Transaction 3. In accounting, we say that the business pays $300 *on account*. The effect on the accounting equation is a decrease in Cash and a decrease in Accounts Payable as shown here:

| | ASSETS | | | | | | | | LIABILITIES + | | EQUITY | | | | | | |
|---|---|---|---|---|---|---|---|---|---|---|---|---|---|---|---|---|---|
| | | | | | | | | | | | Contributed Capital | + | Retained Earnings | | | | |
| | Cash | + | Accounts Receivable | + | Office Supplies | + | Land | = | Accounts Payable | + | Common Stock | + | Service Revenue | − | Rent Expense | − | Salaries Expense |
| Bal. | $12,300 | + | $3,000 | + | $500 | + | $20,000 | | $500 | + | $30,000 | + | $8,500 | − | $2,000 | − | $1,200 |
| (7) | −300 | | | | | | | | −300 | | | | | | | | |
| Bal. | $12,000 | + | $3,000 | + | $500 | + | $20,000 | | $200 | + | $30,000 | + | $8,500 | − | $2,000 | − | $1,200 |

The payment of cash on account has no effect on the amount of Office Supplies (Asset). Smart Touch Learning has not increased the amount of its office supplies; instead, it is paying off a liability (Accounts Payable decreased $300) with cash (Cash decreased $300). **To record an increase to Office Supplies, in this transaction, would be accounting for the purchase of office supplies twice.** We have already recorded the purchase of office supplies in Transaction 3; in this transaction, we are now ready to record only the payment on account.

Why didn't we record an increase to Office Supplies? We are making a payment for the supplies; wouldn't we increase Office Supplies and decrease Cash?

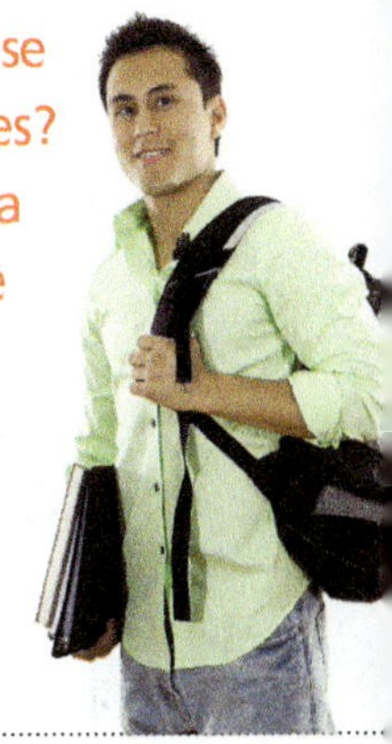

### Transaction 8—Collection on Account (Accounts Receivable)

In Transaction 5, the business performed services for clients on account. Smart Touch Learning now collects $2,000 from a client. We say that Smart Touch Learning collects the cash *on account*. The business will record an increase in the asset Cash. Should it also record an increase in Service Revenue? No, because the business already recorded the revenue when it earned the revenue in Transaction 5. The phrase "collect cash on account" means to record an increase in Cash and a decrease in Accounts Receivable. Accounts Receivable is decreased because the $2,000 that the business was to collect at some point in the future is being collected today. The effect on the accounting equation is as follows:

| | ASSETS | | | | | | | | LIABILITIES + | | EQUITY | | | | | | | |
|---|---|---|---|---|---|---|---|---|---|---|---|---|---|---|---|---|---|---|
| | | | | | | | | | | | Contributed Capital | + | Retained Earnings | | | | | |
| | Cash | + | Accounts Receivable | + | Office Supplies | + | Land | = | Accounts Payable | + | Common Stock | + | Service Revenue | − | Rent Expense | − | Salaries Expense |
| Bal. | $12,000 | + | $3,000 | + | $500 | + | $20,000 | | $200 | + | $30,000 | + | $8,500 | − | $2,000 | − | $1,200 |
| (8) | +2,000 | | −2,000 | | | | | | | | | | | | | | |
| Bal. | $14,000 | + | $1,000 | + | $500 | + | $20,000 | | $200 | + | $30,000 | + | $8,500 | − | $2,000 | − | $1,200 |

This transaction is recorded as an increase in one asset (Cash) and a decrease in another asset (Accounts Receivable). Is the accounting equation still in balance? Yes. **As long as you record an increase and decrease of the same amount on one side of the accounting equation, the accounting equation remains in balance.** In other words, total assets, liabilities, and equity are all unchanged from the preceding total. Why? Because Smart Touch Learning exchanged one asset (Cash) for another (Accounts Receivable), causing a zero effect on the total amount of assets in the accounting equation (+$2,000 − $2,000 = $0).

Don't I have to put an amount on the left side of the accounting equation and an amount on the right side of the accounting equation for the equation to balance?

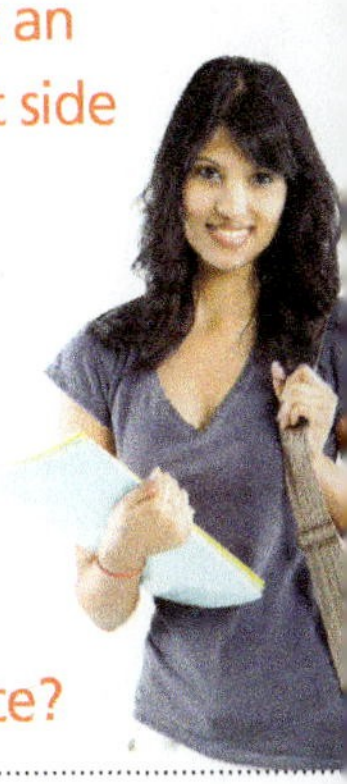

### Transaction 9—Payment of Cash Dividend

Smart Touch Learning distributes a $5,000 cash dividend to the stockholder, Sheena Bright. The effect on the accounting equation is:

| | ASSETS | | | | | | | | LIABILITIES + | | EQUITY | | | | | | | | | |
|---|---|---|---|---|---|---|---|---|---|---|---|---|---|---|---|---|---|---|---|---|
| | | | | | | | | | | | Contributed Capital | + | Retained Earnings | | | | | | | |
| | Cash | + | Accounts Receivable | + | Office Supplies | + | Land | = | Accounts Payable | + | Common Stock | − | Dividends | + | Service Revenue | − | Rent Expense | − | Salaries Expense |
| Bal. | $14,000 | + | $1,000 | + | $500 | + | $20,000 | | $200 | + | $30,000 | | | + | $8,500 | − | $2,000 | − | $1,200 |
| (9) | −5,000 | | | | | | | | | | | | −5,000 | | | | | | |
| Bal. | $ 9,000 | + | $1,000 | + | $500 | + | $20,000 | | $200 | + | $30,000 | − | $5,000 | + | $8,500 | − | $2,000 | − | $1,200 |

The dividend decreases the business's cash and equity. *Dividends do not represent an expense because they are not related to the earning of revenue. Therefore, dividends do not affect the business's net income or net loss.*

A summary of all nine transactions for Smart Touch Learning is presented in Exhibit 1-6.

**Exhibit 1-6** | **Analysis of Transactions, Smart Touch Learning**

1. Smart Touch Learning received $30,000 cash and issued common stock to Sheena Bright, stockholder.
2. Paid $20,000 cash for land.
3. Bought $500 of office supplies on account.
4. Received $5,500 cash from clients for service revenue earned.
5. Performed services for clients on account, $3,000.
6. Paid cash expenses: office rent, $2,000; employee salaries, $1,200.
7. Paid $300 on the accounts payable created in Transaction 3.
8. Collected $2,000 on the accounts receivable created in Transaction 5.
9. Paid cash dividends of $5,000 to stockholder, Sheena Bright.

| | ASSETS | | | | = | LIABILITIES + | EQUITY | | | | |
|---|---|---|---|---|---|---|---|---|---|---|---|
| | | | | | | | Contributed Capital + | Retained Earnings | | | |
| | Cash + | Accounts Receivable + | Office Supplies + | Land | | Accounts Payable + | Common Stock − | Dividends + | Service Revenue − | Rent Expense − | Salaries Expense |
| (1) | +30,000 | | | | | | +30,000 | | | | |
| (2) | −20,000 | | | +20,000 | | | | | | | |
| Bal. | $10,000 | | | $20,000 | | | $30,000 | | | | |
| (3) | | | +500 | | | +500 | | | | | |
| Bal. | $10,000 | | $500 | $20,000 | | $500 | $30,000 | | | | |
| (4) | +5,500 | | | | | | | | +5,500 | | |
| Bal. | $15,500 | | $500 | $20,000 | | $500 | $30,000 | | $5,500 | | |
| (5) | | +3,000 | | | | | | | +3,000 | | |
| Bal. | $15,500 | $3,000 | $500 | $20,000 | | $500 | $30,000 | | $8,500 | | |
| (6) | −3,200 | | | | | | | | | −2,000 | −1,200 |
| Bal. | $12,300 | $3,000 | $500 | $20,000 | | $500 | $30,000 | | $8,500 | $2,000 | $1,200 |
| (7) | −300 | | | | | −300 | | | | | |
| Bal. | $12,000 | $3,000 | $500 | $20,000 | | $200 | $30,000 | | $8,500 | $2,000 | $1,200 |
| (8) | +2,000 | −2,000 | | | | | | | | | |
| Bal. | $14,000 | $1,000 | $500 | $20,000 | | $200 | $30,000 | | $8,500 | $2,000 | $1,200 |
| (9) | −5,000 | | | | | | | −5,000 | | | |
| Bal. | $ 9,000 | $1,000 | $500 | $20,000 | | $200 | $30,000 | $5,000 | $8,500 | $2,000 | $1,200 |
| | $30,500 | | | | | $30,500 | | | | | |

## Try It!

17. Using the information provided, analyze the effects of Lawlor Lawn Service's transactions on the accounting equation.

| | |
|---|---|
| May 1 | Received $1,700 and issued common stock. |
| May 3 | Purchased a mower on account, $1,440. |
| May 5 | Performed lawn services for client on account, $200. |
| May 17 | Paid $60 cash for gas used in mower. |
| May 28 | Paid cash dividends of $300. |

**Check your answers online in MyAccountingLab or at http://www.pearsonhighered.com/Horngren.**

For more practice, see Short Exercises S1-9 and S1-10. MyAccountingLab

## HOW DO YOU PREPARE FINANCIAL STATEMENTS?

**Learning Objective 5**
Prepare financial statements

We have now recorded Smart Touch Learning's transactions, and they are summarized in Exhibit 1-6. Notice how total assets equal total liabilities plus equity ($30,500 = $30,500).

But a basic question remains: How will people actually use this information? The information in Exhibit 1-6 does not tell a lender whether Smart Touch Learning can pay off a loan. The exhibit does not tell whether the business is profitable.

To address these important questions, we need financial statements. **Financial statements** are business documents that are used to communicate information needed to make business decisions. There are four financial statements prepared. These statements are prepared in the order listed in Exhibit 1-7.

**Financial Statements**
Business documents that are used to communicate information needed to make business decisions.

**Exhibit 1-7 | Financial Statements**

| Financial Statement | Information Provided and Purpose | How Is It Prepared? |
|---|---|---|
| **Income Statement** | Provides information about profitability for a particular period for the company. | Revenues − Expenses = Net Income or Net Loss |
| **Statement of Retained Earnings** | Informs users about how much of the earnings were kept and reinvested in the company. | Retained Earnings, Beginning<br>+ Net income or − Net loss for the period<br>− Dividends for the period<br>= Retained Earnings, Ending |
| **Balance Sheet** | Provides valuable information to financial statement users about economic resources the company has (assets) as well as debts the company owes (liabilities). Allows decision makers to determine their opinion about the financial position of the company. | Assets = Liabilities + Stockholders' Equity |
| **Statement of Cash Flows** | Reports on a business's cash receipts and cash payments for a period of time. | Cash flows from operating activities<br>Cash flows from investing activities<br>Cash flows from financing activities |

### Income Statement

Let's start by reviewing the **income statement**. The income statement (also called the *statement of earnings*) presents a summary of a business entity's revenues and expenses for a period of time, such as a month, quarter, or year. The income statement tells us whether the business enjoyed net income or suffered a net loss. Remember:

**Income Statement**
Reports the *net income* or *net loss* of the business for a specific period.

- Net income means total revenues are greater than total expenses.
- Net loss means total expenses are greater than total revenues.

It's important to remember that the only two types of accounts that are reported on the income statement are revenues and expenses. Exhibit 1-8 (on the next page) shows the income statement for Smart Touch Learning. Every income statement contains similar information.

The header includes the name of the business, the title of the statement, and the time period. An income statement always represents a period of time, for example, a month or year.

**Exhibit 1-8 | Income Statement**

| SMART TOUCH LEARNING<br>Income Statement<br>Month Ended November 30, 2016 | | |
|---|---|---|
| Revenues: | | |
| Service Revenue | | $ 8,500 |
| Expenses: | | |
| Rent Expense | $ 2,000 | |
| Salaries Expense | 1,200 | |
| Total Expenses | | 3,200 |
| Net Income | | **$ 5,300** |

The revenue accounts are always listed first and then subtotaled if necessary.

Net income is calculated as total revenues minus total expenses.

Each expense account is listed separately from largest to smallest and then subtotaled if necessary.

## Statement of Retained Earnings

**Statement of Retained Earnings** Reports how the company's retained earnings balance changed from the beginning to the end of the period.

The next statement prepared is the **statement of retained earnings**. The statement of retained earnings shows the changes in retained earnings for a business entity during a time period, such as a month, quarter, or year.

Review the statement of retained earnings for Smart Touch Learning in Exhibit 1-9. Notice that the net income for the month is the net income that was calculated on the income statement. This is the main reason why the income statement is prepared before

The header includes the name of the business, the title of the statement, and the time period. A statement of retained earnings always represents a period of time.

The beginning retained earnings is $0 because Smart Touch Learning began this month; therefore, it had no beginning retained earnings. The beginning retained earnings will always be the ending retained earnings from the previous time period.

**Exhibit 1-9 | Statement of Retained Earnings**

| SMART TOUCH LEARNING<br>Statement of Retained Earnings<br>Month Ended November 30, 2016 | |
|---|---|
| Retained Earnings, November 1, 2016 | $ 0 |
| Net income for the month | 5,300 |
| | 5,300 |
| Dividends | (5,000) |
| Retained Earnings, November 30, 2016 | **$ 300** |

Net income is transferred from the income statement.

The dividends are subtracted from retained earnings. If there had been a net loss rather than a net income, this would also be subtracted.

the statement of retained earnings. The net income must first be calculated on the income statement and then carried to the statement of retained earnings.

**Balance Sheet**
Reports on the assets, liabilities, and stockholders' equity of the business as of a specific date.

## Balance Sheet

The **balance sheet** (also called the *statement of financial position*) lists a business entity's assets, liabilities, and stockholders' equity as of a specific date, usually the end of a month, quarter, or year. **The balance sheet is a snapshot of the entity. An investor or creditor can quickly assess the overall health of a business by viewing the balance sheet.**

Review the balance sheet for Smart Touch Learning in Exhibit 1-10. Every balance sheet is prepared in a similar manner.

What does the balance sheet tell an investor or creditor?

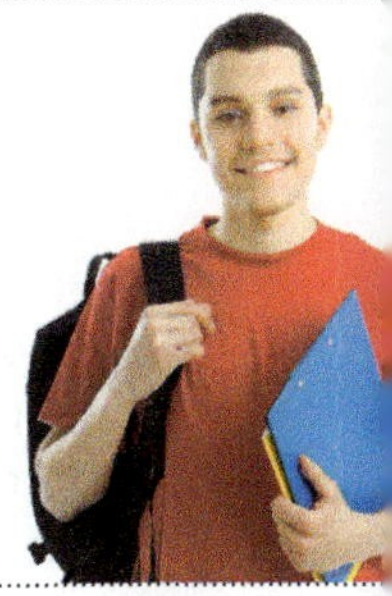

**Exhibit 1-10 | Balance Sheet**

The heading again shows the name of the business and the title of the financial statement. Notice that the date is different. The balance sheet shows the date as a specific date, not a period of time.

Liabilities are listed separately and then totaled. Liabilities that are to be paid first are listed first.

**SMART TOUCH LEARNING**
Balance Sheet
November 30, 2016

| Assets | | Liabilities | |
|---|---|---|---|
| Cash | $ 9,000 | Accounts Payable | $ 200 |
| Accounts Receivable | 1,000 | | |
| Office Supplies | 500 | **Stockholders' Equity** | |
| Land | 20,000 | Common Stock | 30,000 |
| | | Retained Earnings | 300 |
| | | Total Stockholders' Equity | 30,300 |
| Total Assets | **$ 30,500** | Total Liabilities and Stockholders' Equity | **$ 30,500** |

Each asset account is listed separately and then totaled. Cash is always listed first.

The balance sheet must always balance. Assets = Liabilities + Stockholders' Equity

Retained Earnings is taken directly from the statement of retained earnings.

*When you are preparing the financial statements, start by identifying which account goes on which statement. Each account will only go on one statement, except for Retained Earnings and Cash. For example, Service Revenue is only reported on the income statement. Liabilities, such as Accounts Payable, are only reported on the balance sheet. Cash and Retained Earnings appear on two statements. Cash is reported on the balance sheet and statement of cash flows, and Retained Earnings is reported on the statement of retained earnings and balance sheet.*

## ETHICS

### What constitutes manipulating financial statements?

The board of directors of Xiaping Trading Company is meeting to discuss the past year's results before releasing financial statements to the bank. Wai Lee, the company's sole stockholder, comments, "This has not been a good year! Revenue is down, and expenses are way up. If we are not careful, we will report a loss for the third year in a row. I can temporarily transfer some land that I own into the company's name, and that will beef up our balance sheet. Brent, as accountant, can you shave $500,000 from expenses? Then we can probably get the bank loan that we need." What should Brent do? What would you do if you were Brent?

### Solution

Brent should remind Wai Lee that the intent of the financial statements is to tell the truth about the company's performance and financial position. If Wai Lee does not intend to leave the land in the business, then she should not transfer it to the business for the sole intent of increasing the assets and equity of the business.

It is possible that Brent could "shave expenses" legally, if it meant reducing the amount of expenses that the business had. But if Wai Lee meant that Brent should reclassify expenses or delay the recognition of expenses in an effort to boost net income, then this would be false and dishonest.

**Statement of Cash Flows**
Reports on a business's cash receipts and cash payments for a specific period.

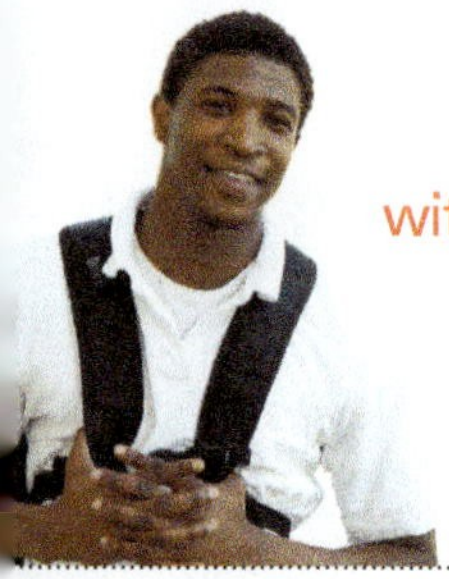

Would the purchase of land with a mortgage be reported on the statement of cash flows?

## Statement of Cash Flows

The **statement of cash flows** reports the cash coming in (positive amounts) and the cash going out (negative amounts) during a period. It only reports transactions that involve cash because it reports the net increase or decrease in *cash* during the period and the ending *cash* balance. **If a transaction does not involve cash, such as the purchase of land with a mortgage, it will not be reported on the statement of cash flows.**

The statement of cash flows is divided into three distinct sections: operating, investing, and financing. *Operating activities* involve cash receipts for services and cash payments for expenses. *Investing activities* include the purchase and sale of land and equipment for cash. The third section, *financing activities*, includes cash contributions by stockholders and cash dividends paid to the stockholders.

Take a look at the statement of cash flows for Smart Touch Learning (Exhibit 1-11). Notice the important items that every statement of cash flows contains.

**Exhibit 1-11 | Statement of Cash Flows**

| SMART TOUCH LEARNING<br>Statement of Cash Flows<br>Month Ended November 30, 2016 | | |
|---|---|---|
| Cash flows from operating activities: | | |
| Receipts: | | |
| Collections from customers | | $ 7,500 |
| Payments: | | |
| For rent | $ (2,000) | |
| For salaries | (1,200) | |
| For office supplies | (300) | (3,500) |
| Net cash provided by operating activities | | 4,000 |
| Cash flows from investing activities: | | |
| Acquisition of land | (20,000) | |
| Net cash used by investing activities | | (20,000) |
| Cash flows from financing activities: | | |
| Issued common stock | 30,000 | |
| Payment of cash dividends | (5,000) | |
| Net cash provided by financing activities | | 25,000 |
| Net increase in cash | | 9,000 |
| Cash balance, November 1, 2016 | | 0 |
| Cash balance, November 30, 2016 | | **$ 9,000** |

The header includes the name of the business, the title of the statement, and the time period. A statement of cash flows always represents a period of time.

Each dollar amount is calculated by evaluating the cash column on Exhibit 1-6. For example, collections from customers is calculated by adding the cash received from customers in Transaction 4 ($5,500) plus Transaction 8 ($2,000).

Operating activities involve cash receipts for services provided and cash payments for expenses paid.

Investing activities include the purchase and sale of land and equipment for cash.

Financing activities include issuance of stock to stockholders and payment of cash dividends.

The ending cash balance must match the cash balance on the balance sheet.

## Try It!

**18.** Using the following information, complete the income statement, statement of retained earnings, and balance sheet for DR Painting for the month of March 2016. The business began operations on March 1, 2016.

| | | | |
|---|---|---|---|
| Accounts Receivable | $ 1,400 | Salaries Expense | 800 |
| Accounts Payable | 1,000 | Service Revenue | 7,000 |
| Cash | 22,300 | Office Supplies | 1,800 |
| Stock issued during March | 40,000 | Truck | 20,000 |
| Dividends paid during March | 1,500 | Utilities Expense | 200 |

**Check your answers online in MyAccountingLab or at http://www.pearsonhighered.com/Horngren.**

For more practice, see Short Exercises S1-11 through S1-15. MyAccountingLab

# HOW DO YOU USE FINANCIAL STATEMENTS TO EVALUATE BUSINESS PERFORMANCE?

**Learning Objective 6**
Use financial statements and return on assets (ROA) to evaluate business performance

Each of the financial statements provides different information about the company to the users of the financial statements. Review Exhibit 1-7 for the information provided and the purpose of each financial statement.

## Green Mountain Coffee Roasters, Inc.

In this chapter, we have reviewed the transactions and financial statements of Smart Touch Learning, a fictitious company. Now it's time to apply what we have learned to a real-world company. In each chapter, we will review the financial statements of **Green Mountain Coffee Roasters, Inc.** You will learn how to analyze its financial statements and apply the concepts presented in the chapter.

Take a moment to review the 2013 financial statements for Green Mountain in Appendix A, located at the end of your book, or online at **http://investor.gmcr.com.** Let's start by identifying the financial statements that we've discussed in this chapter. The income statement is presented on page A-5 of the Annual Report and is called the Consolidated Statements of Operations. Notice that the income statement calculates net income (revenue minus expenses). Green Mountain's net income for the year ending September 28, 2013, was $483,232,000.

Next the balance sheet is presented on page A-4 of the Annual Report. Can you find assets, liabilities, and equity? As we have learned in this chapter, Green Mountain's assets of $3,761,548,000 are equal to its liabilities and equity, $3,761,548,000.

**Return on Assets (ROA)**
Measures how profitably a company uses its assets. Net income / Average total assets.

## Return on Assets (ROA)

One of the many tools that users of financial statements can use to determine how well a company is performing is the company's **return on assets (ROA)**. Return on assets measures

## DECISIONS

### How can individuals make decisions about investing in the stock market?

Lori Cummings just inherited $10,000 from her grandmother. She has decided that she will invest the money in the stock market. She is thinking about investing in one of her favorite clothing stores. The problem is she can't decide between Urban Outfitters or The Gap.

How should Lori decide between the companies? What resources should she use?

### Solution

Lori should begin by reviewing the financial statements of each business. She can locate them on the companies' Web sites or on the Securities and Exchange Commission's Web site (**http://www.sec.gov/edgar.shtml**). She should review the income statements and compare net income. Which business was more profitable? She should look at the balance sheets, carefully reviewing each part of the accounting equation. What was the dollar amount of assets? How much debt does the business have? In addition, she could go online and research the individual companies using a Web site such as Yahoo! Finance. These Web sites provide news and information about the company, such as current headlines, key statistics, and industry comparisons.

Lori should also consider diversifying her investment. Diversifying involves investing in more than one company and in a variety of industries and companies of different sizes. Diversification reduces the risk of an investment. Lori should consider investing half of the $10,000 in a company in a different industry, such as her favorite restaurant or food manufacturer.

how profitably a company uses its assets. Return on assets is calculated by dividing net income by average total assets. Average total assets is calculated by adding the beginning and ending total assets for the time period and then dividing by two.

Return on assets = Net income / Average total assets
Average total assets = (Beginning total assets + Ending total assets) / 2

Let's take a moment to calculate Green Mountain's ROA and measure how profitably it uses its assets. On its 2013 income statement, Green Mountain reported net income of $483,232 (in thousands). The corporation reported beginning total assets (found on the balance sheet) of $3,615,789 (in thousands) and ending total assets of $3,761,548 (in thousands). Green Mountain's return on assets for 2013 is:

Return on assets = $483,232 / (($3,615,789 + $3,761,548) / 2)
= $483,232 / $3,688,669*
= 0.131 = 13.1%*

*rounded

How do we as an investor know if 13.1% is good or bad? We have to compare the return on assets of competing companies such as Caribou Coffee Company, Inc., **Starbucks Corporation**, and Dunkin' Brands Group, Inc. What if we told you that Dunkin' Brands Group, Inc.'s return on assets was 4.5%? Due to Green Mountain's higher ROA, we now know that Green Mountain has a stronger return on its assets than does Dunkin'. What does this mean? It means that Green Mountain produces more profit per every dollar of assets than Dunkin' does. As you learn more about accounting, you will explore more financial tools that are available to help investors evaluate a company's performance. Only after an investor looks at the big picture of a company will he or she have a good sense of the company's investment potential.

## Try It!

**19.** Using the following information, calculate the return on assets (ROA).

| | |
|---|---|
| Net income for November, 2016 | $ 5,000 |
| Total assets, November 1, 2016 | 76,000 |
| Total assets, November 30, 2016 | 80,250 |

**Check your answer online in MyAccountingLab or at http://www.pearsonhighered.com/Horngren.**

For more practice, see Short Exercise S1-16. MyAccountingLab

# REVIEW

## > Things You Should Know

### 1. Why is accounting important?

- It's the language of business.
- Accounting is used by decision makers including individuals, businesses, investors, creditors, and taxing authorities.
- Accounting can be divided into two major fields: financial accounting and managerial accounting.
- Financial accounting is used by external decision makers, and managerial accounting is used by internal decision makers.
- All businesses need accountants. Accountants work in private, public, and governmental jobs.
- Accountants can be licensed as either a certified public accountant (CPA) or certified management accountant (CMA).

### 2. What are the organizations and rules that govern accounting?

- Generally Accepted Accounting Principles (GAAP) are the rules that govern accounting in the United States.
- The Financial Accounting Standards Board (FASB) is responsible for the creation and governance of accounting standards (GAAP).
- Economic entity assumption: Requires an organization to be a separate economic unit such as a sole proprietorship, partnership, corporation, or limited-liability company.
- Cost principle: Acquired assets and services should be recorded at their actual cost.
- Going concern assumption: Assumes that an entity will remain in operation for the foreseeable future.
- Monetary unit assumption: Assumes financial transactions are recorded in a monetary unit.

### 3. What is the accounting equation?

- Assets = Liabilities + Equity
    - Assets: Items the business owns or controls (examples: cash, furniture, land)
    - Liabilities: Items the business owes (examples: accounts payable, notes payable, salaries payable)
    - Equity: Stockholders' claims to the assets through contributed capital and retained earnings (examples: common stock, dividends, revenues, expenses)

### 4. How do you analyze a transaction?

- A transaction affects the financial position of a business and can be measured with faithful representation.
- Transactions are analyzed using three steps:

  **Step 1:** Identify the accounts and account type (Asset, Liability, or Equity).

  **Step 2:** Decide whether each account increases or decreases.

  **Step 3:** Determine whether the accounting equation is in balance.

**5. How do you prepare financial statements?**

- Financial statements are prepared in the following order:
  1. Income Statement:
     - Reports the net income or net loss of a business for a specific period.
     - Revenues − Expenses = Net Income or Net Loss
  2. Statement of Retained Earnings:
     - Reports on the changes in retained earnings for a specific period.
     - Beginning Retained Earnings + Net Income (or − Net Loss) − Dividends = Ending Retained Earnings
  3. Balance Sheet:
     - Reports on an entity's assets, liabilities, and stockholders' equity as of a specific date.
     - Assets = Liabilities + Stockholders' Equity
  4. Statement of Cash Flows:
     - Reports on a business's cash receipts and cash payments for a specific period.
     - Includes three sections:
       - Cash flows from operating activities: Involves cash receipts for services and cash payments for expenses.
       - Cash flows from investing activities: Includes the purchase and sale of land and equipment for cash.
       - Cash flows from financing activities: Includes cash contributions by stockholders and cash dividends paid to the stockholders.

**6. How do you use financial statements to evaluate business performance?**

- Income statement evaluates profitability.
- Statement of retained earnings shows the amount of earnings that were kept and reinvested in the company.
- Balance sheet details the economic resources the company owns as well as debts the company owes.
- Statement of cash flows shows the change in cash.
- Return on assets (ROA) = Net income / Average total assets.

## > Summary Problem

Ron Smith opens an apartment-locator business near a college campus. The company will be named Campus Apartment Locators. During the first month of operations, July 2016, the business completes the following transactions:

a. Smith contributes $35,000 to the business. The business issues common stock to Smith.

b. Purchases $350 of office supplies on account.

c. Pays cash of $30,000 to acquire a lot next to campus.

d. Locates apartments for clients and receives cash of $1,900.

e. Pays $100 on the accounts payable the business created in Transaction (b).

f. Pays cash expenses for office rent, $400, and utilities, $100.

g. Pays cash dividends of $1,200 to stockholders.

**Requirements**

1. Analyze the preceding transactions in terms of their effects on the accounting equation of Campus Apartment Locators. Use Exhibit 1-6 as a guide.
2. Prepare the income statement, statement of retained earnings, and balance sheet of the business after recording the transactions.
3. Calculate the return on assets (ROA).

## > Solution

### Requirement 1

| | ASSETS | | | = | LIABILITIES + | EQUITY | | | | |
|---|---|---|---|---|---|---|---|---|---|---|
| | | | | | | Contributed Capital + | Retained Earnings | | | |
| | Cash | + Office Supplies | + Land | | Accounts Payable | + Common Stock | − Dividends | + Service Revenue | − Rent Expense | − Utilities Expense |
| (a) | +35,000 | | | | | +35,000 | | | | |
| (b) | | +350 | | | +350 | | | | | |
| Bal. | $35,000 | + $350 | | | $350 | + $35,000 | | | | |
| (c) | −30,000 | | +30,000 | | | | | | | |
| Bal. | $5,000 | + $350 | + $30,000 | | $350 | + $35,000 | | | | |
| (d) | +1,900 | | | | | | | +1,900 | | |
| Bal. | $6,900 | + $350 | + $30,000 | | $350 | + $35,000 | | + $1,900 | | |
| (e) | −100 | | | | −100 | | | | | |
| Bal. | $6,800 | + $350 | + $30,000 | | $250 | + $35,000 | | + $1,900 | | |
| (f) | −500 | | | | | | | | −400 | −100 |
| Bal. | $6,300 | + $350 | + $30,000 | | $250 | + $35,000 | | + $1,900 | − $400 | − $100 |
| (g) | −1,200 | | | | | | −1,200 | | | |
| Bal. | $5,100 | + $350 | + $30,000 | | $250 | + $35,000 | − $1,200 | + $1,900 | − $400 | − $100 |
| | $35,450 | | | | $35,450 | | | | | |

### Requirement 2

| CAMPUS APARTMENT LOCATORS<br>Income Statement<br>Month Ended July 31, 2016 | | |
|---|---|---|
| Revenues: | | |
| Service Revenue | | $ 1,900 |
| Expenses: | | |
| Rent Expense | $ 400 | |
| Utilities Expense | 100 | |
| Total Expenses | | 500 |
| Net Income | | **$ 1,400** |

| CAMPUS APARTMENT LOCATORS<br>Statement of Retained Earnings<br>Month Ended July 31, 2016 | |
|---|---|
| Retained Earnings July 1, 2016 | $ 0 |
| Net income for the month | 1,400 |
| | 1,400 |
| Dividends | (1,200) |
| Retained Earnings, July 31, 2016 | **$ 200** |

| CAMPUS APARTMENT LOCATORS<br>Balance Sheet<br>July 31, 2016 | | | |
|---|---|---|---|
| **Assets** | | **Liabilities** | |
| Cash | $ 5,100 | Accounts Payable | $ 250 |
| Office Supplies | 350 | | |
| Land | 30,000 | **Stockholders' Equity** | |
| | | Common Stock | 35,000 |
| | | Retained Earnings | 200 |
| | | Total Stockholders' Equity | 35,200 |
| Total Assets | **$ 35,450** | Total Liabilities and Stockholders' Equity | **$ 35,450** |

**Requirement 3**

ROA = Net income / Average total assets
Average total assets = (Beginning total assets + Ending total assets) / 2
Average total assets = ($0 + $35,450) / 2 = $17,725
ROA = $1,400 / $17,725 = 0.079 = 7.9%*

*rounded

## > Key Terms

**Accounting (p. 2)**

**Accounting Equation (p. 11)**

**Accounts Payable (p. 15)**

**Accounts Receivable (p. 15)**

**Assets (p. 12)**

**Audit (p. 10)**

**Balance Sheet (p. 21)**

**Certified Management Accountants (CMAs) (p. 4)**

**Certified Public Accountants (CPAs) (p. 4)**

**Common Stock (p. 12)**

**Contributed Capital (p. 12)**

**Corporation (p. 7)**

**Cost Principle (p. 9)**

**Creditor (p. 4)**

**Dividend (p. 12)**

**Economic Entity Assumption (p. 6)**

**Equity (p. 12)**

**Expenses (p. 12)**

**Financial Accounting (p. 3)**

**Financial Accounting Standards Board (FASB) (p. 6)**

**Financial Statements (p. 19)**

**Generally Accepted Accounting Principles (GAAP) (p. 6)**

**Going Concern Assumption (p. 10)**

**Income Statement (p. 19)**
**International Accounting Standards Board (IASB) (p. 10)**
**International Financial Reporting Standards (IFRS) (p. 10)**
**Liabilities (p. 12)**
**Limited-Liability Company (LLC) (p. 7)**
**Managerial Accounting (p. 3)**
**Monetary Unit Assumption (p. 10)**
**Net Income (p. 13)**
**Net Loss (p. 13)**
**Partnership (p. 7)**
**Retained Earnings (p. 12)**
**Return on Assets (ROA) (p. 24)**
**Revenues (p. 12)**
**Sarbanes-Oxley Act (SOX) (p. 11)**
**Securities and Exchange Commission (SEC) (p. 6)**
**Sole Proprietorship (p. 7)**
**Statement of Cash Flows (p. 22)**
**Statement of Retained Earnings (p. 20)**
**Stockholder (p. 7)**
**Transaction (p. 13)**

## > Quick Check

**Learning Objective 1**

1. Accounting is the information system that
   a. measures business activities.
   b. communicates the results to decision makers.
   c. processes information into reports.
   d. All of the above.

**Learning Objective 1**

2. Which of the following is not an external user of a business's financial information?
   a. Taxing authorities
   b. Customers
   c. Employees
   d. Investors

**Learning Objective 2**

3. Generally Accepted Accounting Principles (GAAP) are currently formulated by the
   a. Financial Accounting Standards Board (FASB).
   b. Securities and Exchange Commission (SEC).
   c. Institute of Management Accountants (IMA).
   d. American Institute of Certified Public Accountants (AICPA).

**Learning Objective 2**

4. Which type of business organization is owned by only one owner?
   a. Corporation
   b. Partnership
   c. Sole proprietorship
   d. Items a, b, and c are all correct.

**Learning Objective 2**

5. Which of the following characteristics best describes a corporation?
   a. A business with a single owner
   b. Is not taxed
   c. Stockholders not personally liable for entity's debts
   d. Not a separate taxable entity

**Learning Objective 2**

6. Which of the following requires accounting information to be complete, neutral, and free from material error?
   a. Faithful representation concept
   b. Cost principle
   c. Economic entity assumption
   d. Going concern assumption

7. At the end of a recent year, Global Cleaning Service, a full-service house and office cleaning service, had total assets of $3,630 and equity of $2,280. How much were Global Cleaning Service's liabilities? **Learning Objective 3**
   a. $5,910
   b. $3,630
   c. $1,350
   d. $2,280

8. Consider the overall effects on Global Cleaning Service from selling and performing services on account for $6,400 and paying expenses totaling $2,500. What is Global Cleaning Service's net income or net loss? **Learning Objective 3**
   a. Net income of $3,900
   b. Net loss of $3,900
   c. Net income of $6,400
   d. Net income of $8,900

9. Assume that Global Cleaning Service performed cleaning services for a department store on account for $180. How would this transaction affect Global Cleaning Service's accounting equation? **Learning Objective 4**
   a. Increase both assets and liabilities by $180
   b. Increase both assets and equity by $180
   c. Increase both liabilities and equity by $180
   d. Decrease liabilities by $180, and increase equity by $180

10. The balance sheet reports the **Learning Objective 5**
   a. financial position on a specific date.
   b. results of operations on a specific date.
   c. financial position for a specific period.
   d. results of operations for a specific period.

11. Assume Global Cleaning Service had net income of $570 for the year. Global Cleaning Service's beginning and ending total assets were $4,520 and $4,180, respectively. Calculate Global Cleaning Service's return on assets (ROA) for the year. **Learning Objective 6**
   a. 12.6%
   b. 13.6%
   c. 13.1%
   d. 7.63%

**Check your answers at the end of the chapter.**

# ASSESS YOUR PROGRESS

## > Review Questions

1. What is accounting?
2. Briefly describe the two major fields of accounting.
3. Describe the various types of individuals who use accounting information and how they use that information to make important decisions.
4. What are two certifications available for accountants? Briefly explain each certification.
5. What is the role of the Financial Accounting Standards Board (FASB)?
6. Explain the purpose of Generally Accepted Accounting Principles (GAAP), including the organization currently responsible for the creation and governance of these standards.

7. Describe the similarities and differences among the four different types of business entities discussed in the chapter.
8. A business purchases an acre of land for $5,000. The current market value is $5,550, and the land was assessed for property tax purposes at $5,250. What value should the land be recorded at, and which accounting principle supports your answer?
9. What does the going concern assumption mean for a business?
10. Which concept states that accounting information should be complete, neutral, and free from material error?
11. Financial statements in the United States are reported in U.S. dollars. What assumption supports this statement?
12. Explain the role of the International Accounting Standards Board (IASB) in relation to International Financial Reporting Standards (IFRS).
13. What is the accounting equation? Briefly explain each of the three parts.
14. How does retained earnings increase? What are the two ways that retained earnings decreases?
15. How is net income calculated? Define *revenues* and *expenses*.
16. What are the steps used when analyzing a business transaction?
17. List the four financial statements. Briefly describe each statement.
18. What is the calculation for return on assets (ROA)? Explain what ROA measures.

## > Short Exercises

**Learning Objective 1**

### S1-1 Identifying users of accounting information

For each user of accounting information, identify if the user would use financial accounting (FA) or managerial accounting (MA).

a. investor
b. banker
c. Internal Revenue Service
d. manager of the business
e. controller
f. stockholder
g. human resources director
h. creditor

**Learning Objective 2**

### S1-2 Determining organizations that govern accounting

Suppose you are starting a business, Wholly Shirts, to imprint logos on T-shirts. In organizing the business and setting up its accounting records, you take your information to a CPA to prepare financial statements for the bank. Name the organization that governs the majority of the guidelines that the CPA will use to prepare financial statements for Wholly Shirts. What are those guidelines called?

**Learning Objective 2**

### S1-3 Identifying types of business organizations

Chloe Michaels plans on opening Chloe Michaels Floral Designs. She is considering the various types of business organizations and wishes to organize her business with unlimited life and wants owners of the business to not be held personally liable for the business's debts. Additionally, Chloe wants the business to be a separate taxable entity. Which type of business organization will meet Chloe's needs best?

**Learning Objective 2**

### S1-4 Identifying types of business organizations

You would like to start a cellular telephone equipment service business. You are considering organizing the business as a sole proprietorship. Identify the advantages and disadvantages of owning a sole proprietorship.

### S1-5 Applying accounting assumptions and principles

Learning Objective 2

Michael McNamee is the proprietor of a property management company, Apartment Exchange, near the campus of Pensacola State College. The business has cash of $8,000 and furniture that cost $9,000 and has a market value of $13,000. The business debts include accounts payable of $6,000. Michael's personal home is valued at $400,000, and his personal bank account has a balance of $1,200. Consider the accounting principles and assumptions discussed in the chapter, and identify the principle or assumption that best matches the situation:

a. Michael's personal assets are not recorded on the Apartment Exchange's balance sheet.

b. The Apartment Exchange records furniture at its cost of $9,000, not its market value of $13,000.

c. The Apartment Exchange reports its financial statements in U.S. dollars.

d. Michael expects the Apartment Exchange to remain in operation for the foreseeable future.

### S1-6 Using the accounting equation

Learning Objective 3

Kenmore Handyman Services has total assets for the year of $16,400 and total liabilities of $8,680.

**Requirements**

1. Use the accounting equation to solve for equity.
2. If next year assets increased by $3,500 and equity decreased by $2,580, what would be the amount of total liabilities for Kenmore Handyman Services?

### S1-7 Using the accounting equation

Learning Objective 3

Josh's Overhead Doors reports the following financial information:

| | |
|---|---|
| Assets | $ 42,600 |
| Liabilities | 17,220 |
| Common Stock | 26,240 |
| Dividends | 8,500 |
| Revenues | 12,080 |
| Expenses | ? |

**Requirements**

1. Use the accounting equation to solve for the missing information.
2. Did Josh's Overhead Doors report net income or net loss?

### S1-8 Identifying accounts

Learning Objective 3

Consider the following accounts:

a. Accounts Payable
b. Cash
c. Common Stock
d. Accounts Receivable
e. Rent Expense
f. Service Revenue
g. Office Supplies
h. Dividends
i. Land
j. Salaries Expense

Identify each account as Asset (A), Liability (L), or Equity (E).

Learning Objective 4

**S1-9 Using the accounting equation to analyze transactions**

Tiny Town Kennel earns service revenue by caring for the pets of customers. Tiny Town Kennel is organized as a corporation. During the past month, Tiny Town Kennel has the following transactions:

a. Received $520 cash for service revenue earned.
b. Paid $325 cash for salaries expense.
c. Investors contributed $1,000 to the corporation in exchange for common stock.
d. Earned $640 for service revenue, but the customer has not paid Tiny Town Kennel yet.
e. Received utility bill of $85, which will be paid next month.
f. Cash dividends of $100 were paid to stockholders.

Indicate the effects of the business transactions on the accounting equation for Tiny Town Kennel. Transaction (a) is answered as a guide.

*a. Increase asset (Cash); Increase equity (Service Revenue)*

Learning Objective 4

**S1-10 Using the accounting equation to analyze transactions**

Elaine's Inflatables earns service revenue by providing party planning services and inflatable playscapes. Elaine's Inflatables is organized as a corporation. During the past month, Elaine's Inflatables had the following transactions:

a. Investors contributed $10,000 to the corporation in exchange for common stock.
b. Purchased equipment for $5,000 on account.
c. Paid $400 for office supplies.
d. Earned and received $2,500 cash for service revenue.
e. Paid $400 for wages to employees.
f. Cash dividends of $1,000 were paid to stockholders.
g. Earned $1,000 for services provided. Customer has not yet paid.
h. Paid $1,000 for rent.
i. Received a bill for $250 for the monthly utilities. The bill has not yet been paid.

Indicate the effects of the business transactions on the accounting equation for Elaine's Inflatables. Transaction (a) is answered as a guide.

*a. Increase asset (Cash); Increase equity (Common Stock)*

Learning Objective 5

**S1-11 Identifying accounts on the financial statements**

Consider the following accounts:

a. Accounts Payable
b. Cash
c. Common Stock
d. Accounts Receivable
e. Rent Expense
f. Service Revenue
g. Office Supplies
h. Dividends
i. Land
j. Salaries Expense

Identify the financial statement (or statements) that each account would appear on. Use I for Income Statement, RE for Statement of Retained Earnings, and B for Balance Sheet.

***Use the following information to answer Short Exercises S1-12 through S1-14.***

Decorating Arrangements has just completed operations for the year ended December 31, 2016. This is the third year of operations for the company. The following data have been assembled for the business:

| | | | |
|---|---|---|---|
| Insurance Expense | $ 2,000 | Salaries Expense | $ 37,000 |
| Service Revenue | 80,000 | Accounts Payable | 4,300 |
| Utilities Expense | 500 | Office Supplies | 1,500 |
| Rent Expense | 11,000 | Dividends | 4,500 |
| Common Stock | 8,500 | Accounts Receivable | 7,500 |
| Cash | 7,000 | Equipment | 26,600 |
| Retained Earnings, Jan. 1, 2016 | 4,800 | | |

**S1-12 Preparing the income statement**

**Learning Objective 5**

Prepare the income statement of Decorating Arrangements for the year ended December 31, 2016.

**S1-13 Preparing the statement of retained earnings**

**Learning Objective 5**

Prepare the statement of retained earnings of Decorating Arrangements for the year ended December 31, 2016.

**S1-14 Preparing the balance sheet**

**Learning Objective 5**

Prepare the balance sheet of Decorating Arrangements as of December 31, 2016.

**S1-15 Preparing the statement of cash flows**

**Learning Objective 5**

Pushing Daisies Homes had the following cash transactions for the month ended July 31, 2016.

| | |
|---|---|
| **Cash receipts:** | |
| Collections from customers | $ 24,000 |
| Issued common stock | 12,000 |
| **Cash payments:** | |
| Rent | 3,000 |
| Utilities | 900 |
| Salaries | 1,600 |
| Purchase of equipment | 18,000 |
| Payment of cash dividends | 3,500 |
| Cash balance, July 1, 2016 | 11,000 |
| Cash balance, July 31, 2016 | 20,000 |

Prepare the statement of cash flows for Pushing Daisies Homes for the month ended July 31, 2016.

Learning Objective 6

**S1-16 Calculating Return on Assets (ROA)**

Refined Water Services had net income for the month of October of $74,000. Assets as of the beginning and end of the month totaled $350,000, and $390,000, respectively. Calculate Refined Water Services' return on assets (ROA) for the month of October.

## > Exercises

Learning Objective 1

**E1-17 Identifying users of accounting information**

For each of the users of accounting information, identify whether the user is an external decision maker (E) or an internal decision maker (I):

a. customer
b. company manager
c. Internal Revenue Service
d. lender
e. investor
f. controller
g. cost accountant
h. SEC

Learning Objective 2

**E1-18 Using accounting vocabulary**

Consider the following accounting terms and definitions, and match each term to the definition:

1. Sole proprietorship
2. Faithful representation
3. Partnership
4. IFRS
5. Corporation
6. Audit
7. Cost principle
8. FASB
9. Creditors
10. SEC

a. Set of global accounting guidelines, formulated by the IASB
b. Holds that fair market value should not be used over actual costs
c. Stands for Financial Accounting Standards Board
d. Owner is referred to as a proprietor
e. Asserts that accounting information should be complete, neutral, and free from material error
f. An examination of a company's financial statements and records
g. Has two or more owners (called partners)
h. U.S. governmental agency that oversees the U.S. financial markets
i. Type of entity that is designed to limit personal liability exposure of owners to the entity's debts
j. Person or business lending money

## E1-19 Using accounting vocabulary

**Learning Objectives 3, 5**

Consider the following accounting terms and definitions, and match each term to the definition:

1. Accounting equation
2. Asset
3. Balance sheet
4. Expense
5. Income statement
6. Liability
7. Net income
8. Net loss
9. Revenue
10. Statement of cash flows
11. Statement of retained earnings

a. An economic resource that is expected to be of benefit in the future
b. Debts that are owed to creditors
c. Excess of total expenses over total revenues
d. Excess of total revenues over total expenses
e. The basic tool of accounting, stated as Assets = Liabilities + Equity
f. Decreases in equity that occur in the course of selling goods or services
g. Increases in equity that occur in the course of selling goods or services
h. Reports on a business's cash receipts and cash payments during a period
i. Reports on an entity's assets, liabilities, and stockholders' equity as of a specific date
j. Reports on an entity's revenues, expenses, and net income or loss for the period
k. Reports how the company's retained earnings balance changed from the beginning to the end of the period

## E1-20 Using the accounting equation

**Learning Objective 3**

Compute the missing amount in the accounting equation for each entity from the financial information presented:

| | Assets | Liabilities | Equity |
|---|---|---|---|
| Newton Gas | $ ? | $ 64,000 | $ 80,000 |
| Vegas Video Rentals | 65,000 | ? | 25,000 |
| Cline's Grocery | 200,000 | 43,000 | ? |

## E1-21 Using the accounting equation

**Learning Objective 3**

Green City Builders' balance sheet data at May 31, 2016, and June 30, 2016, follow:

| | May 31, 2016 | June 30, 2016 |
|---|---|---|
| Total assets | $ 188,000 | $ 244,000 |
| Total liabilities | 122,000 | 88,000 |

For each of the following situations with regard to common stock and dividends of a corporation, compute the amount of net income or net loss during June 2016.

a. The company issued $7,500 of common stock and paid no dividends.

b. The company issued no common stock. It paid cash dividends of $13,000.

c. The company issued $20,000 of common stock and paid cash dividends of $18,000.

Learning Objective 3

### E1-22 Using the accounting equation

Star Nursery started 2016 with total assets of $24,000 and total liabilities of $5,000. At the end of 2016, Star Nursery's total assets stood at $18,000 and total liabilities were $1,000.

**Requirements**

1. Did the stockholders' equity of Star Nursery increase or decrease during 2016? By how much?
2. Identify the four possible reasons that stockholders' equity can change.

Learning Objective 3

### E1-23 Using the accounting equation

During 2016, Peaceful River Spa reported revenue of $40,000. Total expenses for the year were $35,000. Peaceful River Spa ended the year with total assets of $23,000, and it owed debts totaling $9,000. At year-end 2015, the business reported total assets of $18,000 and total liabilities of $9,000.

**Requirements**

1. Compute Peaceful River Spa's net income for 2016.
2. Did Peaceful River Spa's stockholders' equity increase or decrease during 2016? By how much?

Learning Objective 3

### E1-24 Using the accounting equation

The records of Meehan Company show the following at December 31, 2016:

| **Beginning:** | | **Equity:** | |
|---|---|---|---|
| Assets | $ 64,000 | Common Stock | $ 13,000 |
| Liabilities | 44,000 | Dividends | 4,000 |
| **Ending:** | | Revenues | 257,000 |
| Assets | $ 54,000 | Expenses | ? |
| Liabilities | 39,000 | Retained Earnings, Jan. 1, 2016 | 7,000 |

**Requirements**

1. Compute the missing amount for Meehan Company. You will need to determine Retained Earnings, December 31, 2016, and total stockholders' equity.
2. Did Meehan earn a net income or suffer a net loss for the year? Compute the amount.

**E1-25 Using the accounting equation to analyze transactions** **Learning Objective 4**

As the manager of a Papa Sean's restaurant, you must deal with a variety of business transactions. Give an example of a transaction that has each of the following effects on the accounting equation:

**a.** Increase one asset and decrease another asset.

**b.** Decrease an asset and decrease equity.

**c.** Decrease an asset and decrease a liability.

**d.** Increase an asset and increase equity.

**e.** Increase an asset and increase a liability.

**E1-26 Using the accounting equation to analyze business transactions** **Learning Objective 4**

Indicate the effects of the following business transactions on the accounting equation of Vivian's Online Video store. Transaction (a) is answered as a guide.

**a.** Received cash of $10,000 from issuance of common stock.

*Answer: Increase asset (Cash); Increase equity (Common Stock)*

**b.** Earned video rental revenue on account, $2,800.

**c.** Purchased office furniture on account, $300.

**d.** Received cash on account, $400.

**e.** Paid cash on account, $100.

**f.** Rented videos and received cash of $200.

**g.** Paid monthly office rent of $1,000.

**h.** Paid $100 cash to purchase office supplies.

**E1-27 Using the accounting equation to analyze business transactions** **Learning Objective 4**

Indicate the effects of the following business transactions on the accounting equation for Sam's Snack Foods, a supplier of snack foods. Transaction (a) is answered as a guide.

**a.** Sam's Snack Foods received cash from issuance of common stock to stockholders.

*Answer: Increase asset (Cash); Increase equity (Common Stock)*

**b.** Cash purchase of land for a building site.

**c.** Paid cash on accounts payable.

**d.** Purchased equipment; signed a note payable.

**e.** Performed service for a customer on account.

**f.** Employees worked for the week but will be paid next Tuesday.

**g.** Received cash from a customer on accounts receivable.

**h.** Borrowed money from the bank.

**i.** Cash dividends paid to stockholders.

**j.** Incurred utilities expense on account.

**Learning Objective 4**

## E1-28 Using the accounting equation to analyze business transactions

The analysis of the first eight transactions of Advanced Accounting Service follows. Describe each transaction.

| | ASSETS | | | = | LIABILITIES + | EQUITY | | | |
|---|---|---|---|---|---|---|---|---|---|
| | | | | | | Contributed Capital + | Retained Earnings | | |
| | Cash + | Accounts Receivable + | Equipment | | Accounts Payable + | Common Stock − | Dividends + | Service Revenue − | Salaries Expense |
| 1 | +31,000 | | | | | +31,000 | | | |
| 2 | | +3,800 | | | | | | +3,800 | |
| Bal. | $31,000 + | $3,800 | | | | $31,000 | | + $3,800 | |
| 3 | | | +13,400 | | +13,400 | | | | |
| Bal. | $31,000 + | $3,800 + | $13,400 | | $13,400 + | $31,000 | | + $3,800 | |
| 4 | +190 | −190 | | | | | | | |
| Bal. | $31,190 + | $3,610 + | $13,400 | | $13,400 + | $31,000 | | + $3,800 | |
| 5 | −410 | | +410 | | | | | | |
| Bal. | $30,780 + | $3,610 + | $13,810 | | $13,400 + | $31,000 | | + $3,800 | |
| 6 | −8,000 | | | | −8,000 | | | | |
| Bal. | $22,780 + | $3,610 + | $13,810 | | $5,400 + | $31,000 | | + $3,800 | |
| 7 | +790 | | | | | | | +790 | |
| Bal. | $23,570 + | $3,610 + | $13,810 | | $5,400 + | $31,000 | | + $4,590 | |
| 8 | −1,500 | | | | | | | | −1,500 |
| Bal. | $22,070 + | $3,610 + | $13,810 | | $5,400 + | $31,000 | | + $4,590 − | $1,500 |

**Learning Objective 4**

## E1-29 Using the accounting equation to analyze business transactions

Samantha Stamford opened a medical practice. During July, the first month of operation, the business, titled Samantha Stamford, M.D., experienced the following events:

| | |
|---|---|
| July 6 | Stamford contributed $65,000 in the business by opening a bank account in the name of S. Stamford, M.D. The corporation issued common stock to Stamford. |
| 9 | Paid $52,000 cash for land. |
| 12 | Purchased medical supplies for $1,600 on account. |
| 15 | Officially opened for business. |
| 20 | Paid cash expenses: employees' salaries, $1,500; office rent, $1,300; utilities, $350. |
| 31 | Earned service revenue for the month, $8,000, receiving cash. |
| 31 | Paid $800 on account. |

Analyze the effects of these events on the accounting equation of the medical practice of Samantha Stamford, M.D., using the following format:

| ASSETS | | | = | LIABILITIES + | EQUITY | | | | | |
|---|---|---|---|---|---|---|---|---|---|---|
| | | | | | Contributed Capital + | Retained Earnings | | | | |
| Cash + | Medical Supplies + | Land | | Accounts Payable + | Common Stock − | Dividends + | Service Revenue − | Salaries Expense − | Rent Expense − | Utilities Expense |

### E1-30 Preparing the financial statements

**Learning Objective 5**

Estella Osage publishes an online travel magazine. In need of cash, the business applies for a loan with National Bank. The bank requires borrowers to submit financial statements. With little knowledge of accounting, Estella Osage, a stockholder, does not know how to proceed.

**Requirements**

1. What are the four financial statements that the business will need to prepare?
2. Is there a specific order in which the financial statements must be prepared?
3. Explain how to prepare each statement.

***Use the following information to answer Exercises E1-31 through E1-33.***

The account balances of Wilford Towing Service at June 30, 2016, follow:

| | | | |
|---|---|---|---|
| Equipment | $ 17,500 | Service Revenue | $ 13,000 |
| Office Supplies | 1,300 | Accounts Receivable | 8,200 |
| Notes Payable | 6,900 | Accounts Payable | 6,000 |
| Rent Expense | 800 | Retained Earnings, June 1, 2016 | 3,700 |
| Cash | 1,900 | Salaries Expense | 1,900 |
| Dividends | 2,000 | Common Stock | 4,000 |

### E1-31 Preparing the income statement

**Learning Objective 5**

Net Income $10,300

**Requirements**

1. Prepare the income statement for Wilford Towing Service for the month ending June 30, 2016.
2. What does the income statement report?

### E1-32 Preparing the statement of retained earnings

**Learning Objective 5**

Ending Retained Earnings $12,000

**Requirements**

1. Prepare the statement of retained earnings for Wilford Towing Service for the month ending June 30, 2016.
2. What does the statement of retained earnings report?

### E1-33 Preparing the balance sheet

**Learning Objective 5**

Total Assets $28,900

**Requirements**

1. Prepare the balance sheet for Wilford Towing Service as of June 30, 2016.
2. What does the balance sheet report?

***Use the following information to answer Exercises E1-34 through E1-36.***

The assets, liabilities, and equities of Drought Design Studio have the following balances at December 31, 2016. The retained earnings was $31,000 at the beginning of the year with common stock of $20,000 and dividends of $55,000 at year end.

| | | | |
|---|---|---|---|
| Notes Payable | $ 9,800 | Office Furniture | $ 55,200 |
| Rent Expense | 22,000 | Utilities Expense | 6,500 |
| Cash | 3,100 | Accounts Payable | 3,700 |
| Office Supplies | 4,500 | Service Revenue | 159,200 |
| Salaries Expense | 62,000 | Accounts Receivable | 10,200 |
| Property Tax Expense | 1,200 | Miscellaneous Expense | 4,000 |

**Learning Objective 5**

Net Income $63,500

### E1-34 Preparing the income statement

Prepare the income statement for Drought Design Studio for the year ending December 31, 2016.

**Learning Objective 5**

Ending Retained Earnings $39,500

### E1-35 Preparing the statement of retained earnings

Prepare the statement of retained earnings for Drought Design Studio for the year ending December 31, 2016.

**Learning Objective 5**

Total Assets $73,000

### E1-36 Preparing the balance sheet

Prepare the balance sheet for Drought Design Studio as of December 31, 2016.

**Learning Objective 5**

### E1-37 Preparing the statement of cash flows

For each transaction, identify the appropriate section on the statement of cash flows to report the transaction. Choose from: Cash flows from operating activities (O), Cash flows from investing activities (I), Cash flows from financing activities (F), or Is not reported on the statement of cash flows (X). If reported on the statement, decide whether the transaction should be shown as a positive cash flow (+) or a negative cash flow (–):

**a.** The business received cash from the issuance of common stock.

**b.** Paid cash on accounts payable for office supplies purchased.

**c.** Performed services for a customer on account.

**d.** Cash dividends were paid to stockholders.

**e.** Received cash from a customer for services performed.

**f.** Purchased equipment with cash.

**g.** Paid rent for the month.

**h.** Purchased land; signed a note payable.

**i.** Paid employees wages for the week.

**j.** Incurred utility expense on account.

## E1-38 Preparing the statement of cash flows

**Learning Objective 5**

Decrease in cash $9,300

Bean Town Food Equipment Company had the following transactions for the month ending February 29, 2016. Bean Town's cash balance on February 1, 2016, was $16,400.

| | |
|---|---|
| Feb. 1 | Common stock was issued to stockholders for $7,500 cash. |
| 7 | Purchased equipment for $2,500 on account. |
| 14 | Paid $18,000 cash for land. |
| 17 | Paid cash expenses: employees' salaries, $1,500; office rent, $1,800; utilities, $500. |
| 23 | Paid cash dividends of $3,000. |
| 26 | Earned service revenue for the month, $8,000, receiving cash. |

Prepare the statement of cash flows of Bean Town Food Equipment Company for the month ended February 29, 2016.

## E1-39 Calculating return on assets (ROA)

**Learning Objective 6**

Alec Appliance Service had net income for the year of $18,200. In addition, the balance sheet reports the following balances:

| | Jan. 1, 2016 | Dec. 31, 2016 |
|---|---|---|
| Notes Payable | $ 34,000 | $ 54,000 |
| Cash | 39,000 | 20,200 |
| Office Furniture | 20,000 | 38,000 |
| Building | 155,000 | 155,000 |
| Accounts Payable | 9,500 | 10,000 |
| Total Stockholders' Equity | 198,300 | 214,200 |
| Accounts Receivable | 1,600 | 18,400 |
| Equipment | 22,000 | 46,000 |
| Office Supplies | 4,200 | 600 |

Calculate the return on assets (ROA) for Alec Appliance Service for the year ending December 31, 2016.

# > Problems Group A

## P1-40A Using the accounting equation for transaction analysis

**Learning Objective 4**

Cash $7,350

Missy Mansion opened a public relations firm called Solid Gold on August 1, 2016. The following amounts summarize her business on August 31, 2016:

| | ASSETS | | | | = | LIABILITIES + | EQUITY | | | | |
|---|---|---|---|---|---|---|---|---|---|---|---|
| | | | | | | | Contributed Capital + | Retained Earnings | | | |
| | Cash + | Accounts Receivable + | Office Supplies + | Land | | Accounts Payable + | Common Stock | − Dividends | + Service Revenue | − Rent Expense | − Advertising Expense |
| Bal. | $2,400 + | $2,600 + | $0 + | $15,000 | | $3,000 + | $14,400 | | + $2,600 | | |

During September 2016, the business completed the following transactions:

**a.** Missy Mansion contributed $8,000 cash in exchange for common stock.

**b.** Performed service for a client and received cash of $1,300.

**c.** Paid off the beginning balance of accounts payable.

**d.** Purchased office supplies from OfficeMax on account, $400.

**e.** Collected cash from a customer on account, $2,200.

**f.** Cash dividends of $1,800 were paid to stockholders.

**g.** Consulted for a new band and billed the client for services rendered, $6,500.

**h.** Recorded the following business expenses for the month:
Paid office rent: $1,400.
Paid advertising: $350.

Analyze the effects of the transactions on the accounting equation of Solid Gold using the format presented on page 43.

**Learning Objective 4**

Cash $18,550

## P1-41A Using the accounting equation for transaction analysis

Cameron Turnbull started a new business, Turnbull Gymnastics, and completed the following transactions during December:

| | |
|---|---|
| Dec. 1 | Cameron contributed $21,000 cash in exchange for common stock. |
| 2 | Received $2,400 cash from customers for services performed. |
| 5 | Paid $350 cash for office supplies. |
| 9 | Performed services for a customer and billed the customer for services rendered, $1,500. |
| 10 | Received $100 invoice for utilities due in two weeks. |
| 15 | Paid for advertising in the local paper, $300. |
| 20 | Paid utility invoice received on Dec. 10. |
| 25 | Collected cash in full from customer billed on Dec. 9. |
| 28 | Paid rent for the month, $2,800. |
| 28 | Paid $1,100 to assistant for wages. |
| 30 | Received $2,800 cash from customers for services performed. |
| 31 | Cash dividends of $4,500 were paid to stockholders. |

Analyze the effects of the transactions on the accounting equation of Turnbull Gymnastics using a format similar to Exhibit 1-6.

### P1-42A Preparing financial statements

Learning Objective 5

1. Net Income $97,800

Presented here are the accounts of Golden City Barbershop for the year ended December 31, 2016.

| | | | |
|---|---|---|---|
| Land | $ 5,000 | Common Stock | $ 25,000 |
| Notes Payable | 37,000 | Accounts Payable | 17,000 |
| Property Tax Expense | 2,700 | Accounts Receivable | 900 |
| Dividends | 32,000 | Advertising Expense | 13,000 |
| Rent Expense | 11,000 | Building | 157,000 |
| Salaries Expense | 61,000 | Cash | 3,800 |
| Salaries Payable | 900 | Equipment | 19,000 |
| Service Revenue | 195,000 | Insurance Expense | 2,500 |
| Office Supplies | 9,000 | Interest Expense | 7,000 |
| Retained Earnings, 12/31/15 | 49,000 | | |

**Requirements**

1. Prepare Golden City Barbershop's income statement.
2. Prepare the statement of retained earnings.
3. Prepare the balance sheet.

### P1-43A Preparing financial statements

Learning Objective 5

b. Ending Retained Earnings $76,800

Click a Pix Photography works weddings and prom-type parties. The balance of retained earnings was $26,000 at December 31, 2015. At December 31, 2016, the business's accounting records show these balances:

| | | | |
|---|---|---|---|
| Insurance Expense | $ 11,000 | Accounts Receivable | $ 12,000 |
| Cash | 40,000 | Notes Payable | 9,000 |
| Accounts Payable | 6,000 | Retained Earnings, Dec. 31, 2016 | ? |
| Advertising Expense | 3,200 | Salaries Expense | 20,000 |
| Service Revenue | 95,000 | Equipment | 73,800 |
| Dividends | 10,000 | Common Stock | 34,000 |

Prepare the following financial statements for Click a Pix Photography for the year ended December 31, 2016:

a. Income statement.

b. Statement of retained earnings.

c. Balance sheet.

**Learning Objective 5**

Total Assets $47,100

## P1-44A Preparing financial statements

The bookkeeper of Lone Star Landscaping prepared the company's balance sheet while the accountant was ill. The balance sheet contains numerous errors. In particular, the bookkeeper knew that the balance sheet should balance, so he plugged in the retained earnings amount needed to achieve this balance. The retained earnings is incorrect. All other amounts are correct, but some are out of place or should not be included in this statement. Prepare a corrected balance sheet.

**LONE STAR LANDSCAPING**
Balance Sheet
Month Ended November 30, 2016

| **Assets** | | **Liabilities** | |
|---|---|---|---|
| Cash | $ 4,900 | Accounts Receivable | $ 2,100 |
| Office Supplies | 300 | Dividends | 8,000 |
| Land | 33,800 | Service Revenue | 44,000 |
| Salaries Expense | 3,100 | Property Tax Expense | 2,700 |
| Office Furniture | 6,000 | Accounts Payable | 2,800 |
| Notes Payable | 24,200 | Retained Earnings | 1,150 |
| Rent Expense | 450 | **Stockholders' Equity** | |
| | | Common Stock | 12,000 |
| Total Assets | **$ 72,750** | Total Liabilities | **$ 72,750** |

**Learning Objectives 4, 5**

2b. Ending Retained Earnings $6,900

## P1-45A Using the accounting equation for transaction analysis and preparing financial statements

Alfonso Sheen recently opened his own accounting firm, which he operates as a corporation. The name of the new entity is Alfonso Sheen, CPA. Sheen experienced the following events during the organizing phase of the new business and its first month of operations in 2016:

| | |
|---|---|
| Feb. 5 | Sheen deposited $70,000 in a new business bank account titled Alfonso Sheen, CPA. The business issued common stock to Sheen. |
| 6 | Paid $350 cash for letterhead stationery for new office. |
| 7 | Purchased office furniture for the office on account, $7,000. |
| 10 | Consulted with tax client and received $1,800 for services rendered. |
| 11 | Paid utilities, $400. |
| 12 | Finished tax hearings on behalf of a client and submitted a bill for accounting services, $11,000. |
| 18 | Paid office rent, $1,000. |
| 25 | Received amount due from client that was billed on February 12. |
| 27 | Paid full amount of accounts payable created on February 7. |
| 29 | Cash dividends of $4,500 were paid to stockholders. |

**Requirements**

1. Analyze the effects of the events on the accounting equation of Alfonso Sheen, CPA. Use a format similar to Exhibit 1-6.
2. Prepare the following financial statements:
   a. Income statement.
   b. Statement of retained earnings.
   c. Balance sheet.

### P1-46A Using the accounting equation for transaction analysis and preparing financial statements

**Learning Objectives 4, 5**

2c. Total Assets $94,360

Angela Petrillo recently opened her own law office, which she operates as a corporation. The name of the new entity is Angela Petrillo, Attorney. Petrillo experienced the following events during the organizing phase of the new business and its first month of operation, March 2016. Some of the events were personal and did not affect the law practice. Others were business transactions and should be accounted for by the business.

| | |
|---|---|
| Mar. 1 | Sold personal investment in Amazon stock, which she had owned for several years, receiving $31,000 cash. |
| 2 | Deposited the $31,000 cash from the sale of the Amazon stock in her personal bank account. |
| 3 | Deposited $72,000 cash in a new business bank account titled Angela Petrillo, Attorney. The business issued common stock to Petrillo. |
| 5 | Paid $350 cash for ink cartridges for the printer. |
| 7 | Purchased computer for the law office, agreeing to pay the account, $5,500, within three months. |
| 9 | Received $2,500 cash from customers for services rendered. |
| 15 | Received bill from *The Lawyer* for magazine subscription, $340. (Use Miscellaneous Expense account.) |
| 23 | Finished court hearings on behalf of a client and submitted a bill for legal services, $18,000, on account. |
| 28 | Paid bill from *The Lawyer*. |
| 30 | Paid utilities, $1,300. |
| 31 | Received $1,800 cash from clients billed on Mar. 23. |
| 31 | Cash dividends of $2,000 were paid to stockholders. |

**Requirements**

1. Analyze the effects of the preceding events on the accounting equation of Angela Petrillo, Attorney. Use a format similar to Exhibit 1-6.
2. Prepare the following financial statements:
   a. Income statement.
   b. Statement of retained earnings.
   c. Balance sheet.

# > Problems Group B

**Learning Objective 4**

Cash $8,150

## P1-47B Using the accounting equation for transaction analysis

Meg Clifford opened a public relations firm called Dance Fever on August 1, 2016. The following amounts summarize her business on August 31, 2016:

| | ASSETS | | | | | LIABILITIES + | EQUITY | | | | |
|---|---|---|---|---|---|---|---|---|---|---|---|
| | | | | | | | Contributed Capital + | Retained Earnings | | | |
| | Cash + | Accounts Receivable + | Office Supplies + | Land | = | Accounts Payable + | Common Stock | − Dividends | + Service Revenue | − Rent Expense | − Advertising Expense |
| Bal. | $2,100 + | $2,500 + | $0 + | $11,000 | | $6,000 + | $7,100 | | + $2,500 | | |

During September 2016, the business completed the following transactions:

**a.** Meg Clifford contributed $13,000 cash in exchange for common stock.

**b.** Performed service for a client and received cash of $1,200.

**c.** Paid off the beginning balance of accounts payable.

**d.** Purchased office supplies from OfficeMax on account, $1,000.

**e.** Collected cash from a customer on account, $1,500.

**f.** Cash dividends of $1,900 were paid to stockholders.

**g.** Consulted for a new band and billed the client for services rendered, $6,000.

**h.** Recorded the following business expenses for the month:

Paid office rent: $1,400.

Paid advertising: $350.

Analyze the effects of the transactions on the accounting equation of Dance Fever using the format presented above.

**Learning Objective 4**

Cash $19,775

## P1-48B Using the accounting equation for transaction analysis

Cosmo Timmins started a new business, Timmins Gymnastics, and completed the following transactions during December:

| | | |
|---|---|---|
| Dec. | 1 | Cosmo contributed $20,000 cash in exchange for common stock. |
| | 2 | Received $2,200 cash from customers for services performed. |
| | 5 | Paid $350 cash for office supplies. |
| | 9 | Performed services for a customer and billed the customer for services rendered, $4,500. |
| | 10 | Received $100 invoice for utilities due in two weeks. |
| | 15 | Paid for advertising in the local paper, $475. |
| | 20 | Paid utility invoice received on Dec. 10. |
| | 25 | Collected cash in full from customer billed on Dec. 9. |
| | 28 | Paid rent for the month, $3,000. |
| | 28 | Paid $1,500 to assistant for wages. |
| | 30 | Received $2,000 cash from customers for services performed. |
| | 31 | Cash dividends of $3,500 were paid to stockholders. |

Analyze the effects of the transactions on the accounting equation of Timmins Gymnastics using a format similar to Exhibit 1-6.

## P1-49B Preparing financial statements

Learning Objective 5

1. Net Income $74,900

Presented here are the accounts of Town and Country Realty for the year ended December 31, 2016:

| | | | |
|---|---|---|---|
| Land | $ 5,000 | Common Stock | $ 28,000 |
| Notes Payable | 36,000 | Accounts Payable | 14,000 |
| Property Tax Expense | 3,400 | Accounts Receivable | 1,000 |
| Dividends | 32,000 | Advertising Expense | 14,000 |
| Rent Expense | 10,000 | Building | 144,600 |
| Salaries Expense | 69,000 | Cash | 3,800 |
| Salaries Payable | 1,500 | Equipment | 13,000 |
| Service Revenue | 180,000 | Insurance Expense | 2,200 |
| Office Supplies | 12,000 | Interest Expense | 6,500 |
| Retained Earnings, 12/31/15 | 57,000 | | |

**Requirements**

1. Prepare Town and Country Realty's income statement.
2. Prepare the statement of retained earnings.
3. Prepare the balance sheet.

## P1-50B Preparing financial statements

Learning Objective 5

b. Ending Retained Earnings $86,500

Precision Pics works weddings and prom-type parties. The balance of Retained Earnings was $26,000 at December 31, 2015. At December 31, 2016, the business's accounting records show these balances:

| | | | |
|---|---|---|---|
| Insurance Expense | $ 14,000 | Accounts Receivable | $ 7,000 |
| Cash | 38,000 | Notes Payable | 9,000 |
| Accounts Payable | 13,000 | Retained Earnings, Dec. 31, 2016 | ? |
| Advertising Expense | 3,500 | Salaries Expense | 21,000 |
| Service Revenue | 110,000 | Equipment | 96,500 |
| Dividends | 11,000 | Common Stock | 33,000 |

Prepare the following financial statements for Precision Pics for the year ended December 31, 2016:

a. Income statement.

b. Statement of retained earnings.

c. Balance sheet.

**Learning Objective 5**

Total Assets $47,400

## P1-51B Preparing financial statements

The bookkeeper of Beautiful World Landscaping prepared the company's balance sheet while the accountant was ill. The balance sheet contains numerous errors. In particular, the bookkeeper knew that the balance sheet should balance, so he plugged in the retained earnings amount needed to achieve this balance. The retained earnings is incorrect. All other amounts are correct, but some are out of place or should not be included on this statement. Prepare a corrected balance sheet.

| BEAUTIFUL WORLD LANDSCAPING<br>Balance Sheet<br>Month Ended July 31, 2016 | | | |
|---|---|---|---|
| **Assets** | | **Liabilities** | |
| Cash | $ 5,500 | Accounts Receivable | $ 1,900 |
| Office Supplies | 300 | Dividends | 13,000 |
| Land | 34,100 | Service Revenue | 44,000 |
| Salaries Expense | 2,700 | Property Tax Expense | 2,600 |
| Office Furniture | 5,600 | Accounts Payable | 2,400 |
| Notes Payable | 24,600 | Retained Earnings | 3,300 |
| Rent Expense | 400 | **Stockholders' Equity** | |
| | | Common Stock | 6,000 |
| Total Assets | **$ 73,200** | Total Liabilities | **$ 73,200** |

**Learning Objectives 4, 5**

2c. Total Assets $76,700

## P1-52B Using the accounting equation for transaction analysis and preparing financial statements

Andre Simmon recently opened his own accounting firm, which he operates as a corporation. The name of the new entity is Andre Simmon, CPA. Simmon experienced the following events during the organizing phase of the new business and its first month of operations in 2016.

| | |
|---|---|
| Feb. 5 | Simmon deposited $65,000 in a new business bank account titled Andre Simmon, CPA. The business issued common stock to Simmon. |
| 6 | Paid $300 cash for letterhead stationery for new office. |
| 7 | Purchased office furniture for the office on account, $6,800. |
| 10 | Consulted with tax client and received $3,300 for services rendered. |
| 11 | Paid utilities, $100. |
| 12 | Finished tax hearings on behalf of a client and submitted a bill for accounting services, $12,500. |
| 18 | Paid office rent, $1,000. |
| 25 | Received amount due from client that was billed on February 12. |
| 27 | Paid full amount of accounts payable created on February 7. |
| 29 | Cash dividends of $3,000 were paid to stockholders. |

**Requirements**

1. Analyze the effects of the events on the accounting equation of Andre Simmon, CPA. Use a format similar to Exhibit 1-6.
2. Prepare the following financial statements:
   a. Income statement.
   b. Statement of retained earnings.
   c. Balance sheet.

**P1-53B Using the accounting equation for transaction analysis and preparing financial statements**

**Learning Objectives 4, 5**

2c. Total Assets $89,060

Ariana Peterson recently opened her own law office, which she operates as a corporation. The name of the new entity is Ariana Peterson, Attorney. Peterson experienced the following events during the organizing phase of the new business and its first month of operation, December 2016. Some of the events were personal and did not affect the law practice. Others were business transactions and should be accounted for by the business.

| | |
|---|---|
| Dec. 1 | Sold personal investment in Nike stock, which she had owned for several years, receiving $25,000 cash. |
| 2 | Deposited the $25,000 cash from the sale of the Nike stock in her personal bank account. |
| 3 | Deposited $65,000 cash in a new business bank account titled Ariana Peterson, Attorney. The business issued common stock to Peterson. |
| 5 | Paid $400 cash for ink cartridges for the printer. |
| 7 | Purchased computer for the law office, agreeing to pay the account, $6,800, within three months. |
| 9 | Received $2,900 cash from customers for services rendered. |
| 15 | Received bill from *The Lawyer* for magazine subscription, $300. (Use Miscellaneous Expense account.) |
| 23 | Finished court hearings on behalf of a client and submitted a bill for legal services, $18,000, on account. |
| 28 | Paid bill from *The Lawyer*. |
| 30 | Paid utilities, $840. |
| 31 | Received $2,800 cash from clients billed on Dec. 23. |
| 31 | Cash dividends of $2,500 were paid to stockholders. |

**Requirements**

1. Analyze the effects of the preceding events on the accounting equation of Ariana Peterson, Attorney. Use a format similar to Exhibit 1-6.
2. Prepare the following financial statements:
   a. Income statement.
   b. Statement of retained earnings.
   c. Balance sheet.

## > Continuing Problem

Problem P1-54 is the first problem in a sequence that begins an accounting cycle. The cycle is continued in Chapter 2 and completed in Chapter 5.

### P1-54 Using the accounting equation for transaction analysis, preparing financial statements, and calculating return on assets (ROA)

Daniels Consulting began operations and completed the following transactions during December 2016:

| | |
|---|---|
| Dec. 2 | Stockholders contributed $20,000 cash in exchange for common stock. |
| 2 | Paid monthly office rent, $2,000. |
| 3 | Paid cash for a computer, $3,600. This equipment is expected to remain in service for five years. |
| 4 | Purchased office furniture on account, $3,000. The furniture should last for five years. |
| 5 | Purchased office supplies on account, $800. |
| 9 | Performed consulting service for a client on account, $2,500. |
| 12 | Paid utilities expenses, $150. |
| 18 | Performed service for a client and received cash of $2,100. |
| 21 | Received $2,400 in advance for client service to be performed in the future. (This increases the Unearned Revenue account, which is a liability. This account will be explained in more detail in Chapter 2.) |
| 21 | Hired an administrative assistant to be paid $2,055 on the 20th day of each month. The secretary begins work immediately. |
| 26 | Paid $200 on account. |
| 28 | Collected $400 on account. |
| 30 | Cash dividends of $1,000 were paid to stockholders. |

**Requirements**

1. Analyze the effects of Daniels Consulting's transactions on the accounting equation. Use the format of Exhibit 1-6, and include these headings: Cash; Accounts Receivable; Office Supplies; Equipment; Furniture; Accounts Payable; Unearned Revenue; Common Stock; Dividends; Service Revenue; Rent Expense; and Utilities Expense.
2. Prepare the income statement of Daniels Consulting for the month ended December 31, 2016.
3. Prepare the statement of retained earnings for the month ended December 31, 2016.
4. Prepare the balance sheet as of December 31, 2016.
5. Calculate the return on assets for Daniels Consulting for December, 2016.

# CRITICAL THINKING

## > Decision Case 1-1

Let's examine a case using Greg's Tunes and Sal's Silly Songs. It is now the end of the first year of operations, and the stockholders want to know how well each business came out at the end of the year. Neither business kept complete accounting records, and no dividends were paid. The businesses throw together the following data at year-end:

| | |
|---|---|
| **Sal's Silly Songs:** | |
| Total assets | $ 23,000 |
| Common Stock | 8,000 |
| Total revenues | 35,000 |
| Total expenses | 22,000 |
| **Greg's Tunes:** | |
| Total liabilities | $ 10,000 |
| Common Stock | 6,000 |
| Total expenses | 44,000 |
| Net income | 9,000 |

To gain information for evaluating the businesses, the stockholders ask you several questions. For each answer, you must show your work to convince the stockholders that you know what you are talking about.

**Requirements**

1. Which business has more assets?
2. Which business owes more to creditors?
3. Which business has more stockholders' equity at the end of the year?
4. Which business brought in more revenue?
5. Which business is more profitable?
6. Which of the foregoing questions do you think is most important for evaluating these two businesses? Why?
7. Which business looks better from a financial standpoint?

## > Ethical Issue 1-1

The tobacco companies have paid billions because of smoking-related illnesses. In particular, Philip Morris, a leading cigarette manufacturer, paid more than $3,000,000,000 in settlement payments in one year.

**Requirements**

1. Suppose you are the chief financial officer (CFO) responsible for the financial statements of Philip Morris. What ethical issue would you face as you consider what to report in your company's annual report about the cash payments? What is the ethical course of action for you to take in this situation?
2. What are some of the negative consequences to Philip Morris for not telling the truth? What are some of the negative consequences to Philip Morris for telling the truth?

## > Fraud Case 1-1

Exeter is a building contractor on the Gulf Coast. After losing a number of big lawsuits, it was facing its first annual net loss as the end of the year approached. The owner, Hank Snow, was under intense pressure from the company's creditors to report positive net income for the year. However, he knew that the controller, Alice Li, had arranged a short-term bank loan of $10,000 to cover a temporary shortfall of cash. He told Alice to record the incoming cash as "construction revenue" instead of a loan. That would nudge the company's income into positive territory for the year, and then, he said, the entry could be corrected in January when the loan was repaid.

**Requirements**

1. How would this action affect the year-end income statement? How would it affect the year-end balance sheet?
2. If you were one of the company's creditors, how would this fraudulent action affect you?

## > Financial Statement Case 1-1

This and similar cases in later chapters focus on the financial statements of a real company—**Starbucks Corporation**, a premier roaster and retailer of specialty coffee. As you work each case, you will gain confidence in your ability to use the financial statements of real companies.

Visit **http://www.pearsonhighered.com/Horngren** to view a link to the Starbucks Corporation Fiscal 2013 Annual Report.

**Requirements**

1. How much in cash (including cash equivalents) did Starbucks Corporation have on September 29, 2013?
2. What were the company's total assets at September 29, 2013? At September 30, 2012?
3. Write the company's accounting equation at September 29, 2013, by filling in the dollar amounts:

   Assets = Liabilities + Equity

4. Identify total net sales (revenues) for the year ended September 29, 2013. How much did total revenue increase or decrease from 2012 to 2013?
5. How much net income (net earnings) or net loss did Starbucks earn for 2013 and for 2012? Based on net income, was 2013 better or worse than 2012?
6. Calculate Starbucks Corporation's return on assets for the year ending September 29, 2013.
7. How did Starbucks Corporation's return on assets compare to **Green Mountain Coffee Roasters, Inc.'s** return on assets?



## > Quick Check Answers

**1.** d **2.** c **3.** a **4.** c **5.** c **6.** a **7.** c **8.** a **9.** b **10.** a **11.** c

# Recording Business Transactions

# 2

## Where's the Money?

Rachel Long scoured through the stacks of printouts. She had been hired to work on an embezzlement (stealing cash or assets of an entity) case for a local school district. The chief financial officer had called her because he suspected one of his employees was stealing money from the Parent Teacher Association (PTA). Rachel loved working on embezzlement cases. She enjoyed searching through the financial statements, identifying a problem, and then finding the transactions that documented the embezzlement. Rachel knew that if she looked deeply enough she would find the evidence that money was stolen. She always treated these cases as a puzzle that needed to be solved.

Sometimes businesses are unfortunate enough to have employees steal from them, and they need help in identifying the thief and providing enough evidence to turn the matter over to a law enforcement agency. Businesses often turn to an accountant, such as Rachel, who specializes in fraud, often called a certified fraud examiner. In addition, businesses hire accountants to help protect their assets by identifying potential problems in their recordkeeping and control of cash and assets.

Where will Rachel start looking when she begins searching for the stolen money? She'll start at the source, by reviewing documents such as invoices, sales receipts, and bank deposit slips. She will then review the transactions that were recorded (or not recorded) from those documents. These two pieces will help Rachel determine whether money was stolen from the school district and how the embezzlement occurred. It's important to Rachel that she not only catches the thief but also helps the school district prevent losses in the future. She will use her knowledge and experience in accounting to help her.

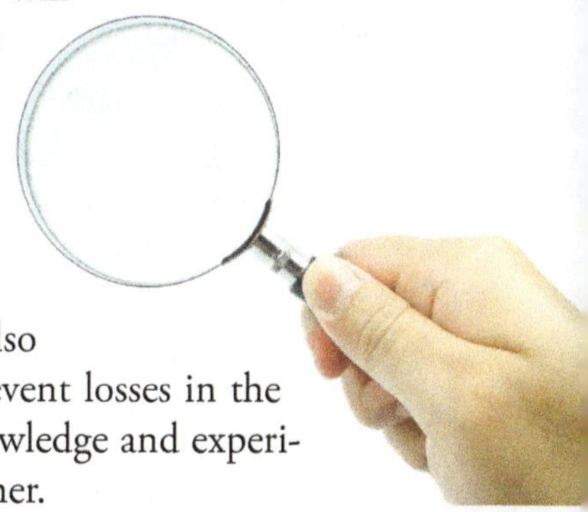

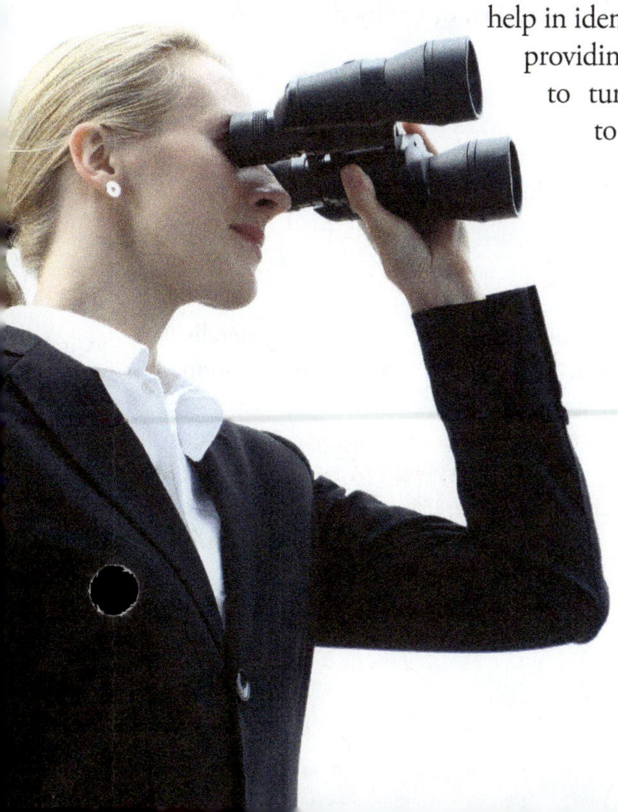

**Why Is Recording Business Transactions Important?**

Accounting is based on transactions. The recording of those transactions is based on source documents that provide the proof of the financial position of the business. The lack of that proof can lead to discoveries of stolen money and fictitious financial statements. As an example, when an employee at WorldCom, Inc., a long distance telephone company, found a $500 million accounting entry without any evidence to support it, it led to the discovery of a $3.8 billion fraud. The recording of transactions from source documents is the first step in the accounting process—and one of the most important. In this chapter, you learn about source documents and how to record transactions.

# Chapter 2 Learning Objectives

1 Explain accounts as they relate to the accounting equation and describe common accounts

2 Define debits, credits, and normal account balances using double-entry accounting and T-accounts

3 Record transactions in a journal and post journal entries to the ledger

4 Prepare the trial balance and illustrate how to use the trial balance to prepare financial statements

5 Use the debt ratio to evaluate business performance

Smart Touch Learning started out by recording the company's business transactions in terms of the accounting equation. That procedure works well when learning how to analyze transactions, but it's not a method in which a real-world business actually records transactions. In this chapter, you learn a more efficient way to capture business transactions. First, we need to start with a review of the accounting equation.

## WHAT IS AN ACCOUNT?

**Learning Objective 1**
Explain accounts as they relate to the accounting equation and describe common accounts

Recall that the basic tool of accounting is the accounting equation:

**Assets = Liabilities + Equity**

**Account**
A detailed record of all increases and decreases that have occurred in an individual asset, liability, or equity during a specific period.

The accounting equation is made up of three parts or categories: assets, liabilities, and equity. Each category contains accounts. An **account** is the detailed record of all increases and decreases that have occurred in an individual asset, liability, or equity during a specified period.

### Assets

*Assets* are economic resources that are expected to benefit the business in the future—something the business owns or has control of that has value. Exhibit 2-1 contains a list of asset accounts that most businesses use.

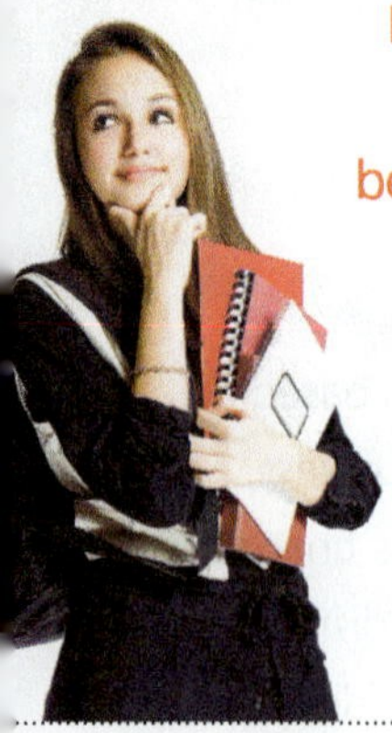

I get confused by the difference between Accounts Receivable and Accounts Payable. Is there an easy way to remember these two accounts?

### Liabilities

Recall that a *liability* is a debt—that is, something the business owes. A business generally has fewer liability accounts than asset accounts. Exhibit 2-2 contains examples of common liability accounts.

**You might be confused by the difference between the asset account, Accounts Receivable, and the liability account, Accounts Payable. An easy way to remember the distinction between these two accounts involves the words *Receivable* and *Payable*. A *receivable* involves a future *receipt* of cash. A *payable* involves a future *payment* of cash.**

**Exhibit 2-1** | **Asset Accounts**

| Account Name | Explanation |
|---|---|
| **Cash** | A business's money. Includes bank balances, bills, coins, and checks. |
| **Accounts Receivable** | A customer's promise to pay in the future for services or goods sold. Often described as "On Account." |
| **Notes Receivable** | A *written* promise that a customer will pay a fixed amount of money and *interest* by a certain date in the future. Usually more formal than an Accounts Receivable. |
| **Prepaid Expense** | A payment of an expense in advance. It is considered an asset because the prepayment provides a benefit in the future. Examples of prepaid expenses are *Prepaid Rent*, *Prepaid Insurance*, and *Office Supplies*. |
| **Equipment, Furniture, and Fixtures** | The cost of equipment, furniture, and fixtures (such as light fixtures and shelving). A business has a separate asset account for each type. |
| **Building** | The cost of an office building, a store, or a warehouse. |
| **Land** | The cost of land a business uses in operations. |

**Notes Receivable**
A written promise that a customer will pay a fixed amount of principal plus interest by a certain date in the future.

**Prepaid Expense**
A payment of an expense in advance.

**Exhibit 2-2** | **Liability Accounts**

| Account Name | Explanation |
|---|---|
| **Accounts Payable** | A promise made by the business to pay a debt in the future. Arises from a credit purchase. |
| **Notes Payable** | A *written* promise made by the business to pay a debt, usually involving *interest,* in the future. |
| **Accrued Liability** | An amount owed but not paid. A specific type of payable such as *Taxes Payable*, *Rent Payable*, and *Salaries Payable*. |
| **Unearned Revenue** | Occurs when a company receives cash from a customer but has not provided the product or service. The promise to provide services or deliver goods in the future. |

**Notes Payable**
A written promise made by the business to pay a debt, usually involving interest, in the future.

**Accrued Liability**
A liability for which the business knows the amount owed but the bill has not been paid.

**Unearned Revenue**
A liability created when a business collects cash from customers in advance of providing services or delivering goods.

## Equity

The stockholders' claim to the assets of the business is called equity or stockholders' equity. As shown in Exhibit 2-3, a company has separate accounts for each element of equity.

**Exhibit 2-3 | Equity Accounts**

| Account Name | Explanation |
|---|---|
| **Common Stock** | Represents the net contributions of the stockholders in the business. Increases equity. |
| **Dividends** | Distributions of cash or other assets to the stockholders. Decreases equity. |
| **Revenues** | Earnings that result from delivering goods or services to customers. Increases equity. Examples include *Service Revenue* and *Rent Revenue*. |
| **Expenses** | The cost of selling goods or services. Decreases equity. Examples include *Rent Expense*, *Salaries Expense*, and *Utilities Expense*. |

## Chart of Accounts

**Chart of Accounts**
A list of all of a company's accounts with their account numbers.

Companies need a way to organize their accounts. They use a **chart of accounts** to do this. A chart of accounts lists all company accounts along with the account numbers. The chart of accounts for Smart Touch Learning appears in Exhibit 2-4. Account numbers are just shorthand versions of the account names. One account number equals one account name—just like your Social Security number is unique to you.

*It can be confusing to choose the correct account to use when there are multiple accounts that sound similar. As an example, let's think about rent. There are four types of rent accounts: Prepaid Rent (asset), Rent Payable (liability), Rent Revenue (equity), or Rent Expense (equity). It is important that we understand the definition of each type of account so that we can use the account correctly. Prepaid Rent represents a prepayment of cash for renting a building in the future. Rent Payable represents a debt owed for renting a building currently, and Rent Expense represents the cost of renting a building currently. Rent Revenue, on the other hand, relates to the earning of revenue related to renting the building to a tenant currently.*

Account numbers usually have two or more digits. Assets are often numbered beginning with 1, liabilities with 2, stockholders' equity with 3, revenues with 4, and expenses with 5. The second and third digits in an account number indicate where the account fits within the category. For example, if Smart Touch Learning is using three-digit account numbers, Cash may be account number 101, the first asset account. Accounts Receivable may be account number 111, the second asset. Accounts Payable may be account number 201, the first liability. When numbers are used, all accounts are numbered by this system. However, each company chooses its own account numbering system.

Notice in Exhibit 2-4 the gap in account numbers between 121 and 141. Smart Touch Learning may need to add another asset account in the future. For example, the business may start selling some type of inventory and want to use account number 131 for Merchandise Inventory. So, the chart of accounts will change as the business evolves.

**Exhibit 2-4** | **Chart of Accounts—Smart Touch Learning**

| Balance Sheet Accounts | | |
|---|---|---|
| **Assets** | **Liabilities** | **Equity** |
| 101 Cash | 201 Accounts Payable | 301 Common Stock |
| 111 Accounts Receivable | 211 Salaries Payable | 311 Retained Earnings |
| 121 Notes Receivable | 221 Interest Payable | 321 Dividends |
| 141 Office Supplies | 231 Unearned Revenue | |
| 151 Furniture | 241 Notes Payable | |
| 171 Building | | |
| 191 Land | | |

| Income Statement Accounts (Part of Equity) | |
|---|---|
| **Revenues** | **Expenses** |
| 401 Service Revenue | 501 Rent Expense |
| 411 Interest Revenue | 511 Salaries Expense |
| | 521 Utilities Expense |
| | 531 Advertising Expense |

**IFRS**

Worldwide, accounting systems are based on the same equation: Assets = Liabilities + Equity. Or, in Spanish: Activos = Pasivos + Patrimonio Neto. And accounts are the building blocks for all accounting systems.

The chart of accounts varies from business to business, though many account names are common to all companies. For example, you will find Cash on every company's chart of accounts. The chart of accounts contains the list of account names you will use to record a transaction.

**Ledger**
The record holding all the accounts of a business, the changes in those accounts, and their balances.

## Ledger

In addition to a chart of accounts, companies need a way to show all of the increases and decreases in each account along with their balances. Companies use a **ledger** to fulfill this task. A ledger is a collection of all the accounts, the changes in those accounts, and their balances.

What are the similarities and differences between a chart of accounts and a ledger?

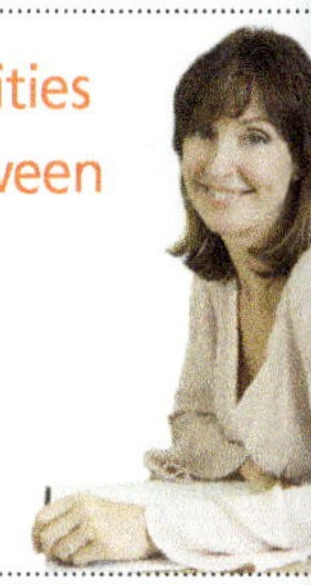

**A chart of accounts and a ledger are similar in that they both list the account names and account numbers of the business. A ledger, though, provides more detail. It includes the increases and decreases of each account for a specific period and the balance of each account at a specific point in time.**

## Try It!

Consider the following accounts and identify each as an asset (A), liability (L), or equity (E).

| | |
|---|---|
| 1. Rent Expense | 6. Accounts Payable |
| 2. Common Stock | 7. Unearned Revenue |
| 3. Furniture | 8. Notes Receivable |
| 4. Service Revenue | 9. Dividends |
| 5. Prepaid Insurance | 10. Insurance Expense |

**Check your answers online in MyAccountingLab or at http://www.pearsonhighered.com/Horngren.**

For more practice, see Short Exercise S2-1. MyAccountingLab

## WHAT IS DOUBLE-ENTRY ACCOUNTING?

**Learning Objective 2**
Define debits, credits, and normal account balances using double-entry accounting and T-accounts

Previously you learned that every transaction must be recorded into at least two accounts. For example, when a stockholder contributes money in exchange for Common Stock, the two accounts involved are Cash and Common Stock. Accounting uses this **double-entry system** to record the dual effects of each transaction. A transaction would be incomplete if only one side were recorded.

**Double-Entry System**
A system of accounting in which every transaction affects at least two accounts.

Consider a cash purchase of office supplies. What are the dual effects? A cash purchase of office supplies:

1. Increases the account Office Supplies (the business received office supplies).
2. Decreases Cash (the business paid cash).

### The T-Account

**T-Account**
A summary device that is shaped like a capital *T* with debits posted on the left side of the vertical line and credits on the right side of the vertical line.

A shortened form of the ledger is called the **T-account** because it takes the form of the capital letter *T*. The vertical line divides the account into its left and right sides, with the account name at the top. For example, the Cash T-account appears as follows:

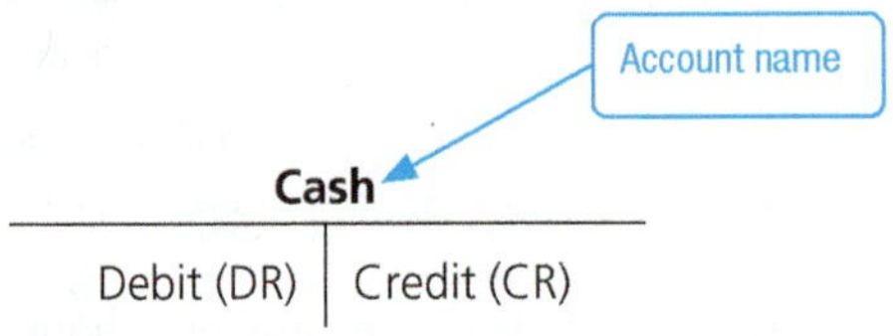


**Debit**
The left side of a T-account.

**Credit**
The right side of a T-account.

The left side of the T-account is called the **debit** side, and the right side is called the **credit** side. To become comfortable using these terms, remember the following: Debits go on the left; credits go on the right. Debit is abbreviated as DR, and Credit is abbreviated as CR.

### Increases and Decreases in the Accounts

How we record increases and decreases to an account is determined by the account type (asset, liability, or equity). For any given account, increases are recorded on one side and decreases are recorded on the opposite side. The following T-accounts provide a summary:

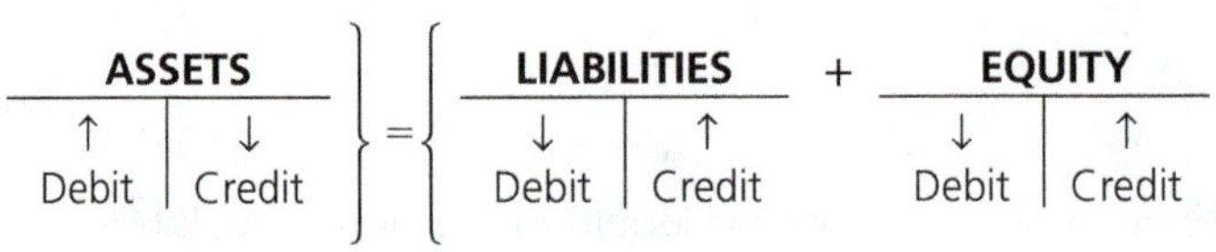


In other words, assets are always increased with a *debit* and decreased with a *credit*. Liabilities and equity are always increased with a *credit* and decreased with a *debit*. Whether an account is increased or decreased by a debit or a credit depends on the type of account. Debits are not "good" or "bad." Neither are credits. Debits are not always increases or always decreases—neither are credits. **The only thing a designation as a debit or credit means is where the item is placed—on the left or right side of the T-account.**

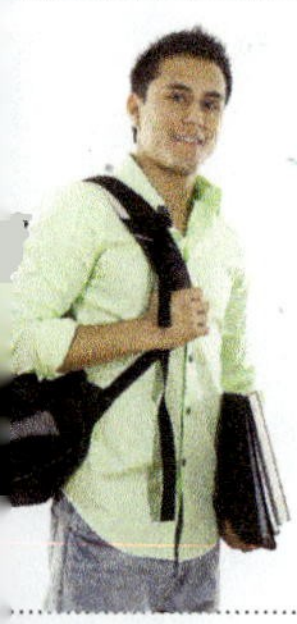

I always thought that a debit meant decrease and a credit meant increase. Am I wrong?

In a computerized accounting information system, the computer interprets debits and credits as increases or decreases, based on the account type. For example, a computer reads a debit to Cash as an increase because it is an asset account. The computer reads a debit to Accounts Payable as a decrease because it is a liability account.

**Example:** Assume a business wants to record an increase of $30,000 to the Cash account. The business would record a debit to Cash as follows:

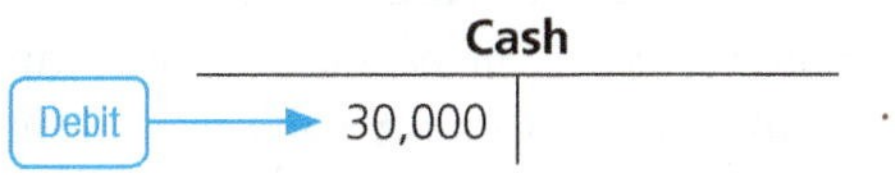


Cash is an asset account and, remember, asset accounts are increased with debits.

**Example:** What if the business, instead, wanted to record a decrease of $20,000 to the Cash account? The business would record a credit to Cash because Cash is an asset account and asset accounts are decreased with credits:

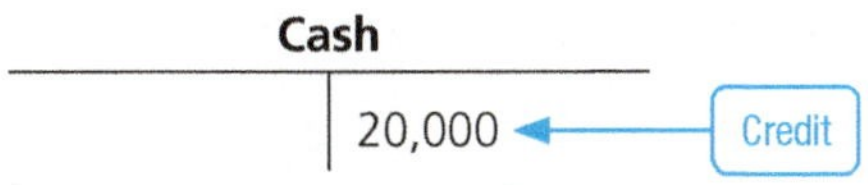


## Expanding the Rules of Debit and Credit

As we have noted, equity contains four account types: Common Stock, Dividends, Revenues, and Expenses. Common Stock and Revenues increase equity, whereas Dividends and Expenses decrease equity. We must now expand the accounting equation and the rules of debits and credits to include all elements of equity:

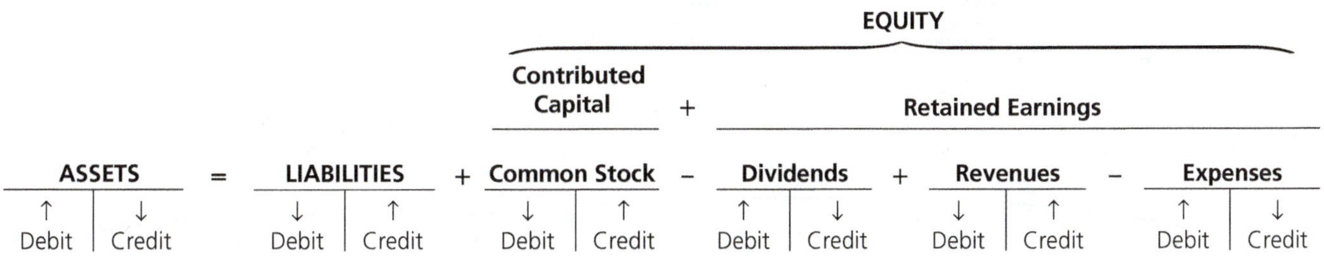


Notice in the expanded accounting equation that Dividends and Expenses record increases and decreases opposite of Common Stock and Revenues. This is because increases in Dividends and Expenses decrease equity.

## The Normal Balance of an Account

All accounts have a normal balance. An account's **normal balance** appears on the side—either debit or credit—where we record an *increase* (↑) in the account's balance. For example, assets are increased with a debit, so the normal balance is a debit. Liabilities and equity are increased with a credit, so the normal balance is a credit. Expenses and Dividends are equity accounts that have normal debit balances—unlike the other equity accounts. They have debit balances because they decrease equity. Common Stock and Revenues have a normal balance of credit. Let's look again at the accounting equation, this time with the normal balances marked:

**Normal Balance**
The balance that appears on the increase side of an account.

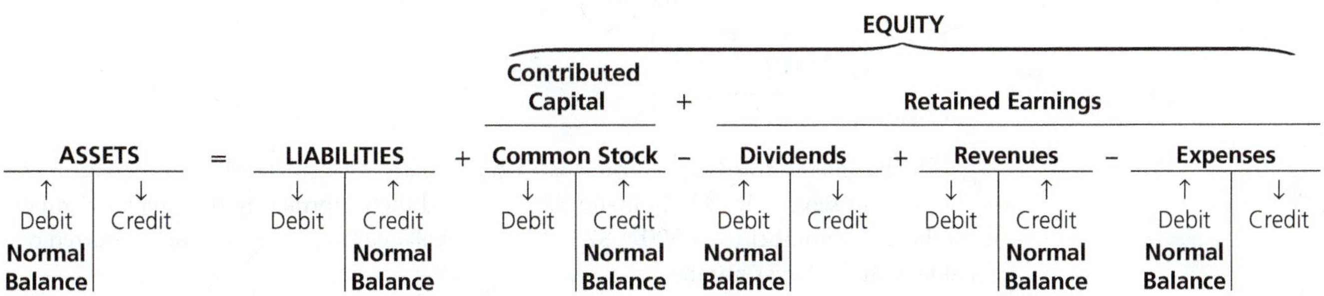

An account with a normal debit balance may occasionally have a credit balance. That indicates a negative amount in the account. For example, Cash will have a credit balance if the business overdraws its bank account. Also, the liability, Accounts Payable—a normal credit balance account—could have a debit balance if the company overpays its accounts payable. In other cases, a non-normal account balance indicates an error. For example, a credit balance in Office Supplies, Furniture, or Buildings is an error because negative amounts of these assets make no sense.

Exhibit 2-5 summarizes the rules of debit and credit and the normal balances for each account type.

**Exhibit 2-5 | Rules of Debit and Credit and Normal Balances for Each Account Type**

| Account Type | Increases | Decreases | Normal Balance |
|---|---|---|---|
| **Assets** | Debit | Credit | Debit |
| **Expenses** | Debit | Credit | Debit |
| **Dividends** | Debit | Credit | Debit |
| **Liabilities** | Credit | Debit | Credit |
| **Revenues** | Credit | Debit | Credit |
| **Common Stock** | Credit | Debit | Credit |

*An easy way to remember the rules of debits and credits is to memorize this helpful sentence. All elephants do love rowdy children. The first three words in the sentence will help you remember that assets, expenses, and dividends all have normal debit balances. The last three words in the sentence will remind you that liabilities, revenues, and common stock all have normal credit balances.*

## Determining the Balance of a T-Account

T-accounts can be used to determine the amount remaining in an account or the *balance* of the account. To illustrate, let's look at the following Cash T-Account:

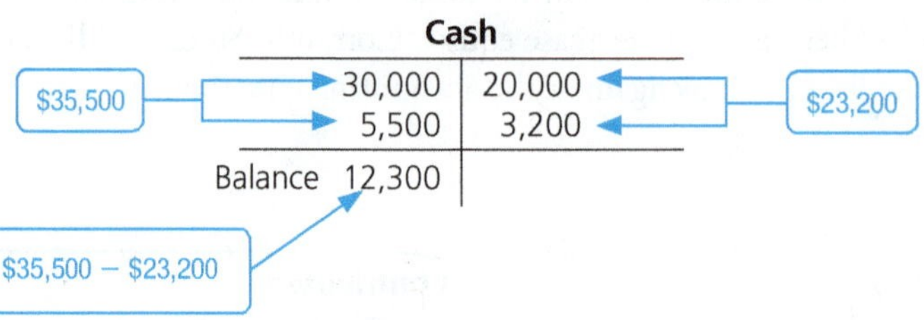


The balance of this Cash account is $12,300. This is calculated by adding each side of the account separately ($35,500 and $23,200) and then subtracting the smaller number from the larger number ($35,500 – $23,200). The balance ($12,300) is always reported on the side with the larger number.

## Try It!

For each account, identify if the change would be recorded as a debit (DR) or credit (CR).

| | |
|---|---|
| **11.** Increase to Cash | **16.** Increase to Interest Revenue |
| **12.** Decrease to Accounts Payable | **17.** Increase to Rent Expense |
| **13.** Increase to Common Stock | **18.** Decrease to Office Supplies |
| **14.** Increase to Unearned Revenue | **19.** Increase to Prepaid Rent |
| **15.** Decrease to Accounts Receivable | **20.** Increase to Notes Payable |

**Check your answers online in MyAccountingLab or at http://www.pearsonhighered.com/Horngren.**

For more practice, see Short Exercises S2-2 and S2-3. MyAccountingLab

# HOW DO YOU RECORD TRANSACTIONS?

When we reviewed the activity for Smart Touch Learning, we provided you with the transactions. In a real-world business, because of the faithful representation concept, accountants would need to provide evidence for those transactions.

**Learning Objective 3**
Record transactions in a journal and post journal entries to the ledger

## Source Documents—The Origin of the Transactions

Accountant use **source documents** to provide the evidence and data for recording transactions. For example, consider Sheena Bright's contribution of $30,000 to the business. Exhibit 2-6 illustrates the transaction. In that exhibit, Smart Touch Learning received $30,000 and deposited it in the bank. The business then gave common stock to Sheena Bright. The check received and the bank deposit slip are the source documents that show the amount of cash received by the business and the equity contribution of the stockholder, Sheena Bright. Based on these documents, the business can determine how to record this transaction.

**Source Document**
Provides the evidence and data for accounting transactions.

**Exhibit 2-6 | Flow of Accounting Data**

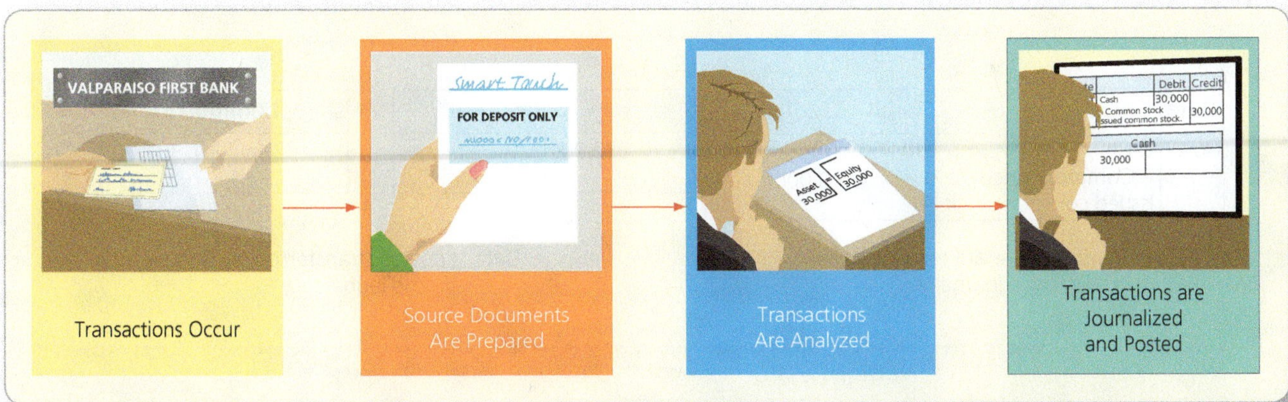

## ETHICS

### Are receipts really important?

Elijah Morris, assistant manager for Red's American Burger Restaurant, is responsible for purchasing equipment and supplies for the restaurant. Elijah recently purchased a $4,000 commercial-grade refrigerator for the restaurant, but he can't find the receipt. Elijah purchased the refrigerator with personal funds and is asking to be reimbursed by the restaurant. Hannah, the restaurant's accountant, has said that she is unsure if the business can reimburse Elijah without a receipt. Elijah suggests: "Hannah, it won't really matter if I have a receipt or not. You've seen the refrigerator in the restaurant, so you know I purchased it. What difference is a little receipt going to make?"

What should Hannah do? What would you do?

#### Solution

Hannah should not reimburse Elijah until she receives the receipt—the source document. Elijah could have purchased the refrigerator for less than the amount he is asking in reimbursement. Source documents provide the evidence of the amount of the transaction. If either an auditor or the owner of the restaurant investigated the $4,000 purchase, he or she would need to see the source document to verify the transaction. If Elijah truly cannot find the receipt, Hannah should ask for an alternative source document such as a credit card or bank statement that shows evidence of the purchase. In addition, Elijah should be warned about using personal funds to purchase equipment for the business.

Other source documents that businesses use include the following:

- **Purchase invoices.** Documents that tell the business how much and when to pay a vendor for purchases on account, such as office supplies.
- **Bank checks.** Documents that illustrate the amount and date of cash payments.
- **Sales invoices.** Documents provided to clients when a business sells services or goods; tells the business how much revenue to record.

## Journalizing and Posting Transactions

**Journal**
A record of transactions in date order.

**Posting**
Transferring data from the journal to the ledger.

After accountants review the source documents, they are then ready to record the transactions. Transactions are first recorded in a **journal**, which is the record of transactions in date order.

Journalizing a transaction records the data only in the journal—not in the ledger (the record holding all of the accounts of a business). The data must also be transferred to the ledger. The process of transferring data from the journal to the ledger is called **posting**. We post from the journal to the ledger. Debits in the journal are posted as debits in the ledger and credits as credits—no exceptions.

The following diagram shows this process:

| Date | | Debit | Credit |
|---|---|---|---|
| Nov. 1 | Cash | 30,000 | |
| | Common Stock | | 30,000 |
| | Issued common stock. | | |

Transactions are recorded in a journal.

| Cash | |
|---|---|
| 30,000 | |

| Common Stock | |
|---|---|
| | 30,000 |

Data is posted (transferred) to the ledger.

You have learned steps to use when analyzing accounting transactions. Use a modified version of those steps to help when recording transactions in the journal and then posting the journal entries to the ledger. The journalizing and posting process has five steps:

**Step 1:** Identify the accounts and the account type (asset, liability, or equity).

**Step 2:** Decide whether each account increases or decreases, then apply the rules of debits and credits.

**Step 3:** Record the transaction in the journal.

**Step 4:** Post the journal entry to the ledger.

**Step 5:** Determine whether the accounting equation is in balance.

Let's begin by journalizing the first transaction of Smart Touch Learning.

## Transaction 1—Stockholder Contribution

On November 1, the e-learning company received $30,000 cash from Sheena Bright and the business issued common stock to her.

**Step 1: Identify the accounts and the account type.** The two accounts involved are Cash (Asset) and Common Stock (Equity).

**Step 2: Decide whether each account increases or decreases, then apply the rules of debits and credits.** Both accounts increase by $30,000. Reviewing the rules of debits and credits, we use the accounting equation to help determine debits and credits for each account. Cash is an asset account and is increasing, so we will record a debit to Cash. Common Stock is an equity account and is increasing, so we will record a credit to Common Stock.

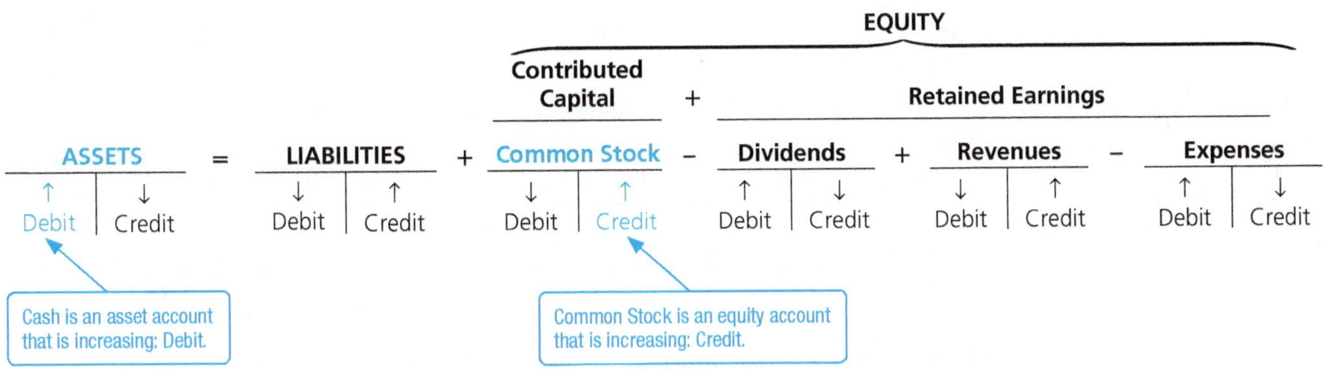


**Step 3: Record the transaction in the journal.** The recording of a transaction in the journal creates a journal entry. The journal entry for Transaction 1 is illustrated below. Notice that each journal entry contains four parts.

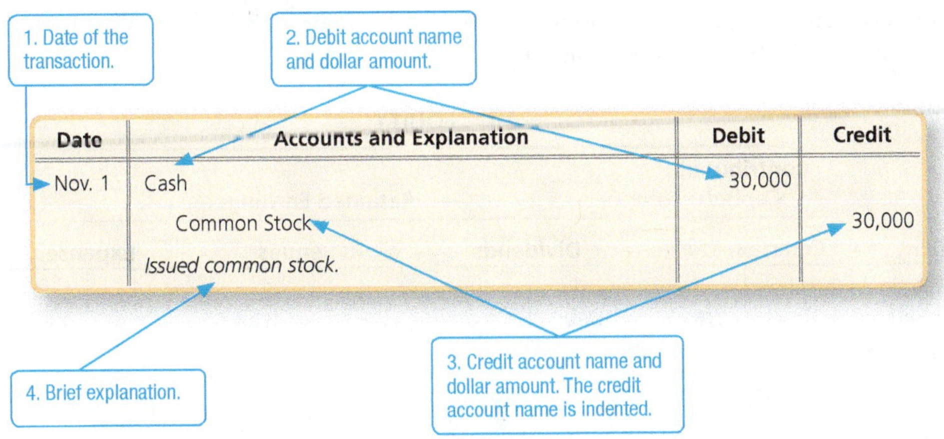


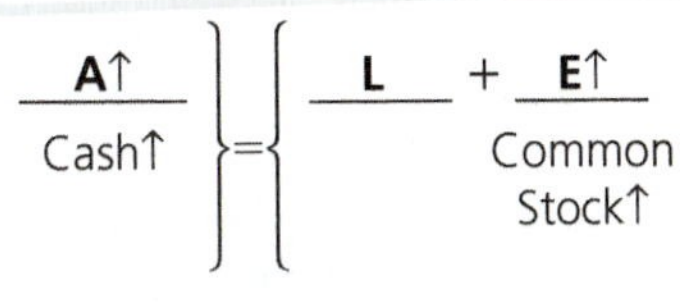

**Step 4: Post the journal entry to the ledger.** When transactions are posted from the journal to the ledger, the dollar amount is transferred from the debit and credit columns to the specific account. The date of the journal entry is also transferred to the T-accounts in the ledger. In a computerized system, this step is completed automatically when the transaction is recorded in the journal.

| Date | Accounts and Explanation | Debit | Credit |
|---|---|---|---|
| Nov. 1 | Cash | 30,000 | |
| | Common Stock | | 30,000 |
| | *Issued common stock.* | | |

**Cash**

| | |
|---|---|
| Nov. 1 30,000 | |

**Common Stock**

| | |
|---|---|
| | 30,000 Nov. 1 |

**Step 5: Determine if the accounting equation is in balance.**

| | ASSETS | | LIABILITIES + EQUITY |
|---|---|---|---|
| | Cash | = | Common Stock |
| (1) | + 30,000 | | + 30,000 |

*To help reinforce your learning of the account types, we will illustrate the transaction in the margin. We will indicate the accounts and account type (Step 1) and whether each account is increasing or decreasing (Step 2). These notations would not normally show up in a journal, but we have included them here to reinforce the rules of debits and credits.*

Let's look at Transaction 2 for Smart Touch Learning and apply the steps we just learned.

## Transaction 2—Purchase of Land for Cash

On November 2, Smart Touch Learning paid $20,000 cash for land.

**Step 1: Identify the accounts and the account type.** The two accounts involved are Cash (Asset) and Land (Asset).

**Step 2: Decide whether each account increases or decreases, then apply the rules of debits and credits.** Cash decreases. The business paid cash. Therefore, we credit Cash. The land increased, so we debit the Land account.

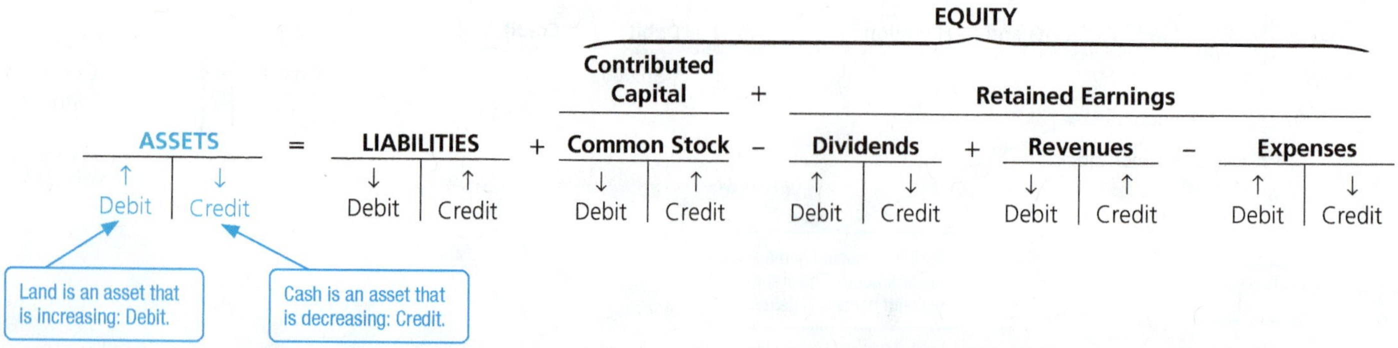

**Step 3: Record the transaction in the journal.**

| Date | Accounts and Explanation | Debit | Credit |
|---|---|---|---|
| Nov. 2 | Land | 20,000 | |
| | Cash | | 20,000 |
| | *Paid cash for land.* | | |

| A↑↓ | | L | + | E |
|---|---|---|---|---|
| Land↑<br>Cash↓ | = | | | |

**Step 4: Post the journal entry to the ledger.**

| Cash | | | |
|---|---|---|---|
| Nov. 1 | 30,000 | 20,000 | Nov. 2 |

| Land | |
|---|---|
| Nov. 2 | 20,000 |

**Step 5: Determine whether the accounting equation is in balance.**

| | ASSETS | | | | LIABILITIES | + | EQUITY |
|---|---|---|---|---|---|---|---|
| | Cash | + | Land | | | + | Common Stock |
| Bal. | $30,000 | | | = | | | $30,000 |
| (2) | −20,000 | | +20,000 | | | | |
| Bal. | $10,000 | + | $20,000 | | | | $30,000 |

We will now record journal entries for several more transactions for Smart Touch Learning. Now that you understand the steps, try to write the steps yourself before looking at the journal entry. Remember, if you need help, we'll provide the effect on the accounting equation in the margin.

## Transaction 3—Purchase of Office Supplies on Account

Smart Touch Learning buys $500 of office supplies on account on November 3.

The supplies will benefit Smart Touch Learning in future periods, so they are an asset to the company until they are used. The asset Office Supplies increased, so we debit Office Supplies. The liability Accounts Payable increased, so we credit Accounts Payable.

| Date | Accounts and Explanation | Debit | Credit |
|---|---|---|---|
| Nov. 3 | Office Supplies | 500 | |
| | Accounts Payable | | 500 |
| | *Purchased office supplies on account.* | | |

| A↑ | | L↑ | + | E |
|---|---|---|---|---|
| Office Supplies↑ | = | Accounts Payable↑ | | |

| Office Supplies | |
|---|---|
| Nov. 3 | 500 |

| Accounts Payable | |
|---|---|
| 500 | Nov. 3 |

## Transcription 4—Earning of Service Revenue for Cash

On November 8, Smart Touch Learning collected cash of $5,500 for service revenue that the business earned by providing e-learning services for clients.

The asset Cash increased, so we debit Cash. Revenue increased, so we credit Service Revenue.

| A↑ | = | L | + | E↑ |
|---|---|---|---|---|
| Cash↑ | = | | | Service Revenue↑ |

| Date | Accounts and Explanation | Debit | Credit |
|---|---|---|---|
| Nov. 8 | Cash | 5,500 | |
| | Service Revenue | | 5,500 |
| | *Performed services and received cash.* | | |

**Cash**

| | Debit | Credit | |
|---|---|---|---|
| Nov. 1 | 30,000 | 20,000 | Nov. 2 |
| Nov. 8 | 5,500 | | |

**Service Revenue**

| | Debit | Credit | |
|---|---|---|---|
| | | 5,500 | Nov. 8 |

## Transaction 5—Earning of Service Revenue on Account

On November 10, Smart Touch Learning performed services for clients, for which the clients will pay the company later. The business earned $3,000 of service revenue on account.

This transaction increased Accounts Receivable, so we debit this asset. Service Revenue is increased with a credit.

| A↑ | = | L | + | E↑ |
|---|---|---|---|---|
| Accounts Receivable↑ | = | | | Service Revenue↑ |

| Date | Accounts and Explanation | Debit | Credit |
|---|---|---|---|
| Nov. 10 | Accounts Receivable | 3,000 | |
| | Service Revenue | | 3,000 |
| | *Performed services on account.* | | |

**Accounts Receivable**

| | Debit | Credit | |
|---|---|---|---|
| Nov. 10 | 3,000 | | |

**Service Revenue**

| | Debit | Credit | |
|---|---|---|---|
| | | 5,500 | Nov. 8 |
| | | 3,000 | Nov. 10 |

Notice the differences and the similarities between Transactions 4 and 5. In both transactions, Service Revenue was increased (credited) because in both cases the company had earned revenue. However, in Transaction 4, the company was paid at the time of service. In Transaction 5, on the other hand, the company will receive cash later (Accounts Receivable). This difference is key because the amount of revenue is not determined by when the company *receives* cash. Revenues are recorded when the company *does* the work or provides the service.

## Transaction 6—Payment of Expenses with Cash

Smart Touch Learning paid the following cash expenses on November 15: office rent, $2,000, and employee salaries, $1,200. We need to debit each expense account to record its increase and credit Cash, an asset, for the total decrease.

| Date | Accounts and Explanation | Debit | Credit |
|---|---|---|---|
| Nov. 15 | Rent Expense | 2,000 | |
| | Salaries Expense | 1,200 | |
| | Cash | | 3,200 |
| | *Paid cash expenses.* | | |

| A↓ | = | L | + | E↓ |
|---|---|---|---|---|
| Cash↓ | | | | Rent Expense↑<br>Salaries Expense↑ |

**Cash**

| | | | |
|---|---|---|---|
| Nov. 1 | 30,000 | 20,000 | Nov. 2 |
| Nov. 8 | 5,500 | 3,200 | Nov. 15 |

**Rent Expense**

| | | |
|---|---|---|
| Nov. 15 | 2,000 | |

**Salaries Expense**

| | | |
|---|---|---|
| Nov. 15 | 1,200 | |

**Compound Journal Entry**
A journal entry that is characterized by having multiple debits and/or multiple credits.

Notice that the journal entry has three accounts involved—two debits and one credit. This is a compound journal entry. A **compound journal entry** has more than two accounts, but total dollar value of the debits still must equal total dollar value of the credits.

Before we move to the next transaction, let's take a moment to carefully look at expenses. In Transaction 6, we recorded a debit to each expense account. The accounting equation and the rules of debits and credits state that a debit to an expense account increases the account.

**We are recording an increase to the expense account because the business has more expenses now than it had before. But, remember, the overall effect on the accounting equation is that increases in expenses decrease equity. An easy way to think about it is that we are increasing a negative account.**

I thought expenses decreased equity, but we are debiting the expense that records an increase to the account.

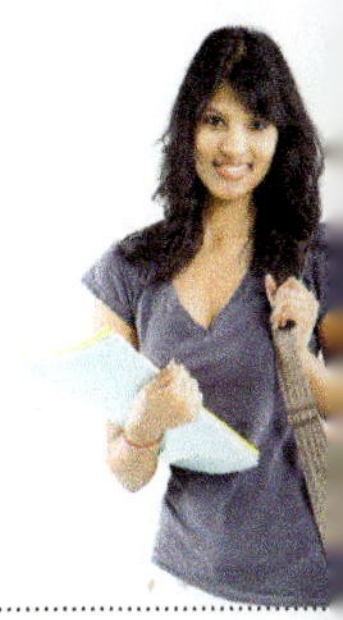

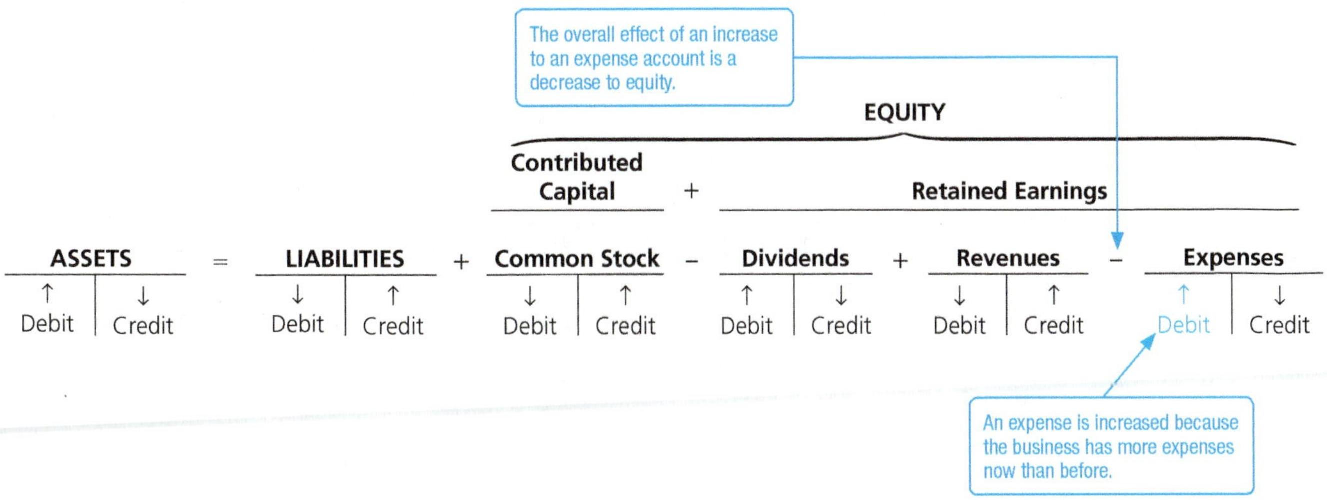

### Transaction 7—Payment on Account (Accounts Payable)

On November 21, Smart Touch Learning paid $300 on the accounts payable created in Transaction 3. The payment decreased cash, an asset, so we credit Cash. The payment decreased Accounts Payable, so we debit that liability.

A↓ = L↓ + E
Cash↓ = Accounts Payable↓

| Date | Accounts and Explanation | Debit | Credit |
|---|---|---|---|
| Nov. 21 | Accounts Payable | 300 | |
| | Cash | | 300 |
| | *Paid cash on account.* | | |

**Cash**

| | | | |
|---|---|---|---|
| Nov. 1 | 30,000 | 20,000 | Nov. 2 |
| Nov. 8 | 5,500 | 3,200 | Nov. 15 |
| | | 300 | Nov. 21 |

**Accounts Payable**

| | | | |
|---|---|---|---|
| Nov. 21 | 300 | 500 | Nov. 3 |

Notice that after recording this transaction and posting to the Accounts Payable account, the balance of Accounts Payable is $200 ($500 – $300). This is the new balance that the business owes to its creditor.

### Transaction 8—Collection on Account (Accounts Receivable)

On November 22, Smart Touch Learning collected $2,000 cash from a client in Transaction 5. Cash is increased, so we debit the asset Cash. Accounts Receivable, also an asset, is decreased, so we credit Accounts Receivable. *Note:* This transaction has no effect on revenue; the related revenue was recorded in Transaction 5.

A↓↑ = L + E
Cash↑
Accounts Receivable↓

| Date | Accounts and Explanation | Debit | Credit |
|---|---|---|---|
| Nov. 22 | Cash | 2,000 | |
| | Accounts Receivable | | 2,000 |
| | *Received cash on account.* | | |

**Cash**

| | | | |
|---|---|---|---|
| Nov. 1 | 30,000 | 20,000 | Nov. 2 |
| Nov. 8 | 5,500 | 3,200 | Nov. 15 |
| Nov. 22 | 2,000 | 300 | Nov. 21 |

**Accounts Receivable**

| | | | |
|---|---|---|---|
| Nov. 10 | 3,000 | 2,000 | Nov. 22 |

## Transaction 9—Payment of Cash Dividend

On November 25, a payment of $5,000 cash was paid for dividends. The dividend decreased the entity's cash, so we credit Cash. The dividend also decreased equity. Decreases in equity that result from dividends are debited to the Dividends account.

| Date | Accounts and Explanation | Debit | Credit |
|---|---|---|---|
| Nov. 25 | Dividends | 5,000 | |
| | Cash | | 5,000 |
| | *Paid dividends.* | | |

| A↓ | = | L | + | E↓ |
|---|---|---|---|---|
| Cash↓ | | | | Dividends↑ |

**Cash**

| | | | |
|---|---|---|---|
| Nov. 1 | 30,000 | 20,000 | Nov. 2 |
| Nov. 8 | 5,500 | 3,200 | Nov. 15 |
| Nov. 22 | 2,000 | 300 | Nov. 21 |
| | | 5,000 | Nov. 25 |

**Dividends**

| | | |
|---|---|---|
| Nov. 25 | 5,000 | |

## Transaction 10—Prepaid Expenses

On December 1, Smart Touch Learning prepays three months' office rent of $3,000 ($1,000 per month × 3 months). The prepayment of the rent is recorded to the Prepaid Rent account (Asset). It is recorded as an asset because Smart Touch Learning will receive a benefit in the future. The asset, Prepaid Rent, is increasing, so we will need to debit it. Cash is decreasing and will be recorded as a credit.

| Date | Accounts and Explanation | Debit | Credit |
|---|---|---|---|
| Dec. 1 | Prepaid Rent | 3,000 | |
| | Cash | | 3,000 |
| | *Paid rent in advance.* | | |

| A↓↑ | = | L | + | E |
|---|---|---|---|---|
| Prepaid Rent↑<br>Cash↓ | | | | |

**Cash**

| | | | |
|---|---|---|---|
| Nov. 1 | 30,000 | 20,000 | Nov. 2 |
| Nov. 8 | 5,500 | 3,200 | Nov. 15 |
| Nov. 22 | 2,000 | 300 | Nov. 21 |
| | | 5,000 | Nov. 25 |
| | | 3,000 | Dec. 1 |

**Prepaid Rent**

| | | |
|---|---|---|
| Dec. 1 | 3,000 | |

### Transaction 11—Payment of Expense with Cash

On December 1, Smart Touch Learning paid employee salaries of $1,200. Salaries Expense will be debited to record its increase, and Cash will be credited for the decrease.

| A↓ | = | L | + | E↓ |
|---|---|---|---|---|
| Cash↓ | | | | Salaries Expense↑ |

| Date | Accounts and Explanation | Debit | Credit |
|---|---|---|---|
| Dec. 1 | Salaries Expense | 1,200 | |
| | Cash | | 1,200 |
| | *Paid salaries.* | | |

**Cash**

| | | | |
|---|---|---|---|
| Nov. 1 | 30,000 | 20,000 | Nov. 2 |
| Nov. 8 | 5,500 | 3,200 | Nov. 15 |
| Nov. 22 | 2,000 | 300 | Nov. 21 |
| | | 5,000 | Nov. 25 |
| | | 3,000 | Dec. 1 |
| | | 1,200 | Dec. 1 |

**Salaries Expense**

| | | | |
|---|---|---|---|
| Nov. 15 | 1,200 | | |
| Dec. 1 | 1,200 | | |

### Transaction 12—Purchase of Building with Notes Payable

On December 1, Smart Touch Learning purchased a $60,000 building in exchange for a note payable. The building will benefit the business in the future, so it is recorded as an asset to the company. The asset Building is increased, so we debit Building. The liability Notes Payable increased, so we credit Notes Payable.

| A↑ | = | L↑ | + | E |
|---|---|---|---|---|
| Building↑ | | Notes Payable↑ | | |

| Date | Accounts and Explanation | Debit | Credit |
|---|---|---|---|
| Dec. 1 | Building | 60,000 | |
| | Notes Payable | | 60,000 |
| | *Purchase of building with note.* | | |

**Building**

| | | | |
|---|---|---|---|
| Dec. 1 | 60,000 | | |

**Notes Payable**

| | | | |
|---|---|---|---|
| | | 60,000 | Dec. 1 |

### Transaction 13—Stockholder Contribution

On December 2, Smart Touch Learning received a contribution of furniture with a fair market value of $18,000 from Sheena Bright. In exchange, Smart Touch Learning issued common stock. The furniture will benefit the company in the future, so it is recorded as an asset. The asset Furniture is increasing, so we debit it. Common Stock, an equity account, is also increasing and is recorded as a credit.

| Date | Accounts and Explanation | Debit | Credit |
|---|---|---|---|
| Dec. 2 | Furniture | 18,000 | |
| | Common Stock | | 18,000 |
| | *Contribution of furniture in exchange for common stock.* | | |

| A↑ | = | L | + | E↑ |
|---|---|---|---|---|
| Furniture↑ | = | | | Common Stock↑ |

**Furniture**

| Debit | | Credit | |
|---|---|---|---|
| Dec. 2 | 18,000 | | |

**Common Stock**

| Debit | | Credit | |
|---|---|---|---|
| | | 30,000 | Nov. 1 |
| | | 18,000 | Dec. 2 |

### Transaction 14—Accrued Liability

On December 15, Smart Touch Learning received a telephone bill for $100 and will pay this expense next month. There is no cash payment now. This is an accrued liability. Remember, an accrued liability is a liability for which the business knows the amount owed, but the bill has not been paid. The Utilities Expense increased, so we debit this expense. The liability (Utilities Payable) increased, so we credit Utilities Payable. Alternatively, we could credit Accounts Payable instead of Utilities Payable.

| Date | Accounts and Explanation | Debit | Credit |
|---|---|---|---|
| Dec. 15 | Utilities Expense | 100 | |
| | Utilities Payable | | 100 |
| | *Accrued utility liability.* | | |

| A | = | L↑ | + | E↓ |
|---|---|---|---|---|
| | = | Utilities Payable↑ | | Utilities Expense↑ |

**Utilities Payable**

| Debit | | Credit | |
|---|---|---|---|
| | | 100 | Dec. 15 |

**Utilities Expense**

| Debit | | Credit | |
|---|---|---|---|
| Dec. 15 | 100 | | |

### Transaction 15—Payment of Expense with Cash

On December 15, Smart Touch Learning paid employee salaries of $1,200. Salaries Expense will be debited to record its increase, and Cash will be credited for the decrease.

| A↓ | = | L | + | E↓ |
|---|---|---|---|---|
| Cash↓ | = | | | Salaries Expense↑ |

| Date | Accounts and Explanation | Debit | Credit |
|---|---|---|---|
| Dec. 15 | Salaries Expense | 1,200 | |
| | Cash | | 1,200 |
| | *Paid salaries.* | | |

**Cash**

| | | | |
|---|---|---|---|
| Nov. 1 | 30,000 | 20,000 | Nov. 2 |
| Nov. 8 | 5,500 | 3,200 | Nov. 15 |
| Nov. 22 | 2,000 | 300 | Nov. 21 |
| | | 5,000 | Nov. 25 |
| | | 3,000 | Dec. 1 |
| | | 1,200 | Dec. 1 |
| | | 1,200 | Dec. 15 |

**Salaries Expense**

| | | | |
|---|---|---|---|
| Nov. 15 | 1,200 | | |
| Dec. 1 | 1,200 | | |
| Dec. 15 | 1,200 | | |

### Transaction 16—Unearned Revenue

On December 21, a law firm engages Smart Touch Learning to provide e-learning services and agrees to pay $600 in advance. Smart Touch Learning received cash but has not yet performed the services. Cash increased, so we debit Cash. The promise to perform services in the future will be recorded as Unearned Revenue, a liability account. Unearned Revenue is increasing, so we credit it. Notice that we did not record revenue. Revenue is not recorded until Smart Touch Learning provides the services.

| A↑ | = | L↑ | + | E |
|---|---|---|---|---|
| Cash↑ | = | Unearned Revenue↑ | | |

| Date | Accounts and Explanation | Debit | Credit |
|---|---|---|---|
| Dec. 21 | Cash | 600 | |
| | Unearned Revenue | | 600 |
| | *Collected cash for future services.* | | |

**Cash**

| | | | |
|---|---|---|---|
| Nov. 1 | 30,000 | 20,000 | Nov. 2 |
| Nov. 8 | 5,500 | 3,200 | Nov. 15 |
| Nov. 22 | 2,000 | 300 | Nov. 21 |
| Dec. 21 | 600 | 5,000 | Nov. 25 |
| | | 3,000 | Dec. 1 |
| | | 1,200 | Dec. 1 |
| | | 1,200 | Dec. 15 |

**Unearned Revenue**

| | | | |
|---|---|---|---|
| | | 600 | Dec. 21 |

### Transaction 17—Earning of Service Revenue for Cash

On December 28, Smart Touch Learning collected cash of $8,000 for Service Revenue that the business earned by providing e-learning services for clients.

| Date | Accounts and Explanation | Debit | Credit |
|---|---|---|---|
| Dec. 28 | Cash | 8,000 | |
| | Service Revenue | | 8,000 |
| | *Performed services and received cash.* | | |

| A↑ | | L + E↑ |
|---|---|---|
| Cash↑ | = | Service Revenue↑ |

**Cash**

| | | | |
|---|---|---|---|
| Nov. 1 | 30,000 | 20,000 | Nov. 2 |
| Nov. 8 | 5,500 | 3,200 | Nov. 15 |
| Nov. 22 | 2,000 | 300 | Nov. 21 |
| Dec. 21 | 600 | 5,000 | Nov. 25 |
| Dec. 28 | 8,000 | 3,000 | Dec. 1 |
| | | 1,200 | Dec. 1 |
| | | 1,200 | Dec. 15 |

**Service Revenue**

| | | | |
|---|---|---|---|
| | | 5,500 | Nov. 8 |
| | | 3,000 | Nov. 10 |
| | | 8,000 | Dec. 28 |

## The Ledger Accounts After Posting

Exhibit 2-7 (on the next page) shows the T-accounts of Smart Touch Learning after posting the journal entries from the journal to the ledger. The accounts are grouped under their headings. Notice that at December 31, Smart Touch Learning has assets of $114,700 ($12,200 + $1,000 + $500 + $3,000 + $18,000 + $60,000 + $20,000), liabilities of $60,900 ($200 + $100 + $600 + $60,000), and equity of $53,800 ($48,000 − $5,000 + $16,500 − $2,000 − $3,600 − $100). The accounting equation is in balance ($114,700 = $60,900 + $53,800).

## Exhibit 2-7 | Smart Touch Learning's Accounts After Posting Journal Entries in November and December

**ASSETS = LIABILITIES + EQUITY**

EQUITY: Contributed Capital + Retained Earnings

### ASSETS

**Cash**

| | | | |
|---|---|---|---|
| Nov. 1 | 30,000 | 20,000 | Nov. 2 |
| Nov. 8 | 5,500 | 3,200 | Nov. 15 |
| Nov. 22 | 2,000 | 300 | Nov. 21 |
| Dec. 21 | 600 | 5,000 | Nov. 25 |
| Dec. 28 | 8,000 | 3,000 | Dec. 1 |
| | | 1,200 | Dec. 1 |
| | | 1,200 | Dec. 15 |
| Bal. | 12,200 | | |

**Accounts Receivable**

| | | | |
|---|---|---|---|
| Nov. 10 | 3,000 | 2,000 | Nov. 22 |
| Bal. | 1,000 | | |

**Office Supplies**

| | | | |
|---|---|---|---|
| Nov. 3 | 500 | | |
| Bal. | 500 | | |

**Prepaid Rent**

| | | | |
|---|---|---|---|
| Dec. 1 | 3,000 | | |
| Bal. | 3,000 | | |

**Furniture**

| | | | |
|---|---|---|---|
| Dec. 2 | 18,000 | | |
| Bal. | 18,000 | | |

**Building**

| | | | |
|---|---|---|---|
| Dec. 1 | 60,000 | | |
| Bal. | 60,000 | | |

**Land**

| | | | |
|---|---|---|---|
| Nov. 2 | 20,000 | | |
| Bal. | 20,000 | | |

### LIABILITIES

**Accounts Payable**

| | | | |
|---|---|---|---|
| Nov. 21 | 300 | 500 | Nov. 3 |
| | | 200 | Bal. |

**Utilities Payable**

| | | | |
|---|---|---|---|
| | | 100 | Dec. 15 |
| | | 100 | Bal. |

**Unearned Revenue**

| | | | |
|---|---|---|---|
| | | 600 | Dec. 21 |
| | | 600 | Bal. |

**Notes Payable**

| | | | |
|---|---|---|---|
| | | 60,000 | Dec. 1 |
| | | 60,000 | Bal. |

### EQUITY

Common Stock − Dividends + Service Revenue − Rent Expense − Salaries Expense − Utilities Expense

**Common Stock**

| | | | |
|---|---|---|---|
| | | 30,000 | Nov. 1 |
| | | 18,000 | Dec. 2 |
| | | 48,000 | Bal. |

**Dividends**

| | | | |
|---|---|---|---|
| Nov. 25 | 5,000 | | |
| Bal. | 5,000 | | |

**Service Revenue**

| | | | |
|---|---|---|---|
| | | 5,500 | Nov. 8 |
| | | 3,000 | Nov. 10 |
| | | 8,000 | Dec. 28 |
| | | 16,500 | Bal. |

**Rent Expense**

| | | | |
|---|---|---|---|
| Nov. 15 | 2,000 | | |
| Bal. | 2,000 | | |

**Salaries Expense**

| | | | |
|---|---|---|---|
| Nov. 15 | 1,200 | | |
| Dec. 1 | 1,200 | | |
| Dec. 15 | 1,200 | | |
| Bal. | 3,600 | | |

**Utilities Expense**

| | | | |
|---|---|---|---|
| Dec. 15 | 100 | | |
| Bal. | 100 | | |

**$114,700 = $60,900 + $53,800**

## The Four-Column Account: An Alternative to the T-Account

The ledger accounts illustrated thus far appear as T-accounts, with the debits on the left and the credits on the right. The T-account clearly separates debits from credits and is used for teaching. An alternative to using the T-account is the four-column account. The four-column account still has debit and credit columns, but it also adds two additional columns that are used to determine a running balance. Exhibit 2-8 shows the Cash T-account and the Cash four-column account for Smart Touch Learning.

The first pair of Debit/Credit columns in the four-column account is for transaction amounts posted to the account from the journal, such as the $30,000 debit. The second pair of Debit/Credit columns shows the balance of the account as of each date. Because the four-column format provides more information, it is used more often in practice than the T-account. Notice that the balance after the last transaction on December 28 is $12,200, which is the same balance calculated in the T-account.

Do you notice the column labeled *Post Ref.* in the four-column account in Exhibit 2-8? This column is used in the posting process. When the information is transferred from the journal to the ledger, a posting reference (Post Ref.) is added. This allows a user of the financial data to trace the amount in the ledger back to the journal. In a computerized system, the user would be able to click on the posting reference to view the

**Exhibit 2-8 | T-Account Versus Four-Column Account**

**Cash**

| | | | |
|---|---|---|---|
| Nov. 1 | 30,000 | 20,000 | Nov. 2 |
| Nov. 8 | 5,500 | 3,200 | Nov. 15 |
| Nov. 22 | 2,000 | 300 | Nov. 21 |
| Dec. 21 | 600 | 5,000 | Nov. 25 |
| Dec. 28 | 8,000 | 3,000 | Dec. 1 |
| | | 1,200 | Dec. 1 |
| | | 1,200 | Dec. 15 |
| Bal. | 12,200 | | |

The Debit or Credit for each transaction.

The balance of the account after each transaction.

| CASH | | | | | Account No. 101 | |
|---|---|---|---|---|---|---|
| Date | Item | Post Ref. | Debit | Credit | Balance | |
| | | | | | Debit | Credit |
| 2016 | | | | | | |
| Nov. 1 | | J1 | 30,000 | | 30,000 | |
| Nov. 2 | | J1 | | 20,000 | 10,000 | |
| Nov. 8 | | J1 | 5,500 | | 15,500 | |
| Nov. 15 | | J1 | | 3,200 | 12,300 | |
| Nov. 21 | | J1 | | 300 | 12,000 | |
| Nov. 22 | | J1 | 2,000 | | 14,000 | |
| Nov. 25 | | J1 | | 5,000 | 9,000 | |
| Dec. 1 | | J2 | | 3,000 | 6,000 | |
| Dec. 1 | | J2 | | 1,200 | 4,800 | |
| Dec. 15 | | J2 | | 1,200 | 3,600 | |
| Dec. 21 | | J2 | 600 | | 4,200 | |
| Dec. 28 | | J2 | 8,000 | | 12,200 | |

related journal entry. Exhibit 2-9 shows the posting and associated posting references for Transaction 1 of Smart Touch Learning. Remember, in a computerized environment, this process is completed automatically when the user enters the journal entry.

**Exhibit 2-9 | Posting References**

The page number from the journal.

**Page 1**

| Date | Accounts and Explanation | Post. Ref. | Debit | Credit |
|---|---|---|---|---|
| Nov. 1 | Cash | 101 | 30,000 | |
| | Common Stock | 301 | | 30,000 |
| | *Issued common stock.* | | | |

The account number from the ledger.

**CASH** **Account No. 101**

| Date | Item | Post. Ref. | Debit | Credit | Balance | |
|---|---|---|---|---|---|---|
| | | | | | Debit | Credit |
| 2016 | | | | | | |
| Nov. 1 | | J1 | 30,000 | | 30,000 | |

**COMMON STOCK** **Account No. 301**

| Date | Item | Post. Ref. | Debit | Credit | Balance | |
|---|---|---|---|---|---|---|
| | | | | | Debit | Credit |
| 2016 | | | | | | |
| Nov. 1 | | J1 | | 30,000 | | 30,000 |

## Try It!

**21.** EMB Consulting Services had the following transactions for the month of November. Journalize the transactions and include an explanation with each entry.

| | |
|---|---|
| Nov. 1 | The business received $10,000 cash and issued common stock. |
| 15 | Purchased office supplies on account, $400. |
| 18 | Paid advertising bill, $150. |
| 20 | Received $1,000 from customers for services rendered. |
| 28 | Cash dividends of $500 were paid to stockholders. |

**Check your answers online in MyAccountingLab or at http://www.pearsonhighered.com/Horngren.**

For more practice, see Short Exercises S2-4 through S2-7. MyAccountingLab

## WHAT IS THE TRIAL BALANCE?

After the transactions are recorded in the journal and then posted to the ledger, a **trial balance** can be prepared. The trial balance summarizes the ledger by listing all the accounts with their balances—assets first, followed by liabilities, and then equity. In a manual accounting system, the trial balance provides an accuracy check by showing whether total debits equal total credits. In all types of systems, the trial balance is a useful summary of the accounts and their balances because it shows the balances on a specific date for all accounts in a company's accounting system. Exhibit 2-10 is the trial balance of Smart Touch Learning at December 31, 2016.

**Learning Objective 4**
Prepare the trial balance and illustrate how to use the trial balance to prepare financial statements

**Trial Balance**
A list of all ledger accounts with their balances at a point in time.

**Exhibit 2-10 | Trial Balance**

SMART TOUCH LEARNING
Trial Balance
December 31, 2016

| | Balance | |
|---|---|---|
| **Account Title** | **Debit** | **Credit** |
| Cash | $ 12,200 | |
| Accounts Receivable | 1,000 | |
| Office Supplies | 500 | |
| Prepaid Rent | 3,000 | |
| Furniture | 18,000 | |
| Building | 60,000 | |
| Land | 20,000 | |
| Accounts Payable | | $ 200 |
| Utilities Payable | | 100 |
| Unearned Revenue | | 600 |
| Notes Payable | | 60,000 |
| Common Stock | | 48,000 |
| Dividends | 5,000 | |
| Service Revenue | | 16,500 |
| Rent Expense | 2,000 | |
| Salaries Expense | 3,600 | |
| Utilities Expense | 100 | |
| Total | **$ 125,400** | **$ 125,400** |

*The trial balance and the balance sheet are not the same. Make sure you understand the differences between these two documents. A trial balance verifies the equality of debits and credits and is an internal document used only by employees of the company. The balance sheet, on the other hand, presents the business's accounting equation and is a financial statement that can be used by both internal and external users.*

### Preparing Financial Statements from the Trial Balance

In addition to proving the equality of debits and credits, the trial balance is also used to prepare the financial statements. The account balances are taken directly from the trial balance and are used to prepare the income statement, statement of retained earnings, and balance sheet. In Exhibit 2-11 (on the next page), we present the financial statements for the two months ended December 31, 2016, for Smart Touch Learning.

**Exhibit 2-11** **Smart Touch Learning's Financial Statements**

| SMART TOUCH LEARNING<br>Income Statement<br>Two Months Ended December 31, 2016 | | |
|---|---|---|
| Revenues: | | |
| Service Revenue | | $ 16,500 |
| Expenses: | | |
| Salaries Expense | $ 3,600 | |
| Rent Expense | 2,000 | |
| Utilities Expense | 100 | |
| Total Expenses | | 5,700 |
| Net Income | | **$ 10,800** |

| SMART TOUCH LEARNING<br>Statement of Retained Earnings<br>Two Months Ended December 31, 2016 | |
|---|---|
| Retained Earnings, November 1, 2016 | $ 0 |
| Net income for the two months | 10,800 |
| | 10,800 |
| Dividends | (5,000) |
| Retained Earnings, December 31, 2016 | **$ 5,800** |

| SMART TOUCH LEARNING<br>Balance Sheet<br>December 31, 2016 | | | |
|---|---|---|---|
| **Assets** | | **Liabilities** | |
| Cash | $ 12,200 | Accounts Payable | $ 200 |
| Accounts Receivable | 1,000 | Utilities Payable | 100 |
| Office Supplies | 500 | Unearned Revenue | 600 |
| Prepaid Rent | 3,000 | Notes Payable | 60,000 |
| Furniture | 18,000 | Total Liabilities | 60,900 |
| Building | 60,000 | | |
| Land | 20,000 | **Stockholders' Equity** | |
| | | Common Stock | 48,000 |
| | | Retained Earnings | 5,800 |
| | | Total Stockholders' Equity | 53,800 |
| Total Assets | **$ 114,700** | Total Liabilities and Stockholders' Equity | **$ 114,700** |

## Correcting Trial Balance Errors

Throughout the accounting process, total debits should always equal total credits. If they do not, there is an error. Computerized accounting systems eliminate many errors because most software will not let you make a journal entry that does not balance. But computers cannot *eliminate* all errors because humans can input the wrong data.

Balancing errors can be detected by computing the difference between total debits and total credits on the trial balance. Then perform one or more of the following actions:

1. **Search the trial balance for a missing account.** For example, suppose the accountant omitted the Dividends account from the trial balance in Exhibit 2-10. Total debits would then be $120,400 ($125,400 − $5,000). Trace each account from the ledger to the trial balance, and you will locate the missing account.
2. **Divide the difference between total debits and total credits by 2.** A debit treated as a credit, or vice versa, doubles the amount of the error. Suppose the accountant posted a $500 credit as a debit. Total debits contain the $500, and total credits omit the $500. The out-of-balance amount is $1,000. Dividing the difference by 2 identifies the $500

amount of the transaction. Then search the journal or ledger for a $500 transaction and trace it to the account affected.

3. **Divide the out-of-balance amount by 9.** If the result is evenly divisible by 9, the error may be a *slide* (example: writing $1,000 as $100 or writing $100 as $1,000) or a *transposition* (example: listing $1,200 as $2,100). Suppose, for example, that the accountant entered the $5,000 Dividends as $50,000 on the trial balance. This is a slide-type error. Total debits would differ from total credits by $45,000 ($50,000 − $5,000 = $45,000). Dividing $45,000 by 9 yields $5,000, the correct amount of the dividends. Look for an account in the ledger with a $5,000 balance until you reach the Dividends account. You have then found the error.

Total debits can equal total credits on the trial balance; however, there still could be errors in individual account balances because an incorrect account might have been selected in an individual journal entry.

**Try It!**

22. Using the following accounts and their balances, prepare the trial balance for Cooper Furniture Repair as of December 31, 2016. All accounts have normal balances.

| | | | |
|---|---|---|---|
| Cash | $ 7,000 | Advertising Expense | $ 1,200 |
| Unearned Revenue | 4,500 | Utilities Expense | 800 |
| Equipment | 10,000 | Rent Expense | 5,000 |
| Service Revenue | 8,000 | Accounts Payable | 2,300 |
| Common Stock | 12,200 | Dividends | 3,000 |

**Check your answers online in MyAccountingLab or at http://www.pearsonhighered.com/Horngren.**

For more practice, see Short Exercise S2-8. MyAccountingLab

## HOW DO YOU USE THE DEBT RATIO TO EVALUATE BUSINESS PERFORMANCE?

**Learning Objective 5**
Use the debt ratio to evaluate business performance

Previously you learned that evaluating a company's return on assets (Net income / Average total assets) can help in determining how well a company is performing. In this chapter, you learn about another tool that can be used when reviewing financial statements. The **debt ratio** shows the proportion of assets financed with debt and is calculated by dividing total liabilities by total assets. It can be used to evaluate a business's ability to pay its debts.

**Debt Ratio**
Shows the proportion of assets financed with debt. Total liabilities / Total assets.

Debt ratio = Total liabilities / Total assets

Think about the accounting equation (Assets = Liabilities + Equity). The equation shows who can claim the assets. The liabilities represent the claims of the creditors, and the equity represents the claims of the stockholders. Companies that have a high percentage of liabilities are at greater risk of default. If they are unable to pay their creditors as the amounts become due, the creditors have the right to claim the assets. The debt ratio calculates the percentage of assets that are financed with liabilities.

Let's look at **Green Mountain Coffee Roasters, Inc.** and evaluate its ability to pay its debts. On its 2013 balance sheet (located in Appendix A), Green Mountain reported (in thousands) total liabilities of $1,125,978 ($597,063 + $160,221 + $76,061 + $252,867 + $28,721 + $11,045) and total assets of $3,761,548. The debt ratio for Green Mountain as of September 28, 2013, follows:

Debt ratio = Total liabilities / Total assets
= $1,125,978 / $3,761,548 = 0.299 = 29.9%*

*rounded

A debt ratio of 29.9% means that approximately thirty percent of the assets of Green Mountain are financed with debt. The other 70.1% (100% − 29.9%) are financed by stockholders of the corporation. The debt ratio indicates the risk of a company. The higher the debt ratio, the higher the risk. All liabilities must eventually be paid, and the debt ratio is one indication of the ability of the company to fulfill these obligations.

## DECISIONS

### Would you purchase equipment with debt?

Jackson Russell works as a district sales manager for a large pharmaceutical sales company. Jackson would like to purchase a new high-tech marketing display that he will be able to use at upcoming medical conferences. The marketing display will allow his customers to access up-to-date information and research statistics on the pharmaceuticals that his company sells by using multiple touch screen computers. He believes that the marketing display will significantly increase the sales revenue of the products he sells. The only problem is that the marketing display will cost $50,000, and he does not have the cash in his budget to purchase the display. Jackson will need to purchase the display using debt, which will increase the district's debt ratio from 20% to 58%. Jackson is aware that his company closely monitors the district's debt ratio and has a policy that the district must maintain a ratio below 55%. Should Jackson purchase the equipment?

#### Solution

If the company has a policy that the district's debt ratio must remain below 55%, then Jackson should not purchase the equipment. However, there might be a way to structure the purchase so that the district's debt ratio would stay below 55%. Jackson either needs to incur less debt or increase his total assets. He could do this in several possible ways. One alternative might be for Jackson to pay for part of the display equipment with cash and only finance part of it with debt. Even putting as little as $10,000 cash down on the equipment would keep the debt ratio below 55%. Another alternative might be for his district to recognize revenue. If there are open sales opportunities that his employees could close, they might be able to increase total assets (and revenue) and, thereby, decrease the debt ratio.

## Try It!

**23.** Using the following accounts and their balances, calculate the debt ratio for Cooper Furniture Repair as of December 31, 2016.

| | | | |
|---|---|---|---|
| Cash | $ 7,000 | Advertising Expense | $ 1,200 |
| Unearned Revenue | 4,500 | Utilities Expense | 800 |
| Equipment | 10,000 | Rent Expense | 5,000 |
| Service Revenue | 8,000 | Accounts Payable | 2,300 |
| Common Stock | 12,200 | Dividends | 3,000 |

**Check your answer online in MyAccountingLab or at http://www.pearsonhighered.com/Horngren.**

For more practice, see Short Exercise S2-9. MyAccountingLab

# REVIEW

## > Things You Should Know

### 1. What is an account?

- An account is a detailed record of all increases and decreases that have occurred in an individual asset, liability, or equity during a specific period.
- Common asset accounts: Cash, Accounts Receivable, Notes Receivable, Prepaid Expenses, Land, Building, Furniture
- Common liability accounts: Accounts Payable, Notes Payable, Taxes Payable, Salaries Payable, Unearned Revenue
- Common equity accounts: Common Stock, Dividends, Revenues, Expenses
- A chart of accounts lists a company's accounts along with account numbers.
- A ledger shows the increases and decreases in each account along with their balances.

### 2. What is double-entry accounting?

- Double-entry accounting requires transactions to be recorded into at least two accounts.
- The T-account is shaped like a capital *T* with debits posted to the left side of the vertical line and credits posted to the right side of the vertical line.
- Debit = Left
- Credit = Right
- Assets, Dividends, and Expenses are increased with a debit and decreased with a credit.
- Liabilities, Common Stock, and Revenues are increased with a credit and decreased with a debit.
- The normal balance of an account is the increase side of an account.

### 3. How do you record transactions?

- Source documents provide the evidence and data for transactions.
- Transactions are recorded in a journal, and then the journal entries are posted (transferred) to the ledger.
- Transactions are journalized and posted using five steps:

  **Step 1:** Identify the accounts and the account type.

  **Step 2:** Decide whether each account increases or decreases, then apply the rules of debits and credits.

  **Step 3:** Record the transaction in the journal.

  **Step 4:** Post the journal entry to the ledger.

  **Step 5:** Determine whether the accounting equation is in balance.

**4. What is the trial balance?**

- The trial balance summarizes the ledger by listing all the accounts with their balances.
- Assets are listed first, followed by liabilities, and then equity.
- The trial balance ensures that debits equal credits and is used to prepare the financial statements.

**5. How do you use the debt ratio to evaluate business performance?**

- The debt ratio can be used to evaluate a business's ability to pay its debts.
- Debt ratio = Total liabilities / Total assets.

## > Summary Problem

The trial balance of Harper Service Center as of February 29, 2016, follows:

**HARPER SERVICE CENTER**
Trial Balance
February 29, 2016

| | Balance | |
|---|---|---|
| **Account Title** | **Debit** | **Credit** |
| Cash | $ 23,900 | |
| Accounts Receivable | 4,500 | |
| Office Supplies | 0 | |
| Land | 0 | |
| Accounts Payable | | $ 2,000 |
| Utilities Payable | | 0 |
| Unearned Revenue | | 0 |
| Notes Payable | | 0 |
| Common Stock | | 18,500 |
| Dividends | 0 | |
| Service Revenue | | 10,000 |
| Salaries Expense | 800 | |
| Rent Expense | 1,000 | |
| Interest Expense | 0 | |
| Utilities Expense | 300 | |
| Total | **$ 30,500** | **$ 30,500** |

During March, the business engaged in the following transactions:

| | |
|---|---|
| Mar. 2 | Borrowed $45,000 from the bank and signed a note payable in the name of the business. |
| 4 | Paid cash of $40,000 to acquire land. |
| 9 | Performed services for a customer and received cash of $5,000. |
| 13 | Purchased office supplies on account, $300. |
| 15 | Performed services for a customer on account, $2,600. |
| 18 | Paid $1,200 on account. |
| 21 | Paid the following cash expenses: salaries, $3,000; rent, $1,500; and interest, $400. |
| 25 | Received $3,100 from a customer on account. |
| 27 | Received a $200 utility bill that will be paid next month. |
| 29 | Received $1,500 for services to be performed next month. |
| 30 | Cash dividends of $1,800 were paid to stockholders. |

**Requirements**

1. Open the accounts listed in the trial balance using the balances indicated. Use the T-account format.
2. Journalize each transaction including explanations.
3. Post the journal entries to the ledger (use T-account format).
4. Prepare the trial balance of Harper Service Center as of March 31, 2016.

## > Solution

**Requirement 1**

| ASSETS | = | LIABILITIES | + | EQUITY | | | | | | |
|---|---|---|---|---|---|---|---|---|---|---|
| | | | | Contributed Capital | + | Retained Earnings | | | | |
| Cash | = | Accounts Payable | + | Common Stock | − | Dividends | + | Service Revenue | − | Salaries Expense |
| Bal. 23,900 \| | | \| 2,000 Bal. | | \| 18,500 Bal. | | Bal. 0 \| | | \| 10,000 Bal. | | Bal. 800 \| |
| Accounts Receivable | | Utilities Payable | | | | | | | | Rent Expense |
| Bal. 4,500 \| | | \| 0 Bal. | | | | | | | | Bal. 1,000 \| |
| Office Supplies | | Unearned Revenue | | | | | | | | Interest Expense |
| Bal. 0 \| | | \| 0 Bal. | | | | | | | | Bal. 0 \| |
| Land | | Notes Payable | | | | | | | | Utilities Expense |
| Bal. 0 \| | | \| 0 Bal. | | | | | | | | Bal. 300 \| |

## Requirement 2

| Date | Accounts and Explanation | Debit | Credit |
|---|---|---|---|
| Mar. 2 | Cash | 45,000 | |
| | Notes Payable | | 45,000 |
| | *Borrowed cash on notes payable.* | | |
| 4 | Land | 40,000 | |
| | Cash | | 40,000 |
| | *Purchased land with cash.* | | |
| 9 | Cash | 5,000 | |
| | Service Revenue | | 5,000 |
| | *Performed services and received cash.* | | |
| 13 | Office Supplies | 300 | |
| | Accounts Payable | | 300 |
| | *Purchased office supplies on account.* | | |
| 15 | Accounts Receivable | 2,600 | |
| | Service Revenue | | 2,600 |
| | *Performed services on account.* | | |
| 18 | Accounts Payable | 1,200 | |
| | Cash | | 1,200 |
| | *Paid cash on account.* | | |
| 21 | Salaries Expense | 3,000 | |
| | Rent Expense | 1,500 | |
| | Interest Expense | 400 | |
| | Cash | | 4,900 |
| | *Paid cash expenses.* | | |
| 25 | Cash | 3,100 | |
| | Accounts Receivable | | 3,100 |
| | *Received cash on account.* | | |
| 27 | Utilities Expense | 200 | |
| | Utilities Payable | | 200 |
| | *Received utility bill.* | | |
| 29 | Cash | 1,500 | |
| | Unearned Revenue | | 1,500 |
| | *Collected cash for future services.* | | |
| 30 | Dividends | 1,800 | |
| | Cash | | 1,800 |
| | *Paid dividends.* | | |

## Requirement 3

ASSETS = LIABILITIES + EQUITY

EQUITY: Contributed Capital + Retained Earnings

Cash = Accounts Payable + Common Stock − Dividends + Service Revenue − Salaries Expense

**Cash**

| | | | |
|---|---|---|---|
| Bal. | 23,900 | 40,000 | Mar. 4 |
| Mar. 2 | 45,000 | 1,200 | Mar. 18 |
| Mar. 9 | 5,000 | 4,900 | Mar. 21 |
| Mar. 25 | 3,100 | 1,800 | Mar. 30 |
| Mar. 29 | 1,500 | | |
| Bal. | 30,600 | | |

**Accounts Receivable**

| | | | |
|---|---|---|---|
| Bal. | 4,500 | 3,100 | Mar. 25 |
| Mar. 15 | 2,600 | | |
| Bal. | 4,000 | | |

**Office Supplies**

| | | | |
|---|---|---|---|
| Bal. | 0 | | |
| Mar. 13 | 300 | | |
| Bal. | 300 | | |

**Land**

| | | | |
|---|---|---|---|
| Bal. | 0 | | |
| Mar. 4 | 40,000 | | |
| Bal. | 40,000 | | |

**Accounts Payable**

| | | | |
|---|---|---|---|
| Mar. 18 | 1,200 | 2,000 | Bal. |
| | | 300 | Mar. 13 |
| | | 1,100 | Bal. |

**Utilities Payable**

| | | | |
|---|---|---|---|
| | | 0 | Bal. |
| | | 200 | Mar. 27 |
| | | 200 | Bal. |

**Unearned Revenue**

| | | | |
|---|---|---|---|
| | | 0 | Bal. |
| | | 1,500 | Mar. 29 |
| | | 1,500 | Bal. |

**Notes Payable**

| | | | |
|---|---|---|---|
| | | 0 | Bal. |
| | | 45,000 | Mar. 2 |
| | | 45,000 | Bal. |

**Common Stock**

| | | | |
|---|---|---|---|
| | | 18,500 | Bal. |
| | | 18,500 | Bal. |

**Dividends**

| | | | |
|---|---|---|---|
| Bal. | 0 | | |
| Mar. 30 | 1,800 | | |
| Bal. | 1,800 | | |

**Service Revenue**

| | | | |
|---|---|---|---|
| | | 10,000 | Bal. |
| | | 5,000 | Mar. 9 |
| | | 2,600 | Mar. 15 |
| | | 17,600 | Bal. |

**Salaries Expense**

| | | | |
|---|---|---|---|
| Bal. | 800 | | |
| Mar. 21 | 3,000 | | |
| Bal. | 3,800 | | |

**Rent Expense**

| | | | |
|---|---|---|---|
| Bal. | 1,000 | | |
| Mar. 21 | 1,500 | | |
| Bal. | 2,500 | | |

**Interest Expense**

| | | | |
|---|---|---|---|
| Bal. | 0 | | |
| Mar. 21 | 400 | | |
| Bal. | 400 | | |

**Utilities Expense**

| | | | |
|---|---|---|---|
| Bal. | 300 | | |
| Mar. 27 | 200 | | |
| Bal. | 500 | | |

## Requirement 4

**HARPER SERVICE CENTER**
Trial Balance
March 31, 2016

| | Balance | |
|---|---|---|
| **Account Title** | **Debit** | **Credit** |
| Cash | $ 30,600 | |
| Accounts Receivable | 4,000 | |
| Office Supplies | 300 | |
| Land | 40,000 | |
| Accounts Payable | | $ 1,100 |
| Utilities Payable | | 200 |
| Unearned Revenue | | 1,500 |
| Notes Payable | | 45,000 |
| Common Stock | | 18,500 |
| Dividends | 1,800 | |
| Service Revenue | | 17,600 |
| Salaries Expense | 3,800 | |
| Rent Expense | 2,500 | |
| Interest Expense | 400 | |
| Utilities Expense | 500 | |
| Total | **$ 83,900** | **$ 83,900** |

## > Key Terms

**Account** (p. 56)
**Accrued Liability** (p. 57)
**Chart of Accounts** (p. 58)
**Compound Journal Entry** (p. 69)
**Credit** (p. 60)
**Debit** (p. 60)
**Debt Ratio** (p. 81)
**Double-Entry System** (p. 60)
**Journal** (p. 64)
**Ledger** (p. 59)
**Normal Balance** (p. 61)
**Notes Payable** (p. 57)
**Notes Receivable** (p. 57)
**Posting** (p. 64)
**Prepaid Expense** (p. 57)
**Source Document** (p. 63)
**T-Account** (p. 60)
**Trial Balance** (p. 79)
**Unearned Revenue** (p. 57)

## > Quick Check

**Learning Objective 1**

1. The detailed record of the changes in a particular asset, liability, or stockholders' equity is called
   a. an account.
   b. a journal.
   c. a ledger.
   d. a trial balance.

**Learning Objective 1**

2. Which of the following accounts is a liability?
   a. Accounts Receivable
   b. Service Revenue
   c. Unearned Revenue
   d. Prepaid Rent Expense

**Learning Objective 2**

3. The left side of an account is used to record which of the following?
   a. Debit or credit, depending on the type of account
   b. Increases
   c. Credits
   d. Debits

**Learning Objective 2**

4. Which of the following statements is correct?
   a. Prepaid Expenses are decreased with a debit.
   b. Unearned Revenue is increased with a debit.
   c. Rent Expense is increased with a credit.
   d. Accounts Payable is increased with a credit.

**Learning Objective 3**

5. Your business purchased office supplies of $2,500 on account. The journal entry to record this transaction is as follows:

| Date | Accounts and Explanation | Debit | Credit |
|---|---|---|---|
| a. | Office Supplies | 2,500 | |
| | Accounts Receivable | | 2,500 |
| b. | Office Supplies | 2,500 | |
| | Accounts Payable | | 2,500 |
| c. | Accounts Payable | 2,500 | |
| | Office Supplies | | 2,500 |
| d. | Cash | 2,500 | |
| | Accounts Payable | | 2,500 |

**Learning Objective 3**

6. Sedlor Properties purchased office supplies on account for $800. Which journal entry records the payment on account of those office supplies?

| Date | Accounts and Explanation | Debit | Credit |
|---|---|---|---|
| a. | Accounts Payable | 800 | |
| | Accounts Receivable | | 800 |
| b. | Accounts Payable | 800 | |
| | Cash | | 800 |
| c. | Cash | 800 | |
| | Accounts Payable | | 800 |
| d. | Office Supplies | 800 | |
| | Cash | | 800 |

**Learning Objective 3**

7. Posting a $2,500 purchase of office supplies on account appears as follows:

a.

| Cash | |
|---|---|
| | 2,500 |

| Office Supplies | |
|---|---|
| 2,500 | |

b.

| Office Supplies | |
|---|---|
| | 2,500 |

| Accounts Payable | |
|---|---|
| 2,500 | |

c.

| Office Supplies | |
|---|---|
| 2,500 | |

| Accounts Receivable | |
|---|---|
| | 2,500 |

d.

| Office Supplies | |
|---|---|
| 2,500 | |

| Accounts Payable | |
|---|---|
| | 2,500 |

**Learning Objective 4**

8. Pixel Copies recorded a cash collection on account by debiting Cash and crediting Accounts Payable. What will the trial balance show for this error?

   a. Cash is overstated
   b. Liabilities are overstated
   c. Expenses are overstated
   d. The trial balance will not balance

**Learning Objectives 3, 4**

9. Which sequence correctly summarizes the accounting process?

   a. Journalize transactions, post to the accounts, prepare a trial balance
   b. Journalize transactions, prepare a trial balance, post to the accounts
   c. Post to the accounts, journalize transactions, prepare a trial balance
   d. Prepare a trial balance, journalize transactions, post to the accounts

**Learning Objective 5**

10. Nathville Laundry reported assets of $800 and equity of $480. What is Nathville's debt ratio?

   a. 60%
   b. 40%
   c. 67%
   d. Not enough information is provided

**Check your answers at the end of the chapter.**

# ASSESS YOUR PROGRESS

## > Review Questions

1. Identify the three categories of the accounting equation, and list at least four accounts associated with each category.
2. What is the purpose of the chart of accounts? Explain the numbering typically associated with the accounts.
3. What does a ledger show? What's the difference between a ledger and the chart of accounts?
4. Accounting uses a double-entry system. Explain what this sentence means.
5. What is a T-account? On which side is the debit? On which side is the credit? Where does the account name go on a T-account?
6. When are debits increases? When are debits decreases?
7. When are credits increases? When are credits decreases?
8. Identify which types of accounts have a normal debit balance and which types of accounts have a normal credit balance.
9. What are source documents? Provide examples of source documents that a business might use.
10. Where are transactions initially recorded?
11. Explain the five steps in journalizing and posting transactions.
12. What are the four parts of a journal entry?
13. What is involved in the posting process?
14. What is the purpose of the trial balance?
15. What is the difference between the trial balance and the balance sheet?
16. If total debits equal total credits on the trial balance, is the trial balance error-free? Explain your answer.
17. What is the calculation for the debt ratio? Explain what the debt ratio evaluates.

## > Short Exercises

**Learning Objective 1**

**S2-1 Identifying accounts**

Consider the following accounts:

a. Notes Receivable
b. Common Stock
c. Prepaid Insurance
d. Notes Payable
e. Rent Revenue
f. Taxes Payable
g. Rent Expense
h. Furniture
i. Dividends
j. Unearned Revenue

Identify each account as an asset (A), liability (L), or equity (E).

### S2-2 Identifying increases and decreases in accounts

**Learning Objective 2**

For each account, identify whether the changes would be recorded as a debit (DR) or credit (CR).

a. Increase to Accounts Receivable
b. Decrease to Unearned Revenue
c. Decrease to Cash
d. Increase to Interest Expense
e. Increase to Salaries Payable
f. Decrease to Prepaid Rent
g. Increase to Common Stock
h. Increase to Notes Receivable
i. Decrease to Accounts Payable
j. Increase to Interest Revenue

### S2-3 Identifying normal balances

**Learning Objective 2**

For each account, identify whether the normal balance is a debit (DR) or credit (CR).

a. Notes Payable
b. Dividends
c. Service Revenue
d. Land
e. Unearned Revenue
f. Common Stock
g. Utilities Expense
h. Office Supplies
i. Advertising Expense
j. Interest Payable

### S2-4 Journalizing transactions

**Learning Objective 3**

Jack Davis opened a medical practice in Sacramento, California, and had the following transactions during the month of January.

| | |
|---|---|
| Jan. 1 | The business received $35,000 cash and issued common stock to Davis. |
| 2 | Purchased medical supplies on account, $13,000. |
| 4 | Performed services for patients receiving $1,900. |
| 12 | Paid monthly office rent of $2,600. |
| 15 | Recorded $10,000 revenue for services rendered to patients on account. |

Journalize the transactions of Jack Davis, M.D. Include an explanation with each entry.

### S2-5 Journalizing transactions

**Learning Objective 3**

Arkansas Sales Consultants completed the following transactions during the latter part of January:

| | |
|---|---|
| Jan. 22 | Performed services for customers on account, $9,000. |
| 30 | Received cash on account from customers, $7,000. |
| 31 | Received a utility bill, $210, which will be paid during February. |
| 31 | Paid monthly salary to salesman, $2,400. |
| 31 | Received $2,475 for three months of consulting service to be performed starting in February. |
| 31 | Cash dividends of $900 were paid to stockholders. |

Journalize the transactions of Arkansas Sales Consultants. Include an explanation with each journal entry.

CHAPTER 2

Learning Objective 2

### S2-6 Calculating the balance of a T-account

| Accounts Payable | | | |
|---|---|---|---|
| May 2 | 6,000 | 14,000 | May 1 |
| May 22 | 12,000 | 1,000 | May 5 |
| | | 7,000 | May 15 |
| | | 500 | May 23 |

Calculate the Accounts Payable balance.

Learning Objective 3

### S2-7 Journalizing transactions and posting to T-accounts

Kenneth Watson Optical Dispensary completed the following transactions during the latter part of March:

| | |
|---|---|
| Mar. 15 | Purchased office supplies on account, $2,600. |
| 28 | Paid $1,300 on account. |

**Requirements**

1. Journalize the transactions of Kenneth Watson Optical Dispensary. Include an explanation with each journal entry.
2. Open the following accounts (use T-account format): Cash (Beginning Balance of $23,000), Office Supplies, and Accounts Payable. Post the journal entries from Requirement 1 to the accounts, and compute the balance in each account.

Learning Objective 4

### S2-8 Preparing a trial balance

Henderson Floor Coverings reported the following summarized data at December 31, 2016. Accounts appear in no particular order, and all have normal balances.

| | | | |
|---|---|---|---|
| Service Revenue | $ 38,000 | Salaries Payable | $ 15,000 |
| Equipment | 45,000 | Salaries Expense | 1,800 |
| Rent Expense | 10,000 | Cash | 12,000 |
| Common Stock | 25,000 | Accounts Receivable | 4,000 |
| Accounts Payable | 1,500 | Interest Payable | 7,500 |
| Dividends | 12,900 | Utilities Expense | 1,300 |

Prepare the trial balance of Henderson Floor Coverings at December 31, 2016.

Learning Objective 5

### S2-9 Calculating debt ratio

Vacuum Magic Carpet Care had the following total assets, liabilities, and equity as of October 31:

| | |
|---|---|
| Assets | $ 240,000 |
| Liabilities | 60,000 |
| Equity | 180,000 |

What is Vacuum Magic Carpet Care's debt ratio as of October 31?

CHAPTER 2

## > Exercises

### E2-10 Using accounting vocabulary

**Learning Objectives 1, 2, 3, 4**

Match the accounting terms with the corresponding definitions.

| | |
|---|---|
| **1.** Posting | **a.** A detailed record of all increases and decreases that have occurred in a particular asset, liability, or equity during a period |
| **2.** Account | **b.** The record holding all the accounts of a business, the changes in those accounts, and their balances |
| **3.** Debit | **c.** A journal entry that is characterized by having multiple debits and/or multiple credits |
| **4.** Journal | **d.** A record of transactions in date order |
| **5.** Chart of accounts | **e.** Left side of a T-account |
| **6.** Trial balance | **f.** Side of an account where increases are recorded |
| **7.** Normal balance | **g.** Transferring amounts from the journal to the ledger |
| **8.** Ledger | **h.** Right side of a T-account |
| **9.** Credit | **i.** A list of all accounts with their balances at a point in time |
| **10.** Compound journal entry | **j.** A list of all accounts with their account numbers |

### E2-11 Creating a chart of accounts

**Learning Objective 1**

Raymond Autobody Shop has the following accounts:

| | |
|---|---|
| Accounts Payable | Service Revenue |
| Cash | Equipment |
| Utilities Expense | Common Stock |
| Automotive Supplies | Advertising Expense |
| Dividends | Unearned Revenue |
| Retained Earnings | |

Create a chart of accounts for Raymond Autobody Shop using the standard numbering system. Each account is separated by a factor of 10. For example, the first asset account will be 100 and the next asset account will 110.

### E2-12 Identifying accounts, increases in accounts, and normal balances

**Learning Objectives 1, 2**

| | |
|---|---|
| a. Interest Revenue | f. Unearned Revenue |
| b. Accounts Payable | g. Prepaid Rent |
| c. Common Stock | h. Utilities Expense |
| d. Office Supplies | i. Dividends |
| e. Advertising Expense | j. Service Revenue |

**Requirements**

1. Identify each account as asset (A), liability (L), or equity (E).
2. Identify whether the account is increased with a debit (DR) or credit (CR).
3. Identify whether the normal balance is a debit (DR) or credit (CR).

**Learning Objective 2**

### E2-13 Identifying increases and decreases in accounts and normal balances

Insert the missing information into the accounting equation. Signify increases as Incr. and decreases as Decr.

| | | | | | | | | | | | | | | | | |
|---|---|---|---|---|---|---|---|---|---|---|---|---|---|---|---|---|
| (a) | | = | LIABILITIES | | + | (b) | | | | | | | | | | |
| | | | | | | Contributed Capital | | + | Retained Earnings | | | | | | | |
| ASSETS | | = | (c) | | + | Common Stock | | − | (d) | | + | Revenues | | − | Expenses | |
| (e) Debit | Decr. (n) | | Decr. (o) | (f) Credit | | (g) (p) | (h) Credit | | (i) (q) | (j) Credit | | (k) Debit | (l) Credit | | Incr. (r) | (m) Credit |

**Learning Objective 3**

### E2-14 Identifying source documents

For each transaction, identify a possible source document.

a. The business received $20,000 cash and issued common stock to stockholders.

b. Purchased office supplies on account, $500.

c. Recorded $1,000 revenue for services rendered to customers.

**Learning Objective 3**

### E2-15 Analyzing and journalizing transactions

As the manager of Margarita Mexican Restaurant, you must deal with a variety of business transactions. Provide an explanation for the following transactions:

a. Debit Equipment and credit Cash.

b. Debit Dividends and credit Cash.

c. Debit Wages Payable and credit Cash.

d. Debit Equipment and credit Common Stock.

e. Debit Cash and credit Unearned Revenue.

f. Debit Advertising Expense and credit Cash.

g. Debit Cash and credit Service Revenue.

***Use the following information to answer Exercises E2-16 and E2-17.***

The following transactions occurred for London Engineering:

| | |
|---|---|
| Jul. 2 | Received $12,000 contribution from Brett London in exchange for common stock. |
| 4 | Paid utilities expense of $410. |
| 5 | Purchased equipment on account, $2,200. |
| 10 | Performed services for a client on account, $2,800. |
| 12 | Borrowed $7,500 cash, signing a notes payable. |
| 19 | Cash dividends of $750 were paid to stockholders. |
| 21 | Purchased office supplies for $860 and paid cash. |
| 27 | Paid the liability from July 5. |

**Learning Objective 3**

### E2-16 Analyzing and journalizing transactions

Journalize the transactions of London Engineering. Include an explanation with each journal entry. Use the following accounts: Cash; Accounts Receivable; Office Supplies; Equipment; Accounts Payable; Notes Payable; Common Stock; Dividends; Service Revenue; Utilities Expense.

### E2-17 Posting journal entries to T-accounts

Learning Objective 3

3. Cash Balance $15,280

**Requirements**

1. Open the following T-accounts for London Engineering: Cash; Accounts Receivable; Office Supplies; Equipment; Accounts Payable; Notes Payable; Common Stock; Dividends; Service Revenue; Utilities Expense.
2. Post the journal entries to the T-accounts. Also transfer the dates to the T-accounts.
3. Compute the July 31 balance for each account.

***Use the following information to answer Exercises E2-18 and E2-19.***

The following transactions occurred for Wilson Technology Solutions:

| | |
|---|---|
| May 1 | The business received cash of $85,000 and issued common stock to Zack Wilson. |
| 2 | Purchased office supplies on account, $550. |
| 4 | Paid $57,000 cash for building and land. The building had a fair market value of $48,000. |
| 6 | Performed services for customers and received cash, $3,600. |
| 9 | Paid $450 on accounts payable. |
| 17 | Performed services for customers on account, $3,400. |
| 19 | Paid rent expense for the month, $1,400. |
| 20 | Received $1,300 from customers for services to be performed next month. |
| 21 | Paid $300 for advertising in next month's *IT Technology* magazine. |
| 23 | Received $2,600 cash on account from a customer. |
| 31 | Incurred and paid salaries, $1,200. |

### E2-18 Analyzing and journalizing transactions

Learning Objective 3

Journalize the transactions of Wilson Technology Solutions. Include an explanation with each journal entry. Use the following accounts: Cash; Accounts Receivable; Office Supplies; Prepaid Advertising; Building; Land; Accounts Payable; Unearned Revenue; Common Stock; Service Revenue; Rent Expense; Salaries Expense.

### E2-19 Posting journal entries to four-column accounts

Learning Objective 3

2. Cash Balance $32,150

**Requirements**

1. Open four-column accounts using the following account numbers: Cash, 110; Accounts Receivable, 120; Office Supplies, 130; Prepaid Advertising, 140; Building, 150; Land, 160; Accounts Payable, 210; Unearned Revenue, 220; Common Stock, 310; Service Revenue, 410; Rent Expense, 510; Salaries Expense, 520.
2. Post the journal entries to the four-column accounts, and determine the balance in the account after each transaction. Assume that the journal entries were recorded on page 10 of the journal. Make sure to complete the Post. Ref. columns in the journal and ledger.

**Learning Objective 3**

## E2-20 Analyzing transactions from T-accounts

The first nine transactions of North-West Airplane Repair have been posted to the T-accounts. Provide an explanation for each of the nine transactions.

ASSETS = LIABILITIES + EQUITY

EQUITY: Contributed Capital + Retained Earnings

Cash = Accounts Payable + Common Stock − Dividends + Service Revenue − Rent Expense

**Cash**

| | | | |
|---|---|---|---|
| (1) | 370,000 | 360,000 | (2) |
| (3) | 260,000 | 1,200 | (5) |
| (9) | 21,000 | 1,500 | (6) |
| | | 3,900 | (7) |
| | | 7,000 | (8) |

**Office Supplies**

| | | | |
|---|---|---|---|
| (4) | 1,500 | | |

**Building**

| | | | |
|---|---|---|---|
| (2) | 360,000 | | |

**Accounts Payable**

| | | | |
|---|---|---|---|
| (5) | 1,200 | 1,500 | (4) |

**Notes Payable**

| | | | |
|---|---|---|---|
| | | 260,000 | (3) |

**Common Stock**

| | | | |
|---|---|---|---|
| | | 370,000 | (1) |

**Dividends**

| | | | |
|---|---|---|---|
| (8) | 7,000 | | |

**Service Revenue**

| | | | |
|---|---|---|---|
| | | 21,000 | (9) |

**Rent Expense**

| | | | |
|---|---|---|---|
| (7) | 1,400 | | |

**Salaries Expense**

| | | | |
|---|---|---|---|
| (7) | 2,500 | | |

**Property Tax Expense**

| | | | |
|---|---|---|---|
| (6) | 1,500 | | |

**Learning Objective 3**

## E2-21 Journalizing transactions from T-accounts

In December 2016, the first five transactions of Atkins' Lawn Care Company have been posted to the T-accounts. Prepare the journal entries that served as the sources for the five transactions. Include an explanation for each entry.

**Cash**

| | | | |
|---|---|---|---|
| (1) | 56,000 | 37,000 | (3) |
| (4) | 49,000 | 5,900 | (5) |

**Office Supplies**

| | | | |
|---|---|---|---|
| (2) | 200 | | |

**Equipment**

| | | | |
|---|---|---|---|
| (5) | 5,900 | | |

**Building**

| | | | |
|---|---|---|---|
| (3) | 37,000 | | |

**Accounts Payable**

| | | | |
|---|---|---|---|
| | | 200 | (2) |

**Notes Payable**

| | | | |
|---|---|---|---|
| | | 49,000 | (4) |

**Common Stock**

| | | | |
|---|---|---|---|
| | | 56,000 | (1) |

**Learning Objective 4**

Total Debits $211,500

## E2-22 Preparing a trial balance

The accounts of Aker Moving Company follow with their normal balances as of August 31, 2016. The accounts are listed in no particular order.

| | | | |
|---|---|---|---|
| Common Stock | $ 53,300 | Trucks | $ 132,000 |
| Insurance Expense | 600 | Fuel Expense | 3,000 |
| Accounts Payable | 4,200 | Dividends | 6,200 |
| Service Revenue | 92,000 | Utilities Expense | 500 |
| Building | 48,000 | Accounts Receivable | 8,700 |
| Advertising Expense | 200 | Notes Payable | 62,000 |
| Salaries Expense | 7,000 | Office Supplies | 300 |
| Cash | 5,000 | | |

Prepare Aker's trial balance as of August 31, 2016.

## E2-23 Preparing a trial balance from T-accounts

Learning Objective 4

Total Debits $85,200

The T-accounts of Morris Farm Equipment Repair follow as of May 31, 2016.

ASSETS = LIABILITIES + EQUITY

EQUITY: Contributed Capital + Retained Earnings

Cash = Salaries Payable + Common Stock − Dividends + Service Revenue − Salaries Expense

**ASSETS**

| Cash | |
|---|---|
| 29,000 | 12,000 |
| 2,800 | 900 |
| 1,300 | 4,400 |
| | 1,200 |
| | 1,920 |

| Accounts Receivable | |
|---|---|
| 4,400 | 1,300 |

| Equipment | |
|---|---|
| 18,000 | |

| Building | |
|---|---|
| 32,000 | |

| Land | |
|---|---|
| 12,000 | |

**LIABILITIES**

| Salaries Payable | |
|---|---|
| 900 | 4,300 |

| Notes Payable | |
|---|---|
| 4,400 | 32,000 |

**EQUITY — Contributed Capital**

| Common Stock | |
|---|---|
| | 29,000 |
| | 18,000 |

**EQUITY — Retained Earnings**

| Dividends | |
|---|---|
| 1,200 | |

| Service Revenue | |
|---|---|
| | 4,400 |
| | 2,800 |

| Salaries Expense | |
|---|---|
| 1,300 | |
| 4,300 | |

| Property Tax Expense | |
|---|---|
| 300 | |

| Advertising Expense | |
|---|---|
| 320 | |

Prepare Morris Farm Equipment Repair's trial balance as of May 31, 2016.

## E2-24 Journalizing transactions, posting journal entries to four-column accounts, and preparing a trial balance

Learning Objectives 3, 4

3. Total Debits $25,250

The following transactions occurred during the month for Tori Peel, CPA:

| | |
|---|---|
| Jun. 1 | Peel opened an accounting firm by contributing $13,500 cash and office furniture with a fair market value of $5,400 in exchange for common stock. |
| 5 | Paid monthly rent of $1,300. |
| 9 | Purchased office supplies on account, $800. |
| 14 | Paid employee's salary, $1,700. |
| 18 | Received a bill for utilities to be paid next month, $250. |
| 21 | Paid $600 of the accounts payable created on June 9. |
| 25 | Performed accounting services on account, $5,900. |
| 28 | Paid cash dividends of $6,900. |

### Requirements

1. Open the following four-column accounts of Tori Peel, CPA: Cash, 110; Accounts Receivable, 120; Office Supplies, 130; Office Furniture, 140; Accounts Payable, 210; Utilities Payable, 220; Common Stock, 310; Dividends, 320; Service Revenue, 410; Salaries Expense, 510; Rent Expense, 520; Utilities Expense, 530.
2. Journalize the transactions, and then post the journal entries to the four-column accounts. Explanations are not required for the journal entries. Keep a running balance in each account. Assume the journal entries are recorded on page 10 of the journal.
3. Prepare the trial balance as of June 30, 2016.

CHAPTER 2

**Learning Objective 4**

## E2-25 Analyzing accounting errors

Bridget Shine has trouble keeping her debits and credits equal. During a recent month, Bridget made the following accounting errors:

**a.** In preparing the trial balance, Bridget omitted a $4,000 Notes Receivable. The credit to Cash was correct.

**b.** Bridget posted a $50 Utilities Expense as $500. The credit to Cash was correct.

**c.** In recording a $300 payment on account, Bridget debited Furniture instead of Accounts Payable.

**d.** In journalizing a receipt of cash for service revenue, Bridget debited Cash for $110 instead of the correct amount of $1,100. The credit was correct.

**e.** Bridget recorded a $320 purchase of office supplies on account by debiting Office Supplies and crediting Accounts Payable for $230.

### Requirements

1. For each of these errors, state whether total debits equal total credits on the trial balance.
2. Identify each account that has an incorrect balance and the amount and direction of the error (such as "Accounts Receivable $500 too high").

**Learning Objective 4**

Total Debits $39,750

## E2-26 Correcting errors in a trial balance

The accountant for Town and Country Painting Specialists is having a hard time preparing the trial balance as of November 30, 2016:

**TOWN AND COUNTRY PAINTING SPECIALISTS**
Trial Balance
November 30, 2016

| | Balance | |
|---|---|---|
| **Account Title** | **Debit** | **Credit** |
| Painting Equipment | $ 13,000 | |
| Cash | 12,900 | |
| Accounts Receivable | 1,100 | |
| Advertising Expense | 450 | |
| Dividends | | $ 7,000 |
| Accounts Payable | | 3,100 |
| Rent Expense | 2,700 | |
| Common Stock | 15,000 | |
| Service Revenue | | 19,650 |
| Unearned Revenue | 2,000 | |
| Salaries Expense | 2,100 | |
| Office Supplies | | 300 |
| Utilities Expense | 200 | |
| Total | **$ 49,450** | **$ 30,050** |

Prepare the corrected trial balance as of November 30, 2016. Assume all amounts are correct and all accounts have normal balances.

## E2-27 Correcting errors in a trial balance

Learning Objective 4

Total Debits $34,900

The following trial balance of Carla Madock Tutoring Service as of May 31, 2016, does not balance.

| CARLA MADOCK TUTORING SERVICE<br>Trial Balance<br>May 31, 2016 | | |
|---|---|---|
| | Balance | |
| **Account Title** | **Debit** | **Credit** |
| Cash | $ 2,900 | |
| Accounts Receivable | 1,800 | |
| Office Supplies | 700 | |
| Computer Equipment | 15,800 | |
| Accounts Payable | | $ 11,100 |
| Utilities Payable | | 500 |
| Common Stock | | 11,600 |
| Dividends | 10,200 | |
| Service Revenue | | 9,600 |
| Salaries Expense | 1,900 | |
| Rent Expense | 800 | |
| Utilities Expense | 500 | |
| Total | **$ 34,600** | **$ 32,800** |

Investigation of the accounting records reveals that the bookkeeper:

a. Recorded a $600 cash revenue transaction by debiting Accounts Receivable. The credit entry was correct.

b. Posted a $1,000 credit to Accounts Payable as $100.

c. Did not record Utilities Expense or the related Utilities Payable in the amount of $300.

d. Understated Common Stock by $900.

Prepare the corrected trial balance as of May 31, 2016, complete with a heading; journal entries are not required.

**Learning Objective 5**

Total Assets $177,800



## E2-28 Calculating the debt ratio

Jason Hilton, M.D., reported the following trial balance as of September 30, 2016:

**JASON HILTON, M.D.**
Trial Balance
September 30, 2016

| | Balance | |
|---|---|---|
| **Account Title** | **Debit** | **Credit** |
| Cash | $ 37,000 | |
| Accounts Receivable | 7,200 | |
| Office Supplies | 2,600 | |
| Office Equipment | 22,000 | |
| Building | 85,000 | |
| Land | 24,000 | |
| Accounts Payable | | $ 1,800 |
| Utilities Payable | | 700 |
| Unearned Revenue | | 18,290 |
| Notes Payable | | 77,000 |
| Common Stock | | 100,000 |
| Dividends | 50,000 | |
| Service Revenue | | 54,810 |
| Salaries Expense | 23,100 | |
| Utilities Expense | 900 | |
| Advertising Expense | 800 | |
| Total | **$ 252,600** | **$ 252,600** |

Calculate the debt ratio for Jason Hilton, M.D.

## > Problems Group A

### P2-29A Journalizing transactions, posting journal entries to T-accounts, and preparing a trial balance

**Learning Objectives 3, 4**

2. Cash Balance $69,060



Vincent Yarwood practices medicine under the business title Vincent Yarwood, M.D. During July, the medical practice completed the following transactions:

| | |
|---|---|
| Jul. 1 | Yarwood contributed $68,000 cash to the business in exchange for common stock. |
| 5 | Paid monthly rent on medical equipment, $550. |
| 9 | Paid $17,000 cash to purchase land to be used in operations. |
| 10 | Purchased office supplies on account, $1,800. |
| 19 | Borrowed $24,000 from the bank for business use. |
| 22 | Paid $1,700 on account. |
| 28 | The business received a bill for advertising in the daily newspaper to be paid in August, $290. |
| 31 | Revenues earned during the month included $6,000 cash and $5,500 on account. |
| 31 | Paid employees' salaries $2,000, office rent $1,000, and utilities $550. Record as a compound entry. |
| 31 | The business received $1,260 for medical screening services to be performed next month. |
| 31 | Paid cash dividends of $7,400. |

The business uses the following accounts: Cash; Accounts Receivable; Office Supplies; Land; Accounts Payable; Advertising Payable; Unearned Revenue; Notes Payable; Common Stock; Dividends; Service Revenue; Salaries Expense; Rent Expense; Utilities Expense; and Advertising Expense.

**Requirements**

1. Journalize each transaction. Explanations are not required.
2. Post the journal entries to the T-accounts, using transaction dates as posting references in the ledger accounts. Label the balance of each account *Bal.*
3. Prepare the trial balance of Vincent Yarwood, M.D., as of July 31, 2017.

**Learning Objectives 3, 4**

4. Total Debits $55,900

**P2-30A Journalizing transactions, posting journal entries to T-accounts, and preparing a trial balance**

Doris Stann started her practice as a design consultant on September 1, 2017. During the first month of operations, the business completed the following transactions:

| | |
|---|---|
| Sep. 1 | Received $47,000 cash and issued common stock to Stann. |
| 4 | Purchased office supplies, $700, and furniture, $1,600, on account. |
| 6 | Performed services for a law firm and received $1,400 cash. |
| 7 | Paid $20,000 cash to acquire land to be used in operations. |
| 10 | Performed services for a hotel and received its promise to pay the $900 within one week. |
| 14 | Paid for the furniture purchased on September 4 on account. |
| 15 | Paid assistant's semimonthly salary, $1,480. |
| 17 | Received cash on account, $700. |
| 20 | Prepared a design for a school on account, $700. |
| 25 | Received $2,200 cash for design services to be performed in October. |
| 28 | Received $2,600 cash for consulting with Plummer & Gordon. |
| 29 | Paid $2,400 cash for a 12-month insurance policy starting on October 1. |
| 30 | Paid assistant's semimonthly salary, $1,480. |
| 30 | Paid monthly rent expense, $500. |
| 30 | Received a bill for utilities, $400. The bill will be paid next month. |
| 30 | Paid cash dividends of $3,000. |

**Requirements**

1. Record each transaction in the journal using the following account titles: Cash; Accounts Receivable; Office Supplies; Prepaid Insurance; Furniture; Land; Accounts Payable; Utilities Payable; Unearned Revenue; Common Stock; Dividends; Service Revenue; Salaries Expense; Rent Expense; Utilities Expense. Explanations are not required.
2. Open a T-account for each of the accounts.
3. Post the journal entries to the T-accounts, using transaction dates as posting references in the ledger accounts. Label the balance of each account *Bal.*
4. Prepare the trial balance of Doris Stann, Designer, as of September 30, 2017.

## P2-31A Journalizing transactions, posting journal entries to four-column accounts, and preparing a trial balance

**Learning Objectives 3, 4**

3. Cash Balance $23,400

Timothy Monroe opened a law office on January 1, 2017. During the first month of operations, the business completed the following transactions:

| | |
|---|---|
| Jan. 1 | Monroe contributed $62,000 cash to the business, Timothy Monroe, Attorney. The business issued common stock to Monroe. |
| 3 | Purchased office supplies, $500, and furniture, $2,000, on account. |
| 4 | Performed legal services for a client and received $1,600 cash. |
| 7 | Purchased a building with a market value of $70,000, and land with a market value of $29,000. The business paid $35,000 cash and signed a note payable to the bank for the remaining amount. |
| 11 | Prepared legal documents for a client on account, $300. |
| 15 | Paid assistant's semimonthly salary, $1,180. |
| 16 | Paid for the office supplies purchased on January 3 on account. |
| 18 | Received $2,000 cash for helping a client sell real estate. |
| 19 | Defended a client in court and billed the client for $1,400. |
| 25 | Received a bill for utilities, $550. The bill will be paid next month. |
| 29 | Received cash on account, $700. |
| 30 | Paid $840 cash for a 12-month insurance policy starting on February 1. |
| 30 | Paid assistant's semimonthly salary, $1,180. |
| 31 | Paid monthly rent expense, $1,300. |
| 31 | Paid cash dividends of $2,900. |

### Requirements

1. Record each transaction in the journal, using the following account titles: Cash; Accounts Receivable; Office Supplies; Prepaid Insurance; Furniture; Building; Land; Accounts Payable; Utilities Payable; Notes Payable; Common Stock; Dividends; Service Revenue; Salaries Expense; Rent Expense; and Utilities Expense. Explanations are not required.
2. Open the following four-column accounts including account numbers: Cash, 101; Accounts Receivable, 111; Office Supplies, 121; Prepaid Insurance, 131; Furniture, 141; Building, 151; Land, 161; Accounts Payable, 201; Utilities Payable, 211; Notes Payable, 221; Common Stock, 301; Dividends, 311; Service Revenue, 411; Salaries Expense, 511; Rent Expense, 521; and Utilities Expense, 531.
3. Post the journal entries to four-column accounts in the ledger, using dates, account numbers, journal references, and posting references. Assume the journal entries were recorded on page 1 of the journal.
4. Prepare the trial balance of Timothy Monroe, Attorney, at January 31, 2017.

CHAPTER 2

**Learning Objectives 3, 4**

3. Cash Balance $16,700

## P2-32A Journalizing transactions, posting journal entries to four-column accounts, and preparing a trial balance

The trial balance of Steve Mentz, CPA, is dated March 31, 2017:

**STEVE MENTZ, CPA**
Trial Balance
March 31, 2017

| | Balance | |
|---|---|---|
| **Account Title** | **Debit** | **Credit** |
| Cash | $ 18,000 | |
| Accounts Receivable | 9,500 | |
| Office Supplies | 1,000 | |
| Furniture | 0 | |
| Automobile | 0 | |
| Land | 26,000 | |
| Accounts Payable | | $ 5,500 |
| Unearned Revenue | | 0 |
| Common Stock | | 44,100 |
| Dividends | 0 | |
| Service Revenue | | 10,800 |
| Salaries Expense | 5,000 | |
| Rent Expense | 900 | |
| Total | **$ 60,400** | **$ 60,400** |

During April, the business completed the following transactions:

| | |
|---|---|
| Apr. 4 | Collected $1,000 cash from a client on account. |
| 8 | Performed tax services for a client on account, $5,800. |
| 13 | Paid $1,500 on account. |
| 14 | Purchased furniture on account, $4,600. |
| 15 | Mentz contributed his personal automobile to the business in exchange for common stock. The automobile had a market value of $8,000. |
| 18 | Purchased office supplies on account, $500. |
| 19 | Received $2,900 for tax services performed on April 8. |
| 20 | Paid cash dividends of $8,000. |
| 21 | Received $5,400 cash for consulting work completed. |
| 24 | Received $1,200 cash for accounting services to be completed next month. |
| 27 | Paid office rent, $700. |
| 28 | Paid employee salary, $1,600. |

**Requirements**

1. Record the April transactions in the journal. Use the following accounts: Cash; Accounts Receivable; Office Supplies; Furniture; Automobile; Land; Accounts Payable; Unearned Revenue; Common Stock; Dividends; Service Revenue; Salaries Expense; and Rent Expense. Include an explanation for each entry.
2. Open the four-column ledger accounts listed in the trial balance, together with their balances as of March 31. Use the following account numbers: Cash, 11; Accounts Receivable, 12; Office Supplies, 13; Furniture, 14; Automobile, 15; Land, 16; Accounts Payable, 21; Unearned Revenue, 22; Common Stock, 31; Dividends, 33; Service Revenue, 41; Salaries Expense, 51; and Rent Expense, 52.
3. Post the journal entries to four-column accounts in the ledger, using dates, account numbers, journal references, and posting references. Assume the journal entries were recorded on page 5 of the journal.
4. Prepare the trial balance of Steve Mentz, CPA, at April 30, 2017.

## P2-33A Correcting errors in a trial balance

**Learning Objective 4**

Total Debits $115,900

The trial balance of Creative Child Care does not balance.

**CREATIVE CHILD CARE**
Trial Balance
August 31, 2017

| | Balance | |
|---|---|---|
| **Account Title** | **Debit** | **Credit** |
| Cash | $ 6,840 | |
| Accounts Receivable | 7,200 | |
| Office Supplies | 1,200 | |
| Prepaid Insurance | 300 | |
| Equipment | 84,300 | |
| Accounts Payable | | $ 3,100 |
| Notes Payable | | 47,000 |
| Common Stock | | 50,000 |
| Dividends | 5,560 | |
| Service Revenue | | 10,000 |
| Salaries Expense | 3,800 | |
| Rent Expense | 700 | |
| Total | **$ 109,900** | **$ 110,100** |

The following errors are detected:

a. Cash is understated by $1,400.

b. A $3,900 debit to Accounts Receivable was posted as a credit.

c. A $1,300 purchase of office supplies on account was neither journalized nor posted.

d. Equipment was incorrectly transferred from the ledger as $84,300. It should have been transferred as $76,500.

e. Salaries Expense is overstated by $300.

f. A $200 cash payment for advertising expense was neither journalized nor posted.

g. A $240 cash dividend was incorrectly journalized as $2,400.

h. Service Revenue was understated by $4,500.

i. A 12-month insurance policy was posted as a $1,800 credit to Prepaid Insurance. Cash was posted correctly.

Prepare the corrected trial balance as of August 31, 2017. Journal entries are not required.

**Learning Objectives 4, 5**

2. Ending Retained Earnings $5,890

**P2-34A Preparing financial statements from the trial balance and calculating the debt ratio**

The trial balance as of July 31, 2017, for Sandra Sousa, Registered Dietician, is presented below:

**SANDRA SOUSA, REGISTERED DIETICIAN**
Trial Balance
July 31, 2017

| | Balance | |
|---|---|---|
| **Account Title** | **Debit** | **Credit** |
| Cash | $ 33,000 | |
| Accounts Receivable | 9,500 | |
| Office Supplies | 1,500 | |
| Prepaid Insurance | 2,000 | |
| Equipment | 15,000 | |
| Accounts Payable | | $ 3,300 |
| Unearned Revenue | | 2,810 |
| Notes Payable | | 25,000 |
| Common Stock | | 24,000 |
| Dividends | 2,600 | |
| Service Revenue | | 11,840 |
| Salaries Expense | 2,300 | |
| Rent Expense | 800 | |
| Utilities Expense | 250 | |
| Total | **$ 66,950** | **$ 66,950** |

## Requirements

1. Prepare the income statement for the month ended July 31, 2017.
2. Prepare the statement of retained earnings for the month ended July 31, 2017. The beginning balance of retained earnings was $0.
3. Prepare the balance sheet as of July 31, 2017.
4. Calculate the debt ratio as of July 31, 2017.

## > Problems Group B

### P2-35B Journalizing transactions, posting journal entries to T-accounts, and preparing a trial balance

**Learning Objectives 3, 4**

2. Cash Balance $70,020



Vito York practices medicine under the business title Vito York, M.D. During March, the medical practice completed the following transactions:

| | |
|---|---|
| Mar. 1 | York contributed $64,000 cash to the business in exchange for common stock. |
| 5 | Paid monthly rent on medical equipment, $630. |
| 9 | Paid $13,000 cash to purchase land to be used in operations. |
| 10 | Purchased office supplies on account, $1,800. |
| 19 | Borrowed $24,000 from the bank for business use. |
| 22 | Paid $1,200 on account. |
| 28 | The business received a bill for advertising in the daily newspaper to be paid in April, $270. |
| 31 | Revenues earned during the month included $6,600 cash and $5,800 on account. |
| 31 | Paid employees' salaries $2,700, office rent $1,500, and utilities $400. Record as a compound entry. |
| 31 | The business received $1,450 for medical screening services to be performed next month. |
| 31 | Paid cash dividends of $6,600. |

The business uses the following accounts: Cash; Accounts Receivable; Office Supplies; Land; Accounts Payable; Advertising Payable; Unearned Revenue; Notes Payable; Common Stock; Dividends; Service Revenue; Salaries Expense; Rent Expense; Utilities Expense; and Advertising Expense.

**Requirements**

1. Journalize each transaction. Explanations are not required.
2. Post the journal entries to the T-accounts, using transaction dates as posting references in the ledger accounts. Label the balance of each account *Bal.*
3. Prepare the trial balance of Vito York, M.D., as of March 31, 2017.

**Learning Objectives 3, 4**

4. Total Debits $49,500

## P2-36B Journalizing transactions, posting journal entries to T-accounts, and preparing a trial balance

Deb Sikes started her practice as a design consultant on November 1, 2017. During the first month of operations, the business completed the following transactions:

| | |
|---|---|
| Nov. 1 | Received $39,000 cash and issued common stock to Sikes. |
| 4 | Purchased office supplies, $900, and furniture, $1,800, on account. |
| 6 | Performed services for a law firm and received $2,000 cash. |
| 7 | Paid $24,000 cash to acquire land to be used in operations. |
| 10 | Performed services for a hotel and received its promise to pay the $1,200 within one week. |
| 14 | Paid for the furniture purchased on November 4 on account. |
| 15 | Paid assistant's semimonthly salary, $1,410. |
| 17 | Received cash on account, $1,000. |
| 20 | Prepared a design for a school on account, $900. |
| 25 | Received $2,100 cash for design services to be performed in December. |
| 28 | Received $2,800 cash for consulting with Plummer & Gordon. |
| 29 | Paid $1,080 cash for a 12-month insurance policy starting on December 1. |
| 30 | Paid assistant's semimonthly salary, $1,410. |
| 30 | Paid monthly rent expense, $800. |
| 30 | Received a bill for utilities, $600. The bill will be paid next month. |
| 30 | Paid cash dividends of $4,000. |

### Requirements

1. Record each transaction in the journal using the following account titles: Cash; Accounts Receivable; Office Supplies; Prepaid Insurance; Furniture; Land; Accounts Payable; Utilities Payable; Unearned Revenue; Common Stock; Dividends; Service Revenue; Salaries Expense; Rent Expense; Utilities Expense. Explanations are not required.
2. Open a T-account for each of the accounts.
3. Post the journal entries to the T-accounts, using transaction dates as posting references in the ledger accounts. Label the balance of each account *Bal.*
4. Prepare the trial balance of Deb Sikes, Designer, as of November 30, 2017.

**Learning Objectives 3, 4**

3. Service Revenue Balance $6,000



## P2-37B Journalizing transactions, posting journal entries to four-column accounts, and preparing a trial balance

Trevor Moore opened a law office on April 1, 2017. During the first month of operations, the business completed the following transactions:

| | |
|---|---|
| Apr. 1 | Moore contributed $76,000 cash to the business, Trevor Moore, Attorney. The business issued common stock to Moore. |
| 3 | Purchased office supplies, $400, and furniture, $2,200, on account. |
| 4 | Performed legal services for a client and received $900 cash. |
| 7 | Purchased a building with a market value of $120,000, and land with a market value of $29,000. The business paid $45,000 cash and signed a note payable to the bank for the remaining amount. |
| 11 | Prepared legal documents for a client on account, $800. |
| 15 | Paid assistant's semimonthly salary, $1,230. |
| 16 | Paid for the office supplies purchased on April 3 on account. |
| 18 | Received $2,800 cash for helping a client sell real estate. |
| 19 | Defended a client in court and billed the client for $1,500. |
| 25 | Received a bill for utilities, $650. The bill will be paid next month. |
| 28 | Received cash on account, $1,700. |
| 29 | Paid $4,800 cash for a 12-month insurance policy starting on May 1. |
| 29 | Paid assistant's semimonthly salary, $1,230. |
| 30 | Paid monthly rent expense, $1,100. |
| 30 | Paid cash dividends of $2,000. |

### Requirements

1. Record each transaction in the journal, using the following account titles: Cash; Accounts Receivable; Office Supplies; Prepaid Insurance; Furniture; Building; Land; Accounts Payable; Utilities Payable; Notes Payable; Common Stock; Dividends; Service Revenue; Salaries Expense; Rent Expense; and Utilities Expense. Explanations are not required.
2. Open the following four-column accounts including account numbers: Cash, 101; Accounts Receivable, 111; Office Supplies, 121; Prepaid Insurance, 131; Furniture, 141; Building, 151; Land, 161; Accounts Payable, 201; Utilities Payable, 211; Notes Payable, 221; Common Stock, 301; Dividends, 311; Service Revenue, 411; Salaries Expense, 511; Rent Expense, 521; and Utilities Expense, 531.
3. Post the journal entries to four-column accounts in the ledger, using dates, account numbers, journal references, and posting references. Assume the journal entries were recorded on page 1 of the journal.
4. Prepare the trial balance of Trevor Moore, Attorney, at April 30, 2017.

CHAPTER 2

**Learning Objectives 3, 4**

3. Cash Balance $11,000

**P2-38B Journalizing transactions, posting journal entries to four-column accounts, and preparing a trial balance**

The trial balance of James Howe, CPA, is dated March 31, 2017:

**JAMES HOWE, CPA**
Trial Balance
March 31, 2017

| | Balance | |
|---|---|---|
| **Account Title** | **Debit** | **Credit** |
| Cash | $ 10,000 | |
| Accounts Receivable | 7,500 | |
| Office Supplies | 400 | |
| Furniture | 0 | |
| Automobile | 0 | |
| Land | 27,000 | |
| Accounts Payable | | $ 4,200 |
| Unearned Revenue | | 0 |
| Common Stock | | 33,300 |
| Dividends | 0 | |
| Service Revenue | | 10,800 |
| Salaries Expense | 2,500 | |
| Rent Expense | 900 | |
| Total | **$ 48,300** | **$ 48,300** |

During April, the business completed the following transactions:

| | |
|---|---|
| Apr. 4 | Collected $2,000 cash from a client on account. |
| 8 | Performed tax services for a client on account, $5,400. |
| 13 | Paid $3,300 on account. |
| 14 | Purchased furniture on account, $4,600. |
| 15 | Howe contributed his personal automobile to the business in exchange for common stock. The automobile had a market value of $10,000. |
| 18 | Purchased office supplies on account, $1,000. |
| 19 | Received $2,700 for tax services performed on April 8. |
| 20 | Paid cash dividends of $4,000. |
| 21 | Received $3,800 cash for consulting work completed. |
| 24 | Received $1,400 cash for accounting services to be completed next month. |
| 27 | Paid office rent, $600. |
| 28 | Paid employee salary, $1,000. |

**Requirements**

1. Record the April transactions in the journal using the following accounts: Cash; Accounts Receivable; Office Supplies; Furniture; Automobile; Land; Accounts Payable; Unearned Revenue; Common Stock; Dividends; Service Revenue; Salaries Expense; and Rent Expense. Include an explanation for each entry.
2. Open the four-column ledger accounts listed in the trial balance, together with their balances as of March 31. Use the following account numbers: Cash, 11; Accounts Receivable, 12; Office Supplies, 13; Furniture, 14; Automobile, 15; Land, 16; Accounts Payable, 21; Unearned Revenue, 22; Common Stock, 31; Dividends, 33; Service Revenue, 41; Salaries Expense, 51; and Rent Expense, 52.
3. Post the journal entries to four-column accounts in the ledger, using dates, account numbers, journal references, and posting references. Assume the journal entries were recorded on page 5 of the journal.
4. Prepare the trial balance of James Howe, CPA, at April 30, 2017.

## P2-39B Correcting errors in a trial balance

**Learning Objective 4**

Total Debits $122,400

The trial balance of Learn for Life Child Care does not balance.

**LEARN FOR LIFE CHILD CARE**
Trial Balance
May 31, 2017

| | Balance | |
|---|---|---|
| **Account Title** | **Debit** | **Credit** |
| Cash | $ 8,400 | |
| Accounts Receivable | 8,100 | |
| Office Supplies | 900 | |
| Prepaid Insurance | 1,000 | |
| Equipment | 89,300 | |
| Accounts Payable | | $ 3,500 |
| Notes Payable | | 48,000 |
| Common Stock | | 54,000 |
| Dividends | 3,600 | |
| Service Revenue | | 11,500 |
| Salaries Expense | 5,100 | |
| Rent Expense | 900 | |
| Total | **$ 117,300** | **$ 117,000** |

The following errors are detected:

a. Cash is understated by $1,800.

b. A $3,900 debit to Accounts Receivable was posted as a credit.

c. A $1,200 purchase of office supplies on account was neither journalized nor posted.

d. Equipment was incorrectly transferred from the ledger as $89,300. It should have been transferred as $81,500.

e. Salaries Expense is overstated by $500.

f. A $600 cash payment for advertising expense was neither journalized nor posted.

g. A $100 cash dividend was incorrectly journalized as $1,000.

h. Service Revenue was understated by $4,200.

i. A 12-month insurance policy was posted as a $1,300 credit to Prepaid Insurance. Cash was posted correctly.

Prepare the corrected trial balance as of May 31, 2017. Journal entries are not required.

**Learning Objectives 4, 5**

1. Net Income $7,508

**P2-40B Preparing financial statements from the trial balance and calculating the debt ratio**

The trial balance as of July 31, 2017, for Sarah Silk, Registered Dietician, is presented below:

**SARAH SILK, REGISTERED DIETICIAN**
Trial Balance
July 31, 2017

| | Balance | |
|---|---|---|
| **Account Title** | **Debit** | **Credit** |
| Cash | $ 30,000 | |
| Accounts Receivable | 9,700 | |
| Office Supplies | 2,200 | |
| Prepaid Insurance | 2,700 | |
| Equipment | 20,000 | |
| Accounts Payable | | $ 3,400 |
| Unearned Revenue | | 5,192 |
| Notes Payable | | 25,000 |
| Common Stock | | 26,000 |
| Dividends | 2,500 | |
| Service Revenue | | 9,858 |
| Salaries Expense | 1,300 | |
| Rent Expense | 800 | |
| Utilities Expense | 250 | |
| Total | **$ 69,450** | **$ 69,450** |

**Requirements**

1. Prepare the income statement for the month ended July 31, 2017.
2. Prepare the statement of retained earnings for the month ended July 31, 2017. The beginning balance of retained earnings was $0.
3. Prepare the balance sheet as of July 31, 2017.
4. Calculate the debt ratio as of July 31, 2017.

## > Continuing Problem

**P2-41 Journalizing transactions, posting to T-accounts, and preparing a trial balance**

Problem P2-41 continues with the consulting business begun in Problem P1-54 in Chapter 1. Here you will account for Daniels Consulting's transactions as it is actually done in practice.

Daniels Consulting completed the following transactions during December 2016:

| | |
|---|---|
| Dec. 2 | Stockholders contributed $20,000 cash in exchange for common stock. |
| 2 | Paid monthly office rent, $2,000. |
| 3 | Paid cash for a computer, $3,600. This equipment is expected to remain in service for five years. |
| 4 | Purchased office furniture on account, $3,000. The furniture should last for five years. |
| 5 | Purchased office supplies on account, $800. |
| 9 | Performed consulting service for a client on account, $2,500. |
| 12 | Paid utilities expenses, $150. |
| 18 | Performed service for a client and received cash of $2,100. |
| 21 | Received $2,400 in advance for client service to be performed in the future. |
| 21 | Hired an administrative assistant to be paid $2,055 on the 20th day of each month. The secretary begins work immediately. |
| 26 | Paid $200 on account. |
| 28 | Collected $400 on account. |
| 30 | Cash dividends of $1,000 were paid to stockholders. |

### Requirements

1. Journalize the transactions, using the following accounts: Cash; Accounts Receivable; Office Supplies; Equipment; Furniture; Accounts Payable; Unearned Revenue; Common Stock; Dividends; Service Revenue; Rent Expense; and Utilities Expense. Explanations are not required.
2. Open a T-account for each of the accounts.
3. Post the journal entries to the T-accounts, and calculate account balances. Formal posting references are not required.
4. Prepare a trial balance as of December 31, 2016.
5. Prepare the income statement of Daniels Consulting for the month ended December 31, 2016.
6. Prepare the statement of retained earnings for the month ended December 31, 2016.
7. Prepare the balance sheet as of December 31, 2016.
8. Calculate the debt ratio for Daniels Consulting at December 31, 2016.

## > Practice Set

### P2-42 Journalizing transactions, posting to T-accounts, and preparing a trial balance

Consider the following transactional data for the first month of operations for Crystal Clear Cleaning.

| | |
|---|---|
| Nov. 1 | Stockholders contributed $35,000 and a truck, with a market value of $7,000, to the business in exchange for common stock. |
| 2 | The business paid $2,000 to Pleasant Properties for November through February rent. (Debit Prepaid Rent) |
| 3 | Paid $1,800 for a business insurance policy for the term November 1, 2017 through October 31, 2018. (Debit Prepaid Insurance) |
| 4 | Purchased cleaning supplies on account, $220. |
| 5 | Purchased on account an industrial vacuum cleaner costing $2,000. The invoice is payable November 25. |
| 7 | Paid $1,200 for a computer and printer. |
| 9 | Performed cleaning services on account in the amount of $3,800. |
| 10 | Received $300 for services rendered on November 9. |
| 15 | Paid employees, $350. |
| 16 | Received $12,000 for a 1-year contract beginning November 16 for cleaning services to be provided. Contract begins November 16, 2017, and ends November 15, 2018. (Credit Unearned Revenue) |
| 17 | Provided cleaning services and received $1,000 cash. |
| 18 | Received a utility bill for $250 with a due date of December 4, 2017. (Use Accounts Payable) |
| 20 | Borrowed $96,000 from bank with interest rate of 9% per year. |
| 21 | Received $900 on account for services performed on November 9. |
| 25 | Paid $1,000 on account for vacuum cleaner purchased on November 5. |
| 29 | Paid $500 for advertising. |
| 30 | Cash dividends of $200 were paid to stockholders. |

**Requirements**

1. Journalize the transactions, using the following accounts: Cash; Accounts Receivable; Cleaning Supplies; Prepaid Rent; Prepaid Insurance; Equipment; Truck; Accounts Payable; Unearned Revenue; Notes Payable; Common Stock; Dividends; Service Revenue; Salaries Expense; Advertising Expense; and Utilities Expense. Explanations are not required.
2. Open a T-account for each account.
3. Post the journal entries to the T-accounts, and calculate account balances. Formal posting references are not required.
4. Prepare a trial balance as of November 30, 2017.

# CRITICAL THINKING

## > Decision Case 2-1

Your friend, Dean McChesney, requested that you advise him on the effects that certain transactions will have on his business, A-Plus Travel Planners. Time is short, so you cannot journalize the transactions. Instead, you must analyze the transactions without a journal. McChesney will continue the business only if he can expect to earn a monthly net income of $6,000. The business completed the following transactions during June:

**a.** McChesney deposited $10,000 cash in a business bank account to start the company. The company issued common stock to McChesney.

**b.** Paid $300 cash for office supplies.

**c.** Incurred advertising expense on account, $700.

**d.** Paid the following cash expenses: administrative assistant's salary, $1,400; office rent, $1,000.

**e.** Earned service revenue on account, $8,800.

**f.** Collected cash from customers on account, $1,200.

**Requirements**

1. Open the following T-accounts: Cash; Accounts Receivable; Office Supplies; Accounts Payable; Common Stock; Service Revenue; Salaries Expense; Rent Expense; and Advertising Expense.
2. Post the transactions directly to the accounts without using a journal. Record each transaction by letter. Calculate account balances.
3. Prepare a trial balance at June 30, 2016.
4. Compute the amount of net income or net loss for this first month of operations. Would you recommend that McChesney continue in business?

## > Ethical Issue 2-1

Better Days Ahead, a charitable organization, has a standing agreement with First National Bank. The agreement allows Better Days Ahead to overdraw its cash balance at the bank when donations are running low. In the past, Better Days Ahead managed funds wisely and rarely used this privilege. Jacob Henson has recently become the president of Better Days. To expand operations, Henson acquired office equipment and spent large amounts on fundraising. During Henson's presidency, Better Days Ahead has maintained a negative bank balance of approximately $10,000.

What is the ethical issue in this situation, if any? State why you approve or disapprove of Henson's management of Better Days Ahead's funds.

## > Fraud Case 2-1

Roy Akins was the accounting manager at Zelco, a tire manufacturer, and he played golf with Hugh Stallings, the CEO, who was something of a celebrity in the community. The CEO stood to earn a substantial bonus if Zelco increased net income by year-end. Roy was eager to get into Hugh's elite social circle; he boasted to Hugh that he knew some accounting tricks that could increase company income by simply revising a few journal entries for rental payments on storage units. At the end of the year, Roy changed the debits from "rent expense" to "prepaid rent" on several entries. Later, Hugh got his bonus, and the deviations were never discovered.

**Requirements**

1. How did the change in the journal entries affect the net income of the company at year-end?
2. Who gained and who lost as a result of these actions?

## > Financial Statement Case 2-1

Visit **http://www.pearsonhighered.com/Horngren** to view a link to the **Starbucks Corporation** Fiscal 2013 Annual Report.

**Requirements**

1. Calculate the debt ratio for Starbucks Corporation as of September 29, 2013.
2. How did the debt ratio for Starbucks Corporation compare to the debt ratio for **Green Mountain Coffee Roasters, Inc.**? Discuss.

## > Communication Activity 2-1

In 35 words or fewer, explain the difference between a debit and a credit, and explain what the normal balance of the six account types is.



## > Quick Check Answers

**1.** a **2.** c **3.** d **4.** d **5.** b **6.** b **7.** d **8.** b **9.** a **10.** b

# The Adjusting Process 3

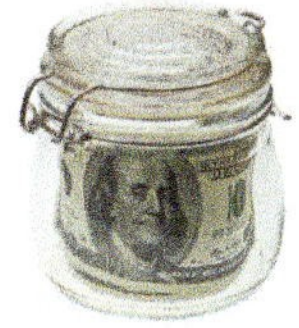

## Where's My Bonus?

Liam Mills was surprised when he opened his mail. He had just received his most recent quarterly bonus check from his employer, Custom Marketing, and the check was smaller than he expected. Liam worked as a sales manager and was responsible for product marketing and implementation in the southwest region of the United States. He was paid a monthly salary but also received a 3% bonus for all revenue generated from advertising services provided to customers in his geographical area. He was counting on his fourth quarter (October–December) bonus check to be large enough to pay off the credit card debt he had accumulated over the holiday break. It had been a great year-end for Liam. He had closed several open accounts, successfully signing several annual advertising contracts. In addition, because of his negotiating skills, he was able to collect half of the payments for services up front instead of waiting for his customers to pay every month. Liam expected that his bonus check would be huge because of this new business, but it wasn't.

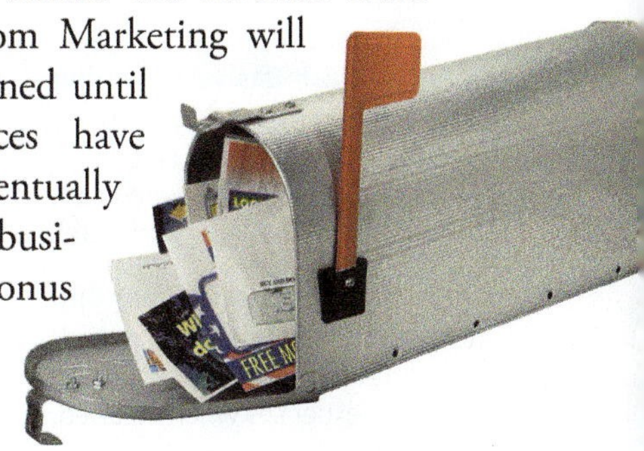

The next day, Liam stopped by the accounting office to discuss his bonus check. He was surprised to learn that his bonus was calculated by the revenue earned by his company through December 31. Although Liam had negotiated to receive half of the payments up front, the business had not yet earned the revenue from those payments. Custom Marketing will not record revenue earned until the advertising services have been performed. Eventually Liam will see the new business reflected in his bonus check, but he'll have to wait until the revenue has been earned.

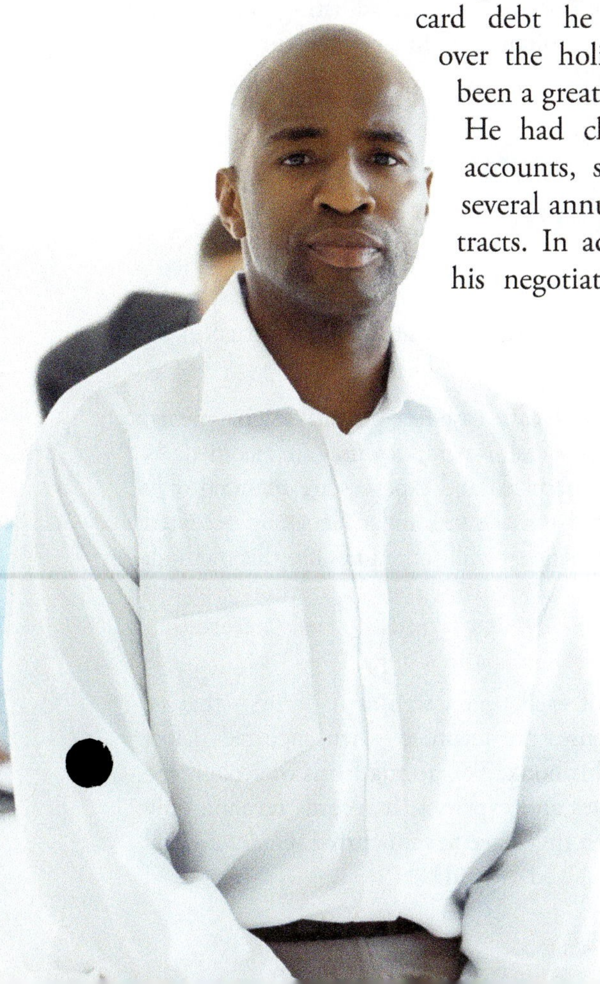

**How Was Revenue Earned Calculated?**

At the end of a time period (often December 31), companies are required to accurately report revenues earned and expenses incurred during that time period. In order to do this, the company reviews the account balances as of the end of the time period and determines whether any adjustments are needed. For example, CC Media Holdings, Inc., the parent company of radio giant Clear Channel Communications and Clear Channel Outdoor Holdings, an outdoor advertising agency, must determine the amount of revenue earned from open advertising contracts. These contracts can cover only a few weeks or as long as several years. Only the amount earned in the current time period is reported as revenue on the income statement. *Adjusting the books* is the process of reviewing and adjusting the account balances so that amounts on the financial statements are reported accurately. This is what we will learn in this chapter.

# Chapter 3 Learning Objectives

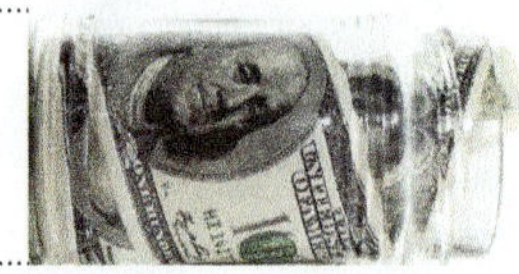

**1** Differentiate between cash basis accounting and accrual basis accounting

**2** Define and apply the time period concept, revenue recognition, and matching principles

**3** Explain the purpose of and journalize and post adjusting entries

**4** Explain the purpose of and prepare an adjusted trial balance

**5** Identify the impact of adjusting entries on the financial statements

**6** Explain the purpose of a worksheet and use it to prepare adjusting entries and the adjusted trial balance

**7** Understand the alternative treatments of recording deferred expenses and deferred revenues (Appendix 3A)

In Chapter 1, we introduced you to the accounting equation and the financial statements. In Chapter 2, you learned about T-accounts, debits, credits, and the trial balance. But have you captured all the transactions for a particular period? Not yet.

In this chapter, we continue our exploration of the accounting cycle by learning how to update the accounts at the end of the period. This process is called adjusting the books, and it requires special journal entries called *adjusting entries.* For example, you learn how, at the end of a particular period, you must determine how many office supplies you have used and how much you owe your employees—and make adjusting entries to account for these amounts. These are just some of the adjusting entries you need to make before you can see the complete picture of how well your company performed during a period of time.

**Cash Basis Accounting**
Accounting method that records revenues only when cash is received and expenses only when cash is paid.

**Accrual Basis Accounting**
Accounting method that records revenues when earned and expenses when incurred.

## WHAT IS THE DIFFERENCE BETWEEN CASH BASIS ACCOUNTING AND ACCRUAL BASIS ACCOUNTING?

**Learning Objective 1**
Differentiate between cash basis accounting and accrual basis accounting

There are two ways to record transactions—cash basis accounting or accrual basis accounting.

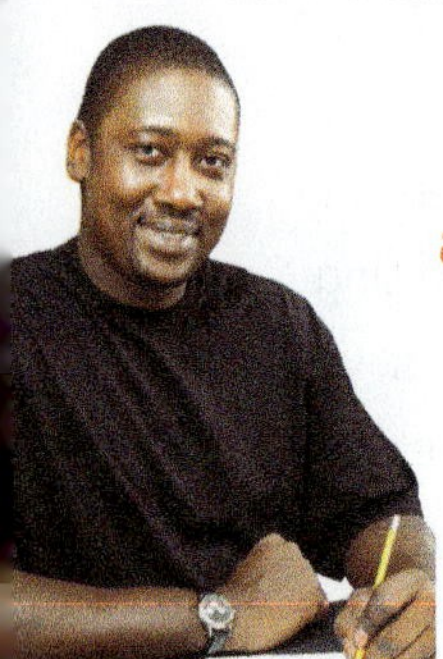

If cash basis accounting is not allowed by GAAP, why would a business choose to use this method?

- **Cash basis accounting** records only transactions with cash: cash receipts and cash payments. When cash is received, revenues are recorded. When cash is paid, expenses are recorded. As a result, revenues are recorded only when cash is received and expenses are recorded only when cash is paid. The cash basis of accounting is not allowed under Generally Accepted Accounting Principles (GAAP); however, small businesses will sometimes use this method. **The cash method is an easier accounting method to follow because it generally requires less knowledge of accounting concepts and principles. The cash basis accounting method also does a good job of tracking a business's cash flow.**
- **Accrual basis accounting** records the effect of each transaction as it occurs—that is, revenues are recorded when earned and expenses are recorded when incurred. Most businesses use the accrual basis as covered in this book. The accrual basis of accounting provides a better picture of a business's revenues and expenses. It records revenue only when it has been earned and expenses only when they have been incurred. Under accrual basis accounting, it is irrelevant when cash is received or paid.

**Example:** Suppose on May 1, Smart Touch Learning paid $1,200 for insurance for the next six months ($200 per month). This prepayment represents insurance coverage for May through October. Under the cash basis method, Smart Touch Learning would record Insurance Expense of $1,200 on May 1. This is because the cash basis method records an expense when cash is paid. Alternatively, accrual basis accounting requires the company to prorate the expense. Smart Touch Learning would record a $200 expense every month from May through October. This is illustrated as follows:

| | Cash basis | | Accrual basis | |
|---|---|---|---|---|
| **Cash Payment Made** | May 1: | $ 1,200 | May 1: | $ 1,200 |
| **Expense Recorded** | May 1: | $ 1,200 | May 31: | $ 200 |
| | | | June 30: | 200 |
| | | | July 31: | 200 |
| | | | August 31: | 200 |
| | | | September 30: | 200 |
| | | | October 31: | 200 |
| **Total Expense Recorded** | | $ 1,200 | | $ 1,200 |

Now let's see how the cash basis and the accrual basis methods account for revenues.

**Example:** Suppose on April 30, Smart Touch Learning received $600 for services to be performed for the next six months (May through October). Under the cash basis method, Smart Touch Learning would record $600 of revenue when the cash is received on April 30. The accrual basis method, though, requires the revenue to be recorded only when it is earned. Smart Touch Learning would record $100 of revenue each month for the next six months beginning in May.

| | Cash basis | | Accrual basis | |
|---|---|---|---|---|
| **Cash Received** | April 30: | $ 600 | April 30: | $ 600 |
| **Revenue Recorded** | April 30: | $ 600 | May 31: | $ 100 |
| | | | June 30: | 100 |
| | | | July 31: | 100 |
| | | | August 31: | 100 |
| | | | September 30: | 100 |
| | | | October 31: | 100 |
| **Total Revenue Recorded** | | $ 600 | | $ 600 |

Notice that under both methods, cash basis and accrual basis, the total amount of revenues and expenses recorded by October 31 was the same. The major difference between a cash basis accounting system and an accrual basis accounting system is the timing of recording the revenue or expense.

## Try It!

Total Pool Services earned $130,000 of service revenue during 2016. Of the $130,000 earned, the business received $105,000 in cash. The remaining amount, $25,000, was still owed by customers as of December 31. In addition, Total Pool Services incurred $85,000 of expenses during the year. As of December 31, $10,000 of the expenses still needed to be paid. In addition, Total Pool Services prepaid $5,000 cash in December 2016 for expenses incurred during the next year.

1. Determine the amount of service revenue and expenses for 2016 using a cash basis accounting system.
2. Determine the amount of service revenue and expenses for 2016 using an accrual basis accounting system.

**Check your answers online in MyAccountingLab or at http://www.pearsonhighered.com/Horngren.**

For more practice, see Short Exercises S3-1 and S3-2. MyAccountingLab

# WHAT CONCEPTS AND PRINCIPLES APPLY TO ACCRUAL BASIS ACCOUNTING?

**Learning Objective 2**
Define and apply the time period concept, revenue recognition, and matching principles.

As we have seen, the timing and recognition of revenues and expenses are the key differences between the cash basis and accrual basis methods of accounting. These differences can be explained by understanding the time period concept and the revenue recognition and matching principles.

## The Time Period Concept

**Time Period Concept**
Assumes that a business's activities can be sliced into small time segments and that financial statements can be prepared for specific periods, such as a month, quarter, or year.

**Fiscal Year**
An accounting year of any 12 consecutive months that may or may not coincide with the calendar year.

Smart Touch Learning will know with 100% certainty how well it has operated only if the company sells all of its assets, pays all of its liabilities, and gives any leftover cash to its stockholders. For obvious reasons, it is not practical to measure income this way. Because businesses need periodic reports on their affairs, the **time period concept** assumes that a business's activities can be sliced into small time segments and that financial statements can be prepared for specific periods, such as a month, quarter, or year.

The basic accounting period is one year, and most businesses prepare annual financial statements. The 12-month accounting period used for the annual financial statements is called a **fiscal year**. For most companies, the annual accounting period is the calendar year, from January 1 through December 31. Other companies use a fiscal year that ends on a date other than December 31. The year-end date is usually the low point in business activity for the year. Retailers are a notable example. For instance, Wal-Mart Stores, Inc., and J. C. Penney Company, Inc., use a fiscal year that ends around January 31 because the low point of their business activity comes about a month after the holidays.

## The Revenue Recognition Principle

**Revenue Recognition Principle**
Requires companies to record revenue when it has been earned and determines the amount of revenue to record.

The **revenue recognition principle** tells accountants the following things:

- *When* to record revenue—that is, when to make a journal entry for revenue
- The *amount* of revenue to record

### When to Record Revenue

The revenue recognition principle requires companies to record revenue when it has been earned—but not before. Revenue has been earned when the business has delivered a good

## COMING SOON

### The NEW Revenue Recognition Principle

On May 28, 2014, the FASB and IASB issued new guidance on accounting for revenue recognition, *Revenue Recognition–Revenue from Contracts with Customers*. Under this new guidance, the previous principle related to revenue recognition will be eliminated.

This new standard will become effective for public business entities with annual reporting periods beginning after December 15, 2016. For all other entities, the new standard will be effective for annual periods beginning after December 15, 2017.

The new revenue recognition principle will apply to most contracts with customers and states that an entity should recognize revenue in an amount that reflects the consideration that the entity expects to be entitled to in exchange for goods or services. The business will recognize revenue by applying five steps:

**Step 1: Identify the contract with the customer.** A contract is an agreement between two or more parties with enforceable rights and obligations.

**Step 2: Identify the performance obligations in the contract.** A performance obligation is a contractual promise with a customer to transfer a distinct good or service.

**Step 3: Determine the transaction price.** The transaction price is the amount that the entity expects to be entitled to as a result of transferring goods or services to the customer.

**Step 4: Allocate the transaction price to the performance obligations in the contract.** If the transaction has multiple performance obligations, the transaction price will be allocated among the different performance obligations.

**Step 5: Recognize revenue when (or as) the entity satisfies a performance obligation.** The business will recognize revenue when (or as) it satisfies a performance obligation by transferring a good or service to a customer.

As this new standard will not be effective until after 2016, the revenue recognition principle discussed in this book is current through December 2016.

or service to the customer, not necessarily when the business receives the cash from the customer. The earnings process is complete when the company has done everything required by the sale agreement regardless of whether cash is received.

### The Amount of Revenue to Record

Revenue is recorded for the actual selling price of the item or service transferred to the customer. Suppose that in order to obtain a new client, Smart Touch Learning performs e-learning services for the discounted price of $100. Ordinarily, the business would have charged $200 for this service. How much revenue should the business record? Smart Touch Learning charged only $100, so the business records $100 of revenue.

## The Matching Principle

The **matching principle** (sometimes called the *expense recognition principle*) guides accounting for expenses and ensures the following:

- All expenses are recorded when they are incurred during the period.
- Expenses are matched against the revenues of the period.

**Matching Principle**
Guides accounting for expenses, ensures that all expenses are recorded when they are incurred during the period, and matches those expenses against the revenues of the period.

To match expenses against revenues means to subtract expenses incurred during one month from revenues earned during that same month. The goal is to compute an accurate net income or net loss for the time period.

There is a natural link between some expenses and revenues. For example, Smart Touch Learning pays a commission to the employee who sells the e-learning company's services. The commission expense is directly related to the e-learning company's revenue earned. Other expenses are not so easy to link to revenues. For example, Smart Touch Learning's monthly rent expense occurs regardless of the revenues earned that month. The matching principle tells us to identify those expenses with a particular period, such as a month or a year, when the related revenue occurred. The business will record rent expense each month based on the rental agreement.

## Try It!

Match the accounting terminology to the definitions.

| | |
|---|---|
| **3.** Time period concept | **a.** requires companies to record revenue when it has been earned and determines the amount of revenue to record |
| **4.** Revenue recognition principle | **b.** assumes that a business's activities can be sliced into small time segments and that financial statements can be prepared for specific periods |
| **5.** Matching principle | **c.** guides accounting for expenses, ensures that all expenses are recorded when they are incurred during the period, and matches those expenses against the revenues of the period. |

**Check your answers online in MyAccountingLab or at http://www.pearsonhighered.com/Horngren.**

For more practice, see Short Exercises S3-3 and S3-4. MyAccountingLab

# WHAT ARE ADJUSTING ENTRIES, AND HOW DO WE RECORD THEM?

**Learning Objective 3**
Explain the purpose of and journalize and post adjusting entries

The end-of-period process begins with the trial balance, which you learned how to prepare in the previous chapter. Exhibit 3-1 is the unadjusted trial balance of Smart Touch Learning at December 31, 2016.

**Exhibit 3-1** | **Unadjusted Trial Balance**

SMART TOUCH LEARNING
Unadjusted Trial Balance
December 31, 2016

| | Balance | |
|---|---|---|
| **Account Title** | **Debit** | **Credit** |
| Cash | $ 12,200 | |
| Accounts Receivable | 1,000 | |
| Office Supplies | 500 | |
| Prepaid Rent | 3,000 | |
| Furniture | 18,000 | |
| Building | 60,000 | |
| Land | 20,000 | |
| Accounts Payable | | $ 200 |
| Utilities Payable | | 100 |
| Unearned Revenue | | 600 |
| Notes Payable | | 60,000 |
| Common Stock | | 48,000 |
| Dividends | 5,000 | |
| Service Revenue | | 16,500 |
| Rent Expense | 2,000 | |
| Salaries Expense | 3,600 | |
| Utilities Expense | 100 | |
| Total | **$ 125,400** | **$ 125,400** |

This *unadjusted trial balance* lists the revenues and expenses of the e-learning company for November and December. But these amounts are incomplete because they omit various revenue and expense transactions. Accrual basis accounting requires the business to review the unadjusted trial balance and determine whether any additional revenues and expenses need to be recorded. Are there revenues that Smart Touch Learning has earned that haven't been recorded yet? Are there expenses that have occurred that haven't been journalized?

For example, consider the Office Supplies account in Exhibit 3-1. Smart Touch Learning uses office supplies during the two months. This reduces the office supplies on hand (an asset) and creates an expense (Supplies Expense). It is a waste of time to record Supplies Expense every time office supplies are used. But by December 31, enough of the $500 of Office Supplies on the unadjusted trial balance (Exhibit 3-1) have probably been used that we need to adjust the Office Supplies account. This is an example of why we need to adjust some accounts at the end of the accounting period.

An **adjusting entry** is completed at the end of the accounting period and records revenues to the period in which they are earned and expenses to the period in which they occur. Adjusting entries also update the asset and liability accounts. Adjustments are needed to properly measure several items such as:

**Adjusting Entry**
An entry made at the end of the accounting period that is used to record revenues to the period in which they are earned and expenses to the period in which they occur.

1. Net income (loss) on the income statement
2. Assets and liabilities on the balance sheet

There are two basic categories of adjusting entries: *deferrals* and *accruals*. In a deferral adjustment, the cash payment occurs before an expense is incurred or the cash receipt occurs before the revenue is earned. Deferrals defer the recognition of revenue or expense to a date after the cash is received or paid. Accrual adjustments are the opposite. An accrual records an expense before the cash is paid, or it records the revenue before the cash is received.

The two basic categories of adjusting entries can be further separated into four types:

1. Deferred expenses (deferral)
2. Deferred revenues (deferral)
3. Accrued expenses (accrual)
4. Accrued revenues (accrual)

The focus of this chapter is on learning how to account for these four types of adjusting entries.

## Deferred Expenses

**Deferred expenses**, also called prepaid expenses, are advance payments of future expenses. They are deferrals because the expense is not recognized at the time of payment but deferred until they are used up. Such payments are considered assets rather than expenses until they are used up. When the prepayment is used up, the used portion of the asset becomes an expense via an adjusting entry.

**Deferred Expense**
An asset created when a business makes advance payments of future expenses.

### Prepaid Rent

Remember Transaction 10 in Chapter 2? Smart Touch Learning prepaid three months' office rent of $3,000 ($1,000 per month × 3 months) on December 1, 2016. The entry to record the payment was as follows:

| Date | Accounts and Explanation | Debit | Credit |
|---|---|---|---|
| Dec. 1 | Prepaid Rent | 3,000 | |
| | Cash | | 3,000 |
| | *Paid rent in advance.* | | |

| A↑↓ | = | L + E |
|---|---|---|
| Prepaid Rent↑ Cash↓ | = | |

After posting, Prepaid Rent has a $3,000 debit balance.

| Prepaid Rent | | | |
|---|---|---|---|
| Dec. 1 | 3,000 | | |

Throughout December, Prepaid Rent maintains this balance. But $3,000 is *not* the amount of Prepaid Rent for the balance sheet at December 31. Why?

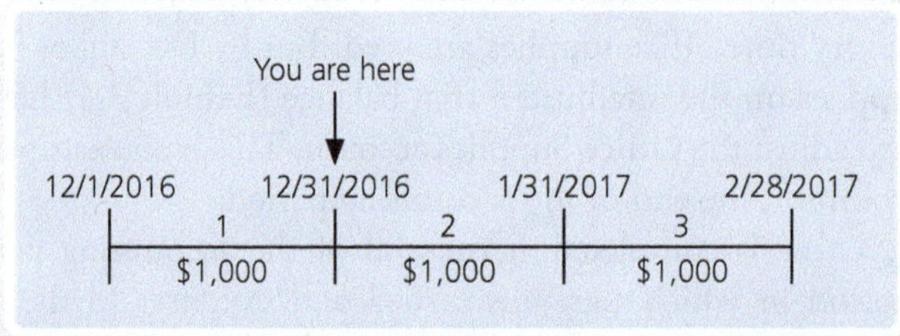


As of December 31, Prepaid Rent should be decreased for the amount that has been used up. The used-up portion is one month of the three months prepaid, or one-third of the prepayment. Recall that an asset that has expired is an *expense*. The adjusting entry transfers $1,000 ($3,000 × 1/3) from Prepaid Rent to Rent Expense. The adjusting entry is as follows:

| A↓ | = | L | + | E↓ |
|---|---|---|---|---|
| Prepaid Rent↓ | = | | | Rent Expense↑ |

| Date | Accounts and Explanation | Debit | Credit |
|---|---|---|---|
| Dec. 31 | Rent Expense | 1,000 | |
| | Prepaid Rent | | 1,000 |
| | *To record rent expense.* | | |

After posting, Prepaid Rent and Rent Expense show correct ending balances:

| Prepaid Rent | | | |
|---|---|---|---|
| Dec. 1 | 3,000 | 1,000 | Dec. 31 |
| Bal. | 2,000 | | |

| Rent Expense | | |
|---|---|---|
| Nov. 15 | 2,000 | |
| Dec. 31 | 1,000 | |
| Bal. | 3,000 | |

Prepaid Rent is an example of an asset that was overstated prior to journalizing and posting the adjusting entry. Notice that the ending balance in Prepaid Rent is now $2,000. Because Prepaid Rent is an asset account for Smart Touch Learning, it should contain only two more months of rent on December 31 (for January and February). So we have $1,000 rent per month times two months equals the $2,000 Prepaid Rent balance.

If Smart Touch Learning had prepaid insurance, the same type of analysis would apply to the prepayment of three months of insurance. The only difference is in the account titles. Prepaid Insurance would be used instead of Prepaid Rent, and Insurance Expense would be used instead of Rent Expense.

## Office Supplies

Office supplies are also accounted for as prepaid expenses. Let's look at another example. On November 3, Smart Touch Learning purchased $500 of office supplies on account.

The December 31 unadjusted trial balance, therefore, still lists Office Supplies with a $500 debit balance. But Smart Touch Learning's December 31 balance sheet should *not* report office supplies of $500. Why not?

During November and December, the e-learning company used office supplies to conduct business. The cost of the supplies used becomes *Supplies Expense*. To measure Supplies Expense, the business first counts the office supplies on hand at the end of December. This is the amount of the asset still owned by the business. Assume that office supplies costing $100 remain on December 31. Then the business uses the Office Supplies T-account to determine the value of the supplies that were used:

**Office Supplies**

| | | |
|---|---|---|
| Nov. 3 | 500 | ? |
| Bal. | 100 | |

Amount of office supplies remaining (→ Bal. 100)

Amount of office supplies used = Supplies Expense (→ ?)

So, we can solve for the office supplies used as follows:

Office Supplies Balance before Adjustment − Office Supplies Used = Office Supplies on Hand
$500 − Office Supplies Used = $100
Office Supplies Used = $400

The December 31 adjusting entry updates Office Supplies and records Supplies Expense for November and December as follows:

| Date | Accounts and Explanation | Debit | Credit |
|---|---|---|---|
| Dec. 31 | Supplies Expense | 400 | |
| | Office Supplies | | 400 |
| | *To record office supplies used.* | | |

A↓ = L + E↓
Office Supplies↓ = Supplies Expense↑

After posting the adjusting entry, the December 31 balance of Office Supplies is correctly reflected as $100 and the Supplies Expense is correctly reflected as $400.

**Office Supplies**

| | | | |
|---|---|---|---|
| Nov. 3 | 500 | 400 | Dec. 31 |
| Bal. | 100 | | |

**Supplies Expense**

| | | |
|---|---|---|
| Dec. 31 | 400 | |
| Bal. | 400 | |

The Office Supplies account then enters January with a $100 balance. If the adjusting entry for Office Supplies had not been recorded, the asset would have been overstated and Supplies Expense would have been understated. In making the adjusting entry, the correct balance of Office Supplies, $100, is now reported on the balance sheet as of December 31 and the income statement is correctly reporting an expense of $400.

## Depreciation

**Plant assets** are long-lived, tangible assets used in the operation of a business. Examples include land, buildings, equipment, furniture, and automobiles. As a business uses these assets, their value and usefulness decline. The decline in usefulness of a plant asset is an expense, and accountants systematically spread the asset's cost over its useful life. The allocation of a plant

**Plant Asset**
Long-lived, tangible asset, such as land, buildings, and equipment, used in the operation of a business.

**Depreciation**
The process by which businesses spread the allocation of a plant asset's cost over its useful life.

asset's cost over its useful life is called **depreciation**. For example, a business might pay cash for an automobile when purchased, but the automobile will last for years, so depreciation allocates the cost spent on the car over the time the business uses the car. All plant assets are depreciated, with the exception of land. We record no depreciation for land because, unlike buildings and equipment, it does not have a definitive or clearly estimable useful life, so it is difficult to allocate the cost of land.

**Similarity to Prepaid Expenses** The concept of accounting for plant assets is similar to that of prepaid expenses. The major difference is the length of time it takes for the asset to be used up. Prepaid expenses usually expire within a year, but plant assets remain useful for several years. As a business uses its plant assets, an adjusting entry is required to allocate the assets' costs. The adjusting entry records the cost allocation to an expense account called Depreciation Expense.

Let's review an example for Smart Touch Learning. On December 2, the business received a contribution of furniture with a market value of $18,000 from Sheena Bright. In exchange, Smart Touch Learning issued shares of stock to Bright and made the following journal entry:

| A↑ | | L | + | E↑ |
|---|---|---|---|---|
| Furniture↑ | = | | | Common Stock↑ |

| Date | Accounts and Explanation | Debit | Credit |
|---|---|---|---|
| Dec. 2 | Furniture | 18,000 | |
| | Common Stock | | 18,000 |
| | *Contribution of furniture in exchange for common stock.* | | |

After posting, the Furniture account has an $18,000 balance:

| Furniture | |
|---|---|
| Dec. 2 18,000 | |

Smart Touch Learning believes the furniture will remain useful for five years, and at the end of five years, Smart Touch Learning believes the furniture will be worthless. The expected value of a depreciable asset at the end of its useful life is called the **residual value**. Smart Touch Learning will use the straight-line method to compute the amount of depreciation. The **straight-line method** allocates an equal amount of depreciation each year and is calculated as:

**Residual Value**
The expected value of a depreciable asset at the end of its useful life.

**Straight-Line Method**
A depreciation method that allocates an equal amount of depreciation each year. (Cost − Residual value) / Useful life.

Straight-line depreciation = (Cost − Residual value) / Useful life

Smart Touch Learning will calculate the depreciation of the furniture for the month of December as:

Straight-line depreciation = (Cost − Residual value) / Useful life
= ($18,000 − $0) / 5 years
= $3,600 per year / 12 months = $300 per month

Depreciation expense for December is recorded by the following adjusting entry:

| Date | Accounts and Explanation | Debit | Credit |
|---|---|---|---|
| Dec. 31 | Depreciation Expense—Furniture | 300 | |
| | Accumulated Depreciation—Furniture | | 300 |
| | *To record depreciation on furniture.* | | |

**A↓** = **L + E↓**

Accumulated Depreciation—Furniture↑ = Depreciation Expense—Furniture↑

**The Accumulated Depreciation Account** **Notice that in the above adjusting entry for depreciation, we credited Accumulated Depreciation—Furniture and *not* the asset account Furniture. Why? We need to keep the original cost of the furniture separate from the accumulated depreciation because of the cost principle. Managers can then refer to the Furniture account to see how much the asset originally cost.** This information may help decide how much to sell the asset for in the future or how much to pay for new furniture. The **Accumulated Depreciation** account is the sum of all depreciation expense recorded for the depreciable asset to date. Accumulated Depreciation will increase (accumulate) over time.

When recording depreciation, why don't we record a credit to the Furniture account?

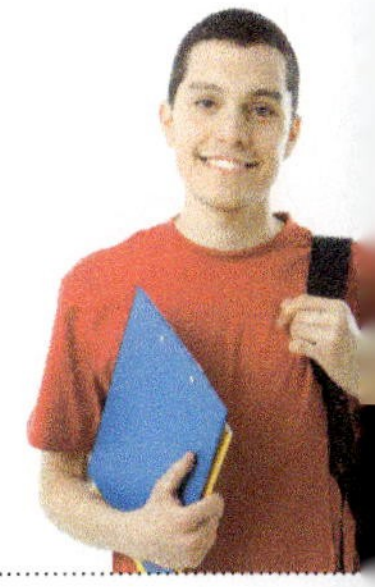

**Accumulated Depreciation**
The sum of all the depreciation expense recorded to date for a depreciable asset.

**Contra Account**
An account that is paired with, and is listed immediately after, its related account in the chart of accounts and associated financial statement and whose normal balance is the opposite of the normal balance of the related account.

Accumulated Depreciation is a contra asset, which means that it is an asset account with a normal credit balance. Contra means opposite. A **contra account** has two main characteristics:

- A contra account is paired with and is listed immediately after its related account in the chart of accounts and associated financial statement.
- A contra account's normal balance (debit or credit) is the opposite of the normal balance of the related account.

For example, Accumulated Depreciation—Furniture is the contra account that follows the Furniture account on the balance sheet. The Furniture account has a normal debit balance, so Accumulated Depreciation—Furniture, a contra asset, has a normal credit balance.

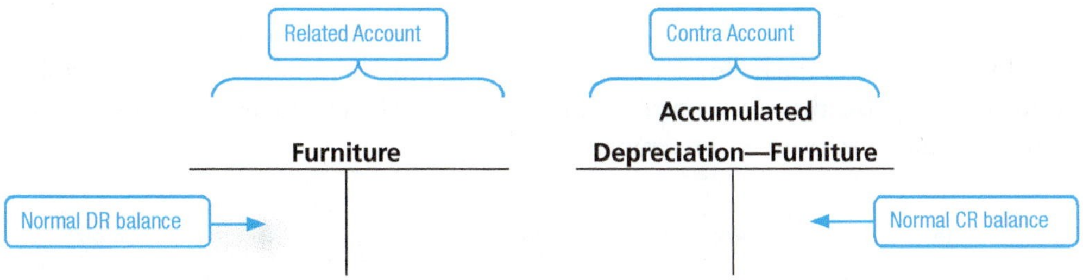


A business may have a separate Accumulated Depreciation account for each depreciable asset. Because Smart Touch Learning has both a Building and a Furniture account, it also has these two accounts: Accumulated Depreciation—Building, and Accumulated Depreciation—Furniture. However, small companies often have only one Accumulated Depreciation account for all of their depreciable assets.

After posting the depreciation, the accounts appear as follows:

| Furniture | |
|---|---|
| Dec. 2 18,000 | |

| Accumulated Depreciation—Furniture | |
|---|---|
| | 300 Dec. 31 |

| Depreciation Expense—Furniture | |
|---|---|
| Dec. 31 300 | |

*The Accumulated Depreciation account accumulates the depreciation expense. This means that next month an additional $300 will be added to the Accumulated Depreciation—Furniture account creating a balance of $600, representing two months of depreciation. At the end of three months, the Accumulated Depreciation—Furniture account will have a balance of $900 ($300 per month x 3 months).*

**Book Value** The balance sheet reports both Furniture and Accumulated Depreciation—Furniture. Because it is a contra account, Accumulated Depreciation—Furniture is subtracted from Furniture. The resulting net amount (cost minus accumulated depreciation) of a plant asset is called its **book value**. The book value represents the cost invested in the asset that the business has not yet expensed. For Smart Touch Learning's furniture, the book value on December 31 is as follows:

**Book Value**
A depreciable asset's cost minus accumulated depreciation.

| Book value of furniture: | |
|---|---|
| Furniture | $ 18,000 |
| Less: Accumulated Depreciation—Furniture | (300) |
| Book value of furniture | $ 17,700 |

Depreciation on the building purchased on December 1 would be recorded in a similar manner. Suppose that the monthly depreciation is $250. The following adjusting entry would record depreciation for December:

| A↓ | = | L | + | E↓ |
|---|---|---|---|---|
| Accumulated Depreciation—Building↑ | = | | | Depreciation Expense—Building↑ |

| Date | Accounts and Explanation | Debit | Credit |
|---|---|---|---|
| Dec. 31 | Depreciation Expense—Building | 250 | |
| | Accumulated Depreciation—Building | | 250 |
| | *To record depreciation on building.* | | |

*Remember, an increase in a contra asset, such as Accumulated Depreciation, decreases total assets. This is because a contra asset has a credit balance and credits decrease assets.*

Had Smart Touch Learning not recorded the adjusting entries for depreciation on the furniture and building, plant assets would have been overstated and expenses would have been understated. After recording the adjusting entries, plant assets are reported at the correct net amount, as shown on the December 31 partial balance sheet in Exhibit 3-2.

**Exhibit 3-2** **Plant Assets on the Balance Sheet of Smart Touch Learning**

| SMART TOUCH LEARNING<br>Balance Sheet (Partial)<br>December 31, 2016 | | |
|---|---|---|
| **Plant Assets:** | | |
| Furniture | $ 18,000 | |
| Less: Accumulated Depreciation—Furniture | (300) | $ 17,700 |
| Building | 60,000 | |
| Less: Accumulated Depreciation—Building | (250) | 59,750 |
| Land | | 20,000 |
| Plant Assets, Net | | **$ 97,450** |

## Deferred Revenues

Remember, deferred (or unearned) revenues occur when the company receives cash before it does the work or delivers a product to earn that cash. The company owes a product or a service to the customer, or it owes the customer his or her money back. Only after completing the job or delivering the product does the business *earn* the revenue. Because of this delay, unearned revenue is a liability and is also called **deferred revenue**. The revenue associated with the work or product is not recognized when the cash is received but is instead deferred until it is earned.

**Deferred Revenue**
A liability created when a business collects cash from customers in advance of completing a service or delivering a product.

Suppose, for example, a law firm engages Smart Touch Learning to provide e-learning services for the next 30 days, agreeing to pay $600 in advance. Smart Touch Learning collected the amount on December 21 and recorded the following entry:

| Date | Accounts and Explanation | Debit | Credit |
|---|---|---|---|
| Dec. 21 | Cash | 600 | |
| | Unearned Revenue | | 600 |
| | *Collected cash for future services.* | | |

| A↑ | = | L↑ | + | E |
|---|---|---|---|---|
| Cash↑ | | Unearned Revenue↑ | | |

The liability account, Unearned Revenue, now shows that Smart Touch Learning owes $600 in services.

| Unearned Revenue | | |
|---|---|---|
| | 600 | Dec. 21 |

During the last 10 days of the month—December 22 through December 31—Smart Touch Learning will *earn* approximately one-third (10 days divided by 30 days) of the $600, or $200. Therefore, Smart Touch Learning makes the following adjusting entry to record earning $200 of revenue:

| A | = | L↓ | + | E↑ |
|---|---|---|---|---|
| | | Unearned Revenue↓ | | Service Revenue↑ |

| Date | Accounts and Explanation | Debit | Credit |
|---|---|---|---|
| Dec. 31 | Unearned Revenue | 200 | |
| | Service Revenue | | 200 |
| | *To record service revenue earned that was collected in advance.* | | |

This adjusting entry shifts $200 from the liability account to the revenue account. Service Revenue increases by $200, and Unearned Revenue decreases by $200. Now both accounts are up to date at December 31:

**Unearned Revenue**

| | | | |
|---|---|---|---|
| Dec. 31 | 200 | 600 | Dec. 21 |
| | | 400 | Bal. |

**Service Revenue**

| | | | |
|---|---|---|---|
| | | 5,500 | Nov. 8 |
| | | 3,000 | Nov. 10 |
| | | 8,000 | Dec. 28 |
| | | 200 | Dec. 31 |
| | | 16,700 | Bal. |

Had the adjusting entry not been made, the liability, Unearned Revenue, would be overstated and Service Revenue would be understated.

## Accrued Expenses

**Accrued Expense**
An expense that the business has incurred but has not yet paid.

Businesses often incur expenses before paying for them. The term **accrued expense** refers to an expense of this type. An accrued expense hasn't been paid for yet. Consider an employee's salary. Salaries Expense grows as the employee works, so the expense is said to *accrue*. Another accrued expense is interest expense on a note payable. Interest accrues as time passes on the note. An accrued expense always creates an accrued liability.

Corporations do not make daily or weekly journal entries to accrue expenses. Instead, they wait until the end of the accounting period. They make an adjusting entry to bring each expense (and the related liability) up to date for the financial statements.

### Accrued Salaries Expense

Smart Touch Learning pays its employee a monthly salary of $2,400—half on the 15th and half on the first day of the next month. On the next page is a calendar for December and the first week in January with the two pay days circled.

**December 2016**

| Sunday | Monday | Tuesday | Wednesday | Thursday | Friday | Saturday |
|---|---|---|---|---|---|---|
| | | | | Dec 1 | 2 | 3 |
| 4 | 5 | 6 | 7 | 8 | 9 | 10 |
| 11 | 12 | 13 | 14 | 15 Pay Day | 16 | 17 |
| 18 | 19 | 20 | 21 | 22 | 23 | 24 |
| 25 | 26 | 27 | 28 | 29 | 30 | 31 |
| Jan 1 Pay Day | 2 | 3 | 4 | 5 | 6 | 7 |

During December, the company paid the first half-month salary on Thursday, December 15, and made this entry:

| Date | Accounts and Explanation | Debit | Credit |
|---|---|---|---|
| Dec. 15 | Salaries Expense | 1,200 | |
| | Cash | | 1,200 |
| | *Paid salaries.* | | |

A↓ (Cash↓) = L + E↓ (Salaries Expense↑)

The December 15 entry records only the first half of December's salaries expense. The second payment of $1,200 will occur on January 1; however, the expense was incurred in December, so the expense must be recorded in December. On December 31, Smart Touch Learning makes the following adjusting entry:

| Date | Accounts and Explanation | Debit | Credit |
|---|---|---|---|
| Dec. 31 | Salaries Expense | 1,200 | |
| | Salaries Payable | | 1,200 |
| | *To accrue salaries expense.* | | |

A = L↑ (Salaries Payable↑) + E↓ (Salaries Expense↑)

After posting, both Salaries Expense and Salaries Payable are up to date:

**Salaries Payable**

| Debit | Credit |
|---|---|
| | 1,200 Dec. 31 |
| | 1,200 Bal. |

**Salaries Expense**

| Debit | Credit |
|---|---|
| Nov. 15 1,200 | |
| Dec. 1 1,200 | |
| Dec. 15 1,200 | |
| Dec. 31 1,200 | |
| Bal. 4,800 | |

Salaries Expense shows a full two months' salary, and Salaries Payable shows the liability owed at December 31. This is an example of a liability that was understated before the adjusting entry was made. It also is an example of the matching principle: We are recording December's Salaries Expense in December so it will be reported on the same income statement as December's revenues.

**Future Payment of Accrued Salaries Expense** The adjusting entry at December 31 creates a liability that will eventually be paid. In this case, Smart Touch Learning will pay its employee the second half of December's wages on January 1. Because the expense has already been recorded, Smart Touch Learning will not record the expense again. To do so would record the expense twice, thus overstating the expense account. Instead, the business will decrease the amount of the liability, Salaries Payable, with a debit and record the cash payment. On January 1, Smart Touch Learning would record the following journal entry:

| A↓ | = | L↓ | + | E |
|---|---|---|---|---|
| Cash↓ | = | Salaries Payable↓ | | |

| Date | Accounts and Explanation | Debit | Credit |
|---|---|---|---|
| Jan. 1 | Salaries Payable | 1,200 | |
| | Cash | | 1,200 |
| | *To record payment of accrued expense.* | | |

*Don't confuse this entry with an adjusting entry. Adjusting entries are recorded only at the end of the accounting period and are used to record either revenue earned or expenses incurred. This entry is a journal entry. It is simply recording an everyday business transaction—the payment of salaries previously accrued. In this example, the amount paid for salaries was equal to the amount of the liability in the adjusting entry. Sometimes, however, the amount paid might be different than the liability in the adjusting entry. For example, assume that instead of making a payment for salaries on January 1, Smart Touch Learning doesn't make the payment until January 15 and pays a full month's salary. By delaying the payment, Smart Touch Learning incurs additional days of salaries expense. The journal entry to record the payment on January 15 will not only decrease the payable recorded in the adjusting entry but will also record any additional expense incurred.*

## Accrued Interest Expense

Borrowing money creates an additional liability for a Note Payable. Remember the purchase of the building on December 1, 2016? Smart Touch Learning purchased a $60,000 building in exchange for a loan. Smart Touch Learning signed a one-year loan and recorded the following entry using the Notes Payable account:

| A↑ | = | L↑ | + | E |
|---|---|---|---|---|
| Building↑ | = | Notes Payable↑ | | |

| Date | Accounts and Explanation | Debit | Credit |
|---|---|---|---|
| Dec. 1 | Building | 60,000 | |
| | Notes Payable | | 60,000 |
| | *Purchase of building with note.* | | |

## ETHICS

### When should accrued expenses be recorded?

Evan is in the process of recording the adjusting entries for Green Landscaping Services. Bob Green, owner and manager, has asked Evan to record all of the adjusting entries except for accrued expenses. Bob has a meeting with the banker on Monday to apply for a business loan. Bob knows that the banker will review his balance sheet and income statement. Bob is concerned that by recording the accrued expenses, the business's liabilities will be significantly higher on the balance sheet and a net loss will be reported on the income statement (due to higher expenses). Bob has instructed Evan to delay recording the accrued expenses until after his meeting with the banker. What should Evan do?

### Solution

Failing to record the adjusting entries for accrued expenses violates the matching principle. Recording the expenses now (before Monday) accurately matches the occurrence of the expenses with the revenues that were created during that period. If Evan does not record the adjusting entries, the financial statements will not accurately represent the financial position or operating performance of the business. The banker could be tricked into lending the company money. Then, if the business could not repay the loan, the bank would lose—all because the banker relied on incorrect accounting information supplied by the company.

Interest on this note is payable one year later, on December 1, 2017. Although the company won't make the interest payment for a year, the company must record the amount of interest expense that has been incurred by December 31, 2016. The company will make an adjusting entry to record interest expense for one month (December 1–December 31). Assume one month's interest expense on this note is $100. The December 31 adjusting entry to accrue interest expense is as follows:

| Date | Accounts and Explanation | Debit | Credit |
|---|---|---|---|
| Dec. 31 | Interest Expense | 100 | |
| | Interest Payable | | 100 |
| | *To accrue interest expense.* | | |

| A | = | L↑ | + | E↓ |
|---|---|---|---|---|
| | | Interest Payable↑ | | Interest Expense↑ |

Notice that the adjusting entry records a credit to the liability, Interest Payable. This is because the interest payment will not be made until next year; therefore, Smart Touch Learning owes interest to the bank. Had the adjusting entry not been recorded, liabilities and expenses would have been understated. After posting, Interest Expense and Interest Payable now have the following correct balances:

| Interest Payable | | | Interest Expense | |
|---|---|---|---|---|
| | 100 Dec. 31 | ←→ | Dec. 31 100 | |
| | 100 Bal. | | Bal. 100 | |

## Accrued Revenues

As we have just seen, expenses can occur before a company makes a cash payment for them, which creates an accrued expense. Similarly, businesses can earn revenue before they receive the cash. This creates an **accrued revenue**, which is a revenue that has been earned but for which the cash has not yet been collected.

**Accrued Revenue**
A revenue that has been earned but for which the cash has not yet been collected.

Assume that Smart Touch Learning is hired on December 15 to perform e-learning services, beginning on December 16. Under this agreement, the business will earn $1,600 monthly and receive payment on January 15. At the date of hiring, Smart Touch Learning does not record a journal entry because revenue has not yet been earned. During December, it will earn half a month's fee, $800, for work December 16 through December 31. On December 31, Smart Touch Learning makes the following adjusting entry to record the revenue earned December 16 through December 31:

| A↑ | = | L | + | E↑ |
|---|---|---|---|---|
| Accounts Receivable↑ | | | | Service Revenue↑ |

| Date | Accounts and Explanation | Debit | Credit |
|---|---|---|---|
| Dec. 31 | Accounts Receivable | 800 | |
| | Service Revenue | | 800 |
| | *To accrue service revenue.* | | |

The adjusting entry records the earned revenue and brings the balance of the Service Revenue account to $17,500. In addition, the adjusting entry records an additional $800 account receivable. Smart Touch Learning did not record cash because the business has not yet received payment on the services provided. The cash will not be received until January 15. Smart Touch Learning's account balances after posting the adjusting entry are:

**Accounts Receivable**

| | | | |
|---|---|---|---|
| Nov. 10 | 3,000 | 2,000 | Nov. 22 |
| Dec. 31 | 800 | | |
| Bal. | 1,800 | | |

**Service Revenue**

| | | | |
|---|---|---|---|
| | | 5,500 | Nov. 8 |
| | | 3,000 | Nov. 10 |
| | | 8,000 | Dec. 28 |
| | | 200 | Dec. 31 |
| | | 800 | Dec. 31 |
| | | 17,500 | Bal. |

Without the adjustment, Smart Touch Learning's financial statements would understate both an asset, Accounts Receivable, and a revenue, Service Revenue.

**Future Receipt of Accrued Revenues** The adjusting entry on December 31 records revenue earned for half a month and also creates an accounts receivable. When Smart Touch Learning receives the payment on January 15, the business will record the following entry:

| A↑ | = | L | + | E↑ |
|---|---|---|---|---|
| Cash↑<br>Accounts Receivable↓ | | | | Service Revenue↑ |

Revenue for Jan. 1–Jan. 15

| Date | Accounts and Explanation | Debit | Credit |
|---|---|---|---|
| Jan. 15 | Cash | 1,600 | |
| | Service Revenue | | 800 |
| | Accounts Receivable | | 800 |
| | *Performed services and received cash.* | | |

Accounts Receivable created from the adjusting entry.

Notice that on January 15, Smart Touch Learning records revenue only for the remaining half of the month (January 1–January 15). Smart Touch Learning recognizes that $800 of revenue was already recorded in December. The entry on January 15 removes the accounts receivable and records the remaining revenue. If the business had incorrectly recorded $1,600 of Service Revenue on January 15, the revenue would have been overstated in January.

Exhibit 3-3 summarizes the adjusting entries for deferrals and accruals.

**Exhibit 3-3 | Deferral and Accrual Adjustments**

**DEFERRALS—Cash receipt or Cash payment occurs first.**

| | ORIGINAL ENTRY | | | ADJUSTING ENTRY | | |
|---|---|---|---|---|---|---|
| **Prepaid Expenses** | Prepaid Rent | XXX | | Rent Expense | XXX | |
| | Cash | | XXX | Prepaid Rent | | XXX |
| | *Pay for rent in advance and record an asset first.* | | | *Adjust for rent used later.* | | |
| **Depreciation** | Furniture | XXX | | Depreciation Expense—Furniture | XXX | |
| | Cash | | XXX | Accumulated Depreciation—Furniture | | XXX |
| | *Pay for furniture in advance and record an asset first.* | | | *Adjust for depreciation (use) of asset later.* | | |
| **Unearned Revenues** | Cash | XXX | | Unearned Revenue | XXX | |
| | Unearned Revenue | | XXX | Service Revenue | | XXX |
| | *Receive cash in advance and record a liability first.* | | | *Adjust for revenue earned later.* | | |

**ACCRUALS—Cash receipt or Cash payment occurs later.**

| | ADJUSTING ENTRY | | |
|---|---|---|---|
| **Accrued Expenses** | Salaries Expense | XXX | |
| | Salaries Payable | | XXX |
| | *Accrual for expense incurred first.* | | |
| **Accrued Revenues** | Accounts Receivable | XXX | |
| | Service Revenue | | XXX |
| | *Accrual for revenue earned first.* | | |

Two rules to remember about adjusting entries:

1. Adjusting entries never involve the Cash account.
2. Adjusting entries either
   a. Increase a revenue account (credit revenue) or
   b. Increase an expense account (debit expense).

The adjusting entries and account balances after posting for Smart Touch Learning at December 31 are shown in Exhibit 3-4.

- Panel A gives the data for each adjustment.
- Panel B shows the adjusting entries.
- Panel C shows the T-accounts and balances after posting.

**Exhibit 3-4 | Journalizing and Posting the Adjusting Entries of Smart Touch Learning**

**Panel A: Information for Adjustments**

a. Prepaid rent expired, $1,000.
b. Supplies used, $400.
c. Depreciation on furniture, $300.
d. Depreciation on building, $250.
e. Service revenue that was collected in advance and now has been earned, $200.
f. Accrued salaries expense, $1,200.
g. Accrued interest on note, $100.
h. Accrued service revenue, $800.

**Panel B: Adjusting Entries**

| Date | Accounts and Explanation | Debit | Credit |
|---|---|---|---|
| (a) Dec. 31 | Rent Expense | 1,000 | |
| | Prepaid Rent | | 1,000 |
| | *To record rent expense.* | | |
| (b) 31 | Supplies Expense | 400 | |
| | Office Supplies | | 400 |
| | *To record office supplies used.* | | |
| (c) 31 | Depreciation Expense—Furniture | 300 | |
| | Accumulated Depreciation—Furniture | | 300 |
| | *To record depreciation on furniture.* | | |
| (d) 31 | Depreciation Expense—Building | 250 | |
| | Accumulated Depreciation—Building | | 250 |
| | *To record depreciation on building.* | | |
| (e) 31 | Unearned Revenue | 200 | |
| | Service Revenue | | 200 |
| | *To record service revenue earned that was collected in advance.* | | |
| (f) 31 | Salaries Expense | 1,200 | |
| | Salaries Payable | | 1,200 |
| | *To accrue salaries expense.* | | |
| (g) 31 | Interest Expense | 100 | |
| | Interest Payable | | 100 |
| | *To accrue interest expense.* | | |
| (h) 31 | Accounts Receivable | 800 | |
| | Service Revenue | | 800 |
| | *To accrue service revenue.* | | |

## Panel C: Account Balances After Posting

**ASSETS = LIABILITIES + EQUITY**

EQUITY: Contributed Capital + Retained Earnings

### ASSETS

**Cash**

| | Debit | Credit | |
|---|---|---|---|
| Nov. 1 | 30,000 | 20,000 | Nov. 2 |
| Nov. 8 | 5,500 | 3,200 | Nov. 15 |
| Nov. 22 | 2,000 | 300 | Nov. 21 |
| Dec. 21 | 600 | 5,000 | Nov. 25 |
| Dec. 28 | 8,000 | 3,000 | Dec. 1 |
| | | 1,200 | Dec. 1 |
| | | 1,200 | Dec. 15 |
| Bal. | 12,200 | | |

**Accounts Receivable**

| | Debit | Credit | |
|---|---|---|---|
| Nov. 10 | 3,000 | 2,000 | Nov. 22 |
| Dec. 31 | 800 | | |
| Bal. | 1,800 | | |

**Office Supplies**

| | Debit | Credit | |
|---|---|---|---|
| Nov. 3 | 500 | 400 | Dec. 31 |
| Bal. | 100 | | |

**Prepaid Rent**

| | Debit | Credit | |
|---|---|---|---|
| Dec. 1 | 3,000 | 1,000 | Dec. 31 |
| Bal. | 2,000 | | |

**Furniture**

| | Debit | Credit | |
|---|---|---|---|
| Dec. 2 | 18,000 | | |
| Bal. | 18,000 | | |

**Accumulated Depreciation—Furniture**

| | Debit | Credit | |
|---|---|---|---|
| | | 300 | Dec. 31 |
| | | 300 | Bal. |

**Building**

| | Debit | Credit | |
|---|---|---|---|
| Dec. 1 | 60,000 | | |
| Bal. | 60,000 | | |

**Accumulated Depreciation—Building**

| | Debit | Credit | |
|---|---|---|---|
| | | 250 | Dec. 31 |
| | | 250 | Bal. |

**Land**

| | Debit | Credit | |
|---|---|---|---|
| Nov. 2 | 20,000 | | |
| Bal. | 20,000 | | |

### LIABILITIES

**Accounts Payable**

| | Debit | Credit | |
|---|---|---|---|
| Nov. 21 | 300 | 500 | Nov. 3 |
| | | 200 | Bal. |

**Utilities Payable**

| | Debit | Credit | |
|---|---|---|---|
| | | 100 | Dec. 15 |
| | | 100 | Bal. |

**Salaries Payable**

| | Debit | Credit | |
|---|---|---|---|
| | | 1,200 | Dec. 31 |
| | | 1,200 | Bal. |

**Interest Payable**

| | Debit | Credit | |
|---|---|---|---|
| | | 100 | Dec. 31 |
| | | 100 | Bal. |

**Unearned Revenue**

| | Debit | Credit | |
|---|---|---|---|
| Dec. 31 | 200 | 600 | Dec. 21 |
| | | 400 | Bal. |

**Notes Payable**

| | Debit | Credit | |
|---|---|---|---|
| | | 60,000 | Dec. 1 |
| | | 60,000 | Bal. |

### EQUITY

#### Contributed Capital

**Common Stock**

| | Debit | Credit | |
|---|---|---|---|
| | | 30,000 | Nov. 1 |
| | | 18,000 | Dec. 2 |
| | | 48,000 | Bal. |

#### Retained Earnings

− **Dividends**

| | Debit | Credit | |
|---|---|---|---|
| Nov. 25 | 5,000 | | |
| Bal. | 5,000 | | |

\+ **Service Revenue**

| | Debit | Credit | |
|---|---|---|---|
| | | 5,500 | Nov. 8 |
| | | 3,000 | Nov. 10 |
| | | 8,000 | Dec. 28 |
| | | 200 | Dec. 31 |
| | | 800 | Dec. 31 |
| | | 17,500 | Bal. |

− **Rent Expense**

| | Debit | Credit | |
|---|---|---|---|
| Nov. 15 | 2,000 | | |
| Dec. 31 | 1,000 | | |
| Bal. | 3,000 | | |

**Salaries Expense**

| | Debit | Credit | |
|---|---|---|---|
| Nov. 15 | 1,200 | | |
| Dec. 1 | 1,200 | | |
| Dec. 15 | 1,200 | | |
| Dec. 31 | 1,200 | | |
| Bal. | 4,800 | | |

**Supplies Expense**

| | Debit | Credit | |
|---|---|---|---|
| Dec. 31 | 400 | | |
| Bal. | 400 | | |

**Utilities Expense**

| | Debit | Credit | |
|---|---|---|---|
| Dec. 15 | 100 | | |
| Bal. | 100 | | |

**Depreciation Expense—Furniture**

| | Debit | Credit | |
|---|---|---|---|
| Dec. 31 | 300 | | |
| Bal. | 300 | | |

**Depreciation Expense—Building**

| | Debit | Credit | |
|---|---|---|---|
| Dec. 31 | 250 | | |
| Bal. | 250 | | |

**Interest Expense**

| | Debit | Credit | |
|---|---|---|---|
| Dec. 31 | 100 | | |
| Bal. | 100 | | |

**$113,550 = $62,000 + $51,550**

## Try It!

Startech Surveillance Services had the following adjustments as of the end of the year:

**a.** Equipment depreciation was $1,500.
**b.** $700 of advertising expense was incurred but not paid. (Use Advertising Payable.)
**c.** Office Supplies on hand at the end of the year totaled $250. The beginning balance of Office Supplies was $600.
**d.** $1,200 of rent revenue was earned but not recorded or received.
**e.** Unearned revenue of $3,000 had been earned.

**6.** For each situation, indicate which category of adjustment (deferral or accrual) is described.
**7.** Journalize the adjusting entry needed.

**Check your answers online in MyAccountingLab or at http://www.pearsonhighered.com/Horngren.**

For more practice, see Short Exercises S3-5 through S3-12. MyAccountingLab

## WHAT IS THE PURPOSE OF THE ADJUSTED TRIAL BALANCE, AND HOW DO WE PREPARE IT?

**Learning Objective 4**
Explain the purpose of and prepare an adjusted trial balance

**Adjusted Trial Balance**
A list of all the accounts with their adjusted balances.

This chapter began with the *unadjusted* trial balance. After the adjustments have been journalized and posted, the account balances are updated and an **adjusted trial balance** can be prepared by listing all the accounts with their adjusted balances. Remember, the purpose of a trial balance is to ensure that total debits equal total credits. Even if the trial balance balances, it does not guarantee that a mistake has not been made. For example, an adjusting entry could have been recorded for the incorrect amount or could have been omitted entirely. The equality of the trial balance ensures only that each posted transaction had an equal debit and credit amount.

The adjusted trial balance for Smart Touch Learning is shown in Exhibit 3-5.

**Exhibit 3-5** | **Adjusted Trial Balance**

**SMART TOUCH LEARNING**
Adjusted Trial Balance
December 31, 2016

| | Balance | |
|---|---|---|
| **Account Title** | **Debit** | **Credit** |
| Cash | $ 12,200 | |
| Accounts Receivable | 1,800 | |
| Office Supplies | 100 | |
| Prepaid Rent | 2,000 | |
| Furniture | 18,000 | |
| Accumulated Depreciation—Furniture | | $ 300 |
| Building | 60,000 | |
| Accumulated Depreciation—Building | | 250 |
| Land | 20,000 | |
| Accounts Payable | | 200 |
| Utilities Payable | | 100 |
| Salaries Payable | | 1,200 |
| Interest Payable | | 100 |
| Unearned Revenue | | 400 |
| Notes Payable | | 60,000 |
| Common Stock | | 48,000 |
| Dividends | 5,000 | |
| Service Revenue | | 17,500 |
| Rent Expense | 3,000 | |
| Salaries Expense | 4,800 | |
| Supplies Expense | 400 | |
| Utilities Expense | 100 | |
| Depreciation Expense—Furniture | 300 | |
| Depreciation Expense—Building | 250 | |
| Interest Expense | 100 | |
| Total | **$ 128,050** | **$ 128,050** |

## Try It!

**8.** Hooten Carpentry had the following accounts and account balances after adjusting entries. Assume all accounts have normal balances. Prepare the adjusted trial balance for Hooten Carpentry as of December 31, 2016.

| | | | |
|---|---|---|---|
| Cash | $ 4,025 | Common Stock | $ ? |
| Land | 5,000 | Accounts Receivable | 660 |
| Utilities Expense | 400 | Office Supplies | 120 |
| Accounts Payable | 225 | Utilities Payable | 210 |
| Accumulated Depreciation—Equipment | 1,000 | Service Revenue | 12,000 |
| Salaries Expense | 550 | Unearned Revenue | 300 |
| Supplies Expense | 80 | Depreciation Expense—Equipment | 800 |
| Equipment | 10,000 | Dividends | 500 |

**Check your answers online in MyAccountingLab or at http://www.pearsonhighered.com/Horngren.**

For more practice, see Short Exercise S3-13. MyAccountingLab

## WHAT IS THE IMPACT OF ADJUSTING ENTRIES ON THE FINANCIAL STATEMENTS?

**Learning Objective 5**
Identify the impact of adjusting entries on the financial statements

The adjusted trial balance is used to prepare the financial statements. If adjusting entries are not recorded, the ledger accounts will not reflect the correct balances and the adjusted trial balance will be incorrect. Remember, adjusting entries are completed to ensure that all revenues and expenses for the accounting period examined have been recorded. In addition, adjusting entries update the balance sheet accounts so that all accounts are properly valued. Exhibit 3-6 summarizes the impact on the financial statements had the adjusting entries not been recorded.

**Exhibit 3-6** | **Impact of Adjusting Entries on Financial Statements**

| Type of Adjusting Entry | Description | Adjusting Entry | Impact on Financial Statement if Adjusting Entries Are Not Made |
|---|---|---|---|
| **Deferred Expenses** | Advance cash payments of future expenses. | Expense DR<br>Asset* CR | Income Statement: expenses understated<br>net income overstated<br>Balance Sheet: assets overstated<br>equity overstated |
| **Deferred Revenues** | Advance cash receipts of future revenues. | Liability DR<br>Revenue CR | Income Statement: revenues understated<br>net income understated<br>Balance Sheet: liabilities overstated<br>equity understated |
| **Accrued Expenses** | An expense that has been incurred but not paid. | Expense DR<br>Liability CR | Income Statement: expenses understated<br>net income overstated<br>Balance Sheet: liabilities understated<br>equity overstated |
| **Accrued Revenues** | A revenue that has been earned but cash has not yet been collected. | Asset DR<br>Revenue CR | Income Statement: revenues understated<br>net income understated<br>Balance Sheet: assets understated<br>equity understated |

*If recording depreciation: the contra asset, Accumulated Depreciation, is credited.

## Try It!

**9.** Identify the impact on the income statement and balance sheet if adjusting entries for the following situations were not recorded.

**a.** Office Supplies used, $800.
**b.** Accrued service revenue, $4,000.
**c.** Depreciation on building, $3,500.
**d.** Prepaid Insurance expired, $650.
**e.** Accrued salaries expense, $2,750.
**f.** Service revenue that was collected in advance has now been earned, $130.

**Check your answers online in MyAccountingLab or at http://www.pearsonhighered.com/Horngren.**

For more practice, see Short Exercise S3-14. MyAccountingLab

## HOW COULD A WORKSHEET HELP IN PREPARING ADJUSTING ENTRIES AND THE ADJUSTED TRIAL BALANCE?

**Learning Objective 6**
Explain the purpose of a worksheet and use it to prepare adjusting entries and the adjusted trial balance

A useful step in preparing adjusting entries and the adjusted trial balance is to create a worksheet. A **worksheet** is an internal document that helps summarize data for the preparation of the financial statements. The worksheet is not a journal, a ledger, or a financial statement. It is merely a summary device that helps identify the accounts that need adjustments. Most worksheets are completed using Microsoft Excel.

Exhibit 3-7 (on the next page) shows the partially completed worksheet for Smart Touch Learning.

**Worksheet**
An internal document that helps summarize data for the preparation of financial statements.

**Exhibit 3-7 | Partially Completed Worksheet**

| | A | B | C | D | E | F | G | H | I | J | K | L | M |
|---|---|---|---|---|---|---|---|---|---|---|---|---|---|
| 1 | SMART TOUCH LEARNING | | | | | | | | | | | | |
| 2 | Worksheet | | | | | | | | | | | | |
| 3 | December 31, 2016 | | | | | | | | | | | | |
| 4 | | | | | | | | | | | | | |
| 5 | Account Names | Unadjusted Trial Balance | | | Adjustments | | | Adjusted Trial Balance | | Income Statement | | Balance Sheet | |
| 6 | | Debit | Credit | | Debit | Credit | | Debit | Credit | Debit | Credit | Debit | Credit |
| 7 | Cash | $ 12,200 | | | | | | $ 12,200 | | | | | |
| 8 | Accounts Receivable | 1,000 | | (h) | $ 800 | | | 1,800 | | | | | |
| 9 | Office Supplies | 500 | | | | $ 400 | (b) | 100 | | | | | |
| 10 | Prepaid Rent | 3,000 | | | | 1,000 | (a) | 2,000 | | | | | |
| 11 | Furniture | 18,000 | | | | | | 18,000 | | | | | |
| 12 | Accumulated Depreciation—Furniture | | | | | 300 | (c) | | $ 300 | | | | |
| 13 | Building | 60,000 | | | | | | 60,000 | | | | | |
| 14 | Accumulated Depreciation—Building | | | | | 250 | (d) | | 250 | | | | |
| 15 | Land | 20,000 | | | | | | 20,000 | | | | | |
| 16 | Accounts Payable | | $ 200 | | | | | | 200 | | | | |
| 17 | Utilities Payable | | 100 | | | | | | 100 | | | | |
| 18 | Salaries Payable | | | | | 1,200 | (f) | | 1,200 | | | | |
| 19 | Interest Payable | | | | | 100 | (g) | | 100 | | | | |
| 20 | Unearned Revenue | | 600 | (e) | 200 | | | | 400 | | | | |
| 21 | Notes Payable | | 60,000 | | | | | | 60,000 | | | | |
| 22 | Common Stock | | 48,000 | | | | | | 48,000 | | | | |
| 23 | Dividends | 5,000 | | | | | | 5,000 | | | | | |
| 24 | Service Revenue | | 16,500 | | | 1,000 | (e,h) | | 17,500 | | | | |
| 25 | Rent Expense | 2,000 | | (a) | 1,000 | | | 3,000 | | | | | |
| 26 | Salaries Expense | 3,600 | | (f) | 1,200 | | | 4,800 | | | | | |
| 27 | Supplies Expense | | | (b) | 400 | | | 400 | | | | | |
| 28 | Utilities Expense | 100 | | | | | | 100 | | | | | |
| 29 | Depreciation Expense—Furniture | | | (c) | 300 | | | 300 | | | | | |
| 30 | Depreciation Expense—Building | | | (d) | 250 | | | 250 | | | | | |
| 31 | Interest Expense | | | (g) | 100 | | | 100 | | | | | |
| 32 | **Total** | **$ 125,400** | **$ 125,400** | | **$ 4,250** | **$ 4,250** | | **$ 128,050** | **$ 128,050** | | | | |
| 33 | | | | | | | | | | | | | |

In this chapter, we complete a part of the worksheet. For now, we will concern ourselves with the first four sections.

**Section 1. Account names:** The account names are taken from and listed in the same order as the chart of accounts. (Cash first, Accounts Receivable second, and so on.)

**Section 2. Unadjusted trial balance:** The account balances are copied directly from the ledger before any adjustments. Total debits must equal total credits.

**Section 3. Adjustments:** Enter the adjusting journal entries that were made on December 31.

**Section 4. Adjusted trial balance:** Gives the account balances after adjustments. Each amount in these columns is computed by combining the unadjusted trial balance amounts plus or minus the adjustments. For example, Accounts Receivable starts with a debit balance of $1,000. Adding the $800 debit from the adjustment gives Accounts Receivable an adjusted balance of $1,800. Service Revenue starts with a $16,500 credit balance. Adding the $1,000 credit from the adjustment gives Service Revenue an adjusted balance of $17,500. As with the unadjusted trial balance, total debits must equal total credits.

The income statement and balance sheet sections of the worksheet remain to be completed. These will be covered in the next chapter.

## Try It!

**10.** The partial worksheet for Sam's Delivery Service follows. Complete the adjusted trial balance columns.

| | A | B | C | D | E | F | G | H | I | J | K | L | M |
|---|---|---|---|---|---|---|---|---|---|---|---|---|---|
| 1 | | | | | **SAM'S DELIVERY SERVICE** | | | | | | | | |
| 2 | | | | | **Worksheet** | | | | | | | | |
| 3 | | | | | **December 31, 2016** | | | | | | | | |
| 4 | | | | | | | | | | | | | |
| 5 | **Account Names** | **Unadjusted Trial Balance** | | | **Adjustments** | | | **Adjusted Trial Balance** | | **Income Statement** | | **Balance Sheet** | |
| 6 | | **Debit** | **Credit** | | **Debit** | **Credit** | | **Debit** | **Credit** | **Debit** | **Credit** | **Debit** | **Credit** |
| 7 | Cash | $ 6,500 | | | | | | | | | | | |
| 8 | Accounts Receivable | 800 | | (g) | $ 225 | | | | | | | | |
| 9 | Office Supplies | 250 | | | | $ 80 | (b) | | | | | | |
| 10 | Prepaid Rent | 1,000 | | | | 800 | (a) | | | | | | |
| 11 | Delivery Van | 23,000 | | | | | | | | | | | |
| 12 | Accumulated Depreciation—Delivery Van | | | | | 750 | (c) | | | | | | |
| 13 | Equipment | 15,000 | | | | | | | | | | | |
| 14 | Accumulated Depreciation—Equipment | | | | | 300 | (d) | | | | | | |
| 15 | Accounts Payable | | $ 800 | | | | | | | | | | |
| 16 | Utilities Payable | | 230 | | | | | | | | | | |
| 17 | Salaries Payable | | | | | 875 | (f) | | | | | | |
| 18 | Unearned Revenue | | 400 | (e) | 130 | | | | | | | | |
| 19 | Common Stock | | 37,800 | | | | | | | | | | |
| 20 | Dividends | 8,000 | | | | | | | | | | | |
| 21 | Delivery Revenue | | 23,000 | | | 355 | (e,g) | | | | | | |
| 22 | Rent Expense | 3,000 | | (a) | 800 | | | | | | | | |
| 23 | Salaries Expense | 4,500 | | (f) | 875 | | | | | | | | |
| 24 | Supplies Expense | | | (b) | 80 | | | | | | | | |
| 25 | Utilities Expense | 180 | | | | | | | | | | | |
| 26 | Depreciation Expense—Delivery Van | | | (c) | 750 | | | | | | | | |
| 27 | Depreciation Expense—Equipment | | | (d) | 300 | | | | | | | | |
| 28 | **Total** | **$ 62,230** | **$ 62,230** | | **$ 3,160** | **$ 3,160** | | | | | | | |
| 29 | | | | | | | | | | | | | |

**Check your answers online in MyAccountingLab or at http://www.pearsonhighered.com/Horngren.**

For more practice, see Short Exercise S3-15. MyAccountingLab

# APPENDIX 3A: Alternative Treatment of Recording Deferred Expenses and Deferred Revenues

Chapters 1–3 illustrate the most popular way to account for deferred expenses and deferred revenues. This appendix illustrates an alternative approach.

**Learning Objective 7**
Understand the alternative treatment of recording deferred expenses and deferred revenues

## WHAT IS AN ALTERNATIVE TREATMENT OF RECORDING DEFERRED EXPENSES AND DEFERRED REVENUES?

### Deferred Expenses

Recall that deferred expenses, also called prepaid expenses, are advance payments of future expenses such as insurance, rent, and advertising. Office supplies are also accounted for as deferred expenses.

When a business prepays an expense—rent, for example—it can debit an *asset* account (Prepaid Rent) and defer the recognition of the expense. For example, Smart Touch Learning prepaid three months of office rent totaling $3,000 on December 1, 2016. The journal entry can be recorded as:

**A↑↓** = **L** + **E**
Prepaid Rent ↑
Cash ↓

| Date | Accounts and Explanation | Debit | Credit |
|---|---|---|---|
| Dec. 1 | Prepaid Rent | 3,000 | |
| | Cash | | 3,000 |
| | *Paid rent in advance.* | | |

## Deferred Expense Recorded Initially as an Expense

Deferring an expense creates an asset. However, the asset may be so short lived that it will expire in the current accounting period—within one year or less. Thus, the accountant may decide to debit the prepayment to an expense account at the time of payment. The entry could, alternatively, be recorded as follows:

**A↓** = **L** + **E↓**
Cash↓ = Rent Expense↑

| Date | Accounts and Explanation | Debit | Credit |
|---|---|---|---|
| Dec. 1 | Rent Expense | 3,000 | |
| | Cash | | 3,000 |
| | *Paid rent in advance.* | | |

As of December 31, only one month's prepayment has expired, leaving two months of rent still prepaid. In this case, the accountant must transfer two-thirds of the original prepayment of $3,000, or $2,000, to the asset account Prepaid Rent. At December 31, 2016, the business still has the benefit of prepayment for January 1 through February 28, 2017. The adjusting entry at December 31 is as follows:

**A↑** = **L** + **E↑**
Prepaid Rent↑ = Rent Expense↓

| Date | Accounts and Explanation | Debit | Credit |
|---|---|---|---|
| Dec. 31 | Prepaid Rent | 2,000 | |
| | Rent Expense | | 2,000 |
| | *To record prepaid rent.* | | |

After posting, the two accounts appear as follows:

**Prepaid Rent**

| | | | |
|---|---|---|---|
| Dec. 31 | 2,000 | | |
| Bal. | 2,000 | | |

**Rent Expense**

| | | | |
|---|---|---|---|
| Dec. 1 | 3,000 | 2,000 | Dec. 31 |
| Bal. | 1,000 | | |

At December 31, the $3,000 prepayment is correctly divided as $2,000 of Prepaid Rent and $1,000 of Rent Expense, regardless of whether the business initially debits the prepayment to an asset or to an expense account.

## Deferred Revenues

Deferred revenues, also called unearned revenues, arise when a business collects cash before earning the revenue. Deferred revenues are liabilities because the business that receives the cash owes the customer goods or services to be delivered later.

When a business receives cash in advance of providing services, a *liability* can be created. As an example, a law firm engages Smart Touch Learning to provide monthly e-learning services, agreeing to pay $600 in advance. Smart Touch Learning received the $600 on December 21. Smart Touch Learning records the following entry, recognizing the liability and deferring the recognition of the revenue.

| Date | Accounts and Explanation | Debit | Credit |
|---|---|---|---|
| Dec. 21 | Cash | 600 | |
| | Unearned Revenue | | 600 |
| | *Collected cash for future services.* | | |

A↑ = L↑ + E
Cash↑ = Unearned Revenue↑

### Deferred Revenues Recorded Initially as a Revenue

Another way to account for the receipt of cash is to credit a *revenue* account when the business receives cash.

| Date | Accounts and Explanation | Debit | Credit |
|---|---|---|---|
| Dec. 21 | Cash | 600 | |
| | Service Revenue | | 600 |
| | *Collected cash for future services.* | | |

A↑ = L + E↑
Cash↑ = Service Revenue↑

If the business then earns all the revenue within the same accounting period, no adjusting entry is needed at the end. However, if the business earns only part of the revenue in that period, it must make an adjusting entry. In our example, Smart Touch Learning has earned only one-third of the $600, or $200, by December 31, 2016. Accordingly, Smart Touch Learning must make an adjusting entry to transfer the unearned portion (2/3 of $600, or $400) from the revenue account to a liability, as follows:

| Date | Accounts and Explanation | Debit | Credit |
|---|---|---|---|
| Dec. 31 | Service Revenue | 400 | |
| | Unearned Revenue | | 400 |
| | *To record unearned revenue.* | | |

A = L↑ + E↓
Unearned Revenue↑ Service Revenue↓

The adjusting entry transfers the unearned portion of service revenue to the liability account because Smart Touch Learning still owes e-learning services next year. After posting, the total amount, $600, is properly divided between the liability account—$400, and the revenue account—$200, as follows:

**Unearned Revenue**

| | | | |
|---|---|---|---|
| | | 400 | Dec. 31 |
| | | 400 | Bal. |

**Service Revenue**

| | | | |
|---|---|---|---|
| Dec. 31 | 400 | 600 | Dec. 21 |
| | | 200 | Bal. |

At December 31, the $600 cash receipt is correctly divided: $400 of Unearned Revenue and $200 of Service Revenue, regardless of whether the business initially credits the cash receipt to a liability or to a revenue account.

## Try It!

**11A.** Iron Horse Printing Services purchased $1,000 of printing supplies for cash, recording the transaction using the alternative treatment for deferred expenses. At the end of the year, Iron Horse had $300 of printing supplies remaining. Record the journal entry for the purchase of printing supplies and the adjusting entry for printing supplies not used.

**Check your answer online in MyAccountingLab or at http://www.pearsonhighered.com/Horngren.**

For more practice, see Short Exercises S3A-16 and S3A-17. MyAccountingLab

# REVIEW

## > Things You Should Know

**1. What is the difference between cash basis accounting and accrual basis accounting?**

- Cash basis accounting: Revenue is recorded only when cash is received, and expenses are recorded only when cash is paid.
  - Not GAAP
  - Often used by small businesses
- Accrual basis accounting: Revenue is recorded when earned, and expenses are recorded when incurred.

**2. What concepts and principles apply to accrual basis accounting?**

- The time period concept assumes that a business's activities can be sliced into small time segments and that financial statements can be prepared for specific periods, such as a month, quarter, or year.
- The revenue recognition principle requires companies to record revenue when it has been earned and determines the amount of revenue to record.
- The matching principle guides accounting for expenses and ensures that all expenses are recorded when they are incurred during the period. It then matches those expenses against the revenues of the period.

**3. What are adjusting entries, and how do we record them?**

- Adjusting entries are completed at the end of the accounting period and record revenues to the period in which they are earned and expenses to the period in which they occur.

- Adjusting entries also update the asset and liability accounts.
- Four types of adjusting entries:
    - Deferred expenses (or prepaid expenses): advance payment of future expenses adjusted for amount used

| Date | Accounts and Explanation | Debit | Credit |
|---|---|---|---|
| | Expense | XXX | |
| | Asset | | XXX |

    - Deferred revenues (or unearned revenues): advance receipts of future revenues adjusted for amount earned

| Date | Accounts and Explanation | Debit | Credit |
|---|---|---|---|
| | Liability | XXX | |
| | Revenue | | XXX |

    - Accrued expenses: expenses that have been incurred but not paid

| Date | Accounts and Explanation | Debit | Credit |
|---|---|---|---|
| | Expense | XXX | |
| | Liability | | XXX |

    - Accrued revenues: revenues that have been earned but not collected

| Date | Accounts and Explanation | Debit | Credit |
|---|---|---|---|
| | Asset | XXX | |
| | Revenue | | XXX |

**4. What is the purpose of the adjusted trial balance, and how do we prepare it?**

- An adjusted trial balance is a list of all the accounts with their adjusted balances.
- It ensures that total debits equal total credits.

**5. What is the impact of adjusting entries on the financial statements?**

- If adjusting entries are not recorded, the balance sheet and income statement accounts will either be overstated or understated.
- Overstating or understating accounts causes the financial statements to be incorrect.

6. **How could a worksheet help in preparing adjusting entries and the adjusted trial balance?**
   - A worksheet is an internal document that helps identify the accounts that need adjustments.
   - In addition, a worksheet helps summarize data for the preparation of the financial statements.

7. **What is an alternative treatment of recording deferred expenses and deferred revenues? (Appendix 3A)**
   - Deferred expenses can be recorded to an expense account at the time of payment. The adjusting entry would transfer any remaining prepayment to the asset account, Prepaid Expenses.
   - Deferred revenues can be recorded to a revenue account at the time of cash receipt. The adjusting entry would transfer any remaining liability to the liability account, Unearned Revenue.



## > Summary Problem 3-1

The unadjusted trial balance as of December 31, 2016, the end of the annual accounting period for Super Employment Services, follows:

**SUPER EMPLOYMENT SERVICES**
Unadjusted Trial Balance
December 31, 2016

| | Balance | |
|---|---|---|
| **Account Title** | **Debit** | **Credit** |
| Cash | $ 6,000 | |
| Accounts Receivable | 5,000 | |
| Office Supplies | 1,000 | |
| Furniture | 10,000 | |
| Accumulated Depreciation—Furniture | | $ 4,000 |
| Building | 40,000 | |
| Accumulated Depreciation—Building | | 30,000 |
| Land | 10,000 | |
| Accounts Payable | | 2,000 |
| Salaries Payable | | |
| Unearned Revenue | | 8,000 |
| Common Stock | | 12,000 |
| Dividends | 25,000 | |
| Service Revenue | | 60,000 |
| Salaries Expense | 16,000 | |
| Supplies Expense | | |
| Depreciation Expense—Furniture | | |
| Depreciation Expense—Building | | |
| Advertising Expense | 3,000 | |
| Total | **$ 116,000** | **$ 116,000** |

Data needed for the adjusting entries include the following:

a. Office Supplies on hand at year-end, $200.
b. Depreciation on furniture, $2,000.
c. Depreciation on building, $1,000.
d. Salaries owed but not yet paid, $500.
e. Accrued service revenue, $1,300.
f. $3,000 of the unearned revenue has been earned.

**Requirements**

1. Open the ledger accounts in T-account form with their unadjusted balances as shown on the unadjusted trial balance.
2. Journalize Super's adjusting entries at December 31, 2016. Use the letter (*a*, *b*, and so on) as the date.
3. Post the adjusting entries to T-accounts. Determine the ending balances in the T-accounts on December 31, 2016.
4. Prepare an adjusted trial balance.
5. Prepare a partial worksheet including the account names, unadjusted trial balance, adjustments, and adjusted trial balance.



## > Solution

**Requirement 1 - See next page**

**Requirement 2**

| Date | Accounts and Explanations | Debit | Credit |
|---|---|---|---|
| 2016 | | | |
| (a) Dec. 31 | Supplies Expense ($1,000 – $200) | 800 | |
| | Office Supplies | | 800 |
| | *To record office supplies used.* | | |
| (b) 31 | Depreciation Expense—Furniture | 2,000 | |
| | Accumulated Depreciation—Furniture | | 2,000 |
| | *To record depreciation expense on furniture.* | | |
| (c) 31 | Depreciation Expense—Building | 1,000 | |
| | Accumulated Depreciation—Building | | 1,000 |
| | *To record depreciation expense on building.* | | |
| (d) 31 | Salaries Expense | 500 | |
| | Salaries Payable | | 500 |
| | *To accrue salaries expense.* | | |
| (e) 31 | Accounts Receivable | 1,300 | |
| | Service Revenue | | 1,300 |
| | *To accrue service revenue.* | | |
| (f) 31 | Unearned Revenue | 3,000 | |
| | Service Revenue | | 3,000 |
| | *To record service revenue earned that was collected in advance.* | | |

## Requirements 1 and 3

### ASSETS

**Cash**

| | |
|---|---|
| Bal. 6,000 | |

**Building**

| | |
|---|---|
| Bal. 40,000 | |

**Accounts Receivable**

| | |
|---|---|
| Bal. 5,000 | |
| (e) 1,300 | |
| Bal. 6,300 | |

**Accumulated Depreciation—Building**

| | |
|---|---|
| | 30,000 Bal. |
| | 1,000 (c) |
| | 31,000 Bal. |

**Office Supplies**

| | |
|---|---|
| Bal. 1,000 | 800 (a) |
| Bal. 200 | |

**Land**

| | |
|---|---|
| Bal. 10,000 | |

**Furniture**

| | |
|---|---|
| Bal. 10,000 | |

**Accumulated Depreciation—Furniture**

| | |
|---|---|
| | 4,000 Bal. |
| | 2,000 (b) |
| | 6,000 Bal. |

### LIABILITIES

**Accounts Payable**

| | |
|---|---|
| | 2,000 Bal. |

**Salaries Payable**

| | |
|---|---|
| | 500 (d) |
| | 500 Bal. |

**Unearned Revenue**

| | |
|---|---|
| (f) 3,000 | 8,000 Bal. |
| | 5,000 Bal. |

### EQUITY

**Common Stock**

| | |
|---|---|
| | 12,000 Bal. |

**Dividends**

| | |
|---|---|
| Bal. 25,000 | |

**Service Revenue**

| | |
|---|---|
| | 60,000 Bal. |
| | 1,300 (e) |
| | 3,000 (f) |
| | 64,300 Bal. |

**Salaries Expense**

| | |
|---|---|
| Bal. 16,000 | |
| (d) 500 | |
| Bal. 16,500 | |

**Supplies Expense**

| | |
|---|---|
| (a) 800 | |
| Bal. 800 | |

**Depreciation Expense—Furniture**

| | |
|---|---|
| (b) 2,000 | |
| Bal. 2,000 | |

**Depreciation Expense—Building**

| | |
|---|---|
| (c) 1,000 | |
| Bal. 1,000 | |

**Advertising Expense**

| | |
|---|---|
| Bal. 3,000 | |

## Requirement 4

| SUPER EMPLOYMENT SERVICES<br>Adjusted Trial Balance<br>December 31, 2016 | | |
|---|---|---|
| | Balance | |
| **Account Title** | **Debit** | **Credit** |
| Cash | $ 6,000 | |
| Accounts Receivable | 6,300 | |
| Office Supplies | 200 | |
| Furniture | 10,000 | |
| Accumulated Depreciation—Furniture | | $ 6,000 |
| Building | 40,000 | |
| Accumulated Depreciation—Building | | 31,000 |
| Land | 10,000 | |
| Accounts Payable | | 2,000 |
| Salaries Payable | | 500 |
| Unearned Revenue | | 5,000 |
| Common Stock | | 12,000 |
| Dividends | 25,000 | |
| Service Revenue | | 64,300 |
| Salaries Expense | 16,500 | |
| Supplies Expense | 800 | |
| Depreciation Expense—Furniture | 2,000 | |
| Depreciation Expense—Building | 1,000 | |
| Advertising Expense | 3,000 | |
| Total | **$ 120,800** | **$ 120,800** |

**Requirement 5**

| | A | B | C | | D | | E | F | G |
|---|---|---|---|---|---|---|---|---|---|
| 1 | SUPER EMPLOYMENT SERVICES | | | | | | | | |
| 2 | Worksheet | | | | | | | | |
| 3 | December 31, 2016 | | | | | | | | |
| 4 | | | | | | | | | |
| 5 | Account Names | Unadjusted Trial Balance | | | Adjustments | | | Adjusted Trial Balance | |
| 6 | | Debit | Credit | | Debit | | Credit | Debit | Credit |
| 7 | Cash | $ 6,000 | | | | | | $ 6,000 | |
| 8 | Accounts Receivable | 5,000 | | (e) | $ 1,300 | | | 6,300 | |
| 9 | Office Supplies | 1,000 | | | | (a) | $ 800 | 200 | |
| 10 | Furniture | 10,000 | | | | | | 10,000 | |
| 11 | Accumulated Depreciation—Furniture | | $ 4,000 | | | (b) | 2,000 | | $ 6,000 |
| 12 | Building | 40,000 | | | | | | 40,000 | |
| 13 | Accumulated Depreciation—Building | | 30,000 | | | (c) | 1,000 | | 31,000 |
| 14 | Land | 10,000 | | | | | | 10,000 | |
| 15 | Accounts Payable | | 2,000 | | | | | | 2,000 |
| 16 | Salaries Payable | | | | | (d) | 500 | | 500 |
| 17 | Unearned Revenue | | 8,000 | (f) | 3,000 | | | | 5,000 |
| 18 | Common Stock | | 12,000 | | | | | | 12,000 |
| 19 | Dividends | 25,000 | | | | | | 25,000 | |
| 20 | Service Revenue | | 60,000 | | | (e) | 1,300 | | |
| 21 | | | | | | (f) | 3,000 | | 64,300 |
| 22 | Salaries Expense | 16,000 | | (d) | 500 | | | 16,500 | |
| 23 | Supplies Expense | | | (a) | 800 | | | 800 | |
| 24 | Depreciation Expense—Furniture | | | (b) | 2,000 | | | 2,000 | |
| 25 | Depreciation Expense—Building | | | (c) | 1,000 | | | 1,000 | |
| 26 | Advertising Expense | 3,000 | | | | | | 3,000 | |
| 27 | **Total** | **$ 116,000** | **$ 116,000** | | **$ 8,600** | | **$ 8,600** | **$ 120,800** | **$ 120,800** |
| 28 | | | | | | | | | |

## > Key Terms

**Accrual Basis Accounting (p. 118)**
**Accrued Expense (p. 130)**
**Accrued Revenue (p. 133)**
**Accumulated Depreciation ( p. 127)**
**Adjusted Trial Balance ( p. 138)**
**Adjusting Entry ( p. 123)**
**Book Value ( p. 128)**
**Cash Basis Accounting ( p. 118)**
**Contra Account ( p. 127)**
**Deferred Expense ( p. 123)**
**Deferred Revenue ( p. 129)**
**Depreciation ( p. 126)**
**Fiscal Year ( p. 120)**
**Matching Principle ( p. 121)**
**Plant Asset ( p. 125)**
**Residual Value ( p. 126)**
**Revenue Recognition Principle ( p. 120)**
**Straight-Line Method ( p. 126)**
**Time Period Concept ( p. 120)**
**Worksheet ( p. 141)**

## > Quick Check

**Learning Objective 1**

1. Which of the following is true of accrual basis accounting and cash basis accounting?
   a. Accrual accounting records revenue only when it is earned.
   b. Accrual accounting is not allowed under GAAP.
   c. Cash basis accounting records all transactions.
   d. All of the above are true.

2. Get Fit Now gains a client who prepays $540 for a package of six physical training sessions. Get Fit Now collects the $540 in advance and will provide the training later. After four training sessions, what should Get Fit Now report on its income statement assuming it uses the accrual basis accounting method?

**Learning Objective 1**

   a. Service revenue of $360
   b. Service revenue of $540
   c. Unearned service revenue of $360
   d. Cash of $180

3. The revenue recognition principle requires

**Learning Objective 2**

   a. time to be divided into annual periods to measure revenue properly.
   b. revenue to be recorded only after the business has earned it.
   c. expenses to be matched with revenue of the period.
   d. revenue to be recorded only after the cash is received.

4. Adjusting the accounts is the process of

**Learning Objective 3**

   a. subtracting expenses from revenues to measure net income.
   b. recording transactions as they occur during the period.
   c. updating the accounts at the end of the period.
   d. zeroing out account balances to prepare for the next period.

5. Which of the following is an example of a deferral (or prepaid) adjusting entry?

**Learning Objective 3**

   a. Recording the usage of office supplies during the period.
   b. Recording salaries expense for employees not yet paid.
   c. Recording revenue that has been earned but not yet received.
   d. Recording interest expense incurred on a notes payable not due until next year.

6. Assume that the weekly payroll of In the Woods Camping Supplies is $300. December 31, end of the year, falls on Tuesday, and In the Woods will pay its employee on Friday for the full week. What adjusting entry will In the Woods make on Tuesday, December 31? (Use five days as a full workweek.)

**Learning Objective 3**

| Date | Accounts and Explanation | Debit | Credit |
|---|---|---|---|
| a. | Salaries Expense | 120 | |
| | Salaries Payable | | 120 |
| b. | Salaries Payable | 300 | |
| | Salaries Expense | | 300 |
| c. | Salaries Expense | 120 | |
| | Cash | | 120 |
| d. | *No adjustment is needed because the company will pay the payroll on Friday.* | | |

7. The adjusted trial balance shows

**Learning Objective 4**

   a. amounts that may be out of balance.
   b. account balances after adjustments.
   c. assets and liabilities only.
   d. revenues and expenses only.

**Learning Objective 5**

8. A & D Window Cleaning performed $450 of services but has not yet billed customers for the month. If A & D fails to record the adjusting entry, what is the impact on the financial statements?
   a. balance sheet: assets understated; equity overstated
   income statement: expense understated
   b. balance sheet: liabilities overstated; equity understated
   income statement: revenues understated
   c. balance sheet: assets overstated, equity understated
   income statement: expenses understated
   d. balance sheet: assets understated, equity understated
   income statement: revenues understated

**Learning Objective 6**

9. A worksheet
   a. is a journal used to record transactions.
   b. is a financial statement that reports net income during the period.
   c. is an internal document that helps summarize data for the preparation of financial statements.
   d. is a ledger listing the account balances and changes in those accounts.

**Learning Objective 7**
**Appendix 3A**

10A. On February 1, Clovis Wilson Law Firm contracted to provide $3,000 of legal services for the next three months and received $3,000 cash from the client. Assuming Wilson records deferred revenues using the alternative treatment, what would be the adjusting entry recorded on February 28?

| Date | Accounts and Explanation | Debit | Credit |
|---|---|---|---|
| a. | Cash | 3,000 | |
| | Unearned Revenue | | 3,000 |
| b. | Service Revenue | 2,000 | |
| | Unearned Revenue | | 2,000 |
| c. | Unearned Revenue | 1,000 | |
| | Service Revenue | | 1,000 |
| d. | Cash | 3,000 | |
| | Service Revenue | | 3,000 |

**Check your answers at the end of the chapter.**

# ASSESS YOUR PROGRESS

## > Review Questions

1. What is the difference between cash basis accounting and accrual basis accounting?
2. Which method of accounting (cash or accrual basis) is consistent with Generally Accepted Accounting Principles?
3. Which accounting concept or principle requires companies to divide their activities into small time segments such as months, quarters, or years?
4. What is a fiscal year? Why might companies choose to use a fiscal year that is not a calendar year?

5. Under the revenue recognition principle, when is revenue recorded?
6. Under the matching principle, when are expenses recorded?
7. When are adjusting entries completed, and what is their purpose?
8. What are the two basic categories of adjusting entries? Provide two examples of each.
9. What is a deferred expense? Provide an example.
10. What is the process of allocating the cost of a plant asset over its useful life called?
11. What is a contra account?
12. In the recording of depreciation expense, which account is credited?
13. What does accumulated depreciation represent?
14. How is book value calculated, and what does it represent?
15. What is a deferred revenue? Provide an example.
16. What is an accrued expense? Provide an example.
17. What is an accrued revenue? Provide an example.
18. What are the two rules to remember about adjusting entries?
19. When is an adjusted trial balance prepared, and what is its purpose?
20. If an accrued expense is not recorded at the end of the year, what is the impact on the financial statements?
21. What is a worksheet, and how is it used to help prepare an adjusted trial balance?

22A. If a payment of a deferred expense was recorded under the alternative treatment, what account would be debited at the time of payment?

23A. If a payment of a deferred expense was recorded under the alternative treatment, what account would be debited in the adjusting entry?



## > Short Exercises

### S3-1 Comparing cash and accrual basis accounting for expenses

**Learning Objective 1**

The Red Roses Law Firm prepays for advertising in the local newspaper. On January 1, the law firm paid $800 for four months of advertising.

How much advertising expense should Red Roses Law Firm record for the two months ending February 28 under the

**a.** cash basis? **b.** accrual basis?

### S3-2 Comparing cash and accrual basis accounting for revenues

**Learning Objective 1**

Peaceful Home provides house-sitting for people while they are away on vacation. Some of its customers pay immediately after the job is finished. Some customers ask that the business send them a bill. As of the end of the year, Peaceful Home has collected $1,000 from cash-paying customers. Peaceful Home's remaining customers owe the business $1,400.

How much service revenue would Peaceful Home have for the year under the

**a.** cash basis? **b.** accrual basis?

**Learning Objective 2**

### S3-3 Applying the revenue recognition principle

*South Shore Magazine* sells subscriptions for $60 for 12 issues. The company collects cash in advance and then mails out the magazines to subscribers each month.

Apply the revenue recognition principle to determine

a. when *South Shore Magazine* should record revenue for this situation.

b. the amount of revenue *South Shore Magazine* should record for eight issues.

**Learning Objective 2**

### S3-4 Applying the matching principle

Suppose on January 1, Antonio's Tavern prepaid rent of $6,000 for the full year.

At June 30, how much rent expense should be recorded for the period January 1 through June 30?

**Learning Objective 3**

### S3-5 Identifying types of adjusting entries

A select list of transactions for Anuradha's Goals follows:

| | | |
|---|---|---|
| Apr. | 1 | Paid six months of rent, $4,800. |
| | 10 | Received $1,200 from customer for six-month service contract that began April 1. |
| | 15 | Purchased a computer for $1,000. |
| | 18 | Purchased $300 of office supplies on account. |
| | 30 | Work performed but not yet billed to customer, $500. |
| | 30 | Employees earned $600 in salaries that will be paid May 2. |

For each transaction, identify what type of adjusting entry would be needed. Select from the following four types of adjusting entries: deferred expense, deferred revenue, accrued expense, accrued revenue.

**Learning Objective 3**

### S3-6 Journalizing and posting adjusting entries for prepaid rent

On April 1, All Star of Toledo prepaid six months of rent, $4,200.

**Requirements**

1. Record the journal entry for the April 1 payment.
2. Record the adjusting entry required at April 30.
3. Using T-accounts, post the journal entry and adjusting entry to the accounts involved and show their balances at April 30. (Ignore the Cash account.)

**Learning Objective 3**

### S3-7 Journalizing and posting an adjusting entry for office supplies

On November 1, Camden Equipment had a beginning balance in the Office Supplies account of $1,300. During the month, Camden purchased $1,400 of office supplies. At November 30, Camden Equipment had $1,200 of office supplies on hand.

**Requirements**

1. Open the Office Supplies T-account, and enter the beginning balance and purchase of office supplies.
2. Record the adjusting entry required at November 30.
3. Post the adjusting entry to the two accounts involved, and show their balances at November 30.

**Learning Objective 3**

**S3-8 Journalizing and posting an adjusting entry for depreciation and determining book value**

On May 1, Chicago Gold Exchange paid cash of $28,800 for computers that are expected to remain useful for four years. At the end of four years, the value of the computers is expected to be zero.

**Requirements**

1. Calculate the amount of depreciation for the month of May using the straight-line depreciation method.
2. Record the adjusting entry for depreciation on May 31.
3. Post the purchase of May 1 and the depreciation on May 31 to T-accounts for the following accounts: Computer Equipment, Accumulated Depreciation—Computer Equipment, and Depreciation Expense—Computer Equipment. Show their balances at May 31.
4. What is the computer equipment's book value on May 31?

**Learning Objective 3**

**S3-9 Journalizing and posting an adjusting entry for unearned revenue**

*Southern Magazine* collects cash from subscribers in advance and then mails the magazines to subscribers over a one-year period.

**Requirements**

1. Record the journal entry to record the original receipt of $150,000 cash.
2. Record the adjusting entry that *Southern Magazine* makes to record earning $9,000 in subscription revenue that was collected in advance.
3. Using T-accounts, post the journal entry and adjusting entry to the accounts involved and show their balances after adjustments. (Ignore the Cash account.)

**Learning Objective 3**

**S3-10 Journalizing and posting an adjusting entry for accrued salaries expense**

Walnut Park Senior Center has a weekly payroll of $7,500. December 31 falls on Wednesday, and Walnut Park Senior Center will pay its employees the following Monday (January 5) for the previous full week. Assume Walnut Park Senior Center has a five-day workweek and has an unadjusted balance in Salaries Expense of $550,000.

**Requirements**

1. Record the adjusting entry for accrued salaries on December 31.
2. Post the adjusting entry to the accounts involved, and show their balances after adjustments.
3. Record the journal entry for payment of salaries made on January 5.

**Learning Objective 3**

**S3-11 Journalizing and posting an adjusting entry for accrued interest expense**

Fly Away Travel borrowed $26,000 on August 1, 2016, by signing a one-year note payable to Region One Bank. Fly Away's interest expense on the note payable for the remainder of the fiscal year (August through October) is $494.

**Requirements**

1. Record the adjusting entry to accrue interest expense at October 31, 2016.
2. Post the adjusting entry to the T-accounts of the two accounts affected by the adjustment.

**Learning Objective 3**

## S3-12 Journalizing an adjusting entry for accrued revenue

At the end of June, Gallio Dental had performed $8,000 of dental services but has not yet billed customers.

Record the adjusting entry for accrued revenue.

**Learning Objective 4**

## S3-13 Preparing an adjusted trial balance

Steve's Tax Services had the following accounts and account balances after adjusting entries. Assume all accounts have normal balances.

| | | | |
|---|---|---|---|
| Cash | $ ? | Equipment | $ 25,000 |
| Land | 24,000 | Accounts Receivable | 4,250 |
| Utilities Payable | 550 | Office Supplies | 900 |
| Accounts Payable | 3,800 | Common Stock | 18,600 |
| Accumulated Depreciation—Equipment | 1,500 | Utilities Expense | 1,550 |
| Service Revenue | 90,000 | Unearned Revenue | 600 |
| Supplies Expense | 700 | Depreciation Expense—Equipment | 1,800 |
| Dividends | 28,000 | Salaries Expense | 5,200 |

Prepare the adjusted trial balance for Steve's Tax Services as of December 31, 2016.

**Learning Objective 5**

## S3-14 Determining the effects on financial statements

In recording adjusting entries, Reagan Financial Advisors failed to record the adjusting entries for the following situations:

a. Office supplies on hand, $100.

b. Accrued revenues, $5,000.

c. Accrued interest expense, $250.

d. Depreciation, $800.

e. Unearned revenue that has been earned, $550.

Determine the effects on the income statement and balance sheet by identifying whether assets, liabilities, equity, revenue, and expenses are either overstated or understated. Use the following table. Adjustment *a* has been provided as an example.

| Adjustment | Balance Sheet | | | Income Statement | |
|---|---|---|---|---|---|
| Not Recorded | Assets | Liabilities | Equity | Revenue | Expenses |
| *(a)* | *Overstated* | | *Overstated* | | *Understated* |

## S3-15 Preparing a partial worksheet

Learning Objective 6

Fabulous Cut Hair Stylists has begun the preparation of its worksheet as follows:

| | A | B | C | D | E | F | G |
|---|---|---|---|---|---|---|---|
| 1 | FABULOUS CUT HAIR STYLISTS | | | | | | |
| 2 | Worksheet | | | | | | |
| 3 | December 31, 2016 | | | | | | |
| 4 | | | | | | | |
| 5 | Account Names | Unadjusted Trial Balance | | Adjustments | | Adjusted Trial Balance | |
| 6 | | Debit | Credit | Debit | Credit | Debit | Credit |
| 7 | Cash | $ 400 | | | | | |
| 8 | Office Supplies | 700 | | | | | |
| 9 | Equipment | 14,700 | | | | | |
| 10 | Accumulated Depreciation—Equipment | | $ 1,100 | | | | |
| 11 | Accounts Payable | | 400 | | | | |
| 12 | Interest Payable | | | | | | |
| 13 | Note Payable | | 3,600 | | | | |
| 14 | Common Stock | | 4,400 | | | | |
| 15 | Service Revenue | | 10,900 | | | | |
| 16 | Rent Expense | 4,400 | | | | | |
| 17 | Supplies Expense | | | | | | |
| 18 | Depreciation Expense—Equipment | | | | | | |
| 19 | Interest Expense | 200 | | | | | |
| 20 | **Total** | **$ 20,400** | **$ 20,400** | | | | |
| 21 | | | | | | | |

Year-end data include the following:

a. Office supplies on hand, $200.

b. Depreciation, $1,100.

c. Accrued interest expense, $200.

Complete Fabulous Cut's worksheet through the adjusted trial balance section. In the adjustments section, mark each adjustment by letter.

## S3A-16 Journalizing the alternative treatment of deferred expenses

Learning Objective 7
Appendix 3A

On August 1, 2016, Blue Design paid $66,000 for store rent covering the 12-month period ending July 31, 2017.

### Requirements

1. Journalize the entry on August 1 by using the alternative treatment of deferred expenses.
2. Record the December 31, 2016 adjusting entry.

## S3A-17 Journalizing the alternative treatment of deferred revenues

Learning Objective 7
Appendix 3A

On October 1, 2016, Amazing Landscaping collected $30,000 in advance from customers for landscaping services. The service revenue will be earned monthly over the six-month period ending March 31, 2017.

### Requirements

1. Journalize the entry on October 1 by using the alternative treatment of deferred revenues.
2. Record the December 31, 2016 adjusting entry.

## > Exercises

**Learning Objectives 1, 2**

**E3-18 Comparing cash and accrual basis accounting and applying the revenue recognition principle**

Momentous Occasions is a photography business that shoots videos at college parties. The freshman class pays $1,000 in advance on March 3 to guarantee services for its party to be held on April 2. The sophomore class promises a minimum of $2,800 for filming its formal dance and actually pays cash of $4,100 on February 28 at the dance.

Answer the following questions about the correct way to account for revenue under the accrual basis:

a. Considering the $1,000 paid by the freshman class, on what date was revenue earned? Did the earnings occur on the same date cash was received?

b. Considering the $4,100 paid by the sophomore class, on what date was revenue earned? Did the earnings occur on the same date cash was received?



**Learning Objectives 1, 2**

2. Cash basis $(3,400)

**E3-19 Comparing cash and accrual basis accounting and applying the revenue recognition principle and the matching principle**

Fantastic Catering completed the following selected transactions during May 2016:

| | | |
|---|---|---|
| May | 1 | Prepaid rent for three months, $1,800. |
| | 5 | Received and paid electricity bill, $200. |
| | 9 | Received cash for meals served to customers, $1,900. |
| | 14 | Paid cash for kitchen equipment, $3,300. |
| | 23 | Served a banquet on account, $3,600. |
| | 31 | Made the adjusting entry for rent (from May 1). |
| | 31 | Accrued salary expense, $1,300. |
| | 31 | Recorded depreciation for May on kitchen equipment, $55. |

**Requirements**

1. Show whether each transaction would be handled as a revenue or an expense using both the cash basis and accrual basis accounting systems by completing the following table. (Expenses should be shown in parentheses.) Also, indicate the dollar amount of the revenue or expense. The May 1 transaction has been completed as an example.

| | Amount of Revenue (Expense) for May | |
|---|---|---|
| Date | Cash Basis Amount of Revenue (Expense) | Accrual Basis Amount of Revenue (Expense) |
| *May 1* | *$(1,800)* | *$0* |

2. After completing the table, calculate the amount of net income or net loss for Fantastic Catering under the accrual basis and cash basis accounting systems for May.
3. Considering your results from Requirement 2, which method gives the best picture of the true earnings of Fantastic Catering? Why?

## E3-20 Determining the amount of prepaid expenses

**Learning Objective 3**

Situation A. Rent Expense $1,200

Consider the facts presented in the following table for Island View:

| | Situation | | | |
|---|---|---|---|---|
| | A | B | C | D |
| Beginning Prepaid Rent | $1,100 | $1,000 | $ 100 | $ 500 |
| Payments for Prepaid Rent during the year | 700 | *b* | 1,300 | *f* |
| Total amount to account for | 1,800 | 1,700 | c | e |
| Subtract: Ending Prepaid Rent | 600 | 400 | *d* | 100 |
| Rent Expense | $ *a* | $1,300 | $1,000 | $1,100 |

Complete the table by filling in the missing values.

## E3-21 Journalizing adjusting entries

**Learning Objective 3**

b. DR Salaries Expense $1,600

Consider the following situations:

a. Business receives $3,800 on January 1 for 10-month service contract for the period January 1 through October 31.

b. Total salaries for all employees is $3,200 per month. Employees are paid on the 1st and 15th of the month.

c. Work performed but not yet billed to customers for the month is $1,000.

d. The company pays interest on its $15,000, 8% note payable of $100 on the first day of each month.

Assume the company records adjusting entries monthly. Journalize the adjusting entries needed as of January 31.

## E3-22 Journalizing adjusting entries

**Learning Objective 3**

e. DR Insurance Expense $750

Consider the following independent situations at December 31:

a. On July 1, a business collected $6,600 rent in advance, debiting Cash and crediting Unearned Revenue. The tenant was paying one year's rent in advance. On December 31, the business must account for the amount of rent it has earned.

b. Salaries expense is $1,300 per day—Monday through Friday—and the business pays employees each Friday. This year, December 31 falls on a Thursday.

c. The unadjusted balance of the Office Supplies account is $2,600. Office supplies on hand total $1,800.

d. Equipment depreciation was $200.

e. On October 1, when the business prepaid $6,000 for a two-year insurance policy, the business debited Prepaid Insurance and credited Cash.

Journalize the adjusting entry needed on December 31 for each situation. Use the letters to label the journal entries.

## E3-23 Journalizing adjusting entries

**Learning Objective 3**

c. DR Supplies Expense $3,300

Consider the following situations for Kirkland Welding Services:

a. Depreciation for the current year includes equipment, $2,700.

b. Each Monday, Kirkland pays employees for the previous week's work. The amount of weekly payroll is $3,500 for a seven-day workweek (Monday to Sunday). This year, December 31 falls on Thursday.

c. The beginning balance of Office Supplies was $2,600. During the year, Kirkland purchased office supplies for $2,500, and at December 31 the office supplies on hand totaled $1,800.

d. Kirkland prepaid a two full years' insurance on October 1 of the current year, $6,480. Record insurance expense for the year ended December 31.

e. Kirkland had earned $3,400 of unearned revenue.

f. Kirkland had incurred (but not recorded) $150 of interest expense on a note payable. The interest will not be paid until February 28.

g. Kirkland billed customers $9,000 for welding services performed.

Journalize the adjusting entry needed on December 31 for each situation. Use the letters to label the journal entries.



**Learning Objective 3**

3. Unearned Revenue bal. $600 CR

### E3-24 Journalizing adjusting entries and posting to T-accounts

The accounting records of Galvin Architects include the following selected, unadjusted balances at March 31: Accounts Receivable, $1,100; Office Supplies, $1,000; Prepaid Rent, $1,000; Equipment, $9,000; Accumulated Depreciation—Equipment, $0; Salaries Payable, $0; Unearned Revenue, $700; Service Revenue, $4,100; Salaries Expense, $1,400; Supplies Expense, $0; Rent Expense, $0; Depreciation Expense—Equipment, $0. The data developed for the March 31 adjusting entries are as follows:

a. Service revenue accrued, $600.

b. Unearned revenue that has been earned, $100.

c. Office Supplies on hand, $500.

d. Salaries owed to employees, $300.

e. One month of prepaid rent has expired, $500.

f. Depreciation on equipment, $135.

**Requirements**

1. Open a T-account for each account using the unadjusted balances given.
2. Journalize the adjusting entries using the letter and March 31 date in the date column.
3. Post the adjustments to the T-accounts, entering each adjustment by letter. Show each account's adjusted balance.

### E3-25 Journalizing adjusting entries and posting to T-accounts

**Learning Objective 3**

3. Office Supplies bal. $1,100 DR

The unadjusted trial balance for First Class Maids Company, a cleaning service, is as follows:

**FIRST CLASS MAIDS COMPANY**
Unadjusted Trial Balance
December 31, 2016

| | Balance | |
|---|---|---|
| **Account Title** | **Debit** | **Credit** |
| Cash | $ 1,200 | |
| Office Supplies | 3,000 | |
| Prepaid Insurance | 700 | |
| Equipment | 20,000 | |
| Accumulated Depreciation—Equipment | | $ 6,000 |
| Accounts Payable | | 2,200 |
| Salaries Payable | | |
| Unearned Revenue | | 600 |
| Common Stock | | 8,100 |
| Dividends | 3,000 | |
| Service Revenue | | 17,000 |
| Salaries Expense | 6,000 | |
| Supplies Expense | | |
| Depreciation Expense—Equipment | | |
| Insurance Expense | | |
| Total | **$ 33,900** | **$ 33,900** |

During the 12 months ended December 31, 2016, First Class Maids:

**a.** used office supplies of $1,900.

**b.** used prepaid insurance of $560.

**c.** depreciated equipment, $510.

**d.** accrued salaries expense of $250 that hasn't been paid yet.

**e.** earned $420 of unearned revenue.

**Requirements**

1. Open a T-account for each account using the unadjusted balances.
2. Journalize the adjusting entries using the letter and December 31 date in the date column.
3. Post the adjustments to the T-accounts, entering each adjustment by letter. Show each account's adjusted balance.

*Note: Exercise E3-26 should be used only in conjunction with Exercise E3-25.*

**Learning Objective 4**

Adjusted trial balance $34,660 total

### E3-26 Preparing an adjusted trial balance

Refer to the data in Exercise E3-25, and prepare an adjusted trial balance.

**Learning Objective 5**

### E3-27 Identifying the impact of adjusting entries on the financial statements

Austin Acoustics recorded the following transactions during October 2016:

a. Received $2,500 cash from customer for three months of service beginning October 1, 2016, and ending December 31, 2016. The company recorded a $2,500 debit to Cash and a $2,500 credit to Unearned Revenue.

b. Employees are paid $3,000 on Monday following the five-day workweek. October 31, 2016, is on Friday.

c. The company pays $440 on October 1, 2016 for its six-month auto insurance policy. The company recorded a $440 debit to Prepaid Insurance and a $440 credit to Cash.

d. The company purchased office furniture for $8,300 on January 2, 2016. The company recorded a $8,300 debit to Office Furniture and a $8,300 credit to Accounts Payable. Annual depreciation for the furniture is $1,000.

e. The company began October with $50 of office supplies on hand. On October 10, the company purchased office supplies on account of $100. The company recorded a $100 debit to Office Supplies and a $100 credit to Accounts Payable. The company used $120 of office supplies during October.

f. The company received its electric bill on October 30 for $325 but did not pay it until November 10.

g. The company paid November's rent of $2,500 on October 30. On October 30, the company recorded an $2,500 debit to Rent Expense and an $2,500 credit to Cash.

Indicate if an adjusting entry is needed for each item on October 31 for the month of October. Assuming the adjusting entry is not made, indicate which specific category or categories of accounts on the financial statements are misstated and if they are overstated or understated. Use the following table as a guide. Item *a* is completed as an example:

| Item | Adjusting Entry Needed? | Specific Category of Accounts on the Balance Sheet | Over / Understated | Specific Category of Accounts on the Income Statement | Over / Understated |
|---|---|---|---|---|---|
| *(a)* | *Yes* | *Liability*<br>*Equity* | *Over*<br>*Under* | *Revenue* | *Under* |

### E3-28 Journalizing adjusting entries and analyzing their effect on the income statement

**Learning Objectives 3, 5**

1. d. DR Salaries Expense $10,400

The following data at July 31, 2016, are given for XYZ:

a. Depreciation, $400.

b. Prepaid rent expires, $800.

c. Interest expense accrued, $600.

d. Employee salaries owed for Monday through Thursday of a five-day workweek; weekly payroll, $13,000.

e. Unearned revenue earned, $1,600.

f. Office supplies used, $100.

**Requirements**

1. Journalize the adjusting entries needed on July 31, 2016.
2. Suppose the adjustments made in Requirement 1 were not made. Compute the overall overstatement or understatement of net income as a result of the omission of these adjustments.



### E3-29 Using the worksheet to record the adjusting journal entries

**Learning Objective 6**

1. Adjustments $3,300 total

The worksheet of Just Jobs Employment Service follows but is incomplete.

| | A | B | C | D | E | F | G |
|---|---|---|---|---|---|---|---|
| 1 | **JUST JOBS EMPLOYMENT SERVICE** | | | | | | |
| 2 | **Worksheet** | | | | | | |
| 3 | **April 30, 2016** | | | | | | |
| 4 | | | | | | | |
| 5 | **Account Names** | **Unadjusted Trial Balance** | | **Adjustments** | | **Adjusted Trial Balance** | |
| 6 | | **Debit** | **Credit** | **Debit** | **Credit** | **Debit** | **Credit** |
| 7 | Cash | $ 1,100 | | | | $ 1,100 | |
| 8 | Accounts Receivable | 4,900 | | | | 6,200 | |
| 9 | Office Supplies | 1,200 | | | | 900 | |
| 10 | Equipment | 32,900 | | | | 32,900 | |
| 11 | Accumulated Depreciation—Equipment | | $ 14,300 | | | | $ 15,200 |
| 12 | Salaries Payable | | | | | | 800 |
| 13 | Common Stock | | 25,100 | | | | 25,100 |
| 14 | Dividends | 5,000 | | | | 5,000 | |
| 15 | Service Revenue | | 9,600 | | | | 10,900 |
| 16 | Salaries Expense | 2,600 | | | | 3,400 | |
| 17 | Rent Expense | 1,300 | | | | 1,300 | |
| 18 | Depreciation Expense—Equipment | | | | | 900 | |
| 19 | Supplies Expense | | | | | 300 | |
| 20 | **Total** | **$ 49,000** | **$ 49,000** | | | **$ 52,000** | **$ 52,000** |
| 21 | | | | | | | |

**Requirements**

1. Calculate and enter the adjustment amounts directly in the Adjustments columns. Use letters *a* through *d* to label the four adjustments.
2. Prepare each adjusting journal entry calculated in Requirement 1. Date the entries, and include explanations.

**Learning Objective 6**

Adjusted trial balance
$216,070 total

### E3-30 Using the worksheet to prepare the adjusted trial balance

The worksheet of Moore's Landscaping Services follows but is incomplete.

| | A | B | C | D | | E | | F | G |
|---|---|---|---|---|---|---|---|---|---|
| 1 | MOORE'S LANDSCAPING SERVICES | | | | | | | | |
| 2 | Worksheet | | | | | | | | |
| 3 | December 31, 2016 | | | | | | | | |
| 4 | | | | | | | | | |
| 5 | Account Names | Unadjusted Trial Balance | | Adjustments | | | | Adjusted Trial Balance | |
| 6 | | Debit | Credit | | Debit | | Credit | Debit | Credit |
| 7 | Cash | $ 27,500 | | | | | | | |
| 8 | Accounts Receivable | 6,600 | | (h) | $ 2,500 | | | | |
| 9 | Office Supplies | 520 | | | | (b) | $ 380 | | |
| 10 | Prepaid Rent | 2,900 | | | | (a) | 1,450 | | |
| 11 | Equipment | 55,000 | | | | | | | |
| 12 | Accumulated Depreciation—Equipment | | | | | (c) | 900 | | |
| 13 | Trucks | 60,000 | | | | | | | |
| 14 | Accumulated Depreciation—Trucks | | | | | (d) | 1,000 | | |
| 15 | Accounts Payable | | $ 4,100 | | | | | | |
| 16 | Utilities Payable | | 750 | | | | | | |
| 17 | Salaries Payable | | | | | (f) | 5,000 | | |
| 18 | Interest Payable | | | | | (g) | 150 | | |
| 19 | Unearned Revenue | | 5,000 | (e) | 3,500 | | | | |
| 20 | Notes Payable | | 30,000 | | | | | | |
| 21 | Common Stock | | 76,670 | | | | | | |
| 22 | Dividends | 12,000 | | | | | | | |
| 23 | Service Revenue | | 90,000 | | | (e, h) | 6,000 | | |
| 24 | Rent Expense | 11,600 | | (a) | 1,450 | | | | |
| 25 | Salaries Expense | 25,600 | | (f) | 5,000 | | | | |
| 26 | Supplies Expense | | | (b) | 380 | | | | |
| 27 | Utilities Expense | 4,800 | | | | | | | |
| 28 | Depreciation Expense—Equipment | | | (c) | 900 | | | | |
| 29 | Depreciation Expense—Trucks | | | (d) | 1,000 | | | | |
| 30 | Interest Expense | | | (g) | 150 | | | | |
| 31 | **Total** | **$ 206,520** | **$ 206,520** | | **$ 14,880** | | **$ 14,880** | | |
| 32 | | | | | | | | | |

Calculate and enter the adjusted account balances in the Adjusted Trial Balance columns.

**Learning Objectives 3, 7**
**Appendix 3A**

2. CR Office Supplies $300

## E3A-31 Understanding the alternative treatment of prepaid expenses

At the beginning of the year, office supplies of $800 were on hand. During the year, Rocket Air Conditioning Service paid $6,000 for more office supplies. At the end of the year, Rocket has $500 of office supplies on hand.

### Requirements

1. Record the adjusting entry assuming that Rocket records the purchase of office supplies by initially debiting an asset account. Post the adjusting entry to the Office Supplies and Supplies Expense T-accounts. Make sure to include the beginning balance and purchase of office supplies in the Office Supplies T-account.
2. Record the adjusting entry assuming that Rocket records the purchase of office supplies by initially debiting an expense account. Post the adjusting entry to the Office Supplies and Supplies Expense T-accounts. Make sure to include the beginning balance in the Office Supplies T-account and the purchase of office supplies in the Supplies Expense T-account.
3. Compare the ending balances of the T-accounts under both approaches. Are they the same?

**Learning Objectives 3, 7**
**Appendix 3A**

2. DR Service Revenue $200

## E3A-32 Understanding the alternative treatment of unearned revenues

At the beginning of the year, Dapper Advertising owed customers $2,400 for unearned revenue collected in advance. During the year, Dapper received advance cash receipts of $7,500 and earned $15,000 of service revenue (exclusive of any amount earned from advance payments). At year-end, the liability for unearned revenue is $2,600 and unadjusted service revenue is $15,000.

### Requirements

1. Record the adjusting entry assuming that Dapper records the cash receipt of unearned revenue by initially crediting a liability account. Post the adjusting entry to the Unearned Revenue and Service Revenue T-accounts. Make sure to include the beginning balance and additional unearned revenue in the Unearned Revenue T-account.
2. Record the adjusting entry assuming that Dapper records the cash receipt of unearned revenue by initially crediting a revenue account. Post the adjusting entry to the Unearned Revenue and Service Revenue T-accounts. Make sure to include the beginning balance in the Unearned Revenue T-account and the additional unearned revenue in the Service Revenue T-account.
3. Compare the ending balances of the T-accounts under both approaches. Are they the same?

# > Problems Group A

**Learning Objective 3**

1. b. DR Insurance Expense $1,250

**P3-33A Journalizing adjusting entries and subsequent journal entries**

Laroche Landscaping has collected the following data for the December 31 adjusting entries:

a. Each Friday, Laroche pays employees for the current week's work. The amount of the weekly payroll is $7,500 for a five-day workweek. This year, December 31 falls on a Wednesday. Laroche will pay its employees on January 2.

b. On January 1 of the current year, Laroche purchases an insurance policy that covers two years, $2,500.

c. The beginning balance of Office Supplies was $3,900. During the year, Laroche purchased office supplies for $5,400, and at December 31 the office supplies on hand total $2,600.

d. During December, Laroche designed a landscape plan and the client prepaid $5,000. Laroche recorded this amount as Unearned Revenue. The job will take several months to complete, and Laroche estimates that the company has earned 60% of the total revenue during the current year.

e. At December 31, Laroche had earned $4,500 for landscape services completed for Turnkey Appliances. Turnkey has stated that it will pay Laroche on January 10.

f. Depreciation for the current year includes Equipment, $3,300; and Trucks, $2,100.

g. Laroche has incurred $400 of interest expense on a $900 interest payment due on January 15.

**Requirements**

1. Journalize the adjusting entry needed on December 31 for each of the previous items affecting Laroche Landscaping. Assume Laroche records adjusting entries only at the end of the year.
2. Journalize the subsequent journal entries for adjusting entries *a, d,* and *g.*

**Learning Objectives 3, 5**

1. d. DR Depreciation Expense $8,000

**P3-34A Journalizing adjusting entries and identifying the impact on financial statements**

Wright Fishing Charters has collected the following data for the December 31 adjusting entries:

a. The company received its electric bill on December 20 for $225 but will not pay it until January 5. (Use the Utilities Payable account.)

b. Wright purchased a nine-month boat insurance policy on November 1 for $9,000. Wright recorded a debit to Prepaid Insurance.

c. As of December 31, Wright had earned $2,000 of charter revenue that has not been recorded or received.

d. Wright's fishing boat was purchased on January 1 at a cost of $44,500. Wright expects to use the boat for five years and that it will have a residual value of $4,500. Determine annual depreciation assuming the straight-line depreciation method is used.

e. On October 1, Wright received $8,000 prepayment for a deep-sea fishing charter to take place in December. As of December 31, Wright has completed the charter.

**Requirements**

1. Journalize the adjusting entries needed on December 31 for Wright Fishing Charters. Assume Wright records adjusting entries only at the end of the year.
2. If Wright had not recorded the adjusting entries, indicate which specific category of accounts on the financial statements would be misstated and if the misstatement is overstated or understated. Use the following table as a guide.

| Adjusting Entry | Specific Category of Accounts on the Balance Sheet | Over / Understated | Specific Category of Accounts on the Income Statement | Over / Understated |
|---|---|---|---|---|

## P3-35A Journalizing and posting adjustments to the T-accounts and preparing an adjusted trial balance

**Learning Objectives 3, 4**

3. Adjusted trial balance $69,750 total

The unadjusted trial balance of Aurora Air Purification System at December 31, 2016, and the data needed for the adjustments follow.

**AURORA AIR PURIFICATION SYSTEM**
Unadjusted Trial Balance
December 31, 2016

| | Balance | |
|---|---|---|
| **Account Title** | **Debit** | **Credit** |
| Cash | $ 7,800 | |
| Accounts Receivable | 19,800 | |
| Prepaid Rent | 2,600 | |
| Office Supplies | 1,100 | |
| Equipment | 19,900 | |
| Accumulated Depreciation—Equipment | | $ 4,100 |
| Accounts Payable | | 3,000 |
| Salaries Payable | | |
| Unearned Revenue | | 2,800 |
| Common Stock | | 39,600 |
| Dividends | 9,300 | |
| Service Revenue | | 15,400 |
| Salaries Expense | 3,100 | |
| Rent Expense | | |
| Depreciation Expense—Equipment | | |
| Advertising Expense | 1,300 | |
| Supplies Expense | | |
| Total | **$ 64,900** | **$ 64,900** |

Adjustment data at December 31 follow:

a. On December 15, Aurora contracted to perform services for a client receiving $2,800 in advance. Aurora recorded this receipt of cash as Unearned Revenue. As of December 31, Aurora has completed $1,800 of the services.

b. Aurora prepaid two months of rent on December 1.

c. Aurora used $600 of office supplies.

d. Depreciation for the equipment is $700.

e. Aurora received a bill for December's online advertising, $1,000. Aurora will not pay the bill until January. (Use Accounts Payable.)

f. Aurora pays its employees on Monday for the previous week's wages. Its employees earn $1,500 for a five-day workweek. December 31 falls on Wednesday this year.

g. On October 1, Aurora agreed to provide a four-month air system check (beginning October 1) for a customer for $3,000. Aurora has completed the system check every month, but payment has not yet been received and no entries have been made.

### Requirements

1. Journalize the adjusting entries on December 31.
2. Using the unadjusted trial balance, open the T-accounts with the unadjusted balances. Post the adjusting entries to the T-accounts.
3. Prepare the adjusted trial balance.
4. How will Aurora Air Purification System use the adjusted trial balance?



**Learning Objectives 3, 4**

3. Adjusted trial balance $555,220 total

### P3-36A Journalizing and posting adjustments to the four-column accounts and preparing an adjusted trial balance

The unadjusted trial balance of Newport Inn Company at December 31, 2016, and the data needed for the adjustments follow.

**NEWPORT INN COMPANY**
Unadjusted Trial Balance
December 31, 2016

| | Balance | |
|---|---|---|
| **Account Title** | **Debit** | **Credit** |
| Cash | $ 11,900 | |
| Accounts Receivable | 13,900 | |
| Prepaid Insurance | 3,500 | |
| Office Supplies | 1,100 | |
| Building | 515,000 | |
| Accumulated Depreciation—Building | | $ 350,000 |
| Accounts Payable | | 4,500 |
| Salaries Payable | | |
| Unearned Revenue | | 2,500 |
| Common Stock | | 175,620 |
| Dividends | 2,170 | |
| Service Revenue | | 18,200 |
| Salaries Expense | 2,500 | |
| Insurance Expense | | |
| Depreciation Expense—Building | | |
| Advertising Expense | 750 | |
| Supplies Expense | | |
| Total | **$ 550,820** | **$ 550,820** |

Adjustment data at December 31 follow:

a. As of December 31, Newport had $600 of Prepaid Insurance remaining.

b. At the end of the month, Newport had $700 of office supplies remaining.

c. Depreciation on the building is $3,500.

d. Newport pays its employees weekly on Friday. Its employees earn $1,500 for a five-day workweek. December 31 falls on Wednesday this year.

e. On November 20, Newport contracted to perform services for a client receiving $2,500 in advance. Newport recorded this receipt of cash as Unearned Revenue. As of December 31, Newport has $1,500 still unearned.

**Requirements**

1. Journalize the adjusting entries on December 31.
2. Using the unadjusted trial balance, open the accounts (use a four-column ledger) with the unadjusted balances. Post the adjusting entries to the ledger accounts.
3. Prepare the adjusted trial balance.
4. Assuming the adjusted trial balance has total debits equal to total credits, does this mean that the adjusting entries have been recorded correctly? Explain.



**P3-37A Using the worksheet to record the adjusting journal entries**

**Learning Objective 6**

2. d. CR Accumulated Depreciation $3,800

Ganville Theater Production Company's partially completed worksheet as of December 31, 2016, follows.

| | A | B | C | D | E | F | G |
|---|---|---|---|---|---|---|---|
| 1 | GANVILLE THEATER PRODUCTION COMPANY | | | | | | |
| 2 | Worksheet | | | | | | |
| 3 | December 31, 2016 | | | | | | |
| 4 | | | | | | | |
| 5 | Account Names | Unadjusted Trial Balance | | Adjustments | | Adjusted Trial Balance | |
| 6 | | Debit | Credit | Debit | Credit | Debit | Credit |
| 7 | Cash | $ 4,000 | | | | $ 4,000 | |
| 8 | Accounts Receivable | 6,000 | | | | 7,000 | |
| 9 | Office Supplies | 1,300 | | | | 400 | |
| 10 | Prepaid Insurance | 3,600 | | | | 3,150 | |
| 11 | Equipment | 28,000 | | | | 28,000 | |
| 12 | Accumulated Depreciation—Equipment | | $ 8,800 | | | | $ 12,600 |
| 13 | Accounts Payable | | 5,000 | | | | 5,000 |
| 14 | Salaries Payable | | | | | | 100 |
| 15 | Common Stock | | 13,500 | | | | 13,500 |
| 16 | Dividends | 31,000 | | | | 31,000 | |
| 17 | Service Revenue | | 76,000 | | | | 77,000 |
| 18 | Depreciation Expense—Equipment | | | | | 3,800 | |
| 19 | Supplies Expense | | | | | 900 | |
| 20 | Utilities Expense | 5,400 | | | | 5,400 | |
| 21 | Salaries Expense | 24,000 | | | | 24,100 | |
| 22 | Insurance Expense | | | | | 450 | |
| 23 | **Total** | **$ 103,300** | **$ 103,300** | | | **$ 108,200** | **$ 108,200** |
| 24 | | | | | | | |

**Requirements**

1. Analyze the worksheet to determine the adjusting entries that account for the differences between the unadjusted trial balance and the adjusted trial balance. Complete the worksheet. Use letters *a* through *e* to label the five adjustments.
2. Journalize the adjusting entries.

**Learning Objectives 3, 7**
**Appendix 3A**

4. Dec 31, CR Insurance Expense $7,500

## P3A-38A Understanding the alternative treatment of prepaid expenses and unearned revenues

Night Flyer Pack'n Mail completed the following transactions during 2016:

| | |
|---|---|
| Nov. 1 | Paid $2,000 store rent covering the four-month period ending February 28, 2017. |
| Nov. 1 | Paid $12,500 insurance covering the five-month period ending March 31, 2017. |
| Dec. 1 | Collected $4,500 cash in advance from customers. The service revenue will be earned $1,500 monthly over the three-month period ending February 28, 2017. |
| Dec. 1 | Collected $9,000 cash in advance from customers. The service revenue will be earned $1,800 monthly over the five-month period ending April 30, 2017. |



### Requirements

1. Journalize the transactions assuming that Night Flyer debits an asset account for prepaid expenses and credits a liability account for unearned revenues.
2. Journalize the related adjusting entries at December 31, 2016.
3. Post the journal and adjusting entries to the T-accounts, and show their balances at December 31, 2016. (Ignore the Cash account.)
4. Repeat Requirements 1–3. This time, debit an expense account for prepaid expenses and credit a revenue account for unearned revenues.
5. Compare the account balances in Requirements 3 and 4. They should be equal.

# > Problems Group B

**Learning Objective 3**

1. b. DR Insurance Expense $2,000

## P3-39B Journalizing adjusting entries and subsequent journal entries

Lorring Landscaping has the following data for the December 31 adjusting entries:

a. Each Friday, Lorring pays employees for the current week's work. The amount of the weekly payroll is $6,000 for a five-day workweek. This year, December 31 falls on a Tuesday. Lorring will pay its employees on January 3.

b. On January 1 of the current year, Lorring purchases an insurance policy that covers two years, $4,000.

c. The beginning balance of Office Supplies was $4,100. During the year, Lorring purchased office supplies for $5,500, and at December 31 the office supplies on hand total $2,200.

d. During December, Lorring designed a landscape plan and the client prepaid $4,000. Lorring recorded this amount as Unearned Revenue. The job will take several months to complete, and Lorring estimates that the company has earned 50% of the total revenue during the current year.

e. At December 31, Lorring had earned $4,500 for landscape services completed for Tomball Appliances. Tomball has stated that it will pay Lorring on January 10.

f. Depreciation for the current year includes Equipment, $3,000; and Trucks, $1,700.

g. Lorring has incurred $800 of interest expense on a $1,200 interest payment due on January 15.

**Requirements**

1. Journalize the adjusting entry needed on December 31 for each of the previous items affecting Lorring Landscaping. Assume Lorring records adjusting entries only at the end of the year.
2. Journalize the subsequent journal entries for adjusting entries *a, d,* and *g*.

## P3-40B Journalizing adjusting entries and identifying the impact on financial statements

**Learning Objectives 3, 5**

1. d. DR Depreciation Expense $15,000

Henderson Fishing Charters has collected the following data for the December 31 adjusting entries:

a. The company received its electric bill on December 20 for $150 but will not pay it until January 5. (Use the Utilities Payable account.)

b. Henderson purchased a nine-month boat insurance policy on November 1 for $8,100. Henderson recorded a debit to Prepaid Insurance.

c. As of December 31, Henderson had earned $4,000 of charter revenue that has not been recorded or received.

d. Henderson's fishing boat was purchased on January 1 at a cost of $80,500. Henderson expects to use the boat for five years and that it will have a residual value of $5,500. Determine annual depreciation assuming the straight-line depreciation method is used.

e. On October 1, Henderson received $5,000 prepayment for a deep-sea fishing charter to take place in December. As of December 31, Henderson has completed the charter.

**Requirements**

1. Journalize the adjusting entries needed on December 31 for Henderson Fishing Charters. Assume Henderson records adjusting entries only at the end of the year.
2. If Henderson had not recorded the adjusting entries, indicate which specific category of accounts on the financial statements would be misstated and if the misstatement is overstated or understated. Use the following table as a guide:

| Adjusting Entry | Specific Category of Accounts on the Balance Sheet | Over / Understated | Specific Category of Accounts on the Income Statement | Over / Understated |
|---|---|---|---|---|

CHAPTER 3

**Learning Objectives 3, 4**

3. Adjusted trial balance $71,700 total

CHAPTER 3

## P3-41B Journalizing and posting adjustments to the T-accounts and preparing an adjusted trial balance

The unadjusted trial balance of Alston Air Purification System at December 31, 2016, and the data needed for the adjustments follow.

**ALSTON AIR PURIFICATION SYSTEM**
Unadjusted Trial Balance
December 31, 2016

| | Balance | |
|---|---|---|
| **Account Title** | **Debit** | **Credit** |
| Cash | $ 7,400 | |
| Accounts Receivable | 19,300 | |
| Prepaid Rent | 2,700 | |
| Office Supplies | 1,100 | |
| Equipment | 20,000 | |
| Accumulated Depreciation—Equipment | | $ 4,000 |
| Accounts Payable | | 3,100 |
| Salaries Payable | | |
| Unearned Revenue | | 2,600 |
| Common Stock | | 40,100 |
| Dividends | 9,900 | |
| Service Revenue | | 15,400 |
| Salaries Expense | 3,400 | |
| Rent Expense | | |
| Depreciation Expense—Equipment | | |
| Advertising Expense | 1,400 | |
| Supplies Expense | | |
| Total | **$ 65,200** | **$ 65,200** |

Adjustment data at December 31 follow:

a. On December 15, Alston contracted to perform services for a client receiving $2,600 in advance. Alston recorded this receipt of cash as Unearned Revenue. As of December 31, Alston has completed $1,200 of the services.

b. Alston prepaid two months of rent on December 1.

c. Alston used $650 of office supplies during the month.

d. Depreciation for the equipment is $500.

e. Alston received a bill for December's online advertising, $600. Alston will not pay the bill until January. (Use Accounts Payable.)

f. Alston pays its employees weekly on Monday for the previous week's wages. Its employees earn $5,500 for a five-day workweek. December 31 falls on Wednesday this year.

g. On October 1, Alston agreed to provide a four-month air system check (beginning October 1) for a customer for $2,800. Alston has completed the system check every month, but payment has not yet been received and no entries have been made.

**Requirements**

1. Journalize the adjusting entries on December 31.
2. Using the unadjusted trial balance, open the T-accounts with the unadjusted balances. Post the adjusting entries to the T-accounts.
3. Prepare the adjusted trial balance.
4. How will Alston Air Purification System use the adjusted trial balance?

**P3-42B Journalizing and posting adjustments to the four-column accounts and preparing an adjusted trial balance**

**Learning Objectives 3, 4**

3. Adjusted trial balance $566,330 total

The unadjusted trial balance of Irvine Inn Company at December 31, 2016, and the data needed for the adjustments follow.

**IRVINE INN COMPANY**
Unadjusted Trial Balance
December 31, 2016

| | Balance | |
|---|---|---|
| **Account Title** | **Debit** | **Credit** |
| Cash | $ 11,200 | |
| Accounts Receivable | 14,600 | |
| Prepaid Insurance | 4,600 | |
| Office Supplies | 700 | |
| Building | 525,000 | |
| Accumulated Depreciation—Building | | $ 240,000 |
| Accounts Payable | | 2,400 |
| Salaries Payable | | |
| Unearned Revenue | | 1,600 |
| Common Stock | | 300,530 |
| Dividends | 1,550 | |
| Service Revenue | | 17,100 |
| Salaries Expense | 3,100 | |
| Insurance Expense | | |
| Depreciation Expense—Building | | |
| Advertising Expense | 880 | |
| Supplies Expense | | |
| Total | **$ 561,630** | **$ 561,630** |

Adjustment data at December 31 follow:

a. As of December 31, Irvine Inn had $500 of Prepaid Insurance remaining.

b. At the end of the month, Irvine Inn had $400 of office supplies remaining.

c. Depreciation on the building is $4,100.

d. Irvine Inn pays its employees on Friday for the weekly salaries. Its employees earn $1,000 for a five-day workweek. December 31 falls on Wednesday this year.

e. On November 20, Irvine Inn contracted to perform services for a client receiving $1,600 in advance. Irvine Inn recorded this receipt of cash as Unearned Revenue. As of December 31, Irvine Inn has $1,100 still unearned.

CHAPTER 3

## Requirements

1. Journalize the adjusting entries on December 31.
2. Using the unadjusted trial balance, open the accounts (use a four-column ledger) with the unadjusted balances. Post the adjusting entries to the ledger accounts.
3. Prepare the adjusted trial balance.
4. Assuming the adjusted trial balance has total debits equal to total credits, does this mean that the adjusting entries have been recorded correctly? Explain.

**Learning Objective 6**

2. d. CR Accumulated Depreciation $4,000

## P3-43B Using the worksheet to record the adjusting journal entries

Grover Theater Production Company's partially completed worksheet as of December 31, 2016, follows.

| | A | B | C | D | E | F | G |
|---|---|---|---|---|---|---|---|
| 1 | GROVER THEATER PRODUCTION COMPANY | | | | | | |
| 2 | Worksheet | | | | | | |
| 3 | December 31, 2016 | | | | | | |
| 4 | | | | | | | |
| 5 | Account Names | Unadjusted Trial Balance | | Adjustments | | Adjusted Trial Balance | |
| 6 | | Debit | Credit | Debit | Credit | Debit | Credit |
| 7 | Cash | $ 3,500 | | | | $ 3,500 | |
| 8 | Accounts Receivable | 6,300 | | | | 6,700 | |
| 9 | Office Supplies | 1,400 | | | | 600 | |
| 10 | Prepaid Insurance | 3,850 | | | | 3,300 | |
| 11 | Equipment | 33,000 | | | | 33,000 | |
| 12 | Accumulated Depreciation—Equipment | | $ 8,500 | | | | $ 12,500 |
| 13 | Accounts Payable | | 4,200 | | | | 4,200 |
| 14 | Salaries Payable | | | | | | 200 |
| 15 | Common Stock | | 22,150 | | | | 22,150 |
| 16 | Dividends | 32,000 | | | | 32,000 | |
| 17 | Service Revenue | | 79,000 | | | | 79,400 |
| 18 | Depreciation Expense—Equipment | | | | | 4,000 | |
| 19 | Supplies Expense | | | | | 800 | |
| 20 | Utilities Expense | 5,300 | | | | 5,300 | |
| 21 | Salaries Expense | 28,500 | | | | 28,700 | |
| 22 | Insurance Expense | | | | | 550 | |
| 23 | **Total** | **$113,850** | **$113,850** | | | **$118,450** | **$118,450** |
| 24 | | | | | | | |

## Requirements

1. Analyze the worksheet to determine the adjusting entries that account for the differences between the unadjusted trial balance and the adjusted trial balance. Complete the worksheet. Use letters *a* through *e* to label the five adjustments.
2. Journalize the adjusting entries.

## P3A-44B Understanding the alternative treatment of prepaid expenses and unearned revenues

**Learning Objectives 3, 7**
**Appendix 3A**

4. Dec 31, CR Insurance Expense $6,400

Speedy Pack'n Mail completed the following transactions during 2016:

| | | |
|---|---|---|
| Nov. | 1 | Paid $5,200 store rent covering the four-month period ending February 28, 2017. |
| | 1 | Paid $9,600 insurance covering the six-month period ending April 30, 2017. |
| Dec. | 1 | Collected $5,400 cash in advance from customers. The service revenue will be earned $1,800 monthly over the three-month period ending February 28, 2017. |
| | 1 | Collected $10,000 cash in advance from customers. The service revenue will be earned $2,000 monthly over the five-month period ending April 30, 2017. |

### Requirements

1. Journalize the transactions assuming that Speedy Pack'n Mail debits an asset account for prepaid expenses and credits a liability account for unearned revenues.
2. Journalize the related adjusting entries at December 31, 2016.
3. Post the journal and adjusting entries to the T-accounts, and show their balances at December 31, 2016. (Ignore the Cash account.)
4. Repeat Requirements 1–3. This time debit an expense account for prepaid expenses and credit a revenue account for unearned revenues.
5. Compare the account balances in Requirements 3 and 4. They should be equal.

## > Continuing Problem

### P3-45 Preparing adjusting entries and preparing an adjusted trial balance

This problem continues the Daniels Consulting situation from Problem P2-41 of Chapter 2. You will need to use the unadjusted trial balance and posted T-accounts that you prepared in Problem P2-41. The unadjusted trial balance at December 31, 2016, is duplicated below:

**DANIELS CONSULTING**
Unadjusted Trial Balance
December 31, 2016

| | Balance | |
|---|---|---|
| **Account Title** | **Debit** | **Credit** |
| Cash | $ 17,950 | |
| Accounts Receivable | 2,100 | |
| Office Supplies | 800 | |
| Equipment | 3,600 | |
| Furniture | 3,000 | |
| Accounts Payable | | $ 3,600 |
| Unearned Revenue | | 2,400 |
| Common Stock | | 20,000 |
| Dividends | 1,000 | |
| Service Revenue | | 4,600 |
| Rent Expense | 2,000 | |
| Utilities Expense | 150 | |
| Total | **$ 30,600** | **$ 30,600** |

At December 31, the business gathers the following information for the adjusting entries:

**a.** Accrued service revenue, $1,500.

**b.** Earned $600 of the service revenue collected in advance on December 21.

**c.** Office supplies on hand, $300.

**d.** Depreciation on equipment, $60; Depreciation on furniture, $50.

**e.** Accrued $685 expense for administrative assistant's salary.

### Requirements

1. Journalize and post the adjusting entries using the T-accounts that you completed in Problem P2-41. In the T-accounts, denote each adjusting amount as *Adj.* and an account balance as *Balance.*
2. Prepare an adjusted trial balance as of December 31, 2016.

## > Practice Set

### P3-46 Preparing adjusting entries and preparing an adjusted trial balance

This problem continues the Crystal Clear Cleaning situation from Problem P2-42 of Chapter 2. Start from the unadjusted trial balance that Crystal Clear Cleaning prepared at November 30, 2017:

**CRYSTAL CLEAR CLEANING**
Unadjusted Trial Balance
November 30, 2017

| | Balance | |
|---|---|---|
| **Account Title** | **Debit** | **Credit** |
| Cash | $138,150 | |
| Accounts Receivable | 2,600 | |
| Cleaning Supplies | 220 | |
| Prepaid Rent | 2,000 | |
| Prepaid Insurance | 1,800 | |
| Equipment | 3,200 | |
| Truck | 7,000 | |
| Accounts Payable | | $ 1,470 |
| Unearned Revenue | | 12,000 |
| Notes Payable | | 96,000 |
| Common Stock | | 42,000 |
| Dividends | 200 | |
| Service Revenue | | 4,800 |
| Salaries Expense | 350 | |
| Advertising Expense | 500 | |
| Utilities Expense | 250 | |
| Total | **$156,270** | **$156,270** |

Consider the following adjustment data:

**a.** Cleaning supplies on hand at the end of November were $30.

**b.** One month's combined depreciation on all depreciable assets was estimated to be $270.

**c.** One month's interest expense is $240.

**Requirements**

1. Using the data provided from the trial balance, the previous adjustment information, and the information from Chapter 2 (P2-42), prepare all required adjusting journal entries at November 30.
2. Prepare an adjusted trial balance as of November 30 for Crystal Clear Cleaning.

CHAPTER 3

# CRITICAL THINKING

## > Decision Case 3-1

One year ago, Tyler Stasney founded Swift Classified Ads. Stasney remembers that you took an accounting course while in college and comes to you for advice. He wishes to know how much net income his business earned during the past year in order to decide whether to keep the company going. His accounting records consist of the T-accounts from his ledger, which were prepared by an accountant who moved to another city. The ledger at December 31 follows. The accounts have *not* been adjusted.

| Account | Debit | Credit |
|---|---|---|
| **Cash** | Dec. 31 5,800 | |
| **Accounts Receivable** | Dec. 31 12,000 | |
| **Prepaid Rent** | Jan. 2 2,800 | |
| **Office Supplies** | Jan. 2 2,600 | |
| **Equipment** | Jan. 2 36,000 | |
| **Accumulated Depreciation—Equipment** | | |
| **Accounts Payable** | | 21,500 Dec. 31 |
| **Unearned Revenue** | | 4,000 Dec. 31 |
| **Salaries Payable** | | |
| **Common Stock** | | 20,000 Dec. 31 |
| **Dividends** | Dec. 31 28,000 | |
| **Service Revenue** | | 59,500 Dec. 31 |
| **Salaries Expense** | Dec. 31 17,000 | |
| **Depreciation Expense—Equipment** | | |
| **Rent Expense** | | |
| **Utilities Expense** | Dec. 31 800 | |
| **Supplies Expense** | | |

Stasney indicates that at year-end, customers owe the business $1,600 for accrued service revenue. These revenues have not been recorded. During the year, Swift Classified Ads collected $4,000 service revenue in advance from customers, but the business earned only $900 of that amount. Rent expense for the year was $2,400, and the business used up $1,700 of the supplies. Swift determines that depreciation on its equipment was $5,000 for the year. At December 31, the business owes an employee $1,200 accrued salary.

Help Swift Classified Ads compute its net income for the year. Advise Stasney whether to continue operating Swift Classified Ads.

## > Ethical Issue 3-1

The net income of Steinbach & Sons, a landscaping company, decreased sharply during 2016. Mort Steinbach, owner and manager of the company, anticipates the need for a bank loan in 2017. Late in 2016, Steinbach instructs the company's accountant to record $2,000 service revenue for landscape services for the Steinbach family, even though the services will not be performed until January 2017. Steinbach also tells the accountant *not* to make the following December 31, 2016, adjusting entries:

| | |
|---|---|
| Salaries owed to employees | $ 900 |
| Prepaid insurance that has expired | 400 |

**Requirements**

1. Compute the overall effects of these transactions on the company's reported net income for 2016.
2. Why is Steinbach taking this action? Is his action ethical? Give your reason, identifying the parties helped and the parties harmed by Steinbach's action.
3. As a personal friend, what advice would you give the accountant?

## > Fraud Case 3-1

XM, Ltd. was a small engineering firm that built high-tech robotic devices for electronics manufacturers. One very complex device was partially completed at the end of 2016. Barb McLauren, head engineer, knew the experimental technology was a failure and XM would not be able to complete the $20,000,000 contract next year. However, the corporation was getting ready to be sold in January. She told the controller that the device was 80% complete at year-end and on track for successful completion the following spring; the controller accrued 80% of the contract revenue at December 31, 2016. McLauren sold the company in January 2017 and retired. By mid-year, it became apparent that XM would not be able to complete the project successfully and the new owner would never recoup his investment.

**Requirements**

1. For complex, high-tech contracts, how does a company determine the percentage of completion and the amount of revenue to accrue?
2. What action do you think was taken by XM in 2017 with regard to the revenue that had been accrued the previous year?

## > Financial Statement Case 3-1

**Starbucks Corporation**—like all other businesses—makes adjusting entries at year-end in order to measure assets, liabilities, revenues, and expenses properly. Examine Starbucks Corporation's Balance Sheet and Income Statement. Visit **http://www.pearsonhighered.com/Horngren** to view a link to Starbucks Corporation's Fiscal 2013 Annual Report.

**Requirements**

1. Which asset accounts might Starbucks record adjusting entries for?
2. Which liability accounts might Starbucks record adjusting entries for?
3. Review Note 1 (Property, Plant, and Equipment) in the Notes to Consolidated Financial Statements. How are property, plant, and equipment carried on the balance sheet? How is depreciation of these assets calculated? What is the range of useful lives used when depreciating these assets?

## > Communication Activity 3-1

In 75 words or fewer, explain adjusting journal entries.



## > Quick Check Answers

**1.** a **2.** a **3.** b **4.** c **5.** a **6.** a **7.** b **8.** d **9.** c **10A.** b

# 4 Completing the Accounting Cycle

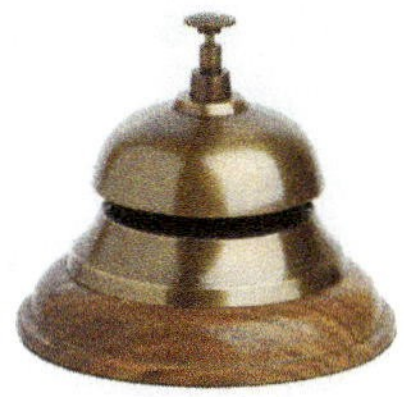

## It's the End of the Year, Now What?

The Bear Paw Inn just celebrated its one-year corporate anniversary. Christina Merthieu, the majority stockholder and manager, is excited that she has one year of experience working for a successful business. Although her previous job of working as a resort manager has helped her in dealing with customers, she has had to learn a lot about the accounting side of the business. Christina attributes her first-year success to always offering exceptional quality and personal service to her customers. In addition, Christina found a great accountant who has been helping her with the books.

From the beginning, Christina relied on her accountant to provide advice about recording transactions throughout the year. Now that the first year of business has been completed, she is ready to perform the final accounting tasks of the year. The corporation's accountant has told her that she can now prepare financial statements to help her evaluate the inn's profit for the year and its financial position. Bear Paw Inn will use those financial statements to assess the business's performance over the past year. The business is also ready to start the next year of business, and in order to do this, Christina must get the books ready for next year by recording closing entries.

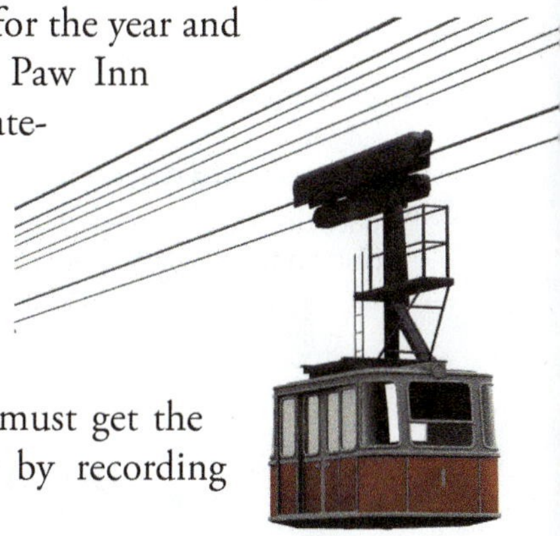

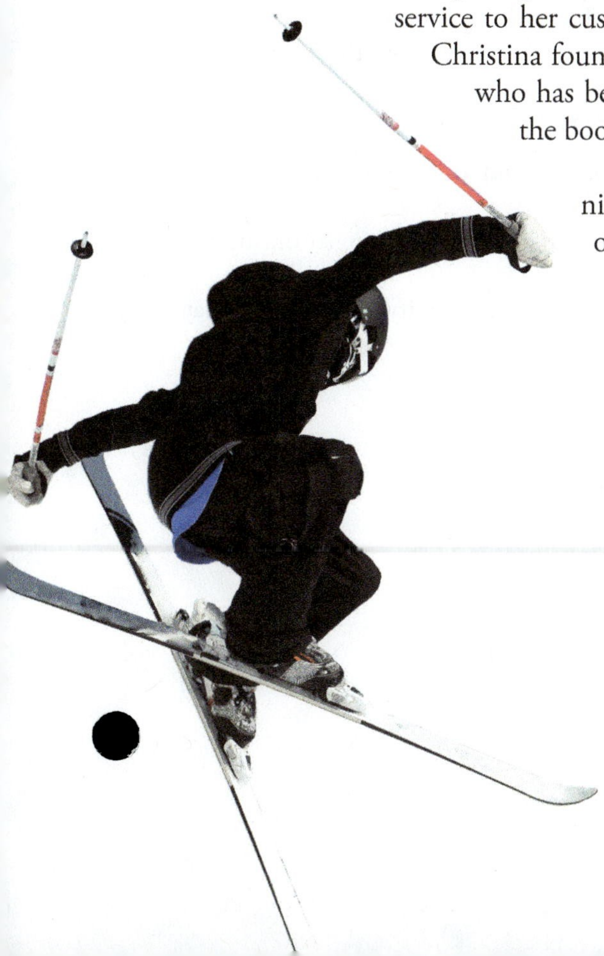

### What Happens at Year-End?

As we saw with Christina and the Bear Paw Inn, businesses have special tasks that have to be completed at the end of the accounting cycle. These tasks help the business in evaluating the past year's operations and also prepare the business to start a new year. For example, Four Seasons Hotels and Resorts must prepare annual financial statements that report on the business's profit or loss for the year and its financial position at the end of the year. In addition, Four Seasons must prepare its books for next year—a process that is called closing the books, which consists of journalizing closing entries and updating the Retained Earnings account for the year. These final tasks in the accounting cycle are what you learn about in this chapter.

# Chapter 4 Learning Objectives

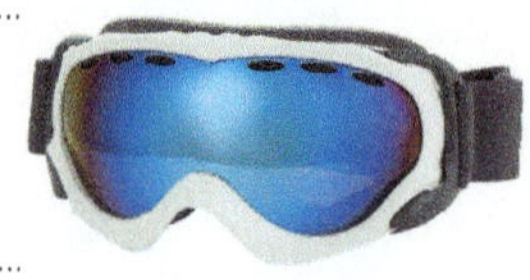

1 Prepare the financial statements including the classified balance sheet

2 Use the worksheet to prepare financial statements

3 Explain the purpose of, journalize, and post closing entries

4 Prepare the post-closing trial balance

5 Describe the accounting cycle

6 Use the current ratio to evaluate business performance

7 Explain the purpose of, journalize, and post reversing entries (Appendix 4A)

In Chapter 3, our fictitious company, Smart Touch Learning, had completed the adjusting entries necessary to properly measure net income on the income statement and assets and liabilities on the balance sheet. Now that its accounts are up to date, Smart Touch Learning is ready to take the next step in the accounting cycle—preparing the financial statements. In this chapter, you review the financial statements that you have already learned about and learn how to prepare a more complete version of the balance sheet. In addition, you complete the accounting cycle by learning how to close the books.

## HOW DO WE PREPARE FINANCIAL STATEMENTS?

**Learning Objective 1**
Prepare the financial statements including the classified balance sheet

The financial statements of Smart Touch Learning are prepared from the adjusted trial balance, which you learned in Chapter 3. Exhibit 4-1 shows the adjusted trial balance for Smart Touch Learning. In the right margin of the exhibit, we see how the accounts are distributed to the financial statements.

As always, the financial statements should be prepared in the following order:

1. **Income statement**—reports revenues and expenses and calculates net income or net loss for the time period.
2. **Statement of retained earnings**—shows how retained earnings changed during the period due to net income (or net loss) and dividends.
3. **Balance sheet**—reports assets, liabilities, and stockholders' equity as of the last day of the period.

IFRS

Following IFRS, companies must present a statement of profit or loss (income statement), statement of financial position (balance sheet), statement of changes in equity (similar to statement of retained earnings) and statement of cash flows—the same as U.S. companies. Yet the statements may look quite different. Revenue may be called "Turnover," and Net Income may be called "Profit." On the balance sheet, assets and liabilities are presented in a different order. Cash is often one of the last assets listed.

**Exhibit 4-1** | **Adjusted Trial Balance**

**SMART TOUCH LEARNING**
Adjusted Trial Balance
December 31, 2016

| | Balance | |
|---|---|---|
| **Account Title** | **Debit** | **Credit** |
| Cash | $ 12,200 | |
| Accounts Receivable | 1,800 | |
| Office Supplies | 100 | |
| Prepaid Rent | 2,000 | |
| Furniture | 18,000 | |
| Accumulated Depreciation—Furniture | | $ 300 |
| Building | 60,000 | |
| Accumulated Depreciation—Building | | 250 |
| Land | 20,000 | |
| Accounts Payable | | 200 |
| Utilities Payable | | 100 |
| Salaries Payable | | 1,200 |
| Interest Payable | | 100 |
| Unearned Revenue | | 400 |
| Notes Payable | | 60,000 |
| Common Stock | | 48,000 |
| Dividends | 5,000 | |
| Service Revenue | | 17,500 |
| Rent Expense | 3,000 | |
| Salaries Expense | 4,800 | |
| Supplies Expense | 400 | |
| Utilities Expense | 100 | |
| Depreciation Expense—Furniture | 300 | |
| Depreciation Expense—Building | 250 | |
| Interest Expense | 100 | |
| Total | **$ 128,050** | **$ 128,050** |

3. Balance Sheet Accounts (Cash through Common Stock)
2. Statement of Retained Earnings Account (Dividends)
1. Income Statement Accounts (Service Revenue through Interest Expense)

The financial statements for Smart Touch Learning are presented in Exhibit 4-2 (on the next page).

## Relationships Among the Financial Statements

The arrows in Exhibit 4-2 (on the next page) show how the financial statements relate to each other.

1. Net income from the income statement increases Retained Earnings. A net loss decreases Retained Earnings.
2. Ending Retained Earnings from the statement of retained earnings goes to the balance sheet and makes total liabilities plus total stockholders' equity equal total assets, satisfying the accounting equation.

To solidify your understanding of these relationships, trace net income from the income statement to the statement of retained earnings. Then trace ending Retained Earnings

**Exhibit 4-2** | **Smart Touch Learning Financial Statements**

**SMART TOUCH LEARNING**
Income Statement
Two Months Ended December 31, 2016

| | | |
|---|---|---|
| **Revenues:** | | |
| Service Revenue | | $ 17,500 |
| **Expenses:** | | |
| Salaries Expense | $ 4,800 | |
| Rent Expense | 3,000 | |
| Supplies Expense | 400 | |
| Depreciation Expense—Furniture | 300 | |
| Depreciation Expense—Building | 250 | |
| Utilities Expense | 100 | |
| Interest Expense | 100 | |
| Total Expenses | | 8,950 |
| Net Income | | $ 8,550 |

1

**SMART TOUCH LEARNING**
Statement of Retained Earnings
Two Months Ended December 31, 2016

| | |
|---|---|
| Retained Earnings, November 1, 2016 | $ 0 |
| Net income for the two months | 8,550 |
| | 8,550 |
| Dividends | (5,000) |
| Retained Earnings, December 31, 2016 | $ 3,550 |

2

**SMART TOUCH LEARNING**
Balance Sheet
December 31, 2016

| **Assets** | | | **Liabilities** | |
|---|---|---|---|---|
| Cash | | $ 12,200 | Accounts Payable | $ 200 |
| Accounts Receivable | | 1,800 | Utilities Payable | 100 |
| Office Supplies | | 100 | Salaries Payable | 1,200 |
| Prepaid Rent | | 2,000 | Interest Payable | 100 |
| Furniture | $ 18,000 | | Unearned Revenue | 400 |
| Less: Acc. Depr.—Furniture | (300) | 17,700 | Notes Payable | 60,000 |
| Building | 60,000 | | Total Liabilities | 62,000 |
| Less: Acc. Depr.—Building | (250) | 59,750 | | |
| Land | | 20,000 | **Stockholders' Equity** | |
| | | | Common Stock | 48,000 |
| | | | Retained Earnings | 3,550 |
| | | | Total Stockholders' Equity | 51,550 |
| Total Assets | | $ 113,550 | Total Liabilities and Stockholders' Equity | $ 113,550 |

to the balance sheet. Note that these are the three main financial statements you learned about in the first chapter. They are always prepared in the order described previously: income statement, then statement of retained earnings, and then balance sheet.

## Classified Balance Sheet

**Classified Balance Sheet**
A balance sheet that places each asset and each liability into a specific category.

**Liquidity**
A measure of how quickly an item can be converted to cash.

So far we have presented the *unclassified* balance sheet of Smart Touch Learning. We are now ready for the balance sheet that is actually used in practice—called a **classified balance sheet**. In a classified balance sheet, each asset and each liability are placed into a specific category or classification.

In a classified balance sheet, assets are shown in order of liquidity and liabilities are classified as either *current* (within one year) or *long-term* (more than one year). **Liquidity** measures how quickly and easily an account can be converted to cash (because cash is the most liquid asset). Accounts Receivable are relatively liquid because receivables are collected quickly. Office Supplies are less liquid, and Furniture and Buildings are even less so because they take longer to convert to cash or to be used up.

## Assets

The balance sheet lists assets in order of liquidity. A classified balance sheet reports two asset categories: *current assets* and *long-term assets.*

**Current assets** will be converted to cash, sold, or used up during the next 12 months or within the business's operating cycle if the cycle is longer than a year. The **operating cycle** is the time span when

1. Cash is used to acquire goods and services.
2. These goods and services are sold to customers.
3. The business collects cash from customers.

For most businesses, the operating cycle is a few months. Cash, Accounts Receivable, Office Supplies, and Prepaid Expenses are examples of current assets.

**Long-term assets** are all the assets that will not be converted to cash or used up within the business's operating cycle or one year, whichever is greater. Long-term assets are typically made up of three categories: long-term investments, plant assets, and intangible assets.

**Long-Term Investments** Notes Receivable and other investments that are held long-term are considered **long-term investments** and include investments in bonds or stocks in which the company intends to hold for longer than one year.

**Plant Assets** Another category of long-term assets is **plant assets** (also called *fixed assets* or *property, plant, and equipment*). Land, Buildings, Furniture, and Equipment used in operations are plant assets. Plant assets are also presented in order of liquidity, with assets such as Furniture and Equipment being presented first and Land presented last.

**Intangible Assets** Assets with no physical form are **intangible assets**. Examples of intangible assets include Patents, Copyrights, and Trademarks. Intangible assets are long-term assets that convey special rights, such as the exclusive right to produce or sell an invention (patent) or book (copyright) or the symbol or image of a distinctive brand (trademark).

## Liabilities

The balance sheet lists liabilities in the order in which they must be paid. The two liability categories reported on the balance sheet are *current liabilities* and *long-term liabilities.*

**Current liabilities** must be paid either with cash or with goods and services within one year or within the entity's operating cycle if the cycle is longer than a year. Accounts Payable, Notes Payable due within one year, Salaries Payable, Interest Payable, and Unearned Revenue are all current liabilities. Any portion of a long-term liability that is due within the next year is also reported as a current liability. Current liabilities are listed in the order that they are due.

**Long-term liabilities** are all liabilities that do not need to be paid within one year or within the entity's operating cycle, whichever is longer. Many Notes Payable are long-term, such as a mortgage on a building.

## Stockholders' Equity

Stockholders' equity represents the stockholders' claims to the assets of the business. The stockholders' equity section reported on the balance sheet is in part transferred from the ending Retained Earnings balance on the statement of retained earnings. The equity balance also reflects the stockholders' contributions through common stock. It represents the amount of assets that is left over after the corporation has paid its liabilities.

**Current Asset**
An asset that is expected to be converted to cash, sold, or used up during the next 12 months or within the business's normal operating cycle if the cycle is longer than a year.

**Operating Cycle**
The time span during which cash is paid for goods and services, which are then sold to customers from whom the business collects cash.

**Long-Term Asset**
An asset that will not be converted to cash or used up within the business's operating cycle or one year, whichever is greater.

**Long-Term Investment**
Investments in bonds (debt securities) or stocks (equity securities) in which the company intends to hold the investment for longer than one year.

**Plant Asset**
Long-lived, tangible asset, such as land, buildings, and equipment, used in the operation of a business.

**Intangible Asset**
An asset with no physical form that is valuable because of the special rights it carries.

**Current Liability**
A liability that must be paid with cash or with goods and services within one year or within the entity's operating cycle if the cycle is longer than a year.

**Long-Term Liability**
A liability that does not need to be paid within one year or within the entity's operating cycle, whichever is longer.

Exhibit 4-3 presents Smart Touch Learning's classified balance sheet. Notice that the company classifies each asset and each liability as either current or long-term, and that the total assets of $113,550 is the same as the total assets on the unclassified balance sheet in Exhibit 4-2.

Compare the balance sheet in Exhibit 4-3 with the balance sheet in Exhibit 4-2. You'll notice two differences. Exhibit 4-3 is a classified balance sheet, but it is also in a different format than Exhibit 4-2. The balance sheet in Exhibit 4-3 is being presented in the *report form*, which lists the assets at the top and liabilities and stockholders' equity below. Smart Touch Learning's balance sheet in Exhibit 4-2 lists the assets on the left and the liabilities and the stockholders' equity on the right in an arrangement known as the *account form*. Although either form is acceptable, the *report form* is more popular.

**Exhibit 4-3 | Classified Balance Sheet**

This classified balance sheet only includes two asset categories: Current Assets and Plant Assets. Other categories that could be included in a company's asset section are Long-Term Investments and Intangible Assets.

| SMART TOUCH LEARNING<br>Balance Sheet<br>December 31, 2016 | | | |
|---|---|---|---|
| **Assets** | | | |
| Current Assets: | | | |
| Cash | | $ 12,200 | |
| Accounts Receivable | | 1,800 | |
| Office Supplies | | 100 | |
| Prepaid Rent | | 2,000 | |
| Total Current Assets | | | $ 16,100 |
| Plant Assets: | | | |
| Furniture | $ 18,000 | | |
| Less: Accumulated Depreciation—Furniture | (300) | 17,700 | |
| Building | 60,000 | | |
| Less: Accumulated Depreciation—Building | (250) | 59,750 | |
| Land | | 20,000 | |
| Total Plant Assets | | | 97,450 |
| Total Assets | | | **$ 113,550** |
| **Liabilities** | | | |
| Current Liabilities: | | | |
| Accounts Payable | | $ 200 | |
| Utilities Payable | | 100 | |
| Salaries Payable | | 1,200 | |
| Interest Payable | | 100 | |
| Unearned Revenue | | 400 | |
| Total Current Liabilities | | | $ 2,000 |
| Long-term Liabilities: | | | |
| Notes Payable | | | 60,000 |
| Total Liabilities | | | 62,000 |
| **Stockholders' Equity** | | | |
| Common Stock | | 48,000 | |
| Retained Earnings | | 3,550 | |
| Total Stockholders' Equity | | | 51,550 |
| Total Liabilities and Stockholders' Equity | | | **$ 113,550** |

## Try It!

For each account listed, identify the category in which it would appear on a classified balance sheet.

1. Patents
2. Mortgage Payable (due in five years)
3. Land
4. Office Supplies
5. Unearned Revenue
6. Investments in stock of another company held long-term
7. Accumulated Depreciation—Furniture

**Check your answers online in MyAccountingLab or at http://www.pearsonhighered.com/Horngren.**

For more practice, see Short Exercises S4-1 through S4-5. MyAccountingLab

# HOW COULD A WORKSHEET HELP IN PREPARING FINANCIAL STATEMENTS?

**Learning Objective 2**
Use the worksheet to prepare financial statements

Previously you learned how a worksheet can be used to help prepare adjusting entries. Now you'll learn how the worksheet can be used to help in the preparation of financial statements. Exhibit 4-4 (on the next page) shows the completed worksheet for Smart Touch Learning. Sections 1 through 4 of the worksheet, shown with a purple background, were completed in Chapter 3. You are now ready to complete the remaining sections that will help in preparing the financial statements.

## Section 5—Income Statement

The income statement section includes only revenue and expense accounts. The revenues and expenses from the adjusted trial balance section will be transferred into the appropriate column in the income statement section. For example, the $17,500 credit balance for Service Revenue in the adjusted trial balance section will be carried over into the credit column in the income statement section. Each debit and credit column will then be totaled.

## Section 6—Balance Sheet

The balance sheet section includes the asset and liability accounts and all equity accounts except revenues and expenses. The balance of each of these accounts will be transferred from the adjusted trial balance section of the worksheet to the appropriate column in the balance sheet section. For example, Accumulated Depreciation—Furniture, a contra-asset, has a $300 credit balance in the adjusted trial balance section. This amount will be reported as a credit of $300 in the balance sheet section. Each debit and credit column will then be totaled.

## Section 7—Determine Net Income or Net Loss

Compute net income or net loss as total revenues minus total expenses ($17,500 − $8,950). Enter net income (loss) as the balancing amount in the income statement and balance sheet sections. If net income exists, the balance will be entered in the *debit* column of the

**Exhibit 4-4** | **Completed Worksheet**

| | A | B | C | D | E | F | G | H | I | J | K | L | M |
|---|---|---|---|---|---|---|---|---|---|---|---|---|---|
| 1 | | | | | | SMART TOUCH LEARNING | | | | | | | |
| 2 | | | | | | Worksheet | | | | | | | |
| 3 | | | | | | December 31, 2016 | | | | | | | |
| 4 | | | | | | | | | | | | | |
| 5 | **Account Names** | **Unadjusted Trial Balance** | | | **Adjustments** | | | **Adjusted Trial Balance** | | **Income Statement** | | **Balance Sheet** | |
| 6 | | **Debit** | **Credit** | | **Debit** | **Credit** | | **Debit** | **Credit** | **Debit** | **Credit** | **Debit** | **Credit** |
| 7 | Cash | $ 12,200 | | | | | | $ 12,200 | | | | $ 12,200 | |
| 8 | Accounts Receivable | 1,000 | | (h) | $ 800 | | | 1,800 | | | | 1,800 | |
| 9 | Office Supplies | 500 | | | | $ 400 | (b) | 100 | | | | 100 | |
| 10 | Prepaid Rent | 3,000 | | | | 1,000 | (a) | 2,000 | | | | 2,000 | |
| 11 | Furniture | 18,000 | | | | | | 18,000 | | | | 18,000 | |
| 12 | Accumulated Depreciation—Furniture | | | | | 300 | (c) | | $ 300 | | | | $ 300 |
| 13 | Building | 60,000 | | | | | | 60,000 | | | | 60,000 | |
| 14 | Accumulated Depreciation—Building | | | | | 250 | (d) | | 250 | | | | 250 |
| 15 | Land | 20,000 | | | | | | 20,000 | | | | 20,000 | |
| 16 | Accounts Payable | | $ 200 | | | | | | 200 | | | | 200 |
| 17 | Utilities Payable | | 100 | | | | | | 100 | | | | 100 |
| 18 | Salaries Payable | | | | | 1,200 | (f) | | 1,200 | | | | 1,200 |
| 19 | Interest Payable | | | | | 100 | (g) | | 100 | | | | 100 |
| 20 | Unearned Revenue | | 600 | (e) | 200 | | | | 400 | | | | 400 |
| 21 | Notes Payable | | 60,000 | | | | | | 60,000 | | | | 60,000 |
| 22 | Common Stock | | 48,000 | | | | | | 48,000 | | | | 48,000 |
| 23 | Dividends | 5,000 | | | | | | 5,000 | | | | 5,000 | |
| 24 | Service Revenue | | 16,500 | | | 1,000 | (e,h) | | 17,500 | | $ 17,500 | | |
| 25 | Rent Expense | 2,000 | | (a) | 1,000 | | | 3,000 | | $ 3,000 | | | |
| 26 | Salaries Expense | 3,600 | | (f) | 1,200 | | | 4,800 | | 4,800 | | | |
| 27 | Supplies Expense | | | (b) | 400 | | | 400 | | 400 | | | |
| 28 | Utilities Expense | 100 | | | | | | 100 | | 100 | | | |
| 29 | Depreciation Expense—Furniture | | | (c) | 300 | | | 300 | | 300 | | | |
| 30 | Depreciation Expense—Building | | | (d) | 250 | | | 250 | | 250 | | | |
| 31 | Interest Expense | | | (g) | 100 | | | 100 | | 100 | | | |
| 32 | **Total** | **$ 125,400** | **$ 125,400** | | **$ 4,250** | **$ 4,250** | | **$ 128,050** | **$ 128,050** | $ 8,950 | $ 17,500 | $ 119,100 | $ 110,550 |
| 33 | | | | | | | | | Net Income | 8,550 | | | 8,550 |
| 34 | **Total** | | | | | | | | | **$ 17,500** | **$ 17,500** | **$ 119,100** | **$ 119,100** |
| 35 | | | | | | | | | | | | | |

Section 5 (columns J–K); Section 6 (columns L–M); Section 7 (rows 33–34); Sections 1–4 (columns A–I)

Net Income = $17,500 − $8,950

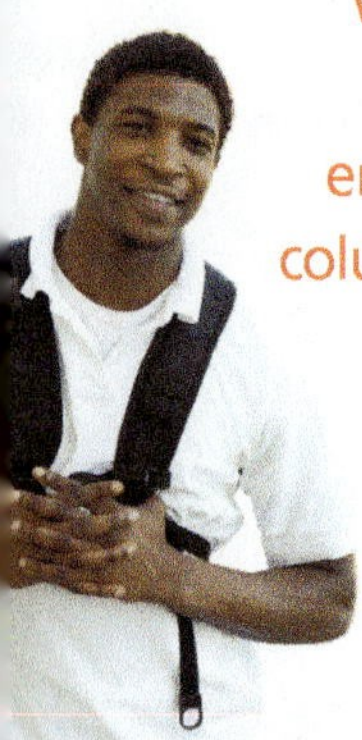

What if Smart Touch Learning had a net loss instead of net income? Would the amount of net loss be entered in the debit column of the income statement section and the credit column of the balance sheet section?

income statement section and the *credit* column of the balance sheet section. For example, Smart Touch Learning has net income of $8,550. This amount should be entered as a debit in the income statement section and a credit in the balance sheet section.

**If expenses exceed revenues, the result is a net loss. In that event, print Net Loss on the worksheet next to the result. The net loss amount should be entered in the *credit* column of the income statement (to balance out) and in the *debit* column of the balance sheet (to balance out).** The main thing to remember is that the net income or net loss is the balancing amount on the worksheet. It should always be entered on the side that makes the debit and credit columns balance.

Smart Touch Learning has now completed the worksheet as of December 31. Remember that the worksheet is an internal tool that can be used to help in recording adjusting entries and preparing financial statements. The adjusting entries still need to be recorded in the journal and posted to the ledger (as shown in Chapter 3), and the financial statements must still be prepared (as shown in Exhibits 4-2 and 4-3).

**Try It!**

For each account listed, identify whether the account would appear in either the income statement section or the balance sheet section of the worksheet. Assuming normal balances, identify if the account would be recorded in the debit (DR) or credit (CR) column.

8. Service Revenue
9. Accounts Payable
10. Cash
11. Depreciation Expense—Building
12. Dividends
13. Accumulated Depreciation—Building

**Check your answers online in MyAccountingLab or at http://www.pearsonhighered.com/Horngren.**

For more practice, see Short Exercises S4-6 through S4-8. MyAccountingLab

## WHAT IS THE CLOSING PROCESS, AND HOW DO WE CLOSE THE ACCOUNTS?

**Learning Objective 3**
Explain the purpose of, journalize, and post closing entries

At the end of the accounting cycle, after the financial statements have been prepared, Smart Touch Learning is ready to close the books. Often referred to as the closing process, this consists of journalizing and posting the closing entries in order to get the accounts ready for the next period. The **closing process** zeroes out all revenue accounts and all expense accounts in order to measure each period's net income separately from all other periods. It also updates the Retained Earnings account balance for net income or loss during the period and any dividends paid to the stockholders. The closing process prepares the accounts for the next time period by setting the balances of revenues, expenses, and dividends to zero. By completing the closing process, the business is following the time period concept in that it is slicing its activities into small time segments and preparing financial statements for only those specific periods.

**Closing Process**
A step in the accounting cycle that occurs at the end of the period. The closing process consists of journalizing and posting the closing entries to set the balances of the revenues, expenses, Income Summary, and Dividends accounts to zero for the next period.

Recall that the income statement reports net income for a specific period. For example, Smart Touch Learning's net income for the two months ended December 31, 2016, relates exclusively to November and December, 2016. At December 31, 2016, Smart Touch Learning closes its revenue and expense accounts for the last two months of the year. For this reason, revenues and expenses are called **temporary accounts** (also known as *nominal accounts*). For example, Smart Touch Learning's balance of Service Revenue at December 31, 2016, is $17,500. This balance relates exclusively to the last two months of 2016 and must be zeroed out before the company records revenue for the next year. Similarly, the various expense account balances are for the last two months of 2016 only and must also be zeroed out at the end of the year.

**Temporary Account**
An account that relates to a particular accounting period and is closed at the end of that period—the revenues, expenses, Income Summary, and Dividends accounts.

The Dividends account is also temporary and must be closed at the end of the period because it measures the payments to stockholders for only that one period. All temporary accounts (revenues, expenses, and dividends) are closed (zeroed). The balances of temporary accounts do not carry forward into the next time period. Instead, the business starts the new time period with a zero beginning balance in the temporary accounts.

**Permanent Account**
An account that is *not* closed at the end of the period—the asset, liability, Common Stock, and Retained Earnings accounts.

**Closing Entries**
Entries that transfer the revenues, expenses, and Dividends balances to the Retained Earnings account to prepare the company's books for the next period.

**Income Summary**
A temporary account into which revenues and expenses are transferred prior to their final transfer into the Retained Earnings account. Summarizes net income (or net loss) for the period.

By contrast, the **permanent accounts** (also known as *real accounts*)—the assets, liabilities, Common Stock, and Retained Earnings—are not closed at the end of the period. Permanent account balances are carried forward into the next time period. All accounts on the balance sheet are permanent accounts.

**Closing entries** transfer the revenues, expenses, and Dividends balances to the Retained Earnings account to prepare the company's books for the next period. This transfer to Retained Earnings also causes the Retained Earnings ledger account to now equal its balance reported on the Balance Sheet.

As an intermediate step, the revenues and the expenses may be transferred first to an account titled **Income Summary**. The Income Summary account *summarizes* the net income (or net loss) for the period by collecting the sum of all the expenses (a debit) and the sum of all the revenues (a credit). The Income Summary account is like a temporary "holding tank" that shows the amount of net income or net loss of the current period. Its ending balance—net income or net loss—is then transferred (closed) to the Retained Earnings account (the final account in the closing process). Exhibit 4-5 summarizes the closing process.

**Exhibit 4-5 | The Closing Process**

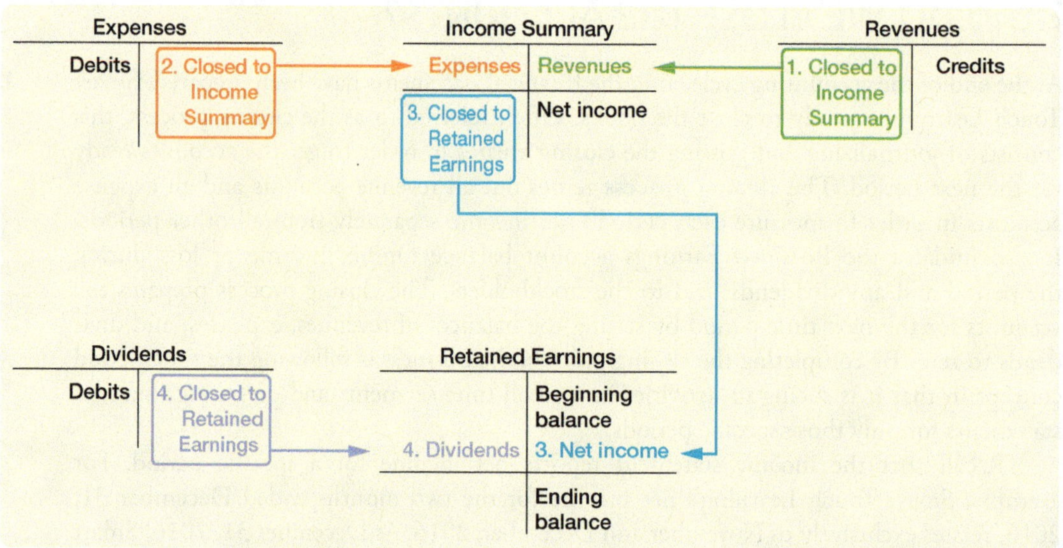


*When thinking about which accounts to close, consider your grades in this class as an example. If you made a failing grade on an exam in this class, would you want your exam grade for this class to carry forward to your next accounting class? Your answer would probably be no, because your exam grade in this class does not necessarily represent your knowledge in your next class. In this example, your exam grades are temporary and should not carry forward to your next accounting class. In the same sense, a business's revenues, expenses, and dividends for a specific time period should not be carried forward to the next time period because doing so does not accurately reflect that future period.*

## DECISIONS

### Why should a business close its books?

Dream Builder is a business that specializes in building custom homes, remodeling existing homes, and creating backyard paradises. Dream Builders has just completed its first year of business, and Shane Wilson, owner and manager, has been very pleased with the first year of operations. The business is growing and even earned a profit. Shane has just met with the company's accountant, Felicia Turner, to go over the books for the year and to get ready for next year. Felicia has told him that he will need to close the books for the current year before he can begin recording transactions for next year. Shane is very confused. He doesn't understand and tells Felicia, "I'm not planning on closing our business. It's doing great. Why would I need to close the books?" What should Felicia tell Shane?

#### Solution

Many new businesses don't realize that they have to close their books each year. Felicia should explain to Shane that closing the books does not imply that the business is closing. Instead, it simply closes the books for the year that has just been completed and prepares the books for a new year. Felicia should explain to Shane that the process of closing the books updates the Retained Earnings account for the net income and any dividends during the year. It allows the business to allocate net income to a specific time period (following the time period concept) and begin the new year with zero balances in all temporary accounts (revenues, expenses, Income Summary, and Dividends).

## Closing Temporary Accounts—Net Income for the Period

As stated previously, all temporary accounts are closed (zeroed out) during the closing process. Revenue, expenses, and dividends accounts are not permanent. Only the balance sheet accounts are permanent. The four steps in closing the books follow (and are illustrated in Exhibit 4-6).

**Step 1:** Make the revenue accounts equal zero via the Income Summary account. This closing entry transfers total revenues to the *credit* side of the Income Summary account.

For example, Smart Touch Learning has a $17,500 credit balance in Service Revenue. To close this account (make it zero), we *debit* Service Revenue and *credit* Income Summary.

**Service Revenue**

| | | | |
|---|---|---|---|
| | | 17,500 | Adj. Bal. |
| Clos. 1 | 17,500 | | |
| | | 0 | Bal. |

**Income Summary**

| | | | |
|---|---|---|---|
| | | 17,500 | Clos. 1 |

| Date | Accounts and Explanation | Debit | Credit |
|---|---|---|---|
| Dec. 31 | Service Revenue | 17,500 | |
| | Income Summary | | 17,500 |
| | *To close revenue.* | | |

A = L + E↑↓
Service Revenue↓
Income Summary↑

**Step 2:** Make expense accounts equal zero via the Income Summary account. This closing entry transfers total expenses to the *debit* side of the Income Summary account.

As an example, we will review the Rent Expense account for Smart Touch Learning, which has a $3,000 debit balance. This account will be closed with a *credit* to Rent Expense.

**Rent Expense**

| | | | |
|---|---|---|---|
| Adj. Bal. | 3,000 | | |
| | | 3,000 | Clos. 2 |
| Bal. | 0 | | |

Smart Touch Learning will close all expense accounts in the same manner. This will most likely be done with a compound closing entry. Each individual expense account will be *credited* and the Income Summary account will be *debited* for the total amount of expenses.

| A | = | L | + | E↑↓ |
|---|---|---|---|---|
| | | | | Income Summary↓ Expenses↓ |

| Date | Accounts and Explanation | Debit | Credit |
|---|---|---|---|
| Dec. 31 | Income Summary | 8,950 | |
| | Rent Expense | | 3,000 |
| | Salaries Expense | | 4,800 |
| | Supplies Expense | | 400 |
| | Utilities Expense | | 100 |
| | Depreciation Expense—Furniture | | 300 |
| | Depreciation Expense—Building | | 250 |
| | Interest Expense | | 100 |
| | *To close expenses.* | | |

The Income Summary account now holds the net income of $8,550 for the period. The Income Summary T-account after closing revenues and expenses is:

**Income Summary**

| | | | |
|---|---|---|---|
| Clos. 2 | 8,950 | 17,500 | Clos. 1 |
| | | 8,550 | Bal. |

**Step 3:** Make the Income Summary account equal zero via the Retained Earnings account. This closing entry transfers net income (or net loss) to the Retained Earnings account.

Smart Touch Learning has an $8,550 credit balance in the Income Summary account. This represents net income for the period. Net income will now be transferred to the Retained Earnings account. We will *debit* Income Summary and *credit* Retained Earnings. Notice that this closing entry, in effect, increases the Retained Earnings account for the net income of the period.

**Income Summary**

| | | | |
|---|---|---|---|
| Clos. 2 | 8,950 | 17,500 | Clos. 1 |
| | | 8,550 | Bal. (Net Income) |
| Clos. 3 | 8,550 | | |
| | | 0 | Bal. |

**Retained Earnings**

| | | | |
|---|---|---|---|
| | | 0 | Adj. Bal. |
| | | 8,550 | Clos. 3 |

| A | = | L | + | E↑↓ |
|---|---|---|---|---|
| | | | | Income Summary↓ Retained Earnings↑ |

| Date | Accounts and Explanation | Debit | Credit |
|---|---|---|---|
| Dec. 31 | Income Summary | 8,550 | |
| | Retained Earnings | | 8,550 |
| | *To close Income Summary.* | | |

**Step 4:** Make the Dividends account equal zero via the Retained Earnings account. This entry transfers the dividends to the *debit* side of the Retained Earnings account.

Smart Touch Learning has a $5,000 debit balance in the Dividends account. This account will be closed with a *debit* to Retained Earnings and a *credit* to Dividends.

**Retained Earnings**

| | | | |
|---|---|---|---|
| | | 0 | Adj. Bal. |
| Clos. 4 | 5,000 | 8,550 | Clos. 3 |
| | | 3,550 | Bal. |

**Dividends**

| | | | |
|---|---|---|---|
| Adj. Bal. | 5,000 | | |
| | | 5,000 | Clos. 4 |
| Bal. | 0 | | |

| Date | Accounts and Explanation | Debit | Credit |
|---|---|---|---|
| Dec. 31 | Retained Earnings | 5,000 | |
| | Dividends | | 5,000 |
| | *To close Dividends.* | | |

A = L + E↑↓
Retained Earnings↓
Dividends↓

## Closing Temporary Accounts—Net Loss for the Period

**If a business had a net loss for the period, closing entries 1, 2, and 4 would be similar to those completed for net income. However, the closing entry to close the Income Summary account would be different.** Consider this example. Suppose a business had a net loss of $2,000. The Income Summary T-account would hold a *debit* balance instead of a *credit* balance. Therefore, the closing entry to close Income Summary would be a *debit* to Retained Earnings and a *credit* to Income Summary.

What if a business had a net loss for the period? Would the closing entries be the same?

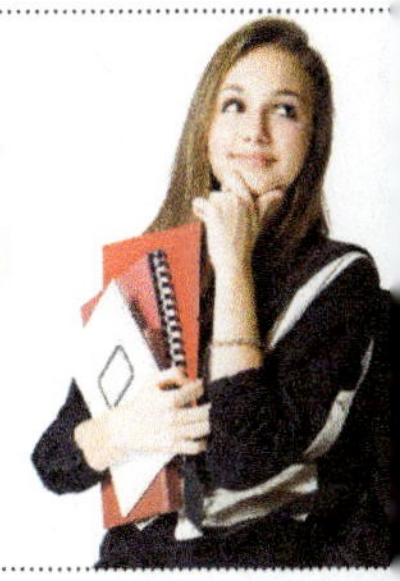

**Income Summary**

| | | | |
|---|---|---|---|
| Clos. 2 | 5,000 | 3,000 | Clos. 1 |
| Bal. | 2,000 | | |
| | | 2,000 | Clos. 3 |
| | | 0 | Bal. |

Net Loss

**Retained Earnings**

| | | | |
|---|---|---|---|
| Clos. 3 | 2,000 | 0 | Adj. Bal. |

| Date | Accounts and Explanation | Debit | Credit |
|---|---|---|---|
| Dec. 31 | Retained Earnings | 2,000 | |
| | Income Summary | | 2,000 |
| | *To close Income Summary.* | | |

A = L + E↑↓
Retained Earnings↓
Income Summary↑

Notice that the effect of this closing entry decreases Retained Earnings. This is because a net loss decreases the Retained Earnings account.

Exhibit 4-6 (on the next page) shows the complete closing process for Smart Touch Learning. Panel A gives the closing entries, and Panel B shows the accounts after posting. After the closing entries, Retained Earnings ends with a balance of $3,550. Trace this balance to the statement of retained earnings and then to the balance sheet in Exhibit 4-2.

## Exhibit 4-6 | Journalizing and Posting Closing Entries

**Panel A: Journalizing**

| Date | Accounts and Explanation | Debit | Credit |
|---|---|---|---|
| Dec. 31 | Service Revenue | 17,500 | |
| | Income Summary | | 17,500 |
| | *To close revenue.* | | |
| 31 | Income Summary | 8,950 | |
| | Rent Expense | | 3,000 |
| | Salaries Expense | | 4,800 |
| | Supplies Expense | | 400 |
| | Utilities Expense | | 100 |
| | Depreciation Expense—Furniture | | 300 |
| | Depreciation Expense—Building | | 250 |
| | Interest Expense | | 100 |
| | *To close expenses.* | | |
| 31 | Income Summary | 8,550 | |
| | Retained Earnings | | 8,550 |
| | *To close Income Summary.* | | |
| 31 | Retained Earnings | 5,000 | |
| | Dividends | | 5,000 |
| | *To close Dividends.* | | |

*When a business uses a computerized accounting system, the software automatically closes the books. The software identifies the temporary accounts, records the closing entries, and posts to the ledger accounts. The closing entries are completed in a matter of seconds.*

**Panel B: Posting**

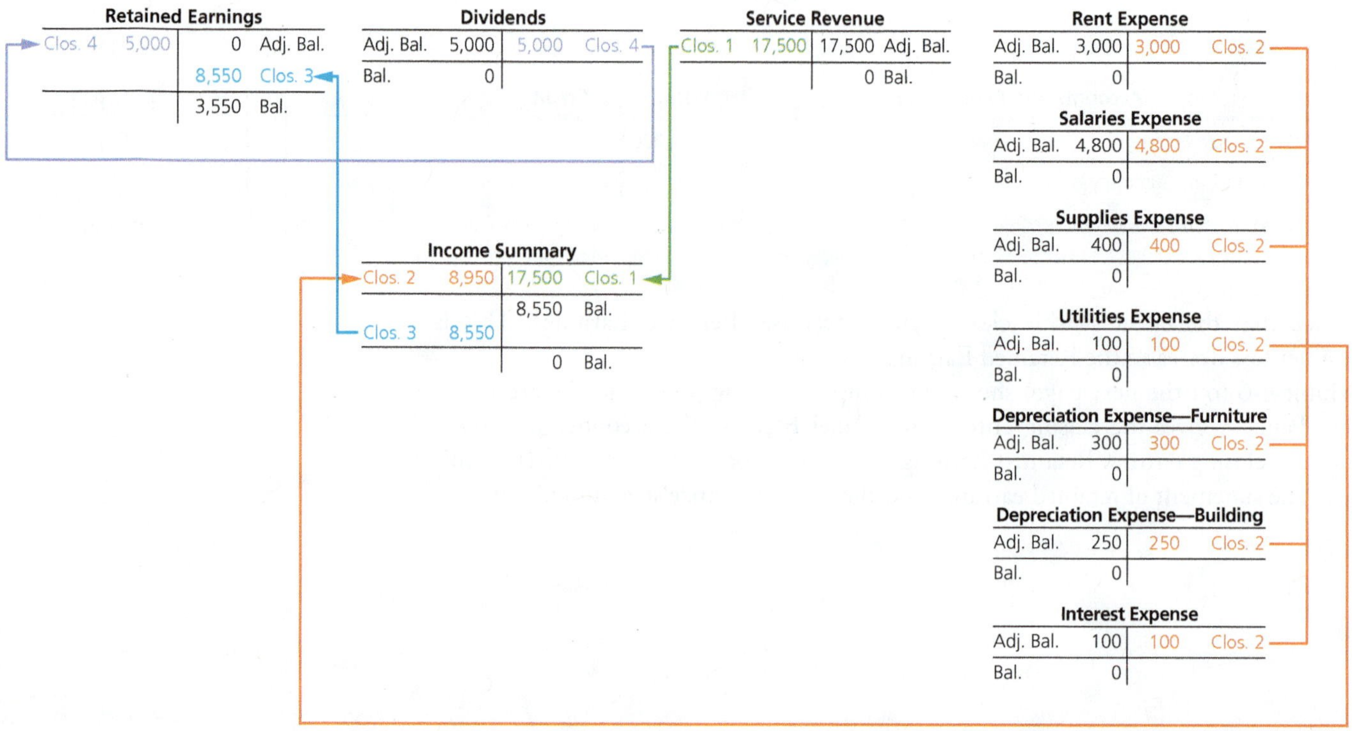

## Try It!

Benson Auto Repair had the following account balances after adjustments. Assume all accounts had normal balances.

| | | | |
|---|---|---|---|
| Cash | $ 4,000 | Common Stock | $ 20,000 |
| Accounts Receivable | 3,200 | Retained Earnings | 15,700 |
| Prepaid Rent | 1,900 | Dividends | 2,100 |
| Office Supplies | 3,000 | Service Revenue | 1,600 |
| Equipment | 34,800 | Depreciation Expense—Equipment | 300 |
| Accumulated Depreciation—Equipment | 1,600 | Salaries Expense | 800 |
| Accounts Payable | 5,400 | Rent Expense | 500 |
| Notes Payable (long-term) | 7,000 | Utilities Expense | 600 |
| | | Supplies Expense | 100 |

**14.** Prepare the closing entries for Benson at December 31.

**15.** What is the balance of Retained Earnings after closing entries have been recorded? (Use a T-account to determine the balance.)

**Check your answers online in MyAccountingLab or at http://www.pearsonhighered.com/Horngren.**

For more practice, see Short Exercises S4-9 and S4-10. MyAccountingLab

## HOW DO WE PREPARE A POST-CLOSING TRIAL BALANCE?

**Learning Objective 4**
Prepare the post-closing trial balance

After closing entries are recorded and posted, the accounting cycle ends with a **post-closing trial balance** (see Exhibit 4-7 on the next page). This step lists the accounts and their balances after closing.

Only assets, liabilities, Common Stock, and Retained Earnings accounts (permanent accounts) appear on the post-closing trial balance. No temporary accounts—revenues, expenses, Income Summary, or Dividends—are included because they have been closed (their balances are zero). Also notice that the Retained Earnings account has been updated to reflect the period's net income (or net loss) and any dividends. The ledger is now up to date and ready for the next period.

**Post-Closing Trial Balance**
A list of the accounts and their balances at the end of the period after journalizing and posting the closing entries. It should include only permanent accounts.

*Notice that the Adjusted Trial Balance for Smart Touch Learning (Exhibit 4-1) and the Post-Closing Trial Balance (Exhibit 4-7) are similar. An easy way to make sure that you didn't make an error in the closing process is to compare the Adjusted Trial Balance to the Post-Closing Trial Balance to ensure that: (1) account balances above Retained Earnings are the same; (2) account balances below Retained Earnings are zero and, therefore, not included; and (3) the Retained Earnings account balance matches Retained Earnings on the balance sheet.*

**Exhibit 4-7** | **Post-Closing Trial Balance**

**SMART TOUCH LEARNING**
Post-Closing Trial Balance
December 31, 2016

| | Balance | |
|---|---|---|
| **Account Title** | **Debit** | **Credit** |
| Cash | $ 12,200 | |
| Accounts Receivable | 1,800 | |
| Office Supplies | 100 | |
| Prepaid Rent | 2,000 | |
| Furniture | 18,000 | |
| Accumulated Depreciation—Furniture | | $ 300 |
| Building | 60,000 | |
| Accumulated Depreciation—Building | | 250 |
| Land | 20,000 | |
| Accounts Payable | | 200 |
| Utilities Payable | | 100 |
| Salaries Payable | | 1,200 |
| Interest Payable | | 100 |
| Unearned Revenue | | 400 |
| Notes Payable | | 60,000 |
| Common Stock | | 48,000 |
| Retained Earnings | | 3,550 |
| Total | **$ 114,100** | **$ 114,100** |

Permanent Accounts

## Try It!

For each account listed, identify whether the account would appear on the post-closing trial balance. Indicate either yes or no.

**16.** Dividends
**17.** Service Revenue
**18.** Cash
**19.** Advertising Expense
**20.** Retained Earnings

**Check your answers online in MyAccountingLab or at http://www.pearsonhighered.com/Horngren.**

For more practice, see Short Exercise S4-11. MyAccountingLab

# WHAT IS THE ACCOUNTING CYCLE?

**Learning Objective 5**
Describe the accounting cycle

We have now completed the accounting cycle for Smart Touch Learning. The **accounting cycle** is the process by which companies produce their financial statements for a specific period. It is the steps that are followed throughout the time period. The accounting cycle starts with the beginning asset, liability, and stockholders' equity account balances left over from the preceding period. Exhibit 4-8 outlines the complete accounting cycle of Smart Touch Learning and every other business. Start with Step 1 and move clockwise.

**Accounting Cycle**
The process by which companies produce their financial statements for a specific period.

Accounting takes place at two different times:

- During the period (Steps 1 through 3)—Journalizing transactions and posting to the accounts
- End of the period (Steps 4 through 10)—Adjusting the accounts, preparing the financial statements, and closing the accounts

**Exhibit 4-8 | The Accounting Cycle**

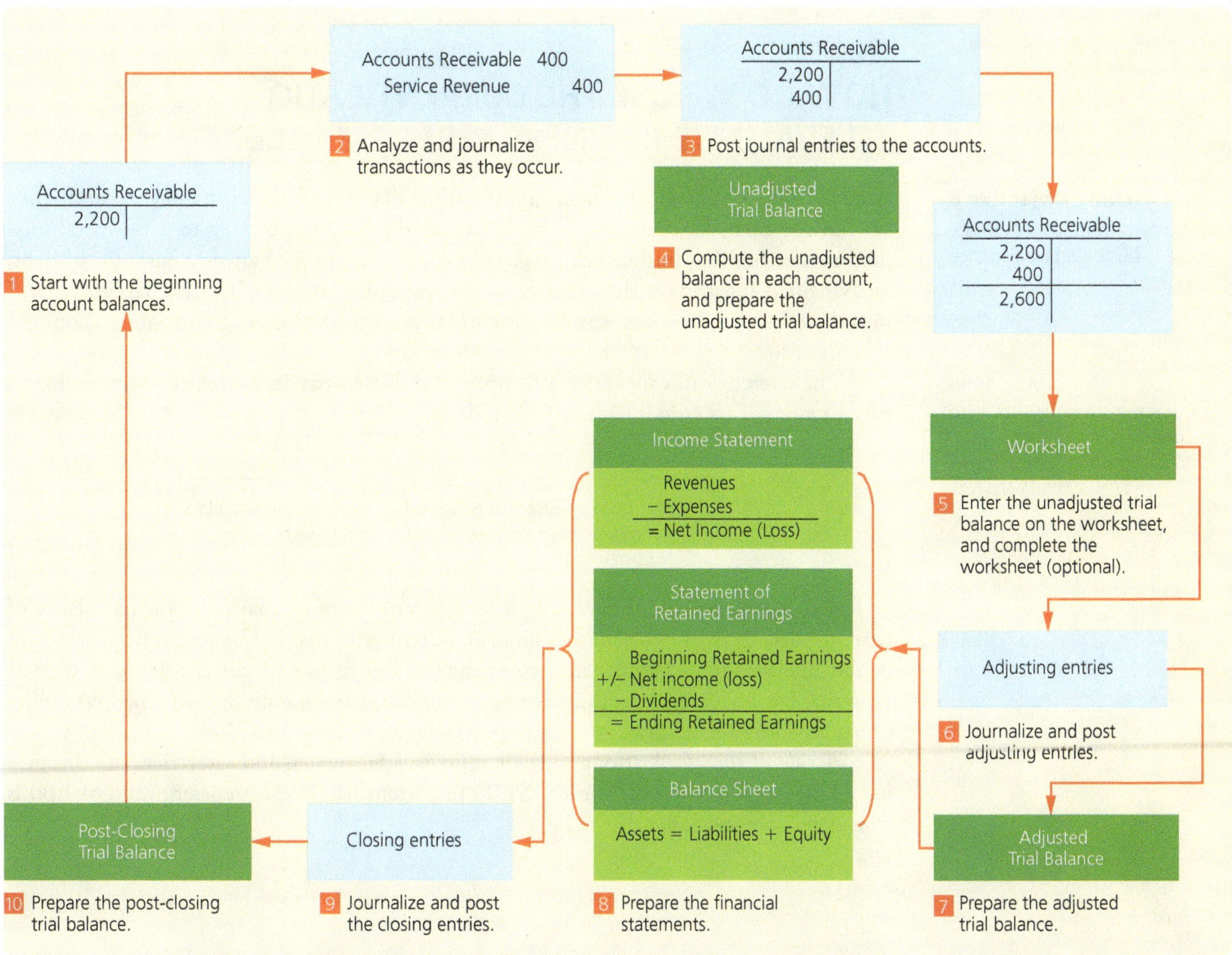

**Try It!**

**21.** The steps of the accounting cycle are presented below. Identify the correct order of the steps.

**a.** Journalize and post the closing entries.
**b.** Start with the beginning account balances.
**c.** Prepare the financial statements.
**d.** Compute the unadjusted balance in each account, and prepare the unadjusted trial balance.
**e.** Journalize and post adjusting entries.
**f.** Enter the unadjusted trial balance on the worksheet, and complete the worksheet (optional).
**g.** Prepare the adjusted trial balance.
**h.** Analyze and journalize transactions as they occur.
**i.** Post journal entries to the accounts.
**j.** Prepare the post-closing trial balance.

**Check your answers online in MyAccountingLab or at http://www.pearsonhighered.com/Horngren.**

For more practice, see Short Exercise S4-12. MyAccountingLab

## HOW DO WE USE THE CURRENT RATIO TO EVALUATE BUSINESS PERFORMANCE?

**Learning Objective 6**
Use the current ratio to evaluate business performance

Accounting is designed to provide information that stockholders, managers, and lenders can use to make decisions. A bank considering lending money to a business must predict whether that business can repay the loan. If a business already has a lot of debt, repayment is less certain than if it does not owe much money. In this chapter, we will introduce another ratio that can be used to measure the business's financial position, the current ratio.

**Current Ratio**
Measures the company's ability to pay current liabilities from current assets. Total current assets / Total current liabilities.

The **current ratio** measures a company's ability to pay its current liabilities with its current assets. This ratio is computed as follows:

Current ratio = Total current assets / Total current liabilities

A company prefers to have a high current ratio because that means it has plenty of current assets to pay its current liabilities. A current ratio that has increased from the prior period indicates improvement in a company's ability to pay its current debts. A current ratio that has decreased from the prior period signals deterioration in the company's ability to pay its current liabilities.

*A rule of thumb:* A strong current ratio is 1.50, which indicates that the business has \$1.50 in current assets for every \$1.00 in current liabilities. A current ratio of 1.00 is considered low and somewhat risky.

Returning to **Green Mountain Coffee Roasters, Inc.** we can now evaluate Green Mountain's current ratio. Green Mountain had the following total current assets and current liabilities, found on the balance sheet located in Appendix A at the back of the book.

| | As of Sep. 28, 2013 | As of Sep. 29, 2012 |
|---|---|---|
| Total current assets (in thousands) | $ 1,521,492 | $ 1,322,956 |
| Total current liabilities (in thousands) | 597,063 | 519,987 |

The current ratio for Green Mountain as of September 28, 2013, follows:

Current ratio = $1,521,492 / $597,063 = 2.55*

*rounded

In comparison, the current ratio as of September 29, 2012, for Green Mountain was:

Current ratio = $1,322,956 / $519,987 = 2.54

The current ratio has increased very little from 2012 to 2013. This indicates that Green Mountain is remaining steady in its ability to pay its current debts. Given that the current ratio is above 1.5 for both years, Green Mountain would be considered a less risky investment than another business with a lower current ratio. Similarly, creditors would be more willing to extend credit to Green Mountain than another company with a lower current ratio.

## ETHICS

### Should revenue be recorded early?

Carnival Custom Painting's controller, Kristi Seay, is hoping to get a loan from a local bank. The business's van engine has just died, and the corporation has no extra cash to replace the engine. It needs a short-term loan of $3,000. A teller at the bank has told Kristi that the bank will only approve the loan if the business has a current ratio that is above 1.2. Currently, Carnival's current ratio is 1.1. The corporation has just received a contract for painting a new commercial building. Kristi has told the teller that she expects revenue of $15,000 from the contract but won't receive payment until the job is completed. The business plans on starting the job next week but won't be finished for another two months, not soon enough to use the cash to replace the engine in the van. The teller has suggested to Kristi that she go ahead and record the revenue and cash receipt of the painting contract even though it hasn't been completed. This, he tells her, will increase the business's current assets and thereby increase the current ratio to 1.4, well above the bank minimum. What should Kristi do? What would you do?

### Solution

Kristi should not record the revenue and cash receipt early. The revenue recognition principle requires that businesses record revenue only when it has been earned. Given that Carnival Custom Painting has not yet started the job, no revenue has been earned. Kristi should look for alternative sources of financing instead of trying to manipulate the current ratio to meet the minimum required by the bank. Another possibility would be for Kristi to renegotiate the contract with the new client to receive $3,000 in advance instead of after the completion of the job. This would allow Kristi to make the repairs on the van and not have to borrow the money from the bank.

## Try It!

**22.** Benson Auto Repair has the following account balances at December 31, 2016, from its adjusted trial balance. Compute Benson's current ratio.

| | | | |
|---|---|---|---|
| Cash | $ 4,000 | Common Stock | $ 20,000 |
| Accounts Receivable | 3,200 | Retained Earnings | 15,700 |
| Prepaid Rent | 1,900 | Dividends | 2,100 |
| Office Supplies | 3,000 | Service Revenue | 1,600 |
| Equipment | 34,800 | Depreciation Expense—Equipment | 300 |
| Accumulated Depreciation—Equipment | 1,600 | Salaries Expense | 800 |
| Accounts Payable | 5,400 | Rent Expense | 500 |
| Notes Payable (long-term) | 7,000 | Utilities Expense | 600 |
| | | Supplies Expense | 100 |

**Check your answer online in MyAccountingLab or at http://www.pearsonhighered.com/Horngren.**

For more practice, see Short Exercise S4-13. MyAccountingLab

# APPENDIX 4A: Reversing Entries: An Optional Step

## WHAT ARE REVERSING ENTRIES?

**Learning Objective 7**
Explain the purpose of, journalize, and post reversing entries

Reversing entries are special journal entries that ease the burden of accounting for transactions in a later period. Reversing entries are the exact opposite of certain adjusting entries. Reversing entries are used in conjunction with accrual-type adjustments, such as accrued salaries expense and accrued service revenue. Generally Accepted Accounting Principles do not require reversing entries. They are used only for convenience and to save time.

### Accounting for Accrued Expenses

To see how reversing entries work, let's return to Smart Touch Learning. In the unadjusted trial balance, Salaries Expense has a debit balance of $3,600 for salaries paid during November and December. At December 31, the business still owes it employees an additional $1,200 for the last half of the month, so the business makes the following adjusting entry:

| A | = | L↑ | + | E↓ |
|---|---|---|---|---|
| | | Salaries Payable↑ | | Salaries Expense↑ |

| Date | Accounts and Explanation | Debit | Credit |
|---|---|---|---|
| Dec. 31 | Salaries Expense | 1,200 | |
| | Salaries Payable | | 1,200 |
| | *To accrue salaries expense.* | | |

After posting, the accounts are updated as of December 31:

**Salaries Payable**

| | | | |
|---|---|---|---|
| | | 1,200 | Adj. |
| | | 1,200 | Adj. Bal. |

**Salaries Expense**

| | | | |
|---|---|---|---|
| Nov. 15 | 1,200 | | |
| Dec. 1 | 1,200 | | |
| Dec. 15 | 1,200 | | |
| Adj. | 1,200 | | |
| Adj. Bal. | 4,800 | | |

After the adjusting entry, the following are noted:

- The income statement reports Salaries Expense of $4,800.
- The balance sheet reports Salaries Payable of $1,200.

The $4,800 debit balance of Salaries Expense is closed at December 31, 2016, with the following closing entry:

| Date | Accounts and Explanation | Debit | Credit |
|---|---|---|---|
| Dec. 31 | Income Summary | 4,800 | |
| | Salaries Expense | | 4,800 |
| | *To close expense.* | | |

| A | = | L | + | E↑↓ |
|---|---|---|---|---|
| | | | | Income Summary↓ Salaries Expense↓ |

After posting the closing entry, Salaries Expense has a zero balance as follows:

**Salaries Expense**

| | | | |
|---|---|---|---|
| Nov. 15 | 1,200 | | |
| Dec. 1 | 1,200 | | |
| Dec. 15 | 1,200 | | |
| Adj. | 1,200 | | |
| Adj. Bal. | 4,800 | | |
| | | 4,800 | Clos. |
| Bal. | 0 | | |

## Accounting Without a Reversing Entry

Assume that Smart Touch Learning will pay its employees the second half of December's salaries along with the first half of January on January 15, 2017. On January 15, the company would record the following journal entry:

| Date | Accounts and Explanation | Debit | Credit |
|---|---|---|---|
| 2017 | | | |
| Jan. 15 | Salaries Payable | 1,200 | |
| | Salaries Expense | 1,200 | |
| | Cash | | 2,400 |
| | *To record payment of salaries.* | | |

| A↓ | = | L↓ | + | E↓ |
|---|---|---|---|---|
| Cash↓ | | Salaries Payable↓ | | Salaries Expense↑ |

After posting the cash payment, the Salaries Payable and Salaries Expense accounts are as follows:

**Salaries Payable**

| | | | |
|---|---|---|---|
| | | 1,200 | Bal. 1/1/17 |
| Jan. 15 | 1,200 | | |
| | | 0 | Bal. |

**Salaries Expense**

| | | |
|---|---|---|
| Jan. 15 | 1,200 | |

This method of recording the cash payment is correct. However, it wastes time because the business must refer back to the December 31 adjustments. Otherwise, the business does not know the amount of the debit to Salaries Payable (in this example $1,200). Searching December's adjusting entries wastes time and money. To save time, accountants can use reversing entries.

## Accounting with a Reversing Entry

**Reversing Entry**
A special journal entry that eases the burden of accounting for transactions in the next period. Such entries are the exact opposite of a prior adjusting entry.

A **reversing entry** switches the debit and the credit of a previous entry. A reversing entry, then, is the exact opposite of a prior adjusting entry. The reversing entry is dated the first day of the new period.

To illustrate reversing entries, recall that on December 31 Smart Touch Learning made the following adjusting entry to accrue Salaries Expense:

A = { L↑ + E↓ : Salaries Payable↑ ; Salaries Expense↑ }

| Date | Accounts and Explanation | Debit | Credit |
|---|---|---|---|
| Dec. 31 | Salaries Expense | 1,200 | |
| | Salaries Payable | | 1,200 |
| | *To accrue salaries expense.* | | |

The reversing entry just reverses the debit and the credit of the adjustment:

A = { L↓ + E↑ : Salaries Payable↓ ; Salaries Expense↓ }

| Date | Accounts and Explanation | Debit | Credit |
|---|---|---|---|
| 2017 | | | |
| Jan. 1 | Salaries Payable | 1,200 | |
| | Salaries Expense | | 1,200 |
| | *To reverse the salaries adjusting entry.* | | |

Observe that the reversing entry is dated the first day of the new period. It is the exact opposite of the adjusting entry. Ordinarily, the accountant who makes the adjusting entries will also prepare reversing entries at the same time. Smart Touch Learning dates the reversing entry as of January 1 so that it affects only the new period. Note how the accounts appear after the accounting clerk posts the reversing entry:

**Salaries Payable**

| | | | |
|---|---|---|---|
| | | 1,200 | Adj. |
| | | 1,200 | Bal. 1/1/17 |
| Rev. Jan. 1 | 1,200 | | |
| | | 0 | Bal. |

**Salaries Expense**

| | | | |
|---|---|---|---|
| Bal. 1/1/17 | 0 | | |
| | | 1,200 | Rev. Jan. 1 |

The arrow between the T-accounts shows the transfer of the $1,200 from Salaries Payable to Salaries Expense. This credit in Salaries Expense does not mean that the entity has negative salaries expense, as you might think. Instead, the odd credit balance in the Salaries Expense account is merely a temporary result of the reversing entry. The credit balance is eliminated on January 15, when Smart Touch Learning pays the payroll and debits Salaries Expense:

| Date | Accounts and Explanation | Debit | Credit |
|---|---|---|---|
| Jan. 15 | Salaries Expense | 2,400 | |
| | Cash | | 2,400 |
| | *To record payment of salaries.* | | |

A↓ = L + E↓

Cash↓ = Salaries Expense↑

This payment is posted to the Salaries Expense account as follows:

**Salaries Expense**

| Debit | | Credit | |
|---|---|---|---|
| Bal. 1/1/17 | 0 | | |
| Jan. 15 | 2,400 | 1,200 | Rev. Jan. 1 |
| Bal. | 1,200 | | |

Now Salaries Expense has a debit balance of $1,200, which is correct and represents only the January salaries. The payment of salaries covered two periods: $1,200 related to 2016 and $1,200 related to 2017. The Salaries Expense account should only contain the amount that relates to 2017.

## Try It!

Winters Landscape Services accrued $4,000 of Salaries Expense at December 31. Winters paid the next payroll at January 10 of $6,000. This payment included the accrued amount at December 31, plus $2,000 for the first few days of January.

**23A.** Record the adjusting entry to accrue Salaries Expense.
**24A.** Record the reversing entry.
**25A.** Journalize the cash payment.

**Check your answers online in MyAccountingLab or at http://www.pearsonhighered.com/Horngren.**

For more practice, see Short Exercise S4A-14. MyAccountingLab

# REVIEW

## > Things You Should Know

### 1. How do we prepare financial statements?

- Financial statements are prepared from the adjusted trial balance in the following order:
  1. Income statement—reports revenues and expenses and calculates net income or net loss during the period
  2. Statement of retained earnings—shows how retained earnings changed during the period due to net income or net loss and dividends
  3. Balance sheet—reports assets, liabilities, and stockholders' equity as of the last day of the period
- A classified balance sheet classifies each asset and each liability into specific categories.

### 2. How could a worksheet help in preparing financial statements?

- The columns of a worksheet can be extended to help in preparing the financial statements.
- The income statement section will include only revenue and expense accounts.
- The balance sheet section will include asset and liability accounts and all equity accounts except revenues and expenses.

### 3. What is the closing process, and how do we close the accounts?

- The closing process consists of zeroing out all temporary accounts (revenues, expenses, Income Summary, and Dividends) in order to get the accounts ready for the next period.
- The closing process also updates the Retained Earnings account balance for net income or net loss during the period and any dividends paid to the stockholders.
- There are four steps in the closing process:
  1. Make the revenue accounts equal zero via the Income Summary account.
  2. Make the expense accounts equal zero via the Income Summary account.
  3. Make the Income Summary account equal zero via the Retained Earnings account.
  4. Make the Dividends account equal zero via the Retained Earnings account.

**4. How do we prepare a post-closing trial balance?**

- A post-closing trial balance is prepared after the closing entries are recorded and posted to the ledger.
- It contains only assets, liabilities, Common Stock, and Retained Earnings accounts (permanent accounts).

**5. What is the accounting cycle?**

- The accounting cycle is the process by which companies produce their financial statements for a specific period.
  1. Start with the beginning account balances.
  2. Analyze and journalize transactions as they occur.
  3. Post journal entries to the accounts.
  4. Compute the unadjusted balance in each account, and prepare the unadjusted trial balance.
  5. Enter the unadjusted trial balance on the worksheet, and complete the worksheet (optional).
  6. Journalize and post adjusting entries.
  7. Prepare the adjusted trial balance.
  8. Prepare the financial statements.
  9. Journalize and post the closing entries.
  10. Prepare the post-closing trial balance.

**6. How do we use the current ratio to evaluate business performance?**

- The current ratio measures a company's ability to pay its current liabilities with its current assets.
- Current ratio = Total current assets / Total current liabilities.

**7. What are reversing entries? (Appendix 4A)**

- Reversing entries are special journal entries that ease the burden of accounting for transactions in a later period.
- Reversing entries are the exact opposite of certain adjusting entries and are used only for accrual adjusting entries.

## > Summary Problem

The adjusted trial balance of Martinez Advertising Services, at December 31, 2016, follows.

**MARTINEZ ADVERTISING SERVICES**
Adjusted Trial Balance
December 31, 2016

| | Balance | |
|---|---|---|
| **Account Title** | **Debit** | **Credit** |
| Cash | $ 6,000 | |
| Accounts Receivable | 6,300 | |
| Office Supplies | 200 | |
| Furniture | 8,000 | |
| Accumulated Depreciation—Furniture | | $ 6,000 |
| Building | 42,000 | |
| Accumulated Depreciation—Building | | 24,000 |
| Land | 10,000 | |
| Accounts Payable | | 2,000 |
| Salaries Payable | | 500 |
| Unearned Revenue | | 5,000 |
| Notes Payable (long-term) | | 7,000 |
| Common Stock | | 12,000 |
| Dividends | 25,000 | |
| Service Revenue | | 64,300 |
| Salaries Expense | 16,500 | |
| Supplies Expense | 800 | |
| Depreciation Expense—Furniture | 2,000 | |
| Depreciation Expense—Building | 1,000 | |
| Advertising Expense | 3,000 | |
| Total | **$ 120,800** | **$ 120,800** |

### Requirements

1. Prepare the income statement for the year ended December 31, 2016.
2. Prepare the statement of retained earnings for the year ended December 31, 2016.
3. Prepare the classified balance sheet at December 31, 2016. Use the report form.
4. Calculate the current ratio at December 31, 2016.
5. Journalize and post the closing entries. Indicate the balance of the Retained Earnings account after the closing entries are posted.
6. Prepare a post-closing trial balance at December 31, 2016.

## > Solution

### Requirement 1

| MARTINEZ ADVERTISING SERVICES<br>Income Statement<br>Year Ended December 31, 2016 | | |
|---|---|---|
| **Revenues:** | | |
| Service Revenue | | $ 64,300 |
| **Expenses:** | | |
| Salaries Expense | $ 16,500 | |
| Advertising Expense | 3,000 | |
| Depreciation Expense—Furniture | 2,000 | |
| Depreciation Expense—Building | 1,000 | |
| Supplies Expense | 800 | |
| Total Expenses | | 23,300 |
| Net Income | | **$ 41,000** |

### Requirement 2

| MARTINEZ ADVERTISING SERVICES<br>Statement of Retained Earnings<br>Year Ended December 31, 2016 | |
|---|---|
| Retained Earnings, January 1, 2016 | $ 0 |
| Net income for the year | 41,000 |
| | 41,000 |
| Dividends | (25,000) |
| Retained Earnings, December 31, 2016 | **$ 16,000** |

## Requirement 3

| | | | |
|---|---|---|---|
| **MARTINEZ ADVERTISING SERVICES**<br>Balance Sheet<br>December 31, 2016 | | | |
| **Assets** | | | |
| Current Assets: | | | |
| Cash | | $ 6,000 | |
| Accounts Receivable | | 6,300 | |
| Office Supplies | | 200 | |
| Total Current Assets | | | $ 12,500 |
| Plant Assets: | | | |
| Furniture | $ 8,000 | | |
| Less: Accumulated Depreciation—Furniture | (6,000) | 2,000 | |
| Building | 42,000 | | |
| Less: Accumulated Depreciation—Building | (24,000) | 18,000 | |
| Land | | 10,000 | |
| Total Plant Assets | | | 30,000 |
| Total Assets | | | **$ 42,500** |
| **Liabilities** | | | |
| Current Liabilities: | | | |
| Accounts Payable | | $ 2,000 | |
| Salaries Payable | | 500 | |
| Unearned Revenue | | 5,000 | |
| Total Current Liabilities | | | $ 7,500 |
| Long-term Liabilities: | | | |
| Notes Payable | | | 7,000 |
| Total Liabilities | | | 14,500 |
| **Stockholders' Equity** | | | |
| Common Stock | | 12,000 | |
| Retained Earnings | | 16,000 | |
| Total Stockholders' Equity | | | 28,000 |
| Total Liabilities and Stockholders' Equity | | | **$ 42,500** |

## Requirement 4

Current ratio = Total current assets / Total current liabilities = $12,500 / $7,500 = 1.67*

*rounded

## Requirement 5

| Date | Accounts and Explanation | Debit | Credit |
|---|---|---|---|
| Dec. 31 | Service Revenue | 64,300 | |
| | Income Summary | | 64,300 |
| | *To close revenue.* | | |
| 31 | Income Summary | 23,300 | |
| | Salaries Expense | | 16,500 |
| | Supplies Expense | | 800 |
| | Depreciation Expense—Furniture | | 2,000 |
| | Depreciation Expense—Building | | 1,000 |
| | Advertising Expense | | 3,000 |
| | *To close expenses.* | | |
| 31 | Income Summary | 41,000 | |
| | Retained Earnings | | 41,000 |
| | *To close Income Summary.* | | |
| 31 | Retained Earnings | 25,000 | |
| | Dividends | | 25,000 |
| | *To close Dividends.* | | |



**Retained Earnings**

| | | | |
|---|---|---|---|
| | | 0 | Adj. Bal. |
| Dec. 31 | 25,000 | 41,000 | Dec. 31 |
| | | 16,000 | Bal. |

**Dividends**

| | | | |
|---|---|---|---|
| Adj. Bal. | 25,000 | 25,000 | Dec. 31 |
| Bal. | 0 | | |

**Service Revenue**

| | | | |
|---|---|---|---|
| Dec. 31 | 64,300 | 64,300 | Adj. Bal. |
| | | 0 | Bal. |

**Salaries Expense**

| | | | |
|---|---|---|---|
| Adj. Bal. | 16,500 | 16,500 | Dec. 31 |
| Bal. | 0 | | |

**Supplies Expense**

| | | | |
|---|---|---|---|
| Adj. Bal. | 800 | 800 | Dec. 31 |
| Bal. | 0 | | |

**Depreciation Expense—Furniture**

| | | | |
|---|---|---|---|
| Adj. Bal. | 2,000 | 2,000 | Dec. 31 |
| Bal. | 0 | | |

**Income Summary**

| | | | |
|---|---|---|---|
| Dec. 31 | 23,300 | 64,300 | Dec. 31 |
| | | 41,000 | Bal. |
| Dec. 31 | 41,000 | | |
| | | 0 | Bal. |

**Depreciation Expense—Building**

| | | | |
|---|---|---|---|
| Adj. Bal. | 1,000 | 1,000 | Dec. 31 |
| Bal. | 0 | | |

**Advertising Expense**

| | | | |
|---|---|---|---|
| Adj. Bal. | 3,000 | 3,000 | Dec. 31 |
| Bal. | 0 | | |

**Requirement 6**

| MARTINEZ ADVERTISING SERVICES<br>Post-Closing Trial Balance<br>December 31, 2016 | | |
|---|---|---|
| | Balance | |
| **Account Title** | **Debit** | **Credit** |
| Cash | $ 6,000 | |
| Accounts Receivable | 6,300 | |
| Office Supplies | 200 | |
| Furniture | 8,000 | |
| Accumulated Depreciation—Furniture | | $ 6,000 |
| Building | 42,000 | |
| Accumulated Depreciation—Building | | 24,000 |
| Land | 10,000 | |
| Accounts Payable | | 2,000 |
| Salaries Payable | | 500 |
| Unearned Revenue | | 5,000 |
| Notes Payable (long-term) | | 7,000 |
| Common Stock | | 12,000 |
| Retained Earnings | | 16,000 |
| Total | **$ 72,500** | **$ 72,500** |



## > Key Terms

**Accounting Cycle (p. 199)**
**Classified Balance Sheet (p. 186)**
**Closing Entries (p. 192)**
**Closing Process (p. 191)**
**Current Asset (p. 187)**
**Current Liability (p. 187)**
**Current Ratio (p. 200)**
**Income Summary (p. 192)**
**Intangible Asset (p. 187)**
**Liquidity (p. 186)**
**Long-Term Asset (p. 187)**
**Long-Term Investment (p. 187)**
**Long-Term Liability (p. 187)**
**Operating Cycle (p. 187)**
**Permanent Account (p. 192)**
**Plant Asset (p. 187)**
**Post-Closing Trial Balance (p. 197)**
**Reversing Entry (p. 204) (Appendix 4A)**
**Temporary Account (p. 191)**

## > Quick Check

**Learning Objective 1**

1. Assets are listed on the balance sheet in the order of their
   a. purchase date.
   b. adjustments.
   c. liquidity.
   d. balance.

**Learning Objective 1**

2. Which of the following accounts would be included in the plant assets category of the classified balance sheet?
   a. Land held for investment
   b. Accumulated Depreciation
   c. Office Supplies
   d. Mortgage Payable

3. Which situation indicates a net loss within the Income Statement section of the worksheet?

**Learning Objective 2**

a. Total credits exceed total debits
b. Total debits exceed total credits
c. Total debits equal total credits
d. None of the above

4. Which of the following accounts is *not* closed?

**Learning Objective 3**

a. Depreciation Expense
b. Dividends
c. Service Revenue
d. Accumulated Depreciation

5. What do closing entries accomplish?

**Learning Objective 3**

a. Zero out the revenues, expenses, and dividends
b. Transfer revenues, expenses, and dividends to the Retained Earnings account
c. Bring the Retained Earnings account to its correct ending balance
d. All of the above

6. Which of the following is *not* a closing entry?

**Learning Objective 3**

| Date | Accounts and Explanation | Debit | Credit |
|---|---|---|---|
| a. | Retained Earnings | xxx | |
| | Dividends | | xxx |
| b. | Service Revenue | xxx | |
| | Income Summary | | xxx |
| c. | Salaries Payable | xxx | |
| | Income Summary | | xxx |
| d. | Income Summary | xxx | |
| | Rent Expense | | xxx |



7. Which of the following accounts may appear on a post-closing trial balance?

**Learning Objective 4**

a. Cash, Salaries Payable, and Retained Earnings
b. Cash, Salaries Payable, and Service Revenue
c. Cash, Service Revenue, and Salaries Expense
d. Cash, Salaries Payable, and Salaries Expense

8. Which of the following steps of the accounting cycle is not completed at the end of the period?

**Learning Objective 5**

a. Journalize transactions as they occur.
b. Journalize and post the closing entries.
c. Prepare the post-closing trial balance.
d. Prepare the financial statements.

9. Clean Water Softener Systems has Cash of $600, Accounts Receivable of $900, and Office Supplies of $400. Clean owes $500 on Accounts Payable and has Salaries Payable of $200. Clean's current ratio is

**Learning Objective 6**

a. 2.71
b. 2.50
c. 0.63
d. 0.37

10A. Which of the following statements concerning reversing entries is true?

**Learning Objective 7**
**Appendix 4A**

a. Reversing entries are required by Generally Accepted Accounting Principles.
b. Reversing entries are most often used with accrual-type adjustments.
c. Reversing entries are dated December 31, the end of the fiscal year.
d. Reversing entries are recorded before adjusting entries.

**Check your answers at the end of the chapter.**

# ASSESS YOUR PROGRESS

## > Review Questions

1. What document are financial statements prepared from?
2. What does the income statement report?
3. What does the statement of retained earnings show?
4. What does the balance sheet report?
5. Why are financial statements prepared in a specific order? What is that order?
6. What is a classified balance sheet?
7. Identify two asset categories on the classified balance sheet, and give examples of each category.
8. Identify two liability categories on the classified balance sheet, and give examples of each category.
9. What does liquidity mean?
10. How could a worksheet help in preparing financial statements?
11. If a business had a net loss for the year, where would the net loss be reported on the worksheet?
12. What is the closing process?
13. What are temporary accounts? Are temporary accounts closed in the closing process?
14. What are permanent accounts? Are permanent accounts closed in the closing process?
15. How is the Income Summary account used? Is it a temporary or permanent account?
16. What are the steps in the closing process?
17. If a business had a net loss for the year, what would be the closing entry to close Income Summary and transfer the net loss to the Retained Earnings account?
18. What types of accounts are listed on the post-closing trial balance?
19. List the steps of the accounting cycle.
20. What is the current ratio, and how is it calculated?

21A. What are reversing entries? Are they required by GAAP?

## > Short Exercises

### S4-1 Preparing an income statement

**Learning Objective 1**

Daylen Hair Stylists's adjusted trial balance follows. Prepare Daylen's income statement for the year ended December 31, 2017.

**DAYLEN HAIR STYLISTS**
Adjusted Trial Balance
December 31, 2017

| | Balance | |
|---|---|---|
| **Account Title** | **Debit** | **Credit** |
| Cash | $ 1,600 | |
| Accounts Receivable | 1,100 | |
| Office Supplies | 2,000 | |
| Equipment | 19,800 | |
| Accumulated Depreciation—Equipment | | $ 1,800 |
| Accounts Payable | | 900 |
| Interest Payable | | 900 |
| Notes Payable | | 3,700 |
| Common Stock | | 12,700 |
| Dividends | 600 | |
| Service Revenue | | 15,100 |
| Rent Expense | 5,300 | |
| Supplies Expense | 800 | |
| Depreciation Expense—Equipment | 1,800 | |
| Interest Expense | 2,100 | |
| Total | **$ 35,100** | **$ 35,100** |

### S4-2 Preparing a statement of retained earnings

**Learning Objective 1**

Refer to the data in Short Exercise S4-1. Prepare Daylen's statement of retained earnings for the year ended December 31, 2017.

### S4-3 Preparing a balance sheet (unclassified, account form)

**Learning Objective 1**

Refer to the data in Short Exercise S4-1. Prepare Daylen's *unclassified* balance sheet at December 31, 2017. Use the account form.

### S4-4 Preparing a balance sheet (classified, report form)

**Learning Objective 1**

Refer to the data in Short Exercise S4-1. Prepare Daylen's classified balance sheet at December 31, 2017. Assume the Notes Payable is due on December 1, 2020. Use the report form.

**Learning Objective 1**

## S4-5 Classifying balance sheet accounts

For each account listed, identify the category in which it would appear on a classified balance sheet.

a. Office Supplies
b. Interest Payable
c. Retained Earnings
d. Copyrights
e. Land
f. Accumulated Depreciation—Furniture
g. Land (held for long-term investment purposes)
h. Unearned Revenue
i. Notes Payable (due in six years)

**Learning Objective 2**

## S4-6 Using the worksheet to prepare financial statements

Answer the following questions:

**Requirements**

1. What type of normal balance does the Retained Earnings account have—debit or credit?
2. Which type of income statement account has the same type of balance as the Retained Earnings account?
3. Which type of income statement account has the opposite type of balance as the Retained Earnings account?
4. What do we call the difference between total debits and total credits on the income statement section of the worksheet?

**Learning Objective 2**

## S4-7 Determining net income using a worksheet

A partial worksheet for Ramson Law Firm is presented below. Solve for the missing information.

| | A | J | K | L | M |
|---|---|---|---|---|---|
| 5 | | Income Statement | | Balance Sheet | |
| 6 | | Debit | Credit | Debit | Credit |
| 32 | Total | (a) | $ 23,475 | $ 217,325 | $ 208,950 |
| 33 | Net (b) | 8,375 | | | (c) |
| 34 | Total | (d) | $ 23,475 | (e) | (f) |
| 35 | | | | | |



**Learning Objective 2**

## S4-8 Determining net loss using a worksheet

A partial worksheet for Akerman Adjusters is presented below. Solve for the missing information.

| | A | J | K | L | M |
|---|---|---|---|---|---|
| 5 | | Income Statement | | Balance Sheet | |
| 6 | | Debit | Credit | Debit | Credit |
| 32 | Total | $ 22,300 | (a) | (b) | $ 60,600 |
| 33 | Net (c) | | 4,800 | (d) | |
| 34 | Total | (e) | (f) | (g) | $ 60,600 |
| 35 | | | | | |

### S4-9 Journalizing closing entries

**Learning Objective 3**

Brett Tamas Enterprises had the following accounts and normal balances listed on its adjusted trial balance: Service Revenue, $21,800; Salaries Expense, $7,200; Rent Expense, $4,400; Advertising Expense, $2,600; Dividends, $6,000.

Journalize the closing entries for Tamas Enterprises.

### S4-10 Posting closing entries directly to T-accounts

**Learning Objective 3**

The following balances appear on the books of Brian Kaufman Enterprises: Retained Earnings, $30,000; Dividends, $5,400; Service Revenue, $20,200; Salaries Expense, $6,800; Rent Expense, $3,000; Advertising Expense, $3,200. All accounts have normal balances.

**Requirements**

1. Open a T-account for each account, and insert its adjusted balance as given (denote as *Adj. Bal.*) at December 31.
2. Post the closing entries to the accounts, denoting posted amounts as *Clos.*
3. Compute the ending balance of Retained Earnings.

### S4-11 Identifying accounts included on a post-closing trial balance

**Learning Objective 4**

For each account listed, identify whether the account would be included on a post-closing trial balance. Signify either Yes (Y) or No (N).

a. Office Supplies
b. Interest Expense
c. Retained Earnings
d. Dividends
e. Service Revenue
f. Accumulated Depreciation—Furniture
g. Rent Expense
h. Unearned Revenue
i. Accounts Payable

CHAPTER 4

### S4-12 Identifying steps in the accounting cycle

**Learning Objective 5**

Review the steps in the accounting cycle, and answer the following questions:

1. What is the first step?
2. Are any steps optional?
3. Which steps are completed throughout the period?
4. Which steps are completed only at the end of the period?
5. What is the last step in the accounting cycle?

### S4-13 Calculating the current ratio

**Learning Objective 6**

Heart of Tennessee Telecom has these account balances at December 31, 2016:

| | | | |
|---|---|---|---|
| Notes Payable, long-term | $ 8,500 | Accounts Payable | $ 3,700 |
| Prepaid Rent | 1,500 | Accounts Receivable | 6,900 |
| Salaries Payable | 1,200 | Cash | 3,400 |
| Service Revenue | 14,900 | Depreciation Expense—Equip. | 1,500 |
| Office Supplies | 500 | Equipment | 19,000 |
| Accumulated Depreciation—Equip. | 3,000 | Common Stock | 3,100 |
| Advertising Expense | 600 | Rent Expense | 1,000 |

### Requirements

1. Calculate Heart of Tennessee Telecom's current ratio.
2. How much in *current* assets does Heart of Tennessee Telecom have for every dollar of *current* liabilities that it owes?

**Learning Objective 7**
**Appendix 4A**

## S4A-14 Journalizing reversing entries

Lake View Associates accrued $7,000 of Service Revenue at December 31. Lake View Associates received $13,500 on January 15, including the accrued revenue recorded on December 31.

### Requirements

1. Record the adjusting entry to accrue Service Revenue.
2. Record the reversing entry.
3. Journalize the cash receipt.

# > Exercises

**Learning Objective 1**

2. Ending Retained Earnings $6,300

## E4-15 Preparing the financial statements

The adjusted trial balance for Burlington Advertising Services is presented below:

**BURLINGTON ADVERTISING SERVICES**
Adjusted Trial Balance
December 31, 2016

| | Balance | |
|---|---|---|
| **Account Title** | **Debit** | **Credit** |
| Cash | $ 14,100 | |
| Accounts Receivable | 14,200 | |
| Office Supplies | 6,200 | |
| Furniture | 19,200 | |
| Accumulated Depreciation—Furniture | | $ 14,400 |
| Building | 51,500 | |
| Accumulated Depreciation—Building | | 35,700 |
| Land | 18,300 | |
| Accounts Payable | | 10,200 |
| Salaries Payable | | 7,400 |
| Unearned Revenue | | 17,500 |
| Common Stock | | 32,000 |
| Retained Earnings | | 37,000 |
| Dividends | 20,100 | |
| Service Revenue | | 40,100 |
| Salaries Expense | 28,000 | |
| Supplies Expense | 8,600 | |
| Depreciation Expense—Furniture | 500 | |
| Depreciation Expense—Building | 2,600 | |
| Advertising Expense | 11,000 | |
| Total | **$ 194,300** | **$ 194,300** |

**Requirements**

1. Prepare the income statement for the year ending December 31, 2016.
2. Prepare the statement of retained earnings for the year ending December 31, 2016.
3. Prepare the classified balance sheet as of December 31, 2016. Use the report form.

## E4-16 Classifying balance sheet accounts

**Learning Objective 1**

For each account listed, identify the category that it would appear on a classified balance sheet. Use the following categories: Current Assets, Long-term Investments, Plant Assets, Intangible Assets, Current Liabilities, Long-term Liabilities, and Stockholders' Equity. If the item does not belong on the classified balance sheet, put an X.

**a.** Land (used in operations)
**b.** Accumulated Depreciation—Equipment
**c.** Common Stock
**d.** Service Revenue
**e.** Investment in Starbucks Corporation (to be held long-term)
**f.** Accounts Receivable
**g.** Equipment
**h.** Buildings
**i.** Notes Payable (due in 10 years)
**j.** Unearned Revenue
**k.** Cash
**l.** Accounts Payable
**m.** Prepaid Rent
**n.** Dividends
**o.** Land (held for investment purposes)
**p.** Depreciation Expense

**Learning Objectives 1, 6**

1. Total Assets $67,000

**E4-17 Preparing a classified balance sheet and calculating the current ratio**

The adjusted trial balance of Penny O'Hara Dance Studio Company follows:

**PENNY O'HARA DANCE STUDIO COMPANY**
Trial Balance
August 31, 2016

| | Balance | |
|---|---|---|
| **Account Title** | **Debit** | **Credit** |
| Cash | $ 14,400 | |
| Office Supplies | 2,600 | |
| Prepaid Rent | 1,400 | |
| Equipment | 54,000 | |
| Accumulated Depreciation—Equipment | | $ 5,400 |
| Accounts Payable | | 4,100 |
| Salaries Payable | | 800 |
| Unearned Revenue | | 4,900 |
| Notes Payable (long-term) | | 4,900 |
| Common Stock | | 20,000 |
| Retained Earnings | | 24,400 |
| Dividends | 1,200 | |
| Service Revenue | | 16,500 |
| Salaries Expense | 4,200 | |
| Rent Expense | 1,900 | |
| Depreciation Expense—Equipment | 400 | |
| Supplies Expense | 200 | |
| Utilities Expense | 700 | |
| Total | **$ 81,000** | **$ 81,000** |

**Requirements**

1. Prepare the classified balance sheet of Penny O'Hara Dance Studio Company at August 31, 2016. Use the report form. You must compute the ending balance of Retained Earnings.
2. Compute O'Hara's current ratio at August 31, 2016. One year ago, the current ratio was 1.57. Indicate whether O'Hara's ability to pay current debts has improved, deteriorated, or remained the same.

## E4-18 Preparing a worksheet

**Learning Objective 2**

The unadjusted trial balance of Voice Link at November 30, 2016, follows:

**VOICE LINK**
Unadjusted Trial Balance
November 30, 2016

| | Balance | |
|---|---|---|
| **Account Title** | **Debit** | **Credit** |
| Cash | $ 3,900 | |
| Accounts Receivable | 3,700 | |
| Prepaid Rent | 1,600 | |
| Office Supplies | 3,900 | |
| Equipment | 33,400 | |
| Accumulated Depreciation—Equipment | | $ 1,500 |
| Accounts Payable | | 5,100 |
| Salaries Payable | | |
| Common Stock | | 36,400 |
| Dividends | 2,400 | |
| Service Revenue | | 8,600 |
| Depreciation Expense—Equipment | | |
| Salaries Expense | 2,000 | |
| Rent Expense | | |
| Utilities Expense | 700 | |
| Supplies Expense | | |
| Total | $ 51,600 | $ 51,600 |

Additional information at November 30, 2016:

a. Accrued service revenue, $600.

b. Depreciation, $300.

c. Accrued salaries expense, $600.

d. Prepaid rent expired, $900.

e. Office Supplies used, $500.

### Requirements

1. Complete Voice Link's worksheet for the month ended November 30, 2016.
2. How much was net income for November?

***Note: Exercise E4-19 should be used only after completing Exercise E4-18.***

**Learning Objectives 1, 2**

2. Ending Retained Earnings $1,800

## E4-19 Preparing financial statements from the completed worksheet

Use your answer from Exercise E4-18 to prepare Voice Link's financial statements.

**Requirements**

1. Complete the income statement for the month ended November 30, 2016.
2. Complete the statement of retained earnings for the month ended November 30, 2016. Assume beginning Retained Earnings was $0.
3. Complete the classified balance sheet as of November 30, 2016. Use the report form.

**Learning Objective 3**

## E4-20 Preparing closing entries from an adjusted trial balance

The adjusted trial balance of Smith Sign Company follows:

**SMITH SIGN COMPANY**
Adjusted Trial Balance
January 31, 2016

| | Balance | |
|---|---|---|
| **Account Title** | **Debit** | **Credit** |
| Cash | $ 15,300 | |
| Office Supplies | 1,800 | |
| Prepaid Rent | 1,000 | |
| Equipment | 51,000 | |
| Accumulated Depreciation—Equipment | | $ 6,600 |
| Accounts Payable | | 4,300 |
| Salaries Payable | | 300 |
| Unearned Revenue | | 4,500 |
| Notes Payable (long-term) | | 4,900 |
| Common Stock | | 38,500 |
| Dividends | 1,000 | |
| Service Revenue | | 17,600 |
| Salaries Expense | 3,800 | |
| Rent Expense | 1,500 | |
| Depreciation Expense—Equipment | 400 | |
| Supplies Expense | 200 | |
| Utilities Expense | 700 | |
| Total | **$ 76,700** | **$ 76,700** |

**Requirements**

1. Assume Smith Sign Company has a January 31 year-end. Journalize Smith's closing entries at January 31.
2. How much net income or net loss did Smith earn for the year ended January 31? How can you tell?

CHAPTER 4

**E4-21 Preparing closing entries from T-accounts** **Learning Objective 3**

Selected accounts for Kennedy Photography at December 31, 2016, follow:

| Retained Earnings | |
|---|---|
| | 60,000 |

| Dividends | |
|---|---|
| 23,000 | |

| Service Revenue | |
|---|---|
| | 36,000 |
| | 7,000 |

| Salaries Expense | |
|---|---|
| 31,600 | |
| 1,300 | |

| Supplies Expense | |
|---|---|
| 3,200 | |

| Depreciation Expense—Furniture | |
|---|---|
| 1,700 | |

| Depreciation Expense—Building | |
|---|---|
| 6,900 | |

**Requirements**

1. Journalize Kennedy Photography's closing entries at December 31, 2016.
2. Determine Kennedy Photography's ending Retained Earnings balance at December 31, 2016.

**E4-22 Determining the effects of closing entries on the Retained Earnings account** **Learning Objective 3**

Allen Insurance Agency started the year with a beginning Retained Earnings balance of $24,500. During the year, Allen earned $34,000 of Service Revenue and incurred $22,500 of various expenses. Dividends of $16,000 from the business were paid to stockholders. After the closing entries are recorded and posted, what will be the balance of Retained Earnings?

**Learning Objectives 2, 3**

1\. Net Income $16,350

(Requirement 1 only)

## E4-23 Preparing a worksheet and closing entries

Cadence Elliot, CPA, had the following partial worksheet:

| | A | B | C | D | E | F | G | H | I | J | K | L | M |
|---|---|---|---|---|---|---|---|---|---|---|---|---|---|
| 1 | CADENCE ELLIOT, CPA | | | | | | | | | | | | |
| 2 | Worksheet | | | | | | | | | | | | |
| 3 | December 31, 2016 | | | | | | | | | | | | |
| 4 | | | | | | | | | | | | | |
| 5 | Account Names | Unadjusted Trial Balance | | | Adjustments | | | Adjusted Trial Balance | | Income Statement | | Balance Sheet | |
| 6 | | Debit | Credit | | Debit | Credit | | Debit | Credit | Debit | Credit | Debit | Credit |
| 7 | Cash | $ 45,500 | | | | | | $ 45,500 | | | | | |
| 8 | Accounts Receivable | 9,300 | | (h) | $ 4,400 | | | 13,700 | | | | | |
| 9 | Office Supplies | 700 | | | | $ 600 | (b) | 100 | | | | | |
| 10 | Prepaid Rent | 10,000 | | | | 2,700 | (a) | 7,300 | | | | | |
| 11 | Furniture | 27,000 | | | | | | 27,000 | | | | | |
| 12 | Accumulated Depreciation—Furniture | | | | | 1,400 | (c) | | $ 1,400 | | | | |
| 13 | Building | 115,000 | | | | | | 115,000 | | | | | |
| 14 | Accumulated Depreciation—Building | | | | | 850 | (d) | | 850 | | | | |
| 15 | Land | 25,000 | | | | | | 25,000 | | | | | |
| 16 | Accounts Payable | | $ 5,200 | | | | | | 5,200 | | | | |
| 17 | Utilities Payable | | 500 | | | | | | 500 | | | | |
| 18 | Salaries Payable | | | | | 4,000 | (f) | | 4,000 | | | | |
| 19 | Interest Payable | | | | | 900 | (g) | | 900 | | | | |
| 20 | Unearned Revenue | | 2,000 | (e) | 400 | | | | 1,600 | | | | |
| 21 | Notes Payable | | 22,000 | | | | | | 22,000 | | | | |
| 22 | Common Stock | | 110,000 | | | | | | 110,000 | | | | |
| 23 | Retained Earnings | | 100,800 | | | | | | 100,800 | | | | |
| 24 | Dividends | 30,000 | | | | | | 30,000 | | | | | |
| 25 | Service Revenue | | 98,000 | | | 4,800 | (e,h) | | 102,800 | | | | |
| 26 | Rent Expense | 25,000 | | (a) | 2,700 | | | 27,700 | | | | | |
| 27 | Salaries Expense | 32,000 | | (f) | 4,000 | | | 36,000 | | | | | |
| 28 | Supplies Expense | | | (b) | 600 | | | 600 | | | | | |
| 29 | Utilities Expense | 19,000 | | | | | | 19,000 | | | | | |
| 30 | Depreciation Expense—Furniture | | | (c) | 1,400 | | | 1,400 | | | | | |
| 31 | Depreciation Expense—Building | | | (d) | 850 | | | 850 | | | | | |
| 32 | Interest Expense | | | (g) | 900 | | | 900 | | | | | |
| 33 | **Total** | **$ 338,500** | **$ 338,500** | | **$ 15,250** | **$ 15,250** | | **$ 350,050** | **$ 350,050** | | | | |
| 34 | | | | | | | | | | | | | |
| 35 | | | | | | | | | | | | | |
| 36 | | | | | | | | | | | | | |

### Requirements

1. Complete the worksheet.
2. Prepare the closing entries for Cadence Elliot, CPA.

**Learning Objectives 3, 4, 6**

**E4-24 Preparing closing entries from an adjusted trial balance; preparing a post-closing trial balance; and calculating the current ratio**

Matthew's Bowling Alley's adjusted trial balance as of December 31, 2016, is presented below:

| MATTHEW'S BOWLING ALLEY<br>Adjusted Trial Balance<br>December 31, 2016 | | |
|---|---|---|
| | Balance | |
| **Account Title** | **Debit** | **Credit** |
| Cash | $ 18,500 | |
| Accounts Receivable | 3,300 | |
| Office Supplies | 650 | |
| Prepaid Insurance | 2,600 | |
| Equipment | 41,000 | |
| Accumulated Depreciation—Equipment | | $ 22,000 |
| Building | 135,000 | |
| Accumulated Depreciation—Building | | 5,500 |
| Land | 30,000 | |
| Accounts Payable | | 3,600 |
| Utilities Payable | | 675 |
| Salaries Payable | | 3,500 |
| Unearned Revenue | | 1,700 |
| Common Stock | | 107,000 |
| Retained Earnings | | 104,825 |
| Dividends | 30,000 | |
| Service Revenue | | 100,000 |
| Insurance Expense | 28,000 | |
| Salaries Expense | 30,000 | |
| Supplies Expense | 1,800 | |
| Utilities Expense | 25,000 | |
| Depreciation Expense—Equipment | 2,500 | |
| Depreciation Expense—Building | 450 | |
| Total | **$ 348,800** | **$ 348,800** |

**Requirements**

1. Prepare the closing entries for Matthew's Bowling Alley.
2. Prepare a post-closing trial balance.
3. Compute the current ratio for Matthew's Bowling Alley.

CHAPTER 4

**Learning Objectives 2, 3, 4**

1. Net Loss $(21,000)

## E4-25 Preparing a worksheet, closing entries, and a post-closing trial balance

San Antonio Veterinary Hospital completed the following worksheet as of December 31, 2016.

| | A | B | C | D | E | F | G | H | I | J | K | L | M |
|---|---|---|---|---|---|---|---|---|---|---|---|---|---|
| 1 | SAN ANTONIO VETERINARY HOSPITAL | | | | | | | | | | | | |
| 2 | Worksheet | | | | | | | | | | | | |
| 3 | December 31, 2016 | | | | | | | | | | | | |
| 4 | | | | | | | | | | | | | |
| 5 | Account Names | Unadjusted Trial Balance | | | Adjustments | | | Adjusted Trial Balance | | Income Statement | | Balance Sheet | |
| 6 | | Debit | Credit | | Debit | Credit | | Debit | Credit | Debit | Credit | Debit | Credit |
| 7 | Cash | $ 28,100 | | | | | | $ 28,100 | | | | | |
| 8 | Accounts Receivable | 9,600 | | (f) | $ 600 | | | 10,200 | | | | | |
| 9 | Office Supplies | 900 | | | | $ 75 | (b) | 825 | | | | | |
| 10 | Prepaid Rent | 9,000 | | | | 950 | (a) | 8,050 | | | | | |
| 11 | Equipment | 23,000 | | | | | | 23,000 | | | | | |
| 12 | Accumulated Depreciation—Equipment | | | | | 1,100 | (c) | | $ 1,100 | | | | |
| 13 | Accounts Payable | | $ 3,600 | | | | | | 3,600 | | | | |
| 14 | Utilities Payable | | 320 | | | | | | 320 | | | | |
| 15 | Salaries Payable | | | | | 875 | (e) | | 875 | | | | |
| 16 | Unearned Revenue | | 10,000 | (d) | 1,400 | | | | 8,600 | | | | |
| 17 | Common Stock | | 39,000 | | | | | | 39,000 | | | | |
| 18 | Retained Earnings | | 56,680 | | | | | | 56,680 | | | | |
| 19 | Dividends | 19,000 | | | | | | 19,000 | | | | | |
| 20 | Service Revenue | | 25,000 | | | 2,000 | (d,f) | | 27,000 | | | | |
| 21 | Rent Expense | 21,000 | | (a) | 950 | | | 21,950 | | | | | |
| 22 | Salaries Expense | 14,000 | | (e) | 875 | | | 14,875 | | | | | |
| 23 | Supplies Expense | | | (b) | 75 | | | 75 | | | | | |
| 24 | Utilities Expense | 10,000 | | | | | | 10,000 | | | | | |
| 25 | Depreciation Expense—Equipment | | | (c) | 1,100 | | | 1,100 | | | | | |
| 26 | **Total** | **$ 134,600** | **$ 134,600** | | **$ 5,000** | **$ 5,000** | | **$ 137,175** | **$ 137,175** | | | | |
| 27 | | | | | | | | | | | | | |
| 28 | | | | | | | | | | | | | |
| 29 | | | | | | | | | | | | | |

### Requirements

1. Complete the worksheet for San Antonio Veterinary Hospital.
2. Prepare the closing entries.
3. Prepare a post-closing trial balance.

**Learning Objective 7**
**Appendix 4A**

## E4A-26 Journalizing reversing entries

Krisp Architects recorded the following adjusting entries as of December 31:

a. Service Revenue accrued, $2,600.

b. Unearned Revenue that has been earned, $400.

c. Office Supplies on hand, $675. The balance of the Office Supplies account was $810.

d. Salaries owed to employees, $850.

e. One month of Prepaid Rent has expired, $2,700.

f. Depreciation on equipment, $12,000.

Journalize any necessary reversing entries for Krisp Architects.

CHAPTER 4

**Learning Objective 7**
**Appendix 4A**

## E4A-27 Journalizing reversing entries

Ocean View Services had the following unadjusted balances at December 31, 2016: Salaries Payable, $0; Salaries Expense, $1,400. The following transactions have taken place at the end of 2016 and beginning of 2017:

| | |
|---|---|
| **2016** | |
| Dec. 31 | Accrued Salaries Expense at December 31, $3,000. |
| 31 | Closed the Salaries Expense account. |
| **2017** | |
| Jan. 1 | Reversed the accrued salaries. (Requirement 3 only) |
| 4 | Paid salaries of $4,400. This payment included the Salaries Payable amount, plus $1,400 for the first few days of January. |

### Requirements

1. Open T-accounts for Salaries Payable and Salaries Expense using their unadjusted balances at December 31, 2016.
2. Journalize the entries assuming Ocean View Services does not use reversing entries. **Do not record the reversing entry on Jan. 1.** Post to the accounts.
3. Open new T-accounts for Salaries Payable and Salaries Expense using their unadjusted balances at December 31, 2016. Journalize the entries assuming Ocean View Services uses reversing entries. **Don't forget to record the reversing entry on Jan. 1.** Post to the accounts. Compare the balances with Requirement 2 balances.

## > Problems Group A

**Learning Objectives 1, 3, 4**

1. Net Loss $(8,700)

**P4-28A Preparing financial statements including a classified balance sheet in report form, preparing and posting closing entries, and preparing a post-closing trial balance**

The adjusted trial balance of Elmo Real Estate Appraisal at June 30, 2016, follows:

| ELMO REAL ESTATE APPRAISAL<br>Adjusted Trial Balance<br>June 30, 2016 | | |
|---|---|---|
| | Balance | |
| **Account Title** | **Debit** | **Credit** |
| Cash | $ 4,900 | |
| Accounts Receivable | 4,800 | |
| Office Supplies | 2,700 | |
| Prepaid Insurance | 1,900 | |
| Building | 79,000 | |
| Accumulated Depreciation—Building | | $ 26,600 |
| Land | 12,600 | |
| Accounts Payable | | 19,300 |
| Interest Payable | | 8,300 |
| Salaries Payable | | 1,700 |
| Unearned Revenue | | 800 |
| Notes Payable (long-term) | | 42,000 |
| Common Stock | | 6,000 |
| Retained Earnings | | 37,000 |
| Dividends | 27,100 | |
| Service Revenue | | 48,400 |
| Insurance Expense | 4,000 | |
| Salaries Expense | 33,900 | |
| Supplies Expense | 200 | |
| Interest Expense | 8,300 | |
| Utilities Expense | 2,800 | |
| Depreciation Expense—Building | 7,900 | |
| Total | **$ 190,100** | **$ 190,100** |

**Requirements**

1. Prepare the company's income statement for the year ended June 30, 2016.
2. Prepare the company's statement of retained earnings for the year ended June 30, 2016.
3. Prepare the company's classified balance sheet in report form at June 30, 2016.
4. Journalize the closing entries.
5. Open the T-accounts using the balances from the adjusted trial balance, and post the closing entries to the T-accounts.
6. Prepare the company's post-closing trial balance at June 30, 2016.

CHAPTER 4

**Learning Objectives 1, 3, 6**

2. Ending Retained Earnings $61,200

## P4-29A Preparing financial statements including a classified balance sheet in report form, preparing closing entries, and using the current ratio to evaluate a company

The adjusted trial balance of Bertrand Irrigation System at December 31, 2016, follows:

| BERTRAND IRRIGATION SYSTEM<br>Adjusted Trial Balance<br>December 31, 2016 | | |
|---|---|---|
| | Balance | |
| **Account Title** | **Debit** | **Credit** |
| Cash | $ 43,700 | |
| Accounts Receivable | 47,600 | |
| Office Supplies | 3,400 | |
| Prepaid Insurance | 6,100 | |
| Equipment | 25,000 | |
| Accumulated Depreciation—Equipment | | $ 6,700 |
| Building | 60,000 | |
| Accumulated Depreciation—Building | | 24,700 |
| Accounts Payable | | 41,600 |
| Interest Payable | | 1,200 |
| Salaries Payable | | 3,600 |
| Unearned Revenue | | 1,600 |
| Notes Payable (long-term) | | 26,200 |
| Common Stock | | 19,000 |
| Retained Earnings | | 13,000 |
| Dividends | 2,400 | |
| Service Revenue | | 74,200 |
| Insurance Expense | 1,300 | |
| Salaries Expense | 16,600 | |
| Supplies Expense | 800 | |
| Interest Expense | 1,200 | |
| Depreciation Expense—Equipment | 2,000 | |
| Depreciation Expense—Building | 1,700 | |
| Total | $ 211,800 | $ 211,800 |

### Requirements

1. Prepare the company's income statement for the year ended December 31, 2016.
2. Prepare the company's statement of retained earnings for the year ended December 31, 2016.
3. Prepare the company's classified balance sheet in report form at December 31, 2016.
4. Journalize the closing entries for Bertrand Irrigation System.
5. Compute the company's current ratio at December 31, 2016. At December 31, 2015, the current ratio was 2.4. Did the company's ability to pay current debts improve or deteriorate, or did it remain the same?

CHAPTER 4

**Learning Objectives 1, 2, 3**

2. Total Assets $88,000

## P4-30A Preparing a worksheet, financial statements, and closing entries

The *unadjusted* trial balance of Frank Investment Advisers at December 31, 2016, follows:

**FRANK INVESTMENT ADVISERS**
Unadjusted Trial Balance
December 31, 2016

| | Balance | |
|---|---|---|
| **Account Title** | **Debit** | **Credit** |
| Cash | $ 28,000 | |
| Accounts Receivable | 47,000 | |
| Office Supplies | 5,000 | |
| Equipment | 21,000 | |
| Accumulated Depreciation—Equipment | | $ 11,000 |
| Accounts Payable | | 16,000 |
| Salaries Payable | | |
| Unearned Revenue | | 2,000 |
| Notes Payable (long-term) | | 23,000 |
| Common Stock | | 19,000 |
| Retained Earnings | | 12,000 |
| Dividends | 27,000 | |
| Service Revenue | | 95,000 |
| Insurance Expense | 3,000 | |
| Salaries Expense | 35,000 | |
| Supplies Expense | | |
| Interest Expense | 4,000 | |
| Rent Expense | 8,000 | |
| Depreciation Expense—Equipment | | |
| Total | **$ 178,000** | **$ 178,000** |

Adjustment data at December 31, 2016:

a. Unearned Revenue earned during the year, $100.
b. Office Supplies on hand, $4,000.
c. Depreciation for the year, $7,000.
d. Accrued Salaries Expense, $2,000.
e. Accrued Service Revenue, $6,000.

### Requirements

1. Prepare a worksheet for Frank Investment Advisers at December 31, 2016.
2. Prepare the income statement, the statement of retained earnings, and the classified balance sheet in account format.
3. Prepare closing entries.

CHAPTER 4

## P4-31A Completing the accounting cycle from adjusting entries to post-closing trial balance with an optional worksheet

**Learning Objectives 1, 2, 3, 4, 5, 6**

5. Net Income $19,890

The *unadjusted* trial balance of Williamson Anvils at December 31, 2016, and the data for the adjustments follow:

**WILLIAMSON ANVILS**
Unadjusted Trial Balance
December 31, 2016

| | Balance | |
|---|---|---|
| **Account Title** | **Debit** | **Credit** |
| Cash | $ 16,370 | |
| Accounts Receivable | 16,500 | |
| Prepaid Rent | 2,530 | |
| Office Supplies | 1,800 | |
| Equipment | 29,000 | |
| Accumulated Depreciation—Equipment | | $ 10,000 |
| Accounts Payable | | 6,600 |
| Salaries Payable | | |
| Unearned Revenue | | 7,200 |
| Common Stock | | 16,000 |
| Retained Earnings | | 12,000 |
| Dividends | 3,500 | |
| Service Revenue | | 20,500 |
| Salaries Expense | 2,600 | |
| Rent Expense | | |
| Depreciation Expense—Equipment | | |
| Supplies Expense | | |
| Total | **$ 72,300** | **$ 72,300** |

Adjustment data:

a. Unearned Revenue still unearned at December 31, $3,300.
b. Prepaid Rent still in force at December 31, $2,400.
c. Office Supplies used, $1,200.
d. Depreciation, $350.
e. Accrued Salaries Expense at December 31, $230.

**Requirements**

1. Open the T-accounts using the balances in the unadjusted trial balance.
2. Complete the worksheet for the year ended December 31, 2016. (optional)
3. Prepare the adjusting entries, and post to the accounts.
4. Prepare an adjusted trial balance.
5. Prepare the income statement, the statement of retained earnings, and the classified balance sheet in report form.

6. Prepare the closing entries, and post to the accounts.
7. Prepare a post-closing trial balance.
8. Calculate the current ratio for the company.

**Learning Objectives 1, 2, 3, 4, 5**

6. Ending Retained Earnings $13,395

**P4-32A Completing the accounting cycle from journal entries to post-closing trial balance with an optional worksheet**

On December 1, Bob Wonder began an auto repair shop, Wonder's Quality Automotive. The following transactions occurred during December:

| | |
|---|---|
| Dec. 1 | Wonder contributed $55,000 cash to the business in exchange for shares of common stock. |
| 1 | Purchased $9,000 of equipment paying cash. |
| 1 | Paid $1,000 for a four-month insurance policy starting on December 1. |
| 9 | Paid $16,000 cash to purchase land to be used in operations. |
| 10 | Purchased office supplies on account, $2,900. |
| 19 | Borrowed $30,000 from the bank for business use. Wonder signed a note payable to the bank in the name of the corporation. The note is due in five years. |
| 22 | Paid $1,200 for advertising expenses. |
| 26 | Paid $500 on account. |
| 28 | The business received a bill for utilities to be paid in January, $230. |
| 31 | Revenues earned during the month included $20,500 cash and $3,300 on account. |
| 31 | Paid employees' salaries $3,100 and building rent $1,000. Record as a compound entry. |
| 31 | The business received $1,050 for auto screening services to be performed next month. |
| 31 | Cash dividends of $3,500 were paid to stockholders. |

The business uses the following accounts: Cash; Accounts Receivable; Office Supplies; Prepaid Insurance; Equipment; Accumulated Depreciation—Equipment; Land; Accounts Payable; Utilities Payable; Interest Payable; Unearned Revenue; Notes Payable; Common Stock; Retained Earnings; Dividends; Income Summary; Service Revenue; Salaries Expense; Rent Expense; Utilities Expense; Advertising Expense; Supplies Expense; Insurance Expense; Interest Expense; and Depreciation Expense—Equipment.

Adjustment data:

a. Office Supplies used during the month, $900.
b. Depreciation for the month, $150.
c. One month insurance has expired.
d. Accrued Interest Expense, $75.

**Requirements**

1. Prepare the journal entries, and post to the T-accounts.
2. Prepare an unadjusted trial balance.
3. Complete the worksheet for the month ended December 31, 2016. (optional)
4. Prepare the adjusting entries, and post to the T-accounts.
5. Prepare an adjusted trial balance.

CHAPTER 4

6. Prepare the income statement, the statement of retained earnings, and the classified balance sheet in report form.
7. Prepare the closing entries, and post to the T-accounts.
8. Prepare a post-closing trial balance.

### P4A-33A Preparing adjusting entries and reversing entries

**Learning Objective 7**
**Appendix 4A**

The unadjusted trial balance and adjustment data of Mildred's Motors at December 31, 2016, follow:

**MILDRED'S MOTORS**
Unadjusted Trial Balance
December 31, 2016

| | Balance | |
|---|---|---|
| **Account Title** | **Debit** | **Credit** |
| Cash | $ 4,900 | |
| Accounts Receivable | 26,700 | |
| Office Supplies | 1,500 | |
| Prepaid Insurance | 1,800 | |
| Equipment | 54,000 | |
| Accumulated Depreciation—Equipment | | $ 36,000 |
| Accounts Payable | | 13,800 |
| Wages Payable | | |
| Unearned Revenue | | 9,600 |
| Common Stock | | 19,600 |
| Dividends | 2,900 | |
| Service Revenue | | 16,000 |
| Depreciation Expense—Equipment | | |
| Wages Expense | 1,800 | |
| Insurance Expense | | |
| Utilities Expense | 1,400 | |
| Supplies Expense | | |
| Total | **$ 95,000** | **$ 95,000** |

Adjustment data at December 31, 2016:

a. Depreciation on equipment, $1,900.
b. Accrued Wages Expense, $800.
c. Office Supplies on hand, $600.
d. Prepaid Insurance expired during December, $200.
e. Unearned Revenue earned during December, $4,000.
f. Accrued Service Revenue, $700.

2017 transactions:

a. On January 4, Mildred's Motors paid wages of $1,200. Of this, $800 related to the accrued wages recorded on December 31.
b. On January 10, Mildred's Motors received $1,300 for Service Revenue. Of this, $700 is related to the accrued Service Revenue recorded on December 31.

**Requirements**

1. Journalize adjusting entries.
2. Journalize reversing entries for the appropriate adjusting entries.
3. Refer to the 2017 data. Journalize the cash payment and the cash receipt that occurred in 2017.

## > Problems Group B

**Learning Objectives 1, 3, 4**

1. Net Loss $(7,200)

**P4-34B Preparing financial statements including a classified balance sheet in report form, preparing and posting closing entries, and preparing a post-closing trial balance**

The adjusted trial balance of Estella Real Estate Appraisal at June 30, 2016, follows:

| ESTELLA REAL ESTATE APPRAISAL<br>Adjusted Trial Balance<br>June 30, 2016 | | |
|---|---|---|
| | Balance | |
| **Account Title** | **Debit** | **Credit** |
| Cash | $ 4,600 | |
| Accounts Receivable | 5,300 | |
| Office Supplies | 1,500 | |
| Prepaid Insurance | 1,600 | |
| Building | 77,000 | |
| Accumulated Depreciation—Building | | $ 26,000 |
| Land | 13,500 | |
| Accounts Payable | | 19,300 |
| Interest Payable | | 8,400 |
| Salaries Payable | | 1,900 |
| Unearned Revenue | | 5,300 |
| Notes Payable (long-term) | | 37,000 |
| Common Stock | | 3,000 |
| Retained Earnings | | 37,000 |
| Dividends | 27,200 | |
| Service Revenue | | 48,900 |
| Insurance Expense | 4,300 | |
| Salaries Expense | 33,000 | |
| Supplies Expense | 200 | |
| Interest Expense | 8,400 | |
| Utilities Expense | 2,500 | |
| Depreciation Expense—Building | 7,700 | |
| Total | **$ 186,800** | **$ 186,800** |

CHAPTER 4

**Requirements**

1. Prepare the company's income statement for the year ended June 30, 2016.
2. Prepare the company's statement of retained earnings for the year ended June 30, 2016.
3. Prepare the company's classified balance sheet in report form at June 30, 2016.
4. Journalize the closing entries.
5. Open the T-accounts using the balances from the adjusted trial balance, and post the closing entries to the T-accounts.
6. Prepare the company's post-closing trial balance at June 30, 2016.

**P4-35B Preparing financial statements including a classified balance sheet in report form, preparing closing entries, and using the current ratio to evaluate a company**

**Learning Objectives 1, 3, 6**

2. Ending Retained Earnings $58,100

The adjusted trial balance of Blume Irrigation System at December 31, 2016, follows:

**BLUME IRRIGATION SYSTEM**
Adjusted Trial Balance
December 31, 2016

| | Balance | |
|---|---|---|
| **Account Title** | **Debit** | **Credit** |
| Cash | $ 49,710 | |
| Accounts Receivable | 47,500 | |
| Office Supplies | 3,790 | |
| Prepaid Insurance | 4,600 | |
| Equipment | 28,000 | |
| Accumulated Depreciation—Equipment | | $ 6,500 |
| Building | 56,100 | |
| Accumulated Depreciation—Building | | 25,000 |
| Accounts Payable | | 42,000 |
| Interest Payable | | 1,200 |
| Salaries Payable | | 3,500 |
| Unearned Revenue | | 1,300 |
| Notes Payable (long-term) | | 30,100 |
| Common Stock | | 22,000 |
| Retained Earnings | | 8,000 |
| Dividends | 2,500 | |
| Service Revenue | | 75,800 |
| Insurance Expense | 800 | |
| Salaries Expense | 15,700 | |
| Supplies Expense | 1,600 | |
| Interest Expense | 1,200 | |
| Depreciation Expense—Equipment | 2,000 | |
| Depreciation Expense—Building | 1,900 | |
| Total | **$ 215,400** | **$ 215,400** |

CHAPTER 4

**Requirements**

1. Prepare the company's income statement for the year ended December 31, 2016.
2. Prepare the company's statement of retained earnings for the year ended December 31, 2016.
3. Prepare the company's classified balance sheet in report form at December 31, 2016.
4. Journalize the closing entries for Blume Irrigation System.
5. Compute the company's current ratio at December 31, 2016. At December 31, 2015, the current ratio was 1.8. Did the company's ability to pay current debts improve or deteriorate, or did it remain the same?

**Learning Objectives 1, 2, 3**

2. Total Assets $84,000

**P4-36B Preparing a worksheet, financial statements, and closing entries**

The *unadjusted* trial balance of Farmer Investment Advisers at December 31, 2016, follows:

**FARMER INVESTMENT ADVISERS**
Unadjusted Trial Balance
December 31, 2016

| | Balance | |
|---|---|---|
| **Account Title** | **Debit** | **Credit** |
| Cash | $ 29,000 | |
| Accounts Receivable | 41,000 | |
| Office Supplies | 7,000 | |
| Equipment | 22,000 | |
| Accumulated Depreciation—Equipment | | $ 14,000 |
| Accounts Payable | | 15,000 |
| Salaries Payable | | |
| Unearned Revenue | | 3,000 |
| Notes Payable (long-term) | | 18,000 |
| Common Stock | | 24,000 |
| Retained Earnings | | 5,000 |
| Dividends | 28,000 | |
| Service Revenue | | 99,000 |
| Insurance Expense | 2,000 | |
| Salaries Expense | 33,000 | |
| Supplies Expense | | |
| Interest Expense | 5,000 | |
| Rent Expense | 11,000 | |
| Depreciation Expense—Equipment | | |
| Total | **$ 178,000** | **$ 178,000** |

Adjustment data at December 31, 2016:

a. Unearned Revenue earned during the year, $700.

b. Office Supplies on hand, $2,000.

c. Depreciation for the year, $2,000.

d. Accrued Salaries Expense, $5,000.

e. Accrued Service Revenue, $6,000.

**Requirements**

1. Prepare a worksheet for Farmer Investment Advisers at December 31, 2016.
2. Prepare the income statement, the statement of retained earnings, and the classified balance sheet in account format.
3. Prepare closing entries.

**P4-37B Completing the accounting cycle from adjusting entries to post-closing trial balance with an optional worksheet**

**Learning Objectives 1, 2, 3, 4, 5, 6**

5. Net Income $19,590

The *unadjusted* trial balance of Walsh Anvils at December 31, 2016, and the data for the adjustments follow:

**WALSH ANVILS**
Unadjusted Trial Balance
December 31, 2016

| | Balance | |
|---|---|---|
| **Account Title** | **Debit** | **Credit** |
| Cash | $ 6,710 | |
| Accounts Receivable | 12,500 | |
| Prepaid Rent | 3,090 | |
| Office Supplies | 2,500 | |
| Equiment | 34,000 | |
| Accumulated Depreciation—Equipment | | $ 4,000 |
| Accounts Payable | | 6,700 |
| Salaries Payable | | |
| Unearned Revenue | | 6,600 |
| Common Stock | | 15,000 |
| Retained Earnings | | 14,100 |
| Dividends | 6,000 | |
| Service Revenue | | 20,500 |
| Salaries Expense | 2,100 | |
| Rent Expense | | |
| Depreciation Expense—Equipment | | |
| Supplies Expense | | |
| Total | **$ 66,900** | **$ 66,900** |

Adjustment data:

a. Unearned Revenue still unearned at December 31, $3,000.

b. Prepaid Rent still in force at December 31, $2,900.

c. Office Supplies used, $1,600.

d. Depreciation, $340.

e. Accrued Salaries Expense at December 31, $280.

CHAPTER 4

**Requirements**

1. Open the T-accounts using the balances in the unadjusted trial balance.
2. Complete the worksheet for the year ended December 31, 2016. (optional)
3. Prepare the adjusting entries, and post to the accounts.
4. Prepare an adjusted trial balance.
5. Prepare the income statement, the statement of retained earnings, and the classified balance sheet in report form.
6. Prepare the closing entries, and post to the accounts.
7. Prepare a post-closing trial balance.
8. Calculate the current ratio for the company.

**Learning Objectives 1, 2, 3, 4, 5**

6. Ending Retained Earnings $4,120

## P4-38B Completing the accounting cycle from journal entries to post-closing trial balance with an optional worksheet

On December 1, Curt Walton began an auto repair shop, Walton's Quality Automotive. The following transactions occurred during December:

| | | |
|---|---|---|
| Dec. | 1 | Walton contributed $55,000 cash to the business in exchange for shares of common stock. |
| | 1 | Purchased $9,000 of equipment paying cash. |
| | 1 | Paid $1,500 for a five-month insurance policy starting on December 1. |
| | 9 | Paid $16,000 cash to purchase land to be used in operations. |
| | 10 | Purchased office supplies on account, $2,000. |
| | 19 | Borrowed $12,000 from the bank for business use. Walton signed a notes payable to the bank in the name of the corporation. The note is due in five years. |
| | 22 | Paid $1,700 for advertising expenses. |
| | 26 | Paid $300 on account. |
| | 28 | The business received a bill for utilities to be paid in January, $180. |
| | 31 | Revenues earned during the month included $14,000 cash and $2,600 on account. |
| | 31 | Paid employees' salaries $3,800 and building rent $1,300. Record as a compound entry. |
| | 31 | The business received $1,400 for auto screening services to be performed next month. |
| | 31 | Cash dividends of $4,000 was paid to stockholders. |

The business uses the following accounts: Cash; Accounts Receivable; Office Supplies; Prepaid Insurance; Equipment; Accumulated Depreciation—Equipment; Land; Accounts Payable; Utilities Payable; Interest Payable; Unearned Revenue; Notes Payable; Common Stock; Retained Earnings; Dividends; Income Summary; Service Revenue; Salaries Expense; Rent Expense; Utilities Expense; Advertising Expense; Supplies Expense; Insurance Expense; Interest Expense; and Depreciation Expense—Equipment.

Adjustment data:

a. Office Supplies used during the month, $1,000.

b. Depreciation for the month, $150.

c. One month insurance has expired.

d. Accrued Interest Expense, $50.

**Requirements**

1. Prepare the journal entries, and post to the T-accounts.
2. Prepare an unadjusted trial balance.
3. Complete the worksheet for the month ended December 31, 2016. (optional)
4. Prepare the adjusting entries, and post to the T-accounts.
5. Prepare an adjusted trial balance.
6. Prepare the income statement, the statement of retained earnings, and the classified balance sheet in report form.
7. Prepare the closing entries, and post to the T-accounts.
8. Prepare a post-closing trial balance.

**P4A-39B Preparing adjusting entries and reversing entries**

**Learning Objective 7**
**Appendix 4A**

The unadjusted trial balance and adjustment data of Mark's Motors at December 31, 2016, follow:

**MARK'S MOTORS**
Unadjusted Trial Balance
December 31, 2016

| | Balance | |
|---|---|---|
| **Account Title** | **Debit** | **Credit** |
| Cash | $ 4,800 | |
| Accounts Receivable | 26,600 | |
| Office Supplies | 600 | |
| Prepaid Insurance | 2,400 | |
| Equiment | 53,900 | |
| Accumulated Depreciation—Equipment | | $ 41,500 |
| Accounts Payable | | 13,500 |
| Wages Payable | | |
| Unearned Revenue | | 5,500 |
| Common Stock | | 18,900 |
| Dividends | 4,200 | |
| Service Revenue | | 16,300 |
| Depreciation Expense—Equipment | | |
| Wages Expense | 1,500 | |
| Insurance Expense | | |
| Utilities Expense | 1,700 | |
| Supplies Expense | | |
| Total | $ 95,700 | $ 95,700 |

Adjustment data at December 31, 2016:

a. Depreciation on equipment, $1,600.
b. Accrued Wages Expense, $1,000.
c. Office Supplies on hand, $100.
d. Prepaid Insurance expired during December, $200.

CHAPTER 4

e. Unearned Revenue earned during December, $4,400.

f. Accrued Service Revenue, $800.

2017 transactions:

a. On January 4, Mark's Motors paid wages of $1,200. Of this, $1,000 related to the accrued wages recorded on December 31.

b. On January 10, Mark's Motors received $1,500 for Service Revenue. Of this, $800 related to the accrued Service Revenue recorded on December 31.

**Requirements**

1. Journalize adjusting entries.
2. Journalize reversing entries for the appropriate adjusting entries.
3. Refer to the 2017 data. Journalize the cash payment and the cash receipt that occurred in 2017.

## > Continuing Problem

This problem continues the Daniels Consulting situation from Problem P3-45 of Chapter 3.



### P4-40 Completing the accounting cycle from adjusted trial balance to post-closing trial balance with an optional worksheet

Start from the posted T-accounts and the adjusted trial balance that Daniels Consulting prepared for the company at December 31.

**Requirements**

1. Complete the worksheet at December 31. (optional)
2. Prepare an income statement for the month ended December 31.
3. Prepare a statement of retained earnings for the month ended December 31.
4. Prepare a classified balance sheet (report form) at December 31.
5. Journalize and post the closing entries at December 31. Denote each closing amount as *Clo.* and each account balance as *Balance*.
6. Prepare a post-closing trial balance.

## > Practice Set

### P4-41 Completing the accounting cycle from adjusted trial balance to post-closing trial balance with an optional worksheet

Refer to the Practice Set data provided in Chapters 2 and 3 for Crystal Clear Cleaning.

**Requirements**

1. Prepare an accounting worksheet. (optional)
2. Prepare an income statement, statement of retained earnings, and classified balance sheet using the report format. Assume the Notes Payable is long-term.
3. Prepare closing entries for the month, and post to the accounts.
4. Prepare a post-closing trial balance.

# COMPREHENSIVE PROBLEMS

## > Comprehensive Problem 1 for Chapters 1–4

Miller Delivery Service completed the following transactions during December 2016:

| | |
|---|---|
| Dec. 1 | Miller Delivery Service began operations by receiving $10,000 cash and a truck with a fair value of $20,000 from Robert Miller. The business issued Miller shares of common stock in exchange for this contribution. |
| 1 | Paid $1,000 cash for a four-month insurance policy. The policy begins December 1. |
| 4 | Paid $500 cash for office supplies. |
| 12 | Performed delivery services for a customer and received $2,000 cash. |
| 15 | Completed a large delivery job, billed the customer, $2,500, and received a promise to collect the $2,500 within one week. |
| 18 | Paid employee salary, $1,000. |
| 20 | Received $15,000 cash for performing delivery services. |
| 22 | Collected $800 in advance for delivery service to be performed later. |
| 25 | Collected $2,500 cash from customer on account. |
| 27 | Purchased fuel for the truck, paying $300 on account. (Credit Accounts Payable) |
| 28 | Performed delivery services on account, $700. |
| 29 | Paid office rent, $1,600, for the month of December. |
| 30 | Paid $300 on account. |
| 31 | Cash dividends of $3,000 were paid to stockholders. |

**Requirements**

1. Record each transaction in the journal using the following chart of accounts. Explanations are not required.

| | |
|---|---|
| Cash | Retained Earnings |
| Accounts Receivable | Dividends |
| Office Supplies | Income Summary |
| Prepaid Insurance | Service Revenue |
| Truck | Salaries Expense |
| Accumulated Depreciation—Truck | Depreciation Expense—Truck |
| Accounts Payable | Insurance Expense |
| Salaries Payable | Fuel Expense |
| Unearned Revenue | Rent Expense |
| Common Stock | Supplies Expense |

2. Post the transactions in the T-accounts.
3. Prepare an unadjusted trial balance as of December 31, 2016.
4. Prepare a worksheet as of December 31, 2016. (optional)
5. Journalize the adjusting entries using the following adjustment data and also by reviewing the journal entries prepared in Requirement 1. Post adjusting entries to the T-accounts.

Adjustment data:

a. Accrued Salaries Expense, $1,000.

b. Depreciation was recorded on the truck using the straight-line method. Assume a useful life of five years and a salvage value of $5,000.

c. Prepaid Insurance for the month has expired.

d. Office Supplies on hand, $100.

e. Unearned Revenue earned during the month, $300.

f. Accrued Service Revenue, $650.

6. Prepare an adjusted trial balance as of December 31, 2016.
7. Prepare Miller Delivery Service's income statement and statement of retained earnings for the month ended December 31, 2016, and the classified balance sheet on that date. On the income statement, list expenses in decreasing order by amount—that is, the largest expense first, the smallest expense last.
8. Journalize the closing entries, and post to the T-accounts.
9. Prepare a post-closing trial balance as of December 31, 2016.



## > Comprehensive Problem 2 for Chapters 1–4

This comprehensive problem is a continuation of Comprehensive Problem 1. Miller Delivery Service has completed closing entries and the accounting cycle for 2016. The business is now ready to record January 2017 transactions.

| | |
|---|---|
| Jan. 3 | Collected $1,000 cash from customer on account. |
| 5 | Purchased office supplies on account, $600. |
| 12 | Performed delivery services for a customer and received $2,000 cash. |
| 15 | Paid employee salary including the amount owed on December 31, $2,500. |
| 18 | Performed delivery services on account, $950. |
| 20 | Paid $200 on account. |
| 24 | Purchased fuel for the truck, paying $250 cash. |
| 27 | Completed the remaining work due for Unearned Revenue. |
| 28 | Paid office rent, $1,600, for the month of January. |
| 30 | Collected $3,200 in advance for delivery service to be performed later. |
| 31 | Cash dividends of $2,000 were paid to stockholders. |

**Requirements**

1. Record each January transaction in the journal. Explanations are not required.
2. Post the transactions in the T-accounts. Don't forget to use the December 31, 2016, ending balances as appropriate.
3. Prepare an unadjusted trial balance as of January 31, 2017.
4. Prepare a worksheet as of January 31, 2017. (optional)
5. Journalize the adjusting entries using the following adjustment data and also by reviewing the journal entries prepared in Requirement 1. Post adjusting entries to the T-accounts.

Adjustment data:

a. Office Supplies on hand, $120.

b. Accrued Service Revenue, $1,200.

c. Accrued Salaries Expense, $1,000.

d. Prepaid Insurance for the month has expired.

e. Depreciation was recorded on the truck for the month.

6. Prepare an adjusted trial balance as of January 31, 2017.

7. Prepare Miller Delivery Service's income statement and statement of retained earnings for the month ended January 31, 2017, and the classified balance sheet on that date. On the income statement, list expenses in decreasing order by amount—that is, the largest expense first, the smallest expense last.

8. Calculate the following ratios as of January 31, 2017, for Miller Delivery Service: return on assets, debt ratio, and current ratio.

# CRITICAL THINKING



## > Ethical Issue 4-1

Grant Film Productions wishes to expand and has borrowed $100,000. As a condition for making this loan, the bank requires that the business maintain a current ratio of at least 1.50.

Business has been good but not great. Expansion costs have brought the current ratio down to 1.40 on December 15. Rita Grant, owner of the business, is considering what might happen if she reports a current ratio of 1.40 to the bank. One course of action for Grant is to record in December $10,000 of revenue that the business will earn in January of next year. The contract for this job has been signed.

**Requirements**

1. Journalize the revenue transaction, and indicate how recording this revenue in December would affect the current ratio.

2. Discuss whether it is ethical to record the revenue transaction in December. Identify the accounting principle relevant to this situation, and give the reasons underlying your conclusion.

## > Fraud Case 4-1

Arthur Chen, a newly minted CPA, was on his second audit job in the Midwest with a new client called Parson Farm Products. He was looking through the past four years of financials and doing a few ratios when he noticed something odd. The current ratio went from 1.9 in 2016 down to 0.3 in 2017, despite the fact that 2017 had record income. He decided to sample a few transactions from December 2017. He found that many of Parson's customers had returned products to the company because of substandard quality. Chen discovered that the company was clearing the receivables (i.e., crediting Accounts Receivable) but "stashing" the debits in an obscure long-term asset account called "grain reserves" rather than debiting Sales Returns and Allowances to keep the company's income "in the black" (i.e., positive income).

**Requirements**

1. How did the fraudulent accounting just described affect the current ratio?
2. Can you think of any reasons why someone in the company would want to take this kind of action?

## > Financial Statement Case 4-1

This case, based on the balance sheet of **Starbucks Corporation**, will familiarize you with some of the assets and liabilities of that company. Visit **http://www.pearsonhighered.com/Horngren** to view a link to the Starbucks Corporation Fiscal 2013 Annual Report. Use the Starbucks Corporation balance sheet to answer the following questions.

**Requirements**

1. Which balance sheet format does Starbucks use?
2. Name the company's largest current asset and largest current liability at September 29, 2013.
3. Compute Starbucks's current ratios at September 29, 2013, and September 30, 2012. Did the current ratio improve, worsen, or hold steady?
4. Under what category does Starbucks report furniture, fixtures, and equipment?
5. What was the cost of the company's fixed assets at September 29, 2013? What was the amount of accumulated depreciation? What was the book value of the fixed assets? See Note 7 for the data.



## > Team Project 4-1

Kathy Wintz formed a lawn service business as a summer job. To start the corporation on May 1, 2016, she deposited $1,000 in a new bank account in the name of the business. The $1,000 consisted of a $600 loan from Bank One to her company, Wintz Lawn Service, and $400 of her own money. The company issued $400 of common stock to Wintz. Wintz rented lawn equipment, purchased supplies, and hired other students to mow and trim customers' lawns.

At the end of each month, Wintz mailed bills to the customers. On August 31, she was ready to dissolve the corporation and return to college. Because she was so busy, she kept few records other than the checkbook and a list of receivables from customers.

At August 31, the business's checkbook shows a balance of $2,000, and customers still owe $750. During the summer, the business collected $5,500 from customers. The business checkbook lists payments for supplies totaling $400, and it still has gasoline, weed trimmer cord, and other supplies that cost a total of $50. The business paid employees $1,800 and still owes them $300 for the final week of the summer.

Wintz rented some equipment from Ludwig's Machine Shop. On May 1, the business signed a six-month rental agreement on mowers and paid $600 for the full rental period in advance. Ludwig's will refund the unused portion of the prepayment if the equipment is returned in good shape. In order to get the refund, Wintz has kept the mowers in excellent condition. In fact, the business had to pay $300 to repair a mower.

To transport employees and equipment to jobs, Wintz used a trailer that the business bought for $300. The business estimates that the summer's work used up one-third of the trailer's service potential. The business checkbook lists a payment of

$500 for cash dividends paid during the summer. The business paid the loan back during August. (For simplicity, ignore any interest expense associated with the loan.)

**Requirements**

1. As a team, prepare the income statement and the statement of retained earnings of Wintz Lawn Service for the four months May 1 through August 31, 2016.
2. Prepare the classified balance sheet (report form) of Wintz Lawn Service at August 31, 2016.
3. Was Wintz's summer work successful? Give your team's reason for your answer.

MyAccountingLab **For a wealth of online resources, including exercises, problems, media, and immediate tutorial help, please visit http://www.myaccountinglab.com.**

## > Quick Check Answers

**1.** c **2.** b **3.** b **4.** d **5.** d **6.** c **7.** a **8.** a **9.** a **10A.** b

# 5 Merchandising Operations

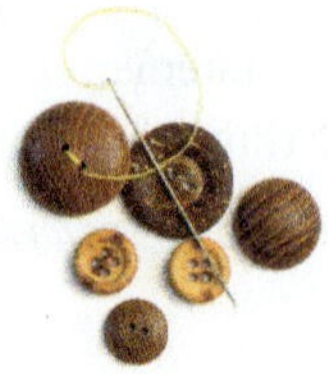

## Will They Buy It?

Julie Ryski studied the model on the catwalk who was wearing the latest spring fashion. As a retail buyer for a nationwide high-end department store, Julie is responsible for selecting merchandise that will be sold in stores across America. Not only must Julie have a keen eye for the latest fashion designs and seasonal variations, but she must also understand the needs of the department store's customers. Julie enjoys attending fashion shows and other fashion-oriented promotions, but she knows that there is more to her responsibilities than simply selecting the newest spring outfits.

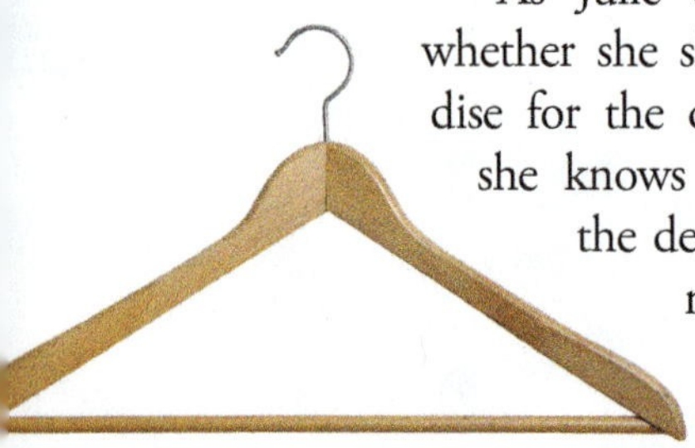

As Julie contemplates the model and whether she should purchase this merchandise for the department store's spring line, she knows that she has to always keep the department store's gross profit in mind. She is responsible for ensuring that the merchandise she buys will be purchased by customers and that it is priced effectively to ensure the highest profit maximization possible. In addition, she must ensure that this merchandise can meet the department store's sales goals and ultimate financial objectives. In the long run, Julie is responsible for all aspects of the merchandise that is sold in the store. She must understand how merchandise is reported on the financial statements, how it is recorded in the accounting records, and how the department store determines gross profit (the difference between the original cost and the retail price). Julie's buying decisions and expertise play a major role in the company's profits. Her pricing decisions ultimately affect the net income of the department store and are a major component of the department store's bottom line.

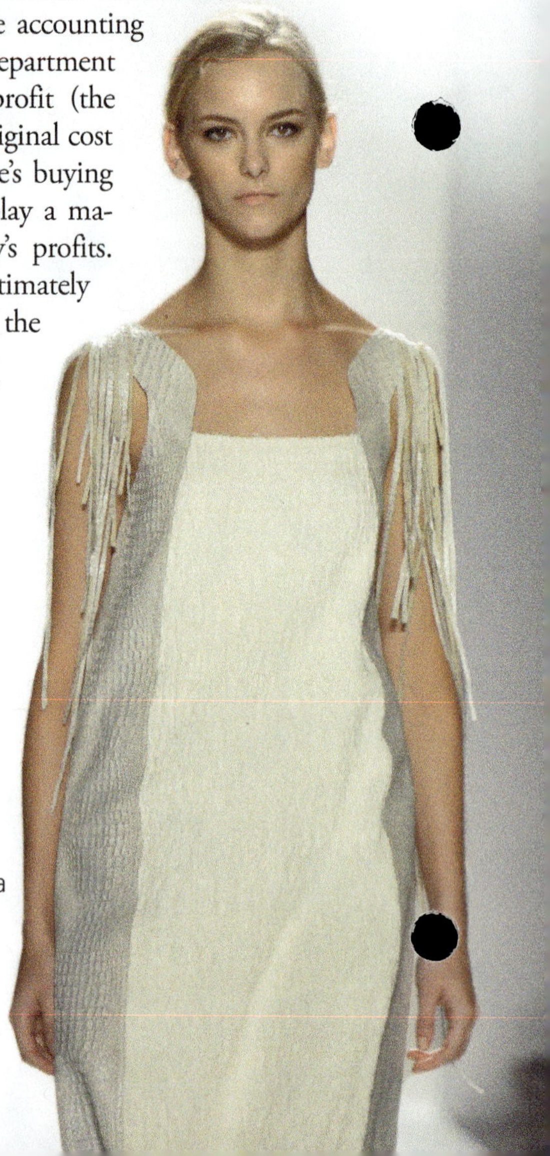

**How Do Businesses Account for Merchandise Inventory?**

In this chapter, we begin our exploration of companies that sell goods (called merchandise inventory) to customers. Although many of the accounting concepts you have learned concerning service businesses apply, merchandisers (businesses that sell inventory) have some unique characteristics you must learn to account for. For example, Macy's, Inc., a nationally known premier retailer of the Macy's and Bloomingdale's brands with nearly 840 stores in 45 states, must have a way of accurately tracking the purchase and sale of its inventory. In addition, Macy's needs to determine if it is selling its merchandise at the right sales prices in order to ensure maximum profit. This chapter explores merchandising operations and how these businesses account for merchandise inventory.

# Chapter 5 Learning Objectives

1 Describe merchandising operations and the two types of merchandise inventory systems
2 Account for the purchase of merchandise inventory using a perpetual inventory system
3 Account for the sale of merchandise inventory using a perpetual inventory system
4 Adjust and close the accounts of a merchandising business
5 Prepare a merchandiser's financial statements
6 Use the gross profit percentage to evaluate business performance
7 Account for the purchase and sale of merchandise inventory using a periodic inventory system (Appendix 5A)

## WHAT ARE MERCHANDISING OPERATIONS?

**Learning Objective 1**
Describe merchandising operations and the two types of merchandise inventory systems

In earlier chapters, you learned about accounting for Smart Touch Learning, an e-learning business that specializes in providing services: online courses in accounting, economics, marketing, and management. In this chapter, you learn about accounting for merchandisers. A **merchandiser** is a business that sells merchandise, or goods, to customers. The merchandise that this type of business sells is called **merchandise inventory**. Merchandisers are often identified as either wholesalers or retailers. A **wholesaler** is a merchandiser that buys goods from a manufacturer and then sells them to retailers. A **retailer** buys merchandise either from a manufacturer or a wholesaler and then sells those goods to consumers.

**Merchandiser**
A business that sells merchandise, or goods, to customers.

**Merchandise Inventory**
The merchandise that a business sells to customers.

**Wholesaler**
A type of merchandiser that buys goods from manufacturers and then sells them to retailers.

**Retailer**
A type of merchandiser that buys merchandise either from a manufacturer or a wholesaler and then sells those goods to consumers.

### The Operating Cycle of a Merchandising Business

The operating cycle of a merchandiser is as follows (see Exhibit 5-1):

**Exhibit 5-1 | Operating Cycle of a Merchandiser**

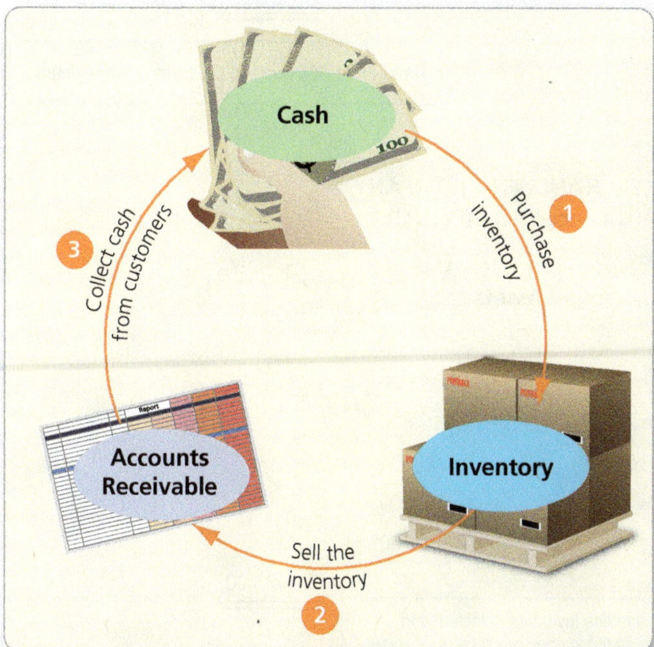

**Vendor**
The individual or business from whom a company purchases goods.

1. It begins when the company purchases inventory from an individual or business, called a **vendor**.
2. The company then sells the inventory to a customer.
3. Finally, the company collects cash from customers.

Because the operating cycle of a merchandiser is different than that of a service company, the financial statements differ. Exhibit 5-2 shows how a service entity's financial statements (on the left) differ from a merchandiser's financial statements (on the right). As you can see, merchandisers have some new balance sheet and income statement items.

**Cost of Goods Sold (COGS)**
The cost of the merchandise inventory that the business has sold to customers.

On the income statement, a merchandising company reports revenues using an account called Sales Revenue rather than the account Service Revenue used by service companies. A merchandiser also reports the cost of merchandise inventory that has been sold to customers, or **Cost of Goods Sold (COGS)**. Cost of Goods Sold is also called *Cost of Sales.* Because COGS is usually a merchandiser's main expense, an intermediary calculation,

**Exhibit 5-2 | Financial Statements of a Service Company and a Merchandising Company**

**SERVICE COMPANY**
**Income Statement**
**Year Ended December 31, 2016**

| | | |
|---|---|---|
| Service Revenue | | $ 230,000 |
| Operating Expenses: | | |
| Salaries Expense | $ 80,000 | |
| Rent Expense | 24,000 | |
| Depreciation Expense—Furniture | 9,000 | |
| Utilities Expense | 3,000 | |
| Total Operating Expenses | | 116,000 |
| Net Income | | $ 114,000 |

Service Revenue − Operating Expenses = Net Income

**MERCHANDISING COMPANY**
**Income Statement**
**Year Ended December 31, 2016**

| | | |
|---|---|---|
| Sales Revenue | | $ 230,000 |
| Cost of Goods Sold | | 100,000 |
| Gross Profit | | 130,000 |
| Operating Expenses: | | |
| Salaries Expense | $ 80,000 | |
| Rent Expense | 24,000 | |
| Depreciation Expense—Furniture | 9,000 | |
| Utilities Expense | 3,000 | |
| Total Operating Expenses | | 116,000 |
| Net Income | | $ 14,000 |

Sales Revenue − Cost of Goods Sold = Gross Profit

A merchandising company reports revenue using Sales Revenue instead of Service Revenue.

Gross Profit − Operating Expenses = Net Income

**SERVICE COMPANY**
**Balance Sheet (Partial)**
**December 31, 2016**

**Assets**

| | | |
|---|---|---|
| Current Assets: | | |
| Cash | $ 34,000 | |
| Accounts Receivable | 10,800 | |
| Office Supplies | 800 | |
| Prepaid Rent | 2,100 | |
| Total Current Assets | | $ 47,700 |

**MERCHANDISING COMPANY**
**Balance Sheet (Partial)**
**December 31, 2016**

**Assets**

| | | |
|---|---|---|
| Current Assets: | | |
| Cash | $ 34,000 | |
| Accounts Receivable | 10,800 | |
| Merchandise Inventory | 60,000 | |
| Office Supplies | 800 | |
| Prepaid Rent | 2,100 | |
| Total Current Assets | | $ 107,700 |

Merchandise Inventory is included in a merchandising company's current assets.

gross profit, is determined before calculating net income. **Gross profit** (also called *gross margin*) is calculated as net Sales Revenue minus Cost of Goods Sold and represents the markup on the merchandise inventory. Gross profit is the extra amount the company receives from the customer (for the merchandise sold) over what the company paid to the vendor. After calculating gross profit, operating expenses are then deducted to determine net income. **Operating expenses** are expenses (other than Cost of Goods Sold) that occur in the entity's major ongoing operations.

**Gross Profit**
Excess of net Sales Revenue over Cost of Goods Sold.

**Operating Expenses**
Expenses, other than Cost of Goods Sold, that are incurred in the entity's major ongoing operations.

On the balance sheet, a merchandiser includes Merchandise Inventory in the current assets section representing the value of inventory that the business has on hand to sell to customers. Remember that the assets in the current asset section are listed in order of liquidity; therefore, Merchandise Inventory is usually listed below Accounts Receivable but before the prepaid assets.

## Merchandise Inventory Systems: Perpetual and Periodic Inventory Systems

Businesses must have a way to determine the value of merchandise inventory on hand and also the value sold. There are two main types of inventory accounting systems that are used:

- Periodic inventory system
- Perpetual inventory system

The **periodic inventory system** requires businesses to obtain a physical count of inventory to determine the quantities on hand. The system is normally used for relatively inexpensive goods, such as in a small, local store without optical-scanning cash registers that does not keep a running record of every loaf of bread and every key chain that it sells. Restaurants and small retail stores often use the periodic inventory system. Appendix 5A covers the periodic inventory system, which is becoming less and less popular because most accounting is done using computerized methods.

**Periodic Inventory System**
An inventory system that requires businesses to obtain a physical count of inventory to determine quantities on hand.

The **perpetual inventory system** keeps a running computerized record of merchandise inventory—that is, the number of inventory units and the dollar amounts associated with the inventory are perpetually (constantly) updated. This system achieves better control over the inventory. A modern perpetual inventory system records the following:

**Perpetual Inventory System**
An inventory system that keeps a running computerized record of merchandise inventory.

- Units purchased and cost amounts.
- Units sold and sales and cost amounts.
- The quantity of merchandise inventory on hand and its cost.

In a perpetual inventory system, merchandise inventory and purchasing systems are integrated with the records for Accounts Receivable and Sales Revenue. For example, major department stores' computers use bar codes to keep up-to-the-minute records and show the current inventory at any time.

In a perpetual inventory system, the "cash register" at the store is a computer terminal that records sales and updates inventory records. **Bar codes are scanned by a laser. The bar coding is linked to merchandise inventory and cost data that are used to keep track of each unique inventory item.** However, note that even in a perpetual inventory system, the business must count inventory at least once a year. The physical count captures inventory transactions that are not recorded by the electronic system (such as misplaced, stolen, or damaged inventory). The count establishes the correct amount of ending inventory for the financial statements and also serves as a check on the perpetual records.

Are the bar codes I see on goods I purchase used to track inventory in the accounting system?

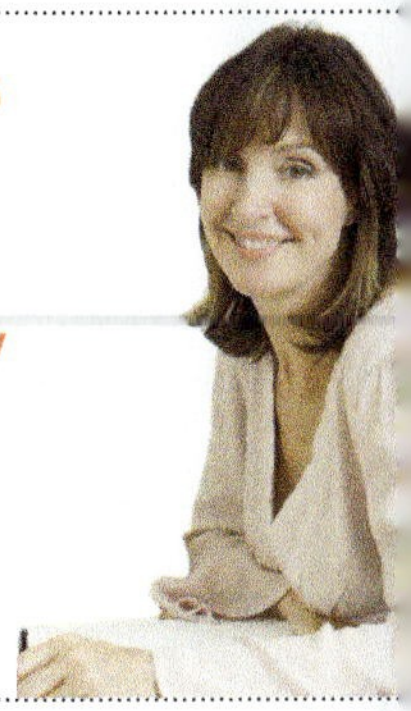

## Try It!

Match the accounting terminology to the definitions.

1. Cost of Goods Sold
2. Perpetual inventory system
3. Vendor
4. Periodic inventory system
5. Operating expenses
6. Gross profit

a. An inventory system that requires businesses to obtain a physical count of inventory to determine quantities on hand.

b. Expenses, other than Cost of Goods Sold, that are incurred in the entity's major ongoing operations.

c. Excess of net Sales Revenue over Cost of Goods Sold.

d. The cost of merchandise inventory that the business has sold to customers.

e. The individual or business from whom a company purchases goods.

f. An inventory system that keeps a running computerized record of merchandise inventory.

**Check your answers online in MyAccountingLab or at http://www.pearsonhighered.com/Horngren.**

For more practice, see Short Exercise S5-1. MyAccountingLab

## HOW ARE PURCHASES OF MERCHANDISE INVENTORY RECORDED IN A PERPETUAL INVENTORY SYSTEM?

**Learning Objective 2**
Account for the purchase of merchandise inventory using a perpetual inventory system

As noted previously, the cycle of a merchandising entity begins with the purchase of merchandise inventory. We will continue to use our fictitious company, Smart Touch Learning, which has now decided to discontinue its service business and instead plans to sell touch screen tablet computers that are preloaded with its e-learning software programs. Smart Touch Learning will purchase these tablets from a vendor. We assume Smart Touch Learning uses a perpetual inventory system.

**Invoice**
A seller's request for payment from the purchaser.

The vendor (Southwest Electronics Direct) ships the tablet computers to Smart Touch Learning and sends an invoice the same day. The **invoice** is the seller's (Southwest Electronics Direct) request for payment from the buyer (Smart Touch Learning). An invoice is also called a *bill.* Exhibit 5-3 is the bill that Smart Touch Learning receives from Southwest Electronics Direct. After the merchandise inventory is received, Smart Touch Learning pays the vendor.

*For Southwest Electronics Direct, the seller, the invoice is called a sales invoice. For Smart Touch Learning, the purchaser, the invoice is called a purchase invoice.*

**Exhibit 5-3 | Purchase Invoice**

1

**Southwest Electronics Direct**
P.O. BOX 101010
HOUSTON, TX 77212

3

| Invoice | |
|---|---|
| Date | Number |
| 6/1/17 | 410 |

2

Shipped To: SMART TOUCH LEARNING
227 LAKE STREET
POMPTON PLAINS, IL 07444

6 *Pd. 6/15/17*

4

| Credit Terms |
|---|
| 3/15, NET 30 DAYS |

| | Description | | Quantity Shipped | Unit Price | Total |
|---|---|---|---|---|---|
| | Touch Screen Tablet Computers | | 100 | $ 350 | $35,000 |
| | | | Sub Total | | $35,000 |
| | | | Ship. or Handl. Chg. | | – |
| | | | Tax (3%) | | – |
| | | | Total(s) | | $35,000 |

5

| Due Date & Due Amount | | | |
|---|---|---|---|
| 06/16/17 | | 07/01/2017 | |
| $33,950 | | $35,000 | |

7

**Explanations:**

1 The seller is Southwest Electronics Direct.

2 The purchaser is Smart Touch Learning.

3 The invoice date is needed to determine whether the purchaser gets a discount for prompt payment (see 4).

4 Credit terms: If Smart Touch Learning pays within 15 days of the invoice date, it can deduct a 3% discount. Otherwise, the full amount—NET—is due in 30 days.

5 Total invoice amount is $35,000.

6 Smart Touch Learning's payment date. How much did Smart Touch Learning pay? (see 7).

7 Payment occurred 14 days after the invoice date—within the discount period—so Smart Touch Learning paid $33,950 ($35,000–3% discount).

## Purchase of Merchandise Inventory

Here we use the actual invoice in Exhibit 5-3 to illustrate the purchasing process. Suppose Smart Touch Learning receives the goods on June 3, 2017, and makes payment on that date (ignore the credit terms on the invoice at this point). Smart Touch Learning records this purchase as follows:

| Date | Accounts and Explanation | Debit | Credit |
|---|---|---|---|
| Jun. 3 | Merchandise Inventory | 35,000 | |
| | Cash | | 35,000 |
| | *Purchased inventory for cash.* | | |

| A↑↓ | | L | + | E |
|---|---|---|---|---|
| Merchandise Inventory↑<br>Cash↓ | = | | | |

*The Merchandise Inventory account, an asset, is used only for goods purchased that the business owns and intends to resell to customers. Office Supplies, Equipment, and other assets are recorded in their own accounts.*

Assume that on June 3, instead of paying cash, Smart Touch Learning receives the merchandise inventory on account. The purchase of inventory on account is recorded as follows:

| A↑ | = | L↑ + E |
|---|---|---|
| Merchandise Inventory↑ | = | Accounts Payable↑ |

| Date | Accounts and Explanation | Debit | Credit |
|---|---|---|---|
| Jun. 3 | Merchandise Inventory | 35,000 | |
| | Accounts Payable | | 35,000 |
| | *Purchased inventory on account.* | | |

## Purchase Discounts

**Purchase Discount**
A discount that businesses offer to purchasers as an incentive for early payment.

**Credit Terms**
The payment terms of purchase or sale as stated on the invoice.

Many businesses offer purchasers a discount for early payment. This is called a **purchase discount** from the purchaser's perspective. Southwest Electronics Direct's **credit terms** of "3/15, NET 30 DAYS" mean that Smart Touch Learning can deduct 3% from the total bill (excluding freight charges, if any) if the company pays within 15 days of the invoice date. Otherwise, the full amount—NET—is due in 30 days. These credit terms can also be expressed as "3/15, n/30."

Terms of "n/30" mean that no discount is offered and payment is due 30 days after the invoice date. Most credit terms express the discount, the discount time period, and the final due date. Occasionally, the credit terms are expressed as EOM, which means payment is due at the end of the current month.

If Smart Touch Learning pays on June 15, 2017, which is within the discount period, the cash payment entry would be as follows:

| A↓ | = | L↓ + E |
|---|---|---|
| Cash↓ Merchandise Inventory↓ | = | Accounts Payable↓ |

| Date | Accounts and Explanation | Debit | Credit |
|---|---|---|---|
| Jun. 15 | Accounts Payable | 35,000 | |
| | Cash ($35,000 − $1,050) | | 33,950 |
| | Merchandise Inventory ($35,000 × 0.03) | | 1,050 |
| | *Paid within discount period.* | | |

*When making payment within a discount period, always debit Accounts Payable for the full amount of the invoice; otherwise there will be a balance remaining in the payable account even though the invoice has been paid in full.*

The purchase discount is credited to the Merchandise Inventory account because the discount for early payment decreases the actual cost paid for Merchandise Inventory, as shown in the T-account:

**Merchandise Inventory**

| | Debit | Credit | |
|---|---|---|---|
| June 3 | 35,000 | 1,050 | June 15 |
| **Bal.** | **33,950** | | |

**Accounts Payable**

| | Debit | Credit | |
|---|---|---|---|
| June 15 | 35,000 | 35,000 | June 3 |
| **Bal.** | | 0 | |

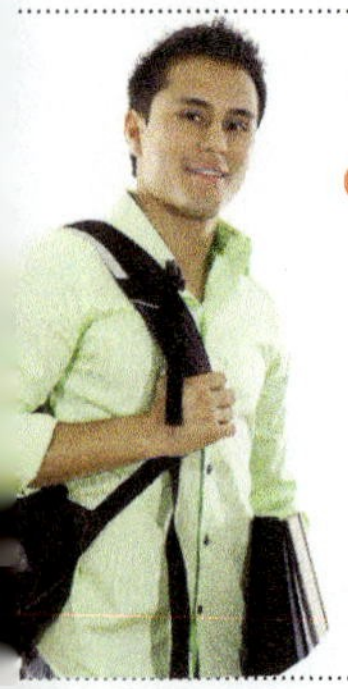

What if a purchaser does not pay for the invoice within the discount period?

Notice that the balance in the Merchandise Inventory account, $33,950, is exactly what was paid for the Merchandise Inventory on June 15, 2017. Also notice that the Accounts Payable account shows that the invoice was paid in full with no remaining balance.

**What if Smart Touch Learning pays this invoice on June 24, 2017, after the discount period ends? Smart Touch Learning must pay the full $35,000.**

In that case, the payment entry is as follows:

| Date | Accounts and Explanation | Debit | Credit |
|---|---|---|---|
| Jun. 24 | Accounts Payable | 35,000 | |
| | Cash | | 35,000 |
| | *Paid after discount period.* | | |

| A↓ | = | L↓ | + | E |
|---|---|---|---|---|
| Cash↓ | = | Accounts Payable↓ | | |

## Purchase Returns and Allowances

Sellers allow purchasers to return merchandise that is defective, damaged, or otherwise unsuitable. This is called a **purchase return** from the purchaser's perspective. Alternatively, the seller may deduct an allowance from the amount the buyer owes. **Purchase allowances** are granted to the purchaser as an incentive to *keep* goods that are not "as ordered." Together, purchase returns and allowances decrease the buyer's cost of the merchandise inventory.

**Purchase Return**
A situation in which sellers allow purchasers to return merchandise that is defective, damaged, or otherwise unsuitable.

**Purchase Allowance**
An amount granted to the purchaser as an incentive to keep goods that are not "as ordered."

Assume that Smart Touch Learning has not yet paid the original bill of June 1. Suppose 20 of the tablets purchased on that invoice (Exhibit 5-3) were damaged in shipment. On June 4, Smart Touch Learning returns the goods (tablets, in this case) valued at $7,000 to the vendor and records the purchase return as follows:

| Date | Accounts and Explanation | Debit | Credit |
|---|---|---|---|
| Jun. 4 | Accounts Payable | 7,000 | |
| | Merchandise Inventory (20 tablets × $350 per tablet) | | 7,000 |
| | *Returned inventory to seller (vendor).* | | |

| A↓ | = | L↓ | + | E |
|---|---|---|---|---|
| Merchandise Inventory↓ | = | Accounts Payable↓ | | |

## ETHICS

### How should you handle gifts from vendors?

Anthony Jackson works as a buyer for a large department store that has decided to expand into selling seasonal home decor. Anthony has been charged with the responsibility of selecting the vendor for the new inventory that the store will sell. His purchasing manager has provided him with two possible vendors to choose from. One vendor, Abbey's Wholesalers, has a long-standing relationship with the department store and can be counted on to provide high-quality goods on a timely basis. The other vendor, Zeta Wholesalers, is a new company that doesn't have much of a track record and is just getting established as a home decor wholesaler. Anthony has contacted both vendors to set up meetings to discuss the new inventory and possible credit terms available. The day before the meeting with the potential vendors, Anthony receives a pair of football tickets to a major NFL game in the mail from Abbey's Wholesalers thanking him for his continued relationship with the wholesaler. What should Anthony do?

### Solution

Anthony should contact his purchasing manager and explain the situation to him or her. By accepting the football tickets, Anthony might unknowingly be violating the code of ethics of the business. Most businesses have a code of ethics that relates to inventory management and purchasing specifically discussing conflicts of interest. Conflicts of interest occur when a vendor is selected above another vendor because of possible personal financial gain such as receiving gifts or entertainment from the selected vendor. Anthony should carefully discuss the situation with his manager before accepting the tickets.

The exact same entry is made for a purchase allowance granted to the buyer from the seller (vendor). The only difference between a purchase return and a purchase allowance is that, in the case of the allowance, Smart Touch Learning keeps the inventory.

Occasionally, a business will return merchandise inventory or receive an allowance before payment has been made. In this scenario, if the payment of the invoice is made within the discount period, the discount should be calculated net of the return or allowance. Let's look at another example. Suppose that on June 10, Smart Touch Learning purchased 15 tablets from Southwest Electronics Direct on account with credit terms of 3/15, n/30 at a cost of $5,250. Five days later, Smart Touch Learning returned five tablets to the vendor because of damages and received a purchase return of $1,750. When Smart Touch Learning makes payment on June 20 (within the discount period), it will calculate the discount on the amount due less the return or $3,500 ($5,250 − $1,750). Smart Touch Learning's discount will be $105 ($3,500 × 0.03). The entries that Smart Touch Learning would record for these transactions follow:

| A↑ | = | L↑ | + | E |
|---|---|---|---|---|
| Merchandise Inventory↑ | = | Accounts Payable↑ | | |

| A↓ | = | L↓ | + | E |
|---|---|---|---|---|
| Merchandise Inventory↓ | = | Accounts Payable↓ | | |

| A↓ | = | L↓ | + | E |
|---|---|---|---|---|
| Cash↓<br>Merchandise Inventory↓ | = | Accounts Payable↓ | | |

| Date | Accounts and Explanation | Debit | Credit |
|---|---|---|---|
| Jun. 10 | Merchandise Inventory | 5,250 | |
| | Accounts Payable | | 5,250 |
| | *Purchased inventory on account.* | | |
| 15 | Accounts Payable | 1,750 | |
| | Merchandise Inventory | | 1,750 |
| | *Returned inventory to the seller (vendor).* | | |
| 20 | Accounts Payable ($5,250 − $1,750) | 3,500 | |
| | Cash ($3,500 − $105) | | 3,395 |
| | Merchandise Inventory ($3,500 × 0.03) | | 105 |
| | *Paid within discount period net of return.* | | |

**DECISIONS**

## Should the business borrow money to make payment within the discount period?

D&B Grocers recently made a large purchase of merchandise inventory on account with credit terms of 5/10, n/30. D&B does not have the cash flow to pay the invoice within the discount period but will have the necessary funds to make payment by the invoice due date. The grocer is considering borrowing money on its line of credit in order to take advantage of the 5% discount. Should D&B borrow the money to make payment within the discount period?

### Solution

D&B should borrow the money only if the amount of interest expense paid on the loan will be less than the discount received. It does not make sense for the grocer to borrow money to make an early payment if in the long run it will end up paying more in interest expense than the discount received.

### Transportation Costs

Either the seller or the buyer must pay the transportation cost of shipping merchandise inventory. The purchase agreement specifies FOB (free on board) terms to determine when title to the goods transfers to the purchaser and who pays the freight. Exhibit 5-4 shows that:

- **FOB shipping point** means the buyer takes ownership (title) to the goods after the goods leave the seller's place of business (shipping point). In most cases, the buyer (owner of the goods while in transit) also pays the freight.
- **FOB destination** means the buyer takes ownership (title) to the goods at the delivery destination point. In most cases, the seller (owner of the goods while in transit) also pays the freight.

When merchandisers are required to pay for shipping costs, those costs are classified as either freight in or freight out as follows:

- **Freight in** is the transportation cost to ship goods into the purchaser's warehouse; thus, it is freight on purchased goods.
- **Freight out** is the transportation cost to ship goods out of the seller's warehouse and to the customer; thus, it is freight on goods sold.

**FOB Shipping Point**
Situation in which the buyer takes ownership (title) to the goods after the goods leave the seller's place of business (shipping point) and the buyer typically pays the freight.

**FOB Destination**
Situation in which the buyer takes ownership (title) to the goods at the delivery destination point and the seller typically pays the freight.

**Freight In**
The transportation cost to ship goods into the purchaser's warehouse; therefore, it is freight on purchased goods.

**Exhibit 5-4 | FOB Terms Determine Who Pays the Freight**

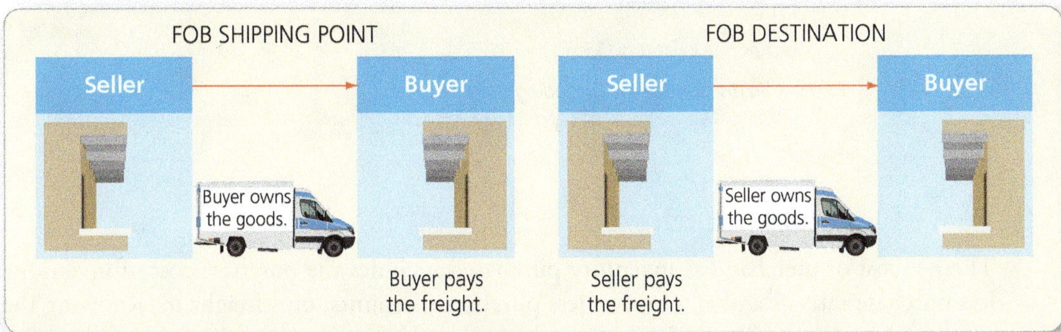


## Freight In

With the terms FOB shipping point, the buyer owns the goods while they are in transit, so the buyer pays the freight. Because the freight is a cost that must be paid to acquire the inventory, freight in becomes part of the cost of merchandise inventory. As a result, freight in costs are debited to the Merchandise Inventory account. Suppose Smart Touch Learning pays a $60 freight charge on June 3 and makes the following entry:

**Freight Out**
The transportation cost to ship goods out of the seller's warehouse; therefore, it is freight on goods sold to a customer.

| Date | Accounts and Explanation | Debit | Credit |
|---|---|---|---|
| Jun. 3 | Merchandise Inventory | 60 | |
| | Cash | | 60 |
| | *Paid a freight bill.* | | |

| A↑↓ | = | L + E |
|---|---|---|
| Merchandise Inventory↑<br>Cash↓ | | |

## Freight In Within Discount Period

Discounts are computed only on the merchandise purchased from the seller. Discounts are not computed on the transportation costs because there is no discount on freight.

Under FOB shipping point, the seller sometimes prepays the transportation cost as a convenience and lists this cost on the invoice. Assume, for example, Smart Touch Learning makes a $5,000 purchase of goods, coupled with a related freight charge of $400, on June 20 on account with terms of 3/5, n/30. The seller prepays the freight charge. The purchase would be recorded as follows:

A↑ (Merchandise Inventory↑) = L↑ (Accounts Payable↑) + E

| Date | Accounts and Explanation | Debit | Credit |
|---|---|---|---|
| Jun. 20 | Merchandise Inventory ($5,000 + $400) | 5,400 | |
| | Accounts Payable | | 5,400 |
| | *Purchased inventory on account, including freight.* | | |

If Smart Touch Learning pays within the discount period, the discount will be computed only on the $5,000 merchandise cost, not on the total invoice of $5,400. The $400 freight is not eligible for the discount. So, the 3% discount would be $150 ($5,000 × 0.03). The entry to record the early payment on June 25 follows:

A↓ (Cash↓, Merchandise Inventory↓) = L↓ (Accounts Payable↓) + E

| Date | Accounts and Explanation | Debit | Credit |
|---|---|---|---|
| Jun. 25 | Accounts Payable | 5,400 | |
| | Cash ($5,400 − $150) | | 5,250 |
| | Merchandise Inventory ($5,000 × 0.03) | | 150 |
| | *Paid within discount period, including freight.* | | |

## Cost of Inventory Purchased

The net cost of merchandise inventory purchased includes the purchase cost of inventory, less purchase returns and allowances, less purchase discounts, plus freight in. Knowing the net cost of inventory allows a business to determine the actual cost of the merchandise purchased and is calculated as follows:

Net Cost of Inventory Purchased = Purchase cost of inventory − Purchase returns and allowances − Purchase discounts + Freight in

Suppose that during the year, Smart Touch Learning buys $281,750 of inventory, returns $61,250 of the goods, and takes a $4,410 early payment discount. The company also pays $14,700 of freight in. The following summary shows Smart Touch Learning's net cost of this merchandise inventory purchased.

| | |
|---|---|
| Purchases | $ 281,750 |
| Less: Purchase Returns and Allowances | 61,250 |
| Purchase Discounts | 4,410 |
| Plus: Freight In | 14,700 |
| Net Cost of Inventory Purchased | $ 230,790 |

## Try It!

**7.** Click Computers has the following transactions in July related to the purchase of merchandise inventory.

| | |
|---|---|
| July 1 | Purchase of $20,500 worth of computers on account, terms of 2/10, n/30. |
| 3 | Return of $4,000 of the computers to the vendor. |
| 9 | Payment made on account. |

Journalize the purchase transactions for Click Computers assuming the company uses the perpetual inventory system.
**Check your answers online in MyAccountingLab or at http://www.pearsonhighered.com/Horngren.**

For more practice, see Short Exercises S5-2 and S5-3. MyAccountingLab

# HOW ARE SALES OF MERCHANDISE INVENTORY RECORDED IN A PERPETUAL INVENTORY SYSTEM?

**Learning Objective 3**
Account for the sale of merchandise inventory using a perpetual inventory system

After a company buys merchandise inventory, the next step is to sell the goods. We shift now to the selling side and follow Smart Touch Learning through a sequence of selling transactions using the perpetual inventory system.

## Sale of Merchandise Inventory

Sales of retailers, such as Smart Touch Learning, are often made for cash. Suppose Smart Touch Learning sold two tablets for cash on June 19, 2017, to a customer and issued the sales invoice in Exhibit 5-5. To the seller, a sales invoice is a bill showing what amount the customer must pay.

**Exhibit 5-5** | **Sales Invoice**

Date: June 19, 2017 Invoice #582

STL SMART TOUCH LEARNING
227 LAKE STREET
POMPTON PLAINS, IL 07444

| Quantity | Item | Unit Price | Total |
|---|---|---|---|
| 2 | Touch Screen Tablet Computers | $500 | $1,000 |
| Total | | | $1,000 |

**Sales Revenue**
The amount that a merchandiser earns from selling its inventory.

The amount a business earns from selling merchandise inventory is called **Sales Revenue** (also called *Sales*). At the time of the sale, two entries must be recorded in the perpetual inventory system. One entry records the Sales Revenue and the Cash (or Accounts Receivable) at the time of the sale. The second entry records Cost of Goods Sold (debit the expense) and reduces the Merchandise Inventory (credit the asset). Remember, Cost of Goods Sold (COGS) is an expense account and represents the cost of inventory that has been sold to customers.

To record the sale by Smart Touch Learning, two journal entries must be recorded. The first journal entry records the cash sale of $1,000 by debiting Cash and crediting Sales Revenue. A second journal entry must also be made to record the expense and decrease the Merchandise Inventory balance. Suppose these goods sold by Smart Touch Learning cost $700. The second journal entry would transfer the $700 from the Merchandise Inventory account to the Cost of Goods Sold account, as follows:

| A↑ | = | L | + | E↑ |
|---|---|---|---|---|
| Cash↑ | | | | Sales Revenue↑ |

| A↓ | = | L | + | E↓ |
|---|---|---|---|---|
| Merchandise Inventory↓ | | | | Cost of Goods Sold↑ |

This entry records the sales revenue.

This entry records the expense and the reduction of merchandise inventory.

| Date | Accounts and Explanation | Debit | Credit |
|---|---|---|---|
| Jun. 19 | Cash | 1,000 | |
| | Sales Revenue | | 1,000 |
| | *Cash sale.* | | |
| 19 | Cost of Goods Sold | 700 | |
| | Merchandise Inventory | | 700 |
| | *Recorded the cost of goods sold.* | | |

The Cost of Goods Sold account keeps a current balance throughout the period in a perpetual inventory system of the cost of merchandise inventory sold. In this example, Cost of Goods Sold is $700 (the cost to Smart Touch Learning) rather than $1,000, the selling price (retail price) of the goods. Cost of Goods Sold is always based on the company's cost, not the retail price.

**Merchandise Inventory**

| | | | |
|---|---|---|---|
| Bal. | xx,xxx | 700 | June 19 |

**Cost of Goods Sold**

| | | |
|---|---|---|
| June 19 | 700 | |

Many sales are made on account (on credit) instead of with cash. Now let's assume that Smart Touch Learning sold 10 tablets for $500 each, making a $5,000 (10 tablets × $500 per tablet) sale on account with terms of 2/10, n/30 on June 21. The goods cost $3,500. The entries to record the sale and cost of goods sold follow:

| A↑ | = | L | + | E↑ |
|---|---|---|---|---|
| Accounts Receivable↑ | | | | Sales Revenue↑ |

| A↓ | = | L | + | E↓ |
|---|---|---|---|---|
| Merchandise Inventory↓ | | | | Cost of Goods Sold↑ |

| Date | Accounts and Explanation | Debit | Credit |
|---|---|---|---|
| Jun. 21 | Accounts Receivable | 5,000 | |
| | Sales Revenue | | 5,000 |
| | *Sale on account.* | | |
| 21 | Cost of Goods Sold | 3,500 | |
| | Merchandise Inventory | | 3,500 |
| | *Recorded the cost of goods sold.* | | |

## Sales Discounts

Many sellers offer customers a discount for early payment. We saw that purchase discounts decrease the cost of inventory purchases. In the same way, **sales discounts** decrease the net amount of revenue earned on sales. The Sales Discounts account is a contra account to Sales Revenue. Recall that a contra account has the opposite normal balance of its companion account. So, Sales Discounts is a contra revenue account and has a normal debit balance.

**Sales Discounts**
Reduction in the amount of cash received from a customer for early payment.

Assume the customer that purchased the tablets on June 21 made payment on June 30, within the discount period. Smart Touch Learning will collect $4,900—the $5,000 amount owed less the 2 percent discount, $100 ($5,000 × 0.02). Smart Touch Learning will record the collection of cash on the receivable and the corresponding sales discount as follows:

| Date | Accounts and Explanation | Debit | Credit |
|---|---|---|---|
| Jun. 30 | Cash ($5,000 − $100) | 4,900 | |
| | Sales Discounts ($5,000 × 0.02) | 100 | |
| | Accounts Receivable | | 5,000 |
| | *Cash collection within the discount period.* | | |

| A↓ | = | L | + | E↓ |
|---|---|---|---|---|
| Cash↑<br>Accounts Receivable↓ | | | | Sales Discounts↑ |

An increase in the Sales Discount contra account is recorded as a debit. This increase reduces the overall Sales Revenue of the company, which decreases equity.

Notice that Smart Touch Learning credited Accounts Receivable for the full amount of the invoice. As shown in the following T-account, by doing this, Smart Touch Learning has accurately shown that the invoice was paid in full with no remaining balance.

| Accounts Receivable | | | |
|---|---|---|---|
| June 21 | 5,000 | 5,000 | June 30 |
| **Bal.** | **0** | | |

Assume instead that the customer did not pay the invoice within the discount period, but paid on July 15. The customer would instead pay the full amount of $5,000 and Smart Touch Learning would record the collection of cash as follows:

| Date | Accounts and Explanation | Debit | Credit |
|---|---|---|---|
| Jul. 15 | Cash | 5,000 | |
| | Accounts Receivable | | 5,000 |
| | *Cash collection after the discount period.* | | |

| A↑↓ | = | L | + | E |
|---|---|---|---|---|
| Cash↑<br>Accounts Receivable↓ | | | | |

## Sales Returns and Allowances

After making a sale, Smart Touch Learning may have customers that return goods, asking for a refund or credit to the customer's account. Or the company may instead grant a sales allowance to encourage the customer to accept the nonstandard goods. Such an allowance reduces the future cash collected from the customer. The return of goods or granting of an allowance is called **Sales Returns and Allowances**. Similar to

**Sales Returns and Allowances**
Decreases in the seller's receivable from a customer's return of merchandise or from granting the customer an allowance from the amount owed to the seller.

Sales Discounts, the Sales Returns and Allowances account is a contra account to Sales Revenue and has a normal debit balance.

## Sales Return

Assume that the customer has not yet paid the original bill of June 21. Suppose, on June 25, the customer returns three of the tablets that were sold for $1,500, with a cost of goods sold of $1,050. When recording a return of merchandise, the seller must record two journal entries: one to record the sales return and decrease the receivable ($1,500) and the other to update the Merchandise Inventory account for the cost of the returned merchandise ($1,050). Smart Touch Learning will record the following two journal entries when the merchandise is returned:

| A↓ | = | L | + | E↓ |
|---|---|---|---|---|
| Accounts Receivable↓ | | | | Sales Returns and Allowances↑ |

| A↑ | = | L | + | E↑ |
|---|---|---|---|---|
| Merchandise Inventory↑ | | | | Cost of Goods Sold↓ |

| Date | Accounts and Explanation | Debit | Credit |
|---|---|---|---|
| Jun. 25 | Sales Returns and Allowances | 1,500 | |
| | Accounts Receivable | | 1,500 |
| | *Received returned goods.* | | |
| 25 | Merchandise Inventory | 1,050 | |
| | Cost of Goods Sold | | 1,050 |
| | *Placed goods back in inventory.* | | |

This entry records the sales returns and allowances.

This entry records the return of the merchandise.

By recording the above journal entries, the Sales Returns and Allowances account increases and the Accounts Receivable account decreases. The seller will not collect cash for the returned goods. In addition, the Merchandise Inventory account increases to reflect the returned goods, but the Cost of Goods Sold account must be decreased because the goods are no longer considered sold.

## Sales Allowance

When a seller grants a sales allowance, there are no returned goods from the customer. Therefore, there is no second entry to adjust the Merchandise Inventory account. Suppose that on June 28 Smart Touch Learning grants a $100 sales allowance for goods damaged in transit. A sales allowance is recorded as follows:

| A↓ | = | L | + | E↓ |
|---|---|---|---|---|
| Accounts Receivable↓ | | | | Sales Returns and Allowances↑ |

| Date | Accounts and Explanation | Debit | Credit |
|---|---|---|---|
| Jun. 28 | Sales Returns and Allowances | 100 | |
| | Accounts Receivable | | 100 |
| | *Granted a sales allowance for damaged goods.* | | |

After the return and allowance have been posted, the Accounts Receivable balance related to the June 21 sale is $3,400, as follows:

**Accounts Receivable**

| | | | |
|---|---|---|---|
| June 21 | 5,000 | 1,500 | June 25 |
| | | 100 | June 28 |
| **Bal.** | **3,400** | | |

## Sales Returns and Allowances Within Discount Period

If sales returns and allowances occur before the discount period has expired, any discount allowed would be calculated net of the returns and allowances. For example, suppose that on June 30, Smart Touch Learning receives payment on the receivable. The company's cash receipt is $3,332, and the entry recorded is as follows:

| Date | Accounts and Explanation | Debit | Credit |
|---|---|---|---|
| Jun. 30 | Cash ($3,400 − $68) | 3,332 | |
| | Sales Discounts ($3,400 × 0.02) | 68 | |
| | Accounts Receivable | | 3,400 |
| | *Cash collection within discount period net of return and allowance.* | | |

A↓ = L + E↓
Cash↑, Accounts Receivable↓ = Sales Discounts↑

## Transportation Costs—Freight Out

Remember that a freight out expense is one in which the seller pays freight charges to ship goods to customers. Freight out is a delivery expense to the seller. Delivery expense is an operating expense and is debited to the Delivery Expense account. For example, assume Smart Touch Learning paid $30 to ship goods to a customer on June 21. The entry to record that payment is as follows:

| Date | Accounts and Explanation | Debit | Credit |
|---|---|---|---|
| Jun. 21 | Delivery Expense | 30 | |
| | Cash | | 30 |
| | *Paid a freight bill.* | | |

A↓ = L + E↓
Cash↓ = Delivery Expense↑

## Net Sales Revenue and Gross Profit

**Net Sales Revenue** is calculated as Sales Revenue less Sales Returns and Allowances and Sales Discounts. Net Sales Revenue is the amount a company has earned on sales of merchandise inventory after sales returns and allowances and sales discounts have been taken out.

**Net Sales Revenue**
The amount a company has earned on sales of merchandise inventory after returns, allowances, and discounts have been taken out. Sales Revenue less Sales Returns and Allowances and Sales Discounts.

Net Sales Revenue = Sales Revenue − Sales Returns and Allowances − Sales Discounts

Suppose during the year Smart Touch Learning sells $297,500 of merchandise inventory, receives $11,200 of sales returns and allowances, and accepts $5,600 of early payment discounts. The following summary shows Smart Touch Learning's net sales revenue.

| | |
|---|---|
| Sales Revenue | $ 297,500 |
| Less: Sales Returns and Allowances | 11,200 |
| Sales Discounts | 5,600 |
| Net Sales Revenue | $ 280,700 |

After determining net sales revenue, Smart Touch Learning can then calculate its gross profit. Remember, gross profit is the markup on the merchandise inventory and is calculated as net sales revenue minus cost of goods sold. For this example, assume Smart Touch Learning's Cost of Goods Sold is $199,500; its gross profit is calculated as follows:

| | |
|---|---|
| Net Sales Revenue | $ 280,700 |
| Less: Cost of Goods Sold | 199,500 |
| Gross Profit | $ 81,200 |

*In this chapter, we provide you with the amount of cost of goods sold. You will learn how to calculate cost of goods sold in the next chapter.*

Gross profit, along with net income, is a measure of a business's success. A sufficiently high gross profit is vital to a merchandiser. The gross profit is reported on the merchandiser's income statement and is the sum of the gross profits on all merchandise sold. The gross profit must cover the company's operating expenses for the company to survive.

## Try It!

**8.** Click Computers has the following transactions in July related to the sale of merchandise inventory.

| | |
|---|---|
| July 12 | Sold computers on account for $8,000 to a customer, terms 3/15, n/30. The cost of the computers is $4,800. |
| 21 | Accepted a $1,000 return from the customer from July 12. The computer returned had a cost of $600. |
| 26 | Received payment from the customer on balance due. |

Journalize the sales transactions for Click Computers assuming the company uses the perpetual inventory system.

**Check your answers online in MyAccountingLab or at http://www.pearsonhighered.com/Horngren.**

For more practice, see Short Exercises S5-4 and S5-5. MyAccountingLab

## WHAT ARE THE ADJUSTING AND CLOSING ENTRIES FOR A MERCHANDISER?

**Learning Objective 4**

Adjust and close the accounts of a merchandising business

A merchandiser adjusts and closes accounts the same way a service entity does. If a worksheet is used, the unadjusted trial balance is entered, and the worksheet is completed to determine net income or net loss.

### Adjusting Merchandise Inventory Based on a Physical Count

The Merchandise Inventory account should stay current at all times in a perpetual inventory system. However, the actual amount of inventory on hand may differ from what the books show. This difference can occur because of theft, damage, and errors and is referred to as **inventory shrinkage**. For this reason, businesses take a physical count of inventory *at least* once a year. The most common time to count inventory is at the end of the fiscal year. The business then adjusts the Merchandise Inventory account based on the physical count. Smart Touch Learning must record an adjusting entry to account for this lost inventory.

**Inventory Shrinkage**
The loss of inventory that occurs because of theft, damage, and errors.

Smart Touch Learning's Merchandise Inventory account shows an unadjusted balance of $31,530. With no shrinkage—due to theft or error—the business should have inventory costing $31,530. But on December 31, Smart Touch Learning counts the inventory on hand, and the total cost comes to only $31,290.

> Adjusting entry = Merchandise inventory balance before adjustment − Actual merchandise inventory on hand = $31,530 − $31,290 = $240

Smart Touch Learning records this adjusting entry for inventory shrinkage:

| Date | Accounts and Explanation | Debit | Credit |
|---|---|---|---|
| Dec. 31 | Cost of Goods Sold | 240 | |
| | Merchandise Inventory | | 240 |
| | *Adjustment for inventory shrinkage.* | | |

A↓ = L + E↓
Merchandise Inventory↓ = Cost of Goods Sold↑

This entry brings Merchandise Inventory to its correct balance.

**Merchandise Inventory**

| | | | | |
|---|---|---|---|---|
| Unadj. Bal. | 31,530 | 240 | Adj. | Dec. 31 |
| **Bal.** | **31,290** | | | |

## Closing the Accounts of a Merchandiser

Exhibit 5-6 (on the next page) presents Smart Touch Learning's adjusted trial balance and closing entries for the year, which are similar to those you have already learned, except for the new accounts (highlighted in blue). Closing still means to zero out all temporary accounts (accounts that aren't on the balance sheet).

The four-step closing process for a merchandising company follows:

**Step 1:** Make the revenue accounts equal zero via the Income Summary account.

**Step 2:** Make expense accounts and other temporary accounts with a debit balance (Sales Returns and Allowances and Sales Discounts) equal zero via the Income Summary account.

**Step 3:** Make the Income Summary account equal zero via the Retained Earnings account. This closing entry transfers net income (or net loss) to Retained Earnings.

**Step 4:** Make the Dividends account equal zero via the Retained Earnings account.

**Exhibit 5-6** | **Adjusted Trial Balance and Closing Entries**

**SMART TOUCH LEARNING**
Adjusted Trial Balance
December 31, 2017

| | Balance | |
|---|---|---|
| **Account Title** | **Debit** | **Credit** |
| Cash | $ 8,810 | |
| Accounts Receivable | 4,400 | |
| Merchandise Inventory | 31,290 | |
| Office Supplies | 100 | |
| Prepaid Rent | 4,000 | |
| Furniture | 18,000 | |
| Accumulated Depreciation—Furniture | | $ 2,100 |
| Building | 60,000 | |
| Accumulated Depreciation—Building | | 1,750 |
| Land | 20,000 | |
| Accounts Payable | | 10,800 |
| Utilities Payable | | 2,500 |
| Salaries Payable | | 1,500 |
| Interest Payable | | 300 |
| Unearned Revenue | | 900 |
| Income Tax Payable | | 3,780 |
| Notes Payable | | 60,000 |
| Common Stock | | 48,000 |
| Retained Earnings | | 3,550 |
| Dividends | 10,000 | |
| Sales Revenue | | 297,500 |
| Sales Returns and Allowances | 11,200 | |
| Sales Discounts | 5,600 | |
| Cost of Goods Sold | 199,500 | |
| Salaries Expense | 15,000 | |
| Rent Expense | 13,000 | |
| Utilities Expense | 11,300 | |
| Insurance Expense | 6,500 | |
| Depreciation Expense—Furniture | 1,800 | |
| Depreciation Expense—Building | 1,500 | |
| Advertising Expense | 2,400 | |
| Interest Expense | 2,300 | |
| Delivery Expense | 1,600 | |
| Supplies Expense | 600 | |
| Income Tax Expense | 3,780 | |
| Total | **$ 432,680** | **$ 432,680** |

Temporary accounts that are closed.

**Exhibit 5-6 | (Continued)**

| Date | Accounts and Explanation | Debit | Credit |
|---|---|---|---|
| Dec. 31 | Sales Revenue | 297,500 | |
| | Income Summary | | 297,500 |
| | *To close revenue.* | | |
| 31 | Income Summary | 276,080 | |
| | Sales Returns and Allowances | | 11,200 |
| | Sales Discounts | | 5,600 |
| | Cost of Goods Sold | | 199,500 |
| | Salaries Expense | | 15,000 |
| | Rent Expense | | 13,000 |
| | Utilities Expense | | 11,300 |
| | Insurance Expense | | 6,500 |
| | Depreciation Expense—Furniture | | 1,800 |
| | Depreciation Expense—Building | | 1,500 |
| | Advertising Expense | | 2,400 |
| | Interest Expense | | 2,300 |
| | Delivery Expense | | 1,600 |
| | Supplies Expense | | 600 |
| | Income Tax Expense | | 3,780 |
| | *To close expenses and other debit accounts.* | | |
| 31 | Income Summary | 21,420 | |
| | Retained Earnings | | 21,420 |
| | *To close Income Summary.* | | |
| 31 | Retained Earnings | 10,000 | |
| | Dividends | | 10,000 |
| | *To close Dividends.* | | |

A } = { L + E↑↓
Sales Revenue↓
Income Summary↑

A } = { L + E↑↓
Income Summary↓
Sales Returns and Allowances↓
Sales Discounts↓
Expenses↓

A } = { L + E↑↓
Income Summary↓
Retained Earnings↑

A } = { L + E↑↓
Retained Earnings↓
Dividends↓

**Income Summary**

| | | | |
|---|---|---|---|
| Clos. 2 | 276,080 | 297,500 | Clos. 1 |
| | | 21,420 | Bal. |
| Clos. 3 | 21,420 | | |
| | | **0** | **Bal.** |

**Retained Earnings**

| | | | |
|---|---|---|---|
| | | 3,550 | Adj. Bal. |
| Clos. 4 | 10,000 | 21,420 | Clos. 3 |
| | | 14,970 | **Bal.** |

**Dividends**

| | | | |
|---|---|---|---|
| Adj. Bal. | 10,000 | | |
| | | 10,000 | Clos. 4 |
| **Bal.** | **0** | | |

## Worksheet for a Merchandising Business—Perpetual Inventory System

The worksheet of a merchandiser is similar to the worksheet for a service business. The main new account is the Merchandise Inventory account, which must be adjusted based on a physical count due to inventory shrinkage. Also, the merchandiser's worksheet carries the other new merchandising accounts (Sales Revenue, Sales Returns and Allowances,

Sales Discounts, Delivery Expense, and Cost of Goods Sold). Worksheet procedures are the same as for a service business. The sum of the unadjusted trial balance amounts, plus or minus the adjustments, equals the adjusted trial balance amounts. The revenues and expenses are then moved to the income statement columns, and the assets, liabilities, and equity amounts are moved to the balance sheet columns.

## Try It!

**9.** Click Computers's Merchandise Inventory account at year-end is showing a balance of $43,000. The physical count of inventory came up with $42,500. Journalize the adjusting entry needed to account for the inventory shrinkage. The company uses the perpetual inventory system.

**Check your answer online in MyAccountingLab or at http://www.pearsonhighered.com/Horngren.**

For more practice, see Short Exercises S5-6 and S5-7. MyAccountingLab

# HOW ARE A MERCHANDISER'S FINANCIAL STATEMENTS PREPARED?

**Learning Objective 5**
Prepare a merchandiser's financial statements

The financial statements that you have learned for a service business are also used by a merchandiser. However, the merchandiser's financial statements will contain the new accounts that have been introduced in this chapter. Let's take a look at some of the differences for a merchandising business.

## Income Statement

As you have learned, the balance sheet can appear in two formats:

- The report format (assets at top, liabilities and stockholders' equity at bottom)
- The account format (assets at left, liabilities and stockholders' equity at right)

There are also two formats for the income statement:

- The single-step format
- The multi-step format

### Single-Step Income Statement

**Single-Step Income Statement**
Income statement format that groups all revenues together and then lists and deducts all expenses together without calculating any subtotals.

The **single-step income statement** is the income statement format that you first learned. It groups all revenues together and all expenses together without calculating other subtotals. Many companies use this format. The single-step format clearly distinguishes revenues from expenses and works well for service entities because they have no gross profit to report. Exhibit 5-7 shows a single-step income statement for Smart Touch Learning.

**Exhibit 5-7 | Single-Step Income Statement**

| SMART TOUCH LEARNING<br>Income Statement<br>Year Ended December 31, 2017 | | |
|---|---|---|
| **Revenues:** | | |
| Net Sales Revenue | | $ 280,700 |
| **Expenses:** | | |
| Cost of Goods Sold | $ 199,500 | |
| Salaries Expense | 15,000 | |
| Rent Expense | 13,000 | |
| Utilities Expense | 11,300 | |
| Insurance Expense | 6,500 | |
| Depreciation Expense—Furniture | 1,800 | |
| Depreciation Expense—Building | 1,500 | |
| Advertising Expense | 2,400 | |
| Interest Expense | 2,300 | |
| Delivery Expense | 1,600 | |
| Supplies Expense | 600 | |
| Income Tax Expense | 3,780 | |
| Total Expenses | | 259,280 |
| Net Income | | **$ 21,420** |

IFRS

Cost of Goods Sold represents a *functional* expense. Such expenses explain the purpose of the cost incurred. IFRS allows companies to present expenses according to their function or nature. For example, expenses are described as salaries, utilities, or advertising expenses.

## Multi-Step Income Statement

A **multi-step income statement** lists several important subtotals. In addition to net income (the bottom line), it also reports subtotals for gross profit, operating income (also called *income from operations*), and income before income tax expense. The multi-step income statement for Smart Touch Learning appears in Exhibit 5-8 (on the next page).

The income statement begins with net sales revenue, cost of goods sold, and gross profit. Next, the operating expenses, those expenses other than cost of goods sold, are listed. Both merchandisers and service companies report operating expenses in two categories:

- **Selling expenses** are expenses related to marketing and selling the company's goods and services. These include sales salaries, sales commissions, advertising, depreciation on store buildings and equipment, store rent, utilities on store buildings, property taxes on store buildings, and delivery expense.
- **Administrative expenses** include expenses *not* related to marketing the company's goods and services. These include office expenses, such as the salaries of the executives and office employees; depreciation on office buildings and equipment; rent other than on stores (for example, rent on the administrative office); utilities other than on stores (for example, utilities on the administrative office); and property taxes on the administrative office building.

Gross profit minus operating expenses equals **operating income** (also called *income from operations*). Operating income measures the results of the entity's major ongoing activities (normal operations).

**Multi-Step Income Statement**
Income statement format that contains subtotals to highlight significant relationships. In addition to net income, it reports gross profit and operating income.

**Selling Expenses**
Expenses related to marketing and selling the company's goods and services.

**Administrative Expenses**
Expenses incurred that are not related to marketing the company's goods and services.

**Operating Income**
Measures the results of the entity's major ongoing activities. Gross profit minus operating expenses.

**Exhibit 5-8 | Multi-Step Income Statement**

| | SMART TOUCH LEARNING<br>Income Statement<br>Year Ended December 31, 2017 | | |
|---|---|---|---|
| | Sales Revenue | $ 297,500 | |
| | Less: Sales Returns and Allowances | 11,200 | |
| Gross Profit | Sales Discounts | 5,600 | |
| | Net Sales Revenue | | $ 280,700 |
| | Cost of Goods Sold | | 199,500 |
| | Gross Profit | | 81,200 |
| | Operating Expenses: | | |
| | Selling Expenses: | | |
| | Salaries Expense | 8,100 | |
| | Rent Expense | 7,300 | |
| | Advertising Expense | 2,400 | |
| | Depreciation Expense | 2,200 | |
| | Delivery Expense | 1,600 | |
| | Total Selling Expenses | 21,600 | |
| Operating Income | Administrative Expenses: | | |
| | Utilities Expense | 11,300 | |
| | Salaries Expense | 6,900 | |
| | Insurance Expense | 6,500 | |
| | Rent Expense | 5,700 | |
| | Depreciation Expense | 1,100 | |
| | Supplies Expense | 600 | |
| | Total Administrative Expenses | 32,100 | |
| | Total Operating Expenses | | 53,700 |
| | Operating Income | | 27,500 |
| | Other Revenues and (Expenses): | | |
| Other Revenues and (Expenses) and Income Before Income Tax Expense | Interest Expense | (2,300) | |
| | Total Other Revenues and (Expenses) | | (2,300) |
| | Income Before Income Tax Expense | | $ 25,200 |
| Income Tax Expense and Net Income | Income Tax Expense | | 3,780 |
| | Net Income | | **$ 21,420** |

**Other Revenues and Expenses**
Revenues or expenses that are outside the normal, day-to-day operations of a business, such as a gain or loss on the sale of plant assets or interest expense.

**Income Tax Expense**
Expense incurred by a corporation related to federal and state income taxes.

The next section of the income statement is **other revenues and expenses**. This category reports revenues and expenses that fall outside the business's main, day-to-day, regular operations. Examples include interest revenue, interest expense, and gains and losses on the sale of plant assets. These examples have nothing to do with the business's "normal" operations. As a result, they are classified as "other" items.

Lastly, corporations are required to pay income tax. Therefore, the last section of the income statement is the **income tax expense** section. This section reports the federal and state income taxes that are incurred by the corporation. The calculation of income tax expense is complicated and will be covered in later accounting courses and is only presented here for informational purposes.

## Statement of Retained Earnings and the Balance Sheet

A merchandiser's statement of retained earnings looks exactly like that of a service business. The balance sheet will also look the same as for a service business, except merchandisers have an additional current asset, Merchandise Inventory. Service businesses do not have merchandise inventory.

### Try It!

**10.** Capital City Motorcycle's selected accounts as of December 31, 2016, follow:

| | |
|---|---|
| Selling Expenses | $ 10,500 |
| Interest Revenue | 1,000 |
| Sales Returns and Allowances | 4,500 |
| Sales Revenue | 120,000 |
| Cost of Goods Sold | 85,000 |
| Sales Discounts | 2,000 |
| Administrative Expenses | 8,000 |

Prepare the multi-step income statement for the year ended December 31, 2016.

**Check your answers online in MyAccountingLab or at http://www.pearsonhighered.com/Horngren.**

For more practice, see Short Exercises S5-8 and S5-9. MyAccountingLab

## HOW DO WE USE THE GROSS PROFIT PERCENTAGE TO EVALUATE BUSINESS PERFORMANCE?

**Learning Objective 6**

Use the gross profit percentage to evaluate business performance

Merchandisers use several ratios to evaluate their operations, and among them is the gross profit percentage. The **gross profit percentage** measures the profitability of each sales dollar above the cost of goods sold and is computed as follows:

**Gross Profit Percentage**
Measures the profitability of each sales dollar above the cost of goods sold. Gross profit / Net sales revenue.

Gross profit percentage = Gross profit / Net sales revenue

The gross profit percentage is one of the most carefully watched measures of profitability. It reflects a business's ability to earn a profit on its merchandise inventory. The gross profit earned on merchandise inventory must be high enough to cover the remaining operating expenses and to earn net income. A small increase in the gross profit percentage from last year to this year may signal an important rise in income. Conversely, a small decrease from last year to this year may signal trouble. Gross profit percentages vary among industries, but in general, a high gross profit percentage is desired.

Returning to **Green Mountain Coffee Roasters, Inc.** we can now calculate the gross profit percentage. Green Mountain had the following total net sales and cost of sales (cost of goods sold), found on the income statement for fiscal year ending September 28, 2013, located in Appendix A.

| | For year ended Sep. 28, 2013 (in thousands) | For year ended Sep. 29, 2012 (in thousands) |
|---|---|---|
| Net sales | $ 4,358,100 | $ 3,859,198 |
| Cost of sales | 2,738,714 | 2,589,799 |

Gross profit is calculated as total net sales less cost of sales. To determine the gross profit percentage, the gross profit is then divided by total net sales. The gross profit percentage for the year ending September 28, 2013, follows:

Gross profit percentage = ($4,358,100 − $2,738,714) / $4,358,100 = 0.372 = 37.2%

In comparison, the gross profit percentage for the year ending September 29, 2012, was:

Gross profit percentage = ($3,859,198 − $2,589,799) / $3,859,198 = 0.329 = 32.9%

The gross profit percentage increased slightly from 2012 to 2013, signifying that Green Mountain is increasing the percentage of gross profit on its sales. However, when compared with the industry average for gross profit percentage, 58.58%, Green Mountain is significantly lower than average. Green Mountain should consider increasing the amount of profit it is earning on its merchandise inventory.

## Try It!

11. Capital City Motorcycle's selected accounts as of December 31, 2016, follow:

| | |
|---|---|
| Selling Expenses | $ 10,500 |
| Interest Revenue | 1,000 |
| Sales Returns and Allowances | 4,500 |
| Sales Revenue | 120,000 |
| Cost of Goods Sold | 85,000 |
| Sales Discounts | 2,000 |
| Administrative Expenses | 8,000 |

Determine the gross profit percentage for the year ended December 31, 2016.

**Check your answer online in MyAccountingLab or at http://www.pearsonhighered.com/Horngren.**

For more practice, see Short Exercise S5-10. MyAccountingLab

# APPENDIX 5A: Accounting for Merchandise Inventory in a Periodic Inventory System

## HOW ARE MERCHANDISE INVENTORY TRANSACTIONS RECORDED IN A PERIODIC INVENTORY SYSTEM?

**Learning Objective 7**

Account for the purchase and sale of merchandise inventory using a periodic inventory system

Some smaller businesses find it too expensive to invest in a perpetual inventory system. These businesses use a periodic inventory system. In a periodic inventory system, businesses must obtain a physical count of inventory to determine quantities on hand.

### Purchases of Merchandise Inventory

All inventory systems use the Merchandise Inventory account. But in a periodic inventory system, purchases, purchase discounts, purchase returns and allowances, and freight in costs are recorded in separate accounts during the year and then the Merchandise Inventory account is updated in the closing process. Let's account for Smart Touch Learning's purchase of the tablet computers from Southwest Electronics Direct as shown in Exhibit 5-3.

The following entries record the receipt of goods on account on June 3 and payment on June 15 (within the discount period) using the periodic inventory system.

| Date | Accounts and Explanation | Debit | Credit |
|---|---|---|---|
| Jun. 3 | Purchases | 35,000 | |
| | Accounts Payable | | 35,000 |
| | *Purchased inventory on account.* | | |
| 15 | Accounts Payable | 35,000 | |
| | Cash ($35,000 − $1,050) | | 33,950 |
| | Purchase Discounts ($35,000 × 0.03) | | 1,050 |
| | *Paid within discount period.* | | |

A = L↑ + E↓ (Accounts Payable↑; Purchases↑)

A↓ = L↓ + E↑ (Cash↓ = Accounts Payable↓; Purchase Discounts↑)

*When using the periodic inventory system, the Merchandise Inventory account is not updated during the period. Therefore, it will never be used when recording purchases, discounts, returns, or sales of inventory.*

Notice that the purchase of merchandise inventory is not recorded directly into the Merchandise Inventory account. Instead, it is recorded in a separate account called Purchases (an expense account). Likewise, when Smart Touch Learning makes payment for the merchandise, the purchase discount is recorded in a separate account called Purchase Discounts (a contra expense account).

## Recording Purchase Returns and Allowances

Suppose that, prior to payment, on June 4, Smart Touch Learning returned 20 tablets to the vendor costing $7,000. The company would record this return as follows:

| A | = | L↓ | + | E↑ |
|---|---|---|---|---|
| | | Accounts Payable↓ | | Purchase Returns and Allowances↑ |

| Date | Accounts and Explanation | Debit | Credit |
|---|---|---|---|
| Jun. 4 | Accounts Payable | 7,000 | |
| | Purchase Returns and Allowances | | 7,000 |
| | *Returned inventory to seller (vendor).* | | |

In the periodic inventory system, instead of recording the return to Merchandise Inventory, a separate account, Purchase Returns and Allowances, is used. Both Purchase Discounts and Purchase Returns and Allowances are contra expense accounts. They are contra accounts to the Purchases account.

During the period, the business records the cost of all inventory bought in the Purchases account. The balance of Purchases is a *gross* amount because it does not include subtractions for discounts, returns, or allowances. **Net purchases** is the remainder after subtracting the contra accounts from Purchases:

**Net Purchases**
Purchases less purchase returns and allowances less purchase discounts.

| |
|---|
| Purchases |
| − Purchase Returns and Allowances |
| − Purchase Discounts |
| = Net Purchases |

## Recording Transportation Costs

Under the periodic inventory system, freight in is debited to a separate Freight In account (an expense account) as opposed to debiting the Merchandise Inventory account. For example, suppose Smart Touch Learning pays a $60 freight charge on June 3. The company would make the following entry:

| A↓ | = | L | + | E↓ |
|---|---|---|---|---|
| Cash↓ | | | | Freight In↑ |

| Date | Accounts and Explanation | Debit | Credit |
|---|---|---|---|
| Jun. 3 | Freight In | 60 | |
| | Cash | | 60 |
| | *Paid a freight bill.* | | |

## Sale of Merchandise Inventory

Recording sales of merchandise inventory is streamlined in the periodic inventory system. With no running record of merchandise inventory to maintain, there is no need to record an entry to Merchandise Inventory and Cost of Goods Sold. Instead, a sale of inventory involves recording only the Sales Revenue portion. Suppose that on June 19, Smart Touch Learning sold 10 tablets for a total sale of $5,000 on account. The company would record the sale as follows:

| Date | Accounts and Explanation | Debit | Credit |
|---|---|---|---|
| Jun. 19 | Accounts Receivable | 5,000 | |
| | Sales Revenue | | 5,000 |
| | *Sale on account.* | | |

A↑ = L + E↑

Accounts Receivable↑ = Sales Revenue↑

Accounting for sales discounts and sales returns and allowances is the same as in a perpetual inventory system, except that there are no entries to Merchandise Inventory or Cost of Goods Sold.

## Adjusting and Closing Entries

When using the periodic inventory system, there is no need to record an adjusting entry for inventory shrinkage. This is because there is no perpetual running balance of the Merchandise Inventory account. Instead, the business determines the ending Merchandise Inventory amount by taking a physical count of inventory. The amount of this physical count is the amount that is recorded as ending Merchandise Inventory ($31,290 for Smart Touch Learning).

The process of recording the ending Merchandise Inventory is completed through the closing entry process. Let's take a look at Smart Touch Learning's adjusted trial balance and closing entries for the year under the periodic inventory system shown in Exhibit 5A-1 (on the next page). The accounts that are used in the periodic inventory system are highlighted in blue.

**Exhibit 5A-1** | **Adjusted Trial Balance and Closing Entries**

**SMART TOUCH LEARNING**
Adjusted Trial Balance
December 31, 2017

| | Balance | |
|---|---|---|
| **Account Title** | **Debit** | **Credit** |
| Cash | $ 8,810 | |
| Accounts Receivable | 4,400 | |
| Merchandise Inventory (beginning) | 0 | |
| Office Supplies | 100 | |
| Prepaid Rent | 4,000 | |
| Furniture | 18,000 | |
| Accumulated Depreciation—Furniture | | $ 2,100 |
| Building | 60,000 | |
| Accumulated Depreciation—Building | | 1,750 |
| Land | 20,000 | |
| Accounts Payable | | 10,800 |
| Utilities Payable | | 2,500 |
| Salaries Payable | | 1,500 |
| Interest Payable | | 300 |
| Unearned Revenue | | 900 |
| Income Tax Payable | | 3,780 |
| Notes Payable | | 60,000 |
| Common Stock | | 48,000 |
| Retained Earnings | | 3,550 |
| Dividends | 10,000 | |
| Sales Revenue | | 297,500 |
| Sales Returns and Allowances | 11,200 | |
| Sales Discounts | 5,600 | |
| Purchases | 281,750 | |
| Purchase Returns and Allowances | | 61,250 |
| Purchase Discounts | | 4,410 |
| Freight In | 14,700 | |
| Salaries Expense | 15,000 | |
| Rent Expense | 13,000 | |
| Utilities Expense | 11,300 | |
| Insurance Expense | 6,500 | |
| Depreciation Expense—Furniture | 1,800 | |
| Depreciation Expense—Building | 1,500 | |
| Advertising Expense | 2,400 | |
| Interest Expense | 2,300 | |
| Delivery Expense | 1,600 | |
| Supplies Expense | 600 | |
| Income Tax Expense | 3,780 | |
| Total | **$ 498,340** | **$ 498,340** |

Temporary accounts that are closed.

**Exhibit 5A-1 | (Continued)**

| Date | Accounts and Explanation | Debit | Credit |
| --- | --- | --- | --- |
| Dec. 31 | Sales Revenue | 297,500 | |
| | Purchase Returns and Allowances | 61,250 | |
| | Purchase Discounts | 4,410 | |
| | Merchandise Inventory (ending) | 31,290 | |
| | Income Summary | | 394,450 |
| | *To close revenue and other credit accounts and record ending merchandise inventory.* | | |
| 31 | Income Summary | 373,030 | |
| | Sales Returns and Allowances | | 11,200 |
| | Sales Discounts | | 5,600 |
| | Purchases | | 281,750 |
| | Freight In | | 14,700 |
| | Merchandise Inventory (beginning) | | 0 |
| | Salaries Expense | | 15,000 |
| | Rent Expense | | 13,000 |
| | Utilities Expense | | 11,300 |
| | Insurance Expense | | 6,500 |
| | Depreciation Expense—Furniture | | 1,800 |
| | Depreciation Expense—Building | | 1,500 |
| | Advertising Expense | | 2,400 |
| | Interest Expense | | 2,300 |
| | Delivery Expense | | 1,600 |
| | Supplies Expense | | 600 |
| | Income Tax Expense | | 3,780 |
| | *To close expenses and other debit accounts and remove beginning merchandise inventory.* | | |
| 31 | Income Summary | 21,420 | |
| | Retained Earnings | | 21,420 |
| | *To close Income Summary.* | | |
| 31 | Retained Earnings | 10,000 | |
| | Dividends | | 10,000 |
| | *To close Dividends.* | | |

| A↑ | = | L | + | E↑ |
| --- | --- | --- | --- | --- |
| Merchandise Inventory↑ | = | | | Sales Revenue↓<br>Purchase Returns and Allowances↓<br>Purchase Discounts↓<br>Income Summary↑ |

| A↓ | = | L | + | E↓ |
| --- | --- | --- | --- | --- |
| Merchandise Inventory↓ | = | | | Income Summary↓<br>Sales Returns and Allowances↓<br>Sales Discounts↓<br>Expenses↓ |

| A | = | L | + | E↑↓ |
| --- | --- | --- | --- | --- |
| | = | | | Income Summary↓<br>Retained Earnings↑ |

| A | = | L | + | E↑↓ |
| --- | --- | --- | --- | --- |
| | = | | | Retained Earnings↓<br>Dividends↓ |

**Income Summary**

| | | | |
| --- | --- | --- | --- |
| Clos. 2 | 373,030 | 394,450 | Clos. 1 |
| | | 21,420 | Bal. |
| Clos. 3 | 21,420 | | |
| | | **0** | **Bal.** |

**Retained Earnings**

| | | | |
| --- | --- | --- | --- |
| | | 3,550 | Adj. Bal. |
| Clos. 4 | 10,000 | 21,420 | Clos. 3 |
| | | 14,970 | **Bal.** |

**Dividends**

| | | | |
| --- | --- | --- | --- |
| Adj. Bal. | 10,000 | | |
| | | 10,000 | Clos. 4 |
| **Bal.** | **0** | | |

The four-step closing process under the periodic inventory system is similar to the perpetual inventory system, but let's take a moment to highlight the differences:

**Step 1:** Using the periodic inventory system, Sales Revenue is still closed with a debit via the Income Summary account, but in addition, all other temporary accounts with credit balances (Purchase Returns and Allowances and Purchase Discounts) are also closed. The ending Merchandise Inventory (determined from the physical count) is recorded as a debit.

**Step 2:** Expense accounts and other temporary accounts with debit balances are still closed via the Income Summary account. In addition, the beginning Merchandise Inventory, Purchases, and Freight In are also closed via the Income Summary account. Notice in the Merchandise Inventory T-account shown below that the ending inventory is recorded with a debit entry and the beginning inventory is removed with a credit entry during the closing process.

**Merchandise Inventory**

| | | | |
|---|---|---|---|
| Adj. Bal. | 0 | | |
| Clos. 1 | 31,290 | 0 | Clos. 2 |
| **Bal.** | **31,290** | | |

*The key difference in the closing process under the periodic inventory system is how merchandise inventory is handled. In the periodic inventory system, the ending merchandise inventory balance must be recorded as a debit during closing and the beginning merchandise inventory balance must be recorded as a credit during closing. The additional Purchases and related contra and adjunct accounts must also be closed.*

**Step 3 and Step 4:** These steps, closing the Income Summary and Dividends accounts, are the same under both methods.

## Preparing Financial Statements

The financial statements under the perpetual and periodic inventory systems are similar. However, the periodic inventory system requires an additional calculation—the cost of goods sold. As we have seen under the perpetual inventory system, cost of goods sold is simply the sum of the amounts posted to that account. Cost of goods sold must be computed separately under the periodic inventory system. At the end of each period, the company combines a number of accounts to compute cost of goods sold for the period, and this calculation is shown on the income statement. Cost of goods sold is calculated as follows for Smart Touch Learning:

| | | |
|---|---|---|
| Beginning Merchandise Inventory | | $ 0 |
| Purchases | $ 281,750 | |
| Less: Purchase Returns and Allowances | 61,250 | |
| Purchase Discounts | 4,410 | |
| Net Purchases | 216,090 | |
| Plus: Freight In | 14,700 | |
| Net Cost of Purchases | | 230,790 |
| Cost of Goods Available for Sale | | 230,790 |
| Less: Ending Inventory | | 31,290 |
| Cost of Goods Sold | | $ 199,500 |

The multi-step income statement for Smart Touch Learning is presented in Exhibit 5A-2. Notice that the net income is the same under both methods.

**Exhibit 5A-2 | Multi-Step Income Statement**

| SMART TOUCH LEARNING<br>Income Statement<br>Year Ended December 31, 2017 | | | |
|---|---|---|---|
| Sales Revenue | | $ 297,500 | |
| Less: Sales Returns and Allowances | | 11,200 | |
| Sales Discounts | | 5,600 | |
| Net Sales Revenue | | | $ 280,700 |
| Cost of Goods Sold: | | | |
| Beginning Merchandise Inventory | | 0 | |
| Purchases | $ 281,750 | | |
| Less: Purchase Returns and Allowances | 61,250 | | |
| Purchase Discounts | 4,410 | | |
| Net Purchases | 216,090 | | |
| Plus: Freight In | 14,700 | | |
| Net Cost of Purchases | | 230,790 | |
| Cost of Goods Available for Sale | | 230,790 | |
| Less: Ending Merchandise Inventory | | 31,290 | |
| Cost of Goods Sold | | | 199,500 |
| Gross Profit | | | 81,200 |
| Operating Expenses: | | | |
| Selling Expenses: | | | |
| Salaries Expense | | 8,100 | |
| Rent Expense | | 7,300 | |
| Advertising Expense | | 2,400 | |
| Depreciation Expense | | 2,200 | |
| Delivery Expense | | 1,600 | |
| Total Selling Expenses | | 21,600 | |
| Administrative Expenses: | | | |
| Utilities Expense | | 11,300 | |
| Salaries Expense | | 6,900 | |
| Insurance Expense | | 6,500 | |
| Rent Expense | | 5,700 | |
| Depreciation Expense | | 1,100 | |
| Supplies Expense | | 600 | |
| Total Administrative Expenses | | 32,100 | |
| Total Operating Expenses | | | 53,700 |
| Operating Income | | | 27,500 |
| Other Revenues and (Expenses): | | | |
| Interest Expense | | (2,300) | |
| Total Other Revenues and (Expenses) | | | (2,300) |
| Income Before Income Tax Expense | | | $ 25,200 |
| Income Tax Expense | | | 3,780 |
| Net Income | | | **$ 21,420** |

Gross Profit

Operating Income

Other Revenues and (Expenses) and Income Before Income Tax Expense

Income Tax Expense and Net Income

Exhibit 5A-3 provides a side-by-side comparison of periodic and perpetual inventory system journal entries for the same company's transactions.

**Exhibit 5A-3** | **Perpetual Versus Periodic Inventory System**

### Purchased inventory on account:

PERPETUAL INVENTORY SYSTEM

| Date | Accounts and Explanation | Debit | Credit |
|---|---|---|---|
| | Merchandise Inventory | 5,250 | |
| | Accounts Payable | | 5,250 |
| | *Purchased inventory on account.* | | |

PERIODIC INVENTORY SYSTEM

| Date | Accounts and Explanation | Debit | Credit |
|---|---|---|---|
| | Purchases | 5,250 | |
| | Accounts Payable | | 5,250 |
| | *Purchased inventory on account.* | | |

### Returned inventory to seller (vendor):

PERPETUAL INVENTORY SYSTEM

| Date | Accounts and Explanation | Debit | Credit |
|---|---|---|---|
| | Accounts Payable | 1,750 | |
| | Merchandise Inventory | | 1,750 |
| | *Returned inventory to seller (vendor).* | | |

PERIODIC INVENTORY SYSTEM

| Date | Accounts and Explanation | Debit | Credit |
|---|---|---|---|
| | Accounts Payable | 1,750 | |
| | Purchase Returns and Allowances | | 1,750 |
| | *Returned inventory to seller (vendor).* | | |

### Paid a freight bill on a purchase:

PERPETUAL INVENTORY SYSTEM

| Date | Accounts and Explanation | Debit | Credit |
|---|---|---|---|
| | Merchandise Inventory | 60 | |
| | Cash | | 60 |
| | *Paid a freight bill.* | | |

PERIODIC INVENTORY SYSTEM

| Date | Accounts and Explanation | Debit | Credit |
|---|---|---|---|
| | Freight In | 60 | |
| | Cash | | 60 |
| | *Paid a freight bill.* | | |

### Paid merchandise invoice within discount period:

PERPETUAL INVENTORY SYSTEM

| Date | Accounts and Explanation | Debit | Credit |
|---|---|---|---|
| | Accounts Payable | 3,500 | |
| | Cash | | 3,395 |
| | Merchandise Inventory | | 105 |
| | *Paid within discount period.* | | |

PERIODIC INVENTORY SYSTEM

| Date | Accounts and Explanation | Debit | Credit |
|---|---|---|---|
| | Accounts Payable | 3,500 | |
| | Cash | | 3,395 |
| | Purchase Discounts | | 105 |
| | *Paid within discount period.* | | |

### Paid merchandise invoice after discount period:

PERPETUAL INVENTORY SYSTEM

| Date | Accounts and Explanation | Debit | Credit |
|---|---|---|---|
| | Accounts Payable | 3,500 | |
| | Cash | | 3,500 |
| | *Paid after discount period.* | | |

PERIODIC INVENTORY SYSTEM

| Date | Accounts and Explanation | Debit | Credit |
|---|---|---|---|
| | Accounts Payable | 3,500 | |
| | Cash | | 3,500 |
| | *Paid after discount period.* | | |

### Sale on account:

PERPETUAL INVENTORY SYSTEM

| Date | Accounts and Explanation | Debit | Credit |
|---|---|---|---|
| | Accounts Receivable | 5,000 | |
| | Sales Revenue | | 5,000 |
| | *Sale on account.* | | |
| | | | |
| | Cost of Goods Sold | 3,500 | |
| | Merchandise Inventory | | 3,500 |
| | *Recorded the cost of goods sold.* | | |

PERIODIC INVENTORY SYSTEM

| Date | Accounts and Explanation | Debit | Credit |
|---|---|---|---|
| | Accounts Receivable | 5,000 | |
| | Sales Revenue | | 5,000 |
| | *Sale on account.* | | |

**Exhibit 5A-3 (Continued)**

**PERPETUAL INVENTORY SYSTEM**

**PERIODIC INVENTORY SYSTEM**

**Paid a freight bill on a sale:**

Perpetual:

| Date | Accounts and Explanation | Debit | Credit |
|---|---|---|---|
| | Delivery Expense | 30 | |
| | Cash | | 30 |
| | *Paid a freight bill.* | | |

Periodic:

| Date | Accounts and Explanation | Debit | Credit |
|---|---|---|---|
| | Delivery Expense | 30 | |
| | Cash | | 30 |
| | *Paid a freight bill.* | | |

**Received returned goods:**

Perpetual:

| Date | Accounts and Explanation | Debit | Credit |
|---|---|---|---|
| | Sales Returns and Allowances | 1,500 | |
| | Accounts Receivable | | 1,500 |
| | *Received returned goods.* | | |
| | | | |
| | Merchandise Inventory | 1,050 | |
| | Cost of Goods Sold | | 1,050 |
| | *Placed goods back in inventory.* | | |

Periodic:

| Date | Accounts and Explanation | Debit | Credit |
|---|---|---|---|
| | Sales Returns and Allowances | 1,500 | |
| | Accounts Receivable | | 1,500 |
| | *Received returned goods.* | | |

**Granted a sales allowance:**

Perpetual:

| Date | Accounts and Explanation | Debit | Credit |
|---|---|---|---|
| | Sales Returns and Allowances | 100 | |
| | Accounts Receivable | | 100 |
| | *Granted a sales allowance for damaged goods.* | | |

Periodic:

| Date | Accounts and Explanation | Debit | Credit |
|---|---|---|---|
| | Sales Returns and Allowances | 100 | |
| | Accounts Receivable | | 100 |
| | *Granted a sales allowance for damaged goods.* | | |

**Collected cash within the discount period:**

Perpetual:

| Date | Accounts and Explanation | Debit | Credit |
|---|---|---|---|
| | Cash | 3,332 | |
| | Sales Discounts | 68 | |
| | Accounts Receivable | | 3,400 |
| | *Cash collection within the discount period.* | | |

Periodic:

| Date | Accounts and Explanation | Debit | Credit |
|---|---|---|---|
| | Cash | 3,332 | |
| | Sales Discounts | 68 | |
| | Accounts Receivable | | 3,400 |
| | *Cash collection within the discount period.* | | |

**Collected cash after the discount period:**

Perpetual:

| Date | Accounts and Explanation | Debit | Credit |
|---|---|---|---|
| | Cash | 3,400 | |
| | Accounts Receivable | | 3,400 |
| | *Cash collection after the discount period.* | | |

Periodic:

| Date | Accounts and Explanation | Debit | Credit |
|---|---|---|---|
| | Cash | 3,400 | |
| | Accounts Receivable | | 3,400 |
| | *Cash collection after the discount period.* | | |

**Adjusted for inventory shrinkage:**

Perpetual:

| Date | Accounts and Explanation | Debit | Credit |
|---|---|---|---|
| | Cost of Goods Sold | 240 | |
| | Merchandise Inventory | | 240 |
| | *Adjustment for inventory shrinkage.* | | |

**Exhibit 5A-3 | (Continued)**

### PERPETUAL INVENTORY SYSTEM

**Closing entries:**

| Date | Accounts and Explanation | Debit | Credit |
|---|---|---|---|
| | Sales Revenue | 297,500 | |
| | Income Summary | | 297,500 |
| | *To close revenue account.* | | |
| | Income Summary | 276,080 | |
| | Sales Returns and Allowances | | 11,200 |
| | Sales Discounts | | 5,600 |
| | Cost of Goods Sold | | 199,500 |
| | Salaries Expense | | 15,000 |
| | Rent Expense | | 13,000 |
| | Utilities Expense | | 11,300 |
| | Insurance Expense | | 6,500 |
| | Depreciation Expense—Furniture | | 1,800 |
| | Depreciation Expense—Building | | 1,500 |
| | Advertising Expense | | 2,400 |
| | Interest Expense | | 2,300 |
| | Delivery Expense | | 1,600 |
| | Supplies Expense | | 600 |
| | Income Tax Expense | | 3,780 |
| | *To close expenses and other debit accounts.* | | |
| | Income Summary | 21,420 | |
| | Retained Earnings | | 21,420 |
| | *To close Income Summary.* | | |
| | Retained Earnings | 10,000 | |
| | Dividends | | 10,000 |
| | *To close Dividends.* | | |

### PERIODIC INVENTORY SYSTEM

| Date | Accounts and Explanation | Debit | Credit |
|---|---|---|---|
| | Sales Revenue | 297,500 | |
| | Purchase Returns and Allowances | 61,250 | |
| | Purchase Discounts | 4,410 | |
| | Merchandise Inventory (ending) | 31,290 | |
| | Income Summary | | 394,450 |
| | *To close revenue and other credit accounts and record ending merchandise inventory.* | | |
| | Income Summary | 373,030 | |
| | Sales Returns and Allowances | | 11,200 |
| | Sales Discounts | | 5,600 |
| | Purchases | | 281,750 |
| | Freight In | | 14,700 |
| | Merchandise Inventory (beginning) | | 0 |
| | Salaries Expense | | 15,000 |
| | Rent Expense | | 13,000 |
| | Utilities Expense | | 11,300 |
| | Insurance Expense | | 6,500 |
| | Depreciation Expense—Furniture | | 1,800 |
| | Depreciation Expense—Building | | 1,500 |
| | Advertising Expense | | 2,400 |
| | Interest Expense | | 2,300 |
| | Delivery Expense | | 1,600 |
| | Supplies Expense | | 600 |
| | Income Tax Expense | | 3,780 |
| | *To close expenses and other debit accounts and remove beginning merchandise inventory.* | | |
| | Income Summary | 21,420 | |
| | Retained Earnings | | 21,420 |
| | *To close Income Summary.* | | |
| | Retained Earnings | 10,000 | |
| | Dividends | | 10,000 |
| | *To close Dividends.* | | |

## Try It!

**12A.** Click Computers has the following transactions in July related to purchase and sale of merchandise inventory.

| | |
|---|---|
| July 1 | Purchase of $20,500 worth of computers on account, terms of 2/10, n/30. |
| 3 | Return of $4,000 of the computers to the vendor. |
| 9 | Payment made on account. |
| 12 | Sold computers on account for $8,000 to a customer, terms 3/15, n/30. |
| 21 | Accepted a $1,000 return from a customer. |
| 26 | Received payment from customer on balance due. |

Journalize the transactions for Click Computers assuming that the company uses the periodic inventory system.

**Check your answers online in MyAccountingLab or at http://www.pearsonhighered.com/Horngren.**

For more practice, see Short Exercises S5A-11, S5A-12, S5A-13, and S5A-14. MyAccountingLab

# REVIEW

## > Things You Should Know

### 1. What are merchandising operations?

- A merchandiser is a business that sells merchandise, or goods, to customers.
- There are two main types of inventory accounting systems that are used by merchandisers:
  - Periodic inventory system—requires businesses to obtain a physical count of inventory to determine quantities on hand
  - Perpetual inventory system—keeps a running computerized record of merchandise inventory

### 2. How are purchases of merchandise inventory recorded in a perpetual inventory system?

- Purchase of merchandise inventory

| Date | Accounts and Explanation | Debit | Credit |
|---|---|---|---|
| | Merchandise Inventory | XXX | |
| | Cash or Accounts Payable | | XXX |

- Purchase return

| Date | Accounts and Explanation | Debit | Credit |
|---|---|---|---|
| | Cash or Accounts Payable | XXX | |
| | Merchandise Inventory | | XXX |

- Payment of freight in

| Date | Accounts and Explanation | Debit | Credit |
|---|---|---|---|
| | Merchandise Inventory | XXX | |
| | Cash | | XXX |

- Payment within discount period

| Date | Accounts and Explanation | Debit | Credit |
|---|---|---|---|
| | Accounts Payable | XXX | |
| | Cash | | XXX |
| | Merchandise Inventory | | XXX |

- Payment after discount period

| Date | Accounts and Explanation | Debit | Credit |
|---|---|---|---|
| | Accounts Payable | XXX | |
| | Cash | | XXX |

**3. How are sales of merchandise inventory recorded in a perpetual inventory system?**

- Sale of merchandise inventory

| Date | Accounts and Explanation | Debit | Credit |
|---|---|---|---|
| | Cash or Accounts Receivable | XXX | |
| | Sales Revenue | | XXX |
| | | | |
| | Cost of Goods Sold | XXX | |
| | Merchandise Inventory | | XXX |

- Sales return

| Date | Accounts and Explanation | Debit | Credit |
|---|---|---|---|
| | Sales Returns and Allowances | XXX | |
| | Cash or Accounts Receivable | | XXX |
| | | | |
| | Merchandise Inventory | XXX | |
| | Cost of Goods Sold | | XXX |

- Sales allowance

| Date | Accounts and Explanation | Debit | Credit |
|---|---|---|---|
| | Sales Returns and Allowances | XXX | |
| | Cash or Accounts Receivable | | XXX |

- Payment of freight out

| Date | Accounts and Explanation | Debit | Credit |
|---|---|---|---|
| | Delivery Expense | XXX | |
| | Cash | | XXX |

- Collection of cash during discount period

| Date | Accounts and Explanation | Debit | Credit |
|---|---|---|---|
| | Cash | XXX | |
| | Sales Discounts | XXX | |
| | Accounts Receivable | | XXX |

- Collection of cash after discount period

| Date | Accounts and Explanation | Debit | Credit |
|---|---|---|---|
| | Cash | XXX | |
| | Accounts Receivable | | XXX |

**4. What are the adjusting and closing entries for a merchandiser?**

- An adjusting entry must be made for inventory shrinkage, the loss of inventory that occurs because of theft, damage, and errors.
- The closing entries are similar to those already learned, except for including the new accounts (Sales Revenue, Sales Returns and Allowances, Sales Discounts, Delivery Expense, and Cost of Goods Sold).

**5. How are a merchandiser's financial statements prepared?**

- There are two formats for the income statement:
  - Single-step income statement—groups all revenues together and all expenses together without calculating other subtotals
  - Multi-step income statement—lists several important subtotals including gross profit, operating income, and income before income tax expense
- A merchandiser's statement of retained earnings looks exactly like that of a service business.
- The balance sheet will also look the same, except merchandisers have an additional current asset, Merchandise Inventory.

**6. How do we use the gross profit percentage to evaluate business performance?**

- The gross profit percentage measures the profitability of each sales dollar above the cost of goods sold.
- Gross profit percentage = Gross profit / Net sales revenue.

**7. How are merchandise inventory transactions recorded in a periodic inventory system? (Appendix 5A)**

- The Merchandise Inventory account is not used when recording purchase transactions. Instead Purchases, Purchase Discounts, Purchase Returns and Allowances, and Freight In are used.
- Sales transactions only involve recording the Sales Revenue. The Merchandise Inventory account is not used.
- An adjustment for inventory shrinkage is not needed.
- Closing entries are similar to the perpetual inventory system with the addition of closing the new accounts discussed. Ending Merchandise Inventory must be recorded, and beginning Merchandise Inventory must be removed.



## > Summary Problem 5-1

Suppose Heat Miser Air Conditioner Company engaged in the following transactions during June of the current year:

| | |
|---|---|
| Jun. 3 | Purchased inventory on account with credit terms of 1/10, n/EOM, $1,600. |
| 9 | Returned 40% of the inventory purchased on June 3. It was defective. |
| 12 | Sold goods for cash, $920 (cost, $550). |
| 15 | Purchased goods for $5,000 on account. Credit terms were 3/15, n/30. |
| 16 | Paid a $260 freight bill on goods purchased. |
| 18 | Sold inventory for $2,000 on account with credit terms of 2/10, n/30 (cost, $1,180). |
| 22 | Received returned goods from the customer of the June 18 sale, $800 (cost, $480). |
| 24 | Paid supplier for goods purchased on June 15. |
| 28 | Received cash in full settlement of the account from the customer who purchased inventory on June 18. |
| 29 | Paid the amount owed on account from the purchase of June 3. |

**Requirements**

1. Journalize the preceding transactions. Assume Heat Miser uses a perpetual inventory system.
2. Set up T-accounts, and post the journal entries to show the ending balances in the Merchandise Inventory and the Cost of Goods Sold accounts only.

## > Solution

### Requirement 1

| Date | Accounts and Explanation | Debit | Credit |
|---|---|---|---|
| Jun. 3 | Merchandise Inventory | 1,600 | |
| | Accounts Payable | | 1,600 |
| | *Purchased inventory on account.* | | |
| 9 | Accounts Payable ($1,600 × 0.40) | 640 | |
| | Merchandise Inventory | | 640 |
| | *Returned inventory to seller (vendor).* | | |
| 12 | Cash | 920 | |
| | Sales Revenue | | 920 |
| | *Cash sale.* | | |
| 12 | Cost of Goods Sold | 550 | |
| | Merchandise Inventory | | 550 |
| | *Recorded the cost of goods sold.* | | |
| 15 | Merchandise Inventory | 5,000 | |
| | Accounts Payable | | 5,000 |
| | *Purchased inventory on account.* | | |
| 16 | Merchandise Inventory | 260 | |
| | Cash | | 260 |
| | *Paid a freight bill.* | | |

| Date | Accounts and Explanation | Debit | Credit |
|---|---|---|---|
| Jun. 18 | Accounts Receivable | 2,000 | |
| | Sales Revenue | | 2,000 |
| | *Sale on account.* | | |
| 18 | Cost of Goods Sold | 1,180 | |
| | Merchandise Inventory | | 1,180 |
| | *Recorded the cost of goods sold.* | | |
| 22 | Sales Returns and Allowances | 800 | |
| | Accounts Receivable | | 800 |
| | *Received returned goods.* | | |
| 22 | Merchandise Inventory | 480 | |
| | Cost of Goods Sold | | 480 |
| | *Placed goods back in inventory.* | | |
| 24 | Accounts Payable | 5,000 | |
| | Cash ($5,000 − $150) | | 4,850 |
| | Merchandise Inventory ($5,000 × 0.03) | | 150 |
| | *Paid within discount period.* | | |
| 28 | Cash ($1,200 − $24) | 1,176 | |
| | Sales Discounts ($1,200 × 0.02) | 24 | |
| | Accounts Receivable ($2,000 − $800) | | 1,200 |
| | *Cash collection within discount period net of return.* | | |
| 29 | Accounts Payable ($1,600 − $640) | 960 | |
| | Cash | | 960 |
| | *Paid after discount period net of return.* | | |

**Requirement 2**

**Merchandise Inventory**

| | | | |
|---|---|---|---|
| Jun. 3 | 1,600 | 640 | Jun. 9 |
| Jun. 15 | 5,000 | 550 | Jun. 12 |
| Jun. 16 | 260 | 1,180 | Jun. 18 |
| Jun. 22 | 480 | 150 | Jun. 24 |
| **Bal.** | **4,820** | | |

**Cost of Goods Sold**

| | | | |
|---|---|---|---|
| Jun. 12 | 550 | 480 | Jun. 22 |
| Jun. 18 | 1,180 | | |
| **Bal.** | **1,250** | | |

## > Summary Problem 5-2

King Cornelius Company uses a perpetual inventory system. The adjusted trial balance of King Cornelius Company follows:

| KING CORNELIUS COMPANY<br>Adjusted Trial Balance<br>December 31, 2016 | | |
|---|---|---|
| | Balance | |
| **Account Title** | **Debit** | **Credit** |
| Cash | $ 5,600 | |
| Accounts Receivable | 37,100 | |
| Merchandise Inventory | 25,800 | |
| Office Supplies | 1,300 | |
| Prepaid Rent | 1,000 | |
| Furniture | 26,500 | |
| Accumulated Depreciation—Furniture | | $ 23,800 |
| Accounts Payable | | 6,300 |
| Salaries Payable | | 2,000 |
| Interest Payable | | 600 |
| Unearned Revenue | | 2,400 |
| Notes Payable, long-term | | 35,000 |
| Common Stock | | 20,000 |
| Retained Earnings | | 2,200 |
| Dividends | 48,000 | |
| Sales Revenue | | 244,000 |
| Sales Returns and Allowances | 10,000 | |
| Sales Discounts | 8,000 | |
| Interest Revenue | | 2,000 |
| Cost of Goods Sold | 81,000 | |
| Salaries Expense | 72,700 | |
| Rent Expense | 7,700 | |
| Utilities Expense | 5,800 | |
| Depreciation Expense—Furniture | 2,700 | |
| Supplies Expense | 2,200 | |
| Interest Expense | 2,900 | |
| Total | **$ 338,300** | **$ 338,300** |

**Requirements**

1. Journalize the closing entries at December 31. Post to the Income Summary account as an accuracy check on net income. Recall that the credit balance closed out of Income Summary should equal net income as computed on the income statement. Also post to Retained Earnings, whose balance should agree with the amount reported on the balance sheet.
2. Prepare the company's multi-step income statement, statement of retained earnings, and balance sheet in report form for year ended December 31, 2016. Note: King Cornelius doesn't separate its operating expenses as either selling or administrative.
3. Compute the gross profit percentage for 2016.

## Requirement 1

| Date | Accounts and Explanation | Debit | Credit |
|---|---|---|---|
| Dec. 31 | Sales Revenue | 244,000 | |
| | Interest Revenue | 2,000 | |
| | Income Summary | | 246,000 |
| | *To close revenue accounts.* | | |
| | | | |
| 31 | Income Summary | 193,000 | |
| | Sales Returns and Allowances | | 10,000 |
| | Sales Discounts | | 8,000 |
| | Cost of Goods Sold | | 81,000 |
| | Salaries Expense | | 72,700 |
| | Rent Expense | | 7,700 |
| | Utilities Expense | | 5,800 |
| | Depreciation Expense—Furniture | | 2,700 |
| | Supplies Expense | | 2,200 |
| | Interest Expense | | 2,900 |
| | *To close expenses and other debit accounts.* | | |
| | | | |
| 31 | Income Summary | 53,000 | |
| | Retained Earnings | | 53,000 |
| | *To close Income Summary.* | | |
| | | | |
| 31 | Retained Earnings | 48,000 | |
| | Dividends | | 48,000 |
| | *To close Dividends.* | | |

**Income Summary**

| | | | |
|---|---|---|---|
| Clos. 2 | 193,000 | 246,000 | Clos. 1 |
| | | 53,000 | Bal. |
| Clos. 3 | 53,000 | | |
| | | **0** | **Bal.** |

**Retained Earnings**

| | | | |
|---|---|---|---|
| | | 2,200 | Adj. Bal. |
| Clos. 4 | 48,000 | 53,000 | Clos. 3 |
| | | **7,200** | **Bal.** |

**Dividends**

| | | | |
|---|---|---|---|
| Adj. Bal. | 48,000 | | |
| | | 48,000 | Clos. 4 |
| **Bal.** | **0** | | |

**Requirement 2**

| KING CORNELIUS COMPANY<br>Income Statement<br>Year Ended December 31, 2016 | | |
|---|---|---|
| Sales Revenue | $ 244,000 | |
| Less: Sales Discounts | 8,000 | |
| Sales Returns and Allowances | 10,000 | |
| Net Sales Revenue | | $ 226,000 |
| Cost of Goods Sold | | 81,000 |
| Gross Profit | | 145,000 |
| Operating Expenses: | | |
| Salaries Expense | 72,700 | |
| Rent Expense | 7,700 | |
| Utilities Expense | 5,800 | |
| Depreciation Expense—Furniture | 2,700 | |
| Supplies Expense | 2,200 | |
| Total Operating Expenses | | 91,100 |
| Operating Income | | 53,900 |
| Other Revenues and (Expenses): | | |
| Interest Revenue | 2,000 | |
| Interest Expense | (2,900) | |
| Total Other Revenues and (Expenses) | | (900) |
| Net Income | | **$ 53,000** |

| KING CORNELIUS COMPANY<br>Statement of Retained Earnings<br>Year Ended December 31, 2016 | |
|---|---|
| Retained Earnings, January 1, 2016 | $ 2,200 |
| Net income for the year | 53,000 |
| | 55,200 |
| Dividends | (48,000) |
| Retained Earnings, December 31, 2016 | **$ 7,200** |

| KING CORNELIUS COMPANY<br>Balance Sheet<br>December 31, 2016 | | |
|---|---|---|
| **Assets** | | |
| Current Assets: | | |
| Cash | $ 5,600 | |
| Accounts Receivable | 37,100 | |
| Merchandise Inventory | 25,800 | |
| Office Supplies | 1,300 | |
| Prepaid Rent | 1,000 | |
| Total Current Assets | | $ 70,800 |
| Plant Assets: | | |
| Furniture | 26,500 | |
| Less: Accumulated Depreciation—Furniture | (23,800) | |
| Total Plant Assets | | 2,700 |
| Total Assets | | **$ 73,500** |
| **Liabilities** | | |
| Current Liabilities: | | |
| Accounts Payable | $ 6,300 | |
| Salaries Payable | 2,000 | |
| Interest Payable | 600 | |
| Unearned Revenue | 2,400 | |
| Total Current Liabilities | | $ 11,300 |
| Long-term Liabilities: | | |
| Notes Payable | | 35,000 |
| Total Liabilities | | 46,300 |
| **Stockholders' Equity** | | |
| Common Stock | | 20,000 |
| Retained Earnings | | 7,200 |
| Total Stockholders' Equity | | 27,200 |
| Total Liabilities and Stockholders' Equity | | **$ 73,500** |

CHAPTER 5

## Requirement 3

Gross profit percentage = Gross profit / Net sales revenue = $145,000 / $226,000 = 0.642 = 64.2%

## > Key Terms

Administrative Expenses (p. 267)
Cost of Goods Sold (COGS) (p. 248)
Credit Terms (p. 252)
FOB Destination (p. 255)
FOB Shipping Point (p. 255)
Freight In (p. 255)
Freight Out (p. 255)
Gross Profit (p. 249)
Gross Profit Percentage (p. 269)
Income Tax Expense (p. 268)
Inventory Shrinkage (p. 263)
Invoice (p. 250)
Merchandise Inventory (p. 247)
Merchandiser (p. 247)
Multi-Step Income Statement (p. 267)
Net Purchases (p. 272) (Appendix 5A)
Net Sales Revenue (p. 261)
Operating Expenses (p. 249)
Operating Income (p. 267)
Other Revenues and Expenses (p. 268)
Periodic Inventory System (p. 249)
Perpetual Inventory System (p. 249)
Purchase Allowance (p. 253)
Purchase Discount (p. 252)
Purchase Return (p. 253)
Retailer (p. 247)
Sales Discounts (p. 259)
Sales Returns and Allowances (p. 259)
Sales Revenue (p. 258)
Selling Expenses (p. 267)
Single-Step Income Statement (p. 266)
Vendor (p. 248)
Wholesaler (p. 247)

## > Quick Check

**Learning Objective 1**

1. Which account does a merchandiser use that a service company does not use?
   a. Cost of Goods Sold
   b. Merchandise Inventory
   c. Sales Revenue
   d. All of the above

**Learning Objective 1**

2. The two main inventory accounting systems are the
   a. perpetual and periodic.
   b. purchase and sale.
   c. returns and allowances.
   d. cash and accrual.

**Learning Objective 2**

3. The journal entry for the purchase of inventory on account *using the perpetual inventory system* is

| Date | Accounts and Explanation | Debit | Credit |
|---|---|---|---|
| a. | Merchandise Inventory | XXX | |
| | Accounts Receivable | | XXX |
| b. | Accounts Payable | XXX | |
| | Merchandise Inventory | | XXX |
| c. | Merchandise Inventory | XXX | |
| | Accounts Payable | | XXX |
| d. | Merchandise Inventory | XXX | |
| | Cash | | XXX |

**Learning Objective 2**

4. JC Manufacturing purchased inventory for $5,300 and also paid a $260 freight bill. JC Manufacturing returned 45% of the goods to the seller and later took a 2% purchase discount. Assume JC Manufacturing uses a perpetual inventory system. What is JC Manufacturing's final cost of the inventory that it kept? (Round your answer to the nearest whole number.)
   a. $2,997
   b. $2,337
   c. $3,117
   d. $2,857

CHAPTER 5

**Learning Objective 3**

5. Suppose Austin Sound had sales of $300,000 and sales returns of $45,000. Cost of goods sold was $152,000. How much gross profit did Austin Sound report?

a. $148,000 b. $103,000 c. $255,000 d. $88,000

**Learning Objective 4**

6. Suppose Dave's Discount's Merchandise Inventory account showed a balance of $8,000 before the year-end adjustments. The physical count of goods on hand totaled $7,400. Dave uses a perpetual inventory system. To adjust the accounts, which entry would the company make?

| Date | Accounts and Explanation | Debit | Credit |
|---|---|---|---|
| a. | Cost of Goods Sold | 600 | |
| | Merchandise Inventory | | 600 |
| b. | Merchandise Inventory | 600 | |
| | Accounts Receivable | | 600 |
| c. | Accounts Payable | 600 | |
| | Merchandise Inventory | | 600 |
| d. | Merchandise Inventory | 600 | |
| | Cost of Goods Sold | | 600 |

**Learning Objective 4**

7. Which of the following accounts would be closed at the end of the year *using the perpetual inventory system*?

a. Cost of Goods Sold
b. Merchandise Inventory
c. Accounts Receivable
d. Accounts Payable

**Learning Objective 5**

8. What is the order of the subtotals that appear on a multi-step income statement?

a. Gross Profit, Operating Income, Net Income, Total Other Revenues and Expenses
b. Operating Income, Gross Profit, Net Income, Total Other Revenues and Expenses
c. Total Other Revenues and Expenses, Operating Income, Gross Profit, Net Income
d. Gross Profit, Operating Income, Total Other Revenues and Expenses, Net Income

**Learning Objective 6**

9. Assume Juniper Natural Dyes made Net Sales Revenue of $90,000 and Cost of Goods Sold totaled $58,000. What was Juniper Natural Dyes's gross profit percentage for this period? (Round your answer to the nearest whole percent.)

a. 36% b. 3.4 times c. 64% d. 17%

**Learning Objective 7 Appendix 5A**

10A. The journal entry for the purchase of inventory on account *using the periodic inventory system* is

| Date | Accounts and Explanation | Debit | Credit |
|---|---|---|---|
| a. | Purchases | XXX | |
| | Accounts Receivable | | XXX |
| b. | Accounts Payable | XXX | |
| | Merchandise Inventory | | XXX |
| c. | Merchandise Inventory | XXX | |
| | Accounts Payable | | XXX |
| d. | Purchases | XXX | |
| | Accounts Payable | | XXX |

**Check your answers at the end of the chapter.**

# ASSESS YOUR PROGRESS

## > Review Questions

1. What is a merchandiser, and what is the name of the merchandise that it sells?
2. What are the two types of merchandisers? How do they differ?
3. Describe the operating cycle of a merchandiser.
4. What is Cost of Goods Sold (COGS), and where is it reported?
5. How is gross profit calculated, and what does it represent?
6. What are the two types of inventory accounting systems? Briefly describe each.
7. What is an invoice?
8. What account is debited when recording a purchase of inventory when using the perpetual inventory system?
9. What would the credit terms of "2/10, n/EOM" mean?
10. What is a purchase return? How does a purchase allowance differ from a purchase return?
11. Describe FOB shipping point and FOB destination. When does the buyer take ownership of the goods, and who typically pays the freight?
12. How is the net cost of inventory calculated?
13. What are the two journal entries involved when recording the sale of inventory when using the perpetual inventory system?
14. When granting a sales allowance, is there a return of merchandise inventory from the customer? Describe the journal entry(ies) that would be recorded.
15. What is freight out, and how is it recorded by the seller?
16. How is net sales revenue calculated?
17. What is inventory shrinkage? Describe the adjusting entry that would be recorded to account for inventory shrinkage.
18. What are the four steps involved in the closing process for a merchandising company?
19. Describe the single-step income statement.
20. Describe the multi-step income statement.
21. What financial statement is merchandise inventory reported on, and in what section?
22. What does the gross profit percentage measure, and how is it calculated?

23A. What account is debited when recording a purchase of inventory when using a periodic inventory system?

24A. When recording purchase returns and purchase allowances under the periodic inventory system, what account is used?

25A. What account is debited when recording the payment of freight in when using the periodic inventory system?

26A. Describe the journal entry(ies) when recording a sale of inventory using the periodic inventory system.

27A. Is an adjusting entry needed for inventory shrinkage when using the periodic inventory system? Explain.

28A. Highlight the differences in the closing process when using the periodic inventory system rather than the perpetual inventory system.

29A. Describe the calculation of cost of goods sold when using the periodic inventory system.

## > Short Exercises

***For all short exercises, assume the perpetual inventory system is used unless stated otherwise. Round all numbers to the nearest whole dollar unless stated otherwise.***

### S5-1 Comparing periodic and perpetual inventory systems

**Learning Objective 1**

For each statement below, identify whether the statement applies to the periodic inventory system or perpetual inventory system.

**a.** Normally used for relatively inexpensive goods.

**b.** Keeps a running computerized record of merchandise inventory.

**c.** Achieves better control over merchandise inventory.

**d.** Requires a physical count of inventory to determine the quantities on hand.

**e.** Uses bar codes to keep up-to-the-minute records of inventory.

### S5-2 Journalizing purchase transactions

**Learning Objective 2**

Consider the following transactions for Partytime Toys:

| | |
|---|---|
| Oct. 8 | Partytime Toys buys $141,800 worth of MegoBlock toys on account with credit terms of 2/10, n/30. |
| 11 | Partytime Toys returns $14,100 of the merchandise to MegoBlock due to damage during shipment. |
| 15 | Partytime Toys paid the amount due, less the return and discount. |

**Requirements**

1. Journalize the purchase transactions. Explanations are not required.
2. In the final analysis, how much did the inventory cost Partytime Toys?

### S5-3 Journalizing purchase transactions

**Learning Objective 2**

Consider the following transactions for Derry Drug Store:

| | |
|---|---|
| Jun. 2 | Derry buys $23,000 worth of inventory on account with credit terms of 2/15, n/30, FOB shipping point. |
| 4 | Derry pays a $110 freight charge. |
| 8 | Derry returns $6,200 of the merchandise due to damage during shipment. |
| 14 | Derry paid the amount due, less return and discount. |

**Requirements**

1. Journalize the purchase transactions. Explanations are not required.
2. In the final analysis, how much did the inventory cost Derry Drug Store?

Learning Objective 3

## S5-4 Journalizing sales transactions

Journalize the following sales transactions for Paul Sportswear. Explanations are not required.

| | |
|---|---|
| Aug. 1 | Paul sold $66,000 of women's sportswear on account, credit terms are 2/10, n/30. Cost of goods is $33,000. |
| 5 | Paul received a $5,000 sales return on damaged goods from the customer. Cost of goods damaged is $2,500. |
| 10 | Paul receives payment from the customer on the amount due, less the return and discount. |

Learning Objectives 2, 3

## S5-5 Journalizing purchase and sales transactions

Suppose Muddyriver.com sells 2,000 books on account for $19 each (cost of these books is $22,800), credit terms 1/20, n/45 on October 10, 2016, to The Salem Store. One hundred of these books (cost $1,140) were damaged in shipment, so Muddyriver.com later received the damaged goods from The Salem Store as sales returns on October 13, 2016. The Salem Store paid the balance to Muddyriver.com on October 22, 2016.

**Requirements**

1. Journalize The Salem Store's October 2016 transactions.
2. Journalize Muddyriver.com's October 2016 transactions.

Learning Objective 4

## S5-6 Adjusting for inventory shrinkage

Carla's Furniture's unadjusted Merchandise Inventory account at year-end is $62,000. The physical count of inventory came up with a total of $60,800. Journalize the adjusting entry needed to account for inventory shrinkage.

Learning Objective 4

## S5-7 Journalizing closing entries

Rockwall RV Center's accounting records include the following accounts at December 31, 2016.

| | | | |
|---|---|---|---|
| Cost of Goods Sold | $ 368,000 | Accumulated Depreciation—Building | $ 40,000 |
| Accounts Payable | 20,000 | Cash | 54,000 |
| Rent Expense | 23,000 | Sales Revenue | 710,000 |
| Building | 115,000 | Depreciation Expense—Building | 16,000 |
| Common Stock | 132,000 | Dividends | 55,000 |
| Retained Earnings | 46,400 | Sales Discounts | 6,000 |
| Merchandise Inventory | 238,400 | Interest Revenue | 4,000 |
| Sales Returns and Allowances | 40,000 | | |
| Notes Receivable | 37,000 | | |

**Requirements**

1. Journalize the required closing entries for Rockwall.
2. Determine the ending balance in the Retained Earnings account.

***Use the following information to answer Short Exercises S5-8 and S5-9.***

Carissa Communications reported the following figures from its adjusted trial balance for its first year of business, which ended on July 31, 2016:

| | | | |
|---|---|---|---|
| Cash | $ 4,100 | Cost of Goods Sold | $ 18,800 |
| Selling Expenses | 1,300 | Equipment, net | 8,500 |
| Accounts Payable | 4,900 | Accrued Liabilities | 2,000 |
| Common Stock | 2,820 | Sales Revenue | 42,000 |
| Notes Payable, long-term | 400 | Accounts Receivable | 3,400 |
| Merchandise Inventory | 1,200 | Interest Expense | 20 |
| Administrative Expenses | 3,100 | Sales Discounts | 4,300 |
| Sales Returns and Allowances | 7,400 | | |

**S5-8 Preparing a merchandiser's income statement** **Learning Objective 5**

Prepare Carissa Communications's multi-step income statement for the year ended July 31, 2016.

**S5-9 Preparing a merchandiser's statement of retained earnings and balance sheet** **Learning Objective 5**

**Requirements**

1. Prepare Carissa Communications's statement of retained earnings for the year ended July 31, 2016. Assume that there were no dividends declared during the year and that the business began on August 1, 2015.
2. Prepare Carissa Communications's classified balance sheet at July 31, 2016. Use the report format.

**S5-10 Computing the gross profit percentage** **Learning Objective 6**

Morris Landscape Supply's selected accounts as of December 31, 2016, follow. Compute the gross profit percentage for 2016.

| | |
|---|---|
| Selling Expenses | $ 13,100 |
| Interest Revenue | 1,500 |
| Sales Returns and Allowances | 5,000 |
| Sales Revenue | 141,000 |
| Cost of Goods Sold | 112,000 |
| Sales Discounts | 1,900 |
| Administrative Expenses | 10,100 |

Learning Objective 7
Appendix 5A

## S5A-11 Journalizing purchase transactions—periodic inventory system

Consider the following transactions for Garnier Packing Supplies:

| | |
|---|---|
| Apr. 10 | Garnier Packing Supplies buys $156,000 worth of merchandise inventory on account with credit terms of 3/10, n/30. |
| 12 | Garnier returns $11,000 of the merchandise to the vendor due to damage during shipment. |
| 19 | Garnier paid the amount due, less the return and discount. |

**Requirements**

1. Journalize the purchase transactions assuming Garnier Packing Supplies uses the periodic inventory system. Explanations are not required.
2. What is the amount of net purchases?

Learning Objective 7
Appendix 5A

## S5A-12 Journalizing sales transactions—periodic inventory system

Journalize the following sales transactions for Sandman Camera Store using the periodic inventory system. Explanations are not required.

| | |
|---|---|
| Dec. 3 | Sandman sold $44,800 of camera equipment on account, credit terms are 3/15, n/EOM. |
| 5 | Sandman received a $900 sales return on damaged goods from the customer. |
| 17 | Sandman receives payment from the customer on the amount due, less the return and discount. |

Learning Objective 7
Appendix 5A

## S5A-13 Journalizing closing entries—periodic inventory system

D & L Printing Supplies's accounting records include the following accounts at December 31, 2016.

| | | | |
|---|---|---|---|
| Purchases | $ 189,600 | Accumulated Depreciation—Building | $ 23,000 |
| Accounts Payable | 7,900 | Cash | 17,900 |
| Rent Expense | 9,000 | Sales Revenue | 295,100 |
| Building | 47,900 | Depreciation Expense—Building | 3,600 |
| Common Stock | 58,000 | Dividends | 27,100 |
| Retained Earnings | 21,800 | Sales Discounts | 4,300 |
| Merchandise Inventory, Beginning | 122,000 | Interest Expense | 2,200 |
| Sales Returns and Allowances | 17,500 | Merchandise Inventory, Ending | 99,500 |
| Notes Payable | 11,500 | Purchase Returns and Allowances | 21,200 |
| Purchase Discounts | 2,600 | | |

**Requirements**

1. Journalize the required closing entries for D & L Printing Supplies assuming that D & L uses the periodic inventory system.
2. Determine the ending balance in the Retained Earnings account.

**S5A-14 Computing cost of goods sold in a periodic inventory system**

**Learning Objective 7 Appendix 5A**

X Wholesale Company began the year with merchandise inventory of $11,000. During the year, X purchased $93,000 of goods and returned $6,700 due to damage. X also paid freight charges of $1,200 on inventory purchases. At year-end, X's ending merchandise inventory balance stood at $17,300. Assume that X uses the periodic inventory system. Compute X's cost of goods sold for the year.

## > Exercises

***For all exercises, assume the perpetual inventory system is used unless stated otherwise. Round all numbers to the nearest whole dollar unless stated otherwise.***

**E5-15 Using accounting vocabulary**

**Learning Objectives 1, 2, 3**

Match the accounting terms with the corresponding definitions.

**1.** Credit Terms
**2.** FOB Destination
**3.** Invoice
**4.** Cost of Goods Sold
**5.** Net Sales Revenue
**6.** Purchase Allowance
**7.** FOB Shipping Point
**8.** Wholesaler
**9.** Purchase Discount
**10.** Retailer

**a.** The cost of the merchandise inventory that the business has sold to customers.
**b.** An amount granted to the purchaser as an incentive to keep goods that are not "as ordered."
**c.** A type of merchandiser that buys merchandise either from a manufacturer or a wholesaler and then sells those goods to consumers.
**d.** A situation in which the buyer takes ownership (title) at the delivery destination point.
**e.** A type of merchandiser that buys goods from manufacturers and then sells them to retailers.
**f.** A discount that businesses offer to purchasers as an incentive for early payment.
**g.** A situation in which the buyer takes title to the goods after the goods leave the seller's place of business.
**h.** The terms of purchase or sale as stated on the invoice.
**i.** The amount a company has made on sales of merchandise inventory after returns and allowances and discounts have been taken out.
**j.** A seller's request for cash from the purchaser.

**Learning Objective 2**

3. Oct. 1 Cash $769.35

## E5-16 Journalizing purchase transactions from an invoice

Kingston Tires received the following invoice from a supplier (Fields Distribution, Inc.):

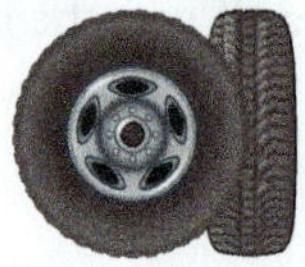

**FIELDS DISTRIBUTION, INC.**
**7290 S. Prospect Street**
**Ravenna, OH 44266**

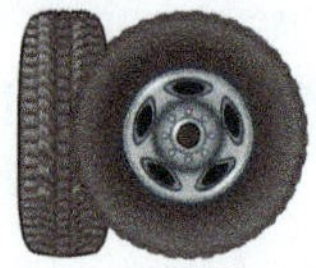

**Invoice date:** September 23, 2016

**Sold to:** Kingston Tires
6678 Diamond Avenue
Ravenna, OH 44266

**Payment terms:** 1/10, n/30

| Description | Quantity Shipped | Price | Amount |
|---|---|---|---|
| D39–X4 Radials | 4 | $38.12 | $152.48 |
| M223 Belted-bias | 10 | 42.84 | 428.40 |
| Q92 Truck tires | 6 | 58.12 | 348.72 |
| Total | | | $929.60 |

| Due date: | Amount: |
|---|---|
| October 3, 2016 | $920.30 |
| October 4 through October 23, 2016 | $929.60 |

### Requirements

1. Journalize the transaction required by Kingston Tires on September 23, 2016. Do not round numbers to the nearest whole dollar. Assume tires are purchased on account.
2. Journalize the return on Kingston's books on September 28, 2016, of the D39–X4 Radials, which were ordered by mistake. Do not round numbers to the nearest whole dollar.
3. Journalize the payment on October 1, 2016, to Fields Distribution, Inc. Do not round numbers to the nearest whole dollar.

CHAPTER 5

**Learning Objective 2**

July 24 Merch. Inv. $90

## E5-17 Journalizing purchase transactions

Hartford Jewelers had the following purchase transactions. Journalize all necessary transactions. Explanations are not required.

| | |
|---|---|
| Jun. 20 | Purchased inventory of $5,400 on account from Surry Diamonds, a jewelry importer. Terms were 3/15, n/45, FOB shipping point. |
| 20 | Paid freight charges, $300. |
| Jul. 4 | Returned $900 of inventory to Surry. |
| 14 | Paid Surry Diamonds, less return. |
| 16 | Purchased inventory of $3,800 on account from Swift Diamonds, a jewelry importer. Terms were 3/10, n/EOM, FOB destination. |
| 18 | Received a $800 allowance from Swift for damaged but usable goods. |
| 24 | Paid Swift Diamonds, less allowance and discount. |

### E5-18 Computing missing amounts

**Learning Objective 3**

Consider the following incomplete table of merchandiser's profit data. Calculate the missing amounts to complete the table.

| | | | | |
|---|---|---|---|---|
| Sales | $ 88,600 | $ 102,500 | $ 65,100 | $ *(f)* |
| Sales Returns and Allowances | 990 | *(b)* | 1,630 | 850 |
| Sales Discounts | 660 | 820 | 440 | 2,000 |
| Net Sales | 86,950 | 98,120 | *(d)* | *(g)* |
| Cost of Goods Sold | 60,200 | *(c)* | 41,200 | 76,200 |
| Gross Profit | *(a)* | 31,720 | *(e)* | 35,950 |

### E5-19 Journalizing sales transactions

**Learning Objective 3**

Jan. 13 Sales Discounts $97

Journalize the following sales transactions for Austin Mall. Explanations are not required.

| | |
|---|---|
| Jan. 4 | Sold $10,000 of antiques on account, credit terms are 1/15, n/30. Cost of goods is $5,000. |
| 8 | Received a $300 sales return on damaged goods from the customer. Cost of goods damaged is $150. |
| 13 | Austin Mall received payment from the customer on the amount due from Jan. 4, less the return and discount. |
| 20 | Sold $5,200 of antiques on account, credit terms are 1/10, n/45, FOB destination. Cost of goods is $2,600. |
| 20 | Austin Mall paid $120 on freight out. |
| 25 | Austin Mall negotiated a $500 allowance on the goods sold on Jan. 20. |
| 29 | Received payment from the customer on the amount due from Jan. 20, less the allowance and discount. |

### E5-20 Journalizing purchase and sales transactions

**Learning Objectives 2, 3**

Feb. 23 Cash $4,653

Journalize the following transactions for Santa Fe Art Gift Shop. Explanations are not required.

| | |
|---|---|
| Feb. 3 | Purchased $2,800 of merchandise inventory on account under terms 3/10, n/EOM and FOB shipping point. |
| 7 | Returned $700 of defective merchandise purchased on February 3. |
| 9 | Paid freight bill of $400 on February 3 purchase. |
| 10 | Sold merchandise inventory on account for $4,800. Payment terms were 1/15, n/30. These goods cost the company $2,400. |
| 12 | Paid amount owed on credit purchase of February 3, less the return and the discount. |
| 16 | Granted a sales allowance of $100 on the February 10 sale. |
| 23 | Received cash from February 10 customer in full settlement of their debt, less the allowance and the discount. |

**Learning Objectives 3, 4**

2. Net Sales $71,400

### E5-21 Journalizing adjusting entries and computing gross profit

Dog-eared Book Shop's accounts at June 30, 2016, included the following unadjusted balances:

| | |
|---|---|
| Merchandise Inventory | $ 5,800 |
| Cost of Goods Sold | 33,750 |
| Sales Revenue | 75,000 |
| Sales Discounts | 1,100 |
| Sales Returns and Allowances | 2,500 |

The cost associated with the physical count of inventory on hand on June 30, 2016, was $5,300.

**Requirements**

1. Journalize the adjustment for inventory shrinkage.
2. Compute the gross profit.

***Use the following information to answer Exercises E5-22 through E5-24.***

The adjusted trial balance of Business Reduction Systems at March 31, 2016, follows:

**BUSINESS REDUCTION SYSTEMS**
Adjusted Trial Balance
March 31, 2016

| | Balance | |
|---|---|---|
| **Account Title** | **Debit** | **Credit** |
| Cash | $ 4,100 | |
| Accounts Receivable | 13,800 | |
| Merchandise Inventory | 31,300 | |
| Office Supplies | 6,100 | |
| Equipment | 42,200 | |
| Accumulated Depreciation—Equipment | | $ 13,100 |
| Accounts Payable | | 9,000 |
| Salaries Payable | | 500 |
| Notes Payable, long-term | | 8,000 |
| Common Stock | | 14,000 |
| Retained Earnings | | 100 |
| Dividends | 40,000 | |
| Sales Revenue | | 234,000 |
| Sales Returns and Allowances | 1,500 | |
| Sales Discounts | 1,900 | |
| Cost of Goods Sold | 93,600 | |
| Selling Expense | 27,600 | |
| Administrative Expense | 14,600 | |
| Interest Expense | 2,000 | |
| Total | **$ 278,700** | **$ 278,700** |

## E5-22 Journalizing closing entries

**Learning Objective 4**

2. Ending Retained Earnings Balance $52,900

### Requirements

1. Journalize the required closing entries at March 31, 2016.
2. Set up T-accounts for Income Summary; Retained Earnings; and Dividends. Post the closing entries to the T-accounts, and calculate their ending balances.
3. How much was Business Reduction's net income or net loss?

## E5-23 Preparing a single-step income statement

**Learning Objective 5**

Net Income $92,800

Prepare Business Reduction's *single-step* income statement for the year ended March 31, 2016.

## E5-24 Preparing a multi-step income statement

**Learning Objective 5**

Gross Profit $137,000

Prepare Business Reduction's *multi-step* income statement for the year ended March 31, 2016.

## E5-25 Computing the gross profit percentage

**Learning Objective 6**

Gross Profit Percentage 39%

Cupcake Queen earned net sales revenue of $67,000,000 in 2016. Cost of goods sold was $40,870,000, and net income reached $8,000,000, the company's highest ever. Compute the company's gross profit percentage for 2016.

## E5A-26 Journalizing purchase transactions—periodic inventory system

**Learning Objective 7 Appendix 5A**

Sep. 17 Cash $5,626

Landry Appliances had the following purchase transactions. Journalize all necessary transactions using the periodic inventory system. Explanations are not required.

| | |
|---|---|
| Sep. 4 | Purchased inventory of $6,200 on account from Max Appliance Wholesale, an appliance wholesaler. Terms were 3/15, n/30, FOB shipping point. |
| 4 | Paid freight charges, $410. |
| 10 | Returned $400 of inventory to Max. |
| 17 | Paid Max Appliance Wholesale, less return and discount. |
| 20 | Purchased inventory of $4,600 on account from MY Appliance, an appliance wholesaler. Terms were 3/10, n/45, FOB destination. |
| 22 | Received a $900 allowance from MY Appliance for damaged but usable goods. |
| 29 | Paid MY Appliance, less allowance and discount. |

## E5A-27 Journalizing sales transactions—periodic inventory system

**Learning Objective 7 Appendix 5A**

Aug. 24 Sales Discounts $50

Journalize the following sales transactions for Double Z Archery using the periodic inventory system. Explanations are not required.

| | |
|---|---|
| Aug. 1 | Sold $7,800 of equipment on account, credit terms are 2/10, n/30. |
| 3 | Received a $300 sales return on damaged goods from the customer. |
| 8 | Double Z received payment from the customer on the amount due from Aug. 1, less the return and discount. |
| 15 | Sold $3,200 of equipment on account, credit terms are 2/10, n/45, FOB destination. |
| 15 | Double Z paid $140 on freight out. |
| 20 | Double Z negotiated a $700 allowance on the goods sold on Aug. 15. |
| 24 | Received payment from the customer on the amount due from Aug. 15, less the allowance and discount. |

**Learning Objective 7**
**Appendix 5A**

Nov. 22 Accounts Receivable $5,800

## E5A-28 Journalizing purchase and sales transactions—periodic inventory system

Journalize the following transactions for Moody Bicycles using the periodic inventory system. Explanations are not required.

| | |
|---|---|
| Nov. 2 | Purchased $3,700 of merchandise inventory on account under terms 3/10, n/EOM and FOB shipping point. |
| 6 | Returned $600 of defective merchandise purchased on November 2. |
| 8 | Paid freight bill of $150 on November 2 purchase. |
| 10 | Sold merchandise inventory on account for $6,200. Payment terms were 1/15, n/45. |
| 11 | Paid amount owed on credit purchase of November 2, less the return and the discount. |
| 15 | Granted a sales allowance of $400 on the November 10 sale. |
| 22 | Received cash from November 10 customer in full settlement of their debt, less the allowance and the discount. |

**Learning Objective 7**
**Appendix 5A**

2. Ending Retained Earnings Balance $72,600

## E5A-29 Journalizing closing entries—periodic inventory system

Nautical Dream Boat Supply uses the periodic inventory method. The adjusted trial balance of Nautical Dream Boat Supply at December 31, 2016, follows:

**NAUTICAL DREAM BOAT SUPPLY**
Adjusted Trial Balance
December 31, 2016

| | Balance | |
|---|---|---|
| **Account Title** | **Debit** | **Credit** |
| Cash | $ 3,700 | |
| Accounts Receivable | 15,700 | |
| Merchandise Inventory (beginning) | 44,700 | |
| Office Supplies | 8,800 | |
| Equipment | 59,900 | |
| Accumulated Depreciation—Equipment | | $ 19,900 |
| Accounts Payable | | 12,000 |
| Salaries Payable | | 1,000 |
| Notes Payable, long-term | | 11,900 |
| Common Stock | | 24,000 |
| Retained Earnings | | 27,500 |
| Dividends | 60,700 | |
| Sales Revenue | | 330,000 |
| Sales Returns and Allowances | 1,900 | |
| Sales Discounts | 2,100 | |
| Interest Revenue | | 3,200 |
| Purchases | 274,600 | |
| Purchase Returns and Allowances | | 94,200 |
| Purchase Discounts | | 8,000 |
| Selling Expense | 38,700 | |
| Administrative Expense | 20,900 | |
| Total | **$ 531,700** | **$ 531,700** |

CHAPTER 5

**Requirements**

1. Journalize the required closing entries at December 31, 2016. Assume ending Merchandise Inventory is $53,300.
2. Set up T-accounts for Income Summary; Retained Earnings; and Dividends. Post the closing entries to the T-accounts, and calculate their ending balances.
3. How much was Nautical Dream's net income or net loss?

**Learning Objective 7**
**Appendix 5A**

## E5A-30 Computing cost of goods sold in a periodic inventory system

Zeta Electric uses the periodic inventory system. Zeta reported the following selected amounts at May 31, 2016:

| | | | |
|---|---|---|---|
| Merchandise Inventory, June 1, 2015 | $ 16,500 | Freight In | $ 7,000 |
| Merchandise Inventory, May 31, 2016 | 24,000 | Sales Revenue | 172,000 |
| Purchases | 90,000 | Sales Discounts | 7,000 |
| Purchase Discounts | 4,500 | Sales Returns and Allowances | 14,000 |
| Purchase Returns and Allowances | 6,500 | Common Stock | 32,000 |
| | | Retained Earnings | 17,000 |

Compute the following for Zeta:

a. Net sales revenue.

b. Cost of goods sold.

c. Gross profit.

## > Problems Group A

***For all problems, assume the perpetual inventory system is used unless stated otherwise. Round all numbers to the nearest whole dollar unless stated otherwise.***

**Learning Objectives 1, 2, 3**

Sep. 10 Cash $2,871

### P5-31A Journalizing purchase and sale transactions

Journalize the following transactions that occurred in September 2016 for Cardinal. No explanations are needed. Identify each accounts payable and accounts receivable with the vendor or customer name.

| | |
|---|---|
| Sep. 3 | Purchased merchandise inventory on account from Sherry Wholesalers, $4,000. Terms 1/15, n/EOM, FOB shipping point. |
| 4 | Paid freight bill of $75 on September 3 purchase. |
| 4 | Purchased merchandise inventory for cash of $1,900. |
| 6 | Returned $1,100 of inventory from September 3 purchase. |
| 8 | Sold merchandise inventory to Houston Company, $5,500, on account. Terms 3/15, n/35. Cost of goods, $2,365. |
| 9 | Purchased merchandise inventory on account from Tarin Wholesalers, $12,000. Terms 3/10, n/30, FOB destination. |
| 10 | Made payment to Sherry Wholesalers for goods purchased on September 3, less return and discount. |
| 12 | Received payment from Houston Company, less discount. |
| 13 | After negotiations, received a $200 allowance from Tarin Wholesalers. |
| 15 | Sold merchandise inventory to Java Company, $3,300, on account. Terms 2/10, n/EOM. Cost of goods, $1,320. |
| 22 | Made payment, less allowance, to Tarin Wholesalers for goods purchased on September 9. |
| 23 | Java Company returned $900 of the merchandise sold on September 15. Cost of goods, $360. |
| 25 | Sold merchandise inventory to Smecker for $1,900 on account that cost $722. Terms of 1/10, n/30 was offered, FOB shipping point. As a courtesy to Smecker, $85 of freight was added to the invoice for which cash was paid by Cardinal. |
| 26 | After negotiations, granted a $200 allowance to Smecker for merchandise purchased on September 25. |
| 29 | Received payment from Smecker, less allowance and discount. |
| 30 | Received payment from Java Company, less return. |

## P5-32A Journalizing purchase and sale transactions

**Learning Objectives 1, 2, 3**

Journalize the following transactions that occurred in November 2016 for May's Adventure Park. No explanations are needed. Identify each accounts payable and accounts receivable with the vendor or customer name.

Nov. 14 Merch. Inv. $40

| | |
|---|---|
| Nov. 4 | Purchased merchandise inventory on account from Valera Company, $8,000. Terms 1/10, n/EOM, FOB shipping point. |
| 6 | Paid freight bill of $160 on November 4 purchase. |
| 8 | Returned half the inventory purchased on November 4 from Valera Company. |
| 10 | Sold merchandise inventory for cash, $1,700. Cost of goods, $680. FOB destination. |
| 11 | Sold merchandise inventory to Garrison Corporation, $10,300, on account, terms of 3/10, n/EOM. Cost of goods, $5,150. FOB shipping point. |
| 12 | Paid freight bill of $30 on November 10 sale. |
| 13 | Sold merchandise inventory to Cain Company, $9,000, on account, terms of 1/15, n/45. Cost of goods, $4,500. FOB shipping point. |
| 14 | Paid the amount owed on account from November 4, less return and discount. |
| 16 | After negotiations, granted a $200 allowance to Garrison Corporation on November 11 sale. |
| 17 | Received defective inventory as a sales return from the November 13 sale, $400. Cost of goods, $200. |
| 18 | Purchased inventory of $3,700 on account from Regan Corporation. Payment terms were 2/10, n/30, FOB destination. |
| 20 | Received cash from Garrison Corporation, less allowance and discount. |
| 26 | Paid amount owed on account from November 18, less discount. |
| 28 | Received cash from Cain Company, less return and discount. |
| 29 | Purchased inventory from Sanders Corporation for cash, $12,000, FOB shipping point. Freight in paid to shipping company, $200. |

**Learning Objectives 4, 5**

1. Operating Income $59,050

**P5-33A Preparing a multi-step income statement, journalizing closing entries, and preparing a post-closing trial balance**

The adjusted trial balance of Big Rita's Music Company at June 30, 2016, follows:

**BIG RITA'S MUSIC COMPANY**
Adjusted Trial Balance
June 30, 2016

| | Balance | |
|---|---|---|
| **Account Title** | **Debit** | **Credit** |
| Cash | $ 3,700 | |
| Accounts Receivable | 38,500 | |
| Merchandise Inventory | 17,100 | |
| Office Supplies | 850 | |
| Furniture | 39,800 | |
| Accumulated Depreciation—Furniture | | $ 8,800 |
| Accounts Payable | | 13,100 |
| Salaries Payable | | 800 |
| Unearned Revenue | | 7,400 |
| Notes Payable, long-term | | 15,000 |
| Common Stock | | 16,000 |
| Retained Earnings | | 23,300 |
| Dividends | 42,500 | |
| Sales Revenue | | 187,000 |
| Sales Returns and Allowances | 4,500 | |
| Sales Discounts | 3,500 | |
| Cost of Goods Sold | 84,150 | |
| Selling Expense | 18,800 | |
| Administrative Expense | 17,000 | |
| Interest Expense | 1,000 | |
| Total | **$ 271,400** | **$ 271,400** |

**Requirements**

1. Prepare Big Rita's multi-step income statement for the year ended June 30, 2016.
2. Journalize Big Rita's closing entries.
3. Prepare a post-closing trial balance as of June 30, 2016.

**P5-34A Journalizing adjusting entries, preparing adjusted trial balance, and preparing financial statements**

**Learning Objectives 4, 5**

2. Total Credits $482,880

The unadjusted trial balance for Travis Electronics Company at March 31, 2016, follows:

**TRAVIS ELECTRONICS COMPANY**
Unadjusted Trial Balance
March 31, 2016

| | Balance | |
|---|---|---|
| **Account Title** | **Debit** | **Credit** |
| Cash | $ 3,700 | |
| Accounts Receivable | 33,300 | |
| Interest Receivable | 0 | |
| Merchandise Inventory | 45,100 | |
| Office Supplies | 6,300 | |
| Equipment | 133,000 | |
| Accumulated Depreciation—Equipment | | $ 36,600 |
| Accounts Payable | | 16,400 |
| Salaries Payable | | 0 |
| Interest Payable | | 0 |
| Unearned Revenue | | 13,600 |
| Notes Payable, long-term | | 44,000 |
| Common Stock | | 40,000 |
| Retained Earnings | | 16,900 |
| Dividends | 21,000 | |
| Sales Revenue | | 310,000 |
| Sales Returns and Allowances | 7,100 | |
| Sales Discounts | 3,000 | |
| Interest Revenue | | 0 |
| Cost of Goods Sold | 170,500 | |
| Salaries Expense (Selling) | 24,000 | |
| Rent Expense (Selling) | 15,000 | |
| Salaries Expense (Administrative) | 5,400 | |
| Utilities Expense (Administrative) | 10,100 | |
| Depreciation Expense—Equipment (Administrative) | 0 | |
| Interest Expense | 0 | |
| Total | $ 477,500 | $ 477,500 |

CHAPTER 5

**Requirements**

1. Journalize the adjusting entries using the following data:
   a. Interest revenue accrued, $450.
   b. Salaries (Selling) accrued, $2,500.
   c. Depreciation expense—Equipment (Administrative), $1,330.
   d. Interest expense accrued, $1,100.
   e. A physical count of inventory was completed. The ending Merchandise Inventory should have a balance of $44,600.
2. Prepare Travis Electronics's adjusted trial balance as of March 31, 2016.
3. Prepare Travis Electronics's *multi-step* income statement for year ended March 31, 2016.
4. Prepare Travis Electronics's statement of retained earnings for year ended March 31, 2016.
5. Prepare Travis Electronics's classified balance sheet in *report form* as of March 31, 2016.

**Learning Objectives 5, 6**

2. Operating Income $80,700

**P5-35A Preparing a single-step income statement, preparing a multi-step income statement, and computing the gross profit percentage**

The records of Quality Cut Steak Company list the following selected accounts for the quarter ended April 30, 2016:

| | | | |
|---|---|---|---|
| Interest Revenue | $ 500 | Accounts Payable | $ 16,900 |
| Merchandise Inventory | 45,300 | Accounts Receivable | 38,000 |
| Notes Payable, long-term | 52,000 | Accumulated Depreciation—Equipment | 36,800 |
| Salaries Payable | 2,400 | Common Stock | 32,000 |
| Sales Discounts | 5,500 | Retained Earnings | 10,200 |
| Sales Returns and Allowances | 8,500 | Dividends | 17,000 |
| Sales Revenue | 306,000 | Cash | 7,400 |
| Rent Expense (Selling) | 21,400 | Cost of Goods Sold | 160,600 |
| Office Supplies | 6,300 | Equipment | 130,000 |
| Unearned Revenue | 13,200 | Interest Payable | 1,000 |
| Interest Expense | 1,700 | Rent Expense (Administrative) | 9,600 |
| Depreciation Expense—Equipment (Administrative) | 1,300 | Utilities Expense (Selling) | 10,600 |
| Utilities Expense (Administrative) | 4,300 | Delivery Expense (Selling) | 3,500 |

**Requirements**

1. Prepare a single-step income statement.
2. Prepare a multi-step income statement.
3. M. Doherty, manager of the company, strives to earn a gross profit percentage of at least 50%. Did Quality Cut achieve this goal? Show your calculations.

CHAPTER 5

**P5A-36A Journalizing purchase and sale transactions—periodic inventory system**

Learning Objective 7
Appendix 5A

Mar. 10 Cash $5,238

Journalize the following transactions that occurred in March 2016 for Dream Line Company. Assume Dream Line uses the periodic inventory system. No explanations are needed. Identify each accounts payable and accounts receivable with the vendor or customer name.

| | |
|---|---|
| Mar. 3 | Purchased merchandise inventory on account from Silton Wholesalers, $6,500. Terms 3/15, n/EOM, FOB shipping point. |
| 4 | Paid freight bill of $45 on March 3 purchase. |
| 4 | Purchased merchandise inventory for cash of $2,100. |
| 6 | Returned $1,100 of inventory from March 3 purchase. |
| 8 | Sold merchandise inventory to Hayes Company, $3,200, on account. Terms 1/15, n/35. |
| 9 | Purchased merchandise inventory on account from Tarin Wholesalers, $5,300. Terms 3/10, n/30, FOB destination. |
| 10 | Made payment to Silton Wholesalers for goods purchased on March 3, less return and discount. |
| 12 | Received payment from Hayes Company, less discount. |
| 13 | After negotiations, received a $100 allowance from Tarin Wholesalers. |
| 15 | Sold merchandise inventory to Julian Company, $2,200, on account. Terms 2/10, n/EOM. |
| 22 | Made payment, less allowance, to Tarin Wholesalers for goods purchased on March 9. |
| 23 | Julian Company returned $100 of the merchandise sold on March 15. |
| 25 | Sold merchandise inventory to Smecker for $800 on account. Terms of 2/10, n/30 was offered, FOB shipping point. |
| 26 | After negotiations, granted a $200 allowance to Smecker for merchandise sold on March 25. |
| 29 | Received payment from Smecker, less allowance and discount. |
| 30 | Received payment from Julian Company, less return. |

**Learning Objective 7**
**Appendix 5A**

1. Gross Profit $200,200

### P5A-37A Preparing a multi-step income statement and journalizing closing entries

Travis Department Store uses a periodic inventory system. The adjusted trial balance of Travis Department Store at December 31, 2016, follows:

**TRAVIS DEPARTMENT STORE**
Adjusted Trial Balance
December 31, 2016

| | Balance | |
|---|---|---|
| **Account Title** | **Debit** | **Credit** |
| Cash | $ 7,700 | |
| Accounts Receivable | 85,200 | |
| Merchandise Inventory (beginning) | 37,500 | |
| Office Supplies | 800 | |
| Furniture | 89,000 | |
| Accumulated Depreciation—Furniture | | $ 18,300 |
| Accounts Payable | | 28,700 |
| Salaries Payable | | 2,600 |
| Unearned Revenue | | 14,200 |
| Notes Payable, long-term | | 33,000 |
| Common Stock | | 70,000 |
| Retained Earnings | | 13,100 |
| Dividends | 89,500 | |
| Sales Revenue | | 387,000 |
| Sales Returns and Allowances | 6,700 | |
| Sales Discounts | 4,300 | |
| Purchases | 294,000 | |
| Purchase Returns and Allowances | | 113,000 |
| Purchase Discounts | | 6,700 |
| Freight In | 500 | |
| Selling Expense | 41,900 | |
| Administrative Expense | 26,500 | |
| Interest Expense | 3,000 | |
| Total | **$ 686,600** | **$ 686,600** |

**Requirements**

1. Prepare Travis Department Store's multi-step income statement for the year ended December 31, 2016. Assume ending Merchandise Inventory is $36,500.
2. Journalize Travis Department Store's closing entries.

CHAPTER 5

## > Problems Group B

***For all problems, assume the perpetual inventory system is used unless stated otherwise. Round all numbers to the nearest whole dollar unless stated otherwise.***

### P5-38B Journalizing purchase and sale transactions

**Learning Objectives 1, 2, 3**

Feb. 12 Cash $5,586

Journalize the following transactions that occurred in February 2016 for Faucet. No explanations are needed. Identify each accounts payable and accounts receivable with the vendor or customer name.

| | |
|---|---|
| Feb. 3 | Purchased merchandise inventory on account from Sidecki Wholesalers, $3,500. Terms 2/15, n/EOM, FOB shipping point. |
| 4 | Paid freight bill of $75 on February 3 purchase. |
| 4 | Purchased merchandise inventory for cash of $2,200. |
| 6 | Returned $800 of inventory from February 3 purchase. |
| 8 | Sold merchandise inventory to Harvey Company, $5,700, on account. Terms 2/15, n/35. Cost of goods, $2,508. |
| 9 | Purchased merchandise inventory on account from Teaton Wholesalers, $6,000. Terms 2/10, n/30, FOB destination. |
| 10 | Made payment to Sidecki Wholesalers for goods purchased on February 3, less return and discount. |
| 12 | Received payment from Harvey Company, less discount. |
| 13 | After negotiations, received a $100 allowance from Teaton Wholesalers. |
| 15 | Sold merchandise inventory to Jackson Company, $2,900, on account. Terms 3/10, n/EOM. Cost of goods, $1,276. |
| 22 | Made payment, less allowance, to Teaton Wholesalers for goods purchased on February 9. |
| 23 | Jackson Company returned $500 of the merchandise sold on February 15. Cost of goods, $220. |
| 25 | Sold merchandise inventory to Secker for $2,000 on account that cost $880. Terms of 2/10, n/30 were offered, FOB shipping point. As a courtesy to Secker, $85 of freight was added to the invoice for which cash was paid by Faucet. |
| 26 | After negotiations, granted a $100 allowance to Secker for merchandise purchased on February 25. |
| 27 | Received payment from Secker, less allowance and discount. |
| 28 | Received payment from Jackson Company, less return. |

**Learning Objectives 1, 2, 3**

Jan. 14 Merch. Inv. $25

## P5-39B Journalizing purchase and sale transactions

Journalize the following transactions that occurred in January 2016 for May's Amusements. No explanations are needed. Identify each accounts payable and accounts receivable with the vendor or customer name.

| | |
|---|---|
| Jan. 4 | Purchased merchandise inventory on account from Vanderbilt Company, $5,000. Terms 1/10, n/EOM, FOB shipping point. |
| 6 | Paid freight bill of $150 on January 4 purchase. |
| 8 | Returned half the inventory purchased on January 4 from Vanderbilt Company. |
| 10 | Sold merchandise inventory for cash, $1,100. Cost of goods, $440. FOB destination. |
| 11 | Sold merchandise inventory to Gilmore Corporation, $10,100, on account, terms of 3/10, n/EOM. Cost of goods, $5,555. FOB shipping point. |
| 12 | Paid freight bill of $30 on January 10 sale. |
| 13 | Sold merchandise inventory to Cadet Company, $8,800, on account, terms of 3/15, n/45. Cost of goods, $4,400. FOB shipping point. |
| 14 | Paid the amount owed on account from January 4, less return and discount. |
| 16 | After negotiations, granted a $800 allowance to Gilmore Corporation on January 11 sale. |
| 17 | Received defective inventory as a sales return from the January 13 sale, $400. Cost of goods, $200. |
| 18 | Purchased inventory of $4,600 on account from Roberts Corporation. Payment terms were1/10, n/30, FOB destination. |
| 20 | Received cash from Gilmore Corporation, less allowance and discount. |
| 26 | Paid amount owed on account from January 18, less discount. |
| 28 | Received cash from Cadet Company, less return and discount. |
| 29 | Purchased inventory from Silk Corporation for cash, $12,000, FOB shipping point. Freight in paid to shipping company, $240. |

## P5-40B Preparing a multi-step income statement, journalizing closing entries, and preparing a post-closing trial balance

**Learning Objectives 4, 5**

1. Operating Income $62,600

The adjusted trial balance of Rachel Rey Dance Company at April 30, 2016, follows:

**RACHEL REY DANCE COMPANY**
Adjusted Trial Balance
April 30, 2016

| | Balance | |
|---|---|---|
| **Account Title** | **Debit** | **Credit** |
| Cash | $ 3,700 | |
| Accounts Receivable | 38,100 | |
| Merchandise Inventory | 17,600 | |
| Office Supplies | 700 | |
| Furniture | 39,800 | |
| Accumulated Depreciation—Furniture | | $ 8,200 |
| Accounts Payable | | 13,600 |
| Salaries Payable | | 500 |
| Unearned Revenue | | 7,100 |
| Notes Payable, long-term | | 17,000 |
| Common Stock | | 16,000 |
| Retained Earnings | | 18,700 |
| Dividends | 42,500 | |
| Sales Revenue | | 180,000 |
| Sales Returns and Allowances | 6,000 | |
| Sales Discounts | 2,500 | |
| Cost of Goods Sold | 72,000 | |
| Selling Expense | 18,900 | |
| Administrative Expense | 18,000 | |
| Interest Expense | 1,300 | |
| Total | **$ 261,100** | **$ 261,100** |

### Requirements

1. Prepare Rachel Rey's multi-step income statement for the year ended April 30, 2016.
2. Journalize Rachel Rey's closing entries.
3. Prepare a post-closing trial balance as of April 30, 2016.

**Learning Objectives 4, 5**

2. Total Credits $490,410

**P5-41B Journalizing adjusting entries, preparing adjusted trial balance, and preparing financial statements**

The unadjusted trial balance for Thomas Electronics Company follows:

**THOMAS ELECTRONICS COMPANY**
Unadjusted Trial Balance
October 31, 2016

| | Balance | |
|---|---|---|
| **Account Title** | **Debit** | **Credit** |
| Cash | $ 4,400 | |
| Accounts Receivable | 35,200 | |
| Interest Receivable | 0 | |
| Merchandise Inventory | 45,600 | |
| Office Supplies | 5,700 | |
| Equipment | 131,000 | |
| Accumulated Depreciation—Equipment | | $ 37,900 |
| Accounts Payable | | 15,800 |
| Salaries Payable | | 0 |
| Interest Payable | | 0 |
| Unearned Revenue | | 13,700 |
| Notes Payable, long-term | | 47,000 |
| Common Stock | | 45,000 |
| Retained Earnings | | 15,700 |
| Dividends | 27,000 | |
| Sales Revenue | | 310,000 |
| Sales Returns and Allowances | 5,500 | |
| Sales Discounts | 4,000 | |
| Interest Revenue | | 0 |
| Cost of Goods Sold | 170,500 | |
| Salaries Expense (Selling) | 25,000 | |
| Rent Expense (Selling) | 15,300 | |
| Salaries Expense (Administrative) | 4,900 | |
| Utilities Expense (Administrative) | 11,000 | |
| Depreciation Expense—Equipment (Administrative) | 0 | |
| Interest Expense | 0 | |
| Total | **$ 485,100** | **$ 485,100** |

CHAPTER 5

**Requirements**

1. Journalize the adjusting entries using the following data:
   a. Interest revenue accrued, $300.
   b. Salaries (Selling) accrued, $2,400.
   c. Depreciation Expense—Equipment (Administrative), $1,310.
   d. Interest expense accrued, $1,300.
   e. A physical count of inventory was completed. The ending Merchandise Inventory should have a balance of $44,900.
2. Prepare Thomas Electronics's adjusted trial balance as of October 31, 2016.
3. Prepare Thomas Electronics's *multi-step* income statement for year ended October 31, 2016.
4. Prepare Thomas Electronics's statement of retained earnings for year ended October 31, 2016.
5. Prepare Thomas Electronics's classified balance sheet in *report form* as of October 31, 2016.

**P5-42B Preparing a single-step income statement, preparing a multi-step income statement, and computing the gross profit percentage**

**Learning Objectives 5, 6**

2. Operating Income $96,595

The records of Farm Fresh Beef Company list the following selected accounts for the quarter ended September 30, 2016:

| | | | |
|---|---|---|---|
| Interest Revenue | $ 700 | Accounts Payable | $ 17,200 |
| Merchandise Inventory | 45,500 | Accounts Receivable | 33,300 |
| Notes Payable, long-term | 44,000 | Accumulated Depreciation—Equipment | 36,800 |
| Salaries Payable | 2,900 | Common Stock | 32,000 |
| Sales Discounts | 4,500 | Retained Earnings | 5,105 |
| Sales Returns and Allowances | 8,300 | Dividends | 25,000 |
| Sales Revenue | 317,800 | Cash | 7,900 |
| Rent Expense (Selling) | 21,800 | Cost of Goods Sold | 158,600 |
| Office Supplies | 6,100 | Equipment | 130,500 |
| Unearned Revenue | 13,900 | Interest Payable | 700 |
| Interest Expense | 1,600 | Rent Expense (Administrative) | 9,000 |
| Depreciation Expense—Equipment (Administrative) | 1,305 | Utilities Expense (Selling) | 10,000 |
| Utilities Expense (Administrative) | 4,300 | Delivery Expense (Selling) | 3,400 |

**Requirements**

1. Prepare a single step income statement.
2. Prepare a multi-step income statement.
3. J. Douglas, manager of the company, strives to earn a gross profit percentage of at least 50%. Did Farm Fresh Beef achieve this goal? Show your calculations.

**Learning Objective 7**
**Appendix 5A**

Jun. 10 Purchase Discount $120

## P5A-43B Journalizing purchase and sale transactions—periodic inventory system

Journalize the following transactions that occurred in June 2016 for Dixie Company. Assume Dixie uses the periodic inventory system. No explanations are needed. Identify each accounts payable and accounts receivable with the vendor or customer name.

| | | |
|---|---|---|
| Jun. 3 | | Purchased merchandise inventory on account from Shue Wholesalers, $4,500. Terms 3/15, n/EOM, FOB shipping point. |
| | 4 | Paid freight bill of $75 on June 3 purchase. |
| | 4 | Purchased merchandise inventory for cash of $1,300. |
| | 6 | Returned $500 of inventory from June 3 purchase. |
| | 8 | Sold merchandise inventory to Herman Company, $3,800, on account. Terms 3/15, n/35. |
| | 9 | Purchased merchandise inventory on account from Tex Wholesalers, $4,700. Terms 2/10, n/30, FOB destination. |
| | 10 | Made payment to Shue Wholesalers for goods purchased on June 3, less return and discount. |
| | 12 | Received payment from Herman Company, less discount. |
| | 13 | After negotiations, received a $500 allowance from Tex Wholesalers. |
| | 15 | Sold merchandise inventory to Jeter Company, $1,800, on account. Terms 3/10, n/EOM. |
| | 22 | Made payment, less allowance, to Tex Wholesalers for goods purchased on June 9. |
| | 23 | Jeter Company returned $100 of the merchandise sold on June 15. |
| | 25 | Sold merchandise inventory to Small for $600 on account. Terms of 2/10, n/30 was offered, FOB shipping point. |
| | 26 | After negotiations, granted a $200 allowance to Small for merchandise sold on June 25. |
| | 29 | Received payment from Small, less allowance and discount. |
| | 30 | Received payment from Jeter Company, less return. |

**Learning Objective 7**
**Appendix 5A**

1. Gross Profit $209,000

**P5A-44B Preparing a multi-step income statement and journalizing closing entries**

Tilton Department Store uses a periodic inventory system. The adjusted trial balance of Tilton Department Store at December 31, 2016, follows:

| TILTON DEPARTMENT STORE<br>Adjusted Trial Balance<br>December 31, 2016 | | |
|---|---|---|
| | Balance | |
| **Account Title** | **Debit** | **Credit** |
| Cash | $ 7,700 | |
| Accounts Receivable | 84,900 | |
| Merchandise Inventory (beginning) | 37,300 | |
| Office Supplies | 700 | |
| Furniture | 81,000 | |
| Accumulated Depreciation—Furniture | | $ 18,100 |
| Accounts Payable | | 29,100 |
| Salaries Payable | | 2,100 |
| Unearned Revenue | | 14,300 |
| Notes Payable, long-term | | 38,000 |
| Common Stock | | 60,000 |
| Retained Earnings | | 1,500 |
| Dividends | 88,700 | |
| Sales Revenue | | 395,000 |
| Sales Returns and Allowances | 6,400 | |
| Sales Discounts | 4,300 | |
| Purchases | 290,000 | |
| Purchase Returns and Allowances | | 109,000 |
| Purchase Discounts | | 7,000 |
| Freight In | 700 | |
| Selling Expense | 42,300 | |
| Administrative Expense | 26,800 | |
| Interest Expense | 3,300 | |
| Total | **$ 674,100** | **$ 674,100** |

**Requirements**

1. Prepare Tilton Department Store's multi-step income statement for the year ended December 31, 2016. Assume ending Merchandise Inventory is $36,700.
2. Journalize Tilton Department Store's closing entries.

## > Continuing Problem

**P5-45 Journalizing purchase and sale transactions, making closing entries, preparing financial statements, and computing the gross profit percentage**

This problem continues the Daniels Consulting situation from Problem P4-40 of Chapter 4. Daniels Consulting performs systems consulting. The company has also begun selling accounting software and uses the perpetual inventory system to account for software inventory. During January, Daniels Consulting completed the following transactions:

| | |
|---|---|
| Jan. 2 | Completed a consulting engagement and received cash of $5,700. |
| 2 | Prepaid three months office rent, $2,400. |
| 7 | Purchased 50 units software inventory on account, $1,050, plus freight in, $50. |
| 18 | Sold 40 software units on account, $2,625 (cost $880). |
| 19 | Consulted with a client for a fee of $2,500 on account. |
| 20 | Paid employee salaries, $1,885, which includes accrued salaries from December. |
| 21 | Paid on account, $1,100. |
| 22 | Purchased 185 units software inventory on account, $4,810. |
| 24 | Paid utilities, $375. |
| 28 | Sold 135 units software for cash, $5,265 (cost $3,470). |
| 31 | Recorded the following adjusting entries:<br>a. Accrued salaries expense, $775<br>b. Depreciation on Equipment, $60; Depreciation on Furniture, $50<br>c. Expiration of prepaid rent, $800<br>d. Physical count of software inventory, 50 units, $1,300 |

**Requirements**

1. Open the following T-accounts in the ledger: Cash, $17,950; Accounts Receivable, $3,600; Software Inventory, $0; Office Supplies, $300; Prepaid Rent, $0; Equipment, $3,600; Accumulated Depreciation—Equipment, $60; Furniture, $3,000; Accumulated Depreciation—Furniture, $50; Accounts Payable, $3,600; Unearned Revenue, $1,800; Salaries Payable, $685; Common Stock, $20,000; Retained Earnings, $2,255; Dividends, $0; Income Summary, $0; Service Revenue, $0; Sales Revenue, $0; Cost of Goods Sold, $0; Salaries Expense, $0; Rent Expense, $0; Utilities Expense, $0; Depreciation Expense—Equipment, $0; and Depreciation Expense—Furniture, $0.
2. Journalize and post the January transactions. Compute each account balance, and denote the balance as *Bal.*
3. Prepare the month ended January 31, 2017, income statement of Daniels Consulting. Use the multi-step format. List Service Revenue under gross profit and ignore classifying the expenses as selling and administrative.
4. Journalize and post the closing entries. Denote each closing amount as *Clo.* After posting all closing entries, prove the equality of debits and credits in the ledger.
5. Compute the gross profit percentage of Daniels Consulting.

CHAPTER 5

## > Practice Set

This problem continues the Crystal Clear Cleaning practice set begun in Chapter 2 and continued through Chapters 3 and 4.

**P5-46 Journalizing purchase and sale transactions, making closing entries, preparing financial statements, and computing the gross profit percentage**

Crystal Clear Cleaning has decided that, in addition to providing cleaning services, it will sell cleaning products. Crystal Clear uses the perpetual inventory system. During December 2017, Crystal Clear completed the following transactions:

| | |
|---|---|
| Dec. 2 | Purchased 475 units of inventory for $2,850 on account from Sparkle, Co. on terms, 3/10, n/20. |
| 5 | Purchased 600 units of inventory from Borax on account with terms 2/10, n/30. The total invoice was for $4,500, which included a $150 freight charge. |
| 7 | Returned 75 units of inventory to Sparkle from the December 2 purchase (cost $450). |
| 9 | Paid Borax. |
| 11 | Sold 285 units of goods to Happy Maids for $3,990 on account with terms 3/10, n/30. Crystal Clear's cost of the goods was $1,710. |
| 12 | Paid Sparkle. |
| 15 | Received 22 units with a retail price of $308 of goods back from customer Happy Maids. The goods cost Crystal Clear $132. |
| 21 | Received payment from Happy Maids, settling the amount due in full. |
| 28 | Sold 265 units of goods to Bridget, Inc. for cash of $3,975 (cost $1,691). |
| 29 | Paid cash for utilities of $415. |
| 30 | Paid cash for Sales Commission Expense of $550. |
| 31 | Recorded the following adjusting entries:<br>a. Physical count of inventory on December 31 showed 428 units of goods on hand, $3,148<br>b. Depreciation, $270<br>c. Accrued salaries expense of $725<br>d. Prepared all other adjustments necessary for December (Hint: You will need to review the adjustment information in Chapter 3 to determine the remaining adjustments). Assume the cleaning supplies left at December 31 are $30. |

**Requirements**

1. Open the following T-accounts in the ledger: Cash, $138,150; Accounts Receivable, $2,600; Merchandise Inventory, $0; Cleaning Supplies, $30; Prepaid Rent, $1,500; Prepaid Insurance, $1,650; Equipment, $3,200; Truck, $7,000; Accumulated Depreciation—Equipment and Truck, $270; Accounts Payable, $1,470; Unearned Revenue, $11,500; Salaries Payable, $0; Interest Payable, $240; Notes Payable (Long-term), $96,000; Common Stock, $42,000; Retained Earnings, $2,650; Dividends, $0; Income Summary, $0; Service Revenue, $0; Sales Revenue, $0; Sales Returns and Allowances, $0; Sales Discounts, $0; Cost of Goods Sold, $0; Sales Commission Expense, $0; Utilities Expense, $0; Depreciation Expense, $0; Salaries Expense, $0; Insurance Expense, $0; Rent Expense, $0; Interest Expense, $0.
2. Journalize and post the December transactions. Compute each account balance, and denote the balance as *Bal.* Identify each accounts payable and accounts receivable with the vendor or customer name.

CHAPTER 5

3. Journalize and post the adjusting entries. Denote each adjusting amount as *Adj.* Compute each account balance, and denote the balance as *Bal.* After posting all adjusting entries, prove the equality of debits and credits in the ledger.
4. Prepare the December multi-step income statement, statement of retained earnings, and classified balance sheet for the company. List Service Revenue under gross profit, and ignore classifying the expenses as selling and administrative.
5. Journalize the December closing entries for the company.
6. Compute the gross profit percentage for the company.

# COMPREHENSIVE PROBLEM

## > Comprehensive Problem for Chapters 1–5

### Completing a Merchandiser's Accounting Cycle

St. John Technology uses a perpetual inventory system. The end-of-month unadjusted trial balance of St. John Technology at January 31, 2016, follows:

**ST. JOHN TECHNOLOGY**
Unadjusted Trial Balance
January 31, 2016

| | Balance | |
|---|---|---|
| **Account** | **Debit** | **Credit** |
| Cash | $ 12,660 | |
| Accounts Receivable | 15,390 | |
| Merchandise Inventory | 58,000 | |
| Office Supplies | 3,330 | |
| Building | 195,000 | |
| Accumulated Depreciation—Building | | $ 45,000 |
| Furniture | 53,000 | |
| Accumulated Depreciation—Furniture | | 6,200 |
| Accounts Payable | | 24,775 |
| Salaries Payable | | 0 |
| Unearned Revenue | | 6,150 |
| Notes Payable, long-term | | 78,000 |
| Common Stock | | 120,000 |
| Retained Earnings | | 42,120 |
| Dividends | 8,200 | |
| Sales Revenue | | 154,795 |
| Sales Discounts | 7,350 | |
| Sales Returns and Allowances | 5,075 | |
| Cost of Goods Sold | 87,665 | |
| Selling Expense | 19,830 | |
| Administrative Expense | 11,540 | |
| Total | **$ 477,040** | **$ 477,040** |

CHAPTER 5

Additional data at January 31, 2016:

a. Office Supplies consumed during the month, $1,780. Half is selling expense, and the other half is administrative expense.
b. Depreciation for the month: building, $4,500; furniture, $2,600. One-fourth of depreciation is selling expense, and three-fourths is administrative expense.
c. Unearned revenue that has been earned during January, $3,825.
d. Accrued salaries, an administrative expense, $975.
e. Merchandise Inventory on hand, $55,375. St. John uses the perpetual inventory system.

**Requirements**

1. Using T-accounts, open the accounts listed on the trial balance, inserting their unadjusted balances. Label the balances as *Bal.* Also open the Income Summary account.
2. Journalize and post the adjusting entries at January 31. Compute the ending balances in the T-accounts, and denote as *Bal.*
3. Enter the unadjusted trial balance on a worksheet, and complete the worksheet for the month ended January 31, 2016. St. John Technology groups all operating expenses under two accounts, Selling Expense and Administrative Expense. Leave two blank lines under Selling Expense and three blank lines under Administrative Expense.
4. Prepare the company's *multi-step* income statement and statement of retained earnings for the month ended January 31, 2016. Also prepare the balance sheet at that date in *report* form.
5. Journalize and post the closing entries at January 31.

# CRITICAL THINKING

## > Decision Case 5-1

Party-Time T-Shirts sells T-shirts for parties at the local college. The company completed the first year of operations, and the shareholders are generally pleased with operating results as shown by the following income statement:

| PARTY-TIME T-SHIRTS<br>Income Statement<br>Year Ended December 31, 2015 | |
|---|---|
| Net Sales Revenue | $ 350,000 |
| Cost of Goods Sold | 210,000 |
| Gross Profit | 140,000 |
| Operating Expenses: | |
| Selling Expense | 40,000 |
| Administrative Expense | 25,000 |
| Net Income | **$ 75,000** |

Bill Hildebrand, the controller, is considering how to expand the business. He proposes two ways to increase profits to $100,000 during 2016.

**a.** Hildebrand believes he should advertise more heavily. He believes additional advertising costing $20,000 will increase net sales by 30% and leave administrative expense unchanged. Assume that Cost of Goods Sold will remain at the same percentage of net sales as in 2015, so if net sales increase in 2016, Cost of Goods Sold will increase proportionately.

**b.** Hildebrand proposes selling higher-margin merchandise, such as party dresses, in addition to the existing product line. An importer can supply a minimum of 1,000 dresses for $40 each; Party-Time can mark these dresses up 100% and sell them for $80. Hildebrand realizes he will have to advertise the new merchandise, and this advertising will cost $5,000. Party-Time can expect to sell only 80% of these dresses during the coming year.

Help Hildebrand determine which plan to pursue. Prepare a single-step income statement for 2016 to show the expected net income under each plan.

## > Ethical Issue 5-1

Dobbs Wholesale Antiques makes all sales under terms of FOB shipping point. The company usually ships inventory to customers approximately one week after receiving the order. For orders received late in December, Kathy Dobbs, the owner, decides when to ship the goods. If profits are already at an acceptable level, Dobbs delays shipment until January. If profits for the current year are lagging behind expectations, Dobbs ships the goods during December.

**Requirements**

1. Under Dobbs's FOB policy, when should the company record a sale?
2. Do you approve or disapprove of Dobbs's manner of deciding when to ship goods to customers and record the sales revenue? If you approve, give your reason. If you disapprove, identify a better way to decide when to ship goods. (There is no accounting rule against Dobbs's practice.)



## > Fraud Case 5-1

Rae Philippe was a warehouse manager for Atkins Oilfield Supply, a business that operated across eight Western states. She was an old pro and had known most of the other warehouse managers for many years. Around December each year, auditors would come to do a physical count of the inventory at each warehouse. Recently, Rae's brother started his own drilling company and persuaded Rae to "loan" him 80 joints of 5-inch drill pipe to use for his first well. He promised to have it back to Rae by December, but the well encountered problems and the pipe was still in the ground. Rae knew the auditors were on the way, so she called her friend Andy, who ran another Atkins warehouse. "Send me over 80 joints of 5-inch pipe tomorrow, and I'll get them back to you ASAP," said Rae. When the auditors came, all the pipe on the books was accounted for, and they filed a "no-exception" report.

**Requirements**

1. Is there anything the company or the auditors could do in the future to detect this kind of fraudulent practice?
2. How would this kind of action affect the financial performance of the company?

## > Financial Statement Case 5-1

This case uses both the income statement (consolidated statement of earnings) and the balance sheet of **Starbucks Corporation**. Visit **http://www.pearsonhighered.com/Horngren** to view a link to the Starbucks Corporation Fiscal 2013 Annual Report.

**Requirements**

1. What was the value of the company's inventory at September 29, 2013, and September 30, 2012?
2. Review Note 5 (specifically Inventories) in the Notes to Consolidated Financial Statements. What do Starbucks' inventories consist of?
3. What was the amount of Starbucks's cost of goods sold (cost of sales) for the year ending September 29, 2013, and the year ending September 30, 2012?
4. What income statement format does Starbucks use? Explain.
5. Compute Starbucks's gross profit percentage for the year ending September 29, 2013, and the year ending September 30, 2012. Did the gross profit percentage improve, worsen, or hold steady? Assuming the industry average for gross profit percentage is 58.58%, how does Starbucks compare in the industry?



## > Quick Check Answers

**1.** d **2.** a **3.** c **4.** c **5.** b **6.** a **7.** a **8.** d **9.** a **10A.** d

# 6 Merchandise Inventory

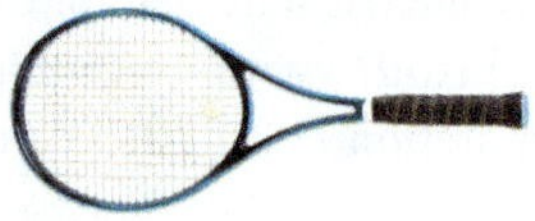

## What Is the Cost of This Merchandise Inventory?

Jorell was excited about the most recent shipment of merchandise inventory that he received today. As the controller of a successful sporting goods store, he has decided to expand the merchandise inventory line by offering outdoor cooking items such as grills, cookers, and accessories. He believes that this new merchandise inventory will draw new customers to the store and eventually bring more profits to the business.

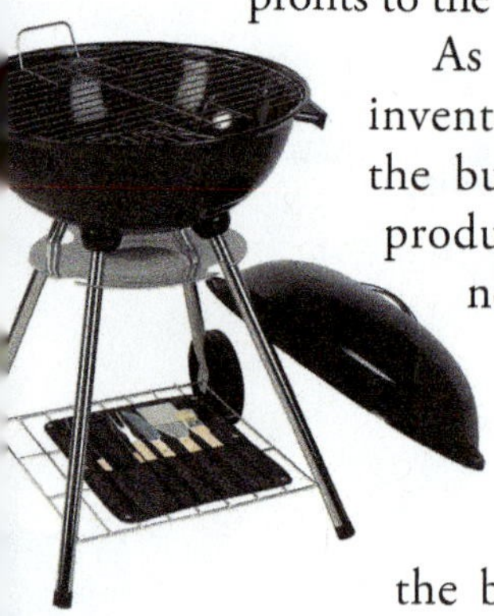

As Jorell prepares the merchandise inventory for sale, he must decide how the business will track the cost of each product sold. For example, if the business sells 500 identical outdoor grills that were purchased at different times and at different costs, how will the business determine the cost of each grill sold? Should the business keep detailed cost records for each specific grill sold? Or should the business use an inventory costing method that will approximate the flow of inventory costs? For example, the business might decide to assign the costs of the first grills purchased to the first grills sold rather than tracking the cost of each grill individually. Or it might decide, instead, to assign the costs of the last grills purchased to the first grills sold.

Jorell understands that he has several options when it comes to selecting an inventory costing method. He wants to select a method that will be relatively easy to implement and maintain. He knows that by selecting the best method for the business, he will be able to easily determine the cost of the goods sold and, ultimately, the gross profit.

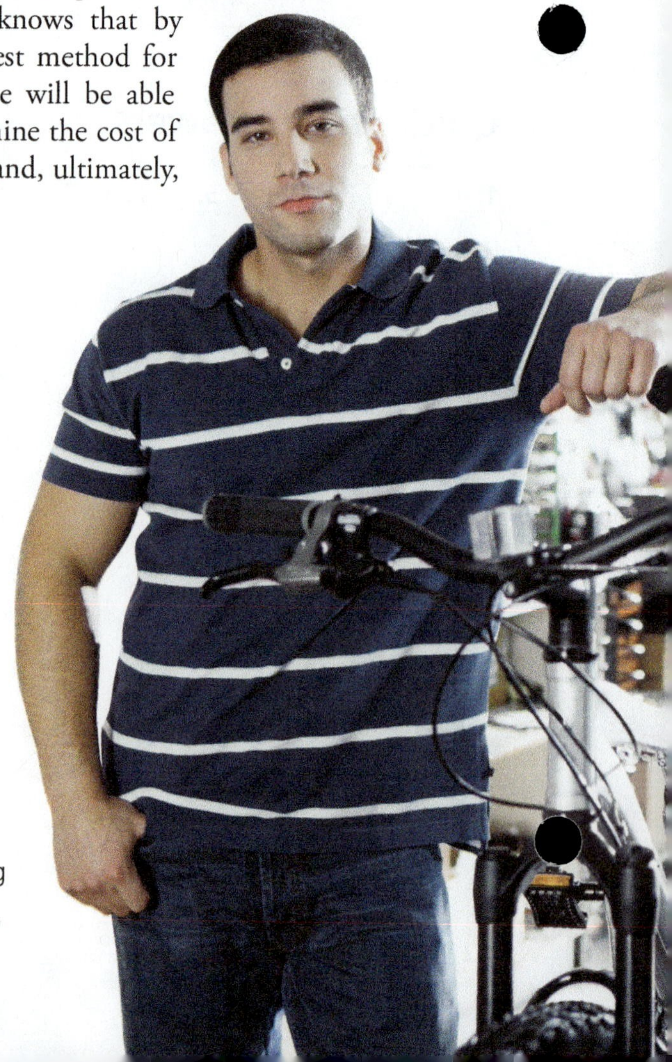

**What Is the Cost of Merchandise Inventory?**

In this chapter, we expand our discussion on merchandise inventory by learning how to account for the cost of inventory. When Dick's Sporting Goods, Inc., a retail chain that sells sporting goods, apparel, and footwear, purchases and sells inventory, the business must account for the inventory appropriately. Dick's must determine the cost of the inventory that is sold in order to calculate gross profit. If a business had only a small amount of inventory, identifying the cost of one particular item would be simple. However, large businesses, such as Dick's, have millions of items of inventory, which makes tracking costs very difficult. In this chapter, you learn that every business must select an inventory costing method that allows it to track costs and determine the cost of goods sold, gross profit, and value of ending merchandise inventory.

# Chapter 6 Learning Objectives

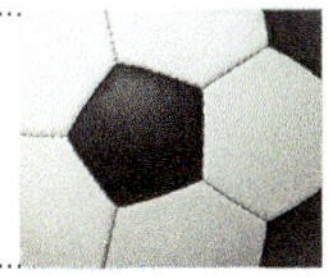

1. Identify accounting principles and controls related to merchandise inventory
2. Account for merchandise inventory costs under a perpetual inventory system
3. Compare the effects on the financial statements when using the different inventory costing methods
4. Apply the lower-of-cost-or-market rule to merchandise inventory
5. Measure the effects of merchandise inventory errors on the financial statements
6. Use inventory turnover and days' sales in inventory to evaluate business performance
7. Account for merchandise inventory costs under a periodic inventory system (Appendix 6A)

## WHAT ARE THE ACCOUNTING PRINCIPLES AND CONTROLS THAT RELATE TO MERCHANDISE INVENTORY?

**Learning Objective 1**
Identify accounting principles and controls related to merchandise inventory

Chapter 5 introduced accounting for merchandise inventory. It showed how Smart Touch Learning, a fictitious merchandiser that sells tablet computers containing e-learning software programs, recorded the purchase and sale of its inventory. The current chapter completes the accounting for merchandise inventory.

### Accounting Principles

Let's begin by learning about several accounting principles that affect merchandise inventories. Among them are consistency, disclosure, materiality, and accounting conservatism.

#### Consistency Principle

The **consistency principle** states that businesses should use the same accounting methods and procedures from period to period. Consistency helps investors and creditors compare a company's financial statements from one period to the next.

**Consistency Principle**
A business should use the same accounting methods and procedures from period to period.

Suppose you are analyzing a company's net income over a two-year period in which there was an increase in net income from the first year to the second. Analysis of the income statement shows Sales Revenue was almost the same for both years, but Cost of Goods Sold decreased significantly, which resulted in increases in gross profit and operating income. Without further information, you might conclude that the company was able to purchase its inventory at a lower cost in the second year and that profits will continue to increase in future years. However, changing inventory costing methods could have caused this one-time change, in which case future profits will not be affected. Therefore, companies must be consistent in the accounting methods they use. If changes are made in accounting methods, these changes must be reported. Investors and creditors need this information to make wise decisions about the company.

#### Disclosure Principle

The **disclosure principle** holds that a company should report enough information for outsiders to make knowledgeable decisions about the company. In short, the company should report information that is relevant and has faithful representation. This includes

**Disclosure Principle**
A business's financial statements must report enough information for outsiders to make knowledgeable decisions about the company.

disclosing the method used to account for merchandise inventories. All major accounting methods and procedures are described in the footnotes to the financial statements. Suppose a banker is comparing two companies—one using inventory method A and the other using inventory method B. The B company reports higher net income but only because of the inventory method it selected. Without knowledge of these accounting methods, the banker could lend money to the wrong business.

*Take a look at Appendix A, which contains the Green Mountain Coffee Roasters, Inc. annual report. After the financial statements, you will find the notes to the financial statements. These footnotes contain important information summarizing the accounting policies that Green Mountain uses and ensure that the company is providing full disclosure to its investors and creditors.*

### Materiality Concept

**Materiality Concept**
A company must perform strictly proper accounting only for items that are significant to the business's financial situation.

The **materiality concept** states that a company must perform strictly proper accounting *only* for significant items. Information is significant—or, in accounting terms, *material*—when it would cause someone to change a decision. The materiality concept frees accountants from having to report every last item in strict accordance with GAAP. For example, $10,000 is material to a small business with annual sales of $100,000. However, $10,000 isn't material to a large company with annual sales of $100,000,000. Therefore, the accounting principles followed for a $10,000 cost in a small company may be different from the accounting principles followed for a $10,000 cost in a large company.

### Conservatism

**Conservatism**
A business should report the least favorable figures in the financial statements when two or more possible options are presented.

**Conservatism** in accounting means exercising caution in reporting items in the financial statements. Conservatism espouses the following ideas:

- Anticipate no gains, but provide for all probable losses.
- If in doubt, record an asset at the lowest reasonable amount and a liability at the highest reasonable amount.
- When there's a question, record an expense rather than an asset.
- When you are faced with a decision between two possible options, you must choose the option that undervalues, rather than overvalues, your business.

The goal of conservatism is to report realistic figures and never overstate assets or net income.

## Control Over Merchandise Inventory

Maintaining good controls over merchandise inventory is very important for a merchandiser. Good controls ensure that inventory purchases and sales are properly authorized and accounted for by the accounting system. This can be accomplished by taking the following measures:

- Ensure merchandise inventory is not purchased without proper authorization, including purchasing only from approved vendors and within acceptable dollar ranges.
- After inventory is purchased, the order should be tracked and properly documented when received. At time of delivery, a count of inventory received should be completed and each item should be examined for damage.
- Damaged inventory should be properly recorded and then should either be used, disposed of, or returned to the vendor.

- A physical count of inventory should be completed at least once a year to track inventory shrinkage due to theft, damage, and errors.
- When sales are made, the inventory sold should be properly recorded and removed from the inventory count. This will prevent the company from running out of inventory, often called a stockout.

## Try It!

Match the accounting terminology to the definitions.

1. Conservatism
2. Materiality concept
3. Disclosure principle
4. Consistency principle

a. A business should report the least favorable figures in the financial statements when two or more possible options are presented.

b. A business's financial statements must report enough information for outsiders to make knowledgeable decisions about the company.

c. A business should use the same accounting methods and procedures from period to period.

d. A company must perform strictly proper accounting only for items that are significant to the business's financial situation.

**Check your answers online in MyAccountingLab or at http://www.pearsonhighered.com/Horngren.**

For more practice, see Short Exercise S6-1. MyAccountingLab

# HOW ARE MERCHANDISE INVENTORY COSTS DETERMINED UNDER A PERPETUAL INVENTORY SYSTEM?

**Learning Objective 2**
Account for merchandise inventory costs under a perpetual inventory system

Previously you learned about merchandise inventory and cost of goods sold. Remember these key equations:

Ending Merchandise Inventory = Number of units *on hand* × Unit cost
Cost of Goods Sold = Number of units *sold* × Unit cost

Companies determine the number of units on hand from perpetual inventory records backed up by a physical count. Exhibit 6-1 (on the next page) gives the inventory data for TAB0503, one model of tablets that Smart Touch Learning sells.

As shown in this exhibit, Smart Touch Learning began August with 2 TAB0503s in inventory. It purchased 4 more tablets on August 5, bringing the total quantity on hand to 6 (2 + 4). On August 15, it sold 4 tablets, leaving 2 remaining on hand (6 − 4). Smart Touch Learning then purchased 12 more on August 26 and sold 10 on August 31. It had 4 TAB0503s at the end of August (2 + 12 − 10). The company sold each tablet for $500 to its customers.

**Exhibit 6-1** | **Perpetual Inventory Record**

**Item:** TAB0503

| Date | Quantity Purchased | Quantity Sold | Cost per Unit | Quantity on Hand |
|---|---|---|---|---|
| Aug. 1 | | | $350 | 2 |
| 5 | 4 | | $350 | 6 ← 2 + 4 |
| 15 | | 4 | | 2 ← 6 − 4 |
| 26 | 12 | | $350 | 14 |
| 31 | | 10 | | 4 |
| Totals | 16 | 14 | | 4 |

Measuring inventory cost is easy when prices do not change. For example, looking at Exhibit 6-1, you can see that Smart Touch Learning's cost per unit remained the same at $350. Therefore ending inventory and cost of goods sold can be calculated easily.

Ending Merchandise Inventory = Number of units *on hand* × Unit cost
= 4 units × $350 per unit
= $1,400

Cost of Goods Sold = Number of units *sold* × Unit cost
= 14 units × $350 per unit
= $4,900

But what if unit cost does change? For example, what if the cost per unit increased to $360 on August 5 and $380 on August 26, as shown in Exhibit 6-2? When inventory is sold on August 31, how many of the tablets sold cost $350? How many cost $360? And how many cost $380? To compute ending inventory and cost of goods sold, Smart Touch Learning must assign a unit cost to each inventory item. This is done by using one of four inventory costing methods: **1.** Specific identification **2.** First-in, first-out (FIFO) **3.** Last-in, first-out (LIFO) **4.** Weighted-average

**Exhibit 6-2** | **Perpetual Inventory Record—Changes in Cost per Unit**

**Item:** TAB0503

| Date | Quantity Purchased | Quantity Sold | Cost per Unit | Quantity on Hand |
|---|---|---|---|---|
| Aug. 1 | | | $350 | 2 |
| 5 | 4 | | $360 | 6 |
| 15 | | 4 | | 2 |
| 26 | 12 | | $380 | 14 |
| 31 | | 10 | | 4 |
| Totals | 16 | 14 | | 4 |

Each **inventory costing method** approximates the flow of inventory costs in a business (with the exception of the specific identification method) and is used to determine the amount of cost of goods sold and ending merchandise inventory.

**Inventory Costing Method**
A method of approximating the flow of inventory costs in a business that is used to determine the amount of cost of goods sold and ending merchandise inventory.

## Specific Identification Method

The **specific identification method** uses the specific cost of each unit of inventory to determine ending inventory and cost of goods sold. In the specific identification method, the company knows exactly which item was sold and exactly what the item cost. This costing method is best for businesses that sell unique, easily identified inventory items, such as automobiles (identified by the vehicle identification number [VIN]), jewels (a specific diamond ring), and real estate (identified by address). For instance, assume that of the 4 tablets sold on August 15, 1 had a cost of $350 and 3 had a cost of $360. As for the August 31 sale, 1 had a cost of $350 and 9 had a cost of $380. Cost of goods sold and ending merchandise inventory can be calculated as shown in Exhibit 6-3.

**Specific Identification Method**
An inventory costing method based on the specific cost of particular units of inventory.

**Exhibit 6-3** | **Perpetual Inventory Record: Specific Identification**

| | Purchases | | | Cost of Goods Sold | | | Inventory on Hand | | |
|---|---|---|---|---|---|---|---|---|---|
| Date | Quantity | Unit Cost | Total Cost | Quantity | Unit Cost | Total Cost | Quantity | Unit Cost | Total Cost |
| Aug. 1 | | | | | | | 2 units | × $ 350 | = $ 700 } $ 700 |
| 5 | 4 units | × $ 360 | = $ 1,440 | | | | 2 units<br>4 units | × $ 350<br>× $ 360 | = $ 700<br>= $ 1,440 } $ 2,140 |
| 15 | | | | 1 unit<br>3 units | × $ 350<br>× $ 360 | = $ 350<br>= $ 1,080 } $ 1,430 | 1 unit<br>1 unit | × $ 350<br>× $ 360 | = $ 350<br>= $ 360 } $ 710 |
| 26 | 12 units | × $ 380 | = $ 4,560 | | | | 1 unit<br>1 unit<br>12 units | × $ 350<br>× $ 360<br>× $ 380 | = $ 350<br>= $ 360<br>= $ 4,560 } $ 5,270 |
| 31 | | | | 1 unit<br>9 units | × $ 350<br>× $ 380 | = $ 350<br>= $ 3,420 } $ 3,770 | 1 unit<br>3 units | × $ 360<br>× $ 380 | = $ 360<br>= $ 1,140 } $ 1,500 |
| Totals | 16 units | | $ 6,000 | 14 units | | $ 5,200 | 4 units | | $ 1,500 |

Notice that under the specific identification method, when inventory is sold, a specific cost is assigned to it. For example, on the August 15 sale, Smart Touch Learning knew that it had sold 1 unit costing $350 and 3 units costing $360. This left 1 unit (2 – 1) at $350 and 1 unit (4 – 3) at $360 in ending inventory. This method requires the business to keep detailed records of inventory sales and purchases and to also be able to carefully identify the inventory that is sold.

## First-In, First-Out (FIFO) Method

**First-In, First-Out (FIFO) Method**
An inventory costing method in which the first costs into inventory are the first costs out to cost of goods sold. Ending inventory is based on the costs of the most recent purchases.

Under the **first-in, first-out (FIFO) method**, the cost of goods sold is based on the oldest purchases—that is, the first units to come in are assumed to be the first units to go out (sold). In Exhibit 6-4, this is illustrated by the cost of goods sold coming from the *first* goods purchased, which are from the August 1 beginning inventory. FIFO costing is consistent with the physical movement of inventory (for most companies). That is, under the FIFO inventory costing method, companies sell their oldest inventory first.

**Exhibit 6-4** | **Perpetual Inventory Record: First-In, First-Out (FIFO)**

| | Purchases | | | Cost of Goods Sold | | | | Inventory on Hand | | | |
|---|---|---|---|---|---|---|---|---|---|---|---|
| Date | Quantity | Unit Cost | Total Cost | Quantity | Unit Cost | Total Cost | | Quantity | Unit Cost | Total Cost | |
| Aug. 1 | | | | | | | | 2 units | × $ 350 | = $ 700 | $ 700 |
| 5 | 4 units | × $ 360 | = $ 1,440 | | | | | 2 units<br>4 units | × $ 350<br>× $ 360 | = $ 700<br>= $ 1,440 | $ 2,140 |
| 15 | | | | 2 units<br>2 units | × $ 350<br>× $ 360 | = $ 700<br>= $ 720 | $ 1,420 | 2 units | × $ 360 | = $ 720 | $ 720 |
| 26 | 12 units | × $ 380 | = $ 4,560 | | | | | 2 units<br>12 units | × $ 360<br>× $ 380 | = $ 720<br>= $ 4,560 | $ 5,280 |
| 31 | | | | 2 units<br>8 units | × $ 360<br>× $ 380 | = $ 720<br>= $ 3,040 | $ 3,760 | 4 units | × $ 380 | = $ 1,520 | $ 1,520 |
| Totals | 16 units | | $ 6,000 | 14 units | | | $ 5,180 | 4 units | | | $ 1,520 |

Smart Touch Learning began August with 2 TAB0503s that cost $350 each. After the August 5 purchase, the inventory on hand consists of 6 units (2 + 4). On August 15, the company sold 4 units. Under FIFO, the first 2 units sold had the oldest cost ($350 per unit). The next 2 units sold cost $360 each. That leaves 2 units in inventory on August 15 at $360 each. The remainder of the inventory record follows the same pattern. Consider the sale on August 31 of 10 units. The oldest cost is from August 5 (2 units @ $360). The next oldest cost is from the August 26 purchase at $380 each (8 units @ $380). This leaves 4 units in inventory on August 31 at $380 each.

The FIFO monthly summary at August 31 is as follows:

- Cost of goods sold: 14 units that cost a total of $5,180.
- Ending inventory: 4 units that cost a total of $1,520.

**Cost of Goods Available for Sale**
The total cost spent on inventory that was available to be sold during a period.

Notice the total cost of goods sold of $5,180 plus the total ending inventory of $1,520 equals the total **cost of goods available for sale** during August of $6,700 [(2 units @ $350) + (4 units @ $360) + (12 units @ $380)]. Cost of goods available for sale represents the total cost of merchandise inventory that is available for sale during the time period. Smart Touch Learning measures cost of goods sold and ending merchandise inventory in this manner to prepare its financial statements.

## Journal Entries Under FIFO

The journal entries under FIFO are presented below. We assume all purchases and sales of inventory are on account. The amounts unique to FIFO are shown in blue for emphasis. All other amounts are the same for all four inventory methods.

| Date | Accounts and Explanation | Debit | Credit | |
|---|---|---|---|---|
| Aug. 5 | Merchandise Inventory (4 × $360) | 1,440 | | A↑ Merchandise Inventory↑ = L↑ Accounts Payable↑ + E |
| | Accounts Payable | | 1,440 | |
| | *Purchased inventory on account.* | | | |
| 15 | Accounts Receivable (4 × $500) | 2,000 | | A↑ Accounts Receivable↑ = L + E↑ Sales Revenue↑ |
| | Sales Revenue | | 2,000 | |
| | *Sale on account.* | | | |
| 15 | Cost of Goods Sold (2 × $350) + (2 × $360) | 1,420 | | A↓ Merchandise Inventory↓ = L + E↓ Cost of Goods Sold↑ |
| | Merchandise Inventory | | 1,420 | |
| | *Recorded the cost of goods sold.* | | | |
| 26 | Merchandise Inventory (12 × $380) | 4,560 | | A↑ Merchandise Inventory↑ = L↑ Accounts Payable↑ + E |
| | Accounts Payable | | 4,560 | |
| | *Purchased inventory on account.* | | | |
| 31 | Accounts Receivable (10 × $500) | 5,000 | | A↑ Accounts Receivable↑ = L + E↑ Sales Revenue↑ |
| | Sales Revenue | | 5,000 | |
| | *Sale on account.* | | | |
| 31 | Cost of Goods Sold (2 × $360) + (8 × $380) | 3,760 | | A↓ Merchandise Inventory↓ = L + E↓ Cost of Goods Sold↑ |
| | Merchandise Inventory | | 3,760 | |
| | *Recorded the cost of goods sold.* | | | |

For example, on August 5, Smart Touch Learning purchased $1,440 of inventory and made the first journal entry. On August 15, the company sold 4 TAB0503s for the sale price of $500 each. Smart Touch Learning recorded the sale, $2,000, and the cost of goods sold, $1,420 (calculated in Exhibit 6-4 as 2 units @ $350 plus 2 units @ $360). The remaining journal entries (August 26 and 31) follow the inventory data in Exhibit 6-4.

## Last-In, First-Out (LIFO) Method

Last-in, first-out (LIFO) is the opposite of FIFO. Under the **last-in, first-out (LIFO) method**, ending inventory comes from the oldest costs (beginning inventory and earliest purchases) of the period. The cost of goods sold is based on the most recent purchases (new

**Last-In, First-Out (LIFO) Method**
An inventory costing method in which the last costs into inventory are the first costs out to cost of goods sold. The method leaves the oldest costs—those of beginning inventory and the earliest purchases of the period—in ending inventory.

costs)—that is, the last units in are assumed to be the first units sold. This is illustrated by the cost of goods sold for the August 31 sale coming from the *last* goods in the warehouse—the August 26 purchase in Exhibit 6-5. Under the LIFO inventory costing method, companies sell their newest inventory first.

**Exhibit 6-5 | Perpetual Inventory Record: Last-In, First-Out (LIFO)**

| Date | Purchases | | | Cost of Goods Sold | | | Inventory on Hand | | |
|---|---|---|---|---|---|---|---|---|---|
| | Quantity | Unit Cost | Total Cost | Quantity | Unit Cost | Total Cost | Quantity | Unit Cost | Total Cost |
| Aug. 1 | | | | | | | 2 units | × $ 350 | = $ 700 } $ 700 |
| 5 | 4 units | × $ 360 | = $ 1,440 | | | | 2 units<br>4 units | × $ 350<br>× $ 360 | = $ 700<br>= $ 1,440 } $ 2,140 |
| 15 | | | | 4 units | × $ 360 | = $ 1,440 } $ 1,440 | 2 units | × $ 350 | = $ 700 } $ 700 |
| 26 | 12 units | × $ 380 | = $ 4,560 | | | | 2 units<br>12 units | × $ 350<br>× $ 380 | = $ 700<br>= $ 4,560 } $ 5,260 |
| 31 | | | | 10 units | × $ 380 | = $ 3,800 } $ 3,800 | 2 units<br>2 units | × $ 350<br>× $ 380 | = $ 700<br>= $ 760 } $ 1,460 |
| Totals | 16 units | | $ 6,000 | 14 units | | $ 5,240 | 4 units | | $ 1,460 |

IFRS

LIFO is not permitted under International Financial Reporting Standards (IFRS). Under IFRS, companies may only use the specific identification, FIFO, and weighted-average methods to cost inventory. If LIFO were eliminated as an acceptable method under GAAP, those U.S. companies currently using the LIFO cost method would experience significant income statement and balance sheet effects. Approximately one-third of U.S. companies use the LIFO method to cost at least part of their inventory.

Again, Smart Touch Learning had 2 TAB0503s at the beginning. After the purchase on August 5, the company holds 6 units of inventory (2 units @ $350 plus 4 units @ $360). On August 15, Smart Touch Learning sells 4 units. Under LIFO, the cost of goods sold always comes from the most recent purchase (4 units @ $360). That leaves 2 TAB0503s in inventory on August 15 (2 units @ $350).

The purchase of 12 units on August 26 adds a new $380 layer to inventory. Now inventory holds 14 units.

Then the sale of 10 units on August 31 peels back units in LIFO order (10 units @ $380). The LIFO monthly summary at August 31 is as follows:

- Cost of goods sold: 14 units that cost a total of $5,240.
- Ending inventory: 4 units that cost a total of $1,460.

Under LIFO, Smart Touch Learning could measure cost of goods sold and ending inventory in this manner to prepare its financial statements.

## Journal Entries Under LIFO

The journal entries under LIFO follow. We assume all purchases and sales of inventory are on account. Amounts unique to LIFO are shown in blue.

| Date | Accounts and Explanation | Debit | Credit |
|---|---|---|---|
| Aug. 5 | Merchandise Inventory (4 × $360) | 1,440 | |
| | Accounts Payable | | 1,440 |
| | *Purchased inventory on account.* | | |
| 15 | Accounts Receivable (4 × $500) | 2,000 | |
| | Sales Revenue | | 2,000 |
| | *Sale on account.* | | |
| 15 | Cost of Goods Sold (4 × $360) | 1,440 | |
| | Merchandise Inventory | | 1,440 |
| | *Recorded the cost of goods sold.* | | |
| 26 | Merchandise Inventory (12 × $380) | 4,560 | |
| | Accounts Payable | | 4,560 |
| | *Purchased inventory on account.* | | |
| 31 | Accounts Receivable (10 × $500) | 5,000 | |
| | Sales Revenue | | 5,000 |
| | *Sale on account.* | | |
| 31 | Cost of Goods Sold (10 × $380) | 3,800 | |
| | Merchandise Inventory | | 3,800 |
| | *Recorded the cost of goods sold.* | | |

| A | = | L | + | E |
|---|---|---|---|---|
| A↑ Merchandise Inventory↑ | = | L↑ Accounts Payable↑ | + | E |
| A↑ Accounts Receivable↑ | = | L | + | E↑ Sales Revenue↑ |
| A↓ Merchandise Inventory↓ | = | L | + | E↓ Cost of Goods Sold↑ |
| A↑ Merchandise Inventory↑ | = | L↑ Accounts Payable↑ | + | E |
| A↑ Accounts Receivable↑ | = | L | + | E↑ Sales Revenue↑ |
| A↓ Merchandise Inventory↓ | = | L | + | E↓ Cost of Goods Sold↑ |

On August 5, Smart Touch Learning purchased inventory of $1,440. The August 15 sale brought in sales revenue (4 units @ $500 = $2,000) and cost of goods sold (4 units @ $360 = $1,440). The August 26 and 31 entries also come from the data in Exhibit 6-5.

*Think about going to the grocery store to buy a gallon of milk. Which gallon is in front of the milk cooler: the older milk or the newer milk? The older milk is in front. That's FIFO. Now visualize reaching all the way to the back of the cooler to get the newer milk. That's LIFO. It's important to understand that although this image represents the physical flow of goods, an inventory costing system may or may not match the physical flow. The costing system is only an assumption about how costs flow. The inventory does not have to actually be sold in the FIFO manner in order to record it as FIFO.*

## Weighted-Average Method

Under the **weighted-average method**, the business computes a new weighted-average cost per unit after each purchase. Ending inventory and cost of goods sold are then based on the same weighted-average cost per unit. After the first purchase on August 5, the weighted-average cost

**Weighted-Average Method**
An inventory costing method based on the weighted-average cost per unit of inventory that is calculated after each purchase. Weighted-average cost per unit is determined by dividing the cost of goods available for sale by the number of units available.

per unit sold falls somewhere between the beginning inventory cost of $350 and the most recent purchase cost of $360.

Exhibit 6-6 shows a perpetual inventory record for the weighted-average method. We round average unit cost to the nearest cent and total cost to the nearest dollar.

**Exhibit 6-6** | **Perpetual Inventory Record: Weighted-Average**

| | Purchases | | | Cost of Goods Sold | | | Inventory on Hand | | | |
|---|---|---|---|---|---|---|---|---|---|---|
| **Date** | **Quantity** | **Unit Cost** | **Total Cost** | **Quantity** | **Unit Cost** | **Total Cost** | **Quantity** | **Unit Cost** | **Total Cost** | |
| Aug. 1 | | | | | | | 2 units | × $ 350 | = $ 700 | |
| 5 | 4 units | × $ 360 | = $ 1,440 | | | | 6 units | × $ 356.67 | = $ 2,140 | $ 2,140 / 6 units = $ 356.67 |
| 15 | | | | 4 units | × $ 356.67 | = $ 1,427 | 2 units | × $ 356.67 | = $ 713 | |
| 26 | 12 units | × $ 380 | = $ 4,560 | | | | 14 units | × $ 376.64 | = $ 5,273 | $ 5,273 / 14 units = $ 376.64 |
| 31 | | | | 10 units | × $ 376.64 | = $ 3,766 | 4 units | × $ 376.64 | = $ 1,507 | |
| Totals | 16 units | | $ 6,000 | 14 units | | $ 5,193 | 4 units | | $ 1,507 | |

As noted previously, after each purchase, Smart Touch Learning computes a new weighted-average cost per unit. For example, on August 5, the new weighted-average unit cost is as follows:

Cost of goods available for sale / Number of units available = ($700 + $1,440) / (2 units + 4 units)
= $2,140 / 6 units
= $356.67 (rounded)

*Under the weighted-average method, the cost per unit is a weighted average. You cannot take the average of the two unit costs ($350 and $360) to determine the new unit cost. Instead, you must use the total cost of goods available for sale ($2,140) divided by the number of units available (6 units).*

The goods sold on August 15 are then costed out at $356.67 per unit. On August 26 when the next purchase is made, the new weighted-average unit cost is as follows:

Cost of goods available for sale / Number of units available = ($713 + $4,560) / (2 units + 12 units)
= $5,273 / 14 units
= $376.64 (rounded)

The weighted-average cost summary at August 31 is as follows:

- Cost of goods sold: 14 units that cost a total of $5,193.
- Ending inventory: 4 units that cost a total of $1,507.

*With the weighted-average cost method, rounding errors can occur. However, this is not the case in this example. Notice that cost of goods sold and ending inventory total $6,700 ($5,193 + $1,507), which equals the total cost of goods available for sale.*

Under the weighted-average cost method, Smart Touch Learning could use these amounts to prepare its financial statements.

## Journal Entries Under Weighted-Average

The journal entries under weighted-average costing follow. We assume all purchases and sales of inventory are on account. Amounts unique to the weighted-average method are shown in blue.

| Date | Accounts and Explanation | Debit | Credit |
|---|---|---|---|
| Aug. 5 | Merchandise Inventory (4 × $360) | 1,440 | |
| | Accounts Payable | | 1,440 |
| | *Purchased inventory on account.* | | |
| 15 | Accounts Receivable (4 × $500) | 2,000 | |
| | Sales Revenue | | 2,000 |
| | *Sale on account.* | | |
| 15 | Cost of Goods Sold (4 × $356.67) | 1,427 | |
| | Merchandise Inventory | | 1,427 |
| | *Recorded the cost of goods sold.* | | |
| 26 | Merchandise Inventory (12 × $380) | 4,560 | |
| | Accounts Payable | | 4,560 |
| | *Purchased inventory on account.* | | |
| 31 | Accounts Receivable (10 × $500) | 5,000 | |
| | Sales Revenue | | 5,000 |
| | *Sale on account.* | | |
| 31 | Cost of Goods Sold (10 × $376.64) | 3,766 | |
| | Merchandise Inventory | | 3,766 |
| | *Recorded the cost of goods sold.* | | |

| A | = | L | + | E |
|---|---|---|---|---|
| A↑ Merchandise Inventory↑ | = | L↑ Accounts Payable↑ | + | E |
| A↑ Accounts Receivable↑ | = | L | + | E↑ Sales Revenue↑ |
| A↓ Merchandise Inventory↓ | = | L | + | E↓ Cost of Goods Sold↑ |
| A↑ Merchandise Inventory↑ | = | L↑ Accounts Payable↑ | + | E |
| A↑ Accounts Receivable↑ | = | L | + | E↑ Sales Revenue↑ |
| A↓ Merchandise Inventory↓ | = | L | + | E↓ Cost of Goods Sold↑ |

On August 5, Smart Touch Learning purchased $1,440 of inventory and made the first journal entry. On August 15, Smart Touch Learning sold 4 TAB0503s for $500 each. The company recorded the sale ($2,000) and the cost of goods sold (4 units at $356.67 = $1,427). The remaining journal entries (August 26 and 31) follow the same procedure.

## Try It!

5. Serenity Books has the following transactions in August related to merchandise inventory.

| | |
|---|---|
| Aug. 1 | Beginning merchandise inventory, 10 books @ $15 each |
| 3 | Sold 3 books @ $20 each |
| 12 | Purchased 8 books @ $18 each |
| 15 | Sold 9 books @ $20 each |
| 20 | Purchased 4 books @ $20 each |
| 28 | Sold 5 books @ $25 each |

a. Determine the cost of goods sold and ending merchandise inventory by preparing a perpetual inventory record using the specific identification method. Assume the following costing information for the books sold during the month:

August 3: 3 books costing $15 each
August 15: 4 books costing $15 each and 5 books costing $18 each
August 28: 2 books costing $18 each and 3 books costing $20 each

b. Determine the cost of goods sold and ending merchandise inventory by preparing a perpetual inventory record using the FIFO inventory costing method.
c. Determine the cost of goods sold and ending merchandise inventory by preparing a perpetual inventory record using the LIFO inventory costing method.
d. Determine the cost of goods sold and ending merchandise inventory by preparing a perpetual inventory record using the weighted-average inventory costing method. Round weighted-average unit cost to the nearest cent and total cost to the nearest dollar.

**Check your answers online in MyAccountingLab or at http://www.pearsonhighered.com/Horngren.**

For more practice, see Short Exercises S6-2 through S6-6. MyAccountingLab

# HOW ARE FINANCIAL STATEMENTS AFFECTED BY USING DIFFERENT INVENTORY COSTING METHODS?

**Learning Objective 3**
Compare the effects on the financial statements when using the different inventory costing methods

What leads Smart Touch Learning to select the specific identification, FIFO, LIFO, or weighted-average inventory costing method? The different methods have different benefits.

## Income Statement

Exhibit 6-7 summarizes the results for the four inventory costing methods for Smart Touch Learning. It shows sales revenue, cost of goods sold, and gross profit for specific identification, FIFO, LIFO, and weighted-average.

Exhibit 6-7 shows that FIFO produces the lowest cost of goods sold and the highest gross profit for Smart Touch Learning. Because operating expenses are the same, regardless of which inventory method a company uses, net income is also the highest under

**Exhibit 6-7** **Comparative Results for Specific Identification, FIFO, LIFO, and Weighted-Average—Income Statement**

| | Specific Identification | FIFO | LIFO | Weighted-Average |
|---|---|---|---|---|
| Sales Revenue (14 units × $500) | $ 7,000 | $ 7,000 | $ 7,000 | $ 7,000 |
| Less: Cost of Goods Sold | 5,200 | 5,180 | 5,240 | 5,193 |
| Gross Profit | $ 1,800 | $ 1,820 | $ 1,760 | $ 1,807 |

FIFO when inventory costs are rising. **Many companies prefer high income in order to attract investors and borrow on favorable terms. FIFO offers this benefit in a period of rising costs.**

When inventory costs are rising, LIFO results in the highest cost of goods sold and the lowest gross profit. **Lower profits mean lower taxable income; thus, LIFO lets companies pay the lowest income taxes when inventory costs are rising.** Low tax payments conserve cash, and that is the main benefit of LIFO. The downside of LIFO is that the company reports lower net income.

The weighted-average method generates amounts that fall between the extremes of FIFO and LIFO. **Therefore, companies that seek a "middle-ground" solution use the weighted-average method for inventory.**

How do businesses decide which inventory costing method to use?

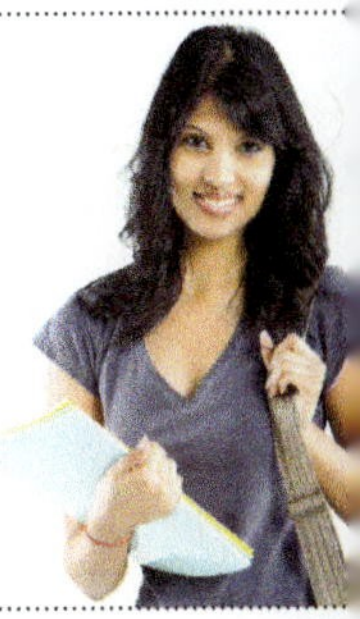

## Balance Sheet

Consider again the purchases made by Smart Touch Learning during August. The company had total inventory in August as follows:

| | | |
|---|---|---|
| Aug. 1 | 2 units × $350 | $ 700 |
| Aug. 5 | 4 units × $360 | 1,440 |
| Aug. 26 | 12 units × $380 | 4,560 |
| Cost of goods available for sale | | $ 6,700 |

Only one of two things can happen to the tablets—either they remain in the warehouse (ending merchandise inventory) or they are sold (Cost of Goods Sold). Ending merchandise inventory can be calculated by determining first the cost of goods available for sale (beginning merchandise inventory plus inventory purchased) and then subtracting merchandise inventory sold (Cost of Goods Sold). Exhibit 6-8 (on the next page) shows the results of Smart Touch Learning's ending merchandise inventory for each of the costing methods for August.

When using the FIFO inventory costing method, ending merchandise inventory will be the highest when costs are increasing. LIFO produces the lowest ending merchandise inventory with weighted-average again in the middle.

So far, we have been ignoring the effects on the income statement and balance sheet when using the specific identification method. This is because under specific identification, the results will vary depending on which costs are assigned to the inventory sold. Most companies will not choose to use the specific identification method unless they want to match each inventory item sold with its exact cost.

**Exhibit 6-8** | **Comparative Results for Specific Identification, FIFO, LIFO, and Weighted-Average—Balance Sheet**

| | Specific Identification | FIFO | LIFO | Weighted-Average |
|---|---|---|---|---|
| Beginning Merchandise Inventory | $ 700 | $ 700 | $ 700 | $ 700 |
| Plus: Net Cost of Purchases | 6,000 | 6,000 | 6,000 | 6,000 |
| Cost of Goods Available for Sale | 6,700 | 6,700 | 6,700 | 6,700 |
| Less: Cost of Goods Sold | 5,200 | 5,180 | 5,240 | 5,193 |
| Ending Merchandise Inventory | $ 1,500 | $ 1,520 | $ 1,460 | $ 1,507 |

*The weighted-average ending merchandise inventory number shown in Exhibit 6-6 may be slightly different than that found in Exhibit 6-8. This is because of rounding. When completing your homework, always read carefully for directions on how to round when using the weighted-average method.*

We have looked at the effects on the financial statements when inventory costs are rising. When inventory costs are instead declining, the effects on the financial statements will be the opposite of those discussed above. Exhibit 6-9 summarizes the effects on the financial statements during periods of rising and declining inventory costs.

**Exhibit 6-9** | **Effects on the Financial Statements During Periods of Rising and Declining Inventory Costs**

| **Period of Rising Inventory Costs:** | | | | |
|---|---|---|---|---|
| | **Specific Identification** | **FIFO** | **LIFO** | **Weighted-Average** |
| **Income Statement:** | | | | |
| Cost of Goods Sold | Varies | Lowest | Highest | Middle |
| Net Income | Varies | Highest | Lowest | Middle |
| **Balance Sheet:** | | | | |
| Ending Merchandise Inventory | Varies | Highest | Lowest | Middle |

| **Period of Declining Inventory Costs:** | | | | |
|---|---|---|---|---|
| | **Specific Identification** | **FIFO** | **LIFO** | **Weighted-Average** |
| **Income Statement:** | | | | |
| Cost of Goods Sold | Varies | Highest | Lowest | Middle |
| Net Income | Varies | Lowest | Highest | Middle |
| **Balance Sheet:** | | | | |
| Ending Merchandise Inventory | Varies | Lowest | Highest | Middle |

## Try It!

6. Antelope Motors is considering which inventory costing method it should use. The business wants to maximize gross profits during a period of declining costs. Which inventory costing method should Antelope Motors select?

**Check your answer online in MyAccountingLab or at http://www.pearsonhighered.com/Horngren.**

For more practice, see Short Exercise S6-7. MyAccountingLab

# HOW IS MERCHANDISE INVENTORY VALUED WHEN USING THE LOWER-OF-COST-OR-MARKET RULE?

**Learning Objective 4**
Apply the lower-of-cost-or-market rule to merchandise inventory

In addition to the specific identification, FIFO, LIFO, and weighted-average inventory costing methods, accountants face other inventory issues, such as the **lower-of-cost-or-market (LCM) rule**. LCM shows accounting conservatism in action and requires that merchandise inventory be reported in the financial statements at whichever is lower of the following:

- The historical cost of the inventory
- The market value of the inventory

**Lower-of-Cost-or-Market (LCM) Rule**
Rule that merchandise inventory should be reported in the financial statements at whichever is lower—its historical cost or its market value.

## Computing the Lower-of-Cost-or-Market

For inventories, market value generally means the current replacement cost (that is, the cost to replace the inventory on hand). If the replacement cost of inventory is less than its historical cost, the business must adjust the inventory value. By adjusting the inventory down (crediting Merchandise Inventory), the balance sheet value of the asset, Merchandise Inventory, is at its correct value (market) rather than its overstated value (cost). If the merchandise inventory's market value is greater than cost, then we don't adjust the Merchandise Inventory account because of the conservatism principle.

**IFRS**

Under International Financial Reporting Standards, inventory must be reported at the lower-of-cost-or-market value. However, "market" is defined differently. Under IFRS, the market value of inventory is defined as the "net realizable value," or essentially its selling price. (What will the company "really" get for its inventory?) If the historical cost is higher than the selling price, then inventory must be written down. The IFRS approach results in fewer write-downs on inventory. In some circumstances, if a write-down is necessary, it may be reversed at a later date. Reversing write-downs of inventory never happens under GAAP.

## Recording the Adjusting Journal Entry to Adjust Merchandise Inventory

Suppose Smart Touch Learning paid $3,000 for its TAB0503 inventory. By December 31, the merchandise inventory can now be replaced for $2,200, and the decline in value appears permanent. Market value is below cost, and the entry to write down the inventory to LCM is as follows:

| Date | Accounts and Explanation | Debit | Credit |
|---|---|---|---|
| Dec. 31 | Cost of Goods Sold | 800 | |
| | Merchandise Inventory ($3,000 − $2,200) | | 800 |
| | *To write merchandise inventory down to market value.* | | |

$$\frac{\mathbf{A}\downarrow}{\text{Merchandise Inventory}\downarrow} = \frac{\mathbf{L}}{} + \frac{\mathbf{E}\downarrow}{\text{Cost of Goods Sold}\uparrow}$$

In this case, Smart Touch Learning's balance sheet would report this inventory as follows:

| SMART TOUCH LEARNING<br>Balance Sheet (Partial)<br>December 31, 2017 | |
|---|---|
| Current Assets: | |
| Merchandise Inventory | $ 2,200 |

Companies often disclose that the LCM rule is followed in notes to their financial statements, as shown here for Smart Touch Learning:

> NOTE 2: STATEMENT OF SIGNIFICANT ACCOUNTING POLICIES
> *Merchandise Inventories.* Merchandise inventories are carried at the *lower-of-cost-or-market*. Cost is determined using the first-in, first-out method.

## DECISIONS

### Should inventory be marked down?

Haley Richardson works for a large retail electronic store, Electronics 'R Us, and is responsible for handling all aspects of merchandise inventory. Earlier in the year, the store had purchased large quantities of the newest laptop computer, counting on the fact that consumers would be rushing into the store to buy them. What Electronics 'R Us didn't know was that the laptops would become obsolete before they were sold. Now, as Haley stares at the laptops sitting on the shelf, she wonders what she should do. What would you do?

### Solution

Generally Accepted Accounting Principles require that companies evaluate the cost of inventory annually to determine whether the current market value is less than the cost of the inventory on the balance sheet. Haley should review the business's stock of laptops and determine the market value. It's important that Haley realize that market value does not mean the value at which the laptops can be sold. Instead, market value represents the current replacement cost or the cost that Electronics 'R Us would incur to replace the laptops on hand. If the replacement cost is less than the historical cost of the laptops, then Haley should record an entry to write down the value of the laptops. This ensures that Electronics 'R Us is not overstating the value of the laptops on its balance sheet.

## Try It!

7. T. J. Jackson Supplies had merchandise inventory that cost $1,300. The market value of the merchandise inventory is $750. What value should Jackson Supplies show on the balance sheet for merchandise inventory? Record the adjusting entry, if one is needed.

**Check your answer online in MyAccountingLab or at http://www.pearsonhighered.com/Horngren.**

For more practice, see Short Exercise S6-8. MyAccountingLab

## WHAT ARE THE EFFECTS OF MERCHANDISE INVENTORY ERRORS ON THE FINANCIAL STATEMENTS?

**Learning Objective 5**
Measure the effects of merchandise inventory errors on the financial statements

Businesses perform a physical count of their merchandise inventory at the end of the accounting period. For the financial statements to be accurate, it is important to get a correct count. This can be difficult for a company with widespread operations.

An error in ending merchandise inventory creates a whole string of errors in other related accounts. To illustrate, suppose Smart Touch Learning accidentally reported $5,000 more ending merchandise inventory than it actually had. In that case, ending merchandise inventory would be overstated by $5,000 on the balance sheet. The following shows how an overstatement of ending inventory affects cost of goods sold, gross profit, and net income:

| | Ending Merchandise Inventory Overstated $5,000 |
|---|---|
| Sales Revenue | Correct |
| Cost of Goods Sold: | |
| Beginning Merchandise Inventory | Correct |
| Net Cost of Purchases | Correct |
| Cost of Goods Available for Sale | Correct |
| Less: Ending Merchandise Inventory | ERROR: Overstated $5,000 |
| Cost of Goods Sold | Understated $5,000 |
| Gross Profit | Overstated $5,000 |
| Operating Expenses | Correct |
| Net Income | Overstated $5,000 |

Understating the ending inventory—reporting the inventory too low—has the opposite effect. If Smart Touch Learning understated the inventory by $1,200, the effect would be as shown here:

| | Ending Merchandise Inventory Understated $1,200 |
|---|---|
| Sales Revenue | Correct |
| Cost of Goods Sold: | |
| Beginning Merchandise Inventory | Correct |
| Net Cost of Purchases | Correct |
| Cost of Goods Available for Sale | Correct |
| Less: Ending Merchandise Inventory | ERROR: Understated $1,200 |
| Cost of Goods Sold | Overstated $1,200 |
| Gross Profit | Understated $1,200 |
| Operating Expenses | Correct |
| Net Income | Understated $1,200 |

Recall that one period's ending merchandise inventory becomes the next period's beginning inventory. As a result, an error in ending merchandise inventory carries over into the next period. Exhibit 6-10 (on the next page) illustrates the effect of an inventory error, assuming all other items on the income statement are unchanged for the three periods. Period 1's ending merchandise inventory is overstated by $5,000; Period 1's ending merchandise inventory should be $10,000. The error carries over to Period 2. Period 3 is correct. In fact, both Period 1 and Period 2 should look like Period 3.

**Exhibit 6-10 | Inventory Errors**

**SAMPLE COMPANY**
Income Statement
For the Years Ended Periods 1, 2, and 3

| | Period 1 | | Period 2 | | Period 3 | |
|---|---|---|---|---|---|---|
| | *Ending* Merchandise Inventory Overstated by $5,000 | | *Beginning* Merchandise Inventory Overstated by $5,000 | | Correct | |
| Sales Revenue | | $ 100,000 | | $ 100,000 | | $ 100,000 |
| Cost of Goods Sold: | | | | | | |
| Beginning Merchandise Inventory | $ 10,000 | | $ 15,000 | | $ 10,000 | |
| Net Cost of Purchases | 50,000 | | 50,000 | | 50,000 | |
| Cost of Goods Available for Sale | 60,000 | | 65,000 | | 60,000 | |
| Less: Ending Merchandise Inventory | 15,000 | | 10,000 | | 10,000 | |
| Cost of Goods Sold | | 45,000 | | 55,000 | | 50,000 |
| Gross Profit | | $ 55,000 | | $ 45,000 | | $ 50,000 |

The correct gross profit is $50,000 for each period. $100,000

Ending merchandise inventory is *subtracted* to compute cost of goods sold in one period and the same amount is *added* as beginning merchandise inventory in the next period. Therefore, an inventory error cancels out after two periods. The overstatement of cost of goods sold in Period 2 counterbalances the understatement for Period 1. Thus, total gross profit for the two periods combined is correct. The effects of inventory errors are summarized in Exhibit 6-11.

**Exhibit 6-11 | Effects of Inventory Errors**

**SAMPLE COMPANY**
Income Statement
For the Years Ended Periods 1 and 2

| | Period 1 | | Period 2 | |
|---|---|---|---|---|
| | Cost of Goods Sold | Gross Profit and Net Income | Cost of Goods Sold | Gross Profit and Net Income |
| Period 1 Ending Merchandise Inventory *overstated* | Understated | Overstated | Overstated | Understated |
| Period 1 Ending Merchandise Inventory *understated* | Overstated | Understated | Understated | Overstated |

## ETHICS

### Should the inventory be included?

One of A'isha Sowell's main responsibilities at the end of the accounting period is to supervise the count of physical inventory for her employer. She knows that it is important that the business get an accurate count of inventory so that its financial statements are reported correctly. In reviewing the inventory count sheet, she realizes that a large crate of inventory that has already been sold but not yet delivered was included in the count of inventory. The crate has left her employer but is still in transit at fiscal year-end. A'isha does not believe that it should be included because the inventory was sold FOB shipping point. When A'isha went to her supervisor with this information, she was told that she shouldn't worry about it because the error would ultimately correct itself. What should A'isha do?

### Solution

Companies whose profits are lagging can be tempted to increase reported income to make the business look more successful. One easy way to do this is to overstate ending inventory. A'isha is correct in her assumption that the inventory should not be included in the physical count of inventory. While this error will ultimately correct itself (in two years), in the current year, the business will be overstating gross profit and net income. This overstatement could cause investors to view the business more favorably than they should. A'isha should stand firm in her decision to not include the inventory in the count.

## Try It!

8. The Shirley's Gourmet Foods' merchandise inventory data for the year ended December 31, 2016, follow:

| | | |
|---|---|---|
| Sales Revenue | | $ 48,000 |
| Cost of Goods Sold: | | |
| Beginning Merchandise Inventory | $ 3,360 | |
| Net Cost of Purchases | 21,280 | |
| Cost of Goods Available for Sale | 24,640 | |
| Less: Ending Merchandise Inventory | 4,960 | |
| Cost of Goods Sold | | 19,680 |
| Gross Profit | | $ 28,320 |

Assume that the ending merchandise inventory was accidentally overstated by $1,920. What are the correct amounts for cost of goods sold and gross profit?

**Check your answers online in MyAccountingLab or at http://www.pearsonhighered.com/Horngren.**

For more practice, see Short Exercise S6-9. MyAccountingLab

## HOW DO WE USE INVENTORY TURNOVER AND DAYS' SALES IN INVENTORY TO EVALUATE BUSINESS PERFORMANCE?

**Learning Objective 6**

Use inventory turnover and days' sales in inventory to evaluate business performance

Businesses strive to sell merchandise inventory quickly because the merchandise inventory generates no profit until it is sold. Further, fast-selling inventory is less likely to become obsolete (worthless) and does not require the business to pay for high storage and insurance costs often associated with keeping inventory on hand. There are two ratios that help businesses monitor their inventory levels: inventory turnover and days' sales in inventory.

## Inventory Turnover

**Inventory Turnover**
Measures the number of times a company sells its average level of merchandise inventory during a period. Cost of goods sold / Average merchandise inventory.

Companies try to manage their inventory levels such that they will have just enough inventory to meet customer demand without investing large amounts of money in inventory sitting on the shelves gathering dust. **Inventory turnover** measures how rapidly merchandise inventory is sold. It is computed as follows:

Inventory turnover = Cost of goods sold / Average merchandise inventory
Average merchandise inventory = (Beginning merchandise inventory + Ending merchandise inventory) / 2

A high rate of turnover indicates ease in selling inventory; a low rate indicates difficulty. For example, an inventory value of 4 means that the company sold its average level of inventory four times—once every three months—during the year. Inventory turnover varies widely with the nature of the business and should be evaluated against industry averages.

## Days' Sales in Inventory

**Days' Sales in Inventory**
Measures the average number of days that inventory is held by a company. 365 days / Inventory turnover.

Another key measure is the **days' sales in inventory** ratio. This ratio measures the average number of days merchandise inventory is held by the company and is calculated as follows:

Days' sales in inventory = 365 days / Inventory turnover

Days' sales in inventory also varies widely, depending on the business. A lower days' sales in inventory is preferable because it indicates that the company is able to sell its inventory quickly, thereby reducing its inventory storage and insurance costs, as well as reducing the risk of holding obsolete inventory.

Let's return to **Green Mountain Coffee Roasters, Inc.** and evaluate the company's inventory levels using the two ratios discussed. Presented below are the cost of goods sold and beginning and ending merchandise inventory figures (in thousands) from Green Mountain's income statement for the year ended September 28, 2013 and balance sheet on September 28, 2013.

| | |
|---|---|
| Cost of goods sold (Cost of sales) | $ 2,738,714 |
| Beginning merchandise inventory | 768,437 |
| Ending merchandise inventory | 676,089 |

Green Mountain's inventory turnover is 3.79 times per year and is calculated as:

Inventory turnover = Cost of goods sold / Average merchandise inventory
= $2,738,714 / [($768,437 + $676,089) / 2]
= 3.79 times per year

Its days' sales in inventory is 96.3 days and is calculated as:

Days' sales in inventory = 365 days / Inventory turnover
= 365 days / 3.79
= 96.3 days

It appears that Green Mountain sells its average inventory 3.79 times per year. A high turnover rate is desirable, and an increase in the turnover rate usually means higher profits. In addition, the days' sales in inventory of Green Mountain indicates that the company, on average, has 96.3 days' supply of inventory on hand. This seems a little high for a consumer beverage company, but it should be evaluated against the industry average.

**Try It!**

9. The Opa's Carving Shop had the following financial data for the year ended December 31, 2016:

| | |
|---|---|
| Cost of Goods Sold | $ 484,000 |
| Beginning Merchandise Inventory | 88,800 |
| Ending Merchandise Inventory | 111,200 |

What are the inventory turnover and days' sales in inventory for the year?

**Check your answers online in MyAccountingLab or at http://www.pearsonhighered.com/Horngren.**

For more practice, see Short Exercise S6-10. MyAccountingLab

# APPENDIX 6A: Merchandise Inventory Costs Under a Periodic Inventory System

## HOW ARE MERCHANDISE INVENTORY COSTS DETERMINED UNDER A PERIODIC INVENTORY SYSTEM?

**Learning Objective 7**
Account for merchandise inventory costs under a periodic inventory system

We described the periodic inventory system briefly in the previous chapter. Accounting is simpler in a periodic inventory system because the company keeps no daily running record of inventory on hand. The only way to determine the ending merchandise inventory and cost of goods sold in a periodic inventory system is to take a physical inventory to count the goods left (on hand)—usually at the end of the fiscal year. The periodic inventory system works well for a small business in which the inventory can be controlled by visual inspection—that is, the inventory usually is not large in size or dollar amount.

The various inventory costing methods (specific identification, FIFO, LIFO, and weighted-average) in a periodic inventory system follow the pattern illustrated earlier for the perpetual inventory system. To show how the periodic inventory system works, we use the same Smart Touch Learning data that we used for the perpetual inventory system (see Exhibit 6A-1, on the next page).

**Exhibit 6A-1** | **Perpetual Inventory Record—Changes in Cost per Unit**

**Item:** TAB0503

| Date | Quantity Purchased | Quantity Sold | Cost per Unit | Quantity on Hand |
|---|---|---|---|---|
| Aug. 1 | | | $350 | 2 |
| 5 | 4 | | $360 | 6 |
| 15 | | 4 | | 2 |
| 26 | 12 | | $380 | 14 |
| 31 | | 10 | | 4 |
| Totals | 16 | 14 | | 4 |

We use these data to illustrate FIFO, LIFO, and weighted-average cost. We will not illustrate the specific identification inventory costing method because it is calculated the same under both the perpetual and periodic inventory systems.

For all four inventory costing methods, cost of goods available for sale is always the sum of beginning inventory plus net purchases:

| | |
|---|---|
| Beginning merchandise inventory (2 units × $350) | $ 700 |
| Plus: Net purchases (4 units × $360) + (12 units × $380) | 6,000 |
| Cost of goods available for sale | $ 6,700 |

The different methods—specific identification, FIFO, LIFO, and weighted-average cost—compute different amounts for ending inventory and cost of goods sold. In other words, the $6,700 invested in cost of goods available for sale will be either on the balance sheet in Merchandise Inventory or expensed on the income statement, as Cost of Goods Sold. The amount on the balance sheet will be the cost of the four tablets that were not sold and are still on hand. The amount on the income statement will be the cost of the 14 tablets sold.

## First-In, First-Out (FIFO) Method

Under FIFO, the ending inventory comes from the newest—the most recent—purchases, which cost $380 per unit as illustrated below:

| | |
|---|---|
| Beginning merchandise inventory (2 units × $350) | $ 700 |
| Net cost of purchases (4 units × $360) + (12 units × $380) | 6,000 |
| Cost of goods available for sale | 6,700 |
| Less: Ending merchandise inventory (4 × $380) | (1,520) |
| Cost of goods sold | $ 5,180 |

*Notice that the FIFO periodic cost of goods sold is $5,180, exactly the same amount as we calculated using the FIFO perpetual inventory method. The amounts obtained for cost of goods sold and ending merchandise inventory are always the same for FIFO perpetual and FIFO periodic. This occurs because FIFO sells the oldest inventory acquisitions first. Therefore, it does not matter when FIFO is calculated; the earliest purchase will always be the same whether we calculate cost of goods sold on the sale date (perpetual) or at the end of the period (periodic).*

## Last-In, First-Out (LIFO) Method

Under LIFO, the ending inventory comes from the oldest costs of the period—in this case, the beginning inventory of two units that cost $350 per unit, plus two from the first purchase at $360. LIFO is calculated as follows:

| | |
|---|---|
| Beginning merchandise inventory (2 units × $350) | $ 700 |
| Net cost purchases (4 units × $360) + (12 units × $380) | 6,000 |
| Cost of goods available for sale | 6,700 |
| Less: Ending merchandise inventory (2 × $350) + (2 × $360) | (1,420) |
| Cost of goods sold | $ 5,280 |

## Weighted-Average Method

In the weighted-average inventory costing method, when using the periodic inventory system, we compute a single weighted-average cost per unit for the entire period:

Cost of goods available for sale (entire period) / Number of units available = $6,700 / 18 units*
= $372.22 (rounded)

*2 units from beginning inventory + 16 units purchased during August

Then apply this weighted-average cost to compute ending merchandise inventory (rounded to the nearest dollar) and cost of goods sold, as shown:

| | |
|---|---|
| Beginning merchandise inventory (2 units × $350) | $ 700 |
| Net cost of purchases (4 units × $360) + (12 units × $380) | 6,000 |
| Cost of goods available for sale | 6,700 |
| Less: Ending merchandise inventory (4 × $372.22) | (1,489) |
| Cost of goods sold | $ 5,211 |

*Notice that when using the periodic system with the LIFO and weighted-average periodic methods, the dollar amounts obtained for the ending merchandise inventory and cost of goods sold are different than those obtained with the perpetual inventory system. This is because the perpetual inventory system keeps a running balance of inventory while the periodic inventory system does not. Under the periodic inventory system, the ending merchandise inventory is determined without regard to when the sales dates of inventory occurred.*

## Try It!

**10A.** Serenity Books has the following transactions in August related to merchandise inventory.

| | |
|---|---|
| Aug. 1 | Beginning merchandise inventory, 10 books @ $15 each |
| 3 | Sold 3 books @ $20 each |
| 12 | Purchased 8 books @ $18 each |
| 15 | Sold 9 books @ $20 each |
| 20 | Purchased 4 books @ $20 each |
| 28 | Sold 5 books @ $25 each |

a. Determine the cost of goods sold and ending merchandise inventory using the FIFO inventory costing method assuming Serenity Books uses the periodic inventory system.
b. Determine the cost of goods sold and ending merchandise inventory using the LIFO inventory costing method assuming Serenity Books uses the periodic inventory system.
c. Determine the cost of goods sold and ending merchandise inventory using the weighted-average inventory costing method assuming Serenity Books uses the periodic inventory system.

**Check your answers online in MyAccountingLab or at http://www.pearsonhighered.com/Horngren.**

For more practice, see Short Exercises S6A-11 through S6A-13. MyAccountingLab

# REVIEW

## > Things You Should Know

### 1. What are the accounting principles and controls that relate to merchandise inventory?

- Consistency principle: Businesses should use the same accounting methods and procedures from period to period.
- Disclosure principle: A company's financial statements should report enough information for outsiders to make knowledgeable decisions about the company.
- Materiality concept: A company must perform strictly proper accounting only for significant items.
- Conservatism: A company should exercise caution in reporting items in the financial statements.
- Controls over merchandise inventory ensure that inventory purchases and sales are properly authorized and accounted for by the accounting system.

**2. How are merchandise inventory costs determined under a perpetual inventory system?**

- Four costing methods can be used to determine merchandise inventory costs:
  - Specific identification method—Uses the specific cost of each unit of inventory to determine ending inventory and cost of goods sold.
  - First-in, first-out (FIFO) method—First costs into inventory are the first costs out to cost of goods sold; ending inventory is based on the costs of the most recent purchases.
  - Last-in, first-out (LIFO) method—Last costs into inventory are the first costs out to cost of goods sold; ending inventory is based on the costs of the oldest inventory.
  - Weighted-average method—Method based on the weighted-average cost per unit of inventory after each purchase. Weighted-average cost per unit is determined by dividing the cost of goods available for sale by the number of units available for sale.

**3. How are financial statements affected by using different inventory costing methods?**

- The FIFO method results in the lowest cost of goods sold and the highest gross profit when costs are rising.
- The LIFO method results in the highest cost of goods sold and the lowest gross profit when costs are rising.
- The weighted-average method generates amounts for cost of goods sold and gross profit that fall between FIFO and LIFO if costs are consistently increasing or decreasing.

**4. How is merchandise inventory valued when using the lower-of-cost-or-market rule?**

- Lower-of-cost-or-market requires that merchandise be reported in the financial statements at whichever is lower of the following:
  - The historical cost of the inventory
  - The market value of the inventory
- An adjusting entry must be recorded to write down merchandise inventory if the market value is lower than the historical cost.

**5. What are the effects of merchandise inventory errors on the financial statements?**

- An error in ending merchandise inventory creates a whole string of errors in other related accounts.
- One period's ending merchandise inventory becomes the next period's beginning merchandise inventory.

**6. How do we use inventory turnover and days' sales in inventory to evaluate business performance?**

- Inventory turnover measures how rapidly merchandise inventory is sold and is calculated as:

  Cost of goods sold / Average merchandise inventory.
- Days' sales in inventory measures the average number of days merchandise inventory is held by the company and is calculated as:

  365 days / Inventory turnover.

**7. How are merchandise inventory costs determined under a periodic inventory system? (Appendix 6A)**

- Specific identification, FIFO, LIFO, and weighted-average can be used in a periodic inventory system.
- Specific identification and FIFO will produce the same amounts for ending merchandise inventory and cost of goods sold under both the perpetual and periodic inventory systems.
- LIFO and weighted-average generally result in different amounts for ending merchandise inventory and cost of goods sold under the perpetual and periodic inventory systems.

## > Summary Problem

Watches R Us specializes in designer watches and leather goods. Watches R Us uses the perpetual inventory system. Assume Watches R Us began June holding 10 wristwatches that cost $50 each. During June, Watches R Us bought and sold inventory as follows:

| | |
|---|---|
| Jun. 3 | Sold 8 units for $100 each. |
| 16 | Purchased 10 units at $56 each. |
| 23 | Sold 8 units for $100 each. |

**Requirements**

1. Prepare a perpetual inventory record for Watches R Us using the FIFO, LIFO, and weighted-average inventory costing methods.
2. Journalize all of Watches R Us's inventory transactions for June under all three costing methods. Assume all sales and purchases are on account. Explanations are not required.
3. Show the computation of gross profit for each method.
4. Which method maximizes net income? Which method minimizes income taxes?

## > Solution

1. Perpetual inventory records:

**FIFO:**

| Date | Purchases Quantity | Purchases Unit Cost | Purchases Total Cost | Cost of Goods Sold Quantity | Cost of Goods Sold Unit Cost | Cost of Goods Sold Total Cost | Inventory on Hand Quantity | Inventory on Hand Unit Cost | Inventory on Hand Total Cost |
|---|---|---|---|---|---|---|---|---|---|
| Jun. 1 | | | | | | | 10 units | × $ 50 | = $ 500 } $ 500 |
| 3 | | | | 8 units | × $ 50 | = $ 400 } $ 400 | 2 units | × $ 50 | = $ 100 } $ 100 |
| 16 | 10 units | × $ 56 | = $ 560 | | | | 2 units<br>10 units | × $ 50<br>× $ 56 | = $ 100<br>= $ 560 } $ 660 |
| 23 | | | | 2 units<br>6 units | × $ 50<br>× $ 56 | = $ 100<br>= $ 336 } $ 436 | 4 units | × $ 56 | = $ 224 } $ 224 |
| Totals | 10 units | | $ 560 | 16 units | | $ 836 | 4 units | | $ 224 |

**LIFO:**

| Date | Purchases Quantity | Purchases Unit Cost | Purchases Total Cost | Cost of Goods Sold Quantity | Cost of Goods Sold Unit Cost | Cost of Goods Sold Total Cost | Inventory on Hand Quantity | Inventory on Hand Unit Cost | Inventory on Hand Total Cost |
|---|---|---|---|---|---|---|---|---|---|
| Jun. 1 | | | | | | | 10 units | × $ 50 | = $ 500 } $ 500 |
| 3 | | | | 8 units | × $ 50 | = $ 400 } $ 400 | 2 units | × $ 50 | = $ 100 } $ 100 |
| 16 | 10 units | × $ 56 | = $ 560 | | | | 2 units<br>10 units | × $ 50<br>× $ 56 | = $ 100<br>= $ 560 } $ 660 |
| 23 | | | | 8 units | × $ 56 | = $ 448 } $ 448 | 2 units<br>2 units | × $ 50<br>× $ 56 | = $ 100<br>= $ 112 } $ 212 |
| Totals | 10 units | | $ 560 | 16 units | | $ 848 | 4 units | | $ 212 |

**Weighted-Average:**

| Date | Purchases Quantity | Purchases Unit Cost | Purchases Total Cost | Cost of Goods Sold Quantity | Cost of Goods Sold Unit Cost | Cost of Goods Sold Total Cost | Inventory on Hand Quantity | Inventory on Hand Unit Cost | Inventory on Hand Total Cost |
|---|---|---|---|---|---|---|---|---|---|
| Jun. 1 | | | | | | | 10 units | × $ 50 | = $ 500 |
| 3 | | | | 8 units | × $ 50 | = $ 400 | 2 units | × $ 50 | = $ 100 |
| 16 | 10 units | × $ 56 | = $ 560 | | | | 12 units | × $ 55 | = $ 660   $ 660 / 12 units = $ 55 |
| 23 | | | | 8 units | × $ 55 | = $ 440 | 4 units | × $ 55 | = $ 220 |
| Totals | 10 units | | $ 560 | 16 units | | $ 840 | 4 units | | $ 220 |

2. Journal entries:

FIFO:

| Date | Accounts and Explanation | Debit | Credit |
|---|---|---|---|
| Jun. 3 | Accounts Receivable | 800 | |
| | Sales Revenue | | 800 |
| 3 | Cost of Goods Sold | 400 | |
| | Merchandise Inventory | | 400 |
| 16 | Merchandise Inventory | 560 | |
| | Accounts Payable | | 560 |
| 23 | Accounts Receivable | 800 | |
| | Sales Revenue | | 800 |
| 23 | Cost of Goods Sold | 436 | |
| | Merchandise Inventory | | 436 |

LIFO:

| Date | Accounts and Explanation | Debit | Credit |
|---|---|---|---|
| Jun. 3 | Accounts Receivable | 800 | |
| | Sales Revenue | | 800 |
| 3 | Cost of Goods Sold | 400 | |
| | Merchandise Inventory | | 400 |
| 16 | Merchandise Inventory | 560 | |
| | Accounts Payable | | 560 |
| 23 | Accounts Receivable | 800 | |
| | Sales Revenue | | 800 |
| 23 | Cost of Goods Sold | 448 | |
| | Merchandise Inventory | | 448 |

Weighted-average:

| Date | Accounts and Explanation | Debit | Credit |
|---|---|---|---|
| Jun. 3 | Accounts Receivable | 800 | |
| | Sales Revenue | | 800 |
| 3 | Cost of Goods Sold | 400 | |
| | Merchandise Inventory | | 400 |
| 16 | Merchandise Inventory | 560 | |
| | Accounts Payable | | 560 |
| 23 | Accounts Receivable | 800 | |
| | Sales Revenue | | 800 |
| 23 | Cost of Goods Sold | 440 | |
| | Merchandise Inventory | | 440 |

3. Gross profit:

| | FIFO | LIFO | Weighted-Average |
|---|---|---|---|
| Sales Revenue ($800 + $800) | $ 1,600 | $ 1,600 | $ 1,600 |
| Less: Cost of Goods Sold ($400 + $436) | 836 | | |
| ($400 + $448) | | 848 | |
| ($400 + $440) | | | 840 |
| Gross Profit | $ 764 | $ 752 | $ 760 |

4. FIFO maximizes net income.
   LIFO minimizes income taxes.

## > Key Terms

**Conservatism (p. 326)**
**Consistency Principle (p. 325)**
**Cost of Goods Available for Sale (p. 330)**
**Days' Sales in Inventory (p. 344)**
**Disclosure Principle (p. 325)**
**First-In, First-Out (FIFO) Method (p. 330)**
**Inventory Costing Method (p. 329)**
**Inventory Turnover (p. 344)**
**Last-In, First-Out (LIFO) Method (p. 331)**
**Lower-of-Cost-or-Market (LCM) Rule (p. 339)**
**Materiality Concept (p. 326)**
**Specific Identification Method (p. 329)**
**Weighted-Average Method (p. 333)**

## > Quick Check

**Learning Objective 1**

1. Which principle or concept states that businesses should use the same accounting methods and procedures from period to period?

   a. Disclosure  b. Conservatism  c. Consistency  d. Materiality

**Learning Objective 2**

2. Which inventory costing method assigns to ending merchandise inventory the newest—the most recent—costs incurred during the period?

   a. First-in, first-out (FIFO)
   b. Weighted-average
   c. Specific identification
   d. Last-in, first-out (LIFO)

**Learning Objective 2**

3. Assume Nile.com began April with 14 units of inventory that cost a total of $266. During April, Nile.com purchased and sold goods as follows:

| | | |
|---|---|---|
| Apr. 8 | Purchase | 42 units @ $ 20 |
| 14 | Sale | 35 units @ $ 40 |
| 22 | Purchase | 28 units @ $ 22 |
| 27 | Sale | 42 units @ $ 40 |

   Under the FIFO inventory costing method and the perpetual inventory system, how much is Nile.com's cost of goods sold for the sale on April 14?

   a. $1,106  b. $686  c. $1,400  d. $700

**Learning Objective 2**

4. Suppose Nile.com used the weighted-average inventory costing method and the perpetual inventory system. Use the Nile.com data in Question 3 to compute the weighted-average unit cost of the company's inventory on hand at April 8. Round weighted-average unit cost to the nearest cent.

   a. $21.00
   b. $19.75
   c. $19.50
   d. Cannot be determined from the data given

**Learning Objective 3**

5. Which inventory costing method results in the lowest net income during a period of rising inventory costs?

   a. Weighted-average
   b. Specific identification
   c. First-in, first-out (FIFO)
   d. Last-in, first-out (LIFO)

**Learning Objective 4**

6. Which of the following is most closely linked to accounting conservatism?

   a. Lower-of-cost-or-market rule
   b. Materiality concept
   c. Disclosure principle
   d. Consistency principle

**Learning Objective 5**

7. At December 31, 2016, Stevenson Company overstated ending inventory by $36,000. How does this error affect cost of goods sold and net income for 2016?

   a. Overstates cost of goods sold and understates net income
   b. Understates cost of goods sold and overstates net income
   c. Leaves both cost of goods sold and net income correct because the errors cancel each other
   d. Overstates both cost of goods sold and net income

**Learning Objective 6**

8. Suppose Maestro's had cost of goods sold during the year of $230,000. Beginning merchandise inventory was $35,000, and ending merchandise inventory was $45,000. Determine Maestro's inventory turnover for the year. Round to the nearest hundredth.

   a. 6.57 times per year
   b. 5.75 times per year
   c. 5.11 times per year
   d. 17.39 times per year

**Learning Objective 7 Appendix 6A**

9A. Suppose Nile.com used the LIFO inventory costing method and the periodic inventory system. Use the Nile.com data in Question 3 to determine Nile.com's cost of goods sold at the end of the month.

   a. $1,568  b. $133  c. $1,589  d. $154

**Check your answers at the end of the chapter.**

# ASSESS YOUR PROGRESS

## > Review Questions

1. Which principle states that businesses should use the same accounting methods and procedures from period to period?
2. What does the disclosure principle require?
3. Discuss the materiality concept. Is the dollar amount that is material the same for a company that has annual sales of $10,000 compared with a company that has annual sales of $1,000,000?
4. What is the goal of conservatism?
5. Discuss some measures that should be taken to maintain control over merchandise inventory.
6. Under a perpetual inventory system, what are the four inventory costing methods and how does each method determine ending merchandise inventory and cost of goods sold?
7. When using a perpetual inventory system and the weighted-average inventory costing method, when does the business compute a new weighted-average cost per unit?
8. During periods of rising costs, which inventory costing method produces the highest gross profit?
9. What does the lower-of-cost-or-market (LCM) rule require?
10. What account is debited when recording the adjusting entry to write down merchandise inventory under the LCM rule?
11. What is the effect on cost of goods sold, gross profit, and net income if ending merchandise inventory is understated?
12. When does an inventory error cancel out, and why?
13. How is inventory turnover calculated, and what does it measure?
14. How is days' sales in inventory calculated, and what does it measure?

15A. When using the periodic inventory system, which inventory costing method(s) always produces the same result as when using the perpetual inventory system?

16A. When using the periodic inventory system and weighted-average inventory costing method, when is the weighted-average cost per unit computed?

## > Short Exercises

***For all short exercises, assume the perpetual inventory system is used unless stated otherwise.***

Learning Objective 1

**S6-1 Determining inventory accounting principles**

Ward Hardware used the FIFO inventory costing method in 2017. Ward plans to continue using the FIFO method in future years. Which accounting principle is most relevant to Ward's decision?

Learning Objective 2

**S6-2 Determining inventory costing methods**

Ward Hardware does not expect costs to change dramatically and wants to use an inventory costing method that averages cost changes.

**Requirements**

1. Which inventory costing method would best meet Ward's goal?
2. Assume Ward wanted to expense out the newer purchases of goods instead. Which inventory costing method would best meet that need?

***Use the following information to answer Short Exercises S6-3 through S6-6.***

Montana Cycles started July with 25 bicycles that cost $36 each. On July 16, Montana bought 35 bicycles at $60 each. On July 31, Montana sold 33 bicycles for $105 each.

Learning Objective 2

**S6-3 Preparing a perpetual inventory record and journal entries—Specific identification**

**Requirements**

1. Prepare Montana Cycle's perpetual inventory record assuming the company uses the specific identification inventory costing method. Assume that Montana sold 20 bicycles that cost $36 each and 13 bicycles that cost $60 each.
2. Journalize the July 16 purchase of merchandise inventory on account and the July 31 sale of merchandise inventory on account.

Learning Objective 2

**S6-4 Preparing a perpetual inventory record and journal entries—FIFO**

**Requirements**

1. Prepare Montana Cycle's perpetual inventory record assuming the company uses the FIFO inventory costing method.
2. Journalize the July 16 purchase of merchandise inventory on account and the July 31 sale of merchandise inventory on account.

Learning Objective 2

**S6-5 Preparing a perpetual inventory record and journal entries—LIFO**

**Requirements**

1. Prepare Montana Cycle's perpetual inventory record assuming the company uses the LIFO inventory costing method.
2. Journalize the July 16 purchase of merchandise inventory on account and the July 31 sale of merchandise inventory on account.

### S6-6 Preparing a perpetual inventory record and journal entries—Weighted-average

**Learning Objective 2**

**Requirements**

1. Prepare Montana Cycle's perpetual inventory record assuming the company uses the weighted-average inventory costing method.
2. Journalize the July 16 purchase of merchandise inventory on account and the July 31 sale of merchandise inventory on account.

***Note: Short Exercises S6-4, S6-5, and S6-6 must be completed before attempting Short Exercise S6-7.***

### S6-7 Comparing Cost of Goods Sold under FIFO, LIFO, and Weighted-average

**Learning Objective 3**

Refer to Short Exercises S6-4 through S6-6. After completing those exercises, answer the following questions:

**Requirements**

1. Which inventory costing method produced the lowest cost of goods sold?
2. Which inventory costing method produced the highest cost of goods sold?
3. If costs had been declining instead of rising, which inventory costing method would have produced the highest cost of goods sold?

### S6-8 Applying the lower-of-cost-or-market rule

**Learning Objective 4**

Assume that a Mega Burger restaurant has the following perpetual inventory record for hamburger patties:

| Date | Purchases | Cost of Goods Sold | Merchandise Inventory on Hand |
|---|---|---|---|
| Jul. 9 | $ 510 | | $ 510 |
| 22 | | $ 300 | 210 |
| 31 | 170 | | 380 |

At July 31, the accountant for the restaurant determines that the current replacement cost of the ending merchandise inventory is $431. Make any adjusting entry needed to apply the lower-of-cost-or-market rule. Merchandise inventory would be reported on the balance sheet at what value on July 31?

### S6-9 Determining the effect of an inventory error

**Learning Objective 5**

Mountain Pool Supplies's merchandise inventory data for the year ended December 31, 2017, follow:

| | | |
|---|---|---|
| Sales Revenue | | $ 46,000 |
| Cost of Goods Sold: | | |
| Beginning Merchandise Inventory | $ 3,500 | |
| Net Cost of Purchases | 30,000 | |
| Cost of Goods Available for Sale | 33,500 | |
| Less: Ending Merchandise Inventory | 5,400 | |
| Cost of Goods Sold | | 28,100 |
| Gross Profit | | **$ 17,900** |

**Requirements**

1. Assume that the ending merchandise inventory was accidentally overstated by $1,300. What are the correct amounts for cost of goods sold and gross profit?
2. How would the inventory error affect Mountain Pool Supplies's cost of goods sold and gross profit for the year ended December 31, 2018, if the error is not corrected in 2017?

**Learning Objective 6**

**S6-10 Computing the rate of inventory turnover and days' sales in inventory**

Clear Communications reported the following figures in its annual financial statements:

| | |
|---|---|
| Cost of Goods Sold | $ 19,000 |
| Beginning Merchandise Inventory | 600 |
| Ending Merchandise Inventory | 460 |

Compute the rate of inventory turnover and days' sales in inventory for Clear Communications. (Round to two decimal places.)

***Use the following information to answer Short Exercises S6A-11 through S6A-13.***

The periodic inventory records of Cambridge Prosthetics indicate the following for the month of July:

| | | |
|---|---|---|
| Jul. 1 | Beginning merchandise inventory | 18 units @ $ 55 each |
| 8 | Purchase | 15 units @ $ 60 each |
| 15 | Purchase | 12 units @ $ 61 each |
| 26 | Purchase | 11 units @ $ 62 each |

At July 31, Cambridge counts nine units of merchandise inventory on hand.

**Learning Objective 7**
**Appendix 6A**

**S6A-11 Computing periodic inventory amounts—FIFO**

Compute ending merchandise inventory and cost of goods sold for Cambridge using the FIFO inventory costing method.

**Learning Objective 7**
**Appendix 6A**

**S6A-12 Computing periodic inventory amounts—LIFO**

Compute ending merchandise inventory and cost of goods sold for Cambridge using the LIFO inventory costing method.

**Learning Objective 7**
**Appendix 6A**

**S6A-13 Computing periodic inventory amounts—Weighted-average**

Compute ending merchandise inventory and cost of goods sold for Cambridge using the weighted-average inventory costing method.

## Exercises

***For all exercises, assume the perpetual inventory system is used unless stated otherwise.***

### E6-14 Using accounting vocabulary

**Learning Objectives 1, 2**

Match the accounting terms with the corresponding definitions.

**1.** Specific Identification
**2.** Materiality Concept
**3.** Last-In, First-Out (LIFO)
**4.** Conservatism
**5.** Consistency Principle
**6.** Weighted-Average
**7.** Disclosure Principle
**8.** First-In, First-Out (FIFO)

**a.** Treats the oldest inventory purchases as the first units sold.
**b.** Requires that a company report enough information for outsiders to make knowledgeable decisions.
**c.** Identifies exactly which inventory item was sold. Usually used for higher cost inventory.
**d.** Calculates a weighted-average cost based on the cost of goods available for sale and the number of units available.
**e.** Principle whose foundation is to exercise caution in reporting financial statement items.
**f.** Treats the most recent/newest purchases as the first units sold.
**g.** Businesses should use the same accounting methods from period to period.
**h.** Principle that states significant items must conform to GAAP.

### E6-15 Comparing inventory methods

**Learning Objective 2**

1\. Ending Merch. Inv. $20.70

Zippy, a regional convenience store chain, maintains milk inventory by the gallon. The first month's milk purchases and sales at its Columbus, Ohio, location follow:

| | |
|---|---|
| Nov. 2 | Purchased 11 gallons @ $2.00 each |
| 6 | Purchased 2 gallons @ $2.65 each |
| 8 | Sold 3 gallons of milk to a customer |
| 13 | Purchased 2 gallons @ $2.70 each |
| 14 | Sold 3 gallons of milk to a customer |

**Requirements**

1. Determine the amount that would be reported in ending merchandise inventory on November 15 using the FIFO inventory costing method.
2. Determine the amount that would be reported in ending merchandise inventory on November 15 using the LIFO inventory costing method.
3. Determine the amount that would be reported in ending merchandise inventory on November 15 using the weighted-average inventory costing method. Round all amounts to the nearest cent.

***Use the following information to answer Exercises E6-16 through E6-18.***

Putter's Choice carries an inventory of putters and other golf clubs. The sales price of each putter is $119. Company records indicate the following for a particular line of Putter's Choice putters:

| Date | Item | Quantity | Unit Cost |
|---|---|---|---|
| Nov. 1 | Balance | 22 | $ 60 |
| 6 | Sale | 12 | |
| 8 | Purchase | 25 | 81 |
| 17 | Sale | 25 | |
| 30 | Sale | 5 | |

**Learning Objective 2**

1. COGS $2,940

**E6-16 Measuring and journalizing merchandise inventory and cost of goods sold—FIFO**

**Requirements**

1. Prepare a perpetual inventory record for the putters assuming Putter's Choice uses the FIFO inventory costing method. Then identify the cost of ending inventory and cost of goods sold for the month.
2. Journalize Putter's Choice's inventory transactions using the FIFO inventory costing method. (Assume purchases and sales are made on account.)

**Learning Objective 2**

1. Ending Merch. Inv. $300

**E6-17 Measuring ending inventory and cost of goods sold in a perpetual inventory system—LIFO**

**Requirements**

1. Prepare Putter's Choice's perpetual inventory record for the putters assuming Putter's Choice uses the LIFO inventory costing method. Then identify the cost of ending inventory and cost of goods sold for the month.
2. Journalize Putter's Choice's inventory transactions using the LIFO inventory costing method. (Assume purchases and sales are made on account.)

**Learning Objective 2**

1. COGS $2,970

**E6-18 Measuring ending inventory and cost of goods sold in a perpetual inventory system—Weighted-average**

**Requirements**

1. Prepare Putter's Choice's perpetual inventory record for the putters assuming Putter's Choice uses the weighted-average inventory costing method. Round weighted-average cost per unit to the nearest cent and all other amounts to the nearest dollar. Then identify the cost of ending inventory and cost of goods sold for the month.
2. Journalize Putter's Choice's inventory transactions using the weighted-average inventory costing method. (Assume purchases and sales are made on account.)

**E6-19 Comparing amounts for cost of goods sold, ending inventory, and gross profit—FIFO and LIFO**

**Learning Objectives 2, 3**

2. Ending Merch. Inv. $70

Assume that Toyland store bought and sold a line of dolls during December as follows:

| | | |
|---|---|---|
| Dec. 1 | Beginning merchandise inventory | 11 units @ $ 8 each |
| 8 | Sale | 6 units @ $ 21 each |
| 14 | Purchase | 17 units @ $ 15 each |
| 21 | Sale | 15 units @ $ 21 each |

**Requirements**

1. Compute the cost of goods sold, cost of ending merchandise inventory, and gross profit using the FIFO inventory costing method.
2. Compute the cost of goods sold, cost of ending merchandise inventory, and gross profit using the LIFO inventory costing method.
3. Which method results in a higher cost of goods sold?
4. Which method results in a higher cost of ending merchandise inventory?
5. Which method results in a higher gross profit?

**E6-20 Comparing cost of goods sold and gross profit—FIFO, LIFO, and weighted-average methods**

**Learning Objectives 2, 3**

1. COGS $2,178

Assume that RK Tire Store completed the following perpetual inventory transactions for a line of tires:

| | | |
|---|---|---|
| May 1 | Beginning merchandise inventory | 24 tires @ $ 61 each |
| 11 | Purchase | 6 tires @ $ 76 each |
| 23 | Sale | 16 tires @ $ 89 each |
| 26 | Purchase | 14 tires @ $ 86 each |
| 29 | Sale | 17 tires @ $ 89 each |

**Requirements**

1. Compute cost of goods sold and gross profit using the FIFO inventory costing method.
2. Compute cost of goods sold and gross profit using the LIFO inventory costing method.
3. Compute cost of goods sold and gross profit using the weighted-average inventory costing method. (Round weighted-average cost per unit to the nearest cent and all other amounts to the nearest dollar.)
4. Which method results in the largest gross profit, and why?

Learning Objective 4

1. CR Merch. Inv. $1,000

## E6-21 Applying the lower-of-cost-or-market rule to merchandise inventories

Rapid Resources, which uses the FIFO inventory costing method, has the following account balances at May 31, 2017, prior to releasing the financial statements for the year:

| | |
|---|---|
| Merchandise Inventory, ending | $ 14,500 |
| Cost of Goods Sold | 70,000 |
| Sales Revenue | 118,000 |

Rapid has determined that the current replacement cost (current market value) of the May 31, 2017, ending merchandise inventory is $13,500.

**Requirements**

1. Prepare any adjusting journal entry required from the information given.
2. What value would Rapid report on the balance sheet at May 31, 2017, for merchandise inventory?

Learning Objective 4

2. GP $69,000

## E6-22 Applying the lower-of-cost-or-market rule to inventories

Nutritional Foods reports merchandise inventory at the lower-of-cost-or-market. Prior to releasing its financial statements for the year ended March 31, 2017, Nutritional's *preliminary* income statement, before the year-end adjustments, appears as follows:

| NUTRITIONAL FOODS<br>Income Statement (Partial)<br>Year Ended March 31, 2017 | |
|---|---|
| Sales Revenue | $ 117,000 |
| Cost of Goods Sold | 45,000 |
| Gross Profit | $ 72,000 |

Nutritional has determined that the current replacement cost of ending merchandise inventory is $17,000. Cost is $20,000.

**Requirements**

1. Journalize the adjusting entry for merchandise inventory, if any is required.
2. Prepare a revised partial income statement to show how Nutritional Foods should report sales, cost of goods sold, and gross profit.

Learning Objective 5

b. Correct GP $25,000

## E6-23 Measuring the effect of an inventory error

La Castle Bakery reported sales revenue of $41,000 and cost of goods sold of $21,000. Compute La Castle's correct gross profit if the company made either of the following independent accounting errors. Show your work.

a. Ending merchandise inventory is overstated by $5,000.
b. Ending merchandise inventory is understated by $5,000.

**Learning Objective 5**

2. 2017, understated $5,000

(Requirement 1 only)

## E6-24 Correcting an inventory error—two years

Natural Bite Grocery reported the following comparative income statements for the years ended June 30, 2017 and 2016:

| NATURAL BITE GROCERY<br>Income Statements<br>Years Ended June 30, 2017 and 2016 | | | | |
|---|---|---|---|---|
| | 2017 | | 2016 | |
| Sales Revenue | | $ 137,000 | | $ 122,000 |
| Cost of Goods Sold: | | | | |
| Beginning Merchandise Inventory | $ 14,000 | | $ 13,000 | |
| Net Cost of Purchases | 79,000 | | 72,000 | |
| Cost of Goods Available for Sale | 93,000 | | 85,000 | |
| Less: Ending Merchandise Inventory | 19,000 | | 14,000 | |
| Cost of Goods Sold | | 74,000 | | 71,000 |
| Gross Profit | | 63,000 | | 51,000 |
| Operating Expenses | | 30,000 | | 19,000 |
| Net Income | | **$ 33,000** | | **$ 32,000** |

During 2017, Natural Bite discovered that ending 2016 merchandise inventory was overstated by $5,000.

### Requirements

1. Prepare corrected income statements for the two years.
2. State whether each year's net income—before your corrections—is understated or overstated, and indicate the amount of the understatement or overstatement.

**Learning Objective 6**

2. 60.43 days

## E6-25 Computing inventory turnover and days' sales in inventory

New Home reported the following income statement for the year ended December 31, 2017:

| NEW HOME<br>Income Statement<br>Year Ended December 31, 2017 | | |
|---|---|---|
| Sales Revenue | | $ 120,000 |
| Cost of Goods Sold: | | |
| Beginning Merchandise Inventory | $ 8,800 | |
| Net Cost of Purchases | 70,000 | |
| Cost of Goods Available for Sale | 78,800 | |
| Less: Ending Merchandise Inventory | 13,000 | |
| Cost of Goods Sold | | 65,800 |
| Gross Profit | | 54,200 |
| Operating Expenses | | 21,300 |
| Net Income | | **$ 32,900** |

**Requirements**

1. Compute New Home's inventory turnover rate for the year. (Round to two decimal places.)
2. Compute New Home's days' sales in inventory for the year. (Round to two decimal places.)

**Learning Objective 7**
**Appendix 6A**

2. COGS $899

### E6A-26 Comparing ending merchandise inventory, cost of goods sold, and gross profit using the periodic inventory system—FIFO, LIFO, and weighted-average methods

Assume that Heavenly Coffee Shop completed the following *periodic* inventory transactions for a line of merchandise inventory:

| | | |
|---|---|---|
| Jun. 1 | Beginning merchandise inventory | 19 units @ $ 27 each |
| 12 | Purchase | 7 units @ $ 28 each |
| 20 | Sale | 11 units @ $ 39 each |
| 24 | Purchase | 14 units @ $ 29 each |
| 29 | Sale | 21 units @ $ 39 each |

**Requirements**

1. Compute ending merchandise inventory, cost of goods sold, and gross profit using the FIFO inventory costing method.
2. Compute ending merchandise inventory, cost of goods sold, and gross profit using the LIFO inventory costing method.
3. Compute ending merchandise inventory, cost of goods sold, and gross profit using the weighted-average inventory costing method. (Round weighted-average cost per unit to the nearest cent and all other amounts to the nearest dollar.)

**Learning Objective 7**
**Appendix 6A**

### E6A-27 Computing periodic inventory amounts

Consider the data of the following companies:

| Company | Net Sales Revenue | Beginning Merchandise Inventory | Net Cost of Purchases | Ending Merchandise Inventory | Cost of Goods Sold | Gross Profit |
|---|---|---|---|---|---|---|
| Ash | $ 103,000 | $ 20,000 | $ 64,000 | $ 19,000 | $ *(a)* | $ 38,000 |
| Elm | *(b)* | 25,000 | 90,000 | *(c)* | 94,000 | 42,000 |
| Fir | 95,000 | *(d)* | 57,000 | 23,000 | 64,000 | *(e)* |
| Oak | 83,000 | 12,000 | *(f)* | 8,000 | *(g)* | 47,000 |

**Requirements**

1. Supply the missing amounts in the preceding table.
2. Prepare the income statement for the year ended December 31, 2017, for Ash Company, which uses the periodic inventory system. Include a complete heading, and show the full computation of cost of goods sold. Ash's operating expenses for the year were $11,000.

## > Problems Group A

***For all problems, assume the perpetual inventory system is used unless stated otherwise.***

### P6-28A Accounting for inventory using the perpetual inventory system—FIFO, LIFO, and weighted-average

**Learning Objectives 2, 3**

2. Ending Merch. Inv., $2,655

Athletic Universe began January with merchandise inventory of 65 crates of vitamins that cost a total of $3,835. During the month, Athletic Universe purchased and sold merchandise on account as follows:

| | | |
|---|---|---|
| Jan. 5 | Purchase | 145 crates @ $ 80 each |
| 13 | Sale | 160 crates @ $ 96 each |
| 18 | Purchase | 170 crates @ $ 90 each |
| 26 | Sale | 175 crates @ $ 110 each |

**Requirements**

1. Prepare a perpetual inventory record, using the FIFO inventory costing method, and determine the company's cost of goods sold, ending merchandise inventory, and gross profit.
2. Prepare a perpetual inventory record, using the LIFO inventory costing method, and determine the company's cost of goods sold, ending merchandise inventory, and gross profit.
3. Prepare a perpetual inventory record, using the weighted-average inventory costing method, and determine the company's cost of goods sold, ending merchandise inventory, and gross profit. (Round weighted-average cost per unit to the nearest cent and all other amounts to the nearest dollar.)
4. If the business wanted to pay the least amount of income taxes possible, which method would it choose?

### P6-29A Accounting for inventory using the perpetual inventory system—FIFO, LIFO, and weighted-average, and comparing FIFO, LIFO, and weighted-average

**Learning Objectives 2, 3**

5. FIFO GP $4,850

Iron Man began August with 65 units of iron inventory that cost $30 each. During August, the company completed the following inventory transactions:

| | | Units | Unit Cost | Unit Sale Price |
|---|---|---|---|---|
| Aug. 3 | Sale | 50 | | $ 81 |
| 8 | Purchase | 85 | $ 50 | |
| 21 | Sale | 80 | | 75 |
| 30 | Purchase | 20 | 45 | |

**Requirements**

1. Prepare a perpetual inventory record for the merchandise inventory using the FIFO inventory costing method.
2. Prepare a perpetual inventory record for the merchandise inventory using the LIFO inventory costing method.

3. Prepare a perpetual inventory record for the merchandise inventory using the weighted-average inventory costing method.
4. Determine the company's cost of goods sold for August using FIFO, LIFO, and weighted-average inventory costing methods.
5. Compute gross profit for August using FIFO, LIFO, and weighted-average inventory costing methods.
6. If the business wanted to maximize gross profit, which method would it select?

**Learning Objectives 1, 4**

3. COGS $420,000

### P6-30A Accounting principles for inventory and applying the lower-of-cost-or-market rule

Some of E and S Electronics's merchandise is gathering dust. It is now December 31, 2016, and the current replacement cost of the ending merchandise inventory is $20,000 below the business's cost of the goods, which was $105,000. Before any adjustments at the end of the period, the company's Cost of Goods Sold account has a balance of $400,000.

**Requirements**

1. Journalize any required entries.
2. At what amount should the company report merchandise inventory on the balance sheet?
3. At what amount should the company report cost of goods sold on the income statement?
4. Which accounting principle or concept is most relevant to this situation?

**Learning Objectives 5, 6**

2. 2017, overstated $7,000

### P6-31A Correcting inventory errors over a three-year period and computing inventory turnover and days' sales in inventory

Lake Air Carpets's books show the following data. In early 2018, auditors found that the ending merchandise inventory for 2015 was understated by $6,000 and that the ending merchandise inventory for 2017 was overstated by $7,000. The ending merchandise inventory at December 31, 2016, was correct.

| | 2017 | | 2016 | | 2015 | |
|---|---|---|---|---|---|---|
| Net Sales Revenue | | $ 208,000 | | $ 164,000 | | $ 177,000 |
| Cost of Goods Sold: | | | | | | |
| Beginning Merchandise Inventory | $ 21,000 | | $ 28,000 | | $ 39,000 | |
| Net Cost of Purchases | 140,000 | | 103,000 | | 91,000 | |
| Cost of Goods Available for Sale | 161,000 | | 131,000 | | 130,000 | |
| Less: Ending Merchandise Inventory | 33,000 | | 21,000 | | 28,000 | |
| Cost of Goods Sold | | 128,000 | | 110,000 | | 102,000 |
| Gross Profit | | 80,000 | | 54,000 | | 75,000 |
| Operating Expenses | | 52,000 | | 25,000 | | 35,000 |
| Net Income | | $ 28,000 | | $ 29,000 | | $ 40,000 |

CHAPTER 6

**Requirements**

1. Prepare corrected income statements for the three years.
2. State whether each year's net income—before your corrections—is understated or overstated, and indicate the amount of the understatement or overstatement.
3. Compute the inventory turnover and days' sales in inventory using the corrected income statements for the three years. (Round all numbers to two decimals.)

**P6A-32A Accounting for inventory using the periodic inventory system—FIFO, LIFO, and weighted-average, and comparing FIFO, LIFO, and weighted-average**

**Learning Objectives 3, 7**
**Appendix 6A**

1. LIFO Ending Merch. Inv., $7,800

Jepson Electronic Center began October with 90 units of merchandise inventory that cost $70 each. During October, the store made the following purchases:

| | |
|---|---|
| Oct. 3 | 20 units @ $ 75 each |
| 12 | 40 units @ $ 78 each |
| 18 | 60 units @ $ 84 each |

Jepson uses the periodic inventory system, and the physical count at October 31 indicates that 110 units of merchandise inventory are on hand.

**Requirements**

1. Determine the ending merchandise inventory and cost of goods sold amounts for the October financial statements using the FIFO, LIFO, and weighted-average inventory costing methods.
2. Sales revenue for October totaled $27,000. Compute Jepson's gross profit for October using each method.
3. Which method will result in the lowest income taxes for Jepson? Why? Which method will result in the highest net income for Jepson? Why?

## > Problems Group B

***For all problems, assume the perpetual inventory system is used unless stated otherwise.***

**P6-33B Accounting for inventory using the perpetual inventory system—FIFO, LIFO, and weighted-average**

**Learning Objectives 2, 3**

2. Ending Merch. Inv., $4,550

Fit World began January with merchandise inventory of 90 crates of vitamins that cost a total of $5,850. During the month, Fit World purchased and sold merchandise on account as follows:

| | | |
|---|---|---|
| Jan. 2 | Purchase | 130 crates @ $ 76 each |
| 5 | Sale | 140 crates @ $ 100 each |
| 16 | Purchase | 170 crates @ $ 86 each |
| 27 | Sale | 180 crates @ $ 104 each |

**Requirements**

1. Prepare a perpetual inventory record, using the FIFO inventory costing method, and determine the company's cost of goods sold, ending merchandise inventory, and gross profit.

2. Prepare a perpetual inventory record, using the LIFO inventory costing method, and determine the company's cost of goods sold, ending merchandise inventory, and gross profit.
3. Prepare a perpetual inventory record, using the weighted-average inventory costing method, and determine the company's cost of goods sold, ending merchandise inventory, and gross profit. (Round weighted-average cost per unit to the nearest cent and all other amounts to the nearest dollar.)
4. If the business wanted to pay the least amount of income taxes possible, which method would it choose?

**Learning Objectives 2, 3**

5. FIFO GP $5,640

### P6-34B Accounting for inventory using the perpetual inventory system—FIFO, LIFO, and weighted-average, and comparing FIFO, LIFO, and weighted-average

Decorative Steel began January with 70 units of iron inventory that cost $25 each. During January, the company completed the following inventory transactions:

| | | Units | Unit Cost | Unit Sale Price |
|---|---|---|---|---|
| Jan. 3 | Sale | 60 | | $ 74 |
| 8 | Purchase | 80 | $ 43 | |
| 21 | Sale | 70 | | 79 |
| 30 | Purchase | 20 | 49 | |

**Requirements**

1. Prepare a perpetual inventory record for the merchandise inventory using the FIFO inventory costing method.
2. Prepare a perpetual inventory record for the merchandise inventory using the LIFO inventory costing method.
3. Prepare a perpetual inventory record for the merchandise inventory using the weighted-average inventory costing method.
4. Determine the company's cost of goods sold for January using FIFO, LIFO, and weighted-average inventory costing methods.
5. Compute gross profit for January using FIFO, LIFO, and weighted-average inventory costing methods.
6. If the business wanted to maximize gross profit, which method would it select?

**Learning Objectives 1, 4**

3. COGS $425,000

### P6-35B Accounting principles for inventory and applying the lower-of-cost-or-market rule

Some of G and A Electronics's merchandise is gathering dust. It is now December 31, 2016, and the current replacement cost of the ending merchandise inventory is $25,000 below the business's cost of the goods, which was $100,000. Before any adjustments at the end of the period, the company's Cost of Goods Sold account has a balance of $400,000.

**Requirements**

1. Journalize any required entries.
2. At what amount should the company report merchandise inventory on the balance sheet?

3. At what amount should the company report cost of goods sold on the income statement?
4. Which accounting principle or concept is most relevant to this situation?

**P6-36B Correcting inventory errors over a three-year period and computing inventory turnover and days' sales in inventory**

**Learning Objectives 5, 6**

2. 2017, overstated $7,000

Evergreen Carpets's books show the following data. In early 2018, auditors found that the ending merchandise inventory for 2015 was understated by $6,000 and that the ending merchandise inventory for 2017 was overstated by $7,000. The ending merchandise inventory at December 31, 2016, was correct.

| | 2017 | | 2016 | | 2015 | |
|---|---|---|---|---|---|---|
| Net Sales Revenue | | $ 218,000 | | $ 161,000 | | $ 176,000 |
| Cost of Goods Sold: | | | | | | |
| Beginning Merchandise Inventory | $ 21,000 | | $ 25,000 | | $ 41,000 | |
| Net Cost of Purchases | 130,000 | | 98,000 | | 83,000 | |
| Cost of Goods Available for Sale | 151,000 | | 123,000 | | 124,000 | |
| Less: Ending Merchandise Inventory | 33,000 | | 21,000 | | 25,000 | |
| Cost of Goods Sold | | 118,000 | | 102,000 | | 99,000 |
| Gross Profit | | 100,000 | | 59,000 | | 77,000 |
| Operating Expenses | | 75,000 | | 29,000 | | 43,000 |
| Net Income | | $ 25,000 | | $ 30,000 | | $ 34,000 |

**Requirements**

1. Prepare corrected income statements for the three years.
2. State whether each year's net income—before your corrections—is understated or overstated, and indicate the amount of the understatement or overstatement.
3. Compute the inventory turnover and days' sales in inventory using the corrected income statements for the three years. (Round all numbers to two decimals.)

**P6A-37B Accounting for inventory using the periodic inventory system—FIFO, LIFO, and weighted-average, and comparing FIFO, LIFO, and weighted-average**

**Learning Objectives 3, 7**
**Appendix 6A**

1. LIFO Ending Merch. Inv., $10,200

Best Yet Electronic Center began October with 100 units of merchandise inventory that cost $78 each. During October, the store made the following purchases:

| | |
|---|---|
| Oct. 3 | 40 units @ $ 80 each |
| 12 | 60 units @ $ 82 each |
| 18 | 40 units @ $ 94 each |

Best Yet uses the periodic inventory system, and the physical count at October 31 indicates that 130 units of merchandise inventory are on hand.

**Requirements**

1. Determine the ending merchandise inventory and cost of goods sold amounts for the October financial statements using the FIFO, LIFO, and weighted-average inventory costing methods.

2. Sales revenue for October totaled $23,000. Compute Best Yet's gross profit for October using each method.
3. Which method will result in the lowest income taxes for Best Yet? Why? Which method will result in the highest net income for Best Yet? Why?

## > Continuing Problem

### P6-38 Accounting for inventory using the perpetual inventory system—FIFO

This problem continues the Daniels Consulting situation from Problem P5-45 in Chapter 5. Consider the January transactions for Daniels Consulting that were presented in Chapter 5. (Cost data have been removed from the sale transactions.) Daniels uses the perpetual inventory system.

| | |
|---|---|
| Jan. 2 | Completed a consulting engagement and received cash of $5,700. |
| 2 | Prepaid three months office rent, $2,400. |
| 7 | Purchased 50 units software inventory on account, $1,050, plus freight in, $50. |
| 18 | Sold 40 software units on account, $2,625. |
| 19 | Consulted with a client for a fee of $2,500 on account. |
| 20 | Paid employee salaries, $1,885, which includes accrued salaries from December. |
| 21 | Paid on account, $1,100. |
| 22 | Purchased 185 units software inventory on account, $4,810. |
| 24 | Paid utilities, $375. |
| 28 | Sold 135 units software for cash, $5,265. |
| 31 | Recorded the following adjusting entries: |
| | a. Accrued salaries expense, $775 |
| | b. Depreciation on Equipment, $60; Depreciation on Furniture, $50 |
| | c. Expiration of prepaid rent, $800 |
| | d. Physical count of software inventory, 50 units |

**Requirements**

1. Prepare perpetual inventory records for January for Daniels using the FIFO inventory costing method. (Note: You must calculate the cost of goods sold on the 18th, 28th, and 31st.)
2. Journalize the transactions for January 18th, 28th, and 31st (adjusting entry d only) using the perpetual inventory record created in Requirement 1.

## Practice Set

This problem continues the Crystal Clear Cleaning problem begun in Chapter 2 and continued through Chapter 5.

### P6-39 Accounting for inventory using the perpetual inventory system—FIFO

Consider the December transactions for Crystal Clear Cleaning that were presented in Chapter 5. (Cost data have been removed from the sale transactions.) Crystal Clear uses the perpetual inventory system.

| | |
|---|---|
| Dec. 2 | Purchased 475 units of inventory for $2,850 on account from Sparkle, Co. on terms, 3/10, n/20. |
| 5 | Purchased 600 units of inventory from Borax on account with terms 2/10, n/30. The total invoice was for $4,500, which included a $150 freight charge. |
| 7 | Returned 75 units of inventory to Sparkle from the December 2 purchase. |
| 9 | Paid Borax. |
| 11 | Sold 285 units of goods to Happy Maids for $3,990 on account with terms 3/10, n/30. |
| 12 | Paid Sparkle. |
| 15 | Received 22 units with a retail price of $308 of goods back from customer Happy Maids. The goods cost Crystal Clear $132. |
| 21 | Received payment from Happy Maids, settling the amount due in full. |
| 28 | Sold 265 units of goods to Bridget, Inc. for cash of $3,975. |
| 29 | Paid cash for utilities of $415. |
| 30 | Paid cash for Sales Commission Expense of $550. |
| 31 | Recorded the following adjusting entries: |
| | a. Physical count of inventory on December 31 showed 428 units of goods on hand. |
| | b. Depreciation, $270 |
| | c. Accrued salaries expense of $725 |
| | d. Prepared all other adjustments necessary for December (Hint: You will need to review the adjustment information in Chapter 3 to determine the remaining adjustments). Assume the cleaning supplies left at December 31 are $30. |

**Requirements**

1. Prepare perpetual inventory records for December for Crystal Clear Cleaning using the FIFO inventory costing method. (Note: You must calculate the cost of goods sold on the 11th, 28th, and 31st.)
2. Journalize the transactions for December 11th, 28th, and 31st (adjusting entry a only) using the perpetual inventory record created in Requirement 1.

CHAPTER 6

# CRITICAL THINKING

## > Decision Case 6-1

Suppose you manage Campbell Appliance. The store's summarized financial statements for 2017, the most recent year, follow:

| CAMPBELL APPLIANCE<br>Income Statement<br>Year Ended December 31, 2017 | |
|---|---|
| Sales | $ 800,000 |
| Cost of Goods Sold | 660,000 |
| Gross Profit | 140,000 |
| Operating Expenses | 100,000 |
| Net Income | **$ 40,000** |

**CAMPBELL APPLIANCE**
**Balance Sheet**
**December 31, 2017**

| Assets | | Liabilities and Stockholders' Equity | |
|---|---|---|---|
| Cash | $ 30,000 | Accounts Payable | $ 35,000 |
| Inventories | 75,000 | Note Payable | 280,000 |
| Land and Buildings, Net | 360,000 | Total Liabilities | 315,000 |
| | | Stockholders' Equity | 150,000 |
| Total Assets | **$ 465,000** | Total Liabilities and Stockholders' Equity | **$ 465,000** |

Assume that you need to double net income. To accomplish your goal, it will be very difficult to raise the prices you charge because there is a discount appliance store nearby. Also, you have little control over your cost of goods sold because the appliance manufacturers set the amount you must pay.

Identify several strategies for doubling net income.

## > Fraud Case 6-1

Ever since he was a kid, Carl Montague wanted to be a pro football player. When that didn't work out, he found another way to channel his natural competitive spirit: He bought a small auto parts store in Kentucky that was deep in red ink (negative earnings). At the end of the year, he created "ghost" inventory by recording fake inventory purchases. He offset these transactions by "adjustments" to Cost of Goods Sold, thereby boosting profit and strengthening the balance sheet. Fortified with great financials, he got bank loans that allowed him to build up a regional chain of stores, buy a local sports franchise, and take on the lifestyle of a celebrity. When the economy in the region tanked, he could no longer cover his losses with new debt or equity infusions, and the whole empire fell like a house of cards.

**Requirements**

1. Name several parties that could have been hurt by the actions of Carl Montague.
2. What kind of adjustment to Cost of Goods Sold (debit or credit) would have the effect of boosting earnings?

## > Financial Statement Case 6-1

The notes are an important part of a company's financial statements, giving valuable details that would clutter the tabular data presented in the statements. This case will help you learn to use a company's inventory notes. Visit **http://www.pearsonhighered.com/Horngren** to view a link to **Starbucks Corporation's** Fiscal 2013 Annual Report. Access the financial statements and related notes, and answer the following questions:

**Requirements**

1. Which inventory costing method does Starbucks use? How does Starbucks value its inventories? See Note 1.
2. By using the cost of goods sold formula, you can compute net purchases, which are not reported in the Starbucks statements. How much were Starbucks's inventory purchases during the year ended September 29, 2013?
3. Determine Starbucks's inventory turnover and days' sales in inventory for the year ended September 29, 2013. (Round each ratio to one decimal place.) How do Starbucks's inventory turnover and days' sales in inventory compare with **Green Mountain Coffee Roasters, Inc.'s** for the year ended September 28, 2013? Explain.

## > Team Project 6-1

Obtain the annual reports of as many companies as you have team members—one company per team member. Most companies post their financial statements on their Web sites.

**Requirements**

1. Identify the inventory method used by each company.
2. Compute each company's gross profit percentage, inventory turnover, and days' sales in inventory for the most recent two years.
3. For the industries of the companies you are analyzing, obtain the industry averages for gross profit percentage and inventory turnover from Robert Morris Associates, *Annual Statement Studies*; Dun and Bradstreet, *Industry Norms and Key Business Ratios*; or Leo Troy, *Almanac of Business and Industrial Financial Ratios*.
4. How well does each of your companies compare with the average for its industry? What insight about your companies can you glean from these ratios?





## Quick Check Answers

**1.** c **2.** a **3.** b **4.** b **5.** d **6.** a **7.** b **8.** b **9A.** c

# 7 Internal Control and Cash

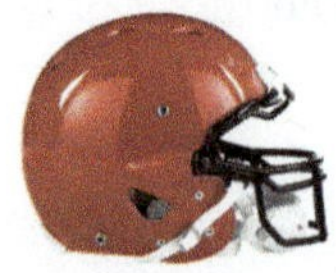

## Where Did the Cash Go?

Andrew Goard, chief financial officer of a sports-themed restaurant located in Brentwood, California, stared at the bank statement on his desk. The business recently experienced record-breaking revenue due to increased customer traffic and expanded menu and drink offerings. Andrew knew that the expenses of the business had also increased, but he had expected the cash in the business's checking account to increase, not decrease, as the bank statement was showing.

Andrew wondered if it was possible that one of his employees was stealing money from the cash register. He really liked all of his employees and didn't think that any of them would steal from the business. But the deposits on the bank statement from customer sales just didn't make sense. Given the increased sales, the cash deposits should have been much higher.

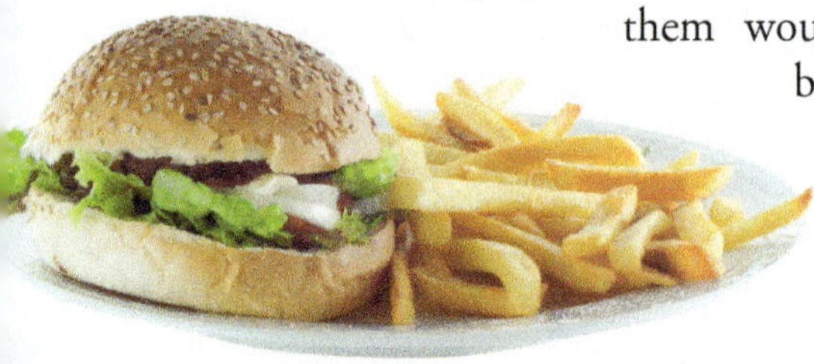

Andrew knew that it was his responsibility to ensure that procedures were put into place to be sure the cash and other assets of the business remained secure. He had thought that completing employee background checks was enough to prevent the theft of the business's assets, but he now suspected that further controls needed to be put into place. Andrew began by reviewing the bank statement and comparing it to the cash records on hand. In doing this, he identified that cash was indeed being stolen from the business by the employee who was responsible for making the daily cash deposits. Andrew realized, though, that it wasn't enough to fire the employee responsible; he needed to put into place security measures that would decrease the likelihood of employee theft happening again.

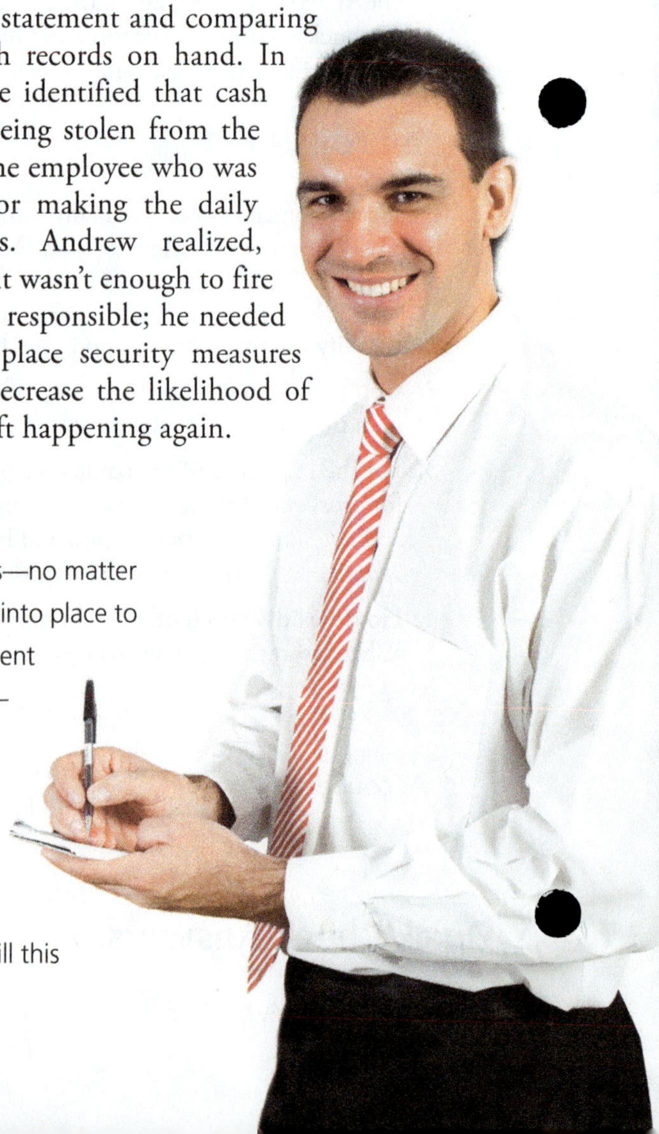

**What Are Internal Controls?**

Safeguarding and securing assets should be a concern of all businesses—no matter how small or large the business is. The procedures that businesses put into place to protect their assets are called *internal controls* and are a key management responsibility. For example, Buffalo Wild Wings Grill & Bar, a New York–style wing restaurant chain that offers a sports bar atmosphere and a full menu featuring everything from salads to wings, must assure its investors that proper controls have been put into place to protect its assets, promote operational efficiency, and ensure accurate and reliable accounting records. In this chapter, we look at the policies and procedures that companies such as Buffalo Wild Wings use to fulfill this responsibility.

# Chapter 7 Learning Objectives

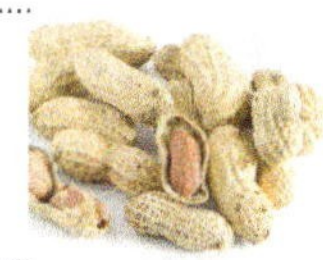

1. Define internal control and describe the components of internal control and control procedures
2. Apply internal controls to cash receipts
3. Apply internal controls to cash payments
4. Explain and journalize petty cash transactions
5. Demonstrate the use of a bank account as a control device and prepare a bank reconciliation and related journal entries
6. Use the cash ratio to evaluate business performance

## WHAT IS INTERNAL CONTROL, AND HOW CAN IT BE USED TO PROTECT A COMPANY'S ASSETS?

**Learning Objective 1**
Define internal control and describe the components of internal control and control procedures

A key responsibility of a business manager is to control operations. Owners set goals, hire managers to lead the way, and hire employees to carry out the business plan. **Internal control** is the organizational plan and all the related measures designed to accomplish the following:

1. **Safeguard assets.** A company must protect its assets; otherwise it is throwing away resources. If you fail to safeguard cash, the most liquid of assets, it will quickly slip away.
2. **Encourage employees to follow company policies.** Everyone in an organization needs to work toward the same goals. It is important for a business to identify policies to help meet the company's goals. These policies are also important for the company to ensure that all customers are treated similarly and that results can be measured effectively.
3. **Promote operational efficiency.** Businesses cannot afford to waste resources. Businesses work hard to make sales and do not want to waste any of the benefits. Promoting operational efficiency reduces expenses and increases business profits.
4. **Ensure accurate, reliable accounting records.** Accurate, reliable accounting records are essential. Without reliable records, managers cannot tell which part of the business is profitable and which part needs improvement. A business could be losing money on every product sold and not realize it—unless it keeps accurate and reliable records.

**Internal Control**
The organizational plan and all the related measures adopted by an entity to safeguard assets, encourage employees to follow company policies, promote operational efficiency, and ensure accurate and reliable accounting records.

### Internal Control and the Sarbanes-Oxley Act

How critical are internal controls for public companies? They are so important that the U.S. Congress passed a law requiring a **public company**—one that sells its stock to the general public—to maintain a system of internal controls.

**Public Company**
A company that sells its stock to the general public.

The Enron Corporation and WorldCom accounting scandals rocked the United States in the early years of this millennium. Enron overstated profits and went out of business almost overnight. WorldCom reported expenses as assets and overstated both profits and assets. The same accounting firm, Arthur Andersen LLP, had audited both companies' financial statements. Arthur Andersen voluntarily closed its doors in 2002 after nearly 90 years in public accounting.

As the scandals unfolded, many people asked, "How could this happen? Where were the auditors?" To address public concern, Congress passed the **Sarbanes-Oxley Act**, abbreviated as **SOX**. This act requires companies to review internal control and take responsibility for the accuracy and completeness of their financial reports. SOX revamped corporate

**Sarbanes-Oxley Act (SOX)**
Requires companies to review internal control and take responsibility for the accuracy and completeness of their financial reports.

**Internal Control Report**
A report by management describing its responsibility for and the adequacy of internal controls over financial reporting.

IFRS

To be IFRS compliant, foreign companies are not required to issue an internal control report or have their internal controls audited by outside auditors. While all companies have internal controls, foreign companies do not have the added expense of an audit of their internal controls. On the other hand, readers of the financial reports of foreign companies have no assurance that the controls are effective.

governance in the United States and affected the accounting profession. Here are some of the SOX provisions:

1. Public companies must issue an **internal control report**, which is a report by management describing its responsibility for and the adequacy of internal controls over financial reporting. Additionally, an outside auditor must evaluate the client's internal controls and report on the internal controls as part of the audit report.
2. A new body, the Public Company Accounting Oversight Board (PCAOB), oversees the work of auditors of public companies.
3. Accounting firms are not allowed to audit a public company and also provide certain consulting services for the same client.
4. Stiff penalties await violators—25 years in prison for securities fraud and 20 years for an executive making false sworn statements.

The Sarbanes-Oxley Act changed the rules for auditors, limiting what services they can perform in addition to the audit and requiring a report on the internal controls of each public company audited. How does a business achieve good internal control? The next section identifies the components of internal control.

## The Components of Internal Control

A business can achieve its internal control objectives by addressing the five components listed below:

- **C**ontrol procedures
- **R**isk assessment
- **I**nformation system
- **M**onitoring of controls
- **E**nvironment

*You can remember the five components of internal control by using the acronym CRIME.*

### Control Procedures

Control procedures are designed to ensure that the business's goals are achieved. The next section, "Internal Control Procedures," discusses the procedures in greater detail.

### Risk Assessment

A company must identify its risks. For example, food manufacturers face the risk that their food products may harm people; airplane carrier businesses face the possibility that planes may crash; music companies face copyright infringement risks; and all companies face the risk of bankruptcy. Companies facing difficulties might be tempted to falsify their financial statements to make themselves look better than they really are. As part of the internal control system, the company's business risk, as well as the risk concerning individual accounts, must be assessed. The higher the risk, the more controls a company must put in place to safeguard its assets and accounting records.

### Information System

As we have seen, the information system is critical. Controls must be in place within the information system to ensure that only authorized users have access to various parts of the accounting information system. Additionally, controls must be in place to ensure adequate approvals for recorded transactions are required. The decision makers need accurate information to keep track of assets and measure profits and losses.

### Monitoring of Controls

Companies hire auditors to monitor their controls. An **internal auditor** is an employee of the business who ensures that the company's employees are following company policies and that operations are running efficiently. Internal auditors also determine whether the company is following legal requirements for internal controls to safeguard assets. An **external auditor** is an outside accountant who is completely independent of the business. External auditors evaluate the controls to ensure that the financial statements are presented fairly, in accordance with Generally Accepted Accounting Principles (GAAP).

**Internal Auditor**
An employee of the business who ensures the company's employees are following company policies, that the company meets all legal requirements, and that operations are running efficiently.

**External Auditor**
An outside accountant, completely independent of the business, who evaluates the controls to ensure that the financial statements are presented fairly in accordance with GAAP.

### Environment

The environment is the "tone at the top" or the culture of the business. It starts with the CFO or CEO and the top managers. They must behave honorably to set a good example for company employees. Each must demonstrate the importance of internal controls if he or she expects the employees to take the controls seriously.

## ETHICS

### Should the liabilities be reported?

Dudley Dorite, CPA, the lead external auditor of Needles Corporation, thinks that Needles may be understating the liabilities on its balance sheet. Needles's transactions are very complex, and outsiders may never figure this out. Dorite asks his CPA firm's audit standards committee how he should handle the situation. The CPA firm's committee replies, "Require Needles to report all its liabilities." Needles is Dorite's most important client, and Needles is pressuring him to certify the liabilities. Dorite can rationalize that Needles's amounts are okay. What should Dorite do? What would you do?

#### Solution

Dorite has three options. He can go along with Needles's liabilities as reported, he can persuade Needles to report higher amounts of liabilities, or, if Needles refuses, he can issue a qualified audit report. A qualified audit report is issued when the auditor disagrees with specific items on the financial statements. Dorite should understand that, when he prepares an audit report, his responsibility is to the investors and the public. He should follow the recommendation of the audit standards committee. If Dorite went along with misrepresenting the liabilities, he might keep a valuable client, but he could face problems in the future for not disclosing flaws in the presentation of liabilities on the balance sheet.

## Internal Control Procedures

Whether the business is a small business that generates less than $10,000 in annual sales or a large business generating $10 billion in annual sales, all companies need the following internal control procedures:

### Competent, Reliable, and Ethical Personnel

Employees should be competent, reliable, and ethical. Paying good salaries will attract high-quality employees. Employees should also be trained to do the job, and their work should be adequately supervised.

### Assignment of Responsibilities

In a business with good internal controls, no duty is overlooked. Each employee has certain, carefully defined responsibilities. For example, in a large company, the person in charge of signing checks is called the *treasurer*. The chief accounting officer is called the *controller*. Even an entry-level bookkeeper, whose job includes recording accounting transactions accurately, has clear responsibilities. This assignment of responsibilities creates job accountability, thus ensuring all important tasks get done.

## Separation of Duties

**Separation of Duties**
Dividing responsibilities between two or more people to limit fraud and promote accuracy of accounting records.

Smart management policies divide responsibilities between two or more people. **Separation of duties** limits fraud and promotes the accuracy of the accounting records. Separation of duties can be divided into two parts:

1. **Separating operations from accounting.** Accounting should be completely separate from the operating departments, such as production and sales. What would happen if sales personnel recorded the company's revenue? Sales figures could be inflated, and then top managers would not know how much the company actually sold.
2. **Separating the custody of assets from accounting.** Accountants must not handle cash, and cashiers must not have access to the accounting records. If one employee has both duties, that employee could steal cash and conceal the theft in the accounting records. The treasurer of a company handles cash, and the controller accounts for the cash. Neither person has both responsibilities. This control applies to all assets, not just cash.

## Audits

To assess the adequacy and accuracy of their accounting records, most companies perform both internal and external audits. Remember that an audit is an examination of a company's financial statements and accounting system by a trained accounting professional called an auditor. Internal audits are performed by employees of the company. External audits are performed by independent auditors who are not employees of the company.

To evaluate the accounting system, auditors must examine the internal controls and test them to ensure the controls are working properly. For example, a control might require authorization by a manager for payments over $50. An auditor would check a sample of payments greater than $50 to determine whether all payments were properly authorized by a manager.

## Documents

Documents provide the details of business transactions and include invoices and orders, which may be paper or electronic. Documents should be prenumbered to prevent theft and inefficiency. A gap in the numbered sequence draws attention.

For example, for Smart Touch Learning, a key document is the sales invoice. The manager can compare the total cash sales on the invoices with the amount of cash received and deposited into the bank account.

## Electronic Devices

Accounting systems are relying less on paper documents and more on electronic documents and digital storage devices. For example, retailers control inventory by attaching an electronic sensor to merchandise. The cashier removes the sensor after a sale is made. If a customer tries to leave the store with the sensor attached, an alarm sounds. Devices such as these can significantly reduce theft.

## E-Commerce

**Encryption**
Rearranging plain-text messages by a mathematical process—the primary method of achieving security in e-commerce.

**Firewall**
A device that enables members of a local network to access the network, while keeping nonmembers out of the network.

E-commerce creates its own unique types of risks. Hackers may gain access to confidential information, such as account numbers and passwords, or introduce computer viruses, Trojans, or phishing expeditions. To address the risks posed by e-commerce, companies have devised a number of security measures. One technique for protecting customer data is encryption. **Encryption** rearranges plain-text messages by a mathematical process. The encrypted message cannot be read by those who do not know the code. An accounting encryption example uses check-sum digits for account numbers. Each account number has its last digit equal to the sum of the previous digits. For example, consider customer number 2237, where $2 + 2 + 3 = 7$. Any account number failing this test triggers an error message.

Another technique for protecting data is firewalls. **Firewalls** limit access into a local network. Members can access the network, but nonmembers cannot. Usually several firewalls are built into the system. At the point of entry, additional security measures, such as passwords, PINs (personal identification numbers), and signatures are used. For additional security, more sophisticated firewalls are used deeper in the network to protect more sensitive data.

## DECISIONS

### What e-commerce internal controls should be put into place?

Jason Kane works as an information technology auditor for Netproducts, a retailer that sells merchandise over the Internet. Jason has been assigned the responsibility of reviewing the existing procedures and suggesting internal controls that could best protect the company. Netproducts sells all its merchandise over the Internet and accepts only credit card payments. Netproducts tracks trend information about its sales and maintains all customer, product, and pricing information on the company's intranet. In addition, Netproducts keeps employee information such as annual leave, payroll deposits, and Social Security numbers on its intranet. What e-commerce controls should Jason suggest?

#### Solution

Jason should suggest that specific controls be put into place, such as using encryption technology and firewalls, to protect customer and employee information. He should recommend that customers be required to create an online account with a password for the site and that the company only use secured Internet networks. In addition, Netproducts should ensure that the customer and employee data are physically secured and that access to the data can be obtained only by authorized individuals.

### Other Controls

The types of other controls are as endless as the types of businesses that employ them. Some examples of other common controls include the following:

- Fireproof vaults to store important documents
- Burglar alarms, fire alarms, and security cameras
- Loss-prevention specialists who train company employees to spot suspicious activity
- Fidelity bonds to reimburse the company for any losses due to employee theft
- Mandatory vacations and job rotation

## The Limitations of Internal Control—Costs and Benefits

Unfortunately, most internal controls can be overcome. **Collusion**—two or more people working together—can beat internal controls. For example, consider the following scenario with Galaxy Theater. Ralph and Lana, employees of Galaxy Theater, can design a scheme in which Ralph, the ticket seller, sells tickets and pockets the cash from 10 customers. Lana, the ticket taker, admits 10 customers to the theater without taking their tickets. Ralph and Lana split the cash. Ralph and Lana have colluded to circumvent controls, resulting in Galaxy Theater losing revenues. To prevent this situation, the manager must take additional steps, such as matching the number of people in the theater against the number of ticket stubs retained, which takes time away from the manager's other duties. It is difficult and costly to plan controls that can prevent collusion.

**Collusion**
Two or more people working together to circumvent internal controls and defraud a company.

The stricter the internal control system, the more it costs. A complex system of internal control can strangle the business with red tape. How tight should the controls be? Internal controls must always be judged in light of their costs versus their benefits. Following is an example of a positive cost–benefit relationship: A security guard at a retail store costs about $28,000 a year. On average, each guard prevents about $50,000 of theft each year. The net savings to the retail store is $22,000. An example of a negative cost–benefit relationship would be paying the same security guard $28,000 a year to guard a $1,000 cash drawer. The cost exceeds the benefit by $27,000.

So far we have discussed what internal control is and how it can be used to protect a company's assets. We will now spend the remainder of the chapter concentrating on cash because it is the asset most likely to be stolen. However, it is important to remember that internal controls should be applied to all assets, not just cash.

## Try It!

Match the accounting terminology to the definitions.

| | |
|---|---|
| 1. Sarbanes-Oxley Act | a. Organizational plan and all the related measures adopted by an entity to safeguard assets, encourage employees to follow company policies, promote operational efficiency, and ensure accurate and reliable accounting records. |
| 2. Internal control | b. Employees of the business who ensure that the company's employees are following company policies and meeting legal requirements and that operations are running efficiently. |
| 3. Encryption | c. Rearranging plain-text messages by a mathematical process—the primary method of achieving security in e-commerce. |
| 4. Separation of duties | d. Requires companies to review internal control and take responsibility for the accuracy and completeness of their financial reports. |
| 5. Internal auditors | e. Dividing responsibilities between two or more people. |

**Check your answers online in MyAccountingLab or at http://www.pearsonhighered.com/Horngren.**

For more practice, see Short Exercise S7-1. MyAccountingLab

## WHAT ARE THE INTERNAL CONTROL PROCEDURES WITH RESPECT TO CASH RECEIPTS?

**Learning Objective 2**
Apply internal controls to cash receipts

Cash receipts occur primarily when a business sells merchandise or services. All cash receipts should be deposited in the bank for safekeeping shortly after the cash is received. Companies receive cash either over the counter, through the mail, or by electronic funds transfer. Each source of cash has its own security measures. We have already discussed internal control procedures for e-commerce, so this section focuses on over-the-counter and mailed cash receipts.

### Cash Receipts Over the Counter

A cash receipt over the counter in a store involves a point-of-sale terminal (cash register) that provides control over the cash receipts. Consider a retail store. For each transaction, the retail store issues a receipt to ensure that each sale is recorded. The cash drawer opens after the clerk enters a transaction, and the machine (cash register) records it. At the end of the day, a manager proves the cash by comparing the cash in the drawer against the machine's record of cash sales. This step helps prevent theft by the clerk.

At the end of the day—or several times a day if business is brisk—the manager deposits the cash in the bank. The machine tape then goes to the accounting department to record the journal entry for cash receipts and sales revenue. These measures, coupled with oversight by a manager, discourage theft.

## Cash Receipts by Mail

Many companies receive checks by mail for payments of services or merchandise. Checks sent via mail are considered to be cash receipts. Exhibit 7-1 shows how companies control cash received by mail.

**Exhibit 7-1 | Cash Receipts by Mail**

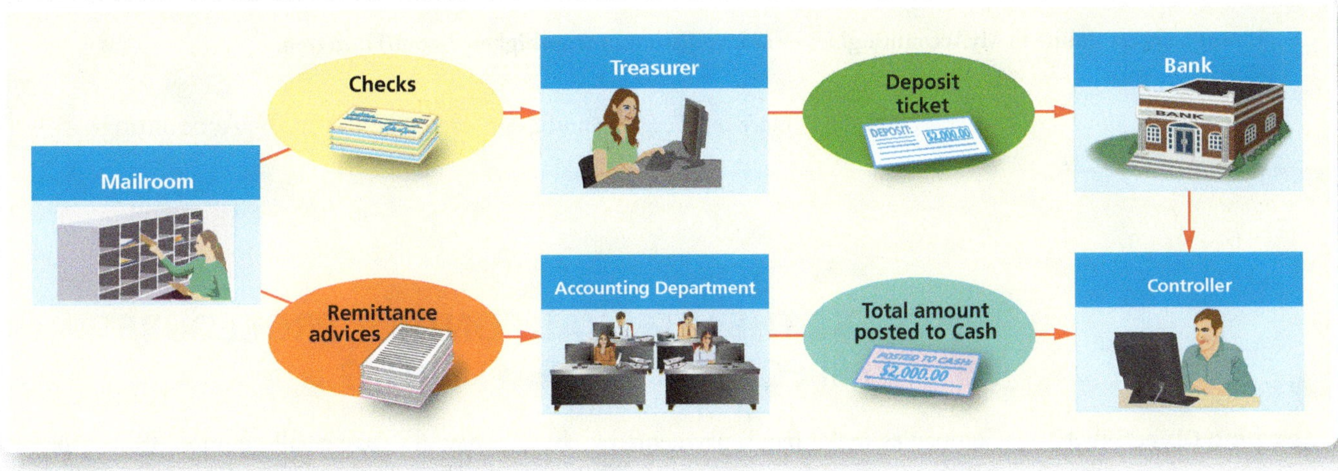


The process works like this:

**Step 1:** All incoming mail is opened by a mailroom employee. The mailroom then sends all customer checks to the treasurer and all remittance advices to the accounting department. A **remittance advice** is an optional attachment to a check that tells the business the reason for the payment.

**Remittance Advice**
An optional attachment to a check that tells the business the reason for the payment.

**Step 2:** The treasurer has the cashier deposit the checks in the bank. The cashier receives a deposit receipt.

**Step 3:** The accounting department (or bookkeeper) uses the remittance advices to record the journal entries to Cash and customer accounts.

**Step 4:** As a final control, the controller compares the following records for the day:

- Bank deposit amount from the treasurer
- Debit to Cash from the accounting department

The debit to Cash should equal the amount deposited in the bank. If it does, all cash receipts are safe in the bank, and the company's books are up to date.

Many companies use a **lock-box system** as an alternative to accepting cash or checks via the mail or over the counter. In a lock-box system, customers send their checks directly to a post office box that belongs to a bank. A bank employee empties the box daily and records the deposits into the company's bank account. Internal control is tight because company personnel never touch incoming cash. The lock-box system puts a business's cash into the company's bank account quickly.

**Lock-Box System**
A system in which customers send their checks to a post office box that belongs to a bank. A bank employee empties the box daily and records the deposits into the company's bank account.

## Try It!

6. Fill in the missing information concerning how companies control cash received by mail.
   a. The ________ opens the mail and sends customer checks to the treasurer.
   b. The ________ deposits the customer checks in the bank.
   c. The ________ uses the remittance advices to record the journal entries for cash receipts.
   d. The ________ compares the bank deposit to the journal entry for cash receipts.

**Check your answers online in MyAccountingLab or at http://www.pearsonhighered.com/Horngren.**

For more practice, see Short Exercises S7-2 and S7-3. MyAccountingLab

# WHAT ARE THE INTERNAL CONTROL PROCEDURES WITH RESPECT TO CASH PAYMENTS?

**Learning Objective 3**
Apply internal controls to cash payments

Companies make many payments by check. They also pay small amounts from a petty cash fund, which is discussed later in the chapter. Let's begin by discussing cash payments by check.

## Controls Over Payment by Check

Companies need a good separation of duties between the operations of the business and writing checks for cash payments. Payment by check is an important internal control for the following reasons:

- The check provides a record of the payment.
- The check must be signed by an authorized official.
- Before signing the check, the official reviews the invoice or other evidence supporting the payment.

### Controls Over Purchases and Payments

To illustrate the internal control over cash payments by check, suppose Smart Touch Learning buys its tablets from an electronics manufacturer. The purchasing and payment process follows these steps, as shown in Exhibit 7-2.

**Step 1:** Smart Touch Learning sends a purchase order to the electronics manufacturer that contains the quantity and type of goods needed.

**Step 2:** The electronics manufacturer ships the inventory and sends an invoice back to Smart Touch Learning.

**Step 3:** Smart Touch Learning receives the inventory and prepares a receiving report.

**Step 4:** After approving all documents, Smart Touch Learning sends a check to the electronics manufacturer.

**Exhibit 7-2 | Cash Payments by Check**

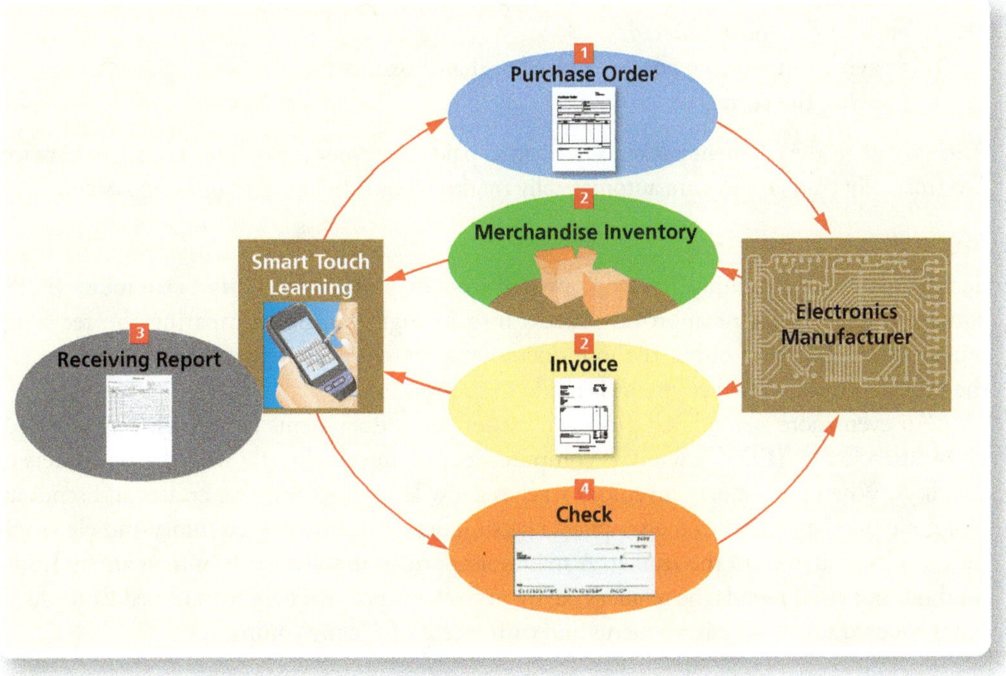


For good internal control, the purchasing agent (the employee who prepares the purchase order) should neither receive the goods nor approve the payment. If these duties are not separated, a purchasing agent could buy goods and have them shipped to his or her home. Or a purchasing agent could spend too much on purchases, approve the payment, and split the excess with the supplier.

Exhibit 7-3 shows Smart Touch Learning's payment packet of documents, which may be in either electronic or paper format. Before signing the check for payment of goods,

**Exhibit 7-3 | Payment Packet**

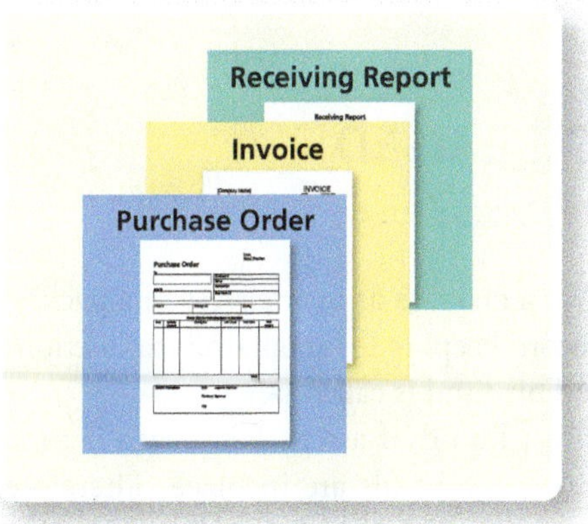

the controller or the treasurer should examine the packet to prove that all the documents agree. Only then does the company know the following:

1. It received the goods ordered.
2. It is paying only for the goods received and authorized.
3. It is paying the correct amount.

After payment, the payment packet is marked as paid to prevent the bill from being paid twice. Electronically paid invoices are automatically marked "paid" by most accounting systems.

**Evaluated Receipts Settlement (ERS)**
A procedure that compresses the payment approval process into a single step by comparing the receiving report to the purchase order.

**Electronic Data Interchange (EDI)**
A streamlined process that bypasses paper documents altogether. Computers of customers communicate directly with the computers of suppliers to automate routine business transactions.

### Streamlined Procedures

Technology is streamlining payment procedures. **Evaluated Receipts Settlement (ERS)** compresses the payment approval process into a single step by comparing the receiving report to the purchase order. If those documents match, then Smart Touch Learning got the tablets it ordered and payment is made to the vendor.

An even more streamlined process bypasses paper documents altogether. In **Electronic Data Interchange (EDI)**, a retailer's computers communicate directly with the computers of suppliers. When the retailer's inventory reaches a low level, the computer creates and sends an electronic purchase order to the supplier. The supplier then ships the inventory and electronically sends an invoice to the retailer. A manager approves the invoice, and then an electronic fund transfer (EFT) sends the retailer's payment to the supplier. These streamlined EDI procedures are used for both cash payments and cash receipts in many companies.

## Try It!

7. Fill in the missing information.
   a. The vendor ships the inventory and sends a(n) ________ back to the purchaser.
   b. After approving all documents, the purchaser sends a(n) ________ to the vendor.
   c. When ordering merchandise inventory, the purchaser sends a(n) ________ to the vendor.
   d. The purchaser receives the inventory and prepares a(n) ________.

**Check your answers online in MyAccountingLab or at http://www.pearsonhighered.com/Horngren.**

For more practice, see Short Exercise S7-4. MyAccountingLab

## HOW CAN A PETTY CASH FUND BE USED FOR INTERNAL CONTROL PURPOSES?

**Learning Objective 4**
Explain and journalize petty cash transactions

**Petty Cash**
A fund containing a small amount of cash that is used to pay for minor expenditures.

It is not cost effective for a business to write a check for a taxi fare or the delivery of a package across town. To meet these needs and to streamline record keeping for small cash transactions, companies keep cash on hand to pay small amounts. This fund is called **petty cash**.

We have already established that cash is the most liquid of assets. Petty cash is more liquid than cash in the bank because none of the bank controls are in place. Therefore, petty cash needs controls such as the following:

- Designate a custodian of the petty cash fund. The custodian is the individual assigned responsibility for the petty cash fund.
- Designate a specific amount of cash to be kept in the petty cash fund.
- Support all petty cash fund payments with a petty cash ticket. These tickets are sequentially numbered. The petty cash ticket serves as an authorization voucher and explanation.

## Setting Up the Petty Cash Fund

The petty cash fund is opened when the company writes a check for the designated amount. The company makes the check payable to Petty Cash. Suppose on August 1, Smart Touch Learning creates a petty cash fund of $200. The custodian cashes the $200 check and places the currency in the fund box. The journal entry is as follows:

| Date | Accounts and Explanation | Debit | Credit |
|---|---|---|---|
| Aug. 1 | Petty Cash | 200 | |
| | Cash | | 200 |
| | *To open the petty cash fund.* | | |

| A↑↓ | | L + E |
|---|---|---|
| Petty Cash↑ Cash↓ | = | |

For each petty cash payment, the custodian prepares a petty cash ticket like the one in Exhibit 7-4.

**Exhibit 7-4 | Petty Cash Ticket**

PETTY CASH TICKET #101

**Date** Aug 25, 2017

**Amount** $60

**For** Letterhead invoices

**Debit** Office Supplies

**Received by** *Lewis Wright* **Fund Custodian** MAR

Signatures (or initials) identify the recipient of the cash and the fund custodian. The custodian keeps the petty cash tickets in the fund box. The sum of the cash plus the total of the petty cash tickets should equal the fund balance, $200, at all times.

Maintaining the Petty Cash account at its designated balance is the nature of an **imprest system**. The imprest system requires that, at any point in time, the petty cash box contain cash and petty cash tickets that total the amount of the imprest balance. This clearly identifies the amount of cash for which the custodian is responsible, and it is the system's main internal control feature.

**Imprest System**
A way to account for petty cash by maintaining a constant balance in the petty cash account. At any time, cash plus petty cash tickets must total the amount allocated to the petty cash fund.

## Replenishing the Petty Cash Fund

Payments decrease the fund, so periodically the fund must be replenished. Suppose that on August 31 the petty cash fund holds $118 in cash and $80 in petty cash tickets (ticket #101 for $60 for office supplies and ticket #102 for $20 for a delivery).

You can see $2 is missing:

| | | |
|---|---|---|
| Fund balance | | $ 200 |
| Cash on hand | $ 118 | |
| Petty cash tickets | 80 | |
| Total accounted for | | 198 |
| Amount of cash missing | | $ 2 |

To replenish the petty cash fund, you need to bring the cash on hand up to $200. The company writes a check, payable to Petty Cash, for $82 ($200 imprest balance – $118 cash on hand). The fund custodian cashes this check and puts $82 back in the fund box. Now the fund box holds $200 cash as it should.

The petty cash tickets tell you what to debit and the check amount tells you what to credit, as shown in this entry to replenish the fund:

| A↓ | | L | + | E↓ |
|---|---|---|---|---|
| Office Supplies↑ Cash↓ | = | | | Delivery Expense↑ Cash Short & Over↑ |

| Date | Accounts and Explanation | Debit | Credit |
|---|---|---|---|
| Aug. 31 | Office Supplies | 60 | |
| | Delivery Expense | 20 | |
| | Cash Short & Over | 2 | |
| | Cash | | 82 |
| | *To replenish the petty cash fund.* | | |

Missing petty cash funds are debited to a new account, Cash Short & Over. In this case, $2 was missing, so we debit Cash Short & Over for the missing petty cash. Another way to look at this is that we needed another $2 debit to make the journal entry balance.

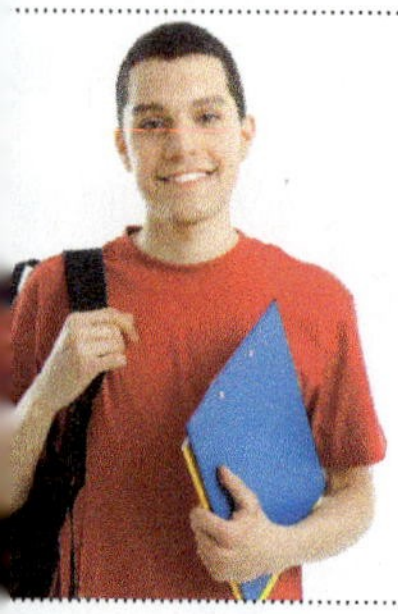

Why wasn't Petty Cash debited when the fund was replenished?

The Petty Cash account keeps its $200 balance at all times. **The Petty Cash account is used in a journal entry only when the fund is started (see the August 1 entry) or when its amount is increased or decreased.** If the business increases the fund amount from $200 to $250, this would require a check to be cashed for $50 and the debit would be to Petty Cash. **When replenishing the fund, the company debits either the associated expense incurred or the asset purchased with the funds.**

At times the sum of cash in the petty cash fund plus the tickets may exceed the fund balance. Consider the previous example. Assume the petty cash ticket #102 for delivery was for $30 instead of $20. Because we know the amount of the petty cash tickets and the amount of cash on hand, we can find out the amount of cash shortage or overage.

| | | |
|---|---|---|
| Fund balance | | $ 200 |
| Cash on hand | $ 118 | |
| Petty cash tickets | 90 | |
| Total accounted for | | 208 |
| Amount of cash overage | | $ 8 |

In this case, the cash on hand plus petty cash tickets ($208) is more than the fund balance ($200). A cash overage exists. The journal entry to replenish the fund would be:

| A↓ | | L | + | E↓ |
|---|---|---|---|---|
| Office Supplies↑ Cash↓ | = | | | Delivery Expense↑ Cash Short & Over↓ |

| Date | Accounts and Explanation | Debit | Credit |
|---|---|---|---|
| Aug. 31 | Office Supplies | 60 | |
| | Delivery Expense | 30 | |
| | Cash Short & Over | | 8 |
| | Cash | | 82 |
| | *To replenish the petty cash fund.* | | |

We know the total debits are $90 ($60 + $30). We know the check to replenish the fund was still $82 (credit to Cash) because the fund balance should total $200 and there was $118 in the petty cash box. For this situation, we need an $8 credit to make the journal entry balance, a gain, which is credited to Cash Short & Over.

## Changing the Amount of the Petty Cash Fund

Suppose that on September 1, Smart Touch Learning decides to increase the amount of the petty cash fund from $200 to $300. In order to increase the fund, Smart Touch Learning must write a check for the additional $100, cash the check, and place the additional currency in the petty cash box. Because the amount of the fund has changed, the company must record the following journal entry showing this change:

| Date | Accounts and Explanation | Debit | Credit |
|---|---|---|---|
| Sep. 1 | Petty Cash | 100 | |
| | Cash | | 100 |
| | *To increase the petty cash fund.* | | |

| A↑↓ | | L + E |
|---|---|---|
| Petty Cash↑<br>Cash↓ | = | |

*Had the Petty Cash fund been decreased, the debit would've been to Cash and the credit to the Petty Cash account. Remember that the only time the Petty Cash account is used in the journal entry is when the account is established, increased, or decreased.*

## Try It!

**8.** The following petty cash transactions of Green Golf Equipment occurred in May:

| | |
|---|---|
| May 1 | Established a petty cash fund with a $200 balance. |
| 31 | The petty cash fund has $18 in cash and $180 in petty cash tickets that were issued to pay for Office Supplies ($81), Delivery Expense ($36), Postage Expense ($54), and Miscellaneous Expense ($9). The petty cash custodian replenished the fund and recorded the expenses. |

Prepare the journal entries.

**Check your answers online in MyAccountingLab or at http://www.pearsonhighered.com/Horngren.**

For more practice, see Short Exercise S7-5. MyAccountingLab

## HOW CAN THE BANK ACCOUNT BE USED AS A CONTROL DEVICE?

**Learning Objective 5**
Demonstrate the use of a bank account as a control device and prepare a bank reconciliation and related journal entries

Cash is the most liquid asset reported on the balance sheet because it is the medium of exchange. Because cash is easy to conceal and relatively easy to steal, businesses keep their cash in a bank account. The bank has established practices for safeguarding the business's money. This section identifies the most common controls applied to a bank account.

**Signature Card**
A card that shows each authorized person's signature for a bank account.

**Deposit Ticket**
A bank form that is completed by the customer and shows the amount of each deposit.

**Check**
A document that instructs a bank to pay the designated person or business a specified amount of money.

**Maker**
The party who issues the check.

**Payee**
The individual or business to whom the check is paid.

## Signature Card

Banks require each person authorized to sign on an account to provide a **signature card**. This helps protect against forgery because the signature card should be checked frequently by bank personnel to authenticate written checks or deposits made by the business.

## Deposit Ticket

Banks supply standard forms such as a deposit ticket. Completed by the customer, the **deposit ticket** shows the amount of each deposit. As proof of the transaction, the customer receives a deposit receipt from the bank.

## Check

To pay cash, the depositor writes a **check**, which is a prenumbered document that tells the bank to pay the designated party a specified amount. Exhibit 7-5 shows a check drawn by Smart Touch Learning. There are three parties to a check: the maker, payee, and bank. The **maker** is the issuer of the check, in this case, Smart Touch Learning. The **payee** (California Office Products) is the individual or business to whom the check is paid.

**Exhibit 7-5** | **Check with Remittance Advice**

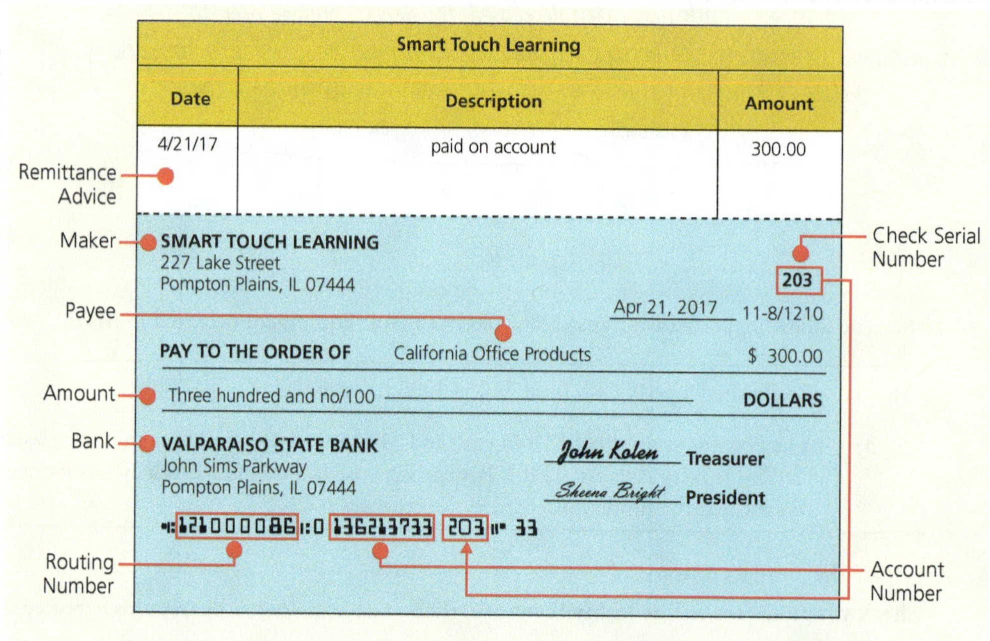


An easy way to remember the difference between the maker and the payee is the maker is the party who is *making* the promise that the cash is available in the bank to settle the check.

**Routing Number**
On a check, the 9-digit number that identifies the bank upon which the payment is drawn.

**Account Number**
On a check, the number that identifies the account upon which the payment is drawn.

This check has two parts, the check itself and the remittance advice. In addition, the check includes the routing number and account number. The **routing number** is a 9-digit number that identifies the bank upon which the payment is drawn. The **account number** identifies the account upon which the payment is drawn.

## Bank Statement

Banks send monthly statements to customers either electronically or in the mail. A **bank statement** reports the activity in the customer's account. The statement shows the account's beginning and ending balances, cash receipts, and cash payments. Included with the statement sometimes are physical or scanned copies of the maker's **canceled checks**, the checks written by the maker that have been cashed (paid) by the bank. Exhibit 7-6 is the April 30, 2017 bank statement of Smart Touch Learning.

**Bank Statement**
A document from the bank that reports the activity in the customer's account. It shows the bank account's beginning and ending balances and lists the month's cash transactions conducted through the bank account.

**Canceled Checks**
Physical or scanned copies of the maker's cashed (paid) checks.

**Exhibit 7-6 | Bank Statement**

BANK STATEMENT

VALPARAISO STATE BANK
JOHN SIMS PARKWAY; POMPTON PLAINS, IL

Smart Touch Learning
227 Lake Street
Pompton Plains, IL 07444

CHECKING ACCOUNT 136–213733
APRIL 30, 2017

| BEGINNING BALANCE | TOTAL DEPOSITS | TOTAL WITHDRAWALS | SERVICE CHARGES | ENDING BALANCE |
|---|---|---|---|---|
| $12,470 | 27,080 | 26,810 | 20 | $12,720 |

TRANSACTIONS

| DEPOSITS | DATE | AMOUNT |
|---|---|---|
| Deposit | 04/01 | 19,450 |
| Deposit | 04/10 | 5,500 |
| Deposit | 04/22 | 2,000 |
| EFT—Collection from customer | 04/27 | 100 |
| Interest | 04/30 | 30 |

| CHARGES | DATE | AMOUNT |
|---|---|---|
| Service Charge | 04/30 | 20 |

CHECKS

| Number | Amount | Number | Amount | Number | Amount |
|---|---|---|---|---|---|
| 202 | 3,200 | 203 | 300 | | |
| 201 | 20,000 | 205 | 150 | | |
| 200 | 1,920 | | | | |

| OTHER DEDUCTIONS | DATE | AMOUNT |
|---|---|---|
| EFT—Water Works | 04/20 | 40 |
| NSF | 04/25 | 1,200 |

## Electronic Funds Transfers

**Electronic funds transfer (EFT)** moves cash by electronic communication. Many bills and other payments, such as salaries, rent, utilities, and insurance, are now paid by EFT. It is much cheaper to pay these items by EFT without having to mail a check. Debit card transactions and direct deposits are also considered EFTs.

**Electronic Funds Transfer (EFT)**
A system that transfers cash by electronic communication rather than by paper documents.

## Bank Reconciliation

**Bank Reconciliation**
A document explaining the reasons for the difference between a depositor's cash records and the depositor's cash balance in its bank account.

The **bank reconciliation** compares and explains the differences between cash on the company's books and cash according to the bank's records on a specific date. There are two records of a business's cash:

1. The Cash account in the company's general ledger. April's Cash T-account for Smart Touch Learning is shown below.

**Cash**

| | | | |
|---|---|---|---|
| Beg. Bal. | 10,550 | 20,000 | Apr. 2 |
| Apr. 1 | 19,450 | 3,200 | Apr. 15 |
| Apr. 8 | 5,500 | 300 | Apr. 21 |
| Apr. 22 | 2,000 | 2,000 | Apr. 30 |
| Apr. 24 | 9,000 | 150 | Apr. 30 |
| End. Bal. | 20,850 | | |

2. The bank statement, which shows the cash receipts and payments transacted through the bank. In Exhibit 7-6, however, the bank shows an ending balance of $12,720 for Smart Touch Learning.

**Timing Difference**
Difference that arises between the balance on the bank statement and the balance on the company's books because of a time lag in recording transactions.

The books and the bank statement usually show different cash balances. Differences may arise because of a time lag in recording transactions, called **timing differences**. Three examples of timing differences follow:

- When a business writes a check, it immediately deducts the amount in its checkbook and Cash account. The bank, however, does not subtract the check from the company's account until the bank pays the check a few days later.
- When a company deposits cash in its account, it immediately adds the cash receipt to the checkbook and Cash account. The bank, however, may take a day or two to add deposits to the company's balance.
- EFT cash payments and EFT cash receipts are often recorded by the bank before a company learns of them.

To obtain accurate cash records, a company must update its Cash account after the company receives its bank statement. A bank reconciliation is used to carry out the updating process. The bank reconciliation explains all differences between the company's cash records and the bank's records of the company's balance. The person who prepares the bank reconciliation should have no other cash duties. This means the reconciler should not be a person who has access to cash or duties that require journalizing cash transactions. Otherwise, he or she could steal cash and manipulate the reconciliation to conceal the theft.

### Preparing the Bank Side of the Bank Reconciliation

Here are the items that appear on the bank side of the bank reconciliation. They all cause differences between the bank balance and the book balance.

The bank side contains items not yet recorded by the bank but recorded by the company or errors made by the bank. These items include the following:

**Deposit in Transit**
A deposit recorded by the company but not yet by its bank.

**Outstanding Check**
A check issued by a company and recorded on its books but not yet paid by its bank.

**Deposits in Transit (Outstanding Deposits)** A **deposit in transit** has been recorded and has already been added to the company's book balance, but the bank has not yet recorded it. These are shown as "Add: Deposits in transit" on the bank side because when the bank does record these deposits, it will increase the bank balance.

**Outstanding Checks** An **outstanding check** is a check that has been recorded and has already been deducted from the company's book balance, but the bank has not yet paid (deducted) it. Such checks are shown as "Less: Outstanding checks" on the bank side because when the bank does make payment for the checks, it will decrease the bank balance.

**Bank Errors** Bank errors are posting errors made by the bank that either incorrectly increase or decrease the bank balance. All bank errors are corrected on the bank side of the reconciliation by reversing the effect of the errors.

*Errors are always recorded on the side of the reconciliation of the party that made the error. If the bank made the error, it is recorded on the bank side. If the business made the error, it is recorded on the book side.*

## Preparing the Book Side of the Bank Reconciliation

The book side contains items not yet recorded by the company on its books but that have been recorded by the bank or errors made by the company. Items to show on the book side include the following:

**Bank Collections** Bank collections are cash receipts the bank has received and recorded for a company's account but that the company has not recorded yet on its books. An example of a bank collection would occur when a business has its customers use a lock-box system. Another example is a bank collecting on a note receivable for a business. A bank collection is often referred to as a credit memorandum. A **credit memorandum** indicates that the customer's account has been increased. A bank collection (which increases the bank balance) that appears on the bank statement will show as "Add: Bank collections" on the book side of the reconciliation because it represents cash receipts not yet recorded by the company.

**Credit Memorandum**
An increase in a bank account.

**Electronic Funds Transfers** The bank may receive or pay cash on a company's behalf. An EFT may be a cash receipt or a cash payment. These will either show up on the book side of the reconciliation as "Add: EFT" for receipts not yet added to the company's books or "Less: EFT" for payments not yet deducted on the company's books.

**Service Charge** This cash payment is the bank's fee for processing a company's transactions. Service charges can also include the cost of printed checks and other bank fees such as ATM fees. A service charge is often referred to as a **debit memorandum** and represents a decrease in the bank account. This will show as "Less: Service charges" on the book side of the reconciliation because it represents a cash payment not yet subtracted from the company's cash balance.

**Debit Memorandum**
A decrease in a bank account.

**Interest Revenue on a Checking Account** A business will sometimes earn interest if it keeps enough cash in its account. The bank statement tells the company of this cash receipt. This will show as "Add: Interest revenue" on the book side of the reconciliation because it represents cash receipts not yet added in the company's cash balance.

**Nonsufficient Funds (NSF) Checks** **Nonsufficient funds (NSF) checks** represent checks received from customers for payment of services rendered or merchandise sold that have turned out to be worthless. NSF checks (sometimes called *hot checks* or *bad checks*) are treated as subtractions on a company's bank reconciliation. NSF checks are customer checks the company has received and deposited for which the customer doesn't have enough money in his or her bank account to cover. NSF checks will show as "Less: NSF checks" on the book side of the reconciliation, as the company previously recorded this receipt as an increase in cash, which now has to be deducted as the funds were not actually received.

**Nonsufficient Funds (NSF) Check**
A check for which the maker's bank account has insufficient money to pay the check.

**Book Errors** Book errors are errors made on the books of the company that either incorrectly increase or decrease the cash balance in the company's general ledger. All book errors are corrected on the book side of the reconciliation by reversing the effect of the errors.

## Completing the Bank Reconciliation

The bank statement in Exhibit 7-6 shows that the April 30 bank balance of Smart Touch Learning is $12,720 (upper-right corner). However, the company's Cash account has a balance of $20,850. This situation calls for a bank reconciliation to explain the difference. In completing the bank reconciliation, Smart Touch Learning will review the bank statement and the business's Cash account to determine the timing differences. Exhibit 7-7, Panel A, lists the reconciling items for your easy reference, and Panel B shows the completed reconciliation.

**Exhibit 7-7 | Bank Reconciliation**

**PANEL A—Reconciling Items**

**Bank side:**

**1.** Deposit in transit, Apr. 24, $9,000.
**2.** Outstanding check no. 204, $2,000.

**Book side:**

**3.** EFT receipt from customer, $100.
**4.** Interest revenue earned on bank balance, $30.
**5.** Bank service charge, $20.
**6.** EFT payment of water bill, $40.
**7.** NSF check, $1,200.

**PANEL B—Bank Reconciliation**

**SMART TOUCH LEARNING**
Bank Reconciliation
April 30, 2017

| BANK | | BOOK | | |
|---|---|---|---|---|
| Balance, April 30, 2017 | $ 12,720 | Balance, April 30, 2017 | | $ 20,850 |
| ADD: | | ADD: | | |
| 1. Deposit in transit | 9,000 | 3. EFT receipt from customer | $ 100 | |
| | 21,720 | 4. Interest revenue earned on bank balance | 30 | 130 |
| | | | | 20,980 |
| LESS: | | LESS: | | |
| | | 5. Service charge | 20 | |
| 2. Outstanding checks | | 6. EFT payment of water bill | 40 | |
| No. 204 | 2,000 | 7. NSF check | 1,200 | 1,260 |
| Adjusted bank balance, April 30, 2017 | **$ 19,720** | Adjusted book balance, April 30, 2017 | | **$ 19,720** |

*These amounts must agree.*

**SUMMARY OF THE VARIOUS RECONCILING ITEMS:**

**BANK BALANCE—ALWAYS**

- *Add* deposits in transit.
- *Subtract* outstanding checks.
- *Add* or *subtract* corrections of bank errors.

**BOOK BALANCE—ALWAYS**

- *Add* bank collections, interest revenue, and EFT receipts.
- *Subtract* service charges, NSF checks, and EFT payments.
- *Add* or *subtract* corrections of book errors.

## Examining a Bank Reconciliation

Let's go through each side of the bank reconciliation for Smart Touch Learning.

### Bank Side of the Reconciliation

Smart Touch Learning begins by recording the bank balance as of April 30, 2017, which is taken from the bank statement, $12,720. The business then identifies any additions or subtractions affecting the bank balance:

1. **Deposit in transit.** Smart Touch Learning reviews the bank statement and the Cash account to determine whether any cash deposits made by the business have not yet been recorded by the bank. Smart Touch Learning identifies that the deposit made on April 24 for $9,000 has not yet been recorded by the bank. This amount is added to the bank balance.
2. **Outstanding check.** The business reviews the canceled checks included with the statement to determine whether any checks written by the business have not yet cleared the bank. Smart Touch Learning identifies check number 204 for $2,000 as outstanding. This amount is subtracted from the bank balance.

After all items affecting the bank side have been identified, the adjusted bank balance is determined.

### Book Side of the Reconciliation

The book side of the reconciliation begins by Smart Touch Learning listing the Cash account balance as of April 30, 2017. This amount—$20,850—is found in the general ledger. Next, Smart Touch Learning reviews the Cash account and bank statement for items that affect the company's Cash account balance but are not recorded by the company:

3. **Electronic funds transfer (EFT).** In reviewing the bank statement, Smart Touch Learning identifies an EFT receipt from a customer in the amount of $100. The company has not recorded this receipt in the Cash account; therefore, it will need to be added to the book balance.
4. **Interest revenue.** Smart Touch Learning identifies a $30 deposit on the bank statement for interest earned that has not yet been recorded in the Cash account. This deposit will be added to the book balance.
5. **Service charge.** The bank statement shows a $20 service charge. Smart Touch Learning has not recorded this charge in the company's Cash account and will, therefore, need to subtract this amount from the book balance.
6. **Electronic funds transfer (EFT).** Listed in the other deductions section on the bank statement, Smart Touch Learning identifies an EFT payment to Water Works for $40. This payment has not been recorded in the company's Cash account. Smart Touch Learning will subtract this amount from the book balance.
7. **Nonsufficient funds (NSF) check.** Smart Touch Learning identifies an NSF check from a customer on the bank statement. The company had recorded the receipt of this check as an increase to cash originally. The bank has now communicated that the customer's check did not clear and that the customer's payment was never deposited into the business's account. Smart Touch Learning must subtract this amount from the book balance.

After recording all of the items that affect the book balance, Smart Touch Learning determines the adjusted book balance and verifies that it equals the adjusted bank balance. This amount represents the correct cash balance as of April 30, 2017.

## Journalizing Transactions from the Bank Reconciliation

The bank reconciliation is an accountant's tool separate from the journals and ledgers. It does *not* account for transactions in the journal. To get the transactions into the accounts, we must make journal entries and post to the ledger. All items on the book side of the bank reconciliation require journal entries. We make no journal entries from the items on the bank side because we have already recorded these items in the business's Cash account.

The bank reconciliation in Exhibit 7-7 requires Smart Touch Learning to make journal entries to bring the Cash account up to date. Numbers in the journal entries correspond to the reconciling items listed in Exhibit 7-7, Panel A, and to the book side of the reconciliation in Panel B. Note that we chose to list each item in a separate journal entry here, but one compound entry could be made instead of the five separate entries illustrated.

| A↑↓ | = | L | + | E |
|---|---|---|---|---|
| Cash↑<br>Accounts Receivable↓ | | | | |

| A↑ | = | L | + | E↑ |
|---|---|---|---|---|
| Cash↑ | | | | Interest Revenue↑ |

| A↓ | = | L | + | E↓ |
|---|---|---|---|---|
| Cash↓ | | | | Bank Expense↑ |

| A↓ | = | L | + | E↓ |
|---|---|---|---|---|
| Cash↓ | | | | Utilities Expense↑ |

| A↑↓ | = | L | + | E |
|---|---|---|---|---|
| Accounts Receivable↑<br>Cash↓ | | | | |

| Date | Accounts and Explanation | Debit | Credit |
|---|---|---|---|
| 3: Apr. 30 | Cash | 100 | |
| | Accounts Receivable | | 100 |
| | *To record account receivable collected by bank.* | | |
| 4: 30 | Cash | 30 | |
| | Interest Revenue | | 30 |
| | *To record interest earned on bank balance.* | | |
| 5: 30 | Bank Expense | 20 | |
| | Cash | | 20 |
| | *To record bank service charges incurred.* | | |
| 6: 30 | Utilities Expense | 40 | |
| | Cash | | 40 |
| | *To record payment of water bill by EFT.* | | |
| 7: 30 | Accounts Receivable | 1,200 | |
| | Cash | | 1,200 |
| | *NSF check returned by bank.* | | |

**Cash**

| | | | |
|---|---|---|---|
| Beg. Bal. | 10,550 | 20,000 | Apr. 2 |
| Apr. 1 | 19,450 | 3,200 | Apr. 15 |
| Apr. 8 | 5,500 | 300 | Apr. 21 |
| Apr. 22 | 2,000 | 2,000 | Apr. 30 |
| Apr. 24 | 9,000 | 150 | Apr. 30 |
| Bal. | 20,850 | | |
| Apr. 30 | 100 | 20 | Apr. 30 |
| Apr. 30 | 30 | 40 | Apr. 30 |
| | | 1,200 | Apr. 30 |
| End. Bal. | 19,720 | | |

## Try It!

For each of the following items, determine whether the item would be:

**a.** added to the bank balance
**b.** subtracted from the bank balance
**c.** added to the book balance
**d.** subtracted from the book balance

**9.** Interest revenue earned
**10.** NSF check
**11.** Deposit in transit
**12.** Service charge
**13.** Outstanding check

**Check your answers online in MyAccountingLab or at http://www.pearsonhighered.com/Horngren.**

For more practice, see Short Exercises S7-6 through S7-9. MyAccountingLab

# HOW CAN THE CASH RATIO BE USED TO EVALUATE BUSINESS PERFORMANCE?

**Learning Objective 6**
Use the cash ratio to evaluate business performance

Cash is an important part of every business. Without an adequate supply of available cash, businesses cannot continue to operate. Businesses, therefore, monitor cash very carefully. One measure that can be used to measure a company's liquidity is the cash ratio. The **cash ratio** helps to determine a company's ability to meet its short-term obligations. It is calculated as follows:

Cash ratio = (Cash + Cash equivalents) / Total current liabilities

**Cash Ratio**
A measure of a company's ability to pay current liabilities from cash and cash equivalents: (Cash + Cash equivalents) / Total current liabilities.

**Cash Equivalent**
A highly liquid investment that can be converted into cash in three months or less.

Notice that the cash ratio includes cash and cash equivalents. **Cash equivalents** are highly liquid investments that can be converted into cash in three months or less. Examples of cash equivalents are money-market accounts and investments in U.S. government securities.

Returning to **Green Mountain Coffee Roasters, Inc.**, let's evaluate the company's liquidity using the cash ratio. Green Mountain's cash and cash equivalents and total current liabilities can be found on the balance sheet located in Appendix A and are presented below (shown in thousands):

| | September 28, 2013 | September 29, 2012 |
|---|---|---|
| Cash and cash equivalents | $ 260,092 | $ 58,289 |
| Total current liabilities | 597,063 | 519,987 |

Green Mountain's cash ratio as of September 28, 2013, follows:

Cash ratio = $260,092 / $597,063 = 0.44*

* rounded

In comparison, the cash ratio as of September 29, 2012, was:

Cash ratio = $58,289 / $519,987 = 0.11

The cash ratio has quadrupled from 2012 to 2013 due to an increase in available cash and cash equivalents. This ratio is the most conservative valuation of liquidity because it looks at only cash and cash equivalents, leaving out other current assets such as merchandise inventory and accounts receivable. Notice that for both years the cash ratio was below 1.0. Having a cash ratio below 1.0 is a good thing. A cash ratio above 1.0 might signify that the company has an unnecessarily large amount of cash supply. This cash could be used to generate higher profits or be paid out for dividends. However, a very low ratio doesn't send a strong message to investors and creditors that the company has the ability to repay its short-term debt.

## Try It!

14. The Scott Sun & Shade Company had the following financial data at December 31, 2016:

| | |
|---|---|
| Cash and cash equivalents | $ 60,000 |
| Total current liabilities | 75,000 |

What is the cash ratio as of December 31, 2016, for Scott Sun & Shade?

**Check your answer online in MyAccountingLab or at http://www.pearsonhighered.com/Horngren.**

For more practice, see Short Exercise S7-10. MyAccountingLab

# REVIEW

## > Things You Should Know

### 1. What is internal control, and how can it be used to protect a company's assets?

- Internal control is the organizational plan and all the related measures designed to safeguard assets, encourage employees to follow company policies, promote operational efficiency, and ensure accurate and reliable accounting records.
- The Sarbanes-Oxley Act was passed by Congress to revamp corporate governance in the United States.
- Internal control includes five components: control procedures, risk assessment, information system, monitoring of controls, and environment.

**2. What are the internal control procedures with respect to cash receipts?**

- A point-of-sale terminal provides control over cash receipts over the counter.
- Companies control cash by mail by ensuring appropriate separation of duties when handling cash and recording the transaction.

**3. What are the internal control procedures with respect to cash payments?**

- Good separation of duties between operations of the business and writing checks for cash payments should exist.
- Many companies use technology to make secure payments.

**4. How can a petty cash fund be used for internal control purposes?**

- A petty cash fund allows a business to keep cash on hand to pay for small miscellaneous items such as postage, office supplies, and taxi fares.
- When the petty cash fund is established, the company records a debit to Petty Cash and a credit to Cash.
- The petty cash fund is replenished by debiting the associated asset and expense accounts and crediting Cash.
- Discrepancies in petty cash funds are either debited or credited to the Cash Short & Over account.

**5. How can the bank account be used as a control device?**

- Bank accounts provide established practices that safeguard a business's money. These controls include use of signature cards, deposit tickets, checks, bank statements, and electronic funds transfers.
- A bank reconciliation can also be used as a form of internal control. The bank reconciliation compares and explains the difference between cash on the company's books and cash according to the bank's records on a specific date.
- After the bank reconciliation has been prepared, journal entries must be completed for all items on the book side of the bank reconciliation.

**6. How can the cash ratio be used to evaluate business performance?**

- The cash ratio measures a company's ability to pay its current liabilities from cash and cash equivalents.
- Cash ratio = (Cash + Cash equivalents) / Total current liabilities.

## > Summary Problem 7-1

Misler Corporation established a $300 petty cash fund on January 12, 2016. Karen Misler (KM) is the fund custodian. At the end of the month, the petty cash fund contains the following:

a. Cash: $163

b. Petty cash tickets, as follows:

| No. | Amount | Issued to | Signed by | Account Debited |
|---|---|---|---|---|
| 44 | $ 14 | B. Jarvis | B. Jarvis and KM | Office Supplies |
| 45 | 39 | S. Bell | S. Bell | Delivery Expense |
| 47 | 43 | R. Tate | R. Tate and KM | — |
| 48 | 33 | L. Blair | L. Blair and KM | Travel Expense |

### Requirements

1. Identify three internal control weaknesses revealed in the given data.
2. Journalize the following transactions:
   a. Establishment of the petty cash fund on January 12, 2016.
   b. Replenishment of the fund on January 31, 2016. Assume petty cash ticket no. 47 was issued for the purchase of office supplies.
3. What is the balance in the Petty Cash account immediately before replenishment? Immediately after replenishment?

## > Solution

### Requirement 1

The three internal control weaknesses are as follows:

1. Petty cash ticket no. 46 is missing. There is no indication of what happened to this ticket. The company should investigate.
2. The petty cash custodian (KM) did not sign petty cash ticket no. 45. This omission may have been an oversight on her part. However, it raises the question of whether she authorized the payment. Both the fund custodian and the recipient of the cash should sign the petty cash ticket.
3. Petty cash ticket no. 47 does not indicate which account to debit on the actual ticket. If Tate or Karen Misler do not remember where the $43 went, then the accountant will not know what account should be debited.

### Requirement 2

Petty cash journal entries:

a. Entry to establish the petty cash fund:

| Date | Accounts and Explanation | Debit | Credit |
|---|---|---|---|
| Jan. 12 | Petty Cash | 300 | |
| | Cash | | 300 |
| | *To open the petty cash fund.* | | |

CHAPTER 7

**b.** Entry to replenish the fund:

| Date | Accounts and Explanation | Debit | Credit |
|---|---|---|---|
| Jan. 31 | Office Supplies | 57 | |
| | Delivery Expense | 39 | |
| | Travel Expense | 33 | |
| | Cash Short & Over | 8 | |
| | Cash | | 137 |
| | *To replenish the petty cash fund.* | | |

**Requirement 3**

The balance in the Petty Cash account is *always* its impres balance, in this case $300.

## > Summary Problem 7-2

The Cash account of Baylor Associates at February 28, 2017, follows:

| | Cash | | |
|---|---|---|---|
| Beg. Bal. | 3,995 | 400 | Feb. 3 |
| Feb. 6 | 800 | 3,100 | Feb. 12 |
| Feb. 15 | 1,800 | 1,100 | Feb. 19 |
| Feb. 23 | 1,100 | 500 | Feb. 25 |
| Feb. 28 | 2,400 | 900 | Feb. 27 |
| End. Bal. | 4,095 | | |

Baylor Associates received the following bank statement on February 28, 2017:

**BANK STATEMENT**

**BANK OF TOMORROW**
123 PETER PAN RD, KISSIMMEE, FL 34747

Baylor Associates
14 W Gadsden St
Pensacola, FL 32501

CHECKING ACCOUNT 136–213734

FEBRUARY 28, 2017

| BEGINNING BALANCE | TOTAL DEPOSITS | TOTAL WITHDRAWALS | SERVICE CHARGES | ENDING BALANCE |
|---|---|---|---|---|
| $3,995 | 4,715 | 5,630 | 10 | $3,070 |

**TRANSACTIONS**

| DEPOSITS | DATE | AMOUNT |
|---|---|---|
| Deposit | 02/07 | 800 |
| Deposit | 02/15 | 1,800 |
| EFT—Collection of note | 02/17 | 1,000 |
| Deposit | 02/24 | 1,100 |
| Interest | 02/28 | 15 |

| CHARGES | DATE | AMOUNT |
|---|---|---|
| Service Charge | 02/28 | 10 |

**CHECKS**

| Number | Amount | Number | Amount | Number | Amount |
|---|---|---|---|---|---|
| 102 | 400 | 103 | 1,100 | | |
| 101 | 3,100 | | | | |

| OTHER DEDUCTIONS | DATE | AMOUNT |
|---|---|---|
| EFT—EZ Rent | 02/01 | 330 |
| NSF Check | 02/13 | 700 |

Additional data:

Baylor deposits all cash receipts in the bank and makes all payments by check.

**Requirements**

1. Prepare the bank reconciliation of Baylor Associates at February 28, 2017.
2. Journalize the entries based on the bank reconciliation.

## > Solution

**Requirement 1**

| BAYLOR ASSOCIATES<br>Bank Reconciliation<br>February 28, 2017 | | |
|---|---|---|
| **Bank:** | | |
| Balance, February 28, 2017 | | $ 3,070 |
| Add: Deposit of February 28 in transit | | 2,400 |
| | | 5,470 |
| Less: Outstanding checks issued on February 25 ($500) | | |
| and February 27 ($900) | | 1,400 |
| Adjusted bank balance, February 28, 2017 | | **$ 4,070** |
| **Books:** | | |
| Balance, February 28, 2017 | | $ 4,095 |
| Add: Bank collection of note receivable | $ 1,000 | |
| Interest revenue earned on bank balance | 15 | 1,015 |
| | | 5,110 |
| Less: Service charge | 10 | |
| NSF check | 700 | |
| EFT—Rent expense | 330 | 1,040 |
| Adjusted book balance, February 28, 2017 | | **$ 4,070** |

***Must be equal.***

**Requirement 2**

| Date | Accounts and Explanation | Debit | Credit |
|---|---|---|---|
| Feb. 28 | Cash | 1,000 | |
| | Notes Receivable | | 1,000 |
| | *Note receivable collected by bank.* | | |
| 28 | Cash | 15 | |
| | Interest Revenue | | 15 |
| | *Interest earned on bank balance.* | | |
| 28 | Bank Expense | 10 | |
| | Cash | | 10 |
| | *Bank service charge.* | | |
| 28 | Accounts Receivable | 700 | |
| | Cash | | 700 |
| | *NSF check returned by bank.* | | |
| 28 | Rent Expense | 330 | |
| | Cash | | 330 |
| | *Monthly rent expense.* | | |

## > Key Terms

**Account Number (p. 388)**
**Bank Reconciliation (p. 390)**
**Bank Statement (p. 389)**
**Canceled Checks (p. 389)**
**Cash Equivalent (p. 395)**
**Cash Ratio (p. 395)**
**Check (p. 388)**
**Collusion (p. 379)**
**Credit Memorandum (p. 391)**
**Debit Memorandum (p. 391)**
**Deposit in Transit (p. 390)**
**Deposit Ticket (p. 388)**
**Electronic Data Interchange (EDI) (p. 384)**
**Electronic Funds Transfer (EFT) (p. 389)**
**Encryption (p. 378)**
**Evaluated Receipts Settlement (ERS) (p. 384)**
**External Auditor (p. 377)**
**Firewall (p. 378)**
**Imprest System (p. 385)**
**Internal Auditor (p. 377)**
**Internal Control (p. 375)**
**Internal Control Report (p. 376)**
**Lock-Box System (p. 381)**
**Maker (p. 388)**
**Nonsufficient Funds (NSF) Check (p. 391)**
**Outstanding Check (p. 390)**
**Payee (p. 388)**
**Petty Cash (p. 384)**
**Public Company (p. 375)**
**Remittance Advice (p. 381)**
**Routing Number (p. 388)**
**Sarbanes-Oxley Act (SOX) (p. 375)**
**Separation of Duties (p. 378)**
**Signature Card (p. 388)**
**Timing Difference (p. 390)**

## > Quick Check

1. Which of the following is *not* part of the definition of internal control? **Learning Objective 1**

   a. Separation of duties
   b. Safeguard assets
   c. Encourage employees to follow company policies
   d. Promote operational efficiency

2. The Sarbanes-Oxley Act **Learning Objective 1**

   a. created the Private Company Accounting Board.
   b. allows accountants to audit and to perform any type of consulting work for a public company.
   c. stipulates that violators of the act may serve 20 years in prison for securities fraud.
   d. requires that an outside auditor must evaluate a public company's internal controls.

3. Encryption **Learning Objective 1**

   a. avoids the need for separation of duties.
   b. creates firewalls to protect data.
   c. cannot be broken by hackers.
   d. rearranges messages by a special process.

4. Separation of duties is important for internal control of **Learning Objective 1**

   a. cash receipts.
   b. cash payments.
   c. Neither of the above
   d. Both a and b

5. Michelle Darby receives cash from customers. Her other assigned job is to post the collections to customer accounts receivable. Her company has weak **Learning Objective 2**

   a. assignment of responsibilities.
   b. ethics.
   c. computer controls.
   d. separation of duties.

6. Payment by check is an important internal control over cash payments because **Learning Objective 3**

   a. the check must be signed by an authorized official.
   b. before signing the check, the official reviews the invoice supporting the payment.
   c. Both a and b
   d. None of the above

7. The petty cash fund had an initial imprest balance of $100. It currently has $20 and petty cash tickets totaling $75 for office supplies. The entry to replenish the fund would contain **Learning Objective 4**

   a. a credit to Cash Short & Over for $5.
   b. a credit to Petty Cash for $80.
   c. a debit to Cash Short & Over for $5.
   d. a debit to Petty Cash for $80.

8. The document that explains all the differences between the company's cash records and the bank's figures is called a(n) **Learning Objective 5**

   a. bank collection.
   b. electronic fund transfer.
   c. bank statement.
   d. bank reconciliation.

**Learning Objective 5**

9. Sahara Company's Cash account shows an ending balance of $650. The bank statement shows a $29 service charge and an NSF check for $150. A $240 deposit is in transit, and outstanding checks total $420. What is Sahara's adjusted cash balance?
   a. $291
   b. $829
   c. $471
   d. $470

**Learning Objective 6**

10. Espinoza Air Conditioning & Heating had the following select financial data as of June 30, 2016.

| | |
|---|---|
| Cash | $ 10,000 |
| Cash Equivalents | 8,850 |
| Accounts Receivable | 3,700 |
| Total current liabilities | 29,000 |

What is Espinoza's cash ratio?

a. 0.34  b. 0.65  c. 0.78  d. 1.54

**Check your answers at the end of the chapter.**

# ASSESS YOUR PROGRESS

## > Review Questions

1. What is internal control?
2. How does the Sarbanes-Oxley Act relate to internal controls?
3. What are the five components of internal control? Briefly explain each component.
4. What is the difference between an internal auditor and external auditor?
5. What is separation of duties?
6. List internal control procedures related to e-commerce.
7. What are some limitations of internal controls?
8. How do businesses control cash receipts over the counter?
9. How do businesses control cash receipts by mail?
10. What are the steps taken to ensure control over purchases and payments by check?
11. What are the controls needed to secure the petty cash fund?
12. When are the only times the Petty Cash account is used in a journal entry?
13. What are some common controls used with a bank account?
14. What is a bank reconciliation?
15. List some examples of timing differences, and for each difference, determine if it would affect the book side of the reconciliation or the bank side of the reconciliation.
16. Why is it necessary to record journal entries after the bank reconciliation has been prepared? Which side of the bank reconciliation requires journal entries?
17. What does the cash ratio help determine, and how is it calculated?

## > Short Exercises

### S7-1 Defining internal control

Learning Objective 1

Internal controls are designed to safeguard assets, encourage employees to follow company policies, promote operational efficiency, and ensure accurate accounting records.

**Requirements**

1. Which objective do you think is most important?
2. Which objective do you think the internal controls must accomplish for the business to survive? Give your reason.

### S7-2 Applying internal control over cash receipts

Learning Objective 2

Sandra Kristof sells furniture for McKinney Furniture Company. Kristof is having financial problems and takes $650 that she received from a customer. She rang up the sale through the cash register. What will alert Megan McKinney, the controller, that something is wrong?

### S7-3 Applying internal control over cash receipts by mail

Learning Objective 2

Review the internal controls over cash receipts by mail presented in the chapter. Exactly what is accomplished by the final step in the process, performed by the controller?

### S7-4 Applying internal control over cash payments by check

Learning Objective 3

A purchasing agent for Franklin Office Supplies receives the goods that he purchases and also approves payment for the goods.

**Requirements**

1. How could this purchasing agent cheat his company?
2. How could Franklin avoid this internal control weakness?

### S7-5 Journalizing petty cash

Learning Objective 4

Prepare the journal entries for the following petty cash transactions of Pawnee Gaming Supplies:

| | |
|---|---|
| Mar. 1 | Established a petty cash fund with a $200 balance. |
| 31 | The petty cash fund has $19 in cash and $188 in petty cash tickets that were issued to pay for Office Supplies ($68) and Entertainment Expense ($120). Replenished the fund and recorded the expenditures. |
| Apr. 15 | Increased the balance of the petty cash fund to $250. |

### S7-6 Understanding bank account controls

Learning Objective 5

Answer the following questions about the controls in bank accounts:

**Requirements**

1. Which bank control protects against forgery?
2. Which bank control reports the activity in the customer's account each period?
3. Which bank control confirms the amount of money put into the bank account?

Learning Objective 5

### S7-7 Identifying timing differences related to a bank reconciliation

For each timing difference listed, identify whether the difference would be reported on the book side of the reconciliation or the bank side of the reconciliation. In addition, identify whether the difference would be an addition or subtraction.

a. Deposit in transit
b. Bank collection
c. Debit memorandum
d. EFT cash receipt
e. Outstanding checks
f. $1,000 deposit erroneously recorded by the bank as $100
g. Service charges
h. Interest revenue
i. $2,500 cash payment for rent expense erroneously recorded by the business as $250
j. Credit memorandum

Learning Objective 5

### S7-8 Preparing a bank reconciliation

The Cash account of Safety Security Systems reported a balance of $2,450 at December 31, 2016. There were outstanding checks totaling $1,700 and a December 31 deposit in transit of $300. The bank statement, which came from Park Cities Bank, listed the December 31 balance of $4,460. Included in the bank balance was a collection of $620 on account from Brendan Ballou, a Safety customer who pays the bank directly. The bank statement also shows a $20 service charge and $10 of interest revenue that Safety earned on its bank balance. Prepare Safety's bank reconciliation at December 31.

***Note: Short Exercise S7-8 must be completed before attempting Short Exercise S7-9.***

Learning Objective 5

### S7-9 Recording transactions from a bank reconciliation

Review your results from preparing Safety Security Systems's bank reconciliation in Short Exercise S7-8. Journalize the company's transactions that arise from the bank reconciliation. Include an explanation with each entry.

Learning Objective 6

### S7-10 Computing the cash ratio

Beautiful Banners reported the following figures in its financial statements:

| | |
|---|---|
| Cash | $ 30,800 |
| Cash Equivalents | 2,000 |
| Total Current Liabilities | 26,240 |

Compute the cash ratio for Beautiful Banners.

## > Exercises

Learning Objective 1

### E7-11 Understanding Sarbanes-Oxley and identifying internal control strengths and weaknesses

The following situations suggest a strength or a weakness in internal control.

a. Top managers delegate all internal control procedures to the accounting department.
b. Accounting department staff (or the bookkeeper) orders merchandise and approves invoices for payment.

c. Cash received over the counter is controlled by the sales clerk, who rings up the sale and places the cash in the register. The sales clerk matches the total recorded by the register to each day's cash sales.

d. The employee who signs checks need not examine the payment packet because he is confident the amounts are correct.

**Requirements**

1. Define *internal control.*
2. The system of internal control must be tested by external auditors. What law or rule requires this testing?
3. Identify each item in the list above as either a strength or a weakness in internal control, and give your reason for each answer.

## E7-12 Identifying internal controls

**Learning Objective 1**

Consider each situation separately. Identify the missing internal control procedure from these characteristics:

- Assignment of responsibilities
- Separation of duties
- Audits
- Electronic devices
- Other controls (specify)

a. While reviewing the records of Quality Pharmacy, you find that the same employee orders merchandise and approves invoices for payment.

b. Business is slow at Amazing Amusement Park on Tuesday, Wednesday, and Thursday nights. To reduce expenses, the business decides not to use a ticket taker on those nights. The ticket seller (cashier) is told to keep the tickets as a record of the number sold.

c. The same trusted employee has served as cashier for 12 years.

d. When business is brisk, Fast Mart deposits cash in the bank several times during the day. The manager at one store wants to reduce the time employees spend delivering cash to the bank, so he starts a new policy. Cash will build up over weekends, and the total will be deposited on Monday.

e. Grocery stores such as Convenience Market and Natural Foods purchase most merchandise from a few suppliers. At another grocery store, the manager decides to reduce paperwork. He eliminates the requirement that the receiving department prepare a receiving report listing the goods actually received from the supplier.

## E7-13 Evaluating internal control over cash receipts

**Learning Objective 2**

Dogtopia sells pet supplies and food and handles all sales with a cash register. The cash register displays the amount of the sale. It also shows the cash received and any change returned to the customer. The register also produces a customer receipt but keeps no internal record of the transactions. At the end of the day, the clerk counts the cash in the register and gives it to the cashier for deposit in the company bank account.

**Requirements**

1. Identify the internal control weakness over cash receipts.
2. What could you do to correct the weakness?

**Learning Objective 3**

## E7-14 Evaluating internal control over cash payments

Gary's Great Cars purchases high-performance auto parts from a Nebraska vendor. Dave Simon, the accountant for Gary's, verifies receipt of merchandise and then prepares, signs, and mails the check to the vendor.

### Requirements

1. Identify the internal control weakness over cash payments.
2. What could the business do to correct the weakness?

**Learning Objectives 1, 2, 3**

## E7-15 Understanding internal control, components, procedures, and laws

Match the following terms with their definitions.

| | |
|---|---|
| **1.** Internal control | **a.** Two or more people working together to overcome internal controls. |
| **2.** Control procedures | **b.** Part of internal control that ensures resources are not wasted. |
| **3.** Firewalls | **c.** Requires companies to review internal control and take responsibility for the accuracy and completeness of their financial reports. |
| **4.** Encryption | **d.** Should be prenumbered to prevent theft and inefficiency. |
| **5.** Environment | **e.** Limits access to a local network. |
| **6.** Information system | **f.** Example: The person who opens the bank statement should not also be the person who is reconciling cash. |
| **7.** Separation of duties | **g.** Identification of uncertainties that may arise due to a company's products, services, or operations. |
| **8.** Collusion | **h.** Examination of a company's financial statements and accounting system by a trained accounting professional. |
| **9.** Documents | **i.** Without a sufficient one of these, information cannot properly be gathered and summarized. |
| **10.** Audits | **j.** The organizational plan and all the related measures that safeguard assets, encourage employees to follow company policies, promote operational efficiency, and ensure accurate and reliable accounting data. |
| **11.** Operational efficiency | **k.** Component of internal control that helps ensure business goals are achieved. |
| **12.** Risk assessment | **l.** Rearranges data by a mathematical process. |
| **13.** Sarbanes-Oxley Act | **m.** To establish an effective one, a company's CEO and top managers must behave honorably to set a good example for employees. |

### E7-16 Accounting for petty cash

Learning Objective 4

2. Cash Short & Over $12

Joy's Dance Studio created a $270 imprest petty cash fund. During the month, the fund custodian authorized and signed petty cash tickets as follows:

| Petty Cash Ticket No. | Item | Account Debited | Amount |
|---|---|---|---|
| 1 | Delivery of programs to customers | Delivery Expense | $ 15 |
| 2 | Mail package | Postage Expense | 10 |
| 3 | Newsletter | Printing Expense | 35 |
| 4 | Key to closet | Miscellaneous Expense | 45 |
| 5 | Copier paper | Office Supplies | 70 |

**Requirements**

1. Make the general journal entry to create the petty cash fund. Include an explanation.
2. Make the general journal entry to record the petty cash fund replenishment. Cash in the fund totals $83. Include an explanation.
3. Assume that Joy's Dance Studio decides to decrease the petty cash fund to $130. Make the general journal entry to record this decrease.

### E7-17 Controlling petty cash

Learning Objective 4

2. March 31, Cash CR $226

Jazzy Night Club maintains an imprest petty cash fund of $250, which is under the control of Sandra Morgan. At March 31, the fund holds $24 cash and petty cash tickets for office supplies, $224, and delivery expense, $15.

**Requirements**

1. Explain how an imprest petty cash system works.
2. Journalize the establishment of the petty cash fund on March 1 and the replenishing of the fund on March 31.
3. Prepare a T-account for Petty Cash, and post to the account. What is the balance of the Petty Cash account at all times?

### E7-18 Classifying bank reconciliation items

Learning Objective 5

The following items could appear on a bank reconciliation:

a. Outstanding checks, $670.

b. Deposits in transit, $1,500.

c. NSF check from customer, #548, for $175.

d. Bank collection of note receivable of $800, and interest of $80.

e. Interest earned on bank balance, $20.

f. Service charge, $10.

g. The business credited Cash for $200. The correct amount was $2,000.

h. The bank incorrectly decreased the business's account by $350 for a check written by another business.

Classify each item as (1) an addition to the book balance, (2) a subtraction from the book balance, (3) an addition to the bank balance, or (4) a subtraction from the bank balance.

**Learning Objective 5**

1. Adjusted Balance $1,270

## E7-19 Preparing a bank reconciliation

Henderson Photography's checkbook lists the following:

| Date | Check No. | Item | Check | Deposit | Balance |
|---|---|---|---|---|---|
| Nov. 1 | | | | | $ 525 |
| 4 | 622 | Quick Mailing | $ 10 | | 515 |
| 9 | | Service Revenue | | $ 130 | 645 |
| 13 | 623 | Photo Supplies | 35 | | 610 |
| 14 | 624 | Utilities | 75 | | 535 |
| 18 | 625 | Cash | 60 | | 475 |
| 26 | 626 | Office Supplies | 85 | | 390 |
| 28 | 627 | Upstate Realty Co. | 270 | | 120 |
| 30 | | Service Revenue | | 1,225 | 1,345 |

Henderson's November bank statement shows the following:

| | | | |
|---|---|---|---|
| Balance | | | $ 525 |
| Deposits | | | 130 |
| Checks: | No. | Amount | |
| | 622 | $ 10 | |
| | 623 | 35 | |
| | 624 | 115* | |
| | 625 | 60 | (220) |
| Other charges: | | | |
| Printed checks | | 30 | |
| Service charge | | 5 | (35) |
| Balance | | | $ 400 |

*This is the correct amount for check number 624.

**Requirements**

1. Prepare Henderson Photography's bank reconciliation at November 30, 2016.
2. How much cash does Henderson actually have on November 30, 2016?
3. Journalize any transactions required from the bank reconciliation.

**Learning Objective 5**

1. Book Deductions $348

## E7-20 Preparing a bank reconciliation

Fred White Corporation operates four bowling alleys. The business just received the October 31, 2016, bank statement from City National Bank, and the statement shows an ending balance of $885. Listed on the statement are an EFT rent collection of $410, a service charge of $10, NSF checks totaling $65, and a $30 charge for printed checks. In reviewing the cash records, the business identified outstanding checks totaling $470 and a deposit in transit of $1,785. During October, the business recorded a $270 check by debiting Salaries Expense and crediting Cash for $27. The business's Cash account shows an October 31 balance of $2,138.

**Requirements**

1. Prepare the bank reconciliation at October 31.
2. Journalize any transactions required from the bank reconciliation.

## > Problems Group A

### P7-21A Identifying internal control weakness in cash receipts

**Learning Objective 2**

Seacrest Productions makes all sales on credit. Cash receipts arrive by mail. Justin Broaddus, the mailroom clerk, opens envelopes and separates the checks from the accompanying remittance advices. Broaddus forwards the checks to another employee, who makes the daily bank deposit but has no access to the accounting records. Broaddus sends the remittance advices, which show cash received, to the accounting department for entry in the accounts. Broaddus's only other duty is to grant sales allowances to customers. (A *sales allowance* decreases the customer's account receivable.) When Broaddus receives a customer check for $225 less a $60 allowance, he records the sales allowance and forwards the document to the accounting department.

**Requirements**

1. Identify the internal control weakness in this situation.
2. Who should record sales allowances?
3. What is the amount that should be shown in the ledger for cash receipts?

### P7-22A Correcting internal control weakness

**Learning Objectives 1, 2, 3**

Each of the following situations has an internal control weakness.

a. Upside-Down Applications develops custom programs to customer's specifications. Recently, development of a new program stopped while the programmers redesigned Upside-Down's accounting system. Upside-Down's accountants could have performed this task.

b. Norma Rottler has been your trusted employee for 24 years. She performs all cash-handling and accounting duties. Ms. Rottler just purchased a new luxury car and a new home in an expensive suburb. As owner of the company, you wonder how she can afford these luxuries because you pay her only $30,000 a year and she has no source of outside income.

c. Izzie Hardwoods, a private company, falsified sales and inventory figures in order to get an important loan. The loan went through, but Izzie later went bankrupt and could not repay the bank.

d. The office supply company where Pet Grooming Goods purchases sales receipts recently notified Pet Grooming Goods that its documents were not prenumbered. Howard Mustro, the owner, replied that he never uses receipt numbers.

e. Discount stores such as Cusco make most of their sales in cash, with the remainder in credit card sales. To reduce expenses, one store manager ceases purchasing fidelity bonds on the cashiers.

f. Cornelius's Corndogs keeps all cash receipts in an empty box for a week because the owner likes to go to the bank on Tuesdays when Joann is working.

**Requirements**

1. Identify the missing internal control characteristics in each situation.
2. Identify the possible problem caused by each control weakness.
3. Propose a solution to each internal control problem.

Learning Objective 4

3. June 30, Cash CR $230

## P7-23A Accounting for petty cash transactions

On June 1, Meadow Salad Dressings creates a petty cash fund with an imprest balance of $400. During June, Al Franklin, the fund custodian, signs the following petty cash tickets:

| Petty Cash Ticket Number | Item | Amount |
|---|---|---|
| 101 | Office supplies | $ 15 |
| 102 | Cab fare for executive | 10 |
| 103 | Delivery of package across town | 20 |
| 104 | Business dinner | 70 |
| 105 | Merchandise inventory | 130 |

On June 30, prior to replenishment, the fund contains these tickets plus cash of $170. The accounts affected by petty cash payments are Office Supplies, Travel Expense, Delivery Expense, Entertainment Expense, and Merchandise Inventory.

### Requirements

1. Explain the characteristics and the internal control features of an imprest fund.
2. On June 30, how much cash should the petty cash fund hold before it is replenished?
3. Journalize all required entries to create the fund and replenish it. Include explanations.
4. Make the July 1 entry to increase the fund balance to $500. Include an explanation, and briefly describe what the custodian does.

Learning Objective 4

2. June 30, Cash CR $158

## P7-24A Accounting for petty cash transactions

Suppose that on June 1, Jammin' Gyrations, a disc jockey service, creates a petty cash fund with an imprest balance of $400. During June, Michael Martell, fund custodian, signs the following petty cash tickets:

| Petty Cash Ticket Number | Item | Amount |
|---|---|---|
| 1 | Postage for package received | $ 20 |
| 2 | Office party | 10 |
| 3 | Two boxes of stationery | 35 |
| 4 | Printer cartridges | 25 |
| 5 | Business dinner | 60 |

On June 30, prior to replenishment, the fund contains these tickets plus cash of $242. The accounts affected by petty cash payments are Office Supplies, Entertainment Expense, and Postage Expense.

### Requirements

1. On June 30, how much cash should this petty cash fund hold before it is replenished?
2. Journalize all required entries to (a) create the fund and (b) replenish it. Include explanations.
3. Make the entry on July 1 to increase the fund balance to $475. Include an explanation.

**Learning Objective 5**

1. Adjusted Balance $17,010

## P7-25A Preparing a bank reconciliation and journal entries

The December cash records of Duffy Insurance follow:

| Cash Receipts | | Cash Payments | |
|---|---|---|---|
| **Date** | **Cash Debit** | **Check No.** | **Cash Credit** |
| Dec. 4 | $ 4,190 | 1416 | $ 840 |
| 9 | 510 | 1417 | 170 |
| 14 | 550 | 1418 | 680 |
| 17 | 2,150 | 1419 | 1,190 |
| 31 | 1,830 | 1420 | 1,470 |
| | | 1421 | 1,200 |
| | | 1422 | 630 |

Duffy's Cash account shows a balance of $17,050 at December 31. On December 31, Duffy Insurance received the following bank statement:

**Bank Statement for December**

| | | | | |
|---|---|---|---|---|
| Beginning Balance | | | | $ 14,000 |
| Deposits and other Credits: | | | | |
| Dec. | 1 | EFT | $ 400 | |
| Dec. | 5 | | 4,190 | |
| Dec. | 10 | | 510 | |
| Dec. | 15 | | 550 | |
| Dec. | 18 | | 2,150 | |
| Dec. | 22 | BC | 1,600 | 9,400 |
| Checks and other Debits: | | | | |
| Dec. | 8 | NSF | 600 | |
| Dec. | 11 (check no. 1416) | | 840 | |
| Dec. | 19 | EFT | 700 | |
| Dec. | 22 (check no. 1417) | | 170 | |
| Dec. | 29 (check no. 1418) | | 680 | |
| Dec. | 31 (check no. 1419) | | 1,910 | |
| Dec. | 31 | SC | 20 | (4,920) |
| Ending Balance | | | | **$ 18,480** |

Explanations: BC–bank collection; EFT–electronic funds transfer; NSF–nonsufficient funds checks; SC–service charge

Additional data for the bank reconciliation follow:

**a.** The EFT credit was a receipt of rent. The EFT debit was an insurance payment.

**b.** The NSF check was received from a customer.

**c.** The $1,600 bank collection was for a note receivable.

**d.** The correct amount of check 1419, for rent expense, is $1,910. Duffy's controller mistakenly recorded the check for $1,190.

**Requirements**

1. Prepare the bank reconciliation of Duffy Insurance at December 31, 2016.
2. Journalize any required entries from the bank reconciliation.

**Learning Objective 5**

1. Book Additions $2,610

## P7-26A Preparing a bank reconciliation and journal entries

The August 31 bank statement of Watson Healthcare has just arrived from United Bank. To prepare the bank reconciliation, you gather the following data:

a. The August 31 bank balance is $5,630.

b. The bank statement includes two charges for NSF checks from customers. One is for $390 (#1), and the other is for $140 (#2).

c. The following Watson checks are outstanding at August 31:

| Check No. | Amount |
|---|---|
| 237 | $ 90 |
| 288 | 160 |
| 291 | 550 |
| 294 | 620 |
| 295 | 10 |
| 296 | 100 |

d. Watson collects from a few customers by EFT. The August bank statement lists a $1,700 EFT deposit for a collection on account.

e. The bank statement includes two special deposits that Watson hasn't recorded yet: $850 for dividend revenue, and $60 for the interest revenue Watson earned on its bank balance during August.

f. The bank statement lists a $70 subtraction for the bank service charge.

g. On August 31, the Watson treasurer deposited $310, but this deposit does not appear on the bank statement.

h. The bank statement includes a $700 deduction for a check drawn by Multi-State Freight Company. Watson notified the bank of this bank error.

i. Watson's Cash account shows a balance of $3,100 on August 31.

**Requirements**

1. Prepare the bank reconciliation for Watson's Healthcare at August 31, 2016.
2. Journalize any required entries from the bank reconciliation. Include an explanation for each entry.

## > Problems Group B

### P7-27B Identifying internal control weakness in cash receipts

**Learning Objective 2**

Black Water Productions makes all sales on credit. Cash receipts arrive by mail. Larry Padgitt, the mailroom clerk, opens envelopes and separates the checks from the accompanying remittance advices. Padgitt forwards the checks to another employee, who makes the daily bank deposit but has no access to the accounting records. Padgitt sends the remittance advices, which show cash received, to the accounting department for entry in the accounts. Padgitt's only other duty is to grant sales allowances to customers. (A *sales allowance* decreases the customer's account receivable.) When Padgitt receives a customer check for $575 less a $45 allowance, he records the sales allowance and forwards the document to the accounting department.

**Requirements**

1. Identify the internal control weakness in this situation.
2. Who should record sales allowances?
3. What is the amount that should be shown in the ledger for cash receipts?

### P7-28B Correcting internal control weakness

**Learning Objectives 1, 2, 3**

Each of the following situations has an internal control weakness.

a. Jade Applications has decided that one way to cut costs in the upcoming year is to fire the external auditor. The business believes that the internal auditor should be able to efficiently monitor the company's internal controls.

b. In an effort to minimize the amount of paperwork, Ross Homes has decided that it will not keep copies of customer invoices related to sales revenue. Ross believes that this effort will minimize the amount of data storage the company will have to pay for.

c. Elle Bee, a trusted employee for many years, has never taken a vacation. The owner believes that he's lucky that she is so committed to her job.

d. The Medicine Chest Company keeps a small petty cash fund to handle small cash transactions. Because no one wants to volunteer to be the custodian, the business manager has decided that all employees should have access to the petty cash. She figures that as long as each employee fills out a petty cash ticket, then there are proper controls in place.

e. Due to the cost of maintaining the security cameras, Wings and More has decided that it will remove the cameras that monitor the cash register.

f. Bryan Miller, manager of Hardware Emporium, prides himself on hiring exceptionally skilled employees who need no training to do their jobs.

**Requirements**

1. Identify the missing internal control characteristics in each situation.
2. Identify the possible problem caused by each control weakness.
3. Propose a solution to each internal control problem.

Learning Objective 4

3. Cash Short & Over CR $10

## P7-29B Accounting for petty cash transactions

On September 1, Top Taste Salad Dressings creates a petty cash fund with an imprest balance of $300. During September, Michael Martell, the fund custodian, signs the following petty cash tickets:

| Petty Cash Ticket Number | Item | Amount |
|---|---|---|
| 101 | Office supplies | $ 30 |
| 102 | Cab fare for executive | 25 |
| 103 | Delivery of package across town | 20 |
| 104 | Business dinner | 45 |
| 105 | Merchandise inventory | 120 |

On September 30, prior to replenishment, the fund contains these tickets plus cash of $70. The accounts affected by petty cash payments are Office Supplies, Travel Expense, Delivery Expense, Entertainment Expense, and Merchandise Inventory.

### Requirements

1. Explain the characteristics and the internal control features of an imprest fund.
2. On September 30, how much cash should the petty cash fund hold before it is replenished?
3. Journalize all required entries to create the fund and replenish it. Include explanations.
4. Make the October 1 entry to increase the fund balance to $350. Include an explanation, and briefly describe what the custodian does.

Learning Objective 4

2. Sep. 30, Cash CR $173

## P7-30B Accounting for petty cash transactions

Suppose that on September 1, Rockin' Gyrations, a disc jockey service, creates a petty cash fund with an imprest balance of $450. During September, Ruth Mangan, fund custodian, signs the following petty cash tickets:

| Petty Cash Ticket Number | Item | Amount |
|---|---|---|
| 1 | Postage for package received | $ 35 |
| 2 | Office party | 25 |
| 3 | Two boxes of stationery | 30 |
| 4 | Printer cartridges | 15 |
| 5 | Business dinner | 65 |

On September 30, prior to replenishment, the fund contains these tickets plus cash of $277. The accounts affected by petty cash payments are Office Supplies, Entertainment Expense, and Postage Expense.

**Requirements**

1. On September 30, how much cash should this petty cash fund hold before it is replenished?
2. Journalize all required entries to (a) create the fund and (b) replenish it. Include explanations.
3. Make the entry on October 1 to increase the fund balance to $525. Include an explanation.

## P7-31B Preparing a bank reconciliation and journal entries

Learning Objective 5

1. Adjusted Balance $16,350

The May cash records of Durkin Insurance follow:

| Cash Receipts | | Cash Payments | |
|---|---|---|---|
| **Date** | **Cash Debit** | **Check No.** | **Cash Credit** |
| May 4 | $ 4,190 | 1416 | $ 840 |
| 9 | 560 | 1417 | 130 |
| 14 | 510 | 1418 | 680 |
| 17 | 2,130 | 1419 | 1,690 |
| 31 | 1,880 | 1420 | 1,470 |
| | | 1421 | 1,300 |
| | | 1422 | 620 |

Durkin's Cash account shows a balance of $16,340 at May 31. On May 31, Durkin Insurance received the following bank statement:

| Bank Statement for May | | | | |
|---|---|---|---|---|
| Beginning Balance | | | | $ 13,800 |
| Deposits and other Credits: | | | | |
| May | 1 | EFT | $ 200 | |
| May | 5 | | 4,190 | |
| May | 10 | | 560 | |
| May | 15 | | 510 | |
| May | 18 | | 2,130 | |
| May | 22 | BC | 1,200 | 8,790 |
| Checks and other Debits: | | | | |
| May | 8 | NSF | 500 | |
| May | 11 (check no. 1416) | | 840 | |
| May | 19 | EFT | 600 | |
| May | 22 (check no. 1417) | | 130 | |
| May | 29 (check no. 1418) | | 680 | |
| May | 31 (check no. 1419) | | 1,960 | |
| May | 31 | SC | 20 | (4,730) |
| Ending Balance | | | | **$ 17,860** |

Explanations: BC–bank collection; EFT–electronic funds transfer; NSF–nonsufficient funds checks; SC–service charge

CHAPTER 7

Additional data for the bank reconciliation follow:

a. The EFT credit was a receipt of rent. The EFT debit was an insurance payment.

b. The NSF check was received from a customer.

c. The $1,200 bank collection was for a note receivable.

d. The correct amount of check 1419, for rent expense, is $1,960. Durkin's controller mistakenly recorded the check for $1,690.

**Requirements**

1. Prepare the bank reconciliation of Durkin Insurance at May 31, 2016.
2. Journalize any required entries from the bank reconciliation.

**Learning Objective 5**

1. Book Deductions $490

**P7-32B Preparing a bank reconciliation and journal entries**

The October 31 bank statement of Wollaston's Healthcare has just arrived from State Bank. To prepare the bank reconciliation, you gather the following data:

a. The October 31 bank balance is $5,580.

b. The bank statement includes two charges for NSF checks from customers. One is for $370 (#1), and the other is for $110 (#2).

c. The following Wollaston's checks are outstanding at October 31:

| Check No. | Amount |
|---|---|
| 237 | $ 90 |
| 288 | 150 |
| 291 | 550 |
| 294 | 630 |
| 295 | 70 |
| 296 | 120 |

d. Wollaston's collects from a few customers by EFT. The October bank statement lists a $1,500 EFT deposit for a collection on account.

e. The bank statement includes two special deposits that Wollaston's hasn't recorded yet: $850 for dividend revenue and $30 for the interest revenue Wollaston's earned on its bank balance during October.

f. The bank statement lists a $10 subtraction for the bank service charge.

g. On October 31, the Wollaston's treasurer deposited $320, but this deposit does not appear on the bank statement.

h. The bank statement includes a $500 deduction for a check drawn by Multi-State Freight Company. Wollaston's notified the bank of this bank error.

i. Wollaston's Cash account shows a balance of $2,900 on October 31.

**Requirements**

1. Prepare the bank reconciliation for Wollaston's Healthcare at October 31, 2016.
2. Journalize any required entries from the bank reconciliation. Include an explanation for each entry.

## Continuing Problem

### P7-33 Preparing a bank reconciliation and journal entries

This problem continues the Daniels Consulting situation from Problem P6-38 of Chapter 6. Daniels's March Cash T-account from its general ledger is as follows:

**Cash**

| | | | |
|---|---|---|---|
| Feb. 28 Bal. | 45,085 | 4,400 | Mar. 1 (ck. 207) |
| Mar. 6 | 2,475 | 730 | Mar. 14 (ck. 208) |
| Mar. 13 | 2,900 | 1,450 | Mar. 14 (ck. 209) |
| Mar. 20 | 4,800 | 190 | Mar. 28 (ck. 210) |
| Mar. 27 | 3,680 | 500 | Mar. 30 (ck. 211) |
| Mar. 31 Bal. | 51,670 | | |

Daniels's bank statement dated March 31, 2017, follows:

| Bank Statement for March 2017 | | |
|---|---|---|
| Beginning Balance, February 28, 2017 | | $ 45,505 |
| Deposits and other Credits: | | |
| Mar. 1 | $ 675 | |
| Mar. 8 | 2,475 | |
| Mar. 14 | 2,900 | |
| Mar. 20 EFT Hip Hop Hats (on account) | 550 | |
| Mar. 22 | 4,800 | |
| Mar. 28 Interest revenue | 25 | 11,425 |
| Checks and other Debits: | | |
| Mar. 2 EFT to Paper Products | 34 | |
| Mar. 2 ck#206 | 1,095 | |
| Mar. 18 ck#207 | 4,400 | |
| Mar. 19 ck#209 | 1,450 | |
| Mar. 28 EFT to The Cable Co. | 85 | |
| Mar. 28 ck#208 | 730 | |
| Bank Service Charge | 13 | (7,807) |
| Ending Balance, March 31, 2017 | | **$ 49,123** |

**Requirements**

1. Prepare the March bank reconciliation.
2. Journalize any transactions required from the bank reconciliation. Compute the adjusted account balance for the Cash T-account, and denote the balance as *End. Bal.*

## > Practice Set

This problem continues the Crystal Clear Cleaning problem from Problem P6-39 of Chapter 6.

### P7-34 Preparing a bank reconciliation and journal entries

The bank statement dated February 28, 2018, for Crystal Clear follows:

| Bank Statement for February 2018 | | | |
|---|---|---|---|
| Beginning Balance, January 31, 2018 | | | $ 0 |
| Deposits and other Credits: | | | |
| Feb. | 2 | $ 30,000 | |
| Feb. | 10 | 100 | |
| Feb. | 18 | 14,000 | |
| Feb. | 20 | 42,000 | |
| Feb. | 23 EFT Weiler's Restaurant | 450 | |
| Feb. | 28 Interest revenue | 10 | 86,560 |
| Checks and other Debits: | | | |
| Feb. | 2 EFT to Check Art | 30 | |
| Feb. | 5 ck#235 | 2,000 | |
| Feb. | 9 ck#237 | 1,600 | |
| Feb. | 9 ck#236 | 2,400 | |
| Feb. | 26 ck#239 | 1,500 | |
| Feb. | 28 EFT to Texas Energy | 140 | |
| Feb. | 28 ck#240 | 200 | |
| Bank Service Charge | | 19 | (7,889) |
| Ending Balance, February 28, 2018 | | | **$ 78,671** |

Additional data for the bank reconciliation follow:

**a.** The company had the following EFT transactions:
- EFT credit on February 23 was a receipt of cash for services on account
- EFT debit on February 2 was a payment for printing of business checks
- EFT debit on February 28 was a payment for utilities

**b.** At February 28, there was a $900 deposit in transit.

**c.** The book balance as of January 31, 2018, was $78,750.

**d.** Check #238, $350, and check #241, $200, were still outstanding at the end of the month.

#### Requirements

1. Prepare the bank reconciliation.
2. Journalize any required entries from the bank reconciliation.

# CRITICAL THINKING

## > Decision Cases

### Decision Case 7-1

Conduct an Internet search for information on internal control and Sarbanes-Oxley. Write a report of your findings. In your report, discuss some of the advantages and disadvantages of Sarbanes-Oxley. Present it to your class (if required by your instructor).

### Decision Case 7-2

This case is based on an actual situation. Centennial Construction Company, headquartered in Dallas, Texas, built a Rodeway Motel 35 miles north of Dallas. The construction foreman, whose name was Slim Chance, hired the 40 workers needed to complete the project. Slim had the construction workers fill out the necessary tax forms, and he sent their documents to the home office.

Work on the motel began on April 1 and ended September 1. Each week, Slim filled out a timecard of hours worked by each employee during the week. Slim faxed the timecards to the home office, which prepared the payroll checks on Friday morning. Slim drove to the home office on Friday, picked up the payroll checks, and returned to the construction site. At 5 p.m. on Friday, Slim distributed payroll checks to the workers.

**Requirements**

1. Describe in detail the main internal control weakness in this situation. Specify what negative result(s) could occur because of the internal control weakness.
2. Describe what you would do to correct the internal control weakness.

## > Fraud Case 7-1

Levon Helm was a kind of one-man mortgage broker. He would drive around Tennessee looking for homes that had second mortgages, and if the criteria were favorable, he would offer to buy the second mortgage for "cash on the barrelhead." Helm bought low and sold high, making sizable profits. Being a small operation, he employed one person, Cindy Patterson, who did all his bookkeeping. Patterson was an old family friend, and he trusted her so implicitly that he never checked up on the ledgers or the bank reconciliations. At some point, Patterson started "borrowing" from the business and concealing her transactions by booking phony expenses. She intended to pay it back someday, but she got used to the extra cash and couldn't stop. By the time the scam was discovered, she had drained the company of funds that it owed to many of its creditors. The company went bankrupt, Patterson did some jail time, and Helm lost everything.

**Requirements**

1. What was the key control weakness in this case?
2. Many small businesses cannot afford to hire enough people for adequate separation of duties. What can they do to compensate for this?

## > Financial Statement Case 7-1

Visit **http://www.pearsonhighered.com/Horngren** to view a link to **Starbucks Corporation's** 2013 Fiscal Year Annual Report. Study the audit opinion (labeled Report of Independent Registered Public Accounting Firm) of Starbucks Corporation and the Starbucks Corporation financial statements. Answer the following questions about the company:

**Requirements**

1. What is the name of Starbucks's outside auditing firm (independent registered public accounting firm)? What office of this firm signed the audit report? How long after the Starbucks year-end did the auditors issue their opinion?
2. Who bears primary responsibility for maintaining effective internal control over financial reporting? How can you tell?
3. Does it appear that Starbucks's internal controls are adequate? How can you tell?
4. What standard of auditing did the outside auditors use in examining the Starbucks financial statements?
5. By how much did Starbucks's cash balance (including cash equivalents) change during year ended September 29, 2013? What were the beginning and ending cash balances?
6. Review the notes to the consolidated financial statements, specifically Note 1 dealing with Cash and Cash Equivalents. What type of instruments does Starbucks consider to be cash equivalents?
7. Determine Starbucks's cash ratio as of September 29, 2013, and September 30, 2012. How do Starbucks's cash ratios compare with **Green Mountain Coffee Roasters** as illustrated in the chapter? Explain.

## > Communication Activity 7-1

In 100 words or fewer, explain why there may be a difference between the bank statement ending cash balance and the ending balance in the Cash account. Give at least two examples each of adjustments to the bank balance and to the book balance.

MyAccountingLab **For a wealth of online resources, including exercises, problems, media, and immediate tutorial help, please visit http://www.myaccountinglab.com.**

## > Quick Check Answers

**1.** a **2.** d **3.** d **4.** d **5.** d **6.** c **7.** c **8.** d **9.** c **10.** b

# Receivables 8

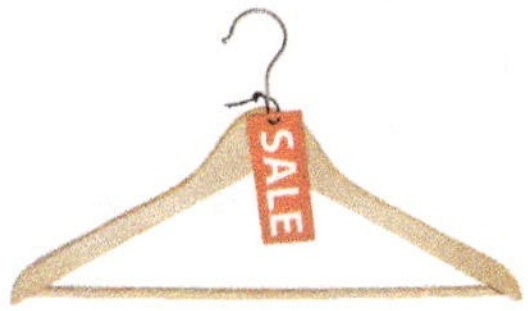


## Should Credit Be Extended?

James Hulsey works for a large department store as a credit manager. His main responsibility is managing all credit sales that generate accounts receivable. James must evaluate each customer's request for credit and determine which customers are allowed to purchase goods on credit. He does this by reviewing the customer's credit history and credit score. James has an important decision to make. He understands that granting credit increases the sales of the department store, but it also has its disadvantages.

One of those disadvantages is that the department store has to wait to receive cash. But, for James, the biggest disadvantage—and the most frustrating part of his job—is when customers don't pay. When this happens, the department store suffers a loss because it will never collect the cash associated with the sale. The department store must have a way to take the accounts of customers who will never make payment off the books; this is called a *write-off.* In addition, James must also help the department store estimate the amount of receivables that will be uncollectible. It's important that the department store have a good idea of the amount of cash that will actually be collected on its receivables so it can estimate future cash flows.

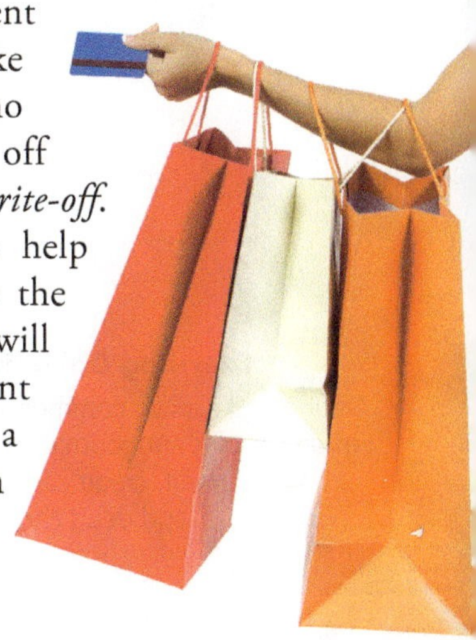

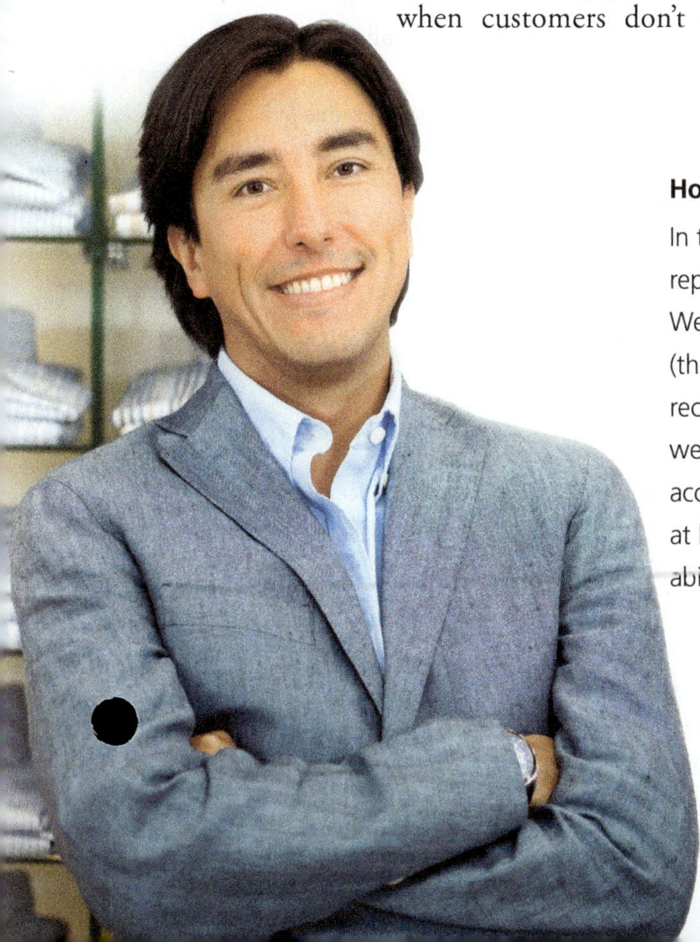

**How Are Receivables Accounted For?**

In this chapter, we determine how companies account for receivables. Receivables represent the right to receive cash in the future from a current transaction. We begin by looking at how companies such as Sears Holdings Corporation (the parent company of Kmart and Sears, Roebuck and Co.) record accounts receivable, including when customers don't make the required payments. Then we review notes receivable, which usually extend over a longer term than accounts receivable and typically involve interest. We finish the chapter by looking at how companies (and investors) can use financial ratios to evaluate a company's ability to collect cash on accounts receivable.

# Chapter 8 Learning Objectives

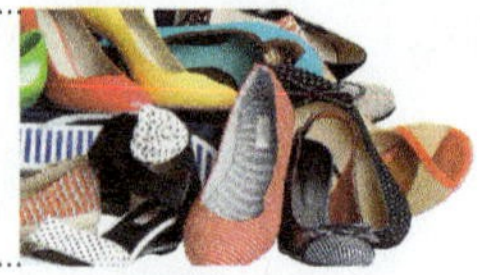

1. Define and explain common types of receivables and journalize sales on credit, credit card sales, and debit card sales
2. Apply the direct write-off method for uncollectibles
3. Apply the allowance method for uncollectibles and estimate bad debts expense based on the percent-of-sales, percent-of-receivables, and aging-of-receivables methods
4. Account for notes receivable including computing interest and recording honored and dishonored notes
5. Use the acid-test ratio, accounts receivable turnover ratio, and days' sales in receivables to evaluate business performance

## WHAT ARE COMMON TYPES OF RECEIVABLES, AND HOW ARE CREDIT SALES RECORDED?

**Learning Objective 1**

Define and explain common types of receivables and journalize sales on credit, credit card sales, and debit card sales

**Receivable**
A monetary claim against a business or an individual.

**Debtor**
The party to a credit transaction who takes on an obligation/payable.

A **receivable** occurs when a business sells goods or services to another party on account (on credit). It is a monetary claim against a business or an individual. The receivable is the seller's claim for the amount of the transaction. Receivables also occur when a business loans money to another party. A receivable is the right to *receive* cash in the future from a current transaction. It is something the business owns; therefore, it is an asset. *Each* receivable transaction involves two parties:

- The creditor, who receives a receivable (an asset). The creditor will collect cash from the customer or borrower.
- The **debtor**, the party to a credit transaction who takes on an obligation/payable (a liability). The debtor will pay cash later.

### Types of Receivables

The three major types of receivables are:

- Accounts receivable
- Notes receivable
- Other receivables

#### Accounts Receivable

**Accounts Receivable**
The right to receive cash in the future from customers for goods sold or for services performed.

**Accounts receivable**, also called *trade receivables*, represent the right to receive cash in the future from customers for goods sold or for services performed. Accounts receivable are usually collected within a short period of time, such as 30 or 60 days, and are therefore reported as a current asset on the balance sheet.

#### Notes Receivable

**Notes Receivable**
A written promise that a customer will pay a fixed amount of principal plus interest by a certain date in the future.

**Maturity Date**
The date when a note is due.

**Notes receivable** usually have longer terms than accounts receivable. Notes receivable, sometimes called promissory notes, represent a written promise that a customer (or another individual or business) will pay a fixed amount of principal plus interest by a certain date in the future—called the **maturity date**. The maturity date is the date on which the notes receivable is due. A written document known as a promissory note serves as evidence of the debt and is signed by the debtor. Notes receivable due within one year or less are considered current assets. Notes receivable due beyond one year are long-term assets.

### Other Receivables

Other receivables make up a miscellaneous category that includes any other type of receivable where there is a right to receive cash in the future. Common examples include dividends receivable, interest receivable, and taxes receivable. These other receivables may be either current or long-term assets, depending on whether they will be received within one year or less.

## Exercising Internal Control Over Receivables

Businesses that sell goods or services on account receive cash (check payments) by mail or online payments (EFT), so internal control over collections is important. As we discussed in the previous chapter, a critical element of internal control is the separation of cash-handling and cash-accounting duties.

Most large companies also have a credit department to evaluate customers' credit applications to determine whether they meet the company's credit approval standards. The extension of credit is a balancing act. The company does not want to lose sales to good customers, but it also wants to avoid receivables that will never be collected. For good internal control over cash collections from receivables, separation of duties must be maintained. The credit department should have no access to cash, and those who handle cash should not be in a position to grant credit to customers. If a credit department employee also handles cash, he or she could pocket money received from a customer. The employee could then label the customer's account as uncollectible, and the company would stop billing that customer. In this scenario, the employee may have covered his or her theft.

## Recording Sales on Credit

As discussed earlier, selling on account (on credit) creates an account receivable. Businesses must maintain a separate accounts receivable account for each customer in order to account for payments received from the customer and amounts still owed.

For example, Smart Touch Learning provides $5,000 in services to customer Brown on account and sells $10,000 (sales price) of merchandise inventory to customer Smith on account on August 8. The revenue is recorded (ignore Cost of Goods Sold) as follows:

| Date | Accounts and Explanation | Debit | Credit |
|---|---|---|---|
| Aug. 8 | Accounts Receivable—Brown | 5,000 | |
| | Service Revenue | | 5,000 |
| | *Performed service on account.* | | |
| 8 | Accounts Receivable—Smith | 10,000 | |
| | Sales Revenue | | 10,000 |
| | *Sold goods on account.* | | |

**A↑** = **L** + **E↑**
Accounts Receivable↑ = Service Revenue↑

**A↑** = **L** + **E↑**
Accounts Receivable↑ = Sales Revenue↑

These separate customer accounts receivable (for example, Accounts Receivable—Brown) are called subsidiary accounts. The sum of all balances in subsidiary accounts receivable equals a control account balance. In this case, Accounts Receivable serves as the control account. This is illustrated as follows:

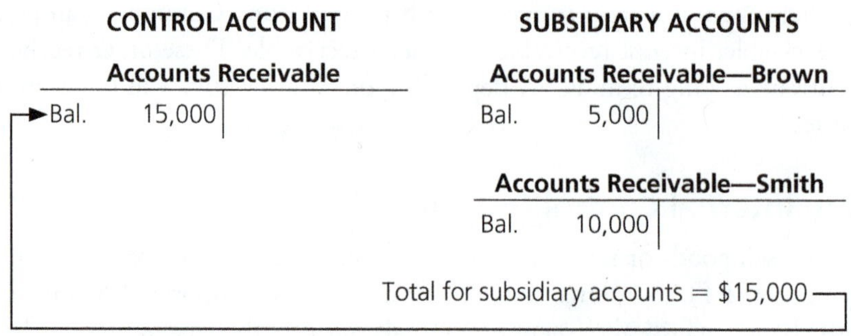


The control account, Accounts Receivable, shows a balance of $15,000. The individual customer accounts in the subsidiary ledger (Accounts Receivable—Brown $5,000 + Accounts Receivable—Smith $10,000) add up to a total of $15,000.

When the business collects cash from both customers on August 29—$4,000 from Brown and $8,000 from Smith—Smart Touch Learning makes the following entry and posts the entry to the T-accounts:

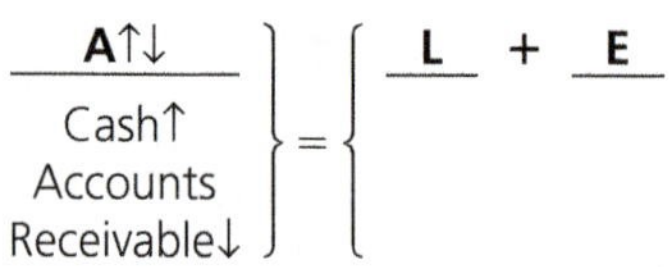


| Date | Accounts and Explanation | Debit | Credit |
|---|---|---|---|
| Aug. 29 | Cash | 12,000 | |
| | Accounts Receivable—Brown | | 4,000 |
| | Accounts Receivable—Smith | | 8,000 |
| | *Collected cash on account.* | | |

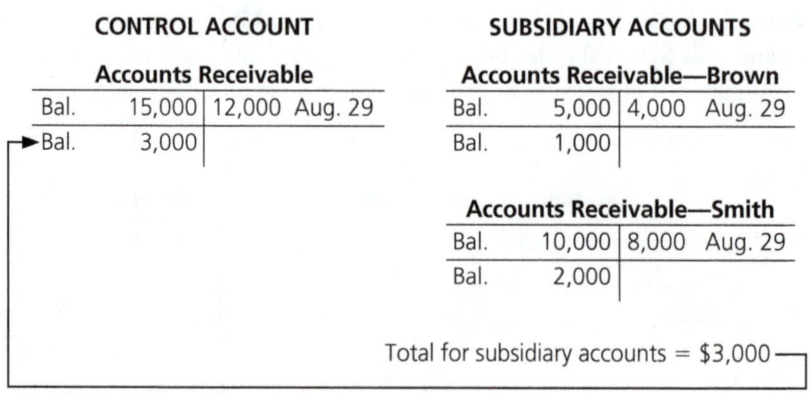


## Recording Credit Card and Debit Card Sales

In addition to selling on account, most companies also accept credit cards and debit cards. By accepting credit cards and debit cards, such as Visa, MasterCard, and American Express, businesses are able to attract more customers. Credit cards offer the customer the convenience of buying something without having to pay cash immediately. Debit cards, on the other hand, reduce the customer's bank account immediately but allow the customer to pay electronically instead of with currency or by writing a check.

Businesses also benefit from accepting payment by credit and debit cards. They do not have to check each customer's credit rating or worry about keeping accounts receivable records or even collecting from the customer. The card issuer has the responsibility of collecting from the customer. Thus, instead of collecting cash from the customer, the seller will receive cash from the card issuer. There is, however, almost always a fee to the seller to cover the processing costs.

Companies hire a third-party processor to process credit and debit card transactions. Transactions are usually entered into an electronic terminal (card scanner) that the company either purchases or rents from the processor. The fees the card processor charges the company for its processing services vary depending on the type of card and the specific agreement the company has with the card processor. The processor agreement specifies how fees are paid to the processor. The following are two common methods of handling the proceeds and processing fees:

- **Net**—The total sale less the processing fee assessed equals the net amount of cash deposited by the processor, usually within a few days of the sale date.
- **Gross**—The total sale is deposited daily within a few days of the actual sale date. The processing fees for all transactions processed for the month are deducted from the company's bank account by the processor, often on the last day of the month.

Proceeds from credit and debit card transactions are usually deposited within a few business days after the sale. Therefore, credit and debit card sales are journalized similar to cash sales. For example, Smart Touch Learning sells merchandise inventory (ignore Cost of Goods Sold) to a customer for $3,000 on August 15. The customer pays with a third-party credit card. Smart Touch Learning would record the entry, assuming the card processor assesses a 4% fee and deposits the net amount, as follows:

| Date | Accounts and Explanation | Debit | Credit |
|---|---|---|---|
| Aug. 15 | Cash | 2,880 | |
| | Credit Card Expense ($3,000 × 0.04) | 120 | |
| | Sales Revenue | | 3,000 |
| | *Recorded credit card sales, net of fee.* | | |

| A↑ | = | L | + | E↑ |
|---|---|---|---|---|
| Cash↑ | | | | Sales Revenue↑<br>Credit Card Expense↑ |

The same entry, assuming the processor uses the gross method, on the sale date would be as follows:

| Date | Accounts and Explanation | Debit | Credit |
|---|---|---|---|
| Aug. 15 | Cash | 3,000 | |
| | Sales Revenue | | 3,000 |
| | *Recorded credit card sales.* | | |

| A↑ | = | L | + | E↑ |
|---|---|---|---|---|
| Cash↑ | | | | Sales Revenue↑ |

At the end of August, the processor would collect the fees assessed for the month. (*Note:* We assume only the one credit card sale for this month.)

| Date | Accounts and Explanation | Debit | Credit |
|---|---|---|---|
| Aug. 31 | Credit Card Expense | 120 | |
| | Cash | | 120 |
| | *Paid fees assessed by credit card processor.* | | |

| A↓ | = | L | + | E↓ |
|---|---|---|---|---|
| Cash↓ | | | | Credit Card Expense↑ |

## Factoring and Pledging Receivables

One of the many drawbacks of accepting sales on account is that the company must wait for the receipt of cash. Sometimes this time period could be delayed as much as 60 to 90 days. In addition, there is always the risk that the company will never collect on the receivable. In the previous section, we looked at credit cards and debit cards as being an option to reduce this risk. Another option for a business is to either factor or pledge its receivables.

When a business factors its receivables, it sells its receivables to a finance company or bank (often called a *factor*). The business receives cash less an applicable fee from the factor for the receivables immediately. The factor, instead of the business, now collects the cash on the receivables. The business no longer has to deal with the collection of the receivable from the customer. The business receives cash associated with the receivable from the factor instead of the customer.

Pledging of receivables is another option for businesses that need cash immediately. In a pledging situation, a business uses its receivables as security for a loan. The business borrows money from a bank and offers its receivables as collateral. The business is still responsible for collecting on the receivables, but it uses this money to pay off the loan along with interest. In pledging, if the loan is not paid, the bank can collect on the receivables.

In both situations, the business has managed to receive cash immediately for the receivables instead of having to wait for collection.

## DECISIONS

### How could we get cash fast?

Peggy Goodman is the bookkeeper of a retail furniture store. Her store accepts credit from customers and lately has accumulated a large amount of accounts receivable instead of cash. Peggy knows that she will eventually receive the cash, but she is concerned about her cash flow. She needs to pay her employees and doesn't think she has enough cash on hand to do so. She is also concerned that she won't receive all of the cash that is due to the business. What should Peggy do?

### Solution

Peggy should consider selling the receivables to a finance company or bank. If the business sells the receivables, it will receive cash immediately, less a fee charged by the finance company or bank. The buyer of the receivables (the finance company or bank) then takes over the receivables and is responsible for collecting the cash when the receivables come due. Peggy's store no longer has the risk of uncollectibles. However, this decision comes at a cost. Peggy must be willing to receive less cash because of the fee the buyer of the receivables charges.

## Try It!

Phoenix Restaurants accepts credit and debit cards as forms of payment. Assume Phoenix had $12,000 of credit and debit card sales on June 30, 2015.

1. Suppose Phoenix's processor charges a 2% fee and deposits sales net of the fee. Journalize the sale transaction for the restaurant.
2. Suppose Phoenix's processor charges a 2% fee and deposits sales using the gross method. Journalize the sale transaction for the restaurant.

**Check your answers online in MyAccountingLab or at http://www.pearsonhighered.com/Horngren.**

For more practice, see Short Exercises S8-1 and S8-2. MyAccountingLab

# HOW ARE UNCOLLECTIBLES ACCOUNTED FOR WHEN USING THE DIRECT WRITE-OFF METHOD?

**Learning Objective 2**

Apply the direct write-off method for uncollectibles

Selling on account brings both a benefit and a cost:

- The benefit to a business is the potential increased revenues and profits by making sales to a wider range of customers.
- The cost, however, is that some customers do not pay, creating uncollectible receivables.

Customers' accounts receivable that are uncollectible must be written off or removed from the books because the company does not expect to receive cash in the future. Instead, the company must record an expense associated with the cost of the uncollectible account. This expense is called **bad debts expense**. Bad debts expense is sometimes called *doubtful accounts expense* or *uncollectible accounts expense*.

**Bad Debts Expense**
The cost to the seller of extending credit. It arises from the failure to collect from some credit customers.

There are two methods of accounting for uncollectible receivables and recording the related bad debts expense:

- Direct write-off method
- Allowance method

## Recording and Writing Off Uncollectible Accounts—Direct Write-off Method

The **direct write-off method** of accounting for uncollectible receivables is primarily used by small, nonpublic companies. Under the direct write-off method, accounts receivable are written off and bad debts expense is recorded when the business determines that it will never collect from a specific customer.

**Direct Write-off Method**
A method of accounting for uncollectible receivables in which the company records bad debts expense when a customer's account receivable is uncollectible.

For example, let's assume that on August 9 Smart Touch Learning determines that it will not be able to collect $200 from customer Dan King for a sale of merchandise inventory made on May 5. The company would write off the customer's account receivable by debiting Bad Debts Expense and crediting the customer's Accounts Receivable as follows:

| Date | Accounts and Explanation | Debit | Credit |
| --- | --- | --- | --- |
| Aug. 9 | Bad Debts Expense | 200 | |
| | Accounts Receivable—King | | 200 |
| | *Wrote off an uncollectible account.* | | |

| A↓ | = | L | + | E↓ |
| --- | --- | --- | --- | --- |
| Accounts Receivable↓ | | | | Bad Debts Expense↑ |

Once an account receivable is written off, the company stops pursuing the collection. Some companies might turn delinquent receivables over to an attorney or other collection agency to recover some of the cash for the company, but generally companies do not expect to receive any future payment.

## Recovery of Accounts Previously Written Off—Direct Write-off Method

Occasionally after a company writes off an account, the customer will decide to make payment. To account for this recovery, the company must reverse the earlier write-off. For example, on September 10, Smart Touch Learning unexpectedly receives $200 cash from

Dan King. The company will reverse the earlier write-off and then record the cash collection as follows:

| A↑ | | L + E↑ |
|---|---|---|
| Accounts Receivable↑ | = | Bad Debts Expense↓ |

| Date | Accounts and Explanation | Debit | Credit |
|---|---|---|---|
| Sep. 10 | Accounts Receivable—King | 200 | |
| | Bad Debts Expense | | 200 |
| | *Reinstated previously written off account.* | | |
| | | | |
| 10 | Cash | 200 | |
| | Accounts Receivable—King | | 200 |
| | *Collected cash on account.* | | |

| A↑↓ | | L + E |
|---|---|---|
| Cash↑ Accounts Receivable↓ | = | |

*In order to keep accurate records about the collection of cash for a previously written off account, the business should reestablish the Accounts Receivable by debiting the receivable account. Then the business can record the receipt of cash for the receivable by debiting Cash and crediting Accounts Receivable. This helps restore the credit history of the customer by showing that the customer did fulfill the promise of payment.*

## Limitations of the Direct Write-off Method

The direct write-off method, as stated earlier, is often used only by small, nonpublic companies. This is because the direct write-off method violates the matching principle. The matching principle requires that the expense of uncollectible accounts be matched with the related revenue. For example, when using the direct write-off method, a company might record sales revenue in 2015 but not record the bad debts expense until 2016. By recording the bad debts expense in a different year than when the revenue was recorded, the company is overstating net income in 2015 and understating net income in 2016. In addition, on the balance sheet at December 31, 2015, Accounts Receivable will be overstated because the company will have some receivables that will be uncollectible but are not yet written off. This method is only acceptable for companies that have very few uncollectible receivables. Most companies must use a method that does a better job of matching expenses to the associated sales revenue. This method is called the *allowance method,* and it is the method required by GAAP.

## Try It!

Williams Company uses the direct write-off method to account for uncollectible receivables. On July 18, Williams wrote off a $6,800 account receivable from customer W. Jennings. On August 24, Williams unexpectedly received full payment from Jennings on the previously written off account.

3. Journalize Williams's write-off on the uncollectible receivable.
4. Journalize Williams's collection of the previously written off receivable.

**Check your answers online in MyAccountingLab or at http://www.pearsonhighered.com/Horngren.**

For more practice, see Short Exercises S8-3 and S8-4. MyAccountingLab

## HOW ARE UNCOLLECTIBLES ACCOUNTED FOR WHEN USING THE ALLOWANCE METHOD?

**Learning Objective 3**

Apply the allowance method for uncollectibles and estimate bad debts expense based on the percent-of-sales, percent-of-receivables, and aging-of-receivables methods

Most companies use the allowance method to measure bad debts. The **allowance method** is based on the matching principle; thus, the key concept is to record bad debts expense in the same period as the sales revenue. The offset to the expense is a contra asset account called **Allowance for Bad Debts** or *Allowance for Doubtful Accounts*. The allowance account reduces the asset Accounts Receivable. The business does not wait to see which customers will not pay. Instead, it records a bad debts expense based on estimates developed from past experience and uses the Allowance for Bad Debts to hold the pool of "unknown" uncollectible accounts.

**Allowance Method**
A method of accounting for uncollectible receivables in which the company estimates bad debts expense instead of waiting to see which customers the company will not collect from.

**Allowance for Bad Debts**
A contra asset account, related to accounts receivable, that holds the estimated amount of uncollectible accounts.

### Recording Bad Debts Expense—Allowance Method

When using the allowance method, companies estimate bad debts expense at the end of the period and then record an adjusting entry. Suppose that as of December 31, 2017, Smart Touch Learning estimates that $80 of its $4,400 accounts receivable are uncollectible. The accounting clerk will record the following adjusting entry:

| Date | Accounts and Explanation | Debit | Credit |
|---|---|---|---|
| 2017 | | | |
| Dec. 31 | Bad Debts Expense | 80 | |
| | Allowance for Bad Debts | | 80 |
| | *Recorded bad debts expense for the period.* | | |

| A↓ | | L | + | E↓ |
|---|---|---|---|---|
| Allowance for Bad Debts↑ | = | | | Bad Debts Expense↑ |

After posting the adjusting entry, Smart Touch Learning has the following balances in its accounts:

**Accounts Receivable**

| | |
|---|---|
| Dec. 31 4,400 | |

**Allowance for Bad Debts**

| | |
|---|---|
| | 80 Dec. 31 |

**Bad Debts Expense**

| | |
|---|---|
| Dec. 31 80 | |

Accounts Receivable will be reported on the balance sheet, but it will now be shown at the net realizable value. **Net realizable value** is the net value the company expects to collect from its accounts receivable (Accounts Receivable less Allowance for Bad Debts). Smart Touch Learning would report the following on its balance sheet:

**Net Realizable Value**
The net value a company expects to collect from its accounts receivable. Accounts Receivable less Allowance for Bad Debts.

| SMART TOUCH LEARNING<br>Balance Sheet (Partial)<br>December 31, 2017 | | |
|---|---|---|
| **Assets** | | |
| Current Assets: | | |
| Accounts Receivable | $ 4,400 | |
| Less: Allowance for Bad Debts | (80) | $ 4,320 |

IFRS

Under IFRS, receivables are recognized and reported similarly to what is required by GAAP. Accounts Receivable must be reported at net realizable value. The allowance method is used to accomplish the matching of bad debt expense to the sales of the period and to report receivables at net realizable value. Under IFRS, the Allowance for Bad Debts may be called the **Provision** for Bad Debts. IFRS provides more detailed criteria than GAAP for determining when an account is uncollectible.

The balance sheet now reports the amount of accounts receivable that Smart Touch Learning expects to collect, $4,320. The contra account, Allowance for Bad Debts, is subtracted from Accounts Receivable showing that although $4,400 is owed to Smart Touch Learning, the company estimates that $80 of accounts receivable will be uncollectible.

## ETHICS

### Should the uncollectible accounts be underestimated?

Norah Wang is in the process of recording adjusting entries for her employer, Happy Kennels. She is evaluating the uncollectible accounts and determining the amount of bad debts expense to record for the year. Her manager, Gillian Tedesco, has asked that Norah underestimate the amount of uncollectible accounts for the year. Gillian is hoping to get a bank loan for an expansion of the kennel facility, and she is concerned that the net income of the company will be too low for a loan to be approved. What should Norah do?

#### Solution

It is important that accounts receivable be reported at the appropriate amount on the balance sheet. This involves determining an accurate estimate of uncollectible accounts and recognizing the associated bad debts expense. In understating the amount of uncollectible accounts, Norah would be misleading the bank on the amount of cash that Happy Kennels expects to collect in the future.

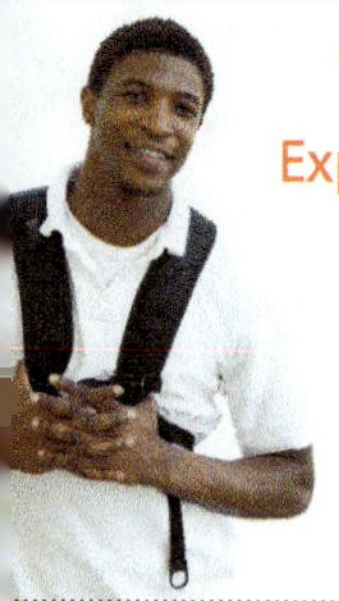

Why isn't Bad Debts Expense debited when writing off an account receivable when using the allowance method?

## Writing Off Uncollectible Accounts—Allowance Method

When using the allowance method, companies still write off accounts receivable that are uncollectible. However, instead of recording a debit to Bad Debts Expense (as done when using the direct write-off method), the company will record a debit to Allowance for Bad Debts. **Bad Debts Expense is not debited when a company writes off an account receivable when using the allowance method because the company has already recorded the Bad Debts Expense as an adjusting entry.** The entry to write off an account under the allowance method has no effect on net income at the time of entry.

For example, on January 10, 2018, Smart Touch Learning determines that it cannot collect a total of $25 from its customer, Shawn Clark. The accounting clerk would record the following entry to write off the account:

| A↑↓ | | L + E |
|---|---|---|
| Allowance for Bad Debts↓<br>Accounts Receivable↓ | = | |

| Date | Accounts and Explanation | Debit | Credit |
|---|---|---|---|
| 2018 | | | |
| Jan. 10 | Allowance for Bad Debts | 25 | |
| | Accounts Receivable—Clark | | 25 |
| | *Wrote off an uncollectible account.* | | |

Smart Touch Learning's account balances after the write-off are:

**Accounts Receivable**

| | | | |
|---|---|---|---|
| Jan. 1, 2018 | 4,400 | | |
| | | 25 | Jan. 10, 2018 |
| Bal. | 4,375 | | |

**Allowance for Bad Debts**

| | | | |
|---|---|---|---|
| | | 80 | Jan. 1, 2018 |
| Jan. 10, 2018 | 25 | | |
| | | 55 | Bal. |

The entry to write off a receivable reduces the amount of the Allowance for Bad Debts account and also the Accounts Receivable account, but it does not affect the net realizable value shown on the balance sheet. This is because both Allowance for Bad Debts (contra asset) and Accounts Receivable (asset) were reduced by the amount of the write-off.

In addition, the write-off of a receivable does not affect net income because the entry does not involve revenue or expenses.

| | Before Write-off | After Write-off |
|---|---|---|
| Accounts Receivable | $ 4,400 | $ 4,375 |
| Less: Allowance for Bad Debts | (80) | (55) |
| Net Realizable Value | $ 4,320 | $ 4,320 |

## Recovery of Accounts Previously Written Off—Allowance Method

After a company has previously written off an account, the company stops attempting to collect on the receivable. Customers will occasionally make payment on receivables that have already been written off. A business will need to reverse the write-off to the Allowance for Bad Debts account and then record the receipt of cash. In reversing the write-off, the business is reestablishing the receivable account and reversing the write-off from the Allowance for Bad Debts account.

Recall that Smart Touch Learning wrote off the $25 receivable from customer Shawn Clark on January 10, 2018. It is now March 4, 2018, and Smart Touch Learning unexpectedly receives $25 cash from Clark. The entries to reverse the write-off and record the receipt of cash are as follows:

| Date | Accounts and Explanation | Debit | Credit |
|---|---|---|---|
| 2018 | | | |
| Mar. 4 | Accounts Receivable—Clark | 25 | |
| | Allowance for Bad Debts | | 25 |
| | *Reinstated previously written off account.* | | |
| 4 | Cash | 25 | |
| | Accounts Receivable—Clark | | 25 |
| | *Collected cash on account.* | | |

| A↑↓ | | L + E |
|---|---|---|
| Accounts Receivable↑<br>Allowance for Bad Debts↑ | = | |

| A↑↓ | | L + E |
|---|---|---|
| Cash↑<br>Accounts Receivable↓ | = | |

## Estimating and Recording Bad Debts Expense—Allowance Method

How do companies determine the amount of bad debts expense when using the allowance method? Companies use their past experience as well as consider the economy, the industry they operate in, and other variables. In short, they make an educated guess, called an *estimate*. There are three basic ways to estimate uncollectibles:

- Percent-of-sales
- Percent-of-receivables
- Aging-of-receivables

### Percent-of-Sales Method

The **percent-of-sales method** computes bad debts expense as a percentage of net credit sales. (Some companies will use all sales, not just credit sales.) This method is also called the *income-statement approach* because it focuses on the amount of expense that is reported on the income statement.

**Percent-of-Sales Method**
A method of estimating uncollectible receivables that calculates bad debts expense based on a percentage of net credit sales.

Let's return to Smart Touch Learning. Based on prior experience, the company's bad debts expense is normally 0.5% of net credit sales, which totaled $60,000 for the year. The accountant calculates bad debts expense using the percent-of-sales method as follows:

**Percent-of-Sales Method:**

Bad Debts Expense = Net credit sales × %

= $60,000 × 0.005

= $300

At December 31, Smart Touch Learning records the following adjusting entry to recognize bad debts expense for the year:

| A↓ | = | L + E↓ |
|---|---|---|
| Allowance for Bad Debts↑ | = | Bad Debts Expense↑ |

| Date | Accounts and Explanation | Debit | Credit |
|---|---|---|---|
| 2018 | | | |
| Dec. 31 | Bad Debts Expense | 300 | |
| | Allowance for Bad Debts | | 300 |
| | *Recorded bad debts expense for the period.* | | |

When using the allowance method, the only time Bad Debts Expense is recorded is as an adjusting entry.

After posting the adjusting entry, Smart Touch Learning has the following balances in its balance sheet and income statement accounts. Ignore the previously recorded reversal of the write-off and assume collections on account during the year are $58,000:

**Balance sheet accounts:**

**Accounts Receivable**

| | Debit | Credit | |
|---|---|---|---|
| Jan. 1, 2018, Bal. | 4,400 | | |
| Net credit sales | 60,000 | 25 | Write-off |
| | | 58,000 | Collections |
| Unadj. Bal. | 6,375 | | |
| **Dec. 31, 2018, Bal.** | **6,375** | | |

**Allowance for Bad Debts**

| | Debit | Credit | |
|---|---|---|---|
| | | 80 | Jan. 1, 2018, Bal. |
| Write-off | 25 | | |
| | | 55 | Unadj. Bal. |
| | | 300 | Adj. |
| | | **355** | **Dec. 31, 2018, Bal.** |

**Income statement account:**

**Bad Debts Expense**

| | Debit | Credit |
|---|---|---|
| Jan. 1, 2018, Bal. | 0 | |
| Adj. | 300 | |
| **Dec. 31, 2018, Bal.** | **300** | |

## Percent-of-Receivables Method

The percent-of-receivables and aging-of-receivables methods are based on the balance of accounts receivable. These approaches are also called *balance-sheet approaches* because they focus on Accounts Receivable (a balance sheet account) and determine a target allowance balance based on a percentage of the receivable balance.

The first balance sheet approach is the **percent-of-receivables method**. In the percent-of-receivables method, the business once again determines a percentage of uncollectible accounts based on past experience. This method is different than the percent-of-sales method because it multiplies the percentage by the *ending* unadjusted balance in the Accounts Receivable account instead of by net credit sales.

**Percent-of-Receivables Method**
A method of estimating uncollectible receivables by determining the balance of the Allowance for Bad Debts account based on a percentage of accounts receivable.

The calculation for bad debts expense under the percent-of-receivables method is a two-step process. First, the company determines the target balance of Allowance for Bad Debts. Then, it uses the target balance to determine the amount of the bad debts expense.

> **Percent-of-Receivables Method:**
>
> Step 1: Determine the target balance of Allowance for Bad Debts.
>
> Target balance = Ending balance of accounts receivable × %
>
> Step 2: Determine the amount of bad debts expense by evaluating the allowance account.
>
> Bad debts expense = Target balance − Unadjusted credit balance of Allowance for Bad Debts
>
> OR
>
> Bad debts expense = Target balance + Unadjusted debit balance of Allowance for Bad Debts

Let's look at an example for Smart Touch Learning. Assume that at December 31, 2018, the company's unadjusted accounts receivable balance is $6,375. Smart Touch Learning estimates that 4% of its accounts receivable will be uncollectible. In step 1, the company determines the target balance for the Allowance for Bad Debts account: $255 ($6,375 × 0.04). Next, its accountant determines the amount of the bad debts expense adjustment: $255 − $55 = $200.

**Allowance for Bad Debts**

| | | | |
|---|---|---|---|
| | | 80 | Jan. 1, 2018, Bal. |
| Write-offs | 25 | | |
| | | 55 | Unadj. Bal. |
| | | 200 | Adj. |
| | | **255** | **Dec. 31, 2018, Bal.** |

Step 2: The bad debts expense adjustment must be calculated based on the target balance. $255 − $55 = $200

Step 1: Calculate the target balance. It is always reported as a credit balance. $6,375 × 0.04 = $255

Smart Touch Learning records the following adjusting entry on December 31 to recognize bad debts expense for the year:

| Date | Accounts and Explanation | Debit | Credit |
|---|---|---|---|
| 2018 | | | |
| Dec. 31 | Bad Debts Expense | 200 | |
| | Allowance for Bad Debts | | 200 |
| | *Recorded bad debts expense for the period.* | | |

| A$\downarrow$ | = | L | + | E$\downarrow$ |
|---|---|---|---|---|
| Allowance for Bad Debts$\uparrow$ | | | | Bad Debts Expense$\uparrow$ |

After posting the adjusting entry, Smart Touch Learning has the following balances in its balance sheet and income statement accounts:

**Balance sheet accounts:**

**Accounts Receivable**

| | | | |
|---|---|---|---|
| Jan. 1, 2018, Bal. | 4,400 | | |
| Net credit sales | 60,000 | 25 | Write-offs |
| | | 58,000 | Collections |
| Unadj. Bal. | 6,375 | | |
| **Dec. 31, 2018, Bal.** | **6,375** | | |

**Allowance for Bad Debts**

| | | | |
|---|---|---|---|
| | | 80 | Jan. 1, 2018, Bal. |
| Write-offs | 25 | | |
| | | 55 | Unadj. Bal. |
| | | 200 | Adj. |
| | | **255** | **Dec. 31, 2018, Bal.** |

**Income statement account:**

**Bad Debts Expense**

| | | |
|---|---|---|
| Jan. 1, 2018, Bal. | 0 | |
| Adj. | 200 | |
| **Dec. 31, 2018, Bal.** | **200** | |

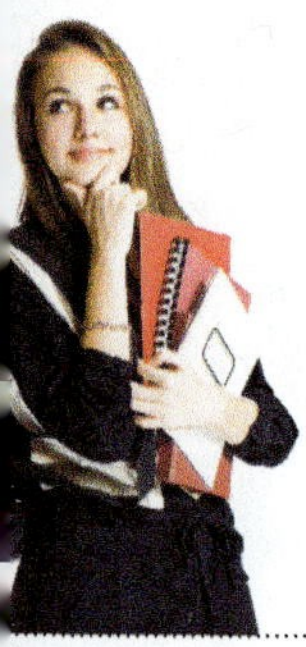

What if a business had a debit balance in the Allowance for Bad Debts account before the adjustment for bad debts expense?

In the preceding example, Smart Touch Learning had an unadjusted *credit* balance in the allowance account. **If a company has a debit balance before the adjustment, the calculation for bad debts expense is a little different. Instead of subtracting the unadjusted balance of the Allowance for Bad Debts from the target balance, the unadjusted balance will be added to the target balance.**

Let's look at an example. Suppose that Martin's Music has a *debit* balance in its Allowance for Bad Debts account of $150. Assume that it estimates its percentage of uncollectible accounts will be 2% of $40,000 of Accounts Receivable. Martin's Music's bad debts expense adjustment would be calculated as follows:

**Allowance for Bad Debts**

| | | | |
|---|---|---|---|
| Unadj. Bal. | 150 | | |
| | | 950 | Adj. |
| | | **800** | **Bal.** |

Step 2: The bad debts expense adjustment must be calculated based on the target balance. $800 + $150 = $950

Step 1: Calculate the target balance. It is always reported as a credit balance. $40,000 × 0.02 = $800

*A company will have a debit balance in the Allowance for Bad Debts account if the company has written off more accounts receivable than it expected to during the year.*

Notice that when the allowance account has an unadjusted debit balance, the target balance must be added to the unadjusted balance of the Allowance for Bad Debts to determine the bad debts expense adjustment. Martin's Music would record the following adjusting entry to recognize bad debts expense:

| Date | Accounts and Explanation | Debit | Credit |
|---|---|---|---|
| Dec. 31 | Bad Debts Expense | 950 | |
| | Allowance for Bad Debts | | 950 |
| | *Recorded bad debts expense for the period.* | | |

| A↓ | | L + E↓ |
|---|---|---|
| Allowance for Bad Debts↑ | = | Bad Debts Expense↑ |

## Aging-of-Receivables Method

The **aging-of-receivables method** is similar to the percent-of-receivables method. However, in the aging method, businesses group individual accounts (Broxson, Andrews, and so on) according to how long the receivable has been outstanding. Then they apply a different percentage uncollectible on each aging category. Exhibit 8-1 shows the aging schedule for Smart Touch Learning.

**Aging-of-Receivables Method**
A method of estimating uncollectible receivables by determining the balance of the Allowance for Bad Debts account based on the age of individual accounts receivable.

**Exhibit 8-1 | Aging of Accounts Receivable**

| Age of Account as of December 31, 2018 | | | | | |
|---|---|---|---|---|---|
| Customer Name | 1–30 Days | 31–60 Days | 61–90 Days | Over 90 Days | Total Balance |
| Broxson | $ 800 | | | | $ 800 |
| Phi Chi Fraternity | 2,100 | | | | 2,100 |
| Andrews | | $ 350 | | | 350 |
| Jones | | 480 | | | 480 |
| Perez | 1,345 | | | | 1,345 |
| Thompson | | | $ 1,200 | | 1,200 |
| Clark | | | | $ 100 | 100 |
| Totals | $ 4,245 | $ 830 | $ 1,200 | $ 100 | $ 6,375 |
| Estimated percentage uncollectible | × 1% | × 2% | × 3% | × 90% | |
| Estimated total uncollectible | $ 42 | $ 17 | $ 36 | $ 90 | $ 185 ← Target balance |

At year-end, Smart Touch Learning will need to record the adjusting entry to recognize bad debts expense. The procedure is similar to the percent-of-receivables method.

**Aging-of-Receivables Method:**

Step 1: Determine the target balance of Allowance for Bad Debts by using the age of each account.

Step 2: Determine the amount of bad debts expense by evaluating the allowance account.

Bad debts expense = Target balance − Unadjusted credit balance of Allowance for Bad Debts

OR

Bad debts expense = Target balance + Unadjusted debit balance of Allowance for Bad Debts

Based on Exhibit 8-1, Smart Touch Learning knows the target balance of the Allowance for Bad Debts account is $185. Smart Touch Learning will determine its bad debts expense by subtracting the $55 unadjusted credit balance in the allowance account from the target balance, $185.

**Allowance for Bad Debts**

| | | | |
|---|---|---|---|
| | | 80 | Jan. 1, 2018, Bal. |
| Write-offs | 25 | | |
| | | 55 | Unadj. Bal. |
| | | 130 | Adj. |
| | | **185** | **Dec. 31, 2018, Bal.** |

Step 2: The bad debts expense adjustment must be calculated based on the target balance. $185 – $55 = $130

Step 1: Calculate the target balance using the aging schedule. It is always reported as a credit balance.

Smart Touch Learning will record the following adjusting entry on December 31 to recognize bad debts expense for the year:

| A↓ | = | L + E↓ |
|---|---|---|
| Allowance for Bad Debts↑ | | Bad Debts Expense↑ |

| Date | Accounts and Explanation | Debit | Credit |
|---|---|---|---|
| 2018 | | | |
| Dec. 31 | Bad Debts Expense | 130 | |
| | Allowance for Bad Debts | | 130 |
| | *Recorded bad debts expense for the period.* | | |

After posting the adjusting entry, Smart Touch Learning has the following balances in its balance sheet and income statement accounts:

**Balance sheet accounts:**

**Accounts Receivable**

| | | | |
|---|---|---|---|
| Jan. 1, 2018, Bal. | 4,400 | | |
| Net credit sales | 60,000 | 25 | Write-offs |
| | | 58,000 | Collections |
| Unadj. Bal. | 6,375 | | |
| **Dec. 31, 2018, Bal.** | **6,375** | | |

**Allowance for Bad Debts**

| | | | |
|---|---|---|---|
| | | 80 | Jan. 1, 2018, Bal. |
| Write-offs | 25 | | |
| | | 55 | Unadj. Bal. |
| | | 130 | Adj. |
| | | **185** | **Dec. 31, 2018, Bal.** |

**Income statement account:**

**Bad Debts Expense**

| | | | |
|---|---|---|---|
| Jan. 1, 2018, Bal. | 0 | | |
| Adj. | 130 | | |
| **Dec. 31, 2018, Bal.** | **130** | | |

## Comparison of Accounting for Uncollectibles

Exhibit 8-2 shows the journal entries that are recorded when using both the direct write-off method and the allowance method of accounting for uncollectibles. Take a moment to review the differences in these two methods. Remember that when using the direct write-off method, the business does not use an allowance account and that this method does not conform with GAAP.

### Exhibit 8-2 | Direct Write-off Method Versus Allowance Method

| DIRECT WRITE-OFF METHOD | | | ALLOWANCE METHOD | | |
|---|---|---|---|---|---|
| **Write-off of an uncollectible account:** | | | | | |
| Bad Debts Expense | 25 | | Allowance for Bad Debts | 25 | |
| Accounts Receivable—Customer Name | | 25 | Accounts Receivable—Customer Name | | 25 |
| *Wrote off an uncollectible account.* | | | *Wrote off an uncollectible account.* | | |
| **Recovery of accounts previously written off:** | | | | | |
| Accounts Receivable—Customer Name | 25 | | Accounts Receivable—Customer Name | 25 | |
| Bad Debts Expense | | 25 | Allowance for Bad Debts | | 25 |
| *Reinstated previously written off account.* | | | *Reinstated previously written off account.* | | |
| Cash | 25 | | Cash | 25 | |
| Accounts Receivable—Customer Name | | 25 | Accounts Receivable—Customer Name | | 25 |
| *Collected cash on account.* | | | *Collected cash on account.* | | |
| **Adjusting entry to recognize bad debts:** | | | | | |
| *No adjusting entry recorded.* | | | Bad Debts Expense | 300 | |
| | | | Allowance for Bad Debts | | 300 |
| | | | *Recorded bad debts expense for the period.* | | |

Under the allowance method of accounting for uncollectibles, businesses must estimate the amount of the bad debts expense at the end of the accounting period. This is done using one of three methods: percent-of-sales, percent-of-receivables, or aging-of-receivables. Exhibit 8-3 summarizes the differences in those three methods.

### Exhibit 8-3 | Comparison of Percent-of-Sales, Percent-of-Receivables, and Aging-of-Receivables Methods

**ALLOWANCE METHOD**

**INCOME STATEMENT APPROACH:**

Percent-of-Sales Method

Bad Debts Expense = Net credit sales × %

**BALANCE SHEET APPROACHES:**

Percent-of-Receivables Method | Aging-of-Receivables Method

Step 1:
Target balance = Ending balance of Accounts Receivable × %

Step 2:
Bad debts expense = Target balance − Unadj. *credit* balance in Allowance for Bad Debts

OR

Bad debts expense = Target balance + Unadj. *debit* balance in Allowance for Bad Debts

## Try It!

Johnson Company uses the allowance method to account for uncollectible receivables. On September 2, Johnson wrote off a $14,000 account receivable from customer J. Mraz. On December 12, Johnson unexpectedly received full payment from Mraz on the previously written off account. Johnson records an adjusting entry for bad debts expense of $800 on December 31.

5. Journalize Johnson's write-off of the uncollectible receivable.
6. Journalize Johnson's collection of the previously written off receivable.
7. Journalize Johnson's adjustment for bad debts expense.

**Check your answers online in MyAccountingLab or at http://www.pearsonhighered.com/Horngren.**

For more practice, see Short Exercises S8-5 through S8-8. MyAccountingLab

## HOW ARE NOTES RECEIVABLE ACCOUNTED FOR?

**Learning Objective 4**

Account for notes receivable including computing interest and recording honored and dishonored notes

**Principal**
The amount loaned out by the payee and borrowed by the maker of the note.

**Interest**
The revenue to the payee for loaning money—the expense to the debtor.

**Interest Period**
The period of time during which interest is computed. It extends from the original date of the note to the maturity date.

**Interest Rate**
The percentage rate of interest specified by the note.

**Maturity Value**
The sum of the principal plus interest due at maturity.

Notes receivable are more formal than accounts receivable. The debtor signs a promissory note as evidence of the transaction. Before launching into the accounting, let's define the special terms used for notes receivable:

- **Promissory note**—A written promise to pay a specified amount of money at a particular future date, usually with interest.
- **Maker of the note (debtor)**—The entity that signs the note and promises to pay the required amount; the maker of the note is the debtor.
- **Payee of the note (creditor)**—The entity to whom the maker promises future payment; the payee of the note is the creditor. The creditor is the company that loans the money.
- **Principal**—The amount loaned by the payee and borrowed by the maker of the note.
- **Interest**—The revenue to the payee for loaning money. Interest is an expense to the debtor and revenue to the creditor.
- **Interest period**—The period of time during which interest is computed. It extends from the original date of the note to the maturity date. Also called the *note term.*
- **Interest rate**—The percentage rate of interest specified by the note. Interest rates are almost always stated for a period of one year.
- **Maturity date**—As stated earlier, this is the date when final payment of the note is due. Also called the *due date.*
- **Maturity value**—The sum of the principal plus interest due at maturity. Maturity value is the total amount that will be paid back.

Exhibit 8-4 illustrates a promissory note.

**Exhibit 8-4 | Promissory Note**

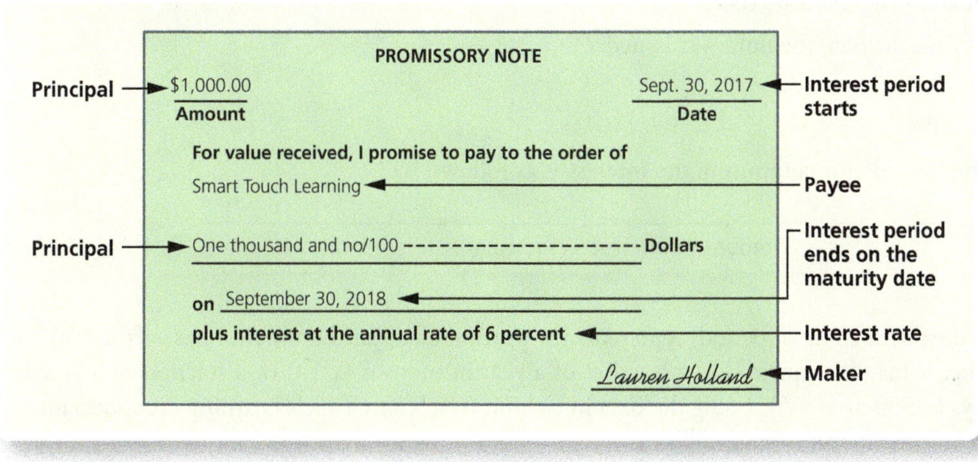


In Exhibit 8-4, we can see Smart Touch Learning is lending Lauren Holland $1,000 on September 30, 2017, for one year at an annual interest rate of 6%. The accounting clerk would record the following journal entry:

| Date | Accounts and Explanation | Debit | Credit |
|---|---|---|---|
| 2017 | | | |
| Sep. 30 | Notes Receivable—Holland | 1,000 | |
| | Cash | | 1,000 |
| | *Accepted note in exchange for cash.* | | |

A↑↓ = L + E
Notes Receivable↑
Cash↓

## Identifying Maturity Date

Some notes specify the maturity date. For example, September 30, 2018, is the maturity date of the note shown in Exhibit 8-4. Other notes state the period of the note in days or months. When the period is given in months, the note's maturity date falls on the same day of the month as the date the note was issued. For example, a six-month note dated February 16, 2017, would mature on August 16, 2017.

When the period is given in days, the maturity date is determined by counting the actual days from the date of issue. A 180-day note dated February 16, 2017, matures on August 15, 2017, as shown here:

| Month | Number of Days | Cumulative Total |
|---|---|---|
| Feb. 2017 | 28 − 16 = 12 | 12 |
| Mar. 2017 | 31 | 43 |
| Apr. 2017 | 30 | 73 |
| May 2017 | 31 | 104 |
| Jun. 2017 | 30 | 134 |
| Jul. 2017 | 31 | 165 |
| Aug. 2017 | 15 | 180 |

In counting the days remaining for a note, remember to

- Count the maturity date.
- Omit the date the note was issued.

## Computing Interest on a Note

The formula for computing the interest is as follows:

Amount of interest = Principal × Interest rate × Time

In the formula, time (period) represents the portion of a year that interest has accrued on the note. It may be expressed as a fraction of a year in months (x/12) or a fraction of a year in days (x/360 or x/365). Using the data in Exhibit 8-4, Smart Touch Learning computes interest revenue for one year as follows:

Amount of interest = Principal × Interest rate × Time
= $1,000 × 0.06 × 12/12
= $60

The maturity value of the note is $1,060 ($1,000 principal + $60 interest). The time element is 12/12 or 1 because the note's term is one year.

When the term of a note is stated in months, we compute the interest based on the 12-month year. Interest on a $2,000 note at 10% for nine months is computed as follows:

Amount of interest = Principal × Interest rate × Time
= $2,000 × 0.10 × 9/12
= $150

When the interest period is stated in days, we sometimes compute interest based on a 360-day year rather than on a 365-day year. (A 360-day year eliminates some rounding and will be used for all calculations in this chapter.) The interest on a $5,000 note at 12% for 60 days can be computed as follows:

Amount of interest = Principal × Interest rate × Time
= $5,000 × 0.12 × 60/360
= $100

Keep in mind that interest rates are stated as an annual rate. Therefore, the time in the interest formula should also be expressed in terms of a fraction of one year.

## Accruing Interest Revenue and Recording Honored Notes Receivable

Some notes receivable may be outstanding at the end of an accounting period. The interest revenue earned on the note up to year-end is part of that year's earnings. Recall that interest revenue is earned over time, not just when cash is received. Because of the revenue recognition principle, we want to record the earnings from the note in the year in which they were earned.

Now, we continue analyzing Smart Touch Learning's note receivable from Exhibit 8-4. Smart Touch Learning's accounting period ends December 31.

- How much of the total interest revenue does Smart Touch Learning earn in 2017 (from September 30 through December 31)? Smart Touch Learning earns three months (October, November, and December) of interest.

$$\$1,000 \times 0.06 \times 3/12 = \$15$$

The accounting clerk makes the following adjusting entry at December 31, 2017:

| Date | Accounts and Explanation | Debit | Credit |
|---|---|---|---|
| 2017 | | | |
| Dec. 31 | Interest Receivable | 15 | |
| | Interest Revenue | | 15 |
| | *Accrued interest revenue.* | | |

A↑ (Interest Receivable↑) = L + E↑ (Interest Revenue↑)

- How much interest revenue does Smart Touch Learning earn in 2018 (for January 1 through September 30)? Smart Touch Learning earns nine months (January through September) of interest.

$$\$1,000 \times 0.06 \times 9/12 = \$45$$

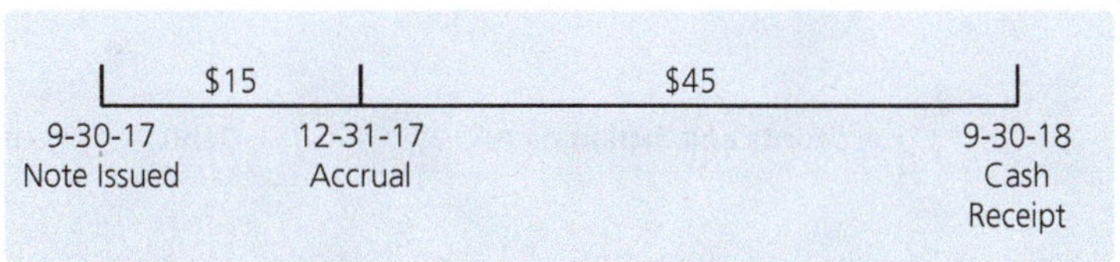


On the maturity date of the note, Smart Touch Learning will receive cash for the principal amount plus interest. The company considers the note honored and makes the following entry:

| Date | Accounts and Explanation | Debit | Credit |
|---|---|---|---|
| 2018 | | | |
| Sep. 30 | Cash ($1,000 + ($1,000 × 0.06 × 12/12)) | 1,060 | |
| | Notes Receivable—Holland | | 1,000 |
| | Interest Receivable | | 15 |
| | Interest Revenue | | 45 |
| | *Collected note receivable plus interest.* | | |

A↑ (Cash↑, Notes Receivable↓, Interest Receivable↓) = L + E↑ (Interest Revenue↑)

Some companies sell merchandise in exchange for notes receivable. Assume that on July 1, 2017, Rosa Electric sells household appliances for $2,000 to Dorman Builders. Dorman signs a nine-month promissory note at 10% annual interest. Rosa's entries to record the sale (ignore Cost of Goods Sold), interest accrual, and collection from Dorman are as follows:

| A↑ | = | L + E↑ |
|---|---|---|
| Notes Receivable↑ | = | Sales Revenue↑ |

| A↑ | = | L + E↑ |
|---|---|---|
| Interest Receivable↑ | = | Interest Revenue↑ |

| A↑ | = | L + E↑ |
|---|---|---|
| Cash↑ Notes Receivable↓ Interest Receivable↓ | = | Interest Revenue↑ |

| Date | Accounts and Explanation | Debit | Credit |
|---|---|---|---|
| 2017 | | | |
| Jul. 1 | Notes Receivable—Dorman Builders | 2,000 | |
| | Sales Revenue | | 2,000 |
| | | | |
| Dec. 31 | Interest Receivable ($2,000 × 0.10 × 6/12) | 100 | |
| | Interest Revenue | | 100 |
| | | | |
| 2018 | | | |
| Apr. 1 | Cash ($2,000 + ($2,000 × 0.10 × 9/12)) | 2,150 | |
| | Notes Receivable—Dorman Builders | | 2,000 |
| | Interest Receivable | | 100 |
| | Interest Revenue ($2,000 × 0.10 × 3/12) | | 50 |

A company may accept a note receivable from a credit customer who fails to pay an account receivable. The customer signs a promissory note and gives it to the creditor. Suppose Sports Club cannot pay Blanding Services the amount due on accounts receivable of $5,000. Blanding may accept a 60-day, $5,000 note receivable, with 12% interest, from Sports Club on November 19, 2017. Blanding's entries are as follows:

| A↑↓ | = | L + E |
|---|---|---|
| Notes Receivable↑ Accounts Receivable↓ | = | |

| A↑ | = | L + E↑ |
|---|---|---|
| Interest Receivable↑ | = | Interest Revenue↑ |

| A↑ | = | L + E↑ |
|---|---|---|
| Cash↑ Notes Receivable↓ Interest Receivable↓ | = | Interest Revenue↑ |

| Date | Accounts and Explanation | Debit | Credit |
|---|---|---|---|
| 2017 | | | |
| Nov. 19 | Notes Receivable—Sports Club | 5,000 | |
| | Accounts Receivable—Sports Club | | 5,000 |
| | | | |
| Dec. 31 | Interest Receivable ($5,000 × 0.12 × 42/360) | 70 | |
| | Interest Revenue | | 70 |
| | | | |
| 2018 | | | |
| Jan. 18 | Cash ($5,000 + ($5,000 × 0.12 × 60/360)) | 5,100 | |
| | Notes Receivable—Sports Club | | 5,000 |
| | Interest Receivable | | 70 |
| | Interest Revenue ($5,000 × 0.12 × 18/360) | | 30 |

## Recording Dishonored Notes Receivable

**Dishonor a Note**
Failure of a note's maker to pay a note receivable at maturity.

If the maker of a note does not pay at maturity, the maker **dishonors a note** (also called *defaulting on a note*). Because the note has expired, it is no longer in force. But the debtor still owes the payee. The payee can transfer the note receivable amount to Accounts Receivable. Suppose Rubinstein Jewelers has a six-month, 10% note receivable for $1,200 from Mark Adair that was signed on March 3, 2017, and Adair defaults. Rubinstein Jewelers will record the default on September 3, 2017, as follows:

| Date | Accounts and Explanation | Debit | Credit |
|---|---|---|---|
| 2017 | | | |
| Sep. 3 | Accounts Receivable—Adair | 1,260 | |
| | Notes Receivable—Adair | | 1,200 |
| | Interest Revenue ($1,200 × 0.10 × 6/12) | | 60 |

| A↑ | = | L | + | E↑ |
|---|---|---|---|---|
| Accounts Receivable↑ Notes Receivable↓ | = | | | Interest Revenue↑ |

Rubinstein will then bill Adair for the account receivable. This also allows Rubinstein to eventually write off the receivable using either the direct write-off method or the allowance method if at a later date Rubinstein can still not collect the account receivable.

## Try It!

On August 1, Taylor Company lent $80,000 to L. King on a 90-day, 5% note.

8. Journalize for Taylor Company the lending of the money on August 1.
9. Journalize the collection of the principal and interest at maturity. Specify the date.

**Check your answers online in MyAccountingLab or at http://www.pearsonhighered.com/Horngren.**

For more practice, see Short Exercises S8-9 through S8-12. MyAccountingLab

## HOW DO WE USE THE ACID-TEST RATIO, ACCOUNTS RECEIVABLE TURNOVER RATIO, AND DAYS' SALES IN RECEIVABLES TO EVALUATE BUSINESS PERFORMANCE?

**Learning Objective 5**

Use the acid-test ratio, accounts receivable turnover ratio, and days' sales in receivables to evaluate business performance

As discussed earlier in the text, the balance sheet lists assets in the order of liquidity (how quickly an asset can be converted to cash). The partial balance sheet of Green Mountain Coffee Roasters, Inc. shown in Exhibit 8-5 (on the next page) provides an example of this. Balance-sheet data become more useful by showing the relationships among assets, liabilities, and revenues. Let's examine three important ratios using Green Mountain Coffee Roasters, Inc.

**Exhibit 8-5 | Green Mountain Coffee Roasters, Inc. Partial Balance Sheet**

**GREEN MOUNTAIN COFFEE ROASTERS, INC.**
Balance Sheet (Partial)
September 28, 2013, and September 29, 2012
(in thousands)

| Assets | Sept. 28, 2013 | Sept. 29, 2012 |
|---|---|---|
| Current Assets: | | |
| Cash and Cash Equivalents | $ 260,092 | $ 58,289 |
| Restricted Cash and Cash Equivalents | 560 | 12,884 |
| Receivables, less uncollectible accounts and return allowances | 467,976 | 363,771 |
| Inventories | 676,089 | 768,437 |
| Income Taxes Receivable | 11,747 | 32,943 |
| Other Current Assets | 46,891 | 35,019 |
| Deferred Income Taxes, Net | 58,137 | 51,613 |
| Total Current Assets | $ 1,521,492 | $ 1,322,956 |
| | | |
| Total Current Liabilities | $ 597,063 | $ 519,987 |

## Acid-Test (or Quick) Ratio

**Acid-Test Ratio**
The ratio of the sum of cash, cash equivalents, short-term investments, and net current receivables to total current liabilities. The ratio tells whether the entity could pay all its current liabilities if they came due immediately. (Cash including cash equivalents + Short-term investments + Net current receivables) / Total current liabilities.

Previously we discussed the current ratio, which measures a company's ability to pay current liabilities with current assets, and the cash ratio, which measures a company's ability to meet its short-term obligations with cash and cash equivalents. We now introduce the **acid-test ratio** (or *quick ratio*), which is also used to measure a company's ability to pay its current liabilities. The acid-test ratio is a more stringent measure than the current ratio but it is not as stringent as the cash ratio. The acid test is a ratio of the sum of a company's quick assets to total current liabilities. Quick assets are defined as cash including cash equivalents, short-term investments, and net current receivables. The acid-test ratio reveals whether the entity could pay all its current liabilities if they were to become due immediately.

The higher the acid-test ratio, the more able the business is to pay its current liabilities. Green Mountain's acid-test ratio of 1.22 means that the business has $1.22 of quick assets to pay each $1.00 of current liabilities.

Acid-test ratio = (Cash including cash equivalents + Short-term investments + Net current receivables*) / Total current liabilities
= ($260,092 + $560 + $467,976) / $597,063
= 1.22 (rounded)

*Income taxes receivable is not part of net current receivables because it is not a quick asset.

What is an acceptable acid-test ratio? That depends on the industry. In general, an acid-test ratio of 1.00 is considered safe.

## Accounts Receivable Turnover Ratio

**Accounts Receivable Turnover Ratio**
A ratio that measures the number of times the company collects the average accounts receivable balance in a year. Net credit sales / Average net accounts receivable.

The **accounts receivable turnover ratio** measures the number of times the company collects the average accounts receivable balance in a year. The higher the ratio, the faster the cash collections. Green Mountain's accounts receivable turnover ratio, presented below, indicates that the business turns over its receivables 10.5 times a year. Green Mountain's net sales are $4,358,100 (in thousands) for the year ended September 28, 2013.

Accounts receivable turnover ratio = Net credit sales / Average net accounts receivable
= $4,358,100 / [($467,976 + $363,771) / 2]
= 10.48 times (rounded)

*In calculating the accounts receivable turnover ratio for Green Mountain, we use net sales instead of net credit sales. This is because most companies don't report the level of detail needed to determine net credit sales.*

## Days' Sales in Receivables

After making a credit sale, the next step is to collect the receivable. **Days' sales in receivables**, also called the *collection period*, indicates how many days it takes to collect the average level of accounts receivable. The number of days' sales in receivables should be close to the number of days customers are allowed to make payment when credit is extended. The shorter the collection period, the more quickly the organization can use its cash. The longer the collection period, the less cash is available for operations. Green Mountain's days' sales in receivables can be computed as follows:

**Days' Sales in Receivables**
The ratio of average net accounts receivable to one day's sales. The ratio tells how many days it takes to collect the average level of accounts receivable. 365 days / Accounts receivable turnover ratio.

Days' sales in receivables = 365 days / Accounts receivable turnover ratio
= 365 days / 10.48
= 35 days (rounded)

On average, it takes Green Mountain 35 days to collect its accounts receivable. The length of the collection period depends on the credit terms of the sale. For example, sales on net 30 terms should be collected within approximately 30 days. When there is a discount, such as 2/10, net 30, the collection period may be shorter than 30 days. Credit terms of net 45 result in a longer collection period than 30 days.

## Try It!

Lovett Company reported the following selected items at February 29, 2016 (last year's—2015—amounts also given as needed):

| | | | |
|---|---|---|---|
| Accounts Payable | $ 128,000 | Accounts Receivable, net: | |
| Cash | 104,000 | February 29, 2016 | $ 108,000 |
| Merchandise Inventory: | | February 28, 2015 | 68,000 |
| February 29, 2016 | 116,000 | Cost of Goods Sold | 460,000 |
| February 28, 2015 | 80,000 | Short-term Investments | 56,000 |
| Net Credit Sales Revenue | 1,168,000 | Other Current Assets | 48,000 |
| Long term Assets | 168,000 | Other Current Liabilities | 72,000 |
| Long-term Liabilities | 52,000 | | |

**10.** Compute Lovett's (a) acid-test ratio, (b) accounts receivable turnover ratio, and (c) days' sales in receivables for 2016.

**Check your answers online in MyAccountingLab or at http://www.pearsonhighered.com/Horngren.**

For more practice, see Short Exercise S8-13. MyAccountingLab

# REVIEW

## > Things You Should Know

### 1. What are common types of receivables, and how are credit sales recorded?

- A receivable is a monetary claim against a business or an individual.
- There are three major types of receivables:
  - Accounts receivable—Represent the right to receive cash in the future from customers for goods sold or for services performed.
  - Notes receivable—Represent a written promise that the customer will pay a fixed amount of principal plus interest by a certain date in the future.
  - Other receivables—A miscellaneous category that includes any other type of receivables where there is a right to receive cash in the future.
- A critical component of internal control over receivables is the separation of cash-handling and cash-accounting duties.
- A separate accounts receivable account (called a subsidiary account) must be maintained for each customer in order to account for payments received from the customer and amounts still owed.
- The sum of all balances in the subsidiary accounts receivable will equal a control account balance, Accounts Receivable.
- Sales by credit cards and debit cards are treated as cash sales and typically include a fee (Credit Card Expense) that is paid by the business to the credit card processor.
- As a way to receive cash before receivables are collected, businesses can factor or pledge their receivables.

### 2. How are uncollectibles accounted for when using the direct write-off method?

- Writing off uncollectible accounts when using the direct write-off method involves a debit to Bad Debts Expense and a credit to Accounts Receivable.
- Recovery of accounts previously written off is recorded by reversing the write-off entry and then recording an entry to receive the cash.
- The direct write-off method violates the matching principle and is not the method required by GAAP.

### 3. How are uncollectibles accounted for when using the allowance method?

- When using the allowance method, companies estimate bad debts expense at the end of the period and record an adjusting entry that debits Bad Debts Expense and credits Allowance for Bad Debts. There are three ways to estimate bad debts expense:
  - Percent-of-sales method—Computes bad debts expense as a percentage of net credit sales.
  - Percent-of-receivables method—Determines the balance of the Allowance for Bad Debts account based on a percentage of accounts receivable.
  - Aging-of-receivables method—Determines the balance of the Allowance for Bad Debts account based on the age of individual accounts receivable.
- Writing off uncollectible accounts involves a debit to Allowance for Bad Debts and a credit to Accounts Receivable.

- Recovery of accounts previously written off is recorded by reversing the write-off entry and then recording an entry to receive the cash.
- The allowance method follows the matching principle and is required by GAAP.

**4. How are notes receivable accounted for?**

- Notes receivable involve interest that is computed as principal times interest rate times time.
- Interest on notes must be accrued at the end of the each period, and an adjusting entry must be recorded by debiting Interest Receivable and crediting Interest Revenue.
- The receipt of cash at a note's maturity includes the principal plus interest.
- When a customer dishonors a note, the business can transfer the note receivable (plus interest earned) to an accounts receivable.

**5. How do we use the acid-test ratio, accounts receivable turnover ratio, and days' sales in receivables to evaluate business performance?**

- The acid-test ratio reveals whether an entity could pay all its current liabilities if they were due immediately. (Cash including cash equivalents + Short-term investments + Net current receivables) / Total current liabilities.
- Accounts receivable turnover ratio measures the number of times the company collects the average accounts receivable balance in a year. Net credit sales / Average net accounts receivable.
- The days' sales in receivables indicates how many days it takes to collect the average level of accounts receivable. 365 days / Accounts receivable turnover ratio.

## > Summary Problem 8-1

Monarch Map Company's balance sheet at December 31, 2015, reported the following:

| | |
|---|---|
| Accounts Receivable | $ 60,000 |
| Less: Allowance for bad debts | 2,000 |

**Requirements**

1. How much of the receivables did Monarch expect to collect? Stated differently, what was the net realizable value of these receivables?
2. Journalize, without explanations, 2016 entries for Monarch and post to the Accounts Receivable and Allowance for Bad Debts T-accounts.
   a. Total credit sales for 2016 were $80,000.
   b. Monarch received cash payments on account during 2016 of $74,300.
   c. Accounts receivable identified to be uncollectible totaled $2,700.
3. Record the adjusting entry to recognize bad debts expense using the following independent situations, and then post to the Bad Debts Expense and Allowance for Bad Debts T-accounts.
   a. 3% of credit sales were estimated to be uncollectible.
   b. An aging of receivables indicates that $2,200 of the receivables are estimated to be uncollectible.

## > Solution

**Requirement 1**

Net realizable value of receivables = $60,000 − $2,000 = $58,000

**Requirement 2**

| Date | Accounts and Explanation | Debit | Credit |
|---|---|---|---|
| 2016 | | | |
| (a) | Accounts Receivable | 80,000 | |
| | Sales Revenue | | 80,000 |
| (b) | Cash | 74,300 | |
| | Accounts Receivable | | 74,300 |
| (c) | Allowance for Bad Debts | 2,700 | |
| | Accounts Receivable | | 2,700 |

**Accounts Receivable**

| | | | |
|---|---|---|---|
| Jan. 1, 2016, Bal. | 60,000 | | |
| (a) | 80,000 | 74,300 | (b) |
| | | 2,700 | (c) |
| Unadj. Bal. | 63,000 | | |

**Allowance for Bad Debts**

| | | | |
|---|---|---|---|
| | | 2,000 | Jan. 1, 2016, Bal. |
| (c) | 2,700 | | |
| Unadj. Bal. | 700 | | |

**Requirement 3a**

Bad debts expense = Net credit sales × % = $80,000 × 0.03 = $2,400

| Date | Accounts and Explanation | Debit | Credit |
|---|---|---|---|
| 2016 | | | |
| Dec. 31 | Bad Debts Expense | 2,400 | |
| | Allowance for Bad Debts | | 2,400 |

**Allowance for Bad Debts**

| | | | |
|---|---|---|---|
| | | 2,000 | Jan. 1, 2016, Bal. |
| (c) | 2,700 | | |
| Unadj. Bal. | 700 | | |
| | | 2,400 | Adj. |
| | | **1,700** | **Dec. 31, 2016, Bal.** |

**Bad Debts Expense**

| | | | |
|---|---|---|---|
| Adj. | 2,400 | | |
| **Dec. 31, 2016, Bal.** | **2,400** | | |

**Requirement 3b**

Bad debts expense = Target balance + Unadj. debit balance = \$2,200 + \$700
= \$2,900

| Date | Accounts and Explanation | Debit | Credit |
|---|---|---|---|
| 2016 | | | |
| Dec. 31 | Bad Debts Expense | 2,900 | |
| | Allowance for Bad Debts | | 2,900 |

**Allowance for Bad Debts**

| | | | |
|---|---|---|---|
| | | 2,000 | Jan. 1, 2016, Bal. |
| (c) | 2,700 | | |
| Unadj. Bal. | 700 | | |
| | | 2,900 | Adj. |
| | | **2,200** | **Dec. 31, 2016, Bal.** |

**Bad Debts Expense**

| | | |
|---|---|---|
| Adj. | 2,900 | |
| **Dec. 31, 2016, Bal.** | **2,900** | |

## > Summary Problem 8-2

Suppose First Fidelity Bank engaged in the following transactions:

| | |
|---|---|
| **2016** | |
| Apr. 1 | Loaned \$8,000 to Bland, Co. Received a six-month, 10% note. |
| Oct. 1 | Collected the Bland note at maturity. |
| Dec. 1 | Loaned \$6,000 to Flores, Inc. on a 180-day, 12% note. |
| 31 | Accrued interest revenue on the Flores note. |
| **2017** | |
| May 30 | Collected the Flores note at maturity. |

Journalize the 2016 and 2017 transactions on First Fidelity's books. Explanations are not needed. Use a 360-day year to compute interest. First Fidelity's accounting period ends on December 31.

## > Solution

| Date | Accounts and Explanation | Debit | Credit |
|---|---|---|---|
| 2016 | | | |
| Apr. 1 | Notes Receivable—Bland, Co. | 8,000 | |
| | Cash | | 8,000 |
| Oct. 1 | Cash ($8,000 + $400) | 8,400 | |
| | Notes Receivable—Bland, Co. | | 8,000 |
| | Interest Revenue ($8,000 × 0.10 × 6/12) | | 400 |
| Dec. 1 | Notes Receivable—Flores, Inc. | 6,000 | |
| | Cash | | 6,000 |
| Dec. 31 | Interest Receivable | 60 | |
| | Interest Revenue ($6,000 × 0.12 × 30/360) | | 60 |
| 2017 | | | |
| May 30 | Cash ($6,000 + ($6,000 × 0.12 × 180/360)) | 6,360 | |
| | Notes Receivable—Flores, Inc. | | 6,000 |
| | Interest Receivable | | 60 |
| | Interest Revenue ($6,000 × 0.12 × 150/360) | | 300 |

## > Key Terms

**Accounts Receivable (p. 424)**
**Accounts Receivable Turnover Ratio (p. 446)**
**Acid-Test Ratio (p. 446)**
**Aging-of-Receivables Method (p. 437)**
**Allowance for Bad Debts (p. 431)**
**Allowance Method (p. 431)**
**Bad Debts Expense (p. 429)**
**Days' Sales in Receivables (p. 447)**
**Debtor (p. 424)**
**Direct Write-off Method (p. 429)**
**Dishonor a Note (p. 444)**
**Interest (p. 440)**
**Interest Period (p. 440)**
**Interest Rate (p. 440)**
**Maturity Date (p. 424)**
**Maturity Value (p. 440)**
**Net Realizable Value (p. 431)**
**Notes Receivable (p. 424)**
**Percent-of-Receivables Method (p. 435)**
**Percent-of-Sales Method (p. 433)**
**Principal (p. 440)**
**Receivable (p. 424)**

## > Quick Check

**Learning Objective 1**

1. With good internal controls, the person who handles cash can also
   a. account for cash payments.
   b. account for cash receipts from customers.
   c. issue credits to customers for sales returns.
   d. None of the above

Learning Objective 1

2. When recording credit card or debit card sales using the net method,
   a. cash received equals sales.
   b. cash received equals sales minus the fee assessed by the card processing company.
   c. cash received equals sales plus the fee assessed by the card processing company.
   d. cash isn't received by the seller until the customer pays his or her credit card statement.

Learning Objective 2

3. Which of the following is a limitation of the direct write-off method of accounting for uncollectibles?
   a. The direct write-off method overstates assets on the balance sheet.
   b. The direct write-off method does not match expenses against revenue very well.
   c. The direct write-off method does not set up an allowance for uncollectibles.
   d. All of the above

Learning Objective 2

4. The entry to record a write-off of an uncollectible account when using the direct write-off method involves a
   a. debit to Allowance for Bad Debts.
   b. credit to Cash.
   c. debit to Accounts Receivable.
   d. debit to Bad Debts Expense.

Learning Objective 3

5. Brickman Corporation uses the allowance method to account for uncollectible receivables. At the beginning of the year, Allowance for Bad Debts had a credit balance of \$1,000. During the year Brickman wrote off uncollectible receivables of \$2,100. Brickman recorded Bad Debts Expense of \$2,700. What is Brickman's year-end balance in Allowance for Bad Debts?
   a. \$1,600 b. \$4,800 c. \$3,700 d. \$600

Learning Objective 3

6. Brickman's ending balance of Accounts Receivable is \$19,500. Use the data in the preceding question to compute the net realizable value of Accounts Receivable at year-end.
   a. \$16,800 b. \$19,500 c. \$17,400 d. \$17,900

Learning Objective 4

7. At December 31 year-end, Crain Corporation has an \$8,400 note receivable from a customer. Interest of 10% has accrued for 10 months on the note. What will Crain's financial statements report for this situation?
   a. The balance sheet will report the note receivable of \$8,400.
   b. The balance sheet will report the note receivable of \$8,400 and interest receivable of \$700.
   c. Nothing because the business has not received the cash yet.
   d. The income statement will report a note receivable of \$8,400.

Learning Objective 4

8. Using the data in the preceding question, what will the income statement for the year ended December 31 report for this situation?
   a. Nothing because the business has not received the cash yet
   b. Note receivable of \$8,400
   c. Interest revenue of \$700
   d. Both b and c

**Learning Objective 5**

9. At year-end, Schultz, Inc. has cash of $11,600, current accounts receivable of $48,900, merchandise inventory of $37,900, and prepaid expenses totaling $5,100. Liabilities of $55,900 must be paid next year. What is Schultz's acid-test ratio?
   a. 1.08
   b. 0.21
   c. 1.76
   d. Cannot be determined from the data given

**Learning Objective 5**

10. Using the data in the preceding question, assume accounts receivable had a beginning balance of $67,400 and net credit sales for the current year totaled $807,800. How many days did it take Schultz to collect its average level of receivables?
    a. 49 b. 35 c. 29 d. 26

**Check your answers at the end of the chapter.**

# ASSESS YOUR PROGRESS

## > Review Questions

1. What is the difference between accounts receivable and notes receivable?
2. List some common examples of other receivables, besides accounts receivable and notes receivable.
3. What is a critical element of internal control in the handling of receivables by a business? Explain how this element is accomplished.
4. When dealing with receivables, give an example of a subsidiary account.
5. What type of account must the sum of all subsidiary accounts be equal to?
6. What are some benefits to a business in accepting credit cards and debit cards?
7. What are two common methods used when accepting deposits for credit card and debit card transactions?
8. What occurs when a business factors its receivables?
9. What occurs when a business pledges its receivables?
10. What is the expense account associated with the cost of uncollectible receivables called?
11. When is bad debts expense recorded when using the direct write-off method?
12. What are some limitations of using the direct write-off method?
13. When is bad debts expense recorded when using the allowance method?
14. When using the allowance method, how are accounts receivable shown on the balance sheet?
15. When using the allowance method, what account is debited when writing off uncollectible accounts? How does this differ from the direct write-off method?
16. When a receivable is written off under the allowance method, how does it affect the net realizable value shown on the balance sheet?
17. How does the percent-of-sales method compute bad debts expense?
18. How do the percent-of-receivables and aging-of-receivables methods compute bad debts expense?

19. What is the difference between the percent-of-receivables and aging-of-receivables methods?
20. What is the formula to compute interest on a note receivable?
21. Why must companies record accrued interest revenue at the end of the accounting period?
22. How is the acid-test ratio calculated, and what does it signify?
23. What does the accounts receivable turnover ratio measure, and how is it calculated?
24. What does the days' sales in receivables indicate, and how is it calculated?

## > Short Exercises

### S8-1 Ensuring internal control over the collection of receivables

**Learning Objective 1**

Consider internal control over receivables collections. What job must be withheld from a company's credit department in order to safeguard its cash? If the credit department does perform this job, what can a credit department employee do to hurt the company?

### S8-2 Recording credit card and debit card sales

**Learning Objective 1**

Restaurants do a large volume of business by credit and debit cards. Suppose Summer, Sand, and Castles Resort restaurant had these transactions on January 28, 2016:

| | |
|---|---|
| National Express credit card sales | $ 10,800 |
| ValueCard debit card sales | 10,000 |

**Requirements**

1. Suppose Summer, Sand, and Castles Resort's processor charges a 2% fee and deposits sales net of the fee. Journalize these sales transactions for the restaurant.
2. Suppose Summer, Sand, and Castles Resort's processor charges a 2% fee and deposits its sales using the gross method. Journalize these sales transactions for the restaurant.

### S8-3 Applying the direct write-off method to account for uncollectibles

**Learning Objective 2**

Susan Knoll is an attorney in Los Angeles. Knoll uses the direct write-off method to account for uncollectible receivables.

At January 31, 2016, Knoll's accounts receivable totaled $18,000. During February, she earned revenue of $21,000 on account and collected $23,000 on account. She also wrote off uncollectible receivables of $1,050 on February 29, 2016.

**Requirements**

1. Use the direct write-off method to journalize Knoll's write-off of the uncollectible receivables.
2. What is Knoll's balance of Accounts Receivable at February 29, 2016?

### S8-4 Collecting a receivable previously written off—direct write-off method

**Learning Objective 2**

Gate City Cycles had trouble collecting its account receivable from Shawna Brown. On June 19, 2016, Gate City finally wrote off Brown's $700 account receivable. On December 31, Brown sent a $700 check to Gate City.

Journalize the entries required for Gate City Cycles, assuming Gate City uses the direct write-off method.

Learning Objective 3

**S8-5 Applying the allowance method to account for uncollectibles**

The Accounts Receivable balance and Allowance for Bad Debts for Turning Leaves Furniture Restoration at December 31, 2015, was $10,800 and $2,000 (credit balance). During 2016, Turning Leaves completed the following transactions:

a. Sales revenue on account, $265,800 (ignore Cost of Goods Sold).

b. Collections on account, $220,000.

c. Write-offs of uncollectibles, $6,100.

d. Bad debts expense of $5,000 was recorded.

**Requirements**

1. Journalize Turning Leaves's transactions for 2016 assuming Turning Leaves uses the allowance method.
2. Post the transactions to the Accounts Receivable, Allowance for Bad Debts, and Bad Debts Expense T-accounts, and determine the ending balance of each account.
3. Show how accounts receivable would be reported on the balance sheet at December 31, 2016.

Learning Objective 3

**S8-6 Applying the allowance method (percent-of-sales) to account for uncollectibles**

During its first year of operations, Signature Lamp Company earned net credit sales of $314,000. Industry experience suggests that bad debts will amount to 4% of net credit sales. At December 31, 2016, accounts receivable total $45,000. The company uses the allowance method to account for uncollectibles.

**Requirements**

1. Journalize Signature's Bad Debts Expense using the percent-of-sales method.
2. Show how to report accounts receivable on the balance sheet at December 31, 2016.

Learning Objective 3

**S8-7 Applying the allowance method (percent-of-receivables) to account for uncollectibles**

The Accounts Receivable balance for Field, Inc. at December 31, 2015, was $25,000. During 2016, Field earned revenue of $457,000 on account and collected $326,000 on account. Field wrote off $5,900 receivables as uncollectible. Industry experience suggests that uncollectible accounts will amount to 4% of accounts receivable.

**Requirements**

1. Assume Field had an unadjusted $2,300 credit balance in Allowance for Bad Debts at December 31, 2016. Journalize Field's December 31, 2016, adjustment to record bad debts expense using the percent-of-receivables method.
2. Assume Field had an unadjusted $1,900 debit balance in Allowance for Bad Debts at December 31, 2016. Journalize Field's December 31, 2016, adjustment to record bad debts expense using the percent-of-receivables method.

## S8-8 Applying the allowance method (aging-of-receivables) to account for uncollectibles

**Learning Objective 3**

World Class Work Shoes had the following balances at December 31, 2016, before the year-end adjustments:

| Accounts Receivable | | Allowance for Bad Debts | |
|---|---|---|---|
| 78,000 | | | 1,060 |

The aging of accounts receivable yields the following data:

| | Age of Accounts Receivable | | |
|---|---|---|---|
| | **0–60 Days** | **Over 60 Days** | **Total Receivables** |
| Accounts Receivable | $ 73,000 | $ 5,000 | $ 78,000 |
| Estimated percent uncollectible | × 2% | × 24% | |

### Requirements

1. Journalize World Class's entry to record bad debts expense for 2016 using the aging-of-receivables method.
2. Prepare a T-account to compute the ending balance of Allowance for Bad Debts.

## S8-9 Computing interest amounts on notes receivable

**Learning Objective 4**

A table of notes receivable for 2016 follows:

| | Principal | Interest Rate | Interest Period During 2016 |
|---|---|---|---|
| Note 1 | $ 30,000 | 4% | 3 months |
| Note 2 | 8,000 | 5% | 180 days |
| Note 3 | 28,000 | 12% | 90 days |
| Note 4 | 110,000 | 10% | 6 months |

For each of the notes receivable, compute the amount of interest revenue earned during 2016. Round to the nearest dollar.

## S8-10 Accounting for a note receivable

**Learning Objective 4**

On June 6, Southside Bank & Trust lent $90,000 to Samantha Michael on a 60-day, 6% note.

### Requirements

1. Journalize for Southside the lending of the money on June 6.
2. Journalize the collection of the principal and interest at maturity. Specify the date.

## S8-11 Accruing interest revenue and recording collection of a note

**Learning Objective 4**

On December 1, Kole Corporation accepted a 120-day, 6%, $17,000 note receivable from J. Peterman in exchange for his account receivable.

### Requirements

1. Journalize the transaction on December 1.
2. Journalize the adjusting entry needed on December 31 to accrue interest revenue.
3. Journalize the collection of the principal and interest at maturity. Specify the date.

Learning Objective 4

**S8-12 Recording a dishonored note receivable**

Midway Corporation has a six-month, $24,000, 3% note receivable from L. Summers that was signed on June 1, 2016. Summers defaults on the loan on December 1.

Journalize the entry for Midway to record the default of the loan.

Learning Objective 5

**S8-13 Using the acid-test ratio, accounts receivable turnover ratio, and days' sales in receivables to evaluate a company**

Gold Clothiers reported the following selected items at September 30, 2016 (last year's—2015—amounts also given as needed):

| | | | |
|---|---|---|---|
| Accounts Payable | $ 331,000 | Accounts Receivable, net: | |
| Cash | 302,900 | September 30, 2016 | $ 303,000 |
| Merchandise Inventory: | | September 30, 2015 | 152,000 |
| September 30, 2016 | 230,000 | Cost of Goods Sold | 1,150,000 |
| September 30, 2015 | 190,000 | Short-term Investments | 151,000 |
| Net Credit Sales Revenue | 3,321,500 | Other Current Assets | 70,000 |
| Long-term Assets | 450,000 | Other Current Liabilities | 191,000 |
| Long-term Liabilities | 100,000 | | |

Compute Gold's (a) acid-test ratio, (b) accounts receivable turnover ratio, and (c) days' sales in receivables for 2016. Evaluate each ratio value as strong or weak. Gold sells on terms of net 30. (Round days' sales in receivables to a whole number.)

## > Exercises

Learning Objective 1

**E8-14 Defining common receivables terms**

Match the terms with their correct definition.

| Terms | Definitions |
|---|---|
| 1. Accounts receivable | a. The party to a credit transaction who takes on an obligation/ payable. |
| 2. Other receivables | b. The party who receives a receivable and will collect cash in the future. |
| 3. Debtor | c. A written promise to pay a specified amount of money at a particular future date. |
| 4. Notes receivable | d. The date when the note receivable is due. |
| 5. Maturity date | e. A miscellaneous category that includes any other type of receivable where there is a right to receive cash in the future. |
| 6. Creditor | f. The right to receive cash in the future from customers for goods sold or for services performed. |

Learning Objective 1

**E8-15 Identifying and correcting internal control weakness**

Suppose The Right Rig Dealership is opening a regional office in Omaha. Cary Regal, the office manager, is designing the internal control system. Regal proposes the following procedures for credit checks on new customers, sales on account, cash collections, and write-offs of uncollectible receivables:

- The credit department runs a credit check on all customers who apply for credit. When an account proves uncollectible, the credit department authorizes the write-off of the accounts receivable.
- Cash receipts come into the credit department, which separates the cash received from the customer remittance slips. The credit department lists all cash receipts by customer name and amount of cash received.
- The cash goes to the treasurer for deposit in the bank. The remittance slips go to the accounting department for posting to customer accounts.
- The controller compares the daily deposit slip to the total amount posted to customer accounts. Both amounts must agree.

Recall the components of internal control. Identify the internal control weakness in this situation, and propose a way to correct it.

**E8-16 Journalizing transactions using the direct write-off method**

**Learning Objectives 1, 2**

On June 1, High Performance Cell Phones sold $19,000 of merchandise to Andrew Trucking Company on account. Andrew fell on hard times and on July 15 paid only $7,000 of the account receivable. After repeated attempts to collect, High Performance finally wrote off its accounts receivable from Andrew on September 5. Six months later, March 5, High Performance received Andrew's check for $12,000 with a note apologizing for the late payment.

**Requirements**

1. Journalize the transactions for High Performance Cell Phones using the direct write-off method. Ignore Cost of Goods Sold.
2. What are some limitations that High Performance will encounter when using the direct write-off method?

***Use the following information to answer Exercises E8-17 and E8-18.***

At January 1, 2016, Hilly Mountain Flagpoles had Accounts Receivable of $31,000, and Allowance for Bad Debts had a credit balance of $3,000. During the year, Hilly Mountain Flagpoles recorded the following:

**a.** Sales of $174,000 ($157,000 on account; $17,000 for cash). Ignore Cost of Goods Sold.

**b.** Collections on account, $131,000.

**c.** Write-offs of uncollectible receivables, $2,200.

**E8-17 Accounting for uncollectible accounts using the allowance method (percent-of-sales) and reporting receivables on the balance sheet**

**Learning Objectives 1, 3**

2. AR, Dec. 31 $54,800

**Requirements**

1. Journalize Hilly's transactions that occurred during 2016. The company uses the allowance method.
2. Post Hilly's transactions to the Accounts Receivable and Allowance for Bad Debts T-accounts.
3. Journalize Hilly's adjustment to record bad debts expense assuming Hilly estimates bad debts as 4% of credit sales. Post the adjustment to the appropriate T-accounts.
4. Show how Hilly Mountain Flagpoles will report net accounts receivable on its December 31, 2016, balance sheet.

**Learning Objectives 1, 3**

3. Bad Debts Expense $844

## E8-18 Accounting for uncollectible accounts using the allowance method (percent-of-receivables) and reporting receivables on the balance sheet

**Requirements**

1. Journalize Hilly's transactions that occurred during 2016. The company uses the allowance method.
2. Post Hilly's transactions to the Accounts Receivable and Allowance for Bad Debts T-accounts.
3. Journalize Hilly's adjustment to record bad debts expense assuming Hilly estimates bad debts as 3% of accounts receivable. Post the adjustment to the appropriate T-accounts.
4. Show how Hilly Mountain Flagpoles will report net accounts receivable on its December 31, 2016, balance sheet.

**Learning Objective 3**

2. Allowance CR Bal. $25,100

## E8-19 Accounting for uncollectible accounts using the allowance method (aging-of-receivables) and reporting receivables on the balance sheet

At December 31, 2016, the Accounts Receivable balance of TM Manufacturer is $230,000. The Allowance for Bad Debts account has a $24,000 debit balance. TM Manufacturer prepares the following aging schedule for its accounts receivable:

| | Age of Accounts | | | |
|---|---|---|---|---|
| | 1–30 Days | 31–60 Days | 61–90 Days | Over 90 Days |
| Accounts Receivable | $ 75,000 | $ 80,000 | $ 35,000 | $ 40,000 |
| Estimated percent uncollectible | 0.8% | 4.0% | 6.0% | 48.0% |

**Requirements**

1. Journalize the year-end adjusting entry for bad debts on the basis of the aging schedule. Show the T-account for the Allowance for Bad Debts at December 31, 2016.
2. Show how TM Manufacturer will report its net accounts receivable on its December 31, 2016, balance sheet.

**Learning Objectives 1, 2, 3**

## E8-20 Journalizing transactions using the direct write-off method versus the allowance method

During August 2016, Ritter Company recorded the following:

- Sales of $62,100 ($55,000 on account; $7,100 for cash). Ignore Cost of Goods Sold.
- Collections on account, $37,800.
- Write-offs of uncollectible receivables, $1,690.
- Recovery of receivable previously written off, $500.

**Requirements**

1. Journalize Ritter's transactions during August 2016, assuming Ritter uses the direct write-off method.
2. Journalize Ritter's transactions during August 2016, assuming Ritter uses the allowance method.

## E8-21 Journalizing credit card sales, note receivable transactions, and accruing interest

**Learning Objectives 1, 4**

Marathon Running Shoes reports the following:

| | |
|---|---|
| **2016** | |
| Feb. 4 | Recorded credit card sales of $96,000, net of processor fee of 1%. Ignore Cost of Goods Sold. |
| Sep. 1 | Loaned $23,000 to Jess Prichett, an executive with the company, on a one-year, 12% note. |
| Dec. 31 | Accrued interest revenue on the Prichett note. |
| **2017** | |
| Sep. 1 | Collected the maturity value of the Prichett note. |

Journalize all entries required for Marathon Running Shoes.

## E8-22 Journalizing note receivable transactions including a dishonored note

**Learning Objective 4**

On September 30, 2016, Regal Bank loaned $92,000 to Kim Warner on a one-year, 6% note. Regal's fiscal year ends on December 31.

### Requirements

1. Journalize all entries for Regal Bank related to the note for 2016 and 2017.
2. Which party has a
   - **a.** note receivable?
   - **b.** note payable?
   - **c.** interest revenue?
   - **d.** interest expense?
3. Suppose that Kim Warner defaulted on the note. What entry would Regal record for the dishonored note?

## E8-23 Journalizing note receivable transactions

**Learning Objective 4**

Feb. 1, 2017 Cash DR $21,200

The following selected transactions occurred during 2016 and 2017 for Mediterranean Importers. The company ends its accounting year on April 30.

| | |
|---|---|
| **2016** | |
| Feb. 1 | Loaned $20,000 cash to Candace Smith on a one-year, 6% note. |
| Apr. 6 | Sold goods to Green Masters, receiving a 90-day, 9% note for $10,000. Ignore Cost of Goods Sold. |
| Apr. 30 | Made a single entry to accrue interest revenue on both notes. |
| ? | Collected the maturity value of the Green Masters note. |
| **2017** | |
| Feb. 1 | Collected the maturity value of the Smith note. |

Journalize all required entries. Make sure to determine the missing maturity date.

**Learning Objective 4**

Oct. 31 Cash DR $24,240

## E8-24 Journalizing note receivable transactions

Like New Steam Cleaning performs services on account. When a customer account becomes four months old, Like New converts the account to a note receivable. During 2016, the company completed the following transactions:

| | |
|---|---|
| Apr. 28 | Performed service on account for Java Club, $24,000. |
| Sep. 1 | Received a $24,000, 60-day, 6% note from Java Club in satisfaction of its past-due account receivable. |
| Oct. 31 | Collected the Java Club note at maturity. |

Record the transactions in Like New's journal.

**Learning Objective 5**

## E8-25 Evaluating ratio data

Chippewa Carpets reported the following amounts in its 2016 financial statements. The 2015 figures are given for comparison.

| | 2016 | | 2015 | |
|---|---|---|---|---|
| Current Assets: | | | | |
| Cash | | $ 3,000 | | $ 9,000 |
| Short-term Investments | | 21,000 | | 10,000 |
| Accounts Receivable | $ 59,000 | | $ 72,000 | |
| Less: Allowance for Bad Debts | (7,000) | 52,000 | (6,000) | 66,000 |
| Merchandise Inventory | | 191,000 | | 187,000 |
| Prepaid Insurance | | 3,000 | | 3,000 |
| Total Current Assets | | $ 270,000 | | $ 275,000 |
| Total Current Liabilities | | $ 105,000 | | $ 107,000 |
| Net Sales (all on account) | | $ 654,900 | | $ 733,000 |

### Requirements

1. Calculate Chippewa's acid-test ratio for 2016. (Round to two decimals.) Determine whether Chippewa's acid-test ratio improved or deteriorated from 2015 to 2016. How does Chippewa's acid-test ratio compare with the industry average of 0.80?
2. Calculate Chippewa's accounts receivable turnover ratio. (Round to two decimals.) How does Chippewa's ratio compare to the industry average accounts receivable turnover of 10?
3. Calculate the days' sales in receivables for 2016. (Round to the nearest day.) How do the results compare with Chippewa's credit terms of net 30?

**E8-26 Computing the collection period for receivables**

Learning Objective 5

New Media Sign Incorporated sells on account. Recently, New reported the following figures:

| | 2016 | 2015 |
|---|---|---|
| Net Credit Sales | $ 539,220 | $ 603,000 |
| Receivables at end of year | 38,600 | 43,100 |

**Requirements**

1. Compute New's days' sales in receivables for 2016. (Round to the nearest day.)
2. Suppose New's normal credit terms for a sale on account are "2/10, net 30." How well does New's collection period compare to the company's credit terms? Is this good or bad for New?

## > Problems Group A

**P8-27A Accounting for uncollectible accounts using the allowance (percent-of-sales) and direct write-off methods and reporting receivables on the balance sheet**

Learning Objectives 1, 2, 3

1. Bad Debts Expense $5,400

On August 31, 2016, Lily Floral Supply had a $145,000 debit balance in Accounts Receivable and a $5,800 credit balance in Allowance for Bad Debts. During September, Lily made

- Sales on account, $540,000. Ignore Cost of Goods Sold.
- Collections on account, $581,000.
- Write-offs of uncollectible receivables, $5,000.

**Requirements**

1. Journalize all September entries using the *allowance* method. Bad debts expense was estimated at 1% of credit sales. Show all September activity in Accounts Receivable, Allowance for Bad Debts, and Bad Debts Expense (post to these T-accounts).
2. Using the same facts, assume that Lily used the direct write-off method to account for uncollectible receivables. Journalize all September entries using the *direct write-off* method. Post to Accounts Receivable and Bad Debts Expense, and show their balances at September 30, 2016.
3. What amount of Bad Debts Expense would Lily report on its September income statement under each of the two methods? Which amount better matches expense with revenue? Give your reason.
4. What amount of *net* accounts receivable would Lily report on its September 30, 2016, balance sheet under each of the two methods? Which amount is more realistic? Give your reason.

**Learning Objective 3**

2. Allowance CR Bal. $7,539 at Dec. 31, 2016

## P8-28A Accounting for uncollectible accounts using the allowance method (aging-of-receivables) and reporting receivables on the balance sheet

At September 30, 2016, the accounts of Park Terrace Medical Center (PTMC) include the following:

| | |
|---|---|
| Accounts Receivable | $ 143,000 |
| Allowance for Bad Debts (credit balance) | 3,300 |

During the last quarter of 2016, PTMC completed the following selected transactions:

| | |
|---|---|
| Dec. 28 | Wrote off accounts receivable as uncollectible: Silver, Co., $1,200; Oscar Wells, $1,000; and Rain, Inc., $600 |
| 31 | Recorded bad debts expense based on the aging of accounts receivable, as follows: |

| | Age of Accounts | | | |
|---|---|---|---|---|
| | 1–30 Days | 31–60 Days | 61–90 Days | Over 90 Days |
| Accounts Receivable | $ 103,000 | $ 41,000 | $ 13,000 | $ 6,000 |
| Estimated percent uncollectible | 0.3% | 3% | 30% | 35% |

### Requirements

1. Journalize the transactions.
2. Open the Allowance for Bad Debts T-account, and post entries affecting that account. Keep a running balance.
3. Show how Park Terrace Medical Center should report net accounts receivable on its December 31, 2016, balance sheet.

**Learning Objectives 1, 3**

3. Net AR $107,300

## P8-29A Accounting for uncollectible accounts using the allowance method (percent-of-sales) and reporting receivables on the balance sheet

Beta Watches completed the following selected transactions during 2016 and 2017:

| | |
|---|---|
| **2016** | |
| Dec. 31 | Estimated that bad debts expense for the year was 3% of credit sales of $400,000 and recorded that amount as expense. The company uses the allowance method. |
| 31 | Made the closing entry for bad debts expense. |
| **2017** | |
| Jan. 17 | Sold merchandise inventory to Marty Viller, $900, on account. Ignore Cost of Goods Sold. |
| Jun. 29 | Wrote off Marty Viller's account as uncollectible after repeated efforts to collect from him. |
| Aug. 6 | Received $900 from Marty Viller, along with a letter apologizing for being so late. Reinstated Viller's account in full and recorded the cash receipt. |
| Dec. 31 | Made a compound entry to write off the following accounts as uncollectible: Bob Keffer, $1,900; Mary Martin, $1,000; and Robert Ronson, $400. |
| 31 | Estimated that bad debts expense for the year was 3% on credit sales of $500,000 and recorded the expense. |
| 31 | Made the closing entry for bad debts expense. |

**Requirements**

1. Open T-accounts for Allowance for Bad Debts and Bad Debts Expense. Keep running balances, assuming all accounts begin with a zero balance.
2. Record the transactions in the general journal, and post to the two T-accounts.
3. Assume the December 31, 2017, balance of Accounts Receivable is $131,000. Show how net accounts receivable would be reported on the balance sheet at that date.

## P8-30A Accounting for uncollectible accounts (aging-of-receivables method), credit card sales, notes receivable, and accrued interest revenue

**Learning Objectives 1, 3, 4**

Dec. 31, 2016 Interest Receivable $3,600

Quality Recliner Chairs completed the following selected transactions:

| | |
|---|---|
| **2016** | |
| Jul. 1 | Sold merchandise inventory to Gray Mart, receiving a $45,000, nine-month, 16% note. Ignore Cost of Goods Sold. |
| Oct. 31 | Recorded credit and debit card sales for the period of $23,000. Use the gross method. Ignore Cost of Goods Sold. |
| Nov. 3 | Card processor drafted company's checking account for processing fee of $460. |
| Dec. 31 | Made an adjusting entry to accrue interest on the Gray Mart note. |
| 31 | Made an adjusting entry to record bad debts expense based on an aging of accounts receivable. The aging schedule shows that $15,200 of accounts receivable will not be collected. Prior to this adjustment, the credit balance in Allowance for Bad Debts is $11,400. |
| **2017** | |
| Apr. 1 | Collected the maturity value of the Gray Mart note. |
| Jun. 23 | Sold merchandise inventory to Artist, Corp., receiving a 60-day, 6% note for $8,000. Ignore Cost of Goods Sold. |
| Aug. 22 | Artist, Corp. dishonored its note at maturity; the business converted the maturity value of the note to an account receivable. |
| Nov. 16 | Loaned $22,000 cash to Creed, Inc., receiving a 90-day, 12% note. |
| Dec. 5 | Collected in full on account from Artist, Corp. |
| 31 | Accrued the interest on the Creed, Inc. note. |

Record the transactions in the journal of Quality Recliner Chairs. Explanations are not required. (For notes stated in days, use a 360-day year. Round to the nearest dollar.)

## P8-31A Accounting for notes receivable and accruing interest

**Learning Objective 4**

1. Note 3 Dec. 18, 2016

Cathy Realty loaned money and received the following notes during 2016.

| Note | Date | Principal Amount | Interest Rate | Term |
|---|---|---|---|---|
| (1) | Jun. 1 | $ 18,000 | 8% | 1 year |
| (2) | Sep. 30 | 24,000 | 12% | 6 months |
| (3) | Oct. 19 | 10,000 | 9% | 60 days |

**Requirements**

1. Determine the maturity date and maturity value of each note.
2. Journalize the entries to establish each Note Receivable and to record collection of principal and interest at maturity. Include a single adjusting entry on December 31, 2016, the fiscal year-end, to record accrued interest revenue on any applicable note. Explanations are not required.

**Learning Objective 4**

Dec. 31, 2016 Income Summary CR $75

**P8-32A Accounting for notes receivable, dishonored notes, and accrued interest revenue**

Consider the following transactions for Jo Jo Music.

| | |
|---|---|
| **2016** | |
| Dec. 6 | Received a $9,000, 90-day, 12% note in settlement of an overdue accounts receivable from Concord Sounds. |
| 31 | Made an adjusting entry to accrue interest on the Concord Sounds note. |
| 31 | Made a closing entry for interest revenue. |
| **2017** | |
| Mar. 6 | Collected the maturity value of the Concord Sounds note. |
| Jun. 30 | Loaned $11,000 cash to Main Street Music, receiving a six-month, 12% note. |
| Oct. 2 | Received a $9,000, 60-day, 12% note for a sale to Salem Sounds. Ignore Cost of Goods Sold. |
| Dec. 1 | Salem Sounds dishonored its note at maturity. |
| 1 | Wrote off the receivable associated with Salem Sounds. (Use the allowance method.) |
| 30 | Collected the maturity value of the Main Street Music note. |

Journalize all transactions for Jo Jo Music. Round all amounts to the nearest dollar. (For notes stated in days, use a 360-day year.)

**Learning Objective 5**

1. Acid-test ratio (2016) 0.86

**P8-33A Using ratio data to evaluate a company's financial position**

The comparative financial statements of Perfection Cosmetic Supply for 2016, 2015, and 2014 include the data shown here:

| | 2016 | 2015 | 2014 |
|---|---|---|---|
| **Balance sheet—partial** | | | |
| Current Assets: | | | |
| Cash | $ 60,000 | $ 80,000 | $ 60,000 |
| Short-term investments | 135,000 | 150,000 | 130,000 |
| Accounts Receivable, Net | 270,000 | 280,000 | 260,000 |
| Merchandise Inventory | 370,000 | 340,000 | 315,000 |
| Prepaid Expenses | 70,000 | 20,000 | 35,000 |
| Total Current Assets | 905,000 | 870,000 | 800,000 |
| Total Current Liabilities | 540,000 | 570,000 | 690,000 |
| **Income statement—partial** | | | |
| Net Sales (all on account) | 5,860,000 | 5,120,000 | 4,200,000 |

**Requirements**

1. Compute these ratios for 2016 and 2015:
   a. Acid-test ratio (Round to two decimals.)
   b. Accounts receivable turnover (Round to two decimals.)
   c. Days' sales in receivables (Round to the nearest whole day.)
2. Considering each ratio individually, which ratios improved from 2015 to 2016 and which ratios deteriorated? Is the trend favorable or unfavorable for the company?

## > Problems Group B

### P8-34B Accounting for uncollectible accounts using the allowance (percent-of-sales) and direct write-off methods and reporting receivables on the balance sheet

**Learning Objectives 1, 2, 3**

1. Sep. 30 Bal. AR $128,000

On August 31, 2016, Bouquet Floral Supply had a $170,000 debit balance in Accounts Receivable and a $6,800 credit balance in Allowance for Bad Debts. During September, Bouquet made the following transactions:

- Sales on account, $550,000. Ignore Cost of Goods Sold.
- Collections on account, $584,000.
- Write-offs of uncollectible receivables, $8,000.

**Requirements**

1. Journalize all September entries using the *allowance* method. Bad debts expense was estimated at 2% of credit sales. Show all September activity in Accounts Receivable, Allowance for Bad Debts, and Bad Debts Expense (post to these T-accounts).
2. Using the same facts, assume that Bouquet used the direct write-off method to account for uncollectible receivables. Journalize all September entries using the *direct write-off* method. Post to Accounts Receivable and Bad Debts Expense, and show their balances at November 30, 2016.
3. What amount of Bad Debts Expense would Bouquet report on its September income statement under each of the two methods? Which amount better matches expense with revenue? Give your reason.
4. What amount of *net* accounts receivable would Bouquet report on its September 30, 2016, balance sheet under each of the two methods? Which amount is more realistic? Give your reason.

### P8-35B Accounting for uncollectible accounts using the allowance method (aging-of-receivables) and reporting receivables on the balance sheet

**Learning Objective 3**

2. Dec. 31, 2016 Allowance CR Bal. $4,616

At September 30, 2016, the accounts of Spring Heights Medical Center (SHMC) include the following:

| | |
|---|---|
| Accounts Receivable | $ 143,000 |
| Allowance for Bad Debts (credit balance) | 3,300 |

During the last quarter of 2016, SHMC completed the following selected transactions:

| | |
|---|---|
| Dec. 28 | Wrote off accounts receivable as uncollectible: Silver, Co., $1,400; Owen Reis, $700; and Pristine, Inc., $700 |
| 31 | Recorded bad debts expense based on the aging of accounts receivable, as follows: |

| | Age of Accounts | | | |
|---|---|---|---|---|
| | 1–30 Days | 31–60 Days | 61–90 Days | Over 90 Days |
| Accounts Receivable | $ 103,000 | $ 43,000 | $ 14,000 | $ 3,000 |
| Estimated percent uncollectible | 0.2% | 2% | 20% | 25% |

**Requirements**

1. Journalize the transactions.
2. Open the Allowance for Bad Debts T-account, and post entries affecting that account. Keep a running balance.
3. Show how Spring Heights Medical Center should report net accounts receivable on its December 31, 2016, balance sheet.

**Learning Objectives 1, 3**

1. Dec. 31, 2017, Allowance CR Bal. $5,900

**P8-36B Accounting for uncollectible accounts using the allowance method (percent-of-sales) and reporting receivables on the balance sheet**

Quality Watches completed the following selected transactions during 2016 and 2017:

| | |
|---|---|
| **2016** | |
| Dec. 31 | Estimated that bad debts expense for the year was 1% of credit sales of $440,000 and recorded that amount as expense. The company uses the allowance method. |
| 31 | Made the closing entry for bad debts expense. |
| **2017** | |
| Jan. 17 | Sold merchandise inventory to Malcom Monet, $500, on account. Ignore Cost of Goods Sold. |
| Jun. 29 | Wrote off Malcom Monet's account as uncollectible after repeated efforts to collect from him. |
| Aug. 6 | Received $500 from Malcom Monet, along with a letter apologizing for being so late. Reinstated Monet's account in full and recorded the cash receipt. |
| Dec. 31 | Made a compound entry to write off the following accounts as uncollectible: Bernard Klaus, $1,800; Mo Vanez, $1,500; and Russell Reeves, $200. |
| 31 | Estimated that bad debts expense for the year was 1% on credit sales of $500,000 and recorded the expense. |
| 31 | Made the closing entry for bad debts expense. |

**Requirements**

1. Open T-accounts for Allowance for Bad Debts and Bad Debts Expense. Keep running balances, assuming all accounts begin with a zero balance.
2. Record the transactions in the general journal, and post to the two T-accounts.
3. Assume the December 31, 2017, balance of Accounts Receivable is $136,000. Show how net accounts receivable would be reported on the balance sheet at that date.

## P8-37B Accounting for uncollectible accounts (aging-of-receivables method), credit card sales, notes receivable, and accrued interest revenue

**Learning Objectives 1, 3, 4**

Dec. 31, 2016 Bad Debts Expense $3,900

Comfy Recliner Chairs completed the following selected transactions:

| | |
|---|---|
| **2016** | |
| Jul. 1 | Sold merchandise inventory to Gray Mart, receiving a $43,000, nine-month, 12% note. Ignore Cost of Goods Sold. |
| Oct. 31 | Recorded credit and debit card sales for the period of $21,000. Use the gross method. Ignore Cost of Goods Sold. |
| Nov. 3 | Card processor drafted company's checking account for processing fee of $400. |
| Dec. 31 | Made an adjusting entry to accrue interest on the Gray Mart note. |
| 31 | Made an adjusting entry to record bad debts expense based on an aging of accounts receivable. The aging schedule shows that $14,600 of accounts receivable will not be collected. Prior to this adjustment, the credit balance in Allowance for Bad Debts is $10,700. |
| **2017** | |
| Apr. 1 | Collected the maturity value of the Gray Mart note. |
| Jun. 23 | Sold merchandise inventory to Aglow, Corp., receiving a 60-day, 9% note for $13,000. Ignore Cost of Goods Sold. |
| Aug. 22 | Aglow, Corp. dishonored its note at maturity; the business converted the maturity value of the note to an account receivable. |
| Nov. 16 | Loaned $22,000 cash to Crowe, Inc., receiving a 90-day, 16% note. |
| Dec. 5 | Collected in full on account from Aglow, Corp. |
| 31 | Accrued the interest on the Crowe, Inc. note. |

Record the transactions in the journal of Comfy Recliner Chairs. Explanations are not required. (For notes stated in days, use a 360-day year. Round to the nearest dollar.)

## P8-38B Accounting for notes receivable and accruing interest

**Learning Objective 4**

1. Note 2 Maturity Value $20,300

Christie Realty loaned money and received the following notes during 2016.

| Note | Date | Principal Amount | Interest Rate | Term |
|---|---|---|---|---|
| (1) | Aug. 1 | $ 24,000 | 7% | 1 year |
| (2) | Nov. 30 | 20,000 | 6% | 3 months |
| (3) | Dec. 19 | 10,000 | 12% | 30 days |

### Requirements

1. Determine the maturity date and maturity value of each note.
2. Journalize the entries to establish each Note Receivable and to record collection of principal and interest at maturity. Include a single adjusting entry on December 31, 2016, the fiscal year-end, to record accrued interest revenue on any applicable note. Explanations are not required.

**Learning Objective 4**

March 6, 2017 Interest Revenue $325

## P8-39B Accounting for notes receivable, dishonored notes, and accrued interest revenue

Consider the following transactions for Smith's Publishing.

| | |
|---|---|
| **2016** | |
| Dec. 6 | Received a $15,000, 90-day, 12% note in settlement of an overdue accounts receivable from Jazz Music. |
| 31 | Made an adjusting entry to accrue interest on the Jazz Music note. |
| 31 | Made a closing entry for interest revenue. |
| **2017** | |
| Mar. 6 | Collected the maturity value of the Jazz Music note. |
| Jun. 30 | Loaned $11,000 cash to RS Publishing, receiving a six-month, 12% note. |
| Oct. 2 | Received a $3,000, 60-day, 12% note for a sale to Tusk Music. Ignore Cost of Goods Sold. |
| Dec. 1 | Tusk Music dishonored its note at maturity. |
| 1 | Wrote off the receivable associated with Tusk Music. (Use the allowance method.) |
| 30 | Collected the maturity value of the RS Publishing note. |

Journalize all transactions for Smith's Publishing. Round all amounts to the nearest dollar. (For notes stated in days, use a 360-day year.)

**Learning Objective 5**

1. Days' sales in receivables (2016) 16 days

## P8-40B Using ratio data to evaluate a company's financial position

The comparative financial statements of True Beauty Cosmetic Supply for 2016, 2015, and 2014 include the data shown here:

| | 2016 | 2015 | 2014 |
|---|---|---|---|
| **Balance sheet—partial** | | | |
| Current Assets: | | | |
| Cash | $ 90,000 | $ 80,000 | $ 60,000 |
| Short-term investments | 140,000 | 150,000 | 125,000 |
| Accounts Receivable, Net | 270,000 | 260,000 | 220,000 |
| Merchandise Inventory | 355,000 | 330,000 | 310,000 |
| Prepaid Expenses | 65,000 | 10,000 | 40,000 |
| Total Current Assets | 920,000 | 830,000 | 755,000 |
| Total Current Liabilities | 540,000 | 580,000 | 670,000 |
| **Income statement—partial** | | | |
| Net Sales (all on account) | 5,880,000 | 5,210,000 | 4,200,000 |

### Requirements

1. Compute these ratios for 2016 and 2015:
   a. Acid-test ratio (Round to two decimals.)
   b. Accounts receivable turnover (Round to two decimals.)
   c. Days' sales in receivables (Round to the nearest whole day.)
2. Considering each ratio individually, which ratios improved from 2015 to 2016 and which ratios deteriorated? Is the trend favorable or unfavorable for the company?

## > Continuing Problem

**P8-41 Accounting for uncollectible accounts using the allowance method**

This problem continues the Daniels Consulting situation from Problem P7-33 of Chapter 7 and Problem P6-38 of Chapter 6. Daniels Consulting reviewed the receivables list from the January transactions. Daniels uses the allowance method for receivables, estimating uncollectibles to be 6% of January sales revenue of $8,180. Daniels identified on February 15 that a customer was not going to pay his receivable of $176.

**Requirements**

1. Journalize the January 31 entry to record and establish the allowance using the percent-of-sales method for January sales revenue.
2. Journalize the entry to record the write-off of the customer's bad debt.

## > Practice Set

This problem continues the Crystal Clear Cleaning problem begun in Chapter 2 and continued through Chapters 3–7.

**P8-42 Accounting for uncollectible accounts using the allowance method and reporting net accounts receivable on the balance sheet**

Crystal Clear Cleaning uses the allowance method to estimate bad debts. Consider the following January transactions for Crystal Clear:

| | |
|---|---|
| Jan. 1 | Performed cleaning service for Debbie's D-list for $9,000 on account with terms 3/10, n/20. |
| 10 | Borrowed money from High Roller Bank, $20,000, making a 180 day, 15% note. |
| 12 | After discussions with Merry Cleaners, Crystal Clear has determined that $275 of the receivable owed will not be collected. Wrote off this portion of the receivable. |
| 15 | Sold goods to Westford for $8,000 on account with terms 5/10, n/30. Cost of Goods Sold was $400. |
| 28 | Sold goods to Meaghan, Inc. for cash of $2,000 (cost $350). |
| 28 | Collected from Merry Cleaners, $275 of receivable previously written off. |
| 29 | Paid cash for utilities of $450. |
| 31 | Created an aging schedule for Crystal Clear for accounts receivable. Crystal Clear determined that $8,100 of receivables were 5% uncollectible, $9,775 of receivables were 15% uncollectible, and $850 of receivables were 30% uncollectible. Crystal Clear determined the total amount of estimated uncollectible receivables and adjusted the Allowance for Bad Debts assuming a credit balance of $240 in the account. (Round to nearest whole dollar.) |

**Requirements**

1. Prepare all required journal entries for Crystal Clear.
2. Show how net accounts receivable would be reported on the balance sheet as of January 31, 2018.

# CRITICAL THINKING

## > Decision Cases

### Decision Case 8-1

Weddings on Demand sells on account and manages its own receivables. Average experience for the past three years has been as follows:

| | |
|---|---|
| Sales | $ 350,000 |
| Cost of Goods Sold | 210,000 |
| Bad Debts Expense | 4,000 |
| Other Expenses | 61,000 |

Unhappy with the amount of bad debts expense she has been experiencing, Aledia Sanchez, controller, is considering a major change in the business. Her plan would be to stop selling on account altogether but accept either cash, credit cards, or debit cards from her customers. Her market research indicates that if she does so, her sales will increase by 10% (i.e., from $350,000 to $385,000), of which $200,000 will be credit or debit card sales and the rest will be cash sales. With a 10% increase in sales, there will also be a 10% increase in Cost of Goods Sold. If she adopts this plan, she will no longer have bad debts expense, but she will have to pay a fee on debit/credit card transactions of 2% of applicable sales. She also believes this plan will allow her to save $5,000 per year in other operating expenses.

Should Sanchez start accepting credit cards and debit cards? Show the computations of net income under her present arrangement and under the plan.

### Decision Case 8-2

Pauline's Pottery has always used the direct write-off method to account for uncollectibles. The company's revenues, bad debt write-offs, and year-end receivables for the most recent year follow:

| Year | Revenues | Write-offs | Receivables at Year-end |
|---|---|---|---|
| 2016 | $ 150,000 | $ 3,900 | $ 14,000 |

The business is applying for a bank loan, and the loan officer requires figures based on the allowance method of accounting for bad debts. In the past, bad debts have run about 4% of revenues.

**Requirements**

Pauline must give the banker the following information:

1. How much more or less would net income be for 2016 if Pauline's Pottery were to use the allowance method for bad debts? Assume Pauline uses the percent-of-sales method.
2. How much of the receivables balance at the end of 2016 does Pauline's Pottery actually expect to collect? (Disregard beginning account balances for the purpose of this question.)
3. Explain why net income is more or less using the allowance method versus the direct write-off method for uncollectibles.

## > Fraud Case 8-1

Dylan worked for a propane gas distributor as an accounting clerk in a small Midwestern town. Last winter, his brother Mike lost his job at the machine plant. By January, temperatures were sub-zero, and Mike had run out of money. Dylan saw that Mike's account was overdue, and he knew Mike needed another delivery to heat his home. He decided to credit Mike's account and debit the balance to the parts inventory because he knew the parts manager, the owner's son, was incompetent and would never notice the extra entry. Months went by, and Dylan repeated the process until an auditor ran across the charges by chance. When the owner fired Dylan, he said, "If you had only come to me and told me about Mike's situation, we could have worked something out."

**Requirements**

1. What can a business like this do to prevent employee fraud of this kind?
2. What effect would Dylan's actions have on the balance sheet? The income statement?
3. How much discretion does a business have with regard to accommodating hardship situations?

## > Financial Statement Case 8-1

Use **Starbucks Corporation**'s Fiscal 2013 Annual Report and the Note 1 data on "Allowance for Doubtful Accounts" to answer the following questions. Visit **http://www.pearsonhighered.com/Horngren** to view a link to Starbucks Corporation's annual report.

**Requirements**

1. How much accounts receivables did Starbucks report as of September 29, 2013? As of September 30, 2012?
2. Refer to Note 1, "Allowance for Doubtful Accounts." How does Starbucks calculate allowance for doubtful accounts? What was the amount of the account as of September 29, 2013? As of September 30, 2012?
3. Compute Starbucks's acid-test ratio at the end of 2013. If all the current liabilities came due immediately, could Starbucks pay them?
4. Compute Starbucks's accounts receivable turnover at the end of 2013. Use total net revenues.
5. Compute Starbucks's days' sales in receivables at the end of 2013.
6. How does Starbucks compare to **Green Mountain Coffee Roasters, Inc.** on the basis of the acid-test ratio, accounts receivable turnover, and days' sales in receivables?



## > Quick Check Answers

**1.** d **2.** b **3.** d **4.** d **5.** a **6.** d **7.** b **8.** c **9.** a **10.** d

# 9 Plant Assets, Natural Resources, and Intangibles

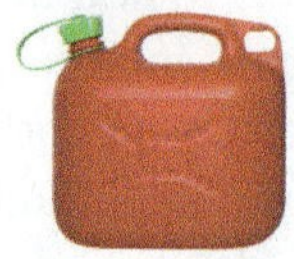

## What Do I Do with This Equipment?

Jerry Drake has been working hard at a new landscaping business for several months. Things are great—sales are increasing every month, and the customer base is increasing. So far, Jerry has been renting lawn equipment or borrowing equipment from his friends. Jerry is now considering buying several new lawn mowers, trimmers, and leaf blowers.

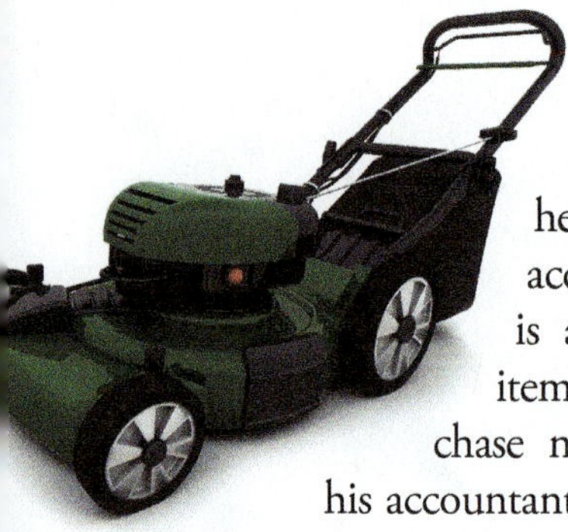

Jerry is trying to figure out how to record the purchase of these items on his books. Should he expense them all or set up asset accounts for each of the items? Jerry is also considering how long each item will last before he needs to purchase new equipment. He knows that his accountant will ask him about depreciation. She has told him there are several methods he should consider. Jerry knows he wants a depreciation method that will match the cost of the equipment with the revenue that the business earns.

In addition, Jerry plans on keeping the equipment as long as he can, which means that he will be making repairs and maintaining the equipment. He is wondering how the cost of the repairs should be recorded. And what happens when he finally sells the equipment? Jerry realizes there is a lot to consider when a business buys equipment. He knows that his accountant will help answer his many questions so he can properly record the cost of the equipment and any future associated costs.

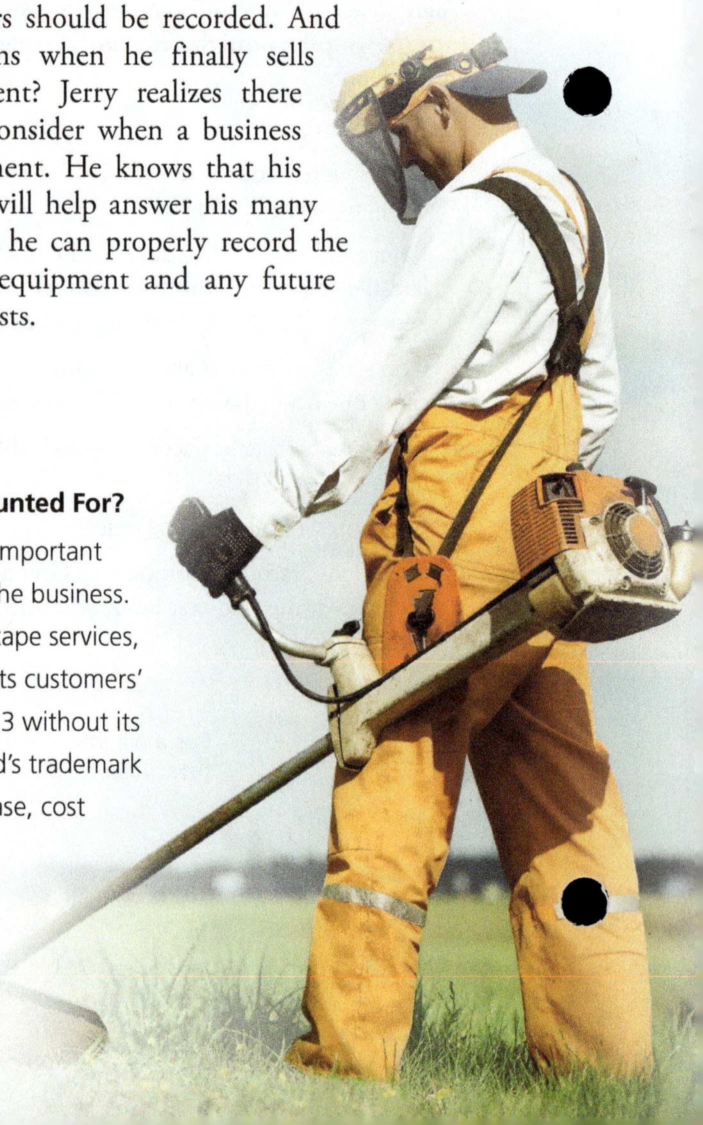

**How Are Plant Assets, Natural Resources, and Intangibles Accounted For?**

Plant assets, natural resources, and intangibles are some of the most important assets on the balance sheet. These assets help create the revenue of the business. For example, TruGreen, a company that specializes in lawn and landscape services, wouldn't earn a profit without the lawn equipment it uses to service its customers' lawns. ConocoPhillips wouldn't have made a $9.1 billion profit in 2013 without its natural resource of oil reserves. And we are all familiar with McDonald's trademark "golden arches." In this chapter, we discuss how to record the purchase, cost allocation, and disposal of these assets.

# Chapter 9 Learning Objectives

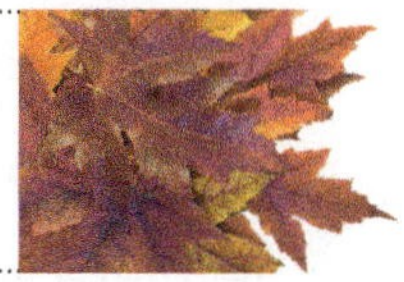

1. Measure the cost of a plant asset
2. Account for depreciation using the straight-line, units-of-production, and double-declining-balance methods
3. Journalize entries for the disposal of plant assets
4. Account for natural resources
5. Account for intangible assets
6. Use the asset turnover ratio to evaluate business performance
7. Journalize entries for the exchange of plant assets (Appendix 9A)

## HOW DOES A BUSINESS MEASURE THE COST OF A PLANT ASSET?

**Learning Objective 1**
Measure the cost of a plant asset

**Plant assets** are long-lived, tangible assets used in the operations of a business. Examples include land, buildings, equipment, furniture, and automobiles. Often, plant assets are referred to as *Property, Plant, and Equipment* or *Fixed Assets* in financial statements.

Plant assets are unique from other assets, such as office supplies, because plant assets are long term (lasting several years). This requires a business to allocate the cost of the asset over the years that the asset is expected to be used. This allocation of a plant asset's cost over its useful life is called **depreciation** and follows the matching principle. The matching principle ensures that all expenses are matched against the revenues of the period. Because plant assets are used over several years, a business will record a portion of the cost of the asset as an expense in each of those years. All plant assets except land are depreciated. We record no depreciation for land because it does not have a definitive or clearly estimable life, so it is difficult to allocate the cost of land.

**Plant Asset**
Long-lived, tangible asset, such as land, buildings, and equipment, used in the operation of a business.

**Depreciation**
The process by which businesses spread the allocation of a plant asset's cost over its useful life.

Plant assets are used in the operations of the business. This means that they are not specifically acquired for resale, but instead they are used to help create the business's revenue. For example, a business that has a vacant building that is not currently being used would classify this asset as a long-term investment instead of as a plant asset. This is because the vacant building is sitting idle and not currently being used in the operations of the business.

Exhibit 9-1 summarizes the life cycle of a plant asset in a business. The business begins by acquiring the asset and recording the asset on its books. This involves determining the asset cost that is reported on the balance sheet. As the business uses the asset, it must record depreciation expense. In addition, the business also incurs additional expenses (such as repairs and maintenance) related to the asset. And lastly, when the asset has reached the end of its useful life, the business disposes of the asset. Each of these stages in the life of a plant asset must be recorded on the business's books.

**Exhibit 9-1 | Life Cycle of a Plant Asset**

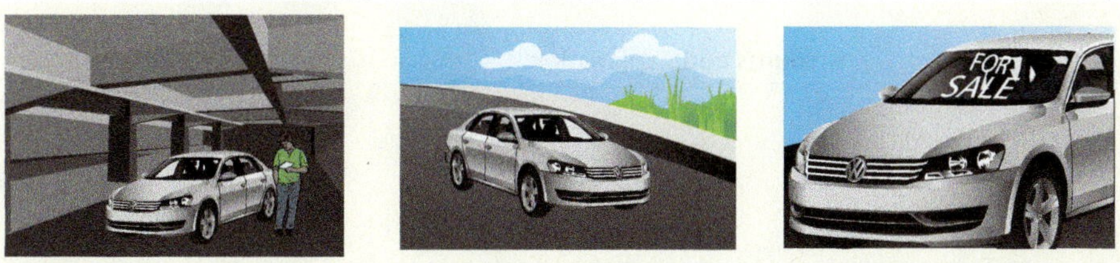


1. Acquisition of asset    2. Usage of asset    3. Disposal of asset

**Cost Principle**
A principle that states that acquired assets and services should be recorded at their actual cost.

Plant assets are recorded at historical cost—the amount paid for the asset. This follows the **cost principle**, which states that acquired assets (and services) should be recorded at their actual cost. The *actual cost of a plant asset* is its purchase price plus taxes, purchase commissions, and all other amounts paid to ready the asset for its intended use. Let's begin by reviewing the different categories of plant assets.

## Land and Land Improvements

The cost of land includes the following amounts paid by the purchaser:

- Purchase price
- Brokerage commission
- Survey and legal fees
- Deliquent property taxes
- Taxes assessed to transfer the ownership (title) on the land
- Cost of clearing the land and removing unwanted buildings

The cost of land does *not* include the following costs:

- Fencing
- Paving
- Sprinkler systems
- Lighting
- Signs

**Land Improvement**
A depreciable improvement to land, such as fencing, sprinklers, paving, signs, and lighting.

These separate plant assets (fencing, paving, and so on) are called **land improvements**. Unlike land, land improvements are subject to depreciation.

Suppose Smart Touch Learning needs property and purchases land on August 1, 2017, for $50,000 with a note payable for the same amount. The company also pays cash as follows: $4,000 in property taxes, $2,000 in transfer taxes, $5,000 to remove an old building, and a $1,000 survey fee. What is the company's cost of this land? Exhibit 9-2 shows all the costs incurred to bring the land to its intended use.

**Exhibit 9-2 | Measuring the Cost of Land**

| | | |
|---|---|---|
| Purchase price of land | | $ 50,000 |
| Add related costs: | | |
| Property taxes | $ 4,000 | |
| Transfer taxes | 2,000 | |
| Removal of building | 5,000 | |
| Survey fee | 1,000 | 12,000 |
| Total cost of land | | $ 62,000 |

The entry to record the purchase of the land on August 1, 2017, follows:

| A↑ | = | L↑ | + E |
|---|---|---|---|
| Land↑ Cash↓ | | Notes Payable↑ | |

| Date | Accounts and Explanation | Debit | Credit |
|---|---|---|---|
| Aug. 1 | Land | 62,000 | |
| | Notes Payable | | 50,000 |
| | Cash | | 12,000 |
| | *To record purchase of land with cash and note payable.* | | |

We would say that Smart Touch Learning *capitalized* the cost of the land at $62,000. **Capitalized** means that an asset account was debited (increased) because the company acquired an asset. So, for our land example, Smart Touch Learning debited the Land account for $62,000, the capitalized cost of the asset.

**Capitalize**
Recording the acquisition of land, building, or other assets by debiting (increasing) an asset account.

Suppose Smart Touch Learning then pays $20,000 for fences, paving, lighting, and signs on August 15, 2017. The following entry records the cost of these land improvements:

| Date | Accounts and Explanation | Debit | Credit |
|---|---|---|---|
| Aug. 15 | Land Improvements | 20,000 | |
| | Cash | | 20,000 |
| | *To record purchase of land improvements for cash.* | | |

| A↑↓ | | L + E |
|---|---|---|
| Land Improvements↑<br>Cash↓ | = | |

Land and land improvements are two entirely separate assets. Recall that land is not depreciated. However, the cost of land improvements *is* depreciated over that asset's useful life.

## Buildings

The cost of a building depends on whether the company is constructing the building itself or is buying an existing one. These costs include the following:

| Constructing a Building | Purchasing an Existing Building |
|---|---|
| • Architectural fees<br>• Building permits<br>• Contractor charges<br>• Payments for materials, labor, and miscellaneous costs | • Purchase price<br>• Costs to renovate the building to ready the building for use, which may include any of the charges listed under "Constructing a Building" |

## Machinery and Equipment

The cost of machinery and equipment includes the following:

- Purchase price (less any discounts)
- Transportation charges
- Insurance while in transit
- Sales tax and other taxes
- Purchase commission
- Installation costs
- Testing costs (prior to use of the asset)

After the asset is up and running, the company no longer capitalizes the cost of insurance, taxes, ordinary repairs, and maintenance to the Equipment account. From that point on, insurance, taxes, repairs, and maintenance costs are recorded as expenses.

## Furniture and Fixtures

Furniture and fixtures include desks, chairs, file cabinets, display racks, shelving, and so forth. The cost of furniture and fixtures includes the basic cost of each asset (less any discounts), plus all other costs to ready the asset for its intended use. For example, for a desk, this may include the cost to ship the desk to the business and the cost paid to a laborer to assemble the desk.

## Lump-Sum Purchase

A company may pay a single price for several assets as a group—a lump-sum purchase (sometimes called a *basket purchase*). For example, Smart Touch Learning may pay a single price for land and a building. For accounting purposes, the company must identify the cost of each asset purchased. The total cost paid (100%) is divided among the assets according to their relative market values. This is called the **relative-market-value method**.

**Relative-Market-Value Method**
A method of allocating the total cost (100%) of multiple assets purchased at one time. Total cost is divided among the assets according to their relative market values.

Suppose Smart Touch Learning paid a combined purchase price of $100,000 on August 1, 2017, for the land and building. An appraisal indicates that the land's market value is $30,000, and the building's market value is $90,000. It is clear that the company got a good deal, paying less than fair market value, which is $120,000 for the combined assets. But how will the accountant allocate the $100,000 paid for both assets?

First, calculate the ratio of each asset's market value to the total market value for both assets. The total appraised value is $120,000.

Total market value = Land market value + Building market value
= $30,000 + $90,000
= $120,000

The land makes up 25% of the total market value and the building 75%, as follows:

Percentage of total value = Land market value / Total market value
= $30,000 / $120,000
= 25%

Percentage of total value = Building market value / Total market value
= $90,000 / $120,000
= 75%

For Smart Touch Learning, the land is assigned the cost of $25,000 and the building is assigned the cost of $75,000. The calculations follow:

| Asset | Market Value | Percentage of Total Value | × Total Purchase Price | = Assigned Cost of Each Asset |
|---|---|---|---|---|
| Land | $ 30,000 | $30,000 / $120,000 = 25% | × $100,000 | = $ 25,000 |
| Building | 90,000 | $90,000 / $120,000 = 75% | × $100,000 | = 75,000 |
| Total | $ 120,000 | 100% | | $ 100,000 |

Suppose the company purchased the assets by signing a note payable. The entry to record the purchase of the land and building is as follows:

| A↑ | = | L↑ | + | E |
|---|---|---|---|---|
| Land↑ Building↑ | = | Notes Payable↑ | | |

| Date | Accounts and Explanation | Debit | Credit |
|---|---|---|---|
| Aug. 1 | Land | 25,000 | |
| | Building | 75,000 | |
| | Notes Payable | | 100,000 |
| | *To record purchase of land and building in exchange for note payable.* | | |

## Capital and Revenue Expenditures

Accountants divide spending on plant assets after the acquisition into two categories:

- Capital expenditures
- Revenue expenditures

A **capital expenditure** is debited to an asset account because it increases the asset's capacity or efficiency or extends the asset's useful life. A capital expenditure is also called a *balance sheet expenditure* because the cost of the expenditure is reported on the balance sheet as an asset.

Examples of capital expenditures include the purchase price plus all the other costs to bring an asset to its intended use, as discussed in the preceding sections. Also, an **extraordinary repair** is a capital expenditure because it extends the asset's capacity or useful life. An example of an extraordinary repair would be spending $3,000 to rebuild the engine on a five-year-old truck. This extraordinary repair would extend the asset's life past the normal expected life. As a result, its cost would be debited to the asset account for the truck as follows:

**Capital Expenditure**
An expenditure that increases the capacity or efficiency of a plant asset or extends its useful life. Capital expenditures are debited to an asset account.

**Extraordinary Repair**
Repair work that generates a capital expenditure because it extends the asset's life past the normal expected life.

| Date | Accounts and Explanation | Debit | Credit |
|---|---|---|---|
| | Truck | 3,000 | |
| | Cash | | 3,000 |
| | *To record cost of rebuilding engine on truck.* | | |

| A↑↓ | | L | + | E |
|---|---|---|---|---|
| Truck↑ | = | | | |
| Cash↓ | | | | |

Expenses incurred to maintain the asset in working order, such as repair or maintenance expense, are *not* debited to an asset account. Examples include the costs of maintaining equipment, such as repairing the air conditioner on a truck, changing the oil filter, and replacing its tires. These ordinary repairs are called **revenue expenditures** and are debited to Repairs and Maintenance Expense. Revenue expenditures, often called *income statement expenditures,* do not increase the capacity or efficiency of an asset or extend its useful life and are reported on the income statement as an expense in the period incurred.

**Revenue Expenditure**
An expenditure that does not increase the capacity or efficiency of an asset or extend its useful life. Revenue expenditures are debited to an expense account.

Suppose that Smart Touch Learning paid $500 cash to replace tires on the truck. This expenditure does not extend the useful life of the truck or increase its efficiency. The company's accounting clerk records this transaction as a revenue expenditure as shown:

| Date | Accounts and Explanation | Debit | Credit |
|---|---|---|---|
| | Repairs and Maintenance Expense | 500 | |
| | Cash | | 500 |
| | *To record repairs and maintenance costs incurred.* | | |

| A↓ | | L | + | E↓ |
|---|---|---|---|---|
| Cash↓ | = | | | Repairs and Maintenance Expense↑ |

Exhibit 9-3 (on the next page) shows some (a) capital expenditures and (b) revenue expenditures for a delivery truck.

**Exhibit 9-3 | Delivery Truck Expenditures—Capital Expenditure or Revenue Expenditure**

| CAPITAL EXPENDITURE: Debit an Asset Account | REVENUE EXPENDITURE: Debit Repairs and Maintenance Expense |
|---|---|
| *Extraordinary Repairs:* | *Revenue Expenditures:* |
| Major engine or transmission overhaul | Repair of transmission or engine |
| Modification for new use | Oil change, lubrication, and so on |
| Addition to storage capacity | Replacement of tires or windshield |
| Anything that increases the life of the asset | Paint job |

Treating a capital expenditure as an expense, or vice versa, creates an accounting error. Suppose a business replaces the engine in the truck. This would be an extraordinary repair because it increases the truck's life. If the company expenses the cost by debiting Repairs and Maintenance Expense rather than capitalizing it (debiting the asset), the company would be making an accounting error. This error has the following effects:

- Overstates Repairs and Maintenance Expense
- Understates net income
- Understates stockholders' equity
- Understates the Truck account (asset) on the balance sheet

Incorrectly capitalizing an expense creates the opposite error. Assume a minor repair, such as replacing the water pump on the truck, was incorrectly debited to the asset account. The error would result in expenses being understated and net income being overstated. Additionally, the cost of the truck would be overstated on the balance sheet by the amount of the repair bill.

## Try It!

1. Budget Banners pays $200,000 cash for a group purchase of land, building, and equipment. At the time of acquisition, the land has a market value of $22,000, the building $187,000, and the equipment $11,000. Journalize the lump-sum purchase.

**Check your answer online in MyAccountingLab or at http://www.pearsonhighered.com/Horngren.**

For more practice, see Short Exercises S9-1 and S9-2. MyAccountingLab

## WHAT IS DEPRECIATION, AND HOW IS IT COMPUTED?

**Learning Objective 2**
Account for depreciation using the straight-line, units-of-production, and double-declining-balance methods

As we learned earlier, depreciation is the allocation of a plant asset's cost to expense over its useful life. Depreciation matches the expense against the revenue generated from using the asset to measure net income.

All assets, except land, wear out as they are used. For example, a business's delivery truck can only go so many miles before it is worn out. As the truck is driven, this use is part of what causes depreciation. Additionally, physical factors, like age and weather, can cause depreciation of assets.

**Obsolete**
An asset is considered obsolete when a newer asset can perform the job more efficiently than the old.

Some assets, such as computers and software, may become *obsolete* before they wear out. An asset is **obsolete** when a newer asset can perform the job more efficiently. As a result, an asset's useful life may be shorter than its physical life. In all cases, the asset's cost is depreciated over its useful life.

Now that we have discussed causes of depreciation, let's discuss what depreciation is *not.*

1. *Depreciation is not a process of valuation.* Businesses do not record depreciation based on changes in the asset's market value.
2. *Depreciation does not mean that the business sets aside cash to replace an asset when it is used up.* Depreciation has nothing to do with cash.

## Factors in Computing Depreciation

Depreciation of a plant asset is based on three main factors:

1. Capitalized cost
2. Estimated useful life
3. Estimated residual value

Capitalized cost is a known cost and, as mentioned earlier in this chapter, includes all items paid for the asset to perform its intended function. The other two factors are estimates.

Estimated **useful life** is how long the company expects it will use the asset. Useful life may be expressed in time, such as months or years, or usage, such as units produced, hours used (for machinery), or miles driven (for a truck). A company's useful life estimate might be shorter than the actual life of the asset. For example, a business might estimate a useful life of five years for a delivery truck because it has a policy that after five years the truck will be traded in for a new vehicle. The business knows that the truck will last longer than five years, but the business uses a useful life of only five years because this is how long the company expects to use the asset.

**Useful Life**
Length of the service period expected from an asset. May be expressed in time, such as months or years, or usage, such as units produced, hours used (for machinery), or miles driven (for a truck).

Useful life is an estimate based on a company's experience and judgment. The goal is to define estimated useful life with the measure (years, units, and so on) that best matches the asset's decline or use. When determining useful life, a company considers how long it will use the asset and when the asset will become obsolete.

Estimated **residual value**—also called *salvage value*—is the asset's expected value at the end of its useful life. When a company decides to dispose of an asset, the company will sell or scrap it. The residual value is the amount the company expects to receive when the company disposes of the asset. Residual value can sometimes be zero if a company does not expect to receive anything when disposing of the asset. If a company plans on trading the asset in for a new asset, the residual value will be the expected trade-in value. Estimated residual value is *not* depreciated because the company expects to receive this amount at the end. Cost minus estimated residual value is called **depreciable cost**.

**Residual Value**
The expected value of a depreciable asset at the end of its useful life.

**Depreciable Cost**
The cost of a plant asset minus its estimated residual value.

Depreciable cost = Cost − Estimated residual value

## Depreciation Methods

There are many depreciation methods for plant assets, but three are used most commonly:

- Straight-line method
- Units-of-production method
- Double-declining-balance method

These methods work differently in *how* they derive the yearly depreciation amount, but they all result in the same total depreciation over the total life of the asset. Exhibit 9-4 (on the next page) gives the data we will use for a truck that Smart Touch Learning purchases and places in service on January 1, 2017.

**Exhibit 9-4 | Data for Truck**

| Data Item | Amount |
|---|---|
| Cost of truck | $ 41,000 |
| Less: Estimated residual value | 1,000 |
| Depreciable cost | $ 40,000 |
| Estimated useful life—Years | 5 years |
| Estimated useful life—Units | 100,000 miles |

## Straight-Line Method

**Straight-Line Method**
A depreciation method that allocates an equal amount of depreciation each year. (Cost − Residual value) / Useful life.

The **straight-line method** allocates an equal amount of depreciation to each year and is calculated as follows:

$$\begin{aligned}\text{Straight-line depreciation} &= (\text{Cost} - \text{Residual value}) / \text{Useful life} \\ &= (\$41{,}000 - \$1{,}000) / 5 \text{ years} \\ &= \$8{,}000 \text{ per year}\end{aligned}$$

Because the asset was placed in service on the first day of the year, the adjusting entry to record each year's depreciation is as follows:

| A↓ | = | L | + | E↓ |
|---|---|---|---|---|
| Accumulated Depreciation—Truck↑ | | | | Depreciation Expense—Truck↑ |

| Date | Accounts and Explanation | Debit | Credit |
|---|---|---|---|
| Dec. 31 | Depreciation Expense—Truck | 8,000 | |
| | Accumulated Depreciation—Truck | | 8,000 |
| | *To record depreciation on truck.* | | |

Depreciation Expense is reported on the income statement. Accumulated Depreciation is a contra asset that is reported on the balance sheet following the Truck account. The **book value** of the plant asset, cost minus accumulated depreciation, is reported on the balance sheet at December 31, 2017, as follows:

**Book Value**
A depreciable asset's cost minus accumulated depreciation.

| **Plant Assets:** | |
|---|---|
| Truck | $ 41,000 |
| Less: Accumulated Depreciation—Truck | (8,000) |
| Truck, Net | $ 33,000 |

A straight-line depreciation schedule for this truck is shown in Exhibit 9-5. The final column on the right shows the asset's book value, which is cost less accumulated depreciation. Notice that the depreciation expense amount is the same every year and that the accumulated depreciation is the sum of all depreciation expense recorded to date for the depreciable asset.

**Exhibit 9-5 | Straight-Line Depreciation Schedule**

| | | Depreciation for the Year | | | | | |
|---|---|---|---|---|---|---|---|
| Date | Asset Cost | Depreciable Cost | Useful Life | | Depreciation Expense | Accumulated Depreciation | Book Value |
| 1-1-2017 | $ 41,000 | | | | | | $ 41,000 |
| 12-31-2017 | | ($41,000 – $1,000) | / 5 years | = | $ 8,000 | $ 8,000 | 33,000 |
| 12-31-2018 | | ($41,000 – $1,000) | / 5 years | = | 8,000 | 16,000 | 25,000 |
| 12-31-2019 | | ($41,000 – $1,000) | / 5 years | = | 8,000 | 24,000 | 17,000 |
| 12-31-2020 | | ($41,000 – $1,000) | / 5 years | = | 8,000 | 32,000 | 9,000 |
| 12-31-2021 | | ($41,000 – $1,000) | / 5 years | = | 8,000 | 40,000 | 1,000 ← Residual value |

As an asset is used, accumulated depreciation increases and book value decreases. (See the Accumulated Depreciation and Book Value columns in Exhibit 9-5.) At the end of its estimated useful life, the asset is said to be fully depreciated. An asset's final book value is its residual value ($1,000 in this example).

**ETHICS**

### Capitalize or expense?

Furniture.com uses automated shipping equipment. Early in the year, Furniture.com purchased equipment at a cost of $400,000. Management expects the equipment to remain in service for five years, with zero residual value. Furniture.com plans on using straight-line depreciation. Mason Green is finalizing the depreciation expense calculation for the year when Furniture.com's controller, Flynn Steel, tells Mason to expense the entire cost of the equipment instead of capitalizing the equipment at the time of purchase. Flynn argues that the company won't have to worry about recording depreciation for the next five years—the accounting will "just be easier." What should Mason do? What would you do?

#### Solution

Mason should explain to Flynn that the cost of an asset that will provide future benefit to the company should be capitalized and then depreciated over the life of the asset. In expensing the entire cost of the equipment in the year of purchase, depreciation expense of $80,000 [($400,000 – $0) / 5 years] that should have been recorded would not have been. This error would make net income understated by $320,000 ($400,000 – $80,000), and the company would not be following GAAP. If the controller still disagrees, Mason should discuss the situation with the company's president.

## Units-of-Production Method

The **units-of-production method** allocates a varying amount of depreciation each year based on an asset's usage. Units-of-production depreciates by units rather than by years. As we noted earlier, a unit of output can be miles, units, hours, or output, depending on which unit type best defines the asset's use. When a plant asset's usage varies every year, the units-of-production method does a better of job of matching expenses with revenues.

**Units-of-Production Method**
A depreciation method that allocates a varying amount of depreciation each year based on an asset's usage.

The truck in our example is estimated to be driven 20,000 miles the first year, 30,000 the second, 25,000 the third, 15,000 the fourth, and 10,000 during the fifth (for a total useful life of 100,000 miles). The units-of-production depreciation for each period varies with the number of units (miles, in the case of the truck) the asset produces. Units-of-production depreciation is calculated as follows:

**Step 1:**

Depreciation per unit = (Cost − Residual value) / Useful life in units
= ($41,000 − $1,000) / 100,000 miles
= $0.40 per mile

**Step 2:**

Units-of-production depreciation = Depreciation per unit × Current year usage
= $0.40 per mile × 20,000 miles
= $8,000 (year 1)

Units-of-production depreciation for the truck is illustrated in Exhibit 9-6.

**Exhibit 9-6 | Units-of-Production Depreciation Schedule**

| | | Depreciation for the Year | | | | | | |
|---|---|---|---|---|---|---|---|---|
| Date | Asset Cost | Depreciation Per Unit | | Number of Units | | Depreciation Expense | Accumulated Depreciation | Book Value |
| 1-1-2017 | $ 41,000 | | | | | | | $ 41,000 |
| 12-31-2017 | | $ 0.40 | × | 20,000 | = | $ 8,000 | $ 8,000 | 33,000 |
| 12-31-2018 | | 0.40 | × | 30,000 | = | 12,000 | 20,000 | 21,000 |
| 12-31-2019 | | 0.40 | × | 25,000 | = | 10,000 | 30,000 | 11,000 |
| 12-31-2020 | | 0.40 | × | 15,000 | = | 6,000 | 36,000 | 5,000 |
| 12-31-2021 | | 0.40 | × | 10,000 | = | 4,000 | 40,000 | 1,000 ← Residual value |

## Double-Declining-Balance Method

**Accelerated Depreciation Method**
A depreciation method that expenses more of the asset's cost near the start of its useful life and less at the end of its useful life.

**Double-Declining-Balance Method**
An accelerated depreciation method that computes annual depreciation by multiplying the depreciable asset's decreasing book value by a constant percent that is two times the straight-line depreciation rate.

An **accelerated depreciation method** expenses more of the asset's cost near the start of an asset's life and less at the end of its useful life. The main accelerated method of depreciation is the **double-declining-balance method**. The double-declining-balance method multiplies an asset's decreasing book value (the asset's cost less its accumulated depreciation) by a constant percentage that is twice the straight-line depreciation rate. The straight-line depreciation rate is calculated as *1 / useful life*. Therefore, the double-declining-balance method rate will be *2 × (1 / useful life)*. Double-declining-balance amounts can be computed using the following formula:

Double-declining-balance depreciation = (Cost − Accumulated depreciation) × 2 × (1 / Useful life)

For the first year of the truck, the calculation would be as shown:

Double-declining-balance depreciation = (Cost − Accumulated depreciation) × 2 × (1 / Useful life)
= ($41,000 − $0) × 2 × (1 / 5 years)
= $16,400 (year 1)

In year 2, the amount of depreciation would decline because the asset has accumulated some depreciation (the $16,400 for the first year). For the second year of the truck, therefore, the calculation would be as shown:

Double-declining-balance depreciation = (Cost − Accumulated depreciation) × 2 × (1 / Useful life)
= ($41,000 − $16,400) × 2 × (1 / 5 years)
= $9,840 (year 2)

*Note that residual value is not included in the formula.* Residual value is ignored until the depreciation expense takes the book value below the residual value. When this occurs, the final year depreciation is calculated as the amount needed to bring the asset to its residual value. In the case of the truck, residual value was given at $1,000. In the double-declining-balance schedule in Exhibit 9-7, notice that, after year 4 (12-31-2020), the truck's book value is $5,314. By definition, the truck is to last five years, which ends on 12-31-2021. At the end of the asset's life, its book value should equal the residual value. Therefore, in the final year, depreciation is book value, $5,314, less the $1,000 residual value, or $4,314 in depreciation expense.

**Exhibit 9-7 | Double-Declining-Balance Depreciation Schedule**

| | | Depreciation for the Year | | | | | | | |
|---|---|---|---|---|---|---|---|---|---|
| **Date** | **Asset Cost** | **Book Value** | | **DDB Rate** | | **Depreciation Expense** | **Accumulated Depreciation** | **Book Value** | |
| 1-1-2017 | $ 41,000 | | | | | | | $ 41,000 | |
| 12-31-2017 | | $41,000 | × | $2 \times \frac{1}{5}$ | = | $ 16,400 | $ 16,400 | 24,600 | |
| 12-31-2018 | | 24,600 | × | $2 \times \frac{1}{5}$ | = | 9,840 | 26,240 | 14,760 | |
| 12-31-2019 | | 14,760 | × | $2 \times \frac{1}{5}$ | = | 5,904 | 32,144 | 8,856 | |
| 12-31-2020 | | 8,856 | × | $2 \times \frac{1}{5}$ | = | 3,542 | 35,686 | 5,314 | |
| 12-31-2021 | | | | | | 4,314* | 40,000 | 1,000 | ← Residual value |

*Last year depreciation is the "plug figure" needed to reduce book value to the residual amount ($5,314 − $1,000 = $4,314).

## Comparing Depreciation Methods

Let's compare the depreciation methods. Annual depreciation expense amounts vary, but total accumulated depreciation is $40,000 for all three methods.

| **Amount of Depreciation per Year** | | | |
|---|---|---|---|
| | | | **Accelerated Method** |
| **Year** | **Straight-Line** | **Units-of-Production** | **Double-Declining-Balance** |
| 1 | $ 8,000 | $ 8,000 | $ 16,400 |
| 2 | 8,000 | 12,000 | 9,840 |
| 3 | 8,000 | 10,000 | 5,904 |
| 4 | 8,000 | 6,000 | 3,542 |
| 5 | 8,000 | 4,000 | 4,314 |
| Total Accumulated Depreciation | $ 40,000 | $ 40,000 | $ 40,000 |

Deciding which method is best depends on the asset. A business should match an asset's expense against the revenue that the asset produces. The following are some guidelines for which method to use:

| Method | Asset Characteristics | Effect on Depreciation | Example Assets |
|---|---|---|---|
| Straight-Line | Generates revenue evenly over time | Equal amount each period | Building |
| Units-of-Production | Depreciates due to wear and tear rather than obsolescence | More usage causes larger depreciation | Vehicles (miles) Machinery (machine hours) |
| Double-Declining-Balance | Produces more revenue in early years | Higher depreciation in early years, less later | Computers |

Exhibit 9-8 shows the three methods in one graph for additional comparison. Notice that the straight-line method produces a straight line on the graph because there is an equal amount of depreciation expense each year. The double-declining-balance method produces a line that is decreasing, and the units-of-production method's line varies based on usage.

**Exhibit 9-8 | Annual Depreciation by Method**

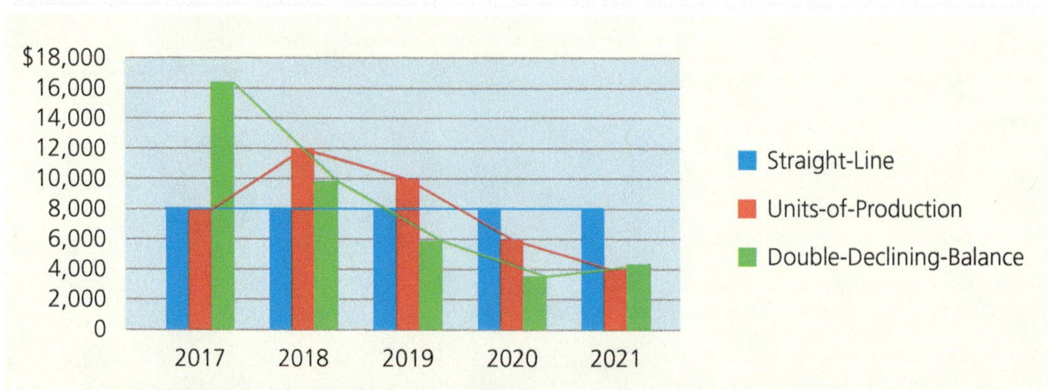

## DECISIONS

### Which depreciation method should be selected?

Three Junes Weaving has just purchased an automated weaving machine and is trying to figure out which depreciation method to use: straight-line, units-of-production, or double-declining-balance. Ira Glasier, the controller, is interested in using a depreciation method that approximates the usage of the weaving machine. He also expects that the weaving machine will have increasing repairs and maintenance as the asset ages. Which method should Ira choose?

### Solution

If Ira is interested in using a depreciation method that approximates the usage of the weaving machine, he should use the units-of-production method to depreciate the asset. He could use number of machine hours as the unit of output. This method would best match the usage of the machine to the amount of expense recorded. Ira should be aware, though, that this method could produce varying amounts of depreciation expense each year. For example, if Three Junes Weaving does not use the weaving machine in one year, no depreciation expense would be recorded. This could cause net income to vary significantly from year to year. Because Ira expects the weaving machine to need more repairs as the asset ages, Ira might consider using the double-declining-balance method instead. The double-declining-balance method records a higher amount of depreciation in the early years and less later. This method works well for assets that are expected to have increasing repairs and maintenance in their later years because the total expense (depreciation and repairs and maintenance) can be spread out equally over the life of the asset.

## Depreciation for Tax Purposes

The Internal Revenue Service (IRS) requires that companies use a specific depreciation method for tax purposes. This method is the **Modified Accelerated Cost Recovery System (MACRS)**.

**Modified Accelerated Cost Recovery System (MACRS)**
A depreciation method that is used for tax purposes.

Under MACRS, assets are divided into specific classes, such as 3-year, 5-year, 7-year, and 39-year property. Businesses do not get to choose the useful life of the asset. Instead, the IRS specifies the useful life based on the specific classes. For example, office furniture has a 7-year life for tax purposes but might only be depreciated for five years for book purposes.

In addition, the MACRS method ignores residual value. For tax purposes, an asset is fully depreciated to a book value of zero. **MACRS is not acceptable for financial reporting under GAAP.** This requires that businesses record depreciation for plant assets under two methods—book method (straight-line, units-of-production, or double-declining-balance) and tax method (MACRS).

Can the MACRS method be used for financial reporting in accordance with GAAP?

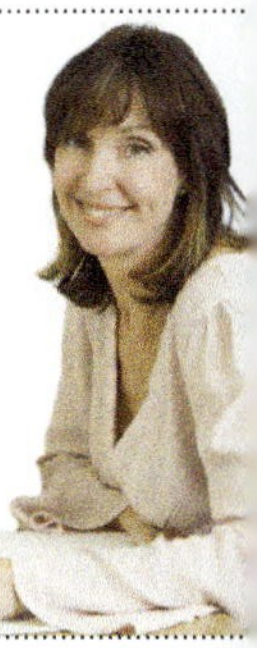

## Partial-Year Depreciation

In the previous examples, we calculated depreciation for the entire year. What would happen if the business placed the truck in service on July 1, 2017, instead of January 1, 2017? Would the depreciation for any of the methods change? Yes, but only the methods that are calculated based on a time period, which means only straight-line and double-declining-balance would change. Units-of-production does not consider years in its formula; thus, that calculation remains the same.

When a business purchases an asset during the year (other than January 1), the business should record depreciation for only the portion of the year that the asset was used in the operations of the business. This partial-year depreciation could be calculated to the nearest day, but this is unnecessary. In this book, we will assume a method called modified half-month convention, which means if an asset is purchased on or before the 15th of the month, the asset will be depreciated for the whole month. If the asset is purchased after the 15th of the month, the asset will not be depreciated until the following month.

Returning to our example, assume that the truck was placed into service on July 1, 2017. The revised straight-line calculation under the altered in-service date is as follows:

Straight-line depreciation = [(Cost − Residual Value) / Useful Life] × (Number of Months / 12 months)
= [($41,000 − $1,000) / 5 years] × (6 / 12)
= $4,000

Because the business used the asset for six months of the year, we only record 6/12 (6 out of 12 months) of straight-line depreciation expense, or $4,000, in 2017.

Partial-year depreciation also applies to disposals of assets (which we will cover later in this chapter). If an asset is disposed of during the year, the business must calculate depreciation for only the time period before the asset was disposed, not the entire year.

## Changing Estimates of a Depreciable Asset

Estimating the useful life and residual value of a plant asset poses a challenge. As the asset is used, the business may change its estimated useful life or estimated residual value. If this happens, the business must recalculate depreciation expense. For example, the business may find that its truck lasts eight years instead of five. This is a change in estimated useful life. Accounting changes like this are common because useful life and residual value are estimates and, as a result, are not based on perfect foresight. When a company makes an accounting change, Generally Accepted Accounting Principles require the business to recalculate the depreciation for the asset in the year of change and in future periods. They do not require that businesses restate prior years' financial statements for this change in estimate.

For a change in either estimated asset life or residual value, the asset's remaining depreciable book value is spread over the asset's remaining life. Suppose Smart Touch Learning used the truck purchased on January 1, 2017, for two full years. Under the straight-line method, accumulated depreciation would be $16,000. (Refer to Exhibit 9-5.)

Straight-line depreciation = (Cost − Residual Value) / Useful Life
= ($41,000 − $1,000) / 5 years
= $8,000 per year × 2 years
= $16,000

Remaining depreciable book value (cost *less* accumulated depreciation) is $25,000 ($41,000 − $16,000). Suppose Smart Touch Learning believes the truck will remain useful for six more years (for a total of eight years). Residual value is unchanged. At the start of 2019, the company would recompute depreciation as follows:

Revised depreciation = (Book value − Revised residual value) / Revised useful life remaining
= ($25,000 − $1,000) / 6 years
= $4,000 per year

*Make sure to use the useful life remaining as the denominator in the formula.*

In years 2019–2024, the yearly depreciation entry based on the new useful life would be as follows:

| Date | Accounts and Explanation | Debit | Credit |
|---|---|---|---|
| Dec. 31 | Depreciation Expense—Truck | 4,000 | |
| | Accumulated Depreciation—Truck | | 4,000 |
| | *To record depreciation on truck.* | | |

$$\frac{\mathbf{A}\downarrow}{\text{Accumulated Depreciation—Truck}\uparrow} = \frac{\mathbf{L} \quad + \quad \mathbf{E}\downarrow}{\text{Depreciation Expense—Truck}\uparrow}$$

IFRS

IFRS permits the presentation of plant assets at their fair market value because market value may be more relevant and thus more useful to readers of financial statements.

## Reporting Plant Assets

Plant assets are reported at book value on the balance sheet. Companies may choose to report plant assets as a single amount, with a note to the financial statements that provides detailed information, or companies may provide detailed information on the face of the statement. The cost of the asset and the related accumulated depreciation should be disclosed. Exhibit 9-9 shows the two alternative reporting treatments for plant assets.

**Exhibit 9-9 | Reporting Plant Assets**

| Treatment 1: Plant Assets on the Balance Sheet of Smart Touch Learning (December 31) | | |
|---|---|---|
| **Plant Assets:** | | |
| Furniture | $ 18,000 | |
| Less: Accumulated Depreciation—Furniture | (300) | $ 17,700 |
| Building | 60,000 | |
| Less: Accumulated Depreciation—Building | (250) | 59,750 |
| Land | | 20,000 |
| Plant Assets, Net | | $ 97,450 |

| Treatment 2: Plant Assets on the Balance Sheet of Smart Touch Learning (December 31) | |
|---|---|
| Plant Assets, Net (See Note 8) | $ 97,450 |

## Try It!

**2.** On January 1, Alamo Cranes purchased a crane for $140,000. Alamo expects the crane to remain useful for six years (1,000,000 lifts) and to have a residual value of $2,000. The company expects the crane to be used for 80,000 lifts the first year.

Compute the first-year depreciation expense on the crane using the following methods:

a. Straight-line
b. Units-of-production (Round *depreciation per unit* to two decimals. Round depreciation expense to the nearest whole dollar.)
c. Double-declining-balance (Round depreciation expense to the nearest whole dollar.)

**Check your answers online in MyAccountingLab or at http://www.pearsonhighered.com/Horngren.**

For more practice, see Short Exercises S9-3 through S9-6. MyAccountingLab

# HOW ARE DISPOSALS OF PLANT ASSETS RECORDED?

**Learning Objective 3**
Journalize entries for the disposal of plant assets

Eventually, an asset wears out or becomes obsolete. The business then has several options:

- Discard the plant asset.
- Sell the plant asset.
- Exchange the plant asset for another plant asset.

In this section, we discuss the first two options. Exchanging a plant asset for another asset is covered in the appendix to this chapter (Appendix 9A).

Plant assets remain on the business's books until they are disposed of. For example, a fully depreciated asset, one that has reached the end of its estimated useful life and is still in service, will still be reported as an asset on the balance sheet. If the asset is still useful, the company may continue using it even though no additional depreciation is recorded. If the asset is no longer useful, it is disposed of. This requires the business to remove the asset and associated accumulated depreciation from the books. In addition, a gain or loss might be recognized by the company.

Regardless of the type of disposal, there are four steps:

1. Bring the depreciation up to date.
2. Remove the old, disposed-of asset and associated accumulated depreciation from the books.
3. Record the value of any cash received (or paid) in the disposal of the asset.
4. Finally, determine the amount of any gain or loss. Gain or loss is determined by comparing the cash received and the market value of any other assets received with the book value of the asset disposed of.

## Discarding Plant Assets

Discarding of plant assets involves disposing of the asset for no cash. If an asset is disposed of when it is fully depreciated and has no residual value, then the business simply removes the asset and contra asset, Accumulated Depreciation, from the books (Step 2). There is no need to bring the depreciation up to date (Step 1) because the asset is already fully depreciated. In addition, no cash was received or paid and no gain or loss is recognized (Steps 3 and 4).

For example, assume that on July 1, Smart Touch Learning discards equipment with a cost of $10,000 and accumulated depreciation of $10,000. The asset and contra asset accounts are shown below before disposal.

| Equipment | |
|---|---|
| 10,000 | |

| Accumulated Depreciation—Equipment | |
|---|---|
| | 10,000 |

To dispose of the equipment, Smart Touch Learning will need to credit the asset account, Equipment, and debit Accumulated Depreciation—Equipment. The accounting clerk will record the transaction as follows:

| A↑↓ | = | L + E |
|---|---|---|
| Equipment↓<br>Accumulated Depreciation—Equipment↓ | = | |

| Date | Accounts and Explanation | Debit | Credit |
|---|---|---|---|
| Jul. 1 | Accumulated Depreciation—Equipment | 10,000 | |
| | Equipment | | 10,000 |
| | *Discarded fully depreciated equipment.* | | |

| | Equipment | | |
|---|---|---|---|
| | 10,000 | 10,000 | July 1 |
| Bal. | 0 | | |

| | Accumulated Depreciation—Equipment | | |
|---|---|---|---|
| July 1 | 10,000 | 10,000 | |
| | | 0 | Bal. |

*After disposal, notice that the Equipment and Accumulated Depreciation—Equipment accounts now have a zero balance. These accounts will no longer be reported on the financial statements because Smart Touch Learning no longer owns the equipment.*

Suppose, instead, that on July 1, Smart Touch Learning discarded the equipment, which has a cost of $10,000 but it is not fully depreciated. As of December 31 of the previous year, accumulated depreciation was $8,000. Annual depreciation expense is $1,000 per year. The first step in recording the disposal is to bring the asset up to date on depreciation. Because Smart Touch Learning disposes of the asset on July 1, one-half of a year's depreciation will be recorded ($1,000 × 1/2 = $500) as follows:

| Date | Accounts and Explanation | Debit | Credit |
|---|---|---|---|
| Jul. 1 | Depreciation Expense—Equipment | 500 | |
| | Accumulated Depreciation—Equipment | | 500 |
| | *To record depreciation on equipment.* | | |

| A↓ | = | L | + | E↓ |
|---|---|---|---|---|
| Accumulated Depreciation—Equipment↑ | | | | Depreciation Expense—Equipment↑ |

Steps 2 through 4 involve recording the disposal of the equipment and accumulated depreciation and calculating any gain or loss. In this situation, there is a $1,500 loss calculated as follows:

| | | |
|---|---|---|
| Market value of assets received | | $ 0 |
| Less: Book value of asset disposed of: | | |
| Cost | $ 10,000 | |
| Less: Accumulated Depreciation ($8,000 + $500) | (8,500) | 1,500 |
| Gain or (Loss) | | $ (1,500) |

*When calculating gain or loss, don't forget to update the Accumulated Depreciation account. In this example, before recording depreciation, the Accumulated Depreciation account was $8,000; $500 of additional depreciation was recorded at disposal, bringing the total accumulated depreciation to $8,500.*

The account, Loss on Disposal, will be used. This account has a normal debit balance and is reported in the Other Revenues and (Expenses) section of the income statement which includes gains and losses on the sale of plant assets.

Smart Touch Learning records the following entry to dispose of the equipment:

| A↓ | = | L | + | E↓ |
|---|---|---|---|---|
| Equipment↓<br>Accumulated Depreciation—Equipment↓ | = | | | Loss on Disposal↑ |

| Date | Accounts and Explanation | Debit | Credit |
|---|---|---|---|
| Jul. 1 | Accumulated Depreciation—Equipment | 8,500 | |
| | Loss on Disposal | 1,500 | |
| | Equipment | | 10,000 |
| | *Discarded equipment with a book value of $1,500.* | | |

**Equipment**

| | | | |
|---|---|---|---|
| | 10,000 | 10,000 | July 1 |
| Bal. | 0 | | |

**Accumulated Depreciation—Equipment**

| | | | |
|---|---|---|---|
| | | 8,000 | |
| July 1 | 8,500 | 500 | July 1 |
| | | 0 | Bal. |

**Loss on Disposal**

| | | |
|---|---|---|
| July 1 | 1,500 | |

## Selling Plant Assets

Companies will often sell a plant asset for cash. We will again use Smart Touch Learning as an example. On July 1, the company sells equipment with a historical cost of $10,000 and accumulated depreciation, as of December 31 of the previous year, of $8,000. Annual depreciation is $1,000. The first step is to bring the depreciation up to date for the six months through the date of disposal.

| A↓ | = | L | + | E↓ |
|---|---|---|---|---|
| Accumulated Depreciation—Equipment↑ | = | | | Depreciation Expense—Equipment↑ |

| Date | Accounts and Explanation | Debit | Credit |
|---|---|---|---|
| Jul. 1 | Depreciation Expense—Equipment | 500 | |
| | Accumulated Depreciation—Equipment | | 500 |
| | *To record depreciation on equipment.* | | |

This entry brings the accumulated depreciation to $8,500 ($8,000 + $500). The equipment now has a book value of $1,500 ($10,000 − $8,500). Now that we have recorded Step 1, let's look at Steps 2 through 4 for several different scenarios.

### Selling a Plant Asset at Book Value

Suppose that Smart Touch Learning sells the equipment for $1,500. Notice that the cash received is equal to the book value of the asset. When a business sells an asset for book value, no gain or loss is recorded. This is because the cash received is equal to the book value of the asset sold.

| | | |
|---|---|---|
| Market value of assets received | | $ 1,500 |
| Less: Book value of asset disposed of: | | |
| Cost | $ 10,000 | |
| Less: Accumulated Depreciation | (8,500) | 1,500 |
| Gain or (Loss) | | $ 0 |

In recording the journal entry, Smart Touch Learning will debit cash for $1,500 and then take the equipment and accumulated depreciation off the books as follows:

| Date | Accounts and Explanation | Debit | Credit |
|---|---|---|---|
| Jul. 1 | Cash | 1,500 | |
| | Accumulated Depreciation—Equipment | 8,500 | |
| | Equipment | | 10,000 |
| | *Sold equipment for cash.* | | |

| A↑↓ | | L + E |
|---|---|---|
| Cash↑<br>Equipment↓<br>Accumulated Depreciation—Equipment↓ | = | |

**Cash**

| | | | |
|---|---|---|---|
| July 1 | 1,500 | | |

**Equipment**

| | | | |
|---|---|---|---|
| | 10,000 | 10,000 | July 1 |
| Bal. | 0 | | |

**Accumulated Depreciation—Equipment**

| | | | |
|---|---|---|---|
| | | 8,000 | |
| July 1 | 8,500 | 500 | July 1 |
| | | 0 | Bal. |

## Selling a Plant Asset Above Book Value

If Smart Touch Learning sells the equipment for $4,000, the company will record a gain on sale of the equipment. Notice that the cash received is more than the book value of the asset. When a business sells an asset for more than its book value, a gain is recorded.

| | | |
|---|---|---|
| Market value of assets received | | $ 4,000 |
| Less: Book value of asset disposed of: | | |
| Cost | $ 10,000 | |
| Less: Accumulated Depreciation | (8,500) | 1,500 |
| Gain or (Loss) | | $ 2,500 |

The account, Gain on Disposal, will be used. This account has a normal credit balance and is reported in the Other Revenues and (Expenses) section of the income statement.

In recording the journal entry, Smart Touch Learning will remove the old equipment and accumulated depreciation from the books (Step 2), record a debit to Cash for $4,000 (Step 3), and then record a credit to Gain on Disposal (Step 4) as follows:

| A↑ | = | L | + | E↑ |
|---|---|---|---|---|
| Cash↑<br>Equipment↓<br>Accumulated Depreciation—Equipment↓ | = | | | Gain on Disposal↑ |

| Date | Accounts and Explanation | Debit | Credit |
|---|---|---|---|
| Jul. 1 | Cash | 4,000 | |
| | Accumulated Depreciation—Equipment | 8,500 | |
| | Equipment | | 10,000 |
| | Gain on Disposal | | 2,500 |
| | *Sold equipment for cash.* | | |

After you have recorded the transaction for disposal of plant assets, it's always a good idea to check that debits equal credits in the journal entry.

**Cash**

| | | | |
|---|---|---|---|
| July 1 | 4,000 | | |

**Equipment**

| | | | |
|---|---|---|---|
| | 10,000 | 10,000 | July 1 |
| Bal. | 0 | | |

**Accumulated Depreciation—Equipment**

| | | | |
|---|---|---|---|
| | | 8,000 | |
| July 1 | 8,500 | 500 | July 1 |
| | | 0 | Bal. |

**Gain on Disposal**

| | | | |
|---|---|---|---|
| | | 2,500 | July 1 |

## Selling a Plant Asset Below Book Value

If Smart Touch Learning sells the equipment for $500, the company will record a loss on the sale of the equipment. Notice that the cash received is less than the book value of the asset. When a business sells an asset for less than its book value, a loss is recorded.

| | | |
|---|---|---|
| Market value of assets received | | $ 500 |
| Less: Book value of asset disposed of: | | |
| Cost | $ 10,000 | |
| Less: Accumulated Depreciation | (8,500) | 1,500 |
| Gain or (Loss) | | ($ 1,000) |

In recording the journal entry, Smart Touch Learning will remove the old equipment and accumulated depreciation from the books (Step 2), record a debit to Cash for $500 (Step 3), and then record a debit to Loss on Disposal (Step 4) as follows:

| A↓ | = | L | + | E↓ |
|---|---|---|---|---|
| Cash↑<br>Equipment↓<br>Accumulated Depreciation—Equipment↓ | = | | | Loss on Disposal↑ |

| Date | Accounts and Explanation | Debit | Credit |
|---|---|---|---|
| Jul. 1 | Cash | 500 | |
| | Accumulated Depreciation—Equipment | 8,500 | |
| | Loss on Disposal | 1,000 | |
| | Equipment | | 10,000 |
| | *Sold equipment for cash.* | | |

**Cash**

| | | | |
|---|---|---|---|
| July 1 | 500 | | |

**Equipment**

| | | | |
|---|---|---|---|
| | 10,000 | 10,000 | July 1 |
| Bal. | 0 | | |

**Accumulated Depreciation—Equipment**

| | | | |
|---|---|---|---|
| | | 8,000 | |
| July 1 | 8,500 | 500 | July 1 |
| | | 0 | Bal. |

**Loss on Disposal**

| | | | |
|---|---|---|---|
| July 1 | 1,000 | | |

In this section, we have reviewed the journal entries for discarding and selling of plant assets. Exhibit 9-10 summarizes what you have learned. Before moving on, take a moment to review the exhibit.

## Exhibit 9-10 | Disposals of Plant Assets

**Discarding of fully depreciated plant asset:**

| Date | Accounts and Explanation | Debit | Credit |
|---|---|---|---|
| | Accumulated Depreciation | 10,000 | |
| | Plant Asset | | 10,000 |

**Discarding of a plant asset that is not fully depreciated:**

| Date | Accounts and Explanation | Debit | Credit |
|---|---|---|---|
| | Accumulated Depreciation | 8,500 | |
| | Loss on Disposal | 1,500 | |
| | Plant Asset | | 10,000 |

**Selling a plant asset at book value:**

| Date | Accounts and Explanation | Debit | Credit |
|---|---|---|---|
| | Cash | 1,500 | |
| | Accumulated Depreciation | 8,500 | |
| | Plant Asset | | 10,000 |

**Selling a plant asset above book value:**

| Date | Accounts and Explanation | Debit | Credit |
|---|---|---|---|
| | Cash | 4,000 | |
| | Accumulated Depreciation | 8,500 | |
| | Plant Asset | | 10,000 |
| | Gain on Disposal | | 2,500 |

**Selling a plant asset below book value:**

| Date | Accounts and Explanation | Debit | Credit |
|---|---|---|---|
| | Cash | 500 | |
| | Accumulated Depreciation | 8,500 | |
| | Loss on Disposal | 1,000 | |
| | Plant Asset | | 10,000 |

## Try It!

3. Counselors of Atlanta purchased equipment on January 1, 2015, for $20,000. Counselors of Atlanta expected the equipment to last for four years and have a residual value of $2,000. Suppose Counselors of Atlanta sold the equipment for $8,000 on December 31, 2017, after using the equipment for three full years. Assume depreciation for 2017 has been recorded. Journalize the sale of the equipment, assuming straight-line depreciation was used.

**Check your answer online in MyAccountingLab or at http://www.pearsonhighered.com/Horngren.**

For more practice, see Short Exercises S9-7 through S9-10. MyAccountingLab

## HOW ARE NATURAL RESOURCES ACCOUNTED FOR?

**Learning Objective 4**
Account for natural resources

**Natural Resource**
An asset that comes from the earth and is consumed.

**Depletion**
The process by which businesses spread the allocation of a natural resource's cost over its usage.

**Natural resources** are assets that come from the earth that are consumed. Examples include iron ore, oil, natural gas, diamonds, gold, coal, and timber. Natural resources are expensed through *depletion*. **Depletion** is the process by which businesses spread the allocation of a natural resource's cost to expense over its usage. It's called depletion because the company is depleting (using up) a natural resource such that at some point in time, there is nothing left to extract. Depletion expense is computed by the units-of-production method.

For example, an oil well cost $700,000 and is estimated to hold 70,000 barrels of oil. There is no residual value. If 3,000 barrels are extracted and sold during the year, then depletion expense is calculated as follows:

**Step 1:**

Depletion per unit = (Cost − Residual value) / Estimated total units
= ($700,000 − $0) / 70,000 barrels
= $10 per barrel

**Step 2:**

Depletion expense = Depletion per unit × Number of units extracted
= $10 per barrel × 3,000 barrels
= $30,000 (year 1)

The depletion entry for the year is as follows:

| A↓ | = | L | + | E↓ |
|---|---|---|---|---|
| Accumulated Depletion—Oil Reserves↑ | | | | Depletion Expense—Oil Reserves↑ |

| Date | Accounts and Explanation | Debit | Credit |
|---|---|---|---|
| Dec. 31 | Depletion Expense—Oil Reserves | 30,000 | |
| | Accumulated Depletion—Oil Reserves | | 30,000 |
| | *To record depletion.* | | |

Accumulated Depletion is a contra asset account similar to Accumulated Depreciation. Natural resources can be reported on the balance sheet as shown for oil reserves in the following example:

| | | |
|---|---|---|
| Oil Reserves | $ 700,000 | |
| Less: Accumulated Depletion—Oil Reserves | (30,000) | $ 670,000 |

**Try It!**

4. Amplify Petroleum holds huge reserves of oil. Assume that at the end of 2015, Amplify Petroleum's cost of oil reserves totaled $80,000,000, representing 100,000,000 barrels of oil. Suppose Amplify Petroleum removed and sold 20,000,000 barrels of oil during 2016. Journalize depletion expense for 2016.

**Check your answer online in MyAccountingLab or at http://www.pearsonhighered.com/Horngren.**

For more practice, see Short Exercise S9-11. MyAccountingLab

## HOW ARE INTANGIBLE ASSETS ACCOUNTED FOR?

**Learning Objective 5**
Account for intangible assets

**Intangible assets** are assets that have no physical form. Instead, these assets convey special rights from patents, copyrights, trademarks, and other creative works.

**Intangible Asset**
An asset with no physical form that is valuable because of the special rights it carries.

In our technology-driven economy, intangibles are very important. The intellectual property of a business is difficult to measure. However, when one company buys another, we get a glimpse of the value of the intellectual property of the acquired company. For example, in 2006, Google acquired YouTube. Google said it would give $1.65 billion even though YouTube had never had a profitable year. Why so much for so little? Because YouTube's intangible assets were extremely valuable. Intangibles can account for most of a company's market value, so companies must value their intangibles just as they value other assets, such as merchandise inventory and equipment.

### Accounting for Intangibles

Intangible assets that are purchased are recorded at cost. If an intangible is not purchased, only some limited costs can be capitalized. Most purchased intangibles are expensed through **amortization**, the allocation of the cost of an intangible asset to expense over its useful life. Amortization applies to intangibles exactly as depreciation applies to equipment and depletion to oil and timber.

**Amortization**
The process by which businesses spread the allocation of an intangible asset's cost over its useful life.

Intangibles either have a definite life or an indefinite life. Intangibles with an indefinite life have no factors (such as legal and contractual obligations) that limit the usage of the intangible asset. Only intangibles that have a definite life are amortized. Intangible assets with an indefinite life are tested for impairment annually. **Impairment** occurs when the fair value of an asset is less than the book value. In other words, there has been a permanent decline in the value of the asset. If an impairment occurs, the company records a loss in the period that the decline is identified.

**Impairment**
A permanent decline in asset value.

### Specific Intangibles

As noted earlier, patents, copyrights, and trademarks are intangible assets. The accounting for the purchase and amortization of each asset is similar.

## Patents

**Patent**
An intangible asset that is a federal government grant conveying an exclusive 20-year right to produce and sell a process, product, or formula.

A **patent** is an intangible asset that is a federal government grant conveying an exclusive 20-year right to produce and sell an invention. The invention may be a process, product, or formula—for example, the Dolby noise-reduction process or a prescription drug formula. The acquisition cost of a patent is debited to the Patent account.

Like any other asset, a patent may be purchased. Suppose Smart Touch Learning pays $200,000 to acquire a patent on January 1. The accounting clerk records the following entry at acquisition:

| A↑↓ | | L | + | E |
|---|---|---|---|---|
| Patent↑<br>Cash↓ | = | | | |

| Date | Accounts and Explanation | Debit | Credit |
|---|---|---|---|
| Jan. 1 | Patent | 200,000 | |
| | Cash | | 200,000 |
| | *To record purchase of patent.* | | |

Smart Touch Learning believes this patent's useful life is only five years because it is likely that a new, more efficient process will be developed within that time. Amortization expense is calculated using the straight-line method as follows:

Amortization expense = (Cost − Residual value) / Useful life
= ($200,000 − $0) / 5 years
= $40,000 per year

*For most intangibles, the residual value will be zero.*

The company's accounting clerk would record the following adjusting entry for amortization:

| A↓ | | L | + | E↓ |
|---|---|---|---|---|
| Patent↓ | = | | | Amortization Expense—Patent↑ |

| Date | Accounts and Explanation | Debit | Credit |
|---|---|---|---|
| Dec. 31 | Amortization Expense—Patent | 40,000 | |
| | Patent | | 40,000 |
| | *To record amortization of patent.* | | |

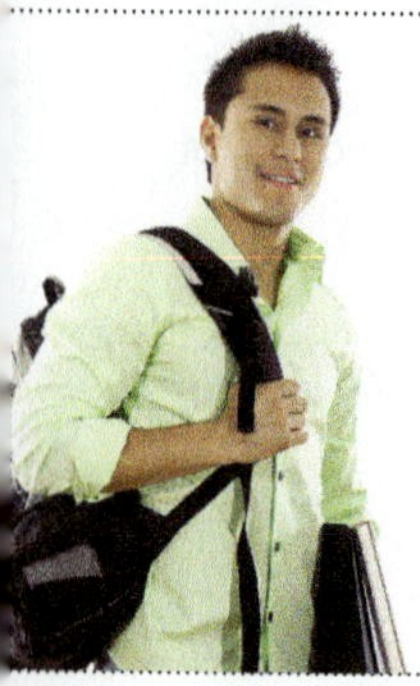

Why was the account Patent credited instead of Accumulated Amortization—Patent?

Notice that Smart Touch Learning credited the amortization directly to the intangible asset, Patent, instead of using an Accumulated Amortization account. A company may credit an intangible asset directly when recording amortization expense, or it may use the account Accumulated Amortization. **Companies frequently choose to credit the asset account directly because the residual value is generally zero and there is no physical asset to dispose of at the end of its useful life, so the asset essentially removes itself from the books through the process of amortization.**

At the end of the first year, Smart Touch Learning will report this patent at $160,000 ($200,000 cost minus first-year amortization of $40,000), the next year at $120,000, and so forth. Each year for five years the value of the patent will be reduced until the end of its five-year life, at which point its book value will be $0.

## Copyrights and Trademarks

**Copyright**
Exclusive right to reproduce and sell a book, musical composition, film, other work of art, or intellectual property.

A **copyright** is the exclusive right to reproduce and sell a book, musical composition, film, other work of art, or intellectual property. Copyrights also protect computer software programs, such as Microsoft® Windows® and the Microsoft® Excel® spreadsheet software. Issued by the federal government, a copyright is granted for the life of the creator plus 70 years.

A company may pay a large sum to purchase an existing copyright. For example, the publisher Simon & Schuster may pay $1 million for the copyright on a popular novel because it thinks it will be able to profit from selling the novel. Even though copyrights have a long legal life (life of creator plus 70 years), most copyrights have short useful lives. Copyrights are amortized over their legal life or useful life, whichever is shorter.

A **trademark** (also called *trade name*) is an asset that represents distinctive identifications of products or services, such as the Nike "swoosh" or the McDonald's "golden arches." Legally protected slogans include Chevrolet's "Like a Rock" and De Beers's "A Diamond Is Forever." The cost of a trademark or trade name is amortized over its useful life.

**Trademark**
An asset that represents distinctive identifications of a product or service.

## Franchises and Licenses

**Franchises** are privileges granted by a business to sell goods or services under specified conditions. The Dallas Cowboys football organization is a franchise granted by the National Football League. McDonald's and Subway are well-known business franchises. **Licenses** are privileges granted by a government to use public property in performing services. A radio station might be granted permission by the federal government to use the airwaves to broadcast its music. The acquisition cost of a franchise or license is amortized over its useful life.

**Franchise**
Privilege granted by a business to sell a product or service under specified conditions.

**License**
Privilege granted by a government to use public property in performing services.

## Goodwill

In accounting, **goodwill** is the excess of the cost to purchase another company over the market value of its net assets (assets minus liabilities). Goodwill is the value paid above the net worth of the company's assets and liabilities.

Suppose White Corporation acquired Mocha, Inc. on January 1, 2016. The sum of the market values of Mocha's assets was $9 million and its liabilities totaled $1 million, so Mocha's net assets totaled $8 million. Suppose White paid $10 million to purchase Mocha. In this case, White paid $2 million above the market value of Mocha's net assets. Therefore, that $2 million is considered goodwill and is computed as follows:

**Goodwill**
Excess of the cost of an acquired company over the sum of the market values of its net assets (assets minus liabilities).

| | | |
|---|---|---|
| Purchase price to acquire Mocha | | $ 10,000,000 |
| Market value of Mocha's assets | $ 9,000,000 | |
| Less: Market value of Mocha's liabilities | (1,000,000) | |
| Less: Market value of Mocha's net assets | | 8,000,000 |
| Goodwill | | $ 2,000,000 |

White's entry to record the purchase of Mocha, including the goodwill that White purchased, would be as follows:

| Date | Accounts and Explanation | Debit | Credit |
|---|---|---|---|
| Jan. 1 | Assets | 9,000,000 | |
| | Goodwill | 2,000,000 | |
| | Liabilities | | 1,000,000 |
| | Cash | | 10,000,000 |
| | *To record purchase of Mocha Company.* | | |

| A↑ | = | L↑ | + | E |
|---|---|---|---|---|
| Assets↑<br>Goodwill↑<br>Cash↓ | = | Liabilities↑ | | |

Goodwill has some special features:

- Goodwill is recorded only by an acquiring company when it purchases another company and pays more for that company than the market value of the net assets acquired (as in our entry above where White purchased Mocha for $2 million more than the market value of Mocha's net assets). An outstanding reputation may create goodwill, but that company never records goodwill for its own business.
- According to Generally Accepted Accounting Principles (GAAP), goodwill is *not* amortized. Instead, the acquiring company measures the fair value of its acquired goodwill each year. If the goodwill has increased in fair value, there is nothing to record. But if goodwill's fair value has decreased, then the company records an impairment loss and writes the goodwill down by debiting (increasing) the Impairment Loss on Goodwill account and crediting (decreasing) the Goodwill account.

## Reporting of Intangible Assets

Intangible assets are reported on the balance sheet similarly to plant assets. If a company uses the contra account, Accumulated Amortization, this account is not typically shown on the balance sheet. Instead, intangible assets are shown only at their net book value. Amortization expense is reported on the income statement as part of operations.

Exhibit 9-11 summarizes our coverage of plant assets, natural resources, and intangibles. Remember that plant assets are those assets that have physical characteristics and are used in operations. Natural resources are assets that come from the physical earth and can be ultimately used up, and intangible assets are assets whose value is not derived from their physical substance.

**Exhibit 9-11 | Assets and Their Related Expenses**

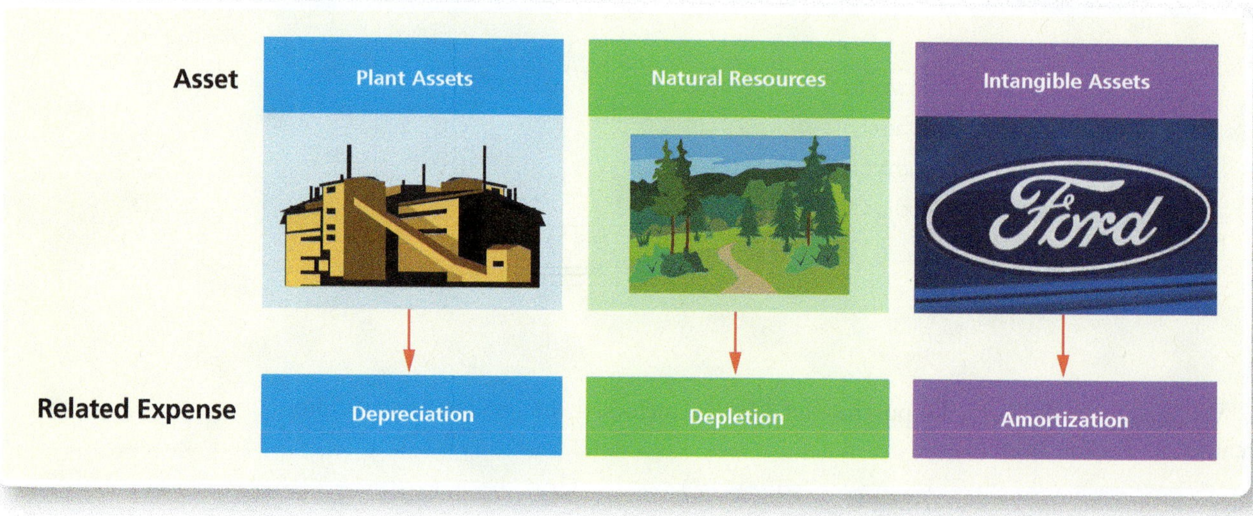

**Try It!**

5. On January 1, Orange Manufacturing paid $40,000 for a patent. Although it gives legal protection for 20 years, the patent is expected to provide a competitive advantage for only eight years. Assuming the straight-line method of amortization, record the journal entry for amortization for year 1.

**Check your answer online in MyAccountingLab or at http://www.pearsonhighered.com/Horngren.**

For more practice, see Short Exercises S9-12 and S9-13. MyAccountingLab

## HOW DO WE USE THE ASSET TURNOVER RATIO TO EVALUATE BUSINESS PERFORMANCE?

**Learning Objective 6**

Use the asset turnover ratio to evaluate business performance

The asset turnover ratio measures the amount of net sales generated for each average dollar of total assets invested. This ratio measures how well a company is using its assets to generate sales revenue. To compute this ratio, we divide net sales by average total assets. Using net sales and total assets (in thousands) from **Green Mountain Coffee Roasters, Inc.'s** 2013 Annual Report (see Appendix A at the end of the book), we can calculate the asset turnover ratio.

**Asset Turnover Ratio**

Measures how efficiently a business uses its average total assets to generate sales. Net sales / Average total assets.

| | September 28, 2013 | September 29, 2012 |
|---|---|---|
| Net sales | $ 4,358,100 | $ 3,859,198 |
| Total assets | 3,761,548 | 3,615,789 |

Asset turnover ratio = Net sales / Average total assets
= $4,358,100 / [($3,761,548 + $3,615,789) / 2]
= 1.18 times (rounded)

Suppose that the asset turnover ratio for the industry is 1.7 times. Green Mountain's asset turnover ratio of 1.18 times is significantly lower than the industry average. This tells us that Green Mountain is producing $1.18 of sales revenue for each dollar ($1.00) of assets invested. Green Mountain should evaluate ways to increase its asset turnover ratio such as increasing net sales or decreasing average total assets. A high asset turnover ratio is desirable.

**Try It!**

6. Maxim Company reported beginning and ending total assets of $140,000 and $160,000, respectively. Its net sales for the year was $240,000. What was Maxim's asset turnover ratio?

**Check your answer online in MyAccountingLab or at http://www.pearsonhighered.com/Horngren.**

For more practice, see Short Exercise S9-14. MyAccountingLab

# Appendix 9A: Exchanging Plant Assets

## HOW ARE EXCHANGES OF PLANT ASSETS ACCOUNTED FOR?

**Learning Objective 7**
Journalize entries for the exchange of plant assets

**Commercial Substance**
A characteristic of a transaction that causes a change in future cash flows.

Earlier in the chapter, we discussed ways that businesses could dispose of plant assets. One way is for a business to exchange a plant asset for another plant asset. In this section, we evaluate how to account for exchanges that have *commercial substance*. An exchange has **commercial substance** if the future cash flows change as a result of the transaction. In other words, an exchange has commercial substance if, in the future, cash flows (receipts of revenue or payment of expenses) of the business will change because of the exchange. For example, exchanging an older asset for a new asset will increase productivity, thereby creating more revenue for the business. Therefore, this exchange has commercial substance.

Exchanges that have commercial substance require any gain or loss on the transaction to be recognized. The old asset will be removed from the books, and the new asset will be recorded at its market value. Exchanges that lack commercial substance ignore any gain or loss on the transaction, except in limited situations. The new asset is recorded at the old asset's book value plus cash paid and minus cash received instead of at market value.

### Exchange of Plant Assets—Gain Situation

Suppose that on December 31, Smart Touch Learning exchanges used equipment for new equipment. The old equipment has a historical cost of $10,000 and accumulated depreciation of $9,000. Its current book value is $1,000 ($10,000 − $9,000). The company acquires the new equipment with a market value of $8,000 and pays cash of $2,000. Assuming this exchange has commercial substance, the gain will be calculated as follows:

| | | |
|---|---|---|
| Market value of assets received | | $ 8,000 |
| Less: | | |
| Book value of asset exchanged | $ 1,000 | |
| Cash paid | 2,000 | 3,000 |
| Gain or (Loss) | | $ 5,000 |

The accounting clerk records the following entry:

| A↑ | = | L | + | E↑ |
|---|---|---|---|---|
| Equipment (new)↑<br>Accumulated Depreciation—Equipment↓<br>Equipment (old)↓<br>Cash↓ | = | | | Gain on Disposal↑ |

| Date | Accounts and Explanation | Debit | Credit |
|---|---|---|---|
| Dec. 31 | Equipment (new) | 8,000 | |
| | Accumulated Depreciation—Equipment | 9,000 | |
| | Equipment (old) | | 10,000 |
| | Cash | | 2,000 |
| | Gain on Disposal | | 5,000 |
| | *Exchanged old equipment and cash for new equipment.* | | |

**Cash**

| | | | |
|---|---|---|---|
| | | 2,000 | Dec. 31 |

**Equipment (new)**

| | | | |
|---|---|---|---|
| Dec. 31 | 8,000 | | |

**Equipment (old)**

| | | | |
|---|---|---|---|
| | 10,000 | 10,000 | Dec. 31 |
| Bal. | 0 | | |

**Accumulated Depreciation—Equipment**

| | | | |
|---|---|---|---|
| | | 9,000 | |
| Dec. 31 | 9,000 | | |
| | | 0 | Bal. |

**Gain on Disposal**

| | | | |
|---|---|---|---|
| | | 5,000 | Dec. 31 |

## Exchange of Plant Assets—Loss Situation

Suppose instead that on December 31, Smart Touch Learning exchanges used equipment for new equipment. The old equipment has a historical cost of $10,000 and accumulated depreciation of $9,000. Its current book value is $1,000 ($10,000 − $9,000). The company acquires the new equipment with a market value of $3,000 and pays cash of $2,500. Assuming this exchange has commercial substance, the loss will be calculated as follows:

| | | |
|---|---|---|
| Market value of assets received | | $ 3,000 |
| Less: | | |
| Book value of asset exchanged | $ 1,000 | |
| Cash paid | 2,500 | 3,500 |
| Gain or (Loss) | | $ (500) |

The accounting clerk records the following entry:

| Date | Accounts and Explanation | Debit | Credit |
|---|---|---|---|
| Dec. 31 | Equipment (new) | 3,000 | |
| | Accumulated Depreciation—Equipment | 9,000 | |
| | Loss on Disposal | 500 | |
| | Equipment (old) | | 10,000 |
| | Cash | | 2,500 |
| | *Exchanged old equipment and cash for new equipment.* | | |

| A↓ | = | L | + | E↓ |
|---|---|---|---|---|
| Equipment (new)↑<br>Accumulated Depreciation—Equipment↓<br>Equipment (old)↓<br>Cash↓ | = | | | Loss on Disposal↑ |

**Cash**

| | | | |
|---|---|---|---|
| | | 2,500 | Dec. 31 |

**Equipment (new)**

| | | | |
|---|---|---|---|
| Dec. 31 | 3,000 | | |

**Equipment (old)**

| | | | |
|---|---|---|---|
| | 10,000 | 10,000 | Dec. 31 |
| Bal. | 0 | | |

**Accumulated Depreciation—Equipment**

| | | | |
|---|---|---|---|
| | | 9,000 | |
| Dec. 31 | 9,000 | | |
| | | 0 | Bal. |

**Loss on Disposal**

| | | | |
|---|---|---|---|
| Dec. 31 | 500 | | |

## Try It!

**7A.** Arca Salvage, Inc. purchased equipment for $10,000. Arca recorded total depreciation of $8,000 on the equipment. Assume that Arca exchanged the old equipment for new equipment, paying $4,000 cash. The fair market value of the new equipment is $5,000. Journalize Arca's exchange of equipment. Assume this exchange has commercial substance.

**Check your answer online in MyAccountingLab or at http://www.pearsonhighered.com/Horngren.**

For more practice, see Short Exercise S9A-15 and S9A-16. MyAccountingLab

# REVIEW

## > Things You Should Know

### 1. How does a business measure the cost of a plant asset?

- Plant assets are long-lived, tangible assets used in the operations of a business.
- Plant assets are recorded at historical cost—the amount paid for the asset. This includes the purchase price plus taxes, purchase commissions, and all other amounts paid to ready the asset for its intended use.
- A lump-sum purchase involves paying a single price for multiple assets. The cost of each asset purchased must be identified based on the relative-market-value method.
- Two additional types of expenditures are often incurred on plant assets:
  - Capital expenditures—debited to an asset account because it increases the asset's capacity or efficiency or extends the asset's useful life
  - Revenue expenditures—debited to Repairs and Maintenance Expense because they are incurred to maintain the asset in working order

### 2. What is depreciation, and how is it computed?

- Depreciation is the allocation of a plant asset's cost to expense over its useful life.
- Three common depreciation methods are:
  - Straight-line method—allocates an equal amount of depreciation to each year
  - Units-of-production method—allocates a varying amount of depreciation each year based on an asset's usage
  - Double-declining-balance method—an accelerated depreciation method that computes annual depreciation by multiplying the depreciable asset's book value by a constant percent that is two times the straight-line rate
- Modified Accelerated Cost Recovery System (MACRS) is used for tax purposes.
- Occasionally a business may change its estimated residual value or estimated useful life of a depreciable asset. This change requires depreciation to be recalculated in the year of change and moving forward.
- Plant assets are reported on the balance sheet at book value (cost – accumulated depreciation).

**3. How are disposals of plant assets recorded?**

- There are four steps to recording disposals.
  - Step 1: Bring the depreciation up to date.
  - Step 2: Remove the old, disposed-of asset and associated accumulated depreciation from the books.
  - Step 3: Record the value of any cash received (or paid) in the disposal of the asset.
  - Step 4: Determine the amount of any gain or loss. (Market value of assets received compared to the book value of the asset disposed of.)
- Review Exhibit 9-10 for a summary of disposal of plant assets journal entries.

**4. How are natural resources accounted for?**

- Natural resources are assets that come from the earth and are consumed.
- Depletion is the process by which businesses spread the allocation of a natural resource's cost over its usage.
- Depletion expense is computed by the units-of-production method.

**5. How are intangible assets accounted for?**

- Intangible assets are assets that have no physical form and are valuable because of special rights they carry.
- Amortization is the process by which businesses spread the allocation of an intangible asset's cost over its useful life.
- Amortization expense is computed by the straight-line method.

**6. How do we use the asset turnover ratio to evaluate business performance?**

- The asset turnover ratio measures the amount of net sales generated for each average dollar of total assets invested.
- Net sales / Average total assets.

**7. How are exchanges of plant assets accounted for? (Appendix 9A)**

- Exchanges that have commercial substance require the recording of any gain or loss on the transaction.
- Exchanges that lack commercial substance ignore any gain or loss on the transaction, except in a few limited cases.

## > Summary Problem

Latté On Demand purchased a coffee drink machine on January 1, 2016, for $44,000. Expected useful life is 10 years or 100,000 drinks. In 2016, 3,000 drinks were sold, and in 2017, 14,000 drinks were sold. Residual value is $4,000.

**Requirements**

1. Determine the depreciation expense for 2016 and 2017 using the following methods:
   a. Straight-line
   b. Units-of-production
   c. Double-declining-balance

2. Prepare a schedule that shows annual depreciation expense, accumulated depreciation, and book value for 2016 and 2017 using the following methods:
   a. Straight-line
   b. Units-of-production
   c. Double-declining-balance
3. Assume that Latté On Demand sold the equipment for $27,000 cash on July 1, 2018. Assume that management has depreciated the equipment by using the double-declining-balance method. Record Latté On Demand's depreciation for 2018 and the sale of the equipment on July 1, 2018.

## > Solution

### Requirement 1

a.

2016: ($44,000 − $4,000) / 10 years = $4,000
2017: ($44,000 − $4,000) / 10 years = $4,000

b.

Depreciation per unit = ($44,000 − $4,000) / 100,000 drinks = $0.40 per drink
2016: $0.40 per drink × 3,000 drinks = $1,200
2017: $0.40 per drink × 14,000 drinks = $5,600

c.

2016: ($44,000 − $0) × 2 × (1 / 10) = $8,800
2017: ($44,000 − $8,800) × 2 × (1 / 10) = $7,040

### Requirement 2

a.

| Year | Annual Depreciation Expense | Accumulated Depreciation | Book Value |
|---|---|---|---|
| 1-1-2016 | | | $ 44,000 |
| 12-31-2016 | $ 4,000 | $ 4,000 | 40,000 |
| 12-31-2017 | 4,000 | 8,000 | 36,000 |

b.

| Year | Annual Depreciation Expense | Accumulated Depreciation | Book Value |
|---|---|---|---|
| 1-1-2016 | | | $ 44,000 |
| 12-31-2016 | $ 1,200 | $ 1,200 | 42,800 |
| 12-31-2017 | 5,600 | 6,800 | 37,200 |

c.

| Year | Annual Depreciation Expense | Accumulated Depreciation | Book Value |
|---|---|---|---|
| 1-1-2016 | | | $ 44,000 |
| 12-31-2016 | $ 8,800 | $ 8,800 | 35,200 |
| 12-31-2017 | 7,040 | 15,840 | 28,160 |

**Requirement 3**

Depreciation expense for 2018:

($44,000 − $15,840) × 2 × (1 / 10) × (6 / 12) = $2,816

| Date | Accounts and Explanation | Debit | Credit |
|---|---|---|---|
| 2018 | | | |
| Jul. 1 | Depreciation Expense—Equipment | 2,816 | |
| | Accumulated Depreciation—Equipment | | 2,816 |
| | *To record depreciation on equipment.* | | |
| | | | |
| 1 | Cash | 27,000 | |
| | Accumulated Depreciation—Equipment ($15,840 + $2,816) | 18,656 | |
| | Gain on Disposal | | 1,656 |
| | Equipment | | 44,000 |
| | *Sold equipment for cash.* | | |

## > Key Terms

**Accelerated Depreciation Method** (p. 484)
**Amortization** (p. 497)
**Asset Turnover Ratio** (p. 501)
**Book Value** (p. 482)
**Capital Expenditure** (p. 479)
**Capitalize** (p. 477)
**Commercial Substance** (p. 502) (Appendix 9A)
**Copyright** (p. 498)
**Cost Principle** (p. 476)
**Depletion** (p. 496)
**Depreciable Cost** (p. 481)
**Depreciation** (p. 475)
**Double-Declining-Balance Method** (p. 484)
**Extraordinary Repair** (p. 479)
**Franchise** (p. 499)
**Goodwill** (p. 499)
**Impairment** (p. 497)
**Intangible Asset** (p. 497)
**Land Improvement** (p. 476)
**License** (p. 499)
**Modified Accelerated Cost Recovery System (MACRS)** (p. 487)
**Natural Resource** (p. 496)
**Obsolete** (p. 480)
**Patent** (p. 498)
**Plant Asset** (p. 475)
**Relative-Market-Value Method** (p. 478)
**Residual Value** (p. 481)
**Revenue Expenditure** (p. 479)
**Straight-Line Method** (p. 482)
**Trademark** (p. 499)
**Units-of-Production Method** (p. 483)
**Useful Life** (p. 481)

## > Quick Check

**Learning Objective 1**

1. Which cost is *not* recorded as part of the cost of a building?
   a. Real estate commission paid to buy the building
   b. Construction materials and labor
   c. Concrete for the building's foundation
   d. Annual building maintenance

**Learning Objective 1**

2. How should you record a capital expenditure?
   a. Debit a liability
   b. Debit capital
   c. Debit an expense
   d. Debit an asset

**Learning Objective 2**

3. Which method almost always produces the most depreciation in the first year?
   a. Units-of-production
   b. Straight-line
   c. Double-declining-balance
   d. All produce the same depreciation in the first year.

**Learning Objective 2**

4. A Celty Airline jet costs $28,000,000 and is expected to fly 200,000,000 miles during its 10-year life. Residual value is expected to be zero because the plane was used when acquired. If the plane travels 1,000,000 miles the first year, how much depreciation should Celty Airline record under the units-of-production method?
   a. $2,800,000
   b. $140,000
   c. $560,000
   d. Cannot be determined from the data given

**Learning Objective 3**

5. A copy machine costs $45,000 when new and has accumulated depreciation of $44,000. Suppose Print and Photo Center junks this machine and receives nothing. What is the result of the disposal transaction?
   a. No gain or loss
   b. Gain of $1,000
   c. Loss of $1,000
   d. Loss of $45,000

**Learning Objective 3**

6. Suppose Print and Photo Center in the preceding question sold the machine for $1,000. What is the result of this disposal transaction?
   a. Loss of $44,000
   b. Gain of $1,000
   c. Loss of $1,000
   d. No gain or loss

**Learning Objective 4**

7. Which method is used to compute depletion?
   a. Double-declining-balance method
   b. Straight-line method
   c. Depletion method
   d. Units-of-production method

**Learning Objective 5**

8. Which intangible asset is recorded only as part of the acquisition of another company?
   a. Patent
   b. Goodwill
   c. Copyright
   d. Franchise

**Learning Objective 6**

9. Liberty Corporation reported beginning and ending total assets of $25,000 and $22,000, respectively. Its net sales for the year were $18,800. What was Liberty's asset turnover ratio?
   a. 0.75
   b. 0.85
   c. 0.80
   d. 1.25

**Learning Objective 7**
**Appendix 9A**

10A. A truck costs $50,000 when new and has accumulated depreciation of $35,000. Suppose Wilson Towing exchanges the truck for a new truck. The new truck has a market value of $60,000, and Wilson pays cash of $40,000. Assume the exchange has commercial substance. What is the result of this exchange?

a. No gain or loss
b. Gain of $5,000
c. Loss of $5,000
d. Gain of $45,000

**Check your answers at the end of the chapter.**



# ASSESS YOUR PROGRESS

## > Review Questions

1. What are plant assets? Provide some examples.
2. Plant assets are recorded at historical cost. What does the historical cost of a plant asset include?
3. How do land improvements differ from land?
4. What does the word *capitalize* mean?
5. What is a lump-sum purchase, and how is it accounted for?
6. What is the difference between a capital expenditure and a revenue expenditure? Give an example of each.
7. What is depreciation? What are the methods described in the chapter that can be used to compute depreciation?
8. Which depreciation method ignores residual value until the last year of depreciation? Why?
9. How does a business decide which depreciation method is best to use?
10. What is the depreciation method that is used for tax accounting purposes? How is it different than the methods that are used for financial accounting purposes?
11. If a business changes the estimated useful life or estimated residual value of a plant asset, what must the business do in regard to depreciation expense?
12. What financial statement is plant assets reported on, and how?
13. How is discarding of a plant asset different from selling a plant asset?
14. How is gain or loss determined when disposing of plant assets? What situation constitutes a gain? What situation constitutes a loss?
15. What is a natural resource? What is the process by which businesses spread the allocation of a natural resource's cost over its usage?
16. What is an intangible asset? Provide some examples.
17. What is the process by which businesses spread the allocation of an intangible asset's cost over its useful life?
18. What is goodwill? Is goodwill amortized? What happens if the value of goodwill has decreased at the end of the year?
19. What does the asset turnover ratio measure, and how is it calculated?

20A. What does it mean if an exchange of plant assets has commercial substance? Are gains and losses recorded on the books because of the exchange?

CHAPTER 9

## > Short Exercises

**Learning Objective 1**

### S9-1 Determining the cost of an asset

Alton Clothing purchased land, paying $88,000 cash plus a $250,000 note payable. In addition, Alton paid delinquent property tax of $1,900, title insurance costing $500, and $4,200 to level the land and remove an unwanted building. Record the journal entry for purchase of the land.

**Learning Objective 1**

### S9-2 Making a lump-sum asset purchase

Foley Distribution Service paid $130,000 for a group purchase of land, building, and equipment. At the time of the acquisition, the land had a market value of $70,000, the building $42,000, and the equipment $28,000. Journalize the lump-sum purchase of the three assets for a total cost of $130,000, the amount for which the business signed a note payable.

**Learning Objective 2**

### S9-3 Computing first-year depreciation and book value

At the beginning of the year, Austin Airlines purchased a used airplane for $33,500,000. Austin Airlines expects the plane to remain useful for five years (4,000,000 miles) and to have a residual value of $5,500,000. The company expects the plane to be flown 1,100,000 miles during the first year.

**Requirements**

1. Compute Austin Airlines's *first-year* depreciation expense on the plane using the following methods:
   a. Straight-line
   b. Units-of-production
   c. Double-declining-balance
2. Show the airplane's book value at the end of the first year for all three methods.

**Learning Objective 2**

### S9-4 Computing second-year depreciation and accumulated depreciation

At the beginning of 2016, Air Asia purchased a used airplane at a cost of $40,000,000. Air Asia expects the plane to remain useful for eight years (5,000,000 miles) and to have a residual value of $5,000,000. Air Asia expects the plane to be flown 1,200,000 miles the first year and 1,400,000 miles the second year.

**Requirements**

1. Compute *second-year (2017)* depreciation expense on the plane using the following methods:
   a. Straight-line
   b. Units-of-production
   c. Double-declining-balance
2. Calculate the balance in Accumulated Depreciation at the end of the second year for all three methods.

**Learning Objective 2**

### S9-5 Calculating partial-year depreciation

On September 30, 2015, Meggie Services purchased a copy machine for $38,000. Meggie Services expects the machine to last for four years and have a residual value of $2,000. Compute depreciation expense on the machine for the year ended December 31, 2015, using the straight-line method.

### S9-6 Changing the estimated life of an asset

**Learning Objective 2**

Assume that ABC Catering Services paid $20,000 for equipment with a 10-year life and zero expected residual value. After using the equipment for four years, the company determines that the asset will remain useful for only three more years.

**Requirements**

1. Record depreciation expense on the equipment for year 5 by the straight-line method.
2. What is accumulated depreciation at the end of year 5?

### S9-7 Discarding of a fully depreciated asset

**Learning Objective 3**

On June 15, 2015, Perfect Furniture discarded equipment that had a cost of $12,000, a residual value of $0, and was fully depreciated. Journalize the disposal of the equipment.

### S9-8 Discarding an asset

**Learning Objective 3**

On May 31, 2016, Choice Landscapes discarded equipment that had a cost of $29,400. Accumulated Depreciation as of December 31, 2015, was $27,000. Assume annual depreciation on the equipment is $2,400. Journalize the partial-year depreciation expense and disposal of the equipment.

### S9-9 Selling an asset at gain or loss

**Learning Objective 3**

Mill Creek Golf Club purchased equipment on January 1, 2016, for $31,500. Suppose Mill Creek Golf Club sold the equipment for $22,000 on December 31, 2018. Accumulated Depreciation as of December 31, 2018, was $21,000. Journalize the sale of the equipment, assuming straight-line depreciation was used.

### S9-10 Selling an asset at gain or loss

**Learning Objective 3**

Pelman Company purchased equipment on January 1, 2016, for $32,000. Suppose Pelman sold the equipment for $5,000 on December 31, 2017. Accumulated Depreciation as of December 31, 2017, was $22,000. Journalize the sale of the equipment, assuming straight-line depreciation was used.

### S9-11 Accounting for depletion of natural resources

**Learning Objective 4**

North Coast Petroleum holds huge reserves of oil assets. Assume that at the end of 2016, North Coast Petroleum's cost of oil reserves totaled $60,000,000,000, representing 5,000,000,000 barrels of oil.

**Requirements**

1. Which method does North Coast Petroleum use to compute depletion?
2. Suppose North Coast Petroleum removed and sold 900,000,000 barrels of oil during 2017. Journalize depletion expense for 2017.

### S9-12 Accounting for an intangible asset

**Learning Objective 5**

On March 1, 2016, Twist Company purchased a patent for $168,000 cash. Although the patent gives legal protection for 20 years, the patent is expected to be used for only five years.

**Requirements**

1. Journalize the purchase of the patent.
2. Journalize the amortization expense for the year ended December 31, 2016. Assume straight-line amortization.

**Learning Objective 5**

### S9-13 Accounting for goodwill

TXL Advertising paid $250,000 to acquire *Seacoast Report*, a weekly advertising paper. At the time of the acquisition, *Seacoast Report*'s balance sheet reported total assets of $140,000 and liabilities of $80,000. The fair market value of *Seacoast Report*'s assets was $110,000. The fair market value of *Seacoast Report's* liabilities was $80,000.

**Requirements**

1. How much goodwill did TXL Advertising purchase as part of the acquisition of *Seacoast Report*?
2. Journalize TXL Advertising's acquisition of *Seacoast Report*.

**Learning Objective 6**

### S9-14 Computing the asset turnover ratio

Balani, Inc. had net sales of $52,000,000 for the year ended May 31, 2016. Its beginning and ending total assets were $53,200,000 and $98,400,000, respectively. Determine Balani's asset turnover ratio for year ended May 31, 2016.

**Learning Objective 7**
**Appendix 9A**

### S9A-15 Exchanging plant assets

Alpha Communications, Inc. purchased a computer for $2,600, debiting Computer Equipment. During 2014 and 2015, Alpha Communications, Inc. recorded total depreciation of $1,800 on the computer. On January 1, 2016, Alpha Communications, Inc. traded in the computer for a new one, paying $2,400 cash. The fair market value of the new computer is $4,300. Journalize Alpha Communications, Inc.'s exchange of computers. Assume the exchange had commercial substance.

**Learning Objective 7**
**Appendix 9A**

### S9A-16 Exchanging plant assets

Orange Corporation purchased equipment for $30,000. Orange recorded total depreciation of $24,000 on the equipment. On January 1, 2016, Orange traded in the equipment for new equipment, paying $23,500 cash. The fair market value of the new equipment is $28,500. Journalize Orange Corporation's exchange of equipment. Assume the exchange had commercial substance.

## > Exercises

**Learning Objective 1**

1. Land $365,000

### E9-17 Determining the cost of assets

Lavallee Furniture purchased land, paying $95,000 cash plus a $260,000 note payable. In addition, Lavallee paid delinquent property tax of $3,000, title insurance costing $2,000, and $5,000 to level the land and remove an unwanted building. The company then constructed an office building at a cost of $450,000. It also paid $55,000 for a fence around the property, $16,000 for a sign near the entrance, and $7,000 for special lighting of the grounds.

**Requirements**

1. Determine the cost of the land, land improvements, and building.
2. Which of these assets will Lavallee depreciate?

CHAPTER 9

### E9-18 Making a lump-sum purchase of assets

Learning Objective 1

Lot 3 $108,750

Dearwood Properties bought three lots in a subdivision for a lump-sum price. An independent appraiser valued the lots as follows:

| Lot | Appraised Value |
|---|---|
| 1 | $ 45,000 |
| 2 | 292,500 |
| 3 | 112,500 |

Dearwood paid $435,000 in cash. Record the purchase in the journal, identifying each lot's cost in a separate Land account. Round decimals to two places, and use the computed percentages throughout.

### E9-19 Distinguishing capital expenditures from revenue expenditures

Learning Objective 1

Consider the following expenditures:

a. Purchase price.
b. Ordinary recurring repairs to keep the machinery in good working order.
c. Lubrication before machinery is placed in service.
d. Periodic lubrication after machinery is placed in service.
e. Major overhaul to extend useful life by three years.
f. Sales tax paid on the purchase price.
g. Transportation and insurance while machinery is in transit from seller to buyer.
h. Installation.
i. Training of personnel for initial operation of the machinery.

Classify each of the expenditures as a capital expenditure or a revenue expenditure related to machinery.

### E9-20 Computing depreciation—three methods

Learning Objective 2

1. Double-declining-balance, 12/31/17, Exp. $5,250

Crackling Fried Chicken bought equipment on January 2, 2016, for $21,000. The equipment was expected to remain in service for four years and to perform 3,600 fry jobs. At the end of the equipment's useful life, Crackling's estimates that its residual value will be $3,000. The equipment performed 360 jobs the first year, 1,080 the second year, 1,440 the third, and 720 the fourth year.

(Requirement 1 only)

**Requirements**

1. Prepare a schedule of *depreciation expense*, *accumulated depreciation*, and *book value* per year for the equipment under the three depreciation methods. Show your computations. *Note:* Three depreciation schedules must be prepared.
2. Which method tracks the wear and tear on the equipment most closely?

### E9-21 Changing an asset's useful life and residual value

Learning Objective 2

Yr. 16 $42,400

Budget Hardware Consultants purchased a building for $452,000 and depreciated it on a straight-line basis over a 35-year period. The estimated residual value is $102,000. After using the building for 15 years, Budget realized that wear and tear on the building would wear it out before 35 years and that the estimated residual value should be $90,000. Starting with the 16th year, Budget began depreciating the building over a revised total life of 20 years using the new residual value. Journalize depreciation expense on the building for years 15 and 16.

**Learning Objectives 2, 3**

Depr. Exp. $2,400

**E9-22 Recording partial-year depreciation and sale of an asset**

On January 2, 2015, Ditto Clothing Consignments purchased showroom fixtures for $12,000 cash, expecting the fixtures to remain in service for five years. Ditto has depreciated the fixtures on a double-declining-balance basis, with zero residual value. On October 31, 2016, Ditto sold the fixtures for $5,900 cash. Record both depreciation expense for 2016 and sale of the fixtures on October 31, 2016.

**Learning Objectives 2, 3**

Loss $(6,000)

**E9-23 Recording partial-year depreciation and sale of an asset**

On January 2, 2014, Pet Salon purchased fixtures for $48,200 cash, expecting the fixtures to remain in service for nine years. Pet Salon has depreciated the fixtures on a straight-line basis, with $5,000 residual value. On May 31, 2016, Pet Salon sold the fixtures for $30,600 cash. Record both depreciation expense for 2016 and sale of the fixtures on May 31, 2016.

**Learning Objective 4**

$1.20 per ton

**E9-24 Journalizing natural resource depletion**

Colorado Mountain Mining paid $507,700 for the right to extract mineral assets from a 500,000-ton deposit. In addition to the purchase price, Colorado also paid a $600 filing fee, a $1,700 license fee to the state of Nevada, and $90,000 for a geological survey of the property. Because Colorado purchased the rights to the minerals only, it expects the asset to have zero residual value. During the first year, Colorado removed and sold 60,000 tons of the minerals. Make journal entries to record (a) purchase of the minerals (debit Minerals), (b) payment of fees and other costs, and (c) depletion for the first year.

**Learning Objectives 2, 5**

2. Amort. Exp. $225,000

**E9-25 Handling acquisition of patent, amortization, and change in useful life**

Medway Printers (MP) manufactures printers. Assume that MP recently paid $900,000 for a patent on a new laser printer. Although it gives legal protection for 20 years, the patent is expected to provide a competitive advantage for only eight years.

**Requirements**

1. Assuming the straight-line method of amortization, make journal entries to record (a) the purchase of the patent and (b) amortization for the first full year.
2. After using the patent for four years, MP learns at an industry trade show that another company is designing a more efficient printer. On the basis of this new information, MP decides, starting with year 5, to amortize the remaining cost of the patent over two remaining years, giving the patent a total useful life of six years. Record amortization for year 5.

**Learning Objective 5**

2. Goodwill $7,000,000

**E9-26 Measuring and recording goodwill**

Princess has acquired several other companies. Assume that Princess purchased Kettle for $11,000,000 cash. The book value of Kettle's assets is $12,000,000 (market value, $16,000,000), and it has liabilities of $12,000,000 (market value, $12,000,000).

**Requirements**

1. Compute the cost of the goodwill purchased by Princess.
2. Record the purchase of Kettle by Princess.

## E9-27 Computing asset turnover ratio

Learning Objective 6

Snap Dragon Photo reported the following figures on its December 31, 2016, income statement and balance sheet:

| | | |
|---|---|---|
| Net sales | $ 440,000 | |
| | **Dec. 31, 2016** | **Dec. 31, 2015** |
| Cash | $ 26,000 | $ 28,000 |
| Accounts Receivable | 56,000 | 58,000 |
| Merchandise Inventory | 79,000 | 76,000 |
| Prepaid Expenses | 8,000 | 14,000 |
| Property, plant, and equipment, net | 180,000 | 11,000 |

Compute the asset turnover ratio for 2016.

## E9A-28 Exchanging assets—two situations

Learning Objective 7
Appendix 9A

2. Loss $(7,000)

Commerce Bank recently traded in office fixtures. Here are the facts:

| **Old fixtures:** | **New fixtures:** |
|---|---|
| Cost, $99,000 | Cash paid, $ 108,000 |
| Accumulated depreciation, $65,000 | Market value, $ 142,000 |

### Requirements

1. Record Commerce Bank's trade-in of old fixtures for new ones. Assume the exchange had commercial substance.
2. Now let's change one fact. Commerce Bank feels compelled to do business with Shoreside Furniture, a bank customer, even though the bank can get the fixtures elsewhere at a better price. Commerce Bank is aware that the new fixtures' market value is only $135,000. Record the trade-in. Assume the exchange had commercial substance.

## E9A-29 Measuring asset cost, units-of-production depreciation, and asset trade

Learning Objectives 1, 2, 7
Appendix 9A

1. $12,870

Pact Trucking Corporation uses the units-of-production depreciation method because units-of-production best measures wear and tear on the trucks. Consider these facts about one Mack truck in the company's fleet.

When acquired in 2013, the rig cost $450,000 and was expected to remain in service for 10 years or 1,000,000 miles. Estimated residual value was $120,000. The truck was driven 82,000 miles in 2013, 122,000 miles in 2014, and 162,000 miles in 2015. After 39,000 miles, on March 15, 2016, the company traded in the Mack truck for a less expensive Freightliner. Pact also paid cash of $27,000. Fair market value of the Mack truck was equal to its net book value on the date of the trade.

### Requirements

1. Record the journal entry for depreciation expense in 2016.
2. Determine Pact's cost of the new truck.
3. Record the journal entry for the exchange of assets on March 15, 2016. Assume the exchange had commercial substance.

CHAPTER 9

## > Problems Group A

**Learning Objectives 1, 2**

1. Bldg. $446,100

### P9-30A Determining asset cost and recording partial-year depreciation

Park and Fly, near an airport, incurred the following costs to acquire land, make land improvements, and construct and furnish a small building:

| | | |
|---|---|---|
| a. | Purchase price of three acres of land | $ 85,000 |
| b. | Delinquent real estate taxes on the land to be paid by Park and Fly | 5,500 |
| c. | Additional dirt and earthmoving | 8,300 |
| d. | Title insurance on the land acquisition | 3,400 |
| e. | Fence around the boundary of the property | 9,400 |
| f. | Building permit for the building | 1,200 |
| g. | Architect's fee for the design of the building | 20,600 |
| h. | Signs near the front of the property | 9,700 |
| i. | Materials used to construct the building | 211,000 |
| j. | Labor to construct the building | 172,000 |
| k. | Interest cost on construction loan for the building | 9,300 |
| l. | Parking lots on the property | 28,800 |
| m. | Lights for the parking lots | 10,600 |
| n. | Salary of construction supervisor (80% to building; 20% to parking lot and concrete walks) | 40,000 |
| o. | Furniture | 11,600 |
| p. | Transportation of furniture from seller to the building | 2,000 |
| q. | Additional fencing | 6,000 |

Park and Fly depreciates land improvements over 20 years, buildings over 40 years, and furniture over eight years, all on a straight-line basis with zero residual value.

**Requirements**

1. Set up columns for Land, Land Improvements, Building, and Furniture. Show how to account for each cost by listing the cost under the correct account. Determine the total cost of each asset.
2. All construction was complete and the assets were placed in service on October 1. Record partial-year depreciation expense for the year ended December 31.

**Learning Objectives 1, 2**

1. Units-of-production, 12/31/16, Dep. Exp. $14,000

### P9-31A Determining asset cost, recording first-year depreciation, and identifying depreciation results that meet management objectives

On January 3, 2016, Fast Delivery Service purchased a truck at a cost of $62,000. Before placing the truck in service, Fast spent $3,000 painting it, $1,500 replacing tires, and $3,500 overhauling the engine. The truck should remain in service for five years and have a residual value of $5,000. The truck's annual mileage is expected to be 28,000 miles in each of the first four years and 18,000 miles in the fifth year—130,000 miles in total. In deciding which depreciation method to use, Steven Kittridge, the general manager, requests a depreciation schedule for each of the depreciation methods (straight-line, units-of-production, and double-declining-balance).

### Requirements

1. Prepare a depreciation schedule for each depreciation method, showing asset cost, depreciation expense, accumulated depreciation, and asset book value.
2. Fast prepares financial statements using the depreciation method that reports the highest net income in the early years of asset use. Consider the first year that Fast uses the truck. Identify the depreciation method that meets the company's objectives.



## P9-32A Recording lump-sum asset purchases, depreciation, and disposals

**Learning Objectives 1, 2, 3**

Sep. 1 Gain $88,000

Grace Carol Associates surveys American eating habits. The company's accounts include Land, Buildings, Office Equipment, and Communication Equipment, with a separate Accumulated Depreciation account for each asset. During 2016, Grace Carol completed the following transactions:

| | |
|---|---|
| Jan. 1 | Purchased office equipment, $112,000. Paid $74,000 cash and financed the remaining with a note payable. |
| Apr. 1 | Acquired land and communication equipment in a lump-sum purchase. Total cost was $340,000 paid in cash. An independent appraisal valued the land at $267,750 and the communication equipment at $89,250. |
| Sep. 1 | Sold a building that cost $540,000 (accumulated depreciation of $240,000 through December 31 of the preceding year). Grace Carol received $380,000 cash from the sale of the building. Depreciation is computed on a straight-line basis. The building has a 40-year useful life and a residual value of $60,000. |
| Dec. 31 | Recorded depreciation as follows: |
| | Communication equipment is depreciated by the straight-line method over a five-year life with zero residual value. |
| | Office equipment is depreciated using the double-declining-balance method over five years with a $2,000 residual value. |

Record the transactions in the journal of Grace Carol Associates.

## P9-33A Accounting for natural resources

**Learning Objective 4**

Dep. Exp. $1,186,250

Chapman Oil, Inc. has an account titled Oil and Gas Properties. Chapman paid $6,300,000 for oil reserves holding an estimated 400,000 barrels of oil. Assume the company paid $560,000 for additional geological tests of the property and $440,000 to prepare for drilling. During the first year, Chapman removed and sold 65,000 barrels of oil. Record all of Chapman's transactions, including depletion for the first year.

## P9-34A Accounting for intangibles

**Learning Objective 5**

1. Goodwill $650,000

Middle Telecom provides communication services in Iowa, Nebraska, the Dakotas, and Montana. Middle purchased goodwill as part of the acquisition of Shipley Wireless Enterprises, which had the following figures:

| | |
|---|---|
| Book value of assets | $ 750,000 |
| Market value of assets | 900,000 |
| Market value of liabilities | 550,000 |

### Requirements

1. Journalize the entry to record Middle's purchase of Shipley Wireless for $400,000 cash plus a $600,000 note payable.
2. What special asset does Middle's acquisition of Shipley Wireless identify? How should Middle Telecom account for this asset after acquiring Shipley Wireless? Explain in detail.

CHAPTER 9

**Learning Objectives 2, 3, 7**
**Appendix 9A**

Jan. 1 Gain $7,000

**P9A-35A Journalizing partial-year depreciation and asset disposals and exchanges**

During 2016, Zora Corporation completed the following transactions:

| | |
|---|---|
| Jan. 1 | Traded in old office equipment with book value of $60,000 (cost of $129,000 and accumulated depreciation of $69,000) for new equipment. Zora also paid $75,000 in cash. Fair value of new equipment is $142,000. Assume the exchange had commercial substance. |
| Apr. 1 | Sold equipment that cost $48,000 (accumulated depreciation of $39,000 through December 31 of the preceding year). Zora received $6,100 cash from the sale of the equipment. Depreciation is computed on a straight-line basis. The equipment has a five-year useful life and a residual value of $0. |
| Dec. 31 | Recorded depreciation as follows:<br>Office equipment is depreciated using the double-declining-balance method over four years with a $4,000 residual value. |

Record the transactions in the journal of Zora Corporation.

## > Problems Group B

**Learning Objectives 1, 2**

1. Bldg. $471,000

**P9-36B Determining asset cost and recording partial-year depreciation**

Park and Go, near an airport, incurred the following costs to acquire land, make land improvements, and construct and furnish a small building:

| | |
|---|---|
| a. Purchase price of three acres of land | $ 88,000 |
| b. Delinquent real estate taxes on the land to be paid by Park and Go | 6,300 |
| c. Additional dirt and earthmoving | 8,100 |
| d. Title insurance on the land acquisition | 3,500 |
| e. Fence around the boundary of the property | 9,200 |
| f. Building permit for the building | 800 |
| g. Architect's fee for the design of the building | 20,800 |
| h. Signs near the front of the property | 9,000 |
| i. Materials used to construct the building | 215,000 |
| j. Labor to construct the building | 174,000 |
| k. Interest cost on construction loan for the building | 9,400 |
| l. Parking lots on the property | 29,500 |
| m. Lights for the parking lots | 10,500 |
| n. Salary of construction supervisor (85% to building; 15% to parking lot and concrete walks) | 60,000 |
| o. Furniture | 11,300 |
| p. Transportation of furniture from seller to the building | 2,200 |
| q. Additional fencing | 6,700 |

Park and Go depreciates land improvements over 20 years, buildings over 50 years, and furniture over eight years, all on a straight-line basis with zero residual value.

**Requirements**

1. Set up columns for Land, Land Improvements, Building, and Furniture. Show how to account for each cost by listing the cost under the correct account. Determine the total cost of each asset.
2. All construction was complete and the assets were placed in service on July 1. Record partial-year depreciation expense for the year ended December 31.

### P9-37B Determining asset cost, recording first-year depreciation, and identifying depreciation results that meet management objectives

**Learning Objectives 1, 2**

1. Units-of-production, 12/31/16, Dep. Exp. $18,900

On January 3, 2016, Quick Delivery Service purchased a truck at a cost of $90,000. Before placing the truck in service, Quick spent $2,500 painting it, $1,800 replacing tires, and $4,700 overhauling the engine. The truck should remain in service for five years and have a residual value of $9,000. The truck's annual mileage is expected to be 21,000 miles in each of the first four years and 16,000 miles in the fifth year—100,000 miles in total. In deciding which depreciation method to use, Harvey Warner, the general manager, requests a depreciation schedule for each of the depreciation methods (straight-line, units-of-production, and double-declining-balance).

**Requirements**

1. Prepare a depreciation schedule for each depreciation method, showing asset cost, depreciation expense, accumulated depreciation, and asset book value.
2. Quick prepares financial statements using the depreciation method that reports the highest net income in the early years of asset use. Consider the first year that Quick uses the truck. Identify the depreciation method that meets the company's objectives.

### P9-38B Recording lump-sum asset purchases, depreciation, and disposals

**Learning Objectives 1, 2, 3**

Sep. 1 Gain $68,000

Granny Carney Associates surveys American eating habits. The company's accounts include Land, Buildings, Office Equipment, and Communication Equipment, with a separate Accumulated Depreciation account for each asset. During 2016, Granny Carney completed the following transactions:

| | |
|---|---|
| Jan. 1 | Purchased office equipment, $112,000. Paid $78,000 cash and financed the remaining with a note payable. |
| Apr. 1 | Acquired land and communication equipment in a lump-sum purchase. Total cost was $410,000 paid in cash. An independent appraisal valued the land at $322,875 and the communication equipment at $107,625. |
| Sep. 1 | Sold a building that cost $540,000 (accumulated depreciation of $240,000 through December 31 of the preceding year). Granny Carney received $360,000 cash from the sale of the building. Depreciation is computed on a straight-line basis. The building has a 40-year useful life and a residual value of $60,000. |
| Dec. 31 | Recorded depreciation as follows: |
| | Communication equipment is depreciated by the straight-line method over a five-year life with zero residual value. |
| | Office equipment is depreciated using the double-declining-balance method over five years with a $5,000 residual value. |

Record the transactions in the journal of Granny Carney Associates.

### P9-39B Accounting for natural resources

**Learning Objective 4**

Dep. Exp. $2,261,000

Gandy Oil Incorporated has an account titled Oil and Gas Properties. Gandy paid $6,100,000 for oil reserves holding an estimated 300,000 barrels of oil. Assume the

CHAPTER 9

company paid $560,000 for additional geological tests of the property and $480,000 to prepare for drilling. During the first year, Gandy removed and sold 95,000 barrels of oil. Record all of Gandy's transactions, including depletion for the first year.

**Learning Objective 5**

1. Goodwill $460,000

### P9-40B Accounting for intangibles

Central States Telecom provides communication services in Iowa, Nebraska, the Dakotas, and Montana. Central States purchased goodwill as part of the acquisition of Shurburn Wireless Company, which had the following figures:

| | |
|---|---|
| Book value of assets | $ 750,000 |
| Market value of assets | 1,000,000 |
| Market value of liabilities | 560,000 |

**Requirements**

1. Journalize the entry to record Central States's purchase of Shurburn Wireless for $360,000 cash plus a $540,000 note payable.
2. What special asset does Central States's acquisition of Shurburn Wireless identify? How should Central States Telecom account for this asset after acquiring Shurburn Wireless? Explain in detail.

**Learning Objectives 2, 3, 7**
**Appendix 9A**

Jan. 1 Gain $8,000

### P9A-41B Journalizing partial-year depreciation and asset disposals and exchanges

During 2016, Dora Company completed the following transactions:

| | |
|---|---|
| Jan. 1 | Traded in old office equipment with book value of $55,000 (cost of $124,000 and accumulated depreciation of $69,000) for new equipment. Dora also paid $100,000 in cash. Fair value of new equipment is $163,000. Assume the exchange had commercial substance. |
| Apr. 1 | Sold equipment that cost $54,000 (accumulated depreciation of $42,000 through December 31 of the preceding year). Dora received $6,300 cash from the sale of the equipment. Depreciation is computed on a straight-line basis. The equipment has a five-year useful life and a residual value of $0. |
| Dec. 31 | Recorded depreciation as follows:<br>Office equipment is depreciated using the double-declining-balance method over four years with a $7,000 residual value. |

Record the transactions in the journal of Dora Company.

## > Continuing Problem

### P9-42 Calculating and journalizing partial-year depreciation

This problem continues the Daniels Consulting situation from Problem P8-41 of Chapter 8. Assume Daniels Consulting had purchased a computer, $3,600, and office furniture, $3,000, on December 3 and 4, 2016, respectively, and that they were expected to last five years. Assume that both assets have a residual value of $0.

**Requirements**

1. Calculate the amount of depreciation expense for each asset for the year ended December 31, 2016, assuming the computer is depreciated using the straight-line method and the office furniture is depreciated using the double-declining-balance method.
2. Record the entry for the one month's depreciation.

# CRITICAL THINKING



## > Ethical Issue 9-1

Western Bank & Trust purchased land and a building for the lump sum of $3,000,000. To get the maximum tax deduction, Western allocated 90% of the purchase price to the building and only 10% to the land. A more realistic allocation would have been 70% to the building and 30% to the land.

**Requirements**

1. Explain the tax advantage of allocating too much to the building and too little to the land.
2. Was Western's allocation ethical? If so, state why. If not, why not? Identify who was harmed.

## > Fraud Case 9-1

Jim Reed manages a fleet of utility trucks for a rural county government. He's been in his job for 30 years, and he knows where the angles are. He makes sure that when new trucks are purchased, the residual value is set as low as possible. Then, when they become fully depreciated, they are sold off by the county at residual value. Jim makes sure his buddies in the construction business are first in line for the bargain sales, and they make sure he gets a little something back. Recently, a new county commissioner was elected with vows to cut expenses for the taxpayers. Unlike other commissioners, this man has a business degree, and he is coming to visit Jim tomorrow.

**Requirements**

1. When a business sells a fully depreciated asset for its residual value, is a gain or loss recognized?
2. How do businesses determine what residual values to use for their various assets? Are there "hard and fast" rules for residual values?
3. How would an organization prevent the kind of fraud depicted here?

## > Financial Statement Case 9-1

Visit **http://www.pearsonhighered.com/Horngren** to view a link to **Starbucks Corporation's** Fiscal 2013 annual report. Refer to the Starbucks Corporation financial statements, including Notes 1 and 7. Answer the following questions.

**Requirements**

1. Which depreciation method does Starbucks Corporation use for reporting in the financial statements? What type of depreciation method does the company probably use for income tax purposes?
2. What was the amount of depreciation and amortization expense for the year ending September 29, 2013? (*Hint:* Review the Statement of Cash Flows.)
3. The statement of cash flows reports the cash purchases of property, plant, and equipment. How much were Starbucks's additions to property, plant, and equipment during the year ending 2013? Did Starbucks record any proceeds from the sale of property, plant, and equipment?

4. What was the amount of accumulated depreciation at September 29, 2013? What was the net book value of property, plant, and equipment for Starbucks as of September 29, 2013?
5. Compute Starbucks's asset turnover ratio for year ending September 29, 2013. How does Starbucks's ratio compare with that of **Green Mountain Coffee Roasters, Inc.**?

## > Communication Activity 9-1

In 150 words or fewer, explain the different methods that can be used to calculate depreciation. Your explanation should include how to calculate depreciation expense using each method.



## > Quick Check Answers

**1.** d **2.** d **3.** c **4.** b **5.** c **6.** d **7.** d **8.** b **9.** c **10A.** b

# 10 Investments

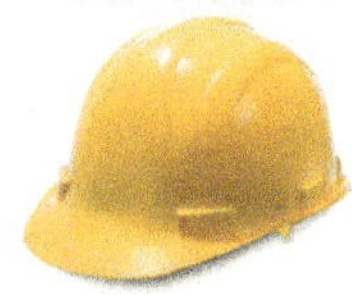

## How Should the Business Invest Its Excess Cash?

Donavon Gill, portfolio manager for GMP Investors, had just finished a meeting with his newest client, Sarah Miller. Sarah is the CEO of Miller Construction, a profitable construction firm with offices throughout the United States. Sarah had requested a meeting with Donavon to discuss an investment plan for the business. Miller Construction was interested in investing its excess cash and, as CEO, Sarah had come to Donavon with a number of questions.

During the meeting, Donavon had shared with Sarah a variety of different investment options that the business could consider. One option might be for Miller Construction to invest in other corporations' stocks (called equity securities). Another option for the business might be investing in bonds (debt securities). He also talked to Sarah about why the business might want to invest in each type of security. Donavon knew that it was his responsibility to provide a custom solution for Miller Construction so that Sarah's business would meet its earnings needs.

Sarah was also interested in how Miller Construction would report these investments on its financial statements. She knew that investments in debt and equity securities were reported as assets on the balance sheet, but she was concerned that there might be some additional reporting requirements. Donavon was glad that Sarah was considering these issues and was happy to help her. He shared with her that the type of security (debt or equity) and the length of time the security was held (short-term versus long-term) determined how it was reported on the financial statements. Donavon also suggested that she talk to her company's accountant before deciding on the business's investment plan. He knew that there were a lot of issues to consider when choosing how to invest excess cash.

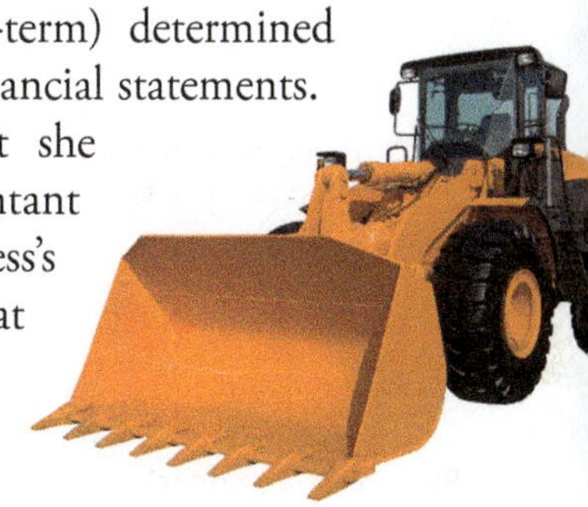

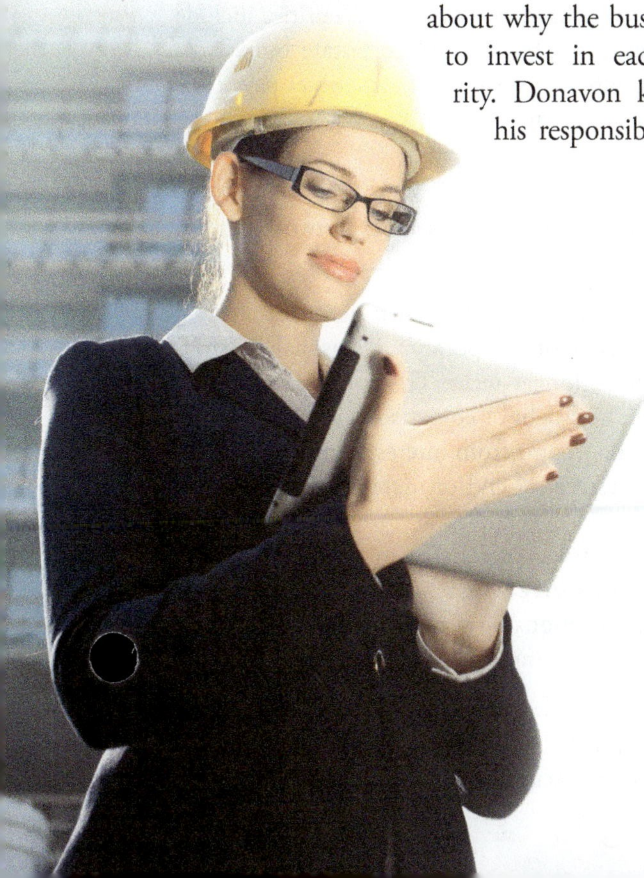

### Why Would a Company Invest?

Many of you are familiar with the famous businessman Warren Buffett, but you might not know that he is the primary stockholder and CEO of Berkshire Hathaway, Inc. Berkshire Hathaway is a holding company that owns a large number of other businesses (called subsidiaries), including the popular automobile insurer GEICO and the railroad system operator Burlington Northern Santa Fe. In addition to owning subsidiaries, Berkshire Hathaway also invests cash in other corporations' stock, such as The Coca-Cola Company (9.1% ownership), Wal-Mart Stores, Inc. (1.8% ownership), and Exxon Mobil Corp. (0.9% ownership). Investing excess cash in corporations' stocks and bonds is a common practice; many businesses (and individuals) do this. In this chapter, you learn why companies might invest in securities and how these investments are reported on the financial statements.

# Chapter 10 Learning Objectives

1. Identify why companies invest in debt and equity securities and classify investments
2. Account for investments in debt securities
3. Account for investments in equity securities
4. Describe and illustrate how debt and equity securities are reported
5. Use the rate of return on total assets to evaluate business performance

## WHY DO COMPANIES INVEST?

**Learning Objective 1**
Identify why companies invest in debt and equity securities and classify investments

Just as individuals invest in a variety of companies' stocks and bonds, the same is true for businesses. Investments in stocks or bonds can range from a few securities to the acquisition of an entire company. In this chapter, we examine debt (bonds) and equity (stock) accounting for the investor who buys them.

### Debt Securities Versus Equity Securities

**Investor**
The owner of a bond or stock of a corporation.

**Investee**
The corporation that issued the bond or stock to the investor.

**Security**
A share or interest representing financial value.

**Debt Security**
Represents a credit relationship with another company or governmental entity that typically pays interest for a fixed period.

**Equity Security**
Represents stock ownership in another company that sometimes pays dividends.

The owner of a bond or stock of a corporation is referred to as the **investor**. The corporation that issued the bond or stock is referred to as the **investee**. For example, if you own shares of Smart Touch Learning's stock, you are the investor and Smart Touch Learning is the investee.

Investors can invest in either debt securities or equity securities. A **security** is a share or interest representing financial value. Securities are represented by a certificate (such as a stock certificate) and are commonly traded on an exchange (such as the New York Stock Exchange). A **debt security** represents a credit relationship with another company or governmental entity, and typically pays interest for a fixed period. Debt securities include U.S. government securities (Treasury bills), municipal bonds, and corporate bonds. An **equity security** represents stock ownership in another company and sometimes pays dividends. Equity securities include common and preferred stock.

### Reasons to Invest

Why would a company invest in debt or equity securities? Let's look at two common reasons:

1. The company may have short-term, excess cash that it doesn't need for normal operations. This excess cash could be the result of temporary or seasonal business fluctuations, or it could be cash available for a longer term. The company wants to make the best use of its excess cash, so it invests in debt or equity securities to generate investment income. This investment income may come from interest earned from debt investments, dividends earned from stock investments, and/or increases in the market value of the security.
2. The company may invest in debt or equity securities of other companies to pursue a certain business strategy. For example, a company may invest in a key vendor's debt or equity securities to further enhance a business relationship with that vendor. Doing so might strengthen the relationship between the investing company and the vendor.

Of course, there are other reasons a company may want to invest in other companies' debt or equity securities, but the reasons we identified above are the most common. Now, let's turn to a few basics of investing in debt or equity securities.

## ETHICS

### It's just a tip, isn't it?

Arlene Barry had just left the most recent board meeting of Panda Toy Manufacturing. Arlene served as chairman of the board and was also a majority stockholder in the business. Panda Toy Manufacturing had just learned that the company was being sued by a multinational retail toy store for failure to use flame-retardant filling in its stuffed panda bears. Arlene knew that the business had been cutting costs and had intentionally used filling that was not up to appropriate standards. She was sure that Panda Toy would lose the lawsuit and knew that the value of her stock would drop considerably. Arlene was considering quickly selling her stock before the lawsuit became public knowledge. What should Arlene do? What would you do?

### Solution

If Arlene sells her investment in Panda Toy Manufacturing, she could be found guilty of illegal insider trading. Insider trading occurs when a corporate officer, director, or employee buys or sells stock after learning information obtained during the performance of the individual's duties that is considered to be nonpublic information about a company. If Arlene wants to sell her shares of Panda Toy, she should wait until after the information has become public. This type of sale would be considered legal insider trading and would need to be reported to the U.S. Securities and Exchange Commission (SEC) to notify the public of a change in ownership of the manufacturer's stock.

## Classification and Reporting of Investments

Investments are first classified based on the length of time the investor intends to hold the investment. The two classifications are similar to the balance sheet classifications you learned previously.

- **Short-term investments**—sometimes called *marketable securities* or *temporary investments*—are current assets. Short-term investments are investments in debt and equity securities that are highly liquid (readily convertible to cash) and that the investor intends to convert to cash within one year.
- **Long-term investments** are all investments that are not short-term. Long-term investments include debt and equity securities that the investor expects to hold longer than one year or debt or equity securities that are not readily marketable—for instance, a stock investment in a small or privately held company that is not traded on any stock exchange.

Debt and equity securities can be further classified into five specific types.

- **Trading investments** are debt securities or equity securities in which the investor holds less than 20% of the voting stock and that the investor plans to sell in the very near future—days, weeks, or only a few months—with the intent of generating a profit on a quick sale. Trading investments are categorized as current assets.
- **Held-to-maturity (HTM) investments** are debt securities the investor intends to hold until they mature. Because equity securities don't "mature" on a specific date, this category of investment applies only to debt securities. Held-to-maturity investments are categorized as current assets or long-term assets on the balance sheet, depending on the maturity date.
- **Available-for-sale (AFS) investments** include all debt securities or equity securities in which the investor holds less than 20% of the voting stock and that aren't trading investments or held-to-maturity investments. In the case of debt securities, AFS investments are not planned to be held until maturity and are reported either as current assets or long-term assets on the balance sheet. AFS investments are reported as current assets if the business expects to sell them within one year. All other AFS investments that are planned to be held longer than a year are reported as long-term assets.

**Short-term Investments**
Investments in debt and equity securities that are highly liquid and that the investor intends to sell in one year or less.

**Long-term Investments**
Investments in bonds (debt securities) or stocks (equity securities) in which the company intends to hold the investment for longer than one year.

**Trading Investment**
A debt security or an equity security in which the investor holds less than 20% of the voting stock and that the investor plans to sell in the very near future.

**Held-to-Maturity (HTM) Investment**
A debt security the investor intends to hold until it matures.

**Available-for-Sale (AFS) Investment**
A debt security or an equity security in which the investor holds less than 20% of the voting stock and that isn't a trading investment or a held-to-maturity investment.

**Significant Interest Investment**
An equity security in which the investor owns from 20% to 50% of the investee's voting stock.

**Controlling Interest Investment**
An equity security in which the investor owns more than 50% of the investee's voting stock.

- **Significant interest investments** are equity securities in which the investor owns from 20% to 50% of the investee's voting stock. Significant interest investments are reported as long-term assets on the balance sheet.
- **Controlling interest investments** are equity securities in which the investor owns more than 50% of the investee's voting stock. Controlling interest investments are consolidated into the investor's financial statements, which is discussed later in the chapter.

Exhibit 10-1 summarizes the five types of investments.

**Exhibit 10-1 | Five Types of Investments**

| Types of Investments | Debt, Equity, or Both | Definition |
|---|---|---|
| **Trading Investments** | Both | Securities in which the investor holds less than 20% of the investee's voting stock (if an equity security) and that the investor plans to sell in the very near future. |
| **Held-to-Maturity Investments** | Debt | Securities the investor intends to hold until they mature. |
| **Available-for-Sale Investments** | Both | Securities in which the investor holds less than 20% of the investee's voting stock (if an equity security) and that the investor does not plan to hold until they mature (if a debt security) or sell in the near future. |
| **Significant Interest Investments** | Equity | Securities in which an investor owns from 20% to 50% of the investee's voting stock. |
| **Controlling Interest Investments** | Equity | Securities in which an investor owns more than 50% of the investee's voting stock. |

## Try It!

Match the key term to the scenario.

| | |
|---|---|
| 1. Available-for-sale investments | a. Jane owns 53% of Richard's Roses's voting stock. |
| 2. Controlling interest investments | b. Joe owns a debt security in Bones, Inc. and intends to hold it until maturity. |
| 3. Trading investments | c. Jeannie owns 18% of Cricket, Inc.'s voting stock and plans on selling the stock after one year. |
| 4. Held-to-maturity investments | d. Jacob owns 24% of Pay, Inc.'s voting stock. |
| 5. Significant interest investments | e. Jim owns 10% of Tag, Inc.'s voting stock and plans on selling the stock next week. |

**Check your answers online in MyAccounting Lab or at http://www.pearsonhighered.com/Horngren.**

For more practice, see Short Exercise S10-1. MyAccountingLab

# HOW ARE INVESTMENTS IN DEBT SECURITIES ACCOUNTED FOR?

**Learning Objective 2**

Account for investments in debt securities

Let's begin by discussing how debt securities are accounted for, including the purchase, interest revenue earned, and disposition of the securities.

## Purchase of Debt Securities

Assume Smart Touch Learning has excess cash to invest and pays $100,000 to buy $100,000 face value, 9%, five-year Neon Company bonds on July 1, 2016. The bonds are issued on July 1, 2016. The bonds pay interest on June 30 and December 31. Smart Touch Learning intends to hold the bonds to maturity and will, therefore, record them as held-to-maturity investments. Smart Touch Learning's accounting clerk will record the investment in debt securities at cost, including any brokerage fees paid, with the following entry:

| Date | Accounts and Explanation | Debit | Credit |
|---|---|---|---|
| 2016 | | | |
| Jul. 1 | Long-term Investments—Held-to-Maturity | 100,000 | |
| | Cash | | 100,000 |
| | *Purchased investment in bonds.* | | |

| A↑↓ | = | L + E |
|---|---|---|
| LT Investments↑<br>Cash↓ | | |

## Interest Revenue

On December 31, 2016, Smart Touch Learning would receive the first interest payment on the bond investment. Smart Touch Learning's entry to record the receipt of interest on December 31, 2016, is as follows:

| Date | Accounts and Explanation | Debit | Credit |
|---|---|---|---|
| 2016 | | | |
| Dec. 31 | Cash | 4,500 | |
| | Interest Revenue ($100,000 × 0.09 × 6/12) | | 4,500 |
| | *Received cash interest.* | | |

| A↑ | = | L | + | E↑ |
|---|---|---|---|---|
| Cash↑ | | | | Interest Revenue↑ |

Smart Touch Learning would repeat this entry every six months for the five years—each time interest payments are received.

## Disposition at Maturity

When Smart Touch Learning disposes of the bonds at maturity (June 30, 2021), it will receive the face value of the bond and record the following entry, assuming the last interest payment has been recorded:

| Date | Accounts and Explanation | Debit | Credit |
|---|---|---|---|
| 2021 | | | |
| Jun. 30 | Cash | 100,000 | |
| | Long-term Investments—Held-to-Maturity | | 100,000 |
| | *Disposed of bond at maturity.* | | |

| A↑↓ | = | L + E |
|---|---|---|
| Cash↑<br>LT Investments↓ | | |

In this example, we illustrated the accounting for held-to-maturity investments. Debt securities can also be trading investments and available-for-sale investments. The accounting for these is the same as illustrated above. The only difference is the use of a different account name. In addition, debt securities can be purchased at face value, at a discount, or at a premium. In our example, we purchased the debt securities at face value. If a debt security is purchased at a discount or at a premium, the discount/premium must be amortized when the interest revenue is earned. This amortization can be done using either the straight-line amortization method or the effective-interest amortization method and is similar to recording the amortization of discount or premium on bonds payable covered in a later chapter.

**Try It!**

6. On January 1, 2016, the College Corporation decides to invest in Small Town bonds. The bonds mature on December 31, 2020, and pay interest of 4% on June 30 and December 31. The market rate of interest was 4% on January 1, 2016, so the $20,000 maturity-value bonds sold for face value. College Corporation intends to hold the bonds until maturity. Journalize the transactions related to College Corporation's investment in Small Town bonds during 2016.

**Check your answers online in MyAccounting Lab or at http://www.pearsonhighered.com/Horngren.**

For more practice, see Short Exercise S10-2. MyAccountingLab

## HOW ARE INVESTMENTS IN EQUITY SECURITIES ACCOUNTED FOR?

**Learning Objective 3**
Account for investments in equity securities

The accounting for equity securities must be separated into three categories based on the percentage of ownership of the investor.

### Equity Securities with Less Than 20% Ownership (Cost Method)

Equity securities in which the investor owns less than 20% ownership in the voting stock of the investee can be either trading investments or available-for-sale investments. Accounting for these types of equity securities is similar to accounting for debt securities. The main difference, though, is that equity securities earn *dividend* revenue instead of *interest* revenue. In the example below, we illustrate the accounting for available-for-sale investments. Trading investments would be recorded in a similar manner.

#### Purchase of Equity Securities

Assume Smart Touch Learning has excess cash to invest and buys 1,000 shares of stock in Yellow Corporation for $26.16 per share on March 1, 2016. Smart Touch Learning owns less than 20% of Yellow's voting stock and intends to hold the stock for two years. This is an available-for-sale investment, which Smart Touch Learning records as follows:

| A↑↓ | = | L + E |
|---|---|---|
| LT Investments↑<br>Cash↓ | | |

| Date | Accounts and Explanation | Debit | Credit |
|---|---|---|---|
| 2016 | | | |
| Mar. 1 | Long-term Investments—Available-for-Sale ($26.16 per share × 1,000 shares) | 26,160 | |
| | Cash | | 26,160 |
| | *Purchased investment in stock.* | | |

### Dividend Revenue

Yellow Corporation declares and pays a cash dividend of $0.16 per share on June 9, 2016. Smart Touch Learning will receive the cash dividend on June 9 and record the entry as follows:

| Date | Accounts and Explanation | Debit | Credit |
|---|---|---|---|
| 2016 | | | |
| Jun. 9 | Cash | 160 | |
| | Dividend Revenue ($0.16 per share × 1,000 shares) | | 160 |
| | *Received cash dividend.* | | |

| A↑ | = | L | + | E↑ |
|---|---|---|---|---|
| Cash↑ | | | | Dividend Revenue↑ |

### Disposition

Assume on July 15, 2016, Smart Touch Learning sells 800 shares of Yellow Stock for $25,000. Smart Touch Learning compares the cash received with the cost of the stock disposed of and determines the amount of gain or loss as follows:

| | |
|---|---|
| Cash received | $ 25,000 |
| Less: Cost of stock disposed of (800 shares × $26.16) | 20,928 |
| Gain or (Loss) | $ 4,072 |

Smart Touch Learning will then record the following journal entry:

| Date | Accounts and Explanation | Debit | Credit |
|---|---|---|---|
| 2016 | | | |
| Jul. 15 | Cash | 25,000 | |
| | Long-term Investments—Available-for-Sale | | 20,928 |
| | Gain on Disposal | | 4,072 |
| | *Disposed of investment in stock.* | | |

| A↑ | = | L | + | E↑ |
|---|---|---|---|---|
| Cash↑<br>LT Investments↓ | | | | Gain on Disposal↑ |

Remember that Gain on Disposal is a temporary equity account and is reported in the Other Revenues and (Expenses) section of the income statement. If the company had sold the stock at a loss, the account Loss on Disposal would be recorded as a debit and also reported in the Other Revenues and (Expenses) section of the income statement.

### Equity Securities with 20% to 50% Ownership (Equity Method)

When a company invests in equity securities with 20% to 50% ownership in the investee's voting stock, the investor can *significantly influence* the investee's decisions. This influence may be helpful if the investee's and investor's businesses are somehow related. These types of investments must be accounted for using the equity method.

## Purchase

Investments accounted for by the equity method are recorded at cost at the time of purchase. Suppose Smart Touch Learning pays $400,000 to purchase 40% of the common stock of Kline, Inc. Smart Touch Learning then refers to Kline as an *affiliated company*. Smart Touch Learning's entry to record the purchase of this investment on January 6, 2016, follows:

A↑↓ = L + E
LT Investments↑
Cash↓

| Date | Accounts and Explanation | Debit | Credit |
|---|---|---|---|
| 2016 | | | |
| Jan. 6 | Long-term Investments—Kline, Inc. | 400,000 | |
| | Cash | | 400,000 |
| | *Purchased investment in stock (equity method).* | | |

## Dividends Received and Share of Net Income

When Smart Touch Learning receives cash dividends from Kline, it records its proportionate part of the cash dividends. Suppose that Kline declares and pays a cash dividend of $50,000 on June 30, 2016. Because Smart Touch Learning owns 40% of the stock, it receives 40%, or $20,000, of the dividend. Smart Touch Learning receives this dividend and makes the following journal entry:

A↑↓ = L + E
Cash↑
LT Investments↓

| Date | Accounts and Explanation | Debit | Credit |
|---|---|---|---|
| 2016 | | | |
| Jun. 30 | Cash ($40,000 × 0.40) | 20,000 | |
| | Long-term Investments—Kline, Inc. | | 20,000 |
| | *Received cash dividend (equity method).* | | |

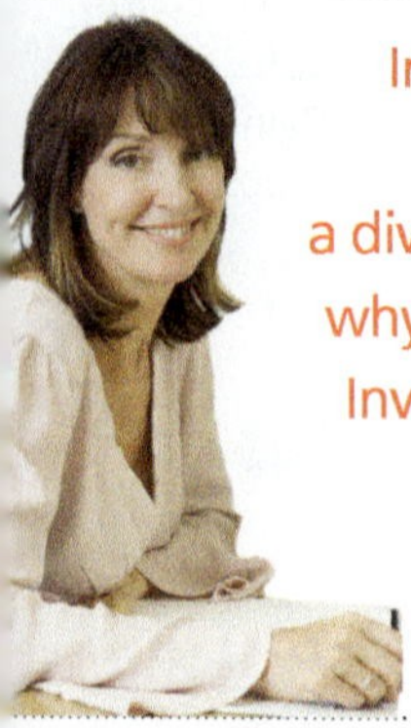

In using the equity method, when a dividend is received, why is the Long-term Investments account credited instead of Dividend Revenue?

**The Long-term Investments account is credited for the receipt of a dividend because it decreases the investor's investment.** In other words, the dividends are treated as if they were a return of capital rather than as earnings.

Under the equity method, the investor also must record annually its share of the investee's net income. The investor debits the Long-term Investments account and credits Revenue from Investments when the investee reports income. As Smart Touch Learning's equity in Kline increases, so does the Long-term Investments account on the investor's books.

Suppose Kline reported net income of $125,000 for the 2016 year. Smart Touch Learning would record 40% of this amount as an increase in the investment account, as follows:

A↑ = L + E↑
LT Investments↑
Revenue from Investments↑

| Date | Accounts and Explanation | Debit | Credit |
|---|---|---|---|
| 2016 | | | |
| Dec. 31 | Long-term Investments—Kline, Inc. | 50,000 | |
| | Revenue from Investments ($125,000 × 0.40) | | 50,000 |
| | *Recorded revenue earned from investment (equity method).* | | |

After the preceding entries are posted, Smart Touch Learning's Long-term Investments T-account shows its equity in the net assets of Kline as follows:

**Long-term Investments—Kline, Inc.**

| | | | |
|---|---|---|---|
| Jan. 6 | 400,000 | 20,000 | Jun. 30 |
| Dec. 31 | 50,000 | | |
| Bal. | 430,000 | | |

Smart Touch Learning would report the long-term investment on the balance sheet and the revenue from investments on the income statement.

### Disposition

When Smart Touch Learning decides to sell its investment in Kline, Inc. it will need to determine whether there is a gain or loss. Suppose Smart Touch Learning sells 10% of the Kline common stock for $40,000 on January 1, 2017. Smart Touch Learning will calculate the gain or loss as follows and record the following journal entry:

| | |
|---|---|
| Cash received | $ 40,000 |
| Less: Book value on date of disposal ($430,000 × 0.10) | 43,000 |
| Gain or (Loss) | $ (3,000) |

| Date | Accounts and Explanation | Debit | Credit |
|---|---|---|---|
| 2017 | | | |
| Jan. 1 | Cash | 40,000 | |
| | Loss on Disposal | 3,000 | |
| | Long-term Investments—Kline, Inc. | | 43,000 |
| | *Disposed of part of investment in stock (equity method).* | | |

A↓ = L + E↓

Cash↑, LT Investments↓ = Loss on Disposal↑

## DECISIONS

### Should the business purchase more stock?

Bath Corporation currently owns 15% of Body Co. Bath has the opportunity to purchase additional shares of stock in Body Co., which would bring Bath's ownership percentage to 25%. Bath Corporation is considering the investment because the purchase would allow Bath Corporation to have some influence over Body, but Bath is not sure about the accounting implications. What should Bath do?

### Solution

If Bath Corporation purchases the additional shares of stock in Body Co., the business will now own from 20% to 50% of Body Co. This is considered significant influence and changes the way the Bath Corporation must account for the investment. If the Bath Corporation investment remains at 15%, the business would record the investment at cost. Any dividends earned would be recorded as dividend revenue. However, if Bath Corporation purchases the additional shares in Body Co., the business would account for the investment using the equity method. The investment would still be recorded initially at cost, but any dividends received would decrease the value of the investment. Also, Bath Corporation would be required to report its share (25%) of Body Co.'s earnings as revenue. Bath Corporation should consider whether the influence gained is worth the additional recording requirements.

**Parent Company**
A company that owns a controlling interest in another company.

**Subsidiary Company**
A company that is controlled by another corporation.

**Consolidation Accounting**
The way to combine the financial statements of two or more companies that have the same owners.

**Consolidated Statements**
Financial statements that combine the balance sheets, income statements, and statements of cash flow of the parent company with those of its controlling interest affiliates.

### Equity Securities with More Than 50% Ownership (Consolidations)

Many large corporations own controlling interests in other companies. An investor owns a controlling interest when the investor owns more than 50% of the investee's voting stock. This type of investment enables the investor to elect a majority of the board of directors and thereby control the investee. The corporation that controls the other company is called the **parent company**, and the company that is controlled by another corporation is called the **subsidiary company**.

In equity securities with more than 50% ownership, the parent usually prepares consolidated financial statements. **Consolidation accounting** is the way to combine the financial statements of two or more companies that have the same owners. Many published financial reports include consolidated statements. **Consolidated statements** combine the financial statements (such as the balance sheets, income statements, and statements of cash flow) of the parent company with those of its controlling interest affiliates. The final outcome is a single set of statements, as if the parent and its subsidiaries were the same entity. This topic is covered in advanced accounting courses.

**Try It!**

7. On May 15, 2016, Mayer Co. invests $8,000 in John, Inc. stock. John pays Mayer a $200 dividend on November 15, 2016. Mayer sells the John stock on December 10, 2016, for $7,500. Assume the investment is categorized as long-term available-for-sale. Journalize the 2016 transactions related to Mayer's investment in John stock.

**Check your answers online in MyAccountingLab or at http://www.pearsonhighered.com/Horngren.**

For more practice, see Short Exercises S10-3 and S10-4. MyAccountingLab

## HOW ARE DEBT AND EQUITY SECURITIES REPORTED?

**Learning Objective 4**
Describe and illustrate how debt and equity securities are reported

Corporations' debt and equity securities are reported on the balance sheet in either the current or the long-term asset section. How they are reported, though, depends upon the type of investment and ownership percentage.

### Trading Investments

**Fair Value**
The price that would be used if the investments were sold on the market.

Trading investments, those that the investor plans to sell in the very near future, are initially recorded at cost. At the end of each period, though, trading securities must be adjusted and reported at fair value. **Fair value** is the price that would be used if the company were to sell the investments on the market. The company will make a year-end adjustment of the trading investment to bring the account to market value. This adjustment is recorded as an unrealized holding gain or loss and is reported in the Other Revenues and (Expenses) section of the income statement.

*It's important to note the distinction between unrealized and realized gains or losses. Unrealized gains or losses occur when a company adjusts an asset to fair value but has not yet disposed of the asset. Realized gains or losses occur when a company disposes of an asset and represents the difference between the cash received at time of disposal and the basis of the asset.*

Suppose that on December 31, 2016, Smart Touch Learning reported trading investments of $26,160. After careful evaluation, Smart Touch Learning concluded that the market value of the trading investments had decreased to $24,000. The company has an unrealized loss of $2,160 on the investments ($24,000 − $26,160). At year-end, Smart Touch Learning would record the following adjusting entry:

| Date | Accounts and Explanation | Debit | Credit |
|---|---|---|---|
| 2016 | | | |
| Dec. 31 | Unrealized Holding Loss—Trading | 2,160 | |
| | Fair Value Adjustment —Trading | | 2,160 |
| | *Adjusted trading investments to market value.* | | |

**A↓** = **L** + **E↓**

Fair Value Adjustment↓ = Unrealized Holding Loss↑

After the adjustment, the investment T-accounts would appear as follows:

| Short-term Investments—Trading | |
|---|---|
| Bal. 26,160 | |

| Fair Value Adjustment—Trading | |
|---|---|
| | 2,160 Dec. 31 |

$26,160 − $2,160 = $24,000

*In this case, the Fair Value Adjustment account is considered a contra account and is subtracted from the Short-term Investments account to determine carrying value when it has a credit balance. If the account has a debit balance, it is considered an adjunct account and is added to the Short-term Investments account to determine carrying value.*

The combined T-accounts show the $24,000 balance for trading investments. Smart Touch Learning would report its trading investments on the balance sheet at $24,000 at December 31, 2016, and the $2,160 unrealized holding loss on the trading investments on the 2016 income statement as follows:

**SMART TOUCH LEARNING**
**Balance Sheet (Partial)**
**December 31, 2016**

| | |
|---|---|
| Current Assets: | |
| Short-term Investments—Trading (at fair value; cost $26,160) | $ 24,000 |

**SMART TOUCH LEARNING**
**Income Statement (Partial)**
**For the Year Ended December 31, 2016**

| | |
|---|---|
| Other Revenues and (Expenses): | |
| Unrealized Holding Loss—Trading | $ (2,160) |

### Disposition

When a trading security is disposed, the fair value adjustment is ignored in determining the calculation of the gain or loss. The disposition is handled as we have shown earlier in the chapter. The amount of gain or loss is calculated as the difference between the cash received and the cost of the stock disposed. At the end of the year, the company would evaluate their remaining trading security investments and make a year-end adjustment to current market value.

## Available-for-Sale Investments

Available-for-sale (AFS) investments are reported as *current assets* on the balance sheet if the business expects to sell them within one year. All other AFS investments that are planned to be held longer than a year are reported as *long-term assets* on the balance sheet. The fair value method is also used to account for AFS investments because they are normally sold in the near future at their current market value.

AFS investments are reported on the balance sheet at current market value. This requires a year-end adjustment of the AFS investment to current market value, much like the treatment of trading investments. However, the unrealized holding gains and losses on AFS investments are not reported on the income statement. They are recorded as an adjustment to the Unrealized Holding Gain—Available-for-Sale account or Unrealized Holding Loss—Available-for-Sale account, which is included in Other Comprehensive Income on the Statement of Comprehensive Income and as a component of Accumulated Other Comprehensive Income in the stockholders' equity section of the balance sheet. Assume on December 31, 2016, Smart Touch Learning reported long-term available-for-sale investments of $60,000. After careful review, the company determines the market value of the AFS investments has increased to $64,000. Smart Touch Learning has an unrealized holding gain of $4,000 on the investment ($64,000 market value minus $60,000 purchase price). At year-end, Smart Touch Learning would make the following adjustment:

| A↑ | = | L | + | E↑ |
|---|---|---|---|---|
| Fair Value Adjustment↑ | | | | Unrealized Holding Gain↑ |

| Date | Accounts and Explanation | Debit | Credit |
|---|---|---|---|
| 2016 | | | |
| Dec. 31 | Fair Value Adjustment—Available-for-Sale | 4,000 | |
| | Unrealized Holding Gain—Available-for-Sale | | 4,000 |
| | *Adjusted available-for-sale investments to market value.* | | |

After posting the December 31, 2016, adjustment, the investment T-accounts would appear as follows:

**Long-term Investments—AFS**

| | | |
|---|---|---|
| Bal. | 60,000 | |

**Fair Value Adjustment—AFS**

| | | |
|---|---|---|
| Dec. 31 | 4,000 | |

$60,000 + $4,000 = $64,000

The combined T-accounts show the $64,000 balance for the AFS investments. Smart Touch Learning would report the investment on the balance sheet at $64,000 at December 31, 2016. The $4,000 Unrealized Holding Gain—Available-for-Sale would be reported in the stockholders' equity section of the balance sheet as Accumulated Other Comprehensive Income as shown here:

| SMART TOUCH LEARNING<br>Balance Sheet (Partial)<br>December 31, 2016 | |
|---|---|
| **Assets** | |
| Long-term Assets: | |
| Long-term Investments—AFS (at fair value; cost $60,000) | $ 64,000 |
| **Stockholders' Equity** | |
| Accumulated Other Comprehensive Income: | |
| Unrealized Holding Gain—AFS | $ 4,000 |

It's important to remember that unrealized holding gains or losses on available-for-sale investments are not included in net income. Instead, they are included as other comprehensive income, which are adjustments to net income to determine comprehensive income. **Comprehensive income** is the company's change in total stockholders' equity from all sources other than owners' investments and dividends. Comprehensive income includes net income plus some specific gains and losses, as follows:

**Comprehensive Income**
A company's change in total stockholders' equity from all sources other than owners' investments and dividends.

- Unrealized holding gains or losses on *available-for-sale investments*
- Foreign currency translation adjustments
- Gains or losses from post-retirement benefit plans
- Deferred gains or losses from derivatives

The calculation of these items is explained in advanced accounting courses. For now, you need to know that these items do not enter into the determination of net income but, instead, are reported as other comprehensive income.

Comprehensive income can be reported one of two ways: as a second income statement or combined with a traditional income statement into a combined statement of comprehensive income. An example of how comprehensive income can be reported is shown in Exhibit 10-2.

**Exhibit 10-2 | Comprehensive Income**

| SMART TOUCH LEARNING<br>Comprehensive Income Statement<br>For the Year Ended December 31, 2016 | |
|---|---|
| Net Income | $ 100,000 |
| Other Comprehensive Income: | |
| Unrealized Holding Gain—AFS | 4,000 |
| Comprehensive Income | $ 104,000 |

## Disposition

It is important to note that disposition of available-for-sale investments is handled in the same manner as trading securities. Any prior period fair value adjustment is ignored when calculating the amount of the gain or loss. The gain or loss is determined as the difference between the amount received and the cost of the investment. At the end of the year, the company would evaluate their remaining available-for-sale investments and make a year-end adjustment to current market value.

## Held-to-Maturity Investments

Held-to-maturity (HTM) investments are normally reported at amortized cost, which is explained in advanced accounting courses. Depending on the maturity date, the HTM investment will be reported as a current asset or a long-term asset on the balance sheet. When the maturity date is within one year of the balance sheet date, the HTM investment is reported as a current asset; otherwise, the asset is reported as long-term. Interest revenue earned on HTM investments is reported on the income statement in the Other Revenues and (Expenses) section.

Exhibit 10-3 summarizes the accounting methods for debt and equity securities and also the financial statement effects.

**Exhibit 10-3** | **Debt and Equity Securities—Accounting Methods and Financial Statement Effects**

| Types of Investments | Accounting Methods | Financial Statement Effects | |
|---|---|---|---|
| | | Balance Sheet | Income Statement |
| **Trading Investments** | Fair Value: Unrealized Holding Gain or Loss is included in net income. | The investment is reported as a current asset on the balance sheet. | Dividend or interest revenue is reported on the income statement. |
| **Held-to-Maturity Investments** | Amortized Cost | Depending on the maturity date, the investment is reported as a current or long-term asset on the balance sheet. | Interest revenue is reported on the income statement. |
| **Available-for-Sale Investments** | Fair Value: Unrealized Holding Gain or Loss is included in Other Comprehensive Income and reported as a separate component of stockholders' equity. | The investment is reported as a current or long-term asset on the balance sheet depending on management's intent. | Dividend or interest revenue is reported on the income statement. |
| **Significant Interest Investments** | Equity | The investment is reported as a long-term asset on the balance sheet. | A percentage share of investee's net income is reported on the income statement. |
| **Controlling Interest Investments** | Consolidation | The balance sheets of the parent and subsidiary are combined. | The income statements of the parent and subsidiary are combined. |

## Try It!

8. On August 20, 2016, Mraz, Co. decides to invest excess cash of $2,500 by purchasing 500 shares of Virginia, Inc. stock at $5 per share. At year-end, December 31, 2016, Virginia's market price was $4 per share. The investment is categorized as available-for-sale. Journalize the adjusting entry needed at December 31, 2016.

**Check your answer online in MyAccountingLab or at http://www.pearsonhighered.com/Horngren.**

For more practice, see Short Exercises S10-5 and S10-6. MyAccountingLab

## HOW DO WE USE THE RATE OF RETURN ON TOTAL ASSETS TO EVALUATE BUSINESS PERFORMANCE?

**Learning Objective 5**

Use the rate of return on total assets to evaluate business performance

The **rate of return on total assets**, or simply return on assets, measures a company's success in using assets to earn a profit. There are two ways that a company can finance its assets:

- Debt—A company can borrow money from creditors to purchase assets. Creditors earn interest on the money that is loaned.
- Equity—A company may receive cash or other assets from stockholders. Stockholders invest in the company and hope to receive a return on their investment.

**Rate of Return on Total Assets**
A ratio that measures the success a company has in using its assets to earn income. (Net income + Interest expense) / Average total assets.

Rate of return on total assets is calculated by adding interest expense to net income and dividing by average total assets. Interest expense is added back to net income to determine the real return on the assets regardless of the corporation's financing choices (debt or equity).

Using **Green Mountain Coffee Roasters, Inc.'s** Fiscal 2013 Annual Report, we can determine its rate of return on total assets. Net income and interest expense are taken from the company's income statement, and total assets is taken from the balance sheet as follows (in thousands):

| | |
|---|---|
| Total Assets, September 28, 2013 | $ 3,761,548 |
| Total Assets, September 29, 2012 | 3,615,789 |
| For Year Ended September 28, 2013: | |
| Interest Expense | 18,177 |
| Net Income | 483,232 |

The rate of return on total assets is calculated as:

Rate of return on total assets = (Net income + Interest expense) / Average total assets
= ($483,232 + $18,177) / [($3,761,548 + $3,615,789) / 2]
= 0.14 = 14%

Green Mountain Coffee Roasters, Inc. has a rate of return on total assets of 14%, which means that for each $1.00 invested in the company's average assets, the company earned $0.14 in profits before considering interest expense. What is a good rate of return on total assets? There is no single answer because rates of return vary widely by industry. Suppose that for the coffee and tea manufacturing industry, an 8% rate of return on total assets is considered good. In that case, Green Mountain's 14% return on assets would be considered very good because it is well above the industry average.

## Try It!

**9.** Lee Co. reported the following items on its 2016 financial statements:

| | |
|---|---|
| Total Assets, December 31, 2016 | $ 10,000 |
| Total Assets, December 31, 2015 | 15,000 |
| For Year Ended December 31, 2016: | |
| Interest Expense | 150 |
| Net Income | 850 |

Determine Lee's rate of return on total assets for 2016.

**Check your answer online in MyAccountingLab or at http://www.pearsonhighered.com/Horngren.**

For more practice, see Short Exercise S10-7. MyAccountingLab

# REVIEW

## > Things You Should Know

### 1. Why do companies invest?

- Companies invest in debt or equity securities to generate investment income or to pursue a certain business strategy.
- A debt security represents a credit relationship with another company or governmental entity, and typically pays interest for a fixed period.
- An equity security represents stock ownership in another company and sometimes pays dividends.
- Investments are classified as either short-term or long-term investments and can be further classified into five categories:
  - Trading investments—debt securities or equity securities in which the investor holds less than 20% of the voting stock and that the investor plans to sell in the very near future
  - Held-to-maturity (HTM) investments—debt securities the investor intends to hold until they mature
  - Available-for-sale (AFS) investments—debt securities or equity securities in which the investor holds less than 20% of the voting stock and that aren't trading investments or held-to-maturity investments
  - Significant interest investments—equity securities in which the investor owns 20% to 50% of the investee's voting stock
  - Controlling interest investments—equity securities in which the investor owns more than 50% of the investee's voting stock

**2. How are investments in debt securities accounted for?**

- Investments in debt securities are recorded at cost, including any brokerage fees paid.
- The receipt of interest revenue is recorded with a debit to Cash and a credit to Interest Revenue.
- Debt securities disposed of at maturity are recorded with a debit to Cash and a credit to the Short-term or Long-term Investments account.

**3. How are investments in equity securities accounted for?**

- Equity securities with less than 20% ownership are recorded using the cost method.
    - The purchase of equity securities is recorded at cost, including any brokerage fees paid.
    - The receipt of dividend revenue is recorded with a debit to Cash and a credit to Dividend Revenue.
    - Equity securities disposed of could involve either a gain or loss on disposal.
- Equity securities with 20% to 50% ownership are recorded using the equity method.
    - The purchase of the equity securities is recorded at cost.
    - Dividends declared and received are recorded with a debit to Cash and a credit to Long-term Investments. A dividend reduces the investor's investment.
    - The investor's share of net income is recorded as a debit to Long-term Investments and a credit to Revenue from Investments. Net income increases the investor's investment.
    - Disposition of equity securities could involve either a gain or loss.
- Equity securities with more than 50% ownership are recorded using the consolidation method, which involves the parent company preparing consolidated statements.

**4. How are debt and equity securities reported?**

- Trading investments and available-for-sale investments are reported at fair value on the balance sheet.
    - The unrealized holding gain or loss incurred on trading investments is reported on the income statement as Other Revenues and (Expenses).
    - The unrealized holding gain or loss incurred on available-for-sale investments is not included in net income. It is, instead, reported as part of accumulated other comprehensive income included in stockholders' equity on the balance sheet.
- Held-to-maturity investments are reported at amortized cost on the balance sheet.

**5. How do we use the rate of return on total assets to evaluate business performance?**

- The rate of return on total assets measures a company's success in using its assets to earn a profit.
- (Net income + Interest expense) / Average total assets.

CHAPTER 10

## > Summary Problem 10-1

**Requirements**

1. Identify the appropriate accounting method for each of the following situations:
   a. Investment in 25% of the investee company's stock
   b. Available-for-sale investment in stock
   c. Investment in more than 50% of the investee company's stock
   d. Bond investment that matures in four years. The investor plans to hold the bond for the full four years.
2. At what amount should the following trading investment portfolio be reported on the December 31, 2016, balance sheet? All the investments represent a 5% investment in the investee's stock.

| Stock | Investment Cost | Current Market Value |
|---|---|---|
| Purple | $ 5,000 | $ 5,500 |
| Yellow | 61,200 | 53,000 |
| Black | 3,680 | 6,230 |
| Totals | $ 69,880 | $ 64,730 |

   Journalize any adjusting entry required on December 31.
3. An investor paid $67,900 on January 1, 2016, to acquire 40% of Finn-Girl, Inc.'s outstanding common stock. During the first year, Finn-Girl's net income was $80,000, and on June 14, the company declared and paid cash dividends of $55,000 to all stockholders. Journalize the investor's transactions related to the Finn-Girl investment: (a) purchase of the investment, (b) receipt of dividends, (c) investor's share of net income, and (d) sale of Finn-Girl stock for $80,100 on January 3, 2017.

## > Solutions

**Requirement 1**

a. Equity
b. Fair value
c. Consolidation
d. Amortized cost

**Requirement 2**

The trading investments should be reported at market value, $64,730, on the balance sheet. The adjusting entry required to report the investments at fair value is as follows:

| Date | Accounts and Explanation | Debit | Credit |
|---|---|---|---|
| 2016 | | | |
| Dec. 31 | Unrealized Holding Loss—Trading ($64,730 − $69,880) | 5,150 | |
| | Fair Value Adjustment—Trading | | 5,150 |
| | *Adjusted trading investments to market value.* | | |

The Unrealized Holding Loss—Trading would be reported as an Other Revenues and (Expenses) item on the income statement.

**Requirement 3**

| Date | Accounts and Explanation | Debit | Credit |
|---|---|---|---|
| 2016 | | | |
| (a) Jan. 1 | Long-term Investments—Finn-Girl, Inc. | 67,900 | |
| | Cash | | 67,900 |
| | *Purchased investment in stock (equity method).* | | |
| (b) Jun. 14 | Cash | 22,000 | |
| | Long-term Investments—Finn-Girl, Inc. ($55,000 × 0.40) | | 22,000 |
| | *Received cash dividends (equity method).* | | |
| (c) Dec. 31 | Long-term Investments—Finn-Girl, Inc. | 32,000 | |
| | Revenue from Investments ($80,000 × 0.40) | | 32,000 |
| | *Recorded revenue earned from investment (equity method).* | | |
| 2017 | | | |
| (d) Jan. 3 | Cash | 80,100 | |
| | Long-term Investments—Finn-Girl, Inc. | | 77,900 |
| | Gain on Disposal | | 2,200 |
| | *Disposed of investment in stock (equity method).* | | |

Calculations for disposal:

**Long-term Investments—Finn-Girl, Inc.**

| | | | |
|---|---|---|---|
| Jan. 1 | 67,900 | 22,000 | Jun. 14 |
| Dec. 31 | 32,000 | | |
| Bal. | 77,900 | | |

| | |
|---|---|
| Cash received | $ 80,100 |
| Less: Book value of stock disposed of | 77,900 |
| Gain or (Loss) | $ 2,200 |

## > Key Terms

**Available-for-Sale (AFS) Investment (p. 525)**
**Comprehensive Income (p. 535)**
**Consolidated Statements (p. 532)**
**Consolidation Accounting (p. 532)**
**Controlling Interest Investment (p. 526)**
**Debt Security (p. 524)**
**Equity Security (p. 524)**
**Fair Value (p. 532)**
**Held-to-Maturity (HTM) Investment (p. 525)**
**Investee (p. 524)**
**Investor (p. 524)**
**Long-term Investments (p. 525)**
**Parent Company (p. 532)**
**Rate of Return on Total Assets (p. 537)**
**Security (p. 524)**
**Short-term Investments (p. 525)**
**Significant Interest Investment (p. 526)**
**Subsidiary Company (p. 532)**
**Trading Investment (p. 525)**

CHAPTER 10

## > Quick Check

**Learning Objective 1**

1. Assume Intervale Railway is considering investing in Pale Co. stock for three months. The investment will represent 5% of the voting stock of Pale Co. How would the investment be classified?

   a. Significant interest investment
   b. Trading investment
   c. Held-to-maturity investment
   d. Controlling interest investment

**Learning Objective 1**

2. Which of the following investments is most likely classified as a held-to-maturity investment?

   a. 80% stock ownership in a subsidiary
   b. 100% ownership in voting stock of a supplier
   c. 10-year bonds
   d. None of the above

**Learning Objective 2**

3. If Intervale Railway invests $100,000 in 5% bonds at face value that the company intends to hold until the bond maturity date, the interest revenue recognized when each semiannual interest payment is received would be recorded as a

   a. credit to Cash, $2,500.
   b. credit to Interest Revenue, $2,500.
   c. debit to Long-term Investments—Held-to-Maturity, $2,500.
   d. debit to Dividend Revenue, $2,500.

**Learning Objective 3**

4. A company invested $45,000 in Yale Co. stock. The investment represented 5% of the voting stock of Yale Co. If the Yale Co. stock investment paid dividends, what account would be credited?

   a. Long-term Investments—Available-for-Sale
   b. Interest Revenue
   c. Dividend Revenue
   d. Cash

**Learning Objective 3**

5. If a company owns 25% of the voting stock of Pink Co., dividends received will be

   a. credited to Long-term Investments—Pink Co.
   b. credited to Dividend Revenue.
   c. debited to Long-term Investments—Pink Co.
   d. credited to Cash.

**Learning Objective 3**

6. Best Appliances owns 90% of the voting stock of Wratchet, Inc. Which of the following is true?

   a. The financial statements of Best would be consolidated into Wratchet.
   b. Wratchet would be considered the parent entity.
   c. Best would be considered the parent entity.
   d. Both a and c are correct.

**Learning Objective 4**

7. Yale Co. purchased an available-for-sale stock investment on October 4 of the current year for $45,000. The market value of the stock investment at year-end is $42,000. What value will be reported in net income for the adjustment, if any?
   a. $42,000
   b. $0
   c. $(3,000)
   d. Not enough information is given to determine the amount included in net income.

**Learning Objective 4**

8. Harvard Co. purchased a trading investment on December 1 of the current year for $30,000. The market value of the stock investment at year-end is $36,000. What value will be reported in net income for the adjustment, if any?
   a. $36,000
   b. $(6,000)
   c. $6,000
   d. $30,000

**Learning Objective 4**

9. Bendi Corp. purchased 1,000 shares of Kala Corp. for $16 per share. The investment represents 5% ownership, and Bendi holds the investment as an available-for-sale investment. The fair value at year-end is $15 per share. Assuming no other transactions occurred where would the $1 per share difference be reported on the year-end financial statements?
   a. Retained Earnings
   b. Other Comprehensive Income
   c. Unrealized Holding Gain—AFS
   d. Both b and c are correct.

**Learning Objective 5**

10. Panjab Company reported the following information on its financial statements

| | |
|---|---|
| Total Assets, December 31, 2016 | $ 400,000 |
| Total Assets, December 31, 2017 | 440,000 |
| For Year Ended December 31, 2017: | |
| Interest Expense | 2,000 |
| Net Income | 40,000 |

What is Panjab's rate of return on total assets?
   a. 10.0%
   b. 9.5%
   c. 10.5%
   d. None of the above

**Check your answers at the end of the chapter.**

CHAPTER 10

# ASSESS YOUR PROGRESS

## > Review Questions

1. What is a debt security?
2. What is an equity security?
3. Why would a company invest in debt or equity securities?
4. Briefly describe the five specific types of debt and equity securities.
5. How is the purchase of a held-to-maturity debt security at face value recorded?
6. When disposing of an available-for-sale investment, where is the gain or loss on disposal reported in the financial statements?
7. What method is used for investments in equity securities with 20% to 50% ownership? Briefly describe how dividends declared and received and share of net income are reported.
8. What method is used for investments in equity securities with more than 50% ownership? Briefly describe this method.
9. What adjustment must be made at the end of the period for trading investments and available-for-sale investments?
10. Where on the financial statements is an unrealized holding gain or loss on trading investments reported?
11. Where on the financial statements is an unrealized holding gain or loss on available-for-sale investments reported?
12. What is comprehensive income, and what does it include?
13. How are held-to-maturity investments reported on the financial statements?
14. What does the rate of return on total assets measure, and how is it calculated?

## > Short Exercises

**Learning Objective 1**

### S10-1 Identifying why companies invest and classifying investments

Garden Haven has excess cash of $15,000 at the end of the harvesting season. Garden Haven will need this cash in four months for normal operations.

**Requirements**

1. What are some reasons why Garden Haven may choose to invest in debt or equity securities?
2. What type of classification would Garden Haven's investment fall within—short-term or long-term? Why?

**Learning Objective 2**

### S10-2 Accounting for held-to-maturity investments

On January 1, 2016, the Warden's Restaurant decides to invest in Lake Turner bonds. The bonds mature on December 31, 2030, and pay interest on June 30 and December 31 at 5% annually. The market rate of interest was 5% on January 1, 2016, so the $150,000 maturity value bonds sold for face value. Warden's intends to hold the bonds until December 31, 2030.

**Requirements**

1. Journalize the transactions related to Warden's investment in Lake Turner bonds during 2016.
2. In what category would Warden's report the investment on the December 31, 2016, balance sheet?

### S10-3 Accounting for trading investments

**Learning Objective 3**

On January 1, 2016, Maple Company invests $16,000 in Sprouts, Inc. stock. Sprouts pays Maple a $300 dividend on August 1, 2016. Maple sells the Sprouts's stock on August 31, 2016, for $16,500. Assume the investment is categorized as a trading investment.

**Requirements**

1. Journalize the transactions for Maple's investment in Sprouts's stock.
2. What was the net effect of the investment on Maple's net income for the year ended December 31, 2016?

### S10-4 Accounting for equity method

**Learning Objective 3**

On January 1, 2016, Staub, Inc. decides to invest in 11,700 shares of Horsepasture stock when the stock is selling for $12 per share. On August 1, 2016, Horsepasture paid a $0.30 per share cash dividend to stockholders. On December 31, 2016, Horsepasture reports net income of $60,000 for 2016. Assume Horsepasture has 26,000 shares of voting stock outstanding during 2016.

**Requirements**

1. Identify what type of investment the Horsepasture stock is for Staub.
2. Journalize the transactions related to Staub's investment in the Horsepasture stock during 2016.
3. In what category and at what value would Staub's report the investment on the December 31, 2016, balance sheet?

### S10-5 Accounting for trading investments

**Learning Objectives 3, 4**

On February 1, 2016, Lee Co. decides to invest excess cash of $21,000 by purchasing 1,400 shares of Hart, Inc. stock at $15 per share. At year-end, December 31, 2016, Hart's market price was $19 per share. The investment is categorized as a trading investment.

**Requirements**

1. Journalize the transactions for Lee's investment in Hart, Inc. for 2016.
2. In what category and at what value would Lee report the asset on the December 31, 2016, balance sheet? In what account would the market price change in Hart's stock be reported, if at all?
3. What was the net effect of the investment on Lee's net income for the year ended December 31, 2016?

### S10-6 Accounting for available-for-sale investments

**Learning Objectives 3, 4**

On June 1, 2016, Rick's Restaurant decides to invest excess cash of $41,800 from the tourist season by purchasing 2,200 shares of Bison, Inc. stock at $19 per share. At year-end, December 31, 2016, Bison's market price was $15 per share. The investment is categorized as an available-for-sale investment and will be held for the short-term.

CHAPTER 10

**Requirements**

1. Journalize the transactions for Rick's investment in Bison, Inc. for 2016.
2. In what category and at what value would Rick report the asset on the December 31, 2016, balance sheet? In what account would the market price change in Bison's stock be reported, if at all?
3. What was the net effect of the investment on Rick's net income for the year ended December 31, 2016?

**Learning Objective 5**

### S10-7 Computing rate of return on total assets

Kabra's 2016 financial statements reported the following items—with 2015 figures given for comparison:

| KABRA, INC.<br>Balance Sheet<br>As of December 31, 2016 and 2015 | | |
|---|---|---|
| | **2016** | **2015** |
| Total Assets | **$ 27,730** | **$ 33,710** |
| Total Liabilities | 12,500 | 15,910 |
| Total Stockholders' Equity (all common) | 15,230 | 17,800 |
| Total Liabilities and Stockholders' Equity | **$ 27,730** | **$ 33,710** |

Net income for 2016 was $4,020, and interest expense was $160. Compute Kabra's rate of return on total assets for 2016. (Round to the nearest percent.)

## > Exercises

**Learning Objective 2**

1. Jun. 30 Int. Rev. CR $2,250

### E10-8 Accounting for bond investments

Bennett purchased a bond on January 1, 2016, for $150,000. The bond has a face value of $150,000 and matures in 15 years. The bond pays interest on June 30 and December 31 at a 3% annual rate. Bennett plans on holding the investment until maturity.

**Requirements**

1. Journalize the 2016 transactions related to Bennett's bond investment. Explanations are not required.
2. Journalize the transaction related to Bennett's disposition of the bond at maturity. Determine the date. (Assume the last interest payment has already been recorded.) Explanations are not required.

**Learning Objective 2**

2. $32,000

### E10-9 Accounting for bond investments

League Up & Co. owns vast amounts of corporate bonds. Suppose League Up buys $800,000 of CocoCorp bonds at face value on January 2, 2016. The CocoCorp bonds pay interest at the annual rate of 4% on June 30 and December 31 and mature on December 31, 2033. League Up intends to hold the investment until maturity.

**Requirements**

1. Journalize any required 2016 entries for the bond investment.
2. How much cash interest will League Up receive each year from CocoCorp?
3. How much interest revenue will League Up report during 2016 on this bond investment?

## E10-10 Accounting for bond investments

**Learning Objective 2**

2a. Int. Rev. CR $18,000

Otter Creek & Co. owns vast amounts of corporate bonds. Suppose Otter Creek buys $1,200,000 of RoastCo bonds at face value on January 2, 2016. The RoastCo bonds pay interest at the annual rate of 3% on June 30 and December 31 and mature on December 31, 2020. Otter Creek intends to hold the investment until maturity.

**Requirements**

1. How would the bond investment be classified on Otter Creek's December 31, 2016, balance sheet?
2. Journalize the following on Otter Creek's books:
   a. Receipt of final interest payment on December 31, 2020
   b. Disposal of the investment at maturity on December 31, 2020

## E10-11 Accounting for stock investments

**Learning Objectives 3, 4**

1. Dec. 31 Unrealized Holding Loss—AFS DR $1,000

Dollar Bill Investments completed these long-term, available-for-sale investment transactions during 2016:

| | |
|---|---|
| Jan. 14 | Purchased 200 shares of Microscape stock, paying $52 per share. The investment represents 4% ownership in Microscape's voting stock. Dollar Bill intends to hold the investment for the indefinite future. |
| Aug. 22 | Received a cash dividend of $0.79 per share on the Microscape stock. |
| Dec. 31 | Adjusted the investment to its current market value of $47 per share. |
| 31 | Microscape reported net income of $400,000 for the year ended 2016. |

**Requirements**

1. Journalize Dollar Bill's investment transactions. Explanations are not required.
2. Classify and prepare partial financial statements for Dollar Bill's Microscape investment as of December 31, 2016. Assume Dollar Bill Investments' net income for the year is $40,000.

## E10-12 Accounting for stock investments

**Learning Objectives 3, 4**

2. Long-term Investments—AFS CR $37,600

Strategic Investments completed the following long-term, available-for-sale investment transactions during 2016:

| | |
|---|---|
| Jan. 14 | Purchased 800 shares of Voltexar stock, paying $47 per share. The investment represents 4% ownership in Voltexar's voting stock. Strategic intends to hold the investment for the indefinite future. |
| Aug. 22 | Received a cash dividend of $0.89 per share on the Voltexar stock. |
| Dec. 31 | Adjusted the Voltexar investment to its current market value of $46. |

On August 4, 2017, Strategic Investments sold its investment in Voltexar stock for $43 per share.

CHAPTER 10

**Requirements**

1. Journalize the entries for 2016. Explanations are not required.
2. Journalize the sale that occurred in 2017. Explanations are not required.
3. What account(s) and amount(s), if any, would be reported on Strategic's income statement for the year ended December 31, 2017?

**Learning Objective 3**

1. Revenue from Investments CR $82,500

### E10-13 Accounting for stock investments

Green Back Investments completed the following transactions during 2016:

| | |
|---|---|
| Jan. 14 | Purchased 1,200 shares of Sysky stock, paying $46 per share. The investment represents 25% ownership in Sysky's voting stock. Green Back intends to hold the investment for the indefinite future. |
| Aug. 22 | Received a cash dividend of $0.34 per share on the Sysky stock. |
| Dec. 31 | Sysky's current market value is $44 per share. |
| 31 | Sysky reported net income of $330,000 for the year ended 2016. |

**Requirements**

1. Journalize Green Back's transactions. Explanations are not required.
2. Classify and prepare partial financial statements for Green Back's 25% Sysky investment for the year ended December 31, 2016.



**Learning Objective 3**

3. $358,000,000 Bal.

### E10-14 Accounting for stock investments

Suppose that on January 6, 2016, Westfall Motors paid $360,000,000 for its 40% investment in Phase Motors. Assume Phase earned net income of $20,000,000 and paid cash dividends of $25,000,000 to all outstanding stockholders during 2016. (Assume all outstanding stock is voting stock.)

**Requirements**

1. What method should Westfall Motors use to account for the investment in Phase Motors? Give your reasoning.
2. Journalize all required 2016 transactions related to Westfall Motors's Phase investment. Include an explanation for each entry.
3. Post all 2016 transactions to the investment T-account. What is its balance after all the transactions are posted? How would this balance be classified on the balance sheet dated December 31, 2016?

**Learning Objectives 1, 3, 4**

1. Dec. 31 Fair Value Adjustment—Trading CR $1,100

### E10-15 Classifying and accounting for stock investments

Hartford Today Publishers completed the following trading investment transactions during 2016 and 2017:

| | |
|---|---|
| **2016** | |
| Dec. 6 | Purchased 1,100 shares of Golden stock at a price of $22.00 per share, intending to sell the investment next month. |
| 23 | Received a cash dividend of $1.10 per share on the Golden stock. |
| 31 | Adjusted the investment to its market value of $21.00 per share. |
| **2017** | |
| Jan. 27 | Sold the Golden stock for $21.60 per share. |

**Requirements**

1. Journalize Hartford Today's investment transactions. Explanations are not required.
2. On December 31, 2016, how would the Golden stock be classified and at what value would it be reported on the balance sheet?

### E10-16 Computing rate of return on total assets

**Learning Objective 5**

Avg. total assets $315,000,000

Winter Exploration Company reported these figures for 2016 and 2015:

| **Income Statement—partial:** | **2016** | **2015** |
|---|---|---|
| Interest Expense | $ 15,600,000 | $ 17,800,000 |
| Net Income | 21,600,000 | 19,600,000 |
| **Balance Sheet—partial:** | **Dec. 31, 2016** | **Dec. 31, 2015** |
| Total Assets | $ 318,000,000 | $ 312,000,000 |

Compute the rate of return on total assets for 2016. (Round to two decimals.)

## > Problems Group A

### P10-17A Accounting for bond investments

**Learning Objective 2**

1. Dec. 31 Int. Rev. CR $15,750

Suppose Jenner and Sons purchases $700,000 of 4.5% annual bonds of McPhee Corporation at face value on January 1, 2016. These bonds pay interest on June 30 and December 31 each year. They mature on December 31, 2020. Jenner intends to hold the McPhee bond investment until maturity.

**Requirements**

1. Journalize Jenner and Sons's transactions related to the bonds for 2016.
2. Journalize the entry required on the McPhee bonds maturity date. (Assume the last interest payment has already been recorded.)

### P10-18A Classifying and accounting for stock investments

**Learning Objectives 1, 3, 4**

2. Sep. 16 Gain on Disposal CR $12,920

Mail 4 You Corporation generated excess cash and invested in securities as follows:

| **2016** | |
|---|---|
| Jul. 2 | Purchased 3,400 shares of Bravo, Inc. common stock at $11.00 per share. Mail 4 You holds the stock in its active trading account and plans to sell the stock within three months, when the company will need the cash for normal operations. |
| Aug. 21 | Received a cash dividend of $0.30 per share on the Bravo stock investment. |
| Sep. 16 | Sold the Bravo stock for $14.80 per share. |
| Oct. 8 | Purchased 400 shares of Zigbo stock at $15.00 per share. The stock is held in the active trading account as Mail 4 You plans to hold the Zigbo stock for less than five months. |
| Dec. 31 | Zigbo stock's current market price is $5.00 per share. |

**Requirements**

1. Classify each of the investments made during 2016. (Assume the investments represent less than 20% of ownership of outstanding voting stock.)
2. Journalize the 2016 transactions. Explanations are not required.
3. Prepare T-accounts for the investment assets, and show how to report the investments on Mail 4 You's balance sheet at December 31, 2016.

**Learning Objectives 3, 4**

1. Dec. 31 Fair Value Adjustment—AFS DR $36,000

### P10-19A Accounting for stock investments

The beginning balance sheet of Desk Source Co. included an $850,000 investment in Parson stock (20% ownership). During the year, Desk Source completed the following investment transactions:

| | |
|---|---|
| Mar. 3 | Purchased 9,000 shares at $9 per share of Andy Software common stock as a long-term, available-for-sale investment, representing 7% ownership. |
| May 15 | Received a cash dividend of $0.57 per share on the Andy investment. |
| Dec. 15 | Received a cash dividend of $80,000 from Parson investment. |
| 31 | Received Parson's annual report showing $300,000 of net income. |
| 31 | Received Andy's annual report showing $500,000 of net income for the year. |
| 31 | Parson's stock fair value at year-end was $830,000. |
| 31 | Andy's common stock fair value at year-end was $13 per share. |

**Requirements**

1. Journalize the transactions for the year of Desk Source.
2. Post transactions to T-accounts to determine the December 31, 2016, balances related to the investment and investment income accounts.
3. Prepare Desk Source's partial balance sheet at December 31, 2016, from your answers in Requirement 2.

## > Problems Group B

**Learning Objective 2**

1. Dec. 31 Int. Rev. CR $10,000

### P10-20B Accounting for bond investments

Suppose Ritter Brothers purchases $400,000 of 5% annual bonds of Clarkson Corporation at face value on January 1, 2016. These bonds pay interest on June 30 and December 31 each year. They mature on December 31, 2020. Ritter intends to hold the Clarkson bond investment until maturity.

**Requirements**

1. Journalize Ritter Brothers's transactions related to the bonds for 2016.
2. Journalize the entry required on the Clarkson bonds maturity date. (Assume the last interest payment has already been recorded.)

CHAPTER 10

## P10-21B Classifying and accounting for stock investments

**Learning Objectives 1, 3, 4**

2. Sep. 16 Gain on Disposal CR $14,760

Ship Your Way Corporation generated excess cash and invested in securities as follows:

| | |
|---|---|
| **2016** | |
| Jul. 2 | Purchased 3,600 shares of TJF, Inc. common stock at $11.00 per share. Ship Your Way holds the stock in its active trading account and plans to sell the stock within three months, when the company will need the cash for normal operations. |
| Aug. 21 | Received a cash dividend of $0.10 per share on the TJF stock investment. |
| Sep. 16 | Sold the TJF stock for $15.10 per share. |
| Oct. 8 | Purchased 400 shares of Seanco stock at $13.00 per share. The stock is held in the active trading account as Ship Your Way plans to hold the Seanco stock for less than five months. |
| Dec. 31 | Seanco stock's current market price is $6.00 per share. |

### Requirements

1. Classify each of the investments made during 2016. (Assume the investments represent less than 20% of ownership of outstanding voting stock.)
2. Journalize the 2016 transactions. Explanations are not required.
3. Prepare T-accounts for the investment assets, and show how to report the investments on Ship Your Way's balance sheet at December 31, 2016.

## P10-22B Accounting for stock investments

**Learning Objectives 3, 4**

1. Dec. 31 Fair Value Adjustment—AFS DR $18,000

The beginning balance sheet of Water Source Co. included a $800,000 investment in Larsen stock (35% ownership).

During the year, Water Source completed the following investment transactions:

| | |
|---|---|
| Mar. 3 | Purchased 6,000 shares at $7 per share of Jack Software common stock as a long-term, available-for-sale investment, representing 3% ownership. |
| May 15 | Received a cash dividend of $0.53 per share on the Jack investment. |
| Dec. 15 | Received a cash dividend of $110,000 from Larsen investment. |
| 31 | Received Larsen's annual report showing $110,000 of net income. |
| 31 | Received Jack's annual report showing $600,000 of net income for the year. |
| 31 | Larsen's stock fair value at year-end was $728,500. |
| 31 | Jack's common stock fair value at year-end was $10 per share. |

### Requirements

1. Journalize the transactions for the year of Water Source.
2. Post transactions to T-accounts to determine the December 31, 2016, balances related to the investment and investment income accounts.
3. Prepare Water Source's partial balance sheet at December 31, 2016, from your answers in Requirement 2.

CHAPTER 10

## > Continuing Problem

**P10-23 Accounting for stock investments**

This problem continues the Daniels Consulting situation from Problem P9-42 of Chapter 9. Daniels Consulting invests its temporary excess cash in a brokerage account. On November 3, 2017, Daniels purchased 300 shares of Mauve Co. common stock for $15 per share. On December 31, 2017, Mauve's common stock was trading at $10 per share. Assume Daniels records the stock as a trading investment.

**Requirements**

1. Journalize the acquisition of Mauve stock on November 3, 2017.
2. Journalize any entries, if required, at December 31, 2017.
3. On January 25, 2018, Daniels sold the Mauve stock for $15.50 per share. Journalize the sale.



# CRITICAL THINKING

## > Decision Case 10-1

Rock Designs, Inc. is a jewelry store located in Miramar Beach, Florida. After Valentine's Day, the store often has excess cash to get it through the three-month slow season. The primary stockholder, Hardy Rock, wants to make this seasonal cash work for the business.

**Requirements**

1. Identify which investment class options are available to Rock Designs, Inc.
2. The company identifies that it wants to invest in the technology sector and has narrowed its choices to three companies: Apple Inc., Google Inc., and Microsoft Corporation. Prepare a brief analysis comparing the three companies, and recommend one of the three based on your analysis.

## > Ethical Issue 10-1

As a result of the recent mortgage crisis, many banks reported record losses to their mortgage receivables and other assets based on the decline in these assets' fair values.

**Requirements**

1. What would the effect be to stakeholders if such losses were not reported in a timely way?
2. If a business chooses not to report these losses, is there an ethical issue involved? Who is hurt?

## > Fraud Case 10-1

Wild Adventure conducts tours of wildlife reserves around the world. The company recently purchased a lodge in Adelaide, Australia, securing a 4% mortgage from First Bank. In addition to monthly payments, Wild Adventure must provide annual reports to the bank showing that the company has a current ratio of 1.2 or better.

After reviewing the annual reports, the CEO, N. O. Scrooge, approached Carl Hauptfleisch, the CFO, and stated, "We've decided we are going to move all our long-term and held-to-maturity investments into our brokerage account so we can sell them soon. Carl, go ahead and make the adjusting entries as of the current year-end."

Carl made the adjustments. The subsequent year, the economy turned, and the company's travel revenues dropped more than 60%. Wild Adventure eventually defaulted on the First Bank loan.

**Requirements**

1. What effect did the adjustments have on the financial statements? What effect did the adjustments have on the current ratio?
2. What type of information in the financial reports would have helped the bank detect this reclassification?
3. Has a fraud occurred? If so, what is the fraud?

## > Financial Statement Case 10-1

Details about a company's investments appear in a number of places in the annual report. Use **Starbucks Corporation's** Fiscal 2013 annual report to answer the following questions. Visit **http://www.pearsonhighered.com/Horngren** to view a link to Starbucks Corporation's Fiscal 2013 annual report.

**Requirements**

1. What classifications of debt and/or equity security investments does Starbucks hold?
2. Review Notes 4 and 6. Give the breakdown of the short-term and long-term investments Starbucks held at September 29, 2013.
3. Review Starbucks's consolidated statement of cash flows for the year ended September 29, 2013. Identify each item related to the company's debt and equity security investments, the amount of the item, and the section of the cash flow statement in which the item appears.
4. Review Note 1, specifically Short-term and Long-term Investments. How are Starbucks's available-for-sale investments reported? How are Starbucks's trading investments reported?

## > Team Project 10-1

Berkshire Hathaway, Inc. is a holding company that owns many diverse companies. Review the company's 2013 annual report. You can access it at **http://www.berkshirehathaway.com/2013ar/2013ar.pdf**.

**Requirements**

With a partner or group, lead your class in a discussion of the following questions or write a report as directed by your instructor.

1. What types of companies does Berkshire Hathaway own?
2. Review Note 3. At December 31, 2013, how much did the company hold in available-for-sale and held-to-maturity investments?
3. Review Berkshire's consolidated statement of cash flows for the year ended December 31, 2013. Identify each item related to the company's debt and equity security investments, the amount of the item, and the section of the cash flow statement in which the item appears.
4. Review Note 1(d). How, if at all, does the company use fair value measurements in regards to its investments?

## > Communication Activity 10-1

In 150 words or fewer, explain the difference between trading investments and available-for-sale investments.



## > Quick Check Answers

**1.** b **2.** c **3.** b **4.** c **5.** a **6.** c **7.** b **8.** c **9.** b **10.** a

# Current Liabilities and Payroll

# 11

## How Much Does One Employee Cost?

Mary Green, MD, recently opened a health care clinic, Family Medicine, that serves low-income families and uninsured individuals. Family Medicine prides itself on keeping its costs low but still providing excellent health care to its patients. When Mary opened the clinic, she hired only one part-time nurse. Now, with the clinic growing, Mary is considering hiring several more nurses and another doctor.

Mary knows that having employees is expensive. Not only does the business have to pay their wages, but there are additional payroll taxes that must be paid. As Mary is deciding what salary to offer her new employees, she must consider these additional costs. She knows that if she offers the new doctor a salary of $100,000, the business will end up paying more than $100,000. This is because of additional payroll taxes such as Social Security and unemployment compensation. In addition, Family Medicine will need to offer health care and retirement benefits to each employee. All of these extra expenses cost money—money she could be saving. But Mary knows that in order to provide the quality of service her patients expect, she must pay the cost of having quality employees.

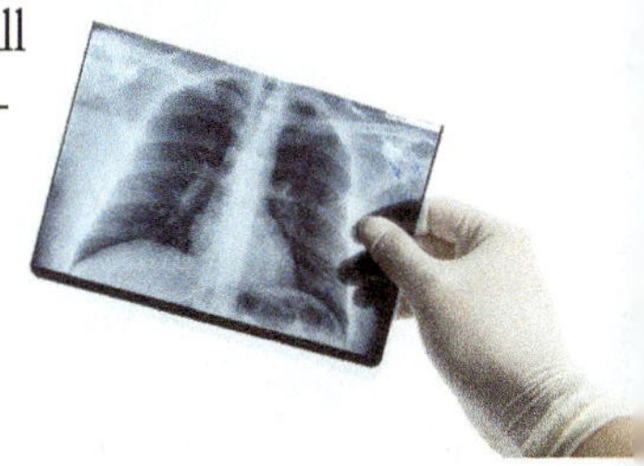

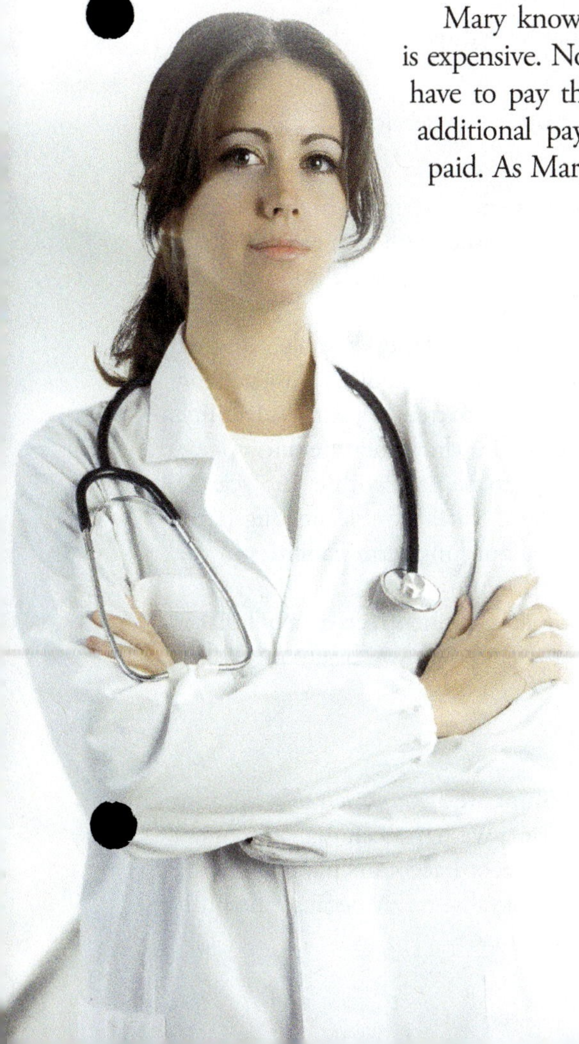

**How Do Businesses Account for Current Liabilities and Payroll?**

We now begin our focus on liabilities, or debts, a business owes. Payroll is one of those liabilities. Companies such as UnitedHealth Group Incorporated, a leading health care company that serves more than 85 million people, value hiring smart, committed, and talented people. Part of UnitedHealth's recruiting package is the salary it offers employees. In addition, UnitedHealth Group also offers benefits such as vacation, health care, and retirement to reward its employees. Payroll and employee benefits are reported as current liabilities on the balance sheet until the company makes payment. In this chapter, we look at how businesses, such as UnitedHealth Group, account for and record payroll and other current liabilities.

# Chapter 11 Learning Objectives

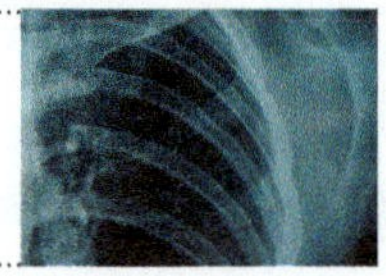

1 Account for current liabilities of known amount
2 Calculate and journalize basic payroll transactions
3 Account for current liabilities that must be estimated
4 Account for contingent liabilities
5 Use the times-interest-earned ratio to evaluate business performance

Up to this point, we've been focusing on all the assets a corporation owns. But what about the bills a business owes? A business needs to know what it owes (liabilities) and by what date they have to be paid. Why? To be sure the business has cash on hand to pay these bills. In this chapter, we focus on some common current liabilities a business may owe. As with other chapters, we'll continue to focus on Smart Touch Learning and see how it manages its current liabilities.

## HOW ARE CURRENT LIABILITIES OF KNOWN AMOUNTS ACCOUNTED FOR?

**Learning Objective 1**
Account for current liabilities of known amount

**Liabilities** are debts that are owed to creditors. Liabilities have three main characteristics:

1. They occur because of a past transaction or event.
2. They create a present obligation for future payment of cash or services.
3. They are an unavoidable obligation.

**Liabilities**
Debts that are owed to creditors.

**Current Liability**
A liability that must be paid with cash or with goods and services within one year or within the entity's operating cycle if the cycle is longer than a year.

Liabilities can be split into two main categories: current and long-term. In this chapter, we discuss current liabilities. **Current liabilities** must be paid either with cash or with goods and services within one year or within the entity's operating cycle if the cycle is longer than a year.

Accounts Payable, Notes Payable due within one year, Salaries Payable, Interest Payable, Unearned Revenue, and Income Tax Payable are all current liabilities. Any portion of a long-term liability that is due within the next year is also reported as a current liability. Current liabilities are listed on the balance sheet in the order in which they are due.

**Long-Term Liability**
A liability that does not need to be paid within one year or within the entity's operating cycle, whichever is longer.

**Long-term liabilities** are liabilities that do not need to be paid within one year or within the entity's operating cycle, whichever is longer. Many Notes Payable are long-term, such as a mortgage on a building. We will explore more about long-term liabilities in the next chapter.

The amounts of most liabilities are known. For example, a business receives a bill that is due in 30 days or a business takes out a 90-day loan from a bank. We will begin our discussion with current liabilities of a known amount.

IFRS

IFRS defines current and long-term liabilities in the same manner as GAAP.

### Accounts Payable

Amounts owed for products or services purchased on account are *accounts payable*. Because these are typically due in 30 days, they are current liabilities. We have seen many accounts payable illustrations in preceding chapters. Businesses can record accounts payable for the purchase of goods or for the receipt of services. Accounts payable occur because the business receives the goods or services before payment has been made.

## Sales Tax Payable

Most states assess sales tax on retail sales. Retailers collect the sales tax in addition to the price of the item sold. Sales Tax Payable is a current liability because the retailer must pay the state in less than a year. Sales tax is usually calculated as a percentage of the amount of the sale.

For example, suppose December's taxable sales for Smart Touch Learning totaled \$10,000. The company collected an additional 6% sales tax, which would equal \$600 (\$10,000 × 0.06). The accounting clerk would record that month's cash sales as follows:

| Date | Accounts and Explanation | Debit | Credit |
|---|---|---|---|
| Dec. 31 | Cash | 10,600 | |
| | Sales Revenue | | 10,000 |
| | Sales Tax Payable (\$10,000 × 0.06) | | 600 |
| | *To record cash sales and the related sales tax.* | | |

| A↑ | = | L↑ | + | E↑ |
|---|---|---|---|---|
| Cash↑ | = | Sales Tax Payable↑ | | Sales Revenue↑ |

Sales tax is not an expense of the business. It is a current liability. Companies collect the sales tax and then forward it to the state at regular intervals. They normally submit it monthly, but they could file it at other intervals, depending on the state and the amount of the tax. To pay the tax, the company debits Sales Tax Payable and credits Cash.

| Date | Accounts and Explanation | Debit | Credit |
|---|---|---|---|
| Jan. 20 | Sales Tax Payable | 600 | |
| | Cash | | 600 |
| | *To record cash payment for sales tax payable.* | | |

| A↓ | = | L↓ | + | E |
|---|---|---|---|---|
| Cash↓ | = | Sales Tax Payable↓ | | |

## Income Tax Payable

The federal government and many state governments require corporations to pay income tax on their net income. Federal income taxes are calculated on a corporate tax return, referred to as a Form 1120. The amount of taxes that the corporation owes but has not yet paid is classified as Income Tax Payable and is reported as a current liability on the balance sheet.

For example, assume that Smart Touch Learning incurred federal income tax payable of \$3,780. Smart Touch Learning would record the following journal entry:

| Date | Accounts and Explanation | Debit | Credit |
|---|---|---|---|
| Dec. 31 | Income Tax Expense | 3,780 | |
| | Income Tax Payable | | 3,780 |
| | *To record income tax expense incurred.* | | |

| A | = | L↑ | + | E↓ |
|---|---|---|---|---|
| | = | Income Tax Payable↑ | | Income Tax Expense↑ |

When Smart Touch Learning files its Form 1120 corporate tax return and makes payment, the corporation will record the following entry:

| A↓ | = | L↓ | + | E |
|---|---|---|---|---|
| Cash↓ | = | Income Tax Payable↓ | | |

| Date | Accounts and Explanation | Debit | Credit |
|---|---|---|---|
| Mar. 15 | Income Tax Payable | 3,780 | |
| | Cash | | 3,780 |
| | *To record cash payment for income tax payable.* | | |

## Unearned Revenues

*Unearned revenue* is also called *deferred revenue*. Unearned revenue arises when a business has received cash in advance of providing goods or performing work and, therefore, has an obligation to provide goods or services to the customer in the future. Unearned revenues are current liabilities until they are earned.

Suppose Smart Touch Learning received $900 in advance on May 21 for a month's work beginning on that date. On May 21, because it received cash before earning the revenue, the company has a liability to perform work for the client. The liability is called Unearned Revenue. The entry made by the accounting clerk on May 21 follows:

| A↑ | = | L↑ | + | E |
|---|---|---|---|---|
| Cash↑ | = | Unearned Revenue↑ | | |

| Date | Accounts and Explanation | Debit | Credit |
|---|---|---|---|
| May 21 | Cash | 900 | |
| | Unearned Revenue | | 900 |
| | *Collected cash for future services.* | | |

During May, Smart Touch Learning delivered one-third of the work and earned $300 ($900 × 1/3) of the revenue. On May 31, the accounting clerk would record the following entry to show that some work had been completed and some revenue had now been earned:

| A | = | L↓ | + | E↑ |
|---|---|---|---|---|
| | = | Unearned Revenue↓ | | Service Revenue↑ |

| Date | Accounts and Explanation | Debit | Credit |
|---|---|---|---|
| May 31 | Unearned Revenue | 300 | |
| | Service Revenue | | 300 |
| | *To record service revenue earned that was collected in advance.* | | |

At this point, Smart Touch Learning has earned $300 of the revenue and still owes $600 of work to the customer as shown in the T-accounts:

**Unearned Revenue**

| | | | |
|---|---|---|---|
| May 31 | 300 | 900 | May 21 |
| | | **600** | **Bal.** |

**Service Revenue**

| | | | |
|---|---|---|---|
| | | 300 | May 31 |

**Short-Term Note Payable**
A written promise made by the business to pay a debt, usually involving interest, within one year or less.

## Short-Term Notes Payable

**Short-term notes payable** are a common form of financing. Short-term notes payable represent a written promise by the business to pay a debt, usually involving interest, within one year or less. Assume on May 1, Smart Touch Learning purchased merchandise inventory with a 10%, 90-day note payable, for $8,000. The company uses the perpetual inventory system. The entry to record the note follows:

| Date | Accounts and Explanation | Debit | Credit |
|---|---|---|---|
| May 1 | Merchandise Inventory | 8,000 | |
| | Notes Payable | | 8,000 |
| | *Purchased merchandise inventory in exchange for 90-day, 10% note.* | | |

| A↑ | = | L↑ | + | E |
|---|---|---|---|---|
| Merchandise Inventory↑ | = | Notes Payable↑ | | |

On July 30, when the note is due, Smart Touch Learning will pay the note plus interest and record the following entry:

| Date | Accounts and Explanation | Debit | Credit |
|---|---|---|---|
| Jul. 30 | Notes Payable | 8,000 | |
| | Interest Expense ($8,000 × 0.10 × 90/360) | 200 | |
| | Cash | | 8,200 |
| | *Paid note and interest at maturity.* | | |

| A↓ | = | L↓ | + | E↓ |
|---|---|---|---|---|
| Cash↓ | = | Notes Payable↓ | | Interest Expense↑ |

*Remember that the calculation for interest is principal × interest rate × time.*

Businesses occasionally borrow cash from banks. The bank requires the business to sign a *promissory note* that states that the business will pay the *principal* plus *interest* at a specified *maturity date.* As an example, assume that on November 1, 2016, Smart Touch Learning borrows $10,000 from First Street Bank at 6% for five months. On November 1, the accounting clerk records the following entry:

| Date | Accounts and Explanation | Debit | Credit |
|---|---|---|---|
| 2016 | | | |
| Nov. 1 | Cash | 10,000 | |
| | Notes Payable | | 10,000 |
| | *Received cash in exchange for 5-month, 6% note.* | | |

| A↑ | = | L↑ | + | E |
|---|---|---|---|---|
| Cash↑ | = | Notes Payable↑ | | |

At year-end, the matching principle requires the business to accrue interest expense for November and December as follows:

| Date | Accounts and Explanation | Debit | Credit |
|---|---|---|---|
| 2016 | | | |
| Dec. 31 | Interest Expense ($10,000 × 0.06 × 2/12) | 100 | |
| | Interest Payable | | 100 |
| | *Accrued interest expense at year-end.* | | |

| A | = | L↑ | + | E↓ |
|---|---|---|---|---|
| | = | Interest Payable↑ | | Interest Expense↑ |

The interest accrual at December 31, 2016, allocated $100 of the interest on this note to 2016. During 2017, the interest on this note for the three remaining months is $150. When Smart Touch Learning records payment for the note, it will record the remaining interest expense and also remove the interest payable and note payable from the books as shown:

| A↓ | = | L↓ | + | E↓ |
|---|---|---|---|---|
| Cash↓ | | Notes Payable↓<br>Interest Payable↓ | | Interest Expense↑ |

| Date | Accounts and Explanation | Debit | Credit |
|---|---|---|---|
| 2017 | | | |
| Apr. 1 | Notes Payable | 10,000 | |
| | Interest Expense ($10,000 × 0.06 × 3/12) | 150 | |
| | Interest Payable | 100 | |
| | Cash | | 10,250 |
| | *Paid note and interest at maturity.* | | |

## Current Portion of Long-Term Notes Payable

**Current Portion of Notes Payable**
The amount of the principal that is payable within one year.

Long-term notes payable are typically reported in the long-term liability section of the balance sheet. If, however, the long-term debt is paid in installments, the business will report the current portion of notes payable (also called *current maturity*) as a current liability. The **current portion of notes payable** is the principal amount that will be paid within one year. The remaining portion of the note will be classified as long-term.

Let's consider a $20,000 note payable that is paid in $5,000 installments over four years. The portion that must be paid within one year, $5,000, is current. The remaining $15,000 will be classified as long-term. No journal entry is needed to reclassify the current portion. It is, instead, only classified as current or long-term for reporting purposes on the balance sheet. Notice that the reclassification does not change the total amount of debt. It only reclassifies $5,000 of the total debt from long-term to current.

### Try It!

On August 10, Swanson Company recorded sales of merchandise inventory on account, $4,000. The sales were subject to sales tax of 4%. The company uses the perpetual inventory system. On September 30, Swanson paid $500 of sales tax to the state.

1. Journalize the transaction to record the sale on August 10. Ignore cost of goods sold.
2. Journalize the transaction to record the payment of sales tax to the state.

**Check your answers online in MyAccountingLab or at http://www.pearsonhighered.com/Horngren.**

For more practice, see Short Exercises S11-1 through S11-5. MyAccountingLab

## HOW DO COMPANIES ACCOUNT FOR AND RECORD PAYROLL?

**Learning Objective 2**
Calculate and journalize basic payroll transactions

Payroll, also called *employee compensation*, also creates liabilities for a business. For service organizations—such as CPA firms and travel agencies—payroll is *the* major expense. Labor cost is so important that most businesses develop a special payroll system.

There are numerous ways to label an employee's pay:

- *Salary* is pay stated at an annual, monthly, or weekly rate, such as $62,400 per year, $5,200 per month, or $1,200 per week.

- *Wages* are pay amounts stated at an hourly rate, such as $15 per hour.
- *Commission* is pay stated as a percentage of a sale amount, such as a 5% commission on a sale. A realtor who earns 5% commission, for example, earns $5,000 on a $100,000 sale of real estate ($100,000 × 5%).
- *Bonus* is pay over and above base salary (or wage or commission). A bonus is usually paid for exceptional performance—in a single amount after year-end.
- *Benefits* are extra compensation—items that are not paid directly to the employee. Benefits cover health, life, and disability insurance. The employer pays the insurance company, which then provides coverage for the employee. Another type of benefit, retirement, sets aside money for the employee for his or her future retirement.

Businesses pay employees at a base rate for a set period—called *straight time*. For additional hours—*overtime*—the employee may get a higher pay rate, depending on the job classification and wage and hour laws.

Assume Ryan Park was hired to work for Smart Touch Learning. His pay is as follows:

- Ryan earns wages of $15 per hour for straight time (40 hours), so his weekly pay is $600 ($15 per hour × 40 hours).
- The company pays *time-and-a-half* for overtime. That rate is 150% (1.5 times) the straight-time pay rate. Thus, Ryan earns $22.50 per hour of overtime ($15.00 × 1.5).
- For working 42 hours during a week, he earns gross pay of $645, computed as follows:

| | |
|---|---|
| Straight-time pay for 40 hours | $ 600 |
| Overtime pay for 2 hours: 2 × $22.50 | 45 |
| Gross Pay | $ 645 |

## Gross Pay and Net (Take-Home) Pay

Two pay amounts are important for accounting purposes. **Gross pay** is the total amount of salary, wages, commissions, and bonuses earned by the employee during a pay period before taxes or any other deductions. Gross pay is an expense to the employer. In the preceding example, Ryan Park's gross pay was $645. **Net pay** is the amount the employee gets to keep. Net pay is also called *take-home pay*. Net pay equals gross pay minus all deductions such as income tax withheld. The employer either writes a paycheck to each employee for his or her take-home pay or directly deposits the employee's take-home pay into the employee's bank account.

**Gross Pay**
The total amount of salary, wages, commissions, and any other employee compensation before taxes and other deductions.

**Net Pay**
Gross pay minus all deductions. The amount of compensation that the employee actually takes home.

## Employee Payroll Withholding Deductions

The federal government, most states, and many municipalities require employers to deduct taxes from employee paychecks. Insurance companies and investment companies may also get some of the employee's gross pay. Amounts withheld from paychecks are called *withholding deductions*. Payroll withholding deductions are the difference between gross pay and take-home pay. These deductions are withheld from paychecks and sent directly to the government, to insurance companies, or to other entities. Payroll withholding deductions fall into two categories:

- *Required deductions*, such as employee federal and state income tax, Social Security tax and other deductions required by federal, state, or local laws. For example, employees pay their income tax and Social Security tax through payroll deductions.
- *Optional deductions*, including insurance premiums, retirement plan contributions, charitable contributions, and other amounts that are withheld at the employee's request.

After being withheld, payroll deductions become the liability of the employer, who then pays the outside party—taxes to the government and contributions to charitable organizations, for example.

## Withholding for Employee Income Tax

**Income Tax Withholding**
Income tax deducted from an employee's gross pay.

U.S. law and some states, cities, and counties require companies to withhold income tax from employee paychecks. The income tax deducted from gross pay is called **income tax withholding**. The amount withheld depends on the employee's gross pay and on the number of *withholding allowances* he or she claims.

For federal tax withholdings, an employee files Form W-4 with his or her employer to indicate the number of allowances claimed for income tax withholding. Each allowance lowers the amount of tax withheld:

**Federal Insurance Contributions Act (FICA)**
The federal act that created the Social Security tax that provides retirement, disability, and medical benefits.

- An unmarried taxpayer usually claims one allowance.
- A childless married couple usually claims two allowances.
- A married couple with one child usually claims three allowances, and so on.

Exhibit 11-1 shows a W-4 for Ryan Park, who claims married with three allowances (lines 3 and 5).

**Exhibit 11-1 | W-4**

Form **W-4**
Department of the Treasury
Internal Revenue Service

**Employee's Withholding Allowance Certificate**

▶ **Whether you are entitled to claim a certain number of allowances or exemption from withholding is subject to review by the IRS. Your employer may be required to send a copy of this form to the IRS.**

OMB No. 1545-0074
**2014**

1 Your first name and middle initial: Ryan G.
Last name: Park
2 **Your social security number**: 123-45-6789

Home address (number and street or rural route): 305 Lost Cove Drive
3 ☐ Single ☑ Married ☐ Married, but withhold at higher Single rate.
**Note.** If married, but legally separated, or spouse is a nonresident alien, check the "Single" box.

City or town, state, and ZIP code: Pompton Plains, IL 07444
4 **If your last name differs from that shown on your social security card, check here. You must call 1-800-772-1213 for a replacement card.** ▶ ☐

5 Total number of allowances you are claiming (from line **H** above **or** from the applicable worksheet on page 2) | 5 | 3
6 Additional amount, if any, you want withheld from each paycheck . . . . . . . . . . . . . . . . . | 6 | $
7 I claim exemption from withholding for 2014, and I certify that I meet **both** of the following conditions for exemption.
- Last year I had a right to a refund of **all** federal income tax withheld because I had **no** tax liability, **and**
- This year I expect a refund of **all** federal income tax withheld because I expect to have **no** tax liability.

If you meet both conditions, write "Exempt" here . . . . . . . . . . . . . . . . . ▶ | 7 |

Under penalties of perjury, I declare that I have examined this certificate and, to the best of my knowledge and belief, it is true, correct, and complete.

**Employee's signature**
(This form is not valid unless you sign it.) ▶ Ryan G. Park **Date** ▶ 11/15/2014

8 Employer's name and address (Employer: Complete lines 8 and 10 only if sending to the IRS.): Smart Touch Learning, 227 Lake Street, Pompton Plains, IL 07444
9 Office code (optional)
10 Employer identification number (EIN): 20-1234567

**For Privacy Act and Paperwork Reduction Act Notice, see page 2.** Cat. No. 10220Q Form **W-4** (2014)

## Withholding for Employee Social Security Tax (FICA)

The **Federal Insurance Contributions Act (FICA)**, also known as the Social Security Act, created the Social Security tax. The Social Security program provides retirement, disability, and medical benefits. The law requires employers to withhold **Social Security (FICA) tax** from employees' paychecks. The FICA tax has two components:

**Social Security (FICA) Tax**
Federal Insurance Contributions Act (FICA) tax, which is withheld from employees' pay and matched by the employer.

1. OASDI (old age, survivors, and disability insurance)
2. Medicare (medical benefits)

OASDI provides retirement benefits to individuals based upon age, benefits to survivors of qualified individuals, and disability insurance to individuals who cannot work because of a medical condition. The amount of tax withheld varies from year to year because the wage base is subject to OASDI tax changes each year. For 2014, the OASDI tax applies to the first $117,000 of employee earnings in a year. The taxable amount of earnings is adjusted annually. The OASDI tax rate for employees at the time of this writing is 6.2%. Therefore, the maximum OASDI tax that an employee paid in 2014 was $7,254 ($117,000 × 0.062).

The Medicare portion of the FICA tax provides health insurance to individuals based on age or disability. Medicare applies to all employee earnings—that means there is no maximum tax. At the time of this writing, this tax rate is 1.45% for earnings up to $200,000. Earnings over $200,000 will be taxed at 2.35%. Therefore, an employee pays a combined FICA tax rate of 7.65% (6.2% + 1.45%) of the first $117,000 of annual earnings ($117,000 is the 2014 cap as it was the most current wage cap at the time of printing), plus 1.45% of earnings above $117,000.

*The percentage used and the wage base for payroll withholdings and taxes vary from year to year. We are using amounts that are current at the time of printing. You should use these numbers when you complete this chapter's assignments.*

Assume that James Kolen, another employee of Smart Touch Learning, earned $112,700 prior to December. Kolen's salary for December is $10,000. Kolen's FICA tax withheld from his paycheck is calculated as follows:

| | OASDI | | Medicare |
|---|---|---|---|
| Employee earnings subject to tax | $ 117,000 | | No Max |
| Employee earnings prior to the current month | − 112,700 | | |
| Current pay subject to tax | $ 4,300 | | $ 10,000 |
| Tax rate | × 0.062 | | × 0.0145 |
| Tax to be withheld from paycheck | $ 267* | | $ 145 |
| Total FICA tax withheld ($267 + $145) | | $412 | |

*Numbers in examples are rounded to nearest dollar for simplicity. Payroll amounts are usually rounded to the nearest cent.

**Notice that only $4,300 of Kolen's $10,000 salary is subject to OASDI tax. This is because in December, Kolen reaches the maximum amount of earnings that is subject to OASDI. Once an employee has earned $117,000, no further earnings are taxed for OASDI in that year.**

Medicare tax, on the other hand, has no maximum. All earnings are subject to the tax. Kolen pays Medicare tax on the entire $10,000 earned in December.

Why did James Kolen only pay OASDI tax on $4,300 of earnings?

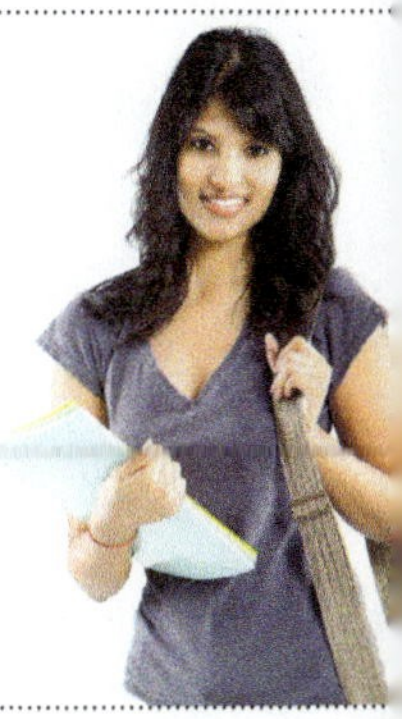

## Optional Withholding Deductions

As a convenience to employees, some companies withhold payroll deductions and then pay designated organizations according to employee instructions. Insurance premiums, retirement savings, union dues, and gifts to charities are examples.

The table on the next page summarizes James Kolen's final pay period on December 31 assuming he authorized a $180 payment for health insurance and a $20 contribution to United Way. Employee income tax is assumed to be 20% of gross pay.

| | | |
|---|---|---|
| Gross pay | | $ 10,000 |
| Withholding deductions: | | |
| Employee income tax (20%) | $ 2,000 | |
| Employee OASDI tax (calculated on prior page) | 267 | |
| Employee Medicare tax (1.45%) | 145 | |
| Employee health insurance | 180 | |
| Employee contribution to United Way | 20 | |
| Total withholdings | | 2,612 |
| Net (take-home) pay | | $ 7,388 |

## Payroll Register

**Payroll Register**
A schedule that summarizes the earnings, withholdings, and net pay for each employee.

Many companies use a **payroll register** to help summarize the earnings, withholdings, and net pay for each employee. Exhibit 11-2 shows the payroll register for Smart Touch Learning for the month of December.

**Exhibit 11-2 | Payroll Register**

| Employee Name | Earnings | | | Withholdings | | | | | | Net Pay | Check No. | Salaries and Wages Expense |
|---|---|---|---|---|---|---|---|---|---|---|---|---|
| | Beginning Cumulative Earnings | Current Period Earnings | Ending Cumulative Earnings | OASDI | Medicare | Income Tax | Health Insurance | Other | Total Withholdings | | | |
| James Kolen | $ 112,700 | $ 10,000 | $ 122,700 | $ 267 | $ 145 | $ 2,000 | $ 180 | $ 20 | $ 2,612 | $ 7,388 | 530 | $ 10,000 |
| Benito Munez | 62,100 | 5,500 | 67,600 | 341 | 80 | 1,100 | 110 | 0 | 1,631 | 3,869 | 531 | 5,500 |
| Ryan Park | 37,400 | 2,580 | 39,980 | 160 | 37 | 516 | 110 | 0 | 823 | 1,757 | 532 | 2,580 |
| Lisa Smart | 0 | 4,000 | 4,000 | 248 | 58 | 800 | 65 | 0 | 1,171 | 2,829 | 533 | 4,000 |
| Sharon Zapato | 71,500 | 6,500 | 78,000 | 403 | 94 | 1,300 | 180 | 40 | 2,017 | 4,483 | 534 | 6,500 |
| Total | $ 283,700 | $ 28,580 | $ 312,280 | $ 1,419 | $ 414 | $ 5,716 | $ 645 | $ 60 | $ 8,254 | $ 20,326 | | $ 28,580 |

*Don't confuse corporate income tax owed by the corporation, which creates Income Tax Payable, and personal income tax withheld from the employees' paychecks, which creates Employee Income Taxes Payable.*

A business's payroll register typically includes the following columns:

1. Employee Name
2. Beginning cumulative earnings—the amount the employee has earned through the last pay period.
3. Current period earnings—earnings for the current period (includes regular and overtime earnings, commissions, and bonuses).
4. Ending cumulative earnings—beginning cumulative earnings plus current period earnings.
5. OASDI—6.2% tax on the first $117,000 earnings.
6. Medicare—1.45% tax on all earnings.
7. Income Tax—includes federal, state, and any local government income tax withheld.
8. Health Insurance—withholdings made for employee-paid health care coverage.
9. Other—employees' voluntary withholdings such as charitable contributions and union dues.

10. Total Withholdings—total of all withholdings.
11. Net Pay—current period earnings less total withholdings. This is the amount that is paid to each employee.
12. Check No.—the check number used to make payment for earnings.
13. Salaries and Wages Expense—the amount debited to Salaries and Wages Expense for the current pay period.

## Journalizing Employee Payroll

The payroll register is used to record the payroll journal entry. Payroll and payroll withholdings are recorded as liabilities until the amounts are paid. The totals from the payroll register will be used to create the journal entry for Smart Touch Learning.

| Date | Accounts and Explanation | Debit | Credit |
|---|---|---|---|
| Dec. 31 | Salaries and Wages Expense | 28,580 | |
| | FICA—OASDI Taxes Payable | | 1,419 |
| | FICA—Medicare Taxes Payable | | 414 |
| | Employee Income Taxes Payable | | 5,716 |
| | Employee Health Insurance Payable | | 645 |
| | United Way Payable | | 60 |
| | Salaries and Wages Payable | | 20,326 |
| | *To record salaries and wages expense and payroll withholdings.* | | |

| A | = | L↑ | + | E↓ |
|---|---|---|---|---|
| | | Various Payables↑<br>Salaries and Wages Payable↑ | | Salaries and Wages Expense↑ |

In the above journal entry, Salaries and Wages Expense ($28,580) represents the gross pay for all employees. Gross pay includes both the amount owed for salaries and wages ($20,326) and payroll withholdings ($1,419 + $414 + $5,716 + $645 + $60).

On payday, Smart Touch Learning will make payment of $20,326 to its employees and record the following journal entry:

| Date | Accounts and Explanation | Debit | Credit |
|---|---|---|---|
| Jan. 5 | Salaries and Wages Payable | 20,326 | |
| | Cash | | 20,326 |
| | *To record payment of salaries.* | | |

| A↓ | = | L↓ | + | E |
|---|---|---|---|---|
| Cash↓ | | Salaries and Wages Payable↓ | | |

The other payable accounts, FICA, Income Taxes Payable, Health Insurance, and any charitable contributions, will be removed from the books when payments are made on those specific payables with debits to the liability accounts and a credit to Cash.

## Employer Payroll Taxes

In addition to income tax and FICA tax, which are withheld from employee paychecks, *employers* must pay at least three payroll taxes. These taxes are not withheld from employees' gross earnings but instead are paid by the employer:

1. Employer FICA tax (OASDI and Medicare)
2. State unemployment compensation tax (SUTA)
3. Federal unemployment compensation tax (FUTA)

### Employer FICA Tax

In addition to the FICA tax withheld from the employee's paycheck, the employer must also pay both OASDI and Medicare. The employer portion of OASDI is 6.2% on the first $117,000 of each employee's annual earnings. The employer's tax rate for Medicare is 1.45% on all earnings. The Social Security system is funded by contributions from both the employer and employee.

### State and Federal Unemployment Compensation Taxes

**Unemployment Compensation Tax**
Payroll tax paid by employers to the government, which uses the cash to pay unemployment benefits to people who are out of work.

The Federal Unemployment Tax Act (FUTA) and the State Unemployment Tax Act (SUTA) finance workers' compensation for people laid off from work. These **unemployment compensation taxes** are paid by the employer; they are not deducted from employees' gross pay. (Some states require employees to contribute to SUTA. For our purposes, we will assume that unemployment compensation taxes are paid only by the employer.) In recent years, employers have paid a combined tax of 6.0% on the first $7,000 of each employee's annual earnings for unemployment tax. The proportion paid to the state depends on the individual state, but for many it is 5.4% to the state plus 0.6% to the federal government. For this payroll tax, the employer uses two liability accounts:

- Federal Unemployment Taxes Payable (FUTA Payable)
- State Unemployment Taxes Payable (SUTA Payable)

Exhibit 11-3 shows the distribution of payroll for an employee who earns $1,000, assuming the employee has not reached the payroll tax limits.

**Exhibit 11-3 | Payroll Costs**

| Employee's taxes and other withholdings | | | | | | | | Employer's taxes | | | | | | |
|---|---|---|---|---|---|---|---|---|---|---|---|---|---|---|
| Net (Take-Home) Pay | | OASDI (6.2% on first $117,000) | | Medicare (1.45% on all earnings) | | Income Tax (20% assumed) | OASDI (6.2% on first $117,000) | | Medicare (1.45% on all earnings) | | FUTA (0.6% on first $7,000) | | SUTA (5.4% on first $7,000) |
| $723 | + | $62 | + | $15 | + | $200 | $62 | + | $15 | + | $6 | + | $54 |
| =$1,000 | | | | | | | =$137 | | | | | | |
| **Employer pays a total of $1,137.** | | | | | | | | | | | | | |

### Journalizing Employer Payroll Taxes

Smart Touch Learning's employer payroll taxes for December will be calculated as follows:

| | Earnings | | | Employer Payroll Taxes | | | | |
|---|---|---|---|---|---|---|---|---|
| **Employee Name** | **Beginning Cumulative Earnings** | **Current Period Earnings** | **Ending Cumulative Earnings** | **OASDI (6.2%)** | **Medicare (1.45%)** | **FUTA (0.6%)** | **SUTA (5.4%)** | **Total Taxes** |
| James Kolen | $ 112,700 | $ 10,000 | $ 122,700 | $ 267 | $ 145 | $ 0 | $ 0 | $ 412 |
| Benito Munez | 62,100 | 5,500 | 67,600 | 341 | 80 | 0 | 0 | 421 |
| Ryan Park | 37,400 | 2,580 | 39,980 | 160 | 37 | 0 | 0 | 197 |
| Lisa Smart | 0 | 4,000 | 4,000 | 248 | 58 | 24 | 216 | 546 |
| Sharon Zapato | 71,500 | 6,500 | 78,000 | 403 | 94 | 0 | 0 | 497 |
| Total | $ 283,700 | $ 28,580 | $ 312,280 | $ 1,419 | $ 414 | $ 24 | $ 216 | $ 2,073 |

As with employee contributions, the federal FICA—OASDI is determined as 6.2% on the first $117,000 earned by each employee. Smart Touch Learning must pay OASDI tax on all employees; however, the amount paid on James Kolen's earnings is limited to the first $117,000 [($117,000 − $112,700) × 6.2% = $267]. FICA—Medicare applies to all earnings at a rate of 1.45%.

FUTA (0.6%) and SUTA (5.4%) tax is only paid on the first $7,000 of each employee's earnings. Smart Touch Learning will only pay unemployment taxes on Lisa Smart because all other employees have earned more than $7,000 to date.

Smart Touch Learning records the employer's payroll tax expense as a debit to Payroll Tax Expense and a credit to the various payable accounts:

| Date | Accounts and Explanation | Debit | Credit |
|---|---|---|---|
| Dec. 31 | Payroll Tax Expense | 2,073 | |
| | FICA—OASDI Taxes Payable | | 1,419 |
| | FICA—Medicare Taxes Payable | | 414 |
| | Federal Unemployment Taxes Payable | | 24 |
| | State Unemployment Taxes Payable | | 216 |
| | *To record employer's payroll tax expense.* | | |

| A | = | L↑ | + | E↓ |
|---|---|---|---|---|
| | | Various Payables↑ | | Payroll Tax Expense↑ |

## Internal Control Over Payroll

There are two main controls for payroll:

- Controls for efficiency
- Controls to safeguard payroll disbursements

### Controls for Efficiency

Payroll transactions are ideal for computer processing. The payroll data are stored in a file, and the computer makes the calculations, prints paychecks, and updates all records electronically. In addition, companies may require direct deposits for employees' pay so that paper checks do not have to be written to each employee. Direct deposits also increase efficiency by reducing the amount of reconciling needed on outstanding checks.

### Controls to Safeguard Payroll Disbursements

A controller of a small business can monitor his or her payroll by personal contact with employees. Large companies cannot. A particular risk is that a paycheck may be written to a fictitious person and cashed by a dishonest employee. To guard against this, large businesses adopt strict internal controls for payroll.

Hiring and firing employees should be separated from accounting and from passing out paychecks. Photo IDs ensure that only actual employees are paid. Employees clock in at the start and clock out at the end of the workday to prove their attendance and hours worked.

The foundation of internal control is the separation of duties. This is why all but the smallest companies have separate departments for the following activities:

- The Human Resources Department hires and fires workers.
- The Payroll Department maintains employee earnings records.
- The Accounting Department records all transactions.
- The Treasurer distributes paychecks to employees.

## Try It!

3. Theodore Simpson works for Blair Company all year and earns a monthly salary of $4,000. There is no overtime pay. Based on Theodore's W-4, Blair withholds income taxes at 15% of his gross pay. As of July 31, Theodore had $28,000 of cumulative earnings.

Journalize the accrual of salary expense for Blair Company related to the employment of Theodore Simpson for the month of August.

**Check your answer online in MyAccountingLab or at http://www.pearsonhighered.com/Horngren.**

For more practice, see Short Exercises S11-6 through S11-8. MyAccountingLab

# HOW ARE CURRENT LIABILITIES THAT MUST BE ESTIMATED ACCOUNTED FOR?

**Learning Objective 3**
Account for current liabilities that must be estimated

A business may know that a liability exists but not know the exact amount. The business cannot simply ignore the liability. It must estimate the amount of the liability and report it on the balance sheet. Common examples of liabilities that are often estimated are bonus plans, vacation pay, health and pension benefits, and warranties.

## Bonus Plans

IFRS

Under IFRS, current liabilities are sometimes called "provisions" rather than payables. For example, IFRS uses Employee Provisions instead of Wages Payable and Provision for Income Tax instead of Income Tax Payable.

Many companies give bonuses to their employees in addition to their regular wages. These bonuses are often based on meeting a specific goal, such as the employee meeting an expected sales goal or the business achieving a target profit. Usually a company does not know the amount of the year-end bonus at year-end; the company instead estimates the amount of the bonus based on a set percentage. For example, assume Smart Touch Learning estimates that it will pay a 5% bonus on annual net income after deducting the bonus. Assume the company reports net income of $315,000 before the calculation of the bonus. The accounting department will calculate the bonus as follows:

Bonus = (Bonus % × Net income before bonus) / (1 + Bonus %)
= (0.05 × $315,000) / (1 + 0.05)
= $15,000

*This formula allows you to back into the bonus amount. For example, net income minus the bonus is $300,000 ($315,000 − $15,000). The bonus of $15,000 is really 5% of net income after the bonus has been subtracted ($300,000 × 0.05 = $15,000).*

Assuming Smart Touch Learning will not make payment until the next year, it must record a liability for the bonus due to its employees. The accounting clerk will record the following entry:

| A | = | L↑ | + | E↓ |
|---|---|---|---|---|
| | = | Employee Bonus Payable↑ | | Employee Bonus Expense↑ |

| Date | Accounts and Explanation | Debit | Credit |
|---|---|---|---|
| Dec. 31 | Employee Bonus Expense | 15,000 | |
| | Employee Bonus Payable | | 15,000 |
| | *To record employee bonus expense.* | | |

When Smart Touch Learning makes payment, it will debit Employee Bonus Payable and credit Cash.

## Vacation, Health, and Pension Benefits

Businesses typically offer vacation, health, and pension benefits to its employees. A **pension plan** provides benefits to retired employees. Vacation, health, and pension benefits must be estimated and recorded as a liability. Suppose Smart Touch Learning employees earn two weeks of vacation throughout the year. The company estimates that the cost of providing vacation benefits is $1,000 per month. The accounting clerk will record the following journal entry monthly:

**Pension Plan**
A plan that provides benefits to retired employees.

| Date | Accounts and Explanation | Debit | Credit |
|---|---|---|---|
| | Vacation Benefits Expense | 1,000 | |
| | Vacation Benefits Payable | | 1,000 |
| | *To record employee vacation benefits expense.* | | |

| A | = | L↑ | + | E↓ |
|---|---|---|---|---|
| | | Vacation Benefits Payable↑ | | Vacation Benefits Expense↑ |

When an employee takes paid vacation, Smart Touch Learning will reduce the liability, Vacation Benefits Payable, with a debit and credit Cash. Other benefits, such as health and pension benefits, are recorded in the same manner.

## Warranties

Many corporations guarantee their products against defects under **warranty** agreements. The time period of warranty agreements varies. The matching principle requires businesses to record Warranty Expense in the same period that the company records the revenue related to that warranty. The expense, therefore, is incurred when the company makes a sale, not when the company pays the warranty claims. At the time of the sale, the company does not know the exact amount of warranty expense but can estimate it.

**Warranty**
An agreement that guarantees a company's product against defects.

Assume that Smart Touch Learning made sales on account of $50,000 (cost of merchandise inventory sold, $35,000) subject to product warranties on June 10 and estimates that warranty costs will be 3% of sales. The company would record the sales revenue, cost of goods sold, and estimated warranty expense as follows:

| Date | Accounts and Explanation | Debit | Credit |
|---|---|---|---|
| Jun. 10 | Accounts Receivable | 50,000 | |
| | Sales Revenue | | 50,000 |
| | *Sale on account.* | | |
| 10 | Cost of Goods Sold | 35,000 | |
| | Merchandise Inventory | | 35,000 |
| | *Recorded the cost of goods sold.* | | |
| 10 | Warranty Expense ($50,000 × 0.03) | 1,500 | |
| | Estimated Warranty Payable | | 1,500 |
| | *To accrue warranty payable.* | | |

| A↑ | = | L | + | E↑ |
|---|---|---|---|---|
| Accounts Receivable↑ | | | | Sales Revenue↑ |

| A↓ | = | L | + | E↓ |
|---|---|---|---|---|
| Merchandise Inventory↓ | | | | Cost of Goods Sold↑ |

| A | = | L↑ | + | E↓ |
|---|---|---|---|---|
| | | Estimated Warranty Payable↑ | | Warranty Expense↑ |

Assume that some of Smart Touch Learning's customers make claims that must be honored through the warranty offered by the company. The warranty costs total $800 and are made on June 27. The company replaces the defective goods and makes the following journal entry:

| A↓ | = | L↓ | + | E |
|---|---|---|---|---|
| Merchandise Inventory↓ | | Estimated Warranty Payable↓ | | |

| Date | Accounts and Explanation | Debit | Credit |
|---|---|---|---|
| Jun. 27 | Estimated Warranty Payable | 800 | |
| | Merchandise Inventory | | 800 |
| | *To replace merchandise inventory under warranty.* | | |

Smart Touch Learning's expense on the income statement is $1,500, the estimated amount, not the $800 actually honored. After honoring these warranties, the company's liability account has a credit balance of $700. This $700 balance represents warranty claims Smart Touch Learning expects to honor in the future based on its estimates; therefore, the $700 is a liability to Smart Touch Learning.

**Estimated Warranty Payable**

| | | | |
|---|---|---|---|
| Jun. 27 | 800 | 1,500 | Jun. 10 |
| | | 700 | Bal. |

## ETHICS

### How much is the warranty expense?

Henry Stevenson works as the manager of Used Car Superstore. The business prides itself on including a three-year bumper-to-bumper warranty on all car sales—no matter how old the car. Henry's job responsibilities include estimating the amount of the warranty on each car sale. Henry knows that the older the car is, the higher the warranty cost will be to the business. Edward Wolf, the CEO, has been criticizing Henry for the amount of warranty expense he has been recording. Edward believes that Henry is overestimating the cost of the warranty and has told Henry that he needs to cut the cost in half. What should Henry do? What would you do?

#### Solution

Accounting for warranties can pose specific ethical challenges because it involves estimates instead of actual proven numbers. Businesses like to show high levels of net income in order to look successful. As a result, upper-level managers, such as Edward, may encourage employees to overlook some expenses and liabilities at the end of the accounting period. If Henry does not record the warranty expense or fails to record it at a reasonable amount, total expenses and total liabilities will be understated and net income will be overstated. This might make the company appear to be in better financial condition than it is. Henry should discuss how he determines the estimated cost with his boss. They should decide on a reasonable and accurate number to record as warranty expense.

## Try It!

4. O'Conner guarantees its vacuums for four years. Prior experience indicates that warranty costs will be approximately 6% of sales. Assume that O'Conner made sales totaling $200,000 during 2016. Record the warranty expense for the year.

**Check your answer online in MyAccountingLab or at http://www.pearsonhighered.com/Horngren.**

For more practice, see Short Exercises S11-9 through S11-11. MyAccountingLab

# HOW ARE CONTINGENT LIABILITIES ACCOUNTED FOR?

**Learning Objective 4**
Account for contingent liabilities

A **contingent liability** is a potential, rather than an actual, liability because it depends on a *future* event. For a contingent liability to be paid, some event (the contingency) must happen in the future. For example, suppose Smart Touch Learning is sued because of alleged patent infringement on one of its online learning videos. The company, therefore, faces a contingent liability, which may or may not become an actual liability. If the outcome of this lawsuit is unfavorable, it could hurt Smart Touch Learning by increasing its liabilities. Therefore, it would be unethical to withhold knowledge of the lawsuit from investors and creditors.

**Contingent Liability**
A potential liability that depends on some future event.

Another contingent liability arises when a company *co-signs a note payable* for another entity. The company co-signing has a contingent liability until the note comes due and is paid by the other entity. If the other company pays off the note, the contingent liability vanishes. If the other company doesn't pay off the note, the co-signing company must pay the debt for the other entity. How businesses record or don't record contingent liabilities is based on one of three likelihoods of the event occurring in the future:

- Remote
- Reasonably possible
- Probable

## Remote Contingent Liability

A contingency that is remote has little chance of the event occurring in the future. If a contingency is remote, the company does not need to record a liability and does not need to disclose it in the notes to the financial statements. An example of a remote contingency would be a frivolous lawsuit.

## Reasonably Possible Contingent Liability

Contingencies that are reasonably possible have a greater chance of occurring but are not likely. A reasonably possible contingency should be described in the notes to the financial statements. For example, consider a company that is the defendant in a significant lawsuit. If the company has been advised by legal counsel that it is reasonably possible that it will lose the lawsuit, then it should report the lawsuit in its notes to the financial statements.

## Probable Contingent Liability

If a contingency is probable, it means that the future event is likely to occur. Only contingencies that are probable *and* can be estimated are recorded as a liability and an expense is accrued. An example of an estimable probable contingency is a warranty.

Contingencies that are probable but *cannot* be estimated are disclosed in the notes to the financial statements. A liability is not recorded because the amount of the contingency cannot be estimated. Exhibit 11-4 (on the next page) summarizes the rules for contingent liabilities.

**IFRS**

Under IFRS, "probable" is defined more broadly as "more likely than not" that the future event will result in a liability. "More likely than not" means more than a 50% chance.

**Exhibit 11-4 | Contingent Liabilities**

| Likelihood of Future Event | How to Report the Contingency |
|---|---|
| Remote | Do not disclose. |
| Reasonably possible | Describe the situation in a note to the financial statements. |
| Probable and the amount of the expense *cannot* be estimated | Describe the situation in a note to the financial statements. |
| Probable and the amount of the expense *can* be estimated | Record an expense and a liability based on estimated amounts. |

## DECISIONS

### How should the contingency be reported?

Emily Gallagher is the independent auditor of Tate Manufacturing, a maker of handheld drills and other carpentry tools. Emily is evaluating current lawsuits for the company to determine whether any contingent liabilities should be disclosed. Tate Manufacturing is currently in litigation for a product liability case. The suit claims that a Tate handheld drill heated up quickly and caused a fire. Tate's attorney has told Emily that it is likely that the manufacturer will lose the case, but he does not want to estimate the amount of damages. The attorney is concerned that estimating the amount of damages would establish a dollar amount for settlement and could place their case in jeopardy. What should Emily do?

### Solution

GAAP requires that businesses report a contingency if it is probable that the event will occur in the future. The issue here is where the reporting should be made. If the attorney cannot reasonably estimate the amount of the possible damage award, Tate should report the contingent liability in the notes to the financial statements. If an amount can be determined, Tate Manufacturing should record an expense and a liability based on the estimated amount. Emily should determine whether the attorney *can* estimate the damages but just doesn't want to. If the damages can be estimated, Emily should require that the company record a contingent liability.

### Alternative Solution

The attorney's concern is understandable. He feels that disclosing the amount of the contingent liability could hurt the determination of the case. If the jury were to find out about the disclosure, it might be more likely to award damages to the plaintiff, or the plaintiff might be able to negotiate a larger settlement with Tate. The attorney has a right to be concerned about the transparency of the financial reporting and potential damage to the outcome of the case. The attorney should provide an estimate only if he is reasonably confident with the amount of damages.

## Try It!

Match the likelihood of a future event with the reporting of the contingency. An answer may be selected more than once.

| Likelihood of Future Event | How to Report the Contingency |
|---|---|
| 5. Remote | a. Do not disclose. |
| 6. Reasonably possible | b. Record an expense and a liability based on estimated amounts. |
| 7. Probable and the amount of the loss *cannot* be estimated | c. Describe the situation in a note to the financial statements. |
| 8. Probable and the amount of the loss *can* be estimated | |

**Check your answers online in MyAccountingLab or at http://www.pearsonhighered.com/Horngren.**

For more practice, see Short Exercise S11-12. MyAccountingLab

# HOW DO WE USE THE TIMES-INTEREST-EARNED RATIO TO EVALUATE BUSINESS PERFORMANCE?

**Learning Objective 5**
Use the times-interest-earned ratio to evaluate business performance

Investors can use the **times-interest-earned ratio** to evaluate a business's ability to pay interest expense. This ratio measures the number of times earnings before interest and taxes (EBIT) can cover (pay) interest expense. The times-interest-earned ratio is also called the *interest-coverage ratio.* A high interest-coverage ratio indicates a business's ease in paying interest expense; a low ratio suggests difficulty. The times-interest-earned ratio is calculated as EBIT (Net income + Income tax expense + Interest expense) divided by Interest expense.

**Times-Interest-Earned Ratio**
Evaluates a business's ability to pay interest expense. (Net income + Income tax expense + Interest expense) / Interest expense.

Let's evaluate **Green Mountain Coffee Roasters, Inc.'s** ability to pay its interest expense. The following amounts (in thousands) are taken from Green Mountain's income statement.

| | Year Ended September 28, 2013 | Year Ended September 29, 2012 |
|---|---|---|
| Net income | $ 483,232 | $ 362,628 |
| Income tax expense | 256,771 | 212,641 |
| Interest expense | 18,177 | 22,983 |

Green Mountain's times-interest-earned ratios for the years ended September 28, 2013, and September 29, 2012, are calculated as follows:

Times-interest-earned ratio = (Net income + Income tax expense + Interest expense) / Interest expense

**2013**

= ($483,232 + $256,771 + $18,177) / $18,177
= 41.71 (rounded)

**2012**

= ($362,628 + $212,641 + $22,983) / $22,983
= 26.03 (rounded)

Notice that from 2012 to 2013, Green Mountain experienced a decrease in interest expense. This is because Green Mountain incurred less debt specifically in its revolving line of credit. This decrease in debt increases Green Mountain's times-interest-earned ratio from 26.03 to 41.71. It would appear that Green Mountain can easily cover its interest expense.

## Try It!

9. Fitzgerald Company reported the following amounts on its 2016 income statement:

| | Year Ended December 31, 2016 |
|---|---|
| Net income | $ 19,300 |
| Income tax expense | 5,800 |
| Interest expense | 900 |

What is Fitzgerald's times-interest-earned ratio for 2016? (Round your answer to two decimals.)

**Check your answer online in MyAccountingLab or at http://www.pearsonhighered.com/Horngren.**

For more practice, see Short Exercise S11-13. MyAccountingLab



# REVIEW

## > Things You Should Know

### 1. How are current liabilities of known amounts accounted for?

- Current liabilities are liabilities that must be paid with cash or with goods and services within one year or within the entity's operating cycle if the cycle is longer than a year.
- Some examples of current liabilities are accounts payable, sales tax payable, income tax payable, unearned revenues, and short-term notes payable.
- Current liabilities also include any current portion of long-term notes payable.

### 2. How do companies account for and record payroll?

- Gross pay is the total amount of salary or wages earned by the employee. Net pay is the amount that each employee gets to keep (take-home pay).
- Payroll withholding deductions are the difference between gross pay and net pay. Examples of payroll deductions that *employees* pay include:
  - Income tax withholding: federal, state, and local income tax
  - Employee FICA tax
    - OASDI: 6.2% on the first $117,000 of annual earnings
    - Medicare: 1.45% on earnings up to $200,000, 2.35% on all earnings above $200,000
  - Optional withholdings: charitable contributions, union dues, and so on
- A payroll register can be used to help summarize the earnings, withholdings, and net pay for each employee.
- Businesses record a journal entry for payroll and payroll withholdings as a debit to Salaries and Wages Expense and a credit to various liabilities until the amounts are paid.

- *Employers* must pay at least three payroll taxes:
  - Employer FICA tax
    - OASDI: 6.2% on the first $117,000 of each employee's annual earnings
    - Medicare: 1.45% on all earnings
  - State unemployment compensation tax (SUTA): varies by state; we will use 5.4% on the first $7,000 of each employee's annual earnings
  - Federal unemployment compensation tax (FUTA): 0.6% on the first $7,000 of each employee's annual earnings
- Payroll taxes are recorded as a debit to Payroll Tax Expense and a credit to various liabilities until they are paid.
- Internal control over payroll involves efficiency and safeguarding of payroll disbursements.

### 3. How are current liabilities that must be estimated accounted for?

- Bonuses are based on meeting a specific goal and are considered liabilities (Employee Bonus Payable) until paid.
- Vacation, health, and pension benefits must be estimated and recorded as liabilities until paid.
- Warranty Expense (DR) and Estimated Warranty Payable (CR) must be recorded in the same period that the company records the revenue related to the warranty.
- As warranties are honored, the Estimated Warranty Payable account is reduced.

### 4. How are contingent liabilities accounted for?

- A contingent liability is a potential liability that depends on some future event.
- Accounting for contingent liabilities is based on the following likelihoods:
  - Remote: Do not disclose.
  - Reasonably possible: Describe the situation in a note to the financial statements.
  - Probable and the amount of loss *cannot* be estimated: Describe the situation in a note to the financial statements.
  - Probable and the amount of the loss *can* be estimated: Record an expense and a liability based on estimated amounts.

### 5. How do we use the times-interest-earned ratio to evaluate business performance?

- The times-interest-earned ratio is calculated as (Net income + Income tax expense + Interest expense) / Interest expense.
- It measures the number of times earnings before interest and taxes (EBIT) can cover (pay) interest expense.

CHAPTER 11

## > Summary Problem 11-1

Answer each question independently.

**Requirements**

1. A restaurant made cash sales of $4,000 subject to a 5% sales tax. Record the sales and the related sales tax. Also record the payment of the tax to the state.

2. On October 1, 2016, Rhodes Company purchased equipment at a cost of $10,000, signing a nine-month, 8% note payable for that amount. Record the October 1 purchase. Also record the adjusting entry needed on December 31, 2016, and payment of the note plus interest at maturity on July 1, 2017.
3. How does a contingent liability differ from a known liability? When would a contingent liability be journalized?

## > Solution

### Requirement 1

| Date | Accounts and Explanation | Debit | Credit |
|---|---|---|---|
| | Cash | 4,200 | |
| | Sales Revenue | | 4,000 |
| | Sales Tax Payable ($4,000 × 0.05) | | 200 |
| | *To record cash sales and the related sales tax.* | | |
| | Sales Tax Payable | 200 | |
| | Cash | | 200 |
| | *To record cash payment for sales tax payable.* | | |



### Requirement 2

| Date | Accounts and Explanation | Debit | Credit |
|---|---|---|---|
| 2016 | | | |
| Oct. 1 | Equipment | 10,000 | |
| | Notes Payable | | 10,000 |
| | *Purchased equipment in exchange for nine-month, 8% note.* | | |
| Dec. 31 | Interest Expense ($10,000 × 0.08 × 3/12) | 200 | |
| | Interest Payable | | 200 |
| | *Accrued interest expense at year-end.* | | |
| 2017 | | | |
| Jul. 1 | Notes Payable | 10,000 | |
| | Interest Expense ($10,000 × 0.08 × 6/12) | 400 | |
| | Interest Payable | 200 | |
| | Cash | | 10,600 |
| | *Paid note and interest at maturity.* | | |

**Requirement 3**

A contingent liability is a *potential*, rather than an actual, liability because it depends on a future event. Some event must happen (the contingency) for a contingent liability to have to be paid. Contingent liabilities are journalized when the likelihood of an actual loss is *probable* and the amount of the expense can be reasonably estimated.

## > Summary Problem 11-2

Rags-to-Riches, a clothing resale store, employs one salesperson, Dee Hunter. Hunter's straight-time wage is $10 per hour, with time-and-a-half pay for hours above 40. Rags-to-Riches withholds income tax (20%), FICA—OASDI (6.2%), and FICA—Medicare (1.45%) from Hunter's pay. Rags-to-Riches also pays payroll taxes for FICA—OASDI (6.2%), FICA—Medicare (1.45%), and state and federal unemployment (5.4% and 0.6%, respectively).

During the week ended December 26, Hunter worked 50 hours. Prior to this week, she had earned $2,000.

**Requirements**

(Round all amounts to the nearest dollar.)

1. Compute Hunter's gross pay and net (take-home) pay for the week.
2. Record the payroll entries that Rags-to-Riches would make for each of the following:
   a. Salaries and wages expense and payment related to Hunter
   b. Employer payroll taxes accrual related to Hunter
   c. Payment of all payroll taxes (employee and employer related)
3. How much was Rags-to-Riches's total payroll expense for the week?

## > Solution

**Requirement 1**

| | | |
|---|---|---|
| Gross pay: | | |
| Straight-time pay (40 hours × $10/hour) | | $ 400 |
| Overtime pay: | | |
| Rate per hour ($10 × 1.5) | $ 15 | |
| Hours (50 hours − 40 hours) | × 10 | |
| | | 150 |
| Gross pay | | $ 550 |
| Net pay: | | |
| Gross pay | | $ 550 |
| Withholding deductions: | | |
| Employee income tax ($550 × 0.20) | $ 110 | |
| Employee OASDI ($550 × 0.062) | 34 | |
| Employee Medicare ($550 × 0.0145) | 8 | |
| Total withholdings | | 152 |
| Net (take-home) pay | | $ 398 |

**Requirement 2**

| Date | Accounts and Explanation | Debit | Credit |
|---|---|---|---|
| a. | Salaries and Wages Expense | 550 | |
| | FICA—OASDI Taxes Payable | | 34 |
| | FICA—Medicare Taxes Payable | | 8 |
| | Employee Income Taxes Payable | | 110 |
| | Salaries and Wages Payable | | 398 |
| | *To record salaries and wages expense and payroll withholdings.* | | |
| | | | |
| | Salaries and Wages Payable | 398 | |
| | Cash | | 398 |
| | *To record payment of salaries and wages.* | | |
| | | | |
| b. | Payroll Tax Expense | 75 | |
| | FICA—OASDI Taxes Payable ($550 × 0.062) | | 34 |
| | FICA—Medicare Taxes Payable ($550 × 0.0145) | | 8 |
| | Federal Unemployment Taxes Payable ($550 × 0.006) | | 3 |
| | State Unemployment Taxes Payable ($550 × 0.054) | | 30 |
| | *To record employer's payroll tax expense.* | | |
| | | | |
| c. | FICA—OASDI Taxes Payable ($34 + $34) | 68 | |
| | FICA—Medicare Taxes Payable ($8 + $8) | 16 | |
| | Employee Income Taxes Payable | 110 | |
| | Federal Unemployment Taxes Payable | 3 | |
| | State Unemployment Taxes Payable | 30 | |
| | Cash | | 227 |
| | *To record payment of payroll tax liabilities.* | | |

**Requirement 3**

Rags-to-Riches incurred *total payroll expense* of $625 (gross pay of $550 + payroll tax expense of $75).

CHAPTER 11

## > Key Terms

**Contingent Liability (p. 571)**
**Current Liability (p. 556)**
**Current Portion of Notes Payable (p. 560)**
**Federal Insurance Contributions Act (FICA) (p. 562)**
**Gross Pay (p. 561)**
**Income Tax Withholding (p. 562)**
**Liabilities (p. 556)**
**Long-Term Liability (p. 556)**
**Net Pay (p. 561)**
**Payroll Register (p. 564)**
**Pension Plan (p. 569)**
**Short-Term Note Payable (p. 558)**
**Social Security (FICA) Tax (p. 562)**
**Times-Interest-Earned Ratio (p. 573)**
**Unemployment Compensation Tax (p. 566)**
**Warranty (p. 569)**

## > Quick Check

Learning Objective 1

1. Known liabilities of estimated amounts are
   - a. ignored. (Record them when paid.)
   - b. reported on the balance sheet.
   - c. reported on the income statement.
   - d. reported only in the notes to the financial statements.

Learning Objective 1

2. On January 1, 2016, a business borrowed $18,000 on a five-year, 5% note payable. At December 31, 2016, the business should *record*
   - a. interest payable of $900.
   - b. note receivable of $18,000.
   - c. cash payment of $18,000.
   - d. nothing. (The note is already on the books.)

Learning Objective 1

3. A company sells $180,000 (selling price) of goods and collects sales tax of 8%. What current liability does the sale create?
   - a. Sales tax payable of $14,400
   - b. Sales revenue of $194,400
   - c. Unearned revenue of $14,400
   - d. None; the company collected cash up front.

Learning Objective 1

4. Jade Larson Antiques owes $20,000 on a truck purchased for use in the business. Assume the company makes timely principal payments of $5,000 each year at December 31 plus interest at 8%. Which of the following is true?
   - a. After the first payment is made, the company owes $15,000 plus three years' interest.
   - b. After the first payment, $15,000 would be shown as a long-term liability.
   - c. After the first payment is made, $5,000 would be shown as the current portion due on the long-term note.
   - d. Just before the last payment is made, $5,000 will appear as a long-term liability on the balance sheet.

Learning Objective 2

5. An employee has year-to-date earnings of $113,900. The employee's gross pay for the next pay period is $5,000. If the FICA—OASDI is 6.2% and the wage base is $117,000, how much FICA—OASDI tax will be withheld from the employee's pay? (Answer is rounded to whole dollar.)

   a. $192 b. $210 c. $310 d. $73

Learning Objective 2

6. The employer is responsible for which of the following payroll taxes?
   - a. 6.2% FICA—OASDI tax
   - b. 1.45% FICA—Medicare tax
   - c. Federal and state unemployment taxes
   - d. All of the above

Learning Objective 3

7. Wells Electric (WE) owed Estimated Warranty Payable of $1,200 at the end of 2015. During 2016, WE made sales of $120,000 and expects product warranties to cost the company 3% of the sales. During 2016, WE paid $2,300 for warranties. What is WE's Estimated Warranty Payable at the end of 2016?

   a. $2,300 b. $2,500 c. $3,600 d. $4,800

**Learning Objective 3**

8. Vega Company expects to pay a 4% bonus on net income of $130,000 after deducting the bonus. The journal entry to record the accrued bonus includes
   - **a.** a debit to Employee Bonus Payable, $5,000.
   - **b.** a debit to Employee Bonus Expense, $5,200.
   - **c.** a credit to Employee Bonus Payable, $5,000.
   - **d.** a credit to Cash, $5,200.

**Learning Objective 4**

9. Swell Company has a lawsuit pending from a customer claiming damages of $100,000. Swell's attorney advises that the likelihood the customer will win is remote. GAAP requires at a minimum that this contingent liability be
   - **a.** disclosed in the footnotes.
   - **b.** disclosed in the footnotes, with ranges of potential loss.
   - **c.** recorded as a journal entry, as well as disclosed in the footnotes.
   - **d.** No disclosure is required.

**Learning Objective 5**

10. McDaniel and Associates reported the following amounts on its 2016 income statement:

| | Year Ended December 31, 2016 |
|---|---|
| Net income | $ 60,500 |
| Income tax expense | 12,100 |
| Interest expense | 5,000 |

What was McDaniel's times-interest-earned ratio for 2016?

**a.** 12.10 **c.** 13.10
**b.** 15.52 **d.** 14.52

**Check your answers at the end of the chapter.**



# ASSESS YOUR PROGRESS

## > Review Questions

1. What are the three main characteristics of liabilities?
2. What is a current liability? Provide some examples of current liabilities.
3. How is sales tax recorded? Is it considered an expense of a business? Why or why not?
4. How do unearned revenues arise?
5. What do short-term notes payable represent?
6. Coltrane Company has a $5,000 note payable that is paid in $1,000 installments over five years. How would the portion that must be paid within the next year be reported on the balance sheet?
7. What is the difference between gross pay and net pay?

8. List the required employee payroll withholding deductions, and provide the tax rate for each.
9. How might a business use a payroll register?
10. What payroll taxes is the employer responsible for paying?
11. What are the two main controls for payroll? Provide an example of each.
12. When do businesses record warranty expense, and why?
13. What is a contingent liability? Provide some examples of contingencies.
14. Curtis Company is facing a potential lawsuit. Curtis's lawyers think that it is reasonably possible that it will lose the lawsuit. How should Curtis report this lawsuit?
15. How is the times-interest-earned ratio calculated, and what does it evaluate?

## > Short Exercises

***For all payroll calculations, use the following tax rates and round amounts to the nearest cent.***

*Employee: OASDI: 6.2% on first $117,000 earned; Medicare: 1.45% up to $200,000, 2.35% on earnings above $200,000.*

*Employer: OASDI: 6.2% on first $117,000 earned; Medicare: 1.45%; FUTA: 0.6% on first $7,000 earned; SUTA: 5.4% on first $7,000 earned.*

CHAPTER 11

### S11-1 Determining current versus long-term liabilities

**Learning Objective 1**

Rios Raft Company had the following liabilities.

a. Accounts Payable
b. Note Payable due in 3 years
c. Salaries Payable
d. Note Payable due in 6 months
e. Sales Tax Payable
f. Unearned Revenue due in 8 months
g. Income Tax Payable

Determine whether each liability would be considered a current liability (CL) or a long-term liability (LTL).

### S11-2 Recording sales tax

**Learning Objective 1**

On July 5, Feather Company recorded sales of merchandise inventory on account, $20,000. The sales were subject to sales tax of 9%. On August 15, Feather Company paid $1,200 of sales tax to the state.

**Requirements**

1. Journalize the transaction to record the sale on July 5. Ignore cost of goods sold.
2. Journalize the transaction to record the payment of sales tax to the state.

### S11-3 Recording unearned revenue

**Learning Objective 1**

On June 1, *Guitar Magazine* collected cash of $51,000 on future annual subscriptions starting on July 1.

**Requirements**

1. Journalize the transaction to record the collection of cash on June 1.
2. Journalize the transaction required at December 31, the magazine's year-end, assuming no revenue earned has been recorded. (Round adjustment to the nearest whole dollar.)

**Learning Objective 1**

### S11-4 Accounting for a note payable

On December 31, 2015, Franklin purchased $7,000 of merchandise inventory on a one-year, 11% note payable. Franklin uses a perpetual inventory system.

**Requirements**

1. Journalize the company's purchase of merchandise inventory on December 31, 2015.
2. Journalize the company's accrual of interest expense on June 30, 2016, its fiscal year-end.
3. Journalize the company's payment of the note plus interest on December 31, 2016.

**Learning Objective 1**

### S11-5 Determining current portion of long-term note payable

On January 1, Garland Company purchased equipment of $120,000 with a long-term note payable. The debt is payable in annual installments of $24,000 due on December 31 of each year. At the date of purchase, how will Garland Company report the note payable?



**Learning Objective 2**

### S11-6 Computing and journalizing an employee's total pay

Jenna Lindsay works at College of Boston and is paid $40 per hour for a 40-hour workweek and time-and-a-half for hours above 40.

**Requirements**

1. Compute Lindsay's gross pay for working 54 hours during the first week of February.
2. Lindsay is single, and her income tax withholding is 10% of total pay. Lindsay's only payroll deductions are payroll taxes. Compute Lindsay's net (take-home) pay for the week. Assume Lindsay's earnings to date are less than the OASDI limit.
3. Journalize the accrual of salaries and wages expense and the payments related to the employment of Jenna Lindsay.

**Learning Objective 2**

### S11-7 Computing payroll amounts considering FICA tax ceilings

Lori Waverly works for MRK all year and earns a monthly salary of $12,000. There is no overtime pay. Lori's income tax withholding rate is 20% of gross pay. In addition to payroll taxes, Lori elects to contribute 4% monthly to United Way. MRK also deducts $125 monthly for co-payment of the health insurance premium. As of September 30, Lori had $108,000 of cumulative earnings.

**Requirements**

1. Compute Lori's net pay for October.
2. Journalize the accrual of salaries expense and the payments related to the employment of Lori Waverly.

**S11-8 Computing and journalizing the payroll expense of an employer** — **Learning Objective 2**

Orchard Company has monthly salaries of $10,000. Assume Orchard pays all the standard payroll taxes and no employees have reached the payroll tax limits. Journalize the accrual and payment of employer payroll taxes for Orchard Company.

**S11-9 Computing bonus payable** — **Learning Objective 3**

On December 31, Peterson Company estimates that it will pay its employees a 3% bonus on $62,000 of net income after deducting the bonus. The bonus will be paid on January 15 of the next year.

**Requirements**

1. Journalize the December 31 transaction for Peterson.
2. Journalize the payment of the bonus on January 15.

**S11-10 Journalizing vacation benefits** — **Learning Objective 3**

Roy Industries has eight employees. Each employee earns two vacation days a month. Roy pays each employee a weekly salary of $1,000 for a five-day workweek.

**Requirements**

1. Determine the amount of vacation expense for one month.
2. Journalize the entry to accrue the vacation expense for the month.

**S11-11 Accounting for warranty expense and warranty payable** — **Learning Objective 3**

Hipster Corrector guarantees its snowmobiles for three years. Company experience indicates that warranty costs will be approximately 3% of sales.

Assume that the Hipster dealer in Colorado Springs made sales totaling $350,000 during 2016. The company received cash for 20% of the sales and notes receivable for the remainder. Warranty payments totaled $8,000 during 2016.

**Requirements**

1. Record the sales, warranty expense, and warranty payments for the company. Ignore cost of goods sold.
2. Post to the Estimated Warranty Payable T-account. At the end of 2016, how much in Estimated Warranty Payable does the company owe? Assume the Estimated Warranty Payable is $0 on January 1, 2016.

**S11-12 Accounting treatment for contingencies** — **Learning Objective 4**

Fernandez Motors, a motorcycle manufacturer, had the following contingencies.

a. Fernandez estimates that it is reasonably possible but not likely that it will lose a current lawsuit. Fernandez's attorneys estimate the potential loss will be $3,200,000.

b. Fernandez received notice that it was being sued. Fernandez considers this lawsuit to be frivolous.

c. Fernandez is currently the defendant in a lawsuit. Fernandez believes it is likely that it will lose the lawsuit and estimates the damages to be paid will be $60,000.

Determine the appropriate accounting treatment for each of the situations Fernandez is facing.

Learning Objective 5

**S11-13 Computing times-interest-earned ratio**

Arnold Electronics reported the following amounts on its 2016 income statement:

| Year Ended December 31, 2016 | |
|---|---|
| Net income | $ 49,000 |
| Income tax expense | 7,350 |
| Interest expense | 5,000 |

What is Arnold's times-interest-earned ratio for 2016? (Round the answer to two decimals.)

## > Exercises

Learning Objective 1

Sales Tax Payable $8,500

**E11-14 Recording sales tax**

Consider the following transactions of Moore Software:

| | |
|---|---|
| Mar. 31 | Recorded cash sales of $170,000, plus sales tax of 5% collected for the state of New Jersey. |
| Apr. 6 | Sent March sales tax to the state. |

Journalize the transactions for the company. Ignore cost of goods sold.

Learning Objective 1

May 1, 2016 Interest Expense $120

**E11-15 Recording note payable transactions**

Consider the following note payable transactions of Concert Video Productions.

| | |
|---|---|
| **2015** | |
| May 1 | Purchased equipment costing $12,000 by issuing a one-year, 3% note payable. |
| Dec. 31 | Accrued interest on the note payable. |
| **2016** | |
| May 1 | Paid the note payable plus interest at maturity. |

Journalize the transactions for the company.

Learning Objective 1

Dec. 31 Subscription Revenue $150

**E11-16 Recording and reporting current liabilities**

Worldly Publishing completed the following transactions during 2016:

| | |
|---|---|
| Oct. 1 | Sold a six-month subscription (starting on November 1), collecting cash of $450, plus sales tax of 6%. |
| Nov. 15 | Remitted (paid) the sales tax to the state of Tennessee. |
| Dec. 31 | Made the necessary adjustment at year-end to record the amount of subscription revenue earned during the year. |

Journalize the transactions (explanations are not required).

CHAPTER 11

**E11-17 Journalizing current liabilities**

**Learning Objectives 1, 2**

Salaries Expense $3,100

Erik O'Hern Associates reported short-term notes payable and salaries payable as follows:

| | 2016 | 2015 |
|---|---|---|
| Current Liabilities—partial: | | |
| Short-Term Notes Payable | $ 16,800 | $ 15,200 |
| Salaries Payable | 3,100 | 3,900 |

During 2016, O'Hern paid off both current liabilities that were left over from 2015, borrowed money on short-term notes payable, and accrued salaries expense. Journalize all four of these transactions for O'Hern during 2016. Assume no interest on short-term notes payable of $15,200.

**E11-18 Computing and recording gross and net pay**

**Learning Objective 2**

1. Net Pay $362.44

Hubert Sollenberger manages a Dairy House drive-in. His straight-time pay is $8 per hour, with time-and-a-half for hours in excess of 40 per week. Sollenberger's payroll deductions include withheld income tax of 20%, FICA tax, and a weekly deduction of $8 for a charitable contribution to United Way. Sollenberger worked 56 hours during the week.

**Requirements**

1. Compute Sollenberger's gross pay and net pay for the week. Assume earnings to date are $11,000.
2. Journalize Dairy Houses wages expense accrual for Sollenberger's work. An explanation is not required.
3. Journalize the subsequent payment of wages to Sollenberger.

**E11-19 Recording employer payroll taxes and employee benefits**

**Learning Objective 2**

Payroll Tax Expense $6,135.00

Diego's Mexican Restaurant incurred salaries expense of $70,000 for 2016. The payroll expense includes employer FICA tax, in addition to state unemployment tax and federal unemployment tax. Of the total salaries, $13,000 is subject to unemployment tax. Also, the company provides the following benefits for employees: health insurance (cost to the company, $2,700), life insurance (cost to the company, $380), and retirement benefits (cost to the company, 10% of salaries expense). Journalize Diego's expenses for employee benefits and for payroll taxes. Explanations are not required.

**Learning Objective 2**

2. Salaries & Wages Payable $17,060.10

## E11-20 Recording employee and employer payroll taxes

District Company had the following partially completed payroll register:

| Earnings | | | Withholdings | | | | | | | | | |
|---|---|---|---|---|---|---|---|---|---|---|---|---|
| Beginning Cumulative Earnings | Current Period Earnings | Ending Cumulative Earnings | OASDI | Medicare | Income Tax | Health Insurance | United Way | Total Withholdings | Net Pay | Check No. | Salaries and Wages Expense |
| $ 83,000 | $ 4,300 | | | | $ 860 | $ 86 | $ 20 | | | 801 | |
| 110,900 | 7,800 | | | | 1,560 | 156 | 15 | | | 802 | |
| 37,000 | 2,100 | | | | 420 | 42 | 0 | | | 803 | |
| 60,500 | 4,500 | | | | 900 | 90 | 35 | | | 804 | |
| 0 | 5,500 | | | | 1,100 | 110 | 0 | | | 805 | |
| $ 291,400 | $ 24,200 | | | | $ 4,840 | $ 484 | $ 70 | | | | |

**Requirements**

1. Complete the payroll register.
2. Journalize District's wages expense accrual for the current pay period.
3. Journalize District's expenses for employer payroll taxes for the current pay period.

**Learning Objective 3**

1. Warranty Expense $14,000

## E11-21 Accounting for warranty expense and warranty payable

The accounting records of Earthtone Ceramics included the following at January 1, 2016:

| Estimated Warranty Payable | |
|---|---|
| | 4,000 Beg. Bal. |

In the past, Earthtone's warranty expense has been 8% of sales. During 2016, Earthtone made sales of $175,000 and paid $9,000 to satisfy warranty claims.

**Requirements**

1. Journalize Earthtone's warranty expense and warranty payments during 2016. Explanations are not required.
2. What balance of Estimated Warranty Payable will Earthtone report on its balance sheet at December 31, 2016?

**Learning Objective 3**

Dec. 31 Employee Bonus Expense $3,283.02

## E11-22 Accounting for warranties, vacation, and bonuses

MacDonald Industries completed the following transactions during 2016:

| | |
|---|---|
| Nov. 1 | Made sales of $32,000. MacDonald estimates that warranty expense is 6% of sales. (Record only the warranty expense.) |
| 20 | Paid $1,400 to satisfy warranty claims. |
| Dec. 31 | Estimated vacation benefits expense to be $4,500. |
| 31 | MacDonald expected to pay its employees a 6% bonus on net income after deducting the bonus. Net income for the year is $58,000. |

Journalize the transactions (explanations are not required).

CHAPTER 11

### E11-23 Accounting treatment for contingencies

**Learning Objective 4**

Analyze the following independent situations.

a. Sophia, Inc. is being sued by a former employee. Sophia believes that there is a remote chance that the employee will win. The employee is suing Sophia for damages of $5,000.

b. Oro Oil Refinery had a gas explosion on one of its oil rigs. Oro believes it is likely that it will have to pay environmental clean-up costs and damages in the future due to the gas explosion. Oro cannot estimate the amount of the damages.

c. Lucky Enterprises estimates that it will have to pay $30,000 in warranty repairs next year.

Determine how each contingency should be treated.

### E11-24 Computing times-interest-earned ratio

**Learning Objective 5**

1. Jameson Ratio 120.3 times

The following financial information was obtained from the year ended 2016 income statements for Jameson Automotive and Bauer Automotive:

| | Jameson | Bauer |
|---|---|---|
| Net income | $ 38,100 | $ 68,930 |
| Income tax expense | 9,620 | 27,970 |
| Interest expense | 400 | 3,000 |

**Requirements**

1. Compute the times-interest-earned ratio for each company.
2. Which company was better able to cover its interest expense?



## > Problems Group A

### P11-25A Journalizing and posting liabilities

**Learning Objectives 1, 2**

1d. Rent Revenue $2,500

The general ledger of Quick Ship at June 30, 2016, the end of the company's fiscal year, includes the following account balances before payroll and adjusting entries.

| | |
|---|---|
| Accounts Payable | $ 114,000 |
| Interest Payable | 0 |
| Salaries Payable | 0 |
| Employee Income Taxes Payable | 0 |
| FICA—OASDI Taxes Payable | 0 |
| FICA—Medicare Taxes Payable | 0 |
| Federal Unemployment Taxes Payable | 0 |
| State Unemployment Taxes Payable | 0 |
| Unearned Rent Revenue | 6,000 |
| Long-term Notes Payable | 300,000 |

The additional data needed to develop the payroll and adjusting entries at June 30 are as follows:

a. The long-term debt is payable in annual installments of $60,000, with the next installment due on July 31. On that date, Quick Ship will also pay one year's interest at 10%. Interest was paid on July 31 of the preceding year. Make the adjusting entry to accrue interest expense at year-end.
b. Gross unpaid salaries for the last payroll of the fiscal year were $4,500. Assume that employee income taxes withheld are $900 and that all earnings are subject to OASDI.
c. Record the associated employer taxes payable for the last payroll of the fiscal year, $4,500. Assume that the earnings are not subject to unemployment.
d. On February 1, the company collected one year's rent of $6,000 in advance.

**Requirements**

1. Using T-accounts, open the listed accounts and insert the unadjusted June 30 balances.
2. Journalize and post the June 30 payroll and adjusting entries to the accounts that you opened. Identify each adjusting entry by letter.
3. Prepare the current liabilities section of the balance sheet at June 30, 2016.



**Learning Objective 2**

1. Net Pay $164,641

## P11-26A Computing and journalizing payroll amounts

Lee Werner is general manager of Stoneybrook Salons. During 2016, Werner worked for the company all year at a $14,000 monthly salary. He also earned a year-end bonus equal to 15% of his annual salary.

Werner's federal income tax withheld during 2016 was $980 per month, plus $1,700 on his bonus check. State income tax withheld came to $60 per month, plus $40 on the bonus. FICA tax was withheld on the annual earnings. Werner authorized the following payroll deductions: Charity Fund contribution of 2% of total earnings and life insurance of $35 per month.

Stoneybrook incurred payroll tax expense on Werner for FICA tax. The company also paid state unemployment tax and federal unemployment tax.

**Requirements**

1. Compute Werner's gross pay, payroll deductions, and net pay for the full year 2016. Round all amounts to the nearest dollar.
2. Compute Stoneybrook's total 2016 payroll tax expense for Werner.
3. Make the journal entry to record Stoneybrook's expense for Werner's total earnings for the year, his payroll deductions, and net pay. Debit Salaries Expense and Bonus Expense as appropriate. Credit liability accounts for the payroll deductions and Cash for net pay. An explanation is not required.
4. Make the journal entry to record the accrual of Stoneybrook's payroll tax expense for Werner's total earnings.

## P11-27A Journalizing liability transactions

**Learning Objectives 1, 3**

Jan. 29 Cash $17,490

The following transactions of Houston Pharmacies occurred during 2015 and 2016:

| | |
|---|---|
| **2015** | |
| Jan. 9 | Purchased computer equipment at a cost of $13,000, signing a six-month, 9% note payable for that amount. |
| 29 | Recorded the week's sales of $66,000, three-fourths on credit and one-fourth for cash. Sales amounts are subject to a 6% state sales tax. Ignore cost of goods sold. |
| Feb. 5 | Sent the last week's sales tax to the state. |
| Jul. 9 | Paid the six-month, 9% note, plus interest, at maturity. |
| Aug. 31 | Purchased merchandise inventory for $6,000, signing a six-month, 10% note payable. The company uses the perpetual inventory system. |
| Dec. 31 | Accrued warranty expense, which is estimated at 3% of sales of $601,000. |
| 31 | Accrued interest on all outstanding notes payable. |
| **2016** | |
| Feb. 29 | Paid the six-month 10% note, plus interest, at maturity. |

Journalize the transactions in Houston's general journal. Explanations are not required.

## P11-28A Journalizing liability transactions

**Learning Objectives 3, 4**

1. June 30 Warranty Expense $8,400

The following transactions of Oscar Landing occurred during 2016:

| | |
|---|---|
| Apr. 30 | Landing is party to a patent infringement lawsuit of $220,000. Landing's attorney is certain it is remote that Landing will lose this lawsuit. |
| Jun. 30 | Estimated warranty expense at 2% of sales of $420,000. |
| Jul. 28 | Warranty claims paid in the amount of $5,800. |
| Sep. 30 | Landing is party to a lawsuit for copyright violation of $110,000. Landing's attorney advises that it is probable Landing will lose this lawsuit. The attorney estimates the loss at $110,000. |
| Dec. 31 | Landing estimated warranty expense on sales for the second half of the year of $460,000 at 2%. |

### Requirements

1. Journalize required transactions, if any, in Landing's general journal. Explanations are not required.
2. What is the balance in Estimated Warranty Payable assuming a beginning balance of $0?

**Learning Objective 5**

1. Net Income $10,950

**P11-29A Computing times-interest-earned ratio**

The income statement for Utah Communications follows. Assume Utah Communications signed a 120-day, 12%, $4,000 note on June 1, 2016, and that this was the only note payable for the company.

| UTAH COMMUNICATIONS<br>Income Statement<br>Year Ended July 31, 2016 | | |
|---|---|---|
| Sales Revenue | $ 33,000 | |
| Less: Sales Returns and Allowances | 5,100 | |
| Sales Discounts | 2,900 | |
| Net Sales Revenue | | $ 25,000 |
| Cost of Goods Sold | | 9,000 |
| Gross Profit | | 16,000 |
| Operating Expenses: | | |
| Selling Expenses | 730 | |
| Administrative Expenses | 1,500 | |
| Total Operating Expenses | | 2,230 |
| Operating Income | | 13,770 |
| Other Revenues and (Expenses): | | |
| Interest Expense | ? | |
| Total Other Revenues and (Expenses) | | ? |
| Net Income before Income Tax Expense | | ? |
| Income Tax Expense | | 2,740 |
| Net Income | | $ ? |

**Requirements**

1. Fill in the missing information for Utah's year ended July 31, 2016, income statement.
2. Compute the times-interest-earned ratio for the company.

## > Problems Group B

### P11-30B Journalizing and posting liabilities

Learning Objectives 1, 2

1d. Rent Revenue $2,625

The general ledger of U-R-Shipping at June 30, 2016, the end of the company's fiscal year, includes the following account balances before payroll and adjusting entries.

| | |
|---|---|
| Accounts Payable | $ 115,000 |
| Interest Payable | 0 |
| Salaries Payable | 0 |
| Employee Income Taxes Payable | 0 |
| FICA—OASDI Taxes Payable | 0 |
| FICA—Medicare Taxes Payable | 0 |
| Federal Unemployment Taxes Payable | 0 |
| State Unemployment Taxes Payable | 0 |
| Unearned Rent Revenue | 6,300 |
| Long-Term Notes Payable | 300,000 |

The additional data needed to develop the payroll and adjusting entries at June 30 are as follows:

a. The long-term debt is payable in annual installments of $60,000, with the next installment due on July 31. On that date, U-R-Shipping will also pay one year's interest at 8%. Interest was paid on July 31 of the preceding year. Make the adjusting entry to accrue interest expense at year-end.

b. Gross unpaid salaries for the last payroll of the fiscal year were $4,100. Assume that employee income taxes withheld are $820 and that all earnings are subject to OASDI.

c. Record the associated employer taxes payable for the last payroll of the fiscal year, $4,100. Assume that the earnings are not subject to unemployment.

d. On February 1, the company collected one year's rent of $6,300 in advance.

**Requirements**

1. Using T-accounts, open the listed accounts and insert the unadjusted June 30 balances.
2. Journalize and post the June 30 payroll and adjusting entries to the accounts that you opened. Identify each adjusting entry by letter.
3. Prepare the current liabilities section of the balance sheet at June 30, 2016.

### P11-31B Computing and journalizing payroll amounts

Learning Objective 2

1. Net Pay $156,895

Len Wilson is general manager of Crossroad Salons. During 2016, Wilson worked for the company all year at a $14,200 monthly salary. He also earned a year-end bonus equal to 10% of his annual salary.

Wilson's federal income tax withheld during 2016 was $1,000 per month, plus $1,200 on his bonus check. State income tax withheld came to $130 per month, plus $70 on the bonus. FICA tax was withheld on the annual earnings. Wilson authorized the following payroll deductions: Charity Fund contribution of 3% of total earnings and life insurance of $10 per month.

Crossroad incurred payroll tax expense on Wilson for FICA tax. The company also paid state unemployment tax and federal unemployment tax.

CHAPTER 11

**Requirements**

1. Compute Wilson's gross pay, payroll deductions, and net pay for the full year 2016. Round all amounts to the nearest dollar.
2. Compute Crossroad's total 2016 payroll tax expense for Wilson.
3. Make the journal entry to record Crossroad's expense for Wilson's total earnings for the year, his payroll deductions, and net pay. Debit Salaries Expense and Bonus Expense as appropriate. Credit liability accounts for the payroll deductions and Cash for net pay. An explanation is not required.
4. Make the journal entry to record the accrual of Crossroad's payroll tax expense for Wilson's total earnings.

**Learning Objectives 1, 3**

Jan. 29 Cash $18,285

## P11-32B Journalizing liability transactions

The following transactions of San Francisco Pharmacies occurred during 2015 and 2016:

| | |
|---|---|
| **2015** | |
| Jan. 9 | Purchased computer equipment at a cost of $9,000, signing a six-month, 6% note payable for that amount. |
| 29 | Recorded the week's sales of $69,000, three-fourths on credit and one-fourth for cash. Sales amounts are subject to a 6% state sales tax. Ignore cost of goods sold. |
| Feb. 5 | Sent the last week's sales tax to the state. |
| Jul. 9 | Paid the six-month, 6% note, plus interest, at maturity. |
| Aug. 31 | Purchased merchandise inventory for $6,000, signing a six-month, 9% note payable. The company uses a perpetual inventory system. |
| Dec. 31 | Accrued warranty expense, which is estimated at 2% of sales of $601,000. |
| 31 | Accrued interest on all outstanding notes payable. |
| **2016** | |
| Feb. 29 | Paid the six-month 9% note, plus interest, at maturity. |

Journalize the transactions in San Francisco's general journal. Explanations are not required.

**Learning Objectives 3, 4**

1. June 30 Warranty Expense $18,000

## P11-33B Journalizing liability transactions

The following transactions of Percy Bowes occurred during 2016:

| | |
|---|---|
| Apr. 30 | Bowes is party to a patent infringement lawsuit of $200,000. Bowes's attorney is certain it is remote that Bowes will lose this lawsuit. |
| Jun. 30 | Estimated warranty expense at 4% of sales of $450,000. |
| Jul. 28 | Warranty claims paid in the amount of $6,300. |
| Sep. 30 | Bowes is party to a lawsuit for copyright violation of $120,000. Bowes's attorney advises that it is probable Bowes will lose this lawsuit. The attorney estimates the loss at $120,000. |
| Dec. 31 | Bowes estimated warranty expense on sales for the second half of the year of $480,000 at 4%. |

**Requirements**

1. Journalize required transactions, if any, in Bowes's general journal. Explanations are not required.
2. What is the balance in Estimated Warranty Payable assuming a beginning balance of $0?

CHAPTER 11

### P11-34B Computing times-interest-earned ratio

**Learning Objective 5**

1. Net Income $5,790

The income statement for Virginia Communications follows. Assume Virginia Communications signed a 120-day, 6%, $10,000 note on June 1, 2016, and that this was the only note payable for the company.

| VIRGINIA COMMUNICATIONS<br>Income Statement<br>Year Ended July 31, 2016 | | |
|---|---|---|
| Sales Revenue | $ 31,000 | |
| Less: Sales Returns and Allowances | 4,700 | |
| Sales Discounts | 3,400 | |
| Net Sales Revenue | | $ 22,900 |
| Cost of Goods Sold | | 13,200 |
| Gross Profit | | 9,700 |
| Operating Expenses: | | |
| Selling Expenses | 710 | |
| Administrative Expenses | 1,650 | |
| Total Operating Expenses | | 2,360 |
| Operating Income | | 7,340 |
| Other Revenues and (Expenses): | | |
| Interest Expense | ? | |
| Total Other Revenues and (Expenses) | | ? |
| Net Income before Income Tax Expense | | ? |
| Income Tax Expense | | 1,450 |
| Net Income | | $ ? |

**Requirements**

1. Fill in the missing information for Virginia's year ended July 31, 2016, income statement.
2. Compute the times-interest-earned ratio for the company.

CHAPTER 11

## > Continuing Problem

### P11-35 Accounting for liabilities of a known amount

This problem continues the Daniels Consulting situation from Problem P10-23 of Chapter 10. Daniels Consulting believes the company will need to borrow $300,000 in order to expand operations. Daniels consults the bank and secures a 6%, five-year note on March 1, 2017. Daniels must pay the bank principal in five equal installments plus interest annually on March 1.

**Requirements**

1. Record the $300,000 note payable on March 1, 2017.
2. Record the entry to accrue interest due on the note at December 31, 2017.
3. Record the entry Daniels would make to record the payment to the bank on March 1, 2018.

# CRITICAL THINKING

## > Decision Cases

### Decision Case 11-1

Golden Bear Construction operates throughout California. The owner, Gaylan Beavers, employs 15 work crews. Construction supervisors report directly to Beavers, and the supervisors are trusted employees. The home office staff consists of an accountant and an office manager.

Because employee turnover is high in the construction industry, supervisors hire and fire their own crews. Supervisors notify the office of all personnel changes. Also, supervisors forward the employee W-4 forms to the home office. Each Thursday, the supervisors submit weekly time sheets for their crews, and the accountant prepares the payroll. At noon on Friday, the supervisors come to the office to get paychecks for distribution to the workers at 5 p.m.

The company accountant prepares the payroll, including the paychecks. Beavers signs all paychecks. To verify that each construction worker is a bona fide employee, the accountant matches the employee's endorsement signature on the back of the canceled paycheck with the signature on that employee's W-4 form.

**Requirements**

1. Identify one way that a supervisor can defraud Golden Bear Construction under the present system.
2. Discuss a control feature that the company can use to *safeguard* against the fraud you identified in Requirement 1.



### Decision Case 11-2

Sell-Soft is the defendant in numerous lawsuits claiming unfair trade practices. Sell-Soft has strong incentives not to disclose these contingent liabilities. However, GAAP requires that companies report their contingent liabilities.

**Requirements**

1. Why would a company prefer *not* to disclose its contingent liabilities?
2. Describe how a bank could be harmed if a company seeking a loan did not disclose its contingent liabilities.
3. What ethical tightrope must companies walk when they report contingent liabilities?

## > Ethical Issue 11-1

Many small businesses have to squeeze down costs any way they can just to survive. One way many businesses do this is by hiring workers as "independent contractors" rather than as regular employees. Unlike rules for regular employees, a business does not have to pay Social Security (FICA) taxes and unemployment insurance payments for independent contractors. Similarly, it does not have to withhold federal, state, or local income taxes or the employee's share of FICA taxes. The IRS has a "20 factor test" that determines whether a worker should be considered an employee or a contractor, but many businesses ignore those rules or interpret them loosely in their favor. When workers are treated as independent contractors, they do not get a W-2 form at tax time (they get a 1099 instead), they do not have any income taxes withheld, and they find themselves subject to "self-employment" taxes, by which they bear the brunt of both the employee's and the employer's shares of FICA taxes.

**Requirements**

1. When a business abuses this issue, how is the independent contractor hurt?
2. If a business takes an aggressive position—that is, interprets the law in a very slanted way—is there an ethical issue involved? Who is hurt?

## > Financial Statement Case 11-1

Details about a company's liabilities appear in a number of places in the annual report. Visit **http://www.pearsonhighered.com/Horngren** to view a link to Starbucks Corporation's Annual Report. Use **Starbucks Corporation**'s fiscal 2013 financial statements to answer the following questions.

**Requirements**

1. Give the breakdown of Starbucks's current liabilities at September 29, 2013.
2. Calculate Starbucks's times-interest-earned ratio for the year ending September 30, 2012.

## > Communication Activity 11-1

In 150 words or fewer, explain how contingent liabilities are accounted for.



## > Quick Check Answers

**1.** b **2.** a **3.** a **4.** c **5.** a **6.** d **7.** b **8.** c **9.** d **10.** b

CHAPTER 11

# 12 Long-Term Liabilities

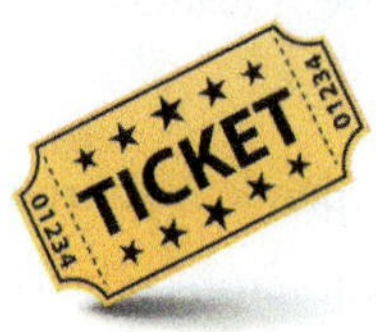


## Should the Business Take on Additional Debt?

Sophie Animations Studios, Inc. specializes in creating animated feature films for children and young-minded adults. The studio was started by founders Steve Lasseter and Lee Bird and has grown to produce many notable films. The corporation's stock is currently sold on a national stock exchange, and the company is widely respected for its consistent earnings each year.

The corporation plans on expanding its existing operations by building a new studio in Canada that will produce short movies and TV specials. In order to fund this expansion, the corporation is considering several options. One option is for the corporation to issue additional stock to raise the necessary cash. Another option is for the corporation to take on additional debt. As majority stockholders, Steve and Lee have expressed their concern over issuing additional shares of stock. The stockholders are concerned that the additional stock will decrease their ownership percentage in the corporation and also cause the market value of the stock to decrease. Due to these concerns, the corporation has decided that the best option would be to explore ways to secure the cash needed for expansion by taking on additional debt.

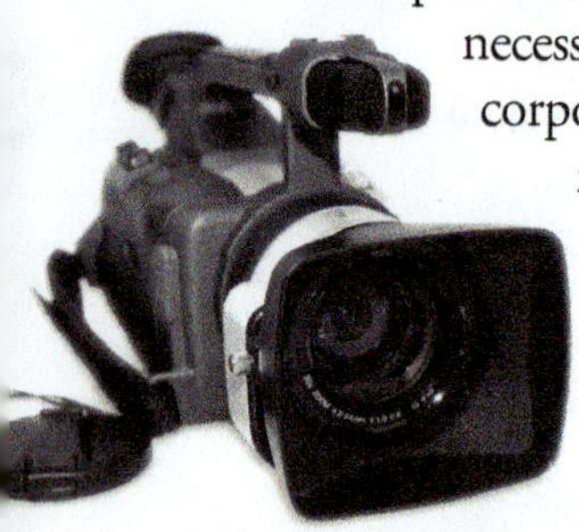

Sophie Animations Studios is currently evaluating different types of long-term liability options such as long-term notes payable and mortgages payable. These debts will most likely be secured by the studio building and will offer a reasonable interest rate and time period for repayment. In addition, Sophie Animations Studios is considering a special type of long-term liability, called a bonds payable. A bonds payable is issued on a bond market and typically provides a larger cash inflow than notes payable and mortgages payable do. In addition, bonds payable also often provide a longer time period for repayment, some even lasting for as long as 100 years. Each of these long-term liabilities is unique and offers advantages and disadvantages that Sophie Animations Studios needs to consider before it can begin the expansion.

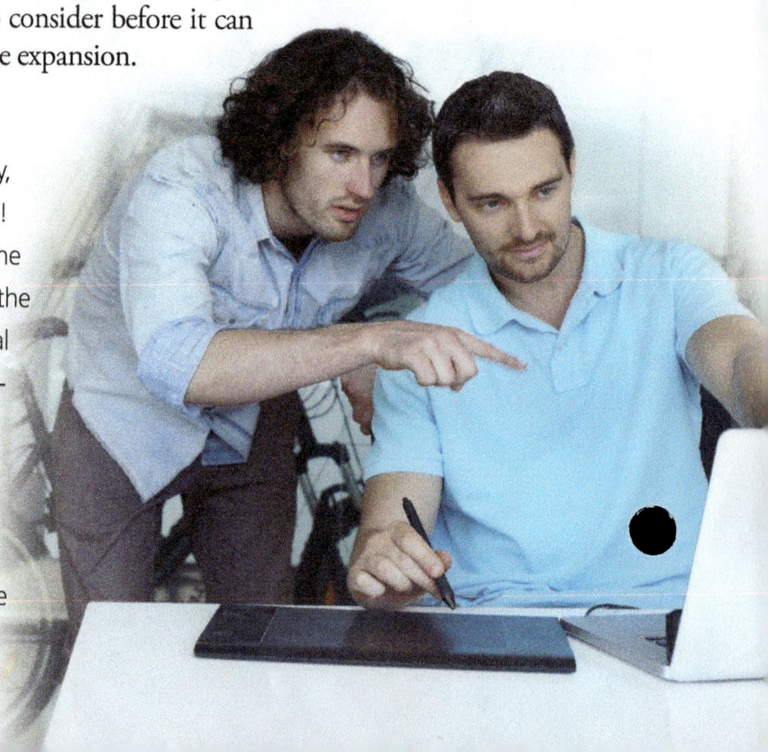

**Why Issue a 100-Year Bond Payable?**

On July 21, 1993, the Walt Disney Company issued a long-term liability, specifically called a bonds payable, that would be payable in 100 years! These bonds were issued with an annual interest rate of 7.55%, and the principal of approximately $300 million was scheduled to be repaid in the year 2093. The Walt Disney Company is well known as an international family entertainment and media enterprise that includes broadcast networks, parks and resorts, the Walt Disney studios, consumer products, and interactive technology and games. Why would the Walt Disney Company issue a debt that wouldn't be paid back for 100 years? How are these types of long-term liabilities accounted for and reported on the balance sheet? In this chapter, you learn why companies might issue bonds payable and also how to account for other long-term liabilities, such as long-term notes payable and mortgages payable.

# Chapter 12 Learning Objectives

1 Journalize transactions for long-term notes payable and mortgages payable

2 Describe bonds payable

3 Journalize transactions for bonds payable and interest expense using the straight-line amortization method

4 Journalize transactions to retire bonds payable

5 Report liabilities on the balance sheet

6 Use the debt to equity ratio to evaluate business performance

7 Use time value of money to compute the present value of future amounts (Appendix 12A)

8 Journalize transactions for bonds payable and interest expense using the effective-interest amortization method (Appendix 12B)

## HOW ARE LONG-TERM NOTES PAYABLE AND MORTGAGES PAYABLE ACCOUNTED FOR?

**Learning Objective 1**
Journalize transactions for long-term notes payable and mortgages payable

You have learned that long-term liabilities are liabilities that do not need to be paid within one year or within the entity's operating cycle, whichever is longer. Both long-term notes payable and mortgages payable are common long-term liabilities.

### Long-Term Notes Payable

Long-term notes payable are typically reported in the long-term liabilities section of the balance sheet. You learned about the current portion of long-term notes payable in a previous chapter. Now, let's focus on the long-term portion of the notes payable and the payments made according to the note contract.

Recall that most long-term notes payable are paid in installments. The *current portion of notes payable* is the principal amount that will be paid within one year—a current liability. The remaining portion is long-term. For example, Smart Touch Learning signed a $20,000 note payable on December 31, 2016. The note will be paid over four years with payments of $5,000 plus 6% interest due each December 31, beginning December 31, 2017. Remember that the current portion of the note, the amount due December 31, 2017, $5,000, is considered a current liability at December 31, 2016. We record the issuance of the note on December 31, 2016, in the following manner:

| Date | Accounts and Explanation | Debit | Credit |
|---|---|---|---|
| 2016 | | | |
| Dec. 31 | Cash | 20,000 | |
| | Notes Payable | | 20,000 |
| | *Received cash in exchange for a 4-year, 6% note.* | | |

| A↑ | } = { | L↑ | + | E |
|---|---|---|---|---|
| Cash↑ | | Notes Payable↑ | | |

On December 31, 2017, Smart Touch Learning will make a $5,000 principal payment plus interest. Exhibit 12-1 (on the next page) shows an **amortization schedule** for the notes payable. An amortization schedule details each loan payment's allocation between principal and interest and also the beginning and ending balances of the loan. Using the calculation for interest that you have already learned, Smart Touch Learning will calculate interest expense

**Amortization Schedule**
A schedule that details each loan payment's allocation between principal and interest and the beginning and ending loan balances.

as beginning balance × interest rate × time. The total cash payment is the principal payment plus interest expense. Notice that at the end of the four years, Smart Touch Learning will have paid total interest of $3,000. Also notice that the interest expense decreases each year, as this expense is based on the principal, which is decreasing with each installment payment.

**Exhibit 12-1 | Long-Term Notes Payable Amortization Schedule**

| | Beginning Balance | Principal Payment | Interest Expense | Total Payment | Ending Balance |
|---|---|---|---|---|---|
| 12/31/2016 | | | | | $ 20,000 |
| 12/31/2017 | $ 20,000 | $ 5,000 | $ 1,200 | $ 6,200 | 15,000 |
| 12/31/2018 | 15,000 | 5,000 | 900 | 5,900 | 10,000 |
| 12/31/2019 | 10,000 | 5,000 | 600 | 5,600 | 5,000 |
| 12/31/2020 | 5,000 | 5,000 | 300 | 5,300 | 0 |
| Total | | $ 20,000 | $ 3,000 | $ 23,000 | |

Beginning balance − Principal payment = $20,000 − $5,000 = $15,000

Beginning balance × Interest rate × Time = $20,000 × 0.06 × 1 year = $1,200

Principal payment + Interest expense = $5,000 + $1,200 = $6,200

Assume it's now December 31, 2017, and Smart Touch Learning must make its first installment payment of $5,000 principal plus interest on the note. The company's accounting clerk will record the following entry:

A↓ Cash↓ } = { L↓ Notes Payable↓ + E↓ Interest Expense↑

| Date | Accounts and Explanation | Debit | Credit |
|---|---|---|---|
| 2017 | | | |
| Dec. 31 | Notes Payable | 5,000 | |
| | Interest Expense | 1,200 | |
| | Cash | | 6,200 |
| | *Paid principal and interest payment.* | | |

After the December 31, 2017, entry, Smart Touch Learning owes $15,000 ($20,000 original note amount minus the $5,000 principal paid on December 31, 2017). The company will record similar entries for the three remaining payments using the amounts calculated in the amortization schedule.

## Mortgages Payable

**Mortgages Payable**
Long-term debts that are backed with a security interest in specific property.

**Mortgages payable** include the borrower's promise to transfer the legal title to specific assets if the mortgage isn't paid on schedule. Mortgages payable are very similar to long-term notes payable. The main difference is the mortgages payable is secured with specific assets, whereas long-term notes are not secured with specific assets. Like long-term notes payable, the total mortgages payable amount has a portion due within one year (current) and a portion that is due more than one year from a specific date.

Commonly, mortgages specify a monthly payment of principal and interest to the lender (usually a bank). The most common type of mortgage is on property—for example, a mortgage on your home. Let's review an example.

Assume that on December 31, 2016, Smart Touch Learning purchases a building for $150,000, paying $49,925 in cash and signing a 30-year mortgage for $100,075, taken out at 6% interest that is payable in $600 monthly payments, which includes principal and interest, beginning January 31, 2017. The following entry is used to record this acquisition:

| Date | Accounts and Explanation | Debit | Credit |
|---|---|---|---|
| 2016 | | | |
| Dec. 31 | Building | 150,000 | |
| | Mortgages Payable | | 100,075 |
| | Cash | | 49,925 |
| | *Purchased building with a mortgage payable and cash payment.* | | |

A↑ = L↑ + E
Building↑ Cash↓ = Mortgages Payable↑

A partial amortization schedule for 2016 and 2017 is shown in Exhibit 12-2.

Beginning balance × Interest rate × Time = $100,075 × 0.06 × 1/12 = $500.38

Total payment − Interest expense = $600.00 − $500.38 = $99.62

**Exhibit 12-2 | Mortgages Payable Amortization Schedule**

| | Beginning Balance | Principal Payment | Interest Expense | Total Payment | Ending Balance |
|---|---|---|---|---|---|
| 12/31/2016 | | | | | $ 100,075.00 |
| 01/31/2017 | $ 100,075.00 | $ 99.62 | $ 500.38 | $ 600.00 | 99,975.38 |
| 02/28/2017 | 99,975.38 | 100.12 | 499.88 | 600.00 | 99,875.26 |
| 03/31/2017 | 99,875.26 | 100.62 | 499.38 | 600.00 | 99,774.64 |
| 04/30/2017 | 99,774.64 | 101.13 | 498.87 | 600.00 | 99,673.51 |
| 05/31/2017 | 99,673.51 | 101.63 | 498.37 | 600.00 | 99,571.88 |
| 06/30/2017 | 99,571.88 | 102.14 | 497.86 | 600.00 | 99,469.74 |
| 07/31/2017 | 99,469.74 | 102.65 | 497.35 | 600.00 | 99,367.09 |
| 08/31/2017 | 99,367.09 | 103.16 | 496.84 | 600.00 | 99,263.93 |
| 09/30/2017 | 99,263.93 | 103.68 | 496.32 | 600.00 | 99,160.25 |
| 10/31/2017 | 99,160.25 | 104.20 | 495.80 | 600.00 | 99,056.05 |
| 11/30/2017 | 99,056.05 | 104.72 | 495.28 | 600.00 | 98,951.33 |
| 12/31/2017 | 98,951.33 | 105.24 | 494.76 | 600.00 | 98,846.09 |
| Total | | $ 1,228.91 | $ 5,971.09 | $ 7,200.00 | |

Beginning balance − Principal payment = $100,075.00 − $99.62 = $99,975.38

*Notice that as time goes by the portion of the payment applied to principal increases and interest expense decreases.*

We can confirm the interest calculations provided in the amortization table. So, for the first payment on the interest is calculated as $100,075.00 × 6% × 1/12, or $500.38. The principal of $99.62 is the difference between the monthly payment of $600.00 and the interest expense of $500.38 ($600.00 − $500.38 = $99.62). The $99.62 reduces the mortgages payable from $100,075.00 to $99,975.38 ($100,075.00 − $99.62 = $99,975.38). So, after reviewing the amortization schedule, Smart Touch Learning records the first mortgage payment as follows:

| A↓ | = | L↓ | + | E↓ |
|---|---|---|---|---|
| Cash↓ | = | Mortgages Payable↓ | | Interest Expense↑ |

| Date | Accounts and Explanation | Debit | Credit |
|---|---|---|---|
| 2017 | | | |
| Jan. 31 | Mortgages Payable | 99.62 | |
| | Interest Expense | 500.38 | |
| | Cash | | 600.00 |
| | *Paid principal and interest payment.* | | |

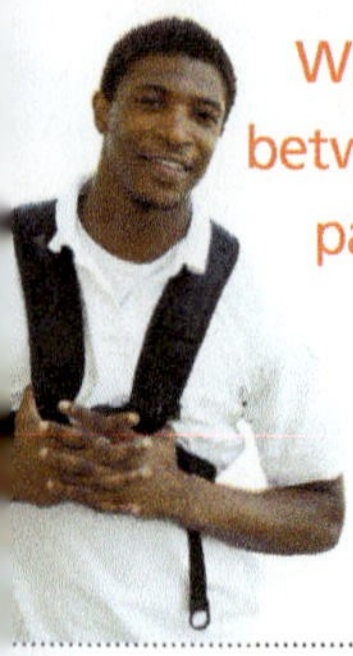

What is the difference between the mortgages payable amortization schedule and the long-term notes payable amortization schedule?

Each mortgage payment will be recorded in a similar journal entry, using the amortization schedule amounts.

Take a moment to review Exhibits 12-1 and 12-2. **In Exhibit 12-1, the principal payment stays the same and the total payment changes. In Exhibit 12-2, the principal payment varies while the total payment stays the same. Long-term liabilities can be structured either way—with an equal principal payment or equal total payment.** One thing that always changes, though, is the amount of interest expense each period. The amount of interest expense is always calculated on the beginning balance of the loan, and because the beginning balance of the loan is decreasing, the amount of interest expense also decreases.

## Try It!

On January 1, 2016, Fox Corporation signed an $80,000, four-year, 4% note. The loan required Fox to make payments annually on December 31 of $20,000 principal plus interest.

1. Journalize the issuance of the note on January 1, 2016.
2. Journalize the first payment on December 31, 2016.

**Check your answers online in MyAccountingLab or at http://www.pearsonhighered.com/Horngren.**

For more practice, see Short Exercises S12-1 and S12-2. MyAccountingLab

## WHAT ARE BONDS?

**Learning Objective 2**
Describe bonds payable

**Bond Payable**
A long-term debt issued to multiple lenders called bondholders, usually in increments of $1,000 per bond.

Large companies need large amounts of money to finance their operations. They may take out long-term loans from banks and/or issue bonds payable to the public to raise the money. **Bonds payable** are long-term debts issued to multiple lenders called bondholders, usually in increments of $1,000 per bond. For example, a company could borrow $100,000 from one lender (the bank), or it could issue 100 bonds payable, each at $1,000, from 100 different lenders. By issuing bonds payable, companies can borrow millions of dollars from thousands of investors rather than depending on a loan from one single bank or lender. Each investor can buy a specified amount of the company's bonds.

Each bondholder gets a bond certificate that shows the name of the company that borrowed the money, exactly like a note payable. The certificate states the face value, which is the amount of the bond issue. The bond's face value is also called *maturity value*, *principal*, or *par value*. The company must then pay each bondholder the face value amount at a specific future date, called the maturity date.

People buy (invest in) bonds to earn interest. The bond certificate states the interest rate that the company will pay and the dates the interest is due, generally semiannually (twice per year). For example, a five-year, 9% bond issued at a face value of \$100,000 on January 1, 2016 will pay 10 semiannual interest payments of \$4,500 (\$100,000 × 0.09 × 6/12) in addition to the face value payment at the maturity date. The cash flow pattern for a bond is as follows:

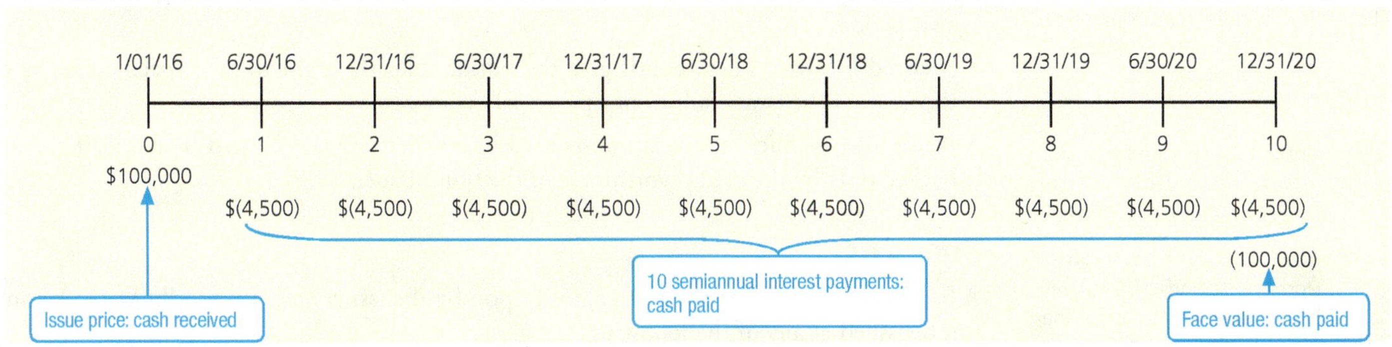


Exhibit 12-3 shows a bond certificate issued by Smart Touch Learning. Review the following bond fundamentals in the exhibit:

- **Face value**: The amount the borrower must pay back to the bondholders on the maturity date (also called *maturity value*, *principal amount*, or *par value*).

**Face Value**
The amount a borrower must pay back to the bondholders on the maturity date.

**Exhibit 12-3 | Bond Certificate**

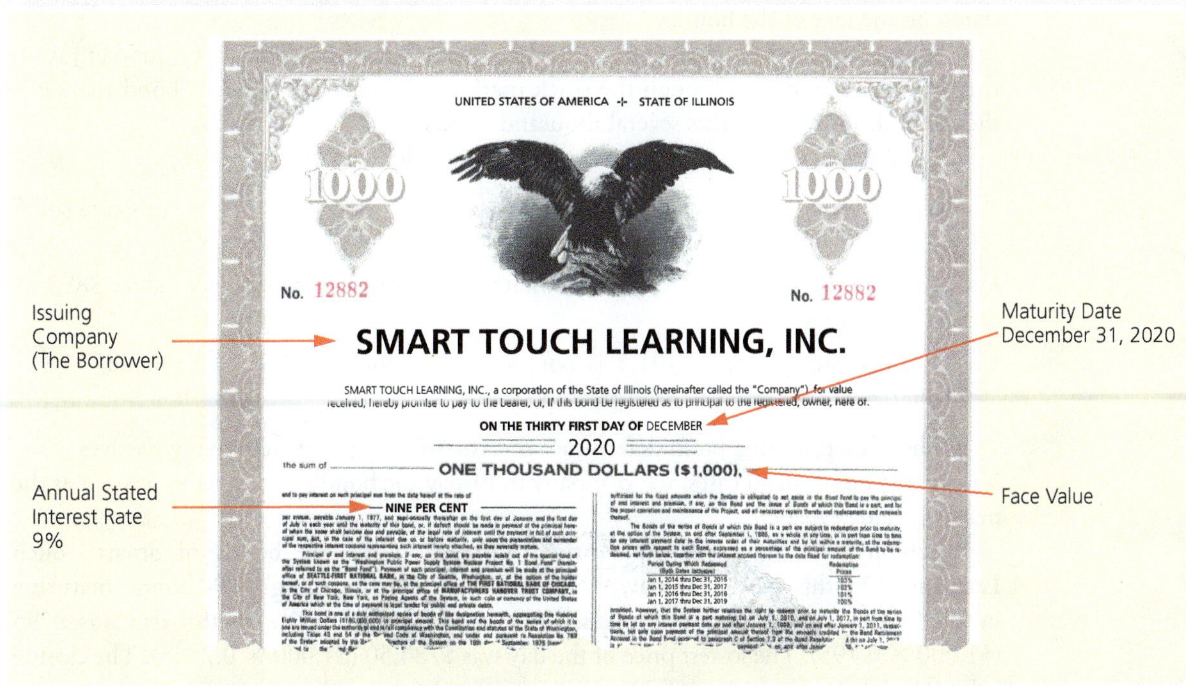

- **Maturity date**: The date on which the borrower must pay the principal amount to the bondholders.
- **Stated interest rate**: The interest rate that determines the amount of cash interest the borrower pays and the investor receives each year (also called *face rate*, *coupon rate*, or *nominal rate*).

**Stated Interest Rate**
The interest rate that determines the amount of cash interest the borrower pays and the investor receives each year.

## Types of Bonds

There are various types of bonds, including the following:

- **Term bonds**—These bonds all mature at the same specified time. For example, $100,000 of term bonds may all mature five years from today.
- **Serial bonds**—Such bonds mature in installments at regular intervals. For example, a $500,000, five-year serial bond may mature in $100,000 annual installments over a five-year period.
- **Secured bonds**—These bonds give the bondholder the right to take specified assets of the issuer if the issuer fails to pay principal or interest.
- **Debentures**—Such bonds are unsecured bonds that are not backed by assets. They are backed only by the credit worthiness of the bond issuer.

**Term Bonds**
Bonds that all mature at the same time.

**Serial Bonds**
Bonds that mature in installments at regular intervals.

**Secured Bonds**
Bonds that give bondholders the right to take specified assets of the issuer if the issuer fails to pay principal or interest.

**Debentures**
Unsecured bonds backed only by the credit worthiness of the bond issuer.

## Bond Prices

A bond can be issued at any price agreed upon by the issuer and the bondholders. A bond can be issued at any of the following:

- **Face value.** Occurs when a bond is issued at face value. Example: A $1,000 bond issued for $1,000.
- **Discount.** A **discount on bonds payable** occurs when the issue price is less than face value. Example: A $1,000 bond issued for $980. The discount is $20 ($1,000 − $980).
- **Premium.** A **premium on bonds payable** occurs when the issue price is above face value. Example: A $1,000 bond issued for $1,015. The premium is $15 ($1,015 − $1,000).

**Discount on Bonds Payable**
Occurs when a bond's issue price is less than face value.

**Premium on Bonds Payable**
Occurs when a bond's issue price is more than face value.

The issue price of a bond does not affect the required payment at maturity. In all of the preceding cases, the company must pay the face value of the bonds at the maturity date stated on the face of the bond.

After a bond is issued, investors may buy and sell it through the bond market just as they buy and sell stocks through the stock market. The most well-known bond market is the NYSE Bonds, which lists several thousand bonds.

Bond prices are quoted as a percentage of face value. For example:

- a $1,000 bond quoted at 100 is bought or sold for 100% of face value, $1,000 ($1,000 × 1.00).
- a $1,000 bond quoted at 88.375 is bought or sold for 88.375% of face value, $883.75 ($1,000 × 0.88375).
- a $1,000 bond quoted at 101.5 is bought or sold for 101.5% of face value, $1,015 ($1,000 × 1.015).

The issue price of a bond determines the amount of cash the company receives when it issues the bond. In all cases, the company must pay the bond's face value to retire it at the maturity date.

Exhibit 12-4 shows example price information for the bonds of Smart Touch Learning. On this particular day, 12 of Smart Touch Learning's 9% bonds maturing in 2021 (indicated by 21) were traded. The bonds' highest price on this day was $795 ($1,000 × 0.795). The lowest price of the day was $784.50 ($1,000 × 0.7845). The closing price (last sale of the day) was $795.

**Exhibit 12-4 | Bond Price Information**

| Bonds | Volume | High | Low | Close |
|---|---|---|---|---|
| SMT 9% of 21 | 12 | 79.5 | 78.45 | 79.5 |

## Present Value

Money earns interest over time, a fact called the **time value of money**. Appendix 12A at the end of this chapter covers the time value of money in detail.

**Time Value of Money**
Recognition that money earns interest over time.

Let's see how the time value of money affects bond prices. Assume that a $1,000 bond reaches maturity three years from now and carries no interest. Would you pay $1,000 to purchase this bond? No, because paying $1,000 today to receive $1,000 later yields no interest on your investment. How much would you pay today in order to receive $1,000 in three years? The answer is some amount less than $1,000. Suppose $750 is a fair price. By investing $750 now to receive $1,000 later, you will earn $250 over the three years. The diagram that follows illustrates the relationship between a bond's price (present value) and its maturity amount (future value).

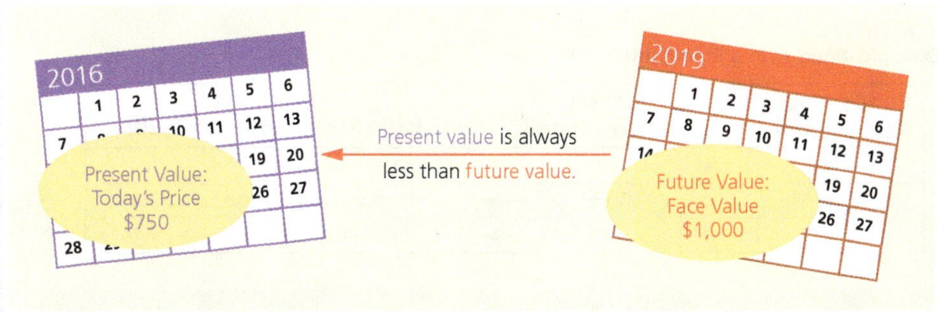


The amount that a person would invest *at the present time* is called the **present value**. The present value is the bond's market price. In our example, $750 is the present value (market price of the bond), and the $1,000 face value to be received in three years is the future amount. We show how to compute the present value of a future amount in Appendix 12A.

**Present Value**
The amount a person would invest now to receive a greater amount in the future.

## Bond Interest Rates

Bonds are sold at their market price (issue price on the date the bonds are first sold), which is the present value of the interest payments the bondholder will receive while holding the bond plus the present value of the bond principal paid at the end of the bond's life. Two interest rates work together to set the price of a bond:

- The stated interest rate determines the amount of cash interest the borrower pays each year. The stated interest rate is printed on the bond and *does not change* from year to year. For example, Smart Touch Learning's 9% bonds payable have a stated interest rate of 9% (see Exhibit 12-3). Therefore, Smart Touch Learning pays $90 of interest annually on each $1,000 bond. The dollar amount of interest paid is not affected by the issue price of the bond.

**Market Interest Rate** The interest rate that investors demand in order to loan their money.

- The **market interest rate** (also known as the *effective interest rate*) is the rate that investors demand to earn for loaning their money. The market interest rate *varies* constantly. A company may issue bonds with a stated interest rate that differs from the market interest rate, due to the time gap between the time the bonds were printed (engraved) showing the stated rate and the actual issuance of the bonds.

Smart Touch Learning may issue its 9% bonds when the market rate has risen to 10%. Will the Smart Touch Learning bonds attract investors in this market? No, because investors can earn 10% on other bonds. Therefore, investors will purchase Smart Touch Learning bonds only at a price *less* than face value. The difference between the lower price and the bonds' face value is a *discount* that will allow the investor to earn 10%, even though Smart Touch Learning's interest checks will be paid at the stated rate of 9%. The difference between what is paid for the bond (less than $1,000) and the bond principal of $1,000 is the interest rate difference between 9% and 10% over the life of the bond.

On the other hand, if the market interest rate is 8%, Smart Touch Learning's 9% bonds will be so attractive that investors will pay more than face value for them because investors will receive more in interest payments than expected. The difference between the higher price and face value is a *premium*. Exhibit 12-5 shows how the stated interest rate and the market interest rate work together to determine the price of a bond.

**Exhibit 12-5** | **Interaction Between Stated Interest Rate, Market Rate, and Price of Bond**

**Example: Bond with a Stated Interest Rate of 9%**

| Bond's Stated Interest Rate | | Market Interest Rate | | Issue Price of Bonds Payable |
|---|---|---|---|---|
| 9% | = | 9% | → | Face value of the bond |
| 9% | < | 10% | → | Discount (price below face value) |
| 9% | > | 8% | → | Premium (price above face value) |

## Issuing Bonds Versus Issuing Stock

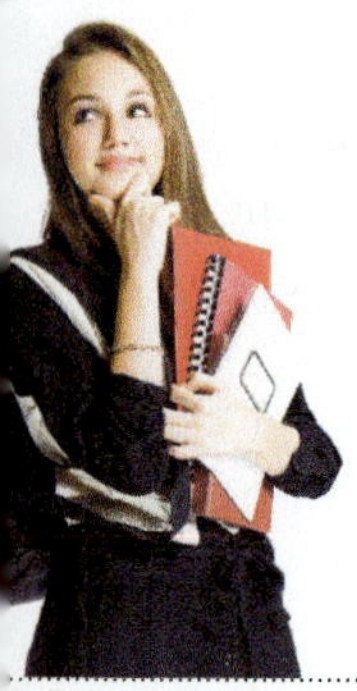

Why would a corporation issue bonds payable instead of issuing stock?

Borrowing by issuing bonds payable carries a risk: The company may be unable to pay off the bonds and the related interest. Why do companies borrow instead of issuing stock? **Debt is a less expensive source of capital than stock, and bonds do not affect the percentage of ownership of the corporation.** Companies face the following decision: How shall we finance a new project—with bonds or with stock?

Suppose Smart Touch Learning has net income of $300,000 and 100,000 shares of common stock outstanding before it begins a new project. Smart Touch Learning needs $500,000 for the project, and the company is considering two plans:

- Plan 1 is to borrow $500,000 at 10% (issue $500,000 of 10% bonds payable).
- Plan 2 is to issue 50,000 shares of common stock for $500,000.

Smart Touch Learning management believes the new cash can be used to increase income before interest and taxes by $200,000 each year. The company estimates income tax expense to be 40%. Exhibit 12-6 shows the advantage of borrowing as it relates to earnings per share.

The earnings per share of stock is higher if Smart Touch Learning issues bonds. If all goes well, the company can earn more on the new project ($90,000) than the interest it pays on the bonds ($50,000). Earning more income on borrowed money than the related interest

**Exhibit 12-6 | Issuing Bonds Payable Versus Issuing Common Stock**

| | Plan 1: Issue $500,000 of 10% Bonds Payable | | Plan 2: Issue $500,000 of Common Stock | |
|---|---|---|---|---|
| Net income before new project | | $ 300,000 | | $ 300,000 |
| Expected income on the new project before interest and income tax expenses | $ 200,000 | | $ 200,000 | |
| Less: Interest expense ($500,000 × 0.10) | 50,000 | | 0 | |
| Project income before income tax | 150,000 | | 200,000 | |
| Less: Income tax expense (40%) | 60,000 | | 80,000 | |
| Project net income | | 90,000 | | 120,000 |
| Net income with new project | | **$ 390,000** | | **$ 420,000** |
| Earnings per share with new project: | | | | |
| Plan 1 ($390,000 / 100,000 shares) | | **$ 3.90** | | |
| Plan 2 ($420,000 / 150,000 shares) | | | | **$ 2.80** |

expense is called **financial leverage**. It is widely used to increase earnings per share of common stock. Notice that, even though net income is higher under Plan 2, the earnings per share is lower. Why? Because the earnings must be shared among 50,000 more shares of stock.

Borrowing can increase the earnings per share, but borrowing has its disadvantages. Debts must be paid during unprofitable years as well as profitable years. A company might not have enough cash flow to make the interest payment, thereby defaulting on the debt. Unlike cash dividends, which are optional payments to stockholders, the interest payment on bonds payable is required. Without the cash necessary to make the interest payment, a company could have to declare bankruptcy.

**Financial Leverage**
Occurs when a company earns more income on borrowed money than the related interest expense.

## Try It!

Determine whether the following bonds payable will be issued at face value, at a premium, or at a discount:

3. A 10% bonds payable is issued when the market interest rate is 8%.
4. A 10% bonds payable is issued when the market interest rate is 10%.
5. A 10% bonds payable is issued when the market interest rate is 12%.

**Check your answers online in MyAccountingLab or at http://www.pearsonhighered.com/Horngren.**

For more practice, see Short Exercises S12-3 and S12-4. MyAccountingLab

## HOW ARE BONDS PAYABLE ACCOUNTED FOR USING THE STRAIGHT-LINE AMORTIZATION METHOD?

**Learning Objective 3**
Journalize transactions for bonds payable and interest expense using the straight-line amortization method

The basic journal entry to record the issuance of bonds payable debits Cash and credits Bonds Payable. As noted previously, a company may issue bonds, a long-term liability, at *face value*, at a *discount*, or at a *premium*. We begin with the simplest case—issuing bonds payable at face value.

## Issuing Bonds Payable at Face Value

Smart Touch Learning has $100,000 of 9% bonds payable that mature in five years. The company issues these bonds at face value on January 1, 2016. The issuance entry is as follows:

| A↑ | = | L↑ | + | E |
|---|---|---|---|---|
| Cash↑ | | Bonds Payable↑ | | |

| Date | Accounts and Explanation | Debit | Credit |
|---|---|---|---|
| 2016 | | | |
| Jan. 1 | Cash | 100,000 | |
| | Bonds Payable | | 100,000 |
| | *Issued bonds at face value.* | | |

Smart Touch Learning, the borrower, makes this one-time journal entry to record the receipt of cash and issuance of bonds payable. Interest payments occur each June 30 and December 31. Smart Touch Learning's first semiannual interest payment is journalized as follows:

| A↓ | = | L | + | E↓ |
|---|---|---|---|---|
| Cash↓ | | | | Interest Expense↑ |

| Date | Accounts and Explanation | Debit | Credit |
|---|---|---|---|
| 2016 | | | |
| Jun. 30 | Interest Expense ($100,000 × 0.09 × 6/12) | 4,500 | |
| | Cash | | 4,500 |
| | *Paid semiannual interest.* | | |

Each semiannual interest payment follows this same pattern.

## Issuing Bonds Payable at a Discount

Now let's see how to issue bonds payable at a discount. This is one of the most common situations.

We know that market conditions may force a company such as Smart Touch Learning to accept a discounted price for its bonds. Suppose Smart Touch Learning issues $100,000 of its 9%, five-year bonds that pay interest semiannually when the market interest rate is 10%. The market price of the bonds drops to 96.149, which means 96.149% of face value. Smart Touch Learning receives $96,149 ($100,000 × 0.96149) at issuance and makes the following journal entry:

| A↑ | = | L↑ | + | E |
|---|---|---|---|---|
| Cash↑ | | Bonds Payable↑<br>Discount on Bonds Payable↑ | | |

| Date | Accounts and Explanation | Debit | Credit |
|---|---|---|---|
| 2016 | | | |
| Jan. 1 | Cash | 96,149 | |
| | Discount on Bonds Payable ($100,000 − $96,149) | 3,851 | |
| | Bonds Payable | | 100,000 |
| | *Issued bonds at a discount.* | | |

After posting, the bond accounts have the following balances:

Main Account → **Bonds Payable**

| Bonds Payable | |
|---|---|
| | 100,000 Jan. 1 |

Contra Account → **Discount on Bonds Payable**

| Discount on Bonds Payable | |
|---|---|
| Jan. 1 3,851 | |

Carrying amount = $100,000 − $3,851 = $96,149

Discount on Bonds Payable is a contra account to Bonds Payable. Bonds Payable *minus* the discount gives the **carrying amount of bonds** (also known as *carrying value*). Smart Touch Learning would report these bonds payable on the balance sheet as follows immediately after issuance:

**Carrying Amount of Bonds**
A bond payable *minus* the discount account current balance or *plus* the premium account current balance.

| | | |
|---|---|---|
| Long-term Liabilities: | | |
| Bonds Payable | $ 100,000 | |
| Less: Discount on Bonds Payable | (3,851) | $ 96,149 |

## Interest Expense on Bonds Payable Issued at a Discount

In this case, we see that a bond's stated interest rate differs from the market interest rate. The market rate was 10% when Smart Touch Learning issued its 9% bonds. This 1% interest rate difference created the $3,851 discount on the bonds. Smart Touch Learning needed to offer this discount because investors were willing to pay only $96,149 for the $100,000, 9% bonds when they could earn 10% on other bonds.

Smart Touch Learning borrowed $96,149 but still must pay $100,000 when the bonds mature five years later. What happens to the $3,851 discount? The discount is additional interest expense to Smart Touch Learning. The discount raises Smart Touch Learning's true interest expense on the bonds to the market interest rate of 10%. The discount becomes interest expense for Smart Touch Learning through a process called *amortization*, the gradual reduction of an item over time.

## Straight-Line Amortization of Bond Discount

We can amortize a bond discount by dividing it into equal amounts for each interest period. This is called the **straight-line amortization method**. It works very much like the straight-line depreciation method we discussed in the Plant Assets chapter. In our example, the initial discount is $3,851 and there are 10 semiannual interest periods during the bonds' five-year life (5 year life × 2 interest payments per year). Therefore, 1/10 of the $3,851 bond discount ($385, rounded) is amortized each interest period. Smart Touch Learning's first semiannual interest entry is as follows:

**Straight-Line Amortization Method**
An amortization method that allocates an equal amount of bond discount or premium to each interest period over the life of the bond.

| Date | Accounts and Explanation | Debit | Credit |
|---|---|---|---|
| 2016 | | | |
| Jun. 30 | Interest Expense ($4,500 + $385) | 4,885 | |
| | Discount on Bonds Payable ($3,851 × 1/10) | | 385 |
| | Cash ($100,000 × 0.09 × 6/12) | | 4,500 |
| | *Paid semiannual interest and amortized discount.* | | |

| A↓ | = | L↑ | + | E↓ |
|---|---|---|---|---|
| Cash↓ | | Discount on Bonds Payable↓ | | Interest Expense↑ |

Interest expense of $4,885 for each six-month period is the sum of the following:

- Stated interest ($4,500, which is paid in cash)
- The amortization of discount, $385

This same entry would be made again on December 31, 2016. So, the bond discount balance would be $3,081 on December 31, 2016.

**Bonds Payable**

| | | | |
|---|---|---|---|
| | | 100,000 | Jan. 1 |

**Discount on Bonds Payable**

| | | | |
|---|---|---|---|
| Jan. 1 | 3,851 | 385 | Jun. 30 |
| | | 385 | Dec. 31 |
| Bal. | 3,081 | | |

So, what would be the balance reported on the December 31, 2016, balance sheet for Bonds Payable?

| | | |
|---|---|---|
| Long-term Liabilities: | | |
| Bonds Payable | $ 100,000 | |
| Less: Discount on Bonds Payable | (3,081) | $ 96,919 |

Discount on Bonds Payable has a debit balance. Therefore, we credit the Discount on Bonds Payable account to amortize (reduce) its balance. Ten amortization entries will decrease the discount to zero (with rounding). Then the carrying amount of the bonds payable will be $100,000 at maturity—$100,000 in Bonds Payable minus $0 in Discount on Bonds Payable. Exhibit 12-7 shows the amortization schedule of the bond.

**Exhibit 12-7 | Bonds Payable—Discount Amortization Schedule**

Face value × Stated interest rate × Time = $100,000 × 0.09 × 6/12 = $4,500

| | Cash Paid | Interest Expense | Discount Amortized | Carrying Amount |
|---|---|---|---|---|
| 01/01/2016 | | | | $ 96,149 |
| 06/30/2016 | $ 4,500 | $ 4,885 | $ 385 | 96,534 |
| 12/31/2016 | 4,500 | 4,885 | 385 | 96,919 |
| 06/30/2017 | 4,500 | 4,885 | 385 | 97,304 |
| 12/31/2017 | 4,500 | 4,885 | 385 | 97,689 |
| 06/30/2018 | 4,500 | 4,885 | 385 | 98,074 |
| 12/31/2018 | 4,500 | 4,885 | 385 | 98,459 |
| 06/30/2019 | 4,500 | 4,885 | 385 | 98,844 |
| 12/31/2019 | 4,500 | 4,885 | 385 | 99,229 |
| 06/30/2020 | 4,500 | 4,885 | 385 | 99,614 |
| 12/31/2020 | 4,500 | 4,886 | 386* | 100,000 |
| Total | $ 45,000 | $ 48,851 | $ 3,851 | |

Cash paid + Discount amortized = $4,500 + $385 = $4,885

Carrying amount + Discount amortized = $96,149 + $385 = $96,534

Discount amortized = $3,851 / 10 = $385

*rounded

## Issuing Bonds Payable at a Premium

To illustrate a bond premium, let's change the Smart Touch Learning example. Assume that the market interest rate is 8% when Smart Touch Learning issues its 9%, five-year bonds. These 9% bonds are attractive in an 8% market, and investors will pay a premium to acquire them. Assume the bonds are priced at 104.1 (104.1% of face value). In that case, Smart Touch Learning receives $104,100 cash upon issuance. Smart Touch Learning's entry to borrow money and issue these bonds is as follows:

| Date | Accounts and Explanation | Debit | Credit |
|---|---|---|---|
| 2016 | | | |
| Jan. 1 | Cash | 104,100 | |
| | Premium on Bonds Payable ($104,100 − $100,000) | | 4,100 |
| | Bonds Payable | | 100,000 |
| | *Issued bonds at a premium.* | | |

| A↑ | | L↑ + E |
|---|---|---|
| Cash↑ | = | Bonds Payable↑ Premium on Bonds Payable↑ |

After posting, the bond accounts have the following balances:

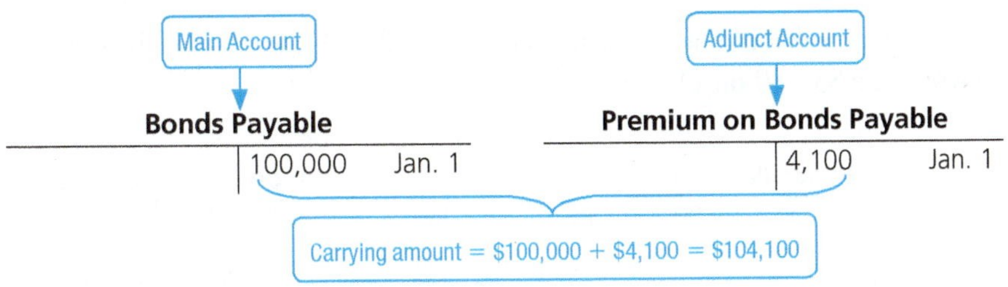


The Bonds Payable account and the Premium on Bonds Payable account each carry a credit balance. The premium is an adjunct account to Bonds Payable. **Adjunct accounts** have the same normal balance as the related account and are added to the related account on the balance sheet. Adjunct accounts work similarly to contra accounts—the only difference is that the adjunct account has the same type of balance as the main account, whereas the contra account has the opposite type of balance of its main account. Therefore, we add the Premium on Bonds Payable to Bonds Payable to determine the bonds' carrying amount. Smart Touch Learning would report these bonds payable as follows immediately after issuance:

**Adjunct Account**
An account that is directly related to another account. Adjunct accounts have the same normal balance as the related account and are added to the related account on the balance sheet.

| | | |
|---|---|---|
| Long-term Liabilities: | | |
| Bonds Payable | $ 100,000 | |
| Add: Premium on Bonds Payable | 4,100 | $ 104,100 |

### Interest Expense on Bonds Payable Issued at a Premium

The 1% difference between the bonds' 9% stated interest rate and the 8% market rate creates the $4,100 premium ($104,100 − $100,000 face value). Smart Touch Learning borrows $104,100 but must pay back only $100,000 at maturity. The premium is like a saving of interest expense to Smart Touch Learning. The premium cuts Smart Touch Learning's cost of borrowing and reduces interest expense to 8%, the market rate. The amortization of bond premium decreases interest expense over the life of the bonds.

## Straight-Line Amortization of Bond Premium

In our example, the beginning premium is $4,100 and there are 10 semiannual interest periods during the bonds' five-year life. Therefore, 1/10 of the $4,100 ($410) of bond premium is amortized each interest period. Smart Touch Learning's first semiannual interest entry is as follows:

| A↓ | | L↓ | + | E↓ |
|---|---|---|---|---|
| Cash↓ | = | Premium on Bonds Payable↓ | | Interest Expense↑ |

| Date | Accounts and Explanation | Debit | Credit |
|---|---|---|---|
| 2016 | | | |
| Jun. 30 | Interest Expense ($4,500 − $410) | 4,090 | |
| | Premium on Bonds Payable ($4,100 × 1/10) | 410 | |
| | Cash ($100,000 × 0.09 × 6/12) | | 4,500 |
| | *Paid semiannual interest and amortized premium.* | | |

Interest expense of $4,090 is

- Stated interest ($4,500, which is paid in cash)
- *Minus* the amortization of the premium of $410

This same entry would be made again on December 31, 2016. So, the bond premium balance would be $3,280 on December 31, 2016.

**Bonds Payable**

| | | | |
|---|---|---|---|
| | | 100,000 | Jan. 1 |

**Premium on Bonds Payable**

| | | | |
|---|---|---|---|
| Jun. 30 | 410 | 4,100 | Jan. 1 |
| Dec. 31 | 410 | | |
| | | 3,280 | Bal. |

At December 31, 2016, immediately after amortizing the bond premium, the bonds have the following carrying amount:

| | | |
|---|---|---|
| Long-term Liabilities: | | |
| Bonds Payable | $ 100,000 | |
| Add: Premium on Bonds Payable | 3,280 | $ 103,280 |

At maturity on December 31, 2020, the bond premium will have been fully amortized (it will have a zero balance), and the bonds' carrying amount will be $100,000 (the amount in the Bonds Payable account). Exhibit 12-8 shows the amortization schedule of the bond.

**Exhibit 12-8 | Bonds Payable—Premium Amortization Schedule**

| | Cash Paid | Interest Expense | Premium Amortized | Carrying Amount |
|---|---|---|---|---|
| 01/01/2016 | | | | $ 104,100 |
| 06/30/2016 | $ 4,500 | $ 4,090 | $ 410 | 103,690 |
| 12/31/2016 | 4,500 | 4,090 | 410 | 103,280 |
| 06/30/2017 | 4,500 | 4,090 | 410 | 102,870 |
| 12/31/2017 | 4,500 | 4,090 | 410 | 102,460 |
| 06/30/2018 | 4,500 | 4,090 | 410 | 102,050 |
| 12/31/2018 | 4,500 | 4,090 | 410 | 101,640 |
| 06/30/2019 | 4,500 | 4,090 | 410 | 101,230 |
| 12/31/2019 | 4,500 | 4,090 | 410 | 100,820 |
| 06/30/2020 | 4,500 | 4,090 | 410 | 100,410 |
| 12/31/2020 | 4,500 | 4,090 | 410 | 100,000 |
| Total | $ 45,000 | $ 40,900 | $ 4,100 | |

Face value × Stated interest rate × Time = $100,000 × 0.09 × 6/12 = $4,500

Carrying amount – Premium amortized = $104,100 – $410 = $103,690

Cash paid – Premium amortized = $4,500 – $410 = $4,090

Premium amortized = $4,100 / 10 = $410

## Try It!

Schmidt Company issued $100,000, 4%, 10-year bonds payable at 98 on January 1, 2016.

6. Journalize the issuance of the bonds payable on January 1, 2016.
7. Journalize the payment of semiannual interest and amortization of the bond discount or premium (using the straight-line amortization method) on July 1, 2016.
8. Assume the bonds payable was instead issued at 106. Journalize the issuance of the bonds payable and the payment of the first semiannual interest and amortization of the bond discount or premium.

**Check your answers online in MyAccountingLab or at http://www.pearsonhighered.com/Horngren.**

For more practice, see Short Exercises S12-5 through S12-8. MyAccountingLab

## HOW IS THE RETIREMENT OF BONDS PAYABLE ACCOUNTED FOR?

**Learning Objective 4**

Journalize transactions to retire bonds payable

Retirement of bonds payable involves paying the face value of the bond. Bonds can be retired at the maturity date or before.

### Retirement of Bonds at Maturity

When the bond is matured, the carrying value always equals the face value. In the case of Smart Touch Learning, with both the discount and premium examples, on December 31,

2020, the carrying amount and face value are $100,000. The entry to retire the bonds, assuming the last interest payment has already been recorded, is as follows:

| A↓ | | L↓ | + | E |
|---|---|---|---|---|
| Cash↓ | = | Bonds Payable↓ | | |

| Date | Accounts and Explanation | Debit | Credit |
|---|---|---|---|
| 2020 | | | |
| Dec. 31 | Bonds Payable | 100,000 | |
| | Cash | | 100,000 |
| | *Retired bonds payable at maturity.* | | |

## Retirement of Bonds Before Maturity

Normally, companies wait until maturity to pay off, or *retire*, their bonds payable. But companies sometimes retire their bonds prior to maturity. The main reason for retiring bonds early is to relieve the pressure of paying the interest payments.

**Callable Bonds**
Bonds that the issuer may call and pay off at a specified price whenever the issuer wants.

Some bonds are **callable**, which means the company may *call*, or pay off, the bonds at a specified price. The call price is usually 100 or a few percentage points above face value, perhaps 101 or 102, to provide an incentive to the bondholder. Callable bonds give the issuer the flexibility to pay off the bonds when it benefits the company. An alternative to calling the bonds is to purchase any available bonds in the open market at their current market price. Whether the bonds are called or purchased in the open market, the same accounts are used in the journal entry.

## DECISIONS

### Should the bonds be callable?

Christina Hoffman, president of Hoffman Corporation, is working with the company's underwriter to define the terms of its upcoming bond issuance. Hoffman Corporation has decided to issue $1,000,000, 6%, 20-year bonds payable. The bonds will be issued at face value. The underwriter is encouraging Christina to offer the bonds as callable bonds instead of noncallable. What should Christina do?

### Solution

Callable bonds provide Hoffman Corporation the right to repay the bonds before the maturity date. Callable bonds protect the corporation from having to pay high interest rates on existing debt if interest rates drop. For example, if the market rate drops to 4%, Hoffman Corporation could call the bonds and replace them with bonds that pay a 4% interest rate. Hoffman would be able to essentially refinance the higher interest debt with a lower interest rate bond. By offering the bonds as callable, Hoffman Corporation prevents itself from being locked into a high interest rate and not being able to change it.

### Alternative Solution

Christina should be careful about offering a callable bond because some investors might not consider the bond a wise investment. An investor typically plans on receiving interest payments from a bond for the life of the bond, and a callable bond does not guarantee a steady stream of payments for the entire period. If the bond were called, investors would no longer receive semiannual interest payments and would be presented with the challenge of investing their money in another investment that offers a comparable return.

Suppose on December 31, 2016, Smart Touch Learning has $100,000 of bonds payable outstanding with a remaining discount balance of $3,081 (the original discount of $3,851 [$100,000 − $96,149] less the straight-line amortization of $385 in June and December [$3,851 − $385 − $385]).

Lower interest rates have convinced management to pay off these bonds now. These bonds are callable at 100. If the market price of the bonds is 95, should Smart Touch Learning call the bonds at 100 or purchase them in the open market at 95? The market price is lower than the call price, so Smart Touch Learning should buy the bonds on the open market at their market price. Retiring the bonds on December 31, 2016, at 95 results in a gain of $1,919, computed as follows:

| | |
|---|---|
| Face value of the bonds being retired | $ 100,000 |
| Less: Discount | (3,081) |
| Carrying amount of bonds payable | 96,919 |
| Less: Market price paid to retire the bonds ($100,000 × 0.95) | (95,000) |
| Gain on retirement of bonds payable | $ 1,919 |

The following entry records retirement of the bonds, immediately after the December 31, 2016, interest payment:

| Date | Accounts and Explanation | Debit | Credit |
|---|---|---|---|
| 2016 | | | |
| Dec. 31 | Bonds Payable | 100,000 | |
| | Discount on Bonds Payable | | 3,081 |
| | Gain on Retirement of Bonds Payable | | 1,919 |
| | Cash | | 95,000 |
| | *Retired bonds payable prior to maturity.* | | |

| A↓ | = | L↓ | + | E↑ |
|---|---|---|---|---|
| Cash↓ | | Bonds Payable↓<br>Discount on Bonds Payable↓ | | Gain on Retirement of Bonds Payable↑ |

After posting, the bond accounts have zero balances.

**Bonds Payable**

| | | | |
|---|---|---|---|
| | | 100,000 | Jan. 1 |
| Dec. 31 | 100,000 | | |
| | | 0 | Bal. |

**Discount on Bonds Payable**

| | | | |
|---|---|---|---|
| Jan. 1 | 3,851 | 385 | Jun. 30 |
| | | 385 | Dec. 31 |
| | | 3,081 | Dec. 31 |
| Bal. | 0 | | |

The journal entry removes the bonds from the books and records a gain on retirement. If the bonds being retired have a premium rather than a discount, any existing premium would be removed with a debit. If Smart Touch Learning retired only half of these bonds, it would remove only half the discount or premium.

When retiring bonds before maturity, follow these steps:

1. Record partial-period amortization of discount or premium and partial-period interest payment if the retirement date does not fall on an interest payment date.
2. Write off the portion of unamortized Discount or Premium that relates to the bonds being retired.
3. Debit Bonds Payable at face value.
4. Credit a gain or debit a loss on retirement.
5. Credit Cash for amount paid to retire the bonds.

**Try It!**

9. Herrera Corporation issued a $400,000, 4.5%, 10-year bond payable on January 1, 2016. Journalize the payment of the bond payable at maturity. (Give the date.)

**Check your answer online in MyAccountingLab or at http://www.pearsonhighered.com/Horngren.**

For more practice, see Short Exercises S12-9 and S12-10. MyAccountingLab

## HOW ARE LIABILITIES REPORTED ON THE BALANCE SHEET?

**Learning Objective 5**
Report liabilities on the balance sheet

At the end of each period, a company reports all of its current and long-term liabilities on the balance sheet. As we have seen throughout the textbook, there are two categories of liabilities, current and long-term. Exhibit 12-9 shows Smart Touch Learning's liabilities portion of its balance sheet (amounts assumed) that we have discussed up to this point.

**Exhibit 12-9** | **Liabilities**

| SMART TOUCH LEARNING<br>Balance Sheet (Partial)<br>December 31, 2016 | | | |
|---|---|---|---|
| **Liabilities** | | | |
| Current Liabilities: | | | |
| Accounts Payable | | $ 12,620 | |
| Employee Income Taxes Payable | | 2,000 | |
| FICA—OASDI Taxes Payable | | 1,158 | |
| FICA—Medicare Taxes Payable | | 855 | |
| Employee Health Insurance Payable | | 180 | |
| United Way Payable | | 20 | |
| Federal Unemployment Taxes Payable | | 15 | |
| State Unemployment Taxes Payable | | 60 | |
| Employee Bonus Payable | | 1,000 | |
| Vacation Benefits Payable | | 800 | |
| Income Tax Payable | | 3,780 | |
| Sales Tax Payable | | 600 | |
| Estimated Warranty Payable | | 700 | |
| Notes Payable (short-term) | | 400 | |
| Current Portion of Mortgage Payable | | 1,305 | |
| Current Portion of Long-term Notes Payable | | 5,000 | |
| Total Current Liabilities | | | $ 30,493 |
| Long-term Liabilities: | | | |
| Notes Payable | | 15,000 | |
| Mortgage Payable | | 97,541 | |
| Bonds Payable | $ 100,000 | | |
| Less: Discount on Bonds Payable | (3,081) | 96,919 | |
| Total Long-term Liabilities | | | 209,460 |
| Total Liabilities | | | **$ 239,953** |

## Try It!

10. Weaver Corporation includes the following selected accounts in its general ledger at December 31, 2016:

| | | | |
|---|---|---|---|
| Notes Payable (long-term) | $ 75,000 | Interest Payable (due next year) | $ 720 |
| Bonds Payable (long-term) | 195,000 | Sales Tax Payable | 480 |
| Accounts Payable | 20,400 | Premium on Bonds Payable | 5,850 |
| Salaries Payable | 1,680 | Estimated Warranty Payable | 1,080 |

Prepare the liabilities section of Weaver Corporation's balance sheet at December 31, 2016.
**Check your answer online in MyAccountingLab or at http://www.pearsonhighered.com/Horngren.**

For more practice, see Short Exercise S12-11. MyAccountingLab

# HOW DO WE USE THE DEBT TO EQUITY RATIO TO EVALUATE BUSINESS PERFORMANCE?

**Learning Objective 6**
Use the debt to equity ratio to evaluate business performance

**Debt to Equity Ratio**
A ratio that measures the proportion of total liabilities relative to total equity. Total liabilities / Total equity.

The relationship between total liabilities and total equity—called the **debt to equity ratio**—shows the proportion of total liabilities relative to the total equity. Thus, this ratio measures financial leverage. If the debt to equity ratio is greater than 1, then the company is financing more assets with debt than with equity. If the ratio is less than 1, then the company is financing more assets with equity than with debt. The higher the debt to equity ratio, the greater the company's financial risk.

**Green Mountain Coffee Roasters, Inc.** reported total liabilities and total equity (in thousands) on its Fiscal 2013 Annual Report as follows:

| | September 28, 2013 | September 29, 2012 |
|---|---|---|
| Total liabilities | $ 1,125,978 | $ 1,354,561 |
| Total equity | 2,635,570 | 2,261,228 |

Green Mountain's debt to equity ratio as of September 28, 2013, can be calculated as follows:

Debt to equity ratio = Total liabilities / Total equity
= $1,125,978 / $2,635,570
= 0.43

Green Mountain's debt to equity ratio as of September 24, 2013, is well below 1, indicating that the company is financing more assets with equity than with debt. Notice that its debt to equity ratio has improved from 2012, when Green Mountain had a debt to equity ratio of 0.60 ($1,354,561 / $2,261,228). This has to do with the fact that Green Mountain experienced an increase in equity and a decrease in liabilities during 2013. Green Mountain's debt to equity ratios for both years indicate a fairly low risk position.

## ETHICS

### Should additional debt be issued?

Phillip Mader is president and majority stockholder of Knightly Corporation. Phillip owns 54% of the stock in the corporation. The corporation is in dire need of additional cash inflow in order to maintain operations. Phillip is urging the board of directors to issue additional debt even though he knows that the corporation already has a substantial amount of debt. Phillip is well aware that by issuing additional debt, the corporation's debt to equity ratio will increase significantly. He believes this will negatively affect the corporation's credit rating and will further limit the company's ability to borrow at low interest rates in the future. Phillip, however, believes all of this is offset by his desire to retain control of the corporation. If the corporation doesn't issue additional debt, it will be forced to issue stock in order to obtain the necessary funds. Phillip does not have the ability to purchase any of the additional shares of stock, and he knows that he will lose his majority stockholder status. What should Phillip do? What would you do?

### Solution

Phillip's overall ethical responsibility lies with the good of the company over what is best for himself. In urging the corporation to issue additional debt, he is putting his needs and desires over the corporation's and the other stockholders' needs. Phillip is aware that by issuing additional debt the corporation will be negatively affected. He should urge the board to issue stock—even though he will not gain personally from the situation. His leadership role as president of the corporation should take precedence over his role as majority stockholder.

## Try It!

**11.** Payne Corporation has the following accounts as of December 31, 2016:

| | |
|---|---|
| Total assets | $ 60,000 |
| Total liabilities | 20,000 |
| Total equity | 40,000 |

Compute the debt to equity ratio at December 31, 2016.

**Check your answer online in MyAccountingLab or at http://www.pearsonhighered.com/Horngren.**

For more practice, see Short Exercise S12-12. MyAccountingLab

# APPENDIX 12A: The Time Value of Money

## WHAT IS THE TIME VALUE OF MONEY, AND HOW IS THE PRESENT VALUE OF A FUTURE AMOUNT CALCULATED?

**Learning Objective 7**
Use time value of money to compute the present value of future amounts

A dollar received today is worth more than a dollar to be received in the future because you can invest today's dollar and earn additional interest so you'll have more cash next year. The fact that invested cash earns interest over time is called the *time value of money*. This concept explains why we would prefer to receive cash sooner rather than later. The time value of money is used to determine the present value of a bond—its market price.

## Time Value of Money Concepts

The time value of money depends on these key factors:

1. The principal amount (*p*)
2. The number of periods (*n*)
3. The interest rate (*i*)

The principal (*p*) refers to the amount of the investment or borrowing. We state the principal as either a single lump sum or an annuity. For example, if you win the lottery, you have the choice of receiving all the winnings now (a single lump sum) or receiving a series of equal payments for a period of time in the future (an annuity). An **annuity** is a stream of *equal cash payments* made at *equal time intervals.*[1] For example, $100 cash received per month for 12 months is an annuity.

**Annuity**
A stream of equal cash payments made at equal time intervals.

The number of periods (*n*) is the length of time from the beginning of the investment or borrowing until termination. All else being equal, the shorter the investment or borrowing period, the lower the total amount of interest earned or paid. If you withdraw your savings after four years rather than five years, you will earn less interest. For bonds, the number of periods is the number of interest payments made. For example, if a five-year bond pays interest semiannually, the number of periods will be 10 (5 years × 2 payments per year).

The interest rate (*i*) is the percentage earned on the investment or paid on the borrowing and can be stated annually or in days, months, or quarters. The interest rate must reflect the number of time periods in the year. A five-year semiannual bond that has an annual market interest rate of 10% will reflect a market interest rate of 5% semiannually (10% per year / 2 periods per year). Interest can be computed as either simple interest or compound interest.

### Simple Interest Versus Compound Interest

**Simple interest** means that interest is calculated *only* on the principal amount. **Compound interest** means that interest is calculated on the principal *and* on all previously earned interest. *Compound interest assumes that all interest earned will remain invested and earn additional interest at the same interest rate.* Exhibit 12A-1 compares simple interest of 6% on a five-year, $10,000 investment with interest compounded yearly (rounded to the nearest

**Simple Interest**
Interest calculated only on the principal amount.

**Compound Interest**
Interest calculated on the principal and on all previously earned interest.

**Exhibit 12A-1** **Simple Interest Versus Compound Interest—$10,000 at 6% for 5 Years**

| Year | Simple Interest Calculation | Simple Interest | Compound Interest Calculation | Compound Interest |
|---|---|---|---|---|
| 1 | $10,000 × 6% | $ 600 | $10,000 × 6% | $ 600 |
| 2 | $10,000 × 6% | 600 | ($10,000 + $600) × 6% | 636 |
| 3 | $10,000 × 6% | 600 | ($10,000 + $600 + $636) × 6% | 674* |
| 4 | $10,000 × 6% | 600 | ($10,000 + $600 + $636 + $674) × 6% | 715 |
| 5 | $10,000 × 6% | 600 | ($10,000 + $600 + $636 + $674 + $715) × 6% | 758 |
| | **Total interest** | **$ 3,000** | **Total interest** | **$ 3,383** |

*all calculations rounded to the nearest dollar for the rest of this chapter

[1] An *ordinary annuity* is an annuity in which the installments occur at the *end* of each period. An *annuity due* is an annuity in which the installments occur at the beginning of each period. Throughout this chapter, we use ordinary annuities.

dollar). As you can see, the amount of compound interest earned yearly grows as the base on which it is calculated (principal plus cumulative interest to date) grows. Over the life of this investment, the total amount of compound interest is more than the total amount of simple interest. Most investments yield compound interest, so we assume compound interest, rather than simple interest, for this chapter.

### Present Value Factors

The future value or present value of an investment simply refers to the value of an investment at different points in time. We can calculate the future value or present value of any investment by knowing (or assuming) information about the three factors we listed earlier: (1) the principal amount, (2) number of periods, and (3) the interest rate. For example, in Exhibit 12A-1, we calculated the interest that would be earned on (1) a $10,000 principal, (2) invested for five years, (3) at 6% interest. The future value of the investment is simply its worth at the end of the five-year time frame—the original principal *plus* the interest earned. In our example, the future value of the investment is as follows:

Future value = Principal + Interest earned
= $10,000 + $3,383
= $13,383

If we invest $10,000 *today*, its *present value* is simply $10,000. So another way of stating the future value is as follows:

Future value = Present value + Interest earned

We can rearrange the equation as follows:

Present value = Future value − Interest earned
$10,000 = $13,383 − $3,383

The only difference between present value and future value is the amount of interest that is earned in the intervening time span.

Calculating each period's compound interest, as we did in Exhibit 12A-1, and then adding it to the present value to determine the future value (or subtracting it from the future value to determine the present value) is tedious. Fortunately, mathematical formulas have been developed that specify future values and present values for unlimited combinations of interest rates ($i$) and time periods ($n$). Separate formulas exist for single lump sum investments and annuities.

These formulas are programmed into most business calculators, so the user only needs to correctly enter the principal amount, interest rate, and number of time periods to find present or future values. These formulas are also programmed into spreadsheet functions in Microsoft Excel. Using Excel to calculate present values is illustrated later in the Capital Investment Decisions chapter. In this chapter, we use present value tables. The present value tables contain the results of the formulas for various interest rate and time period combinations.

The formulas and resulting tables are shown in Appendix B at the end of this book:

1. Present Value of $1 (Appendix B, Table B-1)—*used to calculate the value today of one future amount (a lump sum)*
2. Present Value of Ordinary Annuity of $1 (Appendix B, Table B-2)—*used to calculate the value today of a series of equal future amounts (annuities)*

Take a moment to look at these tables because we are going to use them throughout the rest of the appendix. Note that the columns are interest rates (*i*) and the rows are periods (*n*).

The data in each table, known as present value factors (PV factors), are for an investment (or loan) of $1. To find the present value of an amount other than $1, multiply the PV factor by the future amount.

The annuity tables are derived from the lump sum tables. For example, the Annuity PV factors (in the Present Value of Ordinary Annuity of $1 table) are the *sums* of the PV factors found in the Present Value of $1 tables for a given number of time periods. The annuity tables allow us to perform one-step calculations rather than separately computing the present value of each annual cash installment and then summing the individual present values.

## Present Value of a Lump Sum

The process for calculating present values is often called *discounting future cash flows* because future amounts are discounted (interest removed) to their present value. Let's consider the investment in Exhibit 12A-1. The future value of the investment is $13,383. So the question is "How much would I have to invest today (in the present time) to have $13,383 five years in the future if I invested at 6%?" Let's calculate the present value using PV factors.

$$\text{Present value} = \text{Future value} \times \text{PV factor for } i = 6\%, n = 5$$

We determine the PV factor from the table labeled Present Value of $1 (Appendix B, Table B-1). We use this table for lump sum amounts. We look down the 6% column and across the 5 periods row and find the PV factor is 0.747. We finish our calculation as follows:

$$\begin{aligned}\text{Present value} &= \text{Future value} \times \text{PV factor for } i = 6\%, n = 5\\ &= \$13{,}383 \times 0.747\\ &= \$9{,}997\end{aligned}$$

Notice the calculation is off by $3 due to rounding ($10,000 − $9,997). The PV factors are rounded to three decimal places, so the calculations may not be exact. Also, the interest calculations in Exhibit 12A-1 were rounded to the nearest dollar. Therefore, there are two rounding issues in this calculation. However, we do have the answer to our question: If approximately $9,997 is invested today at 6% for five years, at the end of five years, the investment will grow to $13,383. Or, conversely, if we expect to receive $13,383 five years from now, its equivalent (discounted) value today is $9,997.

## Present Value of an Annuity

Let's now assume that instead of receiving a lump sum at the end of the five years, you will receive $2,000 at the end of each year. This is a series of equal payments ($2,000) over equal intervals (years), so it is an annuity. How much would you have to invest today to receive these payments, assuming an interest rate of 6%?

We determine the annuity PV factor from the table labeled Present Value of Ordinary Annuity of $1 (Appendix B, Table B-2). We use this table for annuities. We look down the 6% column and across the 5 periods row and find the annuity PV factor is 4.212. We finish our calculation as follows:

$$\begin{aligned}\text{Present value} &= \text{Amount of each cash inflow} \times \text{Annuity PV factor for } i = 6\%, n = 5\\ &= \$2{,}000 \times 4.212\\ &= \$8{,}424\end{aligned}$$

This means that an investment today of $8,424 at 6% will yield total payments of $10,000 over 5 years ($2,000 per year × 5 years). The reason is that interest is being earned on principal that is left invested each year. Let's verify the calculation.

| Year | [1] Beginning Balance Previous [4] | [2] Interest [1] × 6% | [3] Withdrawal $2,000 | [4] Ending Balance [1] + [2] – [3] |
|---|---|---|---|---|
| 0 | | | | $ 8,424 |
| 1 | $ 8,424 | $ 505 | $ 2,000 | 6,929 |
| 2 | 6,929 | 416 | $ 2,000 | 5,345 |
| 3 | 5,345 | 321 | $ 2,000 | 3,666 |
| 4 | 3,666 | 220 | $ 2,000 | 1,886 |
| 5 | 1,886 | 114* | $ 2,000 | 0 |

*rounded up by $1

The chart shows that the initial investment of $8,424 is invested for one year, earning $505 in interest. At the end of that period, the first withdrawal of $2,000 takes place, leaving a balance of $6,929 ($8,424 + $505 − $2,000). At the end of the five years, the ending balance is $0 proving that the PV of the $2,000 annuity is $8,424.

## Present Value of Bonds Payable

We can use what we have just learned about the present value of a lump sum and present value of an annuity to calculate the present value of bonds payable. The present value of a bond—its market price—is the sum of:

- the present value of the principal amount to be paid at maturity, a single amount (present value of a lump sum)
- *plus* the present value of the future stated interest payments, an annuity because it occurs in equal amounts over equal time periods (present value of an annuity).

### Present Value of a Bonds Payable Issued at a Discount

Let's compute the present value of Smart Touch Learning's 9%, five-year bonds. The face value of the bonds is $100,000, and they pay (9% × 6/12) or 4.5% stated interest semiannually. At issuance, the annual market interest rate is 10% (5% semiannually). Therefore, the market interest rate for each of the 10 semiannual periods is 5%. We use 5% to compute the present value (PV) of the maturity value and the present value (PV) of the stated interest. The present value of these bonds is $96,149, computed as follows:

**Present value of principal:**

Present value = Future value × PV factor for $i = 5\%, n = 10$
= $100,000 × 0.614
= $61,400

**Present value of stated interest:**

Present value = Amount of each cash flow × Annuity PV factor for $i = 5\%, n = 10$
= ($100,000 × 0.09 × 6/12) × 7.722
= $34,749

**Present value of bonds payable:**

Present value = PV of principal + PV of stated interest
= $61,400 + $34,749
= $96,149

*Notice that the stated interest rate (9% × 6/12 = 4.5%), not the market interest rate (5%), is used to calculate the amount of each cash flow for interest. This is because the bonds payable pay interest based on the rate stated in the contract, not the rate of the market.*

### Present Value of a Bonds Payable Issued at a Premium

Let's consider a premium price for the Smart Touch Learning bonds. Suppose the market interest rate is 8% at issuance (4% for each of the 10 semiannual periods). We would compute the market price of these bonds as follows:

**Present value of principal:**

Present value = Future value × PV factor for $i = 4\%, n = 10$
= $100,000 × 0.676
= $67,600

**Present value of stated interest:**

Present value = Amount of each cash flow × Annuity PV factor for $i = 4\%, n = 10$
= ($100,000 × 0.09 × 6/12) × 8.111
= $36,500

**Present value of bonds payable:**

Present value = PV of principal + PV of stated interest
= $67,600 + $36,500
= $104,100

## Try It!

**12A.** On December 31, 2016, when the market interest rate is 8%, Arnold Corporation issues $200,000 of 6%, 10-year bonds payable. The bonds pay interest semiannually. Determine the present value of the bonds at issuance.

**Check your answer online in MyAccountingLab or at http://www.pearsonhighered.com/Horngren.**

For more practice, see Short Exercises S12A-13 and S12A-14. MyAccountingLab

# APPENDIX 12B: Effective-Interest Method of Amortization

## HOW ARE BONDS PAYABLE ACCOUNTED FOR USING THE EFFECTIVE-INTEREST AMORTIZATION METHOD?

**Learning Objective 8**

Journalize transactions for bonds payable and interest expense using the effective-interest amortization method

**Effective-Interest Amortization Method**

An amortization model that calculates interest expense based on the current carrying amount of the bond and the market interest rate at issuance, then amortizes the difference between the cash interest payment and calculated interest expense as a decrease to the discount or premium.

We began this chapter with straight-line amortization to introduce the concept of amortizing bonds. A more precise way of amortizing bonds used in practice called the **effective-interest amortization method**. This method calculates interest expense based on the current carrying amount of the bond and the market interest rate at issuance, then amortizes the difference between the cash interest payment and calculated interest expense as a decrease to the discount or premium. This appendix explains the present value concepts used to amortize bond discounts and premiums using the effective-interest amortization method.

Generally Accepted Accounting Principles require that interest expense be measured using the *effective-interest amortization method* unless the straight-line amounts are similar. In that case, either method is permitted. Total interest expense over the life of the bonds is the same under both methods; however, interest expense each year is different between the two methods. Let's look at how the effective-interest amortization method works.

### Effective-Interest Amortization for a Bond Discount

Assume that Smart Touch Learning issues $100,000 of 9% bonds at a time when the market rate of interest is 10%. These bonds mature in five years and pay interest semiannually, so there are 10 semiannual interest payments. As you just saw in Appendix 12A, the issue price of the bonds is $96,149, and the discount on these bonds is $3,851 ($100,000 – $96,149).

When using the effective-interest amortization method, the amount of the interest expense is calculated using the *carrying amount* of the bonds and the *market interest rate.* The interest payment is calculated using the *face value* of the bonds and the *stated interest rate.* The amount of discount amortization is the excess of the calculated interest expense over the interest payment. Exhibit 12B-1 shows how to calculate interest expense by the effective-interest amortization method.

**Exhibit 12B-1** | **Bonds Payable—Discount Amortization Schedule; Effective-Interest Amortization Method**

| | Cash Paid | Interest Expense | Discount Amortized | Carrying Amount |
|---|---|---|---|---|
| 01/01/2016 | | | | $ 96,149 |
| 06/30/2016 | $ 4,500 | $ 4,807 | $ 307 | 96,456 |
| 12/31/2016 | 4,500 | 4,823 | 323 | 96,779 |
| 06/30/2017 | 4,500 | 4,839 | 339 | 97,118 |
| 12/31/2017 | 4,500 | 4,856 | 356 | 97,474 |
| 06/30/2018 | 4,500 | 4,874 | 374 | 97,848 |
| 12/31/2018 | 4,500 | 4,892 | 392 | 98,240 |
| 06/30/2019 | 4,500 | 4,912 | 412 | 98,652 |
| 12/31/2019 | 4,500 | 4,933 | 433 | 99,085 |
| 06/30/2020 | 4,500 | 4,954 | 454 | 99,539 |
| 12/31/2020 | 4,500 | 4,961* | 461 | 100,000 |
| Total | $ 45,000 | $ 48,851 | $ 3,851 | |

*rounded

Interest Expense − Cash paid = $4,807 − $4,500 = $307

Carrying amount + Discount amortized = $96,149 + $307 = $96,456

*Face value* × *Stated* Interest rate × Time = $100,000 × 0.09 × 6/12 = $4,500

*Carrying amount* × *Market* interest rate × Time = $96,149 × 0.10 × 6/12 = $4,807

When recording the interest payment for the bonds payable, the *accounts* debited and credited under the effective-interest amortization method and the straight-line amortization method are the same. Only the *amounts* differ. Smart Touch Learning would record the first interest payment on June 30 as follows:

| Date | Accounts and Explanation | Debit | Credit |
|---|---|---|---|
| 2016 | | | |
| Jun. 30 | Interest Expense ($96,149 × 0.10 × 6/12) | 4,807 | |
| | Discount on Bonds Payable ($4,807 − $4,500) | | 307 |
| | Cash ($100,000 × 0.09 × 6/12) | | 4,500 |
| | *Paid semiannual interest and amortized discount.* | | |

| A↓ | = | L↑ + | E↓ |
|---|---|---|---|
| Cash↓ | | Discount on Bonds Payable↓ | Interest Expense↑ |

Regardless of which method is used, the *total* amount of cash paid and *total* interest expense is the same. You can verify this by reviewing the totals from Exhibit 12-7 and Exhibit 12B-1.

## Effective-Interest Amortization of a Bond Premium

Smart Touch Learning may issue its bonds payable at a premium. Assume that Smart Touch Learning issues $100,000 of five-year, 9% bonds when the market interest rate is 8%. The bonds' issue price is $104,100, and the premium is $4,100. When a bond is issued at a premium, the interest expense calculation using the effective-interest amortization method uses the *carrying amount* of the bonds and the *market interest rate* as shown with a discounted bond. The calculation for the amount of premium amortization is calculated as the difference between the cash paid and the calculated interest expense. Exhibit 12B-2 (on the next page) provides the amortization schedule using the effective-interest amortization method for Smart Touch Learning.

**Exhibit 12B-2** **Bonds Payable—Premium Amortization Schedule; Effective-Interest Amortization Method**

| | Cash Paid | Interest Expense | Premium Amortized | Carrying Amount |
|---|---|---|---|---|
| 01/01/2016 | | | | $ 104,100 |
| 06/30/2016 | $ 4,500 | $ 4,164 | $ 336 | 103,764 |
| 12/31/2016 | 4,500 | 4,151 | 349 | 103,415 |
| 06/30/2017 | 4,500 | 4,137 | 363 | 103,052 |
| 12/31/2017 | 4,500 | 4,122 | 378 | 102,674 |
| 06/30/2018 | 4,500 | 4,107 | 393 | 102,281 |
| 12/31/2018 | 4,500 | 4,091 | 409 | 101,872 |
| 06/30/2019 | 4,500 | 4,075 | 425 | 101,447 |
| 12/31/2019 | 4,500 | 4,058 | 442 | 101,005 |
| 06/30/2020 | 4,500 | 4,040 | 460 | 100,545 |
| 12/31/2020 | 4,500 | 3,955* | 545 | 100,000 |
| Total | $ 45,000 | $ 40,900 | $ 4,100 | |

*rounded

Cash paid − Interest expense = $4,500 − $4,164 = $336

Carrying amount − Premium amortized = $104,100 − $336 = $103,764

*Face value* × *Stated* Interest rate × Time = $100,000 × 0.09 × 6/12 = $4,500

*Carrying amount* × *Market* interest rate × Time = $104,100 × 0.08 × 6/12 = $4,164

Smart Touch Learning will record the first interest payment on June 30 as follows:

A↓ / Cash↓ = L↓ + E↓ / Premium on Bonds Payable↓ / Interest Expense↑

| Date | Accounts and Explanation | Debit | Credit |
|---|---|---|---|
| 2016 | | | |
| Jun. 30 | Interest Expense ($104,100 × 0.08 × 6/12) | 4,164 | |
| | Premium on Bonds Payable ($4,500 − $4,164) | 336 | |
| | Cash ($100,000 × 0.09 × 6/12) | | 4,500 |
| | *Paid semiannual interest and amortized premium.* | | |

Regardless of which method is used, the *total* amount of cash paid and *total* interest expense is the same. You can verify this by reviewing the totals from Exhibit 12-8 and Exhibit 12B-2.

## Try It!

**13B.** On January 1, 2016, when the market interest rate is 6%, Hawkins Corporation issues $200,000 of 8%, five-year bonds payable. The bonds pay interest semiannually. Hawkins Corporation received $217,040 in cash at issuance. Assume interest payment dates are June 30 and December 31.

Prepare an effective-interest amortization method amortization table for the first two semiannual interest periods.

**Check your answer online in MyAccountingLab or at http://www.pearsonhighered.com/Horngren.**

For more practice, see Short Exercises S12B-15 and S12B-16. MyAccountingLab

# REVIEW

## > Things You Should Know

### 1. How are long-term notes payable and mortgages payable accounted for?

- Long-term notes payable and mortgages payable are reported in the long-term liabilities section of the balance sheet unless there is a portion due within one year. That portion is shown in the current liabilities section of the balance sheet.
- An amortization schedule should be prepared that details each loan payment's allocation between principal and interest and also the beginning and ending balances of the loan.
- Mortgages payable are long-term debts that are backed with a security interest in specific property.

### 2. What are bonds?

- Bonds payable represent long-term debt issued to multiple lenders called bondholders, usually in increments of $1,000 per bond.
- The bond requires a face value payment at maturity and interest payments based on a stated interest rate over the life of the bond.
- A bond can be issued at face value, a discount, or a premium.
  - Face value—Bond is issued at face value. The stated interest rate is equal to the market interest rate.
  - A discount—Bond is issued at less than face value. The stated interest rate is less than the market interest rate.
  - A premium—Bond is issued for more than face value. The stated interest rate is higher than the market interest rate.

### 3. How are bonds payable accounted for using the straight-line amortization method?

- The basic journal entry to record the issuance of bonds payable debits Cash and credits Bonds Payable.
  - If a bond is issued at a discount, Discount on Bonds Payable will be debited for the difference between the face value and cash received.
  - If a bond is issued at a premium, Premium on Bonds Payable will be credited for the difference between the cash received and face value.
- Interest payments must be recorded with a debit to Interest Expense and a credit to Cash.
  - Discount on Bonds Payable and Premium on Bonds Payable must be amortized over the life of the bond.
  - The straight-line amortization method allocates an equal amount of the bond discount or premium to each interest period.

### 4. How is the retirement of bonds payable accounted for?

- When bonds are retired at maturity, the entry involves a debit to Bonds Payable and a credit to Cash for the face value of the bond.
- Retirement of bonds before maturity involves writing off the remaining portion of the discount or premium account and crediting a gain or debiting a loss on retirement.

5. **How are liabilities reported on the balance sheet?**
   - Current and long-term liabilities are reported separately on the balance sheet.
   - Bonds payable are shown at the carrying amount.

6. **How do we use the debt to equity ratio to evaluate business performance?**
   - The debt to equity ratio shows the proportion of total liabilities relative to the total equity.
   - Total liabilities / Total equity.

7. **What is the time value of money, and how is the present value of a future amount calculated? (Appendix 12A)**
   - The fact that invested money earns interest over time is called the *time value of money*. This concept explains why we would prefer to receive cash sooner rather than later.
   - Lump sum payments are one-time cash payments.
   - Annuities are streams of equal cash payments made at equal time intervals.
   - To calculate the present value of a lump sum:

     Present value = Future value × PV factor for $i$ = ?%, $n$ = ?

   - To calculate the present value of an annuity:

     Present value = Amount of each cash inflow × Annuity PV factor for $i$ = ?%, $n$ = ?

8. **How are bonds payable accounted for using the effective-interest amortization method? (Appendix 12B)**
   - The effective-interest amortization method calculates interest expense based on the current carrying amount of the bond and the market interest rate at issuance, then amortizes the difference between the cash interest payment and calculated interest expense as a decrease to the discount or premium.
   - Using the effective-interest amortization method, the amount of interest expense is calculated using the carrying amount of the bonds and the market interest rate.



## > Summary Problem 12-1

West Virginia Power Company has 8%, 10-year bonds payable that mature on June 30, 2026. The bonds are issued on June 30, 2016, and West Virginia Power pays interest each June 30 and December 31.

### Requirements

1. Will the bonds be issued at face value, at a premium, or at a discount if the market interest rate on the date of issuance is 7%? If the market interest rate is 10%?
2. West Virginia Power issued $100,000 of the bonds at 87.548. Round all calculations to the nearest dollar.
   a. Record issuance of the bonds on June 30, 2016.
   b. Record the payment of interest and amortization of the discount on December 31, 2016. Use the straight-line amortization method.
   c. Compute the bonds' carrying amount at December 31, 2016.
   d. Record the payment of interest and amortization of discount on June 30, 2017.

## > Solution

### Requirement 1

If the market interest rate is 7%, the bonds will be issued at a premium.

If the market interest rate is 10%, the bonds will be issued at a discount.

### Requirement 2

| Date | Accounts and Explanation | Debit | Credit |
|---|---|---|---|
| 2016 | | | |
| (a) Jun. 30 | Cash ($100,000 × 0.87548) | 87,548 | |
| | Discount on Bonds Payable ($100,000 − $87,548) | 12,452 | |
| | Bonds Payable | | 100,000 |
| | *Issued bonds at a discount.* | | |
| (b) Dec. 31 | Interest Expense ($4,000 + $623) | 4,623 | |
| | Discount on Bonds Payable ($12,452 × 1/20) | | 623 |
| | Cash ($100,000 × 0.08 × 6/12) | | 4,000 |

c. Carrying amount at December 31, 2016

| | | |
|---|---|---|
| Long-term Liabilities: | | |
| Bonds Payable | $ 100,000 | |
| Less: Discount on Bonds Payable ($12,452 – $623) | (11,829) | $ 88,171 |

| Date | Accounts and Explanation | Debit | Credit |
|---|---|---|---|
| 2017 | | | |
| (d) Jun. 30 | Interest Expense ($4,000 + $623) | 4,623 | |
| | Discount on Bonds Payable ($12,452 × 1/20) | | 623 |
| | Cash ($100,000 × 0.08 × 6/12) | | 4,000 |

CHAPTER 12

## > Key Terms

## > Quick Check

**Learning Objective 1**

1. Flipco signed a 10-year note payable on January 1, 2016, of $800,000. The note requires annual principal payments each December 31 of $80,000 plus interest at 5%. The entry to record the annual payment on December 31, 2017, includes
   a. a debit to Interest Expense for $36,000.
   b. a debit to Interest Expense for $40,000.
   c. a credit to Notes Payable for $80,000.
   d. a credit to Cash of $120,000.

**Learning Objective 2**

2. Daniels's bonds payable carry a stated interest rate of 5%, and the market rate of interest is 7%. The issue price of the Daniels's bonds will be at
   a. par value.
   b. a premium.
   c. face value.
   d. a discount.

**Learning Objective 2**

3. A bond that matures in installments at regular intervals is a
   a. term bond.
   b. serial bond.
   c. periodic bond.
   d. terminal bond.

**Learning Objective 3**

4. Alan Smith Antiques issued its 7%, 20-year bonds payable at a price of $846,720 (face value is $900,000). The company uses the straight-line amortization method for the bond discount or premium. Interest expense for each year is
   a. $65,664.
   b. $60,336.
   c. $63,000.
   d. $59,270.

**Learning Objective 3**

5. Nicholas Smith Fitness Gym has $700,000 of 20-year bonds payable outstanding. These bonds had a discount of $56,000 at issuance, which was 10 years ago. The company uses the straight-line amortization method. The current carrying amount of these bonds payable is
   a. $672,000.
   b. $644,000.
   c. $700,000.
   d. $728,000.

**Learning Objective 4**

6. Vasquez issued a $400,000 face value, 8%, 20-year bond at 95. Which of the following is the correct journal entry to record the retirement of the bond at maturity?

| Date | Accounts and Explanation | Debit | Credit |
|---|---|---|---|
| a. | Bonds Payable | 380,000 | |
| | Cash | | 380,000 |
| b. | Cash | 400,000 | |
| | Bonds Payable | | 400,000 |
| c. | Bonds Payable | 400,000 | |
| | Cash | | 400,000 |
| d. | Cash | 380,000 | |
| | Bonds Payable | | 380,000 |

Learning Objective 5

7. Sassy's trial balance shows $200,000 face value of bonds with a discount balance of $2,000. The bonds mature in 10 years. How will the bonds be presented on the balance sheet?

   a. Bonds payable $198,000 (net of $2,000 discount) will be listed as a long-term liability.
   b. Bonds payable $200,000 will be listed as a long-term liability. A $2,000 discount on bonds payable will be listed as a contra current liability.
   c. Bonds payable $200,000 will be listed as a long-term liability.
   d. Bonds payable $200,000 will be listed as a long-term liability. A $2,000 discount on bonds payable will be listed as a current liability.

Learning Objective 6

8. The debt to equity ratio is calculated as

   a. Total assets / Total equity.
   b. Current liabilities / Total equity.
   c. Total liabilities / Total assets.
   d. Total liabilities / Total equity.

Learning Objective 7 Appendix 12A

9A. Mike Gordon wishes to have $80,000 in five years. If he can earn annual interest of 2%, how much must he invest today?

   a. $42,170
   b. $72,480
   c. $76,080
   d. $88,320

Learning Objective 8 Appendix 12B

10B. Hicks Corporation issued $500,000 of 5%, 10-year bonds payable at a price of 92. The market interest rate at the date of issuance was 6%, and the bonds pay interest semiannually. The journal entry to record the first semiannual interest payment using the effective-interest amortization method is

| Date | Accounts and Explanation | Debit | Credit |
|---|---|---|---|
| a. | Interest Expense | 14,500 | |
| | Discount on Bonds Payable | | 2,000 |
| | Cash | | 12,500 |
| b. | Interest Expense | 13,800 | |
| | Discount on Bonds Payable | | 1,300 |
| | Cash | | 12,500 |
| c. | Interest Expense | 17,000 | |
| | Discount on Bonds Payable | | 2,000 |
| | Cash | | 15,000 |
| d. | Interest Expense | 16,300 | |
| | Discount on Bonds Payable | | 1,300 |
| | Cash | | 15,000 |

**Check your answers at the end of the chapter.**

# ASSESS YOUR PROGRESS

## > Review Questions

1. Where is the current portion of notes payable reported on the balance sheet?
2. What is an amortization schedule?
3. What is a mortgage payable?
4. What is a bond payable?
5. What is the difference between the stated interest rate and the market interest rate?
6. When does a discount on bonds payable occur?
7. When does a premium on bonds payable occur?
8. When a bond is issued, what is its present value?
9. Why would a company choose to issue bonds instead of issuing stock?
10. What is the carrying amount of a bond?
11. In regard to a bond discount or premium, what is the straight-line amortization method?
12. What is the normal balance of the account Discount on Bonds Payable? Is it added to or subtracted from the Bonds Payable account to determine the carrying amount?
13. What is the normal balance of the account Premium on Bonds Payable? Is it added to or subtracted from the Bonds Payable account to determine the carrying amount?
14. What is the journal entry to retire bonds at maturity?
15. What does it mean when a company calls a bond?
16. What are the two categories of liabilities reported on the balance sheet? Provide examples of each.
17. What does the debt to equity ratio show, and how is it calculated?

18A. Explain each of the key factors that time value of money depends on.

19A. What is an annuity?

20A. How does compound interest differ from simple interest?

21B. In regard to a bond discount or premium, what is the effective-interest amortization method?



## > Short Exercises

***Assume bonds payable are amortized using the straight-line amortization method unless stated otherwise.***

**Learning Objective 1**

**S12-1 Accounting for a long-term note payable**

On January 1, 2016, Locker-Farrell signed a $200,000, 10-year, 13% note. The loan required Locker-Farrell to make annual payments on December 31 of $20,000 principal plus interest.

**Requirements**

1. Journalize the issuance of the note on January 1, 2016.
2. Journalize the first note payment on December 31, 2016.

### S12-2 Accounting for mortgages payable

Learning Objective 1

Elie purchased a building with a market value of $335,000 and land with a market value of $55,000 on January 1, 2016. Elie paid $10,000 cash and signed a 15-year, 12% mortgage payable for the balance.

**Requirements**

1. Journalize the January 1, 2016, purchase.
2. Journalize the first monthly payment of $4,561 on January 31, 2016. (Round to the nearest dollar.)

### S12-3 Determining bond prices

Learning Objective 2

Bond prices depend on the market rate of interest, stated rate of interest, and time. Determine whether the following bonds payable will be issued at face value, at a premium, or at a discount:

a. The market interest rate is 8%. Idaho issues bonds payable with a stated rate of 7.75%.

b. Austin issued 9% bonds payable when the market interest rate was 8.25%.

c. Cleveland's Cars issued 10% bonds when the market interest rate was 10%.

d. Atlanta's Tourism issued bonds payable that pay the stated interest rate of 8.5%. At issuance, the market interest rate was 10.25%.

### S12-4 Pricing bonds

Learning Objective 2

Bond prices depend on the market rate of interest, stated rate of interest, and time.

**Requirements**

1. Compute the price of the following 8% bonds of Allied Telecom.
   a. $500,000 issued at 75.50
   b. $500,000 issued at 102.75
   c. $500,000 issued at 96.50
   d. $500,000 issued at 102.50
2. Which bond will Allied Telecom have to pay the most to retire at maturity? Explain your answer.

### S12-5 Determining bond amounts

Learning Objective 3

Quick Drive-Ins borrowed money by issuing $4,000,000 of 4% bonds payable at 96.5.

**Requirements**

1. How much cash did Quick receive when it issued the bonds payable?
2. How much must Quick pay back at maturity?
3. How much cash interest will Quick pay each six months?

### S12-6 Journalizing bond transactions

Learning Objective 3

Piper Company issued a $800,000, 8%, 10-year bond payable at face value on January 1, 2016.

**Requirements**

1. Journalize the issuance of the bond payable on January 1, 2016.
2. Journalize the payment of semiannual interest on July 1, 2016.

**Learning Objective 3**

### S12-7 Journalizing bond transactions

Ogden issued a $70,000, 12%, 10-year bond payable at 90 on January 1, 2016.

**Requirements**

1. Journalize the issuance of the bond payable on January 1, 2016.
2. Journalize the payment of semiannual interest and amortization of the bond discount or premium on July 1, 2016.

**Learning Objective 3**

### S12-8 Journalizing bond transactions

Watson Mutual Insurance Company issued a $65,000, 11%, 10-year bond payable at 109 on January 1, 2016.

**Requirements**

1. Journalize the issuance of the bond payable on January 1, 2016.
2. Journalize the payment of semiannual interest and amortization of the bond discount or premium on July 1, 2016.

**Learning Objectives 3, 4**

### S12-9 Journalizing bond transactions including retirement at maturity

Deer issued a $125,000, 6.0%, 15-year bond payable. Journalize the following transactions for Deer, and include an explanation for each entry:

a. Issuance of the bond payable at face value on January 1, 2016.

b. Payment of semiannual cash interest on July 1, 2016.

c. Payment of the bond payable at maturity. (Give the date.)

**Learning Objectives 3, 4**

### S12-10 Retiring bonds payable before maturity

On January 1, 2016, Patel issued $400,000 of 7%, five-year bonds payable at 109. Patel has extra cash and wishes to retire the bonds payable on January 1, 2017, immediately after making the second semiannual interest payment. To retire the bonds, Patel pays the market price of 95.

**Requirements**

1. What is Patel's carrying amount of the bonds payable on the retirement date?
2. How much cash must Patel pay to retire the bonds payable?
3. Compute Patel's gain or loss on the retirement of the bonds payable.

**Learning Objective 5**

### S12-11 Preparing the liabilities section of the balance sheet

Master Suites Hotels includes the following selected accounts in its general ledger at December 31, 2016:

| | | | |
|---|---|---|---|
| Notes Payable (long-term) | $ 250,000 | Accounts Payable | $ 41,000 |
| Bonds Payable (due 2022) | 450,000 | Discount on Bonds Payable | 13,500 |
| Interest Payable (due next year) | 1,700 | Salaries Payable | 3,100 |
| Estimated Warranty Payable | 1,500 | Sales Tax Payable | 700 |

Prepare the liabilities section of Master Suites's balance sheet at December 31, 2016.

CHAPTER 12

**S12-12 Computing the debt to equity ratio**

**Learning Objective 6**

Richards Corporation has the following amounts as of December 31, 2016.

| | |
|---|---|
| Total assets | $ 31,500 |
| Total liabilities | 17,500 |
| Total equity | 14,000 |

Compute the debt to equity ratio at December 31, 2016.

**S12A-13 Using the time value of money**

**Learning Objective 7**
**Appendix 12A**

Your grandfather would like to share some of his fortune with you. He offers to give you money under one of the following scenarios (you get to choose):

1. $8,000 per year at the end of each of the next five years
2. $50,250 (lump sum) now
3. $100,250 (lump sum) five years from now

**Requirements**

1. Calculate the present value of each scenario using an 8% discount rate. Which scenario yields the highest present value?
2. Would your preference change if you used a 12% discount rate?

**S12A-14 Determining the present value of bond at issuance**

**Learning Objective 7**
**Appendix 12A**

On December 31, 2016, when the market interest rate is 14%, McCann Realty issues $400,000 of 11.25%, 10-year bonds payable. The bonds pay interest semiannually. Determine the present value of the bonds at issuance.

**S12B-15 Using the effective-interest amortization method**

**Learning Objective 8**
**Appendix 12B**

On December 31, 2016, when the market interest rate is 10%, Timmony Realty issues $450,000 of 7.25%, 10-year bonds payable. The bonds pay interest semiannually. The present value of the bonds at issuance is $372,936.

**Requirements**

1. Prepare an amortization table using the effective interest amortization method for the first two semiannual interest periods. (Round all numbers to the nearest whole dollar.)
2. Using the amortization table prepared in Requirement 1, journalize issuance of the bonds and the first two interest payments.

**S12B-16 Using the effective-interest amortization method**

**Learning Objective 8**
**Appendix 12B**

On December 31, 2016, when the market interest rate is 16%, Bryant Realty issues $700,000 of 17.25%, 10-year bonds payable. The bonds pay interest semiannually. Bryant Realty received $743,262 in cash at issuance.

**Requirements**

1. Prepare an amortization table using the effective interest amortization method for the first two semiannual interest periods. (Round all numbers to the nearest whole dollar.)
2. Using the amortization table prepared in Requirement 1, journalize issuance of the bonds and the first two interest payments.

# > Exercises

***Assume bonds payable are amortized using the straight-line amortization method unless stated otherwise.***

**Learning Objective 1**

2. Total Liabilities $52,680

## E12-17 Accounting for long-term notes payable transactions

Consider the following note payable transactions of Caldwell Video Productions.

| | |
|---|---|
| **2016** | |
| Apr. 1 | Purchased equipment costing $56,000 by issuing a seven-year, 13% note payable. The note requires annual principal payments of $8,000 plus interest each April 1. |
| Dec. 31 | Accrued interest on the note payable. |
| **2017** | |
| Apr. 1 | Paid the first installment on the note. |
| Dec. 31 | Accrued interest on the note payable. |

**Requirements**

1. Journalize the transactions for the company.
2. Considering the given transactions only, what are Caldwell Video Productions' total liabilities on December 31, 2017?

**Learning Objective 1**

3. Interest Expense $4,333.33

## E12-18 Preparing an amortization schedule and recording mortgages payable entries

Keel Company purchased a building and land with a fair market value of $650,000 (building, $550,000, and land, $100,000) on January 1, 2016. Keel signed a 20-year, 8% mortgage payable. Keel will make monthly payments of $5,436.86.

**Requirements**

1. Journalize the mortgage payable issuance on January 1, 2016 (explanations are not required).
2. Prepare an amortization schedule for the first two payments.
3. Journalize the first payment on January 31, 2016 (round to two decimal places).
4. Journalize the second payment on February 29, 2016 (round to two decimal places).

CHAPTER 12

**Learning Objective 2**

## E12-19 Analyzing alternative plans to raise money

AF Electronics is considering two plans for raising $3,000,000 to expand operations. Plan A is to issue 7% bonds payable, and plan B is to issue 100,000 shares of common stock. Before any new financing, AF has net income of $250,000 and 200,000 shares of common stock outstanding. Management believes the company can use the new funds to earn additional income of $500,000 before interest and taxes. The income tax rate is 30%. Analyze the AF Electronics situation to determine which plan will result in higher earnings per share. Use Exhibit 12-6 as a guide.

**Learning Objectives 2, 3**

2. Market price $404,200

## E12-20 Determining bond prices and interest expense

Nooks is planning to issue $470,000 of 5%, 10-year bonds payable to borrow for a major expansion. The owner, Simon Nooks, asks your advice on some related matters.

**Requirements**

1. Answer the following questions:
   a. At what type of bond price will Nooks have total interest expense equal to the cash interest payments?
   b. Under which type of bond price will Nooks' total interest expense be greater than the cash interest payments?
   c. If the market interest rate is 7%, what type of bond price can Nooks expect for the bonds?
2. Compute the price of the bonds if the bonds are issued at 86.
3. How much will Nooks pay in interest each year? How much will Nooks' interest expense be for the first year?

### E12-21 Journalizing bond issuance and interest payments

**Learning Objective 3**

1. June 30 Bonds Payable CR $60,000

On June 30, Paulson Company issues 6%, 10-year bonds payable with a face value of $60,000. The bonds are issued at face value and pay interest on June 30 and December 31.

**Requirements**

1. Journalize the issuance of the bonds on June 30.
2. Journalize the semiannual interest payment on December 31.

### E12-22 Journalizing bond issuance and interest payments

**Learning Objective 3**

1. June 30 Discount DR $7,200

On June 30, Danver Limited issues 5%, 20-year bonds payable with a face value of $120,000. The bonds are issued at 94 and pay interest on June 30 and December 31.

**Requirements**

1. Journalize the issuance of the bonds on June 30.
2. Journalize the semiannual interest payment and amortization of bond discount on December 31.

### E12-23 Journalizing bond transactions

**Learning Objective 3**

2. Interest Expense DR $3,440

Franklin issued $80,000 of 10-year, 8% bonds payable on January 1, 2016. Franklin pays interest each January 1 and July 1 and amortizes discount or premium by the straight-line amortization method. The company can issue its bonds payable under various conditions.

**Requirements**

1. Journalize Franklin's issuance of the bonds and first semiannual interest payment assuming the bonds were issued at face value. Explanations are not required.
2. Journalize Franklin's issuance of the bonds and first semiannual interest payment assuming the bonds were issued at 94. Explanations are not required.
3. Journalize Franklin's issuance of the bonds and first semiannual interest payment assuming the bonds were issued at 103. Explanations are not required.
4. Which bond price results in the most interest expense for Franklin? Explain in detail.

### E12-24 Journalizing bond issuance and interest payments

**Learning Objectives 3, 4**

1. Premium CR $3,600

On January 1, 2016, Dave Unlimited issues 10%, 20-year bonds payable with a face value of $180,000. The bonds are issued at 102 and pay interest on June 30 and December 31.

**Requirements**

1. Journalize the issuance of the bonds on January 1, 2016.
2. Journalize the semiannual interest payment and amortization of bond premium on June 30, 2016.
3. Journalize the semiannual interest payment and amortization of bond premium on December 31, 2016.
4. Journalize the retirement of the bond at maturity. (Give the date.)

**Learning Objective 4**

2. Cash CR $696,900

## E12-25 Retiring bonds payable before maturity

*Parkview Magazine* issued $690,000 of 15-year, 5% callable bonds payable on July 31, 2016, at 95. On July 31, 2019, *Parkview* called the bonds at 101. Assume annual interest payments.

**Requirements**

1. Without making journal entries, compute the carrying amount of the bonds payable at July 31, 2019.
2. Assume all amortization has been recorded properly. Journalize the retirement of the bonds on July 31, 2019. No explanation is required.

**Learning Objectives 2, 3, 5**

## E12-26 Reporting current and long-term liabilities

Optical Dispensary borrowed $330,000 on January 2, 2016, by issuing a 15% serial bond payable that must be paid in three equal annual installments plus interest for the year. The first payment of principal and interest comes due January 2, 2017. Complete the missing information. Assume the bonds are issued at face value.

| | December 31 | | |
|---|---|---|---|
| | **2016** | **2017** | **2018** |
| Current Liabilities: | | | |
| Bonds Payable | $_____ | $_____ | $_____ |
| Interest Payable | _____ | _____ | _____ |
| Long-term Liabilities: | | | |
| Bonds Payable | _____ | _____ | _____ |

**Learning Objectives 2, 3, 5**

Total Liabilities $358,000

## E12-27 Reporting liabilities

At December 31, MediAssist Precision Instruments owes $51,000 on Accounts Payable, Salaries Payable of $12,000, and Income Tax Payable of $10,000. MediAssist also has $280,000 of Bonds Payable that were issued at face value that require payment of a $50,000 installment next year and the remainder in later years. The bonds payable require an annual interest payment of $5,000, and MediAssist still owes this interest for the current year. Report MediAssist's liabilities on its classified balance sheet.

### E12-28 Computing the debt to equity ratio

**Learning Objective 6**

Burkhart Corporation has the following data as of December 31, 2016:

| | | | |
|---|---|---|---|
| Total current liabilities | $ 52,910 | Total stockholders' equity | $ ? |
| Total current assets | 48,100 | Other assets | 42,500 |
| Long-term liabilities | 118,945 | Property, plant, and equipment, net | 208,555 |

Compute the debt to equity ratio at December 31, 2016.

### E12A-29 Determining the present value of bonds payable

**Learning Objective 7**
**Appendix 12A**

2. Present Value $71,329

Interest rates determine the present value of future amounts. (Round all numbers to the nearest whole dollar.)

**Requirements**

1. Determine the present value of six-year bonds payable with face value of $84,000 and stated interest rate of 12%, paid semiannually. The market rate of interest is 12% at issuance.
2. Same bonds payable as in Requirement 1, but the market interest rate is 16%.
3. Same bonds payable as in Requirement 1, but the market interest rate is 10%.

### E12B-30 Journalizing bond transactions using the effective-interest amortization method

**Learning Objective 8**
**Appendix 12B**

2. Interest Expense DR $6,208

Journalize issuance of the bond and the first semiannual interest payment under each of the following three assumptions. The company amortizes bond premium and discount by the effective-interest amortization method. Explanations are not required.

1. Ten-year bonds payable with face value of $86,000 and stated interest rate of 14%, paid semiannually. The market rate of interest is 14% at issuance. The present value of the bonds at issuance is $86,000.
2. Same bonds payable as in assumption 1, but the market interest rate is 16%. The present value of the bonds at issuance is $77,594.
3. Same bonds payable as in assumption 1, but the market interest rate is 8%. The present value of the bonds at issuance is $121,028.

## > Problems Group A

**Learning Objectives 1, 5**

1. Mar. 1, 2017, Mortgage Payable DR $4,710

2. Total Liabilities $345,998

### P12-31A Journalizing liability transactions and reporting them on the balance sheet

The following transactions of Smith Pharmacies occurred during 2016 and 2017:

| | |
|---|---|
| **2016** | |
| Mar. 1 | Borrowed $240,000 from Naples Bank. The eight-year, 7% note requires payments due annually, on March 1. Each payment consists of $30,000 principal plus one year's interest. |
| Dec. 1 | Mortgaged the warehouse for $150,000 cash with Sawyer Bank. The mortgage requires monthly payments of $6,000. The interest rate on the note is 11% and accrues monthly. The first payment is due on January 1, 2017. |
| 31 | Recorded interest accrued on the Sawyer Bank note. |
| 31 | Recorded interest accrued on the Naples Bank note. |
| **2017** | |
| Jan. 1 | Paid Sawyer Bank monthly mortgage payment. |
| Feb. 1 | Paid Sawyer Bank monthly mortgage payment. |
| Mar. 1 | Paid Sawyer Bank monthly mortgage payment. |
| 1 | Paid first installment on note due to Naples Bank. |

**Requirements**

1. Journalize the transactions in the Smith Pharmacies general journal. Round all answers to the nearest dollar. Explanations are not required.
2. Prepare the liabilities section of the balance sheet for Smith Pharmacies on March 1, 2017 after all the journal entries are recorded.

**Learning Objectives 2, 3**

2. Discount CR $4,500

### P12-32A Analyzing, journalizing, and reporting bond transactions

Bob's Hamburgers issued 8%, 10-year bonds payable at 70 on December 31, 2016. At December 31, 2018, Bob reported the bonds payable as follows:

| | | |
|---|---|---|
| Long-term Liabilities: | | |
| Bonds Payable | $ 300,000 | |
| Less: Discount on Bonds Payable | 72,000 | $ 228,000 |

Bob's pays semiannual interest each June 30 and December 31.

**Requirements**

1. Answer the following questions about Bob's bonds payable:
   a. What is the maturity value of the bonds?
   b. What is the carrying amount of the bonds at December 31, 2018?
   c. What is the semiannual cash interest payment on the bonds?
   d. How much interest expense should the company record each year?
2. Record the June 30, 2018, semiannual interest payment and amortization of discount.

CHAPTER 12

**P12-33A Analyzing and journalizing bond transactions**

**Learning Objectives 2, 3, 4**

3. June 30, 2016, Interest Expense DR $16,400

On January 1, 2016, Teacher Credit Union (TCU) issued 8%, 20-year bonds payable with face value of $400,000. The bonds pay interest on June 30 and December 31.

**Requirements**

1. If the market interest rate is 6% when TCU issues its bonds, will the bonds be priced at face value, at a premium, or at a discount? Explain.
2. If the market interest rate is 9% when TCU issues its bonds, will the bonds be priced at face value, at a premium, or at a discount? Explain.
3. The issue price of the bonds is 96. Journalize the following bond transactions:
   a. Issuance of the bonds on January 1, 2016.
   b. Payment of interest and amortization on June 30, 2016.
   c. Payment of interest and amortization on December 31, 2016.
   d. Retirement of the bond at maturity on December 31, 2035.

**P12-34A Analyzing and journalizing bond transactions**

**Learning Objectives 2, 3, 4**

June 30, 2016, Interest Expense DR $20,400

On January 1, 2016, Agricultural Credit Union (ACU) issued 7%, 20-year bonds payable with face value of $600,000. These bonds pay interest on June 30 and December 31. The issue price of the bonds is 104.

Journalize the following bond transactions:

a. Issuance of the bonds on January 1, 2016.
b. Payment of interest and amortization on June 30, 2016.
c. Payment of interest and amortization on December 31, 2016.
d. Retirement of the bond at maturity on December 31, 2035.

**P12-35A Reporting liabilities on the balance sheet and computing debt to equity ratio**

**Learning Objectives 5, 6**

1. Total Liabilities $276,900

The accounting records of Router Wireless include the following as of December 31, 2016:

| | | | |
|---|---|---|---|
| Accounts Payable | $ 69,000 | Salaries Payable | $ 7,500 |
| Mortgages Payable (long-term) | 75,000 | Bonds Payable (current portion) | 25,000 |
| Interest Payable | 21,000 | Premium on Bonds Payable | 13,000 |
| Bonds Payable (long-term) | 63,000 | Unearned Revenue (short-term) | 3,400 |
| Total Stockholders' Equity | 160,000 | | |

**Requirements**

1. Report these liabilities on the Router Wireless balance sheet, including headings and totals for current liabilities and long-term liabilities.
2. Compute Router Wireless's debt to equity ratio at December 31, 2016.

**P12AB-36A Determining the present value of bonds payable and journalizing using the effective-interest amortization method**

**Learning Objectives 7, 8**
**Appendixes 12A, 12B**

3. Jan. 1, 2016, Cash DR $529,170

Ben Norton issued $500,000 of 9%, 8-year bonds payable on January 1, 2016. The market interest rate at the date of issuance was 8%, and the bonds pay interest semiannually.

**Requirements**

1. How much cash did the company receive upon issuance of the bonds payable? (Round all numbers to the nearest whole dollar.)
2. Prepare an amortization table for the bond using the effective-interest method, through the first two interest payments. (Round all numbers to the nearest whole dollar.)
3. Journalize the issuance of the bonds on January 1, 2016, and payment of the first semiannual interest amount and amortization of the bond on June 30, 2016. Explanations are not required.

**Learning Objectives 7, 8**
**Appendixes 12A, 12B**

3. Jan. 1, 2016, Cash DR $557,025

### P12AB-37A Determining the present value of bonds payable and journalizing using the effective-interest amortization method

Serenity, Inc. is authorized to issue 5%, 10-year bonds payable. On January 1, 2016, when the market interest rate is 8%, the company issues $700,000 of the bonds. The bonds pay interest semiannually.

**Requirements**

1. How much cash did the company receive upon issuance of the bonds payable? (Round all numbers to the nearest whole dollar.)
2. Prepare an amortization table for the bond using the effective-interest method, through the first two interest payments. (Round all numbers to the nearest whole dollar.)
3. Journalize the issuance of the bonds on January 1, 2016, and payment of the first semiannual interest amount and amortization of the bond on June 30, 2016. Explanations are not required.

## > Problems Group B

**Learning Objectives 1, 5**

1. Jan. 1, 2017, Interest Payable DR $3,000
2. Total Liabilities $853,895

### P12-38B Journalizing liability transactions and reporting them on the balance sheet

The following transactions of Emergency Pharmacies occurred during 2016 and 2017:

| | |
|---|---|
| **2016** | |
| Mar. 1 | Borrowed $330,000 from Longwood Bank. The six-year, 13% note requires payments due annually, on March 1. Each payment consists of $55,000 principal plus one year's interest. |
| Dec. 1 | Mortgaged the warehouse for $600,000 cash with Sawyer Bank. The mortgage requires monthly payments of $10,000. The interest rate on the note is 6% and accrues monthly. The first payment is due on January 1, 2017. |
| 31 | Recorded interest accrued on the Sawyer Bank note. |
| 31 | Recorded interest accrued on the Longwood Bank note. |
| **2017** | |
| Jan. 1 | Paid Sawyer Bank monthly mortgage payment. |
| Feb. 1 | Paid Sawyer Bank monthly mortgage payment. |
| Mar. 1 | Paid Sawyer Bank monthly mortgage payment. |
| 1 | Paid first installment on note due to Longwood Bank. |

**Requirements**

1. Journalize the transactions in the Emergency Pharmacies general journal. Round all answers to the nearest dollar. Explanations are not required.
2. Prepare the liabilities section of the balance sheet for Emergency Pharmacies on March 1, 2017 after all the journal entries are recorded.

## P12-39B Analyzing, journalizing, and reporting bond transactions

**Learning Objectives 2, 3**

2. Discount CR $2,000

George's Hamburgers issued 8%, 10-year bonds payable at 80 on December 31, 2016. At December 31, 2018, George reported the bonds payable as follows:

| | | |
|---|---|---|
| Long-term Liabilities: | | |
| Bonds Payable | $ 200,000 | |
| Less: Discount on Bonds Payable | 32,000 | $ 168,000 |

George pays semiannual interest each June 30 and December 31.

**Requirements**

1. Answer the following questions about George's bonds payable:
   a. What is the maturity value of the bonds?
   b. What is the carrying amount of the bonds at December 31, 2018?
   c. What is the semiannual cash interest payment on the bonds?
   d. How much interest expense should the company record each year?
2. Record the June 30, 2018, semiannual interest payment and amortization of discount.

## P12-40B Analyzing and journalizing bond transactions

**Learning Objectives 2, 3, 4**

3. June 30 Interest Expense DR $18,600

On January 1, 2016, Texas Credit Union (TCU) issued 6%, 20-year bonds payable with face value of $600,000. The bonds pay interest on June 30 and December 31.

**Requirements**

1. If the market interest rate is 5% when TCU issues its bonds, will the bonds be priced at face value, at a premium, or at a discount? Explain.
2. If the market interest rate is 9% when TCU issues its bonds, will the bonds be priced at face value, at a premium, or at a discount? Explain.
3. The issue price of the bonds is 96. Journalize the following bond transactions:
   a. Issuance of the bonds on January 1, 2016.
   b. Payment of interest and amortization on June 30, 2016.
   c. Payment of interest and amortization on December 31, 2016.
   d. Retirement of the bond at maturity on December 31, 2035.



## P12-41B Analyzing and journalizing bond transactions

**Learning Objectives 2, 3, 4**

June 30 Interest Expense DR $3,300

On January 1, 2016, Technicians Credit Union (TCU) issued 7%, 20-year bonds payable with face value of $100,000. The bonds pay interest on June 30 and December 31. The issue price of the bonds is 108.

Journalize the following bond transactions:

a. Issuance of the bonds on January 1, 2016.

b. Payment of interest and amortization on June 30, 2016.

c. Payment of interest and amortization on December 31, 2016.

d. Retirement of the bond at maturity on December 31, 2035.

**Learning Objectives 5, 6**

1. Total Liabilities $268,900

## P12-42B Reporting liabilities on the balance sheet and computing debt to equity ratio

The accounting records of Path Leader Wireless include the following as of December 31, 2016:

| | | | |
|---|---|---|---|
| Accounts Payable | $ 75,000 | Salaries Payable | $ 7,500 |
| Mortgages Payable (long-term) | 76,000 | Bonds Payable (current portion) | 21,000 |
| Interest Payable | 15,000 | Premium on Bonds Payable | 9,000 |
| Bonds Payable (long-term) | 62,000 | Unearned Revenue (short-term) | 3,400 |
| Total Stockholders' Equity | 180,000 | | |

### Requirements

1. Report these liabilities on the Path Leader Wireless balance sheet, including headings and totals for current liabilities and long-term liabilities.
2. Compute Path Leader Wireless's debt to equity ratio at December 31, 2016.

**Learning Objectives 7, 8**
**Appendixes 12A, 12B**

3. Jan. 1, 2016, Cash DR $595,123

## P12AB-43B Determining the present value of bonds payable and journalizing using the effective-interest amortization method

Ben Nowak issued $500,000 of 11%, 9-year bonds payable on January 1, 2016. The market interest rate at the date of issuance was 8%, and the bonds pay interest semiannually.

### Requirements

1. How much cash did the company receive upon issuance of the bonds payable? (Round all numbers to the nearest whole dollar.)
2. Prepare an amortization table for the bond using the effective-interest method, through the first two interest payments. (Round all numbers to the nearest whole dollar.)
3. Journalize the issuance of the bonds on January 1, 2016, and payment of the first semiannual interest amount and amortization of the bond on June 30, 2016. Explanations are not required.



**Learning Objectives 7, 8**
**Appendixes 12A, 12B**

3. Jan. 1, 2016, Cash DR $565,710

## P12AB-44B Determining the present value of bonds payable and journalizing using the effective-interest amortization method

Spa, Inc. is authorized to issue 11%, 10-year bonds payable. On January 1, 2016, when the market interest rate is 12%, the company issues $600,000 of the bonds. The bonds pay interest semiannually.

### Requirements

1. How much cash did the company receive upon issuance of the bonds payable? (Round all numbers to the nearest whole dollar.)
2. Prepare an amortization table for the bond using the effective-interest method, through the first two interest payments. (Round all numbers to the nearest whole dollar.)
3. Journalize the issuance of the bonds on January 1, 2016, and payment of the first semiannual interest amount and amortization of the bond on June 30, 2016. Explanations are not required.

## > Continuing Problem

**P12-45 Describing bonds and journalizing transactions for bonds payable using the straight-line amortization method**

This problem continues the Daniels Consulting situation from Problem P11-35 of Chapter 11. Daniels Consulting is considering raising additional capital. Daniels plans to raise the capital by issuing $500,000 of 8%, seven-year bonds on January 1, 2017. The bonds pay interest semiannually on June 30 and December 31. On January 1, 2017, the market rate of interest required by investors for similar bonds is 10%.

**Requirements**

1. Will Daniels's bonds issue at face value, a premium, or a discount?
2. Calculate and record the cash received on the bond issue date.
3. Journalize the first interest payment on June 30 and amortize the premium or discount using the straight-line amortization method.

# CRITICAL THINKING

## > Decision Case 12-1

The following questions are not related.

**Requirements**

1. Duncan Brooks needs to borrow $500,000 to open new stores. Brooks can borrow $500,000 by issuing 5%, 10-year bonds at 96. How much will Brooks actually receive in cash under this arrangement? How much must Brooks pay back at maturity? How will Brooks account for the difference between the cash received on the issue date and the amount paid back?
2. Brooks prefers to borrow for longer periods when interest rates are low and for shorter periods when interest rates are high. Why is this a good business strategy?

## > Ethical Issue 12-1

Raffie's Kids, a nonprofit organization that provides aid to victims of domestic violence, low-income families, and special-needs children, has a 30-year, 5% mortgage on the existing building. The mortgage requires monthly payments of $3,000. Raffie's bookkeeper is preparing financial statements for the board and, in doing so, lists the mortgage balance of $287,000 under current liabilities because the board hopes to be able to pay the mortgage off in full next year. Of the mortgage principal, $20,000 will be paid next year if Raffie's pays according to the mortgage agreement. The board members call you, their trusted CPA, to advise them on how Raffie's Kids should report the mortgage on its balance sheet. What is the ethical issue? Provide and discuss the reason for your recommendation.

## > Fraud Case 12-1

Bill and Edna had been married two years and had just reached the point where they had enough savings to start investing. Bill's uncle Dave told them that he had recently inherited some very rare railroad bonds from his grandmother's estate. He wanted to help Bill and Edna get a start in the world and would sell them 50 of the bonds at $100 each. The bonds were dated 1873, beautifully engraved, showing a face value of $1,000 each. Uncle Dave pointed out that "United States of America" was printed prominently at the top and that the U.S. government had established a sinking fund to retire the old railroad bonds. A sinking fund is a fund established for the purpose of repaying the debt. It allows the organization (the U.S. government, in this example) to set aside money over time to retire the bonds. All Bill and Edna needed to do was hold on to them until the government contacted them, and they would eventually get the full $1,000 for each bond. Bill and Edna were overjoyed—until a year later when they saw the exact same bonds for sale at a coin and stamp shop priced as "collectors' items" for $9.95 each!

**Requirements**

1. If a company goes bankrupt, what happens to the bonds it issued and the investors who bought the bonds?
2. When investing in bonds, how can you tell whether the bond issue is a legitimate transaction?
3. Is there a way to determine the relative risk of corporate bonds?

## > Financial Statement Case 12-1

Use the **Starbucks Corporation** financial statements to answer the following questions. Visit **http://www.pearsonhighered.com/Horngren** to view a link to Starbucks Corporation's Fiscal 2013 Annual Report.

**Requirements**

1. How much was Starbucks Corporation's long-term debt at September 29, 2013?
2. Compute Starbucks Corporation's debt to equity ratio at September 29, 2013. How does it compare to **Green Mountain Coffee Roasters, Inc.**?





## > Quick Check Answers

**1.** a **2.** d **3.** b **4.** a **5.** a **6.** c **7.** a **8.** d **9A.** b **10B.** b

# Stockholders' Equity 13

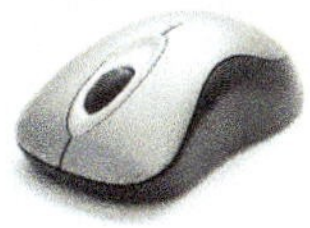

## How Do We Raise More Cash?

Lacey Snyder and Alison Mason, stockholders of Sharemymovie.com, were reviewing the latest financial statements of their business. Sharemymovie .com, a video-sharing Web site in which users can upload, share, and view videos, started five years ago with a cash contribution from each owner and a small bank loan. In the past five years, the site has grown rapidly with more than 1 million video views each day. Lacey and Alison are excited about the success of the business, but the business has recently been experiencing growing pains.

With the increase in the number of users visiting the site and uploading new videos daily, Lacey and Alison know they need to invest in a new Web site design and purchase updated software. But these expansions will take cash, and they are reluctant to borrow more money from the bank. Lacey and Alison considered asking friends and family to invest in the business. They realized that in order to gain enough cash to meet the growing needs of the business, they would need a large influx of money. After talking to their accountant, they are considering expanding their corporation and taking their business public. In other words, the business will offer ownership (through stock) for anyone who is willing to invest.

By offering the opportunity to own a share in the business, Sharemymovie.com can quickly raise the necessary cash to meet its expansion needs. In addition, the corporate form of business offers liability protection for the stockholders. But there are also some disadvantages to the corporate form, such as double taxation and increased government regulation. As Lacey and Alison move forward with their decision, they need to understand the pros and cons of corporations and carefully evaluate the impact of this decision.

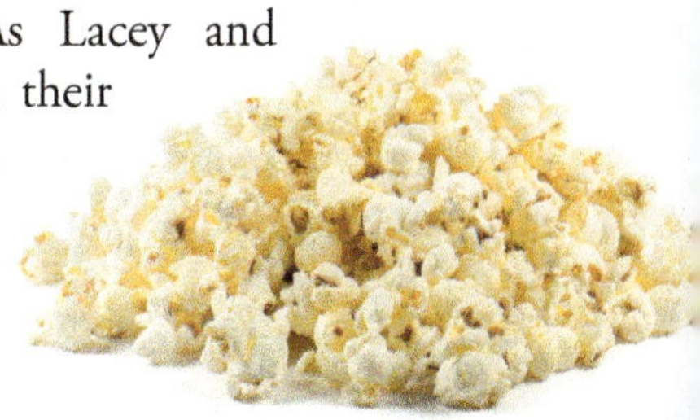

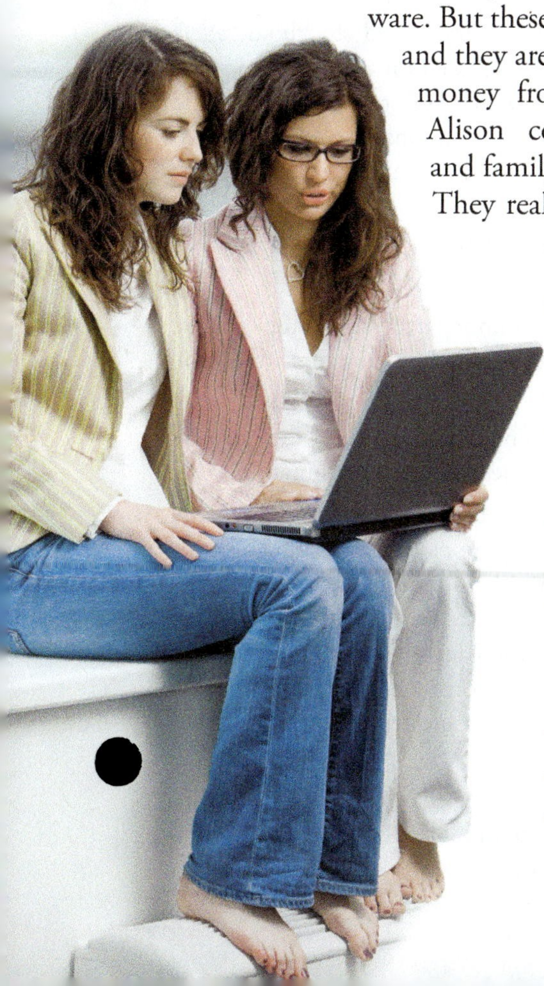

**How Much Is the Business Worth?**

On February 1, 2012, Facebook, Inc., the popular social media Web site, announced that it planned to issue shares of stock on the stock market under the ticker symbol FB. On May 18, Mark Zuckerberg, the mastermind behind Facebook, rang the opening bell of the stock exchange and shares of Facebook stock began selling at $42.05 per share. On that day, more than 500 million shares were sold and exchanged with an estimated market capitalization of more than $104 billion, one of the largest initial public offering (IPO) to date. It's interesting to note that in less than a month after its IPO, Facebook stock lost more than a quarter of its value and continues to fluctuate.

Why did Facebook decide to issue stock? What are the advantages and disadvantages of a corporation? How is stock reported on the financial statements? What does the drop in market price of the stock mean to Facebook? In this chapter, we explore the answers to these questions and many more. You learn why businesses decide to organize as a corporation and how to account for transactions unique to a corporation.

# Chapter 13 Learning Objectives

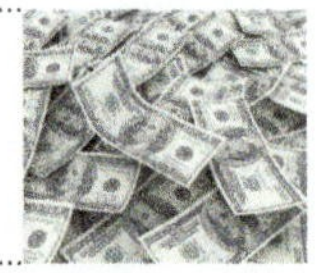

1. Identify the characteristics of a corporation
2. Journalize the issuance of stock
3. Account for the purchase and sale of treasury stock
4. Account for cash dividends, stock dividends, and stock splits
5. Explain how equity is reported for a corporation
6. Use earnings per share, rate of return on common stock, and the price/earnings ratio to evaluate business performance

## WHAT IS A CORPORATION?

**Learning Objective 1**
Identify the characteristics of a corporation

**Corporation**
A business organized under state law that is a separate legal entity.

As introduced in earlier chapters, a **corporation** is a business organized under state law that is a separate legal entity. Corporations dominate business activity in the United States. Most well-known companies are corporations and tend to be large multinational businesses.

### Characteristics of Corporations

A corporation has many unique characteristics:

- **Separate legal entity**—A corporation is a separate legal entity. It is organized independently of its owners.
- **Number of owners**—Corporations have one or more owners (called stockholders). A *public* corporation is a corporation whose stock can be purchased on an organized stock exchange, such as the New York Stock Exchange or the NASDAQ Stock Market. Public corporations often have thousands of owners. Some corporations are *privately held*, which means that the stock cannot be purchased on a stock exchange. These corporations often have only a few stockholders.
- **No personal liability of the owner(s) for business's debts**—Stockholders are not personally liable for the debts of the corporation.
- **Lack of mutual agency**—Unlike a sole proprietorship and partnership, stockholders of the corporation are not mutual agents of the business. Stockholders cannot bind the business to a contract.
- **Indefinite life**—Corporations have an indefinite life. They can exist until the business decides to terminate. Withdrawal or death of an owner does not cause termination.
- **Taxation**—Corporations are separate taxable entities. The corporation pays the income tax on the business earnings and is also responsible for paying payroll taxes on employee salaries and wages. Corporations also experience double taxation. Double taxation occurs when corporations make cash payments (called dividends) to stockholders. These payments are taxed once as earnings of the corporation and then again when the stockholder receives the dividend. The tax is first paid by the corporation on its corporate income tax return, and then the dividends received by the stockholder are reported on the stockholder's personal income tax return.
- **Capital accumulation**—Corporations can raise more money than sole proprietorships and partnerships. This is completed through an initial public offering (IPO) and represents the initial offering of corporate shares of stock to the public.

Exhibit 13-1 summarizes the advantages and disadvantages of a corporation.

**Exhibit 13-1 | Corporations: Advantages and Disadvantages**

| Advantages | Disadvantages |
|---|---|
| 1. Corporations can raise more money than a proprietorship or partnership. | 1. Ownership and management are often separated. |
| 2. A corporation has a continuous life. | 2. The earnings of a corporation may be subject to double taxation. |
| 3. The transfer of corporate ownership is easy. | 3. Government regulation is expensive. |
| 4. There is no mutual agency among the stockholders and the corporation. | 4. Start-up costs are higher than other business forms. |
| 5. Stockholders have limited liability. | |

## Stockholders' Equity Basics

A corporation is created by filing a certificate of formation with a state. The state authorizes the business to be organized as a corporation and grants the entity a charter or articles of incorporation. The corporation then prepares a set of bylaws, which provide the rules and procedures that the corporation will follow.

The corporate charter of a corporation identifies the maximum number of shares of stock the corporation may issue, called **authorized stock**. The charter provides a state's permission for the corporation to operate. Authorized stock can be issued or unissued. **Issued stock** has been issued by the corporation but may or may not be held by stockholders. A corporation issues **stock certificates** to the stockholders when they buy the stock. The stock certificate represents the individual's ownership of the corporation's capital, so it is called **capital stock**. The basic unit of stock is a share. A corporation may issue a physical stock certificate for any number of shares. Today, many corporations issue the stocks electronically rather than printing a paper certificate. Exhibit 13-2 shows a stock certificate for 288 shares of Smart Touch Learning common stock owned by Courtney Edwards.

**Authorized Stock**
The maximum number of shares of stock that the corporate charter allows the corporation to issue.

**Issued Stock**
Stock that has been issued but may or may not be held by stockholders.

**Stock Certificate**
Paper evidence of ownership in a corporation.

**Capital Stock**
Represents the individual's ownership of the corporation's capital.

**Exhibit 13-2 | Stock Certificate**

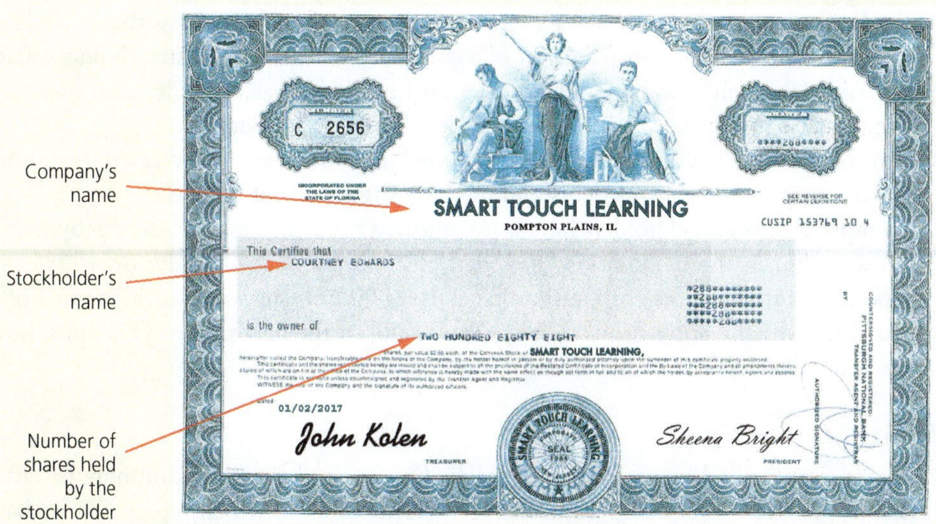

The certificate shows the following:

- Company name
- Stockholder name
- Number of shares owned by the stockholder

**Outstanding Stock**
Issued stock in the hands of stockholders.

Stock that is held by the stockholders is said to be **outstanding stock**. The outstanding stock of a corporation represents 100% of its ownership. The numbers of shares of authorized stock, issued stock, and outstanding stock are most likely going to be different amounts. Exhibit 13-3 explains the differences between these categories of stock.

**Exhibit 13-3 | Categories of Stock**

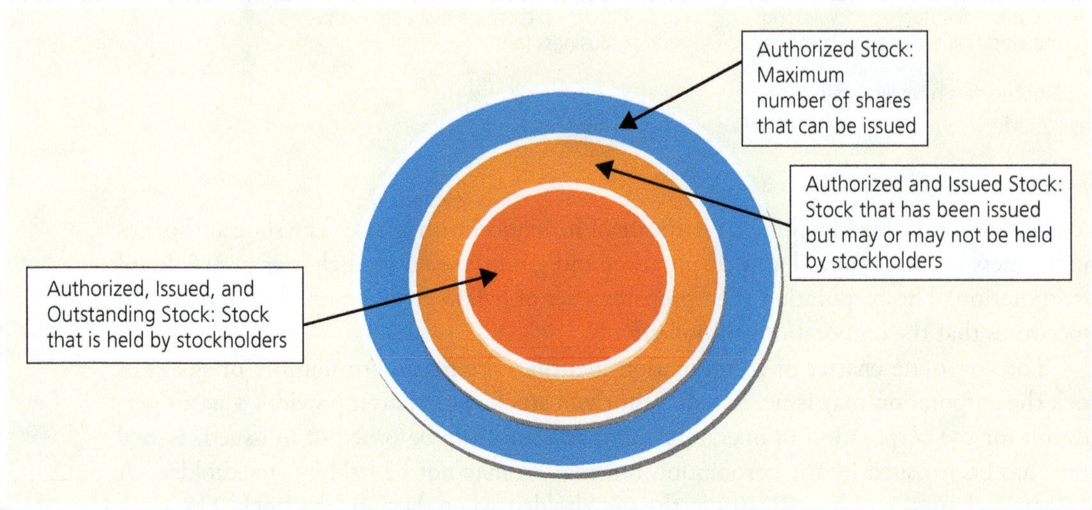


## Stockholders' Rights

A stockholder has four basic rights, unless a right is withheld by contract:

1. **Vote.** Stockholders participate in management indirectly by voting on corporate matters at stockholders' meetings (or sometimes through the mail or electronic voting). This is the only way in which a stockholder can help to manage the corporation. Normally, each share of basic ownership in the corporation carries one vote.
2. **Dividends.** Stockholders receive a proportionate part of any **dividend** that is declared and paid. A dividend is a distribution of a corporation's earnings to stockholders. Each share of stock receives an equal dividend so, for example, a shareholder who owns 1% of the total shares in the company receives 1% of any total dividend.
3. **Liquidation.** Stockholders receive their proportionate share of any assets remaining after the corporation pays its debts and liquidates (goes out of business).
4. **Preemptive right.** Stockholders have a **preemptive right** to maintain their proportionate ownership in the corporation. For example, suppose a stockholder owns 5% of a corporation's stock. If the corporation issues 100,000 new shares of stock, it must offer the stockholder the opportunity to buy 5% (5,000) of the new shares. This right, however, is usually withheld by contract for most corporations.

**Dividend**
A distribution of a corporation's earnings to stockholders.

**Preemptive Right**
Stockholder's right to maintain his or her proportionate ownership in the corporation.

## Capital Stock

Corporations can issue different classes of stock. The stock of a corporation may be either common or preferred. Every corporation issues **common stock**, which represents the basic ownership of the corporation. Some companies issue Class A common stock, which carries

**Common Stock**
Represents the basic ownership of a corporation.

the right to vote. They may also issue Class B common stock, which may be nonvoting. There must be at least one voting class of stock. However, there is no limit as to the number or types of classes of stock that a corporation may issue. Each class of stock has a separate account in the company's ledger.

**Preferred stock** gives its owners certain advantages over common stock. Most notably, preferred stockholders receive a dividend preference over common stockholders. This ensures that if a corporation pays dividends, the preferred stockholders receive their dividends first. They also receive assets before common stockholders if the corporation liquidates. When dividends are declared, corporations pay a fixed dividend on preferred stock. The amount of the preferred dividend is printed on the face of the preferred stock certificate. Investors usually buy preferred stock to earn those fixed dividends. With these advantages, preferred stockholders take less investment risk than common stockholders.

**Preferred Stock**
Stock that gives its owners certain advantages over common stockholders, such as the right to receive dividends before the common stockholders and the right to receive assets before the common stockholders if the corporation liquidates.

**Par Value**
An amount assigned by a company to a share of its stock.

Owners of preferred stock also have the four basic stockholder rights, unless a right is withheld. The right to vote, for example, is usually withheld from preferred stock. Companies may issue different series of preferred stock (Series A and Series B, for example). Each series is recorded in a separate account. Preferred stock is more rare than you might think. Many corporations have the authorization to issue preferred stock, but few actually issue the preferred shares.

Is the par value of a stock the price at which the stock is bought and sold?

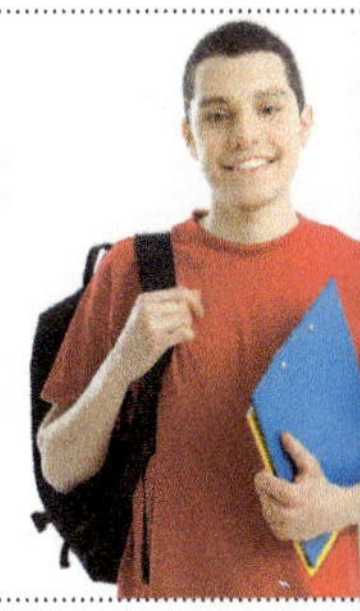

Stock may carry a par value or it may be no-par stock. **Par value is an amount assigned by a company to a share of its stock. Most companies set par value low to avoid issuing their stock below par. The par value of a stock has no relation to the market value, which is the price at which the stock is bought and sold.**

The par value of preferred stock may be higher per share than common stock par values. Par value is arbitrary and is assigned when the organizers file the corporate charter with the state. There is no real reason for why par values vary. It is a choice made by the organizers of the corporation.

Some states allow the issuance of no-par stock. **No-par stock** does not have par value. No-par value stock has an advantage because there is no confusion between the par value and market value of the stock. **Stated value stock** is no-par stock that has been assigned an amount similar to par value. Stated value represents the minimum amount that the corporation can issue the stock for. Usually the state the company incorporates in will determine whether a stock may be par or stated value stock. For accounting purposes, par value stock is treated the same as stated value stock.

**No-Par Stock**
Stock that has no amount (par) assigned to it.

**Stated Value Stock**
No-par stock that has been assigned an amount similar to par value.

## Stockholders' Equity

A corporation's equity is called **stockholders' equity**. State laws require corporations to report their sources of owners' capital because some of the capital must be maintained by the company. The two basic sources of stockholders' equity are as follows:

- **Paid-in capital** (also called *contributed capital*) represents amounts received from the stockholders in exchange for stock. Common stock is the main source of paid-in capital. Paid-in capital is *externally* generated capital and results from transactions with outsiders.
- **Retained earnings** is equity earned by profitable operations that is not distributed to stockholders. Retained earnings is *internally* generated equity because it results from corporate decisions to retain net income to use in future operations or for expansion.

**Stockholders' Equity**
A corporation's equity that includes paid-in capital and retained earnings.

**Paid-In Capital**
Represents amounts received from the stockholders of a corporation in exchange for stock.

**Retained Earnings**
Equity earned by profitable operations of a corporation that is not distributed to stockholders.

## Try It!

Match the key term to the definition.

| | |
|---|---|
| 1. Stock certificate | a. The maximum number of shares of stock that the corporate charter allows the corporation to issue. |
| 2. Preemptive right | b. Stock that gives its owners certain advantages over common stockholders. |
| 3. Authorized stock | c. Stockholders' right to maintain their proportionate ownership in the corporation. |
| 4. Preferred stock | d. Represents amounts received from stockholders of a corporation in exchange for stock. |
| 5. Paid-in capital | e. Paper evidence of ownership in a corporation. |

**Check your answers online in MyAccountingLab or at http://www.pearsonhighered.com/Horngren.**

For more practice, see Short Exercise S13-1. MyAccountingLab

# HOW IS THE ISSUANCE OF STOCK ACCOUNTED FOR?

**Learning Objective 2**
Journalize the issuance of stock

Large corporations such as Intel Corporation and Nike, Inc. need huge quantities of money. They cannot finance all their operations through borrowing, so they raise capital by issuing stock. A company can sell its stock directly to stockholders, or it can use the services of an **underwriter**, such as the brokerage firms of Merrill Lynch & Co., Inc., Morgan Stanley, and JPMorgan Chase & Co. An underwriter usually assumes some of the risk of issuing stock by agreeing to buy all the stock the firm cannot sell to its clients. Stocks of public companies are bought and sold on a stock exchange, such as the New York Stock Exchange (NYSE) or NASDAQ Stock Market.

**Underwriter**
A firm that handles the issuance of a company's stock to the public, usually assuming some of the risk by agreeing to buy the stock if the firm cannot sell all of the stock to its clients.

The amount that the corporation receives from issuing stock is called the **issue price**. Usually, the issue price exceeds par value because par value is normally set quite low.

**Issue Price**
The price the stock initially sells for the first time it is sold.

## Issuing Common Stock at Par Value

In this chapter, we will continue using Smart Touch Learning; however, we will now assume that Smart Touch Learning's common stock carries a par value of $1 per share and that the charter authorizes 20,000,000 shares of common stock. The stock issuance journal entry of 15,000 shares at par value would be as follows:

| A↑ | = | L | + | E↑ |
|---|---|---|---|---|
| Cash↑ | | | | Common Stock↑ |

| Date | Accounts and Explanation | Debit | Credit |
|---|---|---|---|
| | Cash | 15,000 | |
| | Common Stock—$1 Par Value ($1 per share × 15,000 shares) | | 15,000 |
| | *Issued common stock at par.* | | |

## Issuing Common Stock at a Premium

As stated previously, most corporations set par value low and issue common stock for a price above par. The amount above par is called a **premium**. Assume Smart Touch Learning issues an additional 3,000 shares for $5 per share. The $4 difference between the issue price ($5) and par value ($1) is a premium.

**Premium**
The amount above par at which a stock is issued.

A premium on the issue of stock is not a gain, income, or profit for the corporation because the company is dealing with its own stock. This situation illustrates one of the fundamentals of accounting in that a company cannot report a profit or loss when buying or selling its own stock. So, the premium is another type of paid-in capital account known as **Paid-In Capital in Excess of Par**. It is also called *additional paid-in capital.* The Paid-In Capital in Excess of Par account is an equity account that is reported on the balance sheet.

> **Paid-In Capital in Excess of Par**
> Represents amounts received from stockholders in excess of par value.

With a par value of $1, Smart Touch Learning's entry to record the issuance of 3,000 shares of its common stock at $5 per share is as follows:

| Date | Accounts and Explanation | Debit | Credit |
|---|---|---|---|
| | Cash ($5 per share × 3,000 shares) | 15,000 | |
| | Common Stock—$1 Par Value ($1 per share × 3,000 shares) | | 3,000 |
| | Paid-In Capital in Excess of Par—Common ($4 per share × 3,000 shares) | | 12,000 |
| | *Issued common stock at a premium.* | | |

A↑ = L + E↑
Cash↑ = Common Stock↑, Paid-In Capital in Excess of Par↑

*When stock is issued at a premium, common stock is always recorded at the par value. Any amount over par value is recorded to the Paid-In Capital in Excess of Par account.*

Exhibit 13-4 shows how Smart Touch Learning would report stockholders' equity on its balance sheet after the stock issuances, assuming that the balance of Retained Earnings is $3,550.

**Exhibit 13-4 | Stockholders' Equity**

| SMART TOUCH LEARNING, INC.<br>Balance Sheet (Partial)<br>December 31, 2016 | |
|---|---|
| **Stockholders' Equity** | |
| Paid-In Capital: | |
| Common Stock—$1 Par Value; 20,000,000 shares authorized, 18,000 shares issued and outstanding | $ 18,000 |
| Paid-In Capital in Excess of Par—Common | 12,000 |
| Total Paid-In Capital | 30,000 |
| Retained Earnings | 3,550 |
| Total Stockholders' Equity | **$ 33,550** |

## Issuing No-Par Common Stock

When a company issues no-par stock, it debits the asset received and credits the stock account. For no-par stock, there can be no Paid-In Capital in Excess of Par because there is no par to be in excess of.

Assume that, instead of $1 par value, Smart Touch Learning's common stock is no-par. How would that change the recording of the issuance of 15,000 shares for $1 and 3,000 shares for $5? The stock-issuance entries would be as follows:

| A↑ | = | L | + | E↑ |
|---|---|---|---|---|
| Cash↑ | | | | Common Stock↑ |

| Date | Accounts and Explanation | Debit | Credit |
|---|---|---|---|
| | Cash ($1 per share × 15,000 shares) | 15,000 | |
| | Common Stock—No-Par Value | | 15,000 |
| | *Issued no-par common stock.* | | |
| | | | |
| | Cash ($5 per share × 3,000 shares) | 15,000 | |
| | Common Stock— No-Par Value | | 15,000 |
| | *Issued no-par common stock.* | | |

| A↑ | = | L | + | E↑ |
|---|---|---|---|---|
| Cash↑ | | | | Common Stock↑ |

Regardless of the stock's issue price, Cash is debited and Common Stock is credited for the cash received. So, although the total paid-in capital of $30,000 remains the same, the Common Stock account differs from $18,000 (par stock) to $30,000 (no-par stock).

Exhibit 13-5 shows how the stockholders' equity section of the balance sheet would change.

**Exhibit 13-5 | Stockholders' Equity—No-Par Stock**

| SMART TOUCH LEARNING, INC.<br>Balance Sheet (Partial)<br>December 31, 2016 | |
|---|---|
| **Stockholders' Equity** | |
| Paid-In Capital: | |
| Common Stock—No-Par Value; 20,000,000 shares authorized, 18,000 shares issued and outstanding | $ 30,000 |
| Retained Earnings | 3,550 |
| Total Stockholders' Equity | **$ 33,550** |

## Issuing Stated Value Common Stock

Accounting for stated value common stock is almost identical to accounting for par value stock. The only difference is that stated value stock uses an account titled Paid-In Capital in Excess of *Stated* to record amounts received above the stated value.

For example, assume that instead of issuing 3,000 shares of $1 par value stock for $5 per share, Smart Touch Learning issues 3,000 shares of $1 *stated* value stock for $5 per share. Smart Touch Learning would record the following journal entry:

| A↑ | = | L | + | E↑ |
|---|---|---|---|---|
| Cash↑ | | | | Common Stock↑<br>Paid-In Capital in Excess of Stated↑ |

| Date | Accounts and Explanation | Debit | Credit |
|---|---|---|---|
| | Cash ($5 per share × 3,000 shares) | 15,000 | |
| | Common Stock—$1 Stated Value ($1 per share × 3,000 shares) | | 3,000 |
| | Paid-In Capital in Excess of Stated—Common ($4 per share × 3,000 shares) | | 12,000 |
| | *Issued common stock at a premium.* | | |

## Issuing Common Stock for Assets Other Than Cash

A corporation may issue stock for assets other than cash. It records the transaction at the market value of the stock issued or the market value of the assets received, whichever is more clearly determinable. Now let's consider that Smart Touch Learning receives an additional contribution of furniture with a market value of $18,000 in exchange for 5,000 shares of its $1 par common stock. How would the entry be recorded?

| Date | Accounts and Explanation | Debit | Credit |
|---|---|---|---|
| | Furniture | 18,000 | |
| | Common Stock—$1 Par Value ($1 par value × 5,000 shares) | | 5,000 |
| | Paid-In Capital in Excess of Par—Common ($18,000 – $5,000) | | 13,000 |
| | *Issued common stock in exchange for furniture.* | | |

| A↑ | = | L + | E↑ |
|---|---|---|---|
| Furniture↑ | | | Common Stock↑<br>Paid-In Capital in Excess of Par↑ |

As you can see, the common stock is still recorded at its $1 par value and the difference between the market value of the furniture and the par value is recorded to the Paid-In Capital in Excess of Par account. The contributed asset is recorded at its current market value.

### ETHICS

#### What should the building be valued at?

Reed Hiller, the accountant for Snyder Corporation, is trying to decide how to record the company's most recent issuance of stock. Jack Chavez, a majority stockholder, has contributed a building in exchange for common stock. Jack believes that the building should be valued at $4 million, his evaluation of the building's market value. Jack argues that by recording the asset at such a large amount, the business will look more prosperous to investors. Reed is concerned that Jack is overvaluing the asset. What should Reed do?

#### Solution

Issuance of stock for cash poses no ethical challenge because the value of the asset received (cash) is clearly understood. Issuing stock for assets other than cash can pose a challenge, though. A company should record an asset received at its current market value or the market value of the stock issued, whichever is more clearly determinable. One person's evaluation of a building's market value can differ from another's. Reed should encourage the company to hire an independent appraiser to determine the current market value of the building and then record the building at that value. Alternatively, the company can use the market value of the stock issued to determine the value of the building. This would be appropriate if the stock is traded on an organized exchange.

## Issuing Preferred Stock

Accounting for preferred stock follows the pattern illustrated for issuing common stock. Assume that Smart Touch Learning has authorization from the state to issue 2,000 shares of preferred stock. Smart Touch Learning decides to issue 1,000 shares of its $50 par, 6% preferred stock on January 3, 2017, at $55 per share. (The 6% in the description of the preferred stock refers to the stated dividend associated with the stock and is explained later in the chapter.) The issuance entry would be as follows:

| A↑ | = | L + | E↑ |
|---|---|---|---|
| Cash↑ | | | Preferred Stock↑<br>Paid-In Capital in Excess of Par↑ |

| Date | Accounts and Explanation | Debit | Credit |
|---|---|---|---|
| Jan. 3 | Cash ($55 per share × 1,000 shares) | 55,000 | |
| | Preferred Stock—$50 Par Value ($50 per share × 1,000 shares) | | 50,000 |
| | Paid-In Capital in Excess of Par—Preferred ($5 per share × 1,000 shares) | | 5,000 |
| | *Issued preferred stock at a premium.* | | |

Preferred Stock is included in the stockholders' equity section of the balance sheet and is often listed first. Any Paid-In Capital in Excess of Par—Preferred is listed next, followed by Common Stock and Paid-In Capital in Excess of Par—Common. Exhibit 13-6 shows the stockholders' equity section of Smart Touch Learning's balance sheet, assuming both stocks were par value stocks.

**Exhibit 13-6 | Stockholders' Equity**

| SMART TOUCH LEARNING, INC.<br>Balance Sheet (Partial)<br>January 3, 2017 | |
|---|---|
| **Stockholders' Equity** | |
| Paid-In Capital: | |
| Preferred Stock—$50 Par Value; 2,000 shares authorized, 1,000 shares issued and outstanding | $ 50,000 |
| Paid-In Capital in Excess of Par—Preferred | 5,000 |
| Common Stock—$1 Par Value; 20,000,000 shares authorized, 23,000 shares issued and outstanding | 23,000 |
| Paid-In Capital in Excess of Par—Common | 25,000 |
| Total Paid-In Capital | 103,000 |
| Retained Earnings | 3,550 |
| Total Stockholders' Equity | **$ 106,550** |

## Try It!

6. London Corporation has two classes of stock: Common, $1 par value; and Preferred, $4 par value. Journalize the issuance of 10,000 shares of common stock for $8 per share.

**Check your answer online in MyAccountingLab or at http://www.pearsonhighered.com/Horngren.**

For more practice, see Short Exercises S13-2 through S13-5. MyAccountingLab

# HOW IS TREASURY STOCK ACCOUNTED FOR?

**Learning Objective 3**

Account for the purchase and sale of treasury stock

A company's own stock that it has previously issued and later reacquired is called **treasury stock**. In effect, the corporation holds the stock in its treasury. A corporation, such as Smart Touch Learning, may purchase treasury stock for several reasons:

**Treasury Stock**

A corporation's own stock that it has previously issued and later reacquired.

1. Management wants to increase net assets by buying low and selling high.
2. Management wants to support the company's stock price.
3. Management wants to avoid a takeover by an outside party by reducing the number of outstanding shares that have voting rights.
4. Management wants to reward valued employees with stock.

## Treasury Stock Basics

Here are the basics of accounting for treasury stock:

- The Treasury Stock account has a normal debit balance, which is the opposite of the other stockholders' equity accounts. Therefore, *Treasury Stock is a contra equity account.*
- Treasury stock is recorded at cost (what the company paid to reacquire the shares), without reference to par value. (We illustrate the *cost* method of accounting for treasury stock because it is used most widely. Intermediate accounting courses also cover an alternative method.)
- The Treasury Stock account is reported beneath Retained Earnings on the balance sheet as a reduction to total stockholders' equity.

Treasury stock decreases the company's stock that is outstanding—held by outsiders (the stockholders). Therefore, outstanding stock is issued stock less treasury stock. Only outstanding shares have voting rights and receive cash or stock dividends. Treasury stock does not carry a vote, and it receives no cash or stock dividends. Now we illustrate how to account for treasury stock, continuing with Smart Touch Learning.

## Purchase of Treasury Stock

Review Smart Touch Learning's stockholders' equity before purchasing treasury stock as shown in Exhibit 13-6.

Assume that on March 31, Smart Touch Learning purchased 1,000 shares of previously issued common stock, paying $5 per share. To record the purchase, the company debits Treasury Stock—Common and credits Cash:

| Date | Accounts and Explanation | Debit | Credit |
|---|---|---|---|
| Mar. 31 | Treasury Stock—Common ($5 per share × 1,000 shares) | 5,000 | |
| | Cash | | 5,000 |
| | *Purchased treasury stock.* | | |

| A↓ | = | L | + | E↓ |
|---|---|---|---|---|
| Cash↓ | | | | Treasury Stock↑ |

## Sale of Treasury Stock

Companies buy their treasury stock and eventually resell or retire it. A company may resell treasury stock at, above, or below its cost (what the company paid for the shares).

## Sale at Cost

If treasury stock is sold for cost—the same price the corporation paid for it—there is no difference between the cost per share and the sale price per share to journalize. Assume Smart Touch Learning resells 100 of the treasury shares on April 1 for $5 each. The entry follows:

| A↑ | | L | + | E↑ |
|---|---|---|---|---|
| Cash↑ | = | | | Treasury Stock↓ |

| Date | Accounts and Explanation | Debit | Credit |
|---|---|---|---|
| Apr. 1 | Cash | 500 | |
| | Treasury Stock—Common ($5 per share × 100 shares) | | 500 |
| | *Sold treasury stock at cost.* | | |

**Treasury Stock—Common**

| | | | |
|---|---|---|---|
| Mar. 31 | 5,000 | | |
| | | 500 | Apr. 1 |
| Bal. | 4,500 | | |

## Sale Above Cost

If treasury stock is resold for more than cost, the difference is credited to a new stockholders' equity account, Paid-In Capital from Treasury Stock Transactions. This excess is additional paid-in capital because it came from the company's stockholders. It has no effect on net income. Suppose Smart Touch Learning resold 200 of its treasury shares for $6 per share on April 2 (recall that cost was $5 per share). The entry to resell treasury stock for an amount above cost is as follows:

| A↑ | | L | + | E↑ |
|---|---|---|---|---|
| Cash↑ | = | | | Treasury Stock↓<br>Paid-In Capital from Treasury Stock Transactions↑ |

| Date | Accounts and Explanation | Debit | Credit |
|---|---|---|---|
| Apr. 2 | Cash ($6 per share × 200 shares) | 1,200 | |
| | Treasury Stock—Common ($5 per share × 200 shares) | | 1,000 |
| | Paid-In Capital from Treasury Stock Transactions ($1 per share × 200 shares) | | 200 |
| | *Sold treasury stock above cost.* | | |

**Treasury Stock—Common**

| | | | |
|---|---|---|---|
| Mar. 31 | 5,000 | | |
| | | 500 | Apr. 1 |
| | | 1,000 | Apr. 2 |
| Bal. | 3,500 | | |

**Paid-In Capital from Treasury Stock Transactions**

| | | | |
|---|---|---|---|
| | | 200 | Apr. 2 |

Paid-In Capital from Treasury Stock Transactions is reported with the other paid-in capital accounts on the balance sheet, beneath Common Stock and Paid-In Capital in Excess of Par.

## Sale Below Cost

The resale price of treasury stock can be less than cost. The shortfall is debited first to Paid-In Capital from Treasury Stock Transactions. However, this account can only be debited for an amount that brings it to 0 (it can not have a debit balance). If this account's balance is too small, Retained Earnings is debited for the remaining amount. To illustrate, assume Smart Touch Learning had two additional treasury stock sales. First, on April 3,

Smart Touch Learning resold 200 treasury shares for $4.30 each. The entry to record the resale is as follows:

| Date | Accounts and Explanation | Debit | Credit |
|---|---|---|---|
| Apr. 3 | Cash ($4.30 per share × 200 shares) | 860 | |
| | Paid-In Capital from Treasury Stock Transactions ($0.70 per share × 200 shares) | 140 | |
| | Treasury Stock—Common ($5 per share × 200 shares) | | 1,000 |
| | *Sold treasury stock below cost.* | | |

| A↑ | = | L | + | E↑ |
|---|---|---|---|---|
| Cash↑ | | | | Paid-In Capital from Treasury Stock Transactions↓<br>Treasury Stock↓ |

**Treasury Stock—Common**

| | | | |
|---|---|---|---|
| Mar. 31 | 5,000 | | |
| | | 500 | Apr. 1 |
| | | 1,000 | Apr. 2 |
| | | 1,000 | Apr. 3 |
| Bal. | 2,500 | | |

**Paid-In Capital from Treasury Stock Transactions**

| | | | |
|---|---|---|---|
| Apr. 3 | 140 | 200 | Apr. 2 |
| | | 60 | Bal. |

The treasury shares were sold for $140 less than their cost. Smart Touch Learning had previously sold treasury shares for $200 more than their cost, so the $200 credit balance in Paid-In Capital from Treasury Stock Transactions is large enough to cover the $140 debit.

Now, what happens if Smart Touch Learning resells an additional 200 treasury shares for $4.50 each on April 4? Smart Touch Learning records the following entry:

| Date | Accounts and Explanation | Debit | Credit |
|---|---|---|---|
| Apr. 4 | Cash ($4.50 per share × 200 shares) | 900 | |
| | Paid-In Capital from Treasury Stock Transactions | 60 | |
| | Retained Earnings ($1,000 – $900 – $60) | 40 | |
| | Treasury Stock—Common ($5 per share × 200 shares) | | 1,000 |
| | *Sold treasury stock below cost.* | | |

| A↑ | = | L | + | E↑ |
|---|---|---|---|---|
| Cash↑ | | | | Paid-In Capital from Treasury Stock Transactions↓<br>Retained Earnings↓<br>Treasury Stock↓ |

**Treasury Stock—Common**

| | | | |
|---|---|---|---|
| Mar. 31 | 5,000 | | |
| | | 500 | Apr. 1 |
| | | 1,000 | Apr. 2 |
| | | 1,000 | Apr. 3 |
| | | 1,000 | Apr. 4 |
| Bal. | 1,500 | | |

**Paid-In Capital from Treasury Stock Transactions**

| | | | |
|---|---|---|---|
| Apr. 3 | 140 | 200 | Apr. 2 |
| Apr. 4 | 60 | | |
| | | 0 | Bal. |

**Retained Earnings**

| | | | |
|---|---|---|---|
| | | 3,550 | Bal. |
| Apr. 4 | 40 | | |
| | | 3,510 | Bal. |

The 200 treasury shares are sold for $100 less than their cost [($4.50 sales price per share minus $5 cost per share) × 200 shares]. However, only $60 remains in Paid-In Capital from Treasury Stock Transactions. The difference of $40 ($100 – $60) is debited to Retained Earnings because the paid-in capital accounts cannot have debit balances.

Now we can show the revised stockholders' equity for Smart Touch Learning as shown in Exhibit 13-7.

**Exhibit 13-7** | **Stockholders' Equity After Treasury Stock Transactions**

| SMART TOUCH LEARNING, INC.<br>Balance Sheet (Partial)<br>April 4, 2017 | |
|---|---|
| **Stockholders' Equity** | |
| Paid-In Capital: | |
| Preferred Stock—$50 Par Value; 2,000 shares authorized, 1,000 shares issued and outstanding | $ 50,000 |
| Paid-In Capital in Excess of Par—Preferred | 5,000 |
| Common Stock—$1 Par Value; 20,000,000 shares authorized, 23,000 shares issued, 22,700 shares outstanding | 23,000 |
| Paid-In Capital in Excess of Par—Common | 25,000 |
| Total Paid-In Capital | 103,000 |
| Retained Earnings | 3,510 |
| Treasury Stock—Common; 300 shares at cost | (1,500) |
| Total Stockholders' Equity | **$ 105,010** |

So, how many common shares are outstanding on April 4? The 23,000 common shares previously issued minus 300 treasury shares equals 22,700 outstanding common shares.

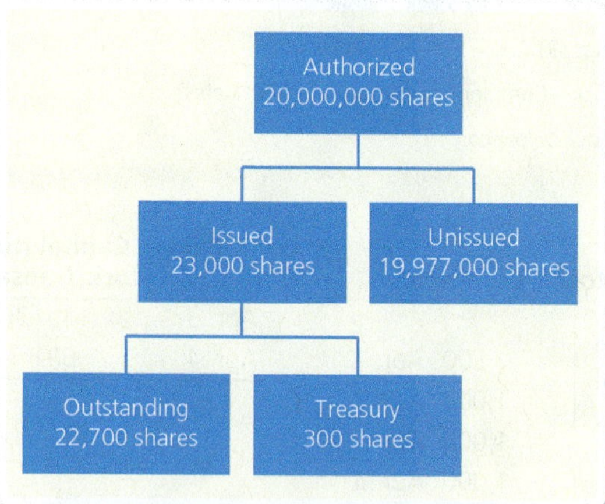


## Retirement of Stock

Not all companies repurchase their previously issued stock to hold it in the treasury. A corporation may retire its stock by canceling the stock certificates. Retired stock cannot be reissued.

Retirements of preferred stock are common as companies seek to avoid paying the preferred dividends. To repurchase previously issued stock for retirement, we debit the stock accounts—for example, Preferred Stock and Paid-In Capital in Excess of Par—Preferred—and credit Cash. That removes the retired stock from the company's books, which reduces total assets and total stockholders' equity.

## Try It!

7. On January 3, Halsall Corporation purchased 2,000 shares of the company's $2 par value common stock as treasury stock, paying cash of $8 per share. On January 30, Halsall sold 1,200 shares of the treasury stock for cash of $10 per share. Journalize these transactions.

**Check your answers online in MyAccountingLab or at http://www.pearsonhighered.com/Horngren.**

For more practice, see Short Exercise S13-6. MyAccountingLab

# HOW ARE DIVIDENDS AND STOCK SPLITS ACCOUNTED FOR?

**Learning Objective 4**
Account for cash dividends, stock dividends, and stock splits

A profitable corporation may make distributions to stockholders in the form of *dividends*. Dividends can be paid in the form of cash, stock, or other property.

## Cash Dividends

Cash dividends cause a decrease in both assets (Cash) and equity (Retained Earnings). Most states prohibit using paid-in capital for dividends. Accountants, therefore, use the term **legal capital** to refer to the portion of stockholders' equity that cannot be used for dividends.

**Legal Capital**
The portion of stockholders' equity that cannot be used for dividends.

A corporation declares a dividend before paying it. Three dividend dates are relevant:

1. **Declaration date.** On the declaration date—say, May 1—the board of directors announces the intention to pay the dividend. The declaration of a cash dividend creates an obligation (liability) for the corporation.
2. **Date of record** (or *record date*). Those stockholders holding the stock at the end of business on the date of record—a week or two after declaration, say, May 15—will receive the dividend check. Date of record is the date the corporation records the stockholders that receive dividend checks.
3. **Payment date.** Payment of the dividend usually follows the record date by a week or two—say, May 30.

### Declaring and Paying Dividends—Common Stock

Suppose on May 1, Smart Touch Learning declares a $0.05 per share cash dividend on 22,700 outstanding shares of common stock (23,000 shares issued less 300 shares of treasury stock). On the date of declaration, Smart Touch Learning records a debit to Cash Dividends and a credit to Dividends Payable—Common (a current liability) as follows:

| Date | Accounts and Explanation | Debit | Credit |
|---|---|---|---|
| May 1 | Cash Dividends ($0.05 per share × 22,700 shares) | 1,135 | |
| | Dividends Payable—Common | | 1,135 |
| | *Declared a cash dividend.* | | |

| A | = | L↑ | + | E↓ |
|---|---|---|---|---|
| | | Dividends Payable↑ | | Cash Dividends↑ |

*Dividends are only paid on outstanding shares. Remember that outstanding stock is issued stock less treasury stock. A corporation will never pay dividends on treasury stock.*

On May 15, the date of record, no journal entry is recorded. This is simply the cutoff point to determine who owns the stock and will, therefore, receive the cash payment. To pay the dividend on the payment date, May 30, Smart Touch Learning debits Dividends Payable—Common and credits Cash:

| A↓ | = | L↓ | + | E |
|---|---|---|---|---|
| Cash↓ | = | Dividends Payable↓ | | |

| Date | Accounts and Explanation | Debit | Credit |
|---|---|---|---|
| May 30 | Dividends Payable—Common | 1,135 | |
| | Cash | | 1,135 |
| | *Payment of cash dividend.* | | |

At the end of the accounting period, Smart Touch Learning will close the Cash Dividends account to Retained Earnings as follows:

| A | = | L | + | E↑↓ |
|---|---|---|---|---|
| | = | | | Retained Earnings↓<br>Cash Dividends↓ |

| Date | Accounts and Explanation | Debit | Credit |
|---|---|---|---|
| Dec. 31 | Retained Earnings | 1,135 | |
| | Cash Dividends | | 1,135 |
| | *To close Cash Dividends.* | | |

## Declaring and Paying Dividends—Preferred Stock

The cash dividend rate on preferred stock is often expressed as a percentage of the preferred stock par value, such as 6%. Sometimes, however, cash dividends on preferred stock are expressed as a flat dollar amount per share, such as $3 per share. Therefore, preferred dividends are computed two ways, depending on how the preferred stock cash dividend rate is stated on the preferred stock certificate. To illustrate, assume a fictitious company, Greg's Games, Inc. has 1,000 outstanding shares of 6%, $50 par value preferred stock. The dividend is computed as follows:

$$
\begin{aligned}
\text{Preferred dividend} &= \text{Outstanding shares} \times \text{Par value} \times \text{Preferred dividend rate} \\
&= 1{,}000 \text{ shares} \times \$50 \text{ par value per share} \times 6\% \\
&= \$3{,}000
\end{aligned}
$$

The journal entries to account for the declaration and payment of a cash dividend on preferred stock are similar to those of common stock. The only difference is that Dividends Payable—Preferred is used instead of Dividends Payable—Common.

Earlier in the chapter, we discussed the dividend preference that preferred stockholders receive. When a company has issued both preferred and common stock, the preferred stockholders receive their dividends first. The common stockholders receive dividends only if the total dividend is large enough to satisfy the preferred requirement. In other words, the common stockholders receive the residual—the amount remaining after the preferred dividends are paid.

For example, if Greg's Games has 1,000 shares of $50 par, 6% preferred stock outstanding and 2,000,000 shares of $1 par common stock outstanding, preferred stockholders will receive $3,000 of any cash dividend declared. So, total declared dividends must exceed $3,000 for the common stockholders to receive a dividend.

If the year's dividend is equal to or less than the annual preferred amount, the preferred stockholders will receive the entire dividend, and the common stockholders will not receive a dividend that year. But, if Greg's Games' dividend is large enough to cover the preferred dividend, the preferred stockholders get their regular dividend of $3,000, and the common stockholders receive any amount remaining.

Remember that a dividend preference on preferred stock does not guarantee that a corporation will pay a dividend equal to the preferred amount. A corporation may fail to pay the preferred dividend if, for example, it does not have cash to fund the dividend. This is called *passing the dividend*, and the dividend is said to be a **dividend in arrears**. In other words, a preferred stock dividend is in arrears if the dividend has not been paid for the year.

**Dividend in Arrears**
A preferred stock dividend is in arrears if the dividend has not been paid for the year and the preferred stock is cumulative.

Preferred stock can be either cumulative or noncumulative. Most preferred stock is cumulative. As a result, preferred stock is assumed to be cumulative unless it is specifically designated as noncumulative. **Cumulative preferred stock** shareholders must receive all dividends in arrears plus the current year dividends before the common stockholders receive a dividend. If the preferred stock is **noncumulative preferred stock**, the corporation will not have any dividends in arrears because the corporation is not required to pay passed dividends.

**Cumulative Preferred Stock**
Preferred stock whose owners must receive all dividends in arrears plus the current year dividend before the corporation pays dividends to the common stockholders.

**Noncumulative Preferred Stock**
Preferred stock whose owners do not receive passed dividends.

Suppose Greg's Games' preferred stock is cumulative and in 2016 the business did not pay any cash dividends. Before paying any common dividend in 2017, Greg's Games must first pay preferred dividends of $3,000 for 2016 and $3,000 for 2017, a total of $6,000. Assume that on September 6, 2017, Greg's Games declares a $50,000 total dividend. How much of this dividend goes to the preferred stockholders? How much goes to the common stockholders? The allocation of this $50,000 dividend is as follows:

| | | |
|---|---|---|
| Total Dividend | | $ 50,000 |
| Dividend to Preferred Stockholders: | | |
| Dividend in Arrears (2016) | $ 3,000 | |
| Current Year Dividend (2017) | 3,000 | |
| Total Dividend to Preferred Stockholders | | (6,000) |
| Dividend to Common Stockholders | | $ 44,000 |

Greg's Games' entry to record the declaration of this dividend on September 6, 2017, is as follows:

| Date | Accounts and Explanation | Debit | Credit |
|---|---|---|---|
| 2017 | | | |
| Sep. 6 | Cash Dividends | 50,000 | |
| | Dividends Payable—Common | | 44,000 |
| | Dividends Payable—Preferred | | 6,000 |
| | *Declared a cash dividend.* | | |

A = { L↑ + E↓ : Dividends Payable↑ ; Cash Dividends↑ }

Dividends in arrears are *not* a liability. A liability for dividends arises only after the board of directors *declares* the dividend. But a corporation reports cumulative preferred dividends in arrears in notes to the financial statements. This shows the common stockholders how big the declared dividend will need to be for them to receive any dividends.

Remember that if the preferred stock is noncumulative preferred stock, the corporation is not required to pay any passed dividends. Keep in mind that this is a risk that the investor bears when investing in noncumulative preferred stock. Suppose Greg's

Games' preferred stock is noncumulative and the company passed the 2016 dividend. The preferred stockholders would lose the 2016 dividend of $3,000 forever. Then, before paying any common dividends in 2017, Greg's Games would have to pay only the 2017 preferred dividend of $3,000, which would leave $47,000 for the common stockholders as follows:

| | | |
|---|---|---|
| Total Dividend | | $ 50,000 |
| Dividend to Preferred Stockholders: | | |
| Current Year Dividend (2017) | $ 3,000 | |
| Total Dividend to Preferred Stockholders | | (3,000) |
| Dividend to Common Stockholders | | $ 47,000 |

## Stock Dividends

**Stock Dividend**
A distribution by a corporation of its own stock to its stockholders.

A **stock dividend** is a distribution of a corporation's own stock to its stockholders. Unlike cash dividends, stock dividends do not give any of the corporation's assets, like cash, to the stockholders. Stock dividends have the following characteristics:

- They affect *only* stockholders' equity accounts (including Retained Earnings, Stock Dividends, Common Stock, and Paid-In Capital in Excess of Par).
- They have *no* effect on total stockholders' equity.
- They have *no* effect on assets or liabilities.

The corporation distributes stock dividends to stockholders in proportion to the number of shares the stockholders already own. Suppose a stockholder owns 1,000 shares of Greg's Games' common stock. If Greg's Games distributes a 10% stock dividend, the stockholder would receive 100 additional shares (1,000 shares × 0.10). The stockholder now owns 1,100 shares of the stock. All other Greg's Games' stockholders also receive additional shares equal to 10% of their stock holdings, so all stockholders are in the same relative position after the stock dividend as they were before. With a stock dividend, the total number of shares issued and outstanding increases, but the percentage of total ownership of individual stockholders stays the same.

### Why Issue Stock Dividends?

A company issues stock dividends for several reasons:

- **To continue dividends but conserve cash.** A company may wish to continue the distribution of dividends to keep stockholders happy but may need to keep its cash for operations. A stock dividend is a way to do so without using corporate cash.
- **To reduce the market price per share of its stock.** Depending on its size, a stock dividend may cause the company's market price per share to fall because of the increased supply of the stock. Suppose that a share of Greg's Games' stock was traded at $50 recently. Doubling the shares issued and outstanding by issuing a stock dividend would likely cause Greg's Games' stock market price per share to drop to closer to $25 per share. One objective behind a stock dividend might be to make the stock less expensive and, therefore, more available and attractive to investors.
- **To reward investors.** Investors often feel like they have received something of value when they get a stock dividend.

## DECISIONS

### Should a cash dividend be paid?

In the past, Valley Mills Construction, Inc. has always paid an annual cash dividend of $0.25 per share. This year, though, the board of directors wants to conserve cash for expansion. The board is considering not paying the cash dividends but is concerned that stockholders will be upset when the announcement to not pay a dividend is made. What should the board do?

### Solution

The board of directors should carefully weigh the benefits of paying a cash dividend versus conserving cash for future expansion. If stockholders are angry enough about the failure to pay a dividend, they might consider selling their stock, causing the market value of the stock to decrease. In addition, the market might perceive the failure to pay a cash dividend as a negative statement on the company's financial health. Investors might perceive Valley Mills Construction, Inc. as having liquidity problems.

### Alternative Solution

Valley Mills Construction, Inc. could consider issuing a stock dividend. Issuing stock dividends is a good alternative to issuing cash dividends when a corporation needs to conserve cash. By issuing a stock dividend, the corporation will issue additional shares of common stock to its stockholders. Stockholders will receive an increase in the number of shares of their stock, but their percentage of total ownership will remain the same. Stockholders will most likely feel that they have received something of value even though they didn't receive cash.

### Recording Stock Dividends

As with a cash dividend, there are three dates for a stock dividend:

- Declaration date
- Record date
- Distribution date

The board of directors announces the stock dividend on the declaration date. The date of record and the distribution date then follow. The declaration of a stock dividend does *not* create a liability because the corporation is not obligated to pay assets. (Recall that a liability is a claim on *assets*.) With a stock dividend, the corporation has declared its intention to distribute its stock. The distribution date is similar to the payment date for a cash dividend. With stock dividends, however, there is no payment of cash—only a distribution of shares of stock.

The entry to record a stock dividend depends on the size of the dividend. Generally Accepted Accounting Principles (GAAP) distinguish between small and large stock dividends in the following manner:

- **Small stock dividend**—less than 20% to 25% of issued and outstanding stock
- **Large stock dividend**—greater than 20% to 25% of issued and outstanding stock

**Small Stock Dividend**
A stock dividend of less than 20% to 25% of the issued and outstanding stock.

**Large Stock Dividend**
A stock dividend greater than 20% to 25% of the issued and outstanding stock.

**Small Stock Dividends—Less than 20% to 25%** Small stock dividends are accounted for at the stock's market value. Here is how the various accounts are affected at the date of declaration:

- Stock Dividends is debited for the *market value* of the dividend shares.
- Common Stock Dividend Distributable is credited for the dividend stock's *par value*.
- Paid-In Capital in Excess of Par is credited for the excess.

Assume, for example, that Greg's Games distributes a 5% common stock dividend on 2,000,000 shares issued and outstanding when the market value of Greg's Games' common stock is $50 per share. Greg's Games will issue 100,000 (2,000,000 shares × 0.05) shares to its stockholders. The entry on the next page illustrates the accounting for this 5% stock dividend on the declaration date of February 1.

| A | = | L + | E↑↓ |
|---|---|---|---|
| | | | Stock Dividends↑ Common Stock Dividend Distributable↑ Paid-In Capital in Excess of Par↑ |

| Date | Accounts and Explanation | Debit | Credit |
|---|---|---|---|
| Feb. 1 | Stock Dividends ($50 per share × 2,000,000 shares × 0.05) | 5,000,000 | |
| | Common Stock Dividend Distributable ($1 per share × 2,000,000 shares × 0.05) | | 100,000 |
| | Paid-In Capital in Excess of Par—Common ($5,000,000 − $100,000) | | 4,900,000 |
| | *Declared a 5% stock dividend.* | | |

*Similar to Cash Dividends, Stock Dividends is closed to Retained Earnings at the end of the accounting period.*

Notice that Common Stock Dividend Distributable is credited for the par value of the common stock. Common Stock Dividend Distributable is an *equity* account, not a liability. It is reported as an addition to paid-in capital in stockholders' equity until the stock is distributed. On February 25, when Greg's Games distributes the common stock, it would record the following entry:

| A | = | L + | E↑↓ |
|---|---|---|---|
| | | | Common Stock Dividend Distributable↓ Common Stock↑ |

| Date | Accounts and Explanation | Debit | Credit |
|---|---|---|---|
| Feb. 25 | Common Stock Dividend Distributable | 100,000 | |
| | Common Stock—$1 Par Value | | 100,000 |
| | *Issued 5% stock dividend.* | | |

After the journal entry for the declaration and issuance of the common stock dividend and the closing entry to close Stock Dividends to Retained Earnings, Greg's Games' accounts are as follows:

**Common Stock—$1 Par Value**

| | | | |
|---|---|---|---|
| | | 2,000,000 | Bal. |
| | | 100,000 | Feb. 25 |
| | | 2,100,000 | Bal. |

**Paid-In Capital in Excess of Par—Common**

| | | | |
|---|---|---|---|
| | | 19,000,000 | Bal. |
| | | 4,900,000 | Feb. 1 |
| | | 23,900,000 | Bal. |

**Common Stock Dividend Distributable**

| | | | |
|---|---|---|---|
| | | 100,000 | Feb. 1 |
| Feb. 25 | 100,000 | | |
| | | 0 | Bal. |

**Retained Earnings**

| | | | |
|---|---|---|---|
| | | 9,000,000 | Bal. |
| Dec. 31 | 5,000,000 | | |
| | | 4,000,000 | Bal. |

*The stock Dividends account is closed with a credit and the corresponding debit to Retained Earnings decreases the equity account.*

Remember that a stock dividend does not affect assets, liabilities, or *total* stockholders' equity. A stock dividend merely rearranges the balances in the stockholders' equity accounts, leaving total stockholders' equity unchanged. Exhibit 13-8 shows what Greg's Games' stockholders' equity looks like before and after the 5% common stock dividend.

**Exhibit 13-8** | **Stockholders' Equity—Small Stock Dividend**

**GREG'S GAMES, INC.**
Balance Sheet (Partial)
February 25, 2017

| **Before Small Stock Dividend:** | | **After Small Stock Dividend:** | |
|---|---|---|---|
| **Stockholders' Equity** | | **Stockholders' Equity** | |
| Paid-In Capital: | | Paid-In Capital: | |
| Preferred Stock—$50 Par Value; 2,000 shares authorized, 1,000 shares issued and outstanding | $ 50,000 | Preferred Stock—$50 Par Value; 2,000 shares authorized, 1,000 shares issued and outstanding | $ 50,000 |
| Paid-In Capital in Excess of Par—Preferred | 5,000 | Paid-In Capital in Excess of Par—Preferred | 5,000 |
| Common Stock—$1 Par Value; 20,000,000 shares authorized, 2,000,000 shares issued and outstanding | 2,000,000 | Common Stock—$1 Par Value; 20,000,000 shares authorized, 2,100,000 shares issued and outstanding | 2,100,000 |
| Paid-In Capital in Excess of Par—Common | 19,000,000 | Paid-In Capital in Excess of Par—Common | 23,900,000 |
| Total Paid-In Capital | 21,055,000 | Total Paid-In Capital | 26,055,000 |
| Retained Earnings | 9,000,000 | Retained Earnings | 4,000,000 |
| Total Stockholders' Equity | **$ 30,055,000** | Total Stockholders' Equity | **$ 30,055,000** |

Note that total stockholders' equity stays at $30,055,000. Total paid-in capital increased $5,000,000 and retained earnings decreased $5,000,000.

**Large Stock Dividends—Greater than 20% to 25%** Large stock dividends are rare, but when they are declared, they are normally accounted for at the stock's par value instead of the stock's market value. Par value is used because the larger number of issued and outstanding shares will reduce market price per share, making market price per share an invalid measurement of the stock dividend value. Assume, for example, on March 2 that Greg's Games declares a second common stock dividend of 50% when the market value of Greg's Games' common stock is $50 per share. The entries to record the large stock dividend on the declaration date (March 2) and distribution date (March 30) are as follows:

| Date | Accounts and Explanation | Debit | Credit |
|---|---|---|---|
| Mar. 2 | Stock Dividends ($1 per share × 2,100,000 shares × 0.50) | 1,050,000 | |
| | Common Stock Dividend Distributable ($1 per share × 2,100,000 shares × 0. 50) | | 1,050,000 |
| | *Declared a 50% stock dividend.* | | |
| 30 | Common Stock Dividend Distributable | 1,050,000 | |
| | Common Stock—$1 Par Value | | 1,050,000 |
| | *Issued 50% stock dividend.* | | |

A = L + E↑↓
Stock Dividends↑
Common Stock Dividend Distributable↑

A = L + E↑↓
Common Stock Dividend Distributable↓
Common Stock↑

*Cash dividends and stock dividends are always declared based on the number of shares issued and outstanding. It's important to keep a running balance of the amount of shares outstanding in order to determine the correct amount of dividends to record. In this case, Greg's Games started with 2,000,000 common shares outstanding and then issued a stock dividend of 100,000 common shares for a total of 2,100,000 common shares issued and outstanding.*

Notice that the large stock dividend also does not change total stockholders' equity. Total paid-in capital increased $1,050,000 and retained earnings decreased $1,050,000 after closing Stock Dividends to Retained Earnings.

## Stock Splits

**Stock Split**
An increase in the number of issued and outstanding shares of stock coupled with a proportionate reduction in the par value of the stock.

A stock split is fundamentally different from a stock dividend. A **stock split** increases the number of issued and outstanding shares of stock. A stock split also decreases par value per share, whereas stock dividends do not affect par value per share. For example, if Greg's Games splits its common stock 2-for-1, the number of issued and outstanding shares is doubled and par value per share is cut in half. A stock split also decreases the market price per share of the stock. A 2-for-1 stock split of a $2 par stock with a $20 market value per share will result in two shares of $1 par value with approximately $10 market value per share.

*A stock split, just like any other stock issuance, cannot involve issuing more shares of stock than authorized in the corporate charter.*

The market value of a share of Greg's Games' common stock has been approximately $50 per share. Assume that Greg's Games wishes to decrease the market price to approximately $25 per share. The company can make the market price drop to around $25 by effecting a 2-for-1 split of its common stock. A 2-for-1 stock split means that Greg's Games will have twice as many shares of stock issued and outstanding after the split as it did before, and each share's par value is cut in half. Assume Greg's Games has 3,150,000 shares issued and outstanding of $1 par common stock before the split. After the stock split, Greg's Games will have 6,300,000 shares (3,150,000 shares × 2) issued and outstanding of $0.50 par value as follows:

| Common Stock Before Stock Split | | Common Stock After Stock Split | |
|---|---|---|---|
| Common Stock—$1 Par Value; 3,150,000 shares issued and outstanding | $ 3,150,000 | Common Stock—$0.50 Par Value; 6,300,000 shares issued and outstanding | $ 3,150,000 |

**Memorandum Entry**
An entry in the journal that notes a significant event, but has no debit or credit amount.

Because the stock split does not affect any account balances, no formal journal entry is needed. Instead, the split is recorded in a **memorandum entry**, an entry in the journal that notes a significant event but has no debit or credit amount.

## Cash Dividends, Stock Dividends, and Stock Splits Compared

Cash dividends, stock dividends, and stock splits have some similarities and some differences. Exhibit 13-9 summarizes their effects on the accounting equation.

**Exhibit 13-9 | Effects of Dividends and Stock Splits on the Accounting Equation**

| Effect On | Cash Dividend | Small Stock Dividend | Large Stock Dividend | Stock Split |
|---|---|---|---|---|
| Total Assets | Decrease | No effect | No effect | No effect |
| Total Liabilities | No effect | No effect | No effect | No effect |
| Common Stock | No effect | Increase | Increase | No effect |
| Paid-In Capital in Excess of Par | No effect | Increase | No effect | No effect |
| Retained Earnings | Decrease | Decrease | Decrease | No effect |
| Total Stockholders' Equity | Decrease | No effect | No effect | No effect |

**Try It!**

8. On August 1, Hagino Corporation declared a $1.50 per share cash dividend on its common stock (20,000 shares) for stockholders on record as of August 15. Hagino paid the dividend on August 31. Journalize the entries declaring the cash dividend and paying the dividend.

**Check your answers online in MyAccountingLab or at http://www.pearsonhighered.com/Horngren.**

For more practice, see Short Exercises S13-7 through S13-11. MyAccountingLab

## HOW IS EQUITY REPORTED FOR A CORPORATION?

**Learning Objective 5**
Explain how equity is reported for a corporation

Earlier, you learned that a corporation's equity contains two basic sources: paid-in capital and retained earnings. Let's explore how stockholders' equity is reported.

### Statement of Retained Earnings

The statement of retained earnings reports how the company's retained earnings balance changed from the beginning of the period to the end of the period. Remember that retained earnings is the equity earned by profitable operations that is not distributed to stockholders. Exhibit 13-10 shows the statement of retained earnings of Smart Touch Learning for 2016.

**Exhibit 13-10 | Statement of Retained Earnings**

| SMART TOUCH LEARNING, INC.<br>Statement of Retained Earnings<br>Year Ended December 31, 2016 | |
|---|---|
| Retained Earnings, January 1, 2016 | $ 0 |
| Net income for the year | 8,550 |
| | 8,550 |
| Dividends declared | (3,000) |
| Retained Earnings, December 31, 2016 | **$ 5,550** |

Companies can report a negative amount in retained earnings. This is called a **deficit** and is reflected by a debit balance in the Retained Earnings account. A deficit occurs when a company has recurring losses and/or declares dividends in excess of retained earnings. Most states prohibit corporations from paying a dividend if a deficit will occur.

**Deficit**
Debit balance in the Retained Earnings account.

### Appropriations of Retained Earnings

Cash dividends and treasury stock purchases require a cash payment. These cash outlays leave fewer resources to pay liabilities. For example, a bank may agree to loan $500,000 to a company only if the company maintains a minimum level of stockholders' equity by limiting both its declaration of dividends and its purchases of treasury stock. The restriction often focuses on the balance of retained earnings. Companies usually report their retained earnings restrictions in notes to the financial statements.

**Appropriations of retained earnings** are retained earnings restrictions recorded by journal entries. A corporation may *appropriate*—that is, segregate in a separate account—a

**Appropriation of Retained Earnings**
Restriction of a portion of retained earnings that is recorded by a journal entry.

portion of retained earnings for a specific use. For example, the board of directors may appropriate part of retained earnings for expansion or contingencies (such as a potential liability associated with a lawsuit).

### Prior-Period Adjustments

Occasionally a company may make an accounting error as a result of mathematical mistakes, misapplying accounting principles, or oversight that is not discovered until the following period. Once discovered, these errors must be corrected because the Retained Earnings account balance is wrong. The error is corrected by adjusting the beginning balance in the Retained Earnings account in the period the error is discovered. Corrections to Retained Earnings for errors of an earlier period are called **prior-period adjustments**. The prior-period adjustment either increases or decreases the beginning balance of the Retained Earnings account and appears on the statement of retained earnings.

**Prior-Period Adjustment**
A correction to Retained Earnings for an error of an earlier period.

To illustrate, assume a fictitious company, Mountain Home, Inc. recorded $30,000 of salaries expense for 2016. The correct amount of salaries expense was $40,000. This error had the following effect:

- Understated Salaries Expense by $10,000
- Overstated net income by $10,000

In 2017, Mountain Home paid the extra $10,000 in salaries owed for the prior year. Mountain Home's prior-period adjustment decreased Retained Earnings as shown in Exhibit 13-11.

**Exhibit 13-11 | Statement of Retained Earnings—Prior Period Adjustment**

| MOUNTAIN HOME, INC.<br>Statement of Retained Earnings<br>Year Ended December 31, 2017 | |
|---|---|
| Retained Earnings, January 1, 2017, as originally reported | $ 140,000 |
| Prior period adjustment | (10,000) |
| Retained Earnings, January 1, 2017, as adjusted | 130,000 |
| Net income for the year | 63,000 |
| | 193,000 |
| Dividends declared | (23,000) |
| Retained Earnings, December 31, 2017 | **$ 170,000** |

## Statement of Stockholders' Equity

IFRS

IFRS requires a Statement of Stockholders' Equity, reporting the changes in all of the equity accounts.

The statement of stockholders' equity is another option for reporting the changes in stockholders' equity of a corporation. This statement has more information than the statement of retained earnings in that it reports the changes in all stockholders' equity accounts, not just Retained Earnings. The statement of stockholders' equity shows the beginning balance, any additions or subtractions, and the ending balance for all equity accounts. In addition, the statement of stockholders' equity also reports on the number of shares and any changes during the year in preferred, common, and treasury stock. Exhibit 13-12 shows a statement of stockholders' equity for Mountain Home, Inc.

**Exhibit 13-12** | **Statement of Stockholders' Equity**

**MOUNTAIN HOME, INC.**
Statement of Stockholders' Equity
Year Ended December 31, 2017

| | Common Stock | | Paid-In Capital in Excess of Par | Retained Earnings | Total Stockholders' Equity |
|---|---|---|---|---|---|
| | Shares | Amount | | | |
| Balances, January 1, 2017, as originally reported | 20,000 | $ 20,000 | $ 80,000 | $ 140,000 | $ 240,000 |
| Prior period adjustment | | | | (10,000) | (10,000) |
| Balances, January 1, 2017, as adjusted | 20,000 | $ 20,000 | $ 80,000 | $ 130,000 | $ 230,000 |
| Net income for the year | | | | 63,000 | 63,000 |
| Dividends declared | | | | (23,000) | (23,000) |
| Balances, December 31, 2017 | **20,000** | **$ 20,000** | **$ 80,000** | **$ 170,000** | **$ 270,000** |

**Try It!**

9. Sjostrom, Inc. had beginning retained earnings of $300,000 on January 1, 2016. During the year, Sjostrom declared and paid $140,000 of cash dividends and earned $200,000 of net income. Prepare a statement of retained earnings for Sjostrom, Inc. for the year ending December 31, 2016.

**Check your answer online in MyAccountingLab or at http://www.pearsonhighered.com/Horngren.**

For more practice, see Short Exercises S13-12 and S13-13. MyAccountingLab

## HOW DO WE USE STOCKHOLDERS' EQUITY RATIOS TO EVALUATE BUSINESS PERFORMANCE?

**Learning Objective 6**
Use earnings per share, rate of return on common stock, and the price/earnings ratio to evaluate business performance

Investors are constantly comparing companies' profits. To compare companies of different sizes, we need some standard profitability measures. Three important ratios to use for comparison are earnings per share, rate of return on common stock, and price/earnings ratio.

### Earnings per Share

The final segment of a corporate income statement reports the company's earnings per share, abbreviated as EPS. EPS is the most widely used of all business statistics. **Earnings per share (EPS)** reports the amount of net income (loss) for each share of the company's *outstanding common stock*. Earnings per share is calculated as net income minus preferred dividends divided by the weighted average number of common shares outstanding. Preferred dividends are subtracted from net income because the preferred stockholders have the first claim to dividends. Therefore, that portion of the company's earnings is not available to the common stockholders and is not included in the EPS calculation on common stock. The computation for the weighted average number of common shares outstanding is covered in advanced accounting courses. For simplicity, we will determine earnings per share on the average number of shares outstanding (beginning balance plus ending balance, divided by two).

**Earnings per Share (EPS)**
Amount of a company's net income (loss) for each share of its outstanding common stock. (Net income − Preferred dividends) / Weighted average number of common shares outstanding.

For example, the **Green Mountain Coffee Roasters, Inc.** Fiscal 2013 Annual Report reports the following amounts:

| | September 28, 2013 | September 29, 2012 |
|---|---|---|
| Net Income (for the year ended) | $ 483,232,000 | $ 362,628,000 |
| Preferred Dividends | 0 | 0 |
| Total Stockholders' Equity | 2,635,570,000 | 2,261,228,000 |
| Stockholders' Equity attributable to Preferred Stock | 0 | 0 |
| Number of Common Shares Outstanding | 150,265,809 shares | 152,680,855 shares |

Green Mountain Coffee Roasters, Inc. earnings per share for 2013 is computed as follows:

Earnings per share = ( Net income − Preferred dividends ) / Average number of common shares outstanding
= ( $483,232,000 − $0 ) / [ ( 150,265,809 shares + 152,680,855 shares ) / 2]
= $3.19 / share

FASB requires that earnings per share be reported on the income statement.

## Price/Earnings Ratio

**Price/Earnings Ratio**
The ratio of the market price of a share of common stock to the company's earnings per share. Measures the value that the stock market places on $1 of a company's earnings. Market price per share of common stock / Earnings per share.

The **price/earnings ratio** is the ratio of the market price of a share of common stock to the company's earnings per share. The price/earnings ratio shows the market price of $1 of earnings. Assuming Green Mountain Coffee Roasters, Inc. has a market price of $75.00 per share of common stock, Green Mountain's price/earnings ratio is calculated as follows:

Price/earnings ratio = Market price per share of common stock / Earnings per share
= $75.00 per share / $3.19 per share
= 23.5

The price/earnings ratio implies that Green Mountain's stock is selling at 23.5 times one year's earnings per share. This ratio is commonly used by investors to evaluate their ability to earn a return on their investment. It tells investors how much they should be willing to pay for $1 of a company's earnings. A higher price/earnings ratio signifies a higher return on investment. As with other ratios, the price/earnings ratio is most useful when comparing one company to another.

## Rate of Return on Common Stock

**Rate of Return on Common Stockholders' Equity**
Shows the relationship between net income available to common stockholders and their average common equity invested in the company. (Net income − Preferred dividends) / Average common stockholders' equity.

**Rate of return on common stockholders' equity**, often shortened to *return on equity*, shows the relationship between net income available to common stockholders and their average common equity invested in the company. The numerator is net income minus preferred dividends. Preferred dividends are subtracted because the preferred stockholders have first claim to any dividends. The demoninator is average common stockholders' equity—total equity minus preferred equity.

Returning to Green Mountain Coffee Roasters, Inc., the rate of return on common stockholders' equity is calculated as follows:

$$\text{Rate of return on common stockholders' equity} = (\text{Net income} - \text{Preferred dividends}) / \text{Average common stockholders' equity}$$
$$= (\$483{,}232{,}000 - \$0) / [(\$2{,}635{,}570{,}000 + \$2{,}261{,}228{,}000) / 2]$$
$$= 0.20 = 20\%$$

Green Mountain has returned $0.20 for each $1 of the average amount invested by common stockholders. A rate of return on common stockholders' equity of 15% to 20% is considered good in most industries. At 20%, Green Mountain has an excellent return on equity.

## Try It!

Vollmer, Inc. had reported the following balances:

| | December 31, 2017 | December 31, 2016 |
|---|---|---|
| Net Income | $ 80,000 | $ 60,000 |
| Preferred Dividends | 2,000 | 5,000 |
| Total Stockholders' Equity | 340,000 | 310,000 |
| Stockholders' Equity attributable to Preferred Stock | 20,000 | 20,000 |
| Number of Common Shares Outstanding | 10,000 | 14,000 |

**10.** Compute Vollmer's earnings per share for 2017.
**11.** Compute Vollmer's price/earnings ratio for 2017, assuming the market price is $40 per share.
**12.** Compute Vollmer's rate of return on common stockholders' equity for 2017.

**Check your answers online in MyAccountingLab or at http://www.pearsonhighered.com/Horngren.**

For more practice, see Short Exercises S13-14 through S13-16. MyAccountingLab

# REVIEW

## > Things You Should Know

### 1. What is a corporation?

- A business organized under state law that is a separate legal entity.
- Corporations have capital stock that represents shares of ownership.
  - Authorized stock is the maximum number of shares of stock that the corporate charter allows the corporation to issue.
  - Outstanding stock is stock that has been issued and is in the hands of stockholders.
- Corporations can have different classes of stock:
  - Common stock represents the basic ownership of a corporation.
  - Preferred stock gives its owners certain advantages, such as the right to receive preferential dividends.
- A corporation's equity is called stockholders' equity. Stockholders' equity consists of two basic sources:
  - Paid-in capital—amounts received from stockholders in exchange for stock.
  - Retained earnings—equity earned by profitable operations that is not distributed to stockholders.

### 2. How is the issuance of stock accounted for?

- Issuance of common stock (and preferred stock) at par value

| Date | Accounts and Explanation | Debit | Credit |
|---|---|---|---|
| | Cash | Par Value | |
| | Common Stock—$1 Par Value | | Par Value |
| | *Issued common stock at par.* | | |

- Issuance of common stock (and preferred stock) at a premium

| Date | Accounts and Explanation | Debit | Credit |
|---|---|---|---|
| | Cash | Issuance Price | |
| | Common Stock—$1 Par Value | | Par Value |
| | Paid-In Capital in Excess of Par—Common | | Difference |
| | *Issued common stock at a premium.* | | |

- Issuing stated value stock is almost identical to accounting for par value stock. The only difference is the use of the Paid-In Capital in Excess of *Stated* account.
- Stock can be issued for assets other than cash. The transaction should be recorded at the market value of the stock issued or the market value of the assets received, whichever is more clearly determinable.

### 3. How is treasury stock accounted for?

- Treasury stock is a corporation's own stock that it has previously issued and later reacquired.
- When treasury stock is purchased, it is recorded at cost, not par value.

| Date | Accounts and Explanation | Debit | Credit |
|---|---|---|---|
| | Treasury Stock—Common | Cost | |
| | Cash | | Cost |
| | *Purchased treasury stock.* | | |

- Treasury Stock is a contra equity account, has a normal debit balance, and is a reduction to total stockholders' equity.
- Treasury stock can be sold at cost, below cost, or above cost.
- As an alternative to treasury stock, corporations can retire stock, which removes the stock from the company's books.

### 4. How are dividends and stock splits accounted for?

- Cash dividends cause a decrease in both assets (Cash) and equity (Retained Earnings).
- Preferred stockholders receive a dividend preference that ensures that the preferred stockholders will receive dividends first. There are two categories of preferred stock:
  - Cumulative preferred stock—owners must receive all dividends in arrears (passed dividends) and current year dividends before the corporation pays dividends to the common stockholders.
  - Noncumulative preferred stock—owners do not receive any passed dividends.
- Stock dividends are distributions of a corporation's stock and have no effect on total stockholders' equity, assets, or liabilities.
  - Small stock dividends (less than 20% to 25%) are recorded at the stock's market value.
  - Large stock dividends (greater than 20% to 25%) are recorded at the stock's par value.
- Stock splits increase the number of issued and outstanding shares of stock coupled with a proportionate reduction in the par value of the stock.
- Stock splits do not affect any account balances, and no journal entry is needed.

### 5. How is equity reported for a corporation?

- The statement of retained earnings reports how the company's retained earnings balance changed from the beginning of the period to the end of the period.
- Retained earnings can be appropriated (set aside) for a specific use.
- Prior-period adjustments must be made to beginning retained earnings for mathematical mistakes, misapplied accounting principles, or oversight.
- The statement of stockholders' equity reports the changes in all stockholders' equity accounts.

### 6. How do we use stockholders' equity ratios to evaluate business performance?

- Earnings per share calculates the amount of a company's net income (loss) for each share of its outstanding common stock. (Net income − Preferred dividends) / Weighted average number of common shares outstanding.

- The price/earnings ratio measures the value that the stock market places on $1 of a company's earnings. Market price per share of common stock / Earnings per share.
- Rate of return on common stockholders' equity shows the relationship between net income available to common stockholders and their average common equity invested in the company. (Net income − Preferred dividends) / Average common stockholders' equity.

## > Summary Problem 13-1

Delphian Corporation's balance sheet as of December 31, 2016, follows:

| DELPHIAN CORPORATION<br>Balance Sheet (Partial)<br>December 31, 2016 | |
|---|---|
| **Stockholders' Equity** | |
| Paid-In Capital: | |
| Common Stock—$1 Par Value; 11,000,000 shares authorized, 8,000,000 shares issued and outstanding | $ 8,000,000 |
| Paid-In Capital in Excess of Par—Common | 200,000 |
| Total Paid-In Capital | 8,200,000 |
| Retained Earnings | 800,000,000 |
| Total Stockholders' Equity | **$ 808,200,000** |

During 2017, Delphian Corporation had the following transactions:

| | |
|---|---|
| Jan. 1 | Issued 10,000 shares of common stock for $10 per share. |
| Feb. 15 | Issued 2,000 shares of common stock for $8 per share. |
| Mar. 1 | Declared a $0.20 per share cash dividend on its common stock to be paid on March 30. Date of record: March 15. |
| 30 | Paid the cash dividend to stockholders. |
| Nov. 1 | Declared a 1% common stock dividend on all common stock outstanding. Current market price of the stock was $8. Date of record: Nov. 15. |
| 30 | Distributed stock to stockholders. |
| Dec. 1 | Purchased 5,000 shares of treasury stock—common at $12 per share. |
| 20 | Sold 3,000 shares of treasury stock—common at $14 per share. |

**Requirements**

1. Journalize Delphian's transactions for 2017.
2. Prepare the stockholders' equity section of the balance sheet as of December 31, 2017. Assume Delphian had net income of $20,000,000 during 2017 and that Cash Dividends and Stock Dividends have been closed to the Retained Earnings account.
3. Determine Delphian's earnings per share for 2017.
4. Assuming Delphian's market value per common share as of December 31, 2017, was $15, calculate Delphian's price/earnings ratio for 2017.

## Solution

1.

| Date | Accounts and Explanation | Debit | Credit |
|---|---|---|---|
| Jan. 1 | Cash ($10 per share × 10,000 shares) | 100,000 | |
| | Common Stock—$1 Par Value ($1 per share × 10,000 shares) | | 10,000 |
| | Paid-In Capital in Excess of Par—Common ($9 per share × 10,000 shares) | | 90,000 |
| | *Issued common stock at a premium.* | | |
| Feb. 15 | Cash ($8 per share × 2,000 shares) | 16,000 | |
| | Common Stock—$1 Par Value ($1 per share × 2,000 shares) | | 2,000 |
| | Paid-In Capital in Excess of Par—Common ($7 per share × 2,000 shares) | | 14,000 |
| | *Issued common stock at a premium.* | | |
| Mar. 1 | Cash Dividends ($0.20 per share × (8,000,000 shares + 10,000 shares + 2,000 shares)) | 1,602,400 | |
| | Dividends Payable—Common | | 1,602,400 |
| | *Declared a cash dividend.* | | |
| 15 | *No entry recorded.* | | |
| 30 | Dividends Payable—Common | 1,602,400 | |
| | Cash | | 1,602,400 |
| | *Payment of cash dividend.* | | |
| Nov. 1 | Stock Dividends ($8 per share × 8,012,000 shares × 0.01) | 640,960 | |
| | Common Stock Dividend Distributable ($1 per share × 8,012,000 shares × 0.01) | | 80,120 |
| | Paid-In Capital in Excess of Par—Common ($640,960 − $80,120) | | 560,840 |
| | *Declared a 1% stock dividend.* | | |
| 15 | *No entry recorded.* | | |
| 30 | Common Stock Dividend Distributable | 80,120 | |
| | Common Stock—$1 Par Value | | 80,120 |
| | *Issued 1% stock dividend.* | | |
| Dec. 1 | Treasury Stock—Common ($12 per share × 5,000 shares) | 60,000 | |
| | Cash | | 60,000 |
| | *Purchased treasury stock.* | | |
| 20 | Cash ($14 per share × 3,000 shares) | 42,000 | |
| | Treasury Stock—Common ($12 per share × 3,000 shares) | | 36,000 |
| | Paid-In Capital from Treasury Stock Transactions ($2 per share × 3,000 shares) | | 6,000 |
| | *Sold treasury stock above cost.* | | |

2.

| DELPHIAN CORPORATION<br>Balance Sheet (Partial)<br>December 31, 2017 | |
|---|---|
| **Stockholders' Equity** | |
| Paid-In Capital: | |
| Common Stock—$1 Par Value; 11,000,000 shares authorized, 8,092,120 shares issued, 8,090,120 outstanding | $ 8,092,120 |
| Paid-In Capital in Excess of Par—Common | 864,840 |
| Paid-In Capital in from Treasury Stock Transactions | 6,000 |
| Total Paid-In Capital | 8,962,960 |
| Retained Earnings | 817,756,640 |
| Treasury Stock at Cost | (24,000) |
| Total Stockholders' Equity | **$ 826,695,600** |

Calculations:

Common stock—number of shares issued and outstanding:

| | |
|---|---|
| Beginning balance, Jan. 1 | 8,000,000 shares |
| Stock issuance on Jan. 1 | 10,000 |
| Stock issuance on Feb. 15 | 2,000 |
| Shares outstanding before dividend | 8,012,000 |
| Stock dividend on Nov. 30 (8,012,000 × 0.01) | 80,120 |
| Common stock issued | 8,092,120 shares |
| Purchase of treasury stock on Dec. 1 | (5,000) |
| Sale of treasury stock on Dec. 20 | 3,000 |
| Common stock outstanding | 8,090,120 shares |

Paid-In Capital in Excess of Par:

| | |
|---|---|
| Beginning balance, Jan. 1 | $ 200,000 |
| Stock issuance on Jan. 1 | 90,000 |
| Stock issuance on Feb. 15 | 14,000 |
| Stock dividend on Nov. 1 | 560,840 |
| Total Paid-In Capital in Excess of Par | $ 864,840 |

Retained Earnings:

| | |
|---|---|
| Beginning balance, Jan. 1 | $ 800,000,000 |
| Cash dividend on Mar. 1 | (1,602,400) |
| Stock dividend on Nov. 1 | (640,960) |
| Net income for the year | 20,000,000 |
| Ending balance, Dec. 31 | $ 817,756,640 |

3. Earnings per share = (Net income − Preferred dividends) / Average number of common shares outstanding = ($20,000,000 − $0) / [(8,000,000 shares + 8,090,120 shares) / 2] = $2.49 per share

4. Price/earnings ratio = Market price per share of common stock / Earnings per share = $15 per share / $2.49 per share = 6.02

## > Key Terms

**Appropriation of Retained Earnings (p. 667)**
**Authorized Stock (p. 647)**
**Capital Stock (p. 647)**
**Common Stock (p. 648)**
**Corporation (p. 646)**
**Cumulative Preferred Stock (p. 661)**
**Deficit (p. 667)**
**Dividend (p. 648)**
**Dividend in Arrears (p. 661)**
**Earnings per Share (EPS) (p. 669)**
**Issue Price (p. 650)**
**Issued Stock (p. 647)**
**Large Stock Dividend (p. 663)**
**Legal Capital (p. 659)**
**Memorandum Entry (p. 666)**
**No-Par Stock (p. 649)**
**Noncumulative Preferred Stock (p. 661)**
**Outstanding Stock (p. 648)**
**Paid-In Capital (p. 649)**
**Paid-In Capital in Excess of Par (p. 651)**
**Par Value (p. 649)**
**Preemptive Right (p. 648)**
**Preferred Stock (p. 649)**
**Premium (p. 650)**
**Price/Earnings Ratio (p. 670)**
**Prior-Period Adjustment (p. 668)**
**Rate of Return on Common Stockholders' Equity (p. 670)**
**Retained Earnings (p. 649)**
**Small Stock Dividend (p. 663)**
**Stated Value Stock (p. 649)**
**Stock Certificate (p. 647)**
**Stock Dividend (p. 662)**
**Stock Split (p. 666)**
**Stockholders' Equity (p. 649)**
**Treasury Stock (p. 655)**
**Underwriter (p. 650)**

## > Quick Check

1. Which characteristic of a corporation is a disadvantage? **Learning Objective 1**
   a. Mutual agency
   b. Double taxation
   c. Limited liability
   d. None are disadvantages.

2. The two basic sources of stockholders' equity are **Learning Objective 1**
   a. assets and equity.
   b. preferred and common.
   c. retained earnings and dividends.
   d. paid-in capital and retained earnings.

3. Suppose Value Home and Garden Imports issued 400,000 shares of $0.10 par common stock at $4 per share. Which journal entry correctly records the issuance of this stock? **Learning Objective 2**

| Date | Accounts and Explanation | Debit | Credit |
|---|---|---|---|
| a. | Common Stock—$0.10 Par Value | 1,600,000 | |
| | Cash | | 40,000 |
| | Paid-In Capital in Excess of Par—Common | | 1,560,000 |
| b. | Common Stock—$0.10 Par Value | 1,600,000 | |
| | Cash | | 1,600,000 |
| c. | Cash | 1,600,000 | |
| | Common Stock—$0.10 Par Value | | 40,000 |
| | Paid-In Capital in Excess of Par—Common | | 1,560,000 |
| d. | Cash | 1,600,000 | |
| | Common Stock—$0.10 Par Value | | 1,600,000 |

**Learning Objective 2**

4. Suppose Yummy Treats Bakery issues common stock in exchange for a building. Yummy Treats Bakery should record the building at
   - **a.** the par value of the stock given.
   - **b.** its book value.
   - **c.** its market value.
   - **d.** a value assigned by the board of directors.

**Learning Objective 3**

5. A company's own stock that it has issued and repurchased is called
   - **a.** outstanding stock.
   - **b.** dividend stock.
   - **c.** issued stock.
   - **d.** treasury stock.

**Learning Objective 3**

6. Assume that a company paid $6 per share to purchase 1,100 shares of its $3 par common stock as treasury stock. The purchase of treasury stock
   - **a.** increased total equity by $3,300.
   - **b.** decreased total equity by $3,300.
   - **c.** decreased total equity by $6,600.
   - **d.** increased total equity by $6,600.

**Learning Objective 4**

7. Winston Corporation has 9,000 shares of 4%, $10 par cumulative preferred stock and 47,000 shares of common stock outstanding. Winston declared no dividends in 2015 and had no dividends in arrears prior to 2015. In 2016, Winston declares a total dividend of $54,000. How much of the dividends go to the common stockholders?
   - **a.** $54,000
   - **b.** $50,400
   - **c.** $46,800
   - **d.** None; it all goes to preferred stockholders.

**Learning Objective 4**

8. A small stock dividend
   - **a.** decreases common stock.
   - **b.** has no effect on total equity.
   - **c.** increases Retained Earnings.
   - **d.** Items a, b, and c are correct.

**Learning Objective 5**

9. Jackson Health Foods has 8,000 shares of $2 par common stock outstanding, which were issued at $15 per share. Jackson also has a deficit balance in Retained Earnings of $86,000. How much is Jackson's total stockholders' equity?
   - **a.** $16,000
   - **b.** $120,000
   - **c.** $206,000
   - **d.** $34,000

**Learning Objective 6**

10. Dale Corporation has the following data:

| | |
|---|---|
| Net income | $ 24,000 |
| Preferred dividends | 12,000 |
| Average common stockholders' equity | 100,000 |

Dale's rate of return on common stockholders' equity is
   - **a.** 24%
   - **b.** 50%
   - **c.** 12%
   - **d.** 36%

**Check your answers at the end of the chapter.**

# ASSESS YOUR PROGRESS

## > Review Questions

1. What is a corporation?
2. List three characteristics of a corporation.
3. How does authorized stock differ from outstanding stock?
4. What are the four basic rights of stockholders?
5. How does preferred stock differ from common stock?
6. What is par value?
7. What are the two basic sources of stockholders' equity? Describe each source.
8. What account is used to record the premium when issuing common stock? What type of account is this?
9. If stock is issued for assets other than cash, describe the recording of this transaction.
10. What is treasury stock? What type of account is Treasury Stock, and what is the account's normal balance?
11. Where and how is treasury stock reported on the balance sheet?
12. What is the effect on the accounting equation when cash dividends are declared? What is the effect on the accounting equation when cash dividends are paid?
13. What are the three relevant dates involving cash dividends? Describe each.
14. How does cumulative preferred stock differ from noncumulative preferred stock?
15. What is a stock dividend?
16. What is the effect on the accounting equation when a stock dividend is declared? What is the effect on the accounting equation when a stock dividend is distributed?
17. What are some reasons corporations issue stock dividends?
18. What is a stock split?
19. What does the statement of retained earnings report?
20. What is a prior-period adjustment?
21. What does the statement of stockholders' equity report? How does the statement of stockholders' equity differ from the statement of retained earnings?
22. What does earnings per share report, and how is it calculated?
23. What is the price/earnings ratio, and how is it calculated?
24. What does the rate of return on common stock show, and how is it calculated?

## > Short Exercises

**S13-1 Describing corporation characteristics**

**Learning Objective 1**

Due to recent beef recalls, Southwest Steakhouse is considering incorporating. Bob, the owner, wants to protect his personal assets in the event the restaurant is sued.

**Requirements**

1. Which advantage of incorporating is most applicable? What are other advantages of organizing as a corporate entity?
2. What are some disadvantages of organizing as a corporation?

Learning Objective 2

### S13-2 Journalizing issuance of stock—at par and at a premium

Coastal Corporation has two classes of stock: common, $4 par value; and preferred, $5 par value.

**Requirements**

1. Journalize Coastal's issuance of 5,500 shares of common stock for $10 per share.
2. Journalize Coastal's issuance of 5,500 shares of preferred stock for a total of $27,500.

Learning Objective 2

### S13-3 Journalizing issuance of stock—no-par

Ashford Corporation issued 10,000 shares of no-par common stock for $5 per share on March 13. Record the stock issuance.

Learning Objective 2

### S13-4 Journalizing issuance of stock—stated value

Turner Corporation issued 6,500 shares of $3 stated value common stock for $11 per share on July 7. Record the stock issuance.

Learning Objective 2

### S13-5 Journalizing issuance of stock for assets other than cash

Miller Corporation issued 30,000 shares of $1 par value common stock in exchange for a building with a market value of $160,000. Record the stock issuance.

Learning Objective 3

### S13-6 Accounting for the purchase and sale of treasury stock

Bottom Dollar Furniture, Inc. completed the following treasury stock transactions in 2016:

| | |
|---|---|
| Dec. 1 | Purchased 1,800 shares of the company's $1 par value common stock as treasury stock, paying cash of $6 per share. |
| 15 | Sold 300 shares of the treasury stock for cash of $9 per share. |
| 20 | Sold 700 shares of the treasury stock for cash of $2 per share. (Assume the balance in Paid-In Capital from Treasury Stock Transactions on December 20 is $2,700.) |

**Requirements**

1. Journalize these transactions. Explanations are not required.
2. How will Bottom Dollar Furniture, Inc. report treasury stock on its balance sheet as of December 31, 2016?

Learning Objective 4

### S13-7 Accounting for cash dividends

Frenchroast Company earned net income of $95,000 during the year ended December 31, 2016. On December 15, Frenchroast declared the annual cash dividend on its 2% preferred stock (par value, $128,000) and a $0.75 per share cash dividend on its common stock (65,000 shares). Frenchroast then paid the dividends on January 4, 2017.

**Requirements**

1. Journalize for Frenchroast the entry declaring the cash dividends on December 15, 2016.
2. Journalize for Frenchroast the entry paying the cash dividends on January 4, 2017.

### S13-8 Dividing cash dividends between preferred and common stock

**Learning Objective 4**

Platinum Trust has the following classes of stock:

| |
|---|
| Preferred Stock—3%, $14 Par Value; 7,000 shares authorized, 5,500 shares issued and outstanding |
| Common Stock—$0.20 Par Value; 2,250,000 shares authorized, 1,650,000 shares issued and outstanding |

**Requirements**

1. Platinum declares cash dividends of $20,000 for 2016. How much of the dividends goes to preferred stockholders? How much goes to common stockholders?
2. Assume the preferred stock is cumulative and Platinum passed the preferred dividend in 2014 and 2015. In 2016, the company declares cash dividends of $50,000. How much of the dividend goes to preferred stockholders? How much goes to common stockholders?
3. Assume the preferred stock is noncumulative and Platinum passed the preferred dividend in 2014 and 2015. In 2016, the company declares cash dividends of $50,000. How much of the dividend goes to preferred stockholders? How much goes to common stockholders?

### S13-9 Journalizing a small stock dividend

**Learning Objective 4**

Greenview Water Sports has 16,000 shares of $1 par value common stock outstanding. Greenview distributes a 5% stock dividend when the market value of its stock is $25 per share.

**Requirements**

1. Journalize Greenview's declaration of the stock dividend on August 15 and distribution on August 31.
2. What is the overall effect of the stock dividend on Greenview's total assets?
3. What is the overall effect on total stockholders' equity?

### S13-10 Journalizing a large stock dividend

**Learning Objective 4**

Billy, Inc. had 270,000 shares of $2 par value common stock issued and outstanding as of December 15, 2016. The company is authorized to issue 1,500,000 common shares. On December 15, 2016, Billy declared a 40% stock dividend when the market value for Billy's common stock was $7 per share. The stock was issued on Dec. 30.

**Requirements**

1. Journalize the declaration and distribution of the stock dividend.
2. How many shares of common stock are outstanding after the dividend?

**Learning Objective 4**

### S13-11 Accounting for a stock split

Decor Plus Imports recently reported the following stockholders' equity:

| Stockholders' Equity | |
|---|---|
| Paid-In Capital: | |
| Common Stock—$1 Par Value; 550,000,000 shares authorized, 110,000,000 shares issued and outstanding | $ 110,000,000 |
| Paid-In Capital in Excess of Par—Common | 154,000,000 |
| Total Paid-In Capital | 264,000,000 |
| Retained Earnings | 645,000,000 |
| Total Stockholders' Equity | **$ 909,000,000** |

Suppose Decor Plus split its common stock 2-for-1 in order to decrease the market price per share of its stock. The company's stock was trading at $21 per share immediately before the split.

**Requirements**

1. Prepare the stockholders' equity section of the Decor Plus Imports balance sheet after the stock split.
2. Were the account balances changed or unchanged after the stock split?

**Learning Objective 5**

### S13-12 Preparing a statement of retained earnings

Tinder, Inc. had beginning retained earnings of $90,000 on January 1, 2016. During the year, Tinder declared and paid $90,000 of cash dividends and earned $95,000 of net income. Prepare a statement of retained earnings for Tinder, Inc. for the year ending December 31, 2016.

**Learning Objective 5**

### S13-13 Analyzing the effect of prior-period adjustments

Taylor Corporation discovered in 2017 that it had incorrectly recorded in 2016 a cash payment of $50,000 for utilities expense. The correct amount of the utilities expense was $60,000.

**Requirements**

1. Determine the effect of the error on the accounting equation in 2016.
2. How should this error be reported in the 2017 financial statements?

**Learning Objective 6**

### S13-14 Computing earnings per share

RUT Corporation had net income for 2016 of $36,400. RUT had 2,400 shares of common stock outstanding at the beginning of the year and 20,000 shares of common stock outstanding as of December 31, 2016. During the year, RUT declared and paid preferred dividends of $5,040. Compute RUT's earnings per share.

***Note: Short Exercise S13-14 must be completed before attempting Short Exercise S13-15.***

**Learning Objective 6**

### S13-15 Computing price/earnings ratio

Refer to the RUT data in Short Exercise S13-14. Assume the market price of RUT's common stock is $18 per share. Compute RUT's price/earnings ratio.

**S13-16 Computing rate of return on common stockholders' equity** Learning Objective 6

Tolman, Inc.'s 2016 balance sheet reported the following items—with 2015 figures given for comparison:

| TOLMAN, INC.<br>Balance Sheet<br>As of December 31, 2016, and December 31, 2015 | | |
|---|---|---|
| | **December 31, 2016** | **December 31, 2015** |
| Total Assets | **$ 24,900** | **$ 26,880** |
| Total Liabilities | 13,400 | 13,380 |
| Total Stockholders' Equity (all common) | 11,500 | 13,500 |
| Total Liabilities and Stockholders' Equity | **$ 24,900** | **$ 26,880** |

Net income for 2016 was $1,750. Compute Tolman's rate of return on common stockholders' equity for 2016.

## > Exercises

**E13-17 Identifying advantages and disadvantages of a corporation** Learning Objective 1

Following is a list of advantages and disadvantages of the corporate form of business. Identify each quality as either an advantage or a disadvantage.

**a.** Ownership and management are separated.

**b.** Entity has continuous life.

**c.** Transfer of ownership is easy.

**d.** Stockholders' liability is limited.

**e.** Exposure to double taxation is evident.

**f.** Entity can raise more money than a partnership or sole proprietorship.

**g.** Government regulation is expensive.

**E13-18 Determining paid-in capital for a corporation** Learning Objective 2

Arilla Corporation recently organized. The company issued common stock to an inventor in exchange for a patent with a market value of $54,000. In addition, Arilla received cash for 3,000 shares of its $10 par preferred stock at par value and 6,000 shares of its no-par common stock at $35 per share. Without making journal entries, determine the total *paid in capital* created by these transactions.

**E13-19 Journaling issuance of stock** Learning Objective 2

Skylar Systems completed the following stock issuance transactions:

| | |
|---|---|
| May 19 | Issued 1,700 shares of $2 par value common stock for cash of $9.50 per share. |
| Jun. 3 | Issued 200 shares of $9, no-par preferred stock for $10,000 cash. |
| 11 | Received equipment with a market value of $76,000 in exchange for 3,000 shares of the $2 par value common stock. |

**Requirements**

1. Journalize the transactions. Explanations are not required.
2. How much paid-in capital did these transactions generate for Skylar Systems?

**Learning Objective 2**

1. a. Cash $16,000

## E13-20 Journalizing issuance of no-par stock

Bates Corp. issued 2,000 shares of no-par common stock for $8 per share.

**Requirements**

1. Record issuance of the stock if the stock:
   a. is true no-par stock.
   b. has stated value of $2 per share.
2. Which type of stock results in more total paid-in capital?

**Learning Objective 2**

2. Total Stockholders' Equity $88,250

## E13-21 Journalizing issuance of stock and preparing the stockholders' equity section of the balance sheet

The charter for WCAP-TV, Inc. authorizes the company to issue 100,000 shares of $2, no-par preferred stock and 500,000 shares of common stock with $1 par value. During its start-up phase, WCAP completed the following transactions:

| | |
|---|---|
| Sep. 6 | Issued 275 shares of common stock to the promoters who organized the corporation, receiving cash of $8,250. |
| 12 | Issued 300 shares of preferred stock for cash of $24,000. |
| 14 | Issued 1,400 shares of common stock in exchange for land with a market value of $19,000. |

**Requirements**

1. Record the transactions in the general journal.
2. Prepare the stockholders' equity section of the WCAP-TV balance sheet at September 30, 2016, assuming WCAP-TV, Inc. had net income of $37,000 for the month.

**Learning Objective 2**

March 23 Common Stock $210 CR

## E13-22 Journalizing issuance of stock and preparing the stockholders' equity section of the balance sheet

The charter of Cherry Blossom Corporation authorizes the issuance of 900 shares of preferred stock and 3,500 shares of common stock. During a two-month period, Cherry Blossom completed these stock-issuance transactions:

| | |
|---|---|
| Mar. 23 | Issued 210 shares of $1 par value common stock for cash of $10 per share. |
| Apr. 12 | Received inventory with a market value of $25,000 and equipment with a market value of $16,000 for 350 shares of the $1 par value common stock. |
| 17 | Issued 900 shares of 6%, $50 par value preferred stock for $50 per share. |

**Requirements**

1. Record the transactions in the general journal.
2. Prepare the stockholders' equity section of the Cherry Blossom balance sheet as of April 30, 2016, for the transactions given in this exercise. Retained Earnings has a balance of $70,000 at April 30, 2016.

## E13-23 Journalizing treasury stock transactions and reporting stockholders' equity

**Learning Objective 3**

2. Total Stockholders' Equity $53,500

Pioneer Amusements Corporation had the following stockholders' equity on November 30:

| Stockholders' Equity | |
|---|---|
| Paid-In Capital: | |
| Common Stock—$5 Par Value; 1,300 shares authorized, 130 shares issued and outstanding | $ 650 |
| Paid-In Capital in Excess of Par—Common | 1,950 |
| Total Paid-In Capital | 2,600 |
| Retained Earnings | 52,000 |
| Total Stockholders' Equity | **$ 54,600** |

On December 30, Pioneer purchased 100 shares of treasury stock at $11 per share.

### Requirements

1. Journalize the purchase of the treasury stock.
2. Prepare the stockholders' equity section of the balance sheet at December 31, 2016. Assume the balance in retained earnings is unchanged from November 30.
3. How many shares of common stock are outstanding after the purchase of treasury stock?

## E13-24 Journalizing issuance of stock and treasury stock transactions

**Learning Objectives 2, 3**

Sept. 22 Treasury Stock $3,300 CR

Stock transactions for Cautious Driving School, Inc. follow:

| | |
|---|---|
| Mar. 4 | Issued 29,000 shares of $1 par value common stock at $8 per share. |
| May 22 | Purchased 900 shares of treasury stock—common at $11 per share. |
| Sep. 22 | Sold 300 shares of treasury stock—common at $25 per share. |
| Oct. 14 | Sold 600 shares of treasury stock—common at $6 per share. |

Journalize the transactions.

## E13-25 Computing dividends on preferred and common stock and journalizing

**Learning Objective 4**

1. Preferred Dividend 2016 $7,680

Horizon Communications has the following stockholders' equity on December 31, 2016:

| Stockholders' Equity | |
|---|---|
| Paid-In Capital: | |
| Preferred Stock—4%, $11 Par Value; 150,000 shares authorized, 22,000 shares issued and outstanding | $ 242,000 |
| Common Stock—$4 Par Value; 575,000 shares authorized, 350,000 shares issued and outstanding | 1,400,000 |
| Paid-In Capital in Excess of Par—Common | 1,050,000 |
| Total Paid-In Capital | 2,692,000 |
| Retained Earnings | 220,000 |
| Total Stockholders' Equity | **$ 2,912,000** |

**Requirements**

1. Assuming the preferred stock is cumulative, compute the amount of dividends to preferred stockholders and to common stockholders for 2016 and 2017 if total dividends are $7,680 in 2016 and $49,000 in 2017. Assume no changes in preferred stock and common stock in 2017.
2. Record the journal entries for 2016, assuming that Horizon Communications declared the dividend on December 1 for stockholders of record on December 10. Horizon Communications paid the dividend on December 20.

**Learning Objective 4**

2. July 1 Cash Dividends $155,000 DR

## E13-26 Computing dividends on preferred and common stock and journalizing

The following elements of stockholders' equity are from the balance sheet of Sacchetti Marketing Corp. at December 31, 2015:

| Stockholders' Equity | |
|---|---|
| Paid-In Capital: | |
| Preferred Stock—5%, $2 Par Value; 90,000 shares authorized, 45,000 shares issued and outstanding | $ 90,000 |
| Common Stock—$0.10 Par Value; 10,000,000 shares authorized, 9,250,000 shares issued and outstanding | 925,000 |

Sacchetti paid no preferred dividends in 2015.

**Requirements**

1. Compute the dividends to the preferred and common shareholders for 2016 if total dividends are $155,000 and assuming the preferred stock is noncumulative.
2. Record the journal entries for 2016 assuming that Sacchetti Marketing Corp. declared the dividends on July 1 for stockholders of record on July 15. Sacchetti paid the dividends on July 31.

**Learning Objective 4**

2. Total Stockholders' Equity $127,600

## E13-27 Journalizing a stock dividend and reporting stockholders' equity

The stockholders' equity of Poolside Occupational Therapy, Inc. on December 31, 2015, follows:

| Stockholders' Equity | |
|---|---|
| Paid-In Capital: | |
| Common Stock—$2 Par Value; 1,600 shares authorized, 600 shares issued and outstanding | $ 1,200 |
| Paid-In Capital in Excess of Par—Common | 2,400 |
| Total Paid-In Capital | 3,600 |
| Retained Earnings | 124,000 |
| Total Stockholders' Equity | **$ 127,600** |

On April 30, 2016, the market price of Poolside's common stock was $15 per share and the company declared a 8% stock dividend. The stock was distributed on May 15.

**Requirements**

1. Journalize the declaration and distribution of the stock dividend.
2. Prepare the stockholders' equity section of the balance sheet as of May 31, 2016. Assume Retained Earnings are $124,000 on April 30, 2016, before the stock dividend, and the only change made to Retained Earnings before preparing the balance sheet was closing the Stock Dividends account.

### E13-28 Journalizing cash and stock dividends

**Learning Objective 4**

1. Common Stock $15,200 CR

Pottery Schools, Inc. is authorized to issue 200,000 shares of $2 par common stock. The company issued 76,000 shares at $4 per share. When the market price of common stock was $6 per share, Pottery declared and distributed a 10% stock dividend. Later, Pottery declared and paid a $0.10 per share cash dividend.

**Requirements**

1. Journalize the declaration and the distribution of the stock dividend.
2. Journalize the declaration and the payment of the cash dividend.

### E13-29 Reporting stockholders' equity after a stock split

**Learning Objective 4**

Total Stockholders' Equity $4,120

Tour Golf Club Corp. had the following stockholders' equity at December 31, 2015:

| Stockholders' Equity | |
|---|---|
| Paid-In Capital: | |
| Common Stock—$2 Par Value; 650 shares authorized, 220 shares issued and outstanding | $ 440 |
| Paid-In Capital in Excess of Par—Common | 880 |
| Total Paid-In Capital | 1,320 |
| Retained Earnings | 2,800 |
| Total Stockholders' Equity | **$ 4,120** |

On June 30, 2016, Tour split its common stock 2-for-1. Prepare the stockholders' equity section of the balance sheet immediately after the split. Assume the balance in retained earnings is unchanged from December 31, 2015.

### E13-30 Determining the effects of cash dividends, stock dividends, and stock splits

**Learning Objective 4**

Complete the following chart by inserting a check mark (√) for each statement that is true.

| | Cash dividend | Stock dividend | Stock split |
|---|---|---|---|
| Decreases retained earnings | | | |
| Has no effect on a liability | | | |
| Increases paid-in capital by the same amount that it decreases retained earnings | | | |
| Decreases both total assets and total stockholders' equity | | | |
| Has no effect on total stockholders' equity | | | |

CHAPTER 13

**Learning Objectives 3, 4**

## E13-31 Determining the effect of stock dividends, stock splits, and treasury stock transactions

Many types of transactions may affect stockholders' equity. Identify the effects of the following transactions on total stockholders' equity. Each transaction is independent.

a. A 10% stock dividend. Before the dividend, 560,000 shares of $1 par value common stock were outstanding; market value was $10 per share at the time of the dividend.

b. A 2-for-1 stock split. Prior to the split, 65,000 shares of $1 par value common stock were outstanding.

c. Purchase of 1,500 shares of $0.50 par treasury stock at $7 per share.

d. Sale of 900 shares of $0.50 par treasury stock for $9 per share. Cost of the treasury stock was $8 per share.

**Learning Objective 5**

Retained Earnings Dec. 31, 2016 $97,000

## E13-32 Preparing a statement of retained earnings

Susan May Bakery, Inc. reported a prior-period adjustment in 2016. An accounting error caused net income of prior years to be overstated by $4,000. Retained Earnings at December 31, 2015, as previously reported, was $42,000. Net income for 2016 was $79,000, and dividends declared were $20,000. Prepare the company's statement of retained earnings for the year ended December 31, 2016.

**Learning Objective 6**

## E13-33 Computing earnings per share and price/earnings ratio

Temple Corp. earned net income of $128,500 and paid the minimum dividend to preferred stockholders for 2016. Assume that there are no changes in common shares outstanding. Temple's books include the following figures:

| | |
|---|---|
| Preferred Stock—5%, $40 Par Value; 2,000 shares authorized, 1,000 shares issued and outstanding | $ 40,000 |
| Common Stock—$10 Par Value; 70,000 shares authorized, 52,000 shares issued, 50,600 shares outstanding | 520,000 |
| Paid-In Capital in Excess of Par—Common | 490,000 |
| Treasury Stock—Common; 1,400 shares at cost | (28,000) |

### Requirements

1. Compute Temple's EPS for the year.
2. Assume Temple's market price of a share of common stock is $8 per share. Compute Temple's price/earnings ratio.

CHAPTER 13

## E13-34 Computing rate of return on common stockholders' equity

Learning Objective 6

Louisville Exploration Company reported these figures for 2016 and 2015:

| | 2016 | 2015 |
|---|---|---|
| **Income Statement—partial:** | | |
| Net Income | $ 15,500,000 | $ 18,800,000 |
| **Balance Sheet—partial:** | | |
| | **Dec. 31, 2016** | **Dec. 31, 2015** |
| Total Assets | $ 324,000,000 | $ 316,000,000 |
| Preferred Stock | 2,600,000 | 2,600,000 |
| Common Stock | 180,000,000 | 171,000,000 |
| Retained Earnings | 7,000,000 | 5,500,000 |
| Total Stockholders' Equity | $ 189,600,000 | $ 179,100,000 |

Compute rate of return on common stockholders' equity for 2016 assuming no dividends were paid to preferred stockholders.

# > Problems Group A

## P13-35A Organizing a corporation and issuing stock

Learning Objectives 1, 2

John and Michael are opening a paint store. There are no competing paint stores in the area. They must decide how to organize the business. They anticipate profits of $100,000 the first year, with the ability to sell franchises in the future. Although they have enough to start the business now as a partnership, cash flow will be an issue as they grow. They feel the corporate form of operation will be best for the long term. They seek your advice.

### Requirements

1. What is the main advantage they gain by selecting a corporate form of business now?
2. Would you recommend they initially issue preferred or common stock? Why?
3. If they decide to issue $10 par common stock and anticipate an initial market price of $40 per share, how many shares will they need to issue to raise $2,250,000?

## P13-36A Identifying sources of equity, stock issuance, and dividends

Learning Objectives 1, 2, 4

4. Common stock dividends $840,000

Travel Comfort Specialists, Inc. reported the following stockholders' equity on its balance sheet at June 30, 2016:

| **Stockholders' Equity** | |
|---|---|
| Paid-In Capital: | |
| Preferred Stock—6%, ? Par Value; 675,000 shares authorized, 200,000 shares issued and outstanding | $ 1,000,000 |
| Common Stock—$1 Par Value; 9,000,000 shares authorized, 1,320,000 shares issued and outstanding | 1,320,000 |
| Paid-In Capital in Excess of Par—Common | 2,700,000 |
| Total Paid-In Capital | 5,020,000 |
| Retained Earnings | 11,900,000 |
| Total Stockholders' Equity | **$ 16,920,000** |

**Requirements**

1. Identify the different classes of stock that Travel has outstanding.
2. What is the par value per share of Travel's preferred stock?
3. Make two summary journal entries to record issuance of all the Travel stock for cash. Explanations are not required.
4. No preferred dividends are in arrears. Journalize the declaration of a $900,000 dividend at June 30, 2016, and the payment of the dividend on July 20, 2016. Use separate Dividends Payable accounts for preferred and common stock. An explanation is not required.

**Learning Objectives 2, 4**

2. Total Stockholders' Equity $323,000

### P13-37A Journalizing stock issuance and cash dividends and preparing the stockholders' equity section of the balance sheet

C-Cell Wireless needed additional capital to expand, so the business incorporated. The charter from the state of Georgia authorizes C-Cell to issue 50,000 shares of 7%, $50 par value cumulative preferred stock and 120,000 shares of $2 par value common stock. During the first month, C-Cell completed the following transactions:

| | |
|---|---|
| Oct. 2 | Issued 22,000 shares of common stock for a building with a market value of $120,000. |
| 6 | Issued 900 shares of preferred stock for $70 per share. |
| 9 | Issued 12,000 shares of common stock for cash of $60,000. |
| 10 | Declared a $16,000 cash dividend for stockholders of record on Oct. 20. Use a separate Dividends Payable account for preferred and common stock. |
| 25 | Paid the cash dividend. |

**Requirements**

1. Record the transactions in the general journal.
2. Prepare the stockholders' equity section of C-Cell's balance sheet at October 31, 2016. Assume C-Cell's net income for the month was $96,000.

**Learning Objectives 3, 4**

Nov. 8 Treasury Stock $6,300 CR

### P13-38A Journalizing dividends and treasury stock transactions and preparing the stockholders' equity section of the balance sheet

Winterborn Manufacturing Co. completed the following transactions during 2016:

| | |
|---|---|
| Jan. 16 | Declared a cash dividend on the 4%, $100 par noncumulative preferred stock (950 shares outstanding). Declared a $0.40 per share dividend on the 95,000 shares of $4 par value common stock outstanding. The date of record is January 31, and the payment date is February 15. |
| Feb. 15 | Paid the cash dividends. |
| Jun. 10 | Split common stock 2-for-1. |
| Jul. 30 | Declared a 50% stock dividend on the common stock. The market value of the common stock was $10 per share. |
| Aug. 15 | Distributed the stock dividend. |
| Oct. 26 | Purchased 1,400 shares of treasury stock at $9 per share. |
| Nov. 8 | Sold 700 shares of treasury stock for $11 per share. |
| 30 | Sold 500 shares of treasury stock for $6 per share. |

**Requirements**

1. Record the transactions in Winterborn's general journal.
2. Prepare the Winterborn's stockholders' equity section of the balance sheet as of December 31, 2016. Assume that Winterborn was authorized to issue 2,400 shares of preferred stock and 500,000 shares of common stock. Both preferred stock and common stock were issued at par. The ending balance of retained earnings as of December 31, 2016, is $2,080,000.

**Learning Objectives 3, 4, 5**

2. Retained Earnings Dec. 31, 2016 $152,240

### P13-39A Journalizing dividend and treasury stock transactions, preparing a statement of retained earnings, and preparing stockholders' equity

The balance sheet of Morrisey Management Consulting, Inc. at December 31, 2015, reported the following stockholders' equity:

| Stockholders' Equity | |
|---|---|
| Paid-In Capital: | |
| Common Stock—$10 Par Value; 300,000 shares authorized, 25,000 shares issued and outstanding | $ 250,000 |
| Paid-In Capital in Excess of Par—Common | 320,000 |
| Total Paid-In Capital | 570,000 |
| Retained Earnings | 158,000 |
| Total Stockholders' Equity | **$ 728,000** |

During 2016, Morrisey completed the following selected transactions:

| | |
|---|---|
| Feb. 6 | Declared a 15% stock dividend on common stock. The market value of Morrisey's stock was $23 per share. |
| 15 | Distributed the stock dividend. |
| Jul. 29 | Purchased 2,100 shares of treasury stock at $23 per share. |
| Nov. 27 | Declared a $0.20 per share cash dividend on the common stock outstanding. |

**Requirements**

1. Record the transactions in the general journal.
2. Prepare a retained earnings statement for the year ended December 31, 2016. Assume Morrisey's net income for the year was $86,000.
3. Prepare the stockholders' equity section of the balance sheet at December 31, 2016.

**Learning Objective 6**

## P13-40A Computing earnings per share, price/earnings ratio, and rate of return on common stockholders' equity

Fowler Company reported these figures for 2016 and 2015:

| | 2016 | 2015 |
|---|---|---|
| **Income Statement—partial:** | | |
| Net Income | $ 21,900 | $ 19,000 |
| **Balance Sheet—partial:** | | |
| | **Dec. 31, 2016** | **Dec. 31, 2015** |
| Total Assets | $ 250,000 | $ 265,000 |
| Paid-In Capital: | | |
| Preferred Stock—10%, $11 Par Value; 95,000 shares authorized, 9,000 shares issued and outstanding | $ 99,000 | $ 99,000 |
| Common Stock—$1 Par Value; 90,000 shares authorized, 60,000 shares issued and outstanding | 60,000 | 60,000 |
| Paid-In Capital in Excess of Par—Common | 25,000 | 25,000 |
| Retained Earnings | 52,000 | 40,000 |
| Total Stockholders' Equity | $ 236,000 | $ 224,000 |

### Requirements

1. Compute Fowler Company's earnings per share for 2016. Assume the company paid the minimum preferred dividend during 2016.
2. Compute Fowler Company's price/earnings ratio for 2016. Assume the company's market price per share of common stock is $5.
3. Compute Fowler Company's rate of return on common stockholders' equity for 2016. Assume the company paid the minimum preferred dividend during 2016.

# > Problems Group B

**Learning Objectives 1, 2**

## P13-41B Organizing a corporation and issuing stock

Phil and Stephen are opening a comic store. There are no competing comic stores in the area. They must decide how to organize the business. They anticipate profits of $200,000 the first year, with the ability to sell franchises in the future. Although they have enough to start the business now as a partnership, cash flow will be an issue as they grow. They feel the corporate form of operation will be best for the long term. They seek your advice.

### Requirements

1. What is the main advantage they gain by selecting a corporate form of business now?
2. Would you recommend they initially issue preferred or common stock? Why?
3. If they decide to issue $3 par common stock and anticipate an initial market price of $45 per share, how many shares will they need to issue to raise $2,025,000?

**P13-42B Identifying sources of equity, stock issuance, and dividends**

**Learning Objectives 1, 2, 4**

4. Common stock dividends $112,000

Terrific Comfort Specialists, Inc. reported the following stockholders' equity on its balance sheet at June 30, 2016:

| Stockholders' Equity | |
|---|---|
| Paid-In Capital: | |
| Preferred Stock—8%, ? Par Value; 600,000 shares authorized, 275,000 shares issued and outstanding | $ 1,100,000 |
| Common Stock—$1 Par Value; 5,000,000 shares authorized, 1,310,000 shares issued and outstanding | 1,310,000 |
| Paid-In Capital in Excess of Par—Common | 2,500,000 |
| Total Paid-In Capital | 4,910,000 |
| Retained Earnings | 12,500,000 |
| Total Stockholders' Equity | **$ 17,410,000** |

**Requirements**

1. Identify the different classes of stock that Terrific has outstanding.
2. What is the par value per share of Terrific's preferred stock?
3. Make two summary journal entries to record issuance of all the Terrific stock for cash. Explanations are not required.
4. No preferred dividends are in arrears. Journalize the declaration of a $200,000 dividend at June 30, 2016, and the payment of the dividend on July 20, 2016. Use separate Dividends Payable accounts for preferred and common stock. An explanation is not required.

**P13-43B Journalizing stock issuance and cash dividends and preparing the stockholders' equity section of the balance sheet**

**Learning Objectives 2, 4**

2. Total Stockholders' Equity $371,000

Waco Wireless needed additional capital to expand, so the business incorporated. The charter from the state of Georgia authorizes Waco to issue 80,000 shares of 10%, $100 par value cumulative preferred stock, and 120,000 shares of $3 par value common stock. During the first month, Waco completed the following transactions:

| | |
|---|---|
| Oct. 2 | Issued 20,000 shares of common stock for a building with a market value of $150,000. |
| 6 | Issued 750 shares of preferred stock for $120 per share. |
| 9 | Issued 15,000 shares of common stock for cash of $60,000. |
| 10 | Declared a $20,000 cash dividend for stockholders of record on Oct. 20. Use a separate Dividends Payable account for preferred and common stock. |
| 25 | Paid the cash dividend. |

**Requirements**

1. Record the transactions in the general journal.
2. Prepare the stockholders' equity section of Waco's balance sheet at October 31, 2016. Assume Waco's net income for the month was $91,000.

**Learning Objectives 3, 4**

1. Nov. 8 Treasury Stock $6,300 CR

## P13-44B Journalizing dividends and treasury stock transactions and preparing the stockholders' equity section of the balance sheet

Summerborn Manufacturing Co. completed the following transactions during 2016:

| | |
|---|---|
| Jan. 16 | Declared a cash dividend on the 6%, $97 par noncumulative preferred stock (1,150 shares outstanding). Declared a $0.25 per share dividend on the 105,000 shares of $8 par value common stock outstanding. The date of record is January 31, and the payment date is February 15. |
| Feb. 15 | Paid the cash dividends. |
| Jun. 10 | Split common stock 2-for-1. |
| Jul. 30 | Declared a 50% stock dividend on the common stock. The market value of the common stock was $11 per share. |
| Aug. 15 | Distributed the stock dividend. |
| Oct. 26 | Purchased 1,400 shares of treasury stock at $9 per share. |
| Nov. 8 | Sold 700 shares of treasury stock for $11 per share. |
| 30 | Sold 500 shares of treasury stock for $6 per share. |

### Requirements

1. Record the transactions in Summerborn's general journal.
2. Prepare the Summerborn's stockholders' equity section of the balance sheet as of December 31, 2016. Assume that Summerborn was authorized to issue 1,500 shares of preferred stock and 500,000 shares of common stock. Both preferred stock and common stock were issued at par. The ending balance of retained earnings as of December 31, 2016, is $2,080,000.

**Learning Objectives 3, 4, 5**

2. Retained Earnings Dec. 31, 2016 $218,740

## P13-45B Journalizing dividend and treasury stock transactions, preparing a statement of retained earnings, and preparing stockholders' equity

The balance sheet of Patrick Management Consulting, Inc. at December 31, 2015, reported the following stockholders' equity:

| Stockholders' Equity | |
|---|---|
| Paid-In Capital: | |
| Common Stock—$12 Par Value; 300,000 shares authorized, 22,000 shares issued and outstanding | $ 264,000 |
| Paid-In Capital in Excess of Par—Common | 340,000 |
| Total Paid-In Capital | 604,000 |
| Retained Earnings | 163,000 |
| Total Stockholders' Equity | **$ 767,000** |

During 2016, Patrick completed the following selected transactions:

| | |
|---|---|
| Feb. 6 | Declared a 5% stock dividend on common stock. The market value of Patrick's stock was $20 per share. |
| 15 | Distributed the stock dividend. |
| Jul. 29 | Purchased 1,800 shares of treasury stock at $20 per share. |
| Nov. 27 | Declared a $0.20 per share cash dividend on the common stock outstanding. |

CHAPTER 13

**Requirements**

1. Record the transactions in the general journal.
2. Prepare a retained earnings statement for the year ended December 31, 2016. Assume Patrick's net income for the year was $82,000.
3. Prepare the stockholders' equity section of the balance sheet at December 31, 2016.

### P13-46B Computing earnings per share, price/earnings ratio, and rate of return on common stockholders' equity

**Learning Objective 6**

Medina Company reported these figures for 2016 and 2015:

| | 2016 | 2015 |
|---|---|---|
| **Income Statement—partial:** | | |
| Net Income | $ 27,000 | $ 17,000 |
| **Balance Sheet—partial:** | | |
| | **Dec. 31, 2016** | **Dec. 31, 2015** |
| Total Assets | $ 260,000 | $ 240,000 |
| Paid-In Capital: | | |
| Preferred Stock—5%, $4 Par Value; 75,000 shares authorized, 10,000 shares issued and outstanding | $ 40,000 | $ 40,000 |
| Common Stock—$2 Par Value; 65,000 shares authorized, 50,000 shares issued and outstanding | 100,000 | 100,000 |
| Paid-In Capital in Excess of Par—Common | 14,000 | 14,000 |
| Retained Earnings | 71,000 | 46,000 |
| Total Stockholders' Equity | $ 225,000 | $ 200,000 |

**Requirements**

1. Compute Medina Company's earnings per share for 2016. Assume the company paid the minimum preferred dividend during 2016.
2. Compute Medina Company's price/earnings ratio for 2016. Assume the company's market price per share of common stock is $7.
3. Compute Medina Company's rate of return on common stockholders' equity for 2016. Assume the company paid the minimum preferred dividend during 2016.

## > Continuing Problem

### P13-47 Sources of equity and journalizing stock issuance

This problem continues the Daniels Consulting situation from Problem P12-45 of Chapter 12. Daniels decides to raise additional capital for a planned business expansion by issuing 8,000 additional $2 par value common shares for $24,000 and by issuing 2,500, 4%, $50 par preferred shares at $55 per share. Assuming total stockholders' equity is $25,422 and includes 200 shares of common stock and 0 shares of preferred stock issued and outstanding immediately before the previously described transactions, journalize the entries related to the issuances of both common and preferred shares.

# CRITICAL THINKING

## > Decision Cases

### Decision Case 13-1

Lena Kay and Kathy Lauder have a patent on a new line of cosmetics. They need additional capital to market the products, and they plan to incorporate the business. They are considering the capital structure for the corporation. Their primary goal is to raise as much capital as possible without giving up control of the business. Kay and Lauder plan to invest the patent (an intangible asset, which will be transferred to the company's ownership in lieu of cash) in the company and receive 100,000 shares of the corporation's common stock. They have been offered $100,000 for the patent, which provides an indication of the fair market value of the patent.

The corporation's plans for a charter include an authorization to issue 5,000 shares of preferred stock and 500,000 shares of $1 par common stock. Kay and Lauder are uncertain about the most desirable features for the preferred stock. Prior to incorporating, they are discussing their plans with two investment groups. The corporation can obtain capital from outside investors under either of the following plans:

- **Plan 1.** Group 1 will invest $150,000 to acquire 1,500 shares of 6%, $100 par nonvoting, noncumulative preferred stock.
- **Plan 2.** Group 2 will invest $100,000 to acquire 1,000 shares of $5, no-par preferred stock and $70,000 to acquire 70,000 shares of common stock. Each preferred share receives 50 votes on matters that come before the common stockholders.

#### Requirements

Assume that the corporation has been chartered (approved) by the state.

1. Journalize the issuance of common stock to Kay and Lauder. Explanations are not required.
2. Journalize the issuance of stock to the outsiders under both plans. Explanations are not required.
3. Net income for the first year is $180,000, and total dividends are $30,000. Prepare the stockholders' equity section of the corporation's balance sheet under both plans at the end of the first year.
4. Recommend one of the plans to Kay and Lauder. Give your reasons.

## > Financial Statement Case 13-1

Use **Starbucks Corporation's** financial statements to answer the following questions. Visit **http://www.pearsonhighered.com/Horngren** to view a link to Starbucks Corporation's Fiscal 2013 Annual Report.

#### Requirements

1. Review the stockholders' equity section of the balance sheet. Did Starbucks have any preferred stock at September 29, 2013?
2. Now review Note 11: Shareholders' Equity. Is Starbucks authorized to issue preferred stock? If so, how much?
3. How much of Starbucks Corporation's common stock was outstanding at September 29, 2013? How can you tell?

4. Examine Starbucks Corporation's consolidated statements of cash flows. Did Starbucks pay any cash dividends during the year ending September 29, 2013? If so, how much?
5. Show how Starbucks Corporation computed basic earnings per share of $0.01 for 2013. (Ignore diluted earnings per share.)

## > Team Project 13-1

Obtain the annual reports (or annual report data) of five well-known companies. You can get the reports either from the companies' Web sites, from your college library, or by mailing a request directly to the company (allow two weeks for delivery). Or you can go online and search the SEC EDGAR database (**http://www.sec.gov/edgar.shtml**), which includes the financial reports of most well-known companies.

**Requirements**

1. After selecting five companies, examine their income statements to search for the following items:
   a. Net income or net loss
   b. Earnings per share data
2. Study the companies' balance sheets to answer the following questions:
   a. What classes of stock has each company issued?
   b. Which item carries a larger balance—the Common Stock account or Paid-In Capital in Excess of Par (also labeled Additional Paid-In Capital)?
   c. What percentage of each company's total stockholders' equity is made up of retained earnings?
   d. Do any of the companies have treasury stock? If so, how many shares and how much is the cost?
3. Examine each company's statement of stockholders' equity for evidence of the following:
   a. Cash dividends
   b. Stock dividends
   c. Treasury stock purchases and sales
4. As directed by your instructor, either write a report or present your findings to your class. You may not be able to understand *everything* you find, but neither can the Wall Street analysts! You will be amazed at how much you have learned.

## > Communication Activity 13-1

In 75 words or fewer, explain the difference between stock dividends and stock splits. Include the effect on stock values.

MyAccountingLab **For a wealth of online resources, including exercises, problems, media, and immediate tutorial help, please visit http://www.myaccountinglab.com.**

## > Quick Check Answers

**1.** b **2.** d **3.** c **4.** c **5.** d **6.** c **7.** c **8.** b **9.** d **10.** c

# 14 The Statement of Cash Flows

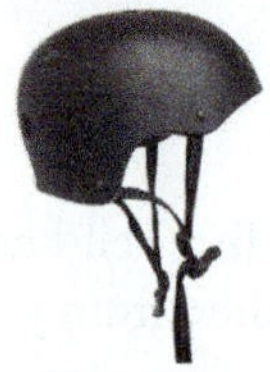

## Why Doesn't the Business Have Any Cash?

David National reviewed his company's income statement with a confused look on his face. The statement reported a net profit of $20,000 for the past quarter. David knew that sales had been increasing in his small sporting equipment retail shop, and he expected this trend to continue through the end of the year. But David didn't understand why the income statement showed a profit. The company's payroll clerk had called him earlier in the day and told him that there wasn't enough cash in the bank to pay the company's monthly salaries.

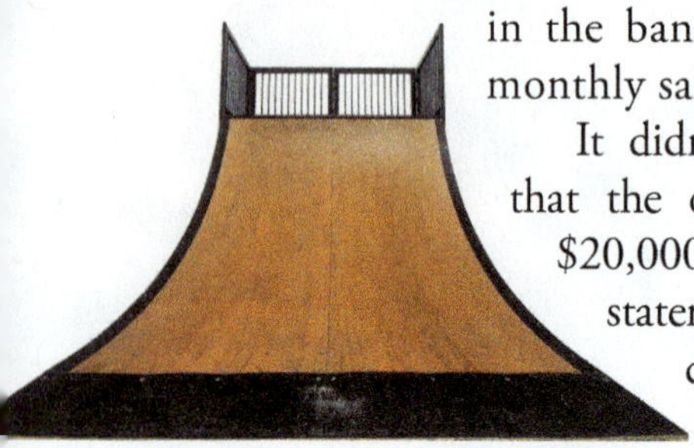

It didn't make sense to David that the company could report a $20,000 profit on the income statement but not have enough cash to pay the payroll. He figured that the newly hired accountant, Mark Maloney, must have made a mistake.

David picked up the phone to call Mark. He had several questions to ask him. Why didn't the company have any cash in the bank? How was the company using its cash? How could the company report a $20,000 profit but not have that much cash in the bank? Where did the cash received from customers go?

After speaking with his accountant, David learned that the profit reported on the income statement didn't represent cash and that it was important that he review the company's statement of cash flows. The statement of cash flows, Mark told him, reports the cash receipts and cash payments of the business. It shows the sources and uses of cash and helps answer the question "Where did the cash go?"

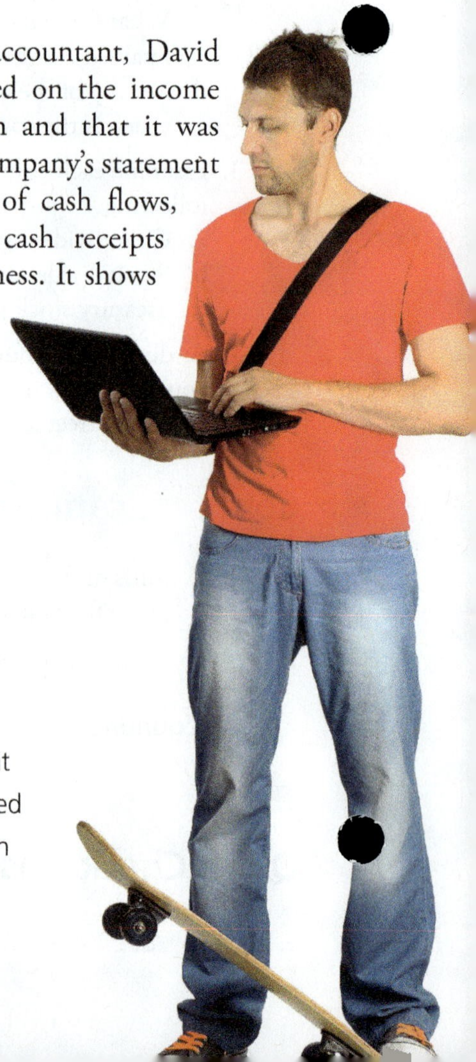

**Why Is Cash So Important?**

You can probably answer that question from your own experience. It takes cash to pay bills and to generate future income for a business. Businesses, such as Target Corporation, a retail corporation that sells everything from sporting equipment to food, closely monitor cash. Target is interested in where its cash came from (receipts) and how its cash is spent (payments). One way for Target to monitor its cash receipts and payments is by preparing a statement of cash flows. For example, on Target's 2013 statement of cash flows, the corporation reported that it paid $3.5 billion purchasing property and equipment and that it received $86 million cash receipts from disposing of property and equipment. It also reported that from 2012 to 2013 the corporation had a decrease in cash of $89 million, even though net income was $1.97 billion. In this chapter, you learn what a statement of cash flows is and why it is useful to a business. In addition, you learn how to prepare the statement and understand why companies and investors carefully monitor the statement of cash flows.

# Chapter 14 Learning Objectives

1 Identify the purposes of the statement of cash flows and distinguish among operating, investing, and financing cash flows

2 Prepare the statement of cash flows by the indirect method

3 Use free cash flow to evaluate business performance

4 Prepare the statement of cash flows by the direct method (Appendix 14A)

5 Prepare the statement of cash flows by the indirect method using a spreadsheet (Appendix 14B)

## WHAT IS THE STATEMENT OF CASH FLOWS?

**Learning Objective 1**
Identify the purposes of the statement of cash flows and distinguish among operating, investing, and financing cash flows

Up to this point, you have learned about three financial statements—the income statement, the statement of retained earnings, and the balance sheet. Each of these financial statements reports specific items about a company. The income statement reports net income or net loss for the time period. The statement of retained earnings reports the changes in retained earnings during the time period, and the balance sheet reports a company's financial position. None of these statements reports specifically on the changes in cash.

When a comparative balance sheet for two periods is presented, it shows whether cash increased or decreased. But the balance sheet does not show *why* cash increased or decreased. We need the statement of cash flows for that. The **statement of cash flows** reports on a business's cash receipts and cash payments for a specific period. This statement does the following:

**Statement of Cash Flows**
Reports on a business's cash receipts and cash payments for a specific period.

**Cash Flows**
Cash receipts and cash payments of a business.

- Reports on the **cash flows** of a business—where cash came from (receipts) and how cash was spent (payments).
- Reports why cash increased or decreased during the period.
- Covers a span of time and is dated the same as the income statement—"Year Ended December 31, 2016," for example.

### Purpose of the Statement of Cash Flows

The statement of cash flows explains why net income as reported on the income statement does not equal the change in the cash balance. In essence, the statement of cash flows is the link between the accrual-based income statement and the cash reported on the balance sheet.

How do people use cash flow information? The statement of cash flows helps do the following:

- **Predict future cash flows.** Past cash receipts and payments help predict future cash flows.
- **Evaluate management.** Wise investment decisions help the business prosper, while unwise decisions cause the business to have problems. Investors and creditors use cash flow information to evaluate managers' decisions.
- **Predict ability to pay debts and dividends.** Lenders want to know whether they will collect on their loans. Stockholders want dividends on their investments. The statement of cash flows helps make these predictions.

## Classification of Cash Flows

There are three basic types of cash flow activities, and the statement of cash flows has a section for each:

- Operating activities
- Investing activities
- Financing activities

Each section reports cash inflows (cash receipts coming into the company) and cash outflows (cash going out of the company) based on these three divisions.

### Operating Activities

**Operating Activities**
Activities that create revenue or expense in the entity's business; a section of the statement of cash flows.

Operating activities is the first section on the statement of cash flows and is often the most important category. The **operating activities** section reports on activities that create revenue or expense in the entity's business. It reflects the day-to-day operations of the business such as cash receipts (cash inflows) from customers for the sales of merchandise inventory and services and the cash outflows for purchases of merchandise inventory or payment of operating expenses. The operating activities section also includes cash receipts (cash inflows) for interest and dividend income and cash payments (cash outflows) for interest expense and income tax expense.

### Investing Activities

**Investing Activities**
Activities that increase or decrease long-term assets; a section of the statement of cash flows.

**Investing activities** is the second category listed on the statement of cash flows. This section reports cash receipts and cash payments that increase or decrease long-term assets such as property, plant, equipment, notes receivable, and investments. It includes the cash inflow from selling and the cash outflow for the purchase of these long-term assets. In addition, it includes the loaning (cash outflow) and collecting (cash inflow) of long-term notes receivable.

### Financing Activities

**Financing Activities**
Activities that increase or decrease long-term liabilities and equity; a section of the statement of cash flows.

The last category on the statement of cash flows is **financing activities**. Financing activities include cash inflows and outflows involved in long-term liabilities and equity. This includes issuing stock, paying dividends, and buying and selling treasury stock. It also includes borrowing money and paying off long-term liabilities such as notes payable, bonds payable, and mortgages payable.

Each section of the statement of cash flows affects a different part of the balance sheet. The operating activities section reports on how cash flows affect the current accounts—current assets and current liabilities. Investing activities affect the long-term assets. And the financing activities affect long-term liabilities and equity. Exhibit 14-1 shows the relationship between operating, investing, and financing cash flows and the various parts of the balance sheet.

**Exhibit 14-1** | **Operating, Investing, and Financing Cash Flows and the Balance Sheet Accounts**

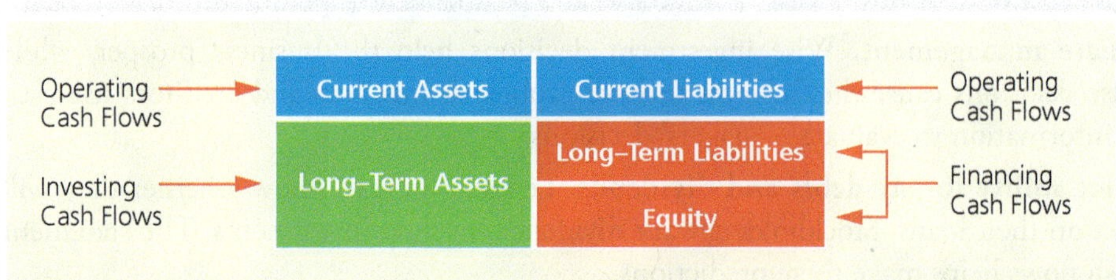

## Non-cash Investing and Financing Activities

The three sections of the statement of cash flows report only activities that involve cash. Companies do make investments that do not require cash. They also obtain financing other than cash. Such transactions are called **non-cash investing and financing activities**. Examples of these activities include the purchase of equipment financed by a long-term note payable or the contribution of equipment by a stockholder in exchange for common stock. These activities are not included in the statement of cash flows. Instead, they appear either as a separate schedule at the bottom of the statement or in the notes to the financial statements.

Exhibit 14-2 summarizes the different sections on the statement of cash flows.

**Non-cash Investing and Financing Activities**
Investing and financing activities that do not involve cash.

**Exhibit 14-2 | Sections of the Statement of Cash Flows**

| | |
|---|---|
| **Operating Activities** | Cash Inflows:<br>• From customers for the sales of merchandise inventory and services<br>• For interest and dividend income<br>Cash Outflows:<br>• For the purchase of merchandise inventory and payment of operating expenses<br>• For interest expense and income tax expense |
| **Investing Activities** | Cash Inflows:<br>• From the sale of property, plant, equipment, and investments<br>• From the collection of long-term notes receivable<br>Cash Outflows:<br>• To purchase property, plant, equipment, and investments<br>• For loans made to borrowers |
| **Financing Activities** | Cash Inflows:<br>• From issuance of stock and selling treasury stock<br>• From receipt of borrowing money<br>Cash Outflows:<br>• For payment of dividends and buying treasury stock<br>• For repayments of loans |
| **Non-cash Investing and Financing Activities** | A separate schedule that includes investing and financing activities that *do not* include cash |

IFRS

Under IFRS, interest and dividend income may be reported either as an operating activity or as an investing activity. Interest and dividends paid may be reported either as an operating activity or as a financing activity.

*The statement of cash flows reports only activities that involve either the receipt of cash or the payment of cash. If a transaction does not involve cash, it will not be included in the operating, investing, or financing sections of the statement of cash flows.*

**Indirect Method**
A format of the operating activities section of the statement of cash flows; starts with net income and reconciles to net cash provided by operating activities.

**Direct Method**
A format of the operating activities section of the statement of cash flows; lists the operating cash receipts and cash payments.

IFRS

IFRS permits the use of either the direct or indirect method.

## Two Formats for Operating Activities

There are two ways to format the operating activities section of the statement of cash flows:

- The **indirect method** starts with net income and adjusts it to net cash provided by operating activities.
- The **direct method** restates the income statement in terms of cash. The direct method shows all the cash receipts and all the cash payments from operating activities.

The indirect and direct methods use different computations but produce the same amount of net cash flow from operating activities. Both methods present investing activities and financing activities in exactly the same format. Only the *operating activities* section is presented differently between the two methods.

We begin with the indirect method because most companies use it. To focus on the direct method, review Appendix 14A, located at the end of this chapter.

### Try It!

Identify each item as operating (O), investing (I), financing (F), or non-cash (N).

1. Cash receipt from the sale of equipment
2. Cash payment for salaries
3. Cash receipt from the collection of long-term notes receivable
4. Purchase of equipment in exchange for notes payable
5. Cash receipt from the issuance of common stock

**Check your answers online in MyAccountingLab or at http://www.pearsonhighered.com/Horngren.**

For more practice, see Short Exercises S14-1 and S14-2. MyAccountingLab

## HOW IS THE STATEMENT OF CASH FLOWS PREPARED USING THE INDIRECT METHOD?

**Learning Objective 2**
Prepare the statement of cash flows by the indirect method

To prepare the statement of cash flows, you need the income statement for the current year, as well as the balance sheets from the current and prior year. In addition, you need to review the transactions for some additional information. For illustrative purposes, we will use ShopMart, Inc., a fictitious retail store that sells electronics, home furnishings, home supplies, and more. ShopMart's comparative balance sheet is shown in Exhibit 14-3, and

**Exhibit 14-3 | Comparative Balance Sheet**

**SHOPMART, INC.**
Comparative Balance Sheet
December 31, 2016 and 2015

| | 2016 | 2015 | Increase (Decrease) |
|---|---|---|---|
| **Assets** | | | |
| Current Assets: | | | |
| Cash | $ 22,000 | $ 42,000 | $ (20,000) |
| Accounts Receivable | 90,000 | 73,000 | 17,000 |
| Merchandise Inventory | 143,000 | 145,000 | (2,000) |
| Long-term Assets: | | | |
| Plants Assets | 507,000 | 252,000 | 255,000 |
| Accumulated Depreciation—Plant Assets | (47,000) | (42,000) | (5,000) |
| Total Assets | **$ 715,000** | **$ 470,000** | **$ 245,000** |
| **Liabilities** | | | |
| Current Liabilities: | | | |
| Accounts Payable | $ 90,000 | $ 50,000 | $ 40,000 |
| Accrued Liabilities | 5,000 | 10,000 | (5,000) |
| Long-term Liabilities: | | | |
| Notes Payable | 160,000 | 80,000 | 80,000 |
| Total Liabilities | 255,000 | 140,000 | 115,000 |
| **Stockholders' Equity** | | | |
| Common Stock, no par | 370,000 | 250,000 | 120,000 |
| Retained Earnings | 110,000 | 80,000 | 30,000 |
| Treasury Stock | (20,000) | 0 | (20,000) |
| Total Stockholders' Equity | 460,000 | 330,000 | 130,000 |
| Total Liabilities and Stockholders' Equity | **$ 715,000** | **$ 470,000** | **$ 245,000** |

its income statement is shown in Exhibit 14-4 (on the next page). Additional information provided by ShopMart includes the following:

- Purchased $310,000 in plant assets by paying cash.
- Sold plant assets with a cost of $55,000 and accumulated depreciation of $15,000, yielding a gain of $10,000.
- Received $90,000 cash from issuance of notes payable.
- Paid $10,000 cash to retire notes payable.
- Received $120,000 cash from issuing shares of common stock.
- Paid $20,000 cash for purchase of shares of treasury stock.

**Exhibit 14-4** | **Income Statement**

**SHOPMART, INC.**
Income Statement
Year Ended December 31, 2016

| | | |
|---|---|---|
| Sales Revenue | | $ 286,000 |
| Cost of Goods Sold | | 156,000 |
| Gross Profit | | 130,000 |
| Operating Expenses: | | |
| Salaries and Wages Expense | $ 56,000 | |
| Depreciation Expense—Plant Assets | 20,000 | |
| Other Operating Expense | 16,000 | |
| Total Operating Expenses | | 92,000 |
| Operating Income | | 38,000 |
| Other Revenue and (Expenses): | | |
| Interest Revenue | 12,000 | |
| Dividend Revenue | 9,000 | |
| Gain on Disposal of Plant Assets | 10,000 | |
| Interest Expense | (15,000) | |
| Total Other Revenues and (Expenses) | | 16,000 |
| Income Before Income Taxes | | 54,000 |
| Income Tax Expense | | 14,000 |
| Net Income | | **$ 40,000** |

To prepare the statement of cash flows by the indirect method, we follow Steps 1–5:

**Step 1:** Complete the cash flows from operating activities section using net income and adjusting for increases or decreases in current assets (other than cash) and current liabilities. Also adjust for gains or losses from long-term assets and non-cash expenses such as depreciation expense.

**Step 2:** Complete the cash flows from investing activities section by reviewing the long-term assets section of the balance sheet.

**Step 3:** Complete the cash flows from financing activities section by reviewing the long-term liabilities and equity sections of the balance sheet.

**Step 4:** Compute the net increase or decrease in cash during the year. The change in cash is the key reconciling figure for the statement of cash flows and must match the change in cash reported on the comparative balance sheet.

**Step 5:** Prepare a separate schedule reporting any non-cash investing and financing activities.

Let's apply these steps to show the operating activities of ShopMart. Exhibit 14-5 depicts the completed statement of cash flows.

**Exhibit 14-5 | Statement of Cash Flows—Indirect Method**

**SHOPMART, INC.**
Statement of Cash Flows
Year Ended December 31, 2016

| | | | |
|---|---|---|---|
| Cash Flows from Operating Activities: | | | Step 1: Operating Activities |
| Net Income | | $ 40,000 | |
| Adjustments to Reconcile Net Income to Net Cash Provided by Operating Activities: | | | |
| Depreciation Expense—Plant Assets | $ 20,000 | | |
| Gain on Disposal of Plant Assets | (10,000) | | |
| Increase in Accounts Receivable | (17,000) | | |
| Decrease in Merchandise Inventory | 2,000 | | |
| Increase in Accounts Payable | 40,000 | | |
| Decrease in Accrued Liabilities | (5,000) | 30,000 | |
| Net Cash Provided by Operating Activities | | 70,000 | |
| Cash Flows from Investing Activities: | | | Step 2: Investing Activities |
| Cash Payment for Acquisition of Plant Assets | (310,000) | | |
| Cash Receipt from Disposal of Plant Assets | 50,000 | | |
| Net Cash Used for Investing Activities | | (260,000) | |
| Cash Flows from Financing Activities: | | | Step 3: Financing Activities |
| Cash Receipt from Issuance of Notes Payable | 90,000 | | |
| Cash Payment of Notes Payable | (10,000) | | |
| Cash Receipt from Issuance of Common Stock | 120,000 | | |
| Cash Payment for Purchase of Treasury Stock | (20,000) | | |
| Cash Payment of Dividends | (10,000) | | |
| Net Cash Provided by Financing Activities | | 170,000 | |
| Net Increase (Decrease) in Cash | | (20,000) | Step 4: Net Increase (Decrease) in Cash |
| Cash Balance, December 31, 2015 | | 42,000 | |
| Cash Balance, December 31, 2016 | | $ 22,000 | |

## Cash Flows from Operating Activities

When using the indirect method, the statement of cash flows operating activities section begins with net income (or net loss) because revenues and expenses, which affect net income, produce cash receipts and cash payments. Revenues bring in cash receipts, and expenses must be paid. But net income as shown on the income statement is accrual-based, and the cash flows (cash basis net income) do not always equal the accrual basis revenues and expenses. For example, sales *on account* generate revenues that increase net income, but the company has not yet collected cash from those sales. Accrued expenses decrease net income, but the company has not paid cash *if the expenses are accrued.*

To go from net income to cash flow from operating activities, we must make some adjustments to net income on the statement of cash flows. These additions and subtractions follow net income and are labeled *Adjustments to Reconcile Net Income to Net Cash Provided by Operating Activities.*

## Depreciation, Depletion, and Amortization Expenses

These adjustments include adding back non-cash expenses such as depreciation, depletion, and amortization expenses. These expenses are added back to net income to reconcile net income to net cash flow from operating activities. Let's see why this occurs. Depreciation is recorded as follows:

| A↓ | = | L | + | E↓ |
|---|---|---|---|---|
| Accumulated Depreciation↑ | | | | Depreciation Expense↑ |

| Date | Accounts and Explanation | Debit | Credit |
|---|---|---|---|
| | Depreciation Expense—Plant Assets | 20,000 | |
| | Accumulated Depreciation—Plant Assets | | 20,000 |

You can see that depreciation does not affect cash as there is no Cash account in the journal entry. Depreciation is a non-cash expense. The cash outflow related to depreciation occurred when the asset was purchased, not as it is depreciated. However, depreciation, like all the other expenses, decreases net income. Therefore, to go from net income to cash flows, we must remove depreciation by adding it back to net income.

| SHOPMART, INC.<br>Statement of Cash Flows (Partial)<br>Year Ended December 31, 2016 | | |
|---|---|---|
| Cash Flows from Operating Activities: | | |
| Net Income | | $ 40,000 |
| Adjustments to Reconcile Net Income to Net Cash Provided by Operating Activities: | | |
| Depreciation Expense—Plant Assets | $ 20,000 | |

Suppose you had only two transactions during the period:

- Cash sale of $60,000
- Depreciation expense of $20,000

Accrual basis net income is $40,000 ($60,000 – $20,000), but cash flow from operations is $60,000. To reconcile from net income, depreciation of $20,000 must be added to net income, $40,000, to determine net cash flow from operations, $60,000. We would also add back any depletion and amortization expenses because they are non-cash expenses, similar to depreciation.

## Gains and Losses on the Disposal of Long-Term Assets

Disposals of long-term assets such as land and buildings are investing activities, and these disposals usually create a gain or a loss. The gain or loss is included in net income, which is already in the operating activities section of the statement of cash flows. The gain or loss must be removed from net income on the statement of cash flows so the total cash receipts from the sale of the asset can be shown in the investing section.

Exhibit 14-4, ShopMart's income statement, includes a gain on disposal of plant assets. During 2016, ShopMart sold equipment, and there was a gain of $10,000 on the sale. The gain was included in the calculation of net income on the income statement, so the gain must be removed from operating cash flows. The gain increased net income, so it is subtracted in the operating activities section.

| SHOPMART, INC.<br>Statement of Cash Flows (Partial)<br>Year Ended December 31, 2016 | | |
|---|---|---|
| Cash Flows from Operating Activities: | | |
| Net Income | | $ 40,000 |
| Adjustments to Reconcile Net Income to Net Cash Provided by Operating Activities: | | |
| Depreciation Expense—Plant Assets | $ 20,000 | |
| Gain on Disposal of Plant Assets | (10,000) | |

**On the other hand, a loss on the disposal of plant assets would decrease net income on the income statement, so the amount of the loss would be reversed to determine the net cash provided by operating activities on the statement of cash flows.** For example, a $5,000 loss on disposal of plant assets would be a $5,000 addition to net income on the statement of cash flows to determine net cash provided by operating activities.

What if there is a loss on disposal of plant assets?

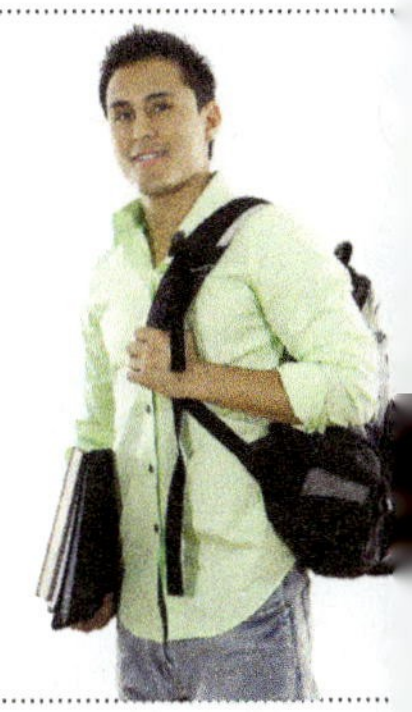

### Changes in Current Assets and Current Liabilities

Most current assets and current liabilities result from operating activities. For example:

- Accounts receivable result from sales.
- Merchandise inventory relates to cost of goods sold, and so on.

Changes in the current asset and current liability accounts create adjustments to net income on the statement of cash flows, as follows:

- **An increase in a current asset other than cash causes a decrease in cash.** If Accounts Receivable, Merchandise Inventory, or Prepaid Expenses increases, then cash decreases. Therefore, we subtract the increase in the current asset from net income to get net cash flow from operating activities. For example, in Exhibit 14-3, ShopMart's Accounts Receivable increased by $17,000. This increase in the current asset shows that there were more sales on account than cash collections from customers and is reported as a decrease in cash on the statement of cash flows.
- **A decrease in a current asset other than cash causes an increase in cash.** ShopMart's Merchandise Inventory decreased by $2,000. What caused the decrease? ShopMart must have sold some merchandise inventory and collected cash. Therefore, we add the decrease in Merchandise Inventory of $2,000 in the statement of cash flows.
- **An increase in a current liability causes an increase in cash.** ShopMart's Accounts Payable increased by $40,000. This means that cash was not spent at the time the expense was incurred, but rather it will be paid at a later time—resulting in a liability. Accordingly, even though net income was reduced by the expense, cash was not reduced. However, cash will be reduced later when ShopMart pays off its liability. Therefore, an increase in a current liability is added to net income in the statement of cash flows.

- **A decrease in a current liability causes a decrease in cash.** The payment of a current liability decreases cash. Therefore, we subtract decreases in current liabilities from net income to get net cash flow from operating activities. ShopMart's Accrued Liabilities decreased by $5,000. That change shows up as a $5,000 decrease in cash flows.

| SHOPMART, INC.<br>Statement of Cash Flows (Partial)<br>Year Ended December 31, 2016 | | |
|---|---|---|
| Cash Flows from Operating Activities: | | |
| Net Income | | $ 40,000 |
| Adjustments to Reconcile Net Income to Net Cash Provided by Operating Activities: | | |
| Depreciation Expense—Plant Assets | $ 20,000 | |
| Gain on Disposal of Plant Assets | (10,000) | |
| Increase in Accounts Receivable | (17,000) | |
| Decrease in Merchandise Inventory | 2,000 | |
| Increase in Accounts Payable | 40,000 | |
| Decrease in Accrued Liabilities | (5,000) | 30,000 |

## DECISIONS

### What can be done to create a positive cash flow?

Meggie Mohamed, CEO, knew that the bank would carefully review her company's most recent statement of cash flows before determining if it would approve the loan needed for expansion. The bank loan officer had told her that it is important that the business show strong operating cash flows. Meggie knows that her company's operating cash flow for this past quarter will most likely be negative. Although the company recorded significant revenue, most of the revenue was recorded as receivables. Meggie expects that the cash will come in soon, but not in time to report a positive operating cash flow. What should Meggie do? What would you do?

### Solution

Meggie could explain to the bank officer that her company is expecting to collect a significant amount of cash in the near future on outstanding receivables. She could provide detailed collection information including the estimated time frame of collection and the amount expected. Meggie also has another option. She could look into selling the receivables to another business, often called a factor. By selling the receivables, the company will be able to decrease its accounts receivable balance, increase its cash balance, and report a positive change in operating cash flows.

### Evaluating Cash Flows from Operating Activities

During 2016, ShopMart's operating activities provided a net cash inflow of $70,000 ($40,000 + $30,000), so the amount is labeled Net Cash *Provided by* Operating Activities. If this amount were a net cash outflow, ShopMart would report Net Cash *Used for* Operating Activities.

| SHOPMART, INC.<br>Statement of Cash Flows (Partial)<br>Year Ended December 31, 2016 | | |
|---|---|---|
| Cash Flows from Operating Activities: | | |
| Net Income | | $ 40,000 |
| Adjustments to Reconcile Net Income to Net Cash Provided by Operating Activities: | | |
| Depreciation Expense—Plant Assets | $ 20,000 | |
| Gain on Disposal of Plant Assets | (10,000) | |
| Increase in Accounts Receivable | (17,000) | |
| Decrease in Merchandise Inventory | 2,000 | |
| Increase in Accounts Payable | 40,000 | |
| Decrease in Accrued Liabilities | (5,000) | 30,000 |
| Net Cash Provided by Operating Activities | | 70,000 |

The operating activities section (indirect method) always starts with accrual basis net income. Adjustments are then made to determine the cash basis net income. Exhibit 14-6 summarizes the adjustments made to reconcile net income to net cash provided by operating activities.

**Exhibit 14-6 | Adjustments Made to Reconcile Net Income to Net Cash Provided by Operating Activities**

| Item | Adjustment on Statement of Cash Flows |
|---|---|
| Depreciation, Depletion, and Amortization Expense | + |
| Gains on Disposal of Long-term Assets | – |
| Losses on Disposal of Long-term Assets | + |
| Increases in Current Assets other than Cash | – |
| Decreases in Current Assets other than Cash | + |
| Increases in Current Liabilities | + |
| Decreases in Current Liabilities | – |

## Cash Flows from Investing Activities

Investing activities affect long-term assets, such as Plant Assets, Investments, and Notes Receivable. These are shown on ShopMart's balance sheet (Exhibit 14-3). Now, let's see how to compute the investing cash flows.

When computing investing cash flows, it is helpful to evaluate the T-accounts for each long-term asset. The T-account will show if there was an acquisition or disposal that happened during the year. Let's look at the Plant Assets and Accumulated Depreciation accounts for ShopMart.

**Plant Assets**

| | | | |
|---|---|---|---|
| 12/31/2015 | 252,000 | | |
| Acquisitions | 310,000 | 55,000 | Disposals |
| 12/31/2016 | 507,000 | | |

**Accumulated Depreciation—Plant Assets**

| | | | |
|---|---|---|---|
| | | 42,000 | 12/31/2015 |
| Disposals | 15,000 | 20,000 | Depr. Exp. |
| | | 47,000 | 12/31/2016 |

Depreciation Expense is from the income statement.

The beginning and ending balances for each account are taken directly from the comparative balance sheet. Depreciation expense has been included in the Accumulated Depreciation account, and this was taken from the income statement. The acquisition and disposal information came from the additional information provided when we introduced the example:

- Purchased $310,000 in plant assets by paying cash.
- Sold plant assets with a cost of $55,000 and accumulated depreciation of $15,000, yielding a gain of $10,000.

We now know that ShopMart paid $310,000 cash to purchase plant assets. This item is listed first in the investing activities section and shown as an outflow of cash, as indicated by the parentheses.

Next we need to determine the amount of cash received for the disposal of plant assets. Using the information provided, we can recreate the journal entry for the disposal and solve for the missing cash amount.

| A↑ | | L | + | E↑ |
|---|---|---|---|---|
| Cash↑<br>Accumulated Depreciation↓<br>Plant Assets↓ | = | | | Gain on Disposal↑ |

| Date | Accounts and Explanation | Debit | Credit |
|---|---|---|---|
| | Cash | ? | |
| | Accumulated Depreciation—Plant Assets | 15,000 | |
| | Gain on Disposal of Plant Assets | | 10,000 |
| | Plant Assets | | 55,000 |

We compute the cash receipt from the disposal as follows:

$$\begin{aligned}\text{Cash received} &= \text{Cost} - \text{Accumulated Depreciation} + \text{Gain} - \text{Loss}\\ &= \$55,000 - \$15,000 + \$10,000\\ &= \$50,000\end{aligned}$$

The cash receipt from the sale of plant assets of $50,000 is shown next in the investing activities section. As there are no other changes to long-term assets, the net cash from investing activities is determined. Notice that this is a net cash outflow, as indicated by the parentheses, and is reported as Net Cash *Used for* Investing Activities.

*In this partial statement, we are showing only the investing activities section of the statement of cash flows. Remember that the investing activities section is reported after the operating activities section.*

| SHOPMART, INC.<br>Statement of Cash Flows (Partial)<br>Year Ended December 31, 2016 | | |
|---|---|---|
| Cash Flows from Investing Activities: | | |
| Cash Payment for Acquisition of Plant Assets | (310,000) | |
| Cash Receipt from Disposal of Plant Assets | 50,000 | |
| Net Cash Used for Investing Activities | | (260,000) |

## Cash Flows from Financing Activities

Financing activities affect the long-term liability and equity accounts, such as Long-Term Notes Payable, Bonds Payable, Common Stock, and Retained Earnings. To determine the cash flows from financing activities, we need to review each of these account types.

### Long-Term Liabilities

The T-account for ShopMart's Notes Payable is shown below. Additional information concerning notes payable is also provided by the company as follows:

- Received $90,000 cash from issuance of notes payable.
- Paid $10,000 cash to retire notes payable.

| Notes Payable | | | |
|---|---|---|---|
| | | 80,000 | 12/31/2015 |
| Payment | 10,000 | 90,000 | Issuance |
| | | 160,000 | 12/31/2016 |

The beginning and ending balances of Notes Payable are taken from the comparative balance sheet. For ShopMart, a new issuance of notes payable is known to be a $90,000 cash receipt and is shown by the following journal entry:

| Date | Accounts and Explanation | Debit | Credit |
|---|---|---|---|
| | Cash | 90,000 | |
| | Notes Payable | | 90,000 |

A↑ Cash↑ } = { L↑ Notes Payable↑ + E

In addition, ShopMart paid $10,000 cash to retire notes payable.

| Date | Accounts and Explanation | Debit | Credit |
|---|---|---|---|
| | Notes Payable | 10,000 | |
| | Cash | | 10,000 |

A↓ Cash↓ } = { L↓ Notes Payable↓ + E

The cash inflow and cash outflow associated with these notes payable are listed first in the cash flows from financing activities section.

| SHOPMART, INC.<br>Statement of Cash Flows (Partial)<br>Year Ended December 31, 2016 | |
|---|---|
| Cash Flows from Financing Activities: | |
| Cash Receipt from Issuance of Notes Payable | 90,000 |
| Cash Payment of Notes Payable | (10,000) |

## ETHICS

### Should the notes payable be reclassified?

Michael Reinstein had just left the office of his supervisor, Scott Medley. The supervisor had mentioned that Michael should reclassify a cash receipt from issuance of long-term notes payable as a short-term notes payable. Scott had shared with Michael that the chairman of the Board of Directors was placing intense pressure on him to report a positive cash flow from operating activities. Michael knew that if the company reclassified the notes payable, the business would no longer report the receipt in the financing activities section of the statement of cash flows. Instead, it would be shown as an increase in current liabilities resulting in a positive cash flow from operating activities. What should Michael do?

### Solution

Michael should not reclassify the notes payable. By reclassifying the note, the company is misleading investors and reporting a positive operating cash flow when it does not have one. This misclassification is a violation of GAAP. If a notes payable is long-term, it should be reported in the financing activities section of the statement of cash flows.

## Common Stock and Treasury Stock

Cash flows for financing activities are also determined by analyzing the stock accounts. For example, the amount of new issuances of stock is determined by analyzing the stock accounts and reviewing the additional information provided:

- Received $120,000 cash from issuing shares of common stock.
- Paid $20,000 cash for purchase of shares of treasury stock.

ShopMart's stock T-accounts are as follows:

**Common Stock**

| | | | |
|---|---|---|---|
| | | 250,000 | 12/31/2015 |
| Retirement | 0 | 120,000 | Issuance |
| | | 370,000 | 12/31/2016 |

**Treasury Stock**

| | | | |
|---|---|---|---|
| 12/31/2015 | 0 | | |
| Purchase | 20,000 | 0 | Disposal |
| 12/31/2016 | 20,000 | | |

The common stock account shows a new stock issuance of $120,000 and would be recorded by the following journal entry:

| Date | Accounts and Explanation | Debit | Credit |
|---|---|---|---|
| | Cash | 120,000 | |
| | Common Stock | | 120,000 |

| A↑ | | L | + | E↑ |
|---|---|---|---|---|
| Cash↑ | = | | | Common Stock↑ |

This is shown as $120,000 cash inflow in the financing activities section of the statement.

Treasury stock also changed on ShopMart's balance sheet. The T-account is showing an acquisition of treasury stock that would be recorded as follows:

| Date | Accounts and Explanation | Debit | Credit |
|---|---|---|---|
| | Treasury Stock | 20,000 | |
| | Cash | | 20,000 |

| A↓ | | L | + | E↓ |
|---|---|---|---|---|
| Cash↓ | = | | | Treasury Stock↑ |

The $20,000 is shown as a cash outflow in the financing section of the statement of cash flows for the purchase of treasury stock.

**SHOPMART, INC.**
Statement of Cash Flows (Partial)
Year Ended December 31, 2016

| | |
|---|---|
| Cash Flows from Financing Activities: | |
| Cash Receipt from Issuance of Notes Payable | 90,000 |
| Cash Payment of Notes Payable | (10,000) |
| Cash Receipt from Issuance of Common Stock | 120,000 |
| Cash Payment for Purchase of Treasury Stock | (20,000) |

## Computing Dividend Payments

The amount of dividend payments can be computed by analyzing the Retained Earnings account. First, we input the balances from the balance sheet:

**Retained Earnings**

| | | | |
|---|---|---|---|
| | | 80,000 | 12/31/2015 |
| Net Loss | ? | ? | Net Income |
| Dividends | ? | | |
| | | 110,000 | 12/31/2016 |

Retained Earnings increases when companies earn net income. Retained Earnings decreases when companies have a net loss and when they declare dividends. We know that ShopMart earned net income of $40,000 from the income statement in Exhibit 14-4.

**Retained Earnings**

| | | | |
|---|---|---|---|
| | | 80,000 | 12/31/2015 |
| Net Loss | ? | 40,000 | Net Income |
| Dividends | ? | | |
| | | 110,000 | 12/31/2016 |

Net Income is from the income statement.

ShopMart can't have both net income and net loss for the same period; therefore, the missing value must be the amount of dividends ShopMart declared. Solving for the dividends follows:

Ending Retained Earnings = Beginning Retained Earnings + Net income − Net loss − Dividends
$110,000 = $80,000 + $40,000 − $0 − Dividends
Dividends = $80,000 + $40,000 − $0 − $110,000
Dividends = $10,000

So our final Retained Earnings T-account shows the following:

**Retained Earnings**

| | | | |
|---|---|---|---|
| | | 80,000 | 12/31/2015 |
| | | 40,000 | Net Income |
| Dividends | 10,000 | | |
| | | 110,000 | 12/31/2016 |

A stock dividend has *no* effect on Cash and is *not* reported in the financing activities section of the statement of cash flows. ShopMart had no stock dividends, only cash dividends, which will be shown as an outflow in the financing activities section of the statement of cash flows.

**SHOPMART, INC.**
**Statement of Cash Flows (Partial)**
**Year Ended December 31, 2016**

| | | |
|---|---|---|
| Cash Flows from Financing Activities: | | |
| Cash Receipt from Issuance of Notes Payable | $ 90,000 | |
| Cash Payment of Notes Payable | (10,000) | |
| Cash Receipt from Issuance of Common Stock | 120,000 | |
| Cash Payment for Purchase of Treasury Stock | (20,000) | |
| Cash Payment of Dividends | (10,000) | |
| Net Cash Provided by Financing Activities | | 170,000 |

## Net Change in Cash and Cash Balances

To complete the statement of cash flows, the net change in cash and its effect on the beginning cash balance must be shown. This represents the total change in cash for the period and reconciles the statement of cash flows. First, the net increase or decrease in cash is computed by combining the cash provided by or used for operating, investing, and financing activities. In the case of ShopMart, there is a net decrease in the cash balance of $20,000 for the year and is calculated as follows:

Net Increase (Decrease) in Cash = Net Cash Provided by Operating Activities − Net Cash Used for Investing Activities + Net Cash Provided by Financing Activities
= $70,000 − $260,000 + $170,000
= $(20,000)

Next, the beginning cash from December 31, 2015, is listed at $42,000, as shown on the comparative balance sheet. The net decrease of $20,000 is subtracted from beginning cash of $42,000, which equals the ending cash balance on December 31, 2016, of $22,000. This is the key to the statement of cash flows—it explains why the cash balance for ShopMart decreased by $20,000, even though the company reported net income for the year.

**SHOPMART, INC.**
Statement of Cash Flows (Partial)
Year Ended December 31, 2016

| | |
|---|---|
| Net Cash Provided by Operating Activities | $ 70,000 |
| Net Cash Used for Investing Activities | (260,000) |
| Net Cash Provided by Financing Activities | 170,000 |
| Net Increase (Decrease) in Cash | (20,000) |
| Cash Balance, December 31, 2015 | 42,000 |
| Cash Balance, December 31, 2016 | **$ 22,000** |

Before moving on, take a moment to review the completed Statement of Cash Flows shown earlier in Exhibit 14-5.

## Non-cash Investing and Financing Activities

The last step in preparing the statement of cash flows is to prepare the non-cash investing and financing activities section. This section appears as a separate schedule of the statement of cash flows or in the notes to the financial statements. Our ShopMart example did not include transactions of this type because the company did not have any non-cash transactions during the year. So, to illustrate them, let's consider three non-cash transactions for another fictitious company, The Outdoors, Inc. How would they be reported? First, we gather the non-cash activities for the company:

1. Acquired $300,000 building by issuing common stock.
2. Acquired $70,000 land by issuing notes payable.
3. Retired $100,000 notes payable by issuing common stock.

Now, we consider each transaction individually.

1. The Outdoors issued common stock of $300,000 to acquire a building. The journal entry to record the purchase would be as follows:

| A↑ | = | L | + | E↑ |
|---|---|---|---|---|
| Building↑ | | | | Common Stock↑ |

| Date | Accounts and Explanation | Debit | Credit |
|---|---|---|---|
| | Building | 300,000 | |
| | Common Stock | | 300,000 |

This transaction would not be reported on the statement of cash flows because no cash was paid or received. But the building and the common stock are important. The purchase of the building is an investing activity. The issuance of common stock is a financing activity. Taken together, this transaction is a *non-cash investing and financing activity.*

2. The second transaction listed indicates that The Outdoors acquired $70,000 of land by issuing a note. The journal entry to record the purchase would be as follows:

| A↑ | = | L↑ | + | E |
|---|---|---|---|---|
| Land↑ | | Notes Payable↑ | | |

| Date | Accounts and Explanation | Debit | Credit |
|---|---|---|---|
| | Land | 70,000 | |
| | Notes Payable | | 70,000 |

This transaction would not be reported on the statement of cash flows because no cash was paid or received. But the land and the notes payable are important. The purchase of the land is an investing activity. The issuance of the note is a financing activity. Taken together, this transaction is a *non-cash investing and financing activity.*

3. The third transaction listed indicates that The Outdoors exchanged $100,000 of debt by issuing common stock. The journal entry to record the transaction would be as follows:

| A | = | L↓ | + | E↑ |
|---|---|---|---|---|
| | | Notes Payable↓ | | Common Stock↑ |

| Date | Accounts and Explanation | Debit | Credit |
|---|---|---|---|
| | Notes Payable | 100,000 | |
| | Common Stock | | 100,000 |

This transaction would not be reported on the statement of cash flows because no cash was paid or received. But the notes payable and the stock issuance are important. The payment on the note and the issuance of the common stock are both financing activities. Taken together, this transaction, even though it is two financing transactions, is reported in the *non-cash investing and financing activities.*

*Non-cash investing and financing activities* are reported in a separate part of the statement of cash flows. Exhibit 14-7 illustrates non-cash investing and financing activities for The Outdoors. This information is either reported as a separate schedule following the statement of cash flows or can be disclosed in a note.

**Exhibit 14-7 | Non-cash Investing and Financing Activities**

| THE OUTDOORS, INC.<br>Statement of Cash Flows (Partial)<br>Year Ended December 31, 2016 | |
|---|---|
| Non-cash Investing and Financing Activities: | |
| Acquisition of building by issuing common stock | $ 300,000 |
| Acquisition of land by issuing notes payable | 70,000 |
| Retirement of notes payable by issuing common stock | 100,000 |
| Total Non-cash Investing and Financing Activities | **$ 470,000** |

## Try It!

6. Owl, Inc.'s accountants have assembled the following data for the year ended December 31, 2016:

| | |
|---|---|
| Cash receipt from sale of equipment | $ 20,000 |
| Depreciation expense | 12,000 |
| Cash payment of dividends | 4,000 |
| Cash receipt from issuance of common stock | 12,000 |
| Net income | 30,000 |
| Cash purchase of land | 25,000 |
| Increase in current liabilities | 10,000 |
| Decrease in current assets other than cash | 8,000 |

Prepare Owl's statement of cash flows using the indirect method for the year ended December 31, 2016. Assume beginning and ending Cash are $12,000 and $75,000 respectively.

**Check your answer online in MyAccountingLab or at http://www.pearsonhighered.com/Horngren.**

For more practice, see Short Exercises S14-3 through S14-9. MyAccountingLab

# HOW DO WE USE FREE CASH FLOW TO EVALUATE BUSINESS PERFORMANCE?

**Learning Objective 3**

Use free cash flow to evaluate business performance

Throughout this chapter, we have focused on cash flows from operating, investing, and financing activities. Some investors want to know how much cash a company can "free up" for new opportunities. **Free cash flow** is the amount of cash available from operating activities after paying for planned investments in long-term assets and after paying cash dividends to shareholders. Free cash flow can be computed as follows:

Free cash flow = Net cash provided by operating activities − Cash payments planned for investments in long-term assets − Cash dividends

**Free Cash Flow**

The amount of cash available from operating activities after paying for planned investments in long-term assets and after paying dividends to shareholders. Net cash provided by operating activities − Cash payments planned for investments in long-term assets − Cash dividends.

Many companies use free cash flow to estimate the amount of cash that would be available for unexpected opportunities. Suppose ShopMart expects net cash provided by operations of $200,000. Assume the company plans to spend $160,000 to modernize its retail facilities and pays $15,000 in cash dividends. In this case, ShopMart's free cash flow would be $25,000 ($200,000 – $160,000 – $15,000). If a good investment opportunity comes along, the company should have $25,000 cash available to invest.

## Try It!

7. Kalapono Company expects the following for 2016:
   - Net cash provided by operating activities of $100,000.
   - Net cash provided by financing activities of $10,000.
   - Net cash used for investing activities of $20,000 (no sales of long-term assets).
   - Cash dividends paid to stockholders was $2,000.

How much free cash flow does Kalapono expect for 2016?

**Check your answer online in MyAccountingLab or at http://www.pearsonhighered.com/Horngren.**

For more practice, see Short Exercise S14-10. MyAccountingLab

# APPENDIX 14A: Preparing the Statement of Cash Flows by the Direct Method

## HOW IS THE STATEMENT OF CASH FLOWS PREPARED USING THE DIRECT METHOD?

**Learning Objective 4**
Prepare the statement of cash flows by the direct method

The Financial Accounting Standards Board (FASB) prefers the direct method of reporting cash flows from operating activities. The direct method provides clearer information about the sources and uses of cash than does the indirect method. However, very few non-public companies use the direct method because it takes more computations than the indirect method. Investing and financing cash flows are exactly the same presentation under both direct and indirect methods. Because only the preparation of the operating activities section differs, it is all we discuss in this appendix.

To illustrate how the operating activities section of the statement of cash flows differs for the direct method, we use the ShopMart data we used within the main chapter.

### Cash Flows from Operating Activities

In the indirect method, we start with accrual basis net income and then adjust it to cash basis through a series of adjusting items. When using the direct method, we take each line item of the income statement and convert it from accrual to cash basis. So, in essence, the operating activities section of the direct-method cash flows statement is really just a cash-basis income statement. Now let's apply this information to ShopMart.

#### Cash Collections from Customers

The first item on the income statement is Sales Revenue. Sales Revenue represents the total of all sales, whether for cash or on account. The balance sheet account related to Sales

Revenue is Accounts Receivable. Accounts Receivable went from $73,000 at December 31, 2015, to $90,000 at December 31, 2016, an increase of $17,000. Sales Revenue can be converted to cash receipts from customers as follows:

| | | |
|---|---|---|
| Cash receipts from customers | = | Sales Revenue + Beginning Accounts Receivable − Ending Accounts Receivable |
| | = | $286,000 + $73,000 − $90,000 |
| | = | $269,000 |

The increase in Accounts Receivable represents the net amount of sales on account not collected from customers.

**Accounts Receivable**

| | | |
|---|---|---|
| 12/31/2015 | 73,000 | |
| Increase | 17,000 | |
| 12/31/2016 | 90,000 | |

**Sales Revenue**

| | |
|---|---|
| | 286,000 |

When a company records a credit to Sales Revenue, it either debits Cash or debits Accounts Receivable.

So, the cash ShopMart received from customers is $269,000. This is the first item in the operating activities section of the direct-method statement of cash flows.

**SHOPMART, INC.**
**Statement of Cash Flows (Partial)**
**Year Ended December 31, 2016**

| | |
|---|---|
| Cash Flows from Operating Activities: | |
| Receipts: | |
| Collections from Customers | $ 269,000 |

Had ShopMart had a decrease in Accounts Receivable, the amount of cash collections from customers would be higher than Sales Revenue.

## Cash Receipts of Interest

The income statement reports interest revenue of $12,000. The balance sheet account related to Interest Revenue is Interest Receivable. Because there is no Interest Receivable account on the balance sheet, the interest revenue must have all been received in cash. So, the statement of cash flows shows interest received of $12,000.

**SHOPMART, INC.**
**Statement of Cash Flows (Partial)**
**Year Ended December 31, 2016**

| | |
|---|---|
| Cash Flows from Operating Activities: | |
| Receipts: | |
| Collections from Customers | $ 269,000 |
| Interest Received | 12,000 |

## Cash Receipts of Dividends

The income statement reports dividend revenue of $9,000. The balance sheet account related to Dividend Revenue is Dividends Receivable. As with the interest, there is no Dividends Receivable account on the balance sheet. Therefore, the dividend revenue must have all been received in cash. So, the statement of cash flows shows cash received from dividends of $9,000.

**SHOPMART, INC.**
Statement of Cash Flows (Partial)
Year Ended December 31, 2016

| | | |
|---|---|---|
| Cash Flows from Operating Activities: | | |
| Receipts: | | |
| Collections from Customers | $ 269,000 | |
| Interest Received | 12,000 | |
| Dividends Received on Investments | 9,000 | |
| Total Cash Receipts | | $ 290,000 |

## Payments to Suppliers

Payments to suppliers include all payments for the following:

- Merchandise inventory
- Operating expenses except employee compensation, interest, and income taxes

*Suppliers*, also called vendors, are those entities that provide the business with its merchandise inventory and essential services. The accounts related to supplier payments for merchandise inventory are Cost of Goods Sold, Merchandise Inventory, and Accounts Payable. Cost of Goods Sold on the income statement was $156,000. Merchandise Inventory decreased from $145,000 at December 31, 2015, to $143,000 at December 31, 2016. Accounts Payable increased from $50,000 at December 31, 2015, to $90,000 at December 31, 2016. We can calculate the cash paid for inventory as follows:

Cash paid for merchandise inventory = Cost of Goods Sold − Beginning Merchandise Inventory + Ending Merchandise Inventory + Beginning Accounts Payable − Ending Accounts Payable
= $156,000 − $145,000 + $143,000 + $50,000 − $90,000
= $114,000

When a company records a debit to Merchandise Inventory, it either credits Cash or credits Accounts Payable.

**Merchandise Inventory**

| | | | |
|---|---|---|---|
| 12/31/2015 | 145,000 | | |
| Purchased | 154,000 | 156,000 | Sold |
| 12/31/2016 | 143,000 | | |

**Accounts Payable**

| | | | |
|---|---|---|---|
| | | 50,000 | 12/31/2015 |
| | | 40,000 | Increase |
| | | 90,000 | 12/31/2016 |

The increase in Accounts Payable represents the net amount of Merchandise Inventory that was purchased on account but not yet paid.

**Cost of Goods Sold**

| | | | |
|---|---|---|---|
| Sold | 156,000 | | |

The accounts related to supplier payments for operating expenses are Other Operating Expense and Accrued Liabilities. Other operating expenses on the income statement were \$16,000. Accrued Liabilities decreased from \$10,000 at December 31, 2015, to \$5,000 at December 31, 2016. Cash paid for operating expenses can be calculated as follows:

Cash paid for operating expenses = Other Operating Expense + Beginning Accrued Liabilities − Ending Accrued Liabilities
= \$16,000 + \$10,000 − \$5,000
= \$21,000

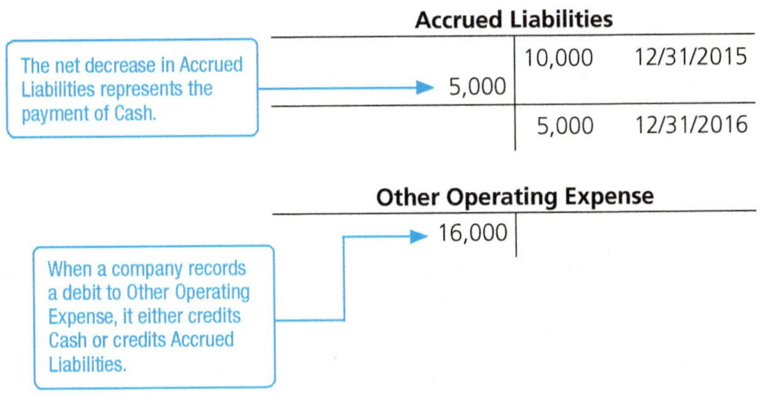


Adding them together, we get total cash paid to suppliers of \$135,000 (\$114,000 + \$21,000).

| SHOPMART, INC.<br>Statement of Cash Flows (Partial)<br>Year Ended December 31, 2016 | | |
|---|---|---|
| Cash Flows from Operating Activities: | | |
| Receipts: | | |
| Collections from Customers | \$ 269,000 | |
| Interest Received | 12,000 | |
| Dividends Received on Investments | 9,000 | |
| Total Cash Receipts | | \$ 290,000 |
| Payments: | | |
| To Suppliers | (135,000) | |

## Payments to Employees

This category includes payments for salaries, wages, and other forms of employee compensation. Accrued amounts are not cash flows because they have not yet been paid. The accounts related to employee payments are Salaries and Wages Expense from the income statement and Salaries and Wages Payable from the balance sheet. Because there is not a Salaries and Wages Payable account on the balance sheet, the Salaries and Wages Expense account must represent all amounts paid in cash to employees. So, the statement of cash flows shows cash payments to employees of \$56,000.

| SHOPMART, INC.<br>Statement of Cash Flows (Partial)<br>Year Ended December 31, 2016 | | |
|---|---|---|
| Cash Flows from Operating Activities: | | |
| Receipts: | | |
| Collections from Customers | $ 269,000 | |
| Interest Received | 12,000 | |
| Dividends Received on Investments | 9,000 | |
| Total Cash Receipts | | $ 290,000 |
| Payments: | | |
| To Suppliers | (135,000) | |
| To Employees | (56,000) | |

## Payments for Interest Expense and Income Tax Expense

These cash payments are reported separately from the other expenses. The accounts related to interest payments are Interest Expense from the income statement and Interest Payable from the balance sheet. Because there is no Interest Payable account on the balance sheet, the Interest Expense account from the income statement must represent all amounts paid in cash for interest. So, the statement of cash flows shows cash payments for interest of $15,000.

The accounts related to income tax payments are Income Tax Expense from the income statement and Income Tax Payable from the balance sheet. Because there is no Income Tax Payable account on the balance sheet, the Income Tax Expense account from the income statement must represent all amounts paid in cash for income tax. So, the statement of cash flows shows cash payments for income tax of $14,000.

| SHOPMART, INC.<br>Statement of Cash Flows (Partial)<br>Year Ended December 31, 2016 | | |
|---|---|---|
| Cash Flows from Operating Activities: | | |
| Receipts: | | |
| Collections from Customers | $ 269,000 | |
| Interest Received | 12,000 | |
| Dividends Received on Investments | 9,000 | |
| Total Cash Receipts | | $ 290,000 |
| Payments: | | |
| To Suppliers | (135,000) | |
| To Employees | (56,000) | |
| For Interest | (15,000) | |
| For Income Tax | (14,000) | |
| Total Cash Payments | | (220,000) |

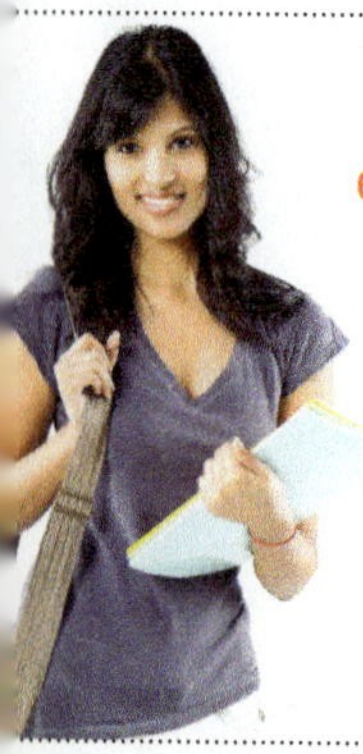

Are depreciation expense and gain or loss on disposal of plant assets included in the operating activities section when using the direct method?

## Non-cash Expenses and Gains or Losses on Disposal of Long-Term Assets

**Non-cash expenses and gains or losses on disposal of long-term assets are reported on the income statement but are not included in the operating activities when using the direct method.** Non-cash expenses are not reported because these items do not affect cash.

The cash received from the disposal of long-term assets is reported in the investing activities section, not the operating activities section.

## Net Cash Provided by Operating Activities

To calculate net cash provided by operating activities using the direct method, we add all the cash receipts and cash payments described previously and find the difference. For ShopMart, total cash receipts were $290,000. Total cash payments were $220,000. So, net cash provided by operating activities is $70,000. If you refer back to the indirect method statement of cash flows shown in Exhibit 14-5, you will find that it showed the same $70,000 for net cash provided by operating activities—only the method by which it was calculated was different.

The remainder of ShopMart's statement of cash flows is exactly the same as what we calculated using the indirect method. Exhibit 14A-1 shows the completed statement of cash flows using the direct method for operating activities.

**Exhibit 14A-1 | Statement of Cash Flows—Direct Method**

**SHOPMART, INC.**
Statement of Cash Flows
Year Ended December 31, 2016

| | | |
|---|---|---|
| Cash Flows from Operating Activities: | | |
| Receipts: | | |
| Collections from Customers | $ 269,000 | |
| Interest Received | 12,000 | |
| Dividends Received on Investments | 9,000 | |
| Total Cash Receipts | | $ 290,000 |
| Payments: | | |
| To Suppliers | (135,000) | |
| To Employees | (56,000) | |
| For Interest | (15,000) | |
| For Income Tax | (14,000) | |
| Total Cash Payments | | (220,000) |
| Net Cash Provided by Operating Activities | | 70,000 |
| Cash Flows from Investing Activities: | | |
| Cash Payment for Acquisition of Plant Assets | (310,000) | |
| Cash Receipt from Disposal of Plant Assets | 50,000 | |
| Net Cash Used for Investing Activities | | (260,000) |
| Cash Flows from Financing Activities: | | |
| Cash Receipt from Issuance of Notes Payable | 90,000 | |
| Cash Payment of Notes Payable | (10,000) | |
| Cash Receipt from Issuance of Common Stock | 120,000 | |
| Cash Payment for Purchase of Treasury Stock | (20,000) | |
| Cash Payment of Dividends | (10,000) | |
| Net Cash Provided by Financing Activities | | 170,000 |
| Net Increase (Decrease) in Cash | | (20,000) |
| Cash Balance, December 31, 2015 | | 42,000 |
| Cash Balance, December 31, 2016 | | **$ 22,000** |

## Try It!

**8A.** Big Island, Inc. began 2016 with cash of $40,000. During the year, Big Island earned revenue of $200,000 and collected $120,000 from customers. Expenses for the year totaled $160,000, of which Big Island paid $65,000 in cash to suppliers and $80,000 in cash to employees. The company received $2,000 cash for interest revenue and paid $10,000 for income taxes. Big Island also paid $35,000 to purchase equipment and a cash dividend of $15,000 to its stockholders during 2016. Prepare the company's operating activities section of the statement of cash flows for the year ended December 31, 2016. Use the direct method.

**Check your answer online in MyAccountingLab or at http://www.pearsonhighered.com/Horngren.**

For more practice, see Short Exercises S14A-11 through S14A-14. MyAccountingLab

# APPENDIX 14B: Preparing the Indirect Statement of Cash Flows Using a Spreadsheet

## HOW IS THE STATEMENT OF CASH FLOWS PREPARED USING THE INDIRECT METHOD AND A SPREADSHEET?

**Learning Objective 5**

Prepare the statement of cash flows by the indirect method using a spreadsheet

This chapter discussed the uses of the statement of cash flows in decision making and showed how to prepare the statement using T-accounts. The T-account approach works well as a learning device. In practice, however, most companies face complex situations. In these cases, a spreadsheet can help in preparing the statement of cash flows.

The spreadsheet starts with the beginning balance sheet and concludes with the ending balance sheet. Two middle columns—one for debit amounts and the other for credit amounts—complete the spreadsheet. These columns, labeled "Transaction Analysis," hold the data for the statement of cash flows. Accountants can prepare the statement directly from the lower part of the spreadsheet. This appendix is based on the ShopMart data used in this chapter. We illustrate this approach only with the indirect method for operating activities. This method could be used for the direct method as well.

The *indirect* method reconciles accrual basis net income to net cash provided by operating activities. Exhibit 14B-1 is the spreadsheet for preparing the statement of cash flows by the *indirect* method. Panel A shows the transaction analysis, and Panel B gives the information to prepare the statement of cash flows.

**Exhibit 14B-1** | **Spreadsheet for Statement of Cash Flows—Indirect Method**

| | A | B | C | D | E | F | G |
|---|---|---|---|---|---|---|---|
| 1 | **SHOPMART, INC.** | | | | | | |
| 2 | **Spreadsheet for Statement of Cash Flows** | | | | | | |
| 3 | **Year Ended December 31, 2016** | | | | | | |
| 4 | | | | | | | |
| 5 | **Panel A—Balance Sheet:** | **Balance** | | **Transaction Analysis** | | | **Balance** |
| 6 | | **12/31/2015** | | **DEBIT** | **CREDIT** | | **12/31/2016** |
| 7 | Cash | $ 42,000 | | | 20,000 | (n) | $ 22,000 |
| 8 | Accounts Receivable | 73,000 | (d) | 17,000 | | | 90,000 |
| 9 | Merchandise Inventory | 145,000 | | | 2,000 | (e) | 143,000 |
| 10 | Plant Assets | 252,000 | (h) | 310,000 | 55,000 | (c) | 507,000 |
| 11 | Accumulated Depreciation—Plant Assets | (42,000) | (c) | 15,000 | 20,000 | (b) | (47,000) |
| 12 | Total Assets | **$ 470,000** | | | | | **$ 715,000** |
| 13 | | | | | | | |
| 14 | Accounts Payable | 50,000 | | | 40,000 | (f) | 90,000 |
| 15 | Accured Liabilities | 10,000 | (g) | 5,000 | | | 5,000 |
| 16 | Notes Payable | 80,000 | (j) | 10,000 | 90,000 | (i) | 160,000 |
| 17 | Total Liabilities | 140,000 | | | | | 255,000 |
| 18 | | | | | | | |
| 19 | Common Stock, no par | 250,000 | | | 120,000 | (k) | 370,000 |
| 20 | Retained Earnings | 80,000 | (m) | 10,000 | 40,000 | (a) | 110,000 |
| 21 | Treasury Stock | 0 | (l) | 20,000 | | | (20,000) |
| 22 | Total Liabilities and Stockholders' Equity | **$ 470,000** | | **$ 387,000** | **$ 387,000** | | **$ 715,000** |
| 23 | | | | | | | |
| 24 | **Panel B—Statement of Cash Flows:** | | | | | | |
| 25 | Cash Flows from Operating Activities: | | | | | | |
| 26 | Net Income | | (a) | 40,000 | | | |
| 27 | Adjustments to Reconcile Net Income to Net Cash Provided by Operating Activities: | | | | | | |
| 28 | Depreciation Expense—Plant Assets | | (b) | 20,000 | | | |
| 29 | Gain on Disposal of Plant Assets | | | | 10,000 | (c) | |
| 30 | Increase in Accounts Receivable | | | | 17,000 | (d) | |
| 31 | Decrease in Merchandise Inventory | | (e) | 2,000 | | | |
| 32 | Increase in Accounts Payable | | (f) | 40,000 | | | |
| 33 | Decrease in Accrued Liabilities | | | | 5,000 | (g) | |
| 34 | Net Cash Provided by Operating Activities | | | | | | |
| 35 | Cash Flows from Investing Activities: | | | | | | |
| 36 | Cash Payment for Acquisition of Plant Assets | | | | 310,000 | (h) | |
| 37 | Cash Receipt from Disposal of Plant Assets | | (c) | 50,000 | | | |
| 38 | Net Cash Used for Investing Activities | | | | | | |
| 39 | Cash Flows from Financing Activities: | | | | | | |
| 40 | Cash Receipt from Issuance of Notes Payable | | (i) | 90,000 | | | |
| 41 | Cash Payment of Notes Payable | | | | 10,000 | (j) | |
| 42 | Cash Receipt from Issuance of Common Stock | | (k) | 120,000 | | | |
| 43 | Cash Payment for Purchase of Treasury Stock | | | | 20,000 | (l) | |
| 44 | Cash Payment of Dividends | | | | 10,000 | (m) | |
| 45 | Net Cash Provided by Financing Activities | | | | | | |
| 46 | Net Increase (Decrease) in Cash | | (n) | 20,000 | | | |
| 47 | **Total** | | | **$ 382,000** | **$ 382,000** | | |
| 48 | | | | | | | |

The following is a listing of the transaction analysis provided on the spreadsheet using the indirect method:

**a.** Net income of $40,000 is the first operating cash inflow. Net income is entered on the spreadsheet (Panel B) as a debit to Net Income under Cash Flows from Operating Activities and as a credit to Retained Earnings on the balance sheet (Panel A).

**b.** Next come the adjustments to net income, starting with depreciation of $20,000—transaction (b)—which is debited to Depreciation Expense—Plant Assets and credited to Accumulated Depreciation—Plant Assets.

**c.** This transaction is the sale of plant assets. The $10,000 gain on the sale is entered as a credit to Gain on Disposal of Plant Assets—a subtraction from net income—under operating cash flows. This credit removes the $10,000 gain from operating activities because the cash proceeds from the sale were $50,000, not $10,000. The $50,000 sale amount is then entered on the spreadsheet under investing activities. Entry (c) is completed by crediting the plant assets' cost of $55,000 to the Plant Assets account and debiting Accumulated Depreciation—Plant Assets for $15,000.

**d.** Entry (d) debits Accounts Receivable for its $17,000 increase during the year. This amount is credited to Increase in Accounts Receivable under operating cash flows.

**e.** This entry credits Merchandise Inventory for its $2,000 decrease during the year. This amount is debited to Decrease in Merchandise Inventory under operating cash flows.

**f.** This entry credits Accounts Payable for its $40,000 increase during the year. Then it is debited to show as Increase in Accounts Payable under operating cash flows.

**g.** This entry debits Accrued Liabilities for its $5,000 decrease during the year. Then it is credited to show as Decrease in Accrued Liabilities under operating cash flows.

**h.** This entry debits Plant Assets for the purchase of $310,000 and credits Cash Payment for Acquisition of Plant Assets under investing cash flows.

**i.** This entry is represented by a credit to Notes Payable and a debit under cash flows from financing activities of $90,000 (Cash Receipt from Issuance of Notes Payable).

**j.** This entry is the opposite of (i). It is represented by a debit (reduction) of $10,000 to Notes Payable and a credit under Cash Flows from Financing Activities for Cash Payment of Notes Payable.

**k.** This entry debits Cash Receipts from Issuance of Common Stock of $120,000 under financing cash flows. The offsetting credit is to Common Stock.

**l.** The purchase of treasury stock debited the Treasury Stock account on the balance sheet $20,000. The corresponding cash flow entry Cash Payment for Purchase of Treasury Stock credits $20,000 to reduce cash flow.

**m.** The $10,000 reduction (debit) to the Retained Earnings account is the result of dividends declared and paid by the company. So, we show Cash Payment of Dividends as a credit in the financing section.

**n.** The final item in Exhibit 14B-1 is the Net Increase (Decrease) in Cash. It is shown as a credit to Cash and a debit to Net Increase (Decrease) in Cash of $20,000.

In Panel B of Exhibit 14B-1, the debits represent increases (or inflows) of cash and the credits represent decreases (or outflows). This is because debits increase Cash and credits decrease Cash.

# Try It!

**9B.** Muench, Inc.'s accountant has partially completed the spreadsheet for the statement of cash flows. Fill in the remaining missing information.

| | A | B | C | D | E | F | G |
|---|---|---|---|---|---|---|---|
| 1 | **MUENCH, INC.** | | | | | | |
| 2 | **Spreadsheet for Statement of Cash Flows** | | | | | | |
| 3 | **Year Ended December 31, 2016** | | | | | | |
| 4 | | | | | | | |
| 5 | **Panel A—Balance Sheet:** | **Balance** | | **Transaction Analysis** | | | **Balance** |
| 6 | | **12/31/2015** | | **DEBIT** | **CREDIT** | | **12/31/2016** |
| 7 | Cash | $ 16,000 | | | | | $ 20,000 |
| 8 | Accounts Receivable | 3,250 | | | | | 5,000 |
| 9 | Plant Assets | 14,000 | | 1,000 | | | 15,000 |
| 10 | Accumulated Depreciation | (100) | | | 100 | | (200) |
| 11 | Total Assets | **$ 33,150** | | | | | **$ 39,800** |
| 12 | | | | | | | |
| 13 | Accounts Payable | 5,000 | | | | | 3,500 |
| 14 | | | | | | | |
| 15 | Common Stock, no par | 24,150 | | | 5,850 | | 30,000 |
| 16 | Retained Earnings | 4,000 | | 5,700 | | | 6,300 |
| 17 | Total Liabilities and Stockholders' Equity | **$ 33,150** | | | | | **$ 39,800** |
| 18 | | | | | | | |
| 19 | **Panel B—Statement of Cash Flows:** | | | | | | |
| 20 | Cash Flows from Operating Activities: | | | | | | |
| 21 | Net Income | | | | | | |
| 22 | Adjustments to Reconcile Net Income to Net Cash Provided by Operating Activities: | | | | | | |
| 23 | Depreciation Expense—Plant Assets | | | 100 | | | |
| 24 | Increase in Accounts Receivable | | | | | | |
| 25 | Decrease in Accounts Payable | | | | | | |
| 26 | Net Cash Provided by Operating Activities | | | | | | |
| 27 | Cash Flows from Investing Activities: | | | | | | |
| 28 | Cash Payment for Acquisition of Plant Assets | | | | 1,000 | | |
| 29 | Net Cash Used for Investing Activities | | | | | | |
| 30 | Cash Flows from Financing Activities: | | | | | | |
| 31 | Cash Receipt from Issuance of Common Stock | | | 5,850 | | | |
| 32 | Cash Payment of Dividends | | | | 5,700 | | |
| 33 | Net Cash Provided by Financing Activities | | | | | | |
| 34 | Net Increase (Decrease) in Cash | | | | | | |
| 35 | | | | | | | |

**Check your answer online in MyAccountingLab or at http://www.pearsonhighered.com/Horngren.**

For more practice, see Short Exercise S14B-15. MyAccountingLab

# REVIEW

## > Things You Should Know

### 1. What is the statement of cash flows?

- The statement of cash flows reports on a business's cash receipts and cash payments for a specific period.
- There are three basic types of cash flow activities:
  - Operating activities—Reports on activities that create revenue or expense in the entity's business
  - Investing activities—Reports cash receipts and cash payments that increase or decrease long-term assets
  - Financing activities—Includes cash receipts and cash payments involved in long-term liabilities and equity
- Non-cash investing and financing activities are not included in the statement of cash flows but appear either as a separate schedule at the bottom of the statement or in the notes to the financial statements.
- There are two ways to format operating activities on the statement of cash flows:
  - Indirect method—Starts with net income and adjusts it to net cash provided by operating activities
  - Direct method—Restates the income statement in terms of cash

### 2. How is the statement of cash flows prepared using the indirect method?

- **Step 1:** Complete the cash flows from operating activities section using net income and adjusting for increases or decreases in current assets (other than cash) and current liabilities. Also adjust for gains or losses on long-term assets and non-cash expenses.
- **Step 2:** Complete the cash flows from investing activities section by reviewing the long-term assets section of the balance sheet.
- **Step 3:** Complete the cash flows from financing activities section by reviewing the long-term liabilities and equity sections of the balance sheet.
- **Step 4:** Compute the net increase or decrease in cash during the year.
- **Step 5:** Prepare a separate schedule reporting any non-cash investing and financing activities.

### 3. How do we use free cash flow to evaluate business performance?

- Free cash flow is the amount of cash available from operating activities after paying for planned investments in long-term assets and after paying cash dividends to shareholders.
- Free cash flow = Net cash provided by operating activities − Cash payments planned for investments in long-term assets − Cash dividends.

### 4. How is the statement of cash flows prepared using the direct method? (Appendix 14A)

- The operating activities section is the only section that differs between the direct and indirect methods.
- When using the direct method, each line item on the income statement is converted from accrual basis to cash basis.

**5. How is the statement of cash flows prepared using the indirect method and a spreadsheet? (Appendix 14B)**

- A spreadsheet can be used to help in preparing the statement of cash flows.
- The spreadsheet helps accountants analyze the changes in balance sheet accounts.

## > Summary Problem 14-1

The Adams Corporation reported the following income statement for 2016 and comparative balance sheet for 2016 and 2015, along with transaction data for 2016:

**ADAMS CORPORATION**
Comparative Balance Sheet
December 31, 2016 and 2015

| | 2016 | 2015 | Increase (Decrease) |
|---|---|---|---|
| **Assets** | | | |
| Current Assets: | | | |
| Cash | $ 22,000 | $ 3,000 | $ 19,000 |
| Accounts Receivable | 22,000 | 23,000 | (1,000) |
| Merchandise Inventory | 35,000 | 34,000 | 1,000 |
| Long-term Assets: | | | |
| Plants Assets | 153,200 | 97,200 | 56,000 |
| Accumulated Depreciation—Plant Assets | (27,200) | (25,200) | (2,000) |
| Total Assets | **$ 205,000** | **$ 132,000** | **$ 73,000** |
| **Liabilities** | | | |
| Current Liabilities: | | | |
| Accounts Payable | $ 35,000 | $ 26,000 | $ 9,000 |
| Accrued Liabilities | 7,000 | 9,000 | (2,000) |
| Income Tax Payable | 10,000 | 10,000 | 0 |
| Long-term Liabilities: | | | |
| Bonds Payable | 84,000 | 53,000 | 31,000 |
| Total Liabilities | 136,000 | 98,000 | 38,000 |
| **Stockholders' Equity** | | | |
| Common Stock, no par | 52,000 | 20,000 | 32,000 |
| Retained Earnings | 27,000 | 19,000 | 8,000 |
| Treasury Stock | (10,000) | (5,000) | (5,000) |
| Total Stockholders' Equity | 69,000 | 34,000 | 35,000 |
| Total Liabilities and Stockholders' Equity | **$ 205,000** | **$ 132,000** | **$ 73,000** |

| ADAMS CORPORATION<br>Income Statement<br>Year Ended December 31, 2016 | | |
|---|---|---|
| Sales Revenue | | $ 662,000 |
| Cost of Goods Sold | | 560,000 |
| Gross Profit | | 102,000 |
| Operating Expenses: | | |
| Salaries and Wages Expense | $ 46,000 | |
| Depreciation Expense—Plant Assets | 10,000 | |
| Rent Expense | 2,000 | |
| Total Operating Expenses | | 58,000 |
| Operating Income | | 44,000 |
| Other Revenue and (Expenses): | | |
| Loss on Disposal of Plant Assets | (2,000) | |
| Total Other Revenues and (Expenses) | | (2,000) |
| Net Income Before Income Taxes | | 42,000 |
| Income Tax Expense | | 16,000 |
| Net Income | | **$ 26,000** |

| Transaction data for 2016 | |
|---|---|
| Cash paid for purchase of equipment | $ 140,000 |
| Cash payment of dividends | 18,000 |
| Issuance of common stock to retire bonds payable | 13,000 |
| Issuance of bonds payable to borrow cash | 44,000 |
| Cash receipt from issuance of common stock | 19,000 |
| Cash receipt from sale of equipment<br>(Cost, $84,000; Accumulated Depreciation, $8,000) | 74,000 |
| Cash paid for purchase of treasury stock | 5,000 |

Prepare Adams Corporation's statement of cash flows for the year ended December 31, 2016. Format cash flows from operating activities by the indirect method.

## > Solution

| ADAMS CORPORATION<br>Statement of Cash Flows<br>Year Ended December 31, 2016 | | |
|---|---|---|
| Cash Flows from Operating Activities: | | |
| Net Income | | $ 26,000 |
| Adjustments to Reconcile Net Income to Net Cash Provided by Operating Activities: | | |
| Depreciation Expense—Plant Assets | $ 10,000 | |
| Loss on Disposal of Plant Assets | 2,000 | |
| Decrease in Accounts Receivable | 1,000 | |
| Increase in Merchandise Inventory | (1,000) | |
| Increase in Accounts Payable | 9,000 | |
| Decrease in Accrued Liabilities | (2,000) | 19,000 |
| Net Cash Provided by Operating Activities | | 45,000 |
| Cash Flows from Investing Activities: | | |
| Cash Payment for Acquisition of Plant Assets | (140,000) | |
| Cash Receipt from Disposal of Plant Assets | 74,000 | |
| Net Cash Used for Investing Activities | | (66,000) |
| Cash Flows from Financing Activities: | | |
| Cash Receipt from Issuance of Bonds Payable | 44,000 | |
| Cash Receipt from Issuance of Common Stock | 19,000 | |
| Cash Payment for Purchase of Treasury Stock | (5,000) | |
| Cash Payment of Dividends | (18,000) | |
| Net Cash Provided by Financing Activities | | 40,000 |
| Net Increase (Decrease) in Cash | | 19,000 |
| Cash Balance, December 31, 2015 | | 3,000 |
| Cash Balance, December 31, 2016 | | **$ 22,000** |
| | | |
| Non-cash Investing and Financing Activities: | | |
| Issuance of Common Stock to Retire Bonds Payable | | $ 13,000 |
| Total Non-cash Investing and Financing Activities | | **$ 13,000** |

Relevant T-accounts:

**Plant Assets**

| | | | |
|---|---|---|---|
| 12/31/2015 | 97,200 | | |
| Acquisitions | 140,000 | 84,000 | Disposals |
| 12/31/2016 | 153,200 | | |

**Accumulated Depreciation—Plant Assets**

| | | | |
|---|---|---|---|
| | | 25,200 | 12/31/2015 |
| Disposals | 8,000 | 10,000 | Depr. Exp. |
| | | 27,200 | 12/31/2016 |

**Bonds Payable**

| | | | |
|---|---|---|---|
| | | 53,000 | 12/31/2015 |
| Retirement | 13,000 | 44,000 | Issuance |
| | | 84,000 | 12/31/2016 |

**Common Stock**

| | | | |
|---|---|---|---|
| | | 20,000 | 12/31/2015 |
| Retirement | 0 | 13,000 | Issuance |
| | | 19,000 | Issuance |
| | | 52,000 | 12/31/2016 |

**Treasury Stock**

| | | | |
|---|---|---|---|
| 12/31/2015 | 5,000 | | |
| Purchase | 5,000 | 0 | Disposal |
| 12/31/2016 | 10,000 | | |

**Retained Earnings**

| | | | |
|---|---|---|---|
| | | 19,000 | 12/31/2015 |
| | | 26,000 | Net Income |
| Dividends | 18,000 | | |
| | | 27,000 | 12/31/2016 |

## > Key Terms

## > Quick Check

1. The purposes of the statement of cash flows are to **Learning Objective 1**

   a. evaluate management decisions.
   b. determine ability to pay debts and dividends.
   c. predict future cash flows.
   d. All of the above

2. The main categories of cash flow activities are **Learning Objective 1**

   a. direct and indirect.
   b. current and long-term.
   c. non-cash investing and financing.
   d. operating, investing, and financing.

3. Operating activities are most closely related to **Learning Objective 1**

   a. long-term assets.
   b. current assets and current liabilities.
   c. long-term liabilities and stockholders' equity.
   d. dividends and treasury stock.

4. Which item does *not* appear on a statement of cash flows prepared by the indirect method? **Learning Objective 2**

   a. Collections from customers
   b. Depreciation expense
   c. Net income
   d. Gain on sale of land

5. Leather Shop earned net income of $57,000 after deducting depreciation of $5,000 and all other expenses. Current assets decreased by $4,000, and current liabilities increased by $8,000. How much was Leather Shop's cash provided by operating activities (indirect method)? **Learning Objective 2**

   a. $40,000
   b. $66,000
   c. $48,000
   d. $74,000

6. The Plant Assets account and Accumulated Depreciation—Plant Assets account of Star Media show the following: **Learning Objective 2**

**Plant Assets**

| | | | |
|---|---|---|---|
| Beg. | 100,000 | | |
| Acquisitions | 428,000 | 52,500 | Disposals |
| End. | 475,500 | | |

**Accumulated Depreciation—Plant Assets**

| | | | |
|---|---|---|---|
| | | 20,000 | 12/31/2015 |
| Disposals | 10,500 | 34,000 | Depr. Exp. |
| | | 43,500 | 12/31/2016 |

Star Media sold plant assets at an $11,000 loss. Where on the statement of cash flows should Star Media report the sale of plant assets? How much should the business report for the sale?

   a. Financing cash flows—cash receipt of $42,000
   b. Investing cash flows—cash receipt of $53,000
   c. Investing cash flows—cash receipt of $31,000
   d. Investing cash flows—cash receipt of $42,000

**Learning Objective 2**

7. Mountain Water Corp. issued common stock of $28,000 to pay off long-term notes payable of $28,000. In what section(s) would these transactions be recorded?
   a. Financing activities payment of note, $(28,000)
   b. Financing activities cash receipt, $28,000
   c. Non-cash investing and financing activities, $28,000
   d. Both a and b are correct.

**Learning Objective 3**

8. Holmes, Inc. expects net cash flow from operating activities to be $160,000, and the company plans purchases of equipment of $83,000 and repurchases of stock of $24,000. What is Holmes's free cash flow?
   a. $53,000 b. $160,000 c. $77,000 d. $83,000

**Learning Objective 4**
**Appendix 14A**

9A. Maxwell Furniture Center had accounts receivable of $20,000 at the beginning of the year and $54,000 at year-end. Revenue for the year totaled $116,000. How much cash did the business collect from customers?
   a. $150,000 b. $62,000 c. $116,000 d. $82,000

**Learning Objective 5**
**Appendix 14B**

10B. If accrued liabilities increased during the year, which of the following is correct when using a spreadsheet to complete the statement of cash flows (indirect method)?
   a. Increase in Accrued Liabilities would be debited
   b. Increase in Accrued Liabilities would be credited
   c. Accrued Liabilities would be debited
   d. None of the above is correct.

**Check your answers at the end of the chapter.**

# ASSESS YOUR PROGRESS

## > Review Questions

1. What does the statement of cash flows report?
2. How does the statement of cash flows help users of financial statements?
3. Describe the three basic types of cash flow activities.
4. What types of transactions are reported in the non-cash investing and financing activities section of the statement of cash flows?
5. Describe the two formats for reporting operating activities on the statement of cash flows.
6. Describe the five steps used to prepare the statement of cash flows by the indirect method.
7. Explain why depreciation expense, depletion expense, and amortization expense are added to net income in the operating activities section of the statement of cash flows when using the indirect method.
8. If a company experienced a loss on disposal of long-term assets, how would this be reported in the operating activities section of the statement of cash flows when using the indirect method? Why?

9. If current assets other than cash increase, what is the effect on cash? What about a decrease in current assets other than cash?
10. If current liabilities increase, what is the effect on cash? What about a decrease in current liabilities?
11. What accounts on the balance sheet must be evaluated when completing the investing activities section of the statement of cash flows?
12. What accounts on the balance sheet must be evaluated when completing the financing activities section of the statement of cash flows?
13. What should the net change in cash section of the statement of cash flows always reconcile with?
14. What is free cash flow, and how is it calculated?

15A. How does the direct method differ from the indirect method when preparing the operating activities section of the statement of cash flows?

16B. Why might a spreadsheet be helpful when completing the statement of cash flows?

## > Short Exercises

### S14-1 Describing the purposes of the statement of cash flows

**Learning Objective 1**

Financial statements all have a goal. The statement of cash flows does as well. Describe how the statement of cash flows helps investors and creditors perform each of the following functions:

a. Predict future cash flows.

b. Evaluate management decisions.

c. Predict the ability to make debt payments to lenders and pay dividends to stockholders.

### S14-2 Classifying items on the statement of cash flows

**Learning Objective 1**

Cash flow items must be categorized into one of four categories. Identify each item as operating (O), investing (I), financing (F), or non-cash (N).

a. Cash purchase of merchandise inventory

b. Cash payment of dividends

c. Cash receipt from the collection of long-term notes receivable

d. Cash payment for income taxes

e. Purchase of equipment in exchange for notes payable

f. Cash receipt from the sale of land

g. Cash received from borrowing money

h. Cash receipt for interest income

i. Cash receipt from the issuance of common stock

j. Cash payment of salaries

Learning Objective 2

**S14-3 Classifying items on the indirect statement of cash flows**

Destiny Corporation is preparing its statement of cash flows by the *indirect* method. Destiny has the following items for you to consider in preparing the statement:

a. Increase in accounts payable
b. Payment of dividends
c. Decrease in accrued liabilities
d. Issuance of common stock
e. Gain on sale of building
f. Loss on sale of land
g. Depreciation expense
h. Increase in merchandise inventory
i. Decrease in accounts receivable
j. Purchase of equipment

Identify each item as a(n):

- Operating activity—addition to net income (O+) or subtraction from net income (O–)
- Investing activity—cash inflow (I+) or cash outflow (I–)
- Financing activity—cash inflow (F+) or cash outflow (F–)
- Activity that is not used to prepare the indirect statement of cash flows (N)

Learning Objective 2

**S14-4 Computing cash flows from operating activities—indirect method**

GDM Equipment, Inc. reported the following data for 2016:

| | |
|---|---|
| Income Statement: | |
| Net Income | $ 44,000 |
| Depreciation Expense | 9,000 |
| Balance Sheet: | |
| Increase in Accounts Receivable | 9,000 |
| Decrease in Accounts Payable | 4,000 |

Compute GDM's net cash provided by operating activities—indirect method.

Learning Objective 2

**S14-5 Computing cash flows from operating activities—indirect method**

Smart Cellular accountants have assembled the following data for the year ended April 30, 2016:

| | | | |
|---|---|---|---|
| Cash receipt from sale of land | $ 26,000 | Net income | $ 62,000 |
| Depreciation expense | 4,000 | Cash purchase of equipment | 36,000 |
| Cash payment of dividends | 5,600 | Decrease in current liabilities | 18,000 |
| Cash receipt from issuance of common stock | 25,000 | Increase in current assets other than cash | 26,000 |

Prepare the *operating* activities section using the indirect method for Smart Cellular's statement of cash flows for the year ended April 30, 2016.

***Note: Short Exercise S14-5 must be completed before attempting Short Exercise S14-6.***

Learning Objective 2

**S14-6 Computing cash flows from investing and financing activities**

Use the data in Short Exercise S14-5 to complete this exercise. Prepare Smart Cellular's statement of cash flows using the indirect method for the year ended April 30, 2016. Assume beginning and ending Cash are $23,300 and $54,700, respectively.

**Learning Objective 2**

**S14-7 Computing investing and financing cash flows**

Stenback Media Corporation had the following income statement and balance sheet for 2016:

| STENBACK MEDIA CORPORATION<br>Income Statement<br>Year Ended December 31, 2016 | |
|---|---|
| Sales Revenue | $ 77,000 |
| Depreciation Expense—Plant Assets | 26,900 |
| Other Expenses | 48,500 |
| Net Income | **$ 1,600** |

| STENBACK MEDIA CORPORATION<br>Comparative Balance Sheet<br>December 31, 2016 and 2015 | | |
|---|---|---|
| | 2016 | 2015 |
| **Assets** | | |
| Current Assets: | | |
| Cash | $ 4,900 | $ 4,100 |
| Accounts Receivable | 9,100 | 8,100 |
| Long-term Assets: | | |
| Plants Assets | 108,250 | 80,350 |
| Accumulated Depreciation—Plant Assets | (33,250) | (6,350) |
| Total Assets | **$ 89,000** | **$ 86,200** |
| **Liabilities** | | |
| Current Liabilities: | | |
| Accounts Payable | $ 6,500 | $ 4,000 |
| Long-term Liabilities: | | |
| Notes Payable | 10,000 | 11,000 |
| Total Liabilities | 16,500 | 15,000 |
| **Stockholders' Equity** | | |
| Common Stock, no par | 24,000 | 19,000 |
| Retained Earnings | 48,500 | 52,200 |
| Total Stockholders' Equity | 72,500 | 71,200 |
| Total Liabilities and Stockholders' Equity | **$ 89,000** | **$ 86,200** |

**Requirements**

1. Compute the acquisition of plant assets for Stenback Media Corporation during 2016. The business sold no plant assets during the year. Assume the company paid cash for the acquisition of plant assets.
2. Compute the payment of a long-term note payable. During the year, the business issued a $4,600 note payable.

***Note: Short Exercise S14-7 must be completed before attempting Short Exercise S14-8.***

**Learning Objective 2**

**S14-8 Preparing the statement of cash flows—indirect method**

Use the Stenback Media Corporation data in Short Exercise S14-7 and the results you calculated from the requirements. Prepare Stenbeck Media's statement of cash flows—indirect method—for the year ended December 31, 2016.

**Learning Objective 2**

**S14-9 Computing the change in cash; identifying non-cash transactions**

Brianna's Wedding Shops earned net income of $25,000, which included depreciation of $16,000. Brianna's acquired a $116,000 building by borrowing $116,000 on a long-term note payable.

**Requirements**

1. How much did Brianna's cash balance increase or decrease during the year?
2. Were there any non-cash transactions for the company? If so, show how they would be reported in the statement of cash flows.

**Learning Objective 3**

**S14-10 Computing free cash flow**

Shauna Lopez Company expects the following for 2016:

- Net cash provided by operating activities of $144,000.
- Net cash provided by financing activities of $60,000.
- Net cash used for investing activities of $84,000 (no sales of long-term assets).
- Cash dividends paid to stockholders of $10,000.

How much free cash flow does Lopez expect for 2016?

**Learning Objective 4**
**Appendix 14A**

**S14A-11 Preparing a statement of cash flows using the direct method**

Green Bean, Inc. began 2016 with cash of $57,000. During the year, Green Bean earned revenue of $596,000 and collected $618,000 from customers. Expenses for the year totaled $433,000, of which Green Bean paid $214,000 in cash to suppliers and $209,000 in cash to employees. Green Bean also paid $146,000 to purchase equipment and a cash dividend of $56,000 to its stockholders during 2016. Prepare the company's statement of cash flows for the year ended December 31, 2016. Format operating activities by the direct method.

**Learning Objective 4**
**Appendix 14A**

**S14A-12 Preparing operating activities using the direct method**

Miss Ella's Learning Center has assembled the following data for the year ended June 30, 2016:

| | |
|---|---|
| Payments to suppliers | $ 118,000 |
| Cash payment for purchase of equipment | 38,000 |
| Payments to employees | 67,000 |
| Payment of notes payable | 26,000 |
| Payment of dividends | 6,500 |
| Cash receipt from issuance of stock | 15,000 |
| Collections from customers | 184,000 |
| Cash receipt from sale of land | 60,000 |
| Cash balance, June 30, 2015 | 39,000 |

Prepare the *operating* activities section of the business's statement of cash flows for the year ended June 30, 2016, using the direct method.

***Note: Short Exercise S14A-12 must be completed before attempting Short Exercise S14A-13.***

**S14A-13 Preparing the direct method statement of cash flows**

**Learning Objective 4**
**Appendix 14A**

Use the data in Short Exercise S14A-12 and your results. Prepare the business's complete statement of cash flows for the year ended June 30, 2016, using the *direct* method for operating activities.

**S14A-14 Preparing the direct method statement of cash flows**

**Learning Objective 4**
**Appendix 14A**

White Toy Company reported the following comparative balance sheet:

| WHITE TOY COMPANY<br>Comparative Balance Sheet<br>December 31, 2016 and 2015 | | |
|---|---|---|
| | 2016 | 2015 |
| **Assets** | | |
| Current Assets: | | |
| Cash | $ 17,000 | $ 15,000 |
| Accounts Receivable | 58,000 | 47,000 |
| Merchandise Inventory | 75,000 | 87,000 |
| Prepaid Expenses | 2,500 | 1,500 |
| Long-term Assets: | | |
| Plants Assets, Net | 228,000 | 183,000 |
| Investments | 79,000 | 90,000 |
| Total Assets | **$ 459,500** | **$ 423,500** |
| **Liabilities** | | |
| Current Liabilities: | | |
| Accounts Payable | $ 45,000 | $ 41,000 |
| Salaries Payable | 21,500 | 19,000 |
| Accrued Liabilities | 5,000 | 15,000 |
| Long-term Liabilities: | | |
| Notes Payable | 66,000 | 70,000 |
| Total Liabilities | 137,500 | 145,000 |
| **Stockholders' Equity** | | |
| Common Stock, no par | 41,000 | 37,000 |
| Retained Earnings | 281,000 | 241,500 |
| Total Stockholders' Equity | 322,000 | 278,500 |
| Total Liabilities and Stockholders' Equity | **$ 459,500** | **$ 423,500** |

**Requirements**

1. Compute the collections from customers during 2016 for White Toy Company. Sales Revenue totaled $136,000.
2. Compute the payments for inventory during 2016. Cost of Goods Sold was $80,000.

**Learning Objective 5**
**Appendix 14B**

**S14B-15 Using a spreadsheet to complete the statement of cash flows—indirect method**

Companies can use a spreadsheet to complete the statement of cash flows. Each item that follows is recorded in the transaction analysis columns of the spreadsheet.

a. Net income
b. Increases in current assets (other than Cash)
c. Decreases in current liabilities
d. Cash payment for acquisition of plant assets
e. Cash receipt from issuance of common stock
f. Depreciation expense

Identify each as being recorded by a Debit or Credit in the *statement of cash flows section* of the spreadsheet.

## > Exercises

**Learning Objective 1**

**E14-16 Classifying cash flow items**

Consider the following transactions:

a. Purchased equipment for $130,000 cash.
b. Issued $14 par preferred stock for cash.
c. Cash received from sales to customers of $35,000.
d. Cash paid to vendors, $17,000.
e. Sold building for $19,000 gain for cash.
f. Purchased treasury stock for $28,000.
g. Retired a notes payable with 1,250 shares of the company's common stock.

Identify the category of the statement of cash flows in which each transaction would be reported.

## E14-17 Classifying transactions on the statement of cash flows—indirect method

**Learning Objective 1**

Consider the following transactions:

| Date | Accounts and Explanation | Debit | Credit |
|---|---|---|---|
| a. | Cash | 72,000 | |
| | Common Stock | | 72,000 |
| b. | Treasury Stock | 16,500 | |
| | Cash | | 16,500 |
| c. | Cash | 88,000 | |
| | Sales Revenue | | 88,000 |
| d. | Land | 103,000 | |
| | Cash | | 103,000 |
| e. | Depreciation Expense—Equipment | 6,800 | |
| | Accumulated Depreciation—Equipment | | 6,800 |
| f. | Dividends Payable | 19,500 | |
| | Cash | | 19,500 |
| g. | Land | 22,000 | |
| | Notes Payable | | 22,000 |
| h. | Cash | 9,600 | |
| | Equipment | | 9,600 |
| i. | Bonds Payable | 51,000 | |
| | Cash | | 51,000 |
| j. | Building | 137,000 | |
| | Notes Payable | | 137,000 |
| k. | Loss on Disposal of Equipment | 1,800 | |
| | Accumulated Depreciation—Equipment | 200 | |
| | Equipment | | 2,000 |

Identify the category of the statement of cash flows in which each transaction would be reported.

## E14-18 Classifying items on the indirect statement of cash flows

**Learning Objectives 1, 2**

The statement of cash flows categorizes like transactions for optimal reporting. Identify each item as a(n):

- Operating activity—addition to net income (O+) or subtraction from net income (O–)
- Investing activity—cash inflow (I+) or cash outflow (I–)
- Financing activity—cash inflow (F+) or cash outflow (F–)
- Non-cash investing and financing activity (NIF)
- Activity that is not used to prepare the indirect statement of cash flows (N)

The *indirect* method is used to report cash flows from operating activities.

a. Loss on sale of land.
b. Acquisition of equipment by issuance of note payable.
c. Payment of long-term debt.
d. Acquisition of building by issuance of common stock.
e. Increase in Salaries Payable.
f. Decrease in Merchandise Inventory.
g. Increase in Prepaid Expenses.
h. Decrease in Accrued Liabilities.
i. Cash sale of land.
j. Issuance of long-term note payable to borrow cash.
k. Depreciation Expense.
l. Purchase of treasury stock.
m. Issuance of common stock.
n. Increase in Accounts Payable.
o. Net income.
p. Payment of cash dividend.

**Learning Objective 2**

Net Cash Prov. by Op. Act. $17,000

### E14-19 Computing operating activities cash flow—indirect method

The records of Paramount Color Engraving reveal the following:

| | | | |
|---|---|---|---|
| Net income | $ 40,000 | Depreciation expense | $ 11,000 |
| Sales revenue | 47,000 | Decrease in current liabilities | 24,000 |
| Loss on sale of land | 5,000 | Increase in current assets other than cash | 15,000 |
| Acquisition of land | 39,000 | | |

Compute cash flows from operating activities by the indirect method for year ended December 31, 2016.

**Learning Objective 2**

Net Cash Prov. by Op. Act. $71,500

### E14-20 Computing operating activities cash flow—indirect method

The accounting records of XYZ Sales, Inc. include the following accounts:

| Account | Beginning Balance | Ending Balance |
|---|---|---|
| Cash | $ 6,500 | $ 4,000 |
| Accounts Receivable | 20,000 | 15,500 |
| Merchandise Inventory | 18,000 | 30,000 |
| Accounts Payable | 14,000 | 19,000 |

**Accumulated Depreciation—Equipment**

| | | |
|---|---|---|
| | 55,000 | Jul. 1 |
| | 4,000 | Depr. Exp. |
| | 59,000 | Jul. 31 |

**Retained Earnings**

| | | | |
|---|---|---|---|
| | | 62,000 | Jul. 1 |
| Dividends | 19,000 | 70,000 | Net Inc. |
| | | 113,000 | Jul. 31 |

Compute XYZ's net cash provided by (used for) operating activities during July 2016. Use the indirect method.

CHAPTER 14

## E14-21 Preparing the statement of cash flows—indirect method

**Learning Objective 2**

Net Cash Prov. by Op. Act. $99,000

The income statement of Supplements Plus, Inc. follows:

| SUPPLEMENTS PLUS, INC.<br>Income Statement<br>Year Ended September 30, 2016 | | |
|---|---|---|
| Sales Revenue | | $ 234,000 |
| Cost of Goods Sold | | 91,000 |
| Gross Profit | | 143,000 |
| Operating Expenses: | | |
| Salaries Expense | $ 55,000 | |
| Depreciation Expense—Plant Assets | 25,000 | |
| Total Operating Expenses | | 80,000 |
| Net Income Before Income Taxes | | 63,000 |
| Income Tax Expense | | 10,000 |
| Net Income | | **$ 53,000** |

Additional data follow:

a. Acquisition of plant assets is $121,000. Of this amount, $104,000 is paid in cash and $17,000 by signing a note payable.

b. Cash receipt from sale of land totals $26,000. There was no gain or loss.

c. Cash receipts from issuance of common stock total $30,000.

d. Payment of notes payable is $16,000.

e. Payment of dividends is $9,000.

f. From the balance sheet:

| | September 30 | |
|---|---|---|
| | **2016** | **2015** |
| Cash | $ 38,000 | $ 12,000 |
| Accounts Receivable | 44,000 | 60,000 |
| Merchandise Inventory | 91,000 | 86,000 |
| Plant Assets | 201,000 | 80,000 |
| Accumulated Depreciation | (35,000) | (10,000) |
| Land | 75,000 | 101,000 |
| Accounts Payable | 31,000 | 15,000 |
| Accrued Liabilities | 20,000 | 26,000 |
| Notes Payable (long-term) | 17,000 | 16,000 |
| Common Stock, no par | 37,000 | 7,000 |
| Retained Earnings | 309,000 | 265,000 |

Prepare Supplements Plus's statement of cash flows for the year ended September 30, 2016, using the indirect method. Include a separate section for non-cash investing and financing activities.

**Learning Objective 2**

2. Book Value on Plant Assets Sold $10,000

## E14-22 Computing cash flows for investing and financing activities

Consider the following facts for Vanilla Valley:

a. Beginning and ending Retained Earnings are $43,000 and $69,000, respectively. Net income for the period is $58,000.

b. Beginning and ending Plant Assets are $120,600 and $126,600, respectively.

c. Beginning and ending Accumulated Depreciation—Plant Assets are $18,600 and $20,600, respectively.

d. Depreciation Expense for the period is $13,000, and acquisitions of new plant assets total $27,000. Plant assets were sold at a $4,000 gain.

### Requirements

1. How much are cash dividends?
2. What was the amount of the cash receipt from the sale of plant assets?

**Learning Objective 2**

2. Payment: $6,000
4. Dividends $32,000

## E14-23 Computing the cash effect

Stenback Exercise Equipment, Inc. reported the following financial statements for 2016:

**STENBACK EXERCISE EQUIPMENT, INC.**
Income Statement
Year Ended December 31, 2016

| | | |
|---|---|---|
| Sales Revenue | | $ 711,000 |
| Cost of Goods Sold | | 343,000 |
| Gross Profit | | 368,000 |
| Operating Expenses: | | |
| Depreciation Expense | $ 51,000 | |
| Other Operating Expenses | 215,000 | |
| Total Operating Expenses | | 266,000 |
| Net Income | | **$ 102,000** |

| STENBACK EXERCISE EQUIPMENT, INC.<br>Comparative Balance Sheet<br>December 31, 2016 and 2015 | | |
|---|---|---|
| | 2016 | 2015 |
| **Assets** | | |
| Current Assets: | | |
| Cash | $ 21,000 | $ 15,000 |
| Accounts Receivable | 56,000 | 50,000 |
| Merchandise Inventory | 84,000 | 88,000 |
| Long-term Assets: | | |
| Plants Assets | 268,700 | 217,200 |
| Accumulated Depreciation—Plant Assets | (41,700) | (34,200) |
| Investments | 93,000 | 75,000 |
| Total Assets | **$ 481,000** | **$ 411,000** |
| **Liabilities** | | |
| Current Liabilities: | | |
| Accounts Payable | $ 75,000 | $ 74,000 |
| Salaries Payable | 2,000 | 4,000 |
| Long-term Liabilities: | | |
| Notes Payable | 59,000 | 65,000 |
| Total Liabilities | 136,000 | 143,000 |
| **Stockholders' Equity** | | |
| Common Stock, no par | 42,000 | 35,000 |
| Retained Earnings | 303,000 | 233,000 |
| Total Stockholders' Equity | 345,000 | 268,000 |
| Total Liabilities and Stockholders' Equity | **$ 481,000** | **$ 411,000** |

**Requirements**

1. Compute the amount of Stenback Exercise's acquisition of plant assets. Assume the acquisition was for cash. Stenback Exercise disposed of plant assets at book value. The cost and accumulated depreciation of the disposed asset was $43,500. No cash was received upon disposal.
2. Compute new borrowing or payment of long-term notes payable, with Stenback Exercise having only one long-term notes payable transaction during the year.
3. Compute the issuance of common stock with Stenback Exercise having only one common stock transaction during the year.
4. Compute the payment of cash dividends.

***Note: Exercise E14-23 must be completed before attempting Exercise E14-24.***

## E14-24 Preparing the statement of cash flows—indirect method

**Learning Objective 2**

Use the Stenback Exercise Equipment data in Exercise E14-23. Prepare the company's statement of cash flows—indirect method—for the year ended December 31, 2016. Assume investments are purchased with cash.

Net Cash Prov. by Op. Act. $150,000

**Learning Objective 2**

Total Non-cash Inv. and Fin. Act. $161,000

### E14-25 Identifying and reporting non-cash transactions

Motorcross, Inc. identified the following selected transactions that occurred during 2016:

**a.** Issued 850 shares of $5 par common stock for cash of $21,000.

**b.** Issued 5,600 shares of $5 par common stock for a building with a fair market value of $99,000.

**c.** Purchased new truck with a fair market value of $36,000. Financed it 100% with a long-term note.

**d.** Retired short-term notes of $26,000 by issuing 2,500 shares of $5 par common stock.

**e.** Paid long-term note of $8,500 to Bank of Tallahassee. Issued new long-term note of $17,000 to Bank of Trust.

Identify any non-cash transactions that occurred during the year, and show how they would be reported in the non-cash investing and financing activities section of the statement of cash flows.

**Learning Objective 3**

### E14-26 Analyzing free cash flow

Use the Stenback Exercise Equipment data in Exercises E14-23 and E14-24. Stenback plans to purchase a truck for $31,000 and a forklift for $120,000 next year. In addition, it plans to pay cash dividends of $1,000. Assuming Stenback plans similar activity for 2017, what would be the amount of free cash flow?

**Learning Objective 4**
**Appendix 14A**

Net Cash Prov. by Op. Act. $1,000

### E14A-27 Preparing operating activities cash flow—direct method

The accounting records of Grand Auto Parts reveal the following:

| | | | |
|---|---|---|---|
| Payment of salaries and wages | $ 33,000 | Net income | $ 24,000 |
| Depreciation expense | 13,000 | Payment of income tax | 15,000 |
| Payment of interest | 14,000 | Collection of dividend revenue | 7,000 |
| Payment of dividends | 7,000 | Payment to suppliers | 57,000 |
| Collections from customers | 113,000 | | |

Compute cash flows from operating activities using the *direct* method for the year ended December 31, 2016.

## E14A-28 Preparing the statement of cash flows—direct method

**Learning Objective 4**
**Appendix 14A**

Net Cash Prov. by Op. Act. $77,000

The income statement and additional data of Rolling Hills Corporation follow:

| ROLLING HILLS CORPORATION<br>Income Statement<br>Year Ended June 30, 2016 | | |
|---|---|---|
| Sales Revenue | | $ 229,000 |
| Cost of Goods Sold | | 107,000 |
| Gross Profit | | 122,000 |
| Operating Expenses: | | |
| Salaries Expense | $ 46,000 | |
| Depreciation Expense—Plant Assets | 28,000 | |
| Advertising Expense | 11,000 | |
| Total Operating Expenses | | 85,000 |
| Operating Income | | 37,000 |
| Other Revenues and (Expenses): | | |
| Dividend Revenue | 10,500 | |
| Interest Expense | (3,000) | |
| Total Other Revenues and (Expenses) | | 7,500 |
| Net Income Before Income Taxes | | 44,500 |
| Income Tax Expense | | 8,000 |
| Net Income | | **$ 36,500** |

a. Collections from customers are $14,000 more than sales.
b. Dividend revenue, interest expense, and income tax expense equal their cash amounts.
c. Payments to suppliers are the sum of cost of goods sold plus advertising expense.
d. Payments to employees are $1,500 more than salaries expense.
e. Cash payment for the acquisition of plant assets is $108,000.
f. Cash receipts from sale of land total $25,000.
g. Cash receipts from issuance of common stock total $31,000.
h. Payment of long-term notes payable is $17,000.
i. Payment of dividends is $12,000.
j. Cash balance at June 30, 2015, was $28,000; at June 30, 2016, it was $24,000.

Prepare Rolling Hills Corporation's statement of cash flows for the year ended June 30, 2016. Use the *direct* method.

## E14A-29 Computing cash flow items—direct method

**Learning Objective 4**
**Appendix 14A**

1. Cash Receipts from Cust. $66,000

Consider the following facts:

a. Beginning and ending Accounts Receivable are $25,000 and $27,000, respectively. Credit sales for the period total $68,000.
b. Cost of goods sold is $81,000.

c. Beginning Merchandise Inventory balance is $25,000, and ending Merchandise Inventory balance is $26,000.

d. Beginning and ending Accounts Payable are $13,000 and $10,000, respectively.

**Requirements**

1. Compute cash collections from customers.
2. Compute cash payments for merchandise inventory.

**Learning Objective 4**
**Appendix 14A**

2. Cash Paid for Merchandise Inventory $18,482
7. Dividends $213

### E14A-30 Computing cash flow items—direct method

Elite Mobile Homes reported the following in its financial statements for the year ended December 31, 2016:

| | 2016 | 2015 |
|---|---|---|
| **Income Statement** | | |
| Net Sales | $ 24,691 | $ 21,555 |
| Cost of Goods Sold | 18,015 | 15,458 |
| Depreciation Expense | 273 | 229 |
| Other Operating Expenses | 4,427 | 4,221 |
| Income Tax Expense | 533 | 489 |
| Net Income | $ 1,443 | $ 1,158 |
| **Balance Sheet** | | |
| Cash | $ 15 | $ 11 |
| Accounts Receivable | 795 | 612 |
| Merchandise Inventory | 3,485 | 2,833 |
| Property and Equipment, net | 4,367 | 3,457 |
| Accounts Payable | 1,543 | 1,358 |
| Accrued Liabilities | 936 | 847 |
| Long-term Liabilities | 478 | 463 |
| Common Stock, no par | 675 | 445 |
| Retained Earnings | 5,030 | 3,800 |

**Requirements**

1. Compute the collections from customers.
2. Compute payments for merchandise inventory.
3. Compute payments of operating expenses.
4. Compute the acquisitions of property and equipment (no sales of property during 2016).
5. Compute the amount of borrowing, with Elite paying no long-term liabilities.
6. Compute the cash receipt from issuance of common stock.
7. Compute the payment of cash dividends.

**Learning Objective 5**
**Appendix 14B**

### E14B-31 Using a spreadsheet to prepare the statement of cash flows—indirect method

Use the Supplements Plus, Inc. data in Exercise E14-21 to prepare the spreadsheet for the 2016 statement of cash flows. Format cash flows from operating activities by the indirect method.

## > Problems Group A

### P14-32A Identifying the purpose and preparing the statement of cash flows—indirect method

**Learning Objectives 1, 2**

2. Net Income $67,700
4. Net Cash Used by Op. Act. $(61,250)

Official Reserve Rare Coins (ORRC) was formed on January 1, 2016. Additional data for the year follow:

a. On January 1, 2016, ORRC issued no par common stock for $500,000.

b. Early in January, ORRC made the following cash payments:
   1. For store fixtures, $54,000
   2. For merchandise inventory, $270,000
   3. For rent expense on a store building, $11,000

c. Later in the year, ORRC purchased merchandise inventory on account for $244,000. Before year-end, ORRC paid $144,000 of this accounts payable.

d. During 2016, ORRC sold 2,300 units of merchandise inventory for $225 each. Before year-end, the company collected 90% of this amount. Cost of goods sold for the year was $320,000, and ending merchandise inventory totaled $194,000.

e. The store employs three people. The combined annual payroll is $88,000, of which ORRC still owes $6,000 at year-end.

f. At the end of the year, ORRC paid income tax of $20,000. There are no income taxes payable.

g. Late in 2016, ORRC paid cash dividends of $35,000.

h. For store fixtures, ORRC uses the straight-line depreciation method, over five years, with zero residual value.

**Requirements**

1. What is the purpose of the statement of cash flows?
2. Prepare ORRC's income statement for the year ended December 31, 2016. Use the single-step format, with all revenues listed together and all expenses listed together.
3. Prepare ORRC's balance sheet at December 31, 2016.
4. Prepare ORRC's statement of cash flows using the indirect method for the year ended December 31, 2016.

### P14-33A Preparing the statement of cash flows—indirect method

**Learning Objective 2**

Net Cash Used for Inv. Act. $(16,000)

Accountants for Smithson, Inc. have assembled the following data for the year ended December 31, 2016:

| | 2016 | 2015 |
|---|---|---|
| Current Assets: | | |
| Cash | $ 102,700 | $ 20,000 |
| Accounts Receivable | 63,500 | 69,500 |
| Merchandise Inventory | 85,000 | 80,000 |
| Current Liabilities: | | |
| Accounts Payable | $ 57,900 | $ 56,000 |
| Income Tax Payable | 14,400 | 17,000 |

| Transaction Data for 2016: | | | |
|---|---|---|---|
| Issuance of common stock for cash | $ 42,000 | Payment of notes payable | $ 42,100 |
| Depreciation expense | 25,000 | Payment of cash dividends | 52,000 |
| Purchase of equipment with cash | 73,000 | Issuance of notes payable to borrow cash | 60,000 |
| Acquisition of land by issuing long-term notes payable | 118,000 | Gain on sale of building | 4,000 |
| Book value of building sold | 53,000 | Net income | 69,500 |

Prepare Smithson's statement of cash flows using the indirect method. Include an accompanying schedule of non-cash investing and financing activities.

**Learning Objective 2**

1. Net Cash Prov. by Op. Act. $132,700

**P14-34A Preparing the statement of cash flows—indirect method with non-cash transactions**

The 2016 income statement and comparative balance sheet of McKnight, Inc. follow:

| MCKNIGHT, INC.<br>Income Statement<br>Year Ended December 31, 2016 | | |
|---|---|---|
| Sales Revenue | | $ 441,000 |
| Cost of Goods Sold | | 202,200 |
| Gross Profit | | 238,800 |
| Operating Expenses: | | |
| Salaries Expense | $ 76,400 | |
| Depreciation Expense—Plant Assets | 14,200 | |
| Other Operating Expenses | 10,500 | |
| Total Operating Expenses | | 101,100 |
| Operating Income | | 137,700 |
| Other Revenues and (Expenses): | | |
| Interest Revenue | 8,800 | |
| Interest Expense | (21,600) | |
| Total Other Revenues and (Expenses) | | (12,800) |
| Net Income Before Income Taxes | | 124,900 |
| Income Tax Expense | | 19,500 |
| Net Income | | **$ 105,400** |

| MCKNIGHT, INC.<br>Comparative Balance Sheet<br>December 31, 2016 and 2015 | | |
|---|---|---|
| | 2016 | 2015 |
| **Assets** | | |
| Current Assets: | | |
| Cash | $ 26,400 | $ 15,100 |
| Accounts Receivable | 26,700 | 25,200 |
| Merchandise Inventory | 79,700 | 91,600 |
| Long-term Assets: | | |
| Plant Assets | 118,510 | 110,310 |
| Accumulated Depreciation—Plant Assets | (19,610) | (15,610) |
| Land | 34,800 | 7,000 |
| Total Assets | **$ 266,500** | **$ 233,600** |
| **Liabilities** | | |
| Current Liabilities: | | |
| Accounts Payable | $ 35,100 | $ 30,500 |
| Accrued Liabilities | 28,200 | 30,100 |
| Long-term Liabilities: | | |
| Notes Payable | 73,000 | 106,000 |
| Total Liabilities | 136,300 | 166,600 |
| **Stockholders' Equity** | | |
| Common Stock, no par | 88,100 | 64,700 |
| Retained Earnings | 42,100 | 2,300 |
| Total Stockholders' Equity | 130,200 | 67,000 |
| Total Liabilities and Stockholders' Equity | **$ 266,500** | **$ 233,600** |

Additionally, McKnight purchased land of $27,800 by financing it 100% with long-term notes payable during 2016. During the year, there were no sales of land, no retirements of stock, and no treasury stock transactions. A plant asset was disposed of for $0. The cost and the accumulated depreciation of the disposed asset was $10,200. The plant acquisition was for cash.

**Requirements**

1. Prepare the 2016 statement of cash flows, formatting operating activities by the *indirect* method.
2. How will what you learned in this problem help you evaluate an investment?

**Learning Objectives 2, 3**

1. Net Cash Used for Inv. Act. $(157,100)

**P14-35A Preparing the statement of cash flows—indirect method, evaluating cash flows, and measuring free cash flows**

The comparative balance sheet of Morston Educational Supply at December 31, 2016, reported the following:

| | 2016 | 2015 |
|---|---|---|
| Current Assets: | | |
| Cash | $ 85,400 | $ 21,500 |
| Accounts Receivable | 14,800 | 21,500 |
| Merchandise Inventory | 63,000 | 59,400 |
| Current Liabilities: | | |
| Accounts Payable | $ 27,100 | $ 26,100 |
| Accrued Liabilities | 10,400 | 10,900 |

Morston's transactions during 2016 included the following:

| | | | |
|---|---|---|---|
| Payment of cash dividends | $ 20,200 | Depreciation expense | $ 17,000 |
| Purchase of equipment with cash | 55,100 | Purchase of building with cash | 102,000 |
| Issuance of long-term notes payable to borrow cash | 47,000 | Net income | 59,600 |
| Issuance of common stock for cash | 114,000 | | |

**Requirements**

1. Prepare the statement of cash flows of Morston Educational Supply for the year ended December 31, 2016. Use the indirect method to report cash flows from operating activities.
2. Evaluate Morston's cash flows for the year. Mention all three categories of cash flows, and give the reason for your evaluation.
3. If Morston plans similar activity for 2017, what is its expected free cash flow?

**Learning Objective 4**
**Appendix 14A**

2. Total Assets $1,177,800
3. Net Cash Prov. by Op. Act. $356,500

**P14A-36A Preparing the statement of cash flows—direct method**

Frontier Rare Coins (FRC) was formed on January 1, 2016. Additional data for the year follow:

a. On January 1, 2016, FRC issued no par common stock for $500,000.
b. Early in January, FRC made the following cash payments:
   1. For store fixtures, $51,000
   2. For merchandise inventory, $300,000
   3. For rent expense on the store building, $16,000
c. Later in the year, FRC purchased merchandise inventory on account for $239,000. Before year-end, FRC paid $139,000 of this accounts payable.
d. During 2016, FRC sold 2,900 units of merchandise inventory for $350 each. Before year-end, the company collected 90% of this amount. Cost of goods sold for the year was $270,000, and ending merchandise inventory totaled $269,000.
e. The store employs three people. The combined annual payroll is $84,000, of which FRC still owes $2,000 at year-end.
f. At the end of the year, FRC paid income tax of $20,000. There are no income taxes payable.

g. Late in 2016, FRC paid cash dividends of $39,000.

h. For store fixtures, FRC uses the straight-line depreciation method, over five years, with zero residual value.

**Requirements**

1. Prepare FRC's income statement for the year ended December 31, 2016. Use the single-step format, with all revenues listed together and all expenses listed together.
2. Prepare FRC's balance sheet at December 31, 2016.
3. Prepare FRC's statement of cash flows for the year ended December 31, 2016. Format cash flows from operating activities by the direct method.

**P14A-37A Preparing the statement of cash flows—direct method**

**Learning Objective 4**
**Appendix 14A**

1. Net Cash Prov. by Op. Act. $132,700
Collections from Cust. $439,500

Use the McKnight, Inc. data from Problem P14-34A.

**Requirements**

1. Prepare the 2016 statement of cash flows by the direct method.
2. How will what you learned in this problem help you evaluate an investment?

**P14B-38A Using a spreadsheet to prepare the statement of cash flows—indirect method**

**Learning Objective 5**
**Appendix 14B**

Cash Pmt. of Div. $28,400
Cash Pmt. for Acq. of Land $25,600

The 2016 comparative balance sheet and income statement of Allentown Group, Inc. follow. Allentown disposed of a plant asset at book value during 2016.

**ALLENTOWN GROUP, INC.**
Income Statement
Year Ended December 31, 2016

| | | |
|---|---|---|
| Sales Revenue | | $ 439,000 |
| Cost of Goods Sold | | 205,300 |
| Gross Profit | | 233,700 |
| Operating Expenses: | | |
| Salaries Expense | $ 76,600 | |
| Depreciation Expense—Plant Assets | 15,600 | |
| Other Operating Expenses | 49,800 | |
| Total Operating Expenses | | 142,000 |
| Operating Income | | 91,700 |
| Other Revenues and (Expenses): | | |
| Interest Revenue | 11,700 | |
| Interest Expense | (24,500) | |
| Total Other Revenues and (Expenses) | | (12,800) |
| Net Income Before Income Taxes | | 78,900 |
| Income Tax Expense | | 16,400 |
| Net Income | | **$ 62,500** |

| ALLENTOWN GROUP, INC.<br>Comparative Balance Sheet<br>December 31, 2016 and 2015 | 2016 | 2015 |
|---|---|---|
| **Assets** | | |
| Current Assets: | | |
| Cash | $ 9,000 | $ 15,100 |
| Accounts Receivable | 42,300 | 43,300 |
| Merchandise Inventory | 97,200 | 93,400 |
| Long-term Assets: | | |
| Plant Assets | 121,540 | 111,140 |
| Accumulated Depreciation—Plant Assets | (20,240) | (16,840) |
| Land | 37,600 | 12,000 |
| Total Assets | **$ 287,400** | **$ 258,100** |
| **Liabilities** | | |
| Current Liabilities: | | |
| Accounts Payable | $ 24,800 | $ 26,400 |
| Accrued Liabilities | 23,300 | 22,100 |
| Long-term Liabilities: | | |
| Notes Payable | 54,000 | 67,000 |
| Total Liabilities | 102,100 | 115,500 |
| **Stockholders' Equity** | | |
| Common Stock, no par | 131,300 | 122,700 |
| Retained Earnings | 54,000 | 19,900 |
| Total Stockholders' Equity | 185,300 | 142,600 |
| Total Liabilities and Stockholders' Equity | **$ 287,400** | **$ 258,100** |

Prepare the spreadsheet for the 2016 statement of cash flows. Format cash flows from operating activities by the indirect method. A plant asset was disposed of for $0. The cost and accumulated depreciation of the disposed asset was $12,200. There were no sales of land, no retirement of common stock, and no treasury stock transactions. Assume plant asset and land acquisitions were for cash.

## > Problems Group B

**Learning Objectives 1, 2**

2. Net Income $521,400
3. Total Assets $1,038,400
4. Net Cash Prov. by Op. Act. $376,000

### P14-39B Identifying the purpose and preparing the statement of cash flows—indirect method

Frank Rare Coins (FRC) was formed on January 1, 2016. Additional data for the year follow:

**a.** On January 1, 2016, FRC issued no par common stock for $450,000.

**b.** Early in January, FRC made the following cash payments:
1. For store fixtures, $48,000
2. For merchandise inventory, $260,000
3. For rent expense on a store building, $14,000

c. Later in the year, FRC purchased merchandise inventory on account for $237,000. Before year-end, FRC paid $137,000 of this accounts payable.

d. During 2016, FRC sold 2,500 units of merchandise inventory for $400 each. Before year-end, the company collected 90% of this amount. Cost of goods sold for the year was $340,000, and ending merchandise inventory totaled $157,000.

e. The store employs three people. The combined annual payroll is $92,000, of which FRC still owes $2,000 at year-end.

f. At the end of the year, FRC paid income tax of $23,000. There was no income taxes payable.

g. Late in 2016, FRC paid cash dividends of $35,000.

h. For store fixtures, FRC uses the straight-line depreciation method, over five years, with zero residual value.

**Requirements**

1. What is the purpose of the statement of cash flows?
2. Prepare FRC's income statement for the year ended December 31, 2016. Use the single-step format, with all revenues listed together and all expenses listed together.
3. Prepare FRC's balance sheet at December 31, 2016.
4. Prepare FRC's statement of cash flows using the indirect method for the year ended December 31, 2016.

**P14-40B Preparing the statement of cash flows—indirect method**

**Learning Objective 2**

Net Cash Prov. by Op. Act. $85,300

Accountants for Carlson, Inc. have assembled the following data for the year ended December 31, 2016:

| | 2016 | 2015 |
|---|---|---|
| Current Assets: | | |
| Cash | $ 89,200 | $ 18,000 |
| Accounts Receivable | 64,600 | 68,800 |
| Merchandise Inventory | 85,000 | 77,000 |
| Current Liabilities: | | |
| Accounts Payable | $ 57,500 | $ 55,400 |
| Income Tax Payable | 14,700 | 16,200 |

| Transaction Data for 2016: | | | |
|---|---|---|---|
| Issuance of common stock for cash | $ 38,000 | Payment of notes payable | $ 51,100 |
| Depreciation expense | 21,000 | Payment of cash dividends | 46,000 |
| Purchase of equipment with cash | 73,000 | Issuance of notes payable to borrow cash | 61,000 |
| Acquisition of land by issuing long-term notes payable | 122,000 | Gain on sale of building | 2,000 |
| Book value of building sold | 55,000 | Net income | 69,500 |

Prepare Carlson's statement of cash flows using the indirect method. Include an accompanying schedule of non-cash investing and financing activities.

**Learning Objective 2**

1. Net Cash Prov. by Op. Act. $132,000

**P14-41B Preparing the statement of cash flows—indirect method with non-cash transactions**

The 2016 income statement and comparative balance sheet of McDonald, Inc. follow:

| MCDONALD, INC.<br>Income Statement<br>Year Ended December 31, 2016 | | |
|---|---|---|
| Sales Revenue | | $ 443,000 |
| Cost of Goods Sold | | 203,200 |
| Gross Profit | | 239,800 |
| Operating Expenses: | | |
| Salaries Expense | $ 78,400 | |
| Depreciation Expense—Plant Assets | 14,800 | |
| Other Operating Expenses | 10,300 | |
| Total Operating Expenses | | 103,500 |
| Operating Income | | 136,300 |
| Other Revenues and (Expenses): | | |
| Interest Revenue | 8,300 | |
| Interest Expense | (21,800) | |
| Total Other Revenues and (Expenses) | | (13,500) |
| Net Income Before Income Taxes | | 122,800 |
| Income Tax Expense | | 19,200 |
| Net Income | | **$ 103,600** |

| MCDONALD, INC.<br>Comparative Balance Sheet<br>December 31, 2016 and 2015 | | |
|---|---|---|
| | 2016 | 2015 |
| **Assets** | | |
| Current Assets: | | |
| Cash | $ 26,200 | $ 15,100 |
| Accounts Receivable | 26,500 | 25,700 |
| Merchandise Inventory | 79,800 | 91,800 |
| Long-term Assets: | | |
| Plant Assets | 117,240 | 109,480 |
| Accumulated Depreciation—Plant Assets | (21,340) | (19,780) |
| Land | 34,500 | 14,000 |
| Total Assets | **$ 262,900** | **$ 236,300** |
| **Liabilities** | | |
| Current Liabilities: | | |
| Accounts Payable | $ 35,000 | $ 30,000 |
| Accrued Liabilities | 28,300 | 30,900 |
| Long-term Liabilities: | | |
| Notes Payable | 75,000 | 105,000 |
| Total Liabilities | 138,300 | 165,900 |
| **Stockholders' Equity** | | |
| Common Stock, no par | 88,800 | 64,300 |
| Retained Earnings | 35,800 | 6,100 |
| Total Stockholders' Equity | 124,600 | 70,400 |
| Total Liabilities and Stockholders' Equity | **$ 262,900** | **$ 236,300** |

Additionally, McDonald purchased land of $20,500 by financing it 100% with long-term notes payable during 2016. During the year, there were no sales of land, no retirements of stock, and no treasury stock transactions. A plant asset was disposed of for $0. The cost and the accumulated depreciation of the disposed asset was $13,240. Plant asset was acquired for cash.

**Requirements**

1. Prepare the 2016 statement of cash flows, formatting operating activities by the *indirect* method.
2. How will what you learned in this problem help you evaluate an investment?

**Learning Objectives 2, 3**

1. Net Cash Used for Inv. Act. $(156,000)

**P14-42B Preparing the statement of cash flows—indirect method, evaluating cash flows, and measuring free cash flows**

The comparative balance sheet of Morris Educational Supply at December 31, 2016, reported the following:

| | 2016 | 2015 |
|---|---|---|
| Current Assets: | | |
| Cash | $ 90,600 | $ 22,500 |
| Accounts Receivable | 15,100 | 21,600 |
| Merchandise Inventory | 63,800 | 58,600 |
| Current Liabilities: | | |
| Accounts Payable | $ 30,600 | $ 29,100 |
| Accrued Liabilities | 10,500 | 11,800 |

Morris's transactions during 2016 included the following:

| | | | |
|---|---|---|---|
| Payment of cash dividends | $ 17,200 | Depreciation expense | $ 17,200 |
| Purchase of equipment with cash | 55,000 | Purchase of building with cash | 101,000 |
| Issuance of long-term notes payable to borrow cash | 50,000 | Net income | 64,600 |
| Issuance of common stock for cash | 108,000 | | |

**Requirements**

1. Prepare the statement of cash flows of Morris Educational Supply for the year ended December 31, 2016. Use the indirect method to report cash flows from operating activities.
2. Evaluate Morris's cash flows for the year. Mention all three categories of cash flows, and give the reason for your evaluation.
3. If Morris plans similar activity for 2017, what is its expected free cash flow?

**Learning Objective 4**
**Appendix 14A**

1. Net Income $115,200
2. Total Assets $612,200
3. Collections from Cust. $464,000

**P14A-43B Preparing the statement of cash flows—direct method**

Official Reserve Rare Coins (ORRC) was formed on January 1, 2016. Additional data for the year follow:

a. On January 1, 2016, ORRC issued no par common stock for $450,000.

b. Early in January, ORRC made the following cash payments:
   1. For store fixtures, $49,000
   2. For merchandise inventory, $280,000
   3. For rent expense on a store building, $10,000

c. Later in the year, ORRC purchased merchandise inventory on account for $238,000. Before year-end, ORRC paid $158,000 of this accounts payable.

d. During 2016, ORRC sold 2,900 units of merchandise inventory for $200 each. Before year-end, the company collected 80% of this amount. Cost of goods sold for the year was $340,000, and ending merchandise inventory totaled $178,000.

e. The store employs three people. The combined annual payroll is $88,000, of which ORRC still owes $5,000 at year-end.

f. At the end of the year, ORRC paid income tax of $17,000. There was no income taxes payable.

g. Late in 2016, ORRC paid cash dividends of $38,000.

h. For store fixtures, ORRC uses the straight-line depreciation method, over five years, with zero residual value.

### Requirements

1. Prepare ORRC's income statement for the year ended December 31, 2016. Use the single-step format, with all revenues listed together and all expenses listed together.
2. Prepare ORRC's balance sheet at December 31, 2016.
3. Prepare ORRC's statement of cash flows for the year ended December 31, 2016. Format cash flows from operating activities by the direct method.

## P14A-44B Preparing the statement of cash flows—direct method

**Learning Objective 4**
**Appendix 14A**

Use the McDonald data from Problem P14-41B.

1. Net Cash Prov. by Op. Act. $132,000
Collections from Cust. $442,200

### Requirements

1. Prepare the 2016 statement of cash flows by the direct method.
2. How will what you learned in this problem help you evaluate an investment?

## P14B-45B Using a spreadsheet to prepare the statement of cash flows—indirect method

**Learning Objective 5**
**Appendix 14B**

Cash Pmt. of Div. $28,900
Cash Pmt. of N/P $17,000

The 2016 comparative balance sheet and income statement of Abilene Group, Inc. follow. Abilene disposed of a plant asset at book value in 2016.

| ABILENE GROUP, INC.<br>Income Statement<br>Year Ended December 31, 2016 | | |
|---|---|---|
| Sales Revenue | | $ 442,000 |
| Cost of Goods Sold | | 205,200 |
| Gross Profit | | 236,800 |
| Operating Expenses: | | |
| Salaries Expense | $ 76,800 | |
| Depreciation Expense | 15,900 | |
| Other Operating Expenses | 49,600 | |
| Total Operating Expenses | | 142,300 |
| Operating Income | | 94,500 |
| Other Revenues and (Expenses): | | |
| Interest Revenue | 11,300 | |
| Interest Expense | (24,200) | |
| Total Other Revenues and (Expenses) | | (12,900) |
| Net Income Before Income Taxes | | 81,600 |
| Income Tax Expense | | 16,600 |
| Net Income | | **$ 65,000** |

CHAPTER 14

| ABILENE GROUP, INC. Comparative Balance Sheet December 31, 2016 and 2015 | | |
|---|---|---|
| | 2016 | 2015 |
| **Assets** | | |
| Current Assets: | | |
| Cash | $ 10,600 | $ 15,700 |
| Accounts Receivable | 41,900 | 43,500 |
| Merchandise Inventory | 96,300 | 93,100 |
| Long-term Assets: | | |
| Plant Assets | 121,860 | 112,060 |
| Accumulated Depreciation—Plant Assets | (21,060) | (17,560) |
| Land | 39,600 | 14,000 |
| Total Assets | **$ 289,200** | **$ 260,800** |
| **Liabilities** | | |
| Current Liabilities: | | |
| Accounts Payable | $ 25,100 | $ 26,300 |
| Accrued Liabilities | 24,100 | 22,400 |
| Long-term Liabilities: | | |
| Notes Payable | 44,000 | 61,000 |
| Total Liabilities | 93,200 | 109,700 |
| **Stockholders' Equity** | | |
| Common Stock, no par | 140,400 | 131,600 |
| Retained Earnings | 55,600 | 19,500 |
| Total Stockholders' Equity | 196,000 | 151,100 |
| Total Liabilities and Stockholders' Equity | **$ 289,200** | **$ 260,800** |

Prepare the spreadsheet for the 2016 statement of cash flows. Format cash flows from operating activities by the indirect method. A plant asset was disposed of for $0. The cost and accumulated depreciation of the disposed asset was $12,400. There were no sales of land, no retirement of common stock, and no treasury stock transactions. Assume plant asset and land acquisitions were for cash.

## > Continuing Problem

### P14-46 Preparing the statement of cash flows—indirect method

This problem continues the Daniels Consulting situation from Problem P13-47 of Chapter 13. Daniels Consulting's comparative balance sheet is shown on the next page.

| DANIELS CONSULTING<br>Comparative Balance Sheet<br>December 31, 2017 and 2016 | | |
|---|---|---|
| | 2017 | 2016 |
| **Assets** | | |
| Current Assets: | | |
| Cash | $ 1,457,524 | $ 31,700 |
| Accounts Receivable | 25,700 | 700 |
| Office Supplies | 2,150 | 50 |
| Long-term Assets: | | |
| Plants Assets | 84,800 | 4,800 |
| Accumulated Depreciation—Plant Assets | (1,696) | (80) |
| Total Assets | **$ 1,568,478** | **$ 37,170** |
| **Liabilities** | | |
| Current Liabilities: | | |
| Accounts Payable | $ 7,300 | $ 4,100 |
| Salaries Payable | 1,800 | 467 |
| Unearned Revenue | 0 | 1,600 |
| Interest Payable | 25,000 | 0 |
| Long-term Liabilities: | | |
| Notes Payable | 500,000 | 0 |
| Bonds Payable | 900,000 | 0 |
| Discount on Bonds Payable | (100,862) | 0 |
| Total Liabilities | 1,333,238 | 6,167 |
| **Stockholders' Equity** | | |
| Common Stock, no par | 115,240 | 240 |
| Retained Earnings | 120,000 | 30,763 |
| Total Stockholders' Equity | 235,240 | 31,003 |
| Total Liabilities and Stockholders' Equity | **$ 1,568,478** | **$ 37,170** |

Additional data follow:

a. Depreciation expense for the year, $1,616.

b. Daniels Consulting had no disposal of plant assets during the year. Plant assets were acquired for cash.

c. Amortization of the discount on bonds payable for the year, $11,206.

d. Daniels Consulting issued a bonds payable with a face value of $900,000, receiving cash of $787,932.

e. Net income for the year was $190,537.

f. Cash receipts from issuance of common stock totaled $115,000.

Prepare the statement of cash flows using the indirect method.

# CRITICAL THINKING

## > Decision Case 14-1

Theater by Design and Show Cinemas are asking you to recommend their stock to your clients. Because Theater by Design and Show Cinemas earn about the same net income and have similar financial positions, your decision depends on their statement of cash flows, summarized as follows:

| | Theater by Design | | Show Cinemas | |
|---|---|---|---|---|
| Net Cash Provided by Operating Activities | | $ 30,000 | | $ 70,000 |
| Cash Provided by (Used for) Investing Activities: | | | | |
| Purchase of Plant Assets | $ (20,000) | | $ (100,000) | |
| Sale of Plant Assets | 40,000 | 20,000 | 10,000 | (90,000) |
| Cash Provided by (Used for) Financing Activities: | | | | |
| Issuance of common stock | | 0 | | 30,000 |
| Payment of long-term debt | | (40,000) | | 0 |
| Net Increase (Decrease) in Cash | | $ 10,000 | | $ 10,000 |

Based on their cash flows, which company looks better? Give your reasons.

## > Ethical Issue 14-1

Moss Exports is having a bad year. Net income is only $60,000. Also, two important overseas customers are falling behind in their payments to Moss, and Moss's accounts receivable are ballooning. The company desperately needs a loan. The Moss Exports Board of Directors is considering ways to put the best face on the company's financial statements. Moss's bank closely examines cash flow from operating activities. Daniel Peavey, Moss's controller, suggests reclassifying the receivables from the slow-paying clients as long-term. He explains to the board that removing the $80,000 increase in accounts receivable from current assets will increase net cash provided by operations. This approach may help Moss get the loan.

**Requirements**

1. Using only the amounts given, compute net cash provided by operations, both without and with the reclassification of the receivables. Which reporting makes Moss look better?
2. Under what condition would the reclassification of the receivables be ethical? Unethical?

## > Financial Statement Case 14-1

Details about a company's cash flows appear in a number of places in the annual report. Use **Starbucks Corporation's** Fiscal 2013 Annual Report to answer the following questions. Visit **http://www.pearsonhighered.com/Horngren** to view a link to Starbucks Corporation's Fiscal 2013 Annual Report.

**Requirements**

1. Which method does Starbucks use to report net cash flows from *operating* activities? How can you tell?
2. Starbucks earned net income during 2013. Did operations *provide* cash or *use* cash during 2013? Give the amount. How did operating cash during 2013 compare with 2012?
3. For the year ended September 29, 2013, did Starbucks pay cash dividends? If so, how much?
4. For the year ended September 29, 2013, did Starbucks use cash to purchase property, plant, and equipment? If so, how much?



## > Quick Check Answers

**1.** d **2.** d **3.** b **4.** a **5.** d **6.** c **7.** c **8.** c **9A.** d **10B.** a

# 15 Financial Statement Analysis

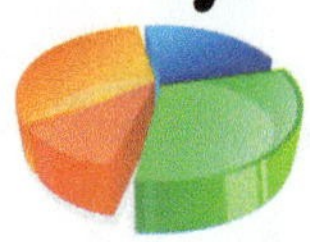

## What Companies Should I Invest In?

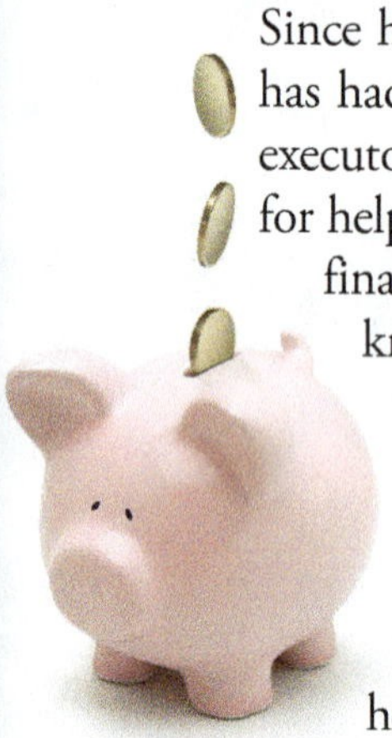

Clara Salerno misses her mom, Sylvia, a lot these days. Her mom always knew just the right words to say when Clara came to visit after a long hard day at work, and her mom's chocolate cookies always worked magic in making her feel better. Since her mom passed away six months ago, Clara has had to make a lot of decisions on her own. As executor of her mom's estate, she was responsible for helping the accountant and attorney finalize the financial details and the estate paperwork. Clara knew that once the estate was settled, she would be receiving a large amount of cash. She knew that deciding what to do with the cash would be a very important decision.

When Clara met with her financial planner, she shared her goals of paying off her student loans and other personal debt and then saving toward her retirement. She wanted to take the cash remaining after paying off her debts and invest it in the stock market. Clara was worried, though. She tried to stay current on the financial markets by reading the business section of the newspaper and listening to the financial news, but she wasn't sure how to decide which companies would be the best investment choices. Clara's financial planner advised her that there are a number of tools that she could use to evaluate companies and determine which company is more profitable. Other tools will be helpful in helping her determine trends across a period of time. Clara knew that with help from her financial planner and these tools she could make sense out of companies' financial statements and invest with a confidence that would make her mom proud.

### What Are the Tools That Help Users Analyze a Business?

In this chapter, you learn about tools that allow users to see beyond the pure numbers on the financial statements and translate them into meaningful analysis. So far you have learned some of what it takes to prepare financial statements; now you will learn how to use financial statements to help manage a company effectively, make wise investments, and compare one company to another. Certified financial planners who work for companies, such as Raymond James Financial, Inc., a financial services holding company that operates a full-service brokerage and investment firm headquartered in Florida, analyze financial statements to compare a company's performance across several periods of time. This comparison helps investors determine how a company is performing over time. In addition, financial planners use another tool, called ratio analysis, to measure one company against other companies in the same industry. Whether you will be an investor, an employee, or a manager of a company, knowing how to evaluate a company's performance accurately will help you make smart business decisions.

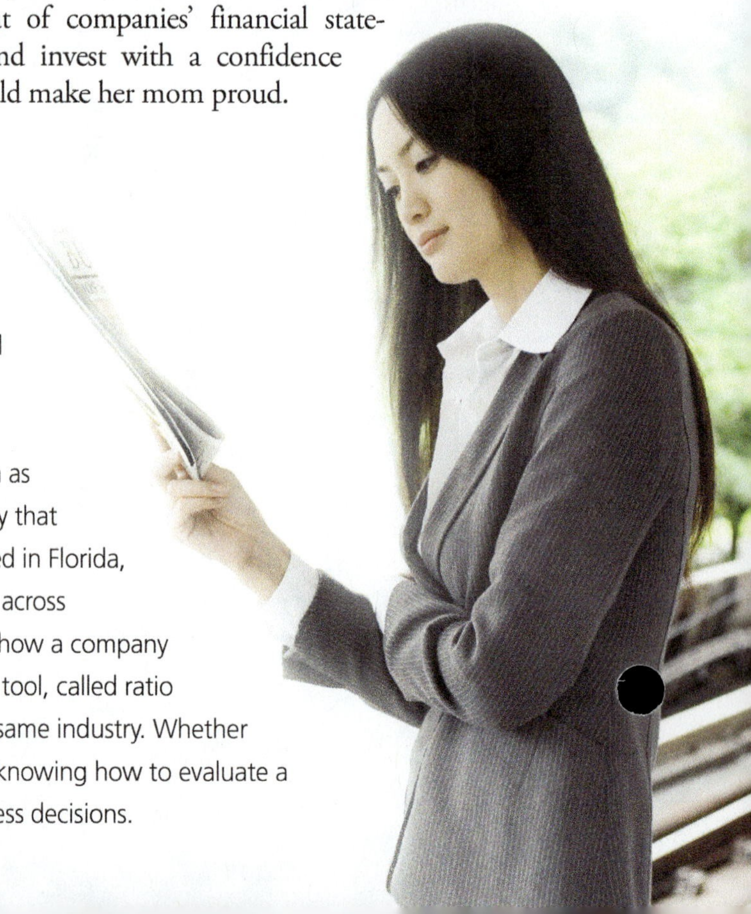

# Chapter 15 Learning Objectives

1. Explain how financial statements are used to analyze a business
2. Perform a horizontal analysis of financial statements
3. Perform a vertical analysis of financial statements
4. Compute and evaluate the standard financial ratios
5. Complete a corporate income statement including earnings per share (Appendix 15A)

## HOW ARE FINANCIAL STATEMENTS USED TO ANALYZE A BUSINESS?

**Learning Objective 1**
Explain how financial statements are used to analyze a business

In this chapter, we use what you have learned about financial statements to analyze Smart Touch Learning. We will determine if it was profitable, as well as its overall financial health.

### Purpose of Analysis

Investors and creditors cannot evaluate a company by examining only one year's data. That is why most financial statements cover at least two periods. In fact, most financial analyses cover trends over three to five years. This chapter shows you how to use some of the analytical tools for charting a company's progress through time. These tools can be used by small business owners to measure performance, by financial analysts to analyze stock investments, by auditors to obtain an overall sense of a company's financial health, by creditors to determine credit risk, or by any other person wanting to compare financial data in relevant terms.

To accurately determine the financial performance of a company, such as Smart Touch Learning, we need to compare its performance in the following ways:

- from year to year
- with a competing company
- with the same industry as a whole

After this comparison, we will have a better idea of how to judge the company's present situation and predict what might happen in the near future.

### Tools of Analysis

There are three main ways to analyze financial statements:

- Horizontal analysis provides a year-to-year comparison of a company's performance in different periods.
- Vertical analysis provides a way to compare different companies.
- Ratio analysis can be used to provide information about a company's performance. It is used most effectively to measure a company against other companies in the same industry and to denote trends within the company.

### Corporate Financial Reports

Before we discuss the different tools available for financial statement analysis, let's review corporate financial reports.

## Annual Reports

**Annual Report**
Provides information about a company's financial condition.

Publicly traded corporations have their stock listed on public stock exchanges, such as the New York Stock Exchange or the NASDAQ. They are required by the Securities and Exchange Commission (SEC) to file annual and quarterly reports (also called a *Form 10-K* and *Form 10-Q*). An **annual report** provides information about a company's financial condition. These reports help investors make informed investment decisions. A typical annual report begins with an overview of the business—including the industry the company is in, its growth strategy, and an overview of the company's brands. It also often discusses the company's competitors and the risks related to the company's business.

## Management's Discussion and Analysis of Financial Condition and Results of Operations

**Management's Discussion and Analysis of Financial Condition and Results of Operations (MD&A)**
The section of the annual report that is intended to help investors understand the results of operations and the financial condition of the company.

Another part of the annual report is **management's discussion and analysis of financial condition and results of operations (MD&A)**. This section of the annual report is intended to help investors understand the results of operations and the financial condition of the company. It is important to realize that this section is written by the company and could present a biased view of the company's financial condition and results. This section of the report is the company's attempt to explain its financial statements and to discuss its performance.

The MD&A section is of interest to investors, though, because it often contains information that is not found in the financial data. Such information might include how a company is planning to spend its cash during the next year for property, plant, and equipment or whether significant changes are expected to occur that would cause revenue or expenses to increase or decrease in the future. This section often provides forward-looking information that can be useful to investors who are trying to estimate what future earnings will be for the company.

## Report of Independent Registered Public Accounting Firm

A report of the independent registered public accounting firm (often referred to as the *auditor's report*) is included in an annual report. The audit report attests to the fairness of the presentation of the financial statements and states whether the financial statements are presented in accordance with Generally Accepted Accounting Principles (GAAP). This report is prepared by an independent external auditor who has performed an audit on the financial statements. In addition, the external auditor is responsible for assessing the effectiveness of the company's internal controls.

Most audit reports have *unqualified opinions*, which means that the financial statements are presented fairly, in all material respects. A *qualified opinion* might be issued if the financial statements include a departure from GAAP. If the auditor finds that the financial statements are not represented fairly, an *adverse opinion* would be given.

## DECISIONS

### Should an unqualified opinion be issued?

Patty Schneider was performing the independent audit for Drake Storage, Inc. Patty was reviewing the work that her staff auditors had completed, and she had several concerns about the company's financial statements. Patty's staff had determined that Drake had underreported its cost of goods sold in order to overstate net income. Patty had spoken to Drake Storage's audit committee and discussed her concerns. The audit committee disagreed with the accounting firm's findings. What should Patty do?

### Solution

Patty's accounting firm should issue either a qualified opinion or an adverse opinion. To issue an unqualified opinion stating that the financial statements are presented fairly in all material respects would be misleading to investors and creditors. As an independent auditor, Patty's primary responsibility is to report on the fairness of the financial statements and assure the public that the financial statements are presented in accordance with GAAP. If they are not, her firm has a responsibility to issue either a qualified or adverse opinion.

### Financial Statements

An annual report contains the four basic financial statements you have learned in this textbook: the balance sheet (sometimes referred to as *statement of financial position)*, the income statement (or *statement of operations)*, the statement of stockholders' equity, and the statement of cash flows. Corporations are required to report multiple-period information for all financial statements. For example, the **Green Mountain Coffee Roasters, Inc.** 2013 Annual Report presents financial data for the past three fiscal periods (2013, 2012, and 2011).

### Notes to Financial Statements

Immediately following the financial statements are the notes to the financial statements. These notes include a summary of significant accounting policies and explanations of specific items on the financial statements. These notes are an important part of the financial statements and are often referred to by investors to understand the information included in the financial statements.

## Try It!

Match the different parts of the annual report with the appropriate description.

| | |
|---|---|
| 1. Includes the income statement, balance sheet, statement of stockholders' equity, and statement of cash flows. | a. Notes to financial statements |
| 2. Attests to the fairness of the presentation of the financial statements. | b. Report of independent registered public accounting firm |
| 3. Includes a summary of significant accounting policies and explanations of specific items on the financial statements. | c. Management's discussion and analysis of financial condition and results of operations (MD&A) |
| 4. Is written by the company to help investors understand the results of operations and the financial condition of the company. | d. Financial statements |

**Check your answers online in MyAccountingLab or at http://www.pearsonhighered.com/Horngren.**

For more practice, see Short Exercise S15-1. MyAccountingLab

## HOW DO WE USE HORIZONTAL ANALYSIS TO ANALYZE A BUSINESS?

**Learning Objective 2**
Perform a horizontal analysis of financial statements

Many decisions hinge on whether the numbers—sales, expenses, and net income, for example—are increasing or decreasing. For example, have sales and other revenues risen from last year? By how much?

Sales may have increased, but considered in isolation, this fact is not very helpful. The *percentage change* in sales over time is more relative and, therefore, more helpful. For example, if a company had sales of $100,000 one year and sales increased by $50,000 the next year, that would be a significant increase. However, if the company had sales of $1 billion and sales increased by $50,000, that would not be significant. Therefore, it is often more relevant to know the percentage increase than the dollar increase.

**Horizontal Analysis**
The study of percentage changes in comparative financial statements. (Dollar amount of change / Base period amount) × 100.

The study of percentage changes in comparative financial statements is called **horizontal analysis**. Horizontal analysis compares one year to the next. Computing a percentage change in comparative statements requires two steps:

1. Compute the dollar amount of the change from the earlier period to the later period.
2. Divide the dollar amount of change by the earlier period amount. We call the earlier period the base period.

Horizontal analysis is illustrated for Smart Touch Learning as:

| | | | Increase (Decrease) | |
|---|---|---|---|---|
| | 2018 | 2017 | Amount | Percentage |
| Net Sales | $858,000 | $803,000 | $55,000 | 6.8% |

Smart Touch Learning's net sales increased by 6.8% during 2018, computed as follows:

**Step 1:** Compute the dollar amount of change in sales from 2017 to 2018:

Dollar amount of change = Later period amount − Earlier period amount
= $858,000 − $803,000
= $55,000

**Step 2:** Divide the dollar amount of change by the base period amount and multiply by 100. This computes the percentage change for the period:

Horizontal analysis % = (Dollar amount of change / Base period amount) × 100
= ($55,000 / $803,000) × 100
= 6.8*

*All percentage calculations are rounded to the nearest tenth for the rest of this chapter.

## Horizontal Analysis of the Income Statement

The horizontal analysis of Smart Touch Learning's income statement is shown in Exhibit 15-1. This comparative income statement reveals a significant amount of growth during 2018. Although gross profit only increased by 17.3%, Smart Touch Learning was able to trim its expenses, creating an 84.6% growth in net income.

Two items on Smart Touch Learning's income statement with the slowest growth rates are Cost of Goods Sold and Administrative Expenses. Cost of Goods Sold increased by only 0.8%, and administrative expenses decreased by 4.1%. On the bottom line, net income grew by an incredible 84.6%. That is real progress!

**Exhibit 15-1 | Comparative Income Statement—Horizontal Analysis**

| SMART TOUCH LEARNING<br>Income Statement<br>Years Ended December 31, 2018 and 2017 | | | | |
|---|---|---|---|---|
| | | | Increase (Decrease) | |
| | 2018 | 2017 | Amount | Percentage |
| Net Sales | $ 858,000 | $ 803,000 | $ 55,000 | 6.8% |
| Cost of Goods Sold | 513,000 | 509,000 | 4,000 | 0.8 |
| Gross Profit | 345,000 | 294,000 | 51,000 | 17.3 |
| Operating Expenses: | | | | |
| Selling Expenses | 126,000 | 114,000 | 12,000 | 10.5 |
| Administrative Expenses | 118,000 | 123,000 | (5,000) | (4.1) |
| Total Operating Expenses | 244,000 | 237,000 | 7,000 | 3.0 |
| Operating Income | 101,000 | 57,000 | 44,000 | 77.2 |
| Other Revenues and (Expenses): | | | | |
| Interest Revenue | 4,000 | 0 | 4,000 | — |
| Interest Expense | (24,000) | (14,000) | 10,000 | 71.4 |
| Total Other Revenues and (Expenses) | (20,000) | (14,000) | 6,000 | 42.9 |
| Income Before Income Taxes | 81,000 | 43,000 | 38,000 | 88.4 |
| Income Tax Expense | 33,000 | 17,000 | 16,000 | 94.1 |
| Net Income | **$ 48,000** | **$ 26,000** | **$ 22,000** | **84.6%** |

## Horizontal Analysis of the Balance Sheet

Horizontal analysis of Smart Touch Learning's comparative balance sheet is shown in Exhibit 15-2 (on the next page). This analysis also shows growth in assets, with total assets increasing by 22.2%. Notice that both Cash and Prepaid Expenses decreased during the year, but this decrease was offset by increases in other assets.

Smart Touch Learning's liabilities also grew. Total liabilities increased by 33.0%, and Accrued Liabilities actually decreased, as indicated by the liability figure in parentheses. This is another indicator of positive growth for Smart Touch Learning.

**Exhibit 15-2** | **Comparative Balance Sheet—Horizontal Analysis**

**SMART TOUCH LEARNING**
Balance Sheet
December 31, 2018 and 2017

| | | | Increase (Decrease) | |
|---|---|---|---|---|
| | **2018** | **2017** | **Amount** | **Percentage** |
| **Assets** | | | | |
| Current Assets: | | | | |
| Cash and Cash Equivalents | $ 29,000 | $ 32,000 | $ (3,000) | (9.4)% |
| Accounts Receivable, Net | 114,000 | 85,000 | 29,000 | 34.1 |
| Merchandise Inventory | 113,000 | 111,000 | 2,000 | 1.8 |
| Prepaid Expenses | 6,000 | 8,000 | (2,000) | (25.0) |
| Total Current Assets | 262,000 | 236,000 | 26,000 | 11.0 |
| Long-term Investments | 18,000 | 9,000 | 9,000 | 100.0 |
| Property, Plant, and Equipment, Net | 507,000 | 399,000 | 108,000 | 27.1 |
| Total Assets | **$ 787,000** | **$ 644,000** | **$ 143,000** | **22.2%** |
| **Liabilities** | | | | |
| Current Liabilities: | | | | |
| Accounts Payable | $ 73,000 | $ 68,000 | $ 5,000 | 7.4 |
| Accrued Liabilities | 27,000 | 31,000 | (4,000) | (12.9) |
| Notes Payable | 42,000 | 27,000 | 15,000 | 55.6 |
| Total Current Liabilities | 142,000 | 126,000 | 16,000 | 12.7 |
| Long-term Liabilities | 289,000 | 198,000 | 91,000 | 46.0 |
| Total Liabilities | 431,000 | 324,000 | 107,000 | 33.0% |
| **Stockholders' Equity** | | | | |
| Common Stock, no par | 186,000 | 186,000 | 0 | 0.0% |
| Retained Earnings | 170,000 | 134,000 | 36,000 | 26.9% |
| Total Stockholders' Equity | 356,000 | 320,000 | 36,000 | 11.3% |
| Total Liabilities and Stockholders' Equity | **$ 787,000** | **$ 644,000** | **$ 143,000** | **22.2%** |

## Trend Analysis

**Trend Analysis**
A form of horizontal analysis in which percentages are computed by selecting a base period as 100% and expressing amounts for following periods as a percentage of the base period amount. (Any period amount / Base period amount) × 100.

**Trend analysis** is a form of horizontal analysis. Trend percentages indicate the direction a business is taking. For example, how have sales changed over a five-year period? What trend does net income show? These questions can be answered by trend analysis over a period, such as three to five years.

Trend analysis percentages are computed by selecting a base period (for example, the earliest year). The base period amounts are set equal to 100%. The amounts for each subsequent year are expressed as a percentage of the base amount. To compute trend analysis percentages, we divide each item for the following years by the base period amount and multiply by 100.

Trend % = (Any period amount / Base period amount) × 100

Assume Smart Touch Learning's Net Sales were $750,000 in 2014 and rose to $858,000 in 2018. To illustrate trend analysis, review the trend of net sales during 2014–2018. The base year is 2014, so that year's percentage is set equal to 100.

| | 2018 | 2017 | 2016 | 2015 | 2014 |
|---|---|---|---|---|---|
| Net Sales | $ 858,000 | $ 803,000 | $ 780,000 | $ 748,000 | $ 750,000 |
| Trend Percentages | 114% | 107% | 104% | 99.7% | 100% |

We want percentages for the five-year period 2014–2018. We compute these by dividing each year's net sales amount by the 2014 net sales amount and multiply by 100. For example, the trend percentage for 2015 is calculated as follows:

$$\begin{aligned} \text{Trend } \% &= (\text{Any period amount} / \text{Base period amount}) \times 100 \\ &= (\$748{,}000 / \$750{,}000) \times 100 \\ &= 99.7\% \end{aligned}$$

Notice that net sales decreased slightly in 2015, and then the rate of growth increased from 2016–2018. You can perform a trend analysis on any one or multiple item(s) you consider important. Trend analysis is widely used to predict the future health of a company.

Trend analysis and horizontal analysis are very similar, but they can be used to indicate different things for a company. **Horizontal analysis allows a company to see the percentage change from one year to the next. Trend analysis shows the percentage change from a base year forward to determine whether the trend in net sales, for example, is positive or negative over a longer period of time.**

What is the difference between horizontal analysis and trend analysis?

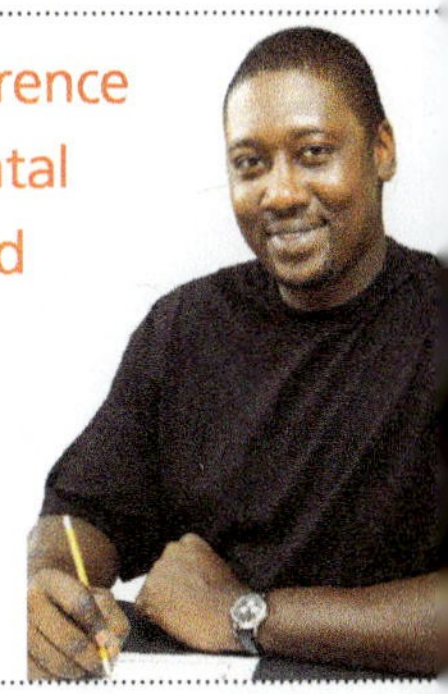

## Try It!

5. Freedom Corp. reported the following on its comparative income statement:

| *(In millions)* | 2017 | 2016 |
|---|---|---|
| Revenue | $ 10,000 | $ 8,000 |
| Cost of Goods Sold | 4,500 | 3,000 |

Prepare a horizontal analysis of revenues, cost of goods sold, and gross profit—both in dollar amounts and in percentages.

**Check your answers online in MyAccountingLab or at http://www.pearsonhighered.com/Horngren.**

For more practice, see Short Exercises S15-2 and S15-3. MyAccountingLab

## HOW DO WE USE VERTICAL ANALYSIS TO ANALYZE A BUSINESS?

**Learning Objective 3**
Perform a vertical analysis of financial statements

As you have seen, horizontal analysis and trend analysis percentages highlight changes in an item from year to year, or over *time*. But no single technique gives a complete picture of a business, so we also need vertical analysis.

**Vertical Analysis**
An analysis of a financial statement that reveals the relationship of each statement item to its base amount, which is the 100% figure. (Specific item / Base amount) × 100.

**Vertical analysis** of a financial statement shows the relationship of each item to its base amount, which is the 100% figure. Every other item on the statement is then reported as a percentage of that base. For the income statement, net sales the base. For the balance sheet, total assets the base.

Vertical analysis % = (Specific item / Base amount) × 100

## Vertical Analysis of the Income Statement

Exhibit 15-3 shows the completed vertical analysis of Smart Touch Learning's 2018 and 2017 comparative income statement.

**Exhibit 15-3 | Comparative Income Statement—Vertical Analysis**

SMART TOUCH LEARNING
Income Statement
Years Ended December 31, 2018 and 2017

| | 2018 | Percent of Total | 2017 | Percent of Total |
|---|---|---|---|---|
| Net Sales | $ 858,000 | 100.0% | $ 803,000 | 100.0% |
| Cost of Goods Sold | 513,000 | 59.8 | 509,000 | 63.4 |
| Gross Profit | 345,000 | 40.2 | 294,000 | 36.6 |
| Operating Expenses: | | | | |
| Selling Expenses | 126,000 | 14.7 | 114,000 | 14.2 |
| Administrative Expenses | 118,000 | 13.8 | 123,000 | 15.3 |
| Total Operating Expenses | 244,000 | 28.4 | 237,000 | 29.5 |
| Operating Income | 101,000 | 11.8 | 57,000 | 7.1 |
| Other Revenues and (Expenses): | | | | |
| Interest Revenue | 4,000 | 0.5 | 0 | 0.0 |
| Interest Expense | (24,000) | (2.8) | (14,000) | (1.7) |
| Total Other Revenues and (Expenses) | (20,000) | (2.3) | (14,000) | (1.7) |
| Income Before Income Taxes | 81,000 | 9.4 | 43,000 | 5.4 |
| Income Tax Expense | 33,000 | 3.8 | 17,000 | 2.1 |
| Net Income | **$ 48,000** | **5.6%** | **$ 26,000** | **3.2%** |

The vertical analysis percentage for Smart Touch Learning's cost of goods sold is 59.8% of net sales (($513,000 / $858,000) × 100 = 59.8%) in 2018 and 63.4% (($509,000 / $803,000) × 100 = 63.4%) in 2017. This means that for every $1 in net sales, almost $0.60 in 2018 and approximately $0.63 in 2017 is spent on cost of goods sold.

Smart Touch Learning's net income is 5.6% of net sales in 2018 and 3.2% of net sales in 2017. That improvement from 2017 to 2018 is extremely good. Suppose under normal conditions a company's net income is 10% of revenues. A drop to 4% may cause the investors to be alarmed and sell their stock.

## Vertical Analysis of the Balance Sheet

Exhibit 15-4 depicts the vertical analysis of Smart Touch Learning's balance sheet. The base amount (100%) is total assets. The base amount is also total liabilities and stockholders' equity because they are exactly the same number (remember the accounting equation); in 2018, that's $787,000.

**Exhibit 15-4 | Comparative Balance Sheet—Vertical Analysis**

**SMART TOUCH LEARNING**
Balance Sheet
December 31, 2018 and 2017

| | 2018 | Percent of Total | 2017 | Percent of Total |
|---|---|---|---|---|
| **Assets** | | | | |
| Current Assets: | | | | |
| Cash and Cash Equivalents | $ 29,000 | 3.7% | $ 32,000 | 5.0% |
| Accounts Receivable, Net | 114,000 | 14.5 | 85,000 | 13.2 |
| Merchandise Inventory | 113,000 | 14.4 | 111,000 | 17.2 |
| Prepaid Expenses | 6,000 | 0.8 | 8,000 | 1.2 |
| Total Current Assets | 262,000 | 33.3 | 236,000 | 36.6 |
| Long-term Investments | 18,000 | 2.3 | 9,000 | 1.4 |
| Property, Plant, and Equipment, Net | 507,000 | 64.4 | 399,000 | 62.0 |
| Total Assets | **$ 787,000** | **100.0%** | **$ 644,000** | **100.0%** |
| **Liabilities** | | | | |
| Current Liabilities: | | | | |
| Accounts Payable | $ 73,000 | 9.3% | $ 68,000 | 10.6% |
| Accrued Liabilities | 27,000 | 3.4 | 31,000 | 4.8 |
| Notes Payable | 42,000 | 5.3 | 27,000 | 4.2 |
| Total Current Liabilities | 142,000 | 18.0 | 126,000 | 19.6 |
| Long-term Liabilities | 289,000 | 36.7 | 198,000 | 30.7 |
| Total Liabilities | 431,000 | 54.8 | 324,000 | 50.3 |
| **Stockholders' Equity** | | | | |
| Common Stock, no par | 186,000 | 23.6 | 186,000 | 28.9 |
| Retained Earnings | 170,000 | 21.6 | 134,000 | 20.8 |
| Total Stockholders' Equity | 356,000 | 45.2 | 320,000 | 49.7 |
| Total Liabilities and Stockholders' Equity | **$ 787,000** | **100.0%** | **$ 644,000** | **100.0%** |

The vertical analysis of Smart Touch Learning's balance sheet reveals several interesting things:

- Current assets make up 33.3% of total assets in 2018 and 36.6% of total assets in 2017. This is typical for most companies with current assets representing close to 30% of total assets.
- Total liabilities are 54.8% of total assets in 2018, increasing slightly from 2017, 50.3%.
- Stockholders' equity makes up 45.2% of total assets in 2018 and 49.7% of total assets in 2017. The percentage share of total assets was nearly equally distributed between total liabilities and total equity for both years.

## Common-Size Statements

Horizontal analysis and vertical analysis provide much useful data about a company. As we have seen, Smart Touch Learning's percentages depict a very successful company. But the data apply only to one business.

To compare Smart Touch Learning to another company, we can use a common-size statement. A **common-size statement** reports only percentages—the same percentages that appear in a vertical analysis. By only reporting percentages, it removes dollar value bias when comparing one company to another company. **Dollar value bias** is the bias one sees from comparing numbers in absolute (dollars) rather than relative (percentage) terms. For us, $1 million seems like a large number. For some large companies, it is immaterial.

**Common-Size Statement**
A financial statement that reports only percentages (no dollar amounts).

**Dollar Value Bias**
The bias one sees from comparing numbers in absolute (dollars) rather than relative (percentage) terms.

We could prepare common-size statements for Smart Touch Learning from year to year; however, we will start by preparing common-size income statements for Smart Touch Learning and Learning School, another fictitious company, both of which compete in the same industry. Which company earns a higher percentage of revenues as profits for its shareholders? Exhibit 15-5 gives both companies' common-size income statements for 2018 so that we can compare them on a relative, not absolute, basis.

**Exhibit 15-5 | Common-Size Income Statement—Smart Touch Learning Versus Learning School**

**SMART TOUCH LEARNING Versus LEARNING SCHOOL**
Common-Size Income Statement
Year Ended December 31, 2018

| | Smart Touch Learning | Learning School |
|---|---|---|
| Net Sales | 100.0% | 100.0% |
| Cost of Goods Sold | 59.8 | 36.3 |
| Gross Profit | 40.2 | 63.7 |
| Operating Expenses: | | |
| Selling Expenses | 14.7 | 21.8 |
| Administrative Expenses | 13.8 | 7.3 |
| Total Operating Expenses | 28.4 | 29.1 |
| Operating Income | 11.8 | 34.6 |
| Other Revenues and (Expenses): | | |
| Interest Revenue | 0.5 | 11.5 |
| Interest Expense | (2.8) | (10.3) |
| Total Other Revenues and (Expenses) | (2.3) | 1.2 |
| Income Before Income Taxes | 9.4 | 35.8 |
| Income Tax Expense | 3.8 | 12.3 |
| Net Income | **5.6%** | **23.5%** |

Exhibit 15-5 shows that Learning School was more profitable than Smart Touch Learning in 2018. Learning School's gross profit percentage is 63.7%, compared with Smart Touch Learning's 40.2%. This means that Learning School is earning more gross profit from every dollar of revenue than Smart Touch Learning is earning. And, most importantly, Learning School's percentage of net income to revenues is 23.5%. That means almost one-fourth of Learning School's revenues result in profits for the company's stockholders. Smart Touch Learning's percentage of net income to revenues, on the other hand, is 5.6%, significantly lower than Learning School's. Smart Touch Learning's lower net income is directly attributable to its larger percentage of cost of goods sold to net sales. Smart Touch Learning's cost of goods sold represents 59.8% of net sales, whereas Learning School's cost of goods sold is only 36.3%.

## Benchmarking

**Benchmarking** is the practice of comparing a company with other leading companies. It often uses the common-size percentages in a graphical manner to highlight differences. There are two main types of benchmarks in financial statement analysis: benchmarking against a key competitor and benchmarking against the industry average.

**Benchmarking**
The practice of comparing a company with other leading companies.

### Benchmarking Against a Key Competitor

Exhibit 15-5 uses a key competitor, Learning School, to compare Smart Touch Learning's profitability. The two companies compete in the same industry, so Learning School serves as an ideal benchmark for Smart Touch Learning. The charts in Exhibit 15-6 highlight the profitability difference between the companies. Focus on the segments of the graphs showing net income. Learning School is clearly more profitable than Smart Touch Learning.

**Exhibit 15-6** | **Graphical Analysis of Common-Size Income Statement—Smart Touch Learning Versus Learning School**

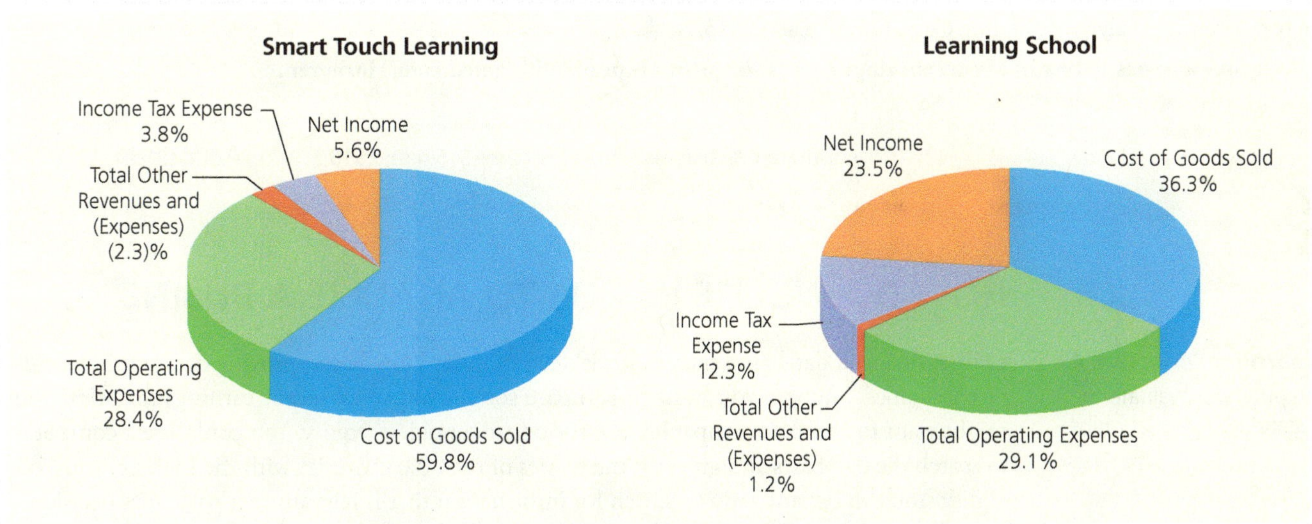


### Benchmarking Against the Industry Average

The industry average can also serve as a very useful benchmark for evaluating a company. An industry comparison would show how Smart Touch Learning is performing alongside the average for the e-learning industry. *Annual Statement Studies*, published by the Risk Management Association, provides common-size statements for most industries. To compare Smart Touch Learning to the industry average, we would simply insert the industry-average common-size income statement in place of Learning School in Exhibit 15-5.

*As you are taking classes toward your degree, how do you know how quickly you can complete your studies? If you knew the average credit hours taken each semester was 12 credit hours, then 12 credit hours would be your benchmark. Comparing the number of classes you take to the average of 12 credit hours a semester is the same concept as benchmarking. Maybe you are taking 15 credit hours a semester. Then you'd be completing your degree faster than the average student. Maybe you take only 3 credit hours in the spring so you can work a part-time job. Then you'd be completing classes at a slower pace than average.*

## Try It!

**6.** Monroe Corp. reported the following amounts on its balance sheet at December 31, 2016 and 2015:

| | 2016 | 2015 |
|---|---|---|
| Cash and Receivables | $ 35,000 | $ 40,000 |
| Merchandise Inventory | 20,000 | 15,000 |
| Property, Plant, and Equipment, Net | 80,000 | 60,000 |
| Total Assets | $ 135,000 | $ 115,000 |

Prepare a vertical analysis of Monroe Corp. for 2016 and 2015.

**Check your answers online in MyAccountingLab or at http://www.pearsonhighered.com/Horngren.**

For more practice, see Short Exercises S15-4 and S15-5. MyAccountingLab

## HOW DO WE USE RATIOS TO ANALYZE A BUSINESS?

**Learning Objective 4**
Compute and evaluate the standard financial ratios

Online financial databases, such as LexisNexis and the Dow Jones, provide data on thousands of companies. Suppose you want to compare some companies' recent earnings histories. You might want to compare companies' returns on stockholders' equity. You could use a computer to search the databases and give you the names of the 20 companies with the highest return on equity. You can use any ratio to search for information that is relevant to a particular decision.

Remember, however, that no single ratio tells the whole picture of any company's performance. Different ratios explain different aspects of a company. The ratios we discuss in this chapter may be classified and used for the following purposes:

- Evaluating the ability to pay current liabilities
- Evaluating the ability to sell merchandise inventory and collect receivables
- Evaluating the ability to pay long-term debt
- Evaluating profitability
- Evaluating stock as an investment

We will use the comparative income statement and balance sheet of Smart Touch Learning, shown in Exhibit 15-7, to discuss the ratios that can be used to evaluate a company. Let's begin by discussing ratios that can be used to evaluate a company's ability to pay its current liabilities.

**Exhibit 15-7 | Comparative Financial Statements**

**SMART TOUCH LEARNING**
Balance Sheet
December 31, 2018 and 2017

| | 2018 | 2017 |
|---|---|---|
| **Assets** | | |
| Current Assets: | | |
| Cash and Cash Equivalents | $ 29,000 | $ 32,000 |
| Accounts Receivable, Net | 114,000 | 85,000 |
| Merchandise Inventory | 113,000 | 111,000 |
| Prepaid Expenses | 6,000 | 8,000 |
| Total Current Assets | 262,000 | 236,000 |
| Long-term Investments | 18,000 | 9,000 |
| Property, Plant, and Equipment, Net | 507,000 | 399,000 |
| Total Assets | **$ 787,000** | **$ 644,000** |
| **Liabilities** | | |
| Current Liabilities: | | |
| Accounts Payable | $ 73,000 | $ 68,000 |
| Accrued Liabilities | 27,000 | 31,000 |
| Notes Payable | 42,000 | 27,000 |
| Total Current Liabilities | 142,000 | 126,000 |
| Long-term Liabilities | 289,000 | 198,000 |
| Total Liabilities | 431,000 | 324,000 |
| **Stockholders' Equity** | | |
| Common Stock, no par | 186,000 | 186,000 |
| Retained Earnings | 170,000 | 134,000 |
| Total Stockholders' Equity | 356,000 | 320,000 |
| Total Liabilities and Stockholders' Equity | **$ 787,000** | **$ 644,000** |

**SMART TOUCH LEARNING**
Income Statement
Years Ended December 31, 2018 and 2017

| | 2018 | 2017 |
|---|---|---|
| Net Sales | $ 858,000 | $ 803,000 |
| Cost of Goods Sold | 513,000 | 509,000 |
| Gross Profit | 345,000 | 294,000 |
| Operating Expenses: | | |
| Selling Expenses | 126,000 | 114,000 |
| Administrative Expenses | 118,000 | 123,000 |
| Total Operating Expenses | 244,000 | 237,000 |
| Operating Income | 101,000 | 57,000 |
| Other Revenues and (Expenses): | | |
| Interest Revenue | 4,000 | 0 |
| Interest Expense | (24,000) | (14,000) |
| Total Other Revenues and (Expenses) | (20,000) | (14,000) |
| Income Before Income Taxes | 81,000 | 43,000 |
| Income Tax Expense | 33,000 | 17,000 |
| Net Income | **$ 48,000** | **$ 26,000** |

## Evaluating the Ability to Pay Current Liabilities

Determining a company's working capital is a good starting place to evaluate a company's ability to pay its current liabilities. **Working capital** measures the ability to meet short-term obligations with current assets. Working capital is defined as follows:

**Working Capital**
A measure of a business's ability to meet its short-term obligations with its current assets. Current assets − Current liabilities.

Working capital = Current assets − Current liabilities

Smart Touch Learning's working capital at December 31, 2018 and 2017, is calculated as follows:

| Working capital | = Current assets | − Current liabilities | |
|---|---|---|---|
| 2018: | $262,000 | − $142,000 | = $120,000 |
| 2017: | $236,000 | − $126,000 | = $110,000 |

Smart Touch Learning's working capital is positive, indicating that the company has more current assets than current liabilities, but additional information would be helpful. Three additional decision tools based on working capital are the current ratio, cash ratio, and acid-test ratio.

## Current Ratio

**Current Ratio**
Measures the company's ability to pay current liabilities from current assets. Total current assets / Total current liabilities.

The most widely used ratio is the **current ratio**, which is calculated as the total current assets divided by total current liabilities. The current ratio measures a company's ability to pay its current liabilities with its current assets.

The current ratios of Smart Touch Learning, at December 31, 2018 and 2017, along with the average for the industry, are as follows:

$$\text{Current ratio} = \frac{\text{Total current assets}}{\text{Total current liabilities}}$$

$$2018: \frac{\$262{,}000}{\$142{,}000} = 1.85$$

$$2017: \frac{\$236{,}000}{\$126{,}000} = 1.87$$

$$\text{Industry average} = 0.60$$

A high current ratio indicates that the business has sufficient current assets to maintain normal business operations. Compare Smart Touch Learning's current ratio of 1.85 for 2018 with the industry average of 0.60.

What is an acceptable current ratio? The answer depends on the industry. The norm for companies in most industries is around 1.50, as reported by the Risk Management Association. Smart Touch Learning's current ratio of 1.85 is strong. Keep in mind that we would not want to see a current ratio that is too high, say 2.5. This would indicate that the company is too liquid and, therefore, is not using its assets effectively. For example, the company may need to reduce merchandise inventory levels so as not to tie up available resources.

**ETHICS**

### Should the debt be reclassified?

Victor Brannon, senior accountant for Moose Corporation, was preparing the latest financial ratios. He knew that the ratios were watched carefully by Moose Corporation's lenders due to strict loan agreements that required the corporation to maintain a minimum current ratio of 1.5. Victor knew that the past quarter's financial ratios would not meet the lenders' requirements. His boss, Cara Romano, suggested that Victor classify a note payable due in 11 months as a long-term liability. What should Victor do? What would you do?

#### Solution

Assets and liabilities are classified as current if they will be used or settled within one year or the operating cycle, whichever is longer. The classification between current and long-term is clear. Victor should not classify the note payable as a long-term liability. It should be classified as current even though the corporation will not meet the lenders' requirements.

## Cash Ratio

**Cash Ratio**
A measure of a company's ability to pay current liabilities from cash and cash equivalents: (Cash + Cash equivalents) / Total current liabilities.

Cash is an important part of every business. Without an adequate supply of available cash, businesses cannot continue to operate. Businesses, therefore, monitor cash very carefully. One measure that can be used to calculate a company's liquidity is the cash ratio. The **cash ratio** helps to determine a company's ability to meet its short-term obligations and is calculated as cash plus cash equivalents divided by total current liabilities.

Notice that the cash ratio includes cash and cash equivalents. As a reminder, cash equivalents are highly liquid investments that can be converted into cash in three months or less. Examples of cash equivalents are money-market accounts and investments in U.S. government securities.

The cash ratios of Smart Touch Learning, at December 31, 2018 and 2017, along with the average for the industry are as follows:

$$\text{Cash ratio} = \frac{\text{Cash} + \text{Cash equivalents}}{\text{Total current liabilities}}$$

$$2018: \frac{\$29,000}{\$142,000} = 0.20$$

$$2017: \frac{\$32,000}{\$126,000} = 0.25$$

$$\text{Industry average} = 0.40$$

The cash ratio has decreased slightly from 2017 to 2018 due to a decrease in available cash and cash equivalents and an increase in total current liabilities. This ratio is the most conservative valuation of liquidity because it looks at only cash and cash equivalents, leaving out other current assets such as merchandise inventory and accounts receivable. Notice that for both years, the cash ratio was below 1.0. Having a cash ratio below 1.0 is a good thing. A cash ratio above 1.0 might signify that the company has an unnecessarily large amount of cash supply. This cash could be used to generate higher profits or be distributed as dividends to stockholders. However, a very low ratio doesn't send a strong message to investors and creditors that the company has the ability to repay its short-term debt.

### Acid-Test (or Quick) Ratio

The **acid-test ratio** (sometimes called the *quick ratio*) tells us whether a company can pay all its current liabilities if they came due immediately. That is, could the company pass the acid test? The acid-test ratio is a more stringent measure than the current ratio, but it is not as stringent as the cash ratio.

To compute the acid-test ratio, we add cash and cash equivalents, short-term investments (those that may be sold in the next 12 months or the business operating cycle, whichever is longer), and net current receivables (accounts and notes receivable, net of allowances) and divide this sum by total current liabilities. Merchandise inventory and prepaid expenses are *not* included in the acid-test ratio because they are the least-liquid current assets. Smart Touch Learning's acid-test ratios for 2018 and 2017 follow:

**Acid-Test Ratio**
The ratio of the sum of cash, cash equivalents, short-term investments, and net current receivables to total current liabilities. The ratio tells whether the entity can pay all its current liabilities if they came due immediately. (Cash including cash equivalents + Short-term investments + Net current receivables) / Total current liabilities.

$$\text{Acid-test ratio} = \frac{\text{Cash including cash equivalents} + \text{Short-term investments} + \text{Net current receivables}}{\text{Total current liabilities}}$$

$$2018: \frac{\$29,000 + \$0 + \$114,000}{\$142,000} = 1.01$$

$$2017: \frac{\$32,000 + \$0 + \$85,000}{\$126,000} = 0.93$$

$$\text{Industry average} = 0.46$$

The company's acid-test ratio improved during 2018 and is significantly better than the industry average. The norm for the acid-test ratio ranges from 0.20 for shoe retailers to 1.20 for manufacturers of equipment, as reported by the Risk Management Association. An acid-test ratio of 0.90 to 1.00 is acceptable in most industries.

## Evaluating the Ability to Sell Merchandise Inventory and Collect Receivables

In this section, we discuss five ratios that measure a company's ability to sell merchandise inventory and collect receivables.

## Inventory Turnover

**Inventory Turnover**
Measures the number of times a company sells its average level of merchandise inventory during a period. Cost of goods sold / Average merchandise inventory.

The **inventory turnover** ratio measures the number of times a company sells its average level of merchandise inventory during a year. A high rate of turnover indicates ease in selling merchandise inventory; a low rate indicates difficulty. A value of 4 means that the company sold its average level of merchandise inventory four times—once every three months—during the year.

To compute inventory turnover, we divide cost of goods sold by the average merchandise inventory for the period. We use the cost of goods sold—not sales—because both cost of goods sold and inventory are stated *at cost.* Sales at *retail* are not comparable with merchandise inventory at *cost.*

Smart Touch Learning's inventory turnover for 2018 is as follows:

$$\text{Inventory turnover} = \frac{\text{Cost of goods sold}}{\text{Average merchandise inventory}}$$

$$2018: \frac{\$513{,}000}{[(\$111{,}000 + \$113{,}000) / 2]} = 4.58$$

$$\text{Industry average} = 27.70$$

Cost of goods sold comes from the income statement (Exhibit 15-7). Average merchandise inventory is figured by adding the beginning merchandise inventory of $111,000 to the ending inventory of $113,000 and dividing by 2. (See the balance sheet, Exhibit 15-7. Remember that 2017's ending balances become 2018's beginning balances.)

Inventory turnover varies widely with the nature of the business. For example, most manufacturers of farm machinery have an inventory turnover close to three times a year. In contrast, companies that remove natural gas from the ground hold their merchandise inventory for a very short period of time and have an average turnover of 30. Smart Touch Learning's turnover of 4.58 times a year means, on average, the company has enough inventory to handle sales for almost 80 days (365 / 4.58 times). This is very low for its industry, which has an average turnover of 27.70 times per year. This ratio has identified an area in which Smart Touch Learning needs to improve.

## Days' Sales in Inventory

**Days' Sales in Inventory**
Measures the average number of days that inventory is held by a company. 365 days / Inventory turnover.

Another key measure is the **days' sales in inventory** ratio. This measures the average number of days merchandise inventory is held by the company. Smart Touch Learning's days' sales in inventory for 2018 is as follows:

$$\text{Days' sales in inventory} = \frac{\text{365 days}}{\text{Inventory turnover}}$$

$$2018: \frac{\text{365 days}}{4.58} = \text{79.7 days}$$

$$\text{Industry average} = \text{13 days}$$

Days' sales in inventory varies widely, depending on the business. Smart Touch Learning's days' sales in inventory is 79.7 days—too high for its industry, which has an average days' sales in inventory ratio of only 13 days. This ratio has identified an area in which Smart Touch Learning needs to improve. Smart Touch Learning should focus on reducing average merchandise inventory held. By decreasing average merchandise inventory, the company can increase inventory turnover and lower the average days' sales in merchandise inventory. Smart Touch Learning will also be able to reduce its merchandise inventory storage and insurance costs as well as reduce the risk of holding obsolete merchandise inventory.

## Gross Profit Percentage

Gross profit (sometimes called *gross margin*) is net sales minus the cost of goods sold. Merchandisers strive to increase the **gross profit percentage** (also called the *gross margin percentage*). This ratio measures the profitability of each net sales dollar above the cost of goods sold and is computed as gross profit divided by net sales revenue.

**Gross Profit Percentage**
Measures the profitability of each sales dollar above the cost of goods sold. Gross profit / Net sales revenue.

The gross profit percentage is one of the most carefully watched measures of profitability. It reflects a business's ability to earn a profit on the merchandise inventory. The gross profit earned on merchandise inventory must be high enough to cover the remaining operating expenses and to earn net income. A small increase in the gross profit percentage from last year to this year may signal an important rise in income. Conversely, a small decrease from last year to this year may signal trouble.

Smart Touch Learning's gross profit percentage for 2018 is as follows:

$$\text{Gross profit percentage} = \frac{\text{Gross profit}}{\text{Net sales revenue}}$$

$$2018: \frac{\$345{,}000}{\$858{,}000} = 0.402 = 40.2\%$$

$$\text{Industry average} = 43\%$$

Gross profit percentage varies widely, depending on the business. Smart Touch Learning's gross profit percentage is 40.2%, which is slightly lower than the industry average of 43%. This ratio has identified an area in which Smart Touch Learning needs to improve. To increase gross profit percentage, Smart Touch Learning needs to decrease the cost of the merchandise inventory and/or increase revenue (selling price). Additionally, addressing Smart Touch Learning's inventory turnover issues will probably help Smart Touch Learning to increase its gross profit percentage.

## Accounts Receivable Turnover Ratio

The **accounts receivable turnover ratio** measures the number of times the company collects the average receivables balance in a year. The higher the ratio, the faster the cash collections. However, a receivable turnover that is too high may indicate that credit is too tight, causing the loss of sales to good customers. To compute accounts receivable turnover, we divide net credit sales (assuming all Smart Touch Learning's sales from Exhibit 15-7 are on account) by average net accounts receivable.

**Accounts Receivable Turnover Ratio**
A ratio that measures the number of times the company collects the average accounts receivable balance in a year. Net credit sales / Average net accounts receivable.

Smart Touch Learning's accounts receivable turnover ratio for 2018 is computed as follows:

$$\text{Accounts receivable turnover ratio} = \frac{\text{Net credit sales}}{\text{Average net accounts receivable}}$$

$$2018: \frac{\$858{,}000}{[(\$85{,}000 + \$114{,}000) / 2]} = 8.6$$

$$\text{Industry average} = 29.1$$

Net credit sales, assumed to equal net sales, comes from the income statement (Exhibit 15-7). Average net accounts receivable is figured by adding the beginning

Accounts Receivable of $85,000 to the ending Accounts Receivable of $114,000 and dividing by 2. (See the balance sheet, Exhibit 15-7.)

Smart Touch Learning's accounts receivable turnover ratio of 8.6 times per year is much slower than the industry average of 29.1. Why the difference? Smart Touch Learning is a fairly new business that sells to established people who pay their accounts over time. Further, this turnover coincides with the lower-than-average inventory turnover. So, Smart Touch Learning may achieve a higher accounts receivable turnover by increasing its inventory turnover ratio.

### Days' Sales in Receivables

**Days' Sales in Receivables**
The ratio of average net accounts receivable to one day's sales. The ratio tells how many days it takes to collect the average level of accounts receivable. 365 days / Accounts receivable turnover ratio.

**Days' sales in receivables**, also called the *collection period*, indicates how many days it takes to collect the average level of receivables and is computed as 365 days divided by the accounts receivable turnover ratio. The number of days in average accounts receivable should be close to the number of days customers are allowed to make payment. The shorter the collection period, the more quickly the organization can use its cash. The longer the collection period, the less cash is available for operations.

To compute this ratio for Smart Touch Learning for 2018, we divide 365 days by the accounts receivable turnover ratio we previously calculated:

$$\text{Days' Sales in Receivables} = \frac{\text{365 days}}{\text{Accounts receivable turnover ratio}}$$

$$\text{2018: } \frac{\text{365 days}}{8.6} = \text{42.4 days}$$

$$\text{Industry average} = \text{25 days}$$

Smart Touch Learning's ratio tells us that 42.4 average days' sales remain in Accounts Receivable and need to be collected. The company's days' sales in receivables ratio is much higher (worse) than the industry average of 25 days. Smart Touch Learning might give its customers a longer time to pay, such as 45 days versus 30 days. Alternatively, Smart Touch Learning's credit department may need to review the criteria it uses to evaluate individual customers' credit. Without the customers' good paying habits, the company's cash flow would suffer.

## Evaluating the Ability to Pay Long-Term Debt

The ratios discussed so far yield insight into current assets and current liabilities. They help us measure ability to sell merchandise inventory, collect receivables, and pay current liabilities. Most businesses also have long-term debt. Three key indicators of a business's ability to pay long-term liabilities are the debt ratio, the debt to equity ratio, and the times-interest-earned ratio.

### Debt Ratio

**Debt Ratio**
Shows the proportion of assets financed with debt. Total liabilities / Total assets.

The relationship between total liabilities and total assets—called the **debt ratio**—shows the proportion of assets financed with debt and is calculated by dividing total liabilities by total assets. If the debt ratio is 100%, then all the assets are financed with debt. A debt ratio of 50% means that half the assets are financed with debt, and the other half are financed by the owners of the business. The higher the debt ratio, the higher the company's financial risk. The debt ratio can be used to evaluate a business's ability to pay its debts.

The debt ratios for Smart Touch Learning at the end of 2018 and 2017 follow:

$$\text{Debt ratio} = \frac{\text{Total liabilities}}{\text{Total assets}}$$

$$2018: \frac{\$431{,}000}{\$787{,}000} = 0.548 = 54.8\%$$

$$2017: \frac{\$324{,}000}{\$644{,}000} = 0.503 = 50.3\%$$

Industry average = 69%

Both total liabilities and total asset amounts are from the balance sheet, presented in Exhibit 15-7. Smart Touch Learning's debt ratio in 2018 of 54.8% is not very high. The Risk Management Association reports that the average debt ratio for most companies ranges from 57% to 67%, with relatively little variation from company to company. Smart Touch Learning's debt ratio indicates a fairly low-risk position compared with the industry average debt ratio of 69%.

### Debt to Equity Ratio

The relationship between total liabilities and total equity—called the **debt to equity ratio**—shows the proportion of total liabilities relative to total equity. Thus, this ratio measures financial leverage. If the debt to equity ratio is greater than 1, then the company is financing more assets with debt than with equity. If the ratio is less than 1, then the company is financing more assets with equity than with debt. The higher the debt to equity ratio, the greater the company's financial risk.

**Debt to Equity Ratio**
A ratio that measures the proportion of total liabilities relative to total equity. Total liabilities / Total equity.

The debt to equity ratios for Smart Touch Learning at the end of 2018 and 2017 follow:

$$\text{Debt to equity ratio} = \frac{\text{Total liabilities}}{\text{Total equity}}$$

$$2018: \frac{\$431{,}000}{\$356{,}000} = 1.21$$

$$2017: \frac{\$324{,}000}{\$320{,}000} = 1.01$$

Industry average = 2.23

Smart Touch Learning's debt to equity ratio in 2018 of 1.21 is not very high. Smart Touch Learning's debt to equity ratio indicates a fairly low-risk position compared with the industry average debt to equity ratio of 2.23.

### Times-Interest-Earned Ratio

The debt ratio and debt to equity ratio say nothing about the ability to pay interest expense. Analysts and investors use the **times-interest-earned ratio** to evaluate a business's ability to pay interest expense. This ratio measures the number of times earnings before interest and taxes (EBIT) can cover (pay) interest expense. This ratio is also called the *interest-coverage ratio*. A high times-interest-earned ratio indicates a business's ease in paying interest expense; a low ratio suggests difficulty. The times-interest-earned ratio is calculated as EBIT (Net income + Income tax expense + Interest expense) divided by interest expense.

**Times-Interest-Earned Ratio**
Evaluates a business's ability to pay interest expense. (Net income + Income tax expense + Interest expense) / Interest expense.

Calculation of Smart Touch Learning's times-interest-earned ratio follows:

$$\text{Times-interest-earned ratio} = \frac{\text{Net income} + \text{Income tax expense} + \text{Interest expense}}{\text{Interest expense}}$$

$$2018: \frac{\$48,000 + \$33,000 + \$24,000}{\$24,000} = 4.38$$

$$2017: \frac{\$26,000 + \$17,000 + \$14,000}{\$14,000} = 4.07$$

$$\text{Industry average} = 7.80$$

The company's times-interest-earned ratios of 4.38 for 2018 and 4.07 for 2017 are significantly lower than the industry average of 7.80 times, but it is slightly better than the ratio for the average U.S. business. The norm for U.S. business, as reported by the Risk Management Association, falls in the range of 2.0 to 3.0. When you consider Smart Touch Learning's debt ratio and its times-interest-earned ratio, Smart Touch Learning appears to have little difficulty paying its liabilities.

## Evaluating Profitability

The fundamental goal of business is to earn a profit. Ratios that measure profitability often are reported in the business press. Let's examine five profitability measures.

### Profit Margin Ratio

**Profit Margin Ratio**
A profitability measure that shows how much net income is earned on every dollar of net sales. Net income / Net sales.

The **profit margin ratio** shows the percentage of each net sales dollar earned as net income. In other words, the profit margin ratio shows how much net income a business earns on every $1.00 of sales. This ratio focuses on the profitability of a business and is calculated as net income divided by net sales.

Smart Touch Learning's profit margin ratio follows:

$$\text{Profit margin ratio} = \frac{\text{Net income}}{\text{Net sales}}$$

$$2018: \frac{\$48,000}{\$858,000} = 0.056 = 5.6\%$$

$$2017: \frac{\$26,000}{\$803,000} = 0.032 = 3.2\%$$

$$\text{Industry average} = 1.7\%$$

Both net income and net sales amounts are from the income statement presented in Exhibit 15-7. Companies strive for a high profit margin. The higher the profit margin, the more sales dollars end up as profit. The increase in Smart Touch Learning's profit margin ratio from 2017 to 2018 is significant and identifies the company as more successful than the average e-learning providers, whose profit margin ratio is 1.7%.

### Rate of Return on Total Assets

**Rate of Return on Total Assets**
A ratio that measures the success a company has in using its assets to earn income. (Net income + Interest expense) / Average total assets.

The **rate of return on total assets** measures a company's success in using assets to earn a profit. There are two ways that a company can finance its assets:

- Debt—A company can borrow cash from creditors to purchase assets. Creditors earn interest on the money that is loaned.
- Equity—A company receives cash or other assets from stockholders. Stockholders invest in the company and hope to receive a return on their investment.

Rate of return on total assets is calculated by adding interest expense to net income and dividing by average total assets. Interest expense is added back to net income to determine the real return on the assets regardless of the corporation's financing choices (debt or equity).

Computation of the rate of return on total assets ratio for Smart Touch Learning follows:

$$\text{Rate of return on total assets} = \frac{\text{Net income} + \text{Interest expense}}{\text{Average total assets}}$$

$$2018\text{: } \frac{\$48{,}000 + \$24{,}000}{[(\$644{,}000 + \$787{,}000)/2]} = 0.101 = 10.1\%$$

Industry average = 6.0%

Net income and interest expense come from the income statement (Exhibit 15-7). Average total assets is figured by adding the beginning total assets of $644,000 to the ending total assets of $787,000 and dividing by 2. (See the balance sheet, Exhibit 15-7.) Smart Touch Learning's rate of return on total assets ratio of 10.1% is much better than the industry average of 6.0%.

## Asset Turnover Ratio

The **asset turnover ratio** measures the amount of net sales generated for each average dollar of total assets invested. This ratio measures how well a company is using its assets to generate sales revenues. To compute this ratio, we divide net sales by average total assets.

Smart Touch Learning's 2018 asset turnover ratio is as follows:

**Asset Turnover Ratio**
Measures how efficiently a business uses its average total assets to generate sales. Net sales / Average total assets.

$$\text{Asset turnover ratio} = \frac{\text{Net sales}}{\text{Average total assets}}$$

$$2018\text{: } \frac{\$858{,}000}{[(\$644{,}000 + \$787{,}000)/2]} = 1.20 \text{ times}$$

Industry average = 3.52 times

Smart Touch Learning's asset turnover ratio of 1.20 is much lower than the industry average of 3.52 times, indicating that Smart Touch Learning is generating less net sales for each average dollar of total assets invested. Recall that Smart Touch Learning's gross profit percentage was lower than the industry's also. Normally, companies with high gross profit percentages will have low asset turnover. Companies with low gross profit percentages will have high asset turnover ratios. This is another area in which Smart Touch Learning's management must consider options to increase sales and decrease its average total assets to improve this ratio.

## Rate of Return on Common Stockholders' Equity

A popular measure of profitability is **rate of return on common stockholders' equity**, often shortened to *return on equity*. This ratio shows the relationship between net income available to common stockholders and their average common equity invested in the company. The rate of return on common stockholders' equity shows how much income is earned for each $1 invested by the common shareholders.

**Rate of Return on Common Stockholders' Equity**
Shows the relationship between net income available to common stockholders and their average common equity invested in the company. (Net income − Preferred dividends) / Average common stockholders' equity.

To compute this ratio, we first subtract preferred dividends from net income to get net income available to the common stockholders. (Smart Touch Learning does not have any preferred stock issued, so preferred dividends are zero.) Then we divide net income available to common stockholders by average common stockholders' equity during the year. Common equity is total stockholders' equity minus preferred equity. Average common stockholders' equity is the average of the beginning and ending common stockholders' equity balances.

The 2018 rate of return on common stockholders' equity for Smart Touch Learning follows:

$$\text{Rate of return on common stockholders' equity} = \frac{\text{Net income} - \text{Preferred dividends}}{\text{Average common stockholders' equity}}$$

$$2018: \frac{\$48{,}000 - \$0}{[(\$320{,}000 + \$356{,}000)\,/\,2]} = 0.142 = 14.2\%$$

$$\text{Industry average} = 10.5\%$$

**Trading on the Equity**
Earning more income on borrowed money than the related interest expense, thereby increasing the earnings for the owners of the business.

Smart Touch Learning's rate of return on common stockholders' equity of 14.2% is higher than its rate of return on total assets of 10.1%. This difference results from borrowing at one rate—say, 8%—and investing the money to earn a higher rate, such as the firm's 14.2% return on equity. This practice is called **trading on the equity**, or using *leverage*. It is directly related to the debt ratio. The higher the debt ratio, the higher the leverage. Companies that finance operations with debt are said to *leverage* their positions.

During good times, leverage increases profitability. But leverage can have a negative impact on profitability as well. Therefore, leverage is a double-edged sword, increasing profits during good times but compounding losses during bad times. Compare Smart Touch Learning's rate of return on common stockholders' equity with the industry average of 10.5%. Once again, Smart Touch Learning is performing much better than the average company in its industry. A rate of return on common stockholders' equity of 15% to 20% year after year is considered good in most industries. At 14.2%, Smart Touch Learning is doing well.

## Earnings per Share (EPS)

**Earnings per Share (EPS)**
Amount of a company's net income (loss) for each share of its outstanding common stock. (Net income − Preferred dividends) / Weighted average number of common shares outstanding.

**Earnings per share (EPS)** is perhaps the most widely quoted of all financial statistics. EPS is the only ratio that must appear on the financial statements. Earnings per share reports the amount of net income (loss) for each share of the company's *outstanding common stock*. Earnings per share is calculated as net income minus preferred dividends divided by the weighted average number of common shares outstanding. Preferred dividends are subtracted from net income because the preferred stockholders have the first claim to dividends. The computation for the weighted average number of common shares outstanding is covered in advanced accounting courses. For simplicity, we will determine earnings per share on the average number of shares outstanding, calculated as the beginning balance plus ending balance divided by two.

FASB requires that earnings per share appear on the income statement. Corporations report a separate EPS figure for each element of income, which is shown in more detail in Appendix 15A at the end of this chapter.

Smart Touch Learning's EPS for 2018 and 2017 follow. (Note that Smart Touch Learning had 10,000 shares of common stock outstanding throughout both years.)

$$\text{Earnings per share} = \frac{\text{Net income} - \text{Preferred dividends}}{\text{Weighted average number of common shares outstanding}}$$

$$2018: \frac{\$48{,}000 - \$0}{10{,}000 \text{ shares}} = \$4.80\,/\,\text{share}$$

$$2017: \frac{\$26{,}000 - \$0}{10{,}000 \text{ shares}} = \$2.60\,/\,\text{share}$$

$$\text{Industry average} = \$9.76\,/\,\text{share}$$

Smart Touch Learning's EPS increased significantly in 2018 (by almost 85%). Its stockholders should not expect this big a boost in EPS every year. Most companies strive to increase EPS by 10% to 15% annually, and leading companies do so. But even the most successful companies have an occasional bad year. EPS for the industry at $9.76 is a little more than twice Smart Touch Learning's 2018 EPS. Therefore, Smart Touch Learning needs to work on continuing to increase EPS by increasing its net income so that it is more competitive with other companies in its industry.

## Evaluating Stock as an Investment

Investors purchase stock to earn a return on their investment. This return consists of two parts: (1) gains (or losses) from selling the stock at a price above (or below) purchase price and (2) dividends. The ratios we examine in this section help analysts evaluate stock investments.

### Price/Earnings Ratio

The **price/earnings ratio** is the ratio of the market price of a share of common stock to the company's earnings per share. The price/earnings ratio shows the market price of $1 of earnings. This ratio, abbreviated P/E, appears in many print or online stock listings and measures the value that the stock market places on a company's earnings.

Calculations for the P/E ratios of Smart Touch Learning follow. These market prices of common stock for real companies can be obtained from a financial Web site, a stockbroker, or the company's Web site. The market price for Smart Touch Learning's common stock was $60 at the end of 2018 and $35 at the end of 2017. The earnings per share values were calculated immediately before the P/E ratio.

**Price/Earnings Ratio**
The ratio of the market price of a share of common stock to the company's earnings per share. Measures the value that the stock market places on $1 of a company's earnings. Market price per share of common stock / Earnings per share.

$$\text{Price/earnings ratio} = \frac{\text{Market price per share of common stock}}{\text{Earnings per share}}$$

$$2018: \frac{\$60 \text{ per share}}{\$4.80 \text{ per share}} = 12.50$$

$$2017: \frac{\$35 \text{ per share}}{\$2.60 \text{ per share}} = 13.46$$

$$\text{Industry average} = 17.79$$

Smart Touch Learning's P/E ratio for 2018 of 12.50 means that the company's stock is selling at 12.5 times one year's earnings. Smart Touch Learning would like to see this ratio increase in future years in order to be more in line with the industry average P/E of 17.79.

### Dividend Yield

**Dividend yield** is the ratio of annual dividends per share to the stock's market price per share. This ratio measures the percentage of a stock's market value that is returned annually as dividends to shareholders. *Preferred* stockholders, who invest primarily to receive dividends, pay special attention to dividend yield.

**Dividend Yield**
Ratio of annual dividends per share of stock to the stock's market price per share. Measures the percentage of a stock's market value that is returned annually as dividends to stockholders. Annual dividend per share / Market price per share.

Assume Smart Touch Learning paid annual cash dividends of \$1.20 per share of common stock in 2018 and \$1.00 in 2017. As noted previously, market prices of the company's common stock were \$60 in 2018 and \$35 in 2017. The firm's dividend yields on common stock follow:

$$\text{Dividend yield} = \frac{\text{Annual dividend per share}}{\text{Market price per share}}$$

$$2018: \frac{\$1.20 \text{ per share}}{\$60 \text{ per share}} = 0.020 = 2.0\%$$

$$2017: \frac{\$1.00 \text{ per share}}{\$35 \text{ per share}} = 0.029 = 2.9\%$$

Industry average = 3.6%

*In this calculation, we are determining the dividend yield for common stock. Dividend yield can also be calculated for preferred stock.*

An investor who buys Smart Touch Learning's common stock for \$60 can expect to receive 2.0% of the investment annually in the form of cash dividends. The industry, however, is paying out 3.6% annually. An investor might be willing to accept lower dividends (cash now) if the stock's market price is growing (cash later when the stock is sold).

## Dividend Payout

**Dividend Payout**
The ratio of dividends declared per common share relative to the earnings per share of the company. Annual dividend per share / Earnings per share.

**Dividend payout** is the ratio of annual dividends declared per common share relative to the earnings per share of the company. This ratio measures the percentage of earnings paid annually to common shareholders as cash dividends.

Recall that Smart Touch Learning paid annual cash dividends of \$1.20 per share of common stock in 2018 and \$1.00 in 2017. Earnings per share were calculated as \$4.80 per share for 2018 and \$2.60 for 2017. So, Smart Touch Learning's dividend payout yields are as follows:

$$\text{Dividend payout} = \frac{\text{Annual dividend per share}}{\text{Earnings per share}}$$

$$2018: \frac{\$1.20 \text{ per share}}{\$4.80 \text{ per share}} = 0.25 = 25\%$$

$$2017: \frac{\$1.00 \text{ per share}}{\$2.60 \text{ per share}} = 0.38 = 38\%$$

Industry average = 63%

Smart Touch Learning's dividend payout ratios of 25% in 2018 and 38% in 2017 are less than the industry average of 63%. Smart Touch Learning, being a fairly new company, might be retaining more of its earnings for growth and expansion. An investor who buys

Smart Touch Learning's common stock may predict annual cash dividends to be about 25% of earnings, based on the 2018 dividend payout ratio. This investor would want to see higher market prices and higher asset turnover for Smart Touch Learning in the future for Smart Touch Learning to stay competitive.

## Red Flags in Financial Statement Analyses

Analysts look for *red flags* in financial statements that may signal financial trouble. Recent accounting scandals highlight the importance of these red flags. The following conditions may reveal that the company is too risky:

- **Movement of sales, merchandise inventory, and receivables.** Sales, merchandise inventory, and receivables generally move together. Increased sales lead to higher receivables and may require more merchandise inventory (or higher inventory turnover) to meet demand. Unexpected or inconsistent movements among sales, merchandise inventory, and receivables make the financial statements look suspect.
- **Earnings problems.** Has net income decreased significantly for several years in a row? Did the company report net income in previous years but now is reporting net loss? Most companies cannot survive losses year after year.
- **Decreased cash flow.** Cash flow validates net income. Is net cash flow from operating activities consistently lower than net income? If so, the company is in trouble. Are the sales of plant assets a major source of cash? If so, the company may face a cash shortage.
- **Too much debt.** How does the company's debt ratio compare to that of major competitors? If the debt ratio is too high, the company may be unable to pay its debts.
- **Inability to collect receivables.** Are days' sales in receivables growing faster than for competitors? If so, a cash shortage may be looming.
- **Buildup of merchandise inventories.** Is inventory turnover too slow? If so, the company may be unable to sell goods, or it may be overstating merchandise inventory.

Do any of these red flags apply to Smart Touch Learning from the analyses we did in the chapter? Although the financial statements depict a strong and growing company, the analysis pointed out several areas of weakness for Smart Touch Learning that include low inventory turnover, low accounts receivable turnover, low gross profit margin, low times interest earned, low asset turnover, and low earnings per share. Smart Touch Learning should continue to carefully monitor its financial statements as it continues to grow. Exhibit 15-8 (on the next page) summarizes the financial ratios that you have learned in this chapter.

**Exhibit 15-8** | **Using Ratios in Financial Statement Analysis**

| Ratio | Computation | Information Provided |
|---|---|---|
| ***Evaluating the ability to pay current liabilities:*** | | |
| **Working capital** | Current assets − Current liabilities | A business's ability to meet its short-term obligations with its current assets. |
| **Current ratio** | $\frac{\text{Total current assets}}{\text{Total current liabilities}}$ | The company's ability to pay current liabilities from current assets. |
| **Cash ratio** | $\frac{\text{Cash + Cash equivalents}}{\text{Total current liabilities}}$ | The company's ability to pay current liabilities from cash and cash equivalents. |
| **Acid-test ratio** | $\frac{\text{Cash including cash equivalents + Short-term investments + Net current receivables}}{\text{Total current liabilities}}$ | The company's ability to pay all its current liabilities if they came due immediately. |
| ***Evaluating the ability to sell merchandise inventory and collect receivables:*** | | |
| **Inventory turnover** | $\frac{\text{Cost of goods sold}}{\text{Average merchandise inventory}}$ | The number of times a company sells its average level of merchandise inventory during a period. |
| **Days' sales in inventory** | $\frac{\text{365 days}}{\text{Inventory turnover}}$ | The average number of days that inventory is held by a company. |
| **Gross profit percentage** | $\frac{\text{Gross profit}}{\text{Net sales revenue}}$ | The profitability of each sales dollar above the cost of goods sold. |
| **Accounts receivable turnover ratio** | $\frac{\text{Net credit sales}}{\text{Average net accounts receivable}}$ | The number of times the company collects the average receivables balance in a year. |
| **Days' sales in receivables** | $\frac{\text{365 days}}{\text{Accounts receivable turnover ratio}}$ | The number of days' sales it takes to collect the average level of receivables. |

**Exhibit 15-8 | Continued**

| Ratio | Computation | Information Provided |
|---|---|---|
| ***Evaluating the ability to pay long-term debt:*** | | |
| **Debt ratio** | $\dfrac{\text{Total liabilities}}{\text{Total assets}}$ | The proportion of assets financed with debt. |
| **Debt to equity ratio** | $\dfrac{\text{Total liabilities}}{\text{Total equity}}$ | The proportion of total liabilities relative to total equity. |
| **Times-interest-earned ratio** | $\dfrac{\text{Net income} + \text{Income tax expense} + \text{Interest expense}}{\text{Interest expense}}$ | A business's ability to pay interest expense. |
| ***Evaluating profitability:*** | | |
| **Profit margin ratio** | $\dfrac{\text{Net income}}{\text{Net sales}}$ | How much net income is earned on every dollar of net sales. |
| **Rate of return on total assets** | $\dfrac{\text{Net income} + \text{Interest expense}}{\text{Average total assets}}$ | The success a company has in using its assets to earn income. |
| **Asset turnover ratio** | $\dfrac{\text{Net sales}}{\text{Average total assets}}$ | How efficiently a business uses its average total assets to generate sales. |
| **Rate of return on common stockholders' equity** | $\dfrac{\text{Net income} - \text{Preferred dividends}}{\text{Average common stockholders' equity}}$ | The relationship between net income available to common stockholders and their average common equity invested in the company. |
| **Earnings per share** | $\dfrac{\text{Net income} - \text{Preferred dividends}}{\text{Weighted average number of common shares outstanding}}$ | Amount of a company's net income (loss) for each share of its outstanding common stock. |
| ***Evaluating stock as an investment:*** | | |
| **Price/earnings ratio** | $\dfrac{\text{Market price per share of common stock}}{\text{Earnings per share}}$ | The value the stock market places on $1 of a company's earnings. |
| **Dividend yield** | $\dfrac{\text{Annual dividend per share}}{\text{Market price per share}}$ | The percentage of a stock's market value that is returned annually as dividends to stockholders. |
| **Dividend payout** | $\dfrac{\text{Annual dividend per share}}{\text{Earnings per share}}$ | Ratio of dividends declared per common share relative to the earnings per share of the company. |

## Try It!

The financial statements of Ion Corporation include the following items:

| | Current Year | Preceding Year |
|---|---|---|
| **Balance Sheet:** | | |
| Cash | $ 6,000 | $ 8,000 |
| Short-term Investments | 4,400 | 10,700 |
| Net Accounts Receivable | 21,600 | 29,200 |
| Merchandise Inventory | 30,800 | 27,600 |
| Prepaid Expenses | 6,000 | 3,600 |
| Total Current Assets | 68,800 | 79,100 |
| Total Current Liabilities | 53,200 | 37,200 |
| **Income Statement:** | | |
| Net Sales Revenue | $ 184,800 | |
| Cost of Goods Sold | 126,000 | |

Compute the following ratios for the current year:

7. Current ratio
8. Acid-test ratio
9. Inventory turnover
10. Gross profit percentage

**Check your answers online in MyAccountingLab or at http://www.pearsonhighered.com/Horngren.**

For more practice, see Short Exercises S15-6 through S15-12. MyAccountingLab

# APPENDIX 15A: The Corporate Income Statement

## HOW IS THE COMPLETE CORPORATE INCOME STATEMENT PREPARED?

**Learning Objective 5**
Complete a corporate income statement including earnings per share

A corporation's income statement includes some unique items that do not often apply to smaller businesses. These unique items are listed after determining the corporation's income from continuing operations. We will review the fictitious company Kevin's Vintage Guitars, Inc.'s income statement for year ended December 31, 2016, shown in Exhibit 15A-1, to illustrate these items.

**Exhibit 15A-1 | Kevin's Vintage Guitars, Inc.—Income Statement**

| KEVIN'S VINTAGE GUITARS, INC.<br>Income Statement<br>Year Ended December 31, 2016 | | |
|---|---|---|
| Net Sales | $ 500,000 | Continuing Operations |
| Cost of Goods Sold | 240,000 | |
| Gross Profit | 260,000 | |
| Operating Expenses | 181,000 | |
| Operating Income | 79,000 | |
| Other Revenues and (Expenses): | | |
| Gain on Sale of Equipment | 11,000 | |
| Income Before Income Taxes | 90,000 | |
| Income Tax Expense | 36,000 | |
| Income from Continuing Operations | 54,000 | |
| Discontinued Operations (less applicable tax of $14,000) | 21,000 | Special Items |
| Income Before Extraordinary Items | 75,000 | |
| Extraordinary Loss (less applicable tax saving of $8,000) | (12,000) | |
| **Net Income** | **$ 63,000** | |
| | | |
| Earnings per Share of Common Stock (20,000 shares outstanding): | | |
| Income from Continuing Operations | $ 2.70 | Earnings per Share |
| Income from Discontinued Operations | 1.05 | |
| Income Before Extraordinary Items | 3.75 | |
| Extraordinary Loss | (0.60) | |
| Net Income | **$ 3.15** | |

## Continuing Operations

In Exhibit 15A-1, the first section reports continuing operations. This part of the business should continue from period to period. Income from continuing operations, therefore, helps investors make predictions about future earnings. We may use this information to predict that Kevin's Vintage Guitars, Inc. may earn approximately $54,000 next year.

The continuing operations of Kevin's Vintage Guitars, Inc. include two items that warrant explanation:

- Kevin's Vintage Guitars had a gain on the sale of equipment, which is outside the company's core business of selling vintage guitars. This is why the gain is reported in the "other" category—separately from Kevin's Vintage Guitars's operating income.
- Income tax expense of $36,000 is subtracted to arrive at income from continuing operations. Kevin's Vintage Guitars's income tax rate is 40% ($90,000 × 0.40 = $36,000).

After continuing operations, an income statement may include two distinctly different gains and losses: discontinued operations and extraordinary items.

## Discontinued Operations

Most corporations engage in several lines of business. For example, General Motors Company is best known for its automobiles, but it also has a financing company and leasing subsidiary called General Motors Financial Company, Inc.

Each identifiable division of a company is called a segment of the business. A company may sell a segment of its business. For example, General Motors Company sold its financing company (GMAC) but continued its automobile segment. The disposal of the financing segment would be reported as discontinued operations for General Motors Company.

Financial analysts are always keeping tabs on companies they follow and predict companies' net income. Most analysts do not include the results of discontinued operations in financial analysis because the discontinued segments will not be around in the future. The income statement reports information on the segments that have been sold under the heading Discontinued Operations. In our example, income from discontinued operations of $35,000 is taxed at 40% and is reported as shown in Exhibit 15A-1. A loss on discontinued operations is reported similarly, but with a subtraction for the income tax *savings* on the loss (the tax savings reduces the loss).

Gains and losses on the normal sale of plant assets are *not* reported as discontinued operations. Instead, they are reported as "Other Revenues and (Expenses)" among continuing operations because companies dispose of old plant assets and equipment more frequently than business segments.

## Extraordinary Items

Extraordinary gains and losses, also called *extraordinary items,* are both unusual and infrequent. GAAP defines *infrequent* as an event that is not expected to recur in the foreseeable future, considering the environment in which the company operates. Losses from natural disasters (floods, earthquakes, and tornadoes) and the taking of company assets by a foreign government (expropriation) could be considered to be extraordinary items. They are reported separately from continuing operations because of their infrequent and unusual nature.

Extraordinary items are reported along with their income tax effect. During 2016, Kevin's Vintage Guitars lost $20,000 of inventory in a flood. This flood loss reduced both Kevin's Vintage Guitars's income and its income tax. The tax effect decreases the net amount of Kevin's Vintage Guitars's loss the same way income tax reduces net income. An extraordinary loss can be reported along with its tax effect, as follows:

| | |
|---|---|
| Extraordinary Flood Loss | $ (20,000) |
| Less: Income Tax Savings ($20,000 × 40%) | 8,000 |
| Extraordinary Flood Loss, Net of Tax | $ (12,000) |

Trace this item to the income statement in Exhibit 15A-1. An extraordinary gain is reported the same as a loss—net of the income tax effect. The following items do *not* qualify as extraordinary:

- Gains and losses on the sale of plant assets
- Losses due to lawsuits
- Losses due to employee labor strikes
- Natural disasters that occur frequently in the area (such as hurricanes in Florida)

These gains and losses fall outside the business's central operations, so they are reported on the income statement as other gains and losses, but they aren't extraordinary. One example for Kevin's Vintage Guitars is the gain on sale of equipment reported in the Other Revenues and (Expenses) section, as part of income from continuing operations in Exhibit 15A-1.

### Earnings per Share

The final segment of a corporate income statement reports the company's earnings per share, abbreviated as EPS. A company that reports a discontinued operation or an extraordinary item must report earnings per share for each of these line items either on the face of the income statement (as shown in Exhibit 15A-1) or in the notes to the financial statements.

**Try It!**

**11A.** Rocky Corporation's accounting records include the following items, listed in no particular order, at December 31, 2016:

| | | | |
|---|---|---|---|
| Other Revenues and (Expenses) | $ (6,000) | Extraordinary Loss | $ 2,800 |
| Net Sales | 70,800 | Cost of Goods Sold | 29,200 |
| Gain on Discontinued Operations | 4,800 | Operating Expenses | 22,000 |

The income tax rate for Rocky Corporation is 30%. Prepare Rocky's income statement for the year ended December 31, 2016. Omit earnings per share. Use a multi-step format.

**Check your answers online in MyAccountingLab or at http://www.pearsonhighered.com/Horngren.**

For more practice, see Short Exercises S15A-13 and S15A-14. MyAccountingLab

# REVIEW

## > Things You Should Know

### 1. How are financial statements used to analyze a business?

- There are three main ways to analyze financial statements:
  - Horizontal analysis
  - Vertical analysis
  - Ratio analysis
- Annual reports provide information about a company's financial condition and include the following:
  - Management's discussion and analysis of financial condition and results of operations (MD&A)
  - Report of independent registered public accounting firm
  - Financial statements
  - Notes to the financial statements

**2. How do we use horizontal analysis to analyze a business?**

- Horizontal analysis is the study of percentage changes in comparative financial statements. It compares one year to the next. (Dollar amount of change / Base period amount) × 100.
- Trend analysis is a form of horizontal analysis in which percentages are computed by selecting a base year as 100% and expressing the amounts for following periods as a percentage of the base period amount. (Any period amount / Base period amount) × 100.

**3. How do we use vertical analysis to analyze a business?**

- Vertical analysis reveals the relationship of each statement item to its base amount, which is the 100% figure. (Specific item / Base amount) × 100.
  - For the income statement, net sales is the base.
  - For the balance sheet, total assets is the base.
- Common-size statements are financial statements that report only percentages—the same percentages that appear in vertical analysis.
- Benchmarking is the practice of comparing a company with other leading companies.

**4. How do we use ratios to analyze a business?**

- Ratios can be used to evaluate a company's:
  - ability to pay current liabilities
  - ability to sell merchandise inventory and collect receivables
  - ability to pay long-term debt
  - profitability
  - stock as an investment
- Exhibit 15-8 summarizes common ratios that can be used to analyze a business.

**5. How is the complete corporate income statement prepared? (Appendix 15A)**

- A corporation's income statement includes the following unique items listed after determining the calculation for income for continuing operations:
  - Discontinued operations—a segment of a business that has been discontinued
  - Extraordinary items—items that are both unusual and infrequent
- Earnings per share must be reported either on the face of the income statement or in the notes to the financial statements.

## > Summary Problem 15-1

Kimball Corporation makes iPod covers and has the following comparative income statement for years ended December 31, 2017 and 2016:

**KIMBALL CORPORATION**
Income Statement
Years Ended December 31, 2017 and 2016

| | 2017 | 2016 |
|---|---|---|
| Revenues: | | |
| Net Sales | $ 300,000 | $ 250,000 |
| Other Revenues | 0 | 1,000 |
| Total Revenues | 300,000 | 251,000 |
| Expenses: | | |
| Cost of Goods Sold | 214,200 | 170,000 |
| Engineering, Selling, and Administrative Expenses | 54,000 | 48,000 |
| Interest Expense | 6,000 | 5,000 |
| Income Tax Expense | 9,000 | 3,000 |
| Other Expenses | 2,700 | 0 |
| Total Expenses | 285,900 | 226,000 |
| Net Income | **$ 14,100** | **$ 25,000** |

### Requirements

Perform a horizontal analysis and a vertical analysis of Kimball Corporation. State whether 2017 was a good year or a bad year, and give your reasons.

## > Solution

**KIMBALL CORPORATION**
Income Statement
Years Ended December 31, 2017 and 2016

| | | | Increase (Decrease) | |
|---|---|---|---|---|
| | 2017 | 2016 | Amount | Percentage |
| Revenues: | | | | |
| Net Sales | $ 300,000 | $ 250,000 | $ 50,000 | 20.0% |
| Other Revenues | 0 | 1,000 | (1,000) | — |
| Total Revenues | 300,000 | 251,000 | 49,000 | 19.5 |
| Expenses: | | | | |
| Cost of Goods Sold | 214,200 | 170,000 | 44,200 | 26.0 |
| Engineering, Selling, and Administrative Expenses | 54,000 | 48,000 | 6,000 | 12.5 |
| Interest Expense | 6,000 | 5,000 | 1,000 | 20.0 |
| Income Tax Expense | 9,000 | 3,000 | 6,000 | 200.0 |
| Other Expenses | 2,700 | 0 | 2,700 | — |
| Total Expenses | 285,900 | 226,000 | 59,900 | 26.5 |
| Net Income | **$ 14,100** | **$ 25,000** | **$ (10,900)** | **(43.6)%** |

The horizontal analysis shows that net sales increased 20.0%. Total expenses increased by 26.5%, and net income decreased 43.6%. So, even though Kimball's net sales increased, the company's expenses increased by a larger percentage, netting an overall 43.6% reduction in net income between the years. That indicates that 2017 was a bad year in comparison to 2016. This analysis identifies areas in which management should review more data. For example, cost of goods sold increased 26.0%. Managers would want to know why this increase occurred to determine whether the company can implement cost-saving strategies (such as purchasing from other, lower-cost vendors).

**KIMBALL CORPORATION**
Income Statement
Years Ended December 31, 2017 and 2016

| | 2017 | Percent | 2016 | Percent |
|---|---|---|---|---|
| Revenues: | | | | |
| Net Sales | $ 300,000 | 100.0% | $ 250,000 | 100.0% |
| Other Revenues | 0 | 0.0 | 1,000 | 0.4 |
| Total Revenues | 300,000 | 100.0 | 251,000 | 100.4 |
| Expenses: | | | | |
| Cost of Goods Sold | 214,200 | 71.4 | 170,000 | 68.0 |
| Engineering, Selling, and Administrative Expenses | 54,000 | 18.0 | 48,000 | 19.2 |
| Interest Expense | 6,000 | 2.0 | 5,000 | 2.0 |
| Income Tax Expense | 9,000 | 3.0 | 3,000 | 1.2 |
| Other Expenses | 2,700 | 0.9 | 0 | 0 |
| Total Expenses | 285,900 | 95.3 | 226,000 | 90.4 |
| Net Income | **$ 14,100** | **4.7%** | **$ 25,000** | **10.0%** |

The vertical analysis shows changes in the line items as percentages of net sales. A few notable items are:

- Cost of Goods Sold increased from 68.0% to 71.4%;
- Engineering, Selling, and Administrative Expenses decreased from 19.2% to 18.0%.

These two items are Kimball's largest dollar expenses, so their percentage changes are important. This indicates that cost controls need to be improved, especially for COGS.

The 2017 net income declined to 4.7% of sales, compared with 10.0% the preceding year. Kimball's increase in cost of goods sold is the biggest factor in the overall decrease in net income as a percentage of sales. The horizontal analysis showed that although net sales increased 20% from 2016 to 2017, the amount of each of those sales dollars resulting in net income decreased.

## > Summary Problem 15-2

**JAVA, INC.**
**Four-Year Selected Financial Data**
**Years Ended January 31, 2017–2014**

| Operating Results: | 2017 | 2016 | 2015 | 2014 |
|---|---|---|---|---|
| Net Sales | $ 13,848 | $ 13,673 | $ 11,635 | $ 9,054 |
| Cost of Goods Sold | 9,704 | 8,599 | 6,775 | 5,318 |
| Interest Expense | 109 | 75 | 45 | 46 |
| Income from Operations | 338 | 1,455 | 1,817 | 1,333 |
| Income Tax Expense | 100 | 263 | 338 | 247 |
| Net Income (Net Loss) | (8) | 877 | 1,127 | 824 |
| Cash Dividends | 76 | 75 | 76 | 77 |
| **Financial Position:** | | | | |
| Merchandise Inventory | 1,677 | 1,904 | 1,462 | 1,056 |
| Total Assets | 7,591 | 7,012 | 5,189 | 3,963 |
| Current Ratio | 1.48:1 | 0.95:1 | 1.25:1 | 1.20:1 |
| Stockholders' Equity | 3,010 | 2,928 | 2,630 | 1,574 |
| Average Number of Shares of Common Stock Outstanding | 860 | 879 | 895 | 576 |

**Requirements**

Using the financial data presented above, compute the following ratios and evaluate Java's results for 2017–2015:

1. Profit margin ratio
2. Earnings per share
3. Inventory turnover
4. Times-interest-earned ratio
5. Rate of return on common stockholders' equity
6. Gross profit percentage

## > Solution

| | 2017 | 2016 | 2015 |
|---|---|---|---|
| **1.** Profit margin ratio | $\frac{\$(8)}{\$13,848} = (0.06\%)$ | $\frac{\$877}{\$13,673} = 6.4\%$ | $\frac{\$1,127}{\$11,635} = 9.7\%$ |
| **2.** Earnings per share | $\frac{\$(8)}{860 \text{ shares}} = \$(0.01)$ per share | $\frac{\$877}{879 \text{ shares}} = \$1.00$ per share | $\frac{\$1,127}{895 \text{ shares}} = \$1.26$ per share |
| **3.** Inventory turnover | $\frac{\$9,704}{(\$1,904 + \$1,677)/2} = 5.4$ times | $\frac{\$8,599}{(\$1,462 + \$1,904)/2} = 5.1$ times | $\frac{\$6,775}{(\$1,056 + \$1,462)/2} = 5.4$ times |
| **4.** Times-interest-earned ratio | $\frac{[\$(8) + \$100 + \$109]}{\$109} = 1.8$ times | $\frac{(\$877 + \$263 + \$75)}{\$75} = 16.2$ times | $\frac{(\$1,127 + \$338 + \$45)}{\$45} = 33.6$ times |
| **5.** Rate of return on common stockholders' equity | $\frac{\$(8)}{(\$2,928 + \$3,010)/2} = (0.3\%)$ | $\frac{\$877}{(\$2,630 + \$2,928)/2} = 31.6\%$ | $\frac{\$1,127}{(\$1,574 + \$2,630)/2} = 53.6\%$ |
| **6.** Gross profit percentage | $\frac{(\$13,848 - \$9,704)}{\$13,848} = 29.9\%$ | $\frac{(\$13,673 - \$8,599)}{\$13,673} = 37.1\%$ | $\frac{(\$11,635 - \$6,775)}{\$11,635} = 41.8\%$ |

*Evaluation:* During this period, Java's operating results deteriorated on all these measures except inventory turnover. The times-interest-earned ratio and rate of return on common stockholders' equity percentages are down sharply. From these data, it is clear that Java could sell its coffee, but not at the markups the company enjoyed in the past. The final result, in 2017, was a net loss for the year.

## > Key Terms

**Accounts Receivable Turnover Ratio (p. 781)**
**Acid-Test Ratio (p. 779)**
**Annual Report (p. 766)**
**Asset Turnover Ratio (p. 785)**
**Benchmarking (p. 775)**
**Cash Ratio (p. 778)**
**Common-Size Statement (p. 774)**
**Current Ratio (p. 778)**
**Days' Sales in Inventory (p. 780)**
**Days' Sales in Receivables (p. 782)**
**Debt Ratio (p. 782)**
**Debt to Equity Ratio (p. 783)**
**Dividend Payout (p. 788)**
**Dividend Yield (p. 787)**
**Dollar Value Bias (p. 774)**
**Earnings per Share (EPS) (p. 786)**
**Gross Profit Percentage (p. 781)**
**Horizontal Analysis (p. 768)**
**Inventory Turnover (p. 780)**
**Management's Discussion and Analysis of Financial Condition and Results of Operations (MD&A) (p. 766)**
**Price/Earnings Ratio (p. 787)**
**Profit Margin Ratio (p. 784)**
**Rate of Return on Common Stockholders' Equity (p. 785)**
**Rate of Return on Total Assets (p. 784)**
**Times-Interest-Earned Ratio (p. 783)**
**Trading on the Equity (p. 786)**
**Trend Analysis (p. 770)**
**Vertical Analysis (p. 772)**
**Working Capital (p. 777)**

## > Quick Check

Liberty Corporation reported the following financial statements:

**LIBERTY CORPORATION**
Comparative Balance Sheet
December 31, 2017 and 2016

| | 2017 | 2016 |
|---|---|---|
| **Assets** | | |
| Current Assets: | | |
| Cash and Cash Equivalents | $ 2,450 | $ 2,094 |
| Accounts Receivable | 1,813 | 1,611 |
| Merchandise Inventory | 1,324 | 1,060 |
| Prepaid Expenses | 1,709 | 2,120 |
| Total Current Assets | 7,296 | 6,885 |
| Other Assets | 18,500 | 15,737 |
| Total Assets | **$ 25,796** | **$ 22,622** |
| **Liabilities** | | |
| Current Liabilities | $ 7,230 | $ 8,467 |
| Long-term Liabilities | 4,798 | 3,792 |
| Total Liabilities | 12,028 | 12,259 |
| **Stockholders' Equity** | | |
| Common Stock, no par | 6,568 | 4,363 |
| Retained Earnings | 7,200 | 6,000 |
| Total Stockholders' Equity | 13,768 | 10,363 |
| Total Liabilities and Stockholders' Equity | **$ 25,796** | **$ 22,622** |

**LIBERTY CORPORATION**
Income Statement
Year Ended December 31, 2017

| | |
|---|---|
| Net Sales | $ 20,941 |
| Cost of Goods Sold | 7,055 |
| Gross Profit | 13,886 |
| Operating Expenses | 7,065 |
| Operating Income | 6,821 |
| Interest Expense | 210 |
| Income Before Income Taxes | 6,611 |
| Income Tax Expense | 2,563 |
| Net Income | **$ 4,048** |

**Learning Objective 1**

1. What part of the Liberty's annual report is written by the company and could present a biased view of financial conditions and results?
   a. Balance Sheet
   b. Management's Discussion and Analysis of Financial Condition and Results of Operations (MD&A)
   c. Auditor's Report
   d. Income Statement

**Learning Objective 2**

2. Horizontal analysis of Liberty's balance sheet for 2017 would report
   a. Cash as 9.50% of total assets.
   b. a 17% increase in Cash and Cash Equivalents.
   c. a current ratio of 1.01.
   d. inventory turnover of 6 times.

**Learning Objective 3**

3. Vertical analysis of Liberty's balance sheet for 2017 would report
   a. Cash as 9.50% of total assets.
   b. inventory turnover of 6 times.
   c. a current ratio of 1.01.
   d. a 17% increase in Cash.

**Learning Objective 4**

4. Which statement best describes Liberty's acid-test ratio for 2017?
   a. Greater than 1
   b. Equal to 1
   c. Less than 1
   d. None of the above

**Learning Objective 4**

5. Liberty's inventory turnover during 2017 was (amounts rounded)
   a. 6 times.
   b. 7 times.
   c. 8 times.
   d. not determinable from the data given.

**Learning Objective 4**

6. Assume all sales are on credit. During 2017, Liberty's days' sales in receivables ratio was (amounts rounded)
   a. 34 days.
   b. 30 days.
   c. 32 days.
   d. 28 days.

**Learning Objective 4**

7. Which measure expresses Liberty's times-interest-earned ratio? (amounts rounded)
   a. 54.7%
   b. 19 times
   c. 34.5%
   d. 32 times

**Learning Objective 4**

8. Liberty's rate of return on common stockholders' equity can be described as
   a. weak.
   b. normal.
   c. strong.
   d. average.

**Learning Objective 4**

9. The company has 2,500 shares of common stock outstanding. What is Liberty's earnings per share?
   a. $1.62
   b. $1.75
   c. $2.73
   d. 2.63 times

**Learning Objective 5**
**Appendix 15A**

10A. In order for an item to be reported in the extraordinary items section of the income statement, it must be
   a. unusual.
   b. infrequent.
   c. unusual or infrequent.
   d. unusual and infrequent.

**Check your answers at the end of the chapter.**

# ASSESS YOUR PROGRESS

## > Review Questions

1. What are the three main ways to analyze financial statements?
2. What is an annual report? Briefly describe the key parts of the annual report.
3. What is horizontal analysis, and how is a percentage change computed?
4. What is trend analysis, and how does it differ from horizontal analysis?
5. What is vertical analysis? What item is used as the base for the income statement? What item is used as the base for the balance sheet?
6. Describe a common-size statement and how it might be helpful in evaluating a company.
7. What is benchmarking, and what are the two main types of benchmarks in financial statement analysis?
8. Briefly describe the ratios that can be used to evaluate a company's ability to pay current liabilities.
9. Briefly describe the ratios that can be used to evaluate a company's ability to sell merchandise inventory and collect receivables.
10. Briefly describe the ratios that can be used to evaluate a company's ability to pay long-term debt.
11. Briefly describe the ratios that can be used to evaluate a company's profitability.
12. Briefly describe the ratios that can be used to evaluate a company's stock as an investment.
13. What are some common red flags in financial statement analysis?

14A. What is reported in the discontinued operations section of the income statement?

15A. Describe the types of items that would be reported in the extraordinary items section of the income statement.

## > Short Exercises

**Learning Objective 1**

### S15-1 Explaining financial statements

Caleb King is interested in investing in Orange Corporation. What types of tools should Caleb use to evaluate the company?

**Learning Objective 2**

### S15-2 Performing horizontal analysis

McDonald Corp. reported the following on its comparative income statement:

| *(In millions)* | 2017 | 2016 | 2015 |
|---|---|---|---|
| Revenue | $ 9,910 | $ 9,700 | $ 9,210 |
| Cost of Goods Sold | 7,210 | 6,900 | 6,125 |

Prepare a horizontal analysis of revenues and gross profit—both in dollar amounts and in percentages—for 2017 and 2016.

**Learning Objective 2**

## S15-3 Calculating trend analysis

Variline Corp. reported the following revenues and net income amounts:

| *(In millions)* | 2017 | 2016 | 2015 | 2014 |
|---|---|---|---|---|
| Revenue | $ 9,990 | $ 9,890 | $ 9,290 | $ 9,090 |
| Net Income | 7,750 | 7,570 | 5,670 | 4,990 |

### Requirements

1. Calculate Variline's trend analysis for revenues and net income. Use 2014 as the base year, and round to the nearest percent.
2. Which measure increased at a higher rate during 2015–2017?

**Learning Objective 3**

## S15-4 Performing vertical analysis

Hoosier Optical Company reported the following amounts on its balance sheet at December 31, 2016 and 2015:

| | 2016 | 2015 |
|---|---|---|
| Cash and Receivables | $ 77,825 | $ 70,200 |
| Merchandise Inventory | 55,825 | 52,780 |
| Property, Plant, and Equipment, Net | 141,350 | 137,020 |
| Total Assets | $ 275,000 | $ 260,000 |

Prepare a vertical analysis of Hoosier assets for 2016 and 2015.

**Learning Objective 3**

## S15-5 Preparing common-size income statement

Data for Martinez, Inc. and Rosario Corp. follow:

| | Martinez | Rosario |
|---|---|---|
| Net Sales | $ 10,000 | $ 17,000 |
| Cost of Goods Sold | 6,210 | 12,359 |
| Other Expenses | 3,180 | 3,825 |
| Net Income | $ 610 | $ 816 |

### Requirements

1. Prepare common-size income statements.
2. Which company earns more net income?
3. Which company's net income is a higher percentage of its net sales?

***Use the following information for Short Exercises S15-6 through S15-10.***

Shine's Companies, a home improvement store chain, reported the following summarized figures:

**SHINE'S COMPANIES**
Income Statement
Years Ended May 31, 2016 and 2015

| | 2016 | 2015 |
|---|---|---|
| Net Sales | $ 57,200,000 | $ 41,100,000 |
| Cost of Goods Sold | 20,600,000 | 29,300,000 |
| Interest Expense | 700,000 | 630,000 |
| All Other Expenses | 6,900,000 | 8,400,000 |
| Net Income | **$ 29,000,000** | **$ 2,770,000** |

**SHINE'S COMPANIES**
Balance Sheet
May 31, 2016 and 2015

| **Assets** | **2016** | **2015** | **Liabilities** | **2016** | **2015** |
|---|---|---|---|---|---|
| Cash | $ 2,200,000 | $ 1,800,000 | Total Current Liabilities | $ 24,000,000 | $ 12,900,000 |
| Short-term Investments | 26,000,000 | 10,000,000 | Long-term Liabilities | 13,400,000 | 10,800,000 |
| Accounts Receivable | 7,200,000 | 5,400,000 | Total Liabilities | 37,400,000 | 23,700,000 |
| Merchandise Inventory | 7,100,000 | 8,200,000 | **Stockholders' Equity** | | |
| Other Current Assets | 9,000,000 | 1,800,000 | Common Stock | 13,000,000 | 13,000,000 |
| Total Current Assets | 51,500,000 | 27,200,000 | Retained Earnings | 33,100,000 | 18,500,000 |
| All Other Assets | 32,000,000 | 28,000,000 | Total Equity | 46,100,000 | 31,500,000 |
| Total Assets | **$ 83,500,000** | **$ 55,200,000** | Total Liabilities and Equity | **$ 83,500,000** | **$ 55,200,000** |

Shine's has 100,000 common shares outstanding during 2016.

## S15-6 Evaluating current ratio

**Learning Objective 4**

**Requirements**

1. Compute Shine's Companies' current ratio at May 31, 2016 and 2015.
2. Did Shine's Companies' current ratio improve, deteriorate, or hold steady during 2016?

**Learning Objective 4**

## S15-7 Computing inventory, gross profit, and receivables ratios

**Requirements**

1. Compute the inventory turnover, days' sales in inventory, and gross profit percentage for Shine's Companies for 2016.
2. Compute days' sales in receivables during 2016. Round dollar amounts to three decimal places. Assume all sales were on account.
3. What do these ratios say about Shine's Companies' ability to sell inventory and collect receivables?

**Learning Objective 4**

## S15-8 Measuring ability to pay liabilities

**Requirements**

1. Compute the debt ratio and the debt to equity ratio at May 31, 2016, for Shine's Companies.
2. Is Shine's ability to pay its liabilities strong or weak? Explain your reasoning.

**Learning Objective 4**

## S15-9 Measuring profitability

**Requirements**

1. Compute the profit margin ratio for Shine's Companies for 2016.
2. Compute the rate of return on total assets for 2016.
3. Compute the asset turnover ratio for 2016.
4. Compute the rate of return on common stockholders' equity for 2016.
5. Are these rates of return strong or weak? Explain your reasoning.

**Learning Objective 4**

## S15-10 Computing EPS and P/E ratio

**Requirements**

1. Compute earnings per share (EPS) for 2016 for Shine's. Round to the nearest cent.
2. Compute Shine's Companies' price/earnings ratio for 2016. The market price per share of Shine's stock is $65.50.
3. What do these results mean when evaluating Shine's Companies' profitability?

**Learning Objective 4**

## S15-11 Using ratios to reconstruct an income statement

Vintage Mills's income statement appears as follows (amounts in thousands):

**VINTAGE MILLS**
Income Statement
Year Ended December 31, 2016

| | |
|---|---|
| Net Sales | $ 7,300 |
| Cost of Goods Sold | (*a*) |
| Selling and Administrative Expenses | 1,700 |
| Interest Expense | (*b*) |
| Other Expenses | 135 |
| Income Before Income Taxes | 1,325 |
| Income Tax Expense | (*c*) |
| Net Income | (*d*) |

Use the following ratio data to complete Vintage Mills's income statement:

1. Inventory turnover is 4.70 (beginning Merchandise Inventory was $750; ending Merchandise Inventory was $710).
2. Profit margin ratio is 0.16.

**S15-12 Using ratios to reconstruct a balance sheet** **Learning Objective 4**

Walsham Mills's balance sheet appears as follows (amounts in thousands):

**WALSHAM MILLS**
Balance Sheet
December 31, 2016

| **Assets** | | **Liabilities** | |
|---|---|---|---|
| Cash | $ 60 | Total Current Liabilities | $ 1,800 |
| Accounts Receivables | *(a)* | Long-term Note Payable | *(e)* |
| Merchandise Inventory | 725 | Other Long-term Liabilities | 770 |
| Prepaid Expenses | *(b)* | Total Liabilities | *(f)* |
| Total Current Assets | *(c)* | | |
| Plant Assets, Net | *(d)* | **Stockholders' Equity** | |
| Other Assets | 2,000 | Stockholders' Equity | 2,675 |
| Total Assets | **$ 6,500** | Total Liabilities and Stockholders' Equity | **$ *(g)*** |

Use the following ratio data to complete Walsham Mills's balance sheet.

**a.** Current ratio is 0.86.

**b.** Acid-test ratio is 0.40.

**S15A-13 Preparing a corporate income statement** **Learning Objective 5 Appendix 15A**

TST Corporation's accounting records include the following items, listed in no particular order, at December 31, 2016:

| | | | |
|---|---|---|---|
| Other Revenues and (Expenses) | $ (10,000) | Extraordinary Loss | $ 16,600 |
| Net Sales | 266,000 | Cost of Goods Sold | 79,000 |
| Gain on Discontinued Operations | 34,500 | Operating Expenses | 65,000 |

The income tax rate for TST Corporation is 50%.

Prepare TST's income statement for the year ended December 31, 2016. Omit earnings per share. Use the multi-step format.

**S15A-14 Reporting earnings per share** **Learning Objective 5 Appendix 15A**

Return to the TST data in Short Exercise S15A-13. TST had 8,000 shares of common stock outstanding during 2016. TST declared and paid preferred dividends of $4,000 during 2016.

Show how TST reports EPS data on its 2016 income statement.

## > Exercises

Learning Objective 2

1. Net Income 35.7%

### E15-15 Performing horizontal analysis—income statement

Data for McCormick Designs, Inc. follow:

**MCCORMICK DESIGNS, INC.**
Comparative Income Statement
Years Ended December 31, 2016 and 2015

| | 2016 | 2015 |
|---|---|---|
| Net Sales Revenue | $ 431,250 | $ 373,000 |
| Expenses: | | |
| Cost of Goods Sold | 202,000 | 189,000 |
| Selling and Administrative Expenses | 100,050 | 92,550 |
| Other Expenses | 8,000 | 2,150 |
| Total Expenses | 310,050 | 283,700 |
| Net Income | **$ 121,200** | **$ 89,300** |

**Requirements**

1. Prepare a horizontal analysis of the comparative income statement of McCormick Designs, Inc. Round percentage changes to one decimal place.
2. Why did 2016 net income increase by a higher percentage than net sales revenue?

Learning Objective 2

1. 2017 Net Income 166%

### E15-16 Computing trend analysis

Grand Oaks Realty's net revenue and net income for the following five-year period, using 2013 as the base year, follow:

| | 2017 | 2016 | 2015 | 2014 | 2013 |
|---|---|---|---|---|---|
| Net Revenue | $ 1,315,000 | $ 1,188,000 | $ 1,160,000 | $ 1,011,000 | $ 1,038,000 |
| Net Income | 126,000 | 115,000 | 82,000 | 77,000 | 76,000 |

**Requirements**

1. Compute a trend analysis for net revenue and net income. Round to the nearest full percent.
2. Which grew faster during the period, net revenue or net income?

## E15-17 Performing vertical analysis of a balance sheet

Learning Objective 3

2016 Current Assets: 15.7%

Tri Designs, Inc. has the following data:

| TRI DESIGNS, INC.<br>Comparative Balance Sheet<br>December 31, 2016 and 2015 | | |
|---|---|---|
| | **2016** | **2015** |
| **Assets** | | |
| Total Current Assets | $ 54,950 | $ 72,250 |
| Property, Plant, and Equipment, Net | 250,250 | 158,950 |
| Other Assets | 44,800 | 57,800 |
| Total Assets | **$ 350,000** | **$ 289,000** |
| **Liabilities** | | |
| Total Current Liabilities | $ 49,700 | $ 47,685 |
| Long-term Debt | 118,300 | 196,520 |
| Total Liabilities | 168,000 | 244,205 |
| **Stockholders' Equity** | | |
| Total Stockholders' Equity | 182,000 | 44,795 |
| Total Liabilities and Stockholders' Equity | **$ 350,000** | **$ 289,000** |

Perform a vertical analysis of Tri Designs's balance sheet for each year.

## E15-18 Preparing common-size income statements

Learning Objective 3

1. 2016 Net Income 28.1%

Refer to the data presented for McCormick Designs, Inc. in Exercise E15-15.

### Requirements

1. Prepare a comparative common-size income statement for McCormick Designs, Inc. using the 2016 and 2015 data. Round percentages to one-tenth percent (three decimal places).
2. To an investor, how does 2016 compare with 2015? Explain your reasoning.

## E15-19 Computing working capital changes

Learning Objective 4

2017 Working Capital $200,000

Data for Outreach Enterprises follows:

| | 2017 | 2016 | 2015 |
|---|---|---|---|
| Total Current Assets | $ 380,000 | $ 330,000 | $ 290,000 |
| Total Current Liabilities | 180,000 | 165,000 | 145,000 |

Compute the dollar amount of change and the percentage of change in Outreach Enterprises's working capital each year during 2017 and 2016. What do the calculated changes indicate?

Learning Objective 4

e. 78 days

## E15-20 Computing key ratios

The financial statements of Victory's Natural Foods include the following items:

| | Current Year | Preceding Year |
|---|---|---|
| **Balance Sheet:** | | |
| Cash | $ 20,000 | $ 24,000 |
| Short-term Investments | 18,000 | 26,000 |
| Net Accounts Receivable | 50,000 | 78,000 |
| Merchandise Inventory | 70,000 | 66,000 |
| Prepaid Expenses | 12,000 | 10,000 |
| Total Current Assets | 170,000 | 204,000 |
| Total Current Liabilities | 129,000 | 92,000 |
| **Income Statement:** | | |
| Net Credit Sales | $ 478,000 | |
| Cost of Goods Sold | 318,000 | |

Compute the following ratios for the current year:

**a.** Current ratio

**b.** Cash ratio

**c.** Acid-test ratio

**d.** Inventory turnover

**e.** Days' sales in inventory

**f.** Days' sales in receivables

**g.** Gross profit percentage (assume all sales are on credit)

Learning Objective 4

d. 2016 0.61

## E15-21 Analyzing the ability to pay liabilities

Big Bend Photo Shop has asked you to determine whether the company's ability to pay current liabilities and total liabilities improved or deteriorated during 2016. To answer this question, you gather the following data:

| | 2016 | 2015 |
|---|---|---|
| Cash | $ 56,000 | $ 51,000 |
| Short-term Investments | 31,000 | 0 |
| Net Accounts Receivable | 134,000 | 136,000 |
| Merchandise Inventory | 257,000 | 297,000 |
| Total Assets | 540,000 | 550,000 |
| Total Current Liabilities | 285,000 | 202,000 |
| Long-term Notes Payable | 46,000 | 58,000 |
| Income from Operations | 170,000 | 178,000 |
| Interest Expense | 54,000 | 45,000 |

Compute the following ratios for 2016 and 2015, and evaluate the company's ability to pay its current liabilities and total liabilities:

**a.** Current ratio

**b.** Cash ratio

**c.** Acid-test ratio

**d.** Debt ratio

**e.** Debt to equity ratio

## E15-22 Analyzing profitability

**Learning Objective 4**

1. 2017 11.6%

Varsity, Inc.'s comparative income statement follows. The 2015 data are given as needed.

**VARSITY, INC.**
Comparative Income Statement
Years Ended December 31, 2017 and 2016

| *Dollars in thousands* | 2017 | 2016 | 2015 |
|---|---|---|---|
| Net Sales | $ 185,000 | $ 153,000 | |
| Cost of Goods Sold | 96,000 | 87,000 | |
| Selling and Administrative Expenses | 46,500 | 39,500 | |
| Interest Expense | 9,500 | 10,500 | |
| Income Tax Expense | 11,500 | 9,000 | |
| Net Income | **$ 21,500** | **$ 7,000** | |
| *Additional data:* | | | |
| Total Assets | $ 200,000 | $ 188,000 | $ 169,000 |
| Common Stockholders' Equity | 92,000 | 87,500 | 80,000 |
| Preferred Dividends | 2,000 | 2,000 | 0 |
| Common Shares Outstanding During the Year | 20,000 | 20,000 | 10,000 |

### Requirements

1. Calculate the profit margin ratio for 2017 and 2016.
2. Calculate the rate of return on total assets for 2017 and 2016.
3. Calculate the asset turnover ratio for 2017 and 2016.
4. Calculate the rate of return on common stockholders' equity for 2017 and 2016.
5. Calculate the earnings per share for 2017 and 2016.
6. Calculate the 2017 dividend payout on common stock. Assume dividends per share for common stock are equal to $0.75 per share.
7. Did the company's operating performance improve or deteriorate during 2017?

## E15-23 Evaluating a stock as an investment

**Learning Objective 4**

Dividend Yield 2016 1.2%

Data for Regal State Bank follow:

| | 2016 | 2015 |
|---|---|---|
| Net Income | $ 56,000 | $ 47,200 |
| Dividends—Common | 16,000 | 16,000 |
| Dividends—Preferred | 16,000 | 16,000 |
| Total Stockholders' Equity at Year-End (includes 80,000 shares of common stock) | 770,000 | 580,000 |
| Preferred Stock | 220,000 | 220,000 |
| Market Price per Share of Common Stock | $ 16.50 | $ 11.00 |

Evaluate the common stock of Regal State Bank as an investment. Specifically, use the three stock ratios to determine whether the common stock has increased or decreased in attractiveness during the past year.

**Learning Objective 4**

Total Assets $2,000,000

## E15-24 Using ratios to reconstruct a balance sheet

The following data are adapted from the financial statements of Jim's Shops, Inc.:

| | |
|---|---|
| Total Current Assets | $ 1,054,000 |
| Accumulated Depreciation | 1,600,000 |
| Total Liabilities | 1,480,000 |
| Preferred Stock | 0 |
| Debt Ratio | 74% |
| Current Ratio | 1.55 |

Prepare Jim's condensed balance sheet as of December 31, 2016.

**Learning Objective 5**
**Appendix 15A**

Net Income $155,400

## E15A-25 Preparing a multi-step income statement

Cloud Photographic Supplies, Inc.'s accounting records include the following for 2016:

| | | | |
|---|---|---|---|
| Income Tax Saving—Extraordinary Loss | $ 10,400 | Sales | $ 575,000 |
| Income Tax Saving—Loss on Discontinued Operations | 6,000 | Operating Expenses (Including Income Tax) | 140,000 |
| Extraordinary Loss | 26,000 | Cost of Goods Sold | 255,000 |
| Loss on Discontinued Operations | 15,000 | | |

Prepare Cloud's multi-step income statement for 2016. Omit earnings per share.

**Learning Objective 5**
**Appendix 15A**

Net Income $14.25

## E15A-26 Computing earnings per share

Falconi Academy Surplus had 55,000 shares of common stock and 5,000 shares of 1%, $10 par value preferred stock outstanding through December 31, 2016. Income from continuing operations for 2016 was $679,750, and loss on discontinued operations (net of income tax saving) was $66,000. Falconi also had an extraordinary gain (net of tax) of $170,500.

Compute Falconi's earnings per share for 2016, starting with income from continuing operations.

# > Problems Group A

**Learning Objectives 2, 4**

2. 2017 15.9%

## P15-27A Computing trend analysis and return on common equity

Net sales revenue, net income, and common stockholders' equity for Shawnee Mission Corporation, a manufacturer of contact lenses, follow for a four-year period.

| | 2017 | 2016 | 2015 | 2014 |
|---|---|---|---|---|
| Net Sales Revenue | $ 764,000 | $ 702,000 | $ 642,000 | $ 665,000 |
| Net Income | 57,000 | 45,000 | 38,000 | 47,000 |
| Ending Common Stockholders' Equity | 362,000 | 356,000 | 328,000 | 294,000 |

**Requirements**

1. Compute trend analyses for each item for 2015–2017. Use 2014 as the base year, and round to the nearest whole percent.
2. Compute the rate of return on common stockholders' equity for 2015–2017, rounding to three decimal places.

## P15-28A Performing vertical analysis

Learning Objective 2

1. Net Income 10.7%

The Roost Department Stores, Inc. chief executive officer (CEO) has asked you to compare the company's profit performance and financial position with the averages for the industry. The CEO has given you the company's income statement and balance sheet as well as the industry average data for retailers.

**ROOST DEPARTMENT STORES, INC.**
Income Statement Compared with Industry Average
Year Ended December 31, 2016

| | Roost | Industry Average |
|---|---|---|
| Net Sales | $ 779,000 | 100.0% |
| Cost of Goods Sold | 526,604 | 65.8 |
| Gross Profit | 252,396 | 34.2 |
| Operating Expenses | 163,590 | 19.7 |
| Operating Income | 88,806 | 14.5 |
| Other Expenses | 5,453 | 0.4 |
| Net Income | **$ 83,353** | **14.1%** |

**ROOST DEPARTMENT STORES, INC.**
Balance Sheet Compared with Industry Average
December 31, 2016

| | Roost | Industry Average |
|---|---|---|
| Current Assets | $ 316,780 | 70.9% |
| Fixed Assets, Net | 120,320 | 23.6 |
| Intangible Assets, Net | 7,990 | 0.8 |
| Other Assets | 24,910 | 4.7 |
| Total Assets | **$ 470,000** | **100.0%** |
| Current Liabilities | $ 217,140 | 48.1% |
| Long-term Liabilities | 104,340 | 16.6 |
| Total Liabilities | 321,480 | 64.7 |
| Stockholders' Equity | 148,520 | 35.3 |
| Total Liabilities and Stockholders' Equity | **$ 470,000** | **100.0%** |

### Requirements

1. Prepare a vertical analysis for Roost for both its income statement and balance sheet.
2. Compare the company's profit performance and financial position with the average for the industry.

***Note: Problem P15-28A must be completed before attempting Problem P15-29A.***

## P15-29A Preparing common-size statements, analysis of profitability and financial position, comparison with the industry, and using ratios to evaluate a company

Learning Objectives 3, 4

2. Gross Profit Percentage 32.4%

Consider the data for Roost Department Stores presented in Problem P15-28A.

### Requirements

1. Prepare a common-size income statement and balance sheet for Roost. The first column of each statement should present Roost's common-size statement, and the second column, the industry averages.
2. For the profitability analysis, compute Roost's (a) gross profit percentage and (b) profit margin ratio. Compare these figures with the industry averages. Is Roost's profit performance better or worse than the industry average?
3. For the analysis of financial position, compute Roost's (a) current ratio and (b) debt to equity ratio. Compare these ratios with the industry averages. Assume the current ratio industry average is 1.47, and the debt to equity industry average is 1.83. Is Roost's financial position better or worse than the industry averages?

**Learning Objective 4**

1. Current Ratio 1.49

## P15-30A Determining the effects of business transactions on selected ratios

Financial statement data of *Off Road Traveler Magazine* include the following items:

| | |
|---|---|
| Cash | $ 23,000 |
| Accounts Receivable, Net | 80,000 |
| Merchandise Inventory | 184,000 |
| Total Assets | 637,000 |
| Accounts Payable | 103,000 |
| Accrued Liabilities | 38,000 |
| Short-term Notes Payable | 51,000 |
| Long-term Liabilities | 224,000 |
| Net Income | 74,000 |
| Common Shares Outstanding | 50,000 |

**Requirements**

1. Compute *Off Road Traveler's* current ratio, debt ratio, and earnings per share. Round all ratios to two decimal places, and use the following format for your answer:

| Current Ratio | Debt Ratio | Earnings per Share |
|---|---|---|

2. Compute the three ratios after evaluating the effect of each transaction that follows. Consider each transaction *separately*.
   a. Purchased merchandise inventory of $48,000 on account.
   b. Borrowed $127,000 on a long-term note payable.
   c. Issued 56,000 shares of common stock, receiving cash of $106,000.
   d. Received cash on account, $5,000.

**Learning Objective 4**

1. 2016 e. 49%

## P15-31A Using ratios to evaluate a stock investment

Comparative financial statement data of Dangerfield, Inc. follow:

**DANGERFIELD, INC.**
**Comparative Income Statement**
**Years Ended December 31, 2016 and 2015**

| | 2016 | 2015 |
|---|---|---|
| Net Sales | $ 465,000 | $ 428,000 |
| Cost of Goods Sold | 237,000 | 214,000 |
| Gross Profit | 228,000 | 214,000 |
| Operating Expenses | 138,000 | 136,000 |
| Income from Operations | 90,000 | 78,000 |
| Interest Expense | 10,000 | 16,000 |
| Income Before Income Tax | 80,000 | 62,000 |
| Income Tax Expense | 23,000 | 25,000 |
| Net Income | **$ 57,000** | **$ 37,000** |

**DANGERFIELD, INC.**
Comparative Balance Sheet
December 31, 2016 and 2015

| | 2016 | 2015 | 2014* |
|---|---|---|---|
| **Assets** | | | |
| Current Assets: | | | |
| Cash | $ 94,000 | $ 93,000 | |
| Accounts Receivable, Net | 107,000 | 116,000 | $ 102,000 |
| Merchandise Inventory | 145,000 | 160,000 | 210,000 |
| Prepaid Expenses | 19,000 | 8,000 | |
| Total Current Assets | 365,000 | 377,000 | |
| Property, Plant, and Equipment, Net | 217,000 | 178,000 | |
| Total Assets | **$ 582,000** | **$ 555,000** | 596,000 |
| **Liabilities** | | | |
| Total Current Liabilities | $ 228,000 | $ 242,000 | |
| Long-term Liabilities | 114,000 | 98,000 | |
| Total Liabilities | 342,000 | 340,000 | |
| **Stockholders' Equity** | | | |
| Preferred Stock, 3% | 96,000 | 96,000 | |
| Common Stockholders' Equity, no par | 144,000 | 119,000 | 91,000 |
| Total Liabilities and Stockholders' Equity | **$ 582,000** | **$ 555,000** | |

* Selected 2014 amounts

1. Market price of Dangerfield's common stock: $76.67 at December 31, 2016, and $37.20 at December 31, 2015.
2. Common shares outstanding: 13,000 during 2016 and 11,000 during 2015 and 2014.
3. All sales are on credit.

**Requirements**

1. Compute the following ratios for 2016 and 2015:
   a. Current ratio
   b. Cash ratio
   c. Times-interest-earned ratio
   d. Inventory turnover
   e. Gross profit percentage
   f. Debt to equity ratio
   g. Rate of return on common stockholders' equity
   h. Earnings per share of common stock
   i. Price/earnings ratio
2. Decide (a) whether Dangerfield's ability to pay debts and to sell inventory improved or deteriorated during 2016 and (b) whether the investment attractiveness of its common stock appears to have increased or decreased.

**Learning Objective 4**

1. Best Digital e. $4.67

## P15-32A Using ratios to decide between two stock investments

Assume that you are purchasing an investment and have decided to invest in a company in the digital phone business. You have narrowed the choice to Best Digital Corp. and Very Zone, Inc. and have assembled the following data.

Selected income statement data for the current year:

| | Best Digital | Very Zone |
|---|---|---|
| Net Sales (all on credit) | $ 417,925 | $ 493,845 |
| Cost of Goods Sold | 207,000 | 259,000 |
| Interest Expense | 0 | 14,000 |
| Net Income | 56,000 | 72,000 |

Selected balance sheet and market price data at the *end* of the current year:

| | Best Digital | Very Zone |
|---|---|---|
| Current Assets: | | |
| Cash | $ 23,000 | $ 21,000 |
| Short-term Investments | 38,000 | 15,000 |
| Accounts Receivable, Net | 37,000 | 47,000 |
| Merchandise Inventory | 65,000 | 97,000 |
| Prepaid Expenses | 22,000 | 18,000 |
| Total Current Assets | $ 185,000 | $ 198,000 |
| Total Assets | $ 261,000 | $ 325,000 |
| Total Current Liabilities | 100,000 | 99,000 |
| Total Liabilities | 100,000 | 131,000 |
| Common Stock, $1 par (12,000 shares) | 12,000 | |
| $1 par (17,000 shares) | | 17,000 |
| Total Stockholders' Equity | 161,000 | 194,000 |
| Market Price per Share of Common Stock | $ 70.05 | $ 97.52 |
| Dividends Paid per Common Share | $ 0.60 | $ 0.40 |

Selected balance sheet data at the *beginning* of the current year:

| | Best Digital | Very Zone |
|---|---|---|
| Balance Sheet: | | |
| Accounts Receivable, net | $ 42,000 | $ 49,000 |
| Merchandise Inventory | 81,000 | 90,000 |
| Total Assets | 258,000 | 275,000 |
| Common Stock, $1 par (12,000 shares) | 12,000 | |
| $1 par (17,000 shares) | | 17,000 |

Your strategy is to invest in companies that have low price/earnings ratios but appear to be in good shape financially. Assume that you have analyzed all other factors and that your decision depends on the results of ratio analysis.

**Requirements**

1. Compute the following ratios for both companies for the current year:
   a. Acid-test ratio
   b. Inventory turnover
   c. Days' sales in receivables
   d. Debt ratio
   e. Earnings per share of common stock
   f. Price/earnings ratio
   g. Dividend payout
2. Decide which company's stock better fits your investment strategy.

**Learning Objective 5**
**Appendix 15A**

Net Income $108,600

**P15A-33A Preparing an income statement**

The following information was taken from the records of Grey Motorsports, Inc. at November 30, 2016:

| | | | |
|---|---|---|---|
| Selling Expenses | $ 125,000 | Common Stock, $5 Par Value, 30,500 shares authorized and issued | $ 152,500 |
| Administrative Expenses | 95,000 | Preferred Stock, $3 No-Par Value, 5,000 shares issued | 250,000 |
| Income from Discontinued Operations | 11,000 | Income Tax Expense: Continuing Operations | 35,000 |
| Cost of Goods Sold | 440,000 | Income Tax Expense: Income from Discontinued Operations | 4,400 |
| Treasury Stock—Common (500 shares) | 4,000 | | |
| Net Sales Revenue | 797,000 | | |

Prepare a multi-step income statement for Grey Motorsports for the fiscal year ended November 30, 2016. Include earnings per share.

## > Problems Group B

**Learning Objectives 2, 4**

2. 2016 10.2%

**P15-34B Computing trend analysis and return on common equity**

Net sales revenue, net income, and common stockholders' equity for Atkinson Mission Corporation, a manufacturer of contact lenses, follow for a four-year period.

| | 2017 | 2016 | 2015 | 2014 |
|---|---|---|---|---|
| Net Sales Revenue | $ 763,000 | $ 704,000 | $ 641,000 | $ 661,000 |
| Net Income | 57,000 | 35,000 | 33,000 | 43,000 |
| Ending Common Stockholders' Equity | 370,000 | 358,000 | 330,000 | 298,000 |

**Requirements**

1. Compute trend analyses for each item for 2015–2017. Use 2014 as the base year, and round to the nearest whole percent.
2. Compute the rate of return on common stockholders' equity for 2015–2017, rounding to three decimal places.

**Learning Objective 2**

1. Net Income 10.9%

## P15-35B Performing vertical analysis

The Russell Department Stores, Inc. chief executive officer (CEO) has asked you to compare the company's profit performance and financial position with the averages for the industry. The CEO has given you the company's income statement and balance sheet as well as the industry average data for retailers.

**RUSSELL DEPARTMENT STORES, INC.**
Income Statement Compared with Industry Average
Year Ended December 31, 2016

| | Russell | Industry Average |
|---|---|---|
| Net Sales | $ 780,000 | 100.0% |
| Cost of Goods Sold | 528,060 | 65.8 |
| Gross Profit | 251,940 | 34.2 |
| Operating Expenses | 159,900 | 19.7 |
| Operating Income | 92,040 | 14.5 |
| Other Expenses | 7,020 | 0.4 |
| Net Income | **$ 85,020** | **14.1%** |

**RUSSELL DEPARTMENT STORES, INC.**
Balance Sheet Compared with Industry Average
December 31, 2016

| | Russell | Industry Average |
|---|---|---|
| Current Assets | $ 323,520 | 70.9% |
| Fixed Assets, Net | 124,800 | 23.6 |
| Intangible Assets, Net | 8,160 | 0.8 |
| Other Assets | 23,520 | 4.7 |
| Total Assets | **$ 480,000** | **100.0%** |
| Current Liabilities | $ 221,760 | 48.1% |
| Long-term Liabilities | 108,480 | 16.6 |
| Total Liabilities | 330,240 | 64.7 |
| Stockholders' Equity | 149,760 | 35.3 |
| Total Liabilities and Stockholders' Equity | **$ 480,000** | **100.0%** |

### Requirements

1. Prepare a vertical analysis for Russell for both its income statement and balance sheet.
2. Compare the company's profit performance and financial position with the average for the industry.

***Note: Problem P15-35B must be completed before attempting Problem P15-36B.***

**Learning Objectives 3, 4**

1. Current Assets 67.4%

## P15-36B Preparing common-size statements, analysis of profitability and financial position, comparison with the industry, and using ratios to evaluate a company

Consider the data for Russell Department Stores presented in Problem P15-35B.

### Requirements

1. Prepare a common-size income statement and balance sheet for Russell. The first column of each statement should present Russell's common-size statement, and the second column, the industry averages.
2. For the profitability analysis, compute Russell's (a) gross profit percentage and (b) profit margin ratio. Compare these figures with the industry averages. Is Russell's profit performance better or worse than the industry average?
3. For the analysis of financial position, compute Russell's (a) current ratio and (b) debt to equity ratio. Compare these ratios with the industry averages. Assume the current ratio industry average is 1.47, and the debt to equity industry average is 1.83. Is Russell's financial position better or worse than the industry averages?

## P15-37B Determining the effects of business transactions on selected ratios

**Learning Objective 4**

1. Earnings per Share $1.83

Financial statement data of *Yankee Traveler's Magazine* include the following items:

| | |
|---|---|
| Cash | $ 21,000 |
| Accounts Receivable, Net | 82,000 |
| Merchandise Inventory | 183,000 |
| Total Assets | 634,000 |
| Accounts Payable | 102,000 |
| Accrued Liabilities | 38,000 |
| Short-term Notes Payable | 46,000 |
| Long-term Liabilities | 222,000 |
| Net Income | 73,000 |
| Common Shares Outstanding | 40,000 |

**Requirements**

1. Compute *Yankee Traveler's* current ratio, debt ratio, and earnings per share. Round all ratios to two decimal places, and use the following format for your answer:

| Current Ratio | Debt Ratio | Earnings per Share |
|---|---|---|

2. Compute the three ratios after evaluating the effect of each transaction that follows. Consider each transaction *separately*.
   a. Purchased merchandise inventory of $42,000 on account.
   b. Borrowed $123,000 on a long-term note payable.
   c. Issued 4,000 shares of common stock, receiving cash of $106,000.
   d. Received cash on account, $7,000.

## P15-38B Using ratios to evaluate a stock investment

**Learning Objective 4**

1. 2015 d. 1.15

Comparative financial statement data of Canfield, Inc. follow:

**CANFIELD, INC.**
**Comparative Income Statement**
**Years Ended December 31, 2016 and 2015**

| | 2016 | 2015 |
|---|---|---|
| Net Sales | $ 459,000 | $ 424,000 |
| Cost of Goods Sold | 237,000 | 215,000 |
| Gross Profit | 222,000 | 209,000 |
| Operating Expenses | 137,000 | 135,000 |
| Income from Operations | 85,000 | 74,000 |
| Interest Expense | 12,000 | 14,000 |
| Income Before Income Tax | 73,000 | 60,000 |
| Income Tax Expense | 19,000 | 25,000 |
| Net Income | **$ 54,000** | **$ 35,000** |

| CANFIELD, INC. Comparative Balance Sheet December 31, 2016 and 2015 | | | |
|---|---|---|---|
| | **2016** | **2015** | **2014*** |
| **Assets** | | | |
| Current Assets: | | | |
| Cash | $ 99,000 | $ 96,000 | |
| Accounts Receivable, Net | 110,000 | 116,000 | $ 101,000 |
| Merchandise Inventory | 145,000 | 163,000 | 210,000 |
| Prepaid Expenses | 12,000 | 7,000 | |
| Total Current Assets | 366,000 | 382,000 | |
| Property, Plant, and Equipment, Net | 219,000 | 180,000 | |
| Total Assets | **$ 585,000** | **$ 562,000** | 598,000 |
| **Liabilities** | | | |
| Total Current Liabilities | $ 223,000 | $ 246,000 | |
| Long-term Liabilities | 120,000 | 95,000 | |
| Total Liabilities | 343,000 | 341,000 | |
| **Stockholders' Equity** | | | |
| Preferred Stock, 3% | 98,000 | 98,000 | |
| Common Stockholders' Equity, no par | 144,000 | 123,000 | 85,000 |
| Total Liabilities and Stockholders' Equity | **$ 585,000** | **$ 562,000** | |

* Selected 2014 amounts

1. Market price of Canfield's common stock: $84.32 at December 31, 2016, and $51.75 at December 31, 2015.
2. Common shares outstanding: 10,000 during 2016 and 9,000 during 2015 and 2014.
3. All sales are on credit.

## Requirements

1. Compute the following ratios for 2016 and 2015:
   a. Current ratio
   b. Cash ratio
   c. Times-interest-earned ratio
   d. Inventory turnover
   e. Gross profit percentage
   f. Debt to equity ratio
   g. Rate of return on common stockholders' equity
   h. Earnings per share of common stock
   i. Price/earnings ratio
2. Decide (a) whether Canfield's ability to pay debts and to sell inventory improved or deteriorated during 2016 and (b) whether the investment attractiveness of its common stock appears to have increased or decreased.

**P15-39B Using ratios to decide between two stock investments**

**Learning Objective 4**

1c. Red Zone 36 days

Assume that you are purchasing an investment and have decided to invest in a company in the digital phone business. You have narrowed the choice to Digital Plus Corp. and Red Zone, Inc. and have assembled the following data.

Selected income statement data for the current year:

| | Digital Plus | Red Zone |
|---|---|---|
| Net Sales (all on credit) | $ 416,830 | $ 497,130 |
| Cost of Goods Sold | 207,000 | 259,000 |
| Interest Expense | 0 | 17,000 |
| Net Income | 54,000 | 76,000 |

Selected balance sheet and market price data at the *end* of the current year:

| | Digital Plus | Red Zone |
|---|---|---|
| Current Assets: | | |
| Cash | $ 24,000 | $ 15,000 |
| Short-term Investments | 37,000 | 14,000 |
| Accounts Receivable, Net | 38,000 | 46,000 |
| Merchandise Inventory | 65,000 | 99,000 |
| Prepaid Expenses | 17,000 | 14,000 |
| Total Current Assets | $ 181,000 | $ 188,000 |
| Total Assets | $ 263,000 | $ 324,000 |
| Total Current Liabilities | 102,000 | 95,000 |
| Total Liabilities | 102,000 | 132,000 |
| Common Stock, $1 par (10,000 shares) | 10,000 | |
| $2 par (16,000 shares) | | 32,000 |
| Total Stockholders' Equity | 161,000 | 192,000 |
| Market Price per Share of Common Stock | $ 86.40 | $ 104.50 |
| Dividends Paid per Common Share | $ 1.20 | $ 1.00 |

Selected balance sheet data at the *beginning* of the current year:

| | Digital Plus | Red Zone |
|---|---|---|
| Balance Sheet: | | |
| Accounts Receivable, Net | $ 42,000 | $ 51,000 |
| Merchandise Inventory | 81,000 | 89,000 |
| Total Assets | 259,000 | 275,000 |
| Common Stock, $1 par (10,000 shares) | 10,000 | |
| $2 par (16,000 shares) | | 32,000 |

Your strategy is to invest in companies that have low price/earnings ratios but appear to be in good shape financially. Assume that you have analyzed all other factors and that your decision depends on the results of ratio analysis.

**Requirements**

1. Compute the following ratios for both companies for the current year:
   a. Acid-test ratio
   b. Inventory turnover
   c. Days' sales in receivables
   d. Debt ratio
   e. Earnings per share of common stock
   f. Price/earnings ratio
   g. Dividend payout
2. Decide which company's stock better fits your investment strategy.

**Learning Objective 5**
**Appendix 15A**

Net Income $149,800

### P15A-40B Preparing an income statement

The following information was taken from the records of Shepard Motorsports, Inc. at November 30, 2016:

| | | | |
|---|---|---|---|
| Selling Expenses | $ 150,000 | Common Stock, $8 Par Value, 29,500 shares authorized and issued | $ 236,000 |
| Administrative Expenses | 95,000 | Preferred Stock, $7 No-Par Value, 9,000 shares issued | 630,000 |
| Income from Discontinued Operations | 7,000 | Income Tax Expense: Continuing Operations | 45,000 |
| Cost of Goods Sold | 425,000 | Income Tax Expense: Income from Discontinued Operations | 2,800 |
| Treasury Stock—Common (1,500 shares) | 16,500 | | |
| Net Sales Revenue | 860,600 | | |

Prepare a multi-step income statement for Shepard Motorsports for the fiscal year ended November 30, 2016. Include earnings per share.

## > Continuing Problem

### P15-41 Using ratios to evaluate a stock investment

This problem continues the Daniels Consulting situation from Problem P14-46 of Chapter 14. Assuming Daniels Consulting's net income for the year was $90,537 and knowing that the current market price of Daniels's stock is $200 per share, calculate the following ratios for 2017 for the company:

a. Current ratio
b. Cash ratio
c. Debt ratio
d. Debt to equity ratio
e. Earnings per share
f. Price/earnings ratio
g. Rate of return on common stockholders' equity

**DANIELS CONSULTING**
Comparative Balance Sheet
December 31, 2017 and 2016

| | 2017 | 2016 |
|---|---|---|
| **Assets** | | |
| Current Assets: | | |
| Cash | $ 1,457,524 | $ 31,700 |
| Accounts Receivable | 25,700 | 700 |
| Office Supplies | 2,150 | 50 |
| Long-term Assets: | | |
| Plants Assets | 84,800 | 4,800 |
| Accumulated Depreciation—Plant Assets | (1,696) | (80) |
| Total Assets | **$ 1,568,478** | **$ 37,170** |
| **Liabilities** | | |
| Current Liabilities: | | |
| Accounts Payable | $ 7,300 | $ 4,100 |
| Salaries Payable | 1,800 | 467 |
| Unearned Revenue | 0 | 1,600 |
| Interest Payable | 25,000 | 0 |
| Long-term Liabilities: | | |
| Notes Payable | 500,000 | 0 |
| Bonds Payable | 900,000 | 0 |
| Discount on Bonds Payable | (100,862) | 0 |
| Total Liabilities | 1,333,238 | 6,167 |
| **Stockholders' Equity** | | |
| Common Stock, $1 par | 115,240 | 240 |
| Retained Earnings | 120,000 | 30,763 |
| Total Stockholders' Equity | 235,240 | 31,003 |
| Total Liabilities and Stockholders' Equity | **$ 1,568,478** | **$ 37,170** |

# COMPREHENSIVE PROBLEM

## > Comprehensive Problem for Chapter 15

**Analyzing a company for its investment potential**

In its annual report, WRM Athletic Supply, Inc. includes the following five-year financial summary:

**WRM ATHLETIC SUPPLY, INC.**
**Five-Year Financial Summary (Partial; adapted)**

| ***(Dollar amounts in thousands except per share data)*** | **2020** | **2019** | **2018** | **2017** | **2016** | **2015** |
|---|---|---|---|---|---|---|
| Net Sales | $ 290,000 | $ 215,000 | $ 194,000 | $ 165,000 | $ 139,000 | |
| Net Sales Increase | 35% | 11% | 18% | 19% | 17% | |
| Domestic Comparative Store Sales Increase | 5% | 7% | 5% | 8% | 10% | |
| Other Income—Net | 2,050 | 1,810 | 1,790 | 1,660 | 1,300 | |
| Cost of Goods Sold | 218,660 | 163,400 | 150,350 | 129,360 | 110,227 | |
| Selling and Administrative Expenses | 41,236 | 36,356 | 31,679 | 27,408 | 22,516 | |
| Interest: | | | | | | |
| Interest Expense | (1,010) | (1,360) | (1,370) | (1,060) | (870) | |
| Interest Income | 120 | 160 | 165 | 225 | 155 | |
| Income Tax Expense | 4,430 | 3,830 | 3,690 | 3,380 | 2,760 | |
| Net Income | 26,834 | 12,024 | 8,866 | 5,677 | 4,082 | |
| Per Share of Common Stock: | | | | | | |
| Net Income | 1.80 | 1.50 | 1.40 | 1.20 | 0.98 | |
| Dividends | 0.40 | 0.38 | 0.34 | 0.30 | 0.26 | |
| **Financial Position** | | | | | | |
| Current Assets, Excluding Merchandise Inventory | $ 30,400 | $ 27,500 | $ 26,200 | $ 24,900 | $ 21,700 | |
| Merchandise Inventory at LIFO Cost | 24,200 | 22,500 | 21,400 | 19,900 | 17,100 | $ 16,400 |
| Property, Plant, and Equipment, Net | 51,100 | 45,600 | 40,700 | 35,200 | 25,900 | |
| Total Assets | 105,700 | 95,600 | 88,300 | 80,000 | 64,700 | |
| Current Liabilities | 32,200 | 27,100 | 28,700 | 25,800 | 16,700 | |
| Long-term Debt | 22,600 | 21,700 | 17,100 | 18,300 | 12,600 | |
| Stockholders' Equity | 50,900 | 46,800 | 42,500 | 35,900 | 35,400 | |
| **Financial Ratios** | | | | | | |
| Acid-Test Ratio | 0.9 | 1.0 | 0.9 | 1.0 | 1.3 | |
| Rate of Return on Total Assets | 27.7% | 14.6% | 12.2% | 9.3% | 8.3% | |
| Rate of Return on Common Stockholders' Equity | 54.9% | 26.9% | 22.6% | 15.9% | 15.4% | |

**Requirements**

1. Analyze the company's financial summary for the fiscal years 2016–2020 to decide whether to invest in the common stock of WRM. Include the following sections in your analysis, and fully explain your final decision.
   a. Trend analysis for net sales and net income (use 2016 as the base year).
   b. Profitability analysis.
   c. Evaluation of the ability to sell merchandise inventory (WRM uses the LIFO method).
   d. Evaluation of the ability to pay debts.
   e. Evaluation of dividends.

# CRITICAL THINKING

## > Decision Case 15-1

Lance Berkman is the controller of Saturn, a dance club whose year-end is December 31. Berkman prepares checks for suppliers in December, makes the proper journal entries, and posts them to the appropriate accounts in that month. However, he holds on to the checks and mails them to the suppliers in January.

**Requirements**

1. What financial ratio(s) is(are) most affected by the action?
2. What is Berkman's purpose in undertaking this activity?

## > Ethical Issue 15-1

Ross's Lipstick Company's long-term debt agreements make certain demands on the business. For example, Ross may not purchase treasury stock in excess of the balance of retained earnings. Also, long-term debt may not exceed stockholders' equity, and the current ratio may not fall below 1.50. If Ross fails to meet any of these requirements, the company's lenders have the authority to take over management of the company.

Changes in consumer demand have made it hard for Ross to attract customers. Current liabilities have mounted faster than current assets, causing the current ratio to fall to 1.47. Before releasing financial statements, Ross's management is scrambling to improve the current ratio. The controller points out that an investment can be classified as either long-term or short-term, depending on management's intention. By deciding to convert an investment to cash within one year, Ross can classify the investment as short-term—a current asset. On the controller's recommendation, Ross's board of directors votes to reclassify long-term investments as short-term.

**Requirements**

1. What effect will reclassifying the investments have on the current ratio? Is Ross's true financial position stronger as a result of reclassifying the investments?
2. Shortly after the financial statements are released, sales improve; so, too, does the current ratio. As a result, Ross's management decides not to sell the investments it had reclassified as short-term. Accordingly, the company reclassifies the investments as long-term. Has management behaved unethically? Give the reasoning underlying your answer.

## > Financial Statement Case 15-1

Use **Starbucks Corporation**'s Fiscal 2013 Annual Report to answer the following questions. Visit **http://www.pearsonhighered.com/Horngren** to view a link to the Starbucks Corporation Annual Report.

**Requirements**

1. Compute trend analyses for total net revenues and net earnings. Use October 2, 2011, as the base year. What is the most notable aspect of these data?
2. Perform a vertical analysis for Starbucks Corporation's asset section of the balance sheet as of September 29, 2013, and September 30, 2012.

## > Team Projects

### Team Project 15-1

Select an industry you are interested in, and pick any company in that industry to use as the benchmark. Then select two other companies in the same industry. For each category of ratios, compute all the ratios for the three companies. Write a two-page report that compares the two companies with the benchmark company.

### Team Project 15-2

Select a company and obtain its financial statements. Convert the income statement and the balance sheet to common size, and compare the company you selected to the industry average. The Risk Management Association's *Annual Statement Studies* and Dun & Bradstreet's *Industry Norms & Key Business Ratios* publish common-size statements for most industries.



## > Quick Check Answers

**1.** b **2.** b **3.** a **4.** c **5.** a **6.** b **7.** d **8.** c **9.** a **10A.** d

# UNITED STATES SECURITIES AND EXCHANGE COMMISSION

## Washington, D.C. 20549

## FORM 10-K/A

## Amendment No. 1

(Mark One)

☒ ANNUAL REPORT PURSUANT TO SECTION 13 OR 15(d) OF THE SECURITIES EXCHANGE ACT OF 1934.

For the fiscal year ended September 28, 2013

OR

☐ TRANSITION REPORT PURSUANT TO SECTION 13 OR 15(d) OF THE SECURITIES EXCHANGE ACT OF 1934.

For the transition period from to

Commission file number 1-12340

# GREEN MOUNTAIN COFFEE ROASTERS, INC.

(Exact name of registrant as specified in its charter)

| Delaware | 03-0339228 |
|---|---|
| (State or other jurisdiction of incorporation or organization) | (I.R.S. Employer Identification No.) |

33 Coffee Lane, Waterbury, Vermont 05676
(Address of principal executive offices) (zip code)

(802) 244-5621
(Registrants' telephone number, including area code)

(Former name, former address and former fiscal year, if changed since last report.)

**Securities registered pursuant to Section 12(b) of the Act:**

| Title of each class | Name of each exchange on which registered |
|---|---|
| Common Stock, $0.10 par value per share | The Nasdaq Global Select Market |

**Securities registered pursuant to Section 12(g) of the Act:** NONE

Indicate by check mark if the registrant is a well-known seasoned issuer, as defined in Rule 405 of the Securities Act. Yes ☒ No ☐

Indicate by check mark if the registrant is not required to file reports pursuant to Section 13 or Section 15(d) of the Act. Yes ☐ No ☒

Indicate by check mark whether the registrant (1) has filed all reports required to be filed by Section 13 or 15(d) of the Securities Exchange Act of 1934 during the preceding 12 months (or for such shorter period that the registrant was required to file such reports), and (2) has been subject to such filing requirements for the past 90 days. Yes ☒ No ☐

Indicate by check mark whether the registrant has submitted electronically and posted on its corporate Web site, if any, every Interactive Data File required to be submitted and posted pursuant to Rule 405 of Regulation S-T (§232.405 of this chapter) during the preceding 12 months (or for such shorter period that the registrant was required to submit and post such files). Yes ☒ No ☐

Indicate by check mark if disclosure of delinquent filers pursuant to Item 405 of Regulation S-K is not contained herein, and will not be contained, to the best of registrant's knowledge, in definitive proxy or information statements incorporated by reference in Part III of this Form 10-K or any amendment to this Form 10-K. ☐

Indicate by check mark whether the registrant is a large accelerated filer, an accelerated filer, a non-accelerated filer, or a smaller reporting company. See the definitions of "large accelerated filer," "accelerated filer" and "smaller reporting company" in Rule 12b-2 of the Exchange Act.

| | |
|---|---|
| Large accelerated filer ☒ | Accelerated filer ☐ |
| Non-accelerated filer ☐<br>(Do not check if a smaller reporting company) | Smaller Reporting Company ☐ |

Indicate by check mark whether the registrant is a shell company (as defined in Rule 12b-2 of the Exchange Act). Yes ☐ No ☒

The aggregate market value of the voting stock of the registrant held by non-affiliates of the registrant on March 30, 2013 was approximately $7,923,000,000 based upon the closing price of such stock on March 29, 2013.

As of November 13, 2013, 149,030,940 shares of common stock of the registrant were outstanding.

## EXPLANATORY NOTE

This Amendment No. 1 ("Amendment No. 1") to the Annual Report on Form 10-K of Green Mountain Coffee Roasters, Inc. (together with its subsidiaries, the "Company," "we," "our," or "us") for the fiscal year ended September 28, 2013 as filed with the SEC on November 20, 2013 (the "2013 Annual Report"), is being filed solely to insert conformed signatures to each of Exhibits 23, 31-1, 31-2, 32-1 and 32-2, which conformed signatures were inadvertently omitted from the initial filing.

This Amendment No. 1 does not amend, modify or update any other portion of the 2013 Annual Report. Additionally, except as specifically referenced herein, this Amendment No. 1 does not reflect any event occurring after the time the 2013 Annual Report was filed on November 20, 2013.

## DOCUMENTS INCORPORATED BY REFERENCE

Portions of the registrant's definitive Proxy Statement for the 2014 Annual Meeting of Stockholders to be filed with the Securities and Exchange Commission pursuant to Regulation 14A not later than 120 days after the end of the fiscal year covered by this Form 10-K, are incorporated by reference in Part III, Items 10-14 of this Form 10-K.

**Report of Independent Registered Public Accounting Firm**

To the Board of Directors and the Stockholders
of Green Mountain Coffee Roasters, Inc.

In our opinion, the consolidated financial statements listed in the accompanying index present fairly, in all material respects, the financial position of Green Mountain Coffee Roasters, Inc. and its subsidiaries at September 28, 2013 and September 29, 2012, and the results of their operations and their cash flows for each of the three years in the period ended September 28, 2013 in conformity with accounting principles generally accepted in the United States of America. In addition, in our opinion, the financial statement schedule listed in the accompanying index presents fairly, in all material respects, the information set forth therein when read in conjunction with the related consolidated financial statements. Also in our opinion, the Company maintained, in all material respects, effective internal control over financial reporting as of September 28, 2013, based on criteria established in *Internal Control—Integrated Framework* (1992) issued by the Committee of Sponsoring Organizations of the Treadway Commission (COSO). The Company's management is responsible for these financial statements and financial statement schedule, for maintaining effective internal control over financial reporting and for its assessment of the effectiveness of internal control over financial reporting, included in Management's Report on Internal Control over Financial Reporting appearing under Item 9A. Our responsibility is to express opinions on these financial statements, on the financial statement schedule, and on the Company's internal control over financial reporting based on our integrated audits. We conducted our audits in accordance with the standards of the Public Company Accounting Oversight Board (United States). Those standards require that we plan and perform the audits to obtain reasonable assurance about whether the financial statements are free of material misstatement and whether effective internal control over financial reporting was maintained in all material respects. Our audits of the financial statements included examining, on a test basis, evidence supporting the amounts and disclosures in the financial statements, assessing the accounting principles used and significant estimates made by management, and evaluating the overall financial statement presentation. Our audit of internal control over financial reporting included obtaining an understanding of internal control over financial reporting, assessing the risk that a material weakness exists, and testing and evaluating the design and operating effectiveness of internal control based on the assessed risk. Our audits also included performing such other procedures as we considered necessary in the circumstances. We believe that our audits provide a reasonable basis for our opinions.

A company's internal control over financial reporting is a process designed to provide reasonable assurance regarding the reliability of financial reporting and the preparation of financial statements for external purposes in accordance with generally accepted accounting principles. A company's internal control over financial reporting includes those policies and procedures that (i) pertain to the maintenance of records that, in reasonable detail, accurately and fairly reflect the transactions and dispositions of the assets of the company; (ii) provide reasonable assurance that transactions are recorded as necessary to permit preparation of financial statements in accordance with generally accepted accounting principles, and that receipts and expenditures of the company are being made only in accordance with authorizations of management and directors of the company; and (iii) provide reasonable assurance regarding prevention or timely detection of unauthorized acquisition, use, or disposition of the company's assets that could have a material effect on the financial statements.

Because of its inherent limitations, internal control over financial reporting may not prevent or detect misstatements. Also, projections of any evaluation of effectiveness to future periods are subject to the risk that controls may become inadequate because of changes in conditions, or that the degree of compliance with the policies or procedures may deteriorate.

/s/ PricewaterhouseCoopers LLP

Boston, Massachusetts
November 20, 2013

## GREEN MOUNTAIN COFFEE ROASTERS, INC.

### CONSOLIDATED BALANCE SHEETS
### (Dollars in thousands)

| | September 28, 2013 | September 29, 2012 |
|---|---|---|
| **Assets** | | |
| Current assets: | | |
| Cash and cash equivalents | $ 260,092 | $ 58,289 |
| Restricted cash and cash equivalents | 560 | 12,884 |
| Receivables, less uncollectible accounts and return allowances of $33,640 and $34,517 at September 28, 2013 and September 29, 2012, respectively | 467,976 | 363,771 |
| Inventories | 676,089 | 768,437 |
| Income taxes receivable | 11,747 | 32,943 |
| Other current assets | 46,891 | 35,019 |
| Deferred income taxes, net | 58,137 | 51,613 |
| Total current assets | 1,521,492 | 1,322,956 |
| Fixed assets, net | 985,563 | 944,296 |
| Intangibles, net | 435,216 | 498,352 |
| Goodwill | 788,184 | 808,076 |
| Deferred income taxes, net | 149 | — |
| Other long-term assets | 30,944 | 42,109 |
| Total assets | $ 3,761,548 | $ 3,615,789 |
| **Liabilities and Stockholders' Equity** | | |
| Current liabilities: | | |
| Current portion of long-term debt | $ 12,929 | $ 6,691 |
| Current portion of capital lease and financing obligations | 1,760 | 3,057 |
| Accounts payable | 312,170 | 279,577 |
| Accrued expenses | 242,427 | 171,450 |
| Income tax payable | — | 29,322 |
| Deferred income taxes, net | 233 | 245 |
| Other current liabilities | 27,544 | 29,645 |
| Total current liabilities | 597,063 | 519,987 |
| Long-term debt, less current portion | 160,221 | 466,984 |
| Capital lease and financing obligations, less current portion | 76,061 | 54,794 |
| Deferred income taxes, net | 252,867 | 270,348 |
| Other long-term liabilities | 28,721 | 32,544 |
| Commitments and contingencies (See Notes 5 and 19) | | |
| Redeemable noncontrolling interests | 11,045 | 9,904 |
| Stockholders' equity: | | |
| Preferred stock, $0.10 par value: Authorized—1,000,000 shares; No shares issued or outstanding | — | — |
| Common stock, $0.10 par value: Authorized—500,000,000 shares; Issued and outstanding—150,265,809 and 152,680,855 shares at September 28, 2013 and September 29, 2012, respectively | 15,026 | 15,268 |
| Additional paid-in capital | 1,387,322 | 1,464,560 |
| Retained earnings | 1,252,407 | 771,200 |
| Accumulated other comprehensive (loss) income | (19,185) | 10,200 |
| Total stockholders' equity | $ 2,635,570 | $ 2,261,228 |
| Total liabilities and stockholders' equity | $ 3,761,548 | $ 3,615,789 |

The accompanying Notes to Consolidated Financial Statements are an integral part of these financial statements.

## GREEN MOUNTAIN COFFEE ROASTERS, INC.

## CONSOLIDATED STATEMENTS OF OPERATIONS
**(Dollars in thousands except per share data)**

| | Fiscal years ended | | |
|---|---|---|---|
| | **September 28, 2013** | **September 29, 2012** | **September 24, 2011** |
| Net sales | $ 4,358,100 | $ 3,859,198 | $ 2,650,899 |
| Cost of sales | 2,738,714 | 2,589,799 | 1,746,274 |
| Gross profit | 1,619,386 | 1,269,399 | 904,625 |
| Selling and operating expenses | 560,430 | 481,493 | 348,696 |
| General and administrative expenses | 293,729 | 219,010 | 187,016 |
| Operating income | 765,227 | 568,896 | 368,913 |
| Other income, net | 960 | 1,819 | 648 |
| Gain (loss) on financial instruments, net | 5,513 | (4,945) | (6,245) |
| (Loss) gain on foreign currency, net | (12,649) | 7,043 | (2,912) |
| Gain on sale of subsidiary | — | 26,311 | — |
| Interest expense | (18,177) | (22,983) | (57,657) |
| Income before income taxes | 740,874 | 576,141 | 302,747 |
| Income tax expense | (256,771) | (212,641) | (101,699) |
| Net Income | $ 484,103 | $ 363,500 | $ 201,048 |
| Net income attributable to noncontrolling interests | 871 | 872 | 1,547 |
| Net income attributable to GMCR | $ 483,232 | $ 362,628 | $ 199,501 |
| Basic income per share: | | | |
| Basic weighted average shares outstanding | 149,638,636 | 154,933,948 | 146,214,860 |
| Net income per common share—basic | $ 3.23 | $ 2.34 | $ 1.36 |
| Diluted income per share: | | | |
| Diluted weighted average shares outstanding | 152,801,493 | 159,075,646 | 152,142,434 |
| Net income per common share—diluted | $ 3.16 | $ 2.28 | $ 1.31 |

The accompanying Notes to Consolidated Financial Statements are an integral part of these financial statements.

## GREEN MOUNTAIN COFFEE ROASTERS, INC.

## CONSOLIDATED STATEMENTS OF COMPREHENSIVE INCOME
(Dollars in thousands)

| | Fiscal years ended | | | | | | | | |
|---|---|---|---|---|---|---|---|---|---|
| | September 28, 2013 | | | September 29, 2012 | | | September 24, 2011 | | |
| | Pre-tax | Tax (expense) benefit | After-tax | Pre-tax | Tax (expense) benefit | After-tax | Pre-tax | Tax (expense) benefit | After-tax |
| Net income | | | $ 484,103 | | | $ 363,500 | | | $ 201,048 |
| Other comprehensive income (loss): | | | | | | | | | |
| Cash flow hedges: | | | | | | | | | |
| Unrealized losses arising during the period | $ (3,732) | $ 1,489 | $ (2,243) | $ (1,234) | $ 498 | $ (736) | $ (7,521) | $ 3,035 | $ (4,486) |
| Losses reclassified to net income | 1,484 | (599) | 885 | 1,359 | (549) | 810 | 419 | (169) | 250 |
| Foreign currency translation adjustments | (28,742) | — | (28,742) | 25,353 | — | 25,353 | (8,895) | — | (8,895) |
| Other comprehensive (loss) income | $ (30,990) | $ 890 | $ (30,100) | $ 25,478 | $ (51) | $ 25,427 | $ (15,997) | $ 2,866 | $ (13,131) |
| Total comprehensive income | | | 454,003 | | | 388,927 | | | 187,917 |
| Total comprehensive income attributable to noncontrolling interests | | | 156 | | | 1,524 | | | 1,361 |
| Total comprehensive income attributable to GMCR | | | $ 453,847 | | | $ 387,403 | | | $ 186,556 |

The accompanying Notes to Consolidated Financial Statements are an integral part of these financial statements.

## GREEN MOUNTAIN COFFEE ROASTERS, INC.

### CONSOLIDATED STATEMENTS OF CHANGES IN STOCKHOLDERS' EQUITY

**For the three fiscal years in the period ended September 28, 2013 (Dollars in thousands)**

| | Common stock | | Additional paid-in capital | Retained earnings | Accumulated other comprehensive income (loss) | Stockholders' Equity |
|---|---|---|---|---|---|---|
| | Shares | Amount | | | | |
| Balance at September 25, 2010 | 132,823,585 | $ 13,282 | $ 473,749 | $ 213,844 | $ (1,630) | $ 699,245 |
| Sale of common stock for private placement | 9,174,991 | 918 | 290,178 | — | — | 291,096 |
| Options exercised | 2,839,426 | 284 | 11,096 | — | — | 11,380 |
| Issuance of common stock under employee stock purchase plan | 148,917 | 15 | 5,933 | — | — | 5,948 |
| Issuance of common stock for public equity offering | 9,479,544 | 948 | 646,415 | — | — | 647,363 |
| Stock compensation expense | — | — | 10,361 | — | — | 10,361 |
| Tax benefit from exercise of options | — | — | 61,670 | — | — | 61,670 |
| Deferred compensation expense | — | — | 214 | — | — | 214 |
| Adjustment of redeemable noncontrolling interests to redemption value | — | — | — | (1,618) | — | (1,618) |
| Other comprehensive loss net of tax | — | — | — | — | (12,945) | (12,945) |
| Net income | — | — | — | 199,501 | — | 199,501 |
| Balance at September 24, 2011 | 154,466,463 | $ 15,447 | $ 1,499,616 | $ 411,727 | $ (14,575) | $ 1,912,215 |
| Options exercised | 940,369 | 94 | 3,300 | — | — | 3,394 |
| Issuance of common stock under employee stock purchase plan | 301,971 | 30 | 8,668 | — | — | 8,698 |
| Restricted stock awards and units | 55,747 | 5 | (5) | — | — | — |
| Issuance of common stock under deferred compensation plan | 37,005 | 4 | (4) | — | — | — |
| Repurchase of common stock | (3,120,700) | (312) | (76,158) | — | — | (76,470) |
| Stock compensation expense | — | — | 17,868 | — | — | 17,868 |
| Tax benefit from equity-based compensation plans | — | — | 11,064 | — | — | 11,064 |
| Deferred compensation expense | — | — | 211 | — | — | 211 |
| Adjustment of redeemable noncontrolling interests to redemption value | — | — | — | (3,155) | — | (3,155) |
| Other comprehensive income, net of tax | — | — | — | — | 24,775 | 24,775 |
| Net income | — | — | — | 362,628 | — | 362,628 |
| Balance at September 29, 2012 | 152,680,855 | $ 15,268 | $ 1,464,560 | $ 771,200 | $ 10,200 | $ 2,261,228 |
| Options exercised | 2,849,308 | 285 | 19,532 | — | — | 19,817 |
| Issuance of common stock under employee stock purchase plan | 343,678 | 34 | 9,926 | — | — | 9,960 |
| Restricted stock awards and units | 34,761 | 3 | (3) | — | — | — |
| Repurchase of common stock | (5,642,793) | (564) | (187,714) | — | — | (188,278) |
| Stock compensation expense | — | — | 26,081 | — | — | 26,081 |
| Tax benefit from equity-based compensation plans | — | — | 54,706 | — | — | 54,706 |
| Deferred compensation expense | — | — | 234 | — | — | 234 |
| Adjustment of redeemable noncontrolling interests to redemption value | — | — | — | (2,025) | — | (2,025) |
| Other comprehensive loss, net of tax | — | — | — | — | (29,385) | (29,385) |
| Net income | — | — | — | 483,232 | — | 483,232 |
| Balance at September 28, 2013 | 150,265,809 | $ 15,026 | $ 1,387,322 | $ 1,252,407 | $ (19,185) | $ 2,635,570 |

The accompanying Notes to Consolidated Financial Statements are an integral part of these financial statements.

## GREEN MOUNTAIN COFFEE ROASTERS, INC.

## CONSOLIDATED STATEMENTS OF CASH FLOWS
**(Dollars in thousands)**

| | Fiscal years ended | | |
|---|---|---|---|
| | **September 28, 2013** | **September 29, 2012** | **September 24, 2011** |
| Cash flows from operating activities: | | | |
| Net income | $ 484,103 | $ 363,500 | $ 201,048 |
| Adjustments to reconcile net income to net cash provided by operating activities: | | | |
| Depreciation and amortization of fixed assets | 183,814 | 135,656 | 72,297 |
| Amortization of intangibles | 45,379 | 45,991 | 41,339 |
| Amortization deferred financing fees | 7,125 | 6,050 | 6,158 |
| Loss on extinguishment of debt | — | — | 19,732 |
| Unrealized loss (gain) on foreign currency, net | 9,159 | (6,557) | 1,041 |
| (Gain) loss on disposal of fixed assets | (85) | 2,517 | 884 |
| Gain on sale of subsidiary, excluding transaction costs | — | (28,914) | — |
| Provision for doubtful accounts | 689 | 3,197 | 2,584 |
| Provision for sales returns | 79,747 | 107,436 | 64,457 |
| (Gain) loss on derivatives, net | (4,507) | 6,310 | 3,292 |
| Excess tax benefits from equity-based compensation plans | (54,699) | (12,070) | (67,813) |
| Deferred income taxes | (17,701) | 60,856 | (8,828) |
| Deferred compensation and stock compensation | 26,315 | 18,079 | 10,575 |
| Other | 844 | (672) | (6,142) |
| Changes in assets and liabilities, net of effects of acquisition: | | | |
| Receivables | (187,221) | (159,317) | (157,329) |
| Inventories | 87,677 | (92,862) | (375,709) |
| Income tax payable/receivable, net | 46,290 | 16,457 | 63,487 |
| Other current assets | (12,668) | (6,900) | (715) |
| Other long-term assets, net | 3,915 | (469) | (11,454) |
| Accounts payable and accrued expenses | 133,532 | 17,125 | 134,035 |
| Other current liabilities | 3,100 | (2,718) | (3,118) |
| Other long-term liabilities | 1,161 | 5,090 | 10,964 |
| Net cash provided by operating activities | 835,969 | 477,785 | 785 |
| Cash flows from investing activities: | | | |
| Change in restricted cash | 3,005 | (2,875) | 2,074 |
| Acquisition of LJVH Holdings, Inc. (Van Houtte), net of cash acquired | — | — | (907,835) |
| Proceeds from the sale of subsidiary, net of cash acquired | — | 137,733 | — |
| Capital expenditures for fixed assets | (232,780) | (401,121) | (283,444) |
| Other investing activities | 4,208 | 618 | 1,533 |
| Net cash used in investing activities | (225,567) | (265,645) | (1,187,672) |

The accompanying Notes to Consolidated Financial Statements are an integral part of these financial statements.

## GREEN MOUNTAIN COFFEE ROASTERS, INC.

## CONSOLIDATED STATEMENTS OF CASH FLOWS (CONTINUED)
### (Dollars in thousands)

| | Fiscal years ended | | |
|---|---|---|---|
| | September 28, 2013 | September 29, 2012 | September 24, 2011 |
| Cash flows from financing activities: | | | |
| Net change in revolving line of credit | (226,210) | (108,727) | 333,835 |
| Proceeds from issuance of common stock under compensation plans | 29,777 | 12,092 | 17,328 |
| Proceeds from issuance of common stock for private placement | — | — | 291,096 |
| Proceeds from issuance of common stock for public equity offering | — | — | 673,048 |
| Financing costs in connection with public equity offering | — | — | (25,685) |
| Repurchase of common stock | (188,278) | (76,470) | — |
| Excess tax benefits from equity-based compensation plans | 54,699 | 12,070 | 67,813 |
| Payments on capital lease and financing obligations | (8,288) | (7,558) | (8) |
| Proceeds from borrowings of long-term debt | — | — | 796,375 |
| Deferred financing fees | — | — | (46,009) |
| Repayment of long-term debt | (71,620) | (7,814) | (906,885) |
| Other financing activities | (1,406) | 3,283 | (1,063) |
| Net cash (used in) provided by financing activities | (411,326) | (173,124) | 1,199,845 |
| Change in cash balances included in current assets held for sale | — | 5,160 | (5,160) |
| Effect of exchange rate changes on cash and cash equivalents | 2,727 | 1,124 | 790 |
| Net increase in cash and cash equivalents | 201,803 | 45,300 | 8,588 |
| Cash and cash equivalents at beginning of period | 58,289 | 12,989 | 4,401 |
| Cash and cash equivalents at end of period | $ 260,092 | $ 58,289 | $ 12,989 |
| Supplemental disclosures of cash flow information: | | | |
| Cash paid for interest | $ 9,129 | $ 20,783 | $ 33,452 |
| Cash paid for income taxes | $ 223,580 | $ 136,407 | $ 58,182 |
| Fixed asset purchases included in accounts payable and not disbursed at the end of each year | $ 30,451 | $ 56,127 | $ 25,737 |
| Noncash financing and investing activity: | | | |
| Fixed assets acquired under capital lease and financing obligations | $ 27,791 | $ 66,531 | $ — |
| Settlement of acquisition-related liabilities through release of restricted cash | $ 9,227 | $ 18,788 | $ — |

The accompanying Notes to Consolidated Financial Statements are an integral part of these financial statements.

## GREEN MOUNTAIN COFFEE ROASTERS, INC.

## NOTES TO CONSOLIDATED FINANCIAL STATEMENTS

**1. Nature of Business and Organization**

Green Mountain Coffee Roasters, Inc. (together with its subsidiaries, "the Company") is a leader in the specialty coffee and coffeemaker businesses. Green Mountain Coffee Roasters, Inc. is a Delaware corporation.

The Company manages its operations through two business segments, its United States operations within the Domestic segment and its Canadian operations within the Canada segment. The Company distributes its products in two channels: at-home ("AH") and away-from-home ("AFH").

The Domestic segment sells single cup brewers, accessories, and sources, produces and sells coffee, hot cocoa, teas and other beverages in K-Cup® and Vue® packs ("portion packs") and coffee in more traditional packaging including bags and fractional packs to retailers including supermarkets, department stores, mass merchandisers, club stores, and convenience stores; to restaurants, hospitality accounts, office coffee distributors, and partner brand owners; and to consumers through Company websites. Substantially all of the Domestic segment's distribution to major retailers is processed by fulfillment entities which receive and fulfill sales orders and invoice certain retailers primarily in the AH channel. The Domestic segment also earns royalty income from K-Cup® packs sold by a third-party licensed roaster.

The Canada segment sells single cup brewers, accessories, and sources, produces and sells coffee and teas and other beverages in portion packs and coffee in more traditional packaging including bags, cans and fractional packs under a variety of brands to retailers including supermarkets, department stores, mass merchandisers, club stores, through office coffee services to offices, convenience stores, restaurants, hospitality accounts, and to consumers through its website. The Canada segment included Filterfresh through October 3, 2011, the date of sale (see Note 3, *Acquisitions and Divestitures*).

The Company's fiscal year ends on the last Saturday in September. Fiscal years 2013, 2012 and 2011 represent the years ended September 28, 2013, September 29, 2012 and September 24, 2011, respectively. Fiscal years 2013 and 2011 each consist of 52 weeks and fiscal 2012 consisted of 53 weeks.

**2. Significant Accounting Policies**

*Use of estimates*

The preparation of financial statements in conformity with accounting principles generally accepted in the United States of America requires the Company to make estimates and assumptions that affect amounts reported in the accompanying Consolidated Financial Statements. Significant estimates and assumptions by management affect the Company's inventory, deferred tax assets, allowance for sales returns, warranty reserves and certain accrued expenses, goodwill, intangible and long-lived assets and stock-based compensation.

Although the Company regularly assesses these estimates, actual results could differ from these estimates. Changes in estimates are recorded in the period they become known. The Company bases its estimates on historical experience and various other assumptions that it believes to be reasonable under the circumstances.

*Principles of Consolidation*

The Consolidated Financial Statements include the accounts of the Company and all of the entities in which the Company has a controlling financial interest, most often because the Company holds a majority voting/ownership interest. All significant intercompany transactions and accounts are eliminated in consolidation.

*Noncontrolling Interests*

Noncontrolling interests ("NCI") are evaluated by the Company and are shown as either a liability, temporary equity (shown between liabilities and equity) or as permanent equity depending on the nature of the redeemable features at amounts based on formulas specific to each entity. Generally, mandatorily redeemable NCI's are classified as liabilities and non-mandatorily redeemable NCI's are classified as either temporary or permanent equity. Redeemable NCIs that are not mandatorily redeemable are classified outside of shareholders' equity in the Consolidated Balance Sheets as temporary equity under the caption, *Redeemable noncontrolling interests,* and are measured at their redemption values at the end of each period. If the redemption value is greater than the carrying value, an adjustment is recorded in retained earnings to record the NCI at its redemption value. Redeemable NCIs that are mandatorily redeemable are classified as a liability in the Consolidated Balance Sheets under either *Other current liabilities* or *Other long-term liabilities*, depending on the remaining duration until settlement, and are measured at the amount of cash that would be paid if settlement occurred at the balance sheet date based on the formula in the Share Purchase and Sale Agreement dated June 22, 2012, with any change from the prior period recognized as interest expense. See Note 8, *Noncontrolling Interests* in the Consolidated Financial Statements included in this Annual Report for further information.

## GREEN MOUNTAIN COFFEE ROASTERS, INC.

## NOTES TO CONSOLIDATED FINANCIAL STATEMENTS—(Continued)

Net income attributable to NCIs reflects the portion of the net income (loss) of consolidated entities applicable to the NCI shareholders in the accompanying Consolidated Statements of Operations. The net income attributable to NCIs is classified in the Consolidated Statements of Operations as part of consolidated net income and deducted from total consolidated net income to arrive at the net income attributable to the Company.

If a change in ownership of a consolidated subsidiary results in a loss of control or deconsolidation, any retained ownership interests are remeasured with the gain or loss reported to net earnings.

*Business Combinations*

The Company uses the acquisition method of accounting for business combinations and recognizes assets acquired and liabilities assumed measured at their fair values on the date acquired. Goodwill represents the excess of the purchase price over the fair value of the net assets. The fair values of the assets and liabilities acquired are determined based upon the Company's valuation. The valuation involves making significant estimates and assumptions which are based on detailed financial models including the projection of future cash flows, the weighted average cost of capital and any cost savings that are expected to be derived in the future.

*Cash and Cash Equivalents*

The Company considers all highly liquid investments purchased with an original maturity of three months or less to be cash equivalents. Cash and cash equivalents include money market funds which are carried at cost, plus accrued interest, which approximates fair value. The Company does not believe that it is subject to any unusual credit or market risk.

*Restricted Cash and Cash Equivalents*

Restricted cash and cash equivalents represents cash that is not available for use in our operations. Restricted cash of $0.6 million and $12.9 million as of September 28, 2013 and September 29, 2012, respectively. The restricted cash balance as of September 29, 2012 consisted primarily of cash placed in escrow related to our acquisition of Van Houtte, and was released during fiscal 2013.

*Allowance for Doubtful Accounts*

A provision for doubtful accounts is provided based on a combination of historical experience, specific identification and customer credit risk where there are indications that a specific customer may be experiencing financial difficulties.

*Inventories*

Inventories consist primarily of green and roasted coffee, including coffee in portion packs, purchased finished goods such as coffee brewers, and packaging materials. Inventories are stated at the lower of cost or market. Cost is being measured using an adjusted standard cost method which approximates FIFO (first-in, first-out). The Company regularly reviews whether the net realizable value of its inventory is lower than its carrying value. If the valuation shows that the net realizable value is lower than the carrying value, the Company takes a charge to cost of sales and directly reduces the carrying value of the inventory.

The Company estimates any required write downs for inventory obsolescence by examining its inventories on a quarterly basis to determine if there are indicators that the carrying values exceed net realizable value. Indicators that could result in additional inventory write downs include age of inventory, damaged inventory, slow moving products and products at the end of their life cycles. While management believes that inventory is appropriately stated at the lower of cost or market, significant judgment is involved in determining the net realizable value of inventory.

*Financial Instruments*

The Company enters into various types of financial instruments in the normal course of business. Fair values are estimated based on assumptions concerning the amount and timing of estimated future cash flows and assumed discount rates reflecting varying degrees of perceived risk. Cash, cash equivalents, accounts receivable, accounts payable and accrued expenses are reported at carrying value and approximate fair value due to the short maturity of these instruments. Long-term debt is also reported at carrying value, which approximates fair value due to the fact that the interest rate on the debt is based on variable interest rates.

## GREEN MOUNTAIN COFFEE ROASTERS, INC.

## NOTES TO CONSOLIDATED FINANCIAL STATEMENTS—(Continued)

The fair values of derivative financial instruments have been determined using market information and valuation methodologies. Changes in assumptions or estimates could affect the determination of fair value; however, management does not believe any such changes would have a material impact on the Company's financial condition, results of operations or cash flows. The fair values of short-term investments and derivative financial instruments are disclosed in Note 12, *Fair Value Measurements*, in the Consolidated Financial Statements included in this Annual Report.

*Derivative Instruments*

The Company enters into over-the-counter derivative contracts based on coffee futures ("coffee futures") to hedge against price increases in price-to-be-fixed coffee purchase commitments and anticipated coffee purchases. Coffee purchases are generally denominated in the U.S. dollar. The Company also enters into interest rate swap agreements to mitigate interest rate risk associated with the Company's variable-rate borrowings and foreign currency forward contracts to hedge the purchase and payment of certain green coffee purchase commitments as well as certain recognized liabilities in currencies other than the Company's functional currency. All derivatives are recorded at fair value. Interest rate swaps, coffee futures, and certain foreign currency forward contracts which hedge the purchase and payment of green coffee purchase commitments are designated as cash flow hedges with the effective portion of the change in the fair value of the derivative instrument recorded as a component of other comprehensive income ("OCI") and subsequently reclassified into net earnings when the hedged exposure affects net earnings. Foreign currency forward contracts which hedge certain recognized liabilities denominated in non-functional currencies are designated as fair value hedges with the changes in the fair value of these instruments along with the changes in the fair value of the hedged liabilities recognized in *gain or loss on foreign currency, net* in the Consolidated Statements of Operations.

Effectiveness is determined by how closely the changes in the fair value of the derivative instrument offset the changes in the fair value of the hedged item. The ineffective portion of the change in the fair value of the derivative instrument is recorded directly to earnings.

The Company formally documents hedging instruments and hedged items, and measures at each balance sheet date the effectiveness of its hedges. When it is determined that a derivative is not highly effective, the derivative expires, or is sold or terminated, or the derivative is discontinued because it is unlikely that a forecasted transaction will occur, the Company discontinues hedge accounting prospectively for that specific hedge instrument.

The Company also enters into certain foreign currency and interest rate derivative contracts to hedge certain foreign currency exposures that are not designated as hedging instruments for accounting purposes. These contracts are recorded at fair value, with the changes in fair value recognized in *gain (loss) on financial instruments, net* in the Consolidated Statements of Operations.

The Company does not engage in speculative transactions, nor does it hold derivative instruments for trading purposes. See Note 11, *Derivative Financial Instruments* and Note 14, *Stockholders' Equity* in the Consolidated Financial Statements included in this Annual Report for further information.

*Deferred Financing Costs*

Deferred financing costs consist primarily of commitment fees and loan origination fees and are being amortized over the respective life of the applicable debt using a method that approximates the effective interest rate method. Deferred financing costs included in *Other long-term assets* in the accompanying Consolidated Balance Sheets as of September 28, 2013 and September 29, 2012 were $15.2 million and $22.3 million, respectively.

*Goodwill and Intangibles*

Goodwill is tested for impairment annually at the end of the Company's fiscal year or whenever events or changes in circumstances indicate that the carrying value may not be recoverable. Goodwill is assigned to reporting units for purposes of impairment testing. A reporting unit is the same as an operating segment or one level below an operating segment. The Company may assess qualitative factors to determine if it is more likely than not (i.e., a likelihood of more than 50%) that the fair value of a reporting unit is less than its carrying amount, including goodwill. If the Company determines that it is not more likely than not that the fair value of a reporting unit is less than its carrying amount, no further testing is necessary. If, however, the Company determines that it is more likely than not that the fair value of a reporting unit is less than its carrying amount, the Company performs the first step of a two-step goodwill impairment test. The assessment of qualitative factors is optional and at the Company's discretion. The Company may bypass the qualitative assessment for any reporting unit in any period and perform the first step of the quantitative goodwill impairment test. The Company may resume performing the qualitative assessment in any subsequent period. The first step is a comparison of each reporting unit's fair value to its carrying value. The Company estimates fair value based on discounted cash flows. The reporting unit's discounted cash flows require significant management judgment with respect to sales forecasts, gross margin percentages, selling, operating, general and administrative ("SG&A") expenses, capital expenditures and the selection and use of an appropriate discount rate. The projected sales, gross margin and SG&A expense rate assumptions and capital expenditures are based on the Company's annual business plan or other forecasted results. Discount rates reflect market-based estimates of the risks associated with the projected cash flows directly resulting from the use of those assets in operations. The estimates of fair value of reporting units are based on the best information available as of the date of the assessment. If the carrying value of a reporting unit exceeds its estimated fair value in the first step, a second step is performed, which requires the Company to allocate the fair value of the reporting unit derived in the first step to the fair value of the reporting unit's net assets, with any fair value in excess of amounts allocated to such net assets representing the implied fair value of goodwill for that reporting unit. If the implied fair value of the goodwill is less than the book value, goodwill is impaired and is written down to the implied fair value amount.

Intangible assets that have finite lives are amortized over their estimated economic useful lives on a straight line basis. Intangible assets that have indefinite lives are not amortized and are tested for impairment annually or whenever events or changes in circumstances indicate that the carrying value may not be recoverable. Similar to the qualitative assessment for goodwill, the Company may assess qualitative factors to determine if it is more likely than not (i.e., a likelihood of more than 50%) that the fair value of the indefinite-lived intangible asset is less than its carrying amount. If the Company determines that it is not more likely than not that the fair value of the indefinite-lived intangible asset is less than its carrying amount, no further testing is necessary. If, however, the Company determines that it is more likely than not that the fair value of the indefinite-lived intangible asset is less than its carrying amount, the Company compares the fair value of the indefinite-lived asset with its carrying amount. If the carrying value of an individual indefinite-lived intangible asset exceeds its fair value, the individual indefinite-lived intangible asset is written down by an amount equal to such excess. The assessment of qualitative factors is optional and at the Company's discretion. The Company may bypass the qualitative assessment for any indefinite-lived intangible asset in any period and resume performing the qualitative assessment in any subsequent period.

*Impairment of Long-Lived Assets*

When facts and circumstances indicate that the carrying values of long-lived assets, including fixed assets, may be impaired, an evaluation of recoverability is performed by comparing the carrying value of the assets, at an asset group level, to undiscounted projected future cash flows in addition to other quantitative and qualitative analyses. When assessing impairment, property, plant and equipment assets are grouped at the lowest level for which there are identifiable cash flows that are largely independent of other groups of assets. Upon indication that the carrying value of such assets may not be recoverable, the Company recognizes an impairment loss as a charge against current operations. Long-lived assets to be disposed of are reported at the lower of the carrying amount or fair value, less estimated costs to sell. The Company makes judgments related to the expected useful lives of long-lived assets and its ability to realize undiscounted cash flows in excess of the carrying amounts of such assets which are affected by factors such as the ongoing maintenance and improvements of the assets, changes in economic conditions and changes in operating performance.

*Fixed Assets*

Fixed assets are carried at cost, net of accumulated depreciation. Expenditures for maintenance, repairs and renewals of minor items are expensed as incurred. Expenditures for refurbishments and improvements that significantly improve the productive capacity or extend the useful life of an asset are capitalized. Depreciation is calculated using the straight-line method over the assets' estimated useful lives. The cost and accumulated depreciation for fixed assets sold, retired, or otherwise disposed of are relieved from the accounts, and the resultant gains and losses are reflected in income.

The Company follows an industry-wide practice of purchasing and loaning coffee brewing and related equipment to wholesale customers. These assets are also carried at cost, net of accumulated depreciation.

Depreciation costs of manufacturing and distribution assets are included in cost of sales on the Consolidated Statements of Operations. Depreciation costs of other assets, including equipment on loan to customers, are included in selling and operating expenses on the Consolidated Statements of Operations.

*Leases*

Occasionally, the Company is involved in the construction of leased properties. Due to the extent and nature of that involvement, the Company is deemed the owner during the construction period and is required to capitalize the construction costs on the Consolidated Balance Sheets along with a corresponding financing obligation for the project costs that are incurred by the lessor. Upon completion of the project, a sale-leaseback analysis is performed to determine if the Company can record a sale to remove the assets and related obligation and record the lease as either an operating or capital lease obligation. If the Company is precluded from derecognizing the assets when construction is complete due to continuing involvement beyond a normal leaseback, the lease is accounted for as a financing transaction and the recorded asset and related financing obligation remain on the Consolidated Balance Sheet. Accordingly, the asset is depreciated over its estimated useful life in accordance with the Company's policy. If the Company is not considered the owner of the land, a portion of the lease payments is allocated to ground rent and treated as an operating lease. The portion of the lease payment allocated to ground rental expense is based on the fair value of the land at the commencement of construction. Lease payments allocated to the buildings are recognized as reductions to the financing obligation and interest expense. See Note 19, *Commitments and Contingencies*, for further information.

Leases that qualify as capital leases are recorded at the lower of the fair value of the asset or the present value of the future minimum lease payments over the lease term generally using the Company's incremental borrowing rate. Assets leased under capital leases are included in fixed assets and generally are depreciated over the lease term. Lease payments under capital leases are recognized as a reduction of the capital lease obligation and interest expense.

All other leases are considered operating leases. Assets subject to an operating lease are not recorded on the balance sheet. Lease payments are recognized on a straight-line basis as rent expense over the expected lease term.

*Revenue Recognition*

Revenue from sales of single cup brewer systems, coffee and other specialty beverages in portion packs, and coffee in more traditional packaging including whole bean and ground coffee selections in bags and ground coffee in fractional packs is recognized when title and risk of loss passes to the customer, which generally occurs upon shipment or delivery of the product to the customer as defined by the contractual shipping terms. Shipping charges billed to customers are also recognized as revenue, and the related shipping costs are included in cost of sales. Cash received in advance of product delivery is recorded in deferred revenue, which is included in other current liabilities on the accompanying Consolidated Balance Sheets, until earned.

The majority of the Company's distribution to major retailers is processed by fulfillment entities. The fulfillment entities receive and fulfill sales orders and invoice certain retailers. All product shipped by the Company to the fulfillment entities are owned by the Company and included in inventories on the accompanying consolidated balance sheets. The Company recognizes revenue when delivery of the product from the fulfillment entity to the retailer has occurred based on the contractual shipping terms and when all other revenue recognition criteria are met.

Sales of single cup brewers, portion packs and other products are recognized net of any discounts, returns, allowances and sales incentives, including coupon redemptions and rebates. The Company estimates the allowance for returns using an average return rate based on historical experience and an evaluation of contractual rights or obligations. The Company routinely participates in trade promotion programs with customers, including customers whose sales are processed by the fulfillment entities, whereby customers can receive certain incentives and allowances which are recorded as a reduction to sales when the sales incentive is offered and committed to or, if the incentive relates to specific sales, at the later of when that revenue is recognized or the date at which the sales incentive is offered. These incentives include, but are not limited to, cash discounts and volume based incentive programs. Allowances to customers that are directly attributable and supportable by customer promotional activities are recorded as selling expenses at the time the promotional activity occurs.

Roasters licensed by the Company to manufacture and sell K-Cup® packs, both to the Company for resale and to their other coffee customers, are obligated to pay a royalty to the Company upon shipment to their customer. The Company records royalty revenue upon shipment of K-Cup® packs by licensed roasters to third-party customers as set forth under the terms and conditions of various licensing agreements. For shipments of K-Cup® packs to the Company for resale, this royalty payment is recorded as a reduction to the carrying value of the related K-Cup® packs in inventory and as a reduction to cost of sales when sold through to third-party customers by the Company.

*Cost of Sales*

Cost of sales for the Company consists of the cost of raw materials including coffee beans, hot cocoa, flavorings and packaging materials; a portion of our rental expense; production, warehousing and distribution costs which include salaries; distribution and merchandising personnel; leases and depreciation on facilities and equipment used in production; the cost of brewers manufactured by suppliers; third-party fulfillment charges; receiving, inspection and internal transfer costs; warranty expense; freight, duties and delivery expenses; and certain third-party royalty charges. All shipping and handling expenses are also included as a component of cost of sales.

*Product Warranty*

The Company provides for the estimated cost of product warranties in cost of sales, at the time product revenue is recognized. Warranty costs are estimated primarily using historical warranty information in conjunction with current engineering assessments applied to the Company's expected repair or replacement costs. The estimate for warranties requires assumptions relating to expected warranty claims which can be impacted significantly by quality issues.

*Advertising Costs*

The Company expenses the costs of advertising the first time the advertising takes place, except for direct mail campaigns targeted directly at consumers, which are expensed over the period during which they are expected to generate sales. As of September 28, 2013 and September 29, 2012, prepaid advertising costs of $4.1 million and $2.4 million, respectively, were recorded in *Other current assets* in the accompanying Consolidated Balance Sheets. Advertising expense totaled $193.2 million, $147.7 million, and $90.8 million, for fiscal years 2013, 2012, and 2011, respectively.

*Income Taxes*

The Company recognizes deferred tax assets and liabilities for the expected future tax benefits or consequences of temporary differences between the financial statement carrying amounts of existing assets and liabilities, and their respective tax bases. Deferred tax assets and liabilities are measured using enacted tax rates in effect for the year in which those temporary differences are expected to be recovered or settled. Judgment is required in determining the provision for income taxes and related accruals, deferred tax assets and liabilities. These include establishing a valuation allowance related to the ability to realize certain deferred tax assets. The Company currently believes that future earnings and current tax planning strategies will be sufficient to recover substantially all of the Company's recorded net deferred tax assets. To the extent future taxable income against which these assets may be applied is not sufficient, some portion or all of our recorded deferred tax assets would not be realizable.

Accounting for uncertain tax positions also requires significant judgments, including estimating the amount, timing and likelihood of ultimate settlement. Although the Company believes that its estimates are reasonable, actual results could differ from these estimates. The Company uses a more-likely-than-not measurement attribute for all tax positions taken or expected to be taken on a tax return in order for those tax positions to be recognized in the financial statements.

*Stock-Based Compensation*

The Company measures the cost of employee services received in exchange for an award of equity instruments based on the grant-date fair value of the award. Equity awards consist of stock options, restricted stock units ("RSUs"), restricted stock awards ("RSAs"), and performance stock units ("PSUs"). The cost is recognized over the period during which an employee is required to provide service in exchange for the award.

The Company measures the fair value of stock options using the Black-Scholes model and certain assumptions, including the expected life of the stock options, an expected forfeiture rate and the expected volatility of its common stock. The expected life of options is estimated based on options vesting periods, contractual lives and an analysis of the Company's historical experience. The expected forfeiture rate is based on the Company's historical employee turnover experience and future expectations. The risk-free interest rate is based on the U.S. Treasury rate over the expected life. The Company uses a blended historical volatility to estimate expected volatility at the measurement date. The fair value of RSUs, RSAs and PSUs is based on the closing price of the Company's common stock on the grant date.

## GREEN MOUNTAIN COFFEE ROASTERS, INC.

## NOTES TO CONSOLIDATED FINANCIAL STATEMENTS—(Continued)

*Foreign Currency Translation and Transactions*

The financial statements of the Company's foreign subsidiaries are translated into the reporting currency of the Company which is the U.S. dollar. The functional currency of certain of the Company's foreign subsidiaries is the local currency of the subsidiary. Accordingly, the assets and liabilities of the Company's foreign subsidiaries are translated into U.S. dollars using the exchange rate in effect at each balance sheet date. Revenue and expense accounts are generally translated using the average rate of exchange during the period. Foreign currency translation adjustments are accumulated as a component of other comprehensive income or loss as a separate component of stockholders' equity. Gains and losses arising from transactions denominated in currencies other than the functional currency of the entity are charged directly against earnings in the Consolidated Statement of Operations. Gains and losses arising from transactions denominated in foreign currencies are primarily related to inter- company loans that have been determined to be temporary in nature, cash, long-term debt and accounts payable denominated in non-functional currencies.

*Significant Customer Credit Risk and Supply Risk*

The majority of the Company's customers are located in the U.S. and Canada. With the exception of M.Block & Sons ("MBlock") as described below, concentration of credit risk with respect to accounts receivable is limited due to the large number of customers in various channels comprising the Company's customer base. The Company does not require collateral from customers as ongoing credit evaluations of customers' payment histories are performed. The Company maintains reserves for potential credit losses and such losses, in the aggregate, have not exceeded management's expectations.

The Company procures the majority of the brewers it sells from one third-party brewer manufacturer. Purchases from this brewer manufacturer amounted to approximately $637.0 million, $721.3 million and $545.3 million in fiscal years 2013, 2012 and 2011, respectively.

The Company primarily relies on MBlock to process the majority of sales orders for our AH single serve business with retailers in the United States. The Company is subject to significant credit risk regarding the creditworthiness of MBlock and, in turn, the creditworthiness of the retailers. Sales processed by MBlock to retailers amounted to $1,600.2 million, $1,458.4 million and $997.0 million for fiscal years 2013, 2012 and 2011, respectively. The Company's account receivables due from MBlock amounted to $157.4 million and $133.1 million at September 28, 2013 and September 29, 2012, respectively.

Sales to customers that represented more than 10% of the Company's net sales included Wal-Mart Stores, Inc. and affiliates ("Wal-Mart"), representing approximately 14% and 12% of consolidated net sales for fiscal years 2013 and 2012, respectively; Costco Wholesale Corporation and affiliates ("Costco"), representing approximately 11% of consolidated net sales for fiscal 2013; and Bed Bath & Beyond, Inc., and affiliates ("Bed Bath & Beyond"), representing approximately 11% of consolidated net sales for fiscal 2011. For Wal-Mart and Bed Bath & Beyond, the majority of U.S. sales are processed through MBlock whereby MBlock is the vendor of record. Starting in fiscal 2012, for U.S. sales to Costco, the Company became the vendor of record and although the sales are processed through MBlock, the Company records the account receivables from the customer and pays MBlock for their fulfillment services. The Company's account receivables due from Costco amounted to $65.7 million, net of allowances, at September 28, 2013.

*Research & Development*

Research and development charges are expensed as incurred. These expenses amounted to $57.7 million, $41.7 million and $17.7 million in fiscal years 2013, 2012 and 2011, respectively. These costs primarily consist of salary and consulting expenses and are recorded in selling and operating expenses in each respective segment of the Company.

*Recent Accounting Pronouncements*

In July 2013, the Financial Accounting Standards Board (the "FASB") issued an Accounting Standards Update ("ASU") No. 2013-11, "Presentation of an Unrecognized Tax Benefit When a Net Operating Loss Carryforward, a Similar Tax Loss, or a Tax Credit Carryforward Exists" ("ASU 2013-11"). ASU 2013-11 was issued to eliminate diversity in practice regarding the presentation of unrecognized tax benefits when a net operating loss carryforward, a similar tax loss, or a tax credit carryforward exists. Under ASU 2013-11, an unrecognized tax benefit, or a portion of an unrecognized tax benefit, should be presented in the financial statements as a reduction to a deferred tax asset for a net operating loss carryforward, a similar tax loss, or a tax credit carryforward. Otherwise, to the extent a net operating loss carryforward, a similar tax loss, or a tax credit carryforward is not available at the reporting date under the tax law of the applicable jurisdiction to settle any additional income taxes that would result from the disallowance of a tax position or the tax law of the applicable jurisdiction does not require the entity to use, and the entity does not intend to use, the deferred tax asset for such purpose, the unrecognized tax benefit should be presented in the financial statements as a liability and should not be combined with deferred tax assets. The amendments in this ASU are effective prospectively for reporting periods beginning after December 15, 2013, and early adoption is permitted. The adoption of ASU 2013-11 is not expected to have a material impact on the Company's net income, financial position or cash flows.

In March 2013, the FASB issued ASU No. 2013-05, "Foreign Currency Matters (Topic 830): Parent's Accounting for the Cumulative Translation Adjustment upon Derecognition of Certain Subsidiaries or Groups of Assets within a Foreign Entity or of an Investment in a Foreign Entity" ("ASU 2013-05"). ASU 2013-05 provides clarification regarding whether Subtopic 810-10, Consolidation—Overall, or Subtopic 830-30, Foreign Currency Matters—Translation of Financial Statements, applies to the release of cumulative translation adjustments into net income when a reporting entity either sells a part or all of its investment in a foreign entity or ceases to have a controlling financial interest in a subsidiary or group of assets that constitute a business within a foreign entity. The amendments in this ASU are effective prospectively for reporting periods beginning after December 15, 2013, and early adoption is permitted. The adoption of ASU 2013-05 is not expected to have a material impact on the Company's net income, financial position or cash flows.

In February 2013, the FASB issued ASU No. 2013-04, "Liabilities (Topic 405): Obligations Resulting from Joint and Several Liability Arrangements for Which the Total Amount of the Obligation Is Fixed at the Reporting Date" ("ASU 2013-04"). ASU 2013-04 provides guidance for the recognition, measurement and disclosure of obligations resulting from joint and several liability arrangements for which the total amount of the obligation within the scope of this ASU is fixed at the reporting date. The guidance requires an entity to measure those obligations as the sum of the amount the reporting entity agreed to pay on the basis of its arrangement among its co-obligors as well as any additional amount the reporting entity expects to pay on behalf of its co-obligors. ASU 2013-04 also requires an entity to disclose the nature and amount of those obligations. The amendments in this ASU are effective for reporting periods beginning after December 15, 2013, with early adoption permitted. Retrospective application is required. The adoption of ASU 2013-04 is not expected to have a material impact on the Company's net income, financial position or cash flows.

In February 2013, the FASB issued ASU No. 2013-02, "Comprehensive Income (Topic 220): Reporting of Amounts Reclassified Out of Accumulated Comprehensive Income" ("ASU 2013-02"). ASU 2013-02 requires an entity to report the effect of significant reclassifications out of accumulated other comprehensive income on the respective line items in net income if the amount being reclassified is required under GAAP to be reclassified in its entirety to net income. For significant items not reclassified in their entirety to net income in the same reporting period, an entity is required to cross- reference other disclosures that provide additional detail about those amounts. The amendments in this ASU are effective for annual reporting periods, and interim periods within those annual reporting periods, beginning after December 15, 2012, which for the Company will be the first quarter of fiscal 2014. The adoption of ASU 2013-02 is not expected to have an impact on the Company's net income, financial position or cash flows.

In December 2011, the FASB issued ASU No. 2011-11, "Disclosures about Offsetting Assets and Liabilities," ("ASU 2011-11") that provides amendments for disclosures about offsetting assets and liabilities. The amendments require an entity to disclose information about offsetting and related arrangements to enable users of its financial statements to understand the effect of those arrangements on its financial position. Entities are required to disclose both gross information and net information about both instruments and transactions eligible for offset in the statement of financial position and instruments and transactions subject to an agreement similar to a master netting arrangement. On January 31, 2013, the FASB issued ASU No. 2013-01, "Clarifying the Scope of Disclosures about Offsetting Assets and Liabilities," which clarified that the scope of the disclosures is limited to include derivatives, sale and repurchase agreements and reverse sale and repurchase agreements, and securities borrowing and securities lending arrangements. The amendments are effective for annual reporting periods beginning on or after January 1, 2013, and interim periods within those annual periods. Disclosures required by the amendments should be provided retrospectively for all comparative periods presented. For the Company, the amendments are effective for the fiscal year ending September 27, 2014 (fiscal year 2014). The adoption of ASU 2011-11 is not expected to have a material impact on the Company's disclosures.

**3. Acquisitions and Divestitures**

*Fiscal 2012*

On October 3, 2011, all the outstanding shares of Van Houtte USA Holdings, Inc., also known as the Van Houtte U.S. Coffee Service business or the "Filterfresh" business, were sold to ARAMARK Refreshment Services, LLC ("ARAMARK") in exchange for $149.5 million in cash. Approximately $4.4 million of cash was transferred to ARAMARK as part of the sale and $7.4 million was repaid to ARAMARK upon finalization of the purchase price, resulting in a net cash inflow related to the Filterfresh sale of $137.7 million. The Company recognized a gain on the sale of $26.3 million during the thirteen weeks ended December 24, 2011. Filterfresh had been included in the Canada segment.

As of September 24, 2011, all the assets and liabilities relating to the Filterfresh business were reported in the Consolidated Balance Sheet as assets and liabilities held-for-sale.

Filterfresh revenues and net income included in the Company's consolidated statement of operations were as follows (dollars in thousands, except per share data):

| | For the period September 25, 2011 through October 3, 2011 (date of sale) | For the period December 17, 2010 (date of acquisition through) September 24, 2011 |
|---|---|---|
| Net sales | $ 2,286 | $ 90,855 |
| Net income | $ 229 | $ 12,263 |
| Less income attributable to noncontrolling interests | 20 | 1,051 |
| Net income attributable to GMCR | $ 209 | $ 11,212 |
| Diluted net income per share | $ — | $ 0.07 |

After the disposition, the Company continues to sell coffee and brewers to Filterfresh, which prior to the sale of Filterfresh were eliminated and were not reflected in the Consolidated Statement of Operations. For fiscal 2012, the Company's sales to Filterfresh through October 3, 2011 (date of sale) that were eliminated in consolidation were $0.6 million. For fiscal 2011, the Company's sales to Filterfresh during the period December 17, 2010 (date of acquisition) through September 24, 2011 that were eliminated in consolidation were $22.2 million.

*Fiscal 2011*

*LJVH Holdings, Inc. (including subsidiaries—Van Houtte)*

On December 17, 2010, the Company acquired all of the outstanding capital stock of LJVH Holdings, Inc. ("LJVH" and together with its subsidiaries, "Van Houtte"), a coffee roaster headquartered in Montreal, Quebec, for $907.8 million, net of cash acquired. The acquisition was financed with cash on hand and a $1,450.0 million credit facility. Van Houtte's functional currency is the Canadian dollar. Van Houtte's operations are included in the Canada segment.

At the time of the acquisition, the Company accounted for all the assets relating to the Filterfresh business as held-for-sale.

The Van Houtte acquisition was accounted for under the acquisition method of accounting. The total purchase price of $907.8 million, net of cash acquired, was allocated to Van Houtte's net tangible assets and identifiable intangible assets based on their estimated fair values as of December 17, 2010. The fair value assigned to identifiable intangible assets acquired was determined primarily by using an income approach. The allocation of the purchase price is based upon a valuation determined using management's and the Company's estimates and assumptions. The table below represents the allocation of the purchase price to the acquired net assets of Van Houtte (in thousands):

| | Total | Van Houtte Canadian Operations | Filterfresh Assets Held For Sale |
|---|---|---|---|
| Restricted cash | $ 500 | $ 500 | $ — |
| Accounts receivable | 61,130 | 47,554 | 13,576 |
| Inventories | 42,958 | 36,691 | 6,267 |
| Income taxes receivable | 2,260 | 2,190 | 70 |
| Deferred income taxes | 4,903 | 3,577 | 1,326 |
| Other current assets | 5,047 | 4,453 | 594 |
| Fixed assets | 143,928 | 110,622 | 33,306 |
| Intangible assets | 375,099 | 355,549 | 19,550 |
| Goodwill | 472,331 | 409,493 | 62,838 |
| Other long-term assets | 1,577 | 962 | 615 |
| Accounts payable and accrued expenses | (54,502) | (46,831) | (7,671) |
| Other short-term liabilities | (4,330) | (3,404) | (926) |
| Income taxes payable | (1,496) | (1,496) | — |
| Deferred income taxes | (117,086) | (104,866) | (12,220) |
| Notes payable | (2,914) | (1,770) | (1,144) |
| Other long-term liabilities | (2,452) | (1,683) | (769) |
| Non-controlling interests | (19,118) | (9,529) | (9,589) |
| | $ 907,835 | $ 802,012 | $ 105,823 |

The purchase price allocated to Filterfresh was the fair value, less the estimated direct costs to sell Filterfresh established at the acquisition date. The fair value of Filterfresh was estimated using an income approach, specifically the discounted cash flow ("DCF") method. Under the DCF method the fair value is calculated by discounting the projected after-tax cash flows for the business to present value. The income approach includes assumptions about the amount and timing of future cash flows using projections and other estimates. A discount rate based on an appropriate weighted average cost of capital was applied to the estimated future cash flows to estimate the fair value.

An income approach, specifically the DCF method, was used to value the noncontrolling interests.

Amortizable intangible assets acquired, valued at the date of acquisition, include approximately $263.1 million for customer relationships, $10.9 million for trademarks and trade names, $1.4 million for franchises and $0.3 million for technology. Indefinite-lived intangible assets acquired include approximately $99.4 million for the Van Houtte trademark which is not amortized. The definite lived intangible assets classified as held-for-sale were not amortized and approximated $19.5 million. Amortizable intangible assets are amortized on a straight-line basis over their respective useful lives, and the weighted-average amortization period is 10.8 years.

The cost of the acquisition in excess of the fair market value of the tangible and intangible assets acquired less liabilities assumed represents acquired goodwill. The acquisition of Van Houtte provides the Company with an expanded Canadian presence and manufacturing and distribution synergies, which provide the basis of the goodwill recognized with respect to the Van Houtte Canadian operations. As discussed above, the purchase price allocated to Filterfresh was the fair value, less the estimated direct costs to sell Filterfresh established at the acquisition date. The excess of the purchase price (fair value) allocated to Filterfresh over the fair value of the net tangible and identifiable intangible assets represents goodwill. Goodwill and intangible assets are reported in the Canada segment. The goodwill and intangible assets recognized are not deductible for tax purposes.

Acquisition costs were expensed as incurred and totaled approximately $10.7 million for the fiscal year ended September 24, 2011 and are included in general and administrative expenses for the Company.

Approximately $9.3 million of the purchase price was held in escrow at September 29, 2012 and was included in restricted cash. A corresponding amount of $9.3 million was included in other current liabilities as of September 29, 2012. None of the purchase price remained in escrow as of September 28, 2013, and therefore, there were no corresponding amounts included in other current liabilities.

## GREEN MOUNTAIN COFFEE ROASTERS, INC.



The acquisition was completed on December 17, 2010 and accordingly results of operations from such date have been included in the Company's Statement of Operations. For fiscal 2011, the Van Houtte operations contributed an additional $321.4 million of consolidated revenue and $20.2 million of income before income taxes.

**4. Segment Reporting**

The Company has historically managed its operations through three business segments: the Specialty Coffee business unit ("SCBU"), the Keurig business unit ("KBU") and the Canadian business unit. Effective as of and as initially disclosed on May 8, 2013, the Company's Board of Directors authorized and approved a reorganization which consolidated U.S. operations to bring greater organizational efficiency and coordination across the Company. Due to this combination, the results of U.S. operations, formerly reported in the SCBU and KBU segments, are reported in one segment ("Domestic") and the results of Canadian operations are reported in the "Canada" segment. The Company's Chief Executive Officer ("CEO") serves as the Company's chief operating decision maker ("CODM") and there are two operating and reportable segments, Domestic and Canada.

As a result of the consolidation of U.S. operations, the Company has recast all historical segment results in order to: i) provide data that is on a basis consistent with the Company's new structure; ii) remove total assets from the Company's segment disclosures as only consolidated asset information is provided to and used by the CODM for use in decision making (in connection with the reorganization, segment asset information is neither provided to nor used by the CODM); and iii) reflect all sustainability expenses in Corporate as the Company no longer allocates those expenses to its operating segments.

For a description of the operating segments, see Note 1, *Nature of Business and Organization*.

Management evaluates the performance of the Company's operating segments based on several factors, including net sales to external customers and operating income. Net sales are recorded on a segment basis and intersegment sales are eliminated as part of the financial consolidation process. Operating income represents gross profit less selling, operating, general and administrative expenses. The Company's manufacturing operations occur within both the Domestic and Canada segments, and the costs of manufacturing are recognized in cost of sales in the operating segment in which the sale occurs. Information system technology services are mainly centralized while finance and accounting functions are primarily decentralized. Expenses consisting primarily of compensation and depreciation related to certain centralized administrative functions including information system technology are allocated to the operating segments. Expenses not specifically related to an operating segment are presented under "Corporate Unallocated." Corporate Unallocated expenses are comprised mainly of the compensation and other related expenses of certain of the Company's senior executive officers and other selected employees who perform duties related to the entire enterprise. Corporate Unallocated expenses also include depreciation for corporate headquarters, sustainability expenses, interest expense not directly attributable to an operating segment, the majority of foreign exchange gains or losses, legal expenses and compensation of the Board of Directors. The Company does not disclose assets or property additions by segment as only consolidated asset information is provided to the CODM for use in decision making.

Effective for the first quarter of fiscal 2013, the Company changed its measure for reporting segment profitability and for evaluating segment performance and the allocation of Company resources from income before taxes to operating income (loss). Prior to the first quarter of fiscal 2013, the Company disclosed each operating and reportable segment's income before taxes to report segment profitability. Segment disclosures for prior periods have been recast to reflect operating income by segment in place of income before taxes. The CODM measures segment performance based upon operating income which excludes interest expense and interest expense is not provided to the CODM by segment. Accordingly, interest expense by segment is no longer presented.

Effective with the beginning of the Company's third quarter of fiscal 2011, sales between operating segments are recorded at cost and the Domestic segment no longer records royalty income from the Canada segment on shipments of portion packs. Prior to the third quarter of fiscal 2011, the Company recorded intersegment sales and purchases of brewer and K-Cup® packs at a markup. As a result of the change, intersegment sales have no impact on segment operating income (loss) and effective with the first quarter of fiscal 2013, the Company no longer discloses intersegment sales. Each operating segment's net sales for fiscal years 2013 and 2012 include only net sales to external customers.

The selected financial data for segment disclosures for fiscal 2011 was not recast for the above changes related to intersegment sales and royalty income. The following table summarizes the approximate net effect of the above changes on segment income before taxes for fiscal 2013, 2012 and 2011 as a result of the above changes (in thousands). The net effect represents the net mark-up on sales between the segments as well as the Domestic segment royalty income on the sale of portion packs by the Canada segment. The Company used historical mark-up percentages and royalty rates to calculate the net effect.

| Increase (decrease) in operating income (loss) | Fiscal 2013 | Fiscal 2012 | Fiscal 2011 |
|---|---|---|---|
| Domestic | $ (38,755) | $ 20,068 | $ (29,584) |
| Canada | 39,057 | (19,084) | 22,157 |
| Corporate—Unallocated | — | — | — |
| Eliminations | (302) | (984) | 7,427 |
| Consolidated | $ — | $ — | $ — |

The following tables summarize selected financial data for segment disclosures for fiscal 2013, 2012 and 2011.

| | For Fiscal 2013 (Dollars in thousands) | | | |
|---|---|---|---|---|
| | Domestic | Canada | Corporate-Unallocated | Consolidated |
| Net sales | $ 3,725,008 | $ 633,092 | $ — | $ 4,358,100 |
| Operating income (loss) | $ 826,092 | $ 87,674 | $ (148,539) | $ 765,227 |
| Depreciation and amortization | $ 162,359 | $ 65,334 | $ 1,500 | $ 229,193 |
| Stock compensation expense | $ 9,909 | $ 2,519 | $ 13,653 | $ 26,081 |

| | For Fiscal 2012 (Dollars in thousands) | | | |
|---|---|---|---|---|
| | Domestic | Canada | Corporate-Unallocated | Consolidated |
| Net sales | $ 3,233,674 | $ 625,524 | $ — | $ 3,859,198 |
| Operating Income (loss) | $ 576,949 | $ 76,198 | $ (84,251) | $ 568,896 |
| Depreciation and amortization | $ 116,722 | $ 62,984 | $ 1,941 | $ 181,647 |
| Stock compensation expense | $ 7,808 | $ 1,890 | $ 8,170 | $ 17,868 |

| | For Fiscal 2011 (Dollars in thousands) | | | | |
|---|---|---|---|---|---|
| | Domestic | Canada | Corporate-Unallocated | Eliminations | Consolidated |
| Sales to unaffiliated customers | $ 2,152,432 | $ 498,467 | $ — | $ — | $ 2,650,899 |
| Intersegment sales | $ 36,855 | $ 98,347 | $ — | $ (135,202) | $ — |
| Net sales | $ 2,189,287 | $ 596,814 | $ — | $ (135,202) | $ 2,650,899 |
| Operating Income | $ 399,638 | $ 67,727 | $ (73,259) | $ (25,193) | $ 368,913 |
| Depreciation and amortization | $ 68,439 | $ 45,193 | $ 4 | $ — | $ 113,636 |
| Stock compensation expense | $ 5,519 | $ 470 | $ 4,372 | $ — | $ 10,361 |

*Geographic Information*

Net sales are attributed to countries based on the location of the customer. Information concerning net sales of principal geographic areas is as follows (in thousands):

| | Fiscal 2013 | Fiscal 2012 | Fiscal 2011 |
|---|---|---|---|
| Net Sales: | | | |
| United States | $ 3,721,182 | $ 3,248,543 | $ 2,248,811 |
| Canada | 634,360 | 609,828 | 400,682 |
| Other | 2,558 | 827 | 1,406 |
| | $ 4,358,100 | $ 3,859,198 | $ 2,650,899 |

Sales to customers that represented more than 10% of the Company's net sales included Wal-Mart, representing approximately 14% and 12% of consolidated net sales for fiscal years 2013 and 2012, respectively, Costco, representing approximately 11% of consolidated net sales for fiscal 2013, and Bed Bath & Beyond, representing approximately 11% of consolidated net sales for fiscal 2011. Sales to Wal-Mart in fiscal years 2013 and 2012 were through both segments; sales to Costco in fiscal 2013 were through both segments; and sales to Bed Bath & Beyond, Inc., in fiscal 2011 were primarily through the Domestic segment.

Information concerning long-lived assets of principal geographic area is as follows (in thousands) as of:

| | September 28, 2013 | September 29, 2012 |
|---|---|---|
| Fixed Assets, net: | | |
| United States | $ 844,471 | $ 783,075 |
| Canada | 135,440 | 143,640 |
| Other | 5,652 | 17,581 |
| | $ 985,563 | $ 944,296 |

**Net Sales by Major Product Category**

Net sales by major product category (in thousands):

| | Fiscal 2013 | Fiscal 2012 | Fiscal 2011 |
|---|---|---|---|
| Portion Packs | $ 3,187,350 | $ 2,708,886 | $ 1,704,021 |
| Brewers and Accessories | 827,570 | 759,805 | 524,709 |
| Other Products and Royalties | 343,180 | 390,507 | 422,169 |
| | $ 4,358,100 | $ 3,859,198 | $ 2,650,899 |

**5. Inventories**

Inventories consisted of the following (in thousands) as of:

| | September 28, 2013 | September 29, 2012 |
|---|---|---|
| Raw materials and supplies | $ 182,882 | $ 229,927 |
| Finished goods | 493,207 | 538,510 |
| | $ 676,089 | $ 768,437 |

## GREEN MOUNTAIN COFFEE ROASTERS, INC.

## NOTES TO CONSOLIDATED FINANCIAL STATEMENTS—(Continued)

As of September 28, 2013, the Company had approximately $245.1 million in green coffee purchase commitments, of which approximately 84% had a fixed price. These commitments primarily extend through fiscal 2015. The value of the variable portion of these commitments was calculated using an average "C" price of coffee of $1.24 per pound at September 28, 2013. In addition to its green coffee commitments, the Company had approximately $141.8 million in fixed price brewer and related accessory purchase commitments and $536.1 million in production raw materials commitments at September 28, 2013. The Company believes, based on relationships established with its suppliers, that the risk of non-delivery on such purchase commitments is remote.

As of September 28, 2013, minimum future inventory purchase commitments were as follows (in thousands):

| Fiscal Year | Inventory Purchase Obligations |
|---|---|
| 2014 | $ 456,955 |
| 2015 | 124,588 |
| 2016 | 119,565 |
| 2017 | 110,837 |
| 2018 | 111,086 |
| | $ 923,031 |

**6. Fixed Assets**

Fixed assets consisted of the following (in thousands) as of:

| | Useful Life in Years | September 28, 2013 | September 29, 2012 |
|---|---|---|---|
| Production equipment | 1–15 | $ 680,457 | $ 544,491 |
| Coffee service equipment | 3–7 | 59,169 | 63,722 |
| Computer equipment and software | 1–6 | 146,246 | 111,441 |
| Land | Indefinite | 11,520 | 11,740 |
| Building and building improvements | 4–30 | 134,495 | 83,172 |
| Furniture and fixtures | 1–15 | 33,975 | 28,477 |
| Vehicles | 4–5 | 11,786 | 10,306 |
| Leasehold improvements | 1–20 or remaining life of lease, whichever is less | 98,990 | 72,755 |
| Assets acquired under capital leases | 5–15 | 41,200 | 51,047 |
| Construction-in-progress | | 202,940 | 234,442 |
| Total fixed assets | | $ 1,420,778 | $ 1,211,593 |
| Accumulated depreciation | | (435,215) | (267,297) |
| | | $ 985,563 | $ 944,296 |

Assets acquired under capital leases, net of accumulated amortization, were $36.9 million and $47.0 million at September 28, 2013 and September 29, 2012, respectively.

Total depreciation and amortization expense relating to all fixed assets was $183.8 million, $135.7 million and $72.3 million for fiscal years 2013, 2012, and 2011, respectively.

Assets classified as construction-in-progress are not depreciated, as they are not ready for productive use.

As of September 28, 2013, construction-in-progress includes $21.1 million relating to properties under construction where the Company is deemed to be the accounting owner, even though the Company is not the legal owner. See footnote 19, *Commitments and Contingencies*.

During fiscal years 2013, 2012 and 2011, $6.1 million, $2.8 million, and $2.6 million, respectively, of interest expense was capitalized.

**7. Goodwill and Intangible Assets**

The following represented the change in the carrying amount of goodwill by segment for fiscal 2013 and 2012 (in thousands):

| | Domestic | Canada | Total |
|---|---|---|---|
| Balance as of September 24, 2011 | $ 386,416 | $ 402,889 | $ 789,305 |
| Reassignment of Timothy's goodwill | (17,063) | 17,063 | — |
| Foreign currency effect | — | 18,771 | 18,771 |
| Balance as of September 29, 2012 | $ 369,353 | $ 438,723 | $ 808,076 |
| Foreign currency effect | — | (19,892) | (19,892) |
| Balance as of September 28, 2013 | $ 369,353 | $ 418,831 | $ 788,184 |

Indefinite-lived intangible assets included in the Canada operating segment consisted of the following (in thousands) as of:

| | September 28, 2013 | September 29, 2012 |
|---|---|---|
| Trade names | $ 97,740 | $ 102,381 |

Effective May 8, 2013, the Company combined the results of its U.S. operations, formerly reported in the SCBU and KBU segments, into one Domestic segment.

Effective September 25, 2011, Timothy's is included in the Canada segment. Prior to September 25, 2011, Timothy's was included in the Domestic segment. This resulted in a re-assignment of goodwill of $17.1 million from the Domestic segment to the Canada segment using a relative fair value approach. The amount of goodwill reassigned was determined based on the relative fair values of Timothy's and the Domestic segment.

The Company conducted its annual impairment test of goodwill and indefinite-lived intangible assets as of September 28, 2013, and elected to bypass the optional qualitative assessment and performed a quantitative impairment test. Goodwill was evaluated for impairment at the following reporting unit levels:

- Domestic
- Canada—Roasting and Retail
- Canada—Coffee Services Canada

For the goodwill impairment test, the fair value of the reporting units was estimated using the Discounted Cash Flow ("DCF") method. A number of significant assumptions and estimates are involved in the application of the DCF method including discount rate, sales volume and prices, costs to produce and working capital changes. For the indefinite-lived intangible assets impairment test, the fair value of the trade name was estimated using the Relief-from-Royalty Method. This method estimates the savings in royalties the Company would otherwise have had to pay if it did not own the trade name and had to license the trade name from a third-party with rights of use substantially equivalent to ownership. The fair value of the trade name is the present value of the future estimated after-tax royalty payments avoided by ownership, discounted at an appropriate, risk-adjusted rate of return. For goodwill and indefinite-lived intangible impairment tests, the Company used a royalty rate of 3.0%, an income tax rate of 38.0% for the United States and 27.5% for Canada, and discount rates ranging from 13% to 14%. There was no impairment of goodwill or indefinite-lived intangible assets in fiscal years 2013, 2012, or 2011.

GREEN MOUNTAIN COFFEE ROASTERS, INC.

NOTES TO CONSOLIDATED FINANCIAL STATEMENTS—(Continued)

*Intangible Assets Subject to Amortization*

Definite-lived intangible assets consisted of the following (in thousands) as of:

| | | September 28, 2013 | | September 29, 2012 | |
|---|---|---|---|---|---|
| | Useful Life in Years | Gross Carrying Amount | Accumulated Amortization | Gross Carrying Amount | Accumulated Amortization |
| Acquired technology | 4–10 | $ 21,609 | $ (17,123) | $ 21,622 | $ (15,433) |
| Customer and roaster agreements | 8–11 | 26,977 | (19,750) | 27,323 | (16,796) |
| Customer relationships | 2–16 | 414,967 | (113,061) | 430,178 | (79,168) |
| Trade names | 9–11 | 37,200 | (13,353) | 38,000 | (9,785) |
| Non-compete agreements | 2–5 | 374 | (364) | 374 | (344) |
| Total | | $ 501,127 | $ (163,651) | $ 517,497 | $ (121,526) |

Definite-lived intangible assets are amortized on a straight-line basis over the period of expected economic benefit. Total amortization expense was $45.4 million, $46.0 million, and $41.3 million for fiscal years 2013, 2012, and 2011, respectively. The weighted average remaining life for definite-lived intangibles at September 28, 2013 is 8.3 years.

The estimated aggregate amortization expense over each of the next five years and thereafter, is as follows (in thousands):

| | |
|---|---|
| 2014 | $ 44,361 |
| 2015 | 42,807 |
| 2016 | 42,081 |
| 2017 | 40,686 |
| 2018 | 40,686 |
| Thereafter | 126,855 |

## GREEN MOUNTAIN COFFEE ROASTERS, INC.

## NOTES TO CONSOLIDATED FINANCIAL STATEMENTS—(Continued)

**8. Noncontrolling Interests**

The changes in the liability and temporary equity attributable to redeemable NCIs for the three fiscal years in the period ended September 28, 2013 are as follows (in thousands):

| | Liability attributable to mandatorily redeemable noncontrolling interests | Equity attributable to redeemable noncontrolling interests |
|---|---|---|
| Balance at September 25, 2010 | $ — | $ — |
| Purchase noncontrolling interests | — | 19,118 |
| Net income | — | 1,547 |
| Adjustment to redemption value | — | 1,618 |
| Cash distributions | — | (1,063) |
| Other comprehensive loss, net of tax | — | (186) |
| Balance at September 24, 2011 | $ — | $ 21,034 |
| Disposition of noncontrolling interest | — | (10,331) |
| Redeemable noncontrolling interest reclassified to other long-term liabilities | 4,708 | (4,708) |
| Net income | 60 | 812 |
| Adjustment to redemption value | 167 | 3,155 |
| Cash distributions | (204) | (513) |
| Other comprehensive loss, net of tax | 197 | 455 |
| Balance at September 29, 2012 | $ 4,928 | $ 9,904 |
| Net income | 462 | 409 |
| Adjustment to redemption value | 372 | 2,025 |
| Cash distributions | (583) | (823) |
| Other comprehensive loss, net of tax | (245) | (470) |
| Balance at September 28, 2013 | $ 4,934 | $ 11,045 |

As of September 28, 2013 and September 29, 2012, the liability attributable to mandatorily redeemable noncontrolling interests was included as a component of *Other current liabilities* and *Other long-term liabilities*, respectively, in the Consolidated Balance Sheets.

**9. Product Warranties**

The Company offers a one-year warranty on all Keurig® Single Cup brewers it sells. The Company provides for the estimated cost of product warranties, primarily using historical information and current repair or replacement costs, at the time product revenue is recognized. Brewer failures may arise in the later part of the warranty period, and actual warranty costs may exceed the reserve. As the Company has grown, it has added significantly to its product testing, quality control infrastructure and overall quality processes. Nevertheless, as the Company continues to innovate, and its products become more complex, both in design and componentry, product performance may tend to modulate, causing warranty rates to possibly fluctuate going forward. As a result, future warranty claims rates may be higher or lower than the Company is currently experiencing and for which the Company is currently providing in its warranty reserve.

The changes in the carrying amount of product warranties for fiscal years 2013 and 2012 are as follows (in thousands):

| | Fiscal 2013 | Fiscal 2012 |
|---|---|---|
| Balance, beginning of year | $ 20,218 | $ 14,728 |
| Provision related to current period | 20,447 | 47,026 |
| Change in estimate | (12,720) | (1,287) |
| Usage | (20,141) | (40,249) |
| Balance, end of year | $ 7,804 | $ 20,218 |

During fiscal years 2013 and 2012, the Company recovered approximately $0.8 million and $8.3 million respectively, as reimbursement from suppliers related to warranty issues. The recoveries are under an agreement with a supplier and are recorded as a reduction to warranty expense. The recoveries are not reflected in the provision charged to income in the table above.

**10. Long-Term Debt**

Long-term debt outstanding consists of the following (in thousands) as of:

| | September 28, 2013 | September 29, 2012 |
|---|---|---|
| Revolving credit facility, USD | $ — | $ 120,000 |
| Revolving credit facility, multicurrency | — | 108,787 |
| Term loan A | 170,937 | 242,188 |
| Other | 2,213 | 2,700 |
| Total long-term debt | $ 173,150 | $ 473,675 |
| Less current portion | 12,929 | 6,691 |
| Long-term portion | $ 160,221 | $ 466,984 |

Under the Company's current credit facility ("Restated Credit Agreement"), the Company maintains senior secured credit facilities consisting of (i) an $800.0 million U.S. revolving credit facility, (ii) a $200.0 million alternative currency revolving credit facility, and (iii) a term loan A facility. The Restated Credit Agreement also provides for an increase option for an aggregate amount of up to $500.0 million.

The term loan A facility requires quarterly principal repayments. The term loan and revolving credit borrowings bear interest at a rate equal to an applicable margin plus, at our option, either (a) a eurodollar rate determined by reference to the cost of funds for deposits for the interest period and currency relevant to such borrowing, adjusted for certain costs, or (b) a base rate determined by reference to the highest of (1) the federal funds rate plus 0.50%, (2) the prime rate announced by Bank of America, N.A. from time to time and (3) the eurodollar rate plus 1.00%. The applicable margin under the Restated Credit Agreement with respect to term loan A and revolving credit facilities is a percentage per annum varying from 0.5% to 1.0% for base rate loans and 1.5% to 2.0% for eurodollar loans, based upon the Company's leverage ratio. The Company's average effective interest rate as of September 28, 2013 and September 29, 2012 was 3.5% and 2.9%, respectively, excluding amortization of deferred financing charges and including the effect of interest swap agreements. The Company also pays a commitment fee of 0.2% on the average daily unused portion of the revolving credit facilities.

All the assets of the Company and its domestic wholly-owned material subsidiaries are pledged as collateral under the Restated Credit Agreement. The Restated Credit Agreement contains customary negative covenants, subject to certain exceptions, including limitations on: liens; investments; indebtedness; merger and consolidations; asset sales; dividends and distributions or repurchases of the Company's capital stock; transactions with affiliates; certain burdensome agreements; and changes in the Company's lines of business.

The Restated Credit Agreement requires the Company to comply on a quarterly basis with a consolidated leverage ratio and a consolidated interest coverage ratio. As of September 28, 2013 and throughout fiscal year 2013, the Company was in compliance with these covenants. In addition, the Restated Credit Agreement contains certain mandatory prepayment requirements and customary events of default.

As of September 28, 2013 and September 29, 2012, outstanding letters of credit under the Restated Credit Agreement, totaled $5.0 million and $3.7 million, respectively. No amounts have been drawn against the letters of credit as of September 28, 2013 and September 29, 2012.

In connection with the Restated Credit Agreement, the Company incurred debt issuance costs of $46.0 million which were deferred and included in *Other Long-Term Assets* on the Consolidated Balance Sheet and amortized as interest expense over the life of the respective loan using a method that approximates the effective interest rate method. The Company incurred a loss of $19.7 million in fiscal 2011 primarily on the extinguishment of the term loan B facility under the credit agreement that immediately preceded the Restated Credit Agreement ("Credit Agreement") and the extinguishment of a former credit facility that preceded the Credit Agreement resulting from the write-off of debt issuance costs and the original issue discount. The loss on the extinguishment of debt is included in *Interest Expense* on the Consolidated Statements of Operations.

The Company enters into interest rate swap agreements to limit a portion of its exposure to variable interest rates by entering into interest rate swap agreements which effectively fix the rates. In accordance with the interest rate swap agreements and on a monthly basis, interest expense is calculated based on the floating 30-day Libor rate and the fixed rate. If interest expense as calculated is greater based on the 30-day Libor rate, the interest rate swap counterparty pays the difference to the Company; if interest expense as calculated is greater based on the fixed rate, the Company pays the difference to the interest rate swap counterparty. See Note 11, *Derivative Financial Instruments*.

Below is a summary of the Company's derivative instruments in effect as of September 28, 2013 mitigating interest rate exposure of variable-rate borrowings (in thousands):

| Derivative Instrument | Hedged Transaction | Notional Amount of Underlying Debt | Fixed Rate Received | Maturity (Fiscal Year) |
|---|---|---|---|---|
| Swap | 30-day Libor | 20,000 | 2.54% | 2016 |
| Swap | 30-day Libor | 30,000 | 2.54% | 2016 |
| Swap | 30-day Libor | 50,000 | 2.54% | 2016 |
| Swap | 30-day Libor | 30,000 | 2.54% | 2016 |
| | | $ 130,000 | | |

In fiscal years 2013, 2012 and 2011 the Company paid approximately $3.4 million, $4.7 million and $3.8 million, respectively, in additional interest expense pursuant to the interest rate swap agreements.

*Maturities*

Scheduled maturities of long-term debt are as follows (in thousands):

| Fiscal Year | |
|---|---|
| 2014 | $ 12,929 |
| 2015 | 19,165 |
| 2016 | 140,064 |
| 2017 | 377 |
| 2018 | 395 |
| Thereafter | 220 |
| | $ 173,150 |

**11. Derivative Financial Instruments**

*Cash Flow Hedges*

The Company is exposed to certain risks relating to ongoing business operations. The primary risks that are mitigated by financial instruments are interest rate risk, commodity price risk and foreign currency exchange rate risk. The Company uses interest rate swaps to mitigate interest rate risk associated with the Company's variable-rate borrowings, enters into coffee futures contracts to hedge future coffee purchase commitments of green coffee with the objective of minimizing cost risk due to market fluctuations, and uses foreign currency forward contracts to hedge the purchase and payment of green coffee purchase commitments denominated in non-functional currencies.

The Company designates these contracts as cash flow hedges and measures the effectiveness of these derivative instruments at each balance sheet date. The changes in the fair value of these instruments are classified in accumulated other comprehensive income (loss). The gains or loss on these instruments is reclassified from OCI into earnings in the same period or periods during which the hedged transaction affects earnings. If it is determined that a derivative is not highly effective, the gain or loss is reclassified into earnings.

## NOTES TO CONSOLIDATED FINANCIAL STATEMENTS—(Continued)

*Fair Value Hedges*

The Company enters into foreign currency forward contracts to hedge certain recognized liabilities in currencies other than the Company's functional currency. The Company designates these contracts as fair value hedges and measures the effectiveness of the derivative instruments at each balance sheet date. The changes in the fair value of these instruments along with the changes in the fair value of the hedged liabilities are recognized in net gains or losses on foreign currency on the consolidated statements of operations.

*Other Derivatives*

The Company is also exposed to certain foreign currency and interest rate risks on an intercompany note with a foreign subsidiary denominated in Canadian currency. At September 28, 2013, the Company has approximately two years remaining on a CDN $120.0 million, Canadian cross currency swap to exchange interest payments and principal on the intercompany note. This cross currency swap is not designated as a hedging instrument for accounting purposes and is recorded at fair value, with the changes in fair value recognized in the Consolidated Statements of Operations. Gains and losses resulting from the change in fair value are largely offset by the financial impact of the remeasurement of the intercompany note. In accordance with the cross currency swap agreement, on a quarterly basis, the Company pays interest based on the three month Canadian Bankers Acceptance rate and receives interest based on the three month U.S. Libor rate. The Company incurred $1.7 million, $1.8 million, and $1.2 million in additional interest expense pursuant to the cross currency swap agreement during fiscal 2013, 2012, and 2011 respectively.

In conjunction with the repayment of the Company's term loan B facility under the Credit Agreement (See Note 10, *Long-Term Debt*), the interest rate cap previously used to mitigate interest rate risk associated with the Company's variable-rate borrowings on the term loan B no longer qualified for hedge accounting treatment. As a result, a loss of $0.4 million, gross of tax, was reclassified from OCI to income during fiscal 2011.

The Company occasionally enters into foreign currency forward contracts and coffee futures contracts that qualify as derivatives, and are not designated as hedging instruments for accounting purposes in addition to the foreign currency forward contracts and coffee futures contracts noted above. Contracts that are not designated as hedging instruments are recorded at fair value with the changes in fair value recognized in the Consolidated Statements of Operations.

The Company does not hold or use derivative financial instruments for trading or speculative purposes.

The Company is exposed to credit loss in the event of nonperformance by the counterparties to these financial instruments, however, nonperformance is not anticipated.

The following table summarizes the fair value of the Company's derivatives included on the Consolidated Balance Sheets (in thousands) as of:

| | September 28, 2013 | September 29, 2012 | Balance Sheet Classification |
|---|---|---|---|
| Derivatives designated as hedges: | | | |
| Interest rate swaps | $ (6,004) | $ (9,019) | Other current liabilities |
| Coffee futures | (3,809) | (342) | Other current liabilities |
| Foreign currency forward contracts | (141) | — | Other current liabilities |
| Foreign currency forward contracts | 13 | — | Other current assets |
| | (9,941) | (9,361) | |
| Derivatives not designated as hedges: | | | |
| Cross currency swap | (1,253) | (7,242) | Other current liabilities |
| | (1,253) | (7,242) | |
| Total | $ (11,194) | $ (16,603) | |

## GREEN MOUNTAIN COFFEE ROASTERS, INC.

## NOTES TO CONSOLIDATED FINANCIAL STATEMENTS—(Continued)

The following table summarizes the coffee futures contracts outstanding as of September 28, 2013 (in thousands, except for average contract price and "C" price):

| Coffee Pounds | Average Contract Price | "C" Price | Maturity | Fair Value of Futures Contracts |
|---|---|---|---|---|
| 375 | $ 1.50 | $ 1.14 | December 2013 | $ (138) |
| 5,887 | $ 1.39 | $ 1.17 | March 2014 | (1,308) |
| 11,438 | $ 1.30 | $ 1.19 | May 2014 | (1,222) |
| 10,875 | $ 1.32 | $ 1.21 | July 2014 | (1,141) |
| 28,575 | | | | $ (3,809) |

The following table summarizes the coffee futures contracts outstanding as of September 29, 2012 (in thousands, except for average contract price and "C" price):

| Coffee Pounds | Average Contract Price | "C" Price | Maturity | Fair Value of Futures Contracts |
|---|---|---|---|---|
| 938 | $ 1.92 | $ 1.74 | December 2012 | $ (169) |
| 938 | $ 1.96 | $ 1.78 | March 2013 | (171) |
| 675 | $ 1.80 | $ 1.80 | May 2013 | (1) |
| 375 | $ 1.83 | $ 1.83 | July 2013 | $ (1) |
| 262 | $ 1.86 | $ 1.86 | September 2013 | $ 0 |
| 3,188 | | | | $ (342) |

The following table summarizes the amount of gain (loss), gross of tax, on financial instruments that qualify for hedge accounting included in OCI (in thousands):

| | Fiscal 2013 | Fiscal 2012 | Fiscal 2011 |
|---|---|---|---|
| Cash Flow Hedges: | | | |
| Interest rate swaps | $ 3,014 | $ 1,250 | $ (7,928) |
| Coffee futures | (6,617) | (2,484) | 407 |
| Forward currency forward contracts | (129) | — | — |
| Total | $ (3,732) | $ (1,234) | $ (7,521) |

The following table summarizes the amount of gain (loss), gross of tax, reclassified from OCI to income (in thousands):

| | Fiscal 2013 | Fiscal 2012 | Fiscal 2011 | |
|---|---|---|---|---|
| Interest rate cap | $ — | $ — | $ (392) | Gain (loss) on financial instruments, net |
| Coffee futures | (1,482) | (1,359) | (27) | Cost of Sales |
| Forward currency forward contracts | (2) | — | — | (Loss) gain on foreign currency, net |
| Total | $ (1,484) | $ (1,359) | $ (419) | |

The Company expects to reclassify $3.5 million of losses, net of tax, from OCI to earnings on coffee derivatives within the next twelve months.

See note 14, *Stockholders' Equity* for a reconciliation of derivatives in beginning accumulated other comprehensive income (loss) to derivatives in ending accumulated other comprehensive income (loss).

The following table summarizes the amount of gain (loss), gross of tax, on fair value hedges and related hedged items (in thousands):

| | Fiscal 2013 | Fiscal 2012 | Fiscal 2011 | Location of gain (loss) recognized in income on derivative |
|---|---|---|---|---|
| Foreign currency forward contracts | | | | |
| Net loss on hedging derivatives | $ (10) | $ (48) | $ — | (Loss) gain on foreign currency, net |
| Net gain on hedged items | $ 10 | $ 48 | $ — | (Loss) gain on foreign currency, net |

Net losses on financial instruments not designated as hedges for accounting purposes recorded in gain (loss) on financial instruments, net, is as follows (in thousands):

| | Fiscal 2013 | Fiscal 2012 | Fiscal 2011 |
|---|---|---|---|
| Net gain (loss) on cross currency swap | $ 5,513 | $ (4,918) | $ (2,324) |
| Net gain (loss) on coffee futures | — | 7 | (250) |
| Net loss on interest rate cap | — | (34) | (615) |
| Net loss on foreign currency option and forward contracts | — | — | (3,056) |
| Total | $ 5,513 | $ (4,945) | $ (6,245) |

The net loss on foreign currency contracts were primarily related to contracts entered into to mitigate the risk associated with the Canadian denominated purchase price of Van Houtte in fiscal 2011.

**12. Fair Value Measurements**

The Company measures fair value as the selling price that would be received for an asset, or paid to transfer a liability, in the principal or most advantageous market on the measurement date. The hierarchy established by the Financial Accounting Standards Board prioritizes fair value measurements based on the types of inputs used in the valuation technique. The inputs are categorized into the following levels:

Level 1—Observable inputs such as quoted prices in active markets for identical assets or liabilities.

Level 2—Inputs other than quoted prices that are observable, either directly or indirectly, which include quoted prices for similar assets or liabilities in active markets and quoted prices for identical assets or liabilities in markets that are not active.

Level 3—Unobservable inputs not corroborated by market data, therefore requiring the entity to use the best available information, including management assumptions.

The following table summarizes the fair values and the levels used in fair value measurements as of September 28, 2013 for the Company's financial (liabilities) assets (in thousands):

| | Fair Value Measurements Using | | |
|---|---|---|---|
| | Level 1 | Level 2 | Level 3 |
| Derivatives: | | | |
| Interest rate swaps | $ — | $ (6,004) | $ — |
| Cross currency swap | — | (1,253) | — |
| Coffee futures | — | (3,809) | — |
| Foreign currency forward contracts | — | (128) | — |
| Total | $ — | $ (11,194) | $ — |

## GREEN MOUNTAIN COFFEE ROASTERS, INC.

## NOTES TO CONSOLIDATED FINANCIAL STATEMENTS—(Continued)

The following table summarizes the fair values and the levels used in fair value measurements as of September 29, 2012 for the Company's financial liabilities (in thousands):

| | Fair Value Measurements Using | | |
|---|---|---|---|
| | Level 1 | Level 2 | Level 3 |
| Derivatives: | | | |
| Interest rate swaps | $ — | $ (9,019) | $ — |
| Cross currency swap | — | (7,242) | — |
| Coffee futures | — | (342) | — |
| Foreign currency forward contracts | — | — | — |
| Total | $ — | $ (16,603) | $ — |

Level 2 derivative financial instruments use inputs that are based on market data of identical (or similar) instruments, including forward prices for commodities, interest rates curves and spot prices that are in observable markets. Derivatives recorded on the balance sheet are at fair value with changes in fair value recorded in OCI for cash flow hedges and in the Consolidated Statements of Operations for fair value hedges and derivatives that do not qualify for hedge accounting treatment.

*Derivatives*

Derivative financial instruments include coffee futures contracts, interest rate swap agreements, a cross-currency swap agreement and foreign currency forward contracts. The Company has identified significant concentrations of credit risk based on the economic characteristics of the instruments that include interest rates, commodity indexes and foreign currency rates and selectively enters into the derivative instruments with counterparties using credit ratings.

To determine fair value, the Company utilizes the market approach valuation technique for coffee futures and foreign currency forward contracts and the income approach for interest rate and cross currency swap agreements. The Company's fair value measurements include a credit valuation adjustment for the significant concentrations of credit risk.

As of September 28, 2013, the amount of loss estimated by the Company due to credit risk associated with the derivatives for all significant concentrations was not material based on the factors of an industry recovery rate and a calculated probability of default.

*Long-Term Debt*

The carrying value of long-term debt was $173.2 million and $473.7 million as of September 28, 2013 and September 29, 2012, respectively. The inputs to the calculation of the fair value of long-term debt are considered to be Level 2 within the fair value hierarchy, as the measurement of fair value is based on the net present value of calculated interest and principal payments, using an interest rate derived from a fair market yield curve adjusted for the Company's credit rating. The carrying value of long-term debt approximates fair value as the interest rate on the debt is based on variable interest rates that reset every 30 days.

**13. Income Taxes**

Income before income taxes and the provision for income taxes for fiscal years 2013, 2012 and 2011, consist of the following (in thousands):

| | Fiscal 2013 | Fiscal 2012 | Fiscal 2011 |
|---|---|---|---|
| Income before income taxes: | | | |
| United States | $ 675,438 | $ 486,258 | $ 248,108 |
| Foreign | 65,436 | 89,883 | 54,639 |
| Total income before income taxes | $ 740,874 | $ 576,141 | $ 302,747 |
| Income tax expense: | | | |
| United States federal: | | | |
| Current | $ 202,006 | $ 75,932 | $ 75,225 |
| Deferred | (8,654) | 74,042 | (3,327) |
| | 193,352 | 149,974 | 71,898 |
| State and local: | | | |
| Current | 47,930 | 40,270 | 13,939 |
| Deferred | (1,695) | (712) | (1,758) |
| | 46,235 | 39,558 | 12,181 |
| Total United States | 239,587 | 189,532 | 84,079 |
| Foreign: | | | |
| Current | 29,901 | 26,860 | 21,306 |
| Deferred | (12,717) | (3,751) | (3,686) |
| Total foreign | 17,184 | 23,109 | 17,620 |
| Total income tax expense | $ 256,771 | $ 212,641 | $ 101,699 |

Net deferred tax liabilities consist of the following (in thousands) as of:

| | September 28, 2013 | September 29, 2012 |
|---|---|---|
| Deferred tax assets: | | |
| Section 263A capitalized expenses | $ 1,876 | $ 2,150 |
| Deferred hedging losses | 4,774 | 3,919 |
| Deferred compensation | 13,632 | 11,534 |
| Net operating loss carryforward | — | 1,017 |
| Capital loss carryforward | 1,418 | 1,418 |
| Valuation allowance—capital loss carryforward | (1,418) | (1,418) |
| Warranty, obsolete inventory and bad debt allowance | 32,692 | 27,421 |
| Tax credit carryforwards | 3,651 | 3,301 |
| Other reserves and temporary differences | 15,558 | 12,412 |
| Gross deferred tax assets | 72,183 | 61,754 |
| Deferred tax liabilities: | | |
| Prepaid expenses | (2,994) | (2,367) |
| Depreciation | (125,504) | (123,044) |
| Intangible assets | (138,262) | (144,329) |
| Other reserves and temporary differences | (237) | (10,994) |
| Gross deferred tax liabilities | (266,997) | (280,734) |
| Net deferred tax liabilities | $ (194,814) | $ (218,980) |

GREEN MOUNTAIN COFFEE ROASTERS, INC.

NOTES TO CONSOLIDATED FINANCIAL STATEMENTS—(Continued)

A reconciliation for continuing operations between the amount of reported income tax expense and the amount computed using the U.S. Federal Statutory rate of 35% is as follows (in thousands):

| | Fiscal 2013 | Fiscal 2012 | Fiscal 2011 |
|---|---|---|---|
| Tax at U.S. Federal Statutory rate | $ 259,306 | $ 201,692 | $ 105,961 |
| Increase (decrease) in rates resulting from: | | | |
| Foreign tax rate differential | (13,087) | (18,072) | (9,289) |
| Non-deductible stock compensation expense | 2,700 | 1,024 | 1,761 |
| State taxes, net of federal benefit | 31,869 | 27,114 | 11,276 |
| Provincial taxes | 7,878 | 10,591 | 6,309 |
| Domestic production activities deduction | (23,558) | (9,245) | (7,831) |
| Acquisition costs | — | — | 4,158 |
| Federal tax credits | (4,506) | (282) | (962) |
| Release of capital loss valuation allowance | — | (3,071) | (6,194) |
| Other | (3,831) | 2,890 | (3,490) |
| Tax at effective rates | $ 256,771 | $ 212,641 | $ 101,699 |

As of September 28, 2013, the Company had a $17.7 million state capital loss carryforward and a state net operating loss carryforward of $11.5 million available to be utilized against future taxable income for years through fiscal 2015 and 2029, respectively, subject to annual limitation pertaining to change in ownership rules under the Internal Revenue Code of 1986, as amended (the "Code"). Based upon earnings history, the Company concluded that it is more likely than not that the net operating loss carryforward will be utilized prior to its expiration but that the capital loss carryforward will not. The Company has recorded a $1.4 million valuation allowance against the entire deferred tax asset balance for the capital loss carryforward

The total amount of unrecognized tax benefits as of September 28, 2013 and September 29, 2012 was $23.3 million and $24.0 million, respectively. The amount of unrecognized tax benefits at September 28, 2013 that would impact the effective tax rate if resolved in favor of the Company is $19.7 million. As a result of prior acquisitions, the Company is indemnified for up to $16.6 million of the total reserve balance, and the indemnification is capped at CDN $37.9 million. If these unrecognized tax benefits are resolved in favor of the Company, the associated indemnification receivable, recorded in other long-term assets would be reduced accordingly. As of September 28, 2013 and September 29, 2012, accrued interest and penalties of $2.0 million and $0.6 million, respectively, were included in the Consolidated Balance Sheets. The Company recognizes interest and penalties in income tax expense. The Company released $1.5 million of unrecognized tax benefits in the fourth quarter of fiscal 2013 due to the expiration of the statute of limitations. Income tax expense included $0.4 million, $0.2 million and $0.3 million of interest and penalties for fiscal 2013, 2012, and 2011, respectively.

A reconciliation of increases and decreases in unrecognized tax benefits, including interest and penalties, is as follows (in thousands):

| | Fiscal 2013 | Fiscal 2012 | Fiscal 2011 |
|---|---|---|---|
| Gross tax contingencies—balance, beginning of year | $ 23,956 | $ 24,419 | $ 5,480 |
| Increases from positions taken during prior periods | 438 | 2,864 | — |
| Decreases from positions taken during prior periods | — | (4,093) | (236) |
| Increases from positions taken during current periods | 2,709 | 906 | 19,175 |
| Decreases resulting from the lapse of the applicable statute of limitations | (3,820) | (140) | — |
| Gross tax contingencies—balance, end of year | $ 23,283 | $ 23,956 | $ 24,419 |

The Company expects to release $3.4 million of unrecognized tax benefits during fiscal 2014 due to the expiration of the statute of limitations.

As of September 28, 2013, the Company had approximately $155.5 million of undistributed international earnings, most of which are Canadian-sourced. With the exception of the repayment of intercompany debt, all earnings of the Company's foreign subsidiaries are considered indefinitely reinvested and no U.S. deferred taxes have been provided on those earnings. If these amounts were distributed to the U.S. in the form of dividends or otherwise, the Company would be subject to additional U.S. income taxes, which could be material. Determination of the amount of any unrecognized deferred income tax on these earnings is not practicable because such liability, if any, is dependent on circumstances existing if and when remittance occurs.

In the normal course of business, the Company is subject to tax examinations by taxing authorities both inside and outside the United States. The Company is currently being examined by the Internal Revenue Service for its fiscal year ended September 25, 2010. With some exceptions, the Company is no longer subject to examinations with respect to returns filed for fiscal years prior to 2006.

**14. Stockholders' Equity**

*Stock Issuances*

On May 11, 2011, the Company issued 9,479,544 shares of its common stock, par value $0.10 per share, at $71.00 per share, which included 1,290,000 shares purchased by the underwriters pursuant to an overallotment option. The Company also completed a concurrent private placement of 608,342 shares of its common stock to Luigi Lavazza S.p.A. ("Lavazza") at $68.34 per share, pursuant to the Common Stock Purchase Agreement entered into between the Company and Lavazza on May 6, 2011 in accordance with the September 28, 2010 agreement discussed below. The aggregate net proceeds to the Company from the public offering and concurrent private placement were approximately $688.9 million, net of underwriting discounts and commissions and offering expenses. The Company used the proceeds to repay a portion of the outstanding debt under its credit facility and for general corporate purposes.

On September 28, 2010, the Company sold 8,566,649 shares of its common stock, par value $0.10 per share, to Lavazza for aggregate gross proceeds of $250.0 million. The sale was recorded to stockholders' equity net of transaction related expenses of approximately $0.5 million. The shares were sold pursuant to a Common Stock Purchase Agreement which contains a five-and-one-half-year standstill period, subject to certain exceptions, during which Lavazza is prohibited from increasing its ownership of Common Stock or making any proposals or announcements relating to extraordinary Company transactions. The standstill is subject to additional exceptions after a one-year period, including Lavazza's right to purchase additional shares up to 15% of the Company's outstanding shares.

*Stock Repurchase Program*

On July 30, 2012, the Board of Directors authorized a program for the Company to repurchase up to $500.0 million of the Company's common shares over the next two years, at such times and prices as determined by the Company's management. Consistent with Delaware law, any repurchased shares are constructively retired and returned to an unissued status. Accordingly, the par value of repurchased shares is deducted from common stock and excess repurchase price over the par value is deducted from additional paid-in capital and from retained earnings if additional paid-in capital is depleted. As of September 28, 2013, $235.3 million remained available for shares to be repurchased under current authorization by our Board of Directors.

| | Fiscal 2013 | Fiscal 2012 |
|---|---|---|
| Number of shares acquired | 5,642,793 | 3,120,700 |
| Average price per share of acquired shares | $ 33.37 | $ 24.50 |
| Total cost of acquired shares (in thousands) | $ 188,278 | $ 76,470 |

Subsequent to the fiscal year ended September 28, 2013, the Company repurchased an additional 1,348,883 of common shares, leaving $137.8 million available for shares to be repurchased under current authorization by the Company's Board of Directors.

*Accumulated Other Comprehensive Income (Loss)*

The following table provides the changes in the components of accumulated other comprehensive income (loss), net of tax (in thousands):

| | Cash Flow Hedges | Translation | Accumulated Other Comprehensive Income (Loss) |
|---|---|---|---|
| Balance at September 25, 2010 | $ (1,630) | $ — | $ (1,630) |
| Other comprehensive loss during the period | (4,236) | (8,709) | (12,945) |
| Balance at September 24, 2011 | (5,866) | (8,709) | (14,575) |
| Other comprehensive income during the period | 74 | 24,701 | 24,775 |
| Balance at September 29, 2012 | (5,792) | 15,992 | 10,200 |
| Other comprehensive loss during the period | (1,358) | (28,027) | (29,385) |
| Balance at September 28, 2013 | $ (7,150) | $ (12,035) | $ (19,185) |

The unfavorable translation adjustment change during fiscal year 2013 and 2011 was primarily due to the weakening of the Canadian dollar against the U.S. dollar. The favorable translation adjustment change during fiscal year 2012 was primarily due to the strengthening of the Canadian against the U.S. dollar. See also Note 11, *Derivative Financial Instruments*.

### 15. Employee Compensation Plans

*Equity-Based Incentive Plans*

On March 16, 2006, stockholders of the Company approved the Company's 2006 Incentive Plan (the "2006 Plan"). The 2006 Plan was amended on March 13, 2008 and on March 11, 2010 to increase the total shares of common stock authorized for issuance to 13,200,000. As of September 28, 2013, 4,537,397 shares of common stock were available for grant for future equity-based compensation awards under the plan.

On September 25, 2001, the Company registered on Form S-8 the 2000 Stock Option Plan (the "2000 Plan"). The plan expired in October 2010. Grants under the 2000 Plan generally expire ten years after the grant date, or earlier if employment terminates. As of September 28, 2013, there were no options for shares of common stock available for grant under this plan.

In connection with the acquisition of Keurig, the Company assumed the existing outstanding unvested option awards of the Keurig, Incorporated Fifth Amended and Restated 1995 Stock Option Plan (the "1995 Plan") and the Keurig, Incorporated 2005 Stock Option Plan (the "2005 Plan"). No shares under either the 1995 Plan or the 2005 Plan were eligible for post-acquisition awards. As of September 28, 2013 and September 29, 2012, 0 and 2,776 options, respectively, out of the 1,386,933 options for shares of common stock granted were outstanding under the 1995 Plan. As of September 28, 2013 and September 29, 2012, 28,749 options and 37,313 options, respectively, out of the 1,490,577 options granted for shares of common stock were outstanding under the 2005 Plan. All awards assumed in the acquisition were initially granted with a four-year vesting schedule.

On May 3, 2007, Mr. Lawrence Blanford commenced his employment as the President and Chief Executive Officer of the Company. Pursuant to the terms of the employment, the Company made an inducement grant on May 4, 2007, to Mr. Blanford of a non-qualified option to purchase 945,000 shares of the Company's common stock, with an exercise price equal to fair market value on the date of the grant. The shares subject to the option vested in 20% installments on each of the first five anniversaries of the date of the grant.

On November 3, 2008, Ms. Michelle Stacy commenced her employment as the President of Keurig, Incorporated. Pursuant to the terms of the employment, the Company made an inducement grant on November 3, 2008, to Ms. Stacy of a non-qualified option to purchase 157,500 shares of the Company's common stock, with an exercise price equal to fair market value on the date of the grant. The shares subject to the option vested in 25% installments on each of the first four anniversaries of the date of the grant.

GREEN MOUNTAIN COFFEE ROASTERS, INC.

NOTES TO CONSOLIDATED FINANCIAL STATEMENTS—(Continued)

On February 9, 2009, Mr. Howard Malovany commenced his employment as the Vice President, Corporate General Counsel and Secretary of the Company. Pursuant to the terms of the employment, the Company made an inducement grant on February 9, 2009, to Mr. Malovany of a non-qualified option to purchase 157,500 shares of the Company's common stock, with an exercise price equal to fair market value on the date of the grant. The shares subject to the option vested in 25% installments on each of the first four anniversaries of the date of the grant.

On December 17, 2010, Mr. Gérard Geoffrion commenced his employment as the President of the Canada segment. Pursuant to the terms of the employment, the Company made an inducement grant on December 17, 2010, to Mr. Geoffrion of a non-qualified option to purchase 35,000 shares of the Company's common stock, with an exercise price equal to fair market value on the date of the grant. The shares subject to the option vest in 25% installments on each of the first four anniversaries of the date of the grant, provided that Mr. Geoffrion remains employed with the Company on each vesting date.

On December 22, 2010, the Company made an inducement grant to Mr. Sylvain Toutant, Chief Operating Officer of the Canada segment, of a non-qualified option to purchase 20,000 shares of the Company's common stock, with an exercise price equal to fair market value on the date of the grant. The shares subject to the option vest in 25% installments on each of the first four anniversaries of the date of the grant, provided that Mr. Toutant remains employed with the Company on each vesting date.

On February 17, 2011, Ms. Linda Longo-Kazanova commenced her employment as the Vice President, Chief Human Resources Officer. Pursuant to the terms of the employment, the Company made an inducement grant on February 17, 2011, to Ms. Longo-Kazanova of a non-qualified option to purchase 30,000 shares of the Company's common stock, with an exercise price equal to fair market value on the date of the grant. The shares subject to the option vest in 25% installments on each of the first four anniversaries of the date of the grant, provided that Ms. Longo-Kazanova remains employed with the Company on each vesting date.

Under the 2000 Plan, the option price for each incentive stock option was not less than the fair market value per share of common stock on the date of grant, with certain provisions which increased the option price of an incentive stock option to 110% of the fair market value of the common stock if the grantee owned in excess of 10% of the Company's common stock at the date of grant. The 2006 Plan requires the exercise price for all awards requiring exercise to be no less than 100% of fair market value per share of common stock on the date of grant, with certain provisions which increase the option price of an incentive stock option to 110% of the fair market value of the common stock if the grantee owns in excess of 10% of the Company's common stock at the date of grant. Options under the 2000 Plan and the 2006 Plan become exercisable over periods determined by the Board of Directors, generally in the range of three to five years.

Option activity is summarized as follows:

| | Number of Shares | Weighted Average Exercise Price (per share) |
|---|---|---|
| Outstanding at September 29, 2012 | 7,470,975 | $ 12.56 |
| Granted | 474,236 | $ 45.48 |
| Exercised | (2,849,308) | $ 6.95 |
| Forfeited/expired | (73,563) | $ 49.53 |
| Outstanding at September 28, 2013 | 5,022,340 | $ 18.30 |
| Exercisable at September 28, 2013 | 3,958,017 | $ 10.70 |

The following table summarizes information about stock options that have vested and are expected to vest at September 28, 2013:

| Number of options outstanding | Weighted average remaining contractual life (in years) | Weighted average exercise price | Intrinsic value at September 28, 2013 (in thousands) |
|---|---|---|---|
| 5,011,076 | 4.81 | $ 18.24 | $ 284,095 |

The following table summarizes information about stock options exercisable at September 28, 2013:

| Number of options exercisable | Weighted average remaining contractual life (in years) | Weighted average exercise price | Intrinsic value at September 28, 2013 (in thousands) |
|---|---|---|---|
| 3,958,017 | 3.90 | $ 10.70 | $ 254,162 |

Compensation expense is recognized only for those options expected to vest, with forfeitures estimated based on the Company's historical employee turnover experience and future expectations.

The Company uses a blend of recent and historical volatility to estimate expected volatility at the measurement date. The expected life of options is estimated based on options vesting periods, contractual lives and an analysis of the Company's historical experience.

The intrinsic values of options exercised during fiscal years 2013, 2012 and 2011 were approximately $165.5 million, $46.6 million and $221.8 million, respectively. The Company's policy is to issue new shares upon exercise of stock options.

The grant-date fair value of employee share options and similar instruments is estimated using the Black-Scholes option-pricing model with the following assumptions for grants issued during fiscal years 2013, 2012 and 2011:

| | Fiscal 2013 | Fiscal 2012 | Fiscal 2011 |
|---|---|---|---|
| Average expected life | 6 years | 6 years | 6 years |
| Average volatility | 81% | 69% | 52% |
| Dividend yield | — | — | — |
| Risk-free interest rate | 1.02% | 1.31% | 2.37% |
| Weighted average fair value | $ 31.23 | $ 30.10 | $ 29.34 |

*Restricted Stock Units and Other Awards*

The Company awards restricted stock units ("RSUs"), restricted stock awards ("RSAs"), and performance stock units ("PSUs") to eligible employees ("Grantee") which entitle the Grantee to receive shares of the Company's common stock. RSUs and PSUs are awards denominated in units that are settled in shares of the Company's common stock upon vesting. RSAs are awards of common stock that are restricted until the shares vest. In general, RSUs and RSAs vest based on a Grantee's continuing employment. The fair value of RSUs, RSAs and PSUs is based on the closing price of the Company's common stock on the grant date. Compensation expense for RSUs and RSAs is recognized ratably over a Grantee's service period. Compensation expense for PSUs is also recognized over a Grantee's service period, but only if and when the Company concludes that it is probable (more than likely) the performance condition(s) will be achieved. The assessment of probability of achievement is performed each period based on the relevant facts and circumstances at that time, and if the estimated grant-date fair value changes as a result of that assessment, the cumulative effect of the change on current and prior periods is recognized in the period of change. In addition, the Company awards deferred cash awards ("DCAs"), to Grantees which entitle a Grantee to receive cash paid over time upon vesting. The vesting of DCAs is conditioned on a Grantee's continuing employment. All awards are reserved for issuance under the Company's 2006 Incentive Plan and vest over periods determined by the Board of Directors, generally in the range of three to four years for RSUs, RSAs and DCAs, and three years for PSUs.

The following table summarizes the number and weighted average grant-date fair value of nonvested RSUs (amounts in thousands except grant date fair value and weighted average remaining contractual life):

| | Share Units | Weighted Average Grant-Date Fair Value | Weighted Average Remaining Contractual Life (in Years) | Intrinsic Value (in Thousands) |
|---|---|---|---|---|
| Nonvested, September 29, 2012 | 81,834 | $ 39.62 | 3.52 | $ 1,943 |
| Granted | 175,789 | $ 45.19 | | |
| Vested | (34,761) | $ 47.22 | | |
| Forfeited | (1,360) | $ 54.12 | | |
| Nonvested, September 28, 2013 | 221,502 | $ 42.74 | 1.71 | $ 16,586 |

As of September 28, 2013, total RSUs expected to vest totaled 218,459 shares with an intrinsic value of $16.4 million. The weighted average grant-date fair value of RSUs granted was $45.19 and $39.73 for fiscal 2013 and fiscal 2012, respectively. There were no RSUs granted prior to fiscal 2012.

The total intrinsic value of RSUs converted to shares of common stock during fiscal 2013 was $2.2 million. There were no RSUs converted to common stock prior to fiscal 2013.

The following table summarizes the number and weighted average grant-date fair value of nonvested PSUs based on the target award amounts in the PSU agreements as of September 28, 2013:

| | Share Units | Weighted Average Grant-Date Fair Value |
|---|---|---|
| Outstanding on September 29, 2012 | — | — |
| Granted | 122,719 | $ 41.28 |
| Forfeited | (2,051) | $ 51.56 |
| Outstanding on September 28, 2013(1) | 120,668 | $ 41.10 |

(1) The outstanding PSUs as of September 28, 2013, at the threshold award and maximum award levels were 96,534 and 144,802, respectively.

The weighted average grant-date fair value of PSUs granted was $41.28 in fiscal 2013. The Company did not issue grants for PSUs prior to fiscal 2013. There were no PSUs converted to shares of common stock during fiscal 2013.

In addition, in fiscal 2012, the Company issued a grant for 55,432 RSAs with an intrinsic value of $1.3 million as of September 29, 2012, which vested in fiscal 2013. The total intrinsic value of RSAs vested during fiscal 2013 was $2.7 million.

*Employee Stock Purchase Plan*

On October 5, 1998, the Company registered on Form S-8 the 1998 Employee Stock Purchase Plan. On March 13, 2008, the plan was amended and renamed the Amended and Restated Employee Stock Purchase Plan ("ESPP"). Under this plan, eligible employees may purchase shares of the Company's common stock, subject to certain limitations, at the lesser of 85 percent of the beginning or ending withholding period fair market value as defined in the plan. There are two six-month withholding periods in each fiscal year. At September 28, 2013, and September 29, 2012, options for 1,216,051 and 1,559,728 shares of common stock were available for purchase under the plan, respectively.

The grant-date fair value of employees' purchase rights granted during fiscal years 2013, 2012 and 2011 under the Company's ESPP is estimated using the Black-Scholes option-pricing model with the following assumptions:

| | Fiscal 2013 | Fiscal 2012 | Fiscal 2011 |
|---|---|---|---|
| Average expected life | 6 months | 6 months | 6 months |
| Average volatility | 86% | 70% | 57% |
| Dividend yield | — | — | — |
| Risk-free interest rate | 0.13% | 0.09% | 0.19% |
| Weighted average fair value | $ 14.38 | $ 11.61 | $ 15.97 |

*Stock-Based Compensation Expense*

Stock-based compensation expense recognized in the Consolidated Statements of Operations in fiscal years 2013, 2012, and 2011 (in thousands):

| | Fiscal 2013 | Fiscal 2012 | Fiscal 2011 |
|---|---|---|---|
| Options | $ 14,151 | $ 12,595 | $ 8,206 |
| RSUs/PSUs/RSAs | 7,529 | 1,861 | — |
| ESPP | 4,401 | 3,412 | 2,155 |
| Total stock-based compensation expense recognized in the Consolidated Statements of Operations | $ 26,081 | $ 17,868 | $ 10,361 |
| Total related tax benefit | $ 9,936 | $ 6,004 | $ 3,147 |

As of September 28, 2013, total unrecognized compensation cost related to all nonvested stock-based compensation arrangements was approximately $30.5 million net of estimated forfeitures. This unrecognized cost is expected to be recognized over a weighted-average period of approximately 1.28 years at September 28, 2013.

**16. Employee Retirement Plans**

*Defined Contribution Plans*

The Company has a defined contribution plan which meets the requirements of section 401(k) of the Internal Revenue Code. All regular full-time U.S. employees of the Company who are at least eighteen years of age and work a minimum of 36 hours per week are eligible to participate in the plan. The plan allows employees to defer a portion of their salary on a pre-tax basis and the Company contributes 50% of amounts contributed by employees up to 6% of their salary. Company contributions to the plan were $5.2 million, $4.4 million, and $2.7 million, for fiscal years 2013, 2012, and 2011, respectively.

In conjunction with the Van Houtte acquisition, the Company also has several Canadian Group Registered Retirement Savings Plans ("GRRSP") and a Deferred Profit Sharing Plan ("DPSP"). Under these plans, employees can contribute a certain percentage of their salary and the Company can also make annual contributions to the plans. Company contributions to the Canadian plans were $1.4 million, $1.0 million and $0.8 million for fiscal years 2013, 2012, and 2011, respectively.

*Defined Benefit Plans*

The Company has a supplementary defined benefit retirement plan and a supplementary employee retirement plan (collectively the "Plans") for certain management employees in the Canada segment. The cost of the Plans is calculated according to actuarial methods that encompass management's best estimate regarding the future evolution of salary levels, the age of retirement of salaried employees and other actuarial factors. These Plans are not funded and there are no plan assets. Future benefits will be paid from the funds of the Company.

The projected benefit obligation was $1.4 million and $1.1 million as of September 28, 2013 and September 29, 2012, which is classified in *other long-term liabilities*. Net periodic pension expense (income) was $0.3 million, $(0.1) million and $0.5 million for fiscal years 2013, 2012, and 2011, respectively.

### 17. Deferred Compensation Plan

The 2002 Deferred Compensation Plan, amended in December 2007, permits certain highly compensated officers and employees of the Company and non-employee directors to defer eligible compensation payable for services rendered to the Company. On March 8, 2013, the Company registered on Form S-8 the 2002 Deferred Compensation Plan. Participants may elect to receive deferred compensation in the form of cash payments or shares of Company Common Stock on the date or dates selected by the participant or on such other date or dates specified in the Deferred Compensation Plan. The Deferred Compensation Plan is in effect for compensation earned on or after September 29, 2002. As of September 28, 2013, and September 29, 2012, 353,434 shares and 357,759 shares of Common Stock were available for future issuance under this Plan, respectively. During fiscal 2013, no rights to shares of Common Stock were exercised under this plan. As of September 28, 2013 and September 29, 2012, rights to acquire 59,561 shares and 55,236 shares of Common Stock were outstanding under this Plan, respectively. As of September 28, 2013, rights to acquire 37,005 shares of Common Stock were committed under this plan. As of September 29, 2012, there were no rights to acquire shares of Common Stock committed under this plan.

### 18. Accrued Expenses

Accrued expenses consisted of the following (in thousands) as of:

| | September 28, 2013 | September 29, 2012 |
|---|---|---|
| Accrued compensation costs | $ 91,418 | $ 38,458 |
| Accrued customer incentives and promotions | 53,689 | 28,374 |
| Accrued freight, fulfillment and transportation costs | 21,941 | 18,455 |
| Accrued sustainability expenses | 9,275 | 11,046 |
| Accrued legal and professional services | 8,278 | 5,010 |
| Warranty reserve | 7,804 | 20,218 |
| Other | 50,022 | 49,889 |
| | $ 242,427 | $ 171,450 |

### 19. Commitments and Contingencies

*Lease Commitments*

The Company leases office and retail space, production, distribution and service facilities, and certain equipment under various non-cancellable operating leases, with terms ranging from one to twenty years. Property leases normally require payment of a minimum annual rental plus a pro-rata share of certain landlord operating expenses. Total rent expense, under all operating leases approximated $23.1 million, $25.1 million, and $18.1 million in fiscal years 2013, 2012, and 2011, respectively. The Company has subleases relating to certain of its operating leases. Sublease income approximated $1.1 million, $0.3 million and $0.3 million for fiscal years 2013, 2012 and 2010, respectively.

In addition, the Company leases a manufacturing facility which is accounted for as a capital lease. The initial term of the lease is 15 years with six additional renewal terms of five years each at the Company's option. The lease requires payment of a minimum annual rental and the Company is responsible for property taxes, insurance and operating expenses.

In June 2012, the Company entered into an arrangement to lease approximately 425,000 square feet located in Burlington, Massachusetts to be constructed. The Burlington facilities will be used by the Domestic segment and will consolidate the three existing Massachusetts facilities that are currently in Reading, Wakefield and Woburn. As of September 28, 2013, approximately 150,000 square feet had been completed and is being used for research and development. The remaining 275,000 square feet is currently under construction and is anticipated to be completed during the summer of 2014.

Due to the Company's involvement in the construction project, including its obligations to fund certain costs of construction exceeding amounts incurred by the lessor, the Company is deemed to be the owner of the project, which includes a pre-existing structure on the site, even though the Company is not the legal owner. Accordingly, total project costs incurred during construction are capitalized as construction-in-progress along with a corresponding financing obligation for the project costs that are incurred by the lessor. In addition, the Company capitalized the estimated fair value of the pre-existing structure of $4.1 million at the date construction commenced as construction-in-progress with a corresponding financing obligation. Upon completion of the project, the Company is expecting to have continuing involvement beyond a normal leaseback, and therefore will not be able to record a sale and derecognize the assets when construction is complete. As a result, the lease will be accounted for as a financing transaction and the recorded asset and related financing obligation will remain on the Balance Sheet.

As of September 28, 2013, future minimum lease payments under financing obligations, capital lease obligations and non-cancellable operating leases as well as minimum payments to be received under non-cancellable subleases are as follows (in thousands):

| Fiscal Year | Capital Leases | Operating Leases | Subleases | Financing Obligations |
|---|---|---|---|---|
| 2014 | $ 3,518 | $ 16,602 | $ (1,021) | $ 2,029 |
| 2015 | 3,838 | 15,534 | (1,012) | 8,661 |
| 2016 | 3,837 | 11,797 | (848) | 9,580 |
| 2017 | 3,837 | 8,631 | (690) | 9,580 |
| 2018 | 3,837 | 5,280 | (634) | 9,665 |
| Thereafter | 31,980 | 20,140 | (2,156) | 113,722 |
| Total | $ 50,847 | $ 77,984 | $ (6,361) | $ 153,237 |
| Less: amount representing interest | (17,075) | | | |
| Present value of future minimum lease payments | $ 33,772 | | | |

The above table for financing obligations represents the portion of the future minimum lease payments which have been allocated to the facility under construction in Burlington, Massachusetts and will be recognized as reductions to the financing obligation and as interest expense upon completion of construction.

*Legal Proceedings*

On October 1, 2010, Keurig, Incorporated, a wholly-owned subsidiary of the Company ("Keurig"), filed suit against Sturm Foods, Inc. ("Sturm") in the United States District Court for the District of Delaware (Civil Action No. 1:10-CV-00841-SLR) for patent and trademark infringement, false advertising, and other claims, related to Sturm's sale of "Grove Square" beverage cartridges that claim to be compatible with Keurig brewers. On September 13, 2012, the District Court rendered a summary judgment decision in favor of Sturm on the patent claims in the suit. On October 17, 2013, the United States Federal Circuit Court of Appeals upheld the District Court's summary judgment decision. Separately, on February 19, 2013, Keurig and Sturm entered into a settlement agreement with respect to the trademark infringement, false advertising, and other claims at issue in the suit, all of which have now been dismissed. The settlement agreement did not materially impact the Company's consolidated financial results of operations.

On November 2, 2011, Keurig filed suit against JBR, INC., d/b/a Rogers Family Company ("Rogers") in the United States District Court for the District of Massachusetts (Civil Action No. 1:11-cv-11941-MBB) for patent infringement related to Rogers' sale of "San Francisco Bay" beverage cartridges for use with Keurig brewers. The suit alleges that the "San Francisco Bay" cartridges infringe certain Keurig patents (U.S. Patent Nos. D502,362, 7,165,488 and 7,347,138). Keurig sought an injunction prohibiting Rogers from selling these cartridges, as well as money damages. In late 2012, Rogers moved for summary judgment of no infringement as to all three asserted patents. On May 24, 2013, the District of Massachusetts granted Rogers' summary judgment motions. Keurig has since appealed the Court's ruling to the Federal Circuit, and that appeal is currently pending.

On May 9, 2011, an organization named Council for Education and Research on Toxics ("CERT"), purporting to act in the public interest, filed suit in Los Angeles Superior Court (*Council for Education and Research on Toxics v. Brad Barry LLC, et al.*, Case No. BC461182.) against several companies, including the Company, that roast, package, or sell coffee in California. The *Brad Barry* complaint alleges that coffee contains the chemical acrylamide and that the Company and the other defendants are required to provide warnings under section 25249.6 of the California Safe Drinking Water and Toxics Enforcement Act, better known as Proposition 65. The Brad Barry action has been consolidated for all purposes with another Proposition 65 case filed by CERT on April 13, 2010 over allegations of acrylamide in "ready to drink" coffee sold in restaurants, convenience stores, and do-nut shops. (*Council for Education and Research on Toxics v. Starbucks Corp., et al.*, Case No. BC 415759). The Company was not named in the *Starbucks* complaint. The Company has joined a joint defense group ("JDG") organized to address CERT's allegations, and the

Company intends to vigorously defend against these allegations. The Court has ordered the case phased for discovery and trial. The first phase of the case, which has been set for trial on September 8, 2014, is limited to three affirmative defenses shared by all defendants in both cases, with other affirmative defenses, plaintiff's prima facie case, and remedies deferred for subsequent phases. Discovery on the first phase of the case is underway. Because this lawsuit is only in a preliminary stage, the Company is unable to predict its outcome, the potential loss or range of loss, if any, associated with its resolution or any potential effect it may have on the Company or its operations.

On January 24, 2012, Teashot, LLC ("Teashot") filed suit against the Company, Keurig and Starbucks Corp. ("Starbucks") in the United States District Court for the District of Colorado (Civil Action No. 12-c v-00189-WJM-KMT) for patent infringement related to the making, using, importing, selling and/or offering for sale of K-Cup packs containing tea. The suit alleges that the Company, Keurig and Starbucks infringe a Teashot patent (U.S. Patent No. 5,895,672). Teashot seeks an injunction prohibiting the Company, Keurig and Starbucks from continued infringement, as well as money damages. Pursuant to the Company's Manufacturing, Sales and Distribution Agreement with Starbucks, the Company is defending and indemnifying Starbucks in connection with the suit. On March 13, 2012, the Company and Keurig, for themselves and Starbucks, filed an answer with the court, generally denying all of Teashot's allegations. The Company and Keurig, for themselves and Starbucks, are vigorously defending this lawsuit. On May 24, 2013, the Company and Keurig, for themselves and Starbucks, filed a motion for summary judgment of non-infringement. On July 19, 2013, Teashot filed a motion for partial summary judgment on certain other, unrelated issues. No hearing on the summary judgment motions has been scheduled. At this time, the Company is unable to predict the outcome of this lawsuit, the potential loss or range of loss, if any, associated with the resolution of this lawsuit or any potential effect it may have on the Company or its operations.

*Securities and Exchange Commission ("SEC") Inquiry*

As first disclosed on September 28, 2010, the staff of the SEC's Division of Enforcement continues to conduct an inquiry into matters at the Company. The Company is cooperating fully with the SEC staff's inquiry.

*Stockholder Litigation*

Two putative securities fraud class actions are presently pending against the Company and certain of its officers and directors, along with two putative stockholder derivative actions. The first pending putative securities fraud class action was filed on November 29, 2011, and the third putative securities fraud class action was filed on May 7, 2012. A consolidated putative stockholder derivative action pending in the United States District Court for the District of Vermont consists of five separate putative stockholder derivative complaints, the first two were filed after the Company's disclosure of the SEC inquiry on September 28, 2010, while the others were filed on February 10, 2012, March 2, 2012, and July 23, 2012, respectively. In addition, a putative stockholder derivative action is pending in the Superior Court of the State of Vermont for Washington County that was commenced following the Company's disclosure of the SEC inquiry on September 28, 2010.

The first pending putative securities fraud class action, captioned Louisiana Municipal Police Employees' Retirement System ("LAMPERS") v. Green Mountain Coffee Roasters, Inc., et al., Civ. No. 2:11-cv-00289, is pending in the United States District Court for the District of Vermont before the Honorable William K. Sessions, III. Plaintiffs' amended complaint alleges violations of the federal securities laws in connection with the Company's disclosures relating to its revenues and its inventory accounting practices. The amended complaint seeks class certification, compensatory damages, attorneys' fees, costs, and such other relief as the court should deem just and proper. Plaintiffs seek to represent all purchasers of the Company's securities between February 2, 2011 and November 9, 2011. The initial complaint filed in the action on November 29, 2011 included counts for alleged violations of (1) Sections 11, 12(a)(2) and 15 of the Securities Act of 1933 (the "Securities Act") against the Company, certain of its officers and directors, and the Company's underwriters in connection with a May 2011 secondary common stock offering; and (2) Section 10(b) of the Exchange Act and Rule 10b-5 against the Company and the officer defendants, and for violation of Section 20(a) of the Exchange Act against the officer defendants. Pursuant to the Private Securities Litigation Reform Act of 1995, 15 U.S.C. § 78u-4(a)(3), plaintiffs had until January 30, 2012 to move the court to serve as lead plaintiff of the putative class. Competing applications were filed and the Court appointed Louisiana Municipal Police Employees' Retirement System, Sjunde AP-Fonden, Board of Trustees of the City of Fort Lauderdale General Employees' Retirements System, Employees' Retirements System of the Government of the Virgin Islands, and Public Employees' Retirement System of Mississippi as lead plaintiffs' counsel on April 27, 2012. Pursuant to a schedule approved by the court, plaintiffs filed their amended complaint on October 22, 2012, and plaintiffs filed a corrected amended complaint on November 5, 2012. Plaintiffs' amended complaint does not allege any claims under the Securities Act against the Company, its officers and directors, or the Company's underwriters in connection with the May 2011 secondary common stock offering. Defendants moved to dismiss the amended complaint on March 1, 2013 and the briefing of their motions was completed on June 26, 2013. An oral argument on the defendants' motions to dismiss was set for August 27, 2013 and has been rescheduled to December 12, 2013. The underwriters previously named as defendants notified the Company of their intent to seek indemnification from the Company pursuant to their underwriting agreement dated May 5, 2011 in regard to the claims asserted in this action.

The second pending consolidated putative securities fraud class action, captioned Fifield v. Green Mountain Coffee Roasters, Inc., Civ. No. 2:12-cv-00091, is also pending in the United States District Court for the District of Vermont before the Honorable William K. Sessions, III. Plaintiffs' amended complaint alleges violations of the federal securities laws in connection with the Company's disclosures relating to its forward guidance. The amended complaint includes counts for alleged violations of Section 10(b) of the Exchange Act and Rule 10b-5 against all defendants, and for alleged violation of Section 20(a) of the Exchange Act against the officer defendants. The amended complaint seeks class certification, compensatory damages, equitable and/or injunctive relief, attorneys' fees, costs, and such other relief as the court should deem just and proper. Plaintiffs seek to represent all purchasers of the Company's securities between February 2, 2012 and May 2, 2012. Pursuant to the Private Securities Litigation Reform Act of 1995, 15 U.S.C. § 78u-4(a)(3), plaintiffs had until July 6, 2012 to move the court to serve as lead plaintiff of the putative class. On July 31, 2012, the court appointed Kambiz Golesorkhi as lead plaintiff and approved his selection of Kahn Swick & Foti LLC as lead counsel. On August 14, 2012, the court granted the parties' stipulated motion for filing of an amended complaint and to set a briefing schedule for defendants' motions to dismiss. Pursuant to a schedule approved by the court, plaintiffs filed their amended complaint on October 23, 2012, adding William C. Daley as an additional lead plaintiff. Defendants moved to dismiss the amended complaint on January 17, 2013 and the briefing of their motions was completed on May 17, 2013. On September 26, 2013, the court issued an order granting defendants' motions and dismissing the amended complaint without prejudice and allowing plaintiffs a 30-day period within which to amend their complaint. On October 18, 2013, plaintiffs filed a notice of intent to appeal the court's September 26, 2013 order to the United States Court of Appeals for the Second Circuit. On November 1, 2013, following the expiration of the 30-day period to amend the complaint, defendants filed a motion for final judgment in District Court. Pursuant to an order issued by the Second Circuit, plaintiff-appellants' brief in the appeal of the District Court's decision is due no later than December 10, 2013 and defendant-appellees' brief is due no later than January 14, 2014.

The first putative stockholder derivative action, a consolidated action captioned In re Green Mountain Coffee Roasters, Inc. Derivative Litigation, Civ. No. 2:10-cv-00233, premised on the same allegations asserted in now-dismissed Horowitz v. Green Mountain Coffee Roasters, Inc., Civ. No. 2:10-cv-00227 securities class action complaint and the other pending putative securities class action complaints described above, is pending in the United States District Court for the District of Vermont before the Honorable William K. Sessions, III. On November 29, 2010, the federal court entered an order consolidating two actions and appointing the firms of Robbins Umeda LLP and Shuman Law Firm as co-lead plaintiffs' counsel. On February 23, 2011, the federal court approved a stipulation filed by the parties providing for a temporary stay of that action until the court rules on defendants' motions to dismiss the consolidated complaint in the Horowitz putative securities fraud class action. On March 7, 2012, the federal court approved a further joint stipulation continuing the temporary stay until the court either denies a motion to dismiss the Horowitz putative securities fraud class action or the Horowitz putative securities fraud class action is dismissed with prejudice. On April 27, 2012, the federal court entered an order consolidating the stockholder derivative action captioned Himmel v. Robert P. Stiller, et al., with two additional putative derivative actions, Musa Family Revocable Trust v. Robert P. Stiller, et al., Civ. No. 2:12-cv-00029, and Laborers Local 235 Benefit Funds v. Robert P. Stiller, et al., Civ. No. 2:12-cv- 00042. On November 14, 2012, the federal court entered an order consolidating an additional stockholder derivative action, captioned as Henry Cargo v. Robert P. Stiller, et al., Civ. No. 2:12-cv-00161, and granting plaintiffs leave to lift the stay for the limited purpose of filing a consolidated complaint. The consolidated complaint is asserted nominally on behalf of the Company against certain of its officers and directors. The consolidated complaint asserts claims for breach of fiduciary duty, waste of corporate assets, unjust enrichment, contribution, and indemnification and seeks compensatory damages, injunctive relief, restitution, disgorgement, attorney's fees, costs, and such other relief as the court should deem just and proper. On May 14, 2013, the court approved a joint stipulation filed by the parties providing for a temporary stay of the proceedings until the conclusion of the appeal in the Horowitz putative securities fraud class action. On August 1, 2013, the parties filed a further joint stipulation continuing the temporary stay until the court either denies a motion to dismiss the LAMPERS putative securities fraud class action or the LAMPERS putative securities fraud class action is dismissed with prejudice, which the court approved on August 2, 2013.

The second putative stockholder derivative action, M. Elizabeth Dickinson v. Robert P. Stiller, et al., Civ. No. 818-11-10, is pending in the Superior Court of the State of Vermont for Washington County. On February 28, 2011, the court approved a stipulation filed by the parties similarly providing for a temporary stay of that action until the federal court rules on defendants' motions to dismiss the consolidated complaint in the Horowitz putative securities fraud class action. As a result of the federal court's ruling in the Horowitz putative securities fraud class action, the temporary stay was lifted. On June 25, 2013, plaintiff filed an amended complaint in the action, which is asserted nominally on behalf of the Company against certain current and former directors and officers. The amended complaint is premised on the same allegations alleged in the Horowitz, LAMPERS, and Fifield putative securities fraud class actions. The amended complaint asserts claims for breach of fiduciary duty, unjust enrichment, waste of corporate assets, and alleged insider selling by certain of the named defendants. The amended complaint seeks compensatory damages, injunctive relief, restitution, disgorgement, attorneys' fees, costs, and such other relief as the court should deem just and proper. On August 7, 2013, the parties filed a further joint stipulation continuing the temporary stay until the court either denies a motion to dismiss the LAMPERS putative securities fraud class action or the LAMPERS putative securities fraud class action is dismissed with prejudice, which the court approved on August 21, 2013.

The Company and the other defendants intend to vigorously defend all the pending lawsuits. Additional lawsuits may be filed and, at this time, the Company is unable to predict the outcome of these lawsuits, the possible loss or range of loss, if any, associated with the resolution of these lawsuits or any potential effect they may have on the Company or its operations.

**20. Related Party Transactions**

The Company, from time to time, used travel services provided by Heritage Flight, a charter air services company acquired in September 2002 by Robert P. Stiller, who previously served on the Company's Board of Directors and who is a security holder of more than 5% of the Company's Common Stock. For fiscal years 2013, 2012, and 2011, the Company incurred expenses of $0.2 million, $0.7 million, and $0.7 million, respectively, for Heritage Flight travel services.

**21. Earnings Per Share**

The following table illustrates the reconciliation of the numerator and denominator of basic and diluted earnings per share computations (dollars in thousands, except share and per share data):

| | Fiscal 2013 | Fiscal 2012 | Fiscal 2011 |
|---|---|---|---|
| Numerator for basic and diluted earnings per share: | | | |
| Net income attributable to GMCR | $ 483,232 | $ 362,628 | $ 199,501 |
| Denominator: | | | |
| Basic weighted average shares outstanding | 149,638,636 | 154,933,948 | 146,214,860 |
| Effect of dilutive securities—stock options | 3,162,857 | 4,141,698 | 5,927,574 |
| Diluted weighted average shares outstanding | 152,801,493 | 159,075,646 | 152,142,434 |
| Basic net income per common share | $ 3.23 | $ 2.34 | $ 1.36 |
| Diluted net income per common share | $ 3.16 | $ 2.28 | $ 1.31 |

For the fiscal years 2013, 2012, and 2011, 822,000, 763,000, and 199,000 equity-based awards for shares of common stock, respectively, have been excluded in the calculation of diluted earnings per share because they were antidilutive.

## GREEN MOUNTAIN COFFEE ROASTERS, INC.

## NOTES TO CONSOLIDATED FINANCIAL STATEMENTS—(Continued)

**22. Unaudited Quarterly Financial Data**

The following table presents the quarterly information for fiscal 2013 (dollars in thousands, except per share data). Each fiscal quarter comprises 13 weeks.

| Fiscal 2013 | December 29, 2012 | March 30, 2013 | June 29, 2013 | September 28, 2013 |
|---|---|---|---|---|
| Net sales | $ 1,339,059 | $ 1,004,792 | $ 967,072 | $ 1,047,177 |
| Gross profit | $ 419,163 | $ 415,146 | $ 407,618 | $ 377,459 |
| Net income attributable to GMCR | $ 107,583 | $ 132,421 | $ 116,272 | $ 126,956 |
| Earnings per share: | | | | |
| Basic | $ 0.72 | $ 0.89 | $ 0.78 | $ 0.84 |
| Diluted | $ 0.70 | $ 0.87 | $ 0.76 | $ 0.83 |

The following table presents the quarterly information for fiscal 2012 (dollars in thousands, except per share data). Each fiscal quarter comprises 13 weeks, except the fiscal quarter ended September 29, 2012 which is comprised of 14 weeks.

| Fiscal 2012 | December 24, 2011 | March 24, 2012 | June 23, 2012 | September 29, 2012 |
|---|---|---|---|---|
| Net sales | $ 1,158,216 | $ 885,052 | $ 869,194 | $ 946,736 |
| Gross profit | $ 336,604 | $ 313,038 | $ 303,311 | $ 316,446 |
| Net income attributable to GMCR | $ 104,414 | $ 93,031 | $ 73,296 | $ 91,887 |
| Earnings per share: | | | | |
| Basic | $ 0.67 | $ 0.60 | $ 0.47 | $ 0.59 |
| Diluted | $ 0.66 | $ 0.58 | $ 0.46 | $ 0.58 |

The following table presents the quarterly information for fiscal 2011 (dollars in thousands, except per share data). Each fiscal quarter comprises 13 weeks.

| Fiscal 2011 | December 25, 2010 | March 26, 2011 | June 25, 2011 | September 24, 2011 |
|---|---|---|---|---|
| Net sales | $ 574,148 | $ 647,658 | $ 717,210 | $ 711,883 |
| Gross profit | $ 143,600 | $ 242,855 | $ 264,080 | $ 254,090 |
| Net income attributable to GMCR | $ 2,412 | $ 65,372 | $ 56,348 | $ 75,369 |
| Earnings per share: | | | | |
| Basic | $ 0.02 | $ 0.46 | $ 0.38 | $ 0.49 |
| Diluted | $ 0.02 | $ 0.44 | $ 0.37 | $ 0.47 |

**23. Subsequent Event**

On November 19, 2013, the Board of Directors declared the Company's first cash dividend of $0.25 per common share, payable on February 14, 2014 to shareholders of record at the close of business on January 17, 2014; and announced an indicated annual dividend of $1.00 per share (payable in $0.25 per quarter).

## SCHEDULE II—VALUATION AND QUALIFYING ACCOUNTS

### For the Fiscal Years Ended September 28, 2013, September 29, 2012, and September 24, 2011 (Dollars in thousands)

| Description | Balance at Beginning of Period | Acquisitions (Dispositions) | Charged to Costs and Expenses | Deductions | Balance at End of Period |
|---|---|---|---|---|---|
| Allowance for doubtful accounts: | | | | | |
| Fiscal 2013 | $ 2,750 | $ — | $ 689 | $ 553 | $ 2,886 |
| Fiscal 2012 | $ 3,404 | $ (299) | $ 3,197 | $ 3,552 | $ 2,750 |
| Fiscal 2011 | $ 1,314 | $ 1,115 | $ 2,584 | $ 1,609 | $ 3,404 |

| Description | Balance at Beginning of Period | Acquisitions (Dispositions) | Charged to Costs and Expenses | Deductions | Balance at End of Period |
|---|---|---|---|---|---|
| Sales returns reserve: | | | | | |
| Fiscal 2013 | $ 31,767 | $— | $ 79,747 | $ 80,760 | $ 30,754 |
| Fiscal 2012 | $ 18,302 | $— | $ 107,436 | $ 93,971 | $ 31,767 |
| Fiscal 2011 | $ 12,742 | $— | $ 64,457 | $ 58,897 | $ 18,302 |

| Description | Balance at Beginning of Period | Acquisitions (Dispositions) | Charged to Costs and Expenses | Deductions | Balance at End of Period |
|---|---|---|---|---|---|
| Warranty reserve(1): | | | | | |
| Fiscal 2013 | $ 20,218 | $— | $ 6,948 | $ 19,362 | $ 7,804 |
| Fiscal 2012 | $ 14,728 | $— | $ 37,390 | $ 31,900 | $ 20,218 |
| Fiscal 2011 | $ 6,694 | $— | $ 35,450 | $ 27,416 | $ 14,728 |

(1) Includes warranty recoveries from suppliers of $0.8 million and $8.3 for fiscal 2013 and 2012, respectively. There were no recoveries during fiscal 2011.

**Item 9. Changes in and Disagreements with Accountants on Accounting and Financial Disclosure**

None.

**Item 9A. Controls and Procedures**

*Evaluation of Disclosure Controls and Procedures*

During the fourth quarter of fiscal 2013, under the supervision of and with the participation of management, including our Chief Executive Officer and Chief Financial Officer, we conducted an evaluation of the effectiveness of the design and operation of our disclosure controls and procedures, as defined in Rules 13a-15(e) and 15d-15(e) of the Securities and Exchange Act of 1934, as amended (the "Exchange Act"). Based on this evaluation, our Chief Executive Officer and Chief Financial Officer have concluded that, as of September 28, 2013, our disclosure controls and procedures were effective to ensure that information required to be disclosed in the reports we file or submit under the Exchange Act was recorded, processed, summarized and reported within the time periods specified in the SEC's rules and forms, and were effective.

*Management's Report on Internal Control over Financial Reporting*

Management is responsible for establishing and maintaining adequate internal control over financial reporting, as defined in Rules 13a-15(f) and 15d-15(f) of the Exchange Act. Internal control over financial reporting is a process designed by, or under the supervision of, the issuer's principal executive and principal financial officers, or persons performing similar functions, and effected by issuer's board of directors, management and other personnel, to provide reasonable assurance regarding the reliability of its financial reporting and the preparation of its financial statements for external purposes in accordance with generally accepted accounting principles and includes those policies and procedures that:

- pertain to the maintenance of records that, in reasonable detail, accurately and fairly reflect the transactions and dispositions of the assets of the Company;
- provide reasonable assurance that transactions are recorded as necessary to permit preparation of financial statements in accordance with generally accepted accounting principles,
- provide reasonable assurance that receipts and expenditures of the Company are being made only in accordance with authorizations of management and directors of the Company; and
- provide reasonable assurance regarding prevention or timely detection of unauthorized acquisition, use, or disposition of the Company's assets that could have a material effect on the financial statements.

Because of its inherent limitations, internal control over financial reporting may not prevent or detect misstatements. Also, projections of any evaluation of effectiveness to future periods are subject to the risk that controls may become inadequate because of changes in conditions or that the degree of compliance with the policies or procedures may deteriorate.

Under the supervision of and with the participation of management, including the Chief Executive Officer and Chief Financial Officer, the Company conducted an evaluation of the effectiveness of its internal control over financial reporting based on the criteria in *Internal Control—Integrated Framework* (1992) issued by the Committee of Sponsoring Organizations of the Treadway Commission ("COSO"). Based upon that evaluation, management concluded we maintained effective internal controls over financial reporting as of September 28, 2013 based on the criteria established in *Internal Control— Integrated Framework* (1992) issued by the COSO.

The effectiveness of the Company's internal control over financial reporting as of September 28, 2013 has been audited by PricewaterhouseCoopers LLP, an independent registered public accounting firm, as stated in their report which appears herein.

*Changes in Internal Control over Financial Reporting*

There have been no changes in our internal control over financial reporting during the fiscal quarter ended September 28, 2013 that have materially affected, or are reasonably likely to materially affect, our internal control over financial reporting.

**Item 9B. Other Information**

None.

# Appendix B

## Present Value Tables

**Table B-1** | **Present Value of $1**

| Periods | Present Value 1% | 2% | 3% | 4% | 5% | 6% | 7% | 8% | 9% | 10% | 12% | 14% | 15% | 16% | 18% | 20% |
|---|---|---|---|---|---|---|---|---|---|---|---|---|---|---|---|---|
| 1 | 0.990 | 0.980 | 0.971 | 0.962 | 0.952 | 0.943 | 0.935 | 0.926 | 0.917 | 0.909 | 0.893 | 0.877 | 0.870 | 0.862 | 0.847 | 0.833 |
| 2 | 0.980 | 0.961 | 0.943 | 0.925 | 0.907 | 0.890 | 0.873 | 0.857 | 0.842 | 0.826 | 0.797 | 0.769 | 0.756 | 0.743 | 0.718 | 0.694 |
| 3 | 0.971 | 0.942 | 0.915 | 0.889 | 0.864 | 0.840 | 0.816 | 0.794 | 0.772 | 0.751 | 0.712 | 0.675 | 0.658 | 0.641 | 0.609 | 0.579 |
| 4 | 0.961 | 0.924 | 0.888 | 0.855 | 0.823 | 0.792 | 0.763 | 0.735 | 0.708 | 0.683 | 0.636 | 0.592 | 0.572 | 0.552 | 0.516 | 0.482 |
| 5 | 0.951 | 0.906 | 0.863 | 0.822 | 0.784 | 0.747 | 0.713 | 0.681 | 0.650 | 0.621 | 0.567 | 0.519 | 0.497 | 0.476 | 0.437 | 0.402 |
| 6 | 0.942 | 0.888 | 0.837 | 0.790 | 0.746 | 0.705 | 0.666 | 0.630 | 0.596 | 0.564 | 0.507 | 0.456 | 0.432 | 0.410 | 0.370 | 0.335 |
| 7 | 0.933 | 0.871 | 0.813 | 0.760 | 0.711 | 0.665 | 0.623 | 0.583 | 0.547 | 0.513 | 0.452 | 0.400 | 0.376 | 0.354 | 0.314 | 0.279 |
| 8 | 0.923 | 0.853 | 0.789 | 0.731 | 0.677 | 0.627 | 0.582 | 0.540 | 0.502 | 0.467 | 0.404 | 0.351 | 0.327 | 0.305 | 0.266 | 0.233 |
| 9 | 0.914 | 0.837 | 0.766 | 0.703 | 0.645 | 0.592 | 0.544 | 0.500 | 0.460 | 0.424 | 0.361 | 0.308 | 0.284 | 0.263 | 0.225 | 0.194 |
| 10 | 0.905 | 0.820 | 0.744 | 0.676 | 0.614 | 0.558 | 0.508 | 0.463 | 0.422 | 0.386 | 0.322 | 0.270 | 0.247 | 0.227 | 0.191 | 0.162 |
| 11 | 0.896 | 0.804 | 0.722 | 0.650 | 0.585 | 0.527 | 0.475 | 0.429 | 0.388 | 0.350 | 0.287 | 0.237 | 0.215 | 0.195 | 0.162 | 0.135 |
| 12 | 0.887 | 0.788 | 0.701 | 0.625 | 0.557 | 0.497 | 0.444 | 0.397 | 0.356 | 0.319 | 0.257 | 0.208 | 0.187 | 0.168 | 0.137 | 0.112 |
| 13 | 0.879 | 0.773 | 0.681 | 0.601 | 0.530 | 0.469 | 0.415 | 0.368 | 0.326 | 0.290 | 0.229 | 0.182 | 0.163 | 0.145 | 0.116 | 0.093 |
| 14 | 0.870 | 0.758 | 0.661 | 0.577 | 0.505 | 0.442 | 0.388 | 0.340 | 0.299 | 0.263 | 0.205 | 0.160 | 0.141 | 0.125 | 0.099 | 0.078 |
| 15 | 0.861 | 0.743 | 0.642 | 0.555 | 0.481 | 0.417 | 0.362 | 0.315 | 0.275 | 0.239 | 0.183 | 0.140 | 0.123 | 0.108 | 0.084 | 0.065 |
| 16 | 0.853 | 0.728 | 0.623 | 0.534 | 0.458 | 0.394 | 0.339 | 0.292 | 0.252 | 0.218 | 0.163 | 0.123 | 0.107 | 0.093 | 0.071 | 0.054 |
| 17 | 0.844 | 0.714 | 0.605 | 0.513 | 0.436 | 0.371 | 0.317 | 0.270 | 0.231 | 0.198 | 0.146 | 0.108 | 0.093 | 0.080 | 0.060 | 0.045 |
| 18 | 0.836 | 0.700 | 0.587 | 0.494 | 0.416 | 0.350 | 0.296 | 0.250 | 0.212 | 0.180 | 0.130 | 0.095 | 0.081 | 0.069 | 0.051 | 0.038 |
| 19 | 0.828 | 0.686 | 0.570 | 0.475 | 0.396 | 0.331 | 0.277 | 0.232 | 0.194 | 0.164 | 0.116 | 0.083 | 0.070 | 0.060 | 0.043 | 0.031 |
| 20 | 0.820 | 0.673 | 0.554 | 0.456 | 0.377 | 0.312 | 0.258 | 0.215 | 0.178 | 0.149 | 0.104 | 0.073 | 0.061 | 0.051 | 0.037 | 0.026 |
| 21 | 0.811 | 0.660 | 0.538 | 0.439 | 0.359 | 0.294 | 0.242 | 0.199 | 0.164 | 0.135 | 0.093 | 0.064 | 0.053 | 0.044 | 0.031 | 0.022 |
| 22 | 0.803 | 0.647 | 0.522 | 0.422 | 0.342 | 0.278 | 0.226 | 0.184 | 0.150 | 0.123 | 0.083 | 0.056 | 0.046 | 0.038 | 0.026 | 0.018 |
| 23 | 0.795 | 0.634 | 0.507 | 0.406 | 0.326 | 0.262 | 0.211 | 0.170 | 0.138 | 0.112 | 0.074 | 0.049 | 0.040 | 0.033 | 0.022 | 0.015 |
| 24 | 0.788 | 0.622 | 0.492 | 0.390 | 0.310 | 0.247 | 0.197 | 0.158 | 0.126 | 0.102 | 0.066 | 0.043 | 0.035 | 0.028 | 0.019 | 0.013 |
| 25 | 0.780 | 0.610 | 0.478 | 0.375 | 0.295 | 0.233 | 0.184 | 0.146 | 0.116 | 0.092 | 0.059 | 0.038 | 0.030 | 0.024 | 0.016 | 0.010 |
| 26 | 0.772 | 0.598 | 0.464 | 0.361 | 0.281 | 0.220 | 0.172 | 0.135 | 0.106 | 0.084 | 0.053 | 0.033 | 0.026 | 0.021 | 0.014 | 0.009 |
| 27 | 0.764 | 0.586 | 0.450 | 0.347 | 0.268 | 0.207 | 0.161 | 0.125 | 0.098 | 0.076 | 0.047 | 0.029 | 0.023 | 0.018 | 0.011 | 0.007 |
| 28 | 0.757 | 0.574 | 0.437 | 0.333 | 0.255 | 0.196 | 0.150 | 0.116 | 0.090 | 0.069 | 0.042 | 0.026 | 0.020 | 0.016 | 0.010 | 0.006 |
| 29 | 0.749 | 0.563 | 0.424 | 0.321 | 0.243 | 0.185 | 0.141 | 0.107 | 0.082 | 0.063 | 0.037 | 0.022 | 0.017 | 0.014 | 0.008 | 0.005 |
| 30 | 0.742 | 0.552 | 0.412 | 0.308 | 0.231 | 0.174 | 0.131 | 0.099 | 0.075 | 0.057 | 0.033 | 0.020 | 0.015 | 0.012 | 0.007 | 0.004 |
| 40 | 0.672 | 0.453 | 0.307 | 0.208 | 0.142 | 0.097 | 0.067 | 0.046 | 0.032 | 0.022 | 0.011 | 0.005 | 0.004 | 0.003 | 0.001 | 0.001 |
| 50 | 0.608 | 0.372 | 0.228 | 0.141 | 0.087 | 0.054 | 0.034 | 0.021 | 0.013 | 0.009 | 0.003 | 0.001 | 0.001 | 0.001 | | |

**Table B-2** | **Present Value of Ordinary Annuity of $1**

| | Present Value | | | | | | | | | | | | | | | |
|---|---|---|---|---|---|---|---|---|---|---|---|---|---|---|---|---|
| **Periods** | **1%** | **2%** | **3%** | **4%** | **5%** | **6%** | **7%** | **8%** | **9%** | **10%** | **12%** | **14%** | **15%** | **16%** | **18%** | **20%** |
| 1 | 0.990 | 0.980 | 0.971 | 0.962 | 0.952 | 0.943 | 0.935 | 0.926 | 0.917 | 0.909 | 0.893 | 0.877 | 0.870 | 0.862 | 0.847 | 0.833 |
| 2 | 1.970 | 1.942 | 1.913 | 1.886 | 1.859 | 1.833 | 1.808 | 1.783 | 1.759 | 1.736 | 1.690 | 1.647 | 1.626 | 1.605 | 1.566 | 1.528 |
| 3 | 2.941 | 2.884 | 2.829 | 2.775 | 2.723 | 2.673 | 2.624 | 2.577 | 2.531 | 2.487 | 2.402 | 2.322 | 2.283 | 2.246 | 2.174 | 2.106 |
| 4 | 3.902 | 3.808 | 3.717 | 3.630 | 3.546 | 3.465 | 3.387 | 3.312 | 3.240 | 3.170 | 3.037 | 2.914 | 2.855 | 2.798 | 2.690 | 2.589 |
| 5 | 4.853 | 4.713 | 4.580 | 4.452 | 4.329 | 4.212 | 4.100 | 3.993 | 3.890 | 3.791 | 3.605 | 3.433 | 3.352 | 3.274 | 3.127 | 2.991 |
| 6 | 5.795 | 5.601 | 5.417 | 5.242 | 5.076 | 4.917 | 4.767 | 4.623 | 4.486 | 4.355 | 4.111 | 3.889 | 3.784 | 3.685 | 3.498 | 3.326 |
| 7 | 6.728 | 6.472 | 6.230 | 6.002 | 5.786 | 5.582 | 5.389 | 5.206 | 5.033 | 4.868 | 4.564 | 4.288 | 4.160 | 4.039 | 3.812 | 3.605 |
| 8 | 7.652 | 7.325 | 7.020 | 6.733 | 6.463 | 6.210 | 5.971 | 5.747 | 5.535 | 5.335 | 4.968 | 4.639 | 4.487 | 4.344 | 4.078 | 3.837 |
| 9 | 8.566 | 8.162 | 7.786 | 7.435 | 7.108 | 6.802 | 6.515 | 6.247 | 5.995 | 5.759 | 5.328 | 4.946 | 4.772 | 4.607 | 4.303 | 4.031 |
| 10 | 9.471 | 8.983 | 8.530 | 8.111 | 7.722 | 7.360 | 7.024 | 6.710 | 6.418 | 6.145 | 5.650 | 5.216 | 5.019 | 4.833 | 4.494 | 4.192 |
| 11 | 10.368 | 9.787 | 9.253 | 8.760 | 8.306 | 7.887 | 7.499 | 7.139 | 6.805 | 6.495 | 5.938 | 5.453 | 5.234 | 5.029 | 4.656 | 4.327 |
| 12 | 11.255 | 10.575 | 9.954 | 9.385 | 8.863 | 8.384 | 7.943 | 7.536 | 7.161 | 6.814 | 6.194 | 5.660 | 5.421 | 5.197 | 4.793 | 4.439 |
| 13 | 12.134 | 11.348 | 10.635 | 9.986 | 9.394 | 8.853 | 8.358 | 7.904 | 7.487 | 7.103 | 6.424 | 5.842 | 5.583 | 5.342 | 4.910 | 4.533 |
| 14 | 13.004 | 12.106 | 11.296 | 10.563 | 9.899 | 9.295 | 8.745 | 8.244 | 7.786 | 7.367 | 6.628 | 6.002 | 5.724 | 5.468 | 5.008 | 4.611 |
| 15 | 13.865 | 12.849 | 11.938 | 11.118 | 10.380 | 9.712 | 9.108 | 8.559 | 8.061 | 7.606 | 6.811 | 6.142 | 5.847 | 5.575 | 5.092 | 4.675 |
| 16 | 14.718 | 13.578 | 12.561 | 11.652 | 10.838 | 10.106 | 9.447 | 8.851 | 8.313 | 7.824 | 6.974 | 6.265 | 5.954 | 5.668 | 5.162 | 4.730 |
| 17 | 15.562 | 14.292 | 13.166 | 12.166 | 11.274 | 10.477 | 9.763 | 9.122 | 8.544 | 8.022 | 7.120 | 6.373 | 6.047 | 5.749 | 5.222 | 4.775 |
| 18 | 16.398 | 14.992 | 13.754 | 12.659 | 11.690 | 10.828 | 10.059 | 9.372 | 8.756 | 8.201 | 7.250 | 6.467 | 6.128 | 5.818 | 5.273 | 4.812 |
| 19 | 17.226 | 15.678 | 14.324 | 13.134 | 12.085 | 11.158 | 10.336 | 9.604 | 8.950 | 8.365 | 7.366 | 6.550 | 6.198 | 5.877 | 5.316 | 4.843 |
| 20 | 18.046 | 16.351 | 14.877 | 13.590 | 12.462 | 11.470 | 10.594 | 9.818 | 9.129 | 8.514 | 7.469 | 6.623 | 6.259 | 5.929 | 5.353 | 4.870 |
| 21 | 18.857 | 17.011 | 15.415 | 14.029 | 12.821 | 11.764 | 10.836 | 10.017 | 9.292 | 8.649 | 7.562 | 6.687 | 6.312 | 5.973 | 5.384 | 4.891 |
| 22 | 19.660 | 17.658 | 15.937 | 14.451 | 13.163 | 12.042 | 11.061 | 10.201 | 9.442 | 8.772 | 7.645 | 6.743 | 6.359 | 6.011 | 5.410 | 4.909 |
| 23 | 20.456 | 18.292 | 16.444 | 14.857 | 13.489 | 12.303 | 11.272 | 10.371 | 9.580 | 8.883 | 7.718 | 6.792 | 6.399 | 6.044 | 5.432 | 4.925 |
| 24 | 21.243 | 18.914 | 16.936 | 15.247 | 13.799 | 12.550 | 11.469 | 10.529 | 9.707 | 8.985 | 7.784 | 6.835 | 6.434 | 6.073 | 5.451 | 4.937 |
| 25 | 22.023 | 19.523 | 17.413 | 15.622 | 14.094 | 12.783 | 11.654 | 10.675 | 9.823 | 9.077 | 7.843 | 6.873 | 6.464 | 6.097 | 5.467 | 4.948 |
| 26 | 22.795 | 20.121 | 17.877 | 15.983 | 14.375 | 13.003 | 11.826 | 10.810 | 9.929 | 9.161 | 7.896 | 6.906 | 6.491 | 6.118 | 5.480 | 4.956 |
| 27 | 23.560 | 20.707 | 18.327 | 16.330 | 14.643 | 13.211 | 11.987 | 10.935 | 10.027 | 9.237 | 7.943 | 6.935 | 6.514 | 6.136 | 5.492 | 4.964 |
| 28 | 24.316 | 21.281 | 18.764 | 16.663 | 14.898 | 13.406 | 12.137 | 11.051 | 10.116 | 9.307 | 7.984 | 6.961 | 6.534 | 6.152 | 5.502 | 4.970 |
| 29 | 25.066 | 21.844 | 19.188 | 16.984 | 15.141 | 13.591 | 12.278 | 11.158 | 10.198 | 9.370 | 8.022 | 6.983 | 6.551 | 6.166 | 5.510 | 4.975 |
| 30 | 25.808 | 22.396 | 19.600 | 17.292 | 15.372 | 13.765 | 12.409 | 11.258 | 10.274 | 9.427 | 8.055 | 7.003 | 6.566 | 6.177 | 5.517 | 4.979 |
| 40 | 32.835 | 27.355 | 23.115 | 19.793 | 17.159 | 15.046 | 13.332 | 11.925 | 10.757 | 9.779 | 8.244 | 7.105 | 6.642 | 6.233 | 5.548 | 4.997 |
| 50 | 39.196 | 31.424 | 25.730 | 21.482 | 18.256 | 15.762 | 13.801 | 12.233 | 10.962 | 9.915 | 8.304 | 7.133 | 6.661 | 6.246 | 5.554 | 4.999 |

# Appendix C
# Accounting Information Systems

## What Should I Do with All This Paperwork?

Sara Faraday stared at the stack of papers on her desk. It was early January, and her accountant had called to remind her that she needed to submit the business's accounting information so that the tax return could be prepared. Sara is a stockholder and manager of a successful gourmet kitchen store that sells specialty food and kitchen products and also offers cooking classes and workshops. Sara loves interacting with her customers, whether she's helping them find the perfect kitchen product or teaching them a new technique. What she doesn't like about her business is the overwhelming amount of paperwork required to keep the business records. When she first started her business, she kept track of sales to customers and bills paid in a notebook. Now, though, her business has grown so much that it is no longer efficient to keep track of her accounting records in this manner.

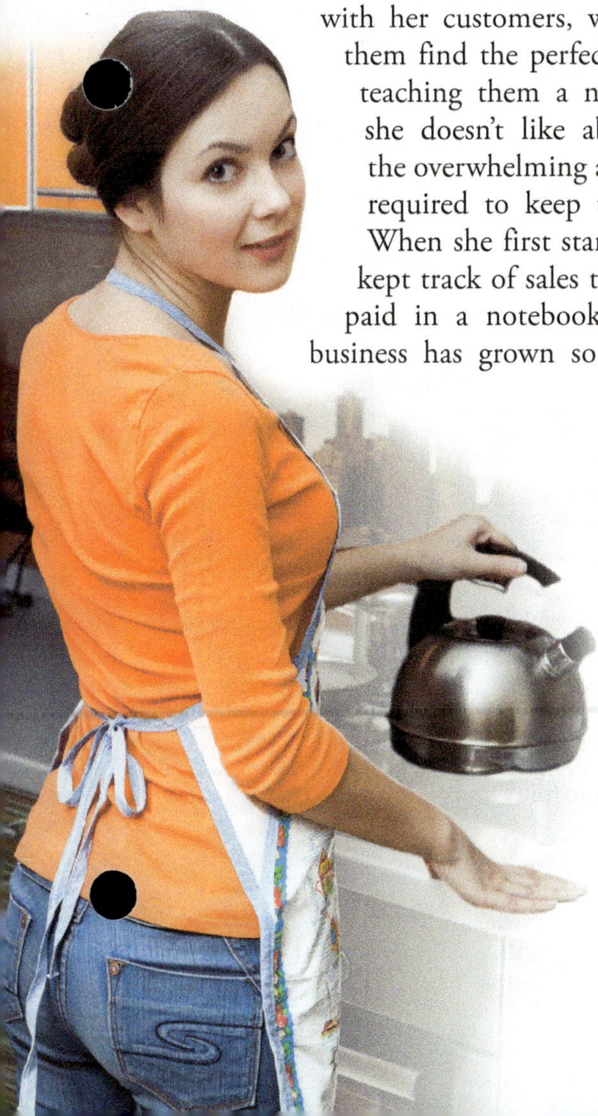

Sara is considering asking her accountant to help her set up a more efficient accounting information system. She wants a system that will save her time and make the recordkeeping process easier. In addition, she would like to find a way to record all of her transactions on the computer so that her business's information is easily accessible. Sara also wants a system that will produce reports, such as financial statements, that can help her make business decisions. She knows that there has to be an easier way to record the transactions than what she is currently doing.

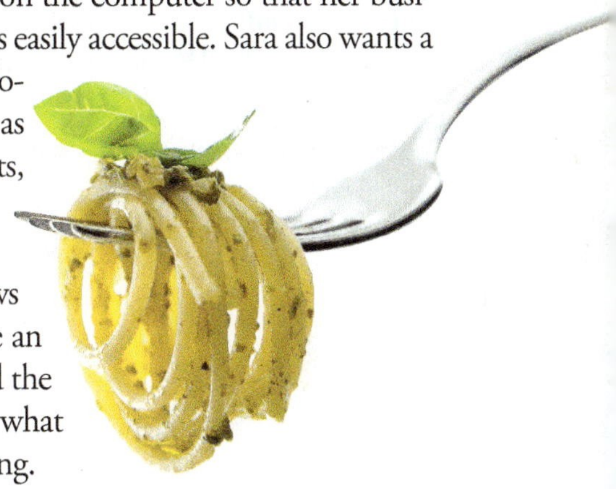

### Is There a More Efficient Way?

Before the advent of computers, businesses had to handle all of their accounting transactions manually—that is, one journal entry at a time using paper and pencil. As computer technology progressed, more and more accounting information was processed using an automated system. Now, most businesses use some form of computerized accounting software. It might be a very basic system that handles only accounting information, or it might be a very advanced system that stores not only accounting information, but also information about human resources, production, and customer services. For example, Dave's Gourmet, Inc. started with a desire to create the world's hottest hot sauce, but as the business grew into the multinational company that it is today, the business had to find a way to keep track of all of the business's accounting information. Dave's Gourmet uses a specialized computerized system that integrates all of its lines of business. In this appendix, we explore how accounting information systems, such as the one that Dave's Gourmet uses, can help a business run more efficiently and effectively.

# Appendix C Learning Objectives

1 Describe an effective accounting information system

2 Journalize and post sales and cash receipts in a manual accounting information system using special journals and subsidiary ledgers

3 Journalize and post purchases, cash payments, and other transactions in a manual accounting information system using special journals and subsidiary ledgers

4 Describe how transactions are recorded in a computerized accounting information system

## WHAT IS AN ACCOUNTING INFORMATION SYSTEM?

**Learning Objective 1**
Describe an effective accounting information system

**Accounting Information System (AIS)**
A system that collects, records, stores, and processes accounting data to produce information that is useful for decision makers.

An **accounting information system (AIS)** collects, records, stores, and processes accounting data to produce information that is useful for decision makers. Businesses must have a way to collect and store data for a large number of transactions and then use those data to produce reports that investors and management can use to make decisions. Exhibit C-1 shows examples of business transactions and activities that are completed when using an accounting information system.

**Exhibit C-1 | Business Transactions and AIS Activities**

| Business Transactions | AIS Activities |
|---|---|
| **Sell merchandise inventory** | Receipt of customer order<br>Approval of credit sale<br>Check availability of merchandise inventory<br>Shipment of inventory to customer<br>Processing of sales invoice<br>Receipt of customer payment |
| **Purchase of goods or services** | Request for purchase of goods or services<br>Approval of vendor<br>Receipt of goods or services<br>Processing of vendor invoice<br>Payment for goods or services |
| **Payroll** | Approval of new employees<br>Collection of time records<br>Preparation and payment of payroll<br>Preparation and payment of payroll taxes |

### Effective Accounting Information Systems

An effective accounting information system provides the following:

- Control
- Compatibility
- Flexibility
- Relevance
- Positive cost/benefit relationship

### Control

An accounting information system must provide adequate controls of the business's assets and data. Internal controls can safeguard a business's assets and reduce the likelihood of fraud and errors. For example, a business needs procedures for making cash payments. An accounting information system creates the structure to encourage adherence to management procedures.

### Compatibility

A compatible system works smoothly with the business's employees and organizational structure. A small business doesn't need a big accounting information system. It could probably do accounting with an entry-level software package such as QuickBooks or Sage 50™ Accounting (formerly called Peachtree). But a large company needs a different system—one that can manage multiple branches and track revenues and expenses in all divisions of the business.

### Flexibility

An accounting information system must be flexible to accommodate changes in a business over time. Businesses might start selling some new products, or they might expand to new locations. This will require a more complicated accounting information system.

### Relevance

An effective accounting information system provides information that is relevant. In other words, it improves decision making and reduces uncertainty. The information produced must be useful to the business in achieving its overall goals.

### Positive Cost/Benefit Relationship

Control, compatibility, flexibility, and relevance can be expensive. A business needs a system that gives the most benefit for the least cost. A relatively inexpensive system, such as QuickBooks, may be the most economical way for a business to do its accounting. Or it may be necessary for a business to invest a large amount of cash in a more complicated system. In addition, the business must consider the cost of training employees to use the system and time spent on entering data into the system. The business must invest only in an accounting information system in which the benefits received outweigh the cost of the system.

An accounting information system can be either manual (completed using paper and pencil) or computerized. All the previously discussed features are needed whether the accounting information system is computerized or manual.

## Components of an Accounting Information System

An accounting information system has three basic components:

- Source documents and input devices
- Processing and storage
- Outputs

### Source Documents and Input Devices

All data must come from **source documents**, which provide the evidence for accounting transactions. Examples of source documents include purchase invoices, bank checks, and sales invoices. Many businesses have paper source documents that require employees to transfer data from the paper source document into the accounting information system. This can be done either by data entry procedures using a keyboard and computer or by using computerized scanning equipment.

**Source Document**
Provides the evidence and data for accounting transactions.

Most businesses now are using computerized accounting information systems to create electronic source documents and capture the data in electronic format. Examples include an electronic invoice and an electronic receiving report.

Source documents also provide control and reliability in an accounting information system. Standardized source documents that require specific data to be input ensure that each transaction is recorded accurately and completely. In addition, prenumbered source documents provide necessary control in a system by automatically assigning a sequential number to each new transaction.

## Processing and Storage

Once data has been input into the system, it must be processed. In a manual accounting information system, processing includes journalizing transactions and posting to the accounts. A computerized system, on the other hand, uses software to process transactions. This software reads and edits transaction data. It allows businesses to process transactions without actually requiring employees to journalize and post to the accounts.

A business's data must also be stored. In a manual system, data are contained in paper documents that are often stored in filing cabinets and off-site document warehouses. Computerized systems now allow businesses to keep data on a main computer, called a **server**, that often allows employees to access information from anywhere in the world. The protection and security of a business's data have become increasingly important. Businesses must be aware of threats to their data such as hacking (unauthorized access) and malware (viruses and spyware). Companies are spending increasingly large amounts of cash to ensure that their data and information are secure.

**Server**
The main computer where data are stored, which can be accessed from many different computers.

## Outputs

Outputs are the reports used for decision making, including the financial statements. In a manual system, reports and financial statements must be created using Word documents, Excel spreadsheets, PowerPoint presentations, or other software applications. In a computerized system, the accounting software can generate reports instantaneously that can be easily manipulated and used to make business decisions.

**DECISIONS**

### How safe are customer data?

Ian Woods had recently been hired as the chief information officer for a start-up Internet-based retail store—ShopUs.com. His main job duties included responsibility for the information technology and computer systems of the business. Ian was reviewing the security of customer data and realized that customer service representatives had access to all customer data including credit card information and billing addresses. What should Ian do?

### Solution

The breach of customer data is a key threat to a business. Not only does a business have to be concerned about employees accessing customer data, but there is also a risk that unauthorized individuals outside of the business might hack into the system to obtain customer information. Ian should evaluate whether customer service representatives should have access to all customer data. It might be possible to encrypt some of the data and allow only managers to have access. In addition, Ian should set up guidelines and procedures for how data should be stored and protected. He should also review the federal and state regulations regarding the security of credit card and personal information to ensure that ShopUs.com is in compliance. Network surveillance, encryption, and software security procedures will all reduce the risk of data breach and abuse.

## Try It!

Match the benefit of an effective accounting information system with the definition.

| Benefit | Definition |
|---|---|
| 1. Control | a. Works smoothly with the business's employees and organization structure |
| 2. Relevance | b. Can accommodate changes in the business over time |
| 3. Flexibility | c. Provides safeguards for a business's assets and reduces the likelihood of fraud and errors |
| 4. Compatibility | d. Benefits received outweigh the cost of the system |
| 5. Positive cost/benefit relationship | e. Provides information that will improve decision making and reduce uncertainty |

**Check your answers online in MyAccountingLab or at http://www.pearsonhighered.com/Horngren.**

For more practice, see Short Exercises SC-1 and SC-2. MyAccountingLab

# HOW ARE SALES AND CASH RECEIPTS RECORDED IN A MANUAL ACCOUNTING INFORMATION SYSTEM?

**Learning Objective 2**
Journalize and post sales and cash receipts in a manual accounting information system using special journals and subsidiary ledgers

We will begin by reviewing how transactions are recorded in a manual accounting information system. You may be wondering why we cover manual accounting information systems when many businesses have computerized systems. There are three main reasons:

1. Learning a manual system equips you to work with both manual and computerized systems. The accounting is the same regardless of the system.
2. Few small businesses have computerized all their accounting. Even companies that use QuickBooks or Sage 50 Accounting, two popular entry-level accounting information systems, keep some manual accounting records.
3. Learning a manual system helps you master accounting.

## Special Journals

In a manual system, transactions are classified by type. It is inefficient to record all transactions in the general journal, so businesses use special journals. A **special journal** is an accounting journal designed to record a specific type of transaction. Sales on account, cash receipts, purchases on account, and cash payments are treated as four separate categories and, therefore, create the four special journals. For example:

**Special Journal**
An accounting journal designed to record one specific type of transaction.

- Sales on account are recorded in a *sales journal*.
- Cash receipts are recorded in a *cash receipts journal*.
- Purchases of inventory and other assets on account are recorded in a *purchases journal*.
- Cash payments are recorded in a *cash payments journal*.
- Transactions that do not fit in any of the special journals, such as adjusting entries, are recorded in the *general journal*, which serves as the "journal of last resort."

The five types of transactions, the related journal, and the posting abbreviations used in a manual system are summarized in Exhibit C-2.

**Exhibit C-2** | **Manual Accounting Information System**

| Transaction | Journal | Posting Abbreviation |
|---|---|---|
| Sale on account | Sales journal | S |
| Cash receipt | Cash receipts journal | CR |
| Purchase on account | Purchases journal | P |
| Cash payment | Cash payments journal | CP |
| All others | General journal | J |

## Subsidiary Ledgers

**Subsidiary Ledger**
Record of accounts that provides supporting details on individual balances, the total of which appears in a general ledger account.

**Accounts Receivable Subsidiary Ledger**
A subsidiary ledger that includes an accounts receivable account for each customer that contains detailed information such as the amount sold, received, and owed.

In addition to special journals, an accounting information system also uses subsidiary ledgers. A **subsidiary ledger** holds individual accounts that support a general ledger account. There are two common subsidiary ledgers: accounts receivable subsidiary ledger and accounts payable subsidiary ledger.

### Accounts Receivable Subsidiary Ledger

The **accounts receivable subsidiary ledger** includes a receivable account for each customer. The customer name and account balance is detailed in the subsidiary ledger. In addition, the subsidiary ledger contains detailed information such as the amount sold, received, and still due for each customer. The total of the accounts in the accounts receivable subsidiary ledger must equal the Accounts Receivable balance in the general ledger. This is demonstrated in Exhibit C-3. The Accounts Receivable balance of $4,319 in the general ledger equals the sum of the accounts in the accounts receivable subsidiary ledger ($935 + $907 + $694 + $1,783).

**Exhibit C-3** | **Accounts Receivable Subsidiary Ledger**

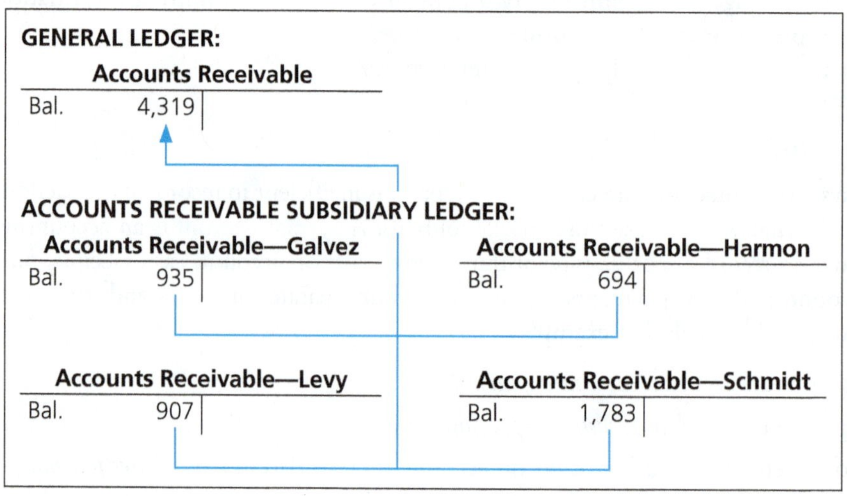

The Accounts Receivable account in the general ledger is called a **control account**. A control account's balance equals the sum of the balances of the accounts in a subsidiary ledger.

**Control Account**
An account whose balance equals the sum of the balances in a group of related accounts in a subsidiary ledger.

### Accounts Payable Subsidiary Ledger

To pay debts on time, a company must know how much it owes each supplier. Accounts Payable in the general ledger shows only a single total for the amount owed on account. It does not indicate the amount owed to each vendor. Companies keep an accounts payable subsidiary ledger that is similar to the accounts receivable subsidiary ledger.

The **accounts payable subsidiary ledger** lists vendors in alphabetical order, along with amounts paid to the vendors and the remaining amounts owed to them. The total of the individual balances in the subsidiary ledger equals the Accounts Payable (control account) balance in the general ledger.

**Accounts Payable Subsidiary Ledger**
A subsidiary ledger that includes an accounts payable account for each vendor that contains detailed information such as the amount purchased, paid, and owed.

*Don't confuse the terms customers and vendors. Remember that a company sells to customers and purchases from vendors.*

## The Sales Journal

Most merchandisers sell merchandise inventory on account. These credit sales are entered in the **sales journal**. The sales journal is used when recording the sale of merchandise inventory *on account.* The sale of merchandise inventory for cash is not recorded in the sales journal, but instead, it is recorded in the cash receipts journal. In addition, credit sales of assets other than merchandise inventory—for example, buildings—occur infrequently and are not recorded in the sales journal. They are, instead, recorded in the general journal.

**Sales Journal**
Special journal used to record credit sales.

### Recording Transactions

Exhibit C-4 illustrates a sales journal (Panel A) and the related posting to the ledgers (Panel B). When a business completes a sale, the accountant enters the following information in the sales journal:

- Date
- Invoice number
- Customer name
- Transaction amount

**Exhibit C-4** | **Sales Journal with Posting**

**PANEL A—Sales Journal:**

| Sales Journal | | | | | Page 3 |
|---|---|---|---|---|---|
| Date | Invoice No. | Customer Account Debited | Post. Ref. | Accounts Receivable DR Sales Revenue CR | Cost of Goods Sold DR Merchandise Inventory CR |
| 2016 | | | | | |
| Nov. 2 | 422 | Maria Galvez | ✓ | 935 | 505 |
| 13 | 423 | Brent Harmon | ✓ | 694 | 361 |
| 18 | 424 | Susan Levy | ✓ | 907 | 517 |
| 27 | 425 | Clay Schmidt | ✓ | 1,783 | 431 |
| Nov. 30 | | Total | | 4,319 | 1,814 |
| | | | | (115/410) | (511/131) |

Individual accounts receivable are posted daily.

Totals are posted at the end of the month.

Totals are posted at the end of the month.

**PANEL B—Posting to the Ledgers:**

**Accounts Receivable Subsidiary Ledger**

| Maria Galvez | | | | | |
|---|---|---|---|---|---|
| | | | | Balance | |
| Date | Post. Ref. | Debit | Credit | Debit | Credit |
| Nov. 2 | S.3 | 935 | | 935 | |

| Brent Harmon | | | | | |
|---|---|---|---|---|---|
| | | | | Balance | |
| Date | Post. Ref. | Debit | Credit | Debit | Credit |
| Nov. 13 | S.3 | 694 | | 694 | |

| Susan Levy | | | | | |
|---|---|---|---|---|---|
| | | | | Balance | |
| Date | Post. Ref. | Debit | Credit | Debit | Credit |
| Nov. 18 | S.3 | 907 | | 907 | |

| Clay Schmidt | | | | | |
|---|---|---|---|---|---|
| | | | | Balance | |
| Date | Post. Ref. | Debit | Credit | Debit | Credit |
| Nov. 27 | S.3 | 1,783 | | 1,783 | |

**General Ledger**

| Accounts Receivable | | | | | No. 115 |
|---|---|---|---|---|---|
| | | | | Balance | |
| Date | Post. Ref. | Debit | Credit | Debit | Credit |
| Nov. 30 | S.3 | 4,319 | | 4,319 | |

| Merchandise Inventory | | | | | No. 131 |
|---|---|---|---|---|---|
| | | | | Balance | |
| Date | Post. Ref. | Debit | Credit | Debit | Credit |
| Nov. 1 | Bal. | | | 3,885 | |
| 30 | S.3 | | 1,814 | 2,071 | |

| Sales Revenue | | | | | No. 410 |
|---|---|---|---|---|---|
| | | | | Balance | |
| Date | Post. Ref. | Debit | Credit | Debit | Credit |
| Nov. 30 | S.3 | | 4,319 | | 4,319 |

| Costs of Goods Sold | | | | | No. 511 |
|---|---|---|---|---|---|
| | | | | Balance | |
| Date | Post. Ref. | Debit | Credit | Debit | Credit |
| Nov. 30 | S.3 | 1,814 | | 1,814 | |

Consider the first transaction in Panel A. On November 2, the business sold merchandise inventory on account to Maria Galvez for $935 with a cost of $505. The invoice number is 422. In Chapter 5, you learned that this transaction was recorded as follows when using the general journal:

| Date | Accounts and Explanation | Debit | Credit |
|---|---|---|---|
| Nov. 2 | Accounts Receivable | 935 | |
| | Sales Revenue | | 935 |
| | *Sale on account.* | | |
| 2 | Cost of Goods Sold | 505 | |
| | Merchandise Inventory | | 505 |
| | *Recorded the cost of goods sold.* | | |

A↑ = L + E↑
Accounts Receivable↑ = Sales Revenue↑

A↓ = L + E↓
Merchandise Inventory↓ = Cost of Goods Sold↑

When using special journals, instead of recording this transaction in the general journal, the business records the transaction in the sales journal. All of the information related to the sale appears on a single line in the sales journal as follows:

**Sales Journal** — Page 3

| Date | Invoice No. | Customer Account Debited | Post. Ref. | Accounts Receivable DR Sales Revenue CR | Cost of Goods Sold DR Merchandise Inventory CR |
|---|---|---|---|---|---|
| 2016 | | | | | |
| Nov. 2 | 422 | Maria Galvez | | 935 | 505 |

The Post. Ref. column is not used until the transaction is posted.

This part of the journal records the sales revenue and associated receivable.

This part of the journal records the expense and the reduction of merchandise inventory.

The entry records the sales revenue and associated accounts receivable by entering the amount of the sale, $935, in the Accounts Receivable DR, Sales Revenue CR column. The entry also records the expense of the sale and the reduction of merchandise inventory by recording the cost of the sale, $505, in the Cost of Goods Sold DR, Merchandise Inventory CR column. By using a sales journal, the recording of sales is streamlined, thus saving a significant amount of time.

*It's important to remember that a transaction is recorded in either the general journal or a special journal, but not in both. We are illustrating the general journal entry as a teaching tool to help you understand how the entry is recorded in the special journal. Transactions are not recorded in both journals. To do so would be to record the entry twice.*

This business, like most other companies, uses a perpetual inventory system. Throughout this appendix, we illustrate the perpetual inventory system. When recording a sale, the business must record the Cost of Goods Sold and the decrease in Merchandise Inventory. If the business, instead, used a periodic inventory system, the sales journal would not need the last column (Cost of Goods Sold DR, Merchandise Inventory CR) because there is no entry recorded to Cost of Goods Sold and Merchandise Inventory at the time of the sale.

In the sales journal that we are using in this example, there are only two columns used for dollar amounts. One column records the sales revenue and accounts receivable, and the other column records the expense of the sale. Businesses that collect sales tax would need to modify the sales journal shown to include an additional column for Sales Taxes Payable. The modified sales journal would have the following headings:

| Sales Journal | | | | | | | Page 3 |
|---|---|---|---|---|---|---|---|
| Date | Invoice No. | Customer Account Debited | Post. Ref. | Accounts Receivable DR | Sales Taxes Payable CR | Sales Revenue CR | Cost of Goods Sold DR Merchandise Inventory CR |
| | | | | | | | |

Each business will modify its sales journal to fit the types of sales it makes. Remember, though, that only sales on account are recorded in the sales journal.

### Posting

Entries in the sales journal are posted to both the accounts receivable subsidiary ledger and the general ledger.

**Posting to the Accounts Receivable Subsidiary Ledger** Individual accounts receivable are posted daily from the sales journal to the accounts receivable subsidiary ledger. For example, on November 2, the accountant posts the $935 receivable to the individual accounts receivable for Maria Galvez. The sales journal is posted daily to the subsidiary ledger to keep a current record of the amount receivable from each customer.

After posting to the subsidiary ledger, the accountant enters a check mark in the posting reference column of the sales journal (see Exhibit C-4). That lets the business know that the transaction was posted to Galvez's account.

**Posting to the General Ledger** At the end of the month, the accountant totals (commonly called *footing*) the Accounts Receivable DR, Sales Revenue CR, and Cost of Goods Sold DR, Merchandise Inventory CR columns. The totals of these columns are posted from the sales journal to the general ledger.

In Exhibit C-4 (Panel A), November's credit sales total $4,319. The $4,319 is posted to the Accounts Receivable and Sales Revenue accounts in the general ledger. The account numbers of each account are then printed beneath the total in the sales journal. In Panel B of Exhibit C-4, the account number for Accounts Receivable is 115 and the account number for Sales Revenue is 410. Entering these account numbers in the sales journal shows that the $4,319 has been posted to the two accounts.

The debit to Cost of Goods Sold and the credit to Merchandise Inventory for the monthly total of $1,814 are also posted at the end of the month. After posting, these accounts' numbers are entered beneath the total to show that Cost of Goods Sold and Merchandise Inventory have been updated.

As the accountant posts to the ledgers, the journal page number and journal name abbreviation are entered in the ledger account to show the source of the data. All transaction data in Exhibit C-4 originated on page 3 of the sales journal, so all posting references are S.3. "S" indicates sales journal. After posting, the Accounts Receivable balance in the general ledger should equal the sum of the individual customer balances in the subsidiary ledger.

Trace all the postings in Exhibit C-4. The way to learn an accounting information system is to study the flow of data. The arrows indicate the direction of the information.

## The Cash Receipts Journal

**Cash Receipts Journal** Special journal used to record cash receipts.

All businesses have lots of cash transactions, and therefore a **cash receipts journal** comes in handy. The cash receipts journal is a special journal that is used to record cash receipts.

Exhibit C-5 illustrates the cash receipts journal. Every transaction recorded in this journal is a cash receipt.

## Exhibit C-5 | Cash Receipts Journal with Posting

**PANEL A—Cash Receipts Journal:**

**Cash Receipts Journal** — Page 5

| Date | Account Credited | Post Ref. | Cash DR | Sales Discounts DR | Accounts Receivable CR | Sales Revenue CR | Other Accounts CR | Cost of Goods Sold DR Merchandise Inventory CR |
|---|---|---|---|---|---|---|---|---|
| 2016 | | | | | | | | |
| Nov. 6 | | | 517 | | | 517 | | 290 |
| 11 | Note Payable to First Bank | 221 | 1,000 | | | | 1,000 | |
| 14 | Maria Galvez | ✓ | 900 | 35 | 935 | | | |
| 19 | | | 853 | | | 853 | | 426 |
| 22 | Brent Harmon | ✓ | 300 | | 300 | | | |
| 25 | Interest Revenue | 460 | 762 | | | | 762 | |
| 28 | | | 1,802 | | | 1,802 | | 991 |
| Nov. 30 | Totals | | 6,134 | 35 | 1,235 | 3,172 | 1,762 | 1,707 |
| | | | (101) | (420) | (115) | (410) | (X) | (511/131) |

Totals are posted at the end of the month.

Individual accounts receivable are posted daily.

Total is not posted.

Total is posted at the end of the month.

Individual amounts are posted at the end of the month.

**PANEL B—Posting to the Ledgers:**

**Accounts Receivable Subsidiary Ledger**

**Maria Galvez**

| Date | Post. Ref. | Debit | Credit | Balance Debit | Balance Credit |
|---|---|---|---|---|---|
| Nov. 2 | S.3 | 935 | | 935 | |
| 14 | CR.5 | | 935 | 0 | |

**Brent Harmon**

| Date | Post. Ref. | Debit | Credit | Balance Debit | Balance Credit |
|---|---|---|---|---|---|
| Nov. 13 | S.3 | 694 | | 694 | |
| 22 | CR.5 | | 300 | 394 | |

**Susan Levy**

| Date | Post. Ref. | Debit | Credit | Balance Debit | Balance Credit |
|---|---|---|---|---|---|
| Nov. 18 | S.3 | 907 | | 907 | |

**Clay Schmidt**

| Date | Post. Ref. | Debit | Credit | Balance Debit | Balance Credit |
|---|---|---|---|---|---|
| Nov. 27 | S.3 | 1,783 | | 1,783 | |

**General Ledger**

**Cash** — No. 101

| Date | Post. Ref. | Debit | Credit | Balance Debit | Balance Credit |
|---|---|---|---|---|---|
| Nov. 30 | CR.5 | 6,134 | | 6,134 | |

**Accounts Receivable** — No. 115

| Date | Post. Ref. | Debit | Credit | Balance Debit | Balance Credit |
|---|---|---|---|---|---|
| Nov. 30 | S.3 | 4,319 | | 4,319 | |
| 30 | CR.5 | | 1,235 | 3,084 | |

**Merchandise Inventory** — No. 131

| Date | Post. Ref. | Debit | Credit | Balance Debit | Balance Credit |
|---|---|---|---|---|---|
| Nov. 1 | Bal. | | | 3,885 | |
| 30 | S.3 | | 1,814 | 2,071 | |
| 30 | CR.5 | | 1,707 | 364 | |

**Note Payable to First Bank** — No. 221

| Date | Post. Ref. | Debit | Credit | Balance Debit | Balance Credit |
|---|---|---|---|---|---|
| Nov. 11 | CR.5 | | 1,000 | | 1,000 |

**Sales Revenue** — No. 410

| Date | Post. Ref. | Debit | Credit | Balance Debit | Balance Credit |
|---|---|---|---|---|---|
| Nov. 30 | S.3 | | 4,319 | | 4,319 |
| 30 | CR.5 | | 3,172 | | 7,491 |

**Sales Discounts** — No. 420

| Date | Post. Ref. | Debit | Credit | Balance Debit | Balance Credit |
|---|---|---|---|---|---|
| Nov. 30 | CR.5 | 35 | | 35 | |

**Interest Revenue** — No. 460

| Date | Post. Ref. | Debit | Credit | Balance Debit | Balance Credit |
|---|---|---|---|---|---|
| Nov. 25 | CR.5 | | 762 | | 762 |

**Cost of Goods Sold** — No. 511

| Date | Post. Ref. | Debit | Credit | Balance Debit | Balance Credit |
|---|---|---|---|---|---|
| Nov. 30 | S.3 | 1,814 | | 1,814 | |
| 30 | CR.5 | 1,707 | | 3,521 | |

The cash receipts journal includes a column for debits to Cash. The next column is for debits to Sales Discounts. The main sources of cash are collections on account and cash sales. Collections on account are recorded in the Accounts Receivable CR column and the Cash DR column. Cash sales are recorded in the Sales Revenue CR column, the Cash DR column, and Cost of Goods Sold DR, Merchandise Inventory CR column. The cash receipts journal also has an Other Accounts CR column that is used to record miscellaneous cash receipt transactions.

## Recording Transactions

In Exhibit C-5, the first cash receipt occurred on November 6 and was a cash sale for $517 (cost of goods sold, $290). If the transaction had been recorded in the general journal, the following entries would have been recorded:

| A↑ | | L | + | E↑ |
|---|---|---|---|---|
| Cash↑ | = | | | Sales Revenue↑ |

| A↓ | | L | + | E↓ |
|---|---|---|---|---|
| Merchandise Inventory↓ | = | | | Cost of Goods Sold↑ |

| Date | Accounts and Explanation | Debit | Credit |
|---|---|---|---|
| Nov. 6 | Cash | 517 | |
| | Sales Revenue | | 517 |
| | *Cash sale.* | | |
| 6 | Cost of Goods Sold | 290 | |
| | Merchandise Inventory | | 290 |
| | *Recorded the cost of goods sold.* | | |

By recording the transaction in the cash receipts journal instead, the entries can be recorded on one line. Observe the debit to Cash and the credit to Sales Revenue ($517) and the debit to Cost of Goods Sold and credit to Merchandise Inventory ($290) for the cost of the merchandise sold.

On November 11, the business borrowed $1,000 from First Bank. If the transaction had been recorded in the general journal, the following entry would have been made:

| A↑ | | L↑ | + | E |
|---|---|---|---|---|
| Cash↑ | = | Notes Payable↑ | | |

| Date | Accounts and Explanation | Debit | Credit |
|---|---|---|---|
| Nov. 11 | Cash | 1,000 | |
| | Note Payable to First Bank | | 1,000 |
| | *Received cash in exchange for note.* | | |

By recording it in the cash receipts journal instead, the accountant would record the $1,000 in the Cash DR column. The Other Accounts CR column is used for the Notes Payable credit because there is no specific credit column for borrowings. For this transaction, the account title, Note Payable to First Bank, is entered in the Account Credited column. The Other Accounts CR column is used when a transaction involves a credit entry that is not listed in the headings (columns) of the cash receipts journal. The entry on November 25 is another example. On November 25, the business received $762 cash of interest revenue. The cash receipts journal does not include a column for credits to interest revenue; therefore, the Other Accounts CR column must be used and the credit account must be written in the Account Credited column.

On November 14, the business collected $900 from Maria Galvez. Back on November 2, the business sold $935 of merchandise to Galvez and recorded the sale in the sales journal. This credit sale allowed a $35 discount for prompt payment, and Galvez paid within the discount period. The business records this cash receipt in the cash receipts journal by debiting Cash for $900 and Sales Discounts for $35 and by crediting Accounts Receivable for $935. The customer's name appears in the Account Credited column.

## Posting

As with the sales journal, entries in the cash receipts journal are posted daily to the accounts receivable subsidiary ledger and monthly to the general ledger.

**Posting to the Accounts Receivable Subsidiary Ledger** Amounts from the cash receipts journal are posted to the accounts receivable subsidiary ledger daily. The postings are credits. Trace the $935 credit to Maria Galvez's account. It reduces her balance to zero. The $300 receipt from Brent Harmon reduces his balance to $394. After posting, the accountant enters a check mark in the posting reference column of the cash receipts journal and shows the CR.5 posting reference in the subsidiary ledger. CR.5 signifies that the posting is transferred from the cash receipts journal, page 5.

*The posting reference CR.5 should not be confused with the abbreviation for credit, CR. The posting reference for the cash receipts journal always includes a page reference while the abbreviation for credit does not.*

**Posting to the General Ledger** At the end of the month, each column in the cash receipts journal is totaled. The equality of the debits and credits is verified by comparing the sum of all debit columns to the sum of all credit columns.

| Debit Columns | | Credit Columns | |
|---|---|---|---|
| Cash | $ 6,134 | Accounts Receivable | $ 1,235 |
| Sales Discounts | 35 | Sales Revenue | 3,172 |
| Cost of Goods Sold | 1,707 | Other Accounts | 1,762 |
| | | Merchandise Inventory | 1,707 |
| Total | $ 7,876 | | $ 7,876 |

All columns, except for the Other Accounts CR column, are posted in total to the general ledger. For example, the total for Cash ($6,134) is posted as a debit in the Cash account in the general ledger. After posting, the account number is printed below the column total in the cash receipts journal. The account number for Cash (101) appears below the column total, and likewise for the other column totals. The journal reference (CR) and page number (5) are shown in the general ledger as reference of the posting. Follow the arrows in Exhibit C-5, which track the posted amounts.

The column total for *Other Accounts* CR is *not* posted. Instead, these credits are posted individually. In Exhibit C-5, the November 11 transaction reads "Note Payable to First Bank." This $1,000 credit entry will need to be posted individually to the Note Payable to First Bank account in the general ledger. The account number (221) in the Post. Ref. column shows that the transaction amount was posted individually. The letter X below the column means that the column total was *not* posted.

After posting, the sum of the individual balances in the accounts receivable subsidiary ledger equals the balance of Accounts Receivable in the general ledger, as follows:

| GENERAL LEDGER | |
|---|---|
| Accounts Receivable debit balance | $ 3,084 |
| **SUBSIDIARY LEDGER: CUSTOMER ACCOUNTS RECEIVABLE** | |
| **Customer** | **Balance** |
| Maria Galvez | $ 0 |
| Brent Harmon | 394 |
| Susan Levy | 907 |
| Clay Schmidt | 1,783 |
| Total Accounts Receivable | $ 3,084 |

**These should be equal.**

## Try It!

6. Evenson Co. sold merchandise inventory on account to Brain Crain, $300. The cost of the goods sold was $240. What special journal should the transaction be recorded in, and what is the column used for the $300?

**Check your answer online in MyAccountingLab or at http://www.pearsonhighered.com/Horngren.**

For more practice, see Short Exercises SC-3 through SC-7. MyAccountingLab

# HOW ARE PURCHASES, CASH PAYMENTS, AND OTHER TRANSACTIONS RECORDED IN A MANUAL ACCOUNTING INFORMATION SYSTEM?

**Learning Objective 3**

Journalize and post purchases, cash payments, and other transactions in a manual accounting information system using special journals and subsidiary ledgers

In the previous section, you learned that when using a manual accounting information system, sales on account are recorded in the sales journal and cash receipts are recorded in the cash receipts journal. We now turn our attention to purchases and cash payments.

## The Purchases Journal

**Purchases Journal**

Special journal used to record all purchases of merchandise inventory, office supplies, and other assets on account.

A merchandising business purchases merchandise inventory and other items, such as office supplies, equipment, and furniture, on account. The **purchases journal** handles these transactions plus other purchases incurred *on account.* Cash purchases are not recorded in the purchases journal; instead, they are recorded in the cash payments journal.

Exhibit C-6 illustrates a purchases journal (Panel A) and posting to the ledgers (Panel B). The purchases journal has special columns for:

- Credits to Accounts Payable
- Debits to Merchandise Inventory, Office Supplies, and Other Accounts

The Other Accounts DR columns are used for purchases on account of items other than merchandise inventory and office supplies. This business uses a perpetual inventory system. In a periodic inventory system, the Merchandise Inventory DR column would be replaced with a column titled Purchases DR.

## Exhibit C-6 | Purchases Journal with Posting

**PANEL A—Purchases Journal:**

**Purchases Journal** — Page 8

| | | | | | | | Other Accounts DR | | |
|---|---|---|---|---|---|---|---|---|---|
| Date | Vendor Account Credited | Terms | Post. Ref. | Accounts Payable CR | Merchandise Inventory DR | Office Supplies DR | Account Title | Post. Ref. | Amount |
| 2016 | | | | | | | | | |
| Nov. 2 | Hanes Textiles | 3/15, n/30 | ✓ | 700 | 700 | | | | |
| 5 | Pioneer Plastics | n/30 | ✓ | 319 | 319 | | | | |
| 9 | City Office Supply | 2/10, n/30 | ✓ | 440 | | | Equipment | 191 | 440 |
| 12 | Advanced Printing | n/30 | ✓ | 236 | 236 | | | | |
| 13 | Hanes Textiles | 3/15, n/30 | ✓ | 451 | 451 | | | | |
| 19 | City Office Supply | 2/10, n/30 | ✓ | 103 | | 103 | | | |
| 23 | O'Leary Furniture | n/60 | ✓ | 627 | | | Furniture | 181 | 627 |
| Nov. 30 | Totals | | | 2,876 | 1,706 | 103 | | | 1,067 |
| | | | | (210) | (131) | (161) | | | (X) |

Individual accounts payable are posted daily.

Totals are posted at the end of the month.

Total is not posted.

Individual amounts are posted at the end of the month.

**PANEL B—Posting to the Ledgers:**

**Accounts Payable Subsidiary Ledger**

**Advanced Printing**

| | | | | Balance | |
|---|---|---|---|---|---|
| Date | Post. Ref. | Debit | Credit | Debit | Credit |
| Nov. 12 | P.8 | | 236 | | 236 |

**City Office Supply**

| | | | | Balance | |
|---|---|---|---|---|---|
| Date | Post. Ref. | Debit | Credit | Debit | Credit |
| Nov. 9 | P.8 | | 440 | | 440 |
| 19 | P.8 | | 103 | | 543 |

**Hanes Textiles**

| | | | | Balance | |
|---|---|---|---|---|---|
| Date | Post. Ref. | Debit | Credit | Debit | Credit |
| Nov. 2 | P.8 | | 700 | | 700 |
| 13 | P.8 | | 451 | | 1,151 |

**O'Leary Furniture**

| | | | | Balance | |
|---|---|---|---|---|---|
| Date | Post. Ref. | Debit | Credit | Debit | Credit |
| Nov. 23 | P.8 | | 627 | | 627 |

**Pioneer Plastics**

| | | | | Balance | |
|---|---|---|---|---|---|
| Date | Post. Ref. | Debit | Credit | Debit | Credit |
| Nov. 5 | P.8 | | 319 | | 319 |

**General Ledger**

**Merchandise Inventory** — No. 131

| | | | | Balance | |
|---|---|---|---|---|---|
| Date | Post. Ref. | Debit | Credit | Debit | Credit |
| Nov. 1 | Bal. | | | 3,885 | |
| 30 | S.3 | | 1,814 | 2,071 | |
| 30 | CR.5 | | 1,707 | 364 | |
| 30 | P.8 | 1,706 | | 2,070 | |

**Office Supplies** — No. 161

| | | | | Balance | |
|---|---|---|---|---|---|
| Date | Post. Ref. | Debit | Credit | Debit | Credit |
| Nov. 30 | P.8 | 103 | | 103 | |

**Furniture** — No. 181

| | | | | Balance | |
|---|---|---|---|---|---|
| Date | Post. Ref. | Debit | Credit | Debit | Credit |
| Nov. 23 | P.8 | 627 | | 627 | |

**Equipment** — No. 191

| | | | | Balance | |
|---|---|---|---|---|---|
| Date | Post. Ref. | Debit | Credit | Debit | Credit |
| Nov. 9 | P.8 | 440 | | 440 | |

**Accounts Payable** — No. 210

| | | | | Balance | |
|---|---|---|---|---|---|
| Date | Post. Ref. | Debit | Credit | Debit | Credit |
| Nov. 30 | P.8 | | 2,876 | | 2,876 |

## Recording Transactions

Let's begin by looking at the first transaction. On November 2, the business purchased merchandise inventory costing $700 from Hanes Textiles. If the transaction had been recorded in the general journal, the following entry would have been recorded:

| A↑ | | L↑ | + | E |
|---|---|---|---|---|
| Merchandise Inventory↑ | = | Accounts Payable↑ | | |

| Date | Accounts and Explanation | Debit | Credit |
|---|---|---|---|
| Nov. 2 | Merchandise Inventory | 700 | |
| | Accounts Payable | | 700 |
| | *Purchased inventory on account.* | | |

By recording the entry in the purchases journal, the transaction can be recorded on one line. The vendor's name (Hanes Textiles) is entered in the Vendor Account Credited column. The purchase terms of 3/15, n/30 are also entered to show the due date and the discount available. Accounts Payable is credited for the transaction amount, and Merchandise Inventory is debited.

Note the November 9 purchase of equipment from City Office Supply. The purchases journal holds no column for equipment, so the business uses the Other Accounts DR columns. Because this was a credit purchase, the accountant enters the vendor name (City Office Supply) in the Vendor Account Credited column and Equipment in the Account Title column.

## Posting

Entries from the purchases journal are posted daily to the accounts payable subsidiary ledger and monthly to the general ledger.

**Accounts Payable Subsidiary Ledger** Individual accounts payable are posted daily from the purchases journal to the accounts payable subsidiary ledger. This allows the business to always have a current record of the accounts payable for each vendor. For example, on November 2, the business would post the $700 accounts payable credit to the Hanes Textiles account in the accounts payable subsidiary ledger. After posting, the accountant enters a check mark in the posting reference column of the purchases journal to indicate that the amount was posted in the subsidiary ledger. In addition, the posting reference (P.8) is printed in the subsidiary ledger.

**Posting to the General Ledger** Posting from the purchases journal is similar to posting from the other special journals. Exhibit C-6, Panel B, illustrates the posting process. At the end of each month, each column in the journal is totaled. All totals, except the Other Accounts DR Amount column, are posted to the general ledger. For example, the $2,876 Accounts Payable CR total is posted to the Accounts Payable account in the general ledger as a credit. After posted, the account number is listed in the purchases journal and the posting reference is listed in the general ledger. The column total for Other Accounts DR Amount is *not* posted. Instead, these debits are posted individually to the specific accounts, as done in the cash receipts journal. After all posting is complete, the Accounts Payable balance in the general ledger should equal the sum of the individual vendor balances in the subsidiary ledger.

# The Cash Payments Journal

**Cash Payments Journal**
Special journal used to record cash payments by check and currency.

Businesses make most cash payments by check, and all checks (and payments of currency) are recorded in the **cash payments journal**. This special journal is also called the *check register* and the *cash disbursements journal*. Exhibit C-7 shows the cash payments journal, with the ledgers in Panel B.

## Exhibit C-7 | Cash Payments Journal with Posting

**PANEL A–Cash Payments Journal:**

**Cash Payments Journal** — Page 6

| Date | Ck. No. | Account Debited | Post. Ref. | Other Accounts DR | Accounts Payable DR | Merchandise Inventory CR | Cash CR |
|---|---|---|---|---|---|---|---|
| 2016 | | | | | | | |
| Nov. 3 | 101 | Rent Expense | 541 | 1,200 | | | 1,200 |
| 8 | 102 | Office Supplies | 161 | 61 | | | 61 |
| 15 | 103 | Hanes Textiles | ✓ | | 700 | 21 | 679 |
| 20 | 104 | Pioneer Plastics | ✓ | | 119 | | 119 |
| 26 | 105 | Merchandise Inventory | 131 | 2,200 | | | 2,200 |
| Nov. 30 | | Totals | | 3,461 | 819 | 21 | 4,259 |
| | | | | (X) | (210) | (131) | (101) |

Total is not posted.

Totals are posted at the end of the month.

Individual accounts payable are posted daily.

Individual accounts are posted at the end of the month.

**PANEL B–Posting to the Ledgers:**

**Accounts Payable Subsidiary Ledger**

**Advanced Printing**

| Date | Post. Ref. | Debit | Credit | Balance Debit | Balance Credit |
|---|---|---|---|---|---|
| Nov. 12 | P.8 | | 236 | | 236 |

**City Office Supply**

| Date | Post. Ref. | Debit | Credit | Balance Debit | Balance Credit |
|---|---|---|---|---|---|
| Nov. 9 | P.8 | | 440 | | 440 |
| 19 | P.8 | | 103 | | 543 |

**Hanes Textiles**

| Date | Post. Ref. | Debit | Credit | Balance Debit | Balance Credit |
|---|---|---|---|---|---|
| Nov. 2 | P.8 | | 700 | | 700 |
| 13 | P.8 | | 451 | | 1,151 |
| 15 | CP.6 | 700 | | | 451 |

**O'Leary Furniture Co.**

| Date | Post. Ref. | Debit | Credit | Balance Debit | Balance Credit |
|---|---|---|---|---|---|
| Nov. 23 | P.8 | | 627 | | 627 |

**Pioneer Plastics**

| Date | Post. Ref. | Debit | Credit | Balance Debit | Balance Credit |
|---|---|---|---|---|---|
| Nov. 5 | P.8 | | 319 | | 319 |
| 20 | CP.6 | 119 | | | 200 |

**General Ledger**

**Cash** — No. 101

| Date | Post. Ref. | Debit | Credit | Balance Debit | Balance Credit |
|---|---|---|---|---|---|
| Nov. 30 | CR. 5 | 6,134 | | 6,134 | |
| 30 | CP. 6 | | 4,259 | 1,875 | |

**Merchandise Inventory** — No. 131

| Date | Post. Ref. | Debit | Credit | Balance Debit | Balance Credit |
|---|---|---|---|---|---|
| Nov. 1 | Bal. | | | 3,885 | |
| 26 | CP.6 | 2,200 | | 6,085 | |
| 30 | S.3 | | 1,814 | 4,271 | |
| 30 | CR.5 | | 1,707 | 2,564 | |
| 30 | P.8 | 1,706 | | 4,270 | |
| 30 | CP.6 | | 21 | 4,249 | |

**Office Supplies** — No. 161

| Date | Post. Ref. | Debit | Credit | Balance Debit | Balance Credit |
|---|---|---|---|---|---|
| Nov. 8 | CP.6 | 61 | | 61 | |
| 30 | P.8 | 103 | | 164 | |

**Accounts Payable** — No. 210

| Date | Post. Ref. | Debit | Credit | Balance Debit | Balance Credit |
|---|---|---|---|---|---|
| Nov. 30 | P.8 | | 2,876 | | 2,876 |
| 30 | CP.6 | 819 | | | 2,057 |

**Rent Expense** — No. 541

| Date | Post. Ref. | Debit | Credit | Balance Debit | Balance Credit |
|---|---|---|---|---|---|
| Nov. 3 | CP.6 | 1,200 | | 1,200 | |

The cash payments journal has two debit columns—one for Other Accounts and one for Accounts Payable. It has two credit columns—one for Merchandise Inventory (for purchase discounts) and one for Cash. This special journal also has columns for the date and check number of each cash payment and the account debited.

## Recording Transactions

Let's review the first transaction listed in the cash payments journal. On November 3, the business paid cash of $1,200 for rent. This payment of cash is recorded in the cash payments journal by entering $1,200 in the Cash CR column and the Other Accounts DR column. The Other Accounts DR column is used to record debits to accounts for which no special column exists. The business enters the name of the other account used, Rent Expense, in the Account Debited column. The Other Accounts DR column was also used on November 8 for the purchase of office supplies for cash and on November 26 for the purchase of Merchandise Inventory with cash.

On November 15, the business paid the vendor, Hanes Textiles, on account, with credit terms of 3/15, n/30 (for details, see the first transaction in the purchases journal, Exhibit C-6). Paying within the discount period allowed a 3% discount ($21), and the business paid the remaining $679 ($700 less the $21 discount). If the business had recorded the transaction in the general journal, the following would have been recorded:

| A↓ | = | L↓ | + | E |
|---|---|---|---|---|
| Cash↓<br>Merchandise Inventory↓ | | Accounts Payable↓ | | |

| Date | Accounts and Explanation | Debit | Credit |
|---|---|---|---|
| Nov. 15 | Accounts Payable | 700 | |
| | Cash | | 679 |
| | Merchandise Inventory | | 21 |
| | *Paid within discount period.* | | |

Instead, the business will record the transaction in the cash payments journal. The entry will be recorded by entering the $679 in the Cash CR column. The Accounts Payable DR column will be recorded for $700, and the discount of $21 will be entered into the Merchandise Inventory CR column. All transactions involving cash payments are recorded in the cash payments journal.

## Posting

Entries in the cash payments journal are posted daily to the accounts payable subsidiary ledger and monthly to the general ledger.

**Posting to the Accounts Payable Subsidiary Ledger** Posting from the cash payments journal is similar to posting from the cash receipts journal. Individual vendor amounts (accounts payable) are posted daily to the accounts payable subsidiary ledger. The postings are debits and reduce the balance in the individual accounts payable account. Trace the $700 payment to Hanes Textiles. The $700 reduces the balance in the Hanes's subsidiary account to $451. After posting, a check mark is entered in the cash payments journal and the posting reference (CP.6) is printed in the subsidiary ledger.

**Posting to the General Ledger** At the end of the month, each column is totaled. The totals, except for the Other Accounts DR column, are posted to the specific general ledger accounts. After posting, the account number is printed below the column total in the cash payments journal and the posting reference is printed in the general ledger.

Amounts in the Other Accounts DR column are posted individually (for example, Rent Expense—debit $1,200). When each Other Account DR is posted to the general ledger, the account number is printed in the Post. Ref. column. The letter X below the column signifies that the total is *not* posted.

To review accounts payable, companies list individual vendor balances in the accounts payable subsidiary ledger. The general ledger and subsidiary ledger totals should agree.

| GENERAL LEDGER | |
|---|---|
| Accounts Payable credit balance | $ 2,057 |
| **SUBSIDIARY LEDGER: ACCOUNTS PAYABLE** | |
| **Vendor** | **Balance** |
| Advanced Printing | $ 236 |
| City Office Supply | 543 |
| Hanes Textiles | 451 |
| O'Leary Furniture Co. | 627 |
| Pioneer Plastics | 200 |
| Total Accounts Payable | $ 2,057 |

**These should be equal.**

## The General Journal

Special journals save time recording repetitive transactions. But some transactions don't fit a special journal. Examples include the adjusting entries for depreciation, the expiration of prepaid insurance, and the accrual of salaries payable at the end of the period. Companies also use the general journal for sales returns and allowances and purchase returns and allowances. All accounting information systems need a general journal. The adjusting entries and the closing entries are recorded in the general journal, along with other nonroutine transactions.

As we have seen, a manual accounting information system involves five journals: sales journal, cash receipts journal, purchases journal, cash payments journal, and the general journal. It's important to remember that transactions are recorded in either one of the special journals or in the general journal, but not both. Exhibit C-8 (on the next page) provides a summary of all five journals that will help you decide which journal to use when recording transactions in a manual system.

**Exhibit C-8** | **Recording Transactions in Special Journals**

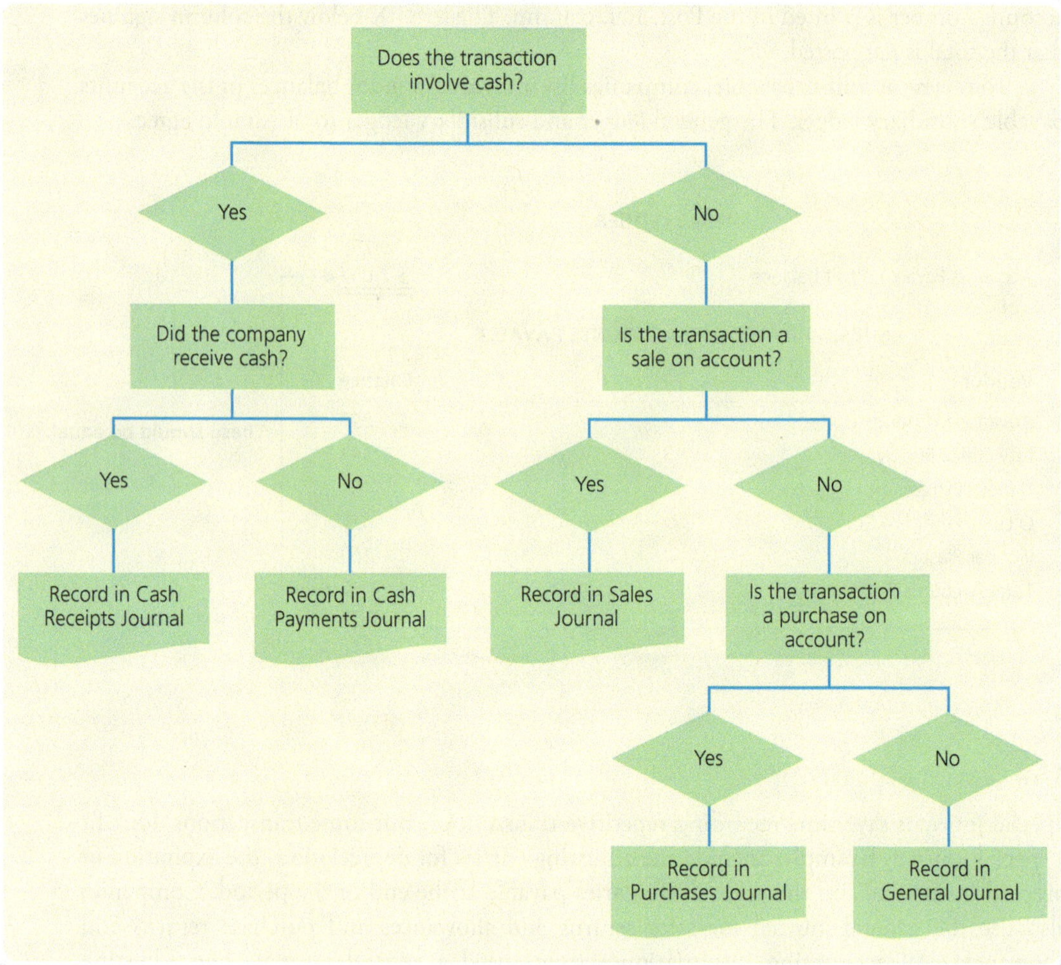


## Try It!

7. Fiscella Co. paid monthly rent of $2,000. What special journal should the transaction be recorded in? What columns will be used?

**Check your answer online in MyAccountingLab or at http://www.pearson.highered.com/Horngren.**

For more practice, see Short Exercises SC-8 through SC-12. MyAccountingLab

# HOW ARE TRANSACTIONS RECORDED IN A COMPUTERIZED ACCOUNTING INFORMATION SYSTEM?

**Learning Objective 4**
Describe how transactions are recorded in a computerized accounting information system

A computerized accounting information system has two basic components:

- Hardware
- Software

**Hardware** is the electronic equipment: computers, monitors, printers, and the network that connects them. Most systems require a **network** to link computers. In a networked system, the server stores the program and the data.

**Software** is the set of programs that drives the computer. Accounting software reads, edits, and stores transaction data. It also generates the reports that businesses can use to make decisions. Many software packages are flexible. For example, a small cleaning business may be only partly computerized. This small business may use the computer for employee payrolls, but other parts of the accounting information system may be manual.

**Hardware**
Electronic equipment that includes computers, monitors, printers, and the network that connects them.

**Network**
The system of electronic linkages that allows different computers to share the same information.

**Software**
Set of programs or instructions that drives the computer to perform the work desired.

## Entry-Level Software

With increased availability of affordable computerized accounting information systems, more and more businesses are completing all of their accounting on the computer. Two popular entry-level software packages are QuickBooks and Sage 50 Accounting. Both of these programs allow businesses to enter sales of services and merchandise inventory. In addition, these programs can record expenses and produce reports such as financial statements. These computerized accounting information systems are relatively easy to use, often requiring little knowledge of accounting or GAAP. Computerized accounting software allows businesses to organize finances, track sales and expenses, and complete recordkeeping. QuickBooks and Sage 50 Accounting, though, work best for small businesses. As businesses grow and expand, they need a software system that can handle more advanced processes and transactions.

## Enterprise Resource Planning (ERP) Systems

Larger companies will often use an **enterprise resource planning (ERP)** system to manage their data. ERP systems such as SAP® and Oracle® can integrate all company data into a single database. ERP feeds the data into software for all company activities—from purchasing to production and customer service.

**Enterprise Resource Planning (ERP)**
Software system that can integrate all of a company's functions, departments, and data into a single system.

Advantages of ERP systems include:

- Reduce operating costs.
- Help companies adjust to changes.
- Replace separate software systems, such as sales and payroll.

Disadvantages of ERP systems include:

- ERP is expensive. Major installations can cost millions of dollars.
- Implementation also requires a large commitment of time and people.

Many ERP systems and entry-level systems can be offered in the "cloud." Cloud computing refers to purchasing software and data storage from a third party. In **cloud computing**, the

**Cloud Computing**
Software and data are stored on a third-party server instead of by the business and can be accessed by employees via the Internet.

software and data are stored on the third-party server instead of by the business. Employees access the software and data via the Internet by using a Web browser. Cloud computing can reduce costs by a significant amount for many businesses.

## QuickBooks

One way to understand how computerized accounting software works is to view how transactions are handled in this type of system. We are now going to look at a common entry-level system, QuickBooks. Although your instructor might not have you complete any assignments using QuickBooks, it will be helpful to view the way QuickBooks handles common accounting entries.

Most computerized accounting information systems are organized by function or task. A user can select a function, such as creating an invoice, from a menu. (A menu is a list of options for choosing computer functions.) QuickBooks uses a navigation panel located on the left-hand side of the screen that allows users to select from a menu of options such as Customers, Vendors, Employees, Transactions, and Reports. The tabs (Customers, Vendors, Employees, Transactions, and Reports) on the navigation panel handle all transactions that a company would use. Transactions involving customers, including invoices (accounts receivable), receipt of payments, and sales returns, would be recorded on the Customers tab. The Vendors tab handles transactions involving vendors, including entering bills (accounts payable), paying bills, and processing refunds. The financial reports of a business such as the income statement and balance sheet are also accessible from the navigation panel.

## ETHICS

### Should I change the transaction?

Girmanesh Landin is responsible for recording all of the transactions for Marshall's Home Care. This is Girmanesh's first job as a staff accountant, and she wants to do a good job. Last week, she recorded several cash payments for bills in the computerized accounting information system. She now realizes that she selected the incorrect cash account. She selected the savings account instead of the checking account. Girmanesh knows that she could go back into each transaction and make the correction without anyone knowing that she made the mistake, but she is unsure of what to do. Should Girmanesh make the correction?

### Solution

Because Girmanesh is new to the job, she should find out the procedure for making corrections in the accounting information system before she changes each transaction. Attempting to hide her mistakes could cause her integrity to be questioned because it would appear that she was trying to cover up things rather than ask for clarification and help. Most businesses will prefer that Girmanesh make a separate correcting entry instead of going back in and changing the incorrect transaction. This procedure allows for businesses to have a record of the original transaction and then the correcting entry. It is generally never a good idea to change transactions that have already been recorded, and many software systems will not allow such actions as a method to prevent fraud.

## Creating a Sales Invoice

Suppose on June 23, Smart Touch Learning performed $3,000 of services for Richard Michura on account. To record this transaction in QuickBooks, Smart Touch Learning would need to create an invoice for Richard. Exhibit C-9 shows the invoice the company created. Notice that there are no debits and credits on the invoice. In a computerized accounting information system, the business does not have to record the transaction in debit and credit format. Instead, by creating the invoice, the software knows automatically to record a debit to Accounts Receivable—Michura and a credit to Sales Revenue. After creating the invoice, the software posts the transaction to the appropriate general ledger accounts. There is no need for the business to manually post the transaction; the software takes care of the posting process.

**Exhibit C-9 | Invoice**

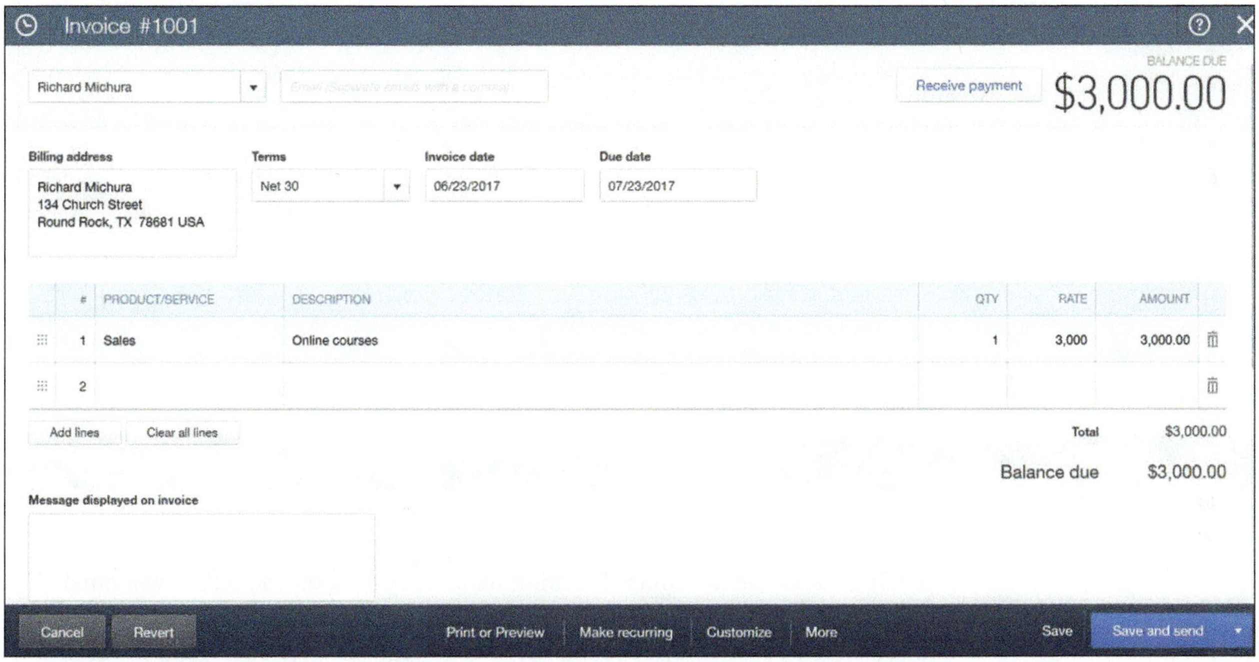


Quickbooks. Reprinted by permission.

When Smart Touch Learning receives the $3,000 from the customer, the accounting clerk will enter the transaction in the Customers tab of QuickBooks by locating the customer's invoice and selecting the "Receive payment" action. By doing this, QuickBooks identifies that the invoice has been paid and that Richard Michura has no further outstanding balance.

## Entering Bills

When a business needs to record a bill received, it will use the Vendors tab of QuickBooks. Suppose that on June 25, Smart Touch Learning receives a $580 bill for utilities. Exhibit C-10 shows the bill that the company will record in QuickBooks. When Smart Touch Learning saves the bill, the software will automatically record a debit to Utilities Expense and credit to Accounts Payable—Smart Energy.

**Exhibit C-10** | **Bill**

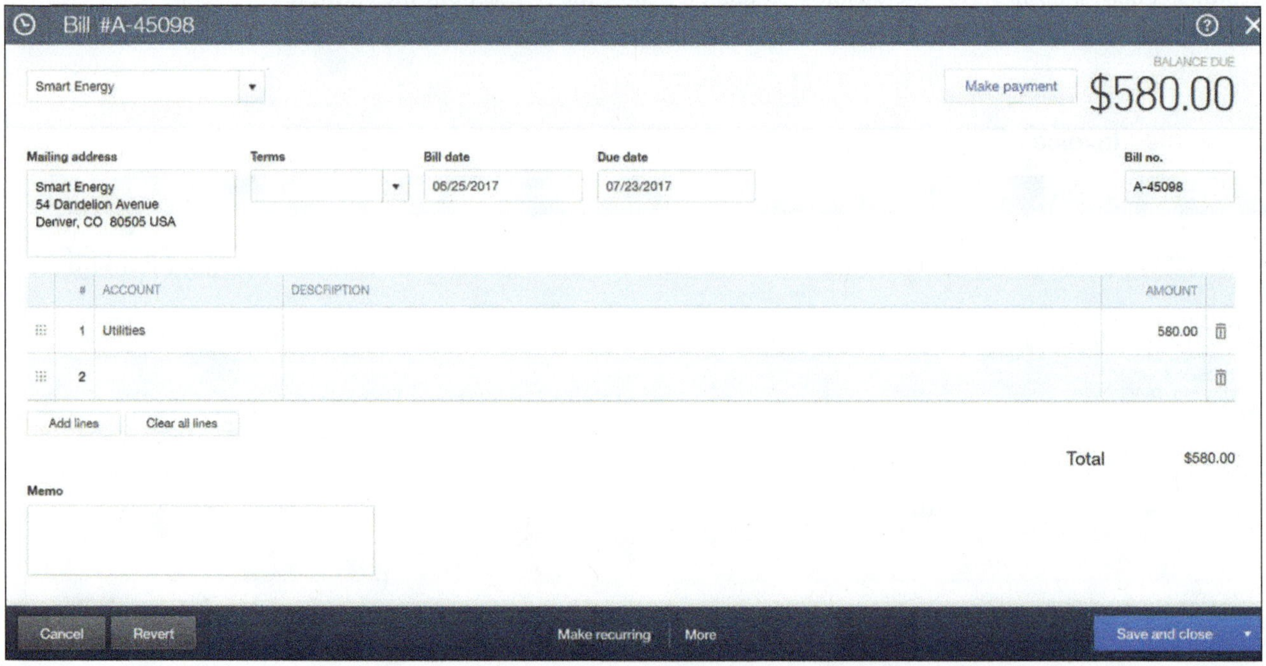


Quickbooks. Reprinted by permission.

On July 5, when Smart Touch Learning makes payment on the bill, it will enter the payment in the Vendors tab of QuickBooks. The accounting clerk will select the bill to be paid and record the payment by selecting the "Make payment" action. Again, the software takes care of recording the journal entry and posting to the ledger accounts.

## Viewing Financial Statements

QuickBooks has the ability to produce numerous reports such as the income statement (called Profit & Loss in QuickBooks), balance sheet, and statement of cash flows. The software can also be used to create accounts receivable and accounts payable aging schedules. Exhibit C-11 shows an example of an income statement for Smart Touch Learning.

**Exhibit C-11 | Income Statement**

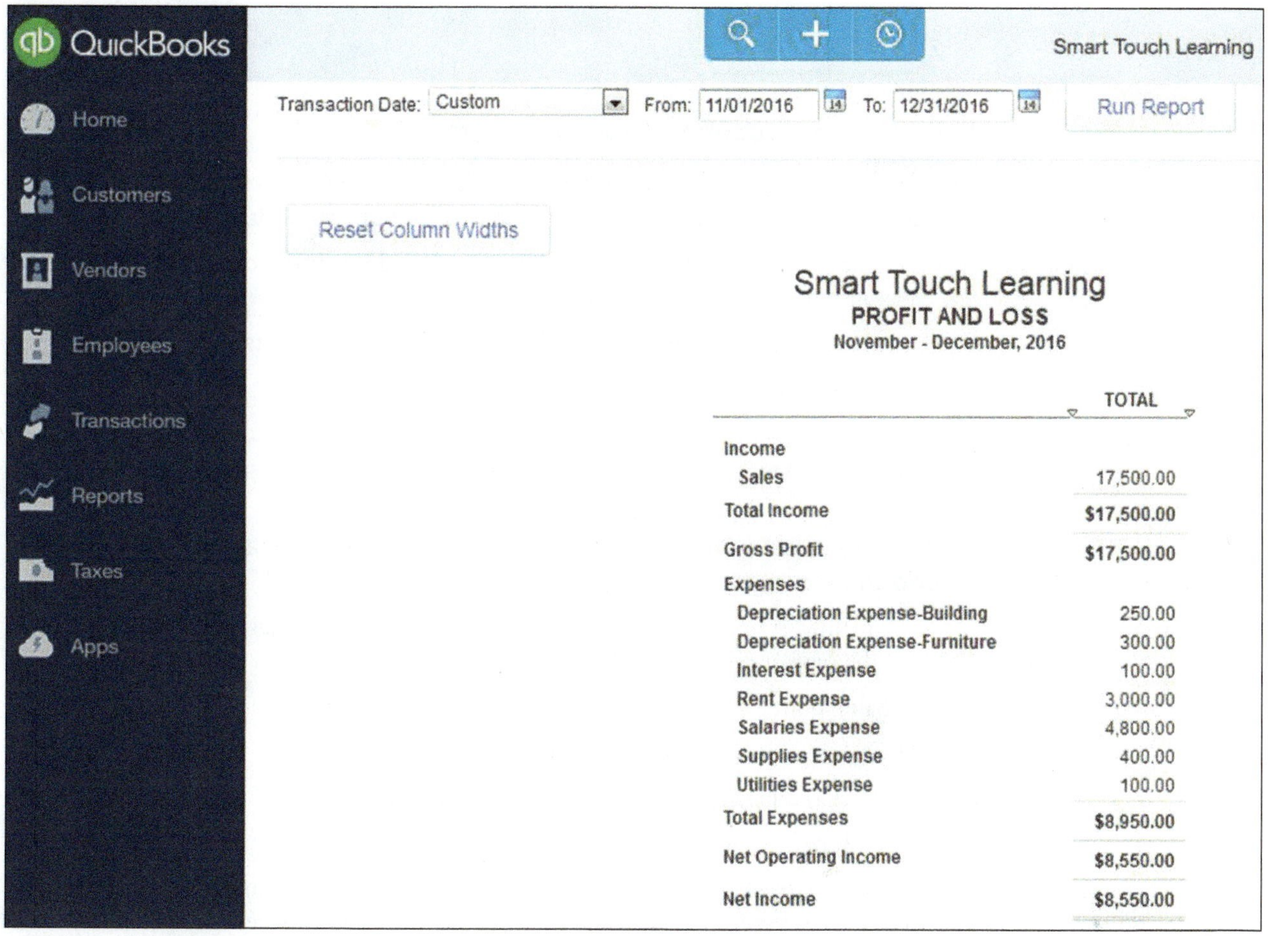


Smart Touch Learning
PROFIT AND LOSS
November - December, 2016

| | TOTAL |
|---|---|
| Income | |
| Sales | 17,500.00 |
| Total Income | $17,500.00 |
| Gross Profit | $17,500.00 |
| Expenses | |
| Depreciation Expense-Building | 250.00 |
| Depreciation Expense-Furniture | 300.00 |
| Interest Expense | 100.00 |
| Rent Expense | 3,000.00 |
| Salaries Expense | 4,800.00 |
| Supplies Expense | 400.00 |
| Utilities Expense | 100.00 |
| Total Expenses | $8,950.00 |
| Net Operating Income | $8,550.00 |
| Net Income | $8,550.00 |

Quickbooks. Reprinted by permission.

One of the many benefits of using a computerized accounting information system is the ease with which reports are created. For most reports needed, the software includes prebuilt templates that can be used. In addition, the software automatically transfers the amounts from the general ledger to the financial statements. The only thing the accountant needs to do is set the correct time period and review the financial statements for accuracy.

## Try It!

**8.** Fill in the missing information.

**a.** ______________ is the set of programs that drives the computer.

**b.** Most systems require a(n) ______________ to link computers.

**c.** ______________ is the electronic equipment used in a computerized accounting information system.

**Check your answers online in MyAccountingLab or at http://www.pearsonhighered.com/Horngren.**

For more practice, see Short Exercise SC-13. MyAccountingLab

# REVIEW

## > Things You Should Know

### 1. What is an accounting information system?

- An accounting information system (AIS) collects, records, stores, and processes accounting data to produce information that is useful for decision makers.
- An effective accounting information system provides control, compatibility, flexibility, relevance, and a positive cost/benefit relationship.
- An accounting information system has three basic components:
  - Source documents and input devices
  - Processing and storage
  - Outputs

### 2. How are sales and cash receipts recorded in a manual accounting information system?

- In a manual system, businesses use special journals that are designed to record a specific type of transaction. The four special journals and their uses are:
  - Sales journal—records sales on account
  - Cash receipts journal—records cash receipts
  - Purchases journal—records purchases on account
  - Cash payments journal—records cash payments
- Subsidiary ledgers are used to hold individual accounts that support a general ledger account. Two common subsidiary ledgers are the accounts receivable subsidiary ledger and accounts payable subsidiary ledger.
- Credit sales are recorded in the sales journal, which uses two columns—Accounts Receivable DR, Sales Revenue CR and Cost of Goods Sold DR, Merchandise Inventory CR.
- Cash receipts are recorded in the cash receipts journal, which includes a Cash DR column and various other debit and credit columns.

### 3. How are purchases, cash payments, and other transactions recorded in a manual accounting information system?

- Purchases on account are recorded in the purchases journal, which includes an Accounts Payable CR column and various other debit columns.
- Cash payments are recorded in the cash payments journal, which includes a Cash CR column and various other debit and credit columns.
- The general journal is used for transactions that aren't recorded in one of the special journals, such as adjusting and closing entries.

**4. How are transactions recorded in a computerized accounting information system?**

- A computerized accounting information system has two basic components:
  - Hardware—the electronic equipment
  - Software—the set of programs that drives the computer
- Entry-level software, such as QuickBooks and Sage 50 Accounting, is often used by small businesses.
- Larger companies use an enterprise resource planning (ERP) system to manage their data.

## > Summary Problem

Houlihan Company completed the following selected transactions during March 2017:

| | |
|---|---|
| Mar. 4 | Received $500 for a cash sale of merchandise inventory to a customer (cost, $319). |
| 6 | Received $60 on account from Brady Lee. The full invoice amount was $65, but Lee paid within the discount period to gain the $5 discount. |
| 9 | Received $1,080 on a note receivable from Beverly Mann. This amount includes the $1,000 note receivable plus interest revenue. |
| 15 | Received $800 for a cash sale of merchandise inventory to a customer (cost, $522). |
| 24 | Borrowed $2,200 by signing a note payable to Interstate Bank. |
| 27 | Received $1,200 on account from Lance Albert. Collection was received after the discount period, as there was no discount. |

### Requirements

The general ledger showed the following balances at February 28: Cash, $1,117; Accounts Receivable, $2,790; Note Receivable—Beverly Mann, $1,000; and Merchandise Inventory, $1,819. The accounts receivable subsidiary ledger at February 28 contained debit balances as follows: Lance Albert, $1,840; Melinda Fultz, $885; Brady Lee, $65.

1. Record the transactions in the cash receipts journal, page 7.
2. Compute column totals at March 31.
3. Post from the cash receipts journal to the general ledger and the accounts receivable subsidiary ledger. Use four-column accounts. Use complete posting references, including the following account numbers: Cash, 11; Accounts Receivable, 12; Note Receivable—Beverly Mann, 13; Merchandise Inventory, 14; Note Payable—Interstate Bank, 22; Sales Revenue, 41; Sales Discounts, 42; Interest Revenue, 46; and Cost of Goods Sold, 51. Insert a check mark (√) in the posting reference column for each February 28 account balance.
4. Balance the Accounts Receivable subsidiary ledger with the Accounts Receivable account in the general ledger.

## > Solution

### Requirements 1 and 2

Cash Receipts Journal — Page 7

| Date | Account Credited | Post. Ref. | Cash DR | Sales Discounts DR | Accounts Receivable CR | Sales Revenue CR | Other Accounts CR | Cost of Goods Sold DR Merchandise Inventory CR |
|---|---|---|---|---|---|---|---|---|
| 2017 | | | | | | | | |
| Mar. 4 | | | 500 | | | 500 | | 319 |
| 6 | Brady Lee | ✓ | 60 | 5 | 65 | | | |
| 9 | Note Receivable-Beverly Mann | 13 | 1,080 | | | | 1,000 | |
| | Interest Revenue | 46 | | | | | 80 | |
| 15 | | | 800 | | | 800 | | 522 |
| 24 | Note Payable-Interstate Bank | 22 | 2,200 | | | | 2,200 | |
| 27 | Lance Albert | ✓ | 1,200 | | 1,200 | | | |
| 31 | | | 5,840 | 5 | 1,265 | 1,300 | 3,280 | 841 |
| | | | (11) | (42) | (12) | (41) | (X) | (51/14) |

### Requirement 3

ACCOUNTS RECEIVABLE SUBSIDIARY LEDGER

**Lance Albert**

| | | | | Balance | |
|---|---|---|---|---|---|
| Date | Post. Ref. | Debit | Credit | Debit | Credit |
| Feb. 28 | ✓ | | | 1,840 | |
| Mar. 27 | CR.7 | | 1,200 | 640 | |

**Melinda Fultz**

| | | | | Balance | |
|---|---|---|---|---|---|
| Date | Post. Ref. | Debit | Credit | Debit | Credit |
| Feb. 28 | ✓ | | | 885 | |

**Brady Lee**

| | | | | Balance | |
|---|---|---|---|---|---|
| Date | Post. Ref. | Debit | Credit | Debit | Credit |
| Feb. 28 | ✓ | | | 65 | |
| Mar. 6 | CR.7 | | 65 | 0 | |

GENERAL LEDGER

| Cash | | | | | No. 11 |
|---|---|---|---|---|---|
| | | | | Balance | |
| Date | Post. Ref. | Debit | Credit | Debit | Credit |
| Feb. 28 | ✓ | | | 1,117 | |
| Mar. 31 | CR.7 | 5,840 | | 6,957 | |

| Accounts Receivable | | | | | No. 12 |
|---|---|---|---|---|---|
| | | | | Balance | |
| Date | Post. Ref. | Debit | Credit | Debit | Credit |
| Feb. 28 | ✓ | | | 2,790 | |
| Mar. 31 | CR.7 | | 1,265 | 1,525 | |

| Note Receivable—Beverly Mann | | | | | No. 13 |
|---|---|---|---|---|---|
| | | | | Balance | |
| Date | Post. Ref. | Debit | Credit | Debit | Credit |
| Feb. 28 | ✓ | | | 1,000 | |
| Mar. 9 | CR.7 | | 1,000 | 0 | |

| Merchandise Inventory | | | | | No. 14 |
|---|---|---|---|---|---|
| | | | | Balance | |
| Date | Post. Ref. | Debit | Credit | Debit | Credit |
| Feb. 28 | ✓ | | | 1,819 | |
| Mar. 31 | CR.7 | | 841 | 978 | |

| Note Payable—Interstate Bank | | | | | No. 22 |
|---|---|---|---|---|---|
| | | | | Balance | |
| Date | Post. Ref. | Debit | Credit | Debit | Credit |
| Mar. 24 | CR.7 | | 2,200 | | 2,200 |

| Sales Revenue | | | | | No. 41 |
|---|---|---|---|---|---|
| | | | | Balance | |
| Date | Post. Ref. | Debit | Credit | Debit | Credit |
| Mar. 31 | CR.7 | | 1,300 | | 1,300 |

| Sales Discounts | | | | | No. 42 |
|---|---|---|---|---|---|
| | | | | Balance | |
| Date | Post. Ref. | Debit | Credit | Debit | Credit |
| Mar. 31 | CR.7 | 5 | | 5 | |

| Interest Revenue | | | | | No. 46 |
|---|---|---|---|---|---|
| | | | | Balance | |
| Date | Post. Ref. | Debit | Credit | Debit | Credit |
| Mar. 9 | CR.7 | | 80 | | 80 |

| Cost of Goods Sold | | | | | No. 51 |
|---|---|---|---|---|---|
| | | | | Balance | |
| Date | Post. Ref. | Debit | Credit | Debit | Credit |
| Mar. 31 | CR.7 | 841 | | 841 | |

## Requirement 4

| GENERAL LEDGER | |
|---|---|
| Accounts Receivable debit balance | $ 1,525 |
| **SUBSIDIARY LEDGER: CUSTOMER ACCOUNTS RECEIVABLE** | |
| **Customer** | **Balance** |
| Lance Albert | $ 640 |
| Melinda Fultz | 885 |
| Brady Lee | 0 |
| Total Accounts Receivable | $ 1,525 |

## > Key Terms

**Accounting Information System (AIS) (p. C-2)**
**Accounts Payable Subsidiary Ledger (p. C-7)**
**Accounts Receivable Subsidiary Ledger (p. C-6)**
**Cash Payments Journal (p. C-16)**
**Cash Receipts Journal (p. C-10)**
**Cloud Computing (p. C-21)**
**Control Account (p. C-7)**
**Enterprise Resource Planning (ERP) (p. C-21)**
**Hardware (p. C-21)**
**Network (p. C-21)**
**Purchases Journal (p. C-14)**
**Sales Journal (p. C-7)**
**Server (p. C-4)**
**Software (p. C-21)**
**Source Document (p. C-3)**
**Special Journal (p. C-5)**
**Subsidiary Ledger (p. C-6)**

## > Quick Check

**Learning Objective 1**

1. Which of the following benefits of an effective accounting information system provides safeguards for a business's assets and reduces the likelihood of fraud and errors?
   **a.** Flexibility
   **b.** Relevance
   **c.** Control
   **d.** Compatibility

**Learning Objective 1**

2. The outputs of a computerized accounting information system are called
   **a.** reports.
   **b.** software.
   **c.** processing.
   **d.** purchase invoices.

**Learning Objective 2**

3. Which of the following is not a special journal?
   **a.** Sales journal
   **b.** General journal
   **c.** Cash receipts journal
   **d.** Purchases journal

**Learning Objective 2**

4. Mountain Day Spa sold merchandise inventory on credit to Marvin Smith, $400. Cost of goods sold was $250. When using a manual accounting information system, where should Mountain record this transaction, and what is the appropriate column in which to record the $250?
   **a.** Sales journal; Accounts Receivable DR, Sales Revenue CR
   **b.** Cash receipts journal; Cash DR, Sales Revenue CR
   **c.** Sales journal; Cost of Goods Sold DR, Merchandise Inventory CR
   **d.** Cash receipts journal; Cash DR, Accounts Receivable CR

**Learning Objective 2**

5. Which of the following correctly describes the posting of transactions from the sales journal?
   **a.** Individual accounts receivable are posted daily to the general ledger.
   **b.** At the end of the month, the totals of the columns are posted to the general ledger.
   **c.** Transactions are posted daily to the general ledger.
   **d.** The total of the Accounts Receivable DR, Sales Revenue CR column is posted to the accounts receivable subsidiary ledger.

**Learning Objective 3**

6. Centex Sound Systems purchased merchandise inventory costing $8,000 from Flower Co. on account. Where should Centex record this transaction, and what account is credited?
   **a.** Cash payments journal; credit Cash
   **b.** Sales journal; credit Sales Revenue

c. Purchases journal; credit Accounts Payable
d. General journal; credit Merchandise Inventory

7. Every transaction recorded in the cash payments journal includes a **Learning Objective 3**
   a. credit to Cash.
   b. debit to Accounts Receivable.
   c. debit to Sales Discounts.
   d. debit to Cash.

8. When using a manual accounting information system, which of the following transactions would be recorded in the general journal? **Learning Objective 3**
   a. Depreciation of office furniture
   b. Cash payment of rent
   c. Sale of merchandise inventory on account
   d. Purchase of merchandise inventory on account

9. Which is a disadvantage of an enterprise resource planning (ERP) system? **Learning Objective 4**
   a. Helps companies adjust to changes
   b. Can replace separate software systems
   c. Can reduce operating costs
   d. Implementation requires a large commitment of time and people

**Check your answers at the end of the chapter.**

# ASSESS YOUR PROGRESS

## > Review Questions

1. What is an accounting information system (AIS)?
2. What does an effective accounting information system provide?
3. Explain the three basic components of an accounting information system.
4. What is a special journal?
5. What is the purpose of a subsidiary ledger?
6. What is a control account?
7. List the four special journals often used in a manual accounting information system. What types of transactions are recorded in each of the special journals?
8. Explain the posting process of the sales journal.
9. Provide some examples of transactions that would be recorded in the Other Accounts CR column of the cash receipts journal.
10. What are the columns that are typically used in the purchases journal?
11. Explain the posting process of the cash payments journal.
12. When is the general journal used in a manual accounting information system? Provide some examples of transactions that would be recorded in the general journal.
13. Explain the two components of a computerized accounting information system.
14. What are two common entry-level accounting software systems used by small businesses?

15. What is an enterprise resource planning (ERP) system? What are the advantages and disadvantages of using an ERP?
16. How is QuickBooks organized?
17. How would a business record a sale of services on account in QuickBooks?
18. How would a business record a bill received in QuickBooks?

## > Short Exercises

**Learning Objective 1**

### SC-1 Evaluating features of an effective accounting information system

In Vogue, a T-shirt business, is growing fast and needs a better accounting information system. Consider the features of an effective system. Which features are most important? Why? Which feature must you consider if your financial resources are limited?

**Learning Objective 1**

### SC-2 Defining components of an accounting information system

Match each component of a computerized accounting information system with an example. Components may be used more than once.

| Example | Component |
|---|---|
| 1. Server | A. Source documents and input devices |
| 2. Bank checks | B. Processing and storage |
| 3. Reports | C. Outputs |
| 4. Keyboard | |
| 5. Software | |
| 6. Financial statements | |
| 7. Bar code scanner | |

**Learning Objective 2**

### SC-3 Identifying special journals

Use the following abbreviations to indicate the journal in which you would record transactions a through n.

J = General journal
S = Sales journal
CR = Cash receipts journal
P = Purchases journal
CP = Cash payments journal

Transactions:

_____ **a.** Cash purchase of merchandise inventory
_____ **b.** Collection of dividend revenue earned on an investment
_____ **c.** Prepayment of insurance
_____ **d.** Borrowing money on a long-term note payable
_____ **e.** Purchase of equipment on account
_____ **f.** Cost of goods sold along with a credit sale
_____ **g.** Cash sale of merchandise inventory
_____ **h.** Payment of rent

_____ i. Depreciation of computer equipment

_____ j. Purchase of merchandise inventory on account

_____ k. Collection of accounts receivable

_____ l. Expiration of prepaid insurance

_____ m. Sale on account

_____ n. Payment on account

## SC-4 Recording transactions in a sales journal

**Learning Objective 2**

| | |
|---|---|
| Jun. 1 | Sold merchandise inventory on account to Flynn Jackson, $1,210. Cost of goods, $920. Invoice no. 101. |
| 8 | Sold merchandise inventory on account to Ike Floyd, $2,100. Cost of goods, $1,660. Invoice no. 102. |
| 13 | Sold merchandise inventory on account to Jessica Till, $400. Cost of goods, $230. Invoice no. 103. |
| 28 | Sold merchandise inventory on account to Greta Ward, $870. Cost of goods, $630. Invoice no. 104. |

Use the following sales journal to record the preceding transactions.

**Sales Journal** — Page 1

| Date | Invoice No. | Customer Account Debited | Post. Ref. | Accounts Receivable DR Sales Revenue CR | Cost of Goods Sold DR Merchandise Inventory CR |
|---|---|---|---|---|---|
| 2016 | | | | | |
| | | | | | |
| | | | | | |
| | | | | | |

***Note: Short Exercise SC-4 must be completed before attempting Short Exercise SC-5.***

## SC-5 Posting transactions from a sales journal to a subsidiary ledger and general ledger

**Learning Objective 2**

Review your results from Short Exercise SC-4.

### Requirements

1. Total each column of the sales journal.
2. Open the following four-column accounts in the accounts receivable subsidiary ledger: Accounts Receivable—Floyd; Accounts Receivable—Jackson; Accounts Receivable—Till; Accounts Receivable—Ward. Post the transactions to the accounts receivable subsidiary ledger.
3. Open the following selected four-column accounts in the general ledger: Accounts Receivable (112); Merchandise Inventory (118), Bal. $5,000; Sales Revenue (411); Cost of Goods Sold (511). Post the total of each column to the general ledger.
4. Balance the total of the customer balances in the accounts receivable subsidiary ledger against Accounts Receivable in the general ledger.

**Learning Objective 2**

## SC-6 Recording transactions in a cash receipts journal

| | |
|---|---|
| Jul. 5 | Sold merchandise inventory for cash, $2,200. Cost of goods, $2,100. |
| 12 | Collected interest revenue of $2,350. |
| 18 | Received cash from Henry Nord, $1,100, on account. There was no discount. |
| 29 | Received $5,400 from Morgan Dexter in full settlement of his account receivable. Dexter earned a $75 discount by paying early. |

Use the following cash receipts journal to record the preceding transactions.

**Cash Receipts Journal** — Page 3

| Date | Account Credited | Post. Ref. | Cash DR | Sales Discounts DR | Accounts Receivable CR | Sales Revenue CR | Other Accounts CR | Cost of Goods Sold DR Merchandise Inventory CR |
|---|---|---|---|---|---|---|---|---|
| 2016 | | | | | | | | |
| | | | | | | | | |
| | | | | | | | | |
| | | | | | | | | |

***Note: Short Exercise SC-6 must be completed before attempting Short Exercise SC-7.***

**Learning Objective 2**

## SC-7 Posting transactions from a cash receipts journal to a subsidiary ledger and general ledger

Review your results from Short Exercise SC-6.

**Requirements**

1. Total each column of the cash receipts journal.
2. Open the following four-column accounts in the accounts receivable subsidiary ledger: Accounts Receivable—Dexter, Bal. $5,475; Accounts Receivable—Nord, Bal. $1,100. Post the transactions to the accounts receivable subsidiary ledger.
3. Open the following selected four-column accounts in the general ledger: Cash (111), Bal. $5,000; Accounts Receivable (112), Bal. $6,575; Merchandise Inventory (118), Bal. $3,000; Sales Revenue (411), Bal. $23,000; Sales Discounts (412); Interest Revenue (419); Cost of Goods Sold (511), Bal. $13,800. Post the total of each column to the general ledger. Also, post the Other Accounts to the general ledger.
4. Balance the total of the customer balances in the accounts receivable subsidiary ledger against Accounts Receivable in the general ledger.

**Learning Objective 3**

## SC-8 Recording transactions in a purchases journal

| | |
|---|---|
| Oct. 1 | Purchased merchandise inventory on account with credit terms of 1/10, n/30 from Milk Co., $2,100. |
| 11 | Purchased office supplies on account from Borris Co., $250. Terms were n/EOM. |
| 24 | Purchased furniture on account with credit terms of 2/10, n/60 from Slip Co., $1,700. |

Use the following purchases journal to record the preceding transactions.

| Purchases Journal | | | | | | | | | Page 6 |
|---|---|---|---|---|---|---|---|---|---|
| | | | | | | | Other Accounts DR | | |
| Date | Vendor Account Credited | Terms | Post. Ref. | Accounts Payable CR | Merchandise Inventory DR | Office Supplies DR | Account Title | Post Ref. | Amount |
| 2016 | | | | | | | | | |
| | | | | | | | | | |
| | | | | | | | | | |
| | | | | | | | | | |

***Note: Short Exercise SC-8 must be completed before attempting Short Exercise SC-9.***

## SC-9 Posting transactions from a purchases journal to a subsidiary ledger and general ledger

**Learning Objective 3**

Review your results from Short Exercise SC-8.

### Requirements

1. Total each column of the purchases journal.
2. Open the following four-column accounts in the accounts payable subsidiary ledger: Accounts Payable—Borris Co.; Accounts Payable—Milk Co.; Accounts Payable—Slip Co. Post the transactions to the accounts payable subsidiary ledger.
3. Open the following selected four-column accounts in the general ledger: Merchandise Inventory (115); Office Supplies (116); Furniture (151); Accounts Payable (211). Post the total of each column to the general ledger. Also, post the Other Accounts to the general ledger.
4. Balance the total of the vendor balances in the accounts payable subsidiary ledger against Accounts Payable in the general ledger.

## SC-10 Recording transactions in a cash payments journal

**Learning Objective 3**

| | |
|---|---|
| Jan. 5 | Issued check no. 430 to purchase equipment for cash, $2,200. |
| 7 | Purchased merchandise inventory for cash, $400, issuing check no. 431. |
| 18 | Paid King Co. amount owed, $1,025, less $60 discount. Issued check no. 432. |
| 28 | Issued check no. 433 to pay utilities, $210. The bill was just received, and there is no liability recorded. |

Use the following cash payments journal to record the preceding transactions.

| Cash Payments Journal | | | | | | | Page 8 |
|---|---|---|---|---|---|---|---|
| Date | Ck. No. | Account Debited | Post. Ref. | Other Accounts DR | Accounts Payable DR | Merchandise Inventory CR | Cash CR |
| 2016 | | | | | | | |
| | | | | | | | |
| | | | | | | | |
| | | | | | | | |

***Note: Short Exercise SC-10 must be completed before attempting Short Exercise SC-11.***

**Learning Objective 3**

**SC-11 Posting transactions from a cash payments journal to a subsidiary ledger and general ledger**

Review your results from Short Exercise SC-10.

**Requirements**

1. Total each column of the cash payments journal.
2. Open the following four-column accounts in the accounts payable subsidiary ledger: Accounts Payable—King Co., Bal. $1,025. Post the transactions to the accounts payable subsidiary ledger.
3. Open the following selected four-column accounts in the general ledger: Cash (111), Bal. $6,500; Merchandise Inventory (118), $1,800; Equipment (150), $10,000; Accounts Payable (211), $1,025; Utilities Expense (541). Post the total of each column to the general ledger. Also, post the Other Accounts to the general ledger.
4. Balance the total of the vendor balances in the accounts payable subsidiary ledger against Accounts Payable in the general ledger.

**Learning Objective 3**

**SC-12 Recording transactions in a general journal**

| | | |
|---|---|---|
| Mar. | 2 | Sold merchandise inventory on account to B. Kamp, issuing invoice no. 501 for $1,100 (cost, $1,090). |
| | 6 | Issued credit memo to B. Kamp for $1,100 for merchandise returned to the business by the customer. Also accounted for receipt of the merchandise inventory at cost. |
| | 21 | Purchased merchandise inventory on credit terms of 3/10, n/30 from Prompt Co., $800. |
| | 28 | Returned damaged merchandise inventory to Prompt Co., issuing a debit memo for $800. |

Journalize the above transactions that should be recorded in the general journal. If a transaction should not be recorded in the general journal, identify the special journal that should be used. Assume the company uses the perpetual inventory system.

### SC-13 Understanding components of a computerized accounting information system

**Learning Objective 4**

Ned Timmons, engineer, is considering using a computerized accounting system for his professional engineering business. Ned has asked that you help him understand the components of a computerized accounting information system by answering the following questions:

**Requirements**

1. What are the two basic components of a computerized accounting information system?
2. Provide examples of each component.
3. If Ned were interested in an entry-level software system, what software might you recommend?

## > Exercises

### EC-14 Recording transactions—sales journal

**Learning Objective 2**

Accounts Receivable DR, Sales Revenue CR column total $1,825

| | |
|---|---|
| Feb. 1 | Sold merchandise inventory on account to Crisp Co., $1,325. Cost of goods, $870. Invoice no. 401. |
| 6 | Sold merchandise inventory for cash, $920 (cost, $660). |
| 12 | Collected interest revenue of $140. |
| 15 | Received cash from Crisp Co. in full settlement of its account receivable. There was no discount. |
| 20 | Sold merchandise inventory on account to Drummer Co., issuing invoice no. 402 for $500 (cost, $425). |
| 22 | Sold merchandise inventory for cash, $570 (cost $450). |
| 26 | Sold office supplies to an employee for cash of $180. |
| 28 | Received $480 from Drummer Co. in full settlement of its account receivable. Drummer earned a discount by paying early. Terms are 4/10, n/15. |

**Requirements**

1. Prepare headings for a sales journal. Journalize the transactions that should be recorded in the sales journal. (Round the sales discount to a whole dollar.) Assume the company uses the perpetual inventory system.
2. Total each column of the sales journal.

### EC-15 Recording transactions—cash receipts journal

**Learning Objective 2**

Accounts Receivable CR column total $1,825

Refer to information in Exercise EC-14.

**Requirements**

1. Prepare headings for a cash receipts journal. Journalize the transactions that should be recorded in the cash receipts journal.
2. Total each column of the cash receipts journal.

**Learning Objective 2**

## EC-16 Using the sales and cash receipts journals

The sales and cash receipts journals of Reynolds Office Products include the following entries:

**Sales Journal** — Page 1

| Date | Invoice No. | Customer Account Debited | Post. Ref. | Accounts Receivable DR Sales Revenue CR | Cost of Goods Sold DR Merchandise Inventory CR |
|---|---|---|---|---|---|
| 2016 | | | | | |
| May 7 | 601 | L. Ellen | ✓ | 145 | 66 |
| 10 | 602 | T. Rex | ✓ | 90 | 34 |
| 10 | 603 | E. Lease | ✓ | 55 | 43 |
| 12 | 604 | B. Gee | ✓ | 170 | 75 |
| May 31 | | Total | | 460 | 218 |
| | | | | | |

**Cash Receipts Journal** — Page 5

| Date | Account Credited | Post. Ref. | Cash DR | Sales Discounts DR | Accounts Receivable CR | Sales Revenue CR | Other Accounts CR | Cost of Goods Sold DR Merchandise Inventory CR |
|---|---|---|---|---|---|---|---|---|
| 2016 | | | | | | | | |
| May 16 | L. Ellen | ✓ | | | | | | |
| 19 | E. Lease | ✓ | | | | | | |
| 24 | | | 350 | | | 350 | | 230 |
| 30 | T. Rex | ✓ | | | | | | |
| May 31 | Total | | | | | | | |
| | | | | | | | | |

Identify the missing information in the cash receipts journal for those transactions listed. There are no sales discounts. Also, total the columns in the cash receipts journal and show that total debits equal total credits.

**Learning Objective 2**

## EC-17 Analyzing postings from the cash receipts journal

The cash receipts journal of Silver Plastics follows.

**Cash Receipts Journal** — Page 7

| Date | Account Credited | Post. Ref. | Cash DR | Sales Discounts DR | Accounts Receivable CR | Sales Revenue CR | Other Accounts CR | Cost of Goods Sold DR Merchandise Inventory CR |
|---|---|---|---|---|---|---|---|---|
| 2016 | | | | | | | | |
| Jan. 2 | Apple, Corp. | *(g)* | 790 | 20 | 810 | | | |
| 9 | Karen, Inc. | *(h)* | 490 | | 490 | | | |
| 19 | Note Receivable | *(i)* | 4,480 | | | | 4,000 | |
| | Interest Revenue | *(j)* | | | | | 480 | |
| 30 | J. T. Fritz | *(k)* | 310 | 10 | 320 | | | |
| 31 | | | 4,230 | | | 4,230 | | 3,500 |
| Jan. 31 | Total | | 10,300 | 30 | 1,620 | 4,230 | 4,480 | 3,500 |
| | | | *(a)* | *(b)* | *(c)* | *(d)* | *(e)* | *(f)* |

Silver's general ledger includes the following selected accounts, along with their account numbers:

| Number | Account | Number | Account |
|---|---|---|---|
| 110 | Cash | 510 | Sales Revenue |
| 115 | Accounts Receivable | 512 | Sales Discounts |
| 118 | Merchandise Inventory | 520 | Interest Revenue |
| 125 | Notes Receivable | 611 | Cost of Goods Sold |

Indicate whether each posting reference (a) through (k) should be a

- Check mark (✓) for a posting to a customer account in the accounts receivable subsidiary ledger.
- Account number for a posting to an account in the general ledger. If so, give the account number.
- Letter (X) for an amount not posted.

## EC-18 Identifying transactions in the accounts receivable subsidiary ledger

**Learning Objective 2**

A customer account in the accounts receivable subsidiary ledger of Landon Old Company follows.

| JACOB WAITS | | | | | |
|---|---|---|---|---|---|
| | | | | Balance | |
| Date | Post. Ref. | Debit | Credit | Debit | Credit |
| Nov. 1 | | | | 400 | |
| 9 | S.5 | 1,180 | | 1,580 | |
| 18 | J.8 | | 190 | 1,390 | |
| 30 | CR.9 | | 700 | 690 | |

Describe the three posted transactions.

## EC-19 Recording transactions—purchases journal

**Learning Objective 3**

Accounts Payable CR column total $4,300

| | |
|---|---|
| Apr. 2 | Purchased merchandise inventory on credit terms of 3/10, n/60 from Viking Co., $2,800. |
| 5 | Issued check no. 820 to purchase equipment for cash, $3,100. |
| 11 | Purchased merchandise inventory for cash, $500, issuing check no. 821. |
| 12 | Issued check no. 822 to pay Viking Co. net amount owed from Apr. 2. |
| 19 | Purchased office supplies on account from Danvers Supplies, $300. Terms were n/EOM. |
| 24 | Purchased merchandise inventory on credit terms of net 30 from Westchester Sales, $1,200. |
| 28 | Issued check no. 823 to pay for insurance coverage, debiting Prepaid Insurance for $1,600. |
| 29 | Issued check no. 824 to pay rent for the month, $1,700. |

### Requirements

1. Prepare headings for a purchases journal. Journalize the transactions that should be recorded in the purchases journal. The company uses the perpetual inventory system.
2. Total each column of the purchases journal.

**Learning Objective 3**

Cash CR column total $9,616

## EC-20 Recording transactions—cash payments journal

Refer to information in Exercise EC-19.

**Requirements**

1. Prepare headings for a cash payments journal. Journalize the transactions that should be recorded in the cash payments journal.
2. Total each column of the cash payments journal.

**Learning Objective 3**

Merchandise Inventory DR column total $2,285

## EC-21 Posting from the purchases journal; balancing the ledgers

The purchases journal of NorthEastern Publishing Company follows.

| Purchases Journal | | | | | | | | | Page 7 |
|---|---|---|---|---|---|---|---|---|---|
| | | | | | | | Other Accounts DR | | |
| Date | Vendor Account Credited | Terms | Post. Ref. | Accounts Payable CR | Merchandise Inventory DR | Office Supplies DR | Account Title | Post. Ref. | Amount |
| 2016 | | | | | | | | | |
| Sep. 2 | Last Tech | n/30 | | 825 | 825 | | | | |
| 5 | Jump Supply | n/30 | | 165 | | 165 | | | |
| 13 | Last Tech | 4/10, n/30 | | 1,460 | 1,460 | | | | |
| 26 | Farrell Equipment | n/30 | | 910 | | | Equipment | | 910 |
| Sep. 30 | Total | | | | | | | | |
| | | | | | | | | | |

**Requirements**

1. Total each column of the purchases journal.
2. Open four-column ledger accounts for Merchandise Inventory (118), Office Supplies (120), Equipment (150), and Accounts Payable (211). Post to these accounts from the purchases journal. Use dates and posting references in the accounts.
3. Open four-column accounts in the accounts payable subsidiary ledger for Farrell Equipment, Jump Supply, and Last Tech. Post from the purchases journal. Use dates and posting references in the ledger accounts.
4. Balance the Accounts Payable control account in the general ledger with the total of the balances in the accounts payable subsidiary ledger.

**Learning Objective 3**

## EC-22 Identifying transactions in the accounts payable subsidiary ledger

A vendor account in the accounts payable subsidiary ledger of Frank Company follows.

| LESLIE CARTER | | | | | |
|---|---|---|---|---|---|
| | | | | Balance | |
| Date | Post. Ref. | Debit | Credit | Debit | Credit |
| Dec. 1 | | | | | 1,800 |
| 12 | P.4 | | 2,340 | | 4,140 |
| 20 | J.10 | 200 | | | 3,940 |
| 29 | CP.6 | 1,500 | | | 2,440 |

Describe the three posted transactions.

### EC-23 Identifying errors in special journals

**Learning Objectives 2, 3**

| Transaction | Recording |
|---|---|
| a. Henry Associates paid $490 on account for an earlier purchase of merchandise inventory. | Purchases journal |
| b. Recorded depreciation expense for the month. | Cash payments journal |
| c. Collected interest revenue. | Cash receipts journal |
| d. Sold merchandise inventory on account. | Cash receipts journal |
| e. Issued check no. 535 for purchase of merchandise inventory. | Purchases journal |
| f. Returned damaged inventory that was purchased on account. | Purchases journal |
| g. Sold merchandise inventory for cash. | Sales journal |

For each transaction listed, identify the recording error and indicate the journal that should have been used.

## > Problems Group A

***All problems can be completed manually or by using either MyAccountingLab General Ledger or QuickBooks.***

### PC-24A Using the sales, cash receipts, and general journals

**Learning Objectives 2, 3, 4**

Cash Receipts Journal, Accounts Receivable CR column total $12,800

Assume Smiling Springs Glass Company uses the perpetual inventory system. The general ledger of Smiling Springs Glass Company includes the following selected accounts, along with their account numbers:

| Number | Account | Number | Account |
|---|---|---|---|
| 11 | Cash | 19 | Land |
| 12 | Accounts Receivable | 41 | Sales Revenue |
| 13 | Notes Receivable | 42 | Sales Discounts |
| 15 | Merchandise Inventory | 43 | Sales Returns and Allowances |
| 16 | Office Supplies | 51 | Cost of Goods Sold |
| 18 | Equipment | | |

All credit sales are on Smiling Springs's standard terms of 2/10, n/30. Sales and cash receipts transactions in July were as follows:

| | |
|---|---|
| Jul. 2 | Sold merchandise inventory on credit to Intelysis, Inc., $1,700. Smiling Springs's cost of these goods was $200. |
| 3 | As an accommodation to a competitor, sold office supplies at cost, $60, receiving cash. |
| 7 | Cash sales for the week totaled $2,000 (cost, $1,500). |
| 9 | Sold merchandise inventory on account to A. B. Moore, $7,500 (cost, $5,400). |
| 10 | Sold land that cost $8,000 for cash of the same amount. |
| 11 | Sold merchandise inventory on account to Smart Electric, $5,800 (cost, $3,250). |
| 12 | Received cash from Intelysis in full settlement of its account receivable from July 2. |
| 14 | Cash sales for the week were $2,500 (cost, $1,700). |
| 15 | Sold merchandise inventory on credit to the partnership of West & Bob, $3,900 (cost, $2,350). |
| 18 | Received merchandise inventory sold on July 9 to A. B. Moore for $300. The goods shipped were unsatisfactory. These goods cost Smiling Springs $200. |
| 20 | Sold merchandise inventory on account to Smart Electric, $650 (cost, $350). |
| 21 | Cash sales for the week were $900 (cost, $650). |
| 22 | Received $4,000 cash from A. B. Moore in partial settlement of his account receivable. There was no discount. |
| 25 | Received cash from West & Bob for its account receivable from July 15. |
| 25 | Sold merchandise inventory on account to Oggie Co., $1,590 (cost, $960). |
| 27 | Collected $5,600 on a note receivable. There was no interest earned. |
| 28 | Cash sales for the week totaled $3,790 (cost, $2,460). |
| 29 | Sold merchandise inventory on account to R. O. Bankston, $200 (cost, $120). |
| 30 | Received merchandise inventory sold on July 25 to Oggie Co. for $40. The cost of these goods was $10. |
| 31 | Received $3,200 cash on account from A. B. Moore. |

## Requirements

1. Use the appropriate journal to record the preceding transactions in a sales journal (omit the Invoice No. column), a cash receipts journal, and a general journal. Smiling Springs Glass Company records sales returns and allowances in the general journal.
2. Total each column of the sales journal and the cash receipts journal. Show that total debits equal total credits.
3. Show how postings would be made by writing the account numbers and check marks in the appropriate places in the journals.

### PC-25A Using the purchases, cash payments, and general journals

**Learning Objectives 3, 4**

Purchases Journal, Accounts Payable CR column total $20,350

The general ledger of Sparkling Lake Golf Shop includes the following selected accounts, along with their account numbers:

| Number | Account | Number | Account |
|---|---|---|---|
| 111 | Cash | 181 | Equipment |
| 131 | Merchandise Inventory | 211 | Accounts Payable |
| 161 | Prepaid Insurance | 564 | Rent Expense |
| 171 | Office Supplies | 583 | Utilities Expense |

Transactions in December that affected purchases and cash payments follow:

| | |
|---|---|
| Dec. 2 | Purchased merchandise inventory on credit from Tighe, $4,300. Terms were 1/10, n/30. |
| 3 | Paid monthly rent, debiting Rent Expense for $2,200. |
| 5 | Purchased office supplies on credit terms of 1/10, n/30 from Ready Supply, $450. |
| 8 | Received and paid electricity utility bill, $570. |
| 9 | Purchased equipment on account from Avery Equipment, $6,800. Payment terms were net 30. |
| 10 | Returned the equipment to Avery Equipment. It was damaged. |
| 11 | Paid Tighe the amount owed on the purchase of December 2. |
| 12 | Purchased merchandise inventory on account from Crystal Golf, $4,500. Terms were 2/10, n/30. |
| 13 | Purchased merchandise inventory for cash, $610. |
| 14 | Paid a semiannual insurance premium, debiting Prepaid Insurance, $1,000. |
| 16 | Paid its account payable to Ready Supply from December 5. |
| 18 | Received and paid gas and water utility bills, $100. |
| 21 | Purchased merchandise inventory on credit terms of 3/10, n/45 from Darling, Inc., $3,800. |
| 21 | Paid its account payable to Crystal Golf from December 12. |
| 22 | Purchased office supplies on account from Office Stuff, Inc., $500. Terms were net 30. |
| 26 | Returned to Darling, Inc. $900 of the merchandise inventory purchased on December 21. |
| 31 | Paid Darling, Inc. the net amount owed from December 21 less the return on December 26. |

#### Requirements

1. Sparkling Lake Golf Shop records purchase returns in the general journal. Use the appropriate journal to record the transactions in a purchases journal, a cash payments journal (omit the Check No. column), and a general journal. The company uses the perpetual inventory system.
2. Total each column of the special journals. Show that total debits equal total credits in each special journal.
3. Show how postings would be made from the journals by writing the account numbers and check marks in the appropriate places in the journals.

**Learning Objectives 2, 3, 4**

Trial balance, total debits $51,000

### PC-26A Using all journals, posting, and balancing the ledgers

Oxford Computer Security uses the perpetual inventory system and makes all credit sales on terms of 2/10, n/30. Oxford completed the following transactions during May:

| | | |
|---|---|---|
| May | 2 | Issued invoice no. 913 for sale on account to K. D. Kerwin, $2,900. Oxford's cost of this merchandise inventory was $1,400. |
| | 3 | Purchased merchandise inventory on credit terms of 3/10, n/60 from Habile Co., $2,800. |
| | 5 | Sold merchandise inventory for cash, $1,500 (cost, $650). |
| | 5 | Issued check no. 532 to purchase furniture for cash, $2,550. |
| | 8 | Collected interest revenue of $1,450. |
| | 9 | Issued invoice no. 914 for sale on account to Burleson Co., $5,400 (cost, $2,600). |
| | 10 | Purchased merchandise inventory for cash, $1,250, issuing check no. 533. |
| | 12 | Received cash from K. D. Kerwin in full settlement of her account receivable from the sale on May 2. |
| | 13 | Issued check no. 534 to pay Habile Co. the net amount owed from May 3. Round to the nearest dollar. |
| | 13 | Purchased office supplies on account from Marszalek, Inc., $400. Terms were n/EOM. |
| | 15 | Sold merchandise inventory on account to M. O. Samson, issuing invoice no. 915 for $900 (cost, $300). |
| | 17 | Issued credit memo to M. O. Samson for $900 for merchandise inventory returned by Samson. Also accounted for receipt of the merchandise inventory at cost. |
| | 18 | Issued invoice no. 916 for credit sale to K. D. Kerwin, $600 (cost, $100). |
| | 19 | Received $5,292 from Burleson Co. in full settlement of its account receivable from May 9. Burleson earned a discount by paying early. |
| | 20 | Purchased merchandise inventory on credit terms of net 30 from Saari Distributing, $2,350. |
| | 22 | Purchased furniture on credit terms of 3/10, n/60 from Habile Co., $600. |
| | 22 | Issued check no. 535 to pay for insurance coverage, debiting Prepaid Insurance for $1,100. |
| | 24 | Sold office supplies to an employee for cash of $75, which was Oxford's cost. |
| | 25 | Received bill and issued check no. 536 to pay utilities, $300. |
| | 28 | Purchased merchandise inventory on credit terms of 2/10, n/30 from Marszalek, Inc., $600. |
| | 29 | Returned damaged merchandise inventory to Marszalek, Inc., issuing a debit memo for $600. |
| | 29 | Sold merchandise inventory on account to Burleson Co., issuing invoice no. 917 for $3,300 (cost, $1,200). |
| | 30 | Issued check no. 537 to pay Marszalek, Inc. in full for May 13 purchase. |
| | 31 | Received cash in full from K. D. Kerwin on credit sale of May 18. There was no discount. |
| | 31 | Issued check no. 538 to pay monthly salaries of $2,050. |

**Requirements**

1. Open four-column general ledger accounts using Oxford's account numbers and balances as of May 1, 2016, that follow. All accounts have normal balances.

| Number | Account | Bal. |
|---|---|---|
| 111 | Cash | $ 15,400 |
| 112 | Accounts Receivable | 1,400 |
| 114 | Merchandise Inventory | 6,700 |
| 116 | Office Supplies | 700 |
| 117 | Prepaid Insurance | 0 |
| 151 | Furniture | 2,700 |
| 211 | Accounts Payable | 1,000 |
| 311 | Common Stock | 19,000 |
| 314 | Retained Earnings | 3,400 |
| 411 | Sales Revenue | 7,500 |
| 412 | Sales Discounts | 0 |
| 413 | Sales Returns and Allowances | 0 |
| 419 | Interest Revenue | 1,100 |
| 511 | Cost of Goods Sold | 2,900 |
| 531 | Salaries Expense | 1,700 |
| 541 | Utilities Expense | 500 |

2. Open four-column accounts in the subsidiary ledgers with beginning balances as of May 1, if any: Accounts receivable subsidiary ledger—Backus Co., $1,400; Burleson Co., $0; M. O. Samson, $0; and K. D. Kerwin, $0. Accounts payable subsidiary ledger—Habile Co., $0; Marszalek, Inc., $0; Saari Distributing, $0; Weaver Co., $1,000.
3. Enter the transactions in a sales journal (page 7), a cash receipts journal (page 5), a purchases journal (page 10), a cash payments journal (page 8), and a general journal (page 6), as appropriate.
4. Post daily to the accounts receivable subsidiary ledger and to the accounts payable subsidiary ledger.
5. Total each column of the special journals. Show that total debits equal total credits in each special journal. On May 31, post to the general ledger.
6. Prepare a trial balance as of May 31, 2016, to verify the equality of the general ledger. Balance the total of the customer account balances in the accounts receivable subsidiary ledger against Accounts Receivable in the general ledger. Do the same for the accounts payable subsidiary ledger and Accounts Payable in the general ledger.

## > Problems Group B

***All problems can be completed manually or by using either MyAccountingLab General Ledger or QuickBooks.***

**Learning Objectives 2, 3, 4**

Cash Receipts Journal, Accounts Receivable CR column total $12,800

### PC-27B Using the sales, cash receipts, and general journals

Assume Brilliant Spring Company uses the perpetual inventory system. The general ledger of Brilliant Springs Company includes the following selected accounts, along with their account numbers:

| Number | Account | Number | Account |
|---|---|---|---|
| 11 | Cash | 19 | Land |
| 12 | Accounts Receivable | 41 | Sales Revenue |
| 13 | Notes Receivable | 42 | Sales Discounts |
| 15 | Merchandise Inventory | 43 | Sales Returns and Allowances |
| 16 | Office Supplies | 51 | Cost of Goods Sold |
| 18 | Equipment | | |

All credit sales are on Brilliant's standard terms of 2/10, n/30. Sales and cash receipts transactions in November were as follows:

| | |
|---|---|
| Nov. 2 | Sold merchandise inventory on credit to Image, Inc., $2,200. Brilliant's cost of these goods was $200. |
| 6 | As an accommodation to another company, sold new equipment for its cost of $85, receiving cash for this amount. |
| 6 | Cash sales for the week totaled $2,300 (cost, $1,500). |
| 8 | Sold merchandise inventory to A. Z. Metz on account, $7,500 (cost, $5,300). |
| 9 | Sold land that cost $9,000 for cash of $9,000. |
| 11 | Sold merchandise inventory on account to Speedy Electric, $5,800 (cost, $3,250). |
| 11 | Received cash from Image in full settlement of its account receivable from November 2. |
| 13 | Cash sales for the week were $2,400 (cost, $1,400). |
| 15 | Sold merchandise inventory on credit to Wilkson and Miller, $3,600 (cost, $2,300). |
| 18 | Received merchandise inventory from A. Z. Metz as a sales return, $500. The goods shipped were unsatisfactory. These goods cost Brilliant $100. |
| 19 | Sold merchandise inventory to Speedy Electric on account, $850 (cost, $350). |
| 20 | Cash sales for the week were $950 (cost, $620). |
| 21 | Received $4,400 cash from A. Z. Metz in partial settlement of its account receivable. There was no discount. |
| 22 | Received cash from Wilkson and Miller for its account receivable from November 15. |
| 22 | Sold merchandise inventory on account to Oliver Co., $1,530 (cost, $980). |
| 25 | Collected $5,000 on a note receivable. There was no interest earned. |
| 27 | Cash sales for the week totaled $3,740 (cost, $2,460). |
| 27 | Sold merchandise inventory on account to R. A. Banks, $210 (cost, $160). |
| 28 | Received merchandise inventory from Oliver Co. as a sales return, $90. The cost of these goods was $60. |
| 30 | Received $2,600 cash on account from A. Z. Metz. There was no discount. |

**Requirements**

1. Use the appropriate journal to record the preceding transactions in a sales journal (omit the Invoice No. column), a cash receipts journal, and a general journal. Record sales returns and allowances in the general journal.
2. Total each column of the sales journal and the cash receipts journal. Determine that total debits equal total credits.
3. Show how postings would be made from the journals by writing the account numbers and check marks in the appropriate places in the journals.

### PC-28B Using the purchases, cash payments, and general journals

**Learning Objectives 3, 4**

Purchases Journal, Accounts Payable CR column total $18,750

The general ledger of Circus Lake Golf Shop includes the following selected accounts, along with their account numbers:

| Number | Account | Number | Account |
|---|---|---|---|
| 111 | Cash | 181 | Equipment |
| 131 | Merchandise Inventory | 211 | Accounts Payable |
| 161 | Prepaid Insurance | 564 | Rent Expense |
| 171 | Office Supplies | 583 | Utilities Expense |

Transactions in December that affected purchases and cash payments were as follows:

| | |
|---|---|
| Dec. 2 | Purchased merchandise inventory on credit from Trudel, $4,200. Terms were 3/10, n/30. |
| 3 | Paid monthly rent, debiting Rent Expense for $2,200. |
| 5 | Purchased office supplies on credit terms of 3/10, n/30 from Rapid Supply, $450. |
| 8 | Received and paid electricity utility bill, $530. |
| 9 | Purchased equipment on account from Alright Equipment, $6,200. Payment terms were net 30. |
| 10 | Returned the equipment to Alright Equipment. It was damaged. |
| 11 | Paid Trudel the amount owed on the purchase of December 2. |
| 12 | Purchased merchandise inventory on account from Callahan Golf, $4,500. Terms were 2/10, n/30. |
| 13 | Purchased merchandise inventory for cash, $640. |
| 14 | Paid a semiannual insurance premium, debiting Prepaid Insurance, $1,300. |
| 16 | Paid its account payable to Rapid Supply from December 5. |
| 18 | Received and paid gas and water utility bills, $700. |
| 21 | Purchased merchandise inventory on credit terms of 2/10, n/45 from Dunnstable, Inc., $3,100. |
| 21 | Paid its account payable to Callahan Golf from December 12. |
| 22 | Purchased office supplies on account from Office Space, Inc., $300. Terms were net 30. |
| 26 | Returned to Dunnstable, Inc. $1,300 of the merchandise inventory purchased on December 21. |
| 31 | Paid Dunnstable, Inc. the net amount owed from December 21 less the return on December 26. |

**Requirements**

1. Use the appropriate journal to record the preceding transactions in a purchases journal, a cash payments journal (omit the Check No. column), and a general journal. Circus Lake Golf Shop records purchase returns in the general journal. The company uses the perpetual inventory system.
2. Total each column of the special journals. Show that total debits equal total credits in each special journal.
3. Show how postings would be made from the journals by writing the account numbers and check marks in the appropriate places in the journals.

**Learning Objectives 2, 3, 4**

Trial balance, total debits $49,400

## PC-29B Using all journals, posting, and balancing the ledgers

Kingston Computer Security uses the perpetual inventory system and makes all credit sales on terms of 2/10, n/30. During March, Kingston completed these transactions:

| | |
|---|---|
| Mar. 2 | Issued invoice no. 191 for sale on account to L. E. Kaeding, $3,200. Kingston's cost of this merchandise inventory was $1,000. |
| 3 | Purchased merchandise inventory on credit terms of 3/10, n/60 from Heard, $3,100. |
| 4 | Sold merchandise inventory for cash, $1,000 (cost, $550). |
| 5 | Issued check no. 473 to purchase furniture for cash $2,650. |
| 8 | Collected interest revenue of $1,250. |
| 9 | Issued invoice no. 192 for sale on account to Cantu Co., $5,700 (cost, $2,600). |
| 10 | Purchased merchandise inventory for cash, $1,150, issuing check no. 474. |
| 12 | Received cash from L. E. Kaeding in full settlement of her account receivable, net of the discount, from the sale of March 2. |
| 13 | Issued check no. 475 to pay Heard net amount owed from March 3. Round to the nearest dollar. |
| 13 | Purchased office supplies on account from Marston Corp., $500. Terms were n/EOM. |
| 15 | Sold merchandise inventory on account to Stenback Co., issuing invoice no. 193 for $650 (cost, $250). |
| 17 | Issued credit memo to Stenback for $650 for defective merchandise inventory returned by Stenback. Also accounted for receipt of the merchandise inventory at cost. |
| 18 | Issued invoice no. 194 for credit sale to L. E. Kaeding, $400 (cost, $100). |
| 19 | Received $5,586 from Cantu Co. in full settlement of its account receivable from March 9. Cantu earned a discount by paying early. |
| 20 | Purchased merchandise inventory on credit terms of net 30 from James Sales, $2,000. |
| 22 | Purchased furniture on credit terms of 3/10, n/60 from Heard, $800. |
| 22 | Issued check no. 476 to pay for insurance coverage, debiting Prepaid Insurance for $1,300. |
| 24 | Sold office supplies to an employee for cash of $125, which was Kingston's cost. |
| 25 | Received bill and issued check no. 477 to pay utilities, $650. |
| 28 | Purchased merchandise inventory on credit terms of 2/10, n/30 from Marston Corp., $700. |
| 29 | Returned damaged merchandise inventory to Marston Corp., issuing a debit memo for $700. |
| 29 | Sold merchandise inventory on account to Cantu Co., issuing invoice no. 195 for $3,400 (cost, $1,100). |
| 30 | Issued check no. 478 to pay Marston Corp. in full for March 13 purchase. |
| 31 | Received cash in full from L. E. Kaeding on credit sale of March 18. There was no discount. |
| 31 | Issued check no. 479 to pay monthly salaries of $1,850. |

**Requirements**

1. Open four-column general ledger accounts using Kingston Computer Security's account numbers and balances as of March 1, 2016, that follow. All accounts have normal balances.

| Number | Account | Bal. |
|---|---|---|
| 111 | Cash | $ 15,200 |
| 112 | Accounts Receivable | 2,000 |
| 114 | Merchandise Inventory | 6,000 |
| 116 | Office Supplies | 900 |
| 117 | Prepaid Insurance | 0 |
| 151 | Furniture | 2,200 |
| 211 | Accounts Payable | 1,000 |
| 311 | Common Stock | 19,000 |
| 314 | Retained Earnings | 2,500 |
| 411 | Sales Revenue | 7,800 |
| 412 | Sales Discounts | 0 |
| 413 | Sales Returns and Allowances | 0 |
| 419 | Interest Revenue | 700 |
| 511 | Cost of Goods Sold | 2,400 |
| 531 | Salaries Expense | 1,700 |
| 541 | Utilities Expense | 600 |

2. Open four-column accounts in the subsidiary ledgers with beginning balances as of March 1, if any. Accounts receivable subsidiary ledger: Abney Co., $2,000; Cantu Co., $0; L. E. Kaeding, $0; and Stenback, $0. Accounts payable subsidiary ledger: Heard, $0; Marston Corp, $0; James Sales, $0; and Yount Co., $1,000.
3. Enter the transactions in a sales journal (page 8), a cash receipts journal (page 3), a purchases journal (page 6), a cash payments journal (page 9), and a general journal (page 4), as appropriate.
4. Post daily to the accounts receivable subsidiary ledger and to the accounts payable subsidiary ledger.
5. Total each column of the special journals. Show that total debits equal total credits in each special journal. On March 31, post to the general ledger.
6. Prepare a trial balance as of March 31, 2016, to verify the equality of the general ledger. Balance the total of the customer account balances in the accounts receivable subsidiary ledger against Accounts Receivable in the general ledger. Do the same for the accounts payable subsidiary ledger and Accounts Payable in the general ledger.

## > Continuing Problem

### PC-30 Using all journals

This problem continues the Daniels Consulting situation. Daniels Consulting performs systems consulting. Daniels has also begun selling accounting software and uses the perpetual inventory system to account for software inventory. During January 2017, Daniels completed the following transactions:

| | |
|---|---|
| Jan. 2 | Completed a consulting engagement and received cash of $5,700. |
| 2 | Prepaid three months office rent, $2,400. |
| 7 | Purchased 50 units software inventory on account from Miller Co., $1,050, plus freight in, $50. |
| 18 | Sold 40 software units on account to Jason Needle, $2,625 (cost, $880). |
| 19 | Consulted with a client, Louis Frank, for a fee of $2,500 on account. (Use general journal.) |
| 20 | Paid employee salaries, $1,885, which includes accrued salaries from December of $685. |
| 21 | Paid Miller Co. on account, $1,100. There was no discount. |
| 22 | Purchased 185 units software inventory on account from Whitestone Co., $4,810. |
| 24 | Received bill and paid utilities, $375. |
| 28 | Sold 135 units software for cash, $5,265 (cost, $3,470). |
| 31 | Recorded the following adjusting entries:<br>a. Accrued salaries expense, $775<br>b. Depreciation on Equipment, $60; Depreciation on Furniture, $50<br>c. Expiration of prepaid rent, $800<br>d. Physical count of software inventory, 50 units, $1,300 |

Daniels Consulting had the following selected accounts with account numbers and normal balances:

| Number | Account | Balances |
|---|---|---|
| 111 | Cash | $ 17,950 |
| 112 | Accounts Receivable | 3,600 |
| 114 | Software Inventory | 0 |
| 116 | Office Supplies | 300 |
| 117 | Prepaid Rent | 0 |
| 170 | Equipment | 3,600 |
| 171 | Accumulated Depreciation—Equipment | 60 |
| 180 | Furniture | 3,000 |
| 181 | Accumulated Depreciation—Furniture | 50 |
| 211 | Accounts Payable | 3,600 |
| 212 | Unearned Revenue | 1,800 |
| 213 | Salaries Payable | 685 |
| 311 | Common Stock | 20,000 |
| 314 | Retained Earnings | 2,255 |
| 411 | Sales Revenue | 0 |
| 412 | Sales Discounts | 0 |
| 419 | Service Revenue | 0 |
| 511 | Cost of Goods Sold | 0 |
| 531 | Salaries Expense | 0 |
| 541 | Utilities Expense | 0 |
| 551 | Depreciation Expense—Equipment | 0 |
| 561 | Depreciation Expense—Furniture | 0 |
| 571 | Rent Expense | 0 |

**Requirements**

1. Use the appropriate journal to record the preceding transactions in a sales journal (omit the Invoice No. column), a cash receipts journal, a purchases journal, a cash payments journal (omit the Check No. column), and a general journal.
2. Total each column of the special journals. Show that total debits equal total credits in each special journal.
3. Show how postings would be made from the journals by writing the account numbers and check marks in the appropriate places in the journals.

## > Practice Set

### PC-31 Using all journals

This problem continues the Crystal Clear Cleaning problem. Crystal Clear Cleaning has decided that, in addition to providing cleaning services, it will sell cleaning products. Crystal Clear uses the perpetual inventory system. During December 2017, Crystal Clear completed the following transactions:

| | |
|---|---|
| Dec. 2 | Purchased 475 units of inventory for $2,850 on account from Sparkle, Co. on terms 3/10, n/20. |
| 5 | Purchased 600 units of inventory from Borax on account with terms 2/10, n/30. The total invoice was for $4,500, which included a $150 freight charge. |
| 7 | Returned 75 units of inventory to Sparkle from the December 2 purchase (cost, $450). |
| 9 | Paid Borax. |
| 11 | Sold 285 units of goods to Happy Maids for $3,990 on account on terms 3/10, n/30. Crystal Clear's cost of the goods was $1,710. |
| 12 | Paid Sparkle. |
| 15 | Received 22 units with a retail price of $308 of goods back from customer Happy Maids. The goods cost Crystal Clear $132. |
| 21 | Received payment from Happy Maids, settling the amount due in full. |
| 28 | Sold 265 units of goods to Bridget, Inc. for cash of $3,975 (cost, $1,691). |
| 29 | Received bill and paid cash for utilities of $415. |
| 30 | Paid cash for Sales Commission Expense of $550. |
| 31 | Recorded the following adjusting entries:<br>a. Physical count of inventory on December 31 showed 428 units of goods on hand, $3,148<br>b. Depreciation, $270<br>c. Accrued salaries expense of $725<br>d. Prepared all other adjustments necessary for December. (Hint: You will need to review the adjustment information in Chapter 3 to determine the remaining adjustments.) Assume cleaning supplies at December 31 are $30. |

Crystal Clear Cleaning had the following selected accounts with account numbers and normal balances:

| Number | Account | Balance |
|---|---|---|
| 111 | Cash | $ 138,150 |
| 112 | Accounts Receivable | 2,600 |
| 114 | Merchandise Inventory | 0 |
| 116 | Cleaning Supplies | 30 |
| 117 | Prepaid Rent | 1,500 |
| 118 | Prepaid Insurance | 1,650 |
| 160 | Equipment | 3,200 |
| 170 | Truck | 7,000 |
| 171 | Accumulated Depreciation | 270 |
| 211 | Accounts Payable | 1,470 |
| 212 | Salaries Payable | 0 |
| 213 | Unearned Revenue | 11,500 |
| 214 | Interest Payable | 240 |
| 216 | Notes Payable | 96,000 |
| 311 | Common Stock | 42,000 |
| 312 | Retained Earnings | 2,650 |
| 411 | Sales Revenue | 0 |
| 412 | Sales Discounts | 0 |
| 413 | Sales Returns and Allowances | 0 |
| 419 | Service Revenue | 0 |
| 511 | Cost of Goods Sold | 0 |
| 531 | Salaries Expense | 0 |
| 541 | Utilities Expense | 0 |
| 551 | Depreciation Expense | 0 |
| 561 | Insurance Expense | 0 |
| 571 | Rent Expense | 0 |
| 581 | Sales Commission Expense | 0 |
| 591 | Interest Expense | 0 |

**Requirements**

1. Use the appropriate journal to record the preceding transactions in a sales journal (omit the Invoice No. column), a cash receipts journal, a purchases journal, a cash payments journal (omit the Check No. column), and a general journal.
2. Total each column of the special journals. Show that total debits equal total credits in each special journal.
3. Show how postings would be made from the journals by writing the account numbers and check marks in the appropriate places in the journals.

# COMPREHENSIVE PROBLEM

## > Comprehensive Problem for Appendix C

### Completing the Accounting Cycle for a Merchandising Entity—Using Special Journals

Quick Networking Systems adjusts and closes its books and then prepares financial statements monthly. Quick uses the perpetual inventory system. The company completed the following transactions during August:

| | |
|---|---|
| Aug. 1 | Issued check no. 682 for August office rent of $2,000. |
| 2 | Issued check no. 683 to pay the salaries payable of $1,250 from July 31. |
| 2 | Issued invoice no. 503 for sale on account to R. T. Lowe, $600. Quick's cost of this merchandise inventory was $190. |
| 3 | Purchased merchandise inventory on credit terms of 1/15, n/60 from Goodman, Inc., $1,400. |
| 4 | Received net amount of cash on account from Finnish Company, $2,156, within the discount period. |
| 4 | Sold merchandise inventory for cash, $330 (cost, $104). |
| 5 | Received from Parkland, Inc. merchandise inventory that had been sold earlier for $550 (cost, $174). |
| 5 | Issued check no. 684 to purchase office supplies for cash, $780. |
| 7 | Issued invoice no. 504 for sale on account to K. D. Statesman, $2,400 (cost, $759). |
| 8 | Issued check no. 685 to pay French Company $2,600 of the amount owed at July 31. This payment occurred after the end of the discount period. |
| 11 | Issued check no. 686 to pay Goodman, Inc. the net amount owed from August 3. |
| 12 | Received cash from R. T. Lowe in full settlement of her account receivable from August 2. |
| 16 | Issued check no. 687 to pay salaries expense of $1,240. |
| 19 | Purchased merchandise inventory for cash, $850, issuing check no. 688. |
| 22 | Purchased furniture on credit terms of 3/15, n/60 from Boxman Corporation, $510. |
| 23 | Sold merchandise inventory on account to Finnish Company, issuing invoice no. 505 for $9,966 (cost, $3,152). |
| 24 | Received half the July 31 amount receivable from K. D. Statesman—after the end of the discount period. |
| 26 | Purchased office supplies on credit terms of 2/10, n/30 from French Company, $180. |
| 30 | Returned damaged merchandise inventory to the company from whom Quick made the cash purchase on August 19, receiving cash of $850. |
| 31 | Purchased merchandise inventory on credit terms of 1/10, n/30 from Sammy Supply, $8,330. |
| 31 | Issued check no. 689 to stockholders, for dividends, $500. |

**Requirements**

1. Open these four-column accounts with their account numbers and July 31 balances in the various ledgers.

**General Ledger:**

| Nbr. | Account Name | Debit | Credit |
|---|---|---|---|
| 101 | Cash | $ 4,490 | |
| 102 | Accounts Receivable | 22,560 | |
| 105 | Merchandise Inventory | 41,800 | |
| 109 | Office Supplies | 1,340 | |
| 117 | Prepaid Insurance | 2,200 | |
| 160 | Furniture | 37,270 | |
| 161 | Accumulated Depreciation—Furniture | | $ 10,550 |
| 201 | Accounts Payable | | 12,600 |
| 204 | Salaries Payable | | 1,250 |
| 220 | Note Payable, Long-term | | 31,000 |
| 301 | Common Stock | | 25,000 |
| 305 | Retained Earnings | | 29,260 |
| 310 | Dividends | | |
| 400 | Income Summary | | |
| 401 | Sales Revenue | | |
| 402 | Sales Discounts | | |
| 403 | Sales Returns and Allowances | | |
| 501 | Cost of Goods Sold | | |
| 510 | Salaries Expense | | |
| 513 | Rent Expense | | |
| 514 | Depreciation Expense—Furniture | | |
| 516 | Insurance Expense | | |
| 519 | Supplies Expense | | |

**Accounts Receivable Subsidiary Ledger:** Finnish Company $2,200; R. T. Lowe, $0; Parkland, Inc., $11,590; K. D. Statesman, $8,770.

**Accounts Payable Subsidiary Ledger:** Boxman Corporation, $0; French Company, $12,600; Goodman, Inc., $0; Sammy Supply, $0.

2. Journalize the August transactions using a sales journal (page 4), a cash receipts journal (page 11), a purchases journal (page 8), a cash payments journal (page 5), and a general journal (page 9). Quick makes all credit sales on terms of 2/10, n/30.
3. Post daily to the accounts receivable subsidiary ledger and the accounts payable subsidiary ledger. On August 31, post to the general ledger.

4. Prepare an unadjusted trial balance for the month ended August 31.
5. Journalize and post the following adjusting entries:
   a. Office supplies on hand, $990.
   b. Prepaid insurance expired, $550.
   c. Depreciation expense, $230.
   d. Accrued salaries expense, $1,030.
6. Prepare an adjusted trial balance.
7. Prepare a multistep income statement, statement of retained earnings, and classified balance sheet.
8. Journalize closing entries and post.
9. Prepare a post-closing trial balance.

# CRITICAL THINKING

## > Decision Case C-1

A fire destroyed certain accounting records of Green Books. The controller, Marilyn Green, asks your help in reconstructing the records. All of the sales are on account, with credit terms of 2/10, n/30. All cash receipts on account reached the store within the 10-day discount period, except as noted. The only accounting record preserved from the fire is the accounts receivable subsidiary ledger, which follows.

**Garcia Sales**

| | | | | Balance | |
|---|---|---|---|---|---|
| **Date** | **Post. Ref.** | **Debit** | **Credit** | **Debit** | **Credit** |
| Apr. 1 | | | | 450 | |
| 3 | CR.8 | | 450 | 0 | |
| 25 | S.6 | 3,600 | | 3,600 | |
| 29 | S.6 | 1,100 | | 4,700 | |

**Leewright, Inc.**

| | | | | Balance | |
|---|---|---|---|---|---|
| **Date** | **Post. Ref.** | **Debit** | **Credit** | **Debit** | **Credit** |
| Apr. 1 | | | | 2,800 | |
| 15 | S.6 | 2,600 | | 5,400 | |
| 29 | CR.8 | | 1,500* | 3,900 | |

*Cash receipt did not occur within the discount period.

**Sally Jones**

| | | | | Balance | |
|---|---|---|---|---|---|
| **Date** | **Post. Ref.** | **Debit** | **Credit** | **Debit** | **Credit** |
| Apr. 1 | | | | 1,100 | |
| 5 | CR.8 | | 1,100 | 0 | |
| 11 | S.6 | 400 | | 400 | |
| 21 | CR.8 | | 400 | 0 | |
| 24 | S.6 | 2,000 | | 2,000 | |

| Jacques LeHavre | | | | | |
|---|---|---|---|---|---|
| | | | | Balance | |
| Date | Post. Ref. | Debit | Credit | Debit | Credit |
| Apr. 1 | | | | 0 | |
| 8 | S.6 | 2,400 | | 2,400 | |
| 16 | S.6 | 900 | | 3,300 | |
| 18 | CR.8 | | 2,400 | 900 | |
| 19 | J.5 | | 200 | 700 | |
| 27 | CR.8 | | 700 | 0 | |

**Requirements**

1. Determine the beginning and ending balances of Accounts Receivable.
2. Determine the sales on account in the month of April.
3. Determine total cash receipts on account from customers during April.

## > Fraud Case C-1

Didrikson Rubin, the auditor of Red Barn Farm Equipment, was verifying cash payments to vendors for the past several months. She noticed that several checks had been paid to a specific vendor, but she couldn't find a record of the transactions in the computerized system. Didrikson suspects that an employee is issuing checks to a fictitious "vendor" and then deleting the transactions from the computerized system. How might Didrikson investigate the suspected fraud?

## > Team Project C-1

Ace Moving is considering investing in an entry-level computerized accounting information system. Ace needs a system that can record customer invoices and cash receipts. In addition, it would like to track all of its bills and cash payments. As a team, investigate the two common entry-level accounting software products: QuickBooks and Sage 50 Accounting. Prepare a PowerPoint presentation that summarizes the similarities and differences between the two software systems.

## > Communication Activity C-1

In 150 words or fewer, explain what an accounting information system is and describe an effective system.



## > Quick Check Answers

**1.** c **2.** a **3.** b **4.** c **5.** b **6.** c **7.** a **8.** a **9.** d

# Glossary

The following Glossary and Index are for all chapters of *Horngren's Financial & Managerial Accounting*, 5/e.

**Absorption Costing.** The product costing method that assigns direct materials, direct labor, variable manufacturing overhead, and fixed manufacturing overhead to products. Required by GAAP for external reporting. (p. 1096)

**Accelerated Depreciation Method.** A depreciation method that expenses more of the asset's cost near the start of its useful life and less at the end of its useful life. (p. 484)

**Account.** A detailed record of all increases and decreases that have occurred in an individual asset, liability, or equity during a specific period. (p. 56)

**Accounting.** The information system that measures business activities, processes the information into reports, and communicates the results to decision makers. (p. 2)

**Accounting Cycle.** The process by which companies produce their financial statements for a specific period. (p. 199)

**Accounting Equation.** The basic tool of accounting, measuring the resources of the business (what the business owns or has control of) and the claims to those resources (what the business owes to creditors and to the owners). Assets = Liabilities + Equity. (p. 11)

**Accounting Information System (AIS).** A system that collects, records, stores, and processes accounting data to produce information that is useful for decision makers. (p. C-2)

**Accounting Rate of Return (ARR).** A capital investment analysis method that measures the profitability of an investment. Average annual operating income / Average amount invested. (p. 1391)

**Account Number.** On a check, the number that identifies the account upon which the payment is drawn. (p. 388)

**Accounts Payable.** A short-term liability that will be paid in the future. (p. 15)

**Accounts Payable Subsidiary Ledger.** A subsidiary ledger that includes an accounts payable account for each vendor that contains detailed information such as the amount purchased, paid, and owed. (p. C-7)

**Accounts Receivable.** The right to receive cash in the future from customers for goods sold or for services performed. (pp. 15, 424)

**Accounts Receivable Subsidiary Ledger.** A subsidiary ledger that includes an accounts receivable account for each customer that contains detailed information such as the amount sold, received, and owed. (p. C-6)

**Accounts Receivable Turnover Ratio.** A ratio that measures the number of times the company collects the average accounts receivable balance in a year. Net credit sales / Average net accounts receivable. (pp. 446, 781)

**Accrual Basis Accounting.** Accounting method that records revenues when earned and expenses when incurred. (p. 118)

**Accrued Expense.** An expense that the business has incurred but has not yet paid. (p. 130)

**Accrued Liability.** A liability for which the business knows the amount owed but the bill has not been paid. (p. 57)

**Accrued Revenue.** A revenue that has been earned but for which the cash has not yet been collected. (p. 133)

**Accumulated Depreciation.** The sum of all the depreciation expense recorded to date for a depreciable asset. (p. 127)

**Acid-Test Ratio.** The ratio of the sum of cash, cash equivalents, short-term investments, and net current receivables to total current liabilities. The ratio tells whether the entity could pay all its current liabilities if they came due immediately. (Cash including cash equivalents + Short-term investments + Net current receivables) / Total current liabilities. (pp. 446, 779)

**Activity-Based Costing (ABC).** Focuses on the costs of activities as the building blocks for allocating indirect costs to products and services. (p. 996)

**Activity-Based Management (ABM).** Using activity-based cost information to make decisions that improve customer satisfaction while also increasing profits. (p. 996)

**Adjunct Account.** An account that is directly related to another account. Adjunct accounts have the same normal balance as the related account and are added to the related account on the balance sheet. (p. 609)

**Adjusted Trial Balance.** A list of all the accounts with their adjusted balances. (p. 138)

**Adjusting Entry.** An entry made at the end of the accounting period that is used to record revenues to the period in which they are earned and expenses to the period in which they occur. (p. 123)

**Administrative Expenses.** Expenses incurred that are not related to marketing the company's goods and services. (p. 267)

**Aging-of-Receivables Method.** A method of estimating uncollectible receivables by determining the balance of the Allowance for Bad Debts account based on the age of individual accounts receivable. (p. 437)

**Allocation Base.** A denominator that links indirect costs to cost objects. Ideally, the allocation base is the primary cost driver of the indirect costs. (p. 882)

**Allowance for Bad Debts.** A contra account, related to accounts receivable, that holds the estimated amount of uncollectible accounts. (p. 431)

**Allowance Method.** A method of accounting for uncollectible receivables in which the company estimates bad debts expense instead of waiting to see which customers the company will not collect from. (p. 431)

**Amortization.** The process by which businesses spread the allocation of an intangible asset's cost over its useful life. (p. 497)

**Amortization Schedule.** A schedule that details each loan payment's allocation between principal and interest and the beginning and ending loan balances. (p. 597)

**Annual Report.** Provides information about a company's financial condition. (p. 766)

**Annuity.** A stream of equal cash payments made at equal time intervals. (pp. 617 Appendix 12A, 1395)

**Appraisal Costs.** Costs incurred to detect poor-quality materials, goods, or services. (p. 1013)

**Appropriation of Retained Earnings.** Restriction of a portion of retained earnings that is recorded by a journal entry. (p. 667)

**Assets.** Economic resources that are expected to benefit the business in the future. Something the business owns or has control of. (p. 12)

**Asset Turnover Ratio.** Measures how efficiently a business uses its average total assets to generate sales. Net sales / Average total assets. (pp. 501, 785, 1297)

**Audit.** An examination of a company's financial statements and records. (p. 10)

**Authorized Stock.** The maximum number of shares of stock that the corporate charter allows the corporation to issue. (p. 647)

**Available-for-Sale (AFS) Investment.** A debt security or an equity security in which the investor holds less than 20% of the voting stock and that isn't a trading investment or a held-to-maturity investment. (p. 525)

**Bad Debts Expense.** The cost to the seller of extending credit. It arises from the failure to collect from some credit customers. (p. 429)

**Balanced Scorecard.** The performance evaluation system that requires management to consider both financial performance measures and operational performance measures when judging the performance of a company and its subunits. (p. 1286)

**Balance Sheet.** Reports on the assets, liabilities, and stockholders' equity of the business as of a specific date. (p. 21)

**Bank Reconciliation.** A document explaining the reasons for the difference between a depositor's cash records and the depositor's cash balance in its bank account. (p. 390)

**Bank Statement.** A document from the bank that reports the activity in the customer's account. It shows the bank account's beginning and ending balances and lists the month's cash transactions conducted through the bank account. (p. 389)

**Benchmarking.** The practice of comparing a company with other leading companies. (p. 775)

**Bond Payable.** A long-term debt issued to multiple lenders called bondholders, usually in increments of $1,000 per bond. (p. 600)

**Book Value.** A depreciable asset's cost minus accumulated depreciation. (pp. 128, 482)

**Breakeven Point.** The sales level at which operating income is zero. Total revenues equal total costs. (p. 1058)

**Budget.** A financial plan that managers use to coordinate a business's activities. (pp. 829, 1137)

**Budgetary Slack.** Occurs when managers intentionally understate expected revenues or overstate expected expenses to increase the chances of receiving favorable performance evaluations. (p. 1140)

**Business Segment.** An identifiable part of the company for which financial information is available. (p. 1108)

**Callable Bonds.** Bonds that the issuer may call and pay off at a specified price whenever the issuer wants. (p. 612)

**Canceled Checks.** Physical or scanned copies of the maker's cashed (paid) checks. (p. 389)
**Capital Asset.** An operational asset used for a long period of time. (p. 1384)
**Capital Budgeting.** The process of planning to invest in long-term assets in a way that returns the most profitability to the company. (p. 1384)
**Capital Expenditure.** An expenditure that increases the capacity or efficiency of a plant asset or extends its useful life. Capital expenditures are debited to an asset account. (p. 479)
**Capital Expenditures Budget.** The budget that presents the company's plan for purchasing property, plant, equipment, and other long-term assets. (p. 1143)
**Capital Investment.** The acquisition of a capital asset. (p. 1384)
**Capital Rationing.** The process of ranking and choosing among alternative capital investments based on the availability of funds. (p. 1386)
**Capital Stock.** Represents the individual's ownership of the corporation's capital. (p. 647)
**Capitalize.** Recording the acquisition of land, building, or other assets by debiting (increasing) an asset account. (p. 477)
**Carrying Amount of Bonds.** A bond payable *minus* the discount account current balance or *plus* the premium account current balance. (p. 607)
**Cash Basis Accounting.** Accounting method that records revenues only when cash is received and expenses only when cash is paid. (p. 118)
**Cash Budget.** The budget that details how the business expects to go from the beginning cash balance to the desired ending cash balance. (p. 1143)
**Cash Equivalent.** A highly liquid investment that can be converted into cash in three months or less. (p. 395)
**Cash Flows.** Cash receipts and cash payments of a business. (p. 699)
**Cash Payments Journal.** Special journal used to record cash payments by check and currency. (p. C-16)
**Cash Ratio.** A measure of a company's ability to pay current liabilities from cash and cash equivalents: (Cash + Cash equivalents) / Total current liabilities. (pp. 395, 778)
**Cash Receipts Journal.** Special journal used to record cash receipts. (p. C-10)
**Centralized Company.** A company in which major planning and controlling decisions are made by top management. (p. 1280)
**Certified Management Accountants (CMAs).** Certified professionals who specialize in accounting and financial management knowledge. They typically work for a single company. (p. 4)
**Certified Public Accountants (CPAs).** Licensed professional accountants who serve the general public. (p. 4)
**Chart of Accounts.** A list of all of a company's accounts with their account numbers. (p. 58)
**Check.** A document that instructs a bank to pay the designated person or business a specified amount of money. (p. 388)
**Classified Balance Sheet.** A balance sheet that places each asset and each liability into a specific category. (p. 186)
**Closing Entries.** Entries that transfer the revenues, expenses, and Dividends balances to the Retained Earnings account to prepare the company's books for the next period. (p. 192)
**Closing Process.** A step in the accounting cycle that occurs at the end of the period. The closing process consists of journalizing and posting the closing entries to set the balances of the revenues, expenses, Income Summary, and Dividends accounts to zero for the next period. (p. 191)
**Cloud Computing.** Software and data are stored on a third-party server instead of by the business and can be accessed by employees via the Internet. (p. C-21)
**Collusion.** Two or more people working together to circumvent internal controls and defraud a company. (p. 379)
**Commercial Substance.** A characteristic of a transaction that causes a change in future cash flows. (p. 502 Appendix 9A)
**Common-Size Statement.** A financial statement that reports only percentages (no dollar amounts). (p. 774)
**Common Stock.** Represents the basic ownership of a corporation. (pp. 12, 648)
**Compound Interest.** Interest calculated on the principal and on all previously earned interest. (pp. 617 Appendix 12A, 1395)
**Compound Journal Entry.** A journal entry that is characterized by having multiple debits and/or multiple credits. (p. 69)
**Comprehensive Income.** A company's change in total stockholders' equity from all sources other than owners' investments and dividends. (p. 535)
**Conservatism.** A business should report the least favorable figures in the financial statements when two or more possible options are presented. (p. 326)
**Consistency Principle.** A business should use the same accounting methods and procedures from period to period. (p. 325)
**Consolidated Statements.** Financial statements that combine the balance sheets, income statements, and statements of cash flow of the parent company with those of its controlling interest affiliates. (p. 532)
**Consolidation Accounting.** The way to combine the financial statements of two or more companies that have the same owners. (p. 532)
**Constraint.** A factor that restricts production or sale of a product. (p. 1345)
**Contingent Liability.** A potential liability that depends on some future event. (p. 571)
**Contra Account.** An account that is paired with, and is listed immediately after, its related account in the chart of accounts and associated financial statement and whose normal balance is the opposite of the normal balance of the related account. (p. 127)
**Contributed Capital.** Owner contributions to a corporation. (p. 12)
**Contribution Margin.** The amount that contributes to covering the fixed costs and then to providing operating income. Net sales revenue − Variable costs. (p. 1053)
**Contribution Margin Income Statement.** The income statement that groups cost by behavior—variable or fixed—and highlights the contribution margin. (p. 1054)
**Contribution Margin Ratio.** The ratio of contribution margin to net sales revenue. Contribution margin / Net sales revenue. (p. 1054)
**Control Account.** An account whose balance equals the sum of the balances in a group of related accounts in a subsidiary ledger. (p. C-7)
**Controllable Cost.** A cost that a manager has the power to influence by his or her decisions. (p. 1290)
**Controlling.** Implementing plans and evaluating the results of business operations by comparing the actual results to the budget. (p. 829)
**Controlling Interest Investment.** An equity security in which the investor owns more than 50% of the investee's voting stock. (p. 526)
**Conversion Costs.** The cost to convert raw materials into finished goods: Direct labor plus manufacturing overhead. (pp. 837, 928)
**Conversion Costs Account.** A temporary account used in JIT management systems to accumulate direct labor and manufacturing overhead costs and then allocate the costs as units are completed. (p. 1009)
**Copyright.** Exclusive right to reproduce and sell a book, musical composition, film, other work of art, or intellectual property. (p. 498)
**Corporation.** A business organized under state law that is a separate legal entity. (pp. 7, 646)
**Cost-Based Transfer Price.** A transfer price based on the cost of producing the goods. (p. 1304)
**Cost/Benefit Analysis.** Weighing costs against benefits to help make decisions. (p. 830)
**Cost Center.** A responsibility center whose manager is only responsible for controlling costs. (p. 1282)
**Cost Driver.** The primary factor that causes a cost to increase or decrease. (p. 882)
**Cost Object.** Anything for which managers want a separate measurement of cost. (p. 836)
**Cost of Goods Available for Sale.** The total cost spent on inventory that was available to be sold during a period. (p. 330)
**Cost of Goods Manufactured.** The manufacturing costs of the goods that finished the production process in a given accounting period. (p. 839)
**Cost of Goods Sold (COGS).** The cost of the merchandise inventory that the business has sold to customers. (p. 248)
**Cost-Plus Pricing.** A method to manage costs and profits by determining the price. Full product cost + Desired profit = Cost-plus price. (p. 1336)
**Cost Principle.** A principle that states that acquired assets and services should be recorded at their actual cost. (pp. 9, 476)
**Cost Structure.** The proportion of fixed costs to variable costs. (p. 1064)
**Cost Variance.** Measures how well the business keeps unit costs of material and labor inputs within standards. (p. 1231)
**Cost-Volume-Profit (CVP) Analysis.** A planning tool that expresses the relationship among costs, volume, and prices and their effects on profits and losses. (p. 1055)
**Credit.** The right side of a T-account. (p. 60)
**Credit Memorandum.** An increase in a bank account. (p. 391)
**Creditor.** Any person or business to whom a business owes money. (p. 4)

**Credit Terms.** The payment terms of purchase or sale as stated on the invoice. (p. 252)

**Cumulative Preferred Stock.** Preferred stock whose owners must receive all dividends in arrears plus the current year dividend before the corporation pays dividends to the common stockholders. (p. 661)

**Current Asset.** An asset that is expected to be converted to cash, sold, or used up during the next 12 months or within the business's normal operating cycle if the cycle is longer than a year. (p. 187)

**Current Liability.** A liability that must be paid with cash or with goods and services within one year or within the entity's operating cycle if the cycle is longer than a year. (pp. 187, 556)

**Current Portion of Notes Payable.** The amount of the principal that is payable within one year. (p. 560)

**Current Ratio.** Measures the company's ability to pay current liabilities from current assets. Total current assets / Total current liabilities. (pp. 200, 778)

**Days' Sales in Inventory.** Measures the average number of days that inventory is held by a company. 365 days / Inventory turnover. (pp. 344, 780)

**Days' Sales in Receivables.** The ratio of average net accounts receivable to one day's sales. The ratio tells how many days it takes to collect the average level of accounts receivable. 365 days / Accounts receivable turnover ratio. (pp. 447, 782)

**Debentures.** Unsecured bonds backed only by the credit worthiness of the bond issuer. (p. 602)

**Debit.** The left side of a T-account. (p. 60)

**Debit Memorandum.** A decrease in a bank account. (p. 391)

**Debtor.** The party to a credit transaction who takes on an obligation/payable. (p. 424)

**Debt Ratio.** Shows the proportion of assets financed with debt. Total liabilities / Total assets. (pp. 81, 782)

**Debt to Equity Ratio.** A ratio that measures the proportion of total liabilities relative to total equity. Total liabilities / Total equity. (pp. 615, 783)

**Debt Security.** Represents a credit relationship with another company or governmental entity that typically pays interest for a fixed period. (p. 524)

**Decentralized Company.** A company that is divided into business segments, with segment managers making planning and controlling decisions for their segments. (p. 1280)

**Deferred Expense.** An asset created when a business makes advance payments of future expenses. (p. 123)

**Deferred Revenue.** A liability created when a business collects cash from customers in advance of completing a service or delivering a product. (p. 129)

**Deficit.** Debit balance in the Retained Earnings account. (p. 667)

**Degree of Operating Leverage.** The ratio that measures the effects that fixed costs have on changes in operating income when sales volume changes. Contribution margin / Operating income. (p. 1065)

**Depletion.** The process by which businesses spread the allocation of a natural resource's cost over its usage. (p. 496)

**Deposit in Transit.** A deposit recorded by the company but not yet by its bank. (p. 390)

**Deposit Ticket.** A bank form that is completed by the customer and shows the amount of each deposit. (p. 388)

**Depreciable Cost.** The cost of a plant asset minus its estimated residual value. (p. 481)

**Depreciation.** The process by which businesses spread the allocation of a plant asset's cost over its useful life. (pp. 126, 475)

**Differential Analysis.** A method that looks at how operating income would differ under each decision alternative; leaves out irrelevant information. (p. 1331)

**Direct Cost.** Cost that can be easily and cost-effectively traced to a cost object. (p. 836)

**Direct Labor (DL).** The labor cost of employees who convert raw materials into finished products. (p. 837)

**Direct Materials (DM).** Materials that become a physical part of a finished product and whose costs are easily traced to the finished product. (p. 837)

**Direct Method.** A format of the operating activities section of the statement of cash flows; lists the operating cash receipts and cash payments. (p. 702)

**Direct Write-off Method.** A method of accounting for uncollectible receivables in which the company records bad debts expense when a customer's account receivable is uncollectible. (p. 429)

**Disclosure Principle.** A business's financial statements must report enough information for outsiders to make knowledgeable decisions about the company. (p. 325)

**Discount on Bonds Payable.** Occurs when a bond's issue price is less than face value. (p. 602)

**Discount Rate.** Management's minimum desired rate of return on a capital investment. (p. 1401)

**Dishonor a Note.** Failure of a note's maker to pay a note receivable at maturity. (p. 444)

**Dividend.** A distribution of a corporation's earnings to stockholders. (pp. 12, 648)

**Dividend in Arrears.** A preferred stock dividend is in arrears if the dividend has not been paid for the year and the preferred stock is cumulative. (p. 661)

**Dividend Payout.** The ratio of dividends declared per common share relative to the earnings per share of the company. Annual dividend per share / Earnings per share. (p. 788)

**Dividend Yield.** Ratio of annual dividends per share of stock to the stock's market price per share. Measures the percentage of a stock's market value that is returned annually as dividends to stockholders. Annual dividend per share / Market price per share. (p. 787)

**Dollar Value Bias.** The bias one sees from comparing numbers in absolute (dollars) rather than relative (percentage) terms. (p. 774)

**Double-Declining-Balance Method.** An accelerated depreciation method that computes annual depreciation by multiplying the depreciable asset's decreasing book value by a constant percent that is two times the straight-line depreciation rate. (p. 484)

**Double-Entry System.** A system of accounting in which every transaction affects at least two accounts. (p. 60)

**Earnings per Share (EPS).** Amount of a company's net income (loss) for each share of its outstanding common stock. (Net income – Preferred dividends) / Weighted average number of common shares outstanding. (pp. 669, 786)

**Economic Entity Assumption.** An organization that stands apart as a separate economic unit. (p. 6)

**Effective-Interest Amortization Method.** An amortization model that calculates interest expense based on the current carrying amount of the bond and the market interest rate at issuance, then amortizes the difference between the cash interest payment and calculated interest expense as a decrease to the discount or premium. (p. 622 Appendix 12B)

**Efficiency Variance.** Measures how well the business uses its materials or human resources. (p. 1231)

**Electronic Data Interchange (EDI).** A streamlined process that bypasses paper documents altogether. Computers of customers communicate directly with the computers of suppliers to automate routine business transactions. (p. 384)

**Electronic Funds Transfer (EFT).** A system that transfers cash by electronic communication rather than by paper documents. (p. 389)

**Encryption.** Rearranging plain-text messages by a mathematical process—the primary method of achieving security in e-commerce. (p. 378)

**Enterprise Resource Planning (ERP).** Software system that can integrate all of a company's functions, departments, and data into a single system. (pp. 831, C-21)

**Equity.** The owners' claims to the assets of the business. (p. 12)

**Equity Security.** Represents stock ownership in another company that sometimes pays dividends. (p. 524)

**Equivalent Units of Production (EUP).** Used to measure the amount of materials added to or work done on partially completed units and expressed in terms of fully completed units. (p. 928)

**Evaluated Receipts Settlement (ERS).** A procedure that compresses the payment approval process into a single step by comparing the receiving report to the purchase order. (p. 384)

**Expenses.** The cost of selling goods or services. (p. 12)

**External Auditor.** An outside accountant, completely independent of the business, who evaluates the controls to ensure that the financial statements are presented fairly in accordance with GAAP. (p. 377)

**External Failure Costs.** Costs incurred when the company does not detect poor-quality goods or services until after delivery to customers. (p. 1013)

**Extraordinary Repair.** Repair work that generates a capital expenditure because it extends the asset's life past the normal expected life. (p. 479)

**Face Value.** The amount a borrower must pay back to the bondholders on the maturity date. (p. 601)

**Fair Value.** The price that would be used if the investments were sold on the market. (p. 532)

**Federal Insurance Contributions Act (FICA).** The federal act that created the Social Security tax that provides retirement, disability, and medical benefits. (p. 562)

**Financial Accounting.** The field of accounting that focuses on providing information for external decision makers. (p. 3)

**Financial Accounting Standards Board (FASB).** The private organization that oversees the creation and governance of accounting standards in the United States. (p. 6)

**Financial Budget.** The budget that includes the cash budget and the budgeted financial statements. (p. 1143)

**Financial Leverage.** Occurs when a company earns more income on borrowed money than the related interest expense. (p. 605)

**Financial Statements.** Business documents that are used to communicate information needed to make business decisions. (p. 19)

**Financing Activities.** Activities that increase or decrease long-term liabilities and equity; a section of the statement of cash flows. (p. 700)

**Finished Goods Inventory (FG).** Completed goods that have not yet been sold. (p. 835)

**Firewall.** A device that enables members of a local network to access the network, while keeping nonmembers out of the network. (p. 378)

**First-In, First-Out (FIFO) Method.** An inventory costing method in which the first costs into inventory are the first costs out to cost of goods sold. Ending inventory is based on the costs of the most recent purchases. (p. 330)

**First-In, First-Out (FIFO) Method (for Process Costing).** Determines the cost of equivalent units of production by accounting for beginning inventory costs separately from current period costs. It assumes the first units started in the production process are the first units completed and sold. (p. 950 Appendix 18A)

**Fiscal Year.** An accounting year of any 12 consecutive months that may or may not coincide with the calendar year. (p. 120)

**Fixed Cost.** A cost that remains the same *in total*, regardless of changes over wide ranges of volume of activity. (p. 1047)

**Flexible Budget.** A budget prepared for various levels of sales volume. (pp. 1141, 1224)

**Flexible Budget Variance.** The difference between actual results and the expected results in the flexible budget for the *actual* units sold. (p. 1225)

**FOB Destination.** Situation in which the buyer takes ownership (title) to the goods at the delivery destination point and the seller typically pays the freight. (p. 255)

**FOB Shipping Point.** Situation in which the buyer takes ownership (title) to the goods after the goods leave the seller's place of business (shipping point) and the buyer typically pays the freight. (p. 255)

**Franchise.** Privilege granted by a business to sell a product or service under specified conditions. (p. 499)

**Free Cash Flow.** The amount of cash available from operating activities after paying for planned investments in long-term assets and after paying dividends to shareholders. Net cash provided by operating activities – Cash payments planned for investments in long-term assets – Cash dividends. (p. 717)

**Freight In.** The transportation cost to ship goods into the purchaser's warehouse; therefore, it is freight on purchased goods. (p. 255)

**Freight Out.** The transportation cost to ship goods out of the seller's warehouse; therefore, it is freight on goods sold to a customer. (p. 255)

**Full Product Cost.** The cost to develop, produce, and deliver the product or service. (p. 1004)

**Generally Accepted Accounting Principles (GAAP).** Accounting guidelines, currently formulated by the *Financial Accounting Standards Board (FASB)*; the main U.S. accounting rule book. (p. 6)

**Goal Congruence.** Aligning the goals of business segment managers and other subordinates with the goals of top management. (p. 1281)

**Going Concern Assumption.** Assumes that the entity will remain in operation for the foreseeable future. (p. 10)

**Goodwill.** Excess of the cost of an acquired company over the sum of the market values of its net assets (assets minus liabilities). (p. 499)

**Gross Pay.** The total amount of salary, wages, commissions, and any other employee compensation before taxes and other deductions. (p. 561)

**Gross Profit.** Excess of net Sales Revenue over Cost of Goods Sold. (p. 249)

**Gross Profit Percentage.** Measures the profitability of each sales dollar above the cost of goods sold. Gross profit / Net sales revenue. (pp. 269, 781)

**Hardware.** Electronic equipment that includes computers, monitors, printers, and the network that connects them. (p. C-21)

**Held-to-Maturity (HTM) Investment.** A debt security the investor intends to hold until it matures. (p. 525)

**High-Low Method.** A method used to separate mixed costs into their variable and fixed components, using the highest and lowest activity levels. (p. 1050)

**Horizontal Analysis.** The study of percentage changes in comparative financial statements. (Dollar amount of change / Base period amount) × 100. (p. 768)

**Impairment.** A permanent decline in asset value. (p. 497)

**Imprest System.** A way to account for petty cash by maintaining a constant balance in the petty cash account. At any time, cash plus petty cash tickets must total the amount allocated to the petty cash fund. (p. 385)

**Income Statement.** Reports the *net income* or *net loss* of the business for a specific period. (p. 19)

**Income Summary.** A temporary account into which revenues and expenses are transferred prior to their final transfer into the Retained Earnings account. Summarizes net income (or net loss) for the period. (p. 192)

**Income Tax Expense.** Expense incurred by a corporation related to federal and state income taxes. (p. 268)

**Income Tax Withholding.** Income tax deducted from an employee's gross pay. (p. 562)

**Indirect Cost.** Cost that cannot be easily or cost-effectively traced to a cost object. (p. 836)

**Indirect Labor.** Labor costs for activities that support the production process but either cannot be conveniently traced directly to specific finished products or are not large enough to justify tracing to the specific product. (p. 837)

**Indirect Materials.** Materials used in making a product but whose costs either cannot be conveniently traced directly to specific finished products or are not large enough to justify tracing to the specific product. (p. 837)

**Indirect Method.** A format of the operating activities section of the statement of cash flows; starts with net income and reconciles to net cash provided by operating activities. (p. 702)

**Intangible Asset.** An asset with no physical form that is valuable because of the special rights it carries. (pp. 187, 497)

**Interest.** The revenue to the payee for loaning money—the expense to the debtor. (p. 440)

**Interest Period.** The period of time during which interest is computed. It extends from the original date of the note to the maturity date. (p. 440)

**Interest Rate.** The percentage rate of interest specified by the note. (p. 440)

**Internal Auditor.** An employee of the business who ensures the company's employees are following company policies, that the company meets all legal requirements, and that operations are running efficiently. (p. 377)

**Internal Control.** The organizational plan and all the related measures adopted by an entity to safeguard assets, encourage employees to follow company policies, promote operational efficiency, and ensure accurate and reliable accounting records. (p. 375)

**Internal Control Report.** A report by management describing its responsibility for and the adequacy of internal controls over financial reporting. (p. 376)

**Internal Failure Costs.** Costs incurred when the company corrects poor-quality goods or services before delivery to customers. (p. 1013)

**Internal Rate of Return (IRR).** The rate of return, based on discounted cash flows, of a capital investment. The interest rate that makes the NPV of the investment equal to zero. (p. 1406)

**International Accounting Standards Board (IASB).** The private organization that oversees the creation and governance of *International Financial Reporting Standards (IFRS)*. (p. 10)

**International Financial Reporting Standards (IFRS).** A set of global accounting guidelines, formulated by the *International Accounting Standards Board (IASB)*. (p. 10)

**Inventory Costing Method.** A method of approximating the flow of inventory costs in a business that is used to determine the amount of cost of goods sold and ending merchandise inventory. (p. 329)

**Inventory Shrinkage.** The loss of inventory that occurs because of theft, damage, and errors. (p. 263)

**Inventory Turnover.** Measures the number of times a company sells its average level of merchandise inventory during a period. Cost of goods sold / Average merchandise inventory. (pp. 344, 780)

**Investee.** The corporation that issued the bond or stock to the investor. (p. 524)

**Investment Center.** A responsibility center whose manager is responsible for generating profits and efficiently managing the center's invested capital. (p. 1282)

**Investing Activities.** Activities that increase or decrease long-term assets; a section of the statement of cash flows. (p. 700)

**Investor.** The owner of a bond or stock of a corporation. (p. 524)

**Invoice.** A seller's request for payment from the purchaser. (p. 250)

**Irrelevant Cost.** A cost that does not affect the decision because it is not in the future or does not differ among alternatives. (p. 1331)

**Issue Price.** The price the stock initially sells for the first time it is sold. (p. 650)

**Issued Stock.** Stock that has been issued but may or may not be held by stockholders. (p. 647)

**Job.** The production of a unique product or specialized service. May be one unit or a batch of units. (p. 873)

**Job Cost Record.** A document that shows the direct materials, direct labor, and manufacturing overhead costs for an individual job. (p. 873)

**Job Order Costing System.** An accounting system that accumulates costs by job. Used by companies that manufacture unique products or provide specialized services. (pp. 873, 924)

**Joint Cost.** A cost of a production process that yields multiple products. (p. 1354)

**Journal.** A record of transactions in date order. (p. 64)

**Just-In-Time Costing.** A costing system that starts with output completed and then assigns manufacturing costs to units sold and to inventories. (p. 1008)

**Just-In-Time (JIT) Management.** A cost management system in which a company produces products just in time to satisfy needs. Suppliers deliver materials just in time to begin production, and finished units are completed just in time for delivery to the customer. (pp. 831, 1006)

**Key Performance Indicator (KPI).** A summary performance measure that helps managers assess whether the company is achieving its goals. (p. 1286)

**Labor Time Record.** A record used to assign direct labor cost to specific jobs. (p. 878)

**Lag Indicator.** A performance measure that indicates past performance. (p. 1286)

**Land Improvement.** A depreciable improvement to land, such as fencing, sprinklers, paving, signs, and lighting. (p. 476)

**Large Stock Dividend.** A stock dividend greater than 20% to 25% of the issued and outstanding stock. (p. 663)

**Last-In, First-Out (LIFO) Method.** An inventory costing method in which the last costs into inventory are the first costs out to cost of goods sold. The method leaves the oldest costs—those of beginning inventory and the earliest purchases of the period—in ending inventory. (p. 331)

**Lead Indicator.** A performance measure that forecasts future performance. (p. 1286)

**Ledger.** The record holding all the accounts of a business, the changes in those accounts, and their balances. (p. 59)

**Legal Capital.** The portion of stockholders' equity that cannot be used for dividends. (p. 659)

**Liabilities.** Debts that are owed to *creditors*. (pp. 12, 556)

**Limited-Liability Company (LLC).** A company in which each member is only liable for his or her own actions. (p. 7)

**Liquidity.** A measure of how quickly an item can be converted to cash. (p. 186)

**License.** Privilege granted by a government to use public property in performing services. (p. 499)

**Lock-Box System.** A system in which customers send their checks to a post office box that belongs to a bank. A bank employee empties the box daily and records the deposits into the company's bank account. (p. 381)

**Long-Term Asset.** An asset that will not be converted to cash or used up within the business's operating cycle or one year, whichever is greater. (p. 187)

**Long-Term Investment.** Investments in bonds (debt securities) or stocks (equity securities) in which the company intends to hold the investment for longer than one year. (pp. 187, 525)

**Long-Term Liability.** A liability that does not need to be paid within one year or within the entity's operating cycle, whichever is longer. (pp. 187, 556)

**Lower-of-Cost-or-Market (LCM) Rule.** Rule that merchandise inventory should be reported in the financial statements at whichever is lower—its historical cost or its market value. (p. 339)

**Maker.** The party who issues the check. (p. 388)

**Management Accountability.** The manager's responsibility to wisely manage the resources of an organization. (p. 830)

**Management by Exception.** When managers concentrate on results that are outside the accepted parameters. (p. 1246)

**Management's Discussion and Analysis of Financial Condition and Results of Operations (MD&A).** The section of the annual report that is intended to help investors understand the results of operations and the financial condition of the company. (p. 766)

**Managerial Accounting.** The field of accounting that focuses on providing information for internal decision makers. (p. 3)

**Manufacturing Company.** A company that uses labor, equipment, supplies, and facilities to convert raw materials into finished products. (p. 835)

**Manufacturing Overhead (MOH).** Manufacturing costs that cannot be easily and cost-effectively traced to a cost object. Includes all manufacturing costs except direct materials and direct labor. (p. 837)

**Margin of Safety.** The excess of expected sales over breakeven sales. The amount sales can decrease before the company incurs an operating loss. (p. 1063)

**Market-Based Transfer Price.** A transfer priced based on the current market value of the goods. (p. 1303)

**Market Interest Rate.** The interest rate that investors demand in order to loan their money. (p. 604)

**Master Budget.** The set of budgeted financial statements and supporting schedules for the entire organization; includes the operating budget, capital expenditures budget, and financial budget. (p. 1142)

**Matching Principle.** Guides accounting for expenses, ensures that all expenses are recorded when they are incurred during the period, and matches those expenses against the revenues of the period. (p. 121)

**Materiality Concept.** A company must perform strictly proper accounting only for items that are significant to the business's financial situation. (p. 326)

**Materials Requisition.** Request for the transfer of raw materials to the production floor. (p. 876)

**Maturity Date.** The date when a note is due. (p. 424)

**Maturity Value.** The sum of the principal plus interest due at maturity. (p. 440)

**Memorandum Entry.** An entry in the journal that notes a significant event but has no debit or credit amount. (p. 666)

**Merchandise Inventory.** The merchandise that a business sells to customers. (p. 247)

**Merchandiser.** A business that sells merchandise, or goods, to customers. (p. 247)

**Merchandising Company.** A company that resells products previously bought from suppliers. (p. 834)

**Mixed Cost.** A cost that has both fixed and variable components. (p. 1049)

**Modified Accelerated Cost Recovery System (MACRS).** A depreciation method that is used for tax purposes. (p. 487)

**Monetary Unit Assumption.** The assumption that requires the items on the financial statements to be measured in terms of a monetary unit. (p. 10)

**Mortgages Payable.** Long-term debts that are backed with a security interest in specific property. (p. 598)

**Multi-Step Income Statement.** Income statement format that contains subtotals to highlight significant relationships. In addition to net income, it reports gross profit and operating income. (p. 267)

**Natural Resource.** An asset that comes from the earth and is consumed. (p. 496)

**Net Income.** The result of operations that occurs when total revenues are greater than total expenses. (p. 13)

**Net Loss.** The result of operations that occurs when total expenses are greater than total revenues. (p. 13)

**Net Pay.** Gross pay minus all deductions. The amount of compensation that the employee actually takes home. (p. 561)

**Net Present Value (NPV).** A capital investment analysis method that measures the net difference between the present value of the investment's net cash inflows and the investment's cost. (p. 1401)

**Net Purchases.** Purchases less purchase returns and allowances less purchase discounts. (p. 272 Appendix 5A)

**Net Realizable Value.** The net value a company expects to collect from its accounts receivable. Accounts Receivable less Allowance for Bad Debts. (p. 431)

**Net Sales Revenue.** The amount a company has earned on sales of merchandise inventory after returns, allowances, and discounts have been taken out. Sales Revenue less Sales Returns and Allowances and Sales Discounts. (p. 261)

**Network.** The system of electronic linkages that allows different computers to share the same information. (p. C-21)

**Non-cash Investing and Financing Activities.** Investing and financing activities that do not involve cash. (p. 701)

**Noncumulative Preferred Stock.** Preferred stock whose owners do not receive passed dividends. (p. 661)

**Nonsufficient Funds (NSF) Check.** A check for which the maker's bank account has insufficient money to pay the check. (p. 391)

**No-Par Stock.** Stock that has no amount (par) assigned to it. (p. 649)

**Normal Balance.** The balance that appears on the increase side of an account. (p. 61)

**Notes Payable.** A written promise made by the business to pay a debt, usually involving interest, in the future. (p. 57)

**Notes Receivable.** A written promise that a customer will pay a fixed amount of principal plus interest by a certain date in the future. (pp. 57, 424)

**Obsolete.** An asset is considered obsolete when a newer asset can perform the job more efficiently than the old. (p. 480)

**Operating Activities.** Activities that create revenue or expense in the entity's business; a section of the statement of cash flows. (p. 700)

**Operating Budget.** The set of budgets that projects sales revenue, cost of goods sold, and selling and administrative expenses, all of which feed into the cash budget and then the budgeted financial statements. (p. 1142)

**Operating Cycle.** The time span during which cash is paid for goods and services, which are then sold to customers from whom the business collects cash. (p. 187)

**Operating Expenses.** Expenses, other than Cost of Goods Sold, that are incurred in the entity's major ongoing operations. (p. 249)

**Operating Income.** Measures the results of the entity's major ongoing activities. Gross profit minus operating expenses. (p. 267)

**Operating Leverage.** Effects that fixed costs have on changes in operating income when sales volume changes. (p. 1065)

**Operational Budget.** A short-term financial plan used to coordinate the activities needed to achieve the short-term goals of the company. (p. 1141)

**Opportunity Cost.** The benefit given up by choosing an alternative course of action. (pp. 1303, 1352)

**Other Revenues and Expenses.** Revenues or expenses that are outside the normal, day-to-day operations of a business, such as a gain or loss on the sale of plant assets or interest expense. (p. 268)

**Outstanding Check.** A check issued by a company and recorded on its books but not yet paid by its bank. (p. 390)

**Outstanding Stock.** Issued stock in the hands of stockholders. (p. 648)

**Overallocated Overhead.** Occurs when the actual manufacturing overhead costs are less than allocated manufacturing overhead costs. (p. 887)

**Paid-In Capital.** Represents amounts received from the stockholders of a corporation in exchange for stock. (p. 649)

**Paid-In Capital in Excess of Par.** Represents amounts received from stockholders in excess of par value. (p. 651)

**Parent Company.** A company that owns a controlling interest in another company. (p. 532)

**Partnership.** A business with two or more owners and not organized as a corporation. (p. 7)

**Par Value.** An amount assigned by a company to a share of its stock. (p. 649)

**Patent.** An intangible asset that is a federal government grant conveying an exclusive 20-year right to produce and sell a process, product, or formula. (p. 498)

**Payback.** A capital investment analysis method that measures the length of time it takes to recover, in net cash inflows, the cost of the initial investment. (p. 1388)

**Payee.** The individual or business to whom the check is paid. (p. 388)

**Payroll Register.** A schedule that summarizes the earnings, withholdings, and net pay for each employee. (p. 564)

**Performance Evaluation System.** A system that provides top management with a framework for maintaining control over the entire organization. (p. 1285)

**Pension Plan.** A plan that provides benefits to retired employees. (p. 569)

**Percent-of-Receivables Method.** A method of estimating uncollectible receivables by determining the balance of the Allowance for Bad Debts account based on a percentage of accounts receivable. (p. 435)

**Percent-of-Sales Method.** A method of estimating uncollectible receivables that calculates bad debts expense based on a percentage of net credit sales. (p. 433)

**Period Cost.** Operating cost that is expensed in the accounting period in which it is incurred. (p. 833)

**Periodic Inventory System.** An inventory system that requires businesses to obtain a physical count of inventory to determine quantities on hand. (p. 249)

**Permanent Account.** An account that is *not* closed at the end of the period—the asset, liability, Common Stock, and Retained Earnings accounts. (p. 192)

**Perpetual Inventory System.** An inventory system that keeps a running computerized record of merchandise inventory. (p. 249)

**Petty Cash.** A fund containing a small amount of cash that is used to pay for minor expenditures. (p. 384)

**Planning.** Choosing goals and deciding how to achieve them. (p. 829)

**Plant Asset.** Long-lived, tangible asset, such as land, buildings, and equipment, used in the operation of a business. (pp. 125, 187, 475)

**Post-Audit.** The comparison of the actual results of capital investments to the projected results. (p. 1386)

**Post-Closing Trial Balance.** A list of the accounts and their balances at the end of the period after journalizing and posting the closing entries. It should include only permanent accounts. (p. 197)

**Posting.** Transferring data from the journal to the ledger. (p. 64)

**Predetermined Overhead Allocation Rate.** Estimated overhead cost per unit of the allocation base, calculated at the beginning of the accounting period. Total estimated overhead costs / Total estimated quantity of the overhead allocation base. (pp. 881, 991)

**Preemptive Right.** Stockholder's right to maintain his or her proportionate ownership in the corporation. (p. 648)

**Preferred Stock.** Stock that gives its owners certain advantages over common stockholders, such as the right to receive dividends before the common stockholders and the right to receive assets before the common stockholders if the corporation liquidates. (p. 649)

**Premium.** The amount above par at which a stock is issued. (p. 650)

**Premium on Bonds Payable.** Occurs when a bond's issue price is more than face value. (p. 602)

**Prepaid Expense.** A payment of an expense in advance. (p. 57)

**Present Value.** The amount a person would invest now to receive a greater amount in the future. (p. 603)

**Prevention Costs.** Costs incurred to avoid poor-quality goods or services. (p. 1013)

**Price/Earnings Ratio.** The ratio of the market price of a share of common stock to the company's earnings per share. Measures the value that the stock market places on $1 of a company's earnings. Market price per share of common stock / Earnings per share. (pp. 670, 787)

**Price-Setter.** A company that has control over the prices of its products and services because its products and services are unique and there is little competition. (p. 1333)

**Price-Taker.** A company that has little control over the prices of its products and services because its products and services are not unique or competition is intense. (p. 1333)

**Prime Costs.** Direct materials plus direct labor. (p. 837)

**Principal.** The amount loaned out by the payee and borrowed by the maker of the note. (p. 440)

**Prior-Period Adjustment.** A correction to Retained Earnings for an error of an earlier period. (p. 668)

**Process.** One of a series of steps in manufacturing production; usually associated with making large quantities of similar items. (p. 924)

**Process Costing System.** An accounting system that accumulates costs by process. Used by companies that manufacture identical units through a series of uniform production steps or processes. (pp. 873, 924)

**Product Cost.** The cost of purchasing or making a product. The cost is recorded as an asset and then expensed when the product is sold. (p. 834)

**Production Cost Report.** A report prepared by a processing department for equivalent units of production, production costs, and the assignment of those costs to the completed and in process units. (p. 930)

**Profitability Index.** Computes the number of dollars returned for every dollar invested, with all calculations performed in present value dollars. Present value of net cash inflows / Initial investment. (p. 1405)

**Profit Center.** A responsibility center whose manager is responsible for generating revenue and controlling costs and, therefore, profits. (p. 1282)

**Profit Margin Ratio.** A profitability measure that shows how much net income is earned on every dollar of net sales. Net income / Net sales. (pp. 784, 1297)

**Public Company.** A company that sells its stock to the general public. (p. 375)

**Purchase Allowance.** An amount granted to the purchaser as an incentive to keep goods that are not "as ordered." (p. 253)

**Purchase Discount.** A discount that businesses offer to purchasers as an incentive for early payment. (p. 252)

**Purchase Return.** A situation in which sellers allow purchasers to return merchandise that is defective, damaged, or otherwise unsuitable. (p. 253)

**Purchases Journal.** Special journal used to record all purchases of merchandise inventory, office supplies, and other assets on account. (p. C-14)

**Quality Management System (QMS).** A system that helps managers improve a business's performance by providing quality products and services. (p. 1012)

**Rate of Return on Common Stockholders' Equity.** Shows the relationship between net income available to common stockholders and their average common equity invested in the company. (Net income − Preferred dividends) / Average common stockholders' equity. (pp. 670, 785)

**Rate of Return on Total Assets.** A ratio that measures the success a company has in using its assets to earn income. (Net income + Interest expense) / Average total assets. (pp. 537, 784)

**Raw and In-Process Inventory.** A combined account for Raw Materials Inventory and Work-In-Process Inventory used in JIT management systems. (p. 1009)

**Raw Materials Inventory (RM).** Materials used to manufacture a product. (p. 835)

**Receivable.** A monetary claim against a business or an individual. (p. 424)

**Relative-Market-Value Method.** A method of allocating the total cost (100%) of multiple assets purchased at one time. Total cost is divided among the assets according to their relative market values. (p. 478)

**Relevant Cost.** A cost that is relevant to a particular decision because it is a future cost and differs among alternatives. (p. 1330)

**Relevant Information.** Expected future data that differ among alternatives. (p. 1330)

**Relevant Range.** The range of volume where total fixed costs and variable cost per unit remain constant. (p. 1052)

**Remittance Advice.** An optional attachment to a check that tells the business the reason for the payment. (p. 381)

**Residual Income (RI).** A measure of profitability and efficiency computed as actual operating income less a specified minimum acceptable operating income. (p. 1298)

**Residual Value.** The expected value of a depreciable asset at the end of its useful life. (pp. 126, 481)

**Responsibility Accounting System.** A system for evaluating the performance of each responsibility center and its manager. (p. 1282)

**Responsibility Center.** A part of the organization for which a manager has decision-making authority and accountability for the results of those decisions. (p. 1281)

**Retailer.** A type of merchandiser that buys merchandise either from a manufacturer or a wholesaler and then sells those goods to consumers. (p. 247)

**Retained Earnings.** Equity earned by profitable operations of a corporation that is not distributed to stockholders. (pp. 12, 649)

**Return on Assets (ROA).** Measures how profitably a company uses its assets. Net income / Average total assets. (p. 24)

**Return on Investment (ROI).** A measure of profitability and efficiency. Operating income / Average total assets. (p. 1296)

**Revenue Center.** A responsibility center whose manager is only responsible for generating revenue. (p. 1282)

**Revenue Expenditure.** An expenditure that does not increase the capacity or efficiency of an asset or extend its useful life. Revenue expenditures are debited to an expense account. (p. 479)

**Revenue Recognition Principle.** Requires companies to record revenue when it has been earned and determines the amount of revenue to record. (p. 120)

**Revenues.** Amounts earned from delivering goods or services to customers. (p. 12)

**Reversing Entry.** A special journal entry that eases the burden of accounting for transactions in the next period. Such entries are the exact opposite of a prior adjusting entry. (p. 204 Appendix 4A)

**Routing Number.** On a check, the 9-digit number that identifies the bank upon which the payment is drawn. (p. 388)

**Sales Discounts.** Reduction in the amount of cash received from a customer for early payment. (p. 259)

**Sales Journal.** Special journal used to record credit sales. (p. C-7)

**Sales Mix.** The combination of products that make up total sales. (p. 1066)

**Sales Returns and Allowances.** Decreases in the seller's receivable from a customer's return of merchandise or from granting the customer an allowance from the amount owed to the seller. (p. 259)

**Sales Revenue.** The amount that a merchandiser earns from selling its inventory. (p. 258)

**Sales Volume Variance.** The difference between the expected results in the flexible budget for the *actual* units sold and the static budget. (p. 1226)

**Sarbanes-Oxley Act (SOX).** Requires companies to review internal control and take responsibility for the accuracy and completeness of their financial reports. (pp. 11, 375)

**Secured Bonds.** Bonds that give bondholders the right to take specified assets of the issuer if the issuer fails to pay principal or interest. (p. 602)

**Securities and Exchange Commission (SEC).** U.S. governmental agency that oversees the U.S. financial markets. (p. 6)

**Security.** A share or interest representing financial value. (p. 524)

**Selling Expenses.** Expenses related to marketing and selling the company's goods and services. (p. 267)

**Sensitivity Analysis.** A "what if " technique that estimates profit or loss results if sales price, costs, volume, or underlying assumptions change. (p. 1061)

**Separation of Duties.** Dividing responsibilities between two or more people to limit fraud and promote accuracy of accounting records. (p. 378)

**Serial Bonds.** Bonds that mature in installments at regular intervals. (p. 602)

**Server.** The main computer where data are stored, which can be accessed from many different computers. (p. C-4)

**Service Company.** A company that sells services—time, skills, and/or knowledge—instead of products. (p. 833)

**Short-Term Investments.** Investments in debt and equity securities that are highly liquid and that the investor intends to sell in one year or less. (p. 525)

**Short-Term Note Payable.** A written promise made by the business to pay a debt, usually involving interest, within one year or less. (p. 558)

**Signature Card.** A card that shows each authorized person's signature for a bank account. (p. 388)

**Significant Interest Investment.** An equity security in which the investor owns from 20% to 50% of the investee's voting stock. (p. 526)

**Simple Interest.** Interest calculated only on the principal amount. (pp. 617 Appendix 12A, 1395)

**Single-Step Income Statement.** Income statement format that groups all revenues together and then lists and deducts all expenses together without calculating any subtotals. (p. 266)

**Small Stock Dividend.** A stock dividend of less than 20% to 25% of the issued and outstanding stock. (p. 663)

**Social Security (FICA) Tax.** Federal Insurance Contributions Act (FICA) tax, which is withheld from employees' pay and matched by the employer. (p. 562)

**Software.** Set of programs or instructions that drives the computer to perform the work desired. (p. C-21)

**Sole Proprietorship.** A business with a single owner. (p. 7)

**Source Document.** Provides the evidence and data for accounting transactions. (pp. 63, C-3)

**Special Journal.** An accounting journal designed to record one specific type of transaction. (p. C-5)

**Specific Identification Method.** An inventory costing method based on the specific cost of particular units of inventory. (p. 329)

**Stakeholder.** An individual or group that has an interest in a business, including customers, creditors, suppliers, and investors. (p. 830)

**Standard.** A price, cost, or quantity that is expected under normal conditions. (p. 1228)
**Standard Cost System.** An accounting system that uses standards for product costs—direct materials, direct labor, and manufacturing overhead. (p. 1228)
**Stated Interest Rate.** The interest rate that determines the amount of cash interest the borrower pays and the investor receives each year. (p. 602)
**Stated Value Stock.** No-par stock that has been assigned an amount similar to par value. (p. 649)
**Statement of Cash Flows.** Reports on a business's cash receipts and cash payments for a specific period. (pp. 22, 699)
**Statement of Retained Earnings.** Reports how the company's retained earnings balance changed from the beginning to the end of the period. (p. 20)
**Static Budget.** A budget prepared for only one level of sales volume. (pp. 1141, 1223)
**Static Budget Variance.** The difference between actual results and the expected results in the static budget. (p. 1223)
**Stock Certificate.** Paper evidence of ownership in a corporation. (p. 647)
**Stock Dividend.** A distribution by a corporation of its own stock to its stockholders. (p. 662)
**Stockholder.** A person who owns stock in a corporation. (p. 7)
**Stockholders' Equity.** A corporation's equity that includes paid-in capital and retained earnings. (p. 649)
**Stock Split.** An increase in the number of issued and outstanding shares of stock coupled with a proportionate reduction in the par value of the stock. (p. 666)
**Straight-Line Method.** A depreciation method that allocates an equal amount of depreciation each year. (Cost - Residual value) / Useful life. (pp. 126, 482)
**Straight-Line Amortization Method.** An amortization method that allocates an equal amount of bond discount or premium to each interest period over the life of the bond. (p. 607)
**Strategic Budget.** A long-term financial plan used to coordinate the activities needed to achieve the long-term goals of the company. (p. 1141)
**Subsidiary Company.** A company that is controlled by another corporation. (p. 532)
**Subsidiary Ledger.** Record of accounts that provides supporting details on individual balances, the total of which appears in a general ledger account. (p. C-6)
**Sunk Cost.** A cost that was incurred in the past and cannot be changed regardless of which future action is taken. (p. 1331)
**T-Account.** A summary device that is shaped like a capital *T* with debits posted on the left side of the vertical line and credits on the right side of the vertical line. (p. 60)
**Target Cost.** The maximum cost to develop, produce, and deliver the product or service *and* earn the desired profit. Target sales price minus desired profit. (p. 1004)
**Target Full Product Cost.** The full cost to develop, produce, and deliver the product or service. (p. 1334)
**Target Price.** The amount customers are willing to pay for a product or service. (p. 1003)
**Target Pricing.** A method to manage costs and profits by determining the target full product cost. Revenue at market price − Desired profit = Target full product cost. (p. 1334)
**Target Profit.** The operating income that results when sales revenue minus variable and fixed costs equals management's profit goal. (p. 1056)
**Temporary Account.** An account that relates to a particular accounting period and is closed at the end of that period—the revenues, expenses, Income Summary, and Dividends accounts. (p. 191)
**Term Bonds.** Bonds that all mature at the same time. (p. 602)
**Time Period Concept.** Assumes that a business's activities can be sliced into small time segments and that financial statements can be prepared for specific periods, such as a month, quarter, or year. (p. 120)
**Times-Interest-Earned Ratio.** Evaluates a business's ability to pay interest expense. (Net income + Income tax expense + Interest expense) / Interest expense. (pp. 573, 783)
**Time Value of Money.** Recognition that money earns interest over time. (p. 603)
**Timing Difference.** Difference that arises between the balance on the bank statement and the balance on the company's books because of a time lag in recording transactions. (p. 390)
**Total Quality Management (TQM).** A philosophy designed to integrate all organizational areas in order to provide customers with superior products and services, while meeting organizational goals throughout the value chain. (p. 831)
**Trademark.** An asset that represents distinctive identifications of a product or service. (p. 499)
**Trading Investment.** A debt security or an equity security in which the investor holds less than 20% of the voting stock and that the investor plans to sell in the very near future. (p. 525)
**Trading on the Equity.** Earning more income on borrowed money than the related interest expense, thereby increasing the earnings for the owners of the business. (p. 786)
**Transaction.** An event that affects the financial position of the business and can be measured with faithful representation. (p. 13)
**Transfer Price.** The transaction amount of one unit of goods when the transaction occurs between divisions within the same company. (p. 1302)
**Transferred In Costs.** Costs that were incurred in a previous process and brought into a later process as part of the product's cost. (p. 936)
**Treasury Stock.** A corporation's own stock that it has previously issued and later reacquired. (p. 655)
**Trend Analysis.** A form of horizontal analysis in which percentages are computed by selecting a base period as 100% and expressing amounts for following periods as a percentage of the base period amount. (Any period amount / Base period amount) × 100. (p. 770)
**Trial Balance.** A list of all ledger accounts with their balances at a point in time. (p. 79)
**Triple Bottom Line.** Evaluating a company's performance by its economic (profits), social (people), and environmental (planet) impact. (p. 831)
**Underallocated Overhead.** Occurs when the actual manufacturing overhead costs are more than allocated manufacturing overhead costs. (p. 887)
**Underwriter.** A firm that handles the issuance of a company's stock to the public, usually assuming some of the risk by agreeing to buy the stock if the firm cannot sell all of the stock to its clients. (p. 650)
**Unearned Revenue.** A liability created when a business collects cash from customers in advance of providing services or delivering goods. (p. 57)
**Unemployment Compensation Tax.** Payroll tax paid by employers to the government, which uses the cash to pay unemployment benefits to people who are out of work. (p. 566)
**Units-of-Production Method.** A depreciation method that allocates a varying amount of depreciation each year based on an asset's usage. (p. 483)
**Useful Life.** Length of the service period expected from an asset. May be expressed in time, such as months or years, or usage, such as units produced, hours used (for machinery), or miles driven (for a truck). (p. 481)
**Value Chain.** Includes all activities that add value to a company's products and services. (p. 831)
**Value Engineering.** Reevaluating activities to reduce costs while satisfying customer needs. (p. 1003)
**Variable Cost.** A cost that increases or decreases *in total* in direct proportion to increases or decreases in the volume of activity. (p. 1046)
**Variable Costing.** The product costing method that assigns only variable manufacturing costs to products: direct materials, direct labor, and variable manufacturing overhead. Used for internal reporting. (p. 1096)
**Variance.** The difference between an actual amount and the budgeted amount; labeled as favorable if it increases operating income and unfavorable if it decreases operating income. (p. 1223)
**Vendor.** The individual or business from whom a company purchases goods. (p. 248)
**Vertical Analysis.** An analysis of a financial statement that reveals the relationship of each statement item to its base amount, which is the 100% figure. (Specific item / Base amount) × 100. (p. 772)
**Warranty.** An agreement that guarantees a company's product against defects. (p. 569)
**Weighted-Average Method.** An inventory costing method based on the weighted-average cost per unit of inventory that is calculated after each purchase. Weighted-average cost per unit is determined by dividing the cost of goods available for sale by the number of units available. (p. 333)
**Weighted-Average Method (for Process Costing).** Determines the average cost of equivalent units of production by combining beginning inventory costs with current period costs. (p. 937)
**Wholesaler.** A type of merchandiser that buys goods from manufacturers and then sells them to retailers. (p. 247)
**Working Capital.** A measure of a business's ability to meet its short-term obligations with its current assets. Current assets – Current liabilities. (p. 777)
**Work-in-Process Inventory (WIP).** Goods that have been started in the manufacturing process but are not yet complete. (p. 835)
**Worksheet.** An internal document that helps summarize data for the preparation of financial statements. (p. 141)

# Subject Index

## F

## Q

# Company Index

# Photo Credits

## Front Matter

Page iii: (top) Bill Woodhull; (middle) Richard Smith; (bottom) Kam-Wah Tsui

## Chapter 1

Page 1: (top) Bragin Alexey/Shutterstock; (middle right) Barbara Tripp/Shutterstock; (bottom left) lightwavemedia/Shutterstock; page 2: (top right) Fotolia; page 4: Monkey Business Images/Shutterstock; page 17: (top) Iodrakon/Shutterstock; page 17: (bottom right) Shutterstock; page 21: Rido/Shutterstock; page 22: Mike Flippo/Shutterstock

## Chapter 2

Page 55: (top) Djordje Radivojevic/Shutterstock; (middle right) Amasterphotographer/Shutterstock; (bottom left) Edyta Pawlowska/Shutterstock; page 56: (top left) Denis Vrublevski/Shutterstock; page 56: (bottom left) Lithian/Shutterstock; page 59: Monkey Business Images/Shutterstock; page 60: Iodrakon/Shutterstock; page 69: Shutterstock

## Chapter 3

Page 117: (top) Ragnarocks/Fotolia; (middle right) Brand X Pictures/Stockbyte/Getty Images; (bottom left) Yuri Arcurs/Fotolia; page 118: (top right) Illustrart/Fotolia; (bottom) Lisa F. Young/Shutterstock; page 127: Rido/Shutterstock

## Chapter 4

Page 183: (top) Dimedrol68/Shutterstock; (middle right) Njaj/Shutterstock; (bottom left) Mountainpix/Shutterstock; page 184 (top right) Andrew Buckin/Shutterstock; page 190: Mike Flippo/Shutterstock; page 195: Lithian/Shutterstock

## Chapter 5

Page 246: (top) Wasanajai/Shutterstock; (middle left) R. Gino Santa Maria/Shutterstock; (bottom right) Pavelbendov/Fotolia; page 247: (top right) Eimantas Buzas/Shutterstock; (middle right) Diana Taliun/Shutterstock; page 249: Monkey Business Images/Shutterstock; page 252: Iodrakon/Shutterstock

## Chapter 6

Page 324: (top) Ari N./Shutterstock;(middle left) K. Miri Photography/Shutterstock (bottom right) Blend Images/Alamy; p. 325: (top right) Tritooth/Fotolia; (middle right) Steshkin Yevgeniy/Shutterstock; page 337: Shutterstock

## Chapter 7

Page 374: (top) Todd Taulman/Shutterstock; (middle left) Eric Gevaert/Shutterstock; (bottom right) Michaeljung/Shutterstock; page 375: (middle right) Krungchingpixs/Shutterstock; page 386: Rido/Shutterstock

## Chapter 8

Page 423: (top) Jmiks/Shutterstock; (middle right) Nenetus/shutterstock; (bottom left) Andresr/ Shutterstock; Artjazz/Shutterstock; page 424: (top right) Photobac/Shutterstock; page 432: Mike Flippo/Shutterstock; page 436: Lithian/Shutterstock

## Chapter 9

Page 474: (top) J. Helgason/Shutterstock; (middle left) Kjpargeter/Shutterstock; (bottom right) Dmitry Kalinovsky/Shutterstock; page 475 (middle right) JPL Designs/Shutterstock; page 487: Monkey Business Images/Shutterstock; page 498: Iodrakon/Shutterstock; page 500: (bottom right) Mim Friday/Alamy

## Chapter 10

Page 523: (top) Iodrakon/Shutterstock; (middle right) Bambuh/Shutterstock; (bottom left) Peter Bernik/Shutterstock; page 504: (top right) Jeka84/Shutterstock; page 530: Monkey Business Images/Shutterstock

## Chapter 11

Page 555: (top) Y.H. Lim/Alamy; (middle right) Elisanth/Shutterstock; (bottom left) Carlo Dapino/Shutterstock; page 556: (top right) Pan Xunbin/Shutterstock; page 563: Shutterstock

## Chapter 12

Page 596: (top) Albachiaraa/Fotolia; (middle right) arfo/Fotolia; (bottom right) PeopleImages.com/Getty; page 597: (top right) Shutterstock; (middle right) Alex Staroseltsev/Shutterstock; page 600: Mike Flippo/Shutterstock; page 604: Lithian/Shutterstock

## Chapter 13

Page 645: (top) AG-Photos/Shutterstock; (middle right) Nuttapong/Shutterstock; (bottom left) StockLite Shutterstock; page 646: (top right) David Castillo DominiciShutterstock; page 649: Rido/Shutterstock

## Chapter 14

Page 698: (top) Nielskliim/Shutterstock; (middle left) Kongsky/Shutterstock; (bottom right) HomeArt/Shutterstock; page 699: (top right) Aaron Amat/Shutterstock; (middle right) Sean Gladwell/Shutterstock; page 707: Iodrakon/Shutterstock; page 722: Shutterstock

## Chapter 15

Page 764: (top) Get4net/Fotolia; (middle left) Rangizzz/Fotolia; (bottom right) Imagemore Co. Ltd./Alamy; page 765: (middle right) Pokomeda/Shutterstock; page 771: Lisa F. Young/Shutterstock

## Appendix C

Page C-1: (top) Zhukov Oleg/Shutterstock; (middle right) Vincent Pen/Fotolia; (bottom left) Nat Ulrich/Shutterstock; page C-2: (top right) Djama/Fotolia